DSN 2000

Proceedings

International Conference on Dependable Systems and Networks

DSN 2000

25-28 June 2000
New York, New York, USA

Sponsored by

IEEE Computer Society Technical Committee on Fault-Tolerant Computing
IFIP Working Group 10.4 on Dependable Computing and Fault Tolerance

In cooperation with

AT&T
Lucent Technologies
Compaq Computer Corp
Georgia Institute of Technology
IBM Corporation
LAAS-CNRS
Microsoft Corporation

IEEE
COMPUTER
SOCIETY

Los Alamitos, California

Washington · Brussels · Tokyo

IEEE Computer Society Order Number PR00707
ISBN 0-7695-0707-7
ISBN 0-7695-0708-5 (case)
ISBN 0-7695-0709-3 (microfiche)
Library of Congress Number 00-102923

Additional copies may be ordered from:

IEEE Computer Society	IEEE Service Center	IEEE Computer Society
Customer Service Center	445 Hoes Lane	Asia/Pacific Office
10662 Los Vaqueros Circle	P.O. Box 1331	Watanabe Bldg., 1-4-2
P.O. Box 3014	Piscataway, NJ 08855-1331	Minami-Aoyama
Los Alamitos, CA 90720-1314	Tel: + 1 732 981 0060	Minato-ku, Tokyo 107-0062
Tel: + 1 714 821 8380	Fax: + 1 732 981 9667	JAPAN
Fax: + 1 714 821 4641	http://shop.ieee.org/store/	Tel: + 81 3 3408 3118
http://computer.org/	customer-service@ieee.org	Fax: + 81 3 3408 3553
csbooks@computer.org		tokyo.ofc@computer.org

Editorial production by Danielle C. Young

Cover art production by Alex Torres

Printed in the United States of America by Technical Communication Services

Table of Contents

International Conference on Dependable Systems and Networks (DSN 2000)

Session 1: Opening Session

Opening Remarks
Presentation of the W.C. Carter Award
Keynote Address: The Challenges for Dependability in E-Business
Dr. Timothy Chou, President and CEO of Oracle Business Online

Session 2A: Embedded Systems

Session 2B: Practical Experience Reports I ♦ Networks

Session 2C: Student Forum

Brief presentations by student travel award winners

Session 3: Panel

EU-USA Program of Research Collaboration on Dependability
    Panel Chair: Brian Randell, University of Newcastle
    Panelists: Frank Anger, NSF; Helen Gill, DARPA; Andrea Servida,
    European Commission; Mark LeBlanc, Department of State

Session 4A: Language Support

Session 4B: Practical Experience Reports II ♦ COTS Evaluation

Session 4C: Student Forum

Brief presentations by student travel award winners

Session 5A: Measurement and Assessment

Session 5B: Practical Experience Reports III ♦ Validation and Evaluation

Session 5C: Student Forum

Brief presentations by student travel award winners

Session 6A: Mobile Agents

Session 6B: Practical Experience Reports IV ♦ System Architecture

Session 6C: Student Forum

Brief presentations by student travel award winners

Session 7: Day 2 ♦ Opening Session

Keynote Address: Internet Performance/Availability from an End User
Perspective
Eric Siegel, Keynote Systems

Session 8A: Analysis and Evaluation

Session 8B: Theory

Session 8C: Software Demonstrations

Session 10B: Group Communication

Session 10C: System Demonstrations

Session 11A: Testing and Applications of Coding

Session 11B: Panel

Statistical or Probabilistic Decision Models: How Dependable Are They?
    Panel Chair: P. Bose, IBM

Session 12: Panel

Running the Bytes without Getting Bitten: Strategies for Dealing with
Malicious Code
    Panel Chair: Carl Landwehr, Mitretek Systems
    Panelists: Crispin Cowan, Oregon Graduate Institute, Gary McGraw,
    Reliable Software Technologies, and Jeannette Wing

Session 13A: Software Fault Injection

Session 13B: Replication

Session 13C: Fast Abstracts

Presentation of work in progress and late-breaking research results

Session 14A: High Performance Architecture

Session 14B: Distributed System Models

Session 14C: Fast Abstracts

Presentation of work in progress and late-breaking research results

Workshop on Dependability of IP Applications Platforms and Networks

Workshop on Dependability of E-Business Systems

Workshop on Dependability Despite Malicious Faults

Message from the Chairs

T. Basil Smith

General Chair

Douglas Blough

Karama Kanoun

Program Chairs

Welcome to New York City and the International Conference on Dependable Systems and Networks (ICDSN). The ICDSN is a new beginning and the successor conference for both the International Symposium on Fault-Tolerant Computing (FTCS), which was sponsored by the IEEE, and the Working Conference on Dependable Computing for Critical Applications (DCCA), which was sponsored by IFIP Working Group 10.4. This year would have been the FTCS-30 and DCCA-8 and it is our hope that ICDSN will combine and add to the tradition of excellence and depth that were the hallmarks of FTCS and DCCA.

Society is now at the brink of unprecedented reliance on the dependability, integrity, security and availability of a global network of computing systems, the Internet. It seems appropriate that we should meet in New York City, at the very heart of global financial networks. These financial networks enable, support and nurture the growing new economy and the resultant global prosperity. At the same time, these financial networks are being transformed and remade by the rush of technology that they finance. It is a good time to consider how fragile and dependent this new world is on the underlying computing technology, and New York City is symbolically the best place to begin this process.

Thus we begin anew. This year the scope of the conference has been expanded to include parallel workshops, which permit a more focused examination of specific problems in dependable computing. There are three of these focused workshops this year, each of which addresses and aspect of providing dependable systems and networks for the new economy. These include a workshop on the dependability of IP applications, platforms and networks, which are the foundation of the new economy, and a workshop on the dependability of e-business systems. Also and very timely, given recent denial of service attacks, we have a workshop on achieving dependability in the face of malicious faults. These workshops add to the traditional tracks of individual papers, and the more informal track of fast abstracts, demonstrations and student papers.

This expanded program was supported by the efforts of an expanded program committee, which included separate and dedicated committees for each of the workshops. In the next several days, we will all come to appreciate the work of these committees as the quality and depth of the program becomes clear. We would like to thank the organizing chairs of the workshops Nicholas Bowen, Yves Deswarte, and Yennun Huang for their contributions. We would also like to thank Rick Harper for his work in putting together the tutorials and demonstrations, and most particularly Farnam Jahanian for his devotion to the duties of publicity chair, a position made more difficult by the expanded scope of this conference. We are also grateful to the local help from Chandra Kintala as registration chair and Ram Chillarege who we leaned on heavily as vice chair. Special thanks go to Chuck Weinstock and Nuno Ferreira Neves for organizing the FastAbstracts track and the Student Forum. The papers of these special sessions appear in separate proceedings.

We express our thanks to all of the 45 Program Committee members for their hard work and continual involvement. Their work began by providing a list of possible referees to the 131 submitted papers. Some papers received as many as 17 suggestions. Based on these suggestions, the referee assignment meeting, attended by a number of PC members, allowed the assignment of paper reviewers to be accomplished in a particularly effective fashion. This effectiveness was demonstrated by an extremely high rate of completed reviews. We are extremely grateful to the 217 reviewers who provided 608 detailed reviews. Their contributions were critical in selection of the 56 excellent papers making up the traditional tracks of the conference.

We express our deep gratitude to the many individuals whose support was crucial in forging a new path for this conference. In particular, Jean Arlat, Kent Fuchs, Jean-Claude Laprie, and Rick Schlichting were always available to provide guidance and to discuss the issues raised by the organization of a new conference, emerging from two existing well-established ones.

We would also like to thank Irith Pomeranz from the University of Iowa and Bill Sanders from the University of Illinois at Urbana Champaign (Program Chairs of FTCS-29) for providing the databases that were central to the review process and for providing welcome advice on many different matters.

Our thanks go to Laurent Blain, Daniel Daurat, Arlette Evrard, Marie-Jo Fontagne, Jackie Furgal, Lili Paigné, Joelle Penavayre and Roger Zittel from LAAS-CNRS, and Pam Halverson, Jamie Brinkley, Weilai Yang, and Stephen Hague from the Georgia Institute of Technology for their help in organizing and preparing various conference-related items.

We would also like to thank AT&T, Compaq, the Georgia Institute of Technology, IBM, LAAS-CNRS, Lucent Technologies, and Microsoft for their financial support, which has made the expense of meeting in New York City somewhat less burdensome.

Finally, we would once again like to welcome you to the heart of New York City. We hope that you take the time not only to enjoy this conference, but also to take in as much of the city that never sleeps as your energy permits.

Program Committee

Algirdas Avizienis, *University of California at Los Angeles, USA*
Dimiter Avresky, *Boston University, USA*
Michel Banatre, *IRISA, France*
Ram Chillarege, *IBM T.J. Watson Research Center, USA*
Mario Dal Cin, *University of Erlangen-Nürnberg, Germany*
Marcelo de Azevedo, *Compaq, USA*
Felicita di Giandomenico, *IEI-CNR, Italy*
Joanne Bechta Dugan, *University of Virginia, USA*
Mootaz Elnozahy, *IBM Austin, USA*
Christof Fetzer, *AT&T Laboratories, USA*
Hideo Fujiwara, *Nara Institute of Science and Technology, Japan*
Rick Harper, *IBM T.J. Watson Research Center, USA*
Guenter Heiner, *Daimler-Chrysler, Germany*
Ravi Iyer, *University of Illinois, USA*
Farnam Jahanian, *University of Michigan, USA*
Nobuyasu Kanekawa, *Hitachi Research Laboratories, Japan*
Johan Karlsson, *Chalmers University of Technology, Sweden*
Tohru Kikuno, *Osaka University, Japan*
Chandra Kintala, *Lucent Bell Laboratories, USA*
Philip Koopman, *Carnegie Mellon University, USA*
Hermann Kopetz, *Technical University of Vienna, Austria*
Jean-Claude Laprie, *LAAS-CNRS, France*
Patrick Lincoln, *SRI, USA*
Michael Lyu, *Chinese University of Hong Kong, China*
Eliane Martins, *University of Campinas, Brazil*
Gerald Masson, *Johns Hopkins University, USA*
Roy Maxion, *Carnegie Mellon University, USA*
John Meyer, *University of Michigan, USA*
Takashi Nanya, *Tokyo University, Japan*
Andrzej Pelc, *University of Quebec at Hull, Canada*
James Plank, *University of Tennessee, USA*
Irith Pomeranz, *University of Iowa, USA*
David Powell, *LAAS-CNRS, France*
Brian Randell, *University of Newcastle upon Tyne, UK*
Sampath Rangarajan, *Lucent Bell Laboratories, USA*
S.S. Ravi, *State University of New York at Albany, USA*
Michel Raynal, *IRISA, France*
G. Robert Redinbo, *University of California at Davis, USA*
Kewal Saluja, *University of Wisconsin at Madison, USA*
William Sanders, *University of Illinois, USA*
Joao Gabriel Silva, *University of Coimbra, Portugal*
Neeraj Suri, *Chalmers University of Technology, Sweden*
Paulo Verissimo, *University of Lisbon, Portugal*
Mladen Vouk, *North Carolina State University, USA*
Yi-Min Wang, *Microsoft Research, USA*

Conference Organization

Conference Chair

T. Basil Smith, *IBM T.J. Watson Research Center, USA*

Conference Vice-Chair

Ram Chillarege, *IBM T.J. Watson Research Center, USA*

Program Chairs

Douglas M. Blough, *Georgia Institute of Technology, USA*

Karama Kanoun, *LAAS-CNRS, France*

Tutorial Chair

Rick Harper, IBM T.J. Watson Research Center, USA

Finance Chair

Neeraj Suri, *Chalmers University of Technology, Sweden*

Registration Chair

Chandra Kintala, *Lucent Bell Laboratories, USA*

Local Arrangements Chairs

Caroline Benveniste, *IBM T.J. Watson Research Center, USA*

Mike Wazlowski, *IBM T.J. Watson Research Center, USA*

Publicity Chair

Farnam Jahanian, *University of Michigan, USA*

Publication Chair

Abhijit Chatterjee, *Georgia Institute of Technology, USA*

Student Forum Chair

Nuno Neves, *University of Lisbon, Portugal*

Ex Officio

Jean Arlat, *LAAS-CNRS, USA*

Rick Schlichting, *University of Arizona, USA*

Fast Abstracts:

Program Chair

Chuck Weinstock, *Carnegie Mellon University, USA*

Program Committee

Dave Bakken, *Washington State University, USA*

Mohamed Kaaniche, *LAAS-CNRS, France*

Workshop on Dependability Despite Malicious Faults:

Program Chair

Yves Deswarte, *LAAS-CNRS, France*

Program Committee

Frederic Cuppens, *ONERA-Toulouse, France*

Marc Dacier, *IBM Zurich Laboratory, Switzerland*

Dieter Gollmann, *Microsoft Research, UK*

Li Gong, *Sun Microsystems, USA*

Sushil Jajodia, *George Mason University, USA*

Carl Landwehr, *Mitretek, USA*

Jean-Claude Laprie, *LAAS-CNRS, France*

Teresa Lunt, *Xerox, USA*

Roy Maxion, *Carnegie-Mellon University, USA*

Brian Randell, *University of Newcastle, UK*

Workshop on Dependability of E-Business Systems:

Program Chair

Nick Bowen, *IBM T.J. Watson Research Center, USA*

Program Committee

Wendy Bartlett, *Compaq, USA*

Linda Ernst, *Intel, USA*

Robert Horst, *3ware, USA*

Brendan Murphy, *Microsoft Research, UK*

Lisa Spainhower, *IBM, USA*

Michael Treese, *Sun Microsystems, USA*

Workshop on Dependability of IP Applications, Platforms and Networks:

Program Chair

Yennun Huang, *AT&T Laboratories, USA*

Program Committee

Christof Fetzer, *AT&T Laboratories, USA*

Rick Harper, *IBM T.J. Watson Research Center, USA*

Craig Labovitz, *University of Michigan, USA*

Haim Levendel, *Motorola, USA*

Sampath Rangarajan, *Lucent Bell Laboratories, USA*

Falguni Sarkar, *Nortel, USA*

Chris Smith, *Ericsson, Sweden*

Kishor Trivedi, *Duke University, USA*

Yi-Min Wang, *Microsoft Research, USA*

Reviewers

Alvisi, L.
Amir, Y.
An, X.
Arlat, J.
Avizienis, A.
Avresky, D.
Baldoni, R.
Banatre, M.
Baratloo, A.
Bauer, G.
Beveridge, M.
Bidoit, M.
Blair, G.
Blough, D.
Bondavalli, A.
Bowen, N.
Burns, A.
Cao, Y.
Chandra, T.
Chen, D.
Chen, P.
Chen, Y.
Chevochot, P.
Chiba, S.
Chillarege, R.
Choi, E.
Correia, M.
Costa, A.
Costes, A.
Courtiat, J.-P.
Crouzet, Y.
Cukier, M.
Cunha, J.
Dacier, M.
Dal Cin, M.
de Azevedo, M.

de Saqui-Sannes, P.
Deswarte, Y.
DeVale, J.
Di Giandomenico, F.
Donandt, J.
Dufour, J.-L.
Dugan, J.
Dutertre, B.
Echtle, K.
Elhakeem, A.K.
Elmenreich, W.
Elnozahy, M.
Fabre, J.-C.
Fantechi, A.
Festor, O.
Fetzer, C.
Fraigniaud, P.
Friedman, R.
Fuchs, E.
Fuchs, W.K.
Fujiwara, E.
Fujiwara, H.
Garcia, I.
Gaudel, M.-C.
Gelembe
Gil Vicente, P.
Guerraoui, R.
Halbwachs, N.
Hamlet, D.
Harper, R.
Heimerdinger, W.
Heiner, G.
Helary, J.-M.
Hiltunen, M.
Huang, Y.
Hurfin, M.

Inoue, T.
Issarny, V.
Iyer, R.
Jahanian, F.
Johnson, S.
Jonsson, J.
Kaaniche, M.
Kaiser, J.
Kalbarczyk, Z.
Kanekawa, N.
Kanoun, K.
Karlsson, J.
Karpovsky, M.
Karr, D.
Kawasaki, K.
Kikuno, T.
Kim, K.
Kintala, C.
Knight, J.
Koopman, P.
Kopetz, H.
Kranakis, E.
Krishna
Krol, T.
Kuo, S.-Y.
Lakamraju, V.
Lakshmanan, K.B.
Lala, J.
Landrault, C.
Laprie, J.-C.
Le Lann, G.
Lee, H.
LeGuin, P.
Leonhardi, A.
Lincoln, P.
Lippman, R.

Little, M.

Littlewood, B.

Lumetta, S.

Lunt, T.

Lyu, M.

Madeira, H.

Maestrini, P.

Malek, M.

Martins, E.

Marzullo, K.

Masson, G.

Mathy, L.

Maxion, R.

Mecella, M.

Melhem, R.

Melliar-Smith, P.M.

Mendelson, A.

Meyer, J.

Morin, C.

Moser, L.

Mostefaoui, A.

Murphy, B.

Mustafa, M.

Nanya, T.

Narasimhan, P.

Neves, N.

Owezarski, P.

Pallierer, R.

Pan, J.

Pasquini, A.

Pelc, A.

Perez, C.

Piestrak, S.

Plank, J.

Popov, P.

Powell, D.

Puaut, Isabelle

Rai, S.

Ramanathan, P.

Randell, B.

Rangarajan, S.

Ravi, S.S.

Raynal, M.

Redinbo, R.

Reis Lagrange, V.

Rennels, D.

Rodrigues, L.

Rodriguez-Moreno, M.

Romanovsky, S.

Rothermel, K.

Rubira, C.

Rushby, J.

Salles, F.

Saluja, K.

Sanders, W.

Schiper, A.

Schlichting, R.

Schneider, F.

Schwarz, J.

Sengupta, A.

Shi, Y.

Shrivastava, S.

Siewiorek, D.

Sifakis, J.

Silva, J.G.

Silva, L.

Simoncini, L.

Singhal, M.

Sinha, P.

Smart, M.

Smith, T.B.

Somani, A.

Spainhower, L.

Sridharan, M.

Ssu, K.-F.

Stankovic, J.

Stott, D.

Strigini, L.

Sundvall, K.-E.

Suri, N.

Tai, A.

Temple, C.

Tillerot, F.

Trivedi, K.

Tsai, T.

Tschaeche, O.

Tsuchiya, T.

Vaidya, N.

van Renesse, R.

Vardanega, T.

Verissimo, P.

Vila-Carbo, J.

Voas, J.

Vouk, M.

Waidner, M.

Wang, Y.-M.

Welch, J.

Werner, M.

Wheater, S.

Whisnant, K.

Wong, A.

Wu, J.

Xie, M.

Yao, B.

Yajnik, S.

Yeh, B.

Yin, M.-L.

Yoneda, T.

Zwaenepoel, W.

William C. Carter Award

William C. Carter

The William C. Carter Award is presented annually to recognize an individual who has made a significant contribution to the field of dependable computing through their graduate dissertation research. The award honors the late William C. Carter, a key figure in the formation and development of the field of dependable computing, and someone who always took the time to encourage, mentor, and inspire newcomers to the field. The award is sponsored by the IEEE Technical Committee on Fault-Tolerant Computing (TC-FTC) in cooperation with the IFIP Working Group on Dependable Computing and Fault Tolerance (WG 10.4).

Requirements for the award were announced in the DSN 2000 Call for Papers. To qualify, a paper based on the student's dissertation must have been submitted to DSN as a regular paper with the student as the first author. Both current graduate students and former graduate students, no more than two years past completion of their dissertations, were eligible.

All Carter Award submissions accepted to DSN 2000 as regular papers were evaluated by the Carter Award Committee established by the TC-FTC Chair. Based on this evaluation, the Committee selected *Wei Chen* as this year's winner based on the research described in:

"On the Quality of Service of Failure Detectors" (Chen, Toueg, Aguilera)

Session 1

Opening Session

Session 2A

Embedded Systems

Transparent Redundancy in the Time-Triggered Architecture

Günther Bauer   Hermann Kopetz

Vienna University of Technology, Real-Time Systems Group
Treitlstr. 3/182-1, A-1040 Vienna, Austria
E-mail: {bauer,hk}@vmars.tuwien.ac.at

Abstract

The time-triggered architecture is an architecture for distributed embedded real-time systems in high dependability applications. The core element of the architecture is the time-triggered communications protocol TTP/C. This paper shows how TTP/C can be extended by a Fault-Tolerance Layer that performs those functions that are necessary for the implementation of application redundancy. The hardware/software interface of the host computer, where the application software is executing, is not changed, neither in the value domain, nor in the temporal domain, by this implementation of fault-tolerance in the communications system. Provided the application software has been properly organized, it is thus possible to implement application redundancy transparently, i.e., without any modification of the function and timing of the application system. The paper also discusses the experiences gained from a prototype implementation of the fault-tolerance layer in the microprogram of a TTP/C controller chip.

1. Introduction

Although the reliability of microelectronics devices has significantly improved over the last decades, the fact remains that any physical component will eventually fail, determined by the intrinsic failure rate of the selected technology. If the consequences of such a component failure on the application service entail the possibility of a severe financial loss, then the implementation of redundancy in order to improve the reliability is economically justified. In safety critical computer applications, such as "fly-by-wire" or "drive-by-wire" systems, it is required by law that no single component failure in the computer control system causes a loss of service at the application level. In other embedded computer applications, such as a robot on a large assembly line, a short outage of a few minutes duration can cause a financial loss that is equivalent to the hardware cost of the complete control system. In these types of applications, the implementation of hardware redundancy is economically imperative.

The implementation of redundancy requires additional hardware and software resources. Because of the impressive price/performance improvements of the computer hardware over the last decades, the relation of the additional software resources to the additional hardware resources that are needed for the implementation of redundancy has drastically changed over the past few years. Whereas ten years ago, the cost of duplicating the complete hardware of an embedded control system was a major issue, today in all but large volume applications the software costs for the implementation of fault-tolerance are dominating. It is therefore economically attractive to provide a hardware architecture where the application software does not have to be modified in case hardware redundancy is introduced in a previously non-redundant configuration.

It is the objective of this paper to show how application-transparent redundancy can be implemented in the time-triggered architecture. In this context application-transparent redundancy means that the hardware/software environment of the application software is not modified – neither in the value domain nor in the time domain – by a change from a non-redundant configuration to a redundant configuration.

The paper is organized as follows. Section 2 introduces the time-triggered architecture (TTA), describes the structure of a Fault-Tolerant Unit (FTU) and explains how input/output is performed in the TTA. Section 3 states the requirements on the organization of the application software in a host computer that must be met if transparency in the implementation of fault-tolerance is to be achieved. Section 4 deals with the services of the fault-tolerance layer. Section 5 reports about the experiences gained from an implementation of the fault-tolerance layer in the microprogram of a communication controller chip of the time-triggered protocol (TTP/C). The paper finishes with a conclusion in Section 6.

2. The Time-Triggered Architecture

The Time-Triggered Architecture (TTA) [17] is an architecture for distributed real-time systems in high-dependability applications, such as computer controlled brakes in an automobile. The time-triggered architecture decomposes a real-time system into clusters, Fault-Tolerant Units (FTU), and nodes. There are two types of nodes in the architecture: a fail-silent TTA system node (Smallest Replaceable Unit – SRU) and a smart sensor node. An SRU consists of two types of subsystems: a communications sub-system and a host computer executing the application soft-ware (Figure 1). The Communication Network Interface (CNI) between a communications subsystem and the host computer is a strict data-sharing interface that is fully spec-ified in the temporal domain and in the value domain and contains state messages [3, p. 32].

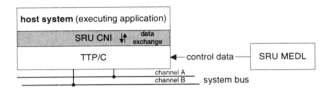

Figure 1. Smallest Replaceable Unit – SRU

The core elements of the TTA are the two time-triggered communication protocols TTP/C [4] and TTP/A [5]. TTP/C controls a replicated system bus intended for the fault-tolerant communication between SRUs, while TTP/A con-trols a sensor bus connecting smart sensors with an SRU. The CNIs of both protocols have the same structure and meaning.

2.1. The TTP/C System Bus

TTP/C is a time-triggered communications system that autonomously and deterministically transmits state mes-sages between the fully specified CNIs in the SRUs. TTP/C provides the following services:

- *Message transport* at known points in time with low latency and minimal jitter (in the present VLSI im-plementation of TTP/C, the jitter is less than one mi-crosecond)

- Fault-tolerant *clock synchronization*

- Provision of a fault-tolerant *membership service*

Media-access in TTP/C is controlled by a conflict-free TDMA (time division multiple access) strategy. The TDMA scheme divides (real) time into slots of not neces-sarily equal length and each SRU is assigned a unique slot

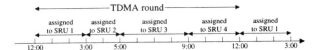

Figure 2. TDMA Round (4 SRUs cluster)

where only this SRU is allowed to send. A lower bound for the length of the slots is determined by the amount of data the assigned SRU has to broadcast and the time needed to execute the TTP/C protocol between two successive data transmissions. Every SRU is equipped with a special piece of hardware (the *bus guardian*) that prevents sending out-side the assigned slot. After all SRUs have sent, the ac-cess pattern is repeated. A single repetition is referred to as *TDMA round* (Figure 2). Every SRU has a copy of the com-mon dispatching table (message descriptor list – MEDL) that contains the TDMA schedule. Because an SRU can only send in its (off-line and statically) assigned sending slot and all SRUs know which slot is assigned to which SRU, there is no need for transmitting a sender ID with the data: the sender ID may be derived from the reception time.

However, the MEDL does not only contain the TDMA access pattern for multiplexing the system bus but also groups several TDMA rounds to a *cluster cycle*. The clus-ter cycle multiplexes the slots of an SRU among several messages (e.g., an SRU can send message A in one TDMA round but message B in the next) and consists of n TDMA rounds, where n is the least common multiple of the num-ber of different messages produced at all SRUs in the clus-ter. Thus, a cluster cycle contains n times the number of SRUs in the cluster entries, each describing an individual message. The cluster cycle layout is also assembled off-line and is static, therefore there is no need for transmitting a message ID either: a receiving SRU can both determine the sender and the message ID from the arrival time. An-other consequence of this is that all messages in TTP/C are broadcast periodically.

To interpret the data correctly, all SRUs must agree on the order of entries in the cluster cycle, the entry assigned to the current slot, and the global time. Agreement on the order is achieved off-line – all SRUs get a local copy of the same global MEDL. To allow for integration of SRUs into a running cluster, the global time at the start of the slot and the MEDL entry assigned to the current slot are periodically broadcast in a specially-formatted data frame (*initialization frame*). Once integrated, the fault-tolerant clock synchro-nization algorithm of TTP/C keeps the SRUs synchronized to each other.

Finally, TTP/C implements *fault isolation* [8]: no fault in any communications subsystem can cause incorrect behav-ior in another communications subsystem; however, if the host application provides incorrect data at the CNI TTP/C will broadcast these data. To prohibit the loss of service of the whole cluster in case of a single bus failure TTP/C uses two replicated channels to communicate data.

2.2. Fault-Tolerance Layer

A fault-tolerant unit (FTU) consists of a defined set of SRUs. The main objective of the fault-tolerance layer (FT layer) is the management of these SRUs forming an FTU in order to mask faults. The number of SRUs of an FTU depends on its type of fault-tolerance, i.e., the number of faults to be masked. In detail, the components of an FTU are:

- the (replicated) applications (each being executed at one of the SRUs forming the FTU) that produce the non-fault-tolerant messages,

- the internal state of each of the application replicas,

- an agreed (reduced) internal application state, and

- the fault-tolerant message.

In the remainder of this paper we will use the term *TTP message* for the data that are transmitted in a single TTP/C frame. A TTP message contains the *replicated message* produced by the application replica executed at the sender SRU (a single SRU hosts a single application replica that produces a single replicated message). Finally, the *FT message* comes into existence by applying an adjudication mechanism to the set of replicated messages each generated by an application replica. The same adjudication mechanism is used to generate an agreed (and thus also fault-tolerant) internal state of the replicated applications from the internal state of each replica.

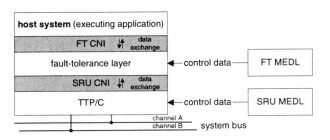

Figure 3. Smallest Replaceable Unit – SRU

Following the basic idea of the time-triggered architecture, the FT layer communicates with both the host system and the TTP/C protocol via a Communication Network Interface (CNI) and is controlled by a message descriptor list (FT MEDL) and the progress of global time (Figure 3). The CNI provided by the FT layer (FT CNI) has similar properties as the CNI provided by TTP/C: it is fully specified

in the temporal and the value domain and consists of two parts:

- The *producer area* contains the replicated message and the internal state information that are produced by the application executed at the host computer system of the respective node.

- The *consumer area* contains all FT messages that are input to the application running at the host system and the agreed version of the internal state of this application.

Whenever an FT message, say A, is contained within the consumer area at two distinct SRUs, it will contain the same data at the same points in (real) time at both SRUs (i.e., the FT message is updated in the same slot) as long as the number of failures in the system does not exceed the number of failures that can be tolerated by the redundancy type of A.

All activities of the FT layer are performed periodically with the period being the cluster cycle of TTP/C introduced in Section 2.1. However, to emphasize the relation to the FT layer we will refer to this period as *fault-tolerance round* (FT round). The FT round consists of two parts: In the first part all applications broadcast their internal states. The FT layer will use the states of all application replicas of an FTU to generate an agreed application state by applying an adjudication mechanism. In the second part, the replicated applications will broadcast the replicated messages they have computed from the input data (using the agreed internal application state).

The fault-tolerance layer is placed in between the CNI provided by TTP/C (the SRU CNI) and the host computer system. Figure 3 shows the structure of an SRU containing an FT layer.

2.3. Input/Output

In the TTA Input/Output is performed using the time-triggered sensor bus TTP/A. TTP/A [5] is based on a multi-master bus that connects one or more SRUs to a set of (fail-consistent) sensor and actuator nodes, as shown in Figure 4. At any point in time, one of the SRUs is the active master while the other SRUs can be shadow masters, which can listen to the traffic on the bus and are in the position to take over the bus control in case the currently active master fails. In a TMR configuration at least two independent TTP/A busses are connected to all three SRUs of a triad. Each SRU can listen to all data exchanged on all busses and can perform an agreement protocol on the acquired input data to generate agreed values out of the measured values. The agreed values are periodically written into the Controlled-Object Interface (COI) of the SRUs at an *a priori* known point in time. Since, in a fault-tolerant configuration, the same value is written at the same point in time into each one of the three COIs of the SRUs forming a triad, the replica deterministic computation of an output message, as explained in Section 2.2, proceeds as with any other message received by an SRU. The host of an SRU is not aware, whether the input value in its COI is the result of an agreement protocol over multiple sensor inputs or the result of a single sensor reading in a non-redundant configuration.

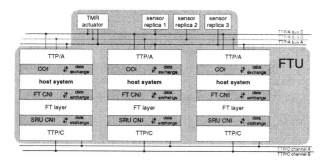

Figure 4. Three SRUs with three TTP/A busses

In case of fault-tolerance an output message is sent at the same point in time from each one of the replicated SRUs of a triad to a fault-tolerant actuator that performs some form of voting [3, p. 205] on its three inputs. In a non-redundant configuration, a single output is sent to a non-fault-tolerant actuator.

3. Host System Requirements

In this section we describe the requirements imposed on the host system and the application software that are necessary to make fault-tolerance transparent in the time-triggered architecture.

3.1. Execution Model

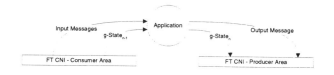

Figure 5. Data Input and Output

The execution model is similar to the one introduced in the SIFT project [18]: all applications are executed periodically where the period is equal to a fraction of the duration of the FT round. The execution of an application instance (e.g., a control algorithm) may start as soon as

all FT messages that are input to the respective application are available at the FT CNI's consumer area (Figures 5, 6). Furthermore, applications must have copied their replicated (output-) message to the FT CNI before it is scheduled for broadcast. In the TTA both of these points are the same (with respect to the start of the FT round) in every FT round and delimit the *execution window*. A correct application instance must both start and terminate within its execution window. However, while the execution window is strictly periodical the application may be executed anywhere within its execution window. It may also be preempted as long as it terminates timely. Consequently, the execution period stated above is only the average interval between the start of two successive application instances.

Of course the TTP/C message transmission schedule will have to obey the constraints imposed by the limited computational resources of the host system to make the applications schedulable. After startup, the application schedule must be started synchronously to the start of the next FT round and must stay synchronous to the communication controller. Finally, application replicas must be executed at distinct nodes and must be replica deterministic [13].

3.2. Ground State

The term *ground state* (g-state) [1] is closely related to the term *history state* (h-state): The output of an application is a function of the input data and the internal state of the application upon invocation. This internal state is called the h-state (in other words, the h-state is input data to an application that is produced by the application itself). If the h-state of one instance of an application is loaded into another "virgin" instance of the same application, this new instance will produce the same output data if it receives the same input as the initial instance does. Further, the generation of the output may alter the h-state; after the generation of the output, the h-state of the two instances will be the same, too. The g-state of an application is an h-state where no task is active and all communication channels are flushed. If an application has no h-state it has no g-state either.

To allow for integration of SRUs and the respective applications being executed by these SRUs, the FT layer provides the g-state information for each application at the FT CNI's consumer area. Upon startup, when the FT layer cannot provide g-state information for an application, the application uses an initial g-state value. After completion of the last instance of an application during an FT round, the g-state information is output to the FT CNI's producer area (Figure 5). However, if the application does not perform any activities (e.g. because not all of the necessary input messages were available) during an FT round it outputs the g-state it received upon start of the round. The FT layer will broadcast the g-state (that has been stored to the

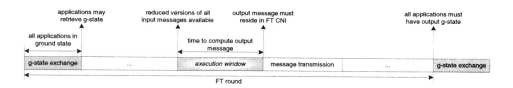

Figure 6. Timing Constraints for Application Execution

FT CNI's producer area) at the begin of the next FT round[1].

The g-state (message) of an application has the same redundancy type as the FT message associated with the application. Consequently, the same adjudication algorithm is used to generate an agreed g-state as is used to generate the FT message.

In fact, application synchronization is the intended purpose of the g-state exchange. Seen from this point of view, the FT round is the re-synchronization period, the g-state messages provide the synchronization information and the adjudication algorithm acts as a fault-tolerant synchronization algorithm. After the g-state exchange part of the FT round application replicas are synchronized. During the rest of the FT round they are free-running and their h-states may diverge in case of a failure. Consequently, the length of an FT round determines both how long it takes an SRU to re-integrate into a running cluster and how long an application may operate using a non-agreed h-state.

3.3. Message Input and Output

An application may have an arbitrary number of input FT messages (Figure 5) but only a single input g-state. It can output one replicated message and one replicated g-state message. However, if an application has a g-state it must both input and output its g-state. No application can only input or output a g-state.

If an application does not have a g-state it simply has to check whether the FT layer can provide all the input FT messages needed to compute the replicated (output) message. If this check evaluates to true (and it will always evaluate to true if an application does not need any input at all), the application computes the replicated output message, copies it to the FT CNI's producer area, and updates the respective message status field to indicate that the content of the replicated message is valid. However, if not all of the necessary input FT messages are available or the application cannot provide a correct replicated message because of any other failure, the application does not output a replicated message to the producer area.

If an application has a g-state, it tries to read the current

g-state from the consumer area upon invocation of its first instance of an FT round. If the FT layer cannot provide a valid g-state the application uses an initial g-state. Once equipped with a g-state the application checks whether all the required input FT messages are available at the consumer area just like an application without g-state. When the last application instance of the FT round has performed all its work and output its results, it stores the new g-state within the FT CNI's producer area. If no instance of the application could perform its work successfully because not all of the input FT messages were available, the g-state will remain unchanged and the initial g-state will be stored in the FT CNI. In case of any other failure, the application does not output the g-state to the producer area.

3.4. Fault Hypothesis

According to the redundancy type of the FT message the computational environment must meet a specified fault hypothesis. E.g., for non-redundant messages, the host system executing the (single) producer application must not exhibit any error neither in the time nor in the value domain during execution of the application. Otherwise, no valid FT message can be provided by the FT layer. TMR FT messages on the other hand allow for a single host executing a replica of the producer application to exhibit arbitrary failures in both the time and the value domain while executing the application without loss of service of the TMR FT message. Application failures in the time domain are either mapped to omission failures (the replicated message is not available when being scheduled for sending) or to value failures (the replicated message was computed using obsolete input); communications system failures in the time domain are prohibited by TTP/C. Both value and omission failures will be masked as long as at least two of the producer applications are executed correctly. However, if the *failure mode assumption* [14] is violated and two replicas of the producer application are affected by a failure, the FT layer cannot provide a correct FT message.

3.5. Transparency

The fault-tolerance layer presented here is designed to provide full transparency in both the time and the value

[1]The communications bandwidth needed for g-state exchange is pure overhead. The timing constraints of the application will determine its maximum size.

9

domain. Transparency in the value domain is provided if applications are implemented respecting the requirements outlined in the previous sections. The FT layer will hide the redundancy type of an FT message from both the producer and the consumer application(s) of this FT message. To achieve transparency in the time domain, the TDMA schedule has to be constructed in a way that allows for the introduction of additional SRUs for all non-redundant messages and for voting.

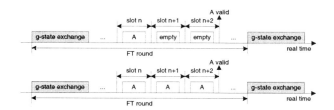

Figure 7. Transparent Fault-Tolerance Extension

Figure 7 gives an example of this. The upper part of Figure 7 shows the initial cluster setup: FT message A is non-redundant and transmitted in slot n. Slots $n + 1$ and $n + 2$ are empty slots and reserved for SRUs that will be introduced to the cluster if the redundancy type of FT message A changes. The FT layer is configured to provide A after all the slots that are assigned to or reserved for A have passed by. The lower part of Figure 7 shows the final cluster setup where A has become a TMR FT message. To achieve this, two new SRUs, both hosting a replica of the application producing a replicated message of A, are inserted into the cluster. The points in time within an FT round where the FT message A becomes valid (i.e., the FT layer provides an agreed value) are the same in the initial and the final cluster setup. In the same way as the redundancy type of an FT message can be changed in order to tolerate more failures, the redundancy type of an FT message can be transparently "downsized".

If a cluster setup is configured respecting the requirements outlined in Sections 3.1 to 3.4 and in this section, fault-tolerance of an FT message is fully transparent to both producer and consumer applications. Consequently, no component above the FT CNI in Figure 3 will have to undergo any changes. Further, changing the redundancy type of a message will also be transparent to the configuration of TTP/C. TTP/C has to provide the additional slots already upon configuration of the initial setup. It follows, that no components below the SRU CNI will have to undergo any changes either. Only the FT layer configuration may be affected if the redundancy type of an FT message changes. However, even the FT layer must only be re-configured if the application being executed above the FT CNI is either

producer or consumer of the respective message. The reserved bandwidth of a non-redundant configuration (Figure 7, upper part) can be used to transmit a replicated message in several slots. This decreases the impact of transient transmission faults.

We are aware of the fact that reserving communication bandwidth is not possible if this is the critical resource. Even if it is not possible to "waste" bandwidth by reserving slots, the FT layer presented here will not require the application implementations to undergo any changes if all timing constraints can also be satisfied in a changed setup. We expect all changes to application scheduling, FT layer configuration, and the configuration of the time-triggered communications system resulting from the change of the redundancy type of one or more FT messages to be executed by extended cluster design tools like the one described in [6]. However, we are looking forward into the future to implements of TTP/C using fiber optics that provide a bit rate of up to 1 GBit. Communication bandwidth should then be no issue any more for most applications.

The requirements on the host system presented in this section are quite restrictive. However, this static structure eases the proof that a system always operates correctly and timely, which is much harder for fully flexible distributed systems. As a consequence of this state of affairs the RTCA (Requirements and Technical Concepts for Aviation) requires the following as a minimum standard for critical airborne computer systems [16, p. 13]: "...The ACR [Avionics Computer Resource] shall include internal hardware and software management methods as necessary to ensure that time, space, and I/O allocations are deterministic and static. 'Deterministic and static' means, in this context, that time, space, and I/O allocations are determined at compilation, assembly, or link time, remain identical at each and every initialisation of a program or process, and are not dynamically altered during runtime. ..." This implies a software structure similar to the one outlined above.

4. Services of the FT Layer

This section introduces the services provided by the FT layer, the input data that are needed by the respective services, and how the FT layer services make use of the services provided by the communications system.

4.1. Message Output

If an SRU is scheduled for sending, the message output service will become active. It first assembles the TTP message by copying the replicated message produced by the application executing at the host system of this SRU from the FT CNI's producer area to the SRU CNI's message area. A replicated message is however only copied to the SRU CNI if its message status indicates that its contents are valid. After having a replicated message transferred, the contents of the message status field are reset to invalid by the FT layer. This forces the producer application to explicitly state the correctness of the replicated message before every transmission.

4.2. Message Reduction

The message reduction service is invoked in every slot (even if the SRU executing reduction sent itself in the respective slot). It inspects the FT MEDL entry of the current slot to find out which FT messages are to be reduced. Reduction of a certain FT message, say A, is performed in the same slots in every FT round. These slots may be chosen arbitrarily as long as all of the replicated messages of A being input to the message reduction service are scheduled for broadcast before the respective slots. The output of the message reduction service is a reduced FT message and the corresponding message status information. The message status of the FT message indicates whether its content is valid or not.

How reduction is performed in detail depends on the fault-tolerance type of the FT message and is outlined in the corresponding sections of the remainder of this paper. The message reduction service utilizes the communications system's message state diagnosis service.

4.3. Membership

Basically, any membership service provides information concerning the operational state of the (distributed) components of a system. Usually, this state information is mapped on to a binary value that indicates whether a component operates correctly (i.e., as expected) or not. E.g., the membership service of TTP/C indicates whether a valid frame was received from an SRU in the last sending slot assigned to this SRU.

Millinger introduces two kinds of fault-tolerant membership semantics [11]: *Association-based* and *node-based* membership. Association-based membership provides information on the status of FT messages. Node-based membership provides information on the status of an FTU as the sum of its constituting SRUs. Because in our approach there is a one-to-one mapping between SRU and message replica, the semantics of these two types of membership information are identical. Consequently, the FT message status information provided by the message reduction service equals the membership information.

4.4. Redundancy Types

This section extends the description of the FT layer services by means of describing the details of these services with respect to the supported types of redundancy. These types of redundancy differ basically in the number of failures that definitely will not lead to the loss of service of the affected FTUs.

No Redundancy of SRUs. For transparency reasons non-redundant units are treated in the same way as "real" FTUs. To tolerate any single fault the system bus of TTP/C contains replicated communication channels. This redundancy type is the only one that also allows for FT messages that do not make use of these redundant channels but only a single one. Thus, non-redundant messages may also be lost if only a single channel of the communications system fails.

However, if a non-redundant FTU makes use of the redundancy provided by the communications system, the FT layer supports it by distributing the replicated message provided by the application to the TTP/C messages for both channels.

An FT message of type *no redundancy* is correct if all the FTUs needing the FT message receive the same correct FT message. However, the receiving FTUs do not need to receive this correct FT message via the same replicated communication path (if the replicated message is transmitted on both channels of TTP/C). Otherwise the FT message is not correct.

Because non-redundant messages are produced by a single application this application does not have to be synchronized with any other application at startup. Using the initial g-state and the actual input FT message values residing in the FT CNI's consumer area suffices to produce correct replicated (output) messages.

For FT messages that are not redundant, reduction is simply copying the replicated message contained in the received TTP message to the consumer area. Besides the FT message itself the message reduction service will provide the message status information. An FT message is valid if at least one of the TTP messages supposed to contain a copy of the associated replicated message was received correctly and contains a valid replicated message. If a copy of the replicated message is transmitted correctly on both channels one will be chosen arbitrarily by the message reduction service. However, if not both of the received copies are equal, no valid FT message can be provided.

Triple Modular Redundancy. A triple-modular-redundant FTU consists of three SRUs. It can tolerate any single failure no matter whether this failure is fail-silent or not. Since the FT layer performs *exact voting*, i.e, replicated messages are considered to be identical if a bit-to-bit comparison evaluates to true [3], this property also extends to asymmetric failures [10]: even a maliciously faulty component will not cause a TMR FTU to fail as long as the remaining two components are correct. $3k + 1$ units –

where k is the number of asymmetric failures – as stated in [12] are needed to arrive at the same vector of input data at all the SRUs. However, a difference in a single element of the vector can be tolerated by the exact voting algorithm in a synchronized TMR unit. Thus, we arrive at the less stringent requirement of $2k + 1$ units stated in [9, 15] to achieve that all non-faulty SRUs arrive at the same FT message[2].

If an application produces a TMR message replica the respective replicated g-state message is also a TMR message replica. If such an application is started and there are already two other replicas of the same application active, the FT layer will provide an agreed g-state of these applications at the FT CNI's consumer area. The application is thus immediately synchronized with its replicas. If there are no other replicas active, the application will use the initial g-state as long as there is no (agreed) g-state available at the FT CNI's consumer area. If another replica is started it will find no valid g-state at the consumer area either and will use the initial g-state as well. However, both replicas will output the g-state after execution of their last instance of the current FT round, this g-state will be broadcast at the begin of the next FT round, and at the end of the g-state exchange of this next FT round the FT layer will provide an agreed g-state at the consumer area. At this point, the applications are synchronized.

In order to make TMR messages insensitive to the loss of a single channel of the communications system it is required to send one copy of a replicated message on each of the two replicated channels of TTP/C.

5. Prototype Implementation

To test the concepts, we have implemented the fault-tolerance layer presented in this paper on a dedicated TTP/C controller chip. The chip was designed to execute the TTP/C protocol but provides enough resources to implement the FT layer as well. This allows to compare the additional overhead introduced by the FT layer functionality to the execution time of the basic TTP/C protocol. The TTP/C controller has a 16 bit architecture, 64 general purpose registers, 1 KWords (2 KBytes) dual-ported RAM (DPRAM) to implement the CNI, and can store 8K instructions (16 bit each) in the instruction memory loaded from an EPROM at power-up time. The processing unit (*Protocol Control*

---

[2]However, a fundamental prerequisite for this is that TTP/C does not allow SRUs to send in any other slot than their own. Consequently, a faulty SRU *A* cannot make other SRUs believe it was SRU *B* (*source address spoofing* [2]). Further, TTP/C messages can be uniquely identified by their time of arrival. All this is a consequence of the static, off-line scheduled, and TDMA-based media access of TTP/C. To enable this access scheme TTP/C provides a Byzantine resilient global time base. However, to allow for tolerating a maliciously faulty SRU the clock synchronization algorithm requires a cluster to contain at least four SRUs.

	Message Output			Message Reduction			TTP/C
	TMR	CSR	NONE	TMR	CSR	NONE	
Static Overhead	4.35			4.35			60.00
1 Byte Message	21.60	18.80	13.45	48.20	20.60	16.00	23.50
Additional Byte	4.20	4.20	2.10	12.60	3.85	2.10	4.00
NBW Violation	2.00			-			-

Table 1. Execution Time Analysis [μs]

Unit – PCU) implements a three-stage pipeline, runs at 20 MHz, and provides 14 different instructions to manipulate the contents of the accumulator register, a "move" instruction, 14 conditional branches and an unconditional "jump" instruction. Besides this, there is a number of dedicated units (e.g., *Time Control Unit* supporting the implementation of a global time base) designed especially to ease the implementation of the TTP/C protocol.

Table 1 provides the results of an execution time analysis. The static overhead of each of the three subsystems (message output, message reduction, and TTP/C) is executed in every slot. The time needed for message output and reduction depends on the type of redundancy of the respective message (CSR stands for *communications system redundancy*, i.e., a copy of the respective message is transmitted on both channels of TTP/C). The time to process the first byte includes all the overhead to prepare the respective action. Every additional byte of message length adds a constant amount of processing time. An NBW [7] violation occurs, if the host system performs write access to a replicated message while the FT layer is copying this replicated message to the SRU CNI.

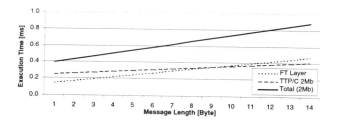

Figure 8. Execution Time Analysis

Figure 8 provides a graph that shows the execution times needed by TTP/C (transmitting at 2MBit/s), the FT layer, and the total execution time of both for TMR messages of all supported lengths from one up to 14 bytes. The graph shows that the communications system and the FT layer need approximately the same execution time. The total time is derived from adding the time to process and transmit three replicated messages and the time to reduce them to an FT message after reception of the last replica. However, the implementation of the FT layer functionality needs only about 25% the number of microprogram instructions that the basic TTP/C protocol needs.

Currently, we are working on an extension to the concept presented in this paper that allows for FTUs to share hardware resources. A single SRU may then be member of distinct FTUs and FTUs will no longer be a simple subset of SRUs of a cluster. In fact, an FTU is then only a logical cluster component that cannot be assigned in an injective manner to a subset of physical components. Furthermore, we are going to extend the set of supported redundancy types and will introduce a leader election service.

6. Conclusion

We have presented an additional layer that introduces fault-tolerance to the time-triggered architecture while preserving all the properties of the other layers. The redundancy type of a message provided by this fault-tolerance layer is fully transparent to both the producer and the consumer application of the respective message if these applications are implemented respecting the requirements outlined in Section 3. These requirements enforce the applications to perform their tasks periodically and to make their internal state externally visible.

We think that these requirements are no restrictions to distributed applications designed for the time-triggered architecture. They enforce the application programmer to explicitly state both the timing characteristics and the internal states of an application at design time. Such an explicit declaration of the internal state has also advantages, e.g., it facilitates testing of an application.

The fault-tolerance layer presented in this paper performs redundancy management in the communication controller. Data exchange with the host system is performed via a – both in the time and the value domain – fully specified interface and error propagation from the host computer system to the communication controller is prohibited by allowing no control signals passing from the host to the communications subsystem. This allows for validation and certification of the redundancy management independently of a particular application.

Acknowledgements

This work has been supported by the Austrian FWF under project No P13010-INF and by the European IST project DSoS under project No IST-1999-11585.

References

[1] M. Ahuja, A. Kshemkalyani, and T. Carlson. A basic unit of computation in distributed systems. In *The 10th International Conference on Distributed Computing Systems*, pages 12–19, June 1990.

[2] F. Cristian and C. Fetzer. The timed asynchronous distributed system model. In *Proc. of the 28th Annual International Symposium on Fault-Tolerant Computing (FTCS-28)*, pages 140–149, June 1998.

[3] H. Kopetz. *Real-Time Systems: Design Principles for Distributed Embedded Applications*. Kluwer Academic Publishers, 1997.

[4] H. Kopetz. *TTP/C Protocol*. TTTech, 1999. Available at http://www.ttpforum.org.

[5] H. Kopetz, M. Holzmann, and W. Elmenreich. A universal smart transducer interface: TTP/A. In *3rd IEEE International Symposium on Object-oriented Real-time Distributed Computing (ISORC'2000)*, June 2000. IEEE Press.

[6] H. Kopetz and R. Nossal. The Cluster Compiler — A Tool for the Design of Time-Triggered Real-Time Systems. In *ACM SIGPLAN Workshop on Languages, Compilers, and Tools for Real-Time Systems*, June 1995.

[7] H. Kopetz and J. Reisinger. The non-blocking write protocol NBW: A solution to a real-time synchronization problem. In *Proc. 14th Real-Time Systems Symposium*, Dec. 1993.

[8] J. H. Lala and R. E. Harper. Architectural principles for safety-critical real-time applications. *Proceedings of the IEEE*, 82(1):25–40, Jan. 1994.

[9] L. Lamport, R. Shostak, and M. Pease. The Byzantine generals problem. *ACM Transactions on Programming Languages and Systems*, 4(3):382–401, July 1982.

[10] J. C. Laprie. *Dependability: Basic Concepts and Terminology*. Springer Verlag, 1992.

[11] D. Millinger. *Design and Implementation of a Communication Network Interface for a Fault-Tolerance Layer*. PhD Thesis, Vienna University of Technology, Institut für Technische Informatik, Dec. 1998.

[12] M. Pease, R. Shostak, and L. Lamport. Reaching agreement in the presence of faults. *Journal of the ACM*, 27(2):228–234, Apr. 1980.

[13] S. Poledna. *Fault Tolerant Real-Time Systems: The Problem of Replica Determinism*. Kluwer Academic Publishers, 1995.

[14] D. Powell. Failure mode assumptions and assumption coverage. In *Proc. of the 22th Annual International Symposium on Fault-Tolerant Computing (FTCS-22)*, pages 386–395, July 1992.

[15] D. Powell, G. Bonn, D. Seaton, P. Verissimo, and F. Waeselynck. The Delta-4 approach to dependability in open distributed computing systems. In *Proc. of the 18th Annual International Symposium on Fault-Tolerant Computing (FTCS-18)*, pages 246–251, June 1988.

[16] Requirements and Technical Concepts for Aviation (RTCA). Minimum operational performance standards for avionics computer resource (ACR). Technical Report RTCA SC-182 / EUROCAE WG-48, RTCA/EUROCAE, June 1999.

[17] C. Scheidler, G. Heiner, R. Sasse, E. Fuchs, H. Kopetz, and C. Temple. Time-triggered architecture (TTA). In *Advances in Information Technologies: The Business Challenge*, Nov. 1997. IOS Press.

[18] J. H. Wensley, L. Lamport, J. Goldberg, M. W. Green, K. N. Levitt, P. M. Melliar-Smith, R. E. Shostak, and C. B. Weinstock. SIFT: Design and analysis of a fault-tolerant computer for aircraft control. *Proceedings of the IEEE*, 66(10):1240–1255, Oct. 1978.

Resource Scheduling in Dependable Integrated Modular Avionics

Yann-Hang Lee and Daeyoung Kim
CISE Department,
University of Florida
{yhlee, dkim}@cise.ufl.edu

Mohamed Younis, Jeff Zhou, James McElroy
Honeywell International Inc.
{mohamed.younis, jeff.zhou, james.mcelroy}
@honeywell.com

Abstract

In the recent development of avionics systems, Integrated Modular Avionics (IMA) is advocated for next generation architecture that needs integration of mixed-criticality real-time applications. These integrated applications meet their own timing constraints while sharing avionics computer resources. To guarantee timing constraints and dependability of each application, an IMA-based system is equipped with the schemes for spatial and temporal partitioning. We refer the model as SP-RTS (Strongly Partitioned Real-Time System), which deals with processor partitions and communication channels as its basic scheduling entities.

This paper presents a partition and channel-scheduling algorithm for the SP-RTS. The basic idea of the algorithm is to use a two-level hierarchical schedule that activates partitions (or channels) following a distance-constraints guaranteed cyclic schedule and then dispatches tasks (or messages) according to a fixed priority schedule. To enhance schedulability, we devised heuristic algorithms for deadline decomposition and channel combining. The simulation results show the schedulability analysis of the two-level scheduling algorithm and the beneficial characteristics of the proposed deadline decomposition and channel combining algorithms.

1. Introduction

Advances in computer and communication technology have introduced new architectures for avionics systems, which emphasize the integration of applications, dependability, and cost reduction. Away from the traditional federated implementation for avionics systems, the new approach, referred to as Integrated Modular Avionics (IMA) [1], utilizes multiple standardized processor modules in building functional components of avionics systems. It allows the applications to be merged into an integrated system. While permitting resource sharing, the approach employs temporal and spatial partitioning to set up the application boundaries needed to maintain system predictability, real-time response, and dependability [2, 6]. For the interactions between applications, it adopts a message model that can easily accommodate replicated executions of mission-critical applications.

Under the IMA architecture, each processor can host multiple partitions in which applications can be executed using the assigned resources. Spatial partitioning implies that a partition cannot access other partition's resources, like memory, buffers, and registers. On the other hand, temporal partitioning guarantees a partition's monopoly use of a pre-allocated processing time without any intervention from other partitions. Thus, a partition is the sole owner of its resources, such as memory segments, I/O devices, and processor time slots. As a result, the applications running in different partitions cannot interfere with each other. To facilitate communications between applications, each partition can be assigned with one or more communication channels. An application can transmit messages during the slots allocated to its channel and access exclusively the channel buffers. In this sense, the channels are spatial and temporal partitions of communication resource and are dedicated to one message-sending application.

An application running within a partition can be with multiple cooperating tasks. For instance, the Honeywell's Enhanced Ground Proximity Warning System (EGPWS) consists of tasks for map loading, terrain threat detection, alert prioritization, display processing, etc. With the spatial and temporal partitioning, the EGPWS application can be developed separately and then integrated with other applications running in different partitions of an IMA-based system. Its execution cannot be affected by any malfunctions of other applications (presumably developed by other manufactures) via wild writes or task overruns. However, sufficient resources must be allocated to the partition and the channels, so that the EGPWS application can ensure a proper execution and meet its real-time constraints.

One apparent advantage of IMA-based systems with spatial and temporal partitioning is that each application is running in its own environment. Thus, as long as the partition environment is not changed, an application's behavior remains constant even if other applications are modified. This leads to a crucial advantage to avionics systems, i.e. when one application is revised, other applications don't need to be re-certified by the FAA. Thus, the integration of applications in a complex system can be upgraded and maintained easily. It is conceivable that such architecture with spatial and temporal partitioning can be useful for integrating general real-time applications, and will be referred to as a strongly partitioned real-time system (SP-RTS) in the paper.

In this paper, we investigate the issues related to the partition and channel scheduling in SP-RTS. To schedule processor execution, we need to determine which partition is active and to select a task from the active partition for execution. According to temporal partitioning, time slots are allocated to partitions. Within each partition, fixed priorities are assigned to tasks based on rate-monotonic or deadline-monotonic algorithms [14, 5]. A lower priority task can be preempted by higher priority tasks of the same partition. In other words, the scheduling approach is hierarchical that partitions are scheduled following a cyclic schedule and tasks are dispatched according to a fixed priority schedule. We can conjecture a real system where partitions are processes with protected memory spaces and tasks are threads in a process. At process level, a cyclic scheduling is employed, whereas, in thread level, thread priorities are compared. The scheme doesn't need to make a global priority comparison between threads of different processes. Similar hierarchical scheduling is also applied to the communication media where channels are scheduled in a cyclic fashion and have enough bandwidth to guarantee message communication. Within each channel, messages are then ordered according to their priorities for transmission.

Given task execution characteristics, we are to determine the cyclic schedules for partitions and channels under which the computation results can be delivered before or on the task deadlines. The problem differs from the typical cyclic scheduling since, at the partition and channel levels, we don't evaluate the invocations for each individual task or message. Only aggregated task execution and message transmission models are considered. In addition, the scheduling for partitions and channels must be done collectively such that tasks can complete their computation and then send out the results without missing any deadlines.

A different two-level hierarchical scheduling scheme has been proposed by Deng and Liu in [8]. The scheme allows real-time applications to share resources in an open environment. The scheduling structure has an earliest-deadline-first (EDF) scheduling at the operating system level. The second level scheduling within each application can be either time-driven or priority-driven. For acceptance test and admission of a new application, the scheme analyzes the application schedulability at a slow processor. Then, the server size is determined and server

deadline of the job at the head of the ready queue is set at run-time. Since the scheme does not rely on fixed allocation of processor time or fine-grain time slicing, it can support various types of applications, such as release time jitters, non-predictable scheduling instances, and stringent timing requirements.

The scheduling approach for avionics applications under the APEX interface of IMA architecture was discussed by Audsley and Wellings [4]. A recurrent solution to analyze task response time in an application domain is derived and the evaluation results show that there is a potential for a large amount of release jitter. However, the paper does not address the issues of constructing cyclic schedules at the operating system level. To remedy the problem, our first step is to establish scheduling requirements for the cyclic schedules such that task schedulability under a given fixed priority schedules within each partition can be ensured. The approach we adopt is similar to the one in [8] of comparing the task execution in SP-RTS environment with that at a dedicated processor. The cyclic schedule then tries to allocate partition execution intervals by "stealing" task inactivity periods. This stealing approach resembles the slack stealer for scheduling soft-aperiodic tasks in fixed priority systems [11]. Once the schedulability requirements are obtained, suitable cyclic schedules can be constructed. Following the partitioning concept of IMA, the operating system level cyclic schedule is flexible to support system upgrade and integration. It is designed in a way that no complete revision of scheduling algorithms is required when the workload or application tasks in one partition are modified.

The rest of the paper is organized as follows. In section 2, we describe the system models that describe tasks, partition servers, messages, and channel servers in SP-RTS. Then, we show the overall system scheduling algorithm and its specific components, such as deadline decomposition, task and message schedulability checking, channel combining, and cyclic scheduling for partition servers and channel servers in section 3. Evaluation results are presented in section 4. A conclusion is then given in section 5.

2. System Models

The SP-RTS system model, as shown in Figure 1, includes multiple processors inter-connected by a time division multiplexing communication bus such as ARINC 659 [3]. Each processor has several execution partitions to which applications can be allocated. An application consists of multiple concurrent tasks that can communicate with each other within the application partition. Task execution is subject to deadlines. Each task must complete its computation and send out the result messages on time in order to meet its timing constraints.

Messages are the only form of communication among applications, regardless of whether their execution partitions are in the same processor or not. For inter-partition communication, the bandwidth of the shared communication media is distributed among all applications by assigning channels to a subset of tasks running in a partition. We assume that there are hardware mechanisms to enforce the partition environment and channel usage by each application, and to prevent any unauthorized accesses. Thus, task computation and message transmission are protected in their application domain. The mechanisms could include memory protection controller, slot/channel mapping, and separate channel buffers.

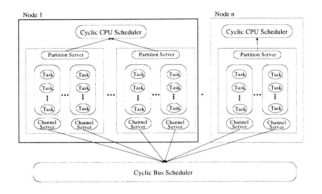

Figure 1. The architecture model for strongly partitioned real-time systems (SP-RTS)

In our task model, we assume that each task arrives periodically and needs to send an output message after its computation. Thus, as illustrated in Figure 2, tasks are specified by several parameters, including invocation period (T_i), worst-case execution time (C_i), deadline (D_i) and message size (M_i). Note that, to model sporadic tasks, we can assign the parameter T_i as the minimum inter-arrival interval between two consecutive invocations.

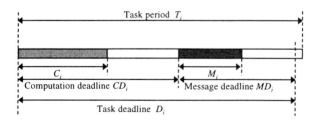

Figure 2. Task model and deadlines

In order to schedule tasks and messages at processors and communication channels, the task deadline, D_i, is decomposed into message deadline (MD_i) and computation deadline (CD_i). The assignment of message deadlines influences the bandwidth allocation for the message. For example, when the message size, M_i, is 1K slots, and the message deadline of 10ms, then the bandwidth requirement is 0.1M slots per second. In the case of the 1ms message deadline, the bandwidth requirement becomes 1M slots per second. However, a tradeoff must be made since a long message deadline implies a less amount of bandwidth to be allocated, thus the task computation has to be completed immediately.

For each processor in SP-RTS architecture, the scheduling is done in a two-level hierarchy. The first level is within each partition server where the application tasks are running and a higher priority task can preempt any lower priority tasks of the same partition. The second level is a cyclic partition schedule that allocates execution time to partition servers of the processor. In other word, each partition server, S_k, is scheduled periodically with a fixed period. We denote this period as the *partition cycle,* η_k. For each partition cycle, the server can execute the tasks in the partition for an interval $\alpha_k \eta_k$ where α_k is less than or equal to 1 and is called *partition capacity*. For the remaining interval of $(1-\alpha_k)\eta_k$, the server is blocked. In Figure 3, an example execution sequence of a partition that consists of three tasks is depicted. During each partition cycle, η_k, the tasks, τ_1, τ_2, and τ_3, are scheduled to be executed for a period of $\alpha_k \eta_k$. If there is no active task in the partition, the processor is idle and cannot run any active tasks from other partitions.

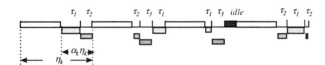

Figure 3. An illustrative task and partition execution sequence

Similarly, a two-level hierarchical scheduling method is applied to the message and channel scheduling. A channel server provides fixed-priority preemptive scheduling for messages. Then, a cyclic schedule assigns a sequence of communication slots to each channel server according to its channel cycle, μ_k, and channel capacity, β_k. A channel may send out messages using $\beta_k \mu_k$ slots during every period of μ_k slots. Note that we use the unit of "slot" to indicate both message length and transmission time, with an assumption that communication bandwidth and slot length are given. For instance, a 64-bit slot in the 30MHz 2-bit wide ARINC 659 bus [3] is equivalent to 1.0667μs, and a message of 1000 bytes will be transmitted in 125 slots. For convenience purposes, we define the conversion factors *ST* as a slot-to-time ratio based on slot length and bus bandwidth.

3. Scheduling Approach

The objective of our scheduling approach is to find feasible cyclic schedules for partition and channel servers which process tasks and transmit messages according to their fixed priorities within the servers. With proper capacity allocation and frequent invocation at each server, the combined delays of task execution and message transmission are bounded by the task deadlines. In Figure 4, we show the overall approach which first applies a heuristic deadline decomposition to divide the problem into two parts: partition-scheduling and channel-scheduling. If either one cannot be done successfully, the approach iterates with a modified deadline assignment. We also assume that the initial task set imposes a processor utilization and a bus utilization less than 100% and each task's deadline is larger than its execution time plus its message transmission time, i.e., $D_i \geq C_i + ST*M_i$ for task i.

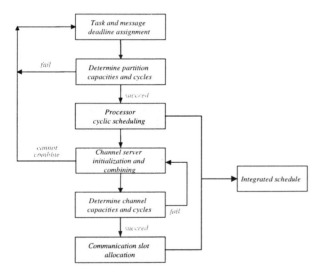

Figure 4. Combined partition and channel scheduling approach

3.1. Deadline Decomposition

It is necessary to decompose the original task deadline, D_i, into computation and message deadline, CD_i and MD_i, for every task, before we can schedule the servers for partition execution and message transmission. A deadline decomposition algorithm is used to assign these deadlines in a heuristic way. If we assign tight message deadlines, messages may not be schedulable. Similarly, if tasks have tight deadlines, processor scheduling can fail. The following equation is used to calculate the message deadline and computation deadline for each task:

Message Deadline, $MD_i = (D_i \dfrac{ST*M_i}{C_i + ST*M_i}) f_i$

Computation Deadline, $CD_i = D_i - MD_i$

where f_i is an adjusting factor for each task. The main idea of deadline decomposition is that it allocates the deadlines, CD_i and MD_i, proportionally to their time requirements needed for task execution and message transmission. In addition, the adjusting factor f_i is used to calibrate the computation and message deadlines based on the result of previous scheduling attempts and the utilization at processor and communication bus. Since the message and task deadlines must be lower-bounded to the transmission time ($ST*M_i$) and computation time (C_i), respectively, and upper-bounded to D_i, we can obtain the lower bound and upper bound of the adjusting factor f as

$$\frac{1}{D_i (\dfrac{1}{C_i + ST*M_i})} \leq f_i \leq \frac{D_i - C_i}{D_i (\dfrac{ST*M_i}{C_i + ST*M_i})}$$

Since an adjusting factor of 1.0 is a fair distribution and always included in the range of f_i, we set the initial value of f_i to be 1. The heuristic deadline decomposition, as show in Figure 5, is similar to a binary search algorithm in the attempt of finding the right proportion of task and message deadlines. If we reach the situation that it cannot assign new value for all tasks, we declare the input set of tasks as unschedulable.

Initialization for all tasks
    *MinF = 1 / (D_i * (1/(C_k+ ST*M_k)));*
    *MaxF = (D_i-C_i) / (D_i * (ST*M_i /(C_i+ ST*M_i)));*
    f_i = 1.0;

Iterative change of f_k when either partition or channel scheduling fails
    If (Partition scheduling fails) {
        MaxF = f_i; f_i = (MinF + f_i) / 2.0;
    }
    else if (Channel scheduling fails) {
        MinF = f_i; f_i = (MaxF + f_i) / 2.0;
    }

Figure 5. The deadline decomposition algorithm

3.2. Partition and Channel Scheduling

In SP-RTS, partitions and channels are cyclically scheduled. The partition cyclic schedule is based on partition cycle, η_k, and partition capacity, α_k. Similarly, a channel cyclic schedule with parameters, β_k and μ_k implies that the channel can utilize $\beta_k \mu_k$ slots during a period of μ_k slot interval. While tasks and messages are scheduled according to their priority within the periodic servers, the cyclic schedule determines the response time of task execution and message transmission. In this subsection, we give a short description of the scheduling theory that can be used to schedule the cyclic partition and channel servers. A full discussion of the scheduling theory and the associated proof are given in our previous paper [10].

Note that, at the system level, the partition server S_k is cyclically scheduled with a fixed partition cycle, η_k. For every partition cycle, the server can execute the task in partition P_k during an interval of $\alpha_k \eta_k$ where $\alpha_k \leq 1$. For the remaining interval of $(1-\alpha_k)\eta_k$, the server is blocked. Suppose that there are n tasks in partition server S_k listed in priority order such that $\tau_1 < \tau_2 < \tau_3 < ... < \tau_n$ where τ_1 has the highest priority and τ_n the lowest. According to deadline monotonic algorithm, we assume that the highest priority is given to the task with shortest task deadline. In order to evaluate the schedulability of the partition server, S_k, we first consider that the task set is executed at a dedicated processor of capacity α_k. Based on the necessary and sufficient condition of schedulability analysis [12, 13], task τ_i is schedulable if there exists a t 0 $H_i = \{CD_i \cup lT_j \mid j=1,2,...,i-1; \; l=1,2,..., \lfloor CD_i/T_j \rfloor \}$ such that:

$$W_i(\alpha_k, t) = \sum_{j=1}^{i} \frac{C_j}{\alpha_k} \left\lceil \frac{t}{T_j} \right\rceil \leq t$$

The expression $W_i(\alpha_k, t)$ indicates the worst cumulative execution time demand on the processor made by the tasks with a priority higher than or equal to τ_i during the interval $[0,t]$. We now define $B_i(\alpha_k) = max_{t \in Hi} \{t - W_i(\alpha_k, t)\}$ and $B_0(\alpha_k) = min_{i=1,2...n} B_i(\alpha_k)$, where n is the total number of tasks in the partition. Note that, when τ_i is schedulable, $B_i(\alpha_k)$ represent the total period in the interval $[0, t]$ that the processor is not running any tasks with a priority higher than or equal to that of τ_i in the partition server. $B_i(\alpha_k)$ is equivalent to the level-i inactivity period in the interval $[0, t]$ [11].

By comparing the task executions at server S_k and at a dedicated processor of capacity α_k, we can obtain the following theorem [10].

Theorem 1. *The partition server S_k is schedulable if S_k is schedulable at a dedicated processor of capacity α_k, and $\eta_k \leq B_0(\alpha_k)/(1-\alpha_k)$*

Note that $B_0(\alpha_k)$ is a non-decreasing function of α_k. There is a minimum α_k such that $B_0(\alpha_k)$ equals to zero, i.e., a zero inactive period for at least one task in the partition. The minimum α_k indicates the minimum processor capacity needed to schedule the partition. Thus,

partition scheduling can fail if the sum of the minimum α_k, for all partitions in a processor, is larger than 1.

With Theorem 1, we can depict the plot of maximum partition cycle vs. the assigned capacity α_k. To illustrate the result, we consider an example in Table 1 in which four application partitions are allocated in a processor. Each partition consists of several periodic tasks and the corresponding parameters of (C_i, T_i) are listed in the Table. Tasks are set to have deadlines equal to their periods and are scheduled within each partition according to a rate-monotonic algorithm. The processor utilization demanded by the 4 partitions, ρ_k, are 0.25, 0.15, 0.27, and 0.03, respectively.

Table 1. Task parameters for the example partitions

	Partition 1 (utilization=0.25)	Partition 2 (utilization=0.15)
tasks (C_i, T_i)	(4, 100) (9, 120) (7, 150) (15, 250) (10, 320)	(2, 50) (1, 70) (8, 110) (4, 150)
	Partition 3 (utilization=0.27)	Partition 4 (utilization=0.03)
tasks (C_i, T_i)	(7,80) (9,100) (16,170)	(1,80) (2,120)

In Figure 6, the curves $\eta_k = B_0(\alpha_k)/(1-\alpha_k)$ are plotted for the example 4 partitions. If the points below the curves are chosen to set up cyclic scheduling parameters for each partition, the tasks in the partition are guaranteed to meet their deadlines.

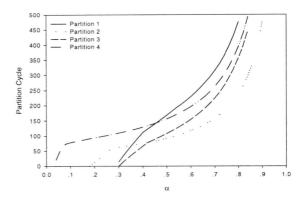

Figure 6. Partition Cycles vs. Processor Capacities for the Example Partitions

For instance, the curve for partition 2 indicates that, if the partition receives 28% of processor capacity, then its tasks are schedulable as long as its partition cycle is less than or equal to 59 time units. Note that the maximum partition cycles increase as we assign more capacity to each partition. This increase is governed by the accumulation of inactivity period when α_k is small. Then, the growth follows by a factor of $1/(1-\alpha_k)$ for a larger α_k. The curves in Figure 6 show that there are sharp rises of the maximum partition cycle when we increase α_k just beyond the minimum required capacities. The rises indicate that a small amount of extra capacity can enlarge the inactive period of a partition server significantly.

According to the design objectives, there are several methods we can use to choose a set of (α_k, η_k) for all partition servers. For instance, we can calculate the minimum α_k first. If the sum of the minimum α_k, for all partition server S_k, and the reserved portion of processor capacity, is less than 100%, the extra capacity can be allocated to all partitions proportionally to their minimum α_k. Then, η_k can be calculated based on Theorem 1. The other approach is to search for the saddle point in the $B_0(\alpha_k)/(1-\alpha_k)$ curve where the initial rise just begins to slow down. The pair (α_k, η_k) at the saddle point is used as the initial capacity allocation and partition cycle. Further increase or reduction can be done proportionally if the total capacity allocated is less than or larger than 1.

We can use the same scheduling method of the partition scheduling for channel scheduling. A channel server, G_k, transmits its messages according to a fixed priority preemptive scheduling method. It provides a bandwidth of $\beta_k\mu_k$ slots to the messages in the channel during every channel cycle, μ_k, where $\beta_k \leq 1$. For the remaining slots of $(1-\beta_k)\mu_k$, the channel server is blocked. Since each channel server follows the identical two-level hierarchical scheduling as partition servers, Theorem 1 can directly applied to obtain the pair of parameters (β_k, μ_k). However, there are several differences. First, only integer number of slots can be assigned to a channel server. Thus, we can use either $\lceil \beta_k\mu_k \rceil$ slots or restrict $\beta_k\mu_k$ to be integer. The second difference is that the message arrivals are not always periodic due to possible release jitters. Release jitters can be included in the schedulability test if they are bounded by some maximum value [15]. The release jitter can also be eliminated if the communication controller incorporates a timed message service that becomes active immediately after the computation deadline is expired. The last difference is the assignment of messages into a channel. According to the principle of partitioning, tasks from different partitions cannot share the same channel for message transmission. For the tasks in a partition, we can group a subset of tasks and let them share a channel server. The grouping can be done based on the semantics of the messages or other engineering constraints. Also, the multiplexing of messages in a shared channel may lead to a saving of bandwidth reservation. We should address this issue in the following subsection.

3.3. Channel Combining

For a channel server that transmits a periodic message with a deadline MD_i and a message size M_i, we must allocate a minimum bandwidth of M_i/MD_i. Since there is a limitation in the total bus bandwidth, we may not always assign one channel server to each message. However, we may be able to combine some messages and let them share a common channel server. This can lead to a bandwidth reduction since the reserved bandwidth can be better utilized by the messages of different deadlines. For example, given two messages 1 and 2 with parameters (M_1, MD_1, T_1) and (M_2, MD_2, T_2), respectively, the minimum bandwidth requirements, in terms of slots per time unit, for separate channels of messages 1 and 2, and for the combined channel, can be computed as following:

$$CB_1 = M_1/MD_1, \quad CB_2 = M_2/MD_2,$$
$$CB_{12} = \max\{ M_1/MD_1, (M_2+M_1* \lceil MD_2/T_1 \rceil)/MD_2 \}$$

We assume that message 1 has a higher priority than message 2 in the above computation. The cost of message preemption is ignored which can be at most one slot per preemption since we assume that slots are the basic transmission units in the communication bus. Notice that CB_{12} is not always less that CB_1+CB_2. However, if message 1 has a much shorter deadline comparing with its period and message 2 has a longer deadline than message 1's period, then the bandwidth reduction $CB_1+CB_2-CB_{12}$ becomes substantial. While we reserve a proper amount of bandwidth for an urgent message, the channel is only partially utilized if the message arrives infrequently. This provides a good chance to accommodate additional messages in the same channel and results in a reduction in the required bandwidth.

The above equation also implies that the maximum bandwidth reduction can be obtained by combining the message with a long deadline and the message with a short deadline where the period of the latter should be greater than message deadline of the former. With this observation, we devise a heuristic channel-combining algorithm which is shown in Figure 7. The computation of the minimum bandwidth requirement of a channel consisting of messages $1,2,...,k-1$, and k, is:

$$CB_{12...k} = \max_{j=1,k}\{((\sum_{i=1}^{j-1} M_i * \left\lceil \frac{MD_j}{T_i} \right\rceil + M_j)/MD_j)\}$$

where we assume that message j has a higher priority then message $j+1$. Note that the real bandwidth allocation must be determined according to the choice of channel cycle as described in Theorem 1. However, in order to calculate channel cycle and capacity, the messages in each channel must be known. The channel-combining algorithm outlined in Figure 7 is developed to allocate messages to channels for each partition and to reduce the minimum bandwidth requirement to a specific threshold. If the combined channels cannot be scheduled, we can further decrease the target threshold until no additional combining can be done.

Initialization (Channel combining is allowed to the tasks in the same partition)

Assign one channel server G_k to the message of each task

Iterate the following steps until the sum of total CB_k is less than the target threshold

determine all pair of combinable channel server G_k and G_j where the max. message deadline in G_k is larger than the min. task period in G_j

For every pair of combinable channel servers G_k and G_j {
*   calculate the bandwidth reduction $CB_k + CB_j - CB_{kj}$*
}

Combine G_j with the server G_k that results in the maximum reduction

---

Figure 7. A heuristic channel combining algorithm

3.4. Cyclic Scheduling for Partition and Channel Servers

Let a feasible set of partition capacities and cycles be $(\alpha_1, \eta_1), (\alpha_2, \eta_2), \ldots, (\alpha_n, \eta_n)$ and the set be sorted in the non-decreasing order of η_k. The set cannot be directly used in a cyclic schedule that guarantees the distance constraint of assigning α_k processor capacity for every η_k period in a partition. To satisfy the distance constraint between any two consecutive invocations, we can adopt the pinwheel scheduling approach [7, 9] and transfer $\{\eta_k\}$ into a harmonic set through a specialization operation. Note that, in [9], a fixed amount of processing time is allocated to each task and would not be reduced even if we invoke the task more frequently. This can lead to a lower utilization after the specialization operations. For our partition-scheduling problem, we allocate a certain percentage of processor capacity to each partition. When the set of partition cycles $\{\eta_k\}$ is transformed in to a harmonic set $\{h_k\}$, this percentage doesn't change. Thus, we can schedule any feasible sets of (α_k, η_k) as long as the total sum of α_k is less than 1.

A simple solution for a harmonic set $\{h_k\}$ is to assign $h_k = \eta_1$ for all k. However, since it chooses a minimal

invocation period for every partition, a substantial number of context switches between partitions could occur. A practical approach of avoiding excessive context switches is to use Han's S_X specialization algorithm with a base 2 [9]. Given a base partition cycle η, the algorithm finds a h_i for each η_i that satisfies:

$$h_i = \eta * 2^j \leq \eta_i < \eta * 2^{j+1} = 2*h_i,$$

To find the optimal base η in the sense of processor utilization, we can test all candidates η in the range of $(\eta_1/2, \eta_1]$ and compute the total capacity $\sum_k \alpha_k$. To obtain the total capacity, the set of η_k is transferred to the set of h_k based on corresponding η and then the least capacity requirement, α_k^h, for partition cycle h_k is obtained from Theorem 1. The optimal η is selected in order to minimize the total capacity. In Figure 8, we show a fixed cyclic processor scheduling example that guarantees distance constraint for the set of partition capacities and cycles, $A(0.1,12)$, $B(0.2,14)$, $C(0.1,21)$, $D(0.2,25)$, $E(0.1,48)$, and $F(0.3,50)$. We use the optimal base of 10 to convert the partition cycles to $10, 10, 20, 20, 40$, and 40, respectively.

Figure 8. Example of processor cyclic scheduling

The basic method of cyclic scheduling for channel servers is same as that of partition server scheduling. The only difference is that we need to consider that channel bandwidth allocation must be done based on integer number of slots. Let the feasible bus bandwidth capacity allocation set be $(\beta_1, \mu_1), (\beta_2, \mu_2), \ldots, (\beta_n, \mu_n)$. Using the S_X specialization, the set $\{\mu_k\}$ will be transformed to a harmonic set $\{m_k\}$. Then, based on Theorem 1 and the reduced m_k, we can adjust the channel capacity β_k to β_k^h subject to $\sum_{i=1}^{n} \lceil \beta_i^h m_k \rceil \leq m_k$. There will be $\lceil \beta_k^h m_k \rceil$ slots allocated to the channel server G_k.

4. Algorithm Evaluation

In this section, we present the evaluation results of the proposed algorithms for SP-RTS. First, we show the percentage of schedulable task sets in terms of processor and bus utilization under the two-level scheduling, deadline decomposition and channel combining algorithms. Then, we show that the penalty of the

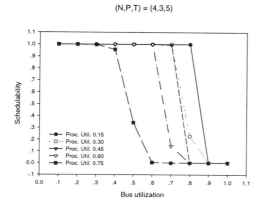

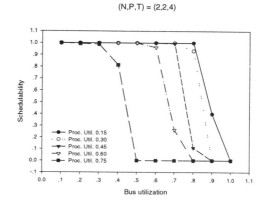

Figure 9. Schedulability test for configurations (4, 3, 5) and (2, 2, 4)

harmonic transformation even if channel server scheduling is negligibly small. Finally, the characteristic behavior of deadline decomposition is illustrated. The evaluations are done with random task and message sets that are generated with specific processor and bus utilization.

4.1. Schedulability Test

A schedulability test of the algorithm is obtained using the simulations of a system model that composes of four processors, three partitions per each processor and five tasks per each partition, i.e., a configuration of (4, 3, 5). The simulations use random task sets that result in variable processor utilization of 15%, 30%, 45%, 60% and 75%. The task periods are uniformly distributed between the minimum and maximum periods. The total processor utilization is randomly distributed to all tasks in each processor and is used to compute the task execution times. To create message sets, we vary the total bus utilization from 10% to 90%. Message lengths are computed with a random distribution of the total bus utilization and task periods.

Using the scheduling procedure of Figure 4, we first assign task and message deadlines for each task. Then the partition capacity and cycle for each partition are computed and the cyclic schedule for each processor is constructed. To schedule message transmission, messages are combined into channels in order to reduce bandwidth requirement. After channel cycle and capacity are determined, a cyclic schedule is formed. For the priority schedules within partitions and channels, we adopt the deadline monotonic approach to order the task and message priorities. With all randomly created task sets, we report the percentage of schedulable task sets among

all sets in Figure 9. The figure shows the algorithms are capable of finding proper deadline assignments and, then, determining feasible partition and channel cyclic schedules. For instance, consider the case of 60% processor and bus utilization. Even if the deadlines are less than task periods, almost 100% of task sets are schedulable. Figure 9 also reports the test results of the configuration (2, 2, 4). The curves have the similar trends as that of the configuration of (4, 3, 5).

4.2. The Effects of Deadline Decomposition and Channel Combining Algorithm

It is worthy to look into how the bus is utilized in the channel schedules resulted from the heuristic algorithms of deadline decomposition and channel combining. Consider the following measures:

1. *Measure1* is the bus utilization which equals to the sum of $(ST*M_i)/T_i$ for all tasks. No real-time constraint of message delivery is considered in this measure.

2. *Measure2* is the total bus capacity needed to transmit messages on time with no channel combining (i.e., each task has a dedicated channel). This capacity will be equal to the summation of $(ST*M_i)/MD_i$ for all tasks and can be computed after message deadlines are assigned.

3. *Measure3* is the minimum bus capacity needed to schedule channels. This measure is equal to the summation of minimum β_k for all channels. Note that, according to Theorem 1, the minimum β_k for a channel is defined as the minimum capacity that results in a zero inactive period for

at least one message in the channel. It can be determined after message deadlines are assigned and messages are combined into the channel.

4. *Measure4* is the total bus capacity selected according to Theorem 1. This measure can be formulated as the summation of β_k for all channels.

5. *Measure5* is the final bus capacity allocated to all channels based on a harmonic set of channel cycles and the integer number of slots for each channel. The capacity is equal to the summation of $\lceil \beta_k^h m_k \rceil / m_k$ for all channels.

We can expect an order of *Measure2> Measure5> Measure4> Measure3> Measure1* among the measures. *Measure2* should be much higher than other measures as we allocate bandwidth for each message independently to ensure on schedule message delivery. With the message multiplexing within each channel, the on schedule message delivery can be achieved with a less amount of bandwidth. However, a bandwidth allocation following *Measure3* cannot be practical since the channel cycles must be infinitely small. According to Theorem 1, *Measure4* contains additional capacity that is added to each channel to allow temporary blocking of message transmission during each channel cycle. Furthermore, in *Measure5*, an extra capacity is allocated as we make integer number of slots for each channel and construct a cyclic schedule with harmonic periods.

The simulation results of the above measures are shown in Figure 10. The results confirm our expectation of the order relationship. However, when we change the bus utilization from 0.1 to 0.8, the curves are not monotonically increasing (except the curve of *Measure1*). This is the consequence of the deadline decomposition (*DD*) algorithm. When channels don't have enough bandwidth to meet short message deadlines, the algorithm adjusts the factor f_k and assigns longer deadlines for message transmission. As shown in Figure 5, the *DD* algorithm uses an approach similar to binary search algorithm and makes a big increase to f_k initially. This results in long deadlines and the reduced capacity allocations in *Measure2-5*. In fact, when the bus utilization is less than 30%, the average number of iterations performed in the *DD* algorithm is slightly larger than 1, i.e., only the initial f_k is used to allocate deadlines. When the bus utilization is raised to 40% to 70%, the average number of iterations jumps to 1.6, 1.98, 2.0, and 2.04, respectively. It further increases to 11.09 when the bus utilization is set to 80%.

Figure 10 also illustrates the magnitude of the measures and the differences among them. The gap between *Measure3* and *Measure2* is very visible. This difference is the product of channel combining algorithm. In order to meet a tight message deadline, we have to

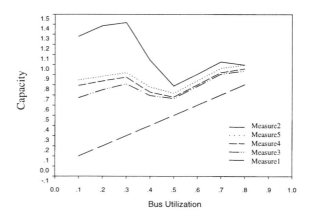

Figure 10. Measures for Bus Utilization and Capacities

reserve a large amount of bandwidth. With channel combining, messages of different deadlines share the allocated slots. As long as the message with a shorter deadline can preempt the on-going transmission, the slots in each channel can be fully utilized by multiplexing and prioritizing message transmissions. There is a moderate gap between *Measure3* and *Measure4*. As indicated in Theorem 1, we search for a channel capacity and a channel cycle located in the knee of the curve $\eta_k \leq B_0(\alpha_k)/(1-\alpha_k)$ after the initial sharp rise. This implies that a small increase of β_k will be added to *Measure3* in order to obtain a reasonable size of channel cycle. Finally, the difference between *Measure4* and *Measure5* is not significant at all. It is caused by the process of converting η_k to a harmonic cycle m_k, and by allocating an integer number of slots $\lceil \beta_k^h m_k \rceil$ for each channel.

The other way of looking into the behavior of the deadline decomposition algorithm is to investigate the resultant decomposition of task deadline, D_i. In Figure 11, we showed the average ratio of message deadline to task deadline, under different processor and bus utilization. If the adjustment factor f_i is constant, the ratio,

$$\frac{MD_i}{D_i} = (\frac{ST * M_i}{C_i + ST * M_i})f_i,$$

should follows a concave curve as we increase bus utilization (by increasing message length, M_i). For instance, when the processor utilization is 15%, there are two segments of concave curves from bus utilization 10% to 70% and from 70% to 90%. The segmentation indicates a jump in the adjustment factors resulted from the deadline decomposition algorithm. In Figure 11, the concavity and the segmentation can also be seen in other curves that represent the message deadline ratios of different processor utilization. When the processor utilization is high, f_i may be modified gradually and partition scheduling may fail if we introduce a sharp increase to f_i. Thus, the concavity and the segmentation are not so obvious as the deadline ratio in an underutilized processor.

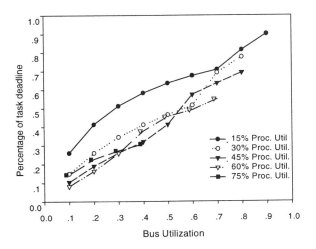

Figure 11. The ratio of message deadline to task deadline

5. Conclusion

In this paper, we present several algorithms in order to produce cyclic partition and channel schedules for the two-level hierarchical scheduling mechanism of IMA-based avionics systems. The system model of the IMA architecture supports spatial and temporal partitioning in all shared resources. Thus, applications can be easily integrated and maintained.

The main idea of our approach is to allocate a proper amount of capacity and to follow a distance constraint on partition and channel invocations. Thus, the tasks (messages) within a partition (channel) can have an inactive period longer than the blocking time of the partition (channel). Also we use a heuristic deadline decomposition technique to find feasible deadlines for both tasks and messages. To reduce bus bandwidth requirement for message transmission, we develop a heuristic channel-combining algorithm which leads to highly utilized channels by multiplexing messages of different deadlines and periods. The simulation analyses show promising results in terms of schedulability and system characteristics.

Based on the work in this paper, we have developed a scheduling tool for the IMA-based avionics systems. The tool includes additional features for practical implementations, such as time-tick based processor scheduling, non-zero context switch overhead, replication

execution and transmission, incremental changes, etc. We are currently looking into different network infrastructures and communication scheduling algorithms that can be employed in the scalable IMA-based systems.

References

[1] "Design Guide for Integrated Modular Avionics," ARINC Report 651, Aeronautical Radio Inc., Annapolis, MD, Nov. 1991.

[2] "Avionics Application Software Standard Interface," ARINC Report 653, Aeronautical Radio Inc., Annapolis, MD, Jan. 1997.

[3] "Backplane Data Bus," ARINC Specification 659, Aeronautical Radio Inc., Annapolis, MD, Dec. 1993.

[4] N. Audsley, and A. Wellings, "Analyzing APEX applications," *Proc. IEEE Real-Time Systems Symposium*, Dec. 1996, pp. 39-44.

[5] N. Audsley, A. Burns, M. Richardson, and A. Wellings, "Hard real-time scheduling: the deadline-monotonic approach," *Eighth IEEE Workshop on Real-time Operating Systems and Software*, 1991, pp. 133-137.

[6] T. Carpenter, "Avionics Integration for CNS/ATM," *Computer*, Dec. 1998, pp. 124-126.

[7] M. Y. Chan and F. Y. L. Chin, "General schedulers for the pinwheel problem based on double-integer reduction," *IEEE Trans. on Computers*, vol. 41, June 1992, pp. 755-768.

[8] Z. Deng and J. W. S. Liu, "Scheduling real-time applications in an open environment," *Proc. IEEE Real-Time Systems Symposium*, Dec. 1997, pp. 308-319.

[9] C.-C. Han, K.-J. Lin, and C.-J. Hou, "Distance-constrained scheduling and its applications to real-time systems," *IEEE Trans. on Computers*, Vol. 45, No. 7, July, 1996, pp. 814--826.

[10] Y. H. Lee, D. Kim, M. Younis, and J. Zhou, "Partition scheduling in APEX runtime environment for embedded avionics software," *Proc. of Real-Time Computing Systems and Applications*, Oct. 1998, pp. 103-109.

[11] J. Lehoczky and S. Ramos-Thuel, "An optimal algorithm for scheduling soft-aperiodic tasks in fixed-priority preemptive systems," *Proc. IEEE Real-Time Systems Symposium*, Dec. 1992, pp. 110-123.

[12] J. Lehoczky, L. Sha, and Y.Ding, "The rate-monotonic scheduling algorithm: exact characteristics and average case behavior," *Proc. IEEE Real-Time Systems Symposium*, Dec. 1989, pp. 166-171.

[13] J. Lehoczky, "Fixed priority scheduling for periodic task sets with arbitrary deadlines," *Proc. IEEE Real-time Systems Symposium*, Dec. 1990, pp. 201-209.

[14] C. L. Liu and J. W. Layland, "Scheduling algorithms for multiprogramming in a hard real-time environment," *JACM*, vol. 20, No. 1, 1973, pp.46-61.

[15] K. W. Tindell, A. Burns, and A. J. Wellings, "An extendible approach for analyzing fixed priority hard real-time tasks," *Real-Time Systems 6(2)*, 1994, pp. 133-151.

Executable Assertions for Detecting Data Errors in Embedded Control Systems[*]

Martin Hiller
Department of Computer Engineering
Chalmers University of Technology
SE-412 96, Göteborg, SWEDEN
hiller@ce.chalmers.se

Abstract

In order to be able to tolerate the effects of faults, we must first detect the symptoms of faults, i.e. the errors. This paper evaluates the error detection properties of an error detection scheme based on the concept of executable assertions aiming to detect data errors in internal signals. The mechanisms are evaluated using error injection experiments in an embedded control system. The results show that using the mechanisms allows one to obtain a fairly high detection probability for errors in the areas monitored by the mechanisms. The overall detection probability for errors injected to the monitored signals was 74%, and if only errors causing failure are taken into account we have a detection probability of over 99%. When subjecting the target system to random error injections in the memory areas of the application, i.e., not only the monitored signals, the detection probability for errors that cause failure was 81%.

Keywords: signal classification scheme, executable assertions, error detection, software implemented fault tolerance, fault injection

1. Introduction

Fault-tolerance is no longer required only in high-end systems such as aircraft, nuclear power plants or spacecraft. Consumer products, such as automobiles, are increasingly dependent on electronics and software and require low-cost techniques for achieving fault-tolerance. Low-cost in this sense means that these techniques are inexpensive to develop and that the product is (relatively) inexpensive to produce.

The first step in tolerating the effects of faults is to detect the symptoms of faults, i.e. the errors. Several techniques and methods have been proposed for error detection. An NVP-style approach to error detection is achieved by running several versions or variants of the system in parallel and then compare their results [1]. If the results differ, an error must have occurred in at least one of the versions. This approach is very effective but tends to be also very expensive. A more inexpensive way of error detection is to explicitly check for errors in the system-state. Several techniques for such self-tests have been proposed (e.g. [2][3][4]), but in many cases little is known about their effectiveness.

Most self-tests are based on the concept of executable assertions [5][6]. Executable assertions are commonly statements, which can be made about the variables in a program. These statements are executed in on-line tests to see if they hold true. If they do not, an error has occurred and processes for assessment and recovery may be invoked. In addition to on-line error detection, executable assertions may be used during the development of a system for testing purposes [7] and to assess the vulnerability of the system.

Self-tests, as for instance executable assertions, also play major roles in software fault tolerance structures such as Recovery Blocks (RB) [8] and its variants (e.g. Consensus RB [9] and Distributed RB [10]), and other structures (e.g. N Self-Checking Components [11], N Copy Programming or Retry Blocks [12]).

The effectiveness of executable assertions is highly application dependant. In order to develop tests with high error detection coverage, the developers require extensive knowledge of the system. Introducing rigorous ways of defining the statements used for executable assertions, or even better, providing generic mechanisms that can be instantiated by parameters alone, reduce the importance of this drawback.

This paper evaluates the detection capabilities of error

---

[*] This research was supported by Volvo and by the National Board for Industrial and Technical Development (NUTEK), Sweden, under contract 1P21-97-4745.

detection mechanisms based on the executable assertion concept, that work on a signal-basis, meaning that only one signal/variable is tested in each individual test routine. The paper also proposes a defined process for incorporating the mechanisms into a system.

In order to evaluate the error detection capabilities of the proposed mechanisms we performed a case study using error injection experiments on an embedded system used for arresting aircraft on a runway. The aim of this study was to investigate the probability of detecting erroneous states induced by internal data errors. We also measured the detection latency as being the time from the first injection of an error to the first detection. Even though the error detection mechanisms may detect errors induced by software faults as well as hardware faults, the case study concentrates on errors induced by hardware faults.

The results show that given that an error is present in a monitored signal, and that this error leads to system failure, the detection probability is over 99%. For error injections into random locations in the memory areas of the target system, the errors that caused system failure were detected with a probability of over 81%. The presented technique is therefore a viable candidate for error detection with reasonably high detection coverage if costs have to be kept low.

Section 2 contains a description of the error detection scheme used for this evaluation. Section 3 describes the case study and the results of the experiments are shown in section 4. Section 5 consists of a discussion of the obtained results and section 6 summarises the study.

2. Executable assertions

Error detection in the form of executable assertions can potentially detect any error in internal data caused by either software faults or hardware faults [13]. When input data arrive at a functional block (e.g. a function or procedure), they are subjected to executable assertions determining whether they are acceptable. Output data from calculations may also be tested to see if the results seem acceptable. Should an error be detected, measures can be taken to recover from the error, and the signal can be returned to a valid state.

2.1. Signal classification

One of the main drawbacks of executable assertions, and indeed of all kinds of acceptance tests, is that they are very application specific. One way of lessening the impact of this specificity is to devise a rigorous way of classifying the data that are to be tested. A classification scheme will

help when determining the valid domain for the signals. The classification scheme used in this investigation is shown in Figure 1. Below is a description of the classification scheme.

The two main categories in the classification scheme are continuous and discrete signals. These categories have subcategories that further classify the signal. For every signal class we can set up a specific set of constraints, such as boundary values and rate limitations, which are then used in the executable assertions. In order to enable a signal to have different behaviours during different modes of operation in the system, a signal may have one set of constraints for each such mode. Which constraints are to be used is defined by the current mode of the signal.

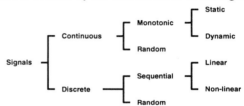

Figure 1. Signal classification scheme.

Error detection is performed as a test of the constraints. A violation of a constraint is interpreted as the detection of an error.

Continuous signals. The continuous signals are often used to model signals in the environment that are of continuous nature. Such signals are typically representations of physical signals such as temperatures, pressures or velocities.

The continuous signals can be divided into monotonic and random continuous signals. Monotonic signals must either increase or decrease their value monotonically and cannot, for example, increase between the first and the second test and then decrease between the second and the third test. However, they may be allowed to remain unchanged between tests. The monotonic signals can have either a static rate or a dynamic rate. A signal with static rate must either increase or decrease its value with a given constant rate. A signal with dynamic rate, however, can change at any rate that is within the specified range. The random continuous signals may decrease or increase (or remain unchanged) between tests (that is, they may randomly increase or decrease between tests).

Also, a signal may be allowed to wrap around, i.e. when it has reached its maximum or minimum value, it may continue "on the other side". This is visualised in Figure 2, which shows examples of the three types of continuous signals.

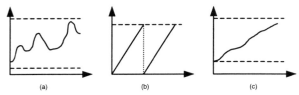

Figure 2. Continuous signals: (a) random, (b) static monotonic (with wrap-around), (c) dynamic monotonic

For the proposed error detection and recovery mechanisms, we assign to each continuous signal a set P_{cont} containing seven different parameters: s_{max} (maximum value), s_{min} (minimum value), $r_{min,incr}$ (minimum increase rate), $r_{max,incr}$ (maximum increase rate), $r_{min,decr}$ (minimum decrease rate), $r_{max,decr}$ (maximum decrease rate), and w (wrap-around allowed/not allowed). Each of these signal classes imposes certain constraints on the parameters, as shown in Table 1.

Table 1. Parameter constraints for continuous signal classes.

Signal class	Parameters
All	$s_{max} > s_{min}$, w = allowed/not allowed
Static monotonic	$(r_{max,incr} = r_{min,incr} = 0, r_{max,decr} = r_{min,decr} > 0)$ or $(r_{max,decr} = r_{min,decr} = 0, r_{max,incr} = r_{min,incr} > 0)$
Dynamic monotonic	$(r_{max,incr} = r_{min,incr} = 0, r_{max,decr} > r_{min,decr} \geq 0)$ or $(r_{max,decr} = r_{min,decr} = 0, r_{max,incr} > r_{min,incr} \geq 0)$
Random	$r_{max,incr} \geq r_{min,incr} \geq 0, r_{max,decr} \geq r_{min,decr} \geq 0$

For statically increasing monotonic signals the change rate limits for decrease are set to zero (i.e. $r_{min,decr} = r_{max,decr} = 0$) and the change rate limits for increase are set to the same value (i.e. $r_{min,incr} = r_{max,incr} > 0$). For a statically decreasing signal, instead the increase rate limits are set to zero and the increase rates are both set to the same value. For random continuous signals we have different values for the change rate limits (i.e. $r_{min,incr} \neq r_{max,incr}$ and/or $r_{min,decr} \neq r_{max,decr}$). These parameters are static, but dynamic constraints as in [4] and [14] may also be considered.

Discrete signals. Discrete signals are allowed to take on a set of discrete values. They often contain information on the settings on an operator panel or the operation mode of the system. Actually, all signals containing some kind of state information internal or external to the system may be classified as discrete signals. For instance, execution sequences that must be followed in a certain order, or state machines with a number of states and a number of transitions between the states, may be modelled as discrete signals. The discrete signals are divided into sequential and random signals.

A sequential signal has constraints on how it may change its value from any given other value, i.e. the order of change is restricted. They are divided into linear and non-linear signals. Linear signals must traverse their valid domain in a fixed predefined order, one value after another. For instance, the execution sequence mentioned above could be modelled as a linear signal. Non-linear signals traverse their valid domain in predefined ways. The random signals are allowed to make any transition from one value to another within the valid domain of the signal.

For the proposed error detection mechanisms we assign to each signal a set P_{disc} containing the following parameters: D (the set of valid values) and $T(d)$ (the set of valid transitions from element d in D; there is one set for each element in D).

A typical example of a discrete signal is a state variable. From any given state, the variable may be set to a (fixed) number of other states. Consider for example the state diagram shown in Figure 3. There are five states ($v1$ through $v5$) and a number of transitions between these states. The valid domain is therefore $D = \{v1, v2, v3, v4, v5\}$ and the transition sets are $T(v1) = \{v2, v4\}$, $T(v2) = \{v3, v4\}$, $T(v3) = \{v4\}$, $T(v4) = \{v5\}$, and $T(v5) = \{v1\}$.

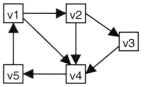

Figure 3. Example state diagram for a non-linear sequential discrete signal.

Signal modes. The behaviour of a signal may differ between different phases of operation of the system. Therefore, a signal can have different modes. A specific set of constraints is generated for each such mode, i.e. a signal with several modes has one parameter set P_{cont} or P_{disc} for each mode. The set used in a certain mode m is $P_{cont}(m)$ or $P_{disc}(m)$. Mode variables (m in this case) can be classified as discrete signals in themselves, so that error detection may be implemented for them as well.

Modes may also be used to model certain dependencies between signals. That is, if the behaviour of signal A is limited due to the operational mode of signal B, these two signals can be grouped by means of signal modes representing this dependency. Furthermore, using different modes may increase the possibility of detecting errors.

2.2. Error detection

Error detection is performed using the configuration parameters of the signals to build executable assertions. An error in a signal is detected as soon as the signal violates the constraints given by the configuration parameters. The executable assertions for continuous and discrete signals are shown in Tables 2 and 3, respectively. In these tables, s is the current signal value and s' is the previous signal value.

Table 2. Executable assertions for continuous signals

Signal status	Test No.	Assertion	Description
-	1	$s \leq s_{max}$	Maximum value
	2	$s \geq s_{min}$	Minimum value
$s > s'$	3a	$s - s' \leq r_{max,incr} \wedge$ $s - s' \geq r_{min,incr}$	Within increase parameters
	4a	$w = $ allowed $\wedge$ $(s' - s_{min}) + (s_{max} - s) \leq r_{max,decr} \wedge$ $(s' - s_{min}) + (s_{max} - s) \geq r_{min,decr}$	Wrap-around is allowed and within decrease parameters
$s < s'$	3b	$s' - s \leq r_{max,decr} \wedge$ $s' - s \geq r_{min,decr}$	Within decrease parameters
	4b	$w = $ allowed $\wedge$ $(s_{max} - s') + (s - s_{min}) \leq r_{max,incr} \wedge$ $(s_{max} - s') + (s - s_{min}) \geq r_{min,incr}$	Wrap-around is allowed and within increase parameters
$s = s'$	3c	$r_{min,incr} = 0 \wedge$ $r_{max,incr} = 0 \wedge$ $r_{min,decr} = 0$	Monotonically decreasing signal and within decrease parameters
	4c	$r_{min,decr} = 0 \wedge$ $r_{max,decr} = 0 \wedge$ $r_{min,incr} = 0$	Monotonically increasing signal and within increase parameters
	5c	$\neg (r_{min,decr} = 0 \wedge r_{max,decr} = 0) \wedge$ $\neg (r_{min,incr} = 0 \wedge r_{max,incr} = 0) \wedge$ $(r_{min,incr} = 0 \vee r_{min,decr} = 0)$	Random signal and within parameters

For continuous signals, there are different validity constraints depending on the relationship between s and s', as indicated by the *Signal status* column. Each set of tests is performed in the order given by the *Test No.* column. The *Assertion* column contains the assertions that the signals must pass. In the *Description* column is a short description of the implications of passing a particular test.

Each time a signal is tested, it is subjected to at most five assertions. The first two tests, Test No. 1 and 2, are always used, regardless of the signal status, whereas the remaining tests are chosen depending on the relationship between the previous signal value and the current signal value. If either of the first two tests fails, the entire test fails. However, if the first two tests are passed, only one of the remaining assertions must be fulfilled.

Table 3. Executable assertions for discrete signals

Signal class	Assertion	Comment
Random	$s \in D$	
Sequential	$s \in D$	
	$s \in T(s')$	*This property actually implies that $s \in D$, but both tests are used nonetheless.*

For discrete signals, the assertions are always executed. If a constraint is violated, the corresponding recovery mechanism is used and the test is terminated.

Since the mechanisms for error detection are general algorithms that are instantiated with parameters, it is possible to formally verify the algorithms, which can totally eliminate the probability of faults in them, although faulty parameters may still be a problem. However, the parameters may be calibrated using fault injection experiments.

2.3. Location and parameters

A number of different methods may be used to determine which signals should be monitored and where the executable assertions should be placed. From system design, the software should already be divided into functional blocks. In safety-critical systems, FMECA (Failure Mode Effect and Criticality Analysis) is widely used as a method for identifying the safety critical parts of the system and assessing the consequences of failures in these parts.

Parameter information may be obtained by the characteristics of the system itself. For instance, sensors naturally have a time constant dictating the maximum rate of change for the data provided by that sensor. Properties of the physical surroundings of the systems are also a source of parameter values. For discrete signals, typical sources of information are allowed settings on user panels, or internal state machines.

The process of gathering information for parameter values for executable assertions forces developers to review the system they have developed. This may assist in identifying contradicting specifications and/or parts that have not yet been properly analysed. The following is our proposed process for equipping a system with error detection mechanisms as described in this paper:

1. Identify the input and output signals of the system.
2. Identify the signal pathways from each input signal through the system and to one or more output signals.
3. Identify internally generated signals that have a direct influence on intermediate and output signals.
4. Determine which of the identified signals are the most crucial for flawless operation of the system and should therefore be monitored by error detection mechanisms, e.g. by using FMECA.
5. Classify each signal found in (4) according to the scheme described above.
6. Determine values for the characterising parameters of the signals. Remember that a signal may behave differently for different modes of operation in the system.
7. Decide on locations for the mechanisms.
8. Incorporate the mechanisms in the system.

2.4. Error detection coverage

The detection coverage that may be obtained with these mechanisms is very dependent on the characteristics of the errors that may occur. If we, given that an error has occurred, define the probabilities $P_{em} = \text{Pr}\{$error location is in a monitored signal$\}$, $P_{en} = \text{Pr}\{$error location is *not* in a monitored signal$\} = 1 - P_{em}$, $P_{prop} = \text{Pr}\{$error propagates to a monitored signal$\}$, and $P_{ds} = \text{Pr}\{$an error is detected given that the error is located in a monitored signal$\}$. The total probability of detecting an error that is present can than be written as $P_{detect} = (P_{en}P_{prop} + P_{em})P_{ds}$. For a given system, the probability P_{ds} can be assessed separately from the other probabilities and is independent of the probability distributions for error occurrence and error location. A common way of performing such an assessment is by conducting error injection experiments. We have performed a case study to assess P_{detect} and P_{ds} for a given target system (see the following sections).

3. Case study

As an assessment of the effectiveness of the error detection mechanisms when employed in an embedded control system, we conducted an evaluation using error injection.

3.1. Target system

The target system is an aircraft-arresting system resembling those found on runways and aircraft carriers. The purpose of this system is to assist incoming aircraft in reducing their velocity to a complete halt. The specifications of the system are based on specifications found in [15]. Our experiments were performed on an actual implementation of this system, i.e. no simulations (other than environment simulations) were used.

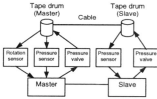

Figure 4. The experiment target: an aircraft arresting system.

System overview. The system consists of a cable strapped between two tape drums, one on each side of the runway (see Figure 4). Two computer nodes control the drums: one master node and one slave node. An incoming aircraft catches the cable by means of a hook, and a rotation sensor on the master drum periodically tells the master node the length of the pulled out cable. The master node calculates the set point pressure to be applied to the drums by means of hydraulic pressure valves. The pressure slows the rotation of the drums and brings the aircraft to a halt. The slave node receives its set point pressure value from the master node and applies this to its drum. Pressure sensors on the valves give feedback to their respective nodes about the pressure that is actually being applied so that a software-implemented PID-regulator can keep the actual pressure as close to the set point as possible.

Software overview. The software of the master node of the system consists of a number of periodic processes and one main background process. An overview of the basic software architecture can be seen in Figure 5.

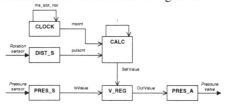

Figure 5. The basic software architecture.

CLOCK provides a clock, *mscnt*, with one millisecond resolution. The signal *ms_slot_nbr* tells the module scheduler (which is a part of the CLOCK module) which the current slot is. The system operates in seven 1-ms-slots. In each slot, one or more of the other modules (except for CALC) are invoked.

DIST_S monitors the rotation sensor and provides a total count of the pulses, *pulscnt*, generated during the arrestment. The rotation sensor reads the number of pulses generated by a tooth wheel on the tape drum.

CALC (which is the main background process) uses the signals *mscnt* and *pulscnt* to calculate a set point value for the pressure valves, *SetValue*, at six predefined checkpoints along the runway. The distance between these checkpoints is constant, and they are detected by comparing the current *pulscnt* with internally stored *pulscnt*-values corresponding to the various checkpoints. The number of the current checkpoint is stored in the checkpoint counter, *i*.

PRES_S monitors the pressure sensor measuring the pressure that is actually being applied by the pressure valves. This value is provided in the signal *IsValue*.

V_REG uses the signals *SetValue* and *IsValue* to control *OutValue*, the output value to the pressure valve. *OutValue* is based on *SetValue* and then modified to compensate for the difference between *SetValue* and *IsValue*. This module contains the software implemented PID-regulator.

PRES_A uses the *OutValue* signal to set the pressure valve.

All modules are periodic except for CALC, which runs when the other modules are dormant, i.e., it runs in the background. CLOCK and DIST_S both have a period of 1 ms and the other modules have periods of 7 ms.

The software of the slave node is slightly different from that of the master node. No calculations of set point values for the applied pressure are performed. The slave node simply receives a set point value from the master node, which it then applies to its tape drum. The modules existing also in the slave node are PRES_S, V_REG, CLOCK, and PRES_A. The modules DIST_S and CALC are not present.

Failure classification. The specifications from which the system is implemented [15] clearly dictate certain physical constraints, which the system must honour. These constraints are that the retardation must not exceed a certain limit in order to not affect either the plane or the pilot in a negative way, and that the force applied to the aircraft by the cable must not exceed certain limits in order to not endangering the aircraft. Also, the length of the runway is limited. However, this constraint may vary from instalment to instalment. The constraints are as follows:

1. Retardation (*r*). The retardation of the aircraft shall not have a negative effect on the pilot. Constraint: $r < 2.8g$

2. Retardation force (F_{ret}). The retarding force shall not exceed the structural limitations of the aircraft. Constraint: $F_{ret} < F_{max}$. The maximum allowed forces (F_{max}) are defined for several aircraft masses and engaging velocities in [15]. Force constraints for combinations of masses and velocities other than those given in [15] are obtained using interpolation and extrapolation.

3. Stopping distance (*d*). The braking distance of the aircraft shall not exceed the length of the runway. Constraint: $d < 335$ m

A violation of one or more of these constraints is defined as a failure. This is a pessimistic failure classification, in the sense that not all arrestments which according to this classification were failures would have turned out to be critical in reality. For instance, in most cases a retardation of up to $3g$ will not significantly damage the aircraft or injure the pilot. The duration of a typical, failure-free, arrestment ranges from about 5 seconds (low kinetic energy) up to about 15 seconds (high kinetic energy).

3.2. Software instrumentation

Using the process described in section 2.3, we identified 7 signals (of a total of 24 signals) in the target system that are service critical, i.e. essential for providing proper service. The signals are shown in Figure 5. The classifications of the signals are seen in Table 4.

Table 4. Classification of the signals.

Signal	Producer	Consumer	Test location	Class
SetValue	CALC	V_REG	V_REG	Co/Ra
IsValue	PRES_S	V_REG	V_REG	Co/Ra
i	CALC	CALC	CALC	Co/Mo/Dy
pulscnt	DIST_S	CALC	DIST_S	Co/Mo/Dy
ms_slot_nbr	CLOCK	CLOCK	CLOCK	Di/Se/Li
mscnt	CLOCK	CALC	CLOCK	Co/Mo/St
OutValue	V_REG	PRES_A	PRES_A	Co/Ra

In Table 4, the *Producer* is the originating module of a signal, the *Consumer* is the receiving module, and the *Test*

Location is where the executable assertions were placed. The *Class* is how the signal was classified (Co = continuous, Ra = random, Mo = monotonic, St = static rate, Dy = dynamic rate, Di = discrete, Se = sequential, Li = linear).

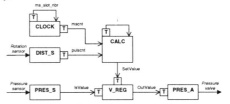

Figure 6. The locations of the executable assertions

Using these classifications, we constructed executable assertions as described in section 2. The locations of these assertions are shown in Figure 6 above (the small boxes with T's inside).

3.3. Fault injection environment

As seen in Figure 7, the target system was hooked up to the fault injection experiment system FIC^3 (Fault Injection Campaign Control Computer, see [16] for details).

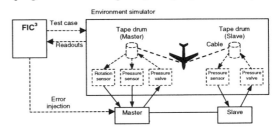

Figure 7. The FIC3 and the target system.

The FIC^3 is capable of injecting errors into the target system by means of SWIFI (SoftWare Implemented Fault Injection). Specifically, before initiating an experiment run, the FIC^3 downloads error parameters to an injection interrupt routine in the target system, which is then, during the experiment run, triggered by the FIC^3 when the actual injection is to be performed. The error detection mechanisms report detection by setting a digital output pin on the target processor high. This is detected by the FIC^3, which records and time-stamps the event. The injected errors consist of modifications of the memory areas where variables and signal values are stored. Previous studies have shown that injecting bit-flips into a system using SWIFI closely resembles the behaviour of hardware failures [17]. The downloaded injection parameters for this type of error are the address and bit position.

An environment simulator acts as the barrier (i.e. cable and tape drums) and as the incoming aircraft. This simulator is initialised using test case data (mass and incoming velocity). The FIC^3 triggers the simulator to start simulating an incoming aircraft. The simulator then feeds the system with sensory data (rotation sensor and pressure sensor) and receives actuator data (pressure value) from the system used for calculating new sensory data. All input to and output from the environment simulator is stored as experiment readouts and is subsequently analysed for system failure.

3.4. Experimental set-up

The experimental set-up calls for two error sets for evaluation purposes. In order to assess the probability P_{ds}, as defined in section 2.4, an error set E_1 containing 112 errors was created. Each error in E_1 is configured as a bit-flip in the monitored signals. Bit-flips can be used to model intermittent hardware faults, and it may be argued that using bit-flips in variables only may also model other faults inducing data errors in variables. Since single-bit errors are uniformly probable in all bit positions we chose to inject errors in each bit position of each signal in order to get a good estimate of the detection probability. Each signal is 16 bits long, hence, we have $7 \cdot 16 = 112$ errors in the error set. The distribution of errors in the error set is shown in Table 6.

Table 6. The distribution of errors in the error set E_1.

Signal	Executable assertion	# errors (n_s)	Error numbers	# injections ($n_s \cdot 25$)
SetValue	EA1	16	S1-S16	400
IsValue	EA2	16	S17-S32	400
i	EA3	16	S33-S48	400
pulscnt	EA4	16	S49-S64	400
ms_slot_nbr	EA5	16	S65-S80	400
mscnt	EA6	16	S81-S96	400
OutValue	EA7	16	S97-S112	400
Total	–	*112*	–	*2800*

The other error set, E_2, contains 200 errors configured as bit-flips in random bit positions in random locations (addresses) in application RAM (417 bytes) and stack (1008 bytes) areas, and is used to assess the total detection probability P_{detect} as described in section 2.4. These errors were selected from a uniform distribution (both location and bit-position), and the sampling was performed with replacement. Of the 200 errors, 150 were located in application RAM areas and 50 in the stack area.

All errors were injected in the master node. For each error in the error set, the system was subjected to 25 test cases, i.e. incoming aircraft, with velocity ranging uniformly from 40 m/s to 70 m/s, and mass ranging uniformly from 8000 kg to 20000 kg. For E_1 we have $112 \cdot 25 = 2800$ different combinations $\langle m, v, e \rangle$ of mass, velocity and error and for E_2 we have $200 \cdot 25 = 5000$ combinations. All test cases are such that if they are run on the target system without error injection, none of the error detection mechanisms report detection.

For E_1, eight different versions of the system were tested – one for each of the seven individual executable assertions and one in which all seven executable assertions were active simultaneously. For each system every combination of mass, velocity and error was exercised, giving us a total of $2800 \cdot 8 = 22400$ experiment runs with error injections for E_1. The error set E_2 was used only on the version containing all seven executable assertions. Therefore we have 5000 experiment runs with error injections for E_2.

The error injections were time triggered and were injected with a period of 20 ms (recall that most modules in the target system have a period of 7 ms). Thus, errors may have been injected during the execution of the executable assertions.

We say that we have successful error detection if an error is detected at least once during the entire observation period (40 seconds). The detection probability is then the probability of detecting an error at least once during the observation period. The detection latency is the time from the first injection of an error to the first reported detection.

4. Results

In Table 7, we can see the estimates of the detection probabilities per signal, per executable assertions and totals, as obtained using error set E_1. The measures are calculated according to the formulas for coverage estimation in [18]. The measure $P(d) = n_d/n_e$ (where n_d is the number of runs in which errors were detected and n_e is the number of runs in which errors were injected) is an estimate of the probability that the error is detected during the observation time, $P(d|fail) = n_{d,fail}/n_{e,fail}$ (where we only take into account those runs in which the system failed) is an estimate of the probability that the error is detected given that a failure occurred, and $P(d|no\ fail) = n_{d,no\ fail}/n_{e,no\ fail}$ (where we only take into account those runs in which the system did not fail) is an estimate of the detection probability given that no failure occurred. The relation $n = n_{fail} + n_{no\ fail}$ holds for both errors and detections. For the individual signals we have $n_e = 400$ and for the totals we have $n_e = 2800$. The *All* column contains the results obtained when using the version of the software, which had all seven executable assertions activated simultaneously. The table also contains the 95% confidence intervals for the estimates of the detection probabilities. We can use the measure $P(d)$ as an estimate of P_{ds} in the expression of the total detection probability for the entire system (see section 2.4). If a cell is empty in the table, this means that no detection was registered for that combination of signal and executable assertion.

The values shown in boldface are those that correspond to the "correct" signal-mechanism pair. For instance, the signal *SetValue* is directly monitored by mechanism EA1, and the signal *IsValue* is directly monitored by EA2

Table 7. Error detection probabilities (%) with confidence intervals at 95%. No confidence interval can be estimated for measured detection probabilities of 100.0%.

Signal	Measure	EA1	EA2	EA3	EA4	EA5	EA6	EA7	All
SetValue	P(d)	55.5±4.1	31.3±3.8	4.0±1.6				44.3±4.1	59.5±4.0
	P(d|fail)	92.6±3.7	72.4±6.4	1.5±1.7				87.9±4.7	97.1±2.4
	P(d|no fail)	36.6±4.9	10.5±3.1	5.3±2.3				22.8±4.2	39.7±5.0
IsValue	P(d)		52.5±4.1					47.0±4.1	54.4±4.1
	P(d|fail)		89.6±7.3					93.3±6.2	100.0
	P(d|no fail)		47.4±4.4					41.1±4.3	47.2±4.4
i	P(d)	26.8±3.6	29.8±3.8	100.0	1.5±1.0	1.0±0.8	0.5±0.6	47.8±4.1	100.0
	P(d|fail)	33.7±7.8	55.4±8.2	100.0	2.0±2.3	2.3±2.1	1.1±1.8	78.0±6.8	100.0
	P(d|no fail)	24.4±4.1	21.1±3.9	100.0	1.3±1.1	0.4±0.6	0.3±0.5	37.7±4.6	100.0
pulscnt	P(d)	50.3±4.1	42.8±4.1	0.3±0.4	12.8±2.7			0.3±0.4	100.0
	P(d|fail)	38.1±5.3	34.5±4.8	0.3±0.5	0.0			0.7±1.2	100.0
	P(d|no fail)	66.9±6.0	58.3±6.9	0.0	16.6±3.5			0.0	100.0
ms_slot_nbr	P(d)		20.0±3.3			100.0		6.8±2.1	100.0
	P(d|fail)		34.6±5.7			100.0		11.6±3.9	100.0
	P(d|no fail)		7.1±2.9			100.0		2.7±1.8	100.0
mscnt	P(d)	8.3±2.3	12.3±2.7				100.0	17.5±3.1	100.0
	P(d|fail)	20.0±13.4	18.2±13.8				100.0	13.0±11.8	100.0
	P(d|no fail)	7.5±2.2	11.9±2.7				100.0	17.8±3.2	100.0
OutValue	P(d)		1.0±0.8					11.3±2.6	4.0±1.6
	P(d|fail)		33.3±34.7					85.7±23.5	100.0
	P(d|no fail)		0.5±0.6					9.9±2.5	3.3±1.5
Total	P(d)	20.1±1.2	27.1±1.4	14.9±1.1	2.0±0.4	14.4±1.1	14.4±1.1	25.0±1.3	74.0±1.4
	P(d|fail)	35.0±2.9	47.0±3.0	12.2±1.9	0.3±0.4	21.7±2.3	3.2±1.0	42.7±3.3	99.6±0.3
	P(d|no fail)	14.9±1.3	19.7±1.4	16.0±1.4	2.5±0.5	11.1±1.2	19.0±1.5	19.9±1.4	60.6±1.9

Table 8. Error detection latencies for all errors (milliseconds).

Signal	Latency	EA1	EA2	EA3	EA4	EA5	EA6	EA7	All
SetValue	Min	160	570	50				20	20
	Average	690	2445	1241				842	692
	Max	6259	5588	6099				5297	6490
IsValue	Min		10					10	20
	Average		612					654	1046
	Max		8142					4466	6630
i	Min	311	270	80	2584	4686	3495	151	100
	Average	2125	2100	210	4381	5538	3891	1900	228
	Max	11397	8272	401	5798	7601	4286	6499	421
pulscnt	Min	390	1182	1563	20			230	20
	Average	1371	1379	1563	239			230	272
	Max	2284	2283	1563	921			230	1803
ms_slot_nbr	Min		1172			20		1703	20
	Average		3654			32		3462	32
	Max		8912			140		5738	80
mscnt	Min	1112	1352				10	1091	20
	Average	2050	1741				25	1673	23
	Max	4196	3525				60	3415	61
OutValue	Min		440					20	2413
	Average		1344					1604	3379
	Max		2704					6179	7781
Total	Min	160	10	50	20	20	10	10	20
	Average	1286	1725	248	727	126	163	1314	511
	Max	11379	8912	6099	5798	7601	4286	6499	7781

Table 9. Results for error set E_2

Area	Detection probability (%, 95% conf. int.)		Detection latency (ms, totals)		Detection latency (ms, failures)	
RAM	P(d)	12.8±0.9	Min	20	Min	20
	P(d|fail)	81.1±6.8	Average	1359	Average	1203
	P(d|no fail)	11.1±0.9	Max	5608	Max	5608
Stack	P(d)	4.2±0.9	Min	20	Min	20
	P(d|fail)	13.7±4.7	Average	250	Average	2077
	P(d|no fail)	2.9±0.8	Max	2684	Max	6449
Total	P(d)	10.6±0.7	Min	20	Min	20
	P(d|fail)	39.4±5.2	Average	1086	Average	1298
	P(d|no fail)	9.2±0.7	Max	5608	Max	6449

In Table 8 are the detection latencies measured during our experiments. The value is the time from the first injection of an error until the first registered detection, and it is measured in milliseconds. The table contains the minimum, average and maximum values for the detection latencies. Again, the boldface values correspond to the primary signal-mechanism pairs. In this table we consider all detected errors, those leading to failure as well as those not leading to failure.

The results from the experiments with error set E_2 are shown in Table 9. The table contains detection coverage with 95% confidence intervals and detection latencies measured in milliseconds. As with the measures for error set E_1, we used the formulas described in [18] to derive the probabilities shown in the table. The probabilities shown in Table 9 are estimates of P_{detect}, whereas the probabilities shown in Table 7 are estimates of P_{ds} (for more information on the definition of these probabilities, see section 2.4).

5. Discussion

The results obtained in this evaluation are specific for the target system, the error model and the test cases we have chosen. For other systems, error models, and/or test cases the results may vary. Having said that, we can now start our discussion of the results shown in the previous section.

5.1. Error detection probability, P_{ds}

This section discusses the results obtained with error set E_1. The results are the estimated values for the probability P_{ds}, i.e. the probability that an error is detected given that an error is present in one of the monitored signals and therefore can be detected by the mechanisms.

The overall detection probability was 74%, and if we

consider the errors that lead to failure, as defined in section 3, the detection probability was over 99%. Roughly, 60% of the errors that did not lead to failure were detected. If we examine the individual executable assertions, we have detection probabilities ranging from just over 11% up to 100%.

The assertions that achieved a 100% detection probability monitored signals that were all essentially counters by nature; they were periodically incremented by some limited (small) amount. This makes errors easy to detect since the freedom of change was very small in these signals. We must remember that it is possible, even probable, that we do not achieve a 100% detection probability for other error models or test cases. However, the results suggest that these mechanisms may be very effective in detecting errors.

The assertions monitoring signals representing continuous values in the environment have a lower detection probability. This can be explained by the fact that these signals have more liberal constraints than the counter signals mentioned above. The liberal constraints let those errors pass which in the value domain constitute a small change in the signal, i.e. the errors most likely to remain undetected are those affecting the least significant bits of the signal. In fact, for continuous signals, errors in the least significant bits may be indistinguishable from noise in the sampling process.

The detection probability for EA7 in the signal *OutValue* was roughly 11%, whereas for all mechanisms it was 4%. This is mainly due to the fact that the behaviour of the target system is not entirely deterministic.

The results of the experiment shows that by using a number of error detection mechanisms covering different parts of the system, a fairly high total coverage may be obtained.

5.2. Total error detection probability, P_{detect}

As shown in section 2.4, the probability of detection given that an error is present in a monitored signal is part of a larger expression for total error detection probability for the entire system: $P_{detect} = (P_{en}P_{prop} + P_{em})P_{ds}$. The value obtained for P_{ds} for the target system in our evaluation was 74%. To obtain $P_{detect} = 74\%$ would mean that all the occurring errors, directly or after propagation, are uniformly distributed over the monitored signals. This is most likely not the case since there probably are some signals that are more dependent on other parts of the system than the remaining signals. If, for example, errors in our target system with a high probability propagate to the *SetValue* signal, P_{detect} would be closer to the detection probability for that signal, which in this case is roughly 59%.

From the experiments performed with error set E_2, we can see that the overall detection coverage for all errors is about 10%. For errors that lead to failures, we obtained detection coverage of 39%. The values differ a lot for the two areas in which we injected errors. Generally, errors injected into the RAM area of the application were detected with a higher probability than were those injected into the stack area. An explanation for this may be that errors in the stack area more often lead to control flow errors. The evaluated mechanisms are not aimed at detecting such errors.

For the errors injected into the RAM area that eventually caused the system to fail, the detection coverage was over 81%, whereas the total detection coverage was just under 13%. We can see that if an error were of such nature that it would cause system failure we can detect it with a fairly high probability using the presented mechanisms.

5.3. Error detection latency

We can see in the results for E_1 that the assertions which monitor signals that are essentially counters in nature have the shortest average detection latency. The three mechanisms that showed a 100% detection probability were also the top three mechanisms when examining the error detection latency.

Looking at the individual mechanisms shows us that the detection latencies are rather short. Most of the mechanisms had average latencies of well below one second, only mechanism EA7 had an average exceeding one second (1.604 seconds). The average of the error detection latency for all mechanisms was 511 milliseconds.

The latencies for errors in E_2 are longer than the latencies for errors in E_1. This, however, is not very surprising since most of the errors in E_2 were not located in the monitored signals and therefore had to propagate to the monitored signals before the mechanisms could have a chance of detecting them. This propagation process increases the total time from injection to detection.

6. Summary

In this paper we investigate the properties of error detection mechanisms based on a classification scheme for signals in software. The mechanisms are generic test algorithms that are instantiated with parameters for each individual signal that is to be monitored. We have also derived an expression for the total error detection probability in a system. Two experiments were performed using error injection experiments. In the first experiment bit-flips were exercised in all bit positions of the monitored signals and in the second experiment we injected bit-flip errors in random bit positions in random memory and stack locations. The first experiment investigated the probability of detecting errors given that the errors are located in the monitored signals, as well as detection latencies. The second experiment investigated the total system detection coverage and detection latencies obtained with the mechanisms.

The detection probability was defined to be the probability of an error being detected at least once during the observation period. The detection latency was defined to be the latency between the first injected error and the first reported detection.

In the first experiment, we achieved an overall detection probability for errors in the monitored signals of 74%, and if we only take into account those errors that lead to failure we had a detection probability of over 99%. The average error detection when all mechanisms were activated simultaneously was 511 milliseconds.

The second experiment showed that for errors in the memory areas of the application we detected over 81% of all errors that caused system failure. Errors in the stack that caused system failure were detected with a probability of 13%. The low detection probability for stack errors is likely due to the fact that errors in the stack often cause control-flow errors, and the evaluated mechanisms are not aimed at detecting such errors. The detection latencies were longer than those obtained in the first experiment. This, however, is not surprising since most injected errors must propagate to the monitored signals in order to be detected. This propagation process increases the detection latency.

The presented mechanisms are good candidates for software-implemented error detection in low-cost embedded systems. They are intuitive and easy to implement and have the potential of providing high detection coverage for data errors in software signals.

Acknowledgement

We would like to thank Dr. Jörgen Christmansson and Dr. Marcus Rimén for their comments on earlier versions of this paper. We are also grateful for the comments of the anonymous reviewers, which helped to increase the quality of this paper.

References

[1] Avizienis A., "The N-Version Approach to Software Fault-Tolerance", *IEEE Transactions on Software Engineering*, Vol. 11, No 12, pp. 1491-1501, 1985

[2] Mahmood A., Andrews D.M., McCluskey E.J., "Executable Assertions and Flight Software", *Proceedings 6th Digital Avionics Systems Conference*, pp. 346-351, Baltimore (MD), USA, AIAA/IEEE, 1984

[3] Rabéjac C., Blanquart J.-P., Queille J.-P., "Executable Assertions and Timed Traces for On-Line Software Error Detection", *Proceedings 26th International Symposium on Fault-Tolerant Computing*, pp.138-147, 1996

[4] Stroph R., Clarke T., "Dynamic Acceptance Tests for Complex Controllers", *Proceedings 24th Euromicro Conference*, pp.411-417, 1998

[5] Hecht H., "Fault-Tolerant Software for Real-Time Applications", *ACM Computing Surveys*, Vol.8, No. 4, pp. 391-407, December 1976

[6] Saib S.H., "Executable Assertions – An Aid To Reliable Software", *Conf. rec. 11th Asilomar Conference on Circuits Systems and Computers*, pp. 277-281, 1978

[7] Andrews D.M., "Using Executable Assertions for Testing and Fault Tolerance", *Proceedings 9th International Symposium on Fault-Tolerant Computing*, pp. 102-105, 1979

[8] Randell B., Xu J., "The evolution of the recovery block concept", *Software Fault Tolerance*, Lyu M.R. (ed.), Chapter 1, Willey, 1995

[9] Scott R.K., Gault J.W., McAllister D.F., "The Consensus Recovery Block", *Proceedings of the Total System Reliability Symposium*, pp. 74-85, 1983

[10] Kim K.H., Welch H.O., "The Distributed Execution of Recovery Blocks: An Approach to Uniform Treatment of Hardware and Software Faults in Real-Time Applications", *IEEE Transactions on Computers*, Vol. C-38, No. 5,pp. 626-636, 1989

[11] Laprie J.C., et al., "Hardware- and Software-Fault-Tolerance: Definition and Analysis of Architectural Solutions", *Proceedings of the 17th International Symposium on Fault-Tolerant Computing*, pp. 116-121, 1987

[12] Ammann P.E., Knight J.C., "Data Diversity: An Approach To Software Fault Tolerance", *IEEE Transactions on Computers*, Vol. C-37, No. 4, pp. 418-425, 1988

[13] Leveson N.G., Cha S.S., Knight J.C., Shimeall T.J., "The Use of Self Checks and Voting in Software Error Detection: An Empirical Study", *IEEE Transactions on Software Engineering*, Vol. 16, No. 4, pp. 432-443, 1990

[14] Clegg M., Marzullo K., "Predicting Physical Processes in the Presence of Faulty Sensor Readings", *Proceedings 27th International Symposium on Fault-Tolerant Computing*, pp.373-378, 1996

[15] US Air Force – 99, "Military specification: Aircraft Arresting System BAK-12A/E32A; Portable, Rotary Friction", *MIL-A-38202C*, Notice 1, US Department of Defence, September 2, 1986

[16] Christmansson J., Hiller M., Rimén M., "An Experimental Comparison of Fault and Error Injection", *Proceedings 9th International Symposium on Software Reliability Engineering*, pp. 369-378, 1998

[17] Rimén M., Ohlsson J., Torin J., "On Microprocessor Error Behavior Modelling", *Proceedings 24th International Symposium on Fault-Tolerant Computing*, pp.76-85, 1994

[18] Powell D., Martins E., Arlat J., Crouzet Y., "Estimators for Fault Tolerance Coverage Evaluation", *IEEE Transactions on Computers*, Vol. 44, No. 2, pp. 261-274, 1995

Session 2B

Practical Experience Reports I ♦ Networks

Experiences with Group Communication Middleware *

Scott Johnson and Farnam Jahanian
Dept. of Electrical Engineering and Computer Science
University of Michigan
1301 Beal Ave.
Ann Arbor, MI 48109-2122
{scottdj,farnam}@eecs.umich.edu

Sunondo Ghosh, Brian Vanvoorst,
Nicholas Weininger, and Walt Heimerdinger
Honeywell Technology Center
3600 Technology Dr.
Minneapolis, MN 55418

Abstract

Group communication is a widely studied paradigm for building fault-tolerant distributed systems. The Armada project at the University of Michigan is a collaborative effort with the Honeywell Technology Center to study how real-world applications use group communication. In this paper, we describe the results of our experience implementing a fault-tolerant distributed radar tracking system, and discuss how we were able to simplify our design and implementation by utilizing additional services built on top of the group communication model.

Keywords: group communication, distributed systems, middleware, fault-tolerant communication

1. Introduction

For the past two years, the Armada project at the University of Michigan has been collaborating with the Honeywell Technology Center on a study of middleware support for fault-tolerant distributed applications. This experience taught us a great deal about how applications use group communication to implement their fault-tolerance and performance requirements. This paper presents the results of our experience, and describes how we were able to simplify our design and implementation by utilizing a service library containing additional abstractions built on top of the group communication model.

The focus of this paper is not to describe a new group communication service or the potential semantic pitfalls associated with the use of a particular protocol. A large body of published research has already provided the community with many intricate protocols, and has explored the subtle ordering and reliability semantics associated with them. But researchers have also observed that group communica-

tion alone is too low-level, and additional services, such as state transfer, may be needed to facilitate the design and implementation of fault-tolerant applications. Our experience confirmed this, as we found that significant functionality had to be added to our application in order to realize its fault-tolerance and functional requirements using basic group communication primitives. We believe that these services are as important as the communication semantics to the distributed application, and must be designed with the same depth and thoroughness. To this end, we collected a variety of services from existing protocols and combined them with additional abstractions of our own design to meet our application's requirements more efficiently.

These abstractions include a process management service, which enables the application to organize processes into specific roles and easily replace failed processes; a set of synchronization and communication primitives, which can simplify complicated message exchanges and synchronize processes at well-known execution points; a failure notification service, which provides alternate mechanisms for notifying the application of process failures; and a group composition service, which enables multiple process groups to be composed together to construct complex, large-scale systems. Although these abstractions were realized in the context of our motivating application, we have designed them based also on experience with other fault-tolerant distributed systems, including interaction with the Naval Surface Warfare Center on the Hiper-D project, and participation in DARPA workgroups on dependability. We therefore believe that they will prove useful in simplifying the design and construction not just of our motivating application, but of fault-tolerant distributed applications in general.

In the following section, we present an overview of the radar tracking application. In section 3 we describe the abstractions in detail, and discuss the motivations behind their use. Section 4 summarizes our results.

---

*This work is supported in part by a research grant from the Defense Advanced Research Projects Agency, monitored by the U.S. Air Force Rome Laboratory under Grant F30602-95-1-0044.

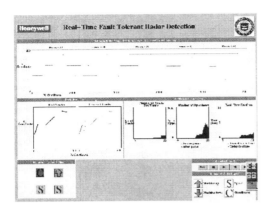

Figure 1. Screenshot of the Hypothesis Testing Application, showing three active tracks and the five most recent frames of radar data.

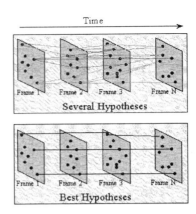

Figure 2. Demonstration of Hypothesis Testing. Originally, there are many possible hypotheses. After scoring and pruning, only the most likely trajectories remain.

2. Application Overview

The application chosen for this study implements a hypothesis testing algorithm, and is part of a larger radar tracking system[9, 8]. Many applications which make statistical predictions based on real-time data use hypothesis testing, including speech recognition algorithms and image understanding algorithms such as medical imaging. The application was implemented using RTCAST, a group communication protocol developed at the University of Michigan. RTCAST provides atomic, totally ordered multicast communication with soft real-time guarantees, and has been ported to Windows NT, Solaris, and Linux. Due to space limitations, we do not describe RTCAST in detail here, but more information is available in [1]. We believe that this method of refining and extending middleware services by implementing a suitable motivating application can be a valuable part of the middleware development process. In addition to the service library we developed, we were able to refine both the interface and the services provided by RTCAST to a degree that would not have been otherwise possible.

Although we selected RTCAST for this implementation, there are a number of group communication protocols which provide similar services and which could also benefit from our experience. Other real-time protocols include TTP [15], and XPA [18]. Non-real-time group communication protocols include ISIS [7], Consul [17], Delta-4 [18], Spinglass [6], and Transis [11].

2.1. Basic Hypothesis Testing Operation

The Hypothesis Testing application takes as input consecutive frames of radar data. Each frame contains both real radar returns and noise. The application then creates hypotheses about which radar returns correspond to real objects, and tracks the trajectories of those objects over time (Figure 1). These hypotheses are then deterministically divided among the available processes for evaluation.

Due to the large number of ways there are to "connect the dots," state explosion can be a significant problem. To mitigate this, each hypothesis is given a score indicating the likelihood that it is correct. After generating and scoring the hypotheses for a radar frame, a group coordinator selects those most likely to be true and the rest are discarded, as shown in Figure 2. At this point, the remaining hypotheses may be redistributed among the available processes to balance the system load before the next frame arrives.

2.2. Fault Tolerance

The Hypothesis Testing application is designed to be run in real-time, mission-critical situations. Because of these requirements, it is imperative that the application be tolerant to process and hardware failures, and be able to recover from those failures while still meeting its deadlines. The primary deadline requirement of each iteration is dictated by the radar frame arrival rate, which is approximately one second. Therefore, if a process fails during the execution of the algorithm, the application must be able to recover the work performed by the failed process up to that point, or else redo it before the deadline. We considered several replication schemes to meet these requirements:

Overlapping Active Replication: Processes are divided into G sub-groups of equal size, and hypotheses are divided equally among all G sub-groups (Figure 3). Every process in a given sub-group maintains the entire hypothesis set for that sub-group. Work is divided round-robin within each sub-group so that no work is duplicated. If a process fails before the current iteration is completed, its work is lost. To recover, the remaining processes in its sub-group first finish their own portion of the hypothesis space. As they finish, they begin working on the failed processor's

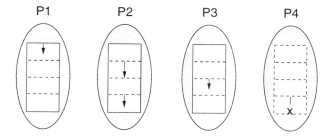

Figure 3. A sub-group performing overlapping active replication. Each process is assigned one quarter of the hypotheses. At this point, process four has failed before finishing. Since process two is done, it has begun working on process four's hypotheses.

hypotheses, starting from separate corners of the hypothesis space, until all hypotheses have been processed. Thus, each sub-group of size S can tolerate up to $S - 1$ failures, depending on available processing time, with no loss of data.

Best K Replication: This scheme is similar to overlapping active replication, but only the top $K\%$ of hypotheses are replicated. Although this does not provide complete recovery, recall that all but the most likely hypotheses are discarded at the end of each round. By carefully choosing K, the application can ensure that hypotheses lost due to failures would likely have been discarded anyway.

Pairwise Active Replication: In this scheme, the processes are organized into non-overlapping pairs. Both processes in each pair analyze the same data on each iteration. If one of the processes in a pair fails no results are lost, since both are doing the same work in parallel. The failed process can then be replaced for the next iteration. One drawback to this approach is that there can be only one failure per pair of processes. However, it is a very simple approach, and is the method used in the final implementation.

3. Higher-level Abstractions and Services

Now that we have described the requirements of hypothesis testing, we discuss the limitations we encountered when trying to implement it using the process group model, and describe the abstractions we propose to address them. These abstractions include some which have been used in other systems, as well as a number of new abstractions we have designed based on our experience.

An important consideration for the abstractions is their integration with the group communication middleware. We have implemented them as a service library which sits on top of RTCAST. It provides a separate application interface, and is implemented as much as possible using services already provided by the underlying middleware. This should enable the abstractions to be ported more easily to other

group communication protocols, since only the part of the library that interfaces to the lower-level middleware would need to be modified. We have tried to use only basic group communication services to maximize portability.

3.1. Application-level Process Management

One of the first things we realized when we began implementing hypothesis testing was that we needed more fine-grained control over the organization of processes within the group than was provided by the group communication model. There were a number of application requirements motivating this: we needed to designate process pairs for active replication, we needed to be able to divide incoming radar data among available processes, we needed to elect a group coordinator, and we needed to replace a process in one of these specific roles if a failure occurred.

Our library supports these tasks through an *Application-level Process Management* service, which allows the application to organize the group at a fine-grained level. With this service, applications can dynamically assign processes to specific roles, and replace failed processes without altering the organization of the group. This service is composed of three related abstractions:

Globally Consistent Process IDs: For an application to be able to assign different roles to individual processes, it must be able to identify those processes in a consistent manner at every group member. Many group communication services use some type of logical addressing to distinguish member processes, but in many cases these logical ids are assigned by the middleware and are either not made available to the application at all, or are made available on a read-only basis. This is sufficient for simple tasks such as selecting a group leader, but is too inflexible to use for more complex role assignments, such as the replication pairs in hypothesis testing, since process identities may change after failures and new processes may be given identifiers that do not match the existing group organization.

To address these limitations, we designed a new process id abstraction, which allows the application to assign a logical id to each group member. Group communication is used to propagate updates and ensure that members have a consistent view of the id assignments. If the middleware enforces total ordering, globally consistent process ids can be guaranteed even if multiple processes set ids simultaneously. If not, a globally consistent view can still be guaranteed if only one process (such as a group leader or replication partner) is responsible for setting the id of each process.

Free Node Management: Resource management has been integrated with group communication in other systems, exemplified by AQuA [10], which manages the availability of communication resources to provide quality of service with Ensemble [13]. Our experience showed us that to reduce the complexity of resource management, the process management service must also support free node management. This service is implemented as an interface to an external resource manager, which is responsible for keeping track of which processors are available in the system, and for implementing a policy to select which processor to use when a new process is requested. This policy can use any metric that meets application requirements, such as CPU utilization or network latency. When the application requests a new process, the service library queries the resource manager for a processor which meets the desired policy. It then creates a new process on that processor using an execution string provided by the application. We have implemented a basic resource manager for the hypothesis testing application, which selects the available processor with the lowest CPU utilization. It would be interesting to explore how this service could be integrated with AQuA's resource management framework.

State Transfer: The final component of application-level process management is a state transfer service. This type of service has been included in other group communication protocols, for example ISIS [7]. It allows the application to specify a buffer which contains state information needed by new members. When a process joins the group, the current contents of this buffer are copied to the new member as part of the join operation. The current mapping of application-assigned process ids can be transferred at the same time, ensuring that new processes will have a current view of the group's application-level organization when they join. This information is guaranteed to be delivered before the process receives any other messages, ensuring that it will be in a consistent and well-known state before processing data or generating new results. This removes most of the burden of state transfer from the application programmer, and provides a much cleaner and simpler semantic for fault-tolerant applications to use when implementing failure recovery. This service can be implemented using a lower-level state transfer service if available, or by intercepting and halting message transmissions to the new member until it has received the state update message.

To illustrate the utility of application-level process management, we now show how it simplified the design and implementation of our application. In hypothesis testing, one application process is initially responsible for creating the group and starting other processes, which is done using the free node management service. This process then assigns each of the N processes an id from 0 to $N - 1$. Process 0 becomes the group coordinator. Process pairs for the pairwise replication scheme are chosen based on the process id modulo 2 (processes 0 and 1 are the first pair, 2 and 3 are the second pair, etc.). Work is divided round robin, such that the first pair gets the first $\frac{2}{N}$ of the data, the next higher pair gets the next $\frac{2}{N}$, etc. Since there is a global view of the process ids, all of these decisions can be made by each

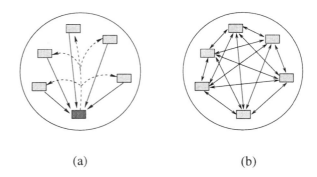

Figure 4. High-level Communication Primitives: (a) Query-Reply (b) Scatter-Gather.

process independently, without explicit communication. If a process fails, its partner uses the free node management service to start a new process, assign it the failed process' identifier, and transfer hypothesis state to it using the state transfer service. Once again, this can be done without explicit coordination among the active processes.

3.2. Synchronization and Communication Primitives

Group communication middleware typically provides a group multicast service, which enables a process to send messages to some or all of the group members with guarantees such as atomicity, reliability, and delivery order with respect to other messages. We have observed that many distributed applications frequently have to perform more complicated exchanges, for example to share results, report information to a group coordinator, or synchronize processes at various execution stages. For example, in hypothesis testing, we needed to enable the group coordinator to query the group for the best hypotheses, allow group members to exchange workload data for load balancing, and ensure that all processes were ready before continuing with the next iteration. Although these forms of communication can be implemented using the group multicast primitive, they often require extra work on the part of the application designer.

In our hypothesis testing implementation, we found that a set of synchronization and communication primitives would simplify the application design. These primitives build on the basic multicast service to provide more robust functionality as a single operation, and have been included in other communication systems such as MPI [16], but are not found in many group communication services that we are aware of. These primitives can be implemented using only a reliable multicast. They include:

Barrier Synchronization: When initializing the application, we needed to ensure that all processes were ready before it could begin accepting radar data. To achieve this, we implemented a barrier synchronization primitive. When executed, it blocks the process until all other processes have reached the same execution point.

Distributed Lock Management: We have also designed a distributed lock management service which implements traditional OS mutual exclusion primitives, such as semaphores and mutexes, between group members, even if they are running on different hosts. One process is responsible for holding each semaphore or mutex, and operations on that object are conducted through reliable multicasts. If the group communication service provides total delivery, then a central coordinator for each object is not necessary, as each member can maintain a local copy and all members will see the same sequence of updates to the object. Although it is certainly possible for an application to implement this functionality, providing it as an abstraction further reduces implementation effort. In addition to serializability, this abstraction also provides a simpler method for atomically conducting operations requiring multiple messages.

Query-Reply: The query-reply primitive allows a process to send a query to the group and collect a response from each group member as a single operation (Figure 4a). In the hypothesis testing application, the group coordinator needs to repeatedly query the members of the group about their hypothesis scores. After each query, the coordinator collects a reply from each member and decides which hypotheses to keep and which to discard. Our experience suggests that this type of operation is fairly common in other fault-tolerant distributed applications as well.

Scatter-Gather: This primitive enables each process to report some information to the group, and collect the information sent by other members as a single operation (Figure 4b. This is similar to the query-reply, but in this case every process receives a copy of the collected responses. We used this to implement replication in hypothesis testing, where Processes need to send updates to their replication partners about their current position in the workload, and to collect the same information from their partners in return. We have observed this form of communication in other applications as well. For example, it can be used for load balancing, where each process could send the size of its current workload to the rest of the group, and collect the same information to use in deciding where to send excess work.

3.3. Failure Notification

For many fault-tolerant applications, failure detection and notification is a key service provided by the middleware. In our experience, some applications use group communication just for failure detection, and do not even need ‍ ‍ multicast service. Traditionally, most group communication protocols have focused on the semantics of failure notification. Although this is important, we found that it is also important to consider the mechanism by which failure notifications are delivered to the application. For example, RTCAST originally only delivered failure notifications in

order with respect to data messages. There may be times when applications can not afford to wait until messages preceding a failure have been delivered. This is true in hypothesis testing with overlapping active replication, since there is no communication during data processing and replicas need to be notified immediately so they can begin recovery.

We have designed a failure notification service which provides several different notification methods that can be used interchangeably by the application, depending on its dynamic failure reporting requirements. Although these mechanisms have been used in other group communication protocols, our experience suggests that it is useful to provide an interface which allows the application to dynamically select its notification methods. However, based on our experience implementing these changes in RTCAST, we believe that the modifications required are minor and relatively easy to make. These methods include:

In-band: Failure notifications are inserted into the message stream, and are delivered to the application like a regular data message. The advantage of this method is that failure notifications can be delivered with the same ordering semantics as data messages. We used this method when selecting the best hypotheses during hypothesis testing.

Callbacks: Some applications may want receive notifications immediately instead of waiting until preceding messages have been delivered. With callbacks, the application provides a function which is called by the service library when a failure occurs. We used callbacks in hypothesis testing to enable replication partners to begin recovery quickly.

Polling: With polling, the application explicitly checks for failures by calling a special function which returns information about the next unreported failure. This is more efficient when the application does not care about immediate failure notification. This method is used during the initialization of hypothesis testing, since any failed processes can be replaced after initialization with no loss of data.

3.4. Group Composition

As mentioned in section 2, hypothesis testing is one component of a larger radar tracking system. This system has a number of components, each of which has its own fault-tolerance and performance requirements. Most of these components could benefit from group communication, especially if it was extended with the services we have described. Unfortunately, there are a number of problems that arise if the system is implemented using a single process group. First, it would be very difficult to manage such a large number of processes working simultaneously on many unrelated tasks. Any failures would be reported to processes in all components, even ones which wouldn't be affected by the failure. In addition, messages for each component would be delivered to all processes in the system, resulting in increased overhead and bandwidth contention. Note that

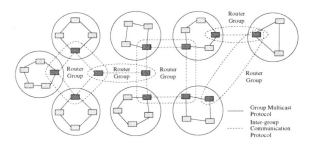

Figure 5. Diagram of the group composition framework, showing several process groups and the inter-group routers used to connect them.

these problems are not specific to the radar tracking system, but have been observed in other large-scale distributed applications and group communication services [1, 4, 3].

To support a more efficient design, we have created a framework[14] which supports the modular composition of process groups (Figure 5). This framework allows composed groups to exchange messages while enforcing end-to-end delivery semantics. Using this method, we were able simplify the design of hypothesis testing's overlapping active replication scheme, by placing each replication subgroup in its own process group.

Other protocols have been proposed which support multiple process groups. These include the Totem multi-ring protocol [2], the Causal daisy architecture [5], and fault-tolerant total order multicast to asynchronous groups [12]. A detailed comparison of these approaches with our group composition framework is available in [14].

4. Conclusion

This paper described our experience with the implementation of a fault-tolerant radar tracking application. It described how we were able to simplify our design and implementation by utilizing a service library containing additional abstractions built on top of the group communication model. We believe that this comprehensive approach to providing higher-level services will make it possible for applications to take full advantage of the group communication paradigm.

References

[1] T. Abdelzaher, A. Shaikh, F. Jahanian, and K. Shin. RT-CAST: Lightweight multicast for real-time process groups. In *Proceedings IEEE Real-Time Technology and Applications Symposium (RTAS '96)*, pages 250–259, June 1996. Additional information is available in a techical report.

[2] D. Agarwal, L. Moser, P. Melliar-Smith, and R. Budhia. A reliable ordered delivery protocol for interconnected local-area networks. In *International Conference on Networking Protocols*, 1995.

[3] Ö. Babaoğlu, A. Bartoli, and G. Dini. Enriched view synchrony: A programming paradigm for partitionable asynchronous distributed systems. *IEEE Transactions on Computers*, 46(6):642–658, June 1997.

[4] Ö. Babaoğlu and A. Schiper. On group communication in large-scale distributed systems. *ACM SIGOPS Operating Systems Review*, 29(1):612–621, Jan. 1995. Also appears as Proceedings ACM SIGOPS European Workshop, September, 1994.

[5] R. Baldoni, R. Friedman, and R. Renesse. Hierarchical daisy architecture for causal delivery. Technical report, Cornell University, 1996.

[6] K. Birman, M. Hayden, O. Ozkasap, Z. Xiao, M. Budiu, and Y. Minsky. Bimodal multicast. *ACM Transactions on Computer Systems*, 17(2), May 1999.

[7] K. Birman, A. Schiper, and P. Stephenson. Lightweight causal and atomic group multicast. *ACM Transactions on Computer Systems*, 9(3):272–314, Aug. 1991.

[8] H. T. Center. Application level benchmark results. Technical Report C0011, Rome Laboratory, New York, Aug. 1998. Contract number F30602-94-C-0084.

[9] H. T. Center. Application level benchmark specifications. Technical Report C0010, Rome Laboratory, New York, Aug. 1998. Contract number F30602-94-C-0084.

[10] M. Cukier, J. Ren, C. Sabnis, D. Henke, J. Pistole, W. Sander, D. Bakken, M. Berman, D. Karr, and R. Schantz. Aqua: An adaptive architecture that provides dependable distributed objects. In *Proceedings of the 17th IEEE Symposium on Reliable Distributed Systems (SRDS 98)*, pages 245–253, Oct. 1996.

[11] D. Dolev and D. Malki. The Transis approach to high availability cluster communication. *Communications of the ACM*, 39(4):64–70, Apr. 1996.

[12] U. Fritzke, Jr., P. Ingels, A. Mostefaoui, and M. Raynal. Fault-tolerant total order multicast to asynchronous groups. Technical report, Centre National de la Recherche Scientifique, Jan. 1998. To appear in SRDS '98.

[13] M. Hayden. *The Ensemble System*. PhD thesis, Cornell University, 1998.

[14] S. Johnson, F. Jahanian, and J. Shah. The inter-group router approach to scalable group composition. In *Proceedings 19th IEEE International Conference on Distributed Computing Systems*, pages 2–13, June 1999.

[15] H. Kopetz and G. Grünsteidl. TTP – a protocol for fault-tolerant real-time systems. *IEEE Computer*, 27(1):14–23, Jan. 1994.

[16] Message Passing Interface Forum. *MPI: A Message-Passing Interface Standard*, 1.1 edition, June 1995. Available at http://www.mpi-forum.org/docs/mpi-11-html/mpi-report.html/.

[17] S. Mishra, L. Peterson, and R. Schlichting. Consul: A communication substrate for fault-tolerant distributed programs. *Distributed Systems Engineering*, 1:87–103, 1993.

[18] P. Verissimo, P. Bond, A. Hilborne, L. Rodrigues, and D. Seaton. The extra performance architecture (xpa). In D. Powell, editor, *Delta-4 - A Generic Architecture for Dependable Dist. Computing*. Springer-Verlag, 1991.

Towards Dependable Home Networking: An Experience Report

Yi-Min Wang
Microsoft Research
Redmond, WA

Wilf Russell
Microsoft Research
Redmond, WA

Anish Arora
Ohio State Univ.
Columbus, OH

Jun Xu
Univ. of Illinois
Urbana, IL

Rajesh K. Jagannathan
Ohio State Univ.
Columbus, OH

Abstract

As the success of the Web increasingly brings us towards a fully connected world, home networking systems that connect and manage home appliances become the natural next step to complete the connectivity. Although there has been fast-growing interest in the design of smart appliances and environments, there has been little study on the dependability issues, which is essential to making home networking part of our daily lives. The heterogeneity of various in-home networks, the undependable nature of consumer devices, and the lack of knowledgeable system administrators in the home environment introduce both opportunities and challenges for dependability research. In this paper, we report the dependability problems we encountered and the solutions we adopted in the deployment of the Aladdin home networking system. We propose the use of a soft-state store as a shared heartbeat infrastructure for monitoring the health of diverse hardware and software entities. We also describe a system architecture for connecting powerline devices to enhance dependability, and a monitoring tool for detecting unusual powerline activities potentially generated by intruders, interferences, or ill-behaved devices.

1. Introduction

With the explosive growth of the Web, we are increasingly moving towards a fully connected world. As broadband communication is being brought to homes with accelerating speed and as small handheld devices get smarter, more popular, and better connected, the notion of being able to communicate with anything at any time from anywhere is bound to become a reality. In this big picture, home networking is a natural next step in which both existing devices and future smart appliances are fully connected inside the house and accessible to the homeowners whenever needed. Starting from the simple scenarios of sharing files, printers, and Internet connections, home networking is also moving towards enabling multi-player, multi-PC games, digital video and audio anywhere in the house, device automation, remote diagnosis of home appliances, etc. An informal survey shows that different people have dramatically different ideas on what the killer applications for home networking should be. It is therefore important to provide an infrastructure for robust device connectivity to allow the construction of versatile applications on top of the infrastructure.

In the *Aladdin* research project [WRA00], we focus on providing the system infrastructure for device connectivity by integrating the seven in-home networks into one dependable home network: powerline, phoneline, RF (Radio Frequency), IR (InfraRed), A/V LAN, security, and temperature control. The goal is to allow the users to plug in a device on any of these networks and make it part of the Aladdin system so that it can be used in conjunction with all the other devices to accomplish higher-level system- or user-directed tasks. To make the whole system good enough to live with, one must pay special attention to the dependability issues, including reliability, availability, security, and manageability. The second goal of the Aladdin project is to support dependable remote home automation and sensing. We believe that home networking adds significant value even when people are away from their homes. Therefore, providing reliable and secure remote access to home networks and providing reliable sensing and control of devices are important parts of the project.

Home networking introduces several new challenges in the area of dependability. First, in the consumer electronics market, selling large volumes in order to drive the price down is a key to success. Manufacturers are therefore led to packaging their products as add-on modules with primitive I/O specifications so that they can be used with a variety of different systems and can be added incrementally to existing systems to control new or existing devices. However, such a design creates dependability problems that must be dealt with by the system. The problems with the powerline-based modules and sensors, which will be described later, are good examples. Second, home networks are heterogeneous and dynamic. Each of the in-home networks has a different characteristic in terms of bandwidth, connectivity, security, interferences, etc. This provides a new opportunity to exploit the redundancy provided by one network to solve dependability problems faced by another network. In addition, compared to the machines in the enterprise environment, consumer devices in the home networking environment are more dynamic in terms of mobility, availability, and extensibility. The system must be able to keep track of all the changes in the entire network in order to support reliable operation. Finally, enterprise environments usually rely on human administrators to perform tasks such as failure diagnosis and recovery, and intrusion detection and defense. But, in the home networking domain, we cannot afford to have the same level of administrator support and so the system must automatically perform those tasks as much as possible. What makes it even more challenging is the fact that consumer devices fail more often and with more different modes, and intrusions and interferences can come from different networks. Building a dependability framework that monitors, diagnoses, and recovers from known dependability problems and allows for extensibility to accommodate new failure modes as they are observed is the centerpiece of the Aladdin project.

In this paper, we focus on three dependability problems and their solutions. First, to robustly track the health of the diverse network entities including devices, sensors, objects, daemon processes, etc., we propose the use of a soft-state store as a shared heartbeat infrastructure. Second, to enhance the dependability of powerline control operation, we describe a system architecture that makes use of private powerline networks and the phoneline network. Finally, to automatically detect and diagnose unreliable device behaviors and even security intrusions, we provide a general tool for monitoring powerline activity.

2. Overview of the Aladdin System

In an ideal home networking system, the house is wired for running Ethernet and most devices are smart, networked devices connected directly to the Ethernet and running device control software themselves. A *home gateway* machine sits between the home network and the external communication infrastructures including the Internet and telephony. *User Access Points (UAPs)* are wall-mounted or stand-alone flat-panel displays deployed throughout the house to allow convenient access to in-home information (calendars, etc.) as well as the Internet from anywhere in the house. UAPs also expose Web-based, natural language-based, and voice-based interfaces for remotely controlling household devices and for monitoring environmental factors through remote sensors. Network bridges are provided for bridging devices on other communication media such as the powerline, RF, IR, and A/V cables to the Ethernet backbone.

Since smart devices are not yet generally available, the current Aladdin system accommodates existing devices by using six Windows 98 PCs and their peripherals to serve as both User Access Points and network bridges. The PCs are all connected by 1Mb/s or 10Mb/s Ethernet over the phoneline [H98]. They also act as device proxies by running device control software on behalf of the devices. The system, currently consisting of about 60 devices, is deployed in the first author's three-story house and used by the author's family on a daily basis.

The software architecture of the Aladdin system is divided into three layers. At the bottom, the *system infrastructure layer* consists of the soft-state store, its associated publish/subscribe eventing component, an Attribute-Based Lookup Service for maintaining a database of all available devices, a Name-Based Lookup Service for maintaining a table of all running object instances, and a device announcement protocol for bridging non-Ethernet devices. These components will be discussed in more details in Section 3. The infrastructure layer also contains the system management daemons for PC failure detection and recovery, which are omitted in this paper due to space limitation.

In the middle, the *application layer* consists of device objects and device daemons that encapsulate device- and network-specific details, and home networking applications for control and sensing. At the top, the *user interface layer* provides a browser-based point-and-click interface, a text-based natural language interface, and a voice recognition interface. To enable remote home automation, Aladdin allows email-based control using natural language and provides emergency notifications through the text messaging support of cell phones. For example, in the current deployment, the homeowner can send a digitally signed and encrypted email to close the garage door, request short video clips from the surveillance cameras, or turn on and off electrical appliances, etc. He will also receive a cell phone call when the garage door is opened, the fish tanks are leaking water, or a power outage occurs, etc.

3. Soft-State Store as a Shared Heartbeat Infrastructure

Home networking systems are more heterogeneous and dynamic than other typical distributed systems. Diverse devices and sensors connected to various in-home networks, and transient objects and long-lived daemon processes running different protocols contribute to the heterogeneity. The consumer-market nature of these network entities implies that they will fail, move, and disconnect more often than their enterprise counterparts, making the system more dynamic. An essential task of any home networking system is therefore to keep track of the status of these network entities. In Aladdin, we use two lookup services to accomplish this task: the *Attribute-Based Lookup Service (ABLS)* maintains a database of available devices and sensors, and supports queries based on device attributes including device type, physical location, etc.; the *Name-Based Lookup Services (NBLS)* maintains a table of running object instances, and provides the name-to-addresses mapping. An object can have multiple addresses including, for example, a distributed object interface pointer in its marshaled, string form and a queued address for asynchronous communication.

To keep track of the health and availability of the network entities, either the system needs to ping them or they need to send periodic heartbeats to the system. The latter approach is the preferred one in home networking for several reasons. First, to reduce cost, many consumer sensors are transmitters only and do not support polling. Also, some of the sensors already periodically send refreshes of their states, which effectively provide heartbeat information. Second, many network protocols and programming paradigms (distributed objects, messaging, etc.) are likely to coexist in home networking systems due to market competition. It will not be practical to require the system to be able to ping all devices and objects with various existing and future protocols and paradigms. Moreover, the ping interface provided by some objects may hang, compromising system robustness. Finally, the pinging approach would require the system to persist information regarding the existence and ping interfaces of all network entities in order to handle system failures. In contrast, the heartbeat approach can simply rely on the refreshes to reconstruct lookup service entries.

Since supporting heartbeats is at the core of building a robust home networking system, we took the approach of building a *Soft-State Store (SSS)* as a shared heartbeat infrastructure and layering lookup services on top of the store. The term *"soft-states"* is defined as *volatile or nonvolatile states that will expire if not refreshed within a pre-determined, but configurable amount of time* [WRA00]. (The notion of soft-states is similar to that of leasing [E99].) The SSS APIs allow programs to create soft-state types and variables, specify heartbeat intervals and maximum number of missing heartbeats, update and retrieve soft-state variable values, and subscribe to events related to changes in the store. The SSS daemon running on each machine is responsible for replicating changes to other machines and for firing events to local subscribers.

The Aladdin system management daemons use the SSS directly to detect the failures of machines and critical daemon processes. Device control objects send heartbeats to the NBLS, which relies on the SSS to maintain the lookup service entries. Sensors emit periodic state refreshes that are received by device daemons and translated into refreshes of corresponding ABLS entries. The ABLS stores the entries in a database to support rich queries, but it relies on the SSS to time out expired entries and fire appropriate events. For example, when a battery-operated garage door sensor runs out of battery, its ABLS entry will eventually be timed out so that the garage door opener object will not utilize incorrect, stale sensor state and an alert can be sent to the homeowner to remind him/her to replace the battery. The interactions between the devices and the SSS are more involved and will be described in more details next.

Aladdin Device Adapter

The most popular off-the-shelf home automation modules today are add-on powerline modules that sit between the electric outlets and the ordinary devices to be controlled remotely. There are two dependability problems in the use of these add-on modules. First, the On/Off status of an add-on module may not be consistent with that of the device that plugs into it. When the device is broken, physically switched off, or unplugged, it is no longer controllable by the system but the add-on module can still be turned on and off. Second, when both the module and the device are unplugged from the outlet, the device may still be incorrectly listed in the lookup service as available.

To achieve dependable operations with add-on modules and to eliminate the need of manual de-registration and re-registration every time a device is physically moved, we introduce the concept of an *Aladdin Device Adapter* as an enhanced add-on module. The key idea is that the Adapter periodically announces the device type, physical location, etc. of the device on its behalf. The Adapter is also responsible for detecting that the device is no longer controllable, and notifying the system to remove its lookup service entry. When both the Adapter and the device are disconnected from the outlet, the missing heartbeats from the Adapter will allow the system to eventually time out its entry.

To demonstrate the Adapter concept, we built a prototype for use with the popular X10 powerline control protocol [S98]. The Adapter consists of (1) an AC current detector that monitors the real working status of the attaching device by measuring the AC current flowing through the device; (2) a regular X10 receiver module that responds to remote On/Off commands by gating the AC current supplied to the device; (3) a state machine that, based on the status of the current detector and the receiver module, decides when to perform device joining and leaving announcements. An initial investigation of the hardware and software requirements suggested that off-the-shelf consumer modules could be modified into the Adapters with minimum additional circuitry.

Initially, when a device (for example, a lamp) is plugged into the Adapter and the Adapter is plugged into a wall outlet, both the power switch on the device and the X10 module in the Adapter are in the Off position. The X10 address of the Adapter is set to that assigned to the outlet. (Every interesting outlet in the house has been assigned a unique X10 address, which maps to a unique physical location, for example, "the garage side of the kitchen on the first floor".) By using the manual override function provided by X10, a user can turn on both the device and the module by simply turning on the power switch on the device. Upon detecting the state change, the state machine sends out a device-joining announcement over the powerline in the form of an *extended X10 code*.

The code contains (1) the X10 address of the outlet that identifies both the powerline address for controlling the device and the physical location of the device; (2) a *device code* that is pre-assigned to represent a particular type of devices; and (3) a *module code* that specifies the valid commands that can be sent to the Adapter to control the device. Upon receiving the announcement, a PC decodes the above information out of the extended X10 code, and registers the device with the ABLS. Afterwards, the Adapter periodically sends out the same announcement as long as the device is still controllable. The PC then performs periodic refreshes of the ABLS entry to prevent it from being timed out by the soft-state store.

When the power switch on the device is turned off or when the device is broken, the state machine detects that the X10 module is still on but the AC current detector does not detect any current flowing through the device. It concludes that the device is no longer controllable by the Aladdin system and so sends out a device-leaving announcement on behalf of the device, again in the form of an extended X10 code over the powerline. Upon receiving the announcement, a PC notifies the ABLS of the device's unavailability to preserve the consistency of the lookup service.

4. System Architecture for Enhancing Powerline Control Dependability

Powerline networking is likely to be an essential part of any home networking systems because it provides the most ubiquitous wired connectivity throughout the majority of the houses. However, due to the quality of the physical wiring and the inherently less secure connection topology [Ev96], powerline networking suffers from more dependability issues than phoneline networking. As a result, the powerline networking industry has advanced less than the phoneline networking industry in terms of both supported bandwidth and programming abstraction.

In the current Aladdin prototype, we use the X10 powerline control protocol and devices because they are the most consumer-ready products at this point, and build system-level solutions to achieve dependability. It remains to be seen whether the next-generation powerline networking protocols can succeed in the consumer market by solving most of the dependability problems at the network level with reasonably low costs in order to compete with other alternatives such as phoneline and wireless networking. With the understanding that X10 has a few inherent weaknesses that cannot be masked by the system, we expect their uses in controlling more critical home appliances will most likely be replaced in the future. In this paper, we focus on the more generic powerline dependability issues and omit discussions on X10-specific issues such as command atomicity and signal collisions.

Security is probably the No. 1 concern. Most houses share the same "powerline subnet" with some neighboring houses connected to the same distribution transformer. Powerline commands from one house can potentially reach the devices in another near-by house and interfere with the controlling of those devices. Conversely, powerline commands and device announcements from one house can potentially be monitored by another house, thus creating privacy concerns. A canonical solution to this problem is to rely on digital signatures and encryptions. But the limited bandwidth currently achievable by low-cost consumer products poses a challenge to the applicability of this solution.

Reliability is also a big issue in powerline networking. Powerline control modules are delicate electrical components and, since they are directly plugged into wall outlets, they are susceptible to the damage by voltage spikes. Signal attenuation may prevent powerline commands generated by a controller connected to one circuit breaker from reliably reaching the target device connected to another circuit breaker. Line noises generated by some household appliances or external sources may transiently interfere with the operation of powerline controls. Finally, since the most common usage of powerline networking is to enable wireless remote control by the users, one or more RF transceivers are almost always present. Unfortunately, such transceivers also provide channels for RF interferences to create either transient, intermittent, or persistent reliability problems.

Figure 1 illustrates the system architecture used in our current deployment for addressing the above dependability issues. We installed an X10 signal blocker at the main electrical panel to block X10 signals from coming into and leaving the house. For critical devices, we rely on the more secure phoneline to provide additional security. The basic idea is to use the phoneline to reach *private powerline networks* to which critical devices are connected. The private powerline networks are constructed by using an X10 signal filter to isolate a power strip from the common powerline (see Figure 1). For example, the garage door opener in Aladdin resides on a private powerline network that is configured as a peripheral of the garage PC. To remotely control the garage door opener, one must go through the phoneline Ethernet to reach the garage PC and send out X10 commands from there. Even as the next-generation powerline networking protocols provide better and better security, the concept of exploiting multiple redundant networks to provide additional security will remain valuable.

On the reliability side, we installed a whole-house surge protector at the main electrical panel to absorb potential power surges. To address the issue of signal attenuation, we again exploit the multiple redundant networks. Suppose PC "Abu" needs to control an Adapter but cannot reach it directly over the powerline. As part of the ABLS lookup operation for locating devices, "Abu" would have identified the subset of other PCs that have been able to receive the announcements from the target Adapter and therefore can directly control the Adapter. "Abu" then issues its control command by first routing the command over the phoneline (in the form of a distributed object method call) to one of those PCs and then sending out a powerline command from there.

Powerline-based motion sensors introduce potential reliability problems. Since they are designed to quickly detect motions and fire events by sending powerline commands, having multiple motion sensors in the presence of persistent motions can exhaust the already limited bandwidth. Our solution is to place each of them on a separate private powerline network as shown in Figure 1, and let each PC be responsible for recording its local motion sensor state. These sensor states are then propagated to other nodes over the phoneline.

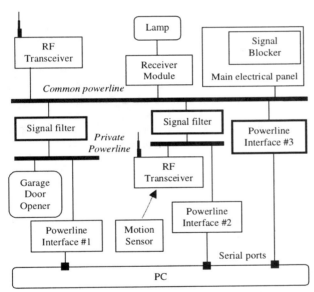

Figure 1. System architecture for enhancing powerline control dependability.

5. Powerline Activity Monitoring

We have also observed reliability problems associated with powerline transmitters. For example, during a 24-hour period, one of the RF transceivers kept receiving RF interferences that resembled valid X10 wireless signals. As a result, it kept converting those interferences to powerline signals and consumed all the bandwidth. In two other incidents, a faulty powerline interface kept generating random X10 signals, again saturating the powerline.

The above observations suggest that consumer device-control transmitters may exhibit non-fail-stop behaviors and create reliability or even security problems if some of the random commands they generate happen to address critical devices. These problems are likely to remain even when the next-generation powerline networking protocols provide better security. The private powerline networking solution mentioned previously can help alleviate this type of problem. But a general tool for monitoring powerline activity is needed to automatically detect and diagnose these problems. We describe such a tool in this subsection. Although the examples are X10-specific, the concept is applicable more generally.

To deal with the RF transceiver interference and faulty powerline interface problems, Aladdin uses *pattern-based detection* [K94]: it monitors X10 powerline transmissions and detects whether they satisfy some specified patterns of bad behaviors. In the X10 system, each receiver module is manually assigned an X10 address consisting of a *house code* (A through P) and a *unit code* (1 through 16). A typical X10 transmission sequence consists of some number of *address commands* (e.g. "A2", "A5", etc.) of the same house code, followed by one or more *function commands* of that same house code (e.g., "A On", "A Off", etc.). Since each transceiver is tuned to receive and transmit X10 commands of exactly one house code, the bad pattern we observed in the RF interference scenario is relatively simple to model as follows.

"Within the last ΔS time, K or more identical function commands were transmitted consecutively on the powerline"

For the faulty interface problem, the pattern of bad behavior is more complex:

"Within the last ΔT time, there were L or more transmission bursts on the powerline in each of which either M or more address commands with the same unit code were transmitted consecutively or N or more identical function commands were transmitted consecutively"

In these two expressions, K, L, M, and N are integer constants (roughly, based on our incidence logs, 25, 15, 5, and 5) and ΔS and ΔT are time constants (roughly, 2 minutes each).

We have chosen not to implement monitors for each observed pattern on a case-by-case basis, since we expect the set of bad behavior patterns to grow as we collect new incidence reports and gain further experience with the fault types in consumer devices. Building upon the SIEFAST monitoring language and its implementation [S], our approach is to express all observed patterns in an extended regular expression language and to automatically generate the monitoring daemon. The extended regular expression language allows (1) parameterized matching of events, for succinct specification of bad behaviors, and (2) event matching in conjunction with satisfaction of state predicates, i.e. Boolean expressions on the system state, for capturing scenarios where transmission sequences are normal but they violate access rights (maintained in system state). For brevity, we omit the description of extension (2) here.

Let Σ be the finite set of events, ε the null event, ev a variable of some type of event, x an event parameter ranging over all possible values in the domain of ev, and E an expression. Atomic expressions have one of the following forms: an event e, the null event ε, and the parameterized event $ev=x$. Expressions have one of the following forms: E^*, which denotes 0 or more occurrences of E; E^+, which denote 1 or more occurrences of E; E^K, which denotes K occurrences of E; $E;F$, which denotes E followed by F; and $E+F$, which denotes nondeterministic choice E or F. The parameterized event $ev=x$ abbreviates nondeterministic choice over an event of type ev. The event parameter x is scoped: multiple occurrences of $ev=x$ within the scope of x in an expression must be matched with the same choice; in other words, x is existentially quantified over its scope. (Unless explicitly specified, the scope of an event parameter is the entire expression.) For example, if $\Sigma=\{a,b,c\}$ and the domain of ev is $\{a,b\}$ then the expression $((ev=x);c;(ev=x)^*)$ abbreviates $(a;c;a^*) + (b;c;b^*)$. Lastly, as a convenience, the symbol Σ is overloaded to abbreviate the expression that denotes a don't-care event, i.e., a nondeterministic choice over all events in Σ; thus, Σ^* denotes 0 or more occurrences of events.

In terms of this language, letting Σ denote the events that can occur on the powerline, the first pattern reduces to witnessing on the powerline the following regular expression within ΔS time:

$$\Sigma^* ; (Function\_Command=x)^K ; \Sigma^*$$

where x is a parameter that ranges over the set of function command values and $Function\_Command=x$ is a parameter expression that matches events which are function commands x. The prefix and suffix Σ^* subexpressions capture the normal transmissions that may occur within the ΔS time interval before and after the bad pattern, which consists of K identical function commands transmitted consecutively. They also capture the case where more than K identical function commands are transmitted consecutively. As another example, the second pattern reduces to witnessing on the powerline within ΔT time:

$$(\Sigma^* ; ((\exists y\ (Address\_Command\_Unitcode=y)^M)+ (\exists z\ (Function\_Command=z)^N)))^L ; \Sigma^*$$

where $Address\_Command\_Unitcode=y$ is an expression that matches events which are address commands with unit code y and $(\exists y ...)$ denotes the scope of parameter y.

6. Summary and Future Work

In this paper, we have focused on the home networking dependability challenges created by the heterogeneity of network entities and the undependable nature of consumer devices for powerline control. We described the use of the soft-state store as a shared heartbeat infrastructure for building robust lookup services that provide eventual consistency in the presence of device/object connecting, disconnecting, and failing. We implemented an Aladdin Device Adapter as an add-on module to allow existing devices to robustly join and leave the system. We described a system architecture that utilizes private powerline networks and exploits the phoneline network to combat the dependability problems in powerline control. Based on actual experiences, we argued for the need to monitor the powerline for unusual activities that could be generated by non-fail-stop devices, radio interferences, and intruders. We described the implementation of a monitoring tool for detecting abnormal powerline command patterns.

Future work includes adding persistence support for soft-states with low-refresh rates in order to enhance data availability upon system failures; modeling all legal powerline command patterns and designing a comprehensive monitoring tool for detecting all bad patterns; and designing a dependability framework to simplify the implementations of dependability solutions and to facilitate the proofs of end-to-end system stabilization [AP95].

References

[AP95] A. Arora and D. Poduska, "A Timing-based Schema for Stabilizing Information Exchange in Networks," in *Proc. Int. Conf. on Computer Networks*, 1995.

[E99] W. K. Edwards, "Core Jini", Prentice-Hall Inc., 1999.

[Ev96] G. Evans, "The CEBus Standard User's Guide", http://www.cebus.com/training.htm#book, May 1996.

[H98] The Home Phoneline Networking Alliance, "Simple, High-Speed Ethernet Technology for the Home," http://www.homepna.org/docs/wp1.pdf, 1998.

[K94] S. Kumar and E. H. Spafford, "A Pattern Matching Model for Misuse Intrusion Detection," In *Proc. National Computer Security Conference*, pp. 11-21, Oct. 1994.

[S] SIEFAST User Guide, http://www.cis.ohio-state.edu/siefast.

[S98] Silent Servant Home Control Inc., "Automated Home Control," 1998.

[WRA00] Y. M. Wang, W. Russell, and A. Arora, "A Toolkit for Building Dependable and Extensible Home Networking Applications," to appear in *Proc. USENIX Windows Systems Symp.*, Aug. 2000.

Design, Implementation, and Performance of Checkpointing in NetSolve

Adnan Agbaria

Department of Computer Science
Technion - Israel Institute of Technology
Haifa 32000, Israel
adnan@cs.technion.ac.il

James S. Plank

Department of Computer Science
University of Tennessee
Knoxville, TN 37996
plank@cs.utk.edu

Abstract

While a variety of checkpointing techniques and systems have been documented for long-running programs, they are typically not available for programmers that are non systems experts. This paper details a project that integrates three technologies, NetSolve, Starfish, and IBP, for the seamless integration of fault-tolerance into long-running applications. We discuss the design and implementation of this project, and present performance results executing on both local and wide-area networks.

1 Introduction

Checkpointing and rollback recovery is a well-studied research area for enabling long-running applications to be fault-tolerant. Many basic checkpointing algorithms [6, 11] and optimization techniques [12] have been developed for uniprocessor and parallel computing systems, and several checkpointing libraries and systems have been implemented [1, 5, 8, 10, 14, 17, 18, 20, 22]. However, for the typical scientific user, actually using a checkpointing system is a difficult task. All systems require the user to port a library and recompile or relink their code subject to a number of restrictions imposed by the library. These restrictions range from strong typing of the source code [17] to restricted file I/O [5, 14] to static linking of runtime libraries [1], to restricted communication patterns [5]. One restriction shared by all checkpointers is that no connections to the outside world may be open while checkpointing is underway.

Because of all of these factors, few scientific users actually employ checkpointing in their applications. This paper describes a research project whose goal is to embed checkpointing seamlessly into long-running applica-

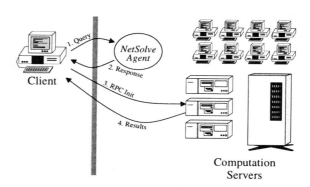

Figure 1. The structure of NetSolve applications

tions for scientific programmers. To achieve this goal, we combine three software systems, NetSolve [2], Starfish [1], and IBP [13]. In this experience report, we describe each software piece and how the pieces are integrated, focusing on the important design decisions. These are:

- A user interface with few complexities.

- An efficient checkpoint library that is fairly simple to embed into server code, and whose restrictions do not limit the user's application.

- A checkpointing storage substrate that facilitates restart and migration across administrative domains, and automatic garbage collection.

We close with a few performance studies in a variety of local and wide area settings.

2   The Components

The system is based on three components: NetSolve, Starfish, and IBP. We first describe these components.

2.1   NetSolve [2]

NetSolve is a brokered remote procedure call (RPC) environment as depicted in Figure 1. The user is termed a *client*, and is typically executing code on a PC or laptop. When the client wishes to perform a computationally complex task, he or she makes a NetSolve client call, specifying the name of the task, plus the arguments. The NetSolve client software (linked to the client in the form of a library) manages the completion of this task, which we will refer to as a "service."

First an *agent* is contacted with a query (step 1), specifying the service name and the size of the arguments. The agent maintains information on a collection of computational servers, which may be uniprocessors, multiprocessors, massively parallel machines, Condor workstation pools [20], etc. This information consists of machine parameters (speed, memory, available software), plus current load information. The agent returns an ordered list of candidate servers to the client (step 2), who then picks a server (typically the first on the list) and initiates a RPC to that server (step 3). The server performs the service, and completes the RPC, returning the results to the client (step 4).

Although not depicted in Figure 1, there may be multiple agents managing overlapping server pools. Additionally, servers may span multiple geographic and administrative domains, of which the clients may or may not be a part. One of NetSolve's strengths is the wide variety of clients that it supports. The NetSolve client code may be linked with C, C++ and Fortran, running on both Unix and Windows platforms. Additionally, it may be used from within the popular scientific toolkits Matlab and Mathematica, and from Microsoft Excel. The NetSolve release contains server software for dense and sparse linear algebra routines and other commonly-used scientific codes (e.g. ARPACK, FitPack, ItPack, MinPack, FFTPACK, LAPACK, QMR, etc.). Users may configure servers to run custom code as well with the aid of some Java tools [3].

2.2   Starfish [1]

Starfish is a transparent checkpointing library originally developed to embed fault-tolerance and migration into MPI applications. The Starfish checkpointing mechanism is a standard core dump mechanism that has served as the basis for many checkpointers (see papers by Tannenbaum [20] and Plank [14] for throrough discussions of these types of checkpointers). Starfish checkpoints periodically, triggering checkpoints by timer interrupts.

This checkpointer is a library to be linked with Solaris-based programs. No recompilation of any source code is required. Starfish implements the copy-on-write optimization [7, 14] so that the act of checkpointing may be overlapped with the execution of server code. Like most checkpointers, Starfish imposes restrictions on file I/O, requires static linking of shared libraries, and prohibits the use of interprocess communication.

2.3   IBP [13]

The **Internet Backplane Protocol (IBP)** is a mechanism for managing storage on the wide area. IBP servers are daemons that provide local storage (disk, tape and physical memory) to remote clients that link the IBP client library. IBP is useful for checkpointing applications because it allows programs to store their checkpoints into a remote storage entity, perhaps one in a different administrative domain. Therefore if the machine executing the program fails and remains inoperative for a long period of time, the program may be restored on a separate machine, again perhaps in a different administrative domain.

IBP has two features that enable it to serve storage on the wide area as a networking resource:

- **There are no user-defined names.** IBP clients allocate storage, and if the allocation is successful, then it returns three *capabilities* to the client — one each for reading, writing, and management. These capabilities are text strings, and may be viewed as server-defined names for the storage. The elimination of user-defined names facilitates scalability, since no global namespace needs to be maintained. To make an IBP client call for reading, writing or management, the client must present the server with the proper capability.

- **Storage may be constrained to be *volatile* or *time-limited*.** An important issue when serving local storage to remote clients is being able to reclaim the storage. IBP servers may be configured so that the storage allocated to IBP clients is *volatile*, meaning it can go away at any time, or *time-limited*, meaning that it goes away after a specified time period.

The transient nature of IBP storage leads us to refer to the units of IBP storage as buffers.

3   Putting it all Together

The structure of NetSolve with checkpointing is depicted in Figure 2. In a nutshell, the NetSolve servers are linked with Starfish and store their checkpoints in IBP buffers.

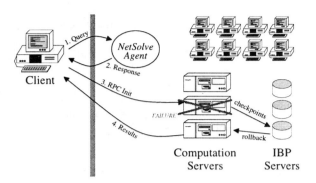

Figure 2. NetSolve with checkpointing

When a server fails, the computation is rolled back to the most recent checkpoint and restored on a new server. The client receives results from whichever server completes the computation. In such a way, the client ends up executing fault-tolerant and migratable code by simply linking with the NetSolve client library.

There is much more detail in the implementation. We first describe the exact client-agent-server interaction. The agent must be aware of server architectures, and whether the server code for a particular computational service has been linked with the Stafish library. This information is returned to the client as part of the response to the client's initial query. Figure 3 illustrates a skeleton of the service code, emphasizing the flow of control for checkpointing and recovery. As part of the service code initiation, the server allocates an IBP buffer on a nearby server. We call this buffer the "naming buffer." The capabilities of the naming buffer are returned to the client.

```
main(int argc, char **argv)
{
    ...
    initialization(&comm, &pd, ...);

    if (chkptState == restart) {
        chkpt_init(argc, argv);       /* Does not return */

    } else if (chkptState == enable) {
        namingBuffer = chkpt_init(argc, argv);
        sendString(comm, namingBuffer); /* Send to client */
        endTransaction(comm);
    }

    /* Perform Service */
    solved = solve(pd, pd->input_objects, pd->output_objects);

    comm = acceptTransaction(sock);
    sendOutputObjects(comm, pd, client_major);
    endTransaction(comm);
}
```

Figure 3. Relevant server source code

When the server initiates both checkpoint and recovery by calling `chkpt_init()`, illustrated in Figure 4.

`Chkpt_init()` sets up periodic checkpointing and the naming buffer, and returns the naming buffer to the server. When it is time to checkpoint, the signal handler calls `chkpt()`, which allocates an IBP buffer for the checkpoint. This is a time-limited allocation for some fixed period of time greater than the checkpoint interval. When the checkpoint is stored in the IBP buffer, the capabilities of this buffer are stored in the naming buffer, and if necessary, the previous checkpoint buffer is deleted.

```
char *chkpt_init(int argc, char **argv)
{
    initialization();
    obtainChkptParams();

    /* Restarts do not return */
    if (chkptState == restart) restartFromIBP(namingBuffer);

    installChkptSignalHandler(chkptInterval);

    /* Allocate the naming buffer */
    namingBuffer = IBP_allocate(ibpMachine, 4*MAXPATHLEN, &ibpAttr);

    return namingBuffer;
}

int chkpt()
{
    if (fork() > 0) {  /* Parent returns while child checkpoints */
        if (chkptSystemInitiated) alarm(chkptInterval);
        return;
    }

    newChkptCap = IBP_allocate(ibpMachine, IBP_CHKPT_SIZE, &ibpAttr);
    rc = ibpWriteChkptData(newChkptCap->write, .....);
    if (rc == CHECKPOINT) {
        removeoldCap(newChkptCap->write, namingBuffer);
    }
}
```

Figure 4. Relevant Starfish source code

The original NetSolve distribution has failure detection and primitive fault-tolerance. Server failures (which may be defined as excessive load) are detected by the NetSolve clients and/or the agent as a result of TCP connection failure. When a failure is detected, the client is reconnected to a new server, which starts the service from scratch. With checkpointing, the client can select a server with the same architecture as the failed server, which can then roll the computation back to the most recent checkpoint. The client presents this new server with the capabilities of the naming buffer, which allow the new server to find the checkpoint buffer and restart the computation. Obviously, this new server may continue checkpointing as well. If there is no server that can restart the computation from the checkpoint, then the client selects the best available server to restart the computation from the beginning.

When the computation completes, the server returns the results to the client and deletes all IBP buffers. Note, however, that if other errors occur, such as NetSolve agent failure, client failure, or NetSolve system shutdown, the time-limited nature of the IBP buffer allocation will make sure that spare checkpoint files are eventually deleted.

As stated above in section 2.2, Starfish places restrictions on the programs that it checkpoints. The only restriction that is a potential problem for NetSolve server code is the prohibition on external connections. While performing a computation, a server only needs to have an open connection to the client when performing the initial RPC interactions and when delivering the results. Thus, Starfish does not start checkpointing until the initial RPC interations are over, and it stops once the server starts delivering results. Typically, NetSolve server codes perform only basic file I/O operations, which are checkpointable by standard means [14].

The selection of checkpointing interval and checkpointing IBP servers is performed by the agent. The optimal checkpoint interval may be approximated by a simple function of checkpoint overhead and failure rate [15, 21], which are both parameters that the agent can estimate. IBP server proximity currently estimated using static metrics. A test implementation of NetSolve integrates the Network Weather Service [23] into the NetSolve system so that the agent can make more accurate predictions of computation server performance and IBP server proximity.

4 Benefits of This Architecture

There are several benefits that this design has in terms of performance, functionality and deployability:

- **The user is insulated from checkpointing details.** In the best case, the user is employing NetSolve to perform common computations such as dense linear algebra. In this case, the NetSolve server setup is trivial, and the user can unknowingly receive the benefits of remote computation and checkpointing even while using Excel on a Windows-based laptop. This is a level of deployability that is typically unheard of in scientific programming.

- **The user's program can have outside connections.** All checkpointing systems restrict connections outside the scope of the programming environment. In other words, while checkpointing systems typically work when all processors are part of the same programming system (for example through the use of PVM or MPI [1, 4, 18]), they only allow programs to interact with the outside world by checkpointing (or logging) before *each* interaction [6, 9]. With NetSolve, the client may initiate a service while maintaining other external connections. This service can checkpoint, fail, rollback, and continue to operate correctly irrespective of the state of the client and its connections to other processing elements. This even works if the client starts the service asynchronously (i.e. in the background while it performs other tasks). Thus, NetSolve's restricted programming model achieves a clean

separation of client and server that allows the server to checkpoint while the client does other things.

- **Migration can occur across the wide area.** NetSolve and IBP both manage resources from different administrative domains, serving cycles and storage to potentially unrelated users and applications. With checkpointing to IBP, it is possible to migrate these services from one domain to another, so long as the server machine architectures are identical.

- **It will work in a lent-resource environment.** Similarly to the above, NetSolve and IBP are both able to manage spare resources (computation and storage) that have limits on their usage. In particular, processors may be revoked due to ownership, and storage may impose time limits on allocation. The inclusion of checkpointing into the NetSolve system means that these resources may be employed by remote computations. This funcationality is similar to that provided by the Condor project [20].

- **Storage ownership is separated from the computation.** Pruyne and Livny have noted that strategic placement of checkpoints at locations external to the computation processors can improve performance [16]. The use of IBP in NetSolve is identical to the use of checkpointing servers in [16] and should improve performance similarly.

5 Performance Case Studies

We briefly detail three performance case studies. In each of these, we have a NetSolve client running Matlab, a Net-Solve agent, two NetSolve servers and one IBP server all running on different machines. The Matlab client makes a NetSolve call to the dmatmul service (matrix multiplication), which gets serviced by one of the NetSolve servers. The server checkpoints to the IBP server, and either it completes without failure, or it fails. When the failure is detected, the second server takes over the service, reading from the checkpoint, and completes the service.

We report results from three separate computing environments: CLUSTER, LOCAL and WIDE. CLUSTER is a tightly-coupled cluster computing environment. The machines are all dual-processor Sun UltraSPARC-2's with 256 Mbytes of RAM, connected by a 155 Mbps ATM network. LOCAL is a department-wide environment, where the NetSolve client and agent are Sun UltraSPARC-1's, and the other machines are lower-end SparcStation-5's. All machines are connected by the Computer Science department's backbone network at the University of Tennessee. Finally WIDE is a wide-area, multi-institutional environment where the client, agent and IBP server are running on

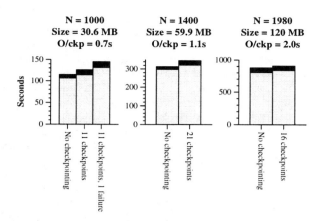

Figure 5. Performance of `dmatmul` **on the** CLUSTER **environment.**

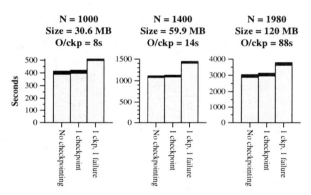

Figure 6. Performance of `dmatmul` **on the** LO-CAL **environment.**

UltraSPARC-1's at Tennessee, while the NetSolve servers are running on two UltraSPARC-1's at Princeton University. Communication between the two institutions is done over the standard Internet. In the CLUSTER test, the machines are dedicated to the experiment. In all other tests, the machines are undedicated.

Results from the CLUSTER environment are displayed in Figure 5. In this and other graphs, The light shaded areas are the server times only. The dark areas add the client interaction times. As expected, the CLUSTER environment exhibits high performance. The ATM network, large physical memories, and copy-on-write optimization combine for extremely high performance. For example, on the $N = 1000$ run, the overhead of checkpointing every ten seconds on the total client/server transaction is 9.7 percent, and the overhead of checkpointing every ten seconds and absorbing one failure is 26 percent.

Results from the LOCAL environment are displayed in Figure 6. As would be expected, the performance of the

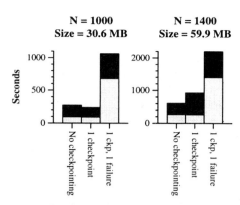

Figure 7. Performance of `dmatmul` **on the** WIDE **environment.**

service is slower due to the slower processors. Likewise, the performance of checkpointing, recovery, and the contact with the client are all worse due to the slower interconnection network. However, in all cases, rolling back from the checkpoint improves performance over restarting from the beginning.

Finally, results from the WIDE environment are displayed in Figure 7. In these graphs, the black boxes are much larger due to the fact that the input and output matrices are being passed across the Internet. Interestingly, even though the checkpoints too are being passed across the Internet, the checkpoint overhead is negligible in comparison to the fluctuation due to non-dedicated access. Once again, this is due to the copy-on-write optimization. However, when a recovery is required, the checkpoint file must be moved across the Internet before recovery may begin, resulting in a severe performance penalty. In this instance, a restart from the beginning would perform better than restarting from the checkpoint. This experiment serves to underscore that it is more important to select the recovering server to be close to the checkpoints than it is to select the checkpointing server to be close to the checkpoints. This is because checkpoints are taken asyncronously, while state restoration is by nature synchronous.

6 Conclusion, Limitations and Deployment

In this paper, we have described a system architecture that brings fault-tolerance and migration to scientific users who need not be computer systems experts. There are two main limitations to this system. First, if a user is not making use of the core NetSolve system services (e.g. linear algebra subroutines) listed in section 2.1, then the "not an expert" label applies less forcefully, as the user must learn how to configure the NetSolve servers. Although this task is made easier by Java-based tools [3], it is a level of complexity higher than simply using NetSolve from Matlab or Excel.

The second limitation is the restriction that the checkpointing and recovering machine must be of the same architecture. This limitation arises from the fact that Starfish is a core-dump style checkpointer. The architecture of the system could easily be extended to use more portable checkpointing substrates, such as applications that implement their own checkpointing and rollback recovery with the help of libraries such as `libft` [10], or a toolkit that embeds portable checkpoints into arbitrary programs [17]. We are exploring using the Porch toolkit [19] to add portable checkpointing to the core NetSolve services.

As described above, this checkpointing system has been implemented and tested. It is anticipated that it will be included as part of the official NetSolve distribution (`http://www.cs.utk.edu/netsolve`) in the year 2000. Starfish and IBP are available from `http://dsl.cs.technion.ac.il/Starfish` and `http://www.cs.utk.edu/~plank/IBP` respectively.

7 Acknowledgements

This material is based upon work supported by the National Science Foundation under grants ACI-9876895, CCR-9703390 and CDA-9529459, and by the Department of Energy under grant DE-FC0299ER25396. The authors thank the anonymous referees for their comments, Dorian Arnold for help with modifying NetSolve, and Roy Friedman and Jack Dongarra for their support.

References

[1] A. Agbaria and R. Friedman. Starfish: Fault-tolerant dynamic MPI programs on clusters of workstations. In *8th IEEE Int. Symp. on High Perf. Dist. Computing*, 1999.

[2] H. Casanova and J. Dongarra. NetSolve: A network server for solving computational science problems. *The International Journal of Supercomputer Applications and High Performance Computing*, 11(3):212–223, 1997.

[3] H. Casanova and J. Dongarra. The use of Java in the NetSolve project. In *15th IMACS World Congress on Scientific Computation, Modeling and Applied Math.*, Berlin, 1997.

[4] J. Casas, D. L. Clark, P. S. Galbiati, R. Konuru, S. W. Otto, R. M. Prouty, and J. Walpole. MIST: PVM with transparent migration and checkpointing. In *3rd Annual PVM Users' Group Meeting*, Pittsburgh, PA, May 1995.

[5] Y. Chen, J. S. Plank, and K. Li. CLIP: A checkpointing tool for message-passing parallel programs. In *SC97: High Performance Networking and Computing*, San Jose, Nov. 1997.

[6] E. N. Elnozahy, L. Alvisi, Y.-M. Wang, and D. B. Johnson. A survey of rollback-recovery protocols in message-passing systems. Technical Report CMU-CS-99-148, Carnegie Mellon University, June 1999.

[7] E. N. Elnozahy, D. B. Johnson, and W. Zwaenepoel. The performance of consistent checkpointing. In *11th Symposium on Reliable Distributed Systems*, pages 39–47, October 1992.

[8] E. N. Elnozahy and W. Zwaenepoel. Manetho: Transparent rollback-recovery with low overhead, limited rollback and fast output commit. *IEEE Transactions on Computers*, 41(5):526–531, May 1992.

[9] E. N. Elnozahy and W. Zwaenepoel. On the use and implementation of message logging. In *24th Int. Symp. on Fault-Tolerant Comp.*, pages 298–307, Austin, TX, June 1994.

[10] Y. Huang, C. Kintala, and Y.-M. Wang. Software tools and libraries for fault tolerance. *IEEE Technical Committee on Operating Systems and Appl. Env.*, 7(4):5–9, Winter 1995.

[11] D. Manivannan and M. Singhal. Quasi-synchronous checkpointing: Models, characterization and classification. *IEEE Transactions on Parallel and Distributed Systems*, 10(7):703–713, July 1999.

[12] J. S. Plank. Program diagnostics. In J. G. Webster, editor, *Wiley Encyclopedia of Electrical and Electronics Engineering*, volume 17, pages 300–310. John Wiley & Sons, Inc., New York, 1999.

[13] J. S. Plank, M. Beck, W. Elwasif, T. Moore, M. Swany, and R. Wolski. The Internet Backplane Protocol: Storage in the network. In *NetStore '99: Network Storage Symposium*. Internet2, http://dsi.internet2.edu/netstore99, October 1999.

[14] J. S. Plank, M. Beck, G. Kingsley, and K. Li. **Libckpt**: Transparent checkpointing under Unix. In *Usenix Winter Technical Conference*, pages 213–223, January 1995.

[15] J. S. Plank and W. R. Elwasif. Experimental assessment of workstation failures and their impact on checkpointing systems. In *28th Int. Symp. on Fault-Tolerant Comp.*, pages 48–57, Munich, June 1998.

[16] J. Pruyne and M. Livny. Managing checkpoints for parallel programs. In *Workshop on Job Scheduling Strategies for Parallel Processing (IPPS '96)*, 1996.

[17] B. Ramkumar and V. Strumpen. Portable checkpointing and recovery in heterogeneous environments. In *27th Int. Symp. on Fault-Tolerant Comp.*, pages 58–97, June 1997.

[18] G. Stellner. CoCheck: Checkpointing and process migration for MPI. In *10th International Parallel Processing Symposium*, pages 526–531. IEEE Computer Society, April 1996.

[19] V. Strumpen. Porch: Portable checkpoint compiler. `http://theory.lcs.mit.edu/~porch/`, 1998.

[20] T. Tannenbaum and M. Litzkow. The Condor distributed processing system. *Dr. Dobb's Journal*, #227:40–48, 1995.

[21] N. H. Vaidya. Impact of checkpoint latency on overhead ratio of a checkpointing scheme. *IEEE Transactions on Computers*, 46(8):942–947, August 1997.

[22] Y.-M. Wang, Y. Huang, K.-P. Vo, P.-Y. Chung, and C. Kintala. Checkpointing and its applications. In *25th Int. Symp. on Fault-Tolerant Comp.*, pages 22–31, Pasadena, CA, June 1995.

[23] R. Wolski, N. Spring, and J. Hayes. The Network Weather Service: A distributed resource performance forecasting service for metacomputing. *Future Generation Computer Systems*, 15, 1999.

Session 2C

Student Forum

Session 3

Panel

Session 4A

Language Support

Efficient Incremental Checkpointing of Java Programs*

Julia L. Lawall[†] and Gilles Muller
COMPOSE group, http://www.irisa.fr/compose
IRISA/INRIA, Campus de Beaulieu, 35042 Rennes Cedex, France
{jll,muller}@irisa.fr
tel:+33.2.99.84.72.87, fax:+33.2.99.84.71.71

Abstract

This paper investigates the optimization of language-level checkpointing of Java programs. First, we describe how to systematically associate incremental checkpoints with Java classes. While being safe, the genericness of this solution induces substantial execution overhead. Second, to solve the dilemma of genericness versus performance, we use automatic program specialization to transform the generic checkpointing methods into highly optimized ones. Specialization exploits two kinds of information: (i) structural properties about the program classes, (ii) knowledge of unmodified data structures in specific program phases. The latter information allows us to generate phase-specific checkpointing methods. We evaluate our approach on two benchmarks, a realistic application which consists of a program analysis engine, and a synthetic program which can serve as a metric. Specialization gives a speedup proportional to the complexity of the object structure and the modification pattern. Measured speedups for the program analysis engine are up to 1.5, and for the synthetic program are up to 15.

1 Introduction

Checkpointing is known to introduce overhead proportional to the checkpoint size [12, 28]. Traditionally, optimizations of the checkpointing process are targeted toward scientific programs written in Fortran or C. Such programs often have good locality and large regions of read-only data. In this environment, an effective optimization technique is *incremental checkpointing*, which uses system-level facilities to identify modified virtual-memory pages [7, 19, 25]. Each checkpoint contains only the pages that have been modified since the previous checkpoint. Additionally, by using a mechanism such as copy-on-write, the application need not be blocked, at the expense of deferring the copy task to the system.

Programs written in an object-oriented language, such as Java, place new demands on checkpointing:

- Object-oriented programming style encourages the creation of many small objects. Each object may have some fields that are read-only, and others that are frequently modified. Thus, object encapsulation conflicts with programmer-based data placement strategies.

- The Java programmer has no control over the location of objects. Thus, it is impossible to ensure that frequently modified objects are all stored in the same page. Furthermore, a single page may contain both live objects and objects awaiting garbage collection.

- Java programs are run on a virtual machine which supports simultaneous processes. Since Java encourages parallelism as a software engineering method, libraries such as the GUI create many processes whose states are not always useful in a checkpoint. Also, object allocation is not usally managed on a per-process basis, thus adding unnecessary memory to a checkpoint. Finally, there is no simple solution to a transparent support of native methods.

These arguments suggest that a user-driven language-level approach may be appropriate for Java programs. Language-level checkpointing augments the source program with code to record the program state [16, 17, 26]. To promote safety, this checkpointing code should be introduced systematically, and interfere as little as possible with the standard behavior of the program. One approach is to add methods to each class to save and restore the local state. Checkpointing is then performed by a generic `checkpoint` method that invokes the checkpointing methods of each checkpointable object. Incremental checkpointing can be implemented by associating a flag with each object, indicating whether the object has been modified since the previous checkpoint. This checkpointing

---

*This research is supported in part by Bull, Alcatel, and by NSF under Grant EIA-9806718

[†]Author's current address: DIKU, University of Copenhagen, Universitetsparken 1, 2100 Copenhagen East, Denmark

code can either be added manually or generated automatically using a preprocessor [16, 17]. In either case, localizing the code for saving and restoring the state of an object in its class definition respects encapsulation, thus enhancing overall program safety, and simplifies program maintenance.

Nevertheless, this generic programming model introduces overheads. First, because the `checkpoint` method is independent of the objects being checkpointed, it must interact with these objects using virtual calls. Virtual calls are less efficient than direct function calls, and block traditional compiler optimizations, such as inlining. Second, although the use of the modified flag reduces the size of checkpoints, it does not eliminate the need to visit each checkpointable object defined by the program.

This checkpointing strategy can be optimized by manually creating specialized checkpointing functions for recurring object structures in the program. When some of the objects are known not to be modified between specific checkpoints, all code relating to the checkpointing of those objects can be removed. Nevertheless, many specialized checkpointing routines may be needed, to account for the range of compound object structures used in different phases of the program. When the program is modified, these manually optimized routines may need to be completely rewritten. Thus, while these kinds of optimizations can yield significant performance improvements, performing them by hand is laborious and error-prone.

Our approach

In this paper, we propose to use *automatic program specialization* to automatically optimize a generic checkpointing algorithm based on programmer-supplied information about the fixed aspects of the object structure. Program specialization is a technique for automatically and aggressively optimizing a generic program with respect to information about the program inputs [11, 15]. This technique has been applied in a wide range of areas, including operating systems [20, 21, 31], and scientific programs [13, 23].

By specializing the checkpointing implementation with respect to recurring structural and modification patterns, we eliminate many tests, virtual calls, and traversals of unmodified data. Because specialization is automatic, these transformations can be performed reliably, and are simple to modify as the program evolves.

To assess the benefits of our approach in a realistic setting, we specialize the checkpointing of an implementation of a program analysis engine, which performs the kinds of analyses that are used in compilation or automatic program specialization. To analyze more precisely the benefits of our approach, we also consider a synthetic program in which we can vary the dimensions and modification pattern of the checkpointed structure. These results can be used as a metric to predict the benefits of specializing the checkpointing process for other applications. We have run the specialized programs on a 300 MHz Sun Ultra2 using the standard JIT of JDK 1.2.2, the HotSpot dynamic compiler, and the Harissa JVM which runs Java-to-C translated programs. We obtain the following results:

- Specializing with respect to the structure of a compound object optimizes the traversal of the subobjects by replacing virtual calls by inlined code.

- Specializing with respect to the modification pattern of a compound object eliminates tests and the traversal of completely unmodified objects.

- The program analysis engine example is divided into phases, each of which reads but does not modify the results of previous phases. We automatically generate a specialized checkpointing routine for each phase. Specializing with respect to both the object structure and the modification pattern gives speedups of up to 1.5 times.

- For the synthetic example, we first specialize with respect to the structure, and then with respect to both the structure and the modification pattern. Specialization with respect to the structure gives speedups up to 3. Specialization with respect to the structure and the modification pattern gives speedups proportional to the percentage of unmodified objects. When three quarters of the objects are unmodified, we obtain speedups up to 15.

The rest of this paper is organized as follows. We begin with a Java implementation of checkpointing, in Section 2. Section 3 then introduces program specialization and identifies opportunities for the specialization of the checkpointing implementation. Sections 4 and 5 assess the benefits of specialization of the checkpointing process on the program analysis engine and the synthetic example. Section 6 describes related work, particularly focusing on complementary approaches to language-level checkpointing. Finally, Section 7 concludes and suggests future work.

2 Incremental Checkpointing of Java Programs

We consider the checkpointing of an object-oriented program in which the state of the program can be recovered from the contents of the object fields. In this context, checkpointing amounts to recursively traversing the objects and recording the local state of each one; the stack is omitted. Similar strategies have been proposed by others, including Kasbekar *et al.* [16] and Killijian *et al.* [17].

2.1 Implementation

The implementation consists of the `Checkpointable` interface, which specifies the methods that must be provided by each object to be checkpointed, and a `Checkpoint` object, which drives the checkpointing process. These are defined in Figure 1. For simplicity, we assume that the checkpointed objects do not contain cycles. We also assume that checkpoints are constructed using a blocking protocol, and are written from the output stream to stable storage asynchronously.

Each checkpointable object contains a unique identifier and methods that describe how to record the state of the object and its children. Additionally, to implement incremental checkpointing, each object contains a flag indicating whether any fields of the object have been modified since the previous checkpoint. This functionality is captured by the `Checkpointable` interface. The unique identifier and the modification flag, which are defined in the same way for all checkpointable objects, are factored into a separate `CheckpointInfo` object, also defined in Figure 1.

```
public interface Checkpointable {
  public CheckpointInfo getCheckpointInfo();
  public void fold(Checkpoint c);
  public void record(OutputStream d);
}

public class Checkpoint {
  OutputStream d;

  public Checkpoint() {
    d = new OutputStream();
  }

  public void checkpoint(Checkpointable o) {
    CheckpointInfo info = o.getCheckpointInfo();
    if (info.modified()) {
      d.writeInt(info.getId());
      o.record(d);
      info.resetModified();
    }
    o.fold(this);
  }
}

public class CheckpointInfo {
  private int id;
  private boolean modified;
  public CheckpointInfo() {
    id = newId();
    modified = true;
  }

  // unique identifier
  public int getId() { return id; }
  private static int newId() { ... }

  // modification flag
  public boolean modified() { return modified; }
  public void setModified() { modified=true; }
  public void resetModified() { modified=false; }
}
```

Figure 1: Incremental checkpointing in Java

The `Checkpointable` interface specifies that each checkpointable object must define the methods `getCheckpointInfo()`, `record()`, and `fold()`. The method `getCheckpointInfo()` accesses the associated `CheckpointInfo` structure. The method `record(OutputStream d)` records the complete local state of the checkpointable object in the output stream d.[1] A value of base type is written directly, while a sub-object is represented by its unique identifier. The method `fold(Checkpoint c)` recursively applies the checkpointing object c to each of the checkpointable sub-objects.

Checkpointing is initiated by creating a `Checkpoint` object, which initializes the output stream. The user program then applies the `checkpoint` method to the root of each compound structure to record in the checkpoint. To implement incremental checkpointing, checkpointing of an object is divided into two steps. First, if the object has been modified, its unique identifier is recorded in the output stream, and its `record()` method is invoked to record its local state. The `modified` field is also reset. Then, regardless of whether the object has been modified since the previous checkpoint, the `fold` method of the object is invoked to recursively apply the checkpointing process to the children.

As in other approaches to checkpointing of object-oriented programs, the state of each object is restored from a checkpoint using a restore method local to the object. The definition of such a method is the inverse of the definition of `record`. The unique identifiers associated with each object are used to reconstruct the state from a sequence of incremental checkpoints. Because restoration is performed rarely, specialization seems unlikely to be interesting here.

2.2 Defining checkpointable objects

The methods required by the `Checkpointable` interface can be systematically defined either manually or automatically, as follows. A class implementing the `Checkpointable` interface creates a `CheckpointInfo` structure and defines the associated `getCheckpointInfo()` accessor function. Such a class also defines `record` and `fold` methods to record its local state and traverse its children, respectively. A class that extends a checkpointable class defines `record` and `fold` methods corresponding to its own local state. These methods invoke the respective methods of the parent class to checkpoint the inherited fields.

As an example, we use part of the implementation of the program analysis engine, presented in Section 4. Each phase of the program analysis engine stores its result in

---

[1] In practice, we instantiate `OutputStream` as a `DataOutputStream` composed with a `ByteArrayOutputStream`, as defined in the `java.io` package.

```
public abstract class Entry
  implements Checkpoint.Checkpointable {
  CheckpointInfo checkpointInfo =
    new Checkpoint.CheckpointInfo();

  public CheckpointInfo getCheckpointInfo() {
    return checkpointInfo;
  }
  public void record(OutputStream d) { }
  public void fold(Checkpoint c) { }
}

public class BTEntry extends Entry {
  BT bt;

  public void record(OutputStream d) {
    super.record(d);
    d.writeInt(bt.getCheckpointInfo().getId());
  }

  public void fold(Checkpoint c) {
    super.fold(c);
    c.checkpoint(bt);
  }

  // Other methods for manipulating the
  // BTEntry object
  ...
}
```

Figure 2: The `Entry` and `BTEntry` classes

a corresponding object. To capture the commonality between these objects, the class of each such object extends an abstract class `Entry`. The class `Entry` and an extension `BTEntry` are shown in Figure 2. The `Entry` class explicitly implements the `Checkpointable` interface. Thus, it creates the `CheckpointInfo` structure and defines the `getCheckpointInfo()` method. The `Entry` class also defines `record()` and `fold()` methods. These methods are trivial, because the `Entry` class has no local state. The `BTEntry` class inherits the `CheckpointInfo` structure of the `Entry` class. It defines its own `record()` and `fold()` methods, to carry out the checkpointing of its child `bt`. The `record()` method first invokes the `record()` method of the superclass, and then accesses the `CheckpointInfo` structure of the child to record the child's unique identifier. The `fold()` method first invokes the `fold()` method of the superclass, and then recursively applies the `checkpoint` method to the child.

3 Program Specialization

Program specialization is the optimization of a program based on supplementary information about its input. We first describe this technique, and then consider how to use it to optimize the checkpointing process.

3.1 Overview of program specialization

Program specialization optimizes a program to a specific usage context. This technique restricts the applicability of a program, in exchange for a more efficient implemen-

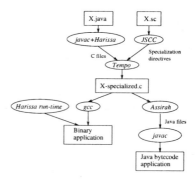

Figure 3: Structure of JSpec, specialization of class x

tation. Specialization of programs written in imperative languages, such as C and Fortran, achieves optimizations such as constant folding and loop unrolling [2, 3, 11]. Specialization of Java programs has been shown to reduce the overhead of data encapsulation, virtual calls, and run-time type and array-bounds checks [27]. Our implementation of checkpointing benefits from these optimizations.

In the context of an object-oriented language, such as Java, the usage context can be described by *specialization classes* [32]. A specialization class describes how a class should be specialized, by declaring properties of the fields and methods of the specialized class. The declared methods are then specialized with respect to this information. Specialization classes are compiled by the *Java Specialization Class Compiler* (JSCC) into directives for the program specializer, and are thus not part of the program execution. We rely on the programmer to specify specialization classes that safely describe the execution context, just as we rely on the programmer to identify points at which specialized checkpointing can be useful.

We specialize the checkpointing process using the *JSpec* program specializer [27], illustrated in Figure 3. JSpec is based on *Tempo*, a program specializer for C [11]. To perform specialization of Java programs, the Java bytecode is first translated into C using the Harissa bytecode-to-C compiler [22]. The specialized C code can be compiled using any C compiler, and then executed in the Harissa JVM. At the C level, the specialized code can express optimizations of the virtual machine, such as the elimination of array-bounds checks, that cannot be expressed in Java. Alternatively, for portability, the specialized C code can be converted back to an ordinary Java program using the Harissa tool *Assirah*.

3.2 Specialization opportunities

The implementation of checkpointing offers two significant opportunities for specialization: specialization with respect to the structure of the checkpointed data and spe-

64

cialization with respect to the data modification pattern of the program. We now describe the benefits of these two kinds of specialization for the checkpointing process.

When there are recurring compound objects having the same structure, we can specialize the `checkpoint` method for this structure. Specialization replaces the virtual calls to the methods of the `Checkpointable` interface by direct calls. These direct calls can be inlined, or otherwise optimized by the compiler. Concretely, inlining generates a monolithic specialized checkpointing implementation for each compound object.

The use of the `modified` field can also be optimized by specialization. Suppose a program initializes a set of objects in one phase, and subsequently only reads their values. When this behavior can be determined before execution, the checkpointing process can be specialized to the fact that in the later phases the `modified` field of such objects is always `false`. This optimization eliminates the test in the `checkpoint` method, which in turn eliminates all reference to the `CheckpointInfo` structure. When combined with specialization to the structure of complex objects, this optimization can eliminate all traversal of compound objects that are completely unmodified between checkpoints.

4 A Realistic Application

Our approach to the optimization of checkpointing is targeted towards complex, long-running programs that manipulate many instances of similar compound structures. We achieve additional benefits when the program is organized in phases, each of which is known to modify only specific kinds of structures. We now describe such a program, a Java implementation of the analyses performed by the program specializer Tempo, and assess the benefits of specialization of the checkpointing process.

4.1 Overview of the program analysis engine

Effective program specialization demands precise, and often time-consuming, analyses. Following the structure of many compilers [1], these analyses are organized in phases, each of which uses, but does not modify, the results of the previous analyses. This kind of program can benefit from specialization of incremental checkpointing.

Concretely, we consider three of the analyses performed by Tempo: *side-effect analysis*, *binding-time analysis*, and *evaluation-time analysis*. Side-effect analysis determines the set of global variables read and written by each program statement. Binding-time analysis identifies expressions that can be evaluated using only the information available to the specializer [15]. Evaluation-time analysis ensures that variables referenced by the specialized program are

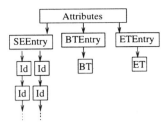

Figure 4: Organization of the `Attributes` structure

properly initialized [14]. Our prototype implementation in Java of these analyses treats a simplified version of C.

Each statement of the analyzed program is associated with an `Attributes` structure, which contains a field for the results of each phase of the analysis. Side-effect analysis collects sets of variables, while binding-time analysis and evaluation-time analysis each record only a single annotation. Thus, most of the information recorded in the `Attributes` structure comes from the side-effect analysis, and is fixed during subsequent phases. Consequently, specialization of the checkpointing process to eliminate the traversal of unmodified objects is most useful for the binding-time and evaluation-time analyses. These analyses are also typically longer than side-effect analysis, making checkpointing more desirable for these phases.

To treat loops, each analysis phase performs repeated iterations over the abstract syntax tree. At the end of each iteration, the local state is captured by the annotations stored at each node. Thus, the end of an iteration is a natural time at which to take a checkpoint.

4.2 Specialization opportunities

We now illustrate the specialization opportunities identified in Section 3.2 in the context of the program analysis engine. We specialize with respect to information about the `Attributes` structure, illustrated in Figure 4. Note that the `BTEntry` class was defined in Figure 2.

We first specialize the checkpointing implementation to the structure of an `Attributes` object. The specialization class `Checkpoint_Attributes` shown below declares that a specialized variant of the `checkpoint` method should be created for the `Attributes` class.

```
specclass Checkpoint_Attributes
  specializes Checkpoint {
  public void checkpoint(Checkpointable o),
    Attributes o;
}
```

Declaring such a specialization of the `Checkpoint` class for each class used in the program makes the types of the checkpointed objects explicit. Specialization replaces virtual calls by direct calls and field references. Virtual calls

```
checkpoint_attr(Checkpointable o) {
 Attributes attr = (Attributes)o;
 CheckpointInfo attrInfo = attr.getCheckpointInfo();
 if (attrInfo.modified()) {
  d.writeInt(attrInfo.getId());
  attr.record(d);
  attrInfo.resetModified();
 }
 SEEntry seEntry = attr.se;
 CheckpointInfo seEntryInfo = SEEntry.getCheckpointInfo();
 if (seEntryInfo.modified()) {
  d.writeInt(seEntryInfo.getId());
  seEntry.record(d); /* records both lists */
  seEntryInfo.resetModified();
 }
 BTEntry btEntry = attr.bt;
 CheckpointInfo btEntryInfo = btEntry.getCheckpointInfo();
 if (btEntryInfo.modified()) {
  d.writeInt(btEntryInfo.getId());
  btEntry.record(d);
  btEntryInfo.resetModified();
 }
 BT bt = btEntry.bt;
 CheckpointInfo btInfo = bt.getCheckpointInfo();
 if (btInfo.modified()) {
  d.writeInt(btInfo.getId());
  bt.record(d); /* virtual call */
  btInfo.resetModified();
 }
 ETEntry etEntry = attr.et;
 CheckpointInfo etEntryInfo = etEntry.getCheckpointInfo();
 if (etEntryInfo.modified()) {
  d.writeInt(etEntryInfo.getId());
  etEntry.record(d);
  etEntryInfo.resetModified();
 }
 ET et = etEntry.et;
 CheckpointInfo etInfo = et.getCheckpointInfo();
 if (etInfo.modified()) {
  d.writeInt(etInfo.getId());
  et.record(d); /* virtual call */
  etInfo.resetModified();
 }
}
```

Figure 5: Specialization of `checkpoint` w.r.t. the structure of an `Attributes` object

```
checkpoint_attr_btmodif(Checkpointable o) {
 Attributes attr = (Attributes)o;
 CheckpointInfo attrInfo = attr.getCheckpointInfo();
 if (info.modified()) {
  d.writeInt(attrInfo.getId());
  attr.record(d);
  attrInfo.resetModified();
 }
 BTEntry btEntry = attr.bt;
 CheckpointInfo btEntryInfo = btEntry.getCheckpointInfo();
 if (btEntryInfo.modified()) {
  d.writeInt(btEntryInfo.getId());
  btEntry.record(d);
  btEntryInfo.resetModified();
 }
 BT bt = btEntry.bt;
 CheckpointInfo btInfo = bt.getCheckpointInfo();
 if (btInfo.modified()) {
  d.writeInt(btInfo.getId());
  bt.record(d); /* virtual call */
  btInfo.resetModified();
 }
}
```

Figure 6: Specialization of `checkpoint` w.r.t. the modification properties of an `Attributes` object for the binding-time analysis

only remain for the methods of the `bt` (binding time) and `et` (evaluation time) objects, whose values are not known during specialization. Subsequent inlining and translation of the specialized C code back to Java produces the optimized implementation shown in Figure 5.

The program analysis engine also has the property that each phase only modifies its corresponding field of the `Attributes` structure. To describe this property, we define a specialization class indicating that the `modified()` method of the `CheckpointInfo` class should be specialized for the case where the `modified` flag has not been set to `true`. To create a specialized checkpointing implementation for use during the binding-time analysis phase, we define a specialization classes for the `Attributes`, `SEEntry`, and `ETEntry` classes indicating that the specialized `modified()` method should be used. The result of specializing according to these declarations is shown in Figure 6. The specialized checkpointing implementation for the evaluation-time analysis phase is specified similarly.

4.3   Performance assessment

Table 1 summarizes the performance of the checkpointing of the binding-time analysis and evaluation-time analysis phases. In a program specializer that treats full C, such as Tempo, these analyses can take up to several hours, depending on the complexity of the analyzed program. Since we treat a simplified version of C, the analyses are considerably faster. We have analyzed a 750-line image manipulation program: without checkpointing, binding-time analysis runs for 62.2 seconds and evaluation-time analysis runs for 6.4 seconds. We compare full checkpointing, incremental checkpointing, and specialized incremental checkpointing. A checkpoint is taken for each iteration of the analyses. The binding-time analysis requires nine iterations, while the evaluation-time analysis requires only three. For full checkpointing, we show the performance for the iterations with the minimum and maximum checkpoint sizes. For unspecialized and specialized incremental checkpointing, the checkpoints all have roughly the same size, so we give average figures. For the binding-time analysis phase, specialization gives speedups of over 1.3, and for the evaluation-time analysis phase specialization gives speedups of almost 1.5 over incremental checkpointing.

We have noted that specialization eliminates the traversal of unmodified objects. Thus, the traversal time represents the limit of the cost that can be eliminated by specialization. The last line of the table compares the traversal time for incremental and specialized incremental checkpointing. For the binding-time analysis phase, specialization reduces the traversal time by 1.8 times, and for the evaluation-time analysis phase specialization reduces the traversal time by over 2 times.

	Binding-time analysis (BTA)				Evaluation-time analysis (ETA)			
	full ckp. min. size	full ckp. max. size	incremental	specialized incremental (speedup)		full ckp. min. size	full ckp. max. size	incremental	specialized incremental (speedup)
Ckp. size (Mb)	12.52	21.88	1.40	1.40		11.04	11.17	0.55	0.55
Ckp. time (s)	5.3	9.08	1.34	1.00 (**1.34**)		4.56	4.65	0.71	0.48 (**1.49**)
Traversal time (s)	-	-	0.74	0.40 (**1.85**)		-	-	0.46	0.23 (**2.03**)

Table 1: Checkpoint size (in Mb) and execution time (in seconds). (JDK 1.2.2 JVM, Sun Ultra2 300MHz)

5 A synthetic application

To assess the benefits of our approach independent of a particular application, we consider a synthetic example, in which we can vary the structure of the checkpointed objects. The goal of these tests is to provide a metric for determining to what degree other applications can benefit from our approach. We consider checkpointing a set of compound structures, each containing five linked lists. We vary properties of these structures such as the length of the lists, the percentage of modified list elements, and the number of integer-typed fields stored in each list element.

The test program constructs 20,000 compound structures, randomly chooses constituent list elements to be modified according to the constraints of the experiment, and performs a single checkpoint. Our benchmarks present the time to construct the checkpoint. Unless otherwise stated, the Java programs were translated to C before specialization and then run in the Harissa JVM.

We first compare incremental checkpointing to full checkpointing. When some objects are not modified, incremental checkpointing reduces the cost of recording the current state. Nevertheless, incremental checkpointing also introduces tests into the traversal of the compound structures. Figure 7 shows that even when all of the objects are modified the added cost is negligible. The speedup obtained by incremental checkpointing increases as the number of modified objects decreases, and as the cost of recording the state of each object increases. When only a quarter of the objects are modified, and when 10 integers are recorded for each modified object, incremental checkpointing is over 3 times faster than full checkpointing.

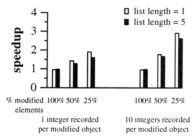

Figure 7: Incremental checkpointing (Harissa JVM)

Incremental checkpointing reduces the number of objects recorded in the checkpoint, but still requires a complete traversal of the compound structures to identify modified objects. Specialization with respect to properties of the object structure optimizes the traversal. In particular, we specialize with respect to the following structural information.

- The shape of the compound structures.
- The set of lists that may contain modified objects.
- The positions in these lists where a modified object may occur.

The speedups with respect to incremental checkpointing achieved by these specialization opportunities are summarized in Figures 8 through 11. The percentages in each figure indicate the percentage of possibly modified objects that are actually modified. For example, in Figure 9, in which the number of lists that contain modified objects is constrained, the case labelled "50%" where there are three modified lists means that among those three lists, half of the objects have been modified since the previous checkpoint.

Specialization with respect to the shape of each compound structure eliminates virtual calls and permits inlining. These optimizations give the most speedup when there are few modified objects, and thus the cost of the structure traversal dominates. Figure 8 shows that the speedup as compared to unspecialized incremental checkpointing ranges from 1.5 when all objects are modified and 10 integers are written for each modified object, to over 3 when each list has length 5, only 25% of the objects are modified, and only one integer is written for each modified object.

When some lists are known to be completely unmodified, specialization with respect to this information eliminates the traversal of such lists. Here, the greatest speedup is obtained when there are long lists, of which few may contain modified objects (see Figure 9). For lists of length 5, when only one value is recorded for each modified object, the speedup ranges from 2 to 9, as the number of lists that may contain modified objects decreases. When 10 integers are recorded for each modified object, the speedup is reduced by up to half.

Specializing with respect to the specific positions within each list at which modified objects can occur eliminates the need to test the other objects. We consider the case where a modified object can only occur as the last element of each list. This is the worst case, because only tests, but not object traversals, are eliminated. Because the number of eliminated tests depends on the length of the lists, we achieve the best speedup for long lists. Figure 10 shows that for lists of length 5, when only one value is recorded for each modified object, the speedup over unspecialized incremental checkpointing ranges from 5 to 15, depending on the number of lists that may contain modified objects. When 10 integers are recorded for each object, these speedups range from 2 to 11.

So far, we have assessed the performance of specialized C code. For portability, we can also translate the specialized C code back to Java using the Assirah tool. In our third specialization experiment above (c.f. Figure 10), we specialize with respect to both the number of lists that may contain a modified object and the position at which a modified object may occur in each list. Figure 11 compares the performance of the Java specialized code with the performance of the unspecialized Java implementation of incremental checkpointing, for lists of length 5. As shown in Figure 11a, using the JDK 1.2.2 JIT compiler, we obtain speedups of up to 12. As shown in Figure 11b, combining JDK 1.2.2 with the state-of-the art dynamic compiler HotSpot, we obtain speedups of up to 6 over the performance of the unspecialized code, also running on HotSpot. As shown in Table 2, the Harissa code is significantly faster than the code produced by the JDK 1.2.2 JIT compiler or HotSpot. Table 2 also shows that the unspecialized code run with HotSpot can be faster than the specialized code run without HotSpot. Thus, one may wonder whether HotSpot subsumes program specialization. Nevertheless, Figure 11b shows that the specialization further improves performance under HotSpot, demonstrating that specialization and dynamic compilation are complementary.

6 Related work

Automatic program-transformation techniques have already been used to improve the reliability and performance of source-level checkpointing. The C-to-C compilers c2ftc and porch, developed by Ramkumar and Strumpen [26, 30] and by Strumpen [29], respectively, add code around each procedure call to enable a program to manage the checkpointing and recovery of its control stack. A preprocessor in the Dome system provides a similar facility for parallel C++ programs [5, 6]. Plank *et al.* propose to use data-flow analysis to determine automatically, based on hints from the user, the regions of memory that are not modified between checkpoints [4, 24]. Calls to functions in a checkpointing library (libckpt for Sparc or CLIP for Intel Paragon) are then automatically inserted into the source program. Killijian *et al.* and Kasbekar *et al.* use compile-time reflection provided by OpenC++ [10] to add check-

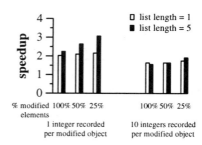

Figure 8: Specialization w.r.t. the object structure (Harissa JVM)

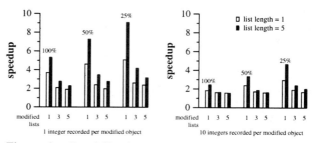

Figure 9: Specialization w.r.t. the object structure and the number of lists that may contain modified elements (Harissa JVM)

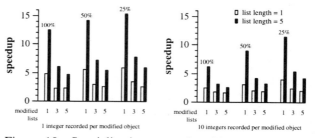

Figure 10: Specialization w.r.t. the object structure and the number of lists whose last element can be modified (Harissa JVM)

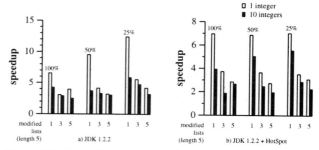

Figure 11: Specialization w.r.t. the object structure and the number of lists whose last element can be modified (Sun JVM)

	Possibly mod. lists	Harissa			JDK 1.2.2			JDK 1.2.2 + HotSpot		
		100%	50%	25%	100%	50%	25%	100%	50%	25%
Unspecialized code	1	1.05	0.98	0.95	3.99	1.98	1.76	1.80	1.56	1.32
	5	1.80	1.36	1.14	10.92	7.05	4.03	4.51	2.41	1.71
Specialized code	1	0.17	0.10	0.08	0.95	0.54	0.30	0.46	0.31	0.24
	5	0.70	0.42	0.27	4.39	2.33	1.27	1.70	1.23	0.76

Table 2: Checkpoint execution time (in seconds), 10 integers written for each element

pointing code at the source level to the definitions of C++ objects [16, 17]. The reflection-based approaches are most closely related to ours. Essentially, we use program specialization to optimize checkpointing methods of the form generated by reflection.

Several of these source-level approaches address the problem of incremental checkpointing. The analysis proposed by Plank *et al.* to detect unmodified regions of memory is performed at compile time, and is thus necessarily approximate. The reflective approach of Killijian *et al.* associates a modification flag with each object field. Maintaining and testing these flags at run time adds substantial overhead: extra space to store the modification flags, extra time on every assignment to update the associated flag, and extra time during checkpointing to test the flags. Our approach exploits both compile-time and run-time information. When it is possible to determine at compile time that an object is not modified between checkpoints, specialization eliminates the code to save the state of the object. When it is not possible to determine this information at compile time, the modified flag is retained in the specialized program and tested at run time. Because specialization is automatic, it is feasible to create many implementations, to account for the modification patterns of each phase of the program, without changing the source code.

Language-level checkpointing for Java provides independence from the virtual machine. Other approaches have simplified the checkpointing process and reduced checkpoint size by omitting aspects of the underlying language implementation. The Stardust [9] and Dome [5, 6] systems for SIMD parallelism in heterogeneous environments restrict checkpointing to synchronization points in the `main` function, eliminating the need to record the stack. In the context of Java, Killijian *et al.* also record only object fields, and thus omit the stack [17].

Checkpointing is conceptually similar to *serialization*, the conversion of an object structure into a flat representation. In Java, serialization is implemented using run-time reflection. Reflection is used both to determine the static structure of each object (its type, field names, etc.), and to access the recorded field values. The structure of an object, however, does not change during execution. Thus, repetitively determining this information at run time is inefficient. Braux and Noyé propose to eliminate the over-

heads of Java reflection using program specialization [8]. These techniques could useful in extending our approach to a checkpointing implementation based on reflection.

Several Java-based mobile agent systems use serialization to transmit the state of an agent to another host [18, 33]. The Concordia system also provides extensive checkpointing facilities based on serialization to recover from transmission failures [33]. Specialization of the checkpointing process could improve the performance of these systems as well.

7 Conclusion and future work

We have shown that automatic program specialization can significantly improve the incremental checkpointing of Java programs. Because specialization is automatic, the generated code is correct. This approach has several advantages: (i) multiple checkpoint procedures can be generated for a single program, permitting to exploit per-phase modification patterns, and (ii) checkpointing can be implemented straightforwardly to facilitate program evolution and maintenance, without sacrificing performance.

This work can fit into a series of automated tools to improve the performance of language-level checkpointing. In the approach we have presented, the user must identify which compound structures are used frequently in the program, and the regions in which such structures are not modified. To automate this process, we propose to automatically construct specialization classes based on an analysis of the data modification pattern of the program. If we additionally use reflection as proposed by Kasbekar *et al.* and by Killijian *et al.* to automatically generate the checkpointing methods for each class [16, 17] and automatically modify the source code as proposed in the `c2ftc` and `porch` systems to save and restore the stack [26, 29, 30], we obtain an efficient and transparent language-level implementation of checkpointing for Java programs.

Acknowledgments

We thank Ulrik Pagh Schultz and Miroslav Malek for helpful comments, and James Plank for shepherding the final version of this paper. We also thank the other members of the Compose group who participated in the design and the implementation of JSpec.

Availability

Examples described in this paper are available at
`http://www.irisa.fr/compose/jspec/checkpoint`.
Tempo, Harissa, JSpec and the Java Specialization Class
Compiler are available at the Compose web page
`http://www.irisa.fr/compose/`.

References

[1] A.V. Aho, R. Sethi, and J.D. Ullman. *Compilers Principles, Techniques, and Tools.* Addison-Wesley, 1986.

[2] L.O. Andersen. *Program Analysis and Specialization for the C Programming Language.* PhD thesis, Computer Science Department, University of Copenhagen, May 1994. DIKU Technical Report 94/19.

[3] R. Baier, R. Glück, and R. Zöchling. Partial evaluation of numerical programs in Fortran. In *ACM SIGPLAN Workshop on Partial Evaluation and Semantics-Based Program Manipulation*, pages 119–132, Orlando, FL, USA, June 1994. Technical Report 94/9, University of Melbourne, Australia.

[4] M. Beck, J.S. Plank, and G. Kingsley. Compiler-assisted checkpointing. Technical Report CS-94-269, University of Tennessee, December 1994.

[5] A. Beguelin, E. Seligman, and E. Stephan. Application level fault tolerance in heterogeneous networks of workstations. Technical Report CMU-CS-96-157, School of Computer Science, Carnegie Mellon University, August 1996.

[6] A. Beguelin, E. Seligman, and P. Stephan. Application level fault tolerance in heterogeneous networks of workstations. *Journal of Parallel and Distributed Computing*, 43(2):147–155, June 1997.

[7] A. Borg, W. Blau, W. Graetsch, F. Herrmann, and W. Oberle. Fault tolerance under UNIX. *ACM Transactions on Computer Systems*, 7(1):1–24, 1989.

[8] M. Braux and J. Noyé. Towards partial evaluating reflection in Java. In *ACM SIGPLAN Workshop on Partial Evaluation and Semantics-Based Program Manipulation*, Boston, MA, USA, January 2000. ACM Press.

[9] G. Cabillic and I. Puaut. Stardust: an environment for parallel programming on networks of heterogeneous workstations. *Journal of Parallel and Distributed Computing*, 40:65–80, February 1997.

[10] S. Chiba. A metaobject protocol for C++. In *OOPSLA'95 Conference Proceedings*, pages 285–299, Austin, TX, USA, October 1995. ACM Press.

[11] C. Consel, L. Hornof, F. Noël, J. Noyé, and E.N. Volanschi. A uniform approach for compile-time and run-time specialization. In O. Danvy, R. Glück, and P. Thiemann, editors, *Partial Evaluation, International Seminar, Dagstuhl Castle*, number 1110 in Lecture Notes in Computer Science, pages 54–72, February 1996.

[12] E.N. Elnozahy, D.B. Johnson, and W. Zwaenpoel. The Performance of Consistent Checkpointing. In *Proceedings of the 11th IEEE Symposium on Reliable Distributed Systems*, Houston, Texas, 1992.

[13] R. Glück, R. Nakashige, and R. Zöchling. Binding-time analysis applied to mathematical algorithms. In J. Doležal and J. Fidler, editors, *System Modelling and Optimization*, pages 137–146. Chapman & Hall, 1995.

[14] L. Hornof and J. Noyé. Accurate binding-time analysis for imperative languages: Flow, context, and return sensitivity. *Theoretical Computer Science*, 248(1–2), 2000.

[15] N.D. Jones, C. Gomard, and P. Sestoft. *Partial Evaluation and Automatic Program Generation.* International Series in Computer Science. Prentice-Hall, June 1993.

[16] M. Kasbekar, S. Yajnik, R. Klemm, Y. Huang, and C.R. Das. Issues in the design of a reflective library for checkpointing C++ objects. In *18th IEEE Symposium on Reliable Distributed Systems*, pages 224–233, Lausanne, Switzerland, October 1999.

[17] M.-O. Killijian, J.-C. Fabre, and J.-C. Ruiz-Garcia. Using compile-time reflection for object checkpointing. Technical Report Noo99049, LAAS, February 1999.

[18] D.B. Lange and M. Oshima. Mobile agents with Java: The Aglet API. *World Wide Web*, 1(3):111–121, 1998.

[19] G. Muller, M. Banâtre, N. Peyrouze, and B. Rochat. Lessons from FTM: an experiment in the design & implementation of a low cost fault tolerant system. *IEEE Transactions on Reliability*, pages 332–340, June 1996. Extended version available as IRISA report 913.

[20] G. Muller, R. Marlet, and E.N. Volanschi. Accurate program analyses for successful specialization of legacy system software. *Theoretical Computer Science*, 248(1–2), 2000.

[21] G. Muller, R. Marlet, E.N. Volanschi, C. Consel, C. Pu, and A. Goel. Fast, optimized Sun RPC using automatic program specialization. In *Proceedings of the 18th International Conference on Distributed Computing Systems*, pages 240–249, Amsterdam, The Netherlands, May 1998. IEEE Computer Society Press.

[22] G. Muller and U. Schultz. Harissa: A hybrid approach to Java execution. *IEEE Software*, pages 44–51, March 1999.

[23] F. Noël, L. Hornof, C. Consel, and J. Lawall. Automatic, template-based run-time specialization : Implementation and experimental study. In *International Conference on Computer Languages*, pages 132–142, Chicago, IL, May 1998. IEEE Computer Society Press. Also available as IRISA report PI-1065.

[24] J.S. Plank, M. Beck, and G. Kingsley. Compiler-Assisted Memory Exclusion for Fast Checkpointing. *IEEE Technical Committee on Operating Systems and Application Environments, Special Issue on Fault-Tolerance*, Winter 1995.

[25] J.S. Plank, Y. Chen, K. Li, M. Beck, and G. Kingsley. Memory exclusion: Optimizing the performance of checkpointing systems. *Software—Practice and Experience*, 29(2):125–142, 1999.

[26] B. Ramkumar and V. Strumpen. Portable checkpointing for heterogeneous architectures. In *Proceedings of The Twenty-Seventh Annual International Symposium on Fault-Tolerant Computing (FTCS'97)*, pages 58–67, Seattle, WA, June 1997. IEEE.

[27] U. Schultz, J. Lawall, C. Consel, and G. Muller. Towards automatic specialization of Java programs. In *Proceedings of the European Conference on Object-oriented Programming (ECOOP'99)*, volume 1628 of *Lecture Notes in Computer Science*, pages 367–390, Lisbon, Portugal, June 1999.

[28] L.M. Silva and J.G. Silva. An experimental evaluation of coordinated checkpointing in a parallel machine. In J. Hlavicka, E. Maehle, and A. Paticza, editors, *Proceedings of The Third European Dependable Computing Conference (EDCC-3)*, volume 1667 of *Lecture Notes in Computer Science*, pages 124–139, Prague, Czech Republic, September 1999. Springer.

[29] V. Strumpen. Compiler technology for portable checkpoints. http://theory.lcs.mit.edu/ strumpen/porch.ps.gz, 1998.

[30] V. Strumpen and B. Ramkumar. *Fault-Tolerant Parallel and Distributed Systems*, chapter Portable Checkpointing for Heterogeneous Architectures, pages 73–92. Kluwer Academic Press, 1998.

[31] S. Thibault, J. Marant, and G. Muller. Adapting distributed applications using extensible networks. In *Proceedings of the 19th International Conference on Distributed Computing Systems*, pages 234–243, Austin, Texas, May 1999. IEEE Computer Society Press.

[32] E.N. Volanschi, C. Consel, G. Muller, and C. Cowan. Declarative specialization of object-oriented programs. In *OOPSLA'97 Conference Proceedings*, pages 286–300, Atlanta, USA, October 1997. ACM Press.

[33] T. Walsh, N. Paciorek, and D. Wong. Security and reliability in concordia(tm). In *Proceedings of the 31st Hawaii International Conference on System Sciences (HICSS'98)*, pages 44–53, Kona, Hawaii, January 1998. IEEE Computer Society Press.

A C/C++ Source-to-Source Compiler for Dependable Applications

A. Benso, S. Chiusano, P. Prinetto, L. Tagliaferri

Politecnico di Torino
Dipartimento di Automatica e Informatica
Email: *{benso, chiusano, prinetto}@polito.it*
http://www.testgroup.polito.it

Abstract

The present paper proposes a C/C++ Source-to-Source Compiler able to increase the dependability properties of a given application. The adopted strategies are based on two main techniques: code re-ordering and variables duplication. The proposed approach is portable to any platform, it can be applied to any C/C++ source code, and it introduces code modifications that are transparent to the original program functionality. The RECCO tool, which fully automates the process, allows the user to trade-off between the level of dependability improvement and the performance degradation due to the code modification.

1. Introduction

The increasing complexity and quality required by the market is making the design of dependable digital systems a key problem from an economical point of view. Recently, several researches started to investigate the possibility of assembling dependable systems using commercial hardware and software components off-the-shelf (COTS) not designed, individually, to guarantee the required dependability level. Since from an economical point of view hardware redundancy is not always the most practical solution, it is straightforward that designing hardware using COTS moves the dependability issue at the software layer, now in charge of also guaranteeing high levels of availability and maintainability. In this context, *software fault tolerance* techniques aim at addressing system failures caused by a *hard* or *soft error* appearing in the system hardware.

This paper proposes a *pure software* and *fully automated* approach based on *code re-ordering* and *variable duplication* to detect data errors appearing in the system memory or microprocessor registers. *RECCO (REliable Code COmpliler)*, an ad-hoc Source-to-Source C++ compiler, has been implemented in order to transform any input *source code* into an output *reliable code,* properly modified to increase its dependability characteristics.

The proposed approach proved to have a high detection capability of faults occurring in the program data segment. The source-code modifications are completely *transparent* to the target program functionality, and can be applied to any target program. Moreover, the generated reliable C/C++ code is *portable*, i.e., it is independent from the native compiler used subsequently to generate the executable file. Both the time and memory overhead introduced by the approach are acceptable and, in any case, controllable by the user on the basis of a trade-off between fault coverage and performances. In particular, *RECCO* supports the designer in identifying both the most critical portions of the *code* and its most critical *variables*, suggesting the best modifications towards a more reliable code.

The proposed techniques have been evaluated on a complete set of benchmarks using BOND, a proprietary Fault Injection tool running under Windows NT 4.0.

The present paper is organized as follows: after presenting some related research in Section 2, the global architecture of the tool is sketched in Section 3. Section 4 presents the evaluation parameters used by RECCO to estimate the criticality of a variable, whereas Sections 5 and 6 focus on the source code modification algorithms. A complete set of experimental results is reported in Section 7, and Section 8 eventually draws some conclusions.

2. Related research

Many researchers [1][2] showed that, in computer-based systems, a high percentage of faults cause a *Fail-Silent Violation* behavior, e.g., the system produces incorrect results while the application seems to terminate correctly. This behavior is mostly caused by pure data errors, i.e., errors appearing in memory locations storing the data or in the microprocessor's user registers. For the sake of clarity, a computer-based system is said to be *Fail-Silent* if it outputs only correct results, i.e., the system does not output incorrect results even if they are generated internally as a consequence of a fault.

[3] showed that it is possible to achieve a high degree of fail-silent behavior in ordinary computers (i.e., not specifically designed to always produce a Fail-Silent behavior) by coupling the intrinsic Error Detection Mechanisms (EDMs) of the system (exceptions, memory protection, etc.) with a set of carefully chosen software error detection techniques. These techniques include *Algorithm Based Fault Tolerance* (ABFT), *Assertions, Time redundancy,* and *Control Flow* checking [4] [5] [6] [7] [8].

ABFT is a very effective approach but lacks of generality. It is well suited for applications using regular structures, and therefore its applicability is valid for a limited set of problems [3].

The use of *Assertions*, i.e., logic statements inserted at different points in the program code to reflect invariant relationships among program variables, can lead to different problems, since assertions are not transparent to the programmer and their effectiveness largely depends on the nature of the application and on the programmer's skills.

Techniques based on *time redundancy* approaches, instead, exploit idle times in the program execution to repeat computations, and detect faults comparing the computations results [9] [10].

The basic idea of *Control Flow checking* is to partition the application program in *basic blocks*, i.e., branch-free slices of code. For each block a deterministic signature is computed and errors can be detected by comparing the run-time signature with a pre-computed one. In most control-flow checking techniques one of the main problems is to tune the test granularity to be used. In [11] is presented PORCH, a Source-to-Source compiler able to automatically insert into the source code of the application, instructions to save and recover from portable checkpoints. Portable checkpoints, which capture the state of a computation in a machine-independent format, provide a potential solution to fault-tolerant software developed for networks of binary incompatible machines.

Finally, a systematic approach for introducing data and code redundancy into an existing source code written in C language is presented in [12]. The simple code transformation rules proposed by the authors are quite effective from the reliability improvement point of view, but are not automated and introduce a very high overhead in terms of memory and execution time.

3. The RECCO Tool

Figure 1 sketches the overall architecture of RECCO. The tool receives the *original source code*, both the C and C++ ANSI languages are supported, and outputs two different "reliable" versions of that code.

The RECCO Source-to-Source compilation process runs through the following three phases:

- *Code Reliability Analysis*. RECCO evaluates the *dependability properties* of the variables, sorting them according to their criticality w.r.t. a correct program execution. For each variable a *reliability-weight* is computed, which takes into account the variable *lifetime* and its *functional dependencies* with other variables. The evaluation performed in this phase allows identifying the most *reliability-critical* variables and correctly driving the next two phases of the RECCO compiling process.

- *Code Re-ordering Phase*. In this phase, RECCO modifies the original C/C++ code and generates a more *reliable code,* functionally equivalent to the original one, but significantly improved in terms of dependability characteristics. The adopted approach consists in performing *local optimizations* aiming at reducing the reliability-weight of the variables identified during the Code Reliability Analysis.

Variable Duplication Phase. In this last phase, the dependability properties of the application source code are further improved by resorting to *variable duplication*. RECCO generates a more reliable code (*Reliable^2 C/C++ code* in

- Figure 1), introducing ad-hoc modifications in the code outputted by the previous phase, still guaranteeing the functional equivalence with the original code. Although the *variable duplication technique* is extremely effective from a reliability point of view, it usually has an evident impact on the system performances and memory overhead. RECCO allows the user to trade-off between *Code Reliability Level* and performance degradation, appropriately setting the *Reliability Requirements*. In the actual implementation of the tool, the user specifies the percentage of variables to be duplicated, and RECCO selects, among all the variables, the ones that are more critical for the application fault tolerance.

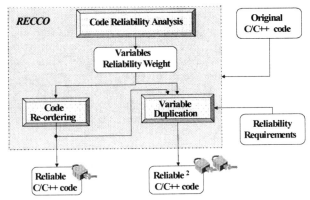

Figure 1: The RECCO tool

In the following three sections we detail the three phases of the Source-to-Source compilation process.

4. Code Reliability Analysis

In our approach, the *reliability-weight* of a given variable *v* is evaluated according to the following parameters: the variable *lifetime* and its *functional dependencies*.

We define *life period* of a variable each period starting from a write operation and ending with the last read operation on the same data preceding the next write operation or the end of the program execution. The *lifetime* is then defined as the sum of all the variable life periods. Data stored in variables with higher lifetime have higher probability of being corrupted, since they are stored in memory for a longer period of time. RECCO evaluates the life time parameter as the number of *lines of code* between the write and the read operation.

Obviously the weight of global variables can not be correctly computed if they are used inside functions. It is therefore necessary to pass their values to procedure and functions as parameters. Moreover, since RECCO performs a static analysis of the code, we assume a loop-free code structure, and we therefore consider all the loops executed only once. Experiments will prove that this assumption does not affect the quality of the results. In case of recursive routines, we again assume they are executed only once.

The second key parameter used to compute the reliability-weight is the *functional dependency* of a variable.

We define as *descendant* of a given variable *v*, any variable loaded with the result of an expression which includes *v*. In the following example *a* and *b* are both descendant of *v*.

```
a = v
b = log(v/w)
```

Variables with a lot of descendants represent a potential criticality for the system: faulty data stored in them are in fact propagated to a large set of other variables. RECCO computes the list of descendants for each variable, analyzing the whole program and building a *Variables Dependencies Graph* (VDG). Figure 2 shows the VDG for a small piece of code. The VDG is a *direct graph*, in which *nodes* represent variables and *direct edges* represent variable dependencies: an edge $(v_i \rightarrow v_j)$ exist if v_j is a *descendant* of v_i.

It is now possible to quantify the *reliability-weight* (RelWeight) that RECCO assigns to each variable after the Code Reliability Analysis phase as a linear function of the two parameters listed above:

$$RelWeight_v = K_l * lifetime_v + K_w * \Sigma \, Relweight_{descendants(v)}$$

Variables with high *reliability-weights* are usually *critical* for the reliability of the application. First of all, faults occurring in these variables are easily propagated to their descendant. Moreover, since they store data for a longer period of time, the probability of a fault appearing in them is higher. This consideration is particularly relevant in space applications, where the most common fault induced by space radiation, i.e., the Single-Event-Upset, appears in the 90% of the cases in the memory elements of the systems.

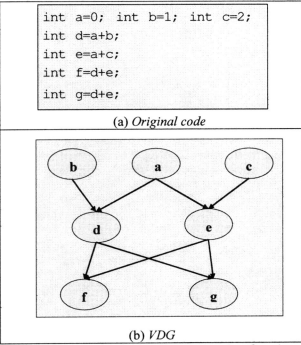

(a) *Original code*

(b) *VDG*

Figure 2: The Variables Dependencies Graph

5. Code Re-ordering Phase

The *code re-ordering* technique aims at *re-scheduling* the code execution flow in order to reduce the reliability-weight of the variables.

RECCO applies the code re-ordering technique on portions of code named *domains*. No read/write dependencies exists among operations belonging to the same domain, i.e., inside a domain no operation reads/writes a variable that is written/read by another operation in the same domain. Therefore, within a *domain* all the operations can be freely re-ordered without affecting the global program behavior. The decomposition of the original code into a set of disjoint domains is performed by RECCO resorting to analysis techniques common in *program-slicing* [6] [13]. Since domains can include function calls, the compiler always checks if the code reordering operations maintain the original semantic of the program [14].

Inside a given domain, each operation is labeled with a reliability-weight, which is function of the reliability-weights of the involved variables. Let's consider an operation *op*, updating a variable *v*; a weight $Relweight_{op,v}$ is computed according to the following relation:

$$Relweight_{op,v} = \Sigma\, Relweight_{ancestors\ of\ v\ in\ op} - Relweight_v$$

where:

- $\Sigma\, Relweight_{ancestors\ of\ v\ in\ op}$ includes the reliability-weights of the variables used to update v in op;
- $Relweight_v$ is the Reliability Weight of the variable v updated in op.

The two terms allow taking into account how the variables lifetime is modified when the operation *op* is scheduled in an instant different from the original one. It is easy to understand how $Relweight_{op,v}$ increases with $\Sigma\, Relweight_{ancestors\ of\ v\ in\ op}$ and decreases with $Relweight_v$. Moreover, if the read variables are more important than the written one, the $Relweight_{op}$ is higher. From the formula it is therefore possible to understand if it is better to shorten the lifetime of the ancestors or the lifetime of the variable itself.

To execute the code re-ordering, the operations are sorted for decreasing reliability-weights and then re-scheduled inside the domain itself. When the procedure is completed, the final reliability-weight values associated to each operation will be lower than the original ones, at least for one of the operations in the domain.

Figure 3 reports a slice of code to briefly show how the procedure works. Let consider a domain *I*, containing five assignment operations. As shown in Figure 3 (a), RECCO labels each variable of the code with a reliability-weight $Relweight_v$, and each operation inside the domain with a reliability-weight $Relweight_{op,v}$. In the proposed example, the variables *f*, *g*, *h*, *i*, and *l* have reliability weight equal to zero. When performing the code re-ordering, the operation with highest weight, *op5*, is moved up to the top of the domain. As a consequence (Figure 3 (b)) the lifetime of at least one of the variable involved in the operation *op5* is decreased: in our case the lifetime of both *a* and *d* is decreased. Moreover, the weight of the operation itself decreases: in our example it moves from 40 to 35.

In the actual implementation of the tool, the loop constructs (e.g., *for* and *while* statements) as well as each branch of an *if* statement correspond to different domains. The computation of the different domains is not always an easy task and therefore the *code-reordering* approach works better in programs with weak data dependencies.

Operations	I-th Domain	Op. Weights:
op1:	int f=b+c+d;	$weight_{op1,f}$ =24
op2:	int g=c+d+e;	$weight_{op2,g}$ =24
op3:	int h=d+e+b;	$weight_{op3,h}$ =24
op4:	int i=e+b+c;	$weight_{op4,g}$ =24
op5:	int l=a+b+c+d+e;	$weight_{op5,g}$ =40

Variables Weights:
$weight_a$,$weight_b$,$weight_c$,$weight_d$,$weight_e$ =8
$weight_f$,$weight_g$,$weight_h$,$weight_i$,$weight_l$ =0

(a) *Domains identification*

Operations	I-th Domain	Op. Weights:
op5:	int l=a+b+c+d+e;	$weight_{op5,f}$ =35
op1:	int f=b+c+d;	$weight_{op1,g}$ =23
op2:	int g=c+d+e;	$weight_{op2,h}$ =23
op3:	int h=d+e+b;	$weight_{op3,g}$ =23
op4:	int i=e+b+c;	$weight_{op4,g}$ =24

Variables Weights:
$weight_a$ =4
$weight_b$, $weight_c$, $weight_e$ =8
$weight_d$ =7
$weight_f$, $weight_g$, $weight_h$, $weight_i$, $weight_l$ =0

(b) *After code-reordering*

Figure 3: Code-reordering method

6. Variable Duplication Phase

The *variable duplication* phase consists in coupling some of the variables of the program with *shadow* variables. The original and the shadow variables behave in the same way, storing the same type of data and being updated, with the same values, at the same time. Periodically monitoring the consistency between the two copies of the variables, it is possible to detect the occurrence of faults in one of the two replicas of the data. Variables coupled with a shadow variable are therefore *reliable* variables.

In our approach the variable duplication technique is supported by three procedures: *Check_Consistency*, *Errorhandle*, and *Write_Shadow*. At compile time, RECCO modifies the code produced in the second phase, i.e., the code re-ordering phase, automatically inserting the declaration, the initialization, and the managing procedures of the *shadow* variables. Figure 4 shows the code modifications introduced to manage the duplication of variables *a* and *c*. The *Check_Consistency* procedure is always invoked after reading data stored into a *reliable variable*. The procedure verifies the correspondence between the content of the original variable and its shadow copy; if a discrepancy is detected the *Errorhandle* procedure is executed to notify the data corruption and, according to the user specification, to stop the program execution or to log the fail silent violation.

The *Write_Shadow* procedure is used to update the content of a shadow copy every time the corresponding variable is modified. Although in the current implementation both variables are updated with the same value, it is also possible to implement more complex coding procedures, able to provide error detection and correction capabilities.

Using *variables duplication*, faults occurring into the data memory segment are detected before being propagated through the program. The main disadvantages of this approach are the *memory overhead* and the *performance degradation* introduced by the shadow variable management.

```
int a=0, b=1, c
......
c=sin(a+b);
```
Unmodified code

```
int a=0, b=1, c
int shadow_a=a;
int shadow_c;
......
        c=sin(a+b);
        if (!Check_consistency(a, shadow_a))
                Errorhandle();
        Else
                Write_Shadow(shadow_c, c);
```
Modified code

Figure 4: Code modification for Variables duplication

6.1. Variable selection

To reduce memory overhead and performance degradation, the user can specify how to select the variables to be duplicated. We implemented three different strategies:

- *Full duplication*: all the variables of the code are duplicated. This solution allows the highest fault detection but introduces the highest execution time overhead.
- *Partial duplication*: only a specified percentage of variables is duplicated. RECCO selects them among the most critical ones, i.e., the ones having the highest reliability-weight. This solution allows the user to trade-off between fault detection and performance degradation.
- *Forced duplication*: the user can specify *super-varibles*, i.e., variables that he wants to be duplicated in any case. This feature gives the user another level of freedom in selecting variables that are critical from his point of view.
- *Temporal duplication*: the reliability weight of a variable may not be constant during the program execution. RECCO is able to duplicate a variable only during the most critical periods of its lifetime. In this way, in each moment only the optimal set of critical variables is duplicated, increasing the dependability of the system without increasing the overheads.

6.2. Consistency Check

The *Check_Consistency* procedure is always invoked before reading data stored into a *reliable variable*. The procedure verifies the correspondence between the content of the original variable and its shadow copy; if a discrepancy is detected the *Errorhandle* procedure is executed to notify to the user the data corruption. According to the user specification, *Errorhandle* can either stop the program execution, or just trace on a log file the fail silent violation.

RECCO can use two different strategies to place the *Check_Consistency* procedure in the code (Figure 5):

- *Intensive*: a *Check_Consistency* function call is placed after each read operation on a duplicated variable. This strategy minimizes the fault detection latency but maximizes the execution time overhead.
- *One-shot*: the *Check_Consistency* function call is only placed before the end of each variable life period. In this way the fault detection is still guaranteed, but the performance overhead decreases since the Check_Consistency function is executed once

for each life period instead of once for each read operation on the variable.

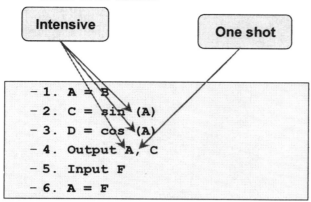

Figure 5: Code modification for Variables duplication

Bench-mark	Code Lines	Number of Variables	Type of Variables	Characteristics
Matrix product	10	3	int	strong read-write dependencies; re-scheduling not allowed
Elliptic Filter	a cycle of 40 code lines	45	long int	medium read-write dependencies
Ex#1	a cycle of $\cong$ 1k code lines	$\cong$ 1k	double	Many read-write dependencies
Ex#2	a cycle of 50 code lines	15	double	Few read-write dependencies

Table 1: Benchmarks characteristics

7. Experimental Results

RECCO has been developed resorting to the C/C++ parser and lexical analyzer developed by James Roskind [15]: the parser is realized with YACC and the lexical analyzer using FLEX. RECCO is able to process any source code written in ANSI C and C++; the generated *reliable code* is still a C or C++ file. The tool currently supports the entire ANSI C standard data types.

To assess the effectiveness of the proposed techniques in improving the dependability properties of the code, a complete set of Fault Injection experiments has been performed on the source code of four benchmark programs. Results were obtained executing RECCO on a 333Mhz Pentium II with 64Megabytes of RAM and running under Windows NT 4.0.

Table 1 summarizes the main characteristics of the four benchmarks. For each of them we reported the *code length*, and the *number* and *type* of *variables*. Moreover, we point out few *characteristics* that can influence the powerfulness of the code modification introduced by RECCO, e.g., if the variables are highly correlated and consequently the corresponding VDG is strongly connected.

Since our approach mainly aims at increasing data dependability, our benchmarks are *data dominated* examples: they are characterized by a quite simple control flow, but include a large number of variables, and a lot of arithmetic operations executed on them. Our test cases comprehend a *matrix product*, an *elliptical filter*, and two ad-hoc developed examples, *Ex#1* and *Ex#2*, executing a sequence of floating point operations.

To evaluate RECCO performances it has been necessary to analyze the system behavior in presence of faulty data. We therefore executed the benchmark programs under the control of a proprietary *Fault Injection environment (BOND)*: concurrently with the program execution, the Fault Injector emulates the appearance of data faults corrupting memory locations storing data. The adopted fault model is the *Single Event Upset* (SEU), consisting in flipping one bit in one data memory location. SEU are *transient faults*, affecting data without physically damaging the memory: the fault effect therefore disappears when the fault location is overwritten. Each experiment involved the injection of a *fault list* including 1,000 faults, each characterized by an *injection location* (i.e., a bit position inside the memory array), and an *injection time* expressed as the elapsed time from the beginning of the program execution. The number of injections and the *injection time* have been chosen in order to statistically cover the whole memory area and to change variables value in different moments of the program execution. Both the parameters have been randomly selected. The system reaction to the injected faults has been eventually classified in one of the following categories: *Fail Silent* (FS), *Fail-Silent Violation* (FSV), or *Detected* thanks to the introduced code modifications.

In order to estimate the improvements introduced by RECCO, the Fault Injection experiments have been performed on both the original code and the two different versions of the code generated by the tool.

The Fault Injection experiments results collected in Table 2 show that, using code re-ordering, the occurrences of *Fail-Silent Violations* (FSVs) decreases: part of the faults causing FSVs in the original program is moved to the *Fail Silent* (FS) condition. The FSVs is reduced about 5% for the *elliptic filter* and 9% for the *Ex#2*. On the *Ex#1*, where few dependencies existing among the variables allow RECCO to fully re-scheduling the execution flow, the FSVs reduction reaches the 65%. On the *matrix product*, instead, the code re-ordering is not applicable, since the existing high dependencies do not allow effective code relocation. Summarizing, the code re-ordering methodology allows adequately re-scheduling the program execution flow: tuning the optimal life time value for the most critical variables, it efficiently reduces the probability of propagating faulty data through the program.

The FSVs further decrease when the code re-ordering technique is coupled with the variable duplication one: the reduction of FSVs ranges from 96% to 100%. With respect to the code re-ordering, variable duplication does not allow the appearance of faulty data, which is *detected* before propagating errors through the program. According to the percentage of duplicated variables, a subset of the FSVs is intercepted and the occurrence is notified to the external application. Results shown in Table 2 are obtained duplicating all the variables; under this assumption any occurrence of faulty data is detected. The number of FSVs could however be still different from zero if a fault affects a variable immediately after its correctness has been verified, but before it is read by other variables (for example in the case of *matrix product* and *Ex#1*).

	Original	Code re-ordering		Code re-ordering & all variables duplications	
Bench-mark	**FSV**	**FSV**	**Red.**	**FSV**	**Red.**
Matrix prod.	249	249	0 %	1	99.6 %
Elliptic Filt.	43	41	4.6 %	0	100 %
Ex#1	205	185	9.7 %	7	96.6 %
Ex#2	162	56	65.4 %	0	100 %

Table 2: Improvement of dependability properties using RECCO

Figure 6, Figure 7, and Figure 8 deeply analyze the trade-off between the improvement in dependability properties, and costs in terms of memory overhead and performance degradation. In particular, we take into consideration example Ex#1 and we analyze performances and overheads when duplicating different percentage of program variables.

Figure 6 shows that, only duplicating 30% of the variables, the FSVs occurrences are already reduced of the 68% w.r.t. the original code; duplicating the 70%, instead, the FSVs reduction is about the 89%. To further underline the quality of the proposed approach, Figure 6 also reports the FSV reduction when the variables to be duplicated are randomly selected. Experiments proved that RECCO always significantly outperforms the random approach.

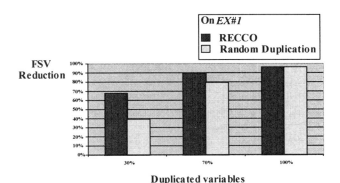

Figure 6: Reduction of Fail-Silent Violations (FSVs) via Variable Duplication

Figure 7 draws the performance degradation introduced by the consistency checking performed on the duplicated variables. Performance degradation ranges from the 6% (30% of variables duplicated) to the 16% (all the variables duplicated).

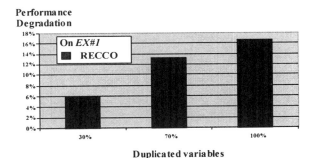

Figure 7: Performance degradation using RECCO

Finally, Figure 8 reports the memory overhead for storing and managing the duplicated variables; the values range from 18% (30% of variables duplicated) to 37% (all the variables duplicated).

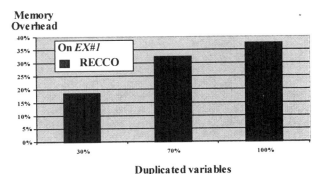

Figure 8: Data memory overhead using RECCO

Although the compiler has not been designed to address faults appearing in the code segment, we evaluated the fault detection capabilities of the approach injecting faults in the code segment of the program as well. The results are shown in Table 3. The number of silent faults is substantially reduced (50% in the best case) except for the Matrix Multiplication benchmark. It is straightforward to understand that the detected faults are those that cause a difference in one of the program variables. However, since not all the code injections affect tha data memory, even duplicating all the variables a certain number of faults remains undetected. Different techniques are required to provide a higher fault detection to code faults.

Bench-mark	FS	FSV	FS	De-tected	FSV	Reduc-tion
Matrix	921	79	915	42	43	45.56 %
Ellip. Filter	932	68	899	48	53	22.05 %
Ex#1	986	14	974	12	14	0.00 %
Ex#2	990	10	990	2	8	20.00 %

Table 3: *Fault Injections on code*

8. Conclusions

We presented RECCO, a REliable Code COmpiler able to automatically generate a reliable version of any C/C++ source code. The tool exploits an effective *code re-ordering* algorithm and a customizable *variable duplication* technique to generate a reliable code able to detect the occurrence of critical data faults. The modifications introduced by the tool are completely transparent to the programmer and do not affect the original functionality of the target program. Moreover, the tool offers the user the possibility of choosing the percentage of duplicated variables in order to keep the overhead under the desired limits. Experimental results demonstrated the effectiveness of the approach and the low overhead introduced in the reliable code in terms of both memory occupancy and execution time. We are currently performing experiments on larger benchmark programs and improving the re-ordering algorithm in order to further increase the detection capabilities of the approach.

9. References

[1]   A. M. Amendola, A. Benso, F. Corno, L. Impagliazzo, P. Marmo, P. Prinetto, M. Rebaudengo, M. Sonza Reorda, *Fault Behavior Observation of a Microprocessor System through a VHDL Simulation-Based Fault Injection Experiment*, EURO-VHDL'96, September 1996, Geneva (CH), pp. 536-541

[2]   J. G. Silva, J. Carreira, H. Madeira, D. Costa, F. Moreira, *Experimental Assessment of Parallel Systems*, Proc. FTCS-26, Sendaj (J), 1996, pp. 415-424

[3]   M. Zenha Rela, H. Madeira, J. G. Silva, *Experimental Evaluation of the Fail-Silent Behavior in Programs with Consistency Checks*, Proc. FTCS-26, Sendaj (J), 1996, pp. 394-403

[4]   K. H. Huang, J. A. Abraham, *Algorithm-Based Fault Tolerance for Matrix Operations*, IEEE Trans. Computers, vol. 33, Dec 1984, pp. 518-528

[5]   V. Strumpen, *Portable and Fault-Tolerant Software Systems*, IEEE Micro, September-October 1998, pp. 22-32

[6]   K. Wilken, J.P. Shen, "*Continuous Signature Monitoring: Low-Cost Concurrent-Detection of Processor Control errors*", IEEE Transaction on Computer Aided Design, vol. 9, No. 6, pp. 629-641, June 1990

[7]   H. Madeira, J.G. Silva, "*On-line Signature Leraning and Checking*", Dependable Computing for Critical Applications 2, Springer-Verlag, pp. 395-420, 1992

[8]   D.J. Lu, "*Watchdog Processor and Structural Integrity Checking*", IEEE Transaction on Computers, vol. C-31, No. 7, pp. 681-685, July 1982

[9]   J.H. Patel et al., "*Concurrent Error Detection in ALUs by Recomputing with Shifted Operands*", IEEE Transaction on Computers, vol. C-31, No. 7, pp. 589-595, July 1982

[10]   Y.M. Hsu et al., "*Time redundancy for error detecting neural networks*", Proc. IEEE Int. Conf. on Wafer Scale Integration, pp. 111-121, Jan. 1995

[11]   V. Strumpen, *Portable and Fault-Tolerant Software Systems*, IEEE Micro, September-October 1998, pp. 22-32

[12]   M. Rebaudengo, M. Sonza Reorda, M. Torchiano, M. Violante, *Soft-error Detection through Software Fault-Tolerance techniques*, DFT'99: IEEE International Symposium on Defect and Fault Tolerance in VLSI Systems, November 1-3, 1999 - Albuquerque, New Mexico, USA, pp. 210-218

[13]   M.Weiser, *Program Sliceing*, IEEE Transaction on Software Engineering, vol. SE-10, No. 4, July 1984, pp 352-357

[14]   S. Horwitz, T. Reps, D. Binkley, *Interprocedural Slicing using Dependence GraphsI*, ACM Transactions on Programming Languages and Systems, Vol. 12, No. 1,January 1990

[15]   ftp://ftp.sra.co.jp/.a/pub/cmd/c++grammar2.0.tar.gz

Session 4B

Practical Experience Reports II ♦ COTS Evaluation

Assessment of The Applicability of COTS Microprocessors in High-Confidence Computing Systems: A Case Study

Yutao He* and Algirdas Avižienis
Computer Science Department
University of California, Los Angeles, CA 90095-1596
E-mail: {yutao, aviz}@cs.ucla.edu

Abstract

Commercial-Off-The-Shelf (COTS) components are increasingly used in building high-confidence systems to assure their dependability in an affordable way. The effectiveness of such a COTS-based design critically depends on the design of the COTS components. Their dependability attributes need a thorough understanding and rigorous assessment yet has received relatively little attention. The research presented in this paper investigates the error detection and recovery faetures of contemporary high-performance COTS microprocessors. A method of assessment is proposed and two state-of-the-art microprocessors are studied and compared.

1 Introduction

COTS-based fault tolerance techniques have gained increasing use in building high-confidence systems in order to reduce the cost and development time. This design style uses COTS hardware or software components as basic building blocks. As a result, system dependability relies critically on the dependability of those COTS components and requires a thorough understanding and rigorous assessment of their error detection and recovery techniques.

Research has been published that evaluates the dependability of COTS operating systems [1, 2], a COTS high-speed network [3], and error detection effectiveness in COTS microprocessors [4]. This paper presents the results of a comprehensive assessment [5] of the "confidence" aspect of two high-performance COTS microprocessors. Two fundamental questions are: (1) Which built-in fault tolerance features in COTS microprocessors are available to assure high confidence? (2) How effective are these built-in fault tolerance features? Based on the concepts of *confidence assurance architecture (CAA)* and *coverage matrix*, a systematic evaluation procedure has been applied to the Intel Pentium II processor and the IBM S/390 G5 processor.

---

*Now with SoHaR Inc., Beverly Hills, CA

The paper is organized as follows: Section 2 describes the method of assessment. Case studies of the Intel Pentium II processor and the IBM S/390 G5 processor are presented in Sections 3 and 4, respectively. Section 5 gives results and analysis. Conclusions are drawn in Section 6.

2 The Methodology

In order to assess rigorously the coverage of hardware faults provided by the built-in mechanisms in COTS processors, a systematic approach has been developed in [5] that consists of three elements: *the fault model, the system model*, and *the effectiveness measure*, as shown in Figure 1. The method is characterized by two constraints: (1) It is a qualitative analysis, and (2) It is based only upon publicly accessible technical documetation on the COTS processors.

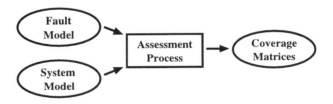

Figure 1: The Assessment Method

The Fault Model specifies the faults to be tolerated in a high-confidence system and is essential for assessment of design of a fault-tolerant system.

The System Model is composed of four parts: *the performance delivery architecture (PDA), the confidence assurance architecture (CAA), the operation modes*, and *the configuration*. PDA is the logic part of a processor that aims to deliver the desired performance and CAA is the logic part of a processor that aims to assure the ability of the PDA to deliver the expected performance in the presence of faults. The Confidence Assurance (CA) functions consists of error detection (ED), error recovery (ER), error logging/reporting(ELR), and fault diagnosis (FD).

The Effectiveness Measure. The concept of *coverage* has long been recognized as the key parameter for designing and evaluating a highly dependable system [6]. It is formulated in [5] as the *PDA coverage matrix* and the *CAA coverage matrix* that are defined as follows:

The PDA (CAA) coverage matrix indicates how much of the PDA (CAA) is protected by CA functions and indicates the confidence level of the PDA (CAA). Each row in the *PDA (CAA) coverage matrix* corresponds to one PDA (CAA) element, as identified in the PDA (CAA) model of the target system. Each column corresponds to one CA function as defined in the CAA model.

Based upon the concepts described above, the assessment problem can be formulated as follows: *Derive the entries for the* PDA coverage matrix *and the* CAA coverage matrix *from the technical documentation of a COTS processor, using its system model and its fault model.*

The assessment is conducted as follows:

1. Establish the system model of a COTS processor with sufficient detail from its publicly assessible technical documentations and partition it into the PDA and the CAA at the top level.

2. Establish the fault model from the documentation.

3. For each identified element of the PDA and CAA, determine if it is covered with respect to the fault model.

4. Repeat the process until the coverage is determine as much as allowed by the available documentation.

3 Case Study 1: Intel Pentium II Processor

Pentium II is a member of the Intel P6 processor family and is one of the most popular high-performance processors intended for a wide range of applications. The assessment is based entirely on publicly available Intel technical documentation [7–12].

3.1 The Fault Model

The faults are classified by Intel in terms of errors they cause (called *hardware errors*, or *machine errors*) that are divided into three types with different levels of severity: (1) *recoverable error (RE)*, (2) *unrecoverable error (UE)*, and (3) *fatal error (FE)*.

3.2 The System Model

The PDA/CAA Model: The PDA and CAA models are shown in Figures 2 and 3, respectively. Note that the figures

were not provided by Intel and that the PDA/CAA partitioning is our own.

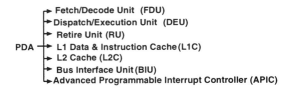

Figure 2: The Pentium II PDA

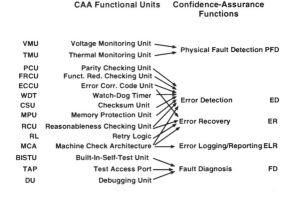

Figure 3: The Pentium II CAA

Operation Modes: Five modes are provided in the Pentium II processor: *start*, *test*, *normal*, *system management mode (SMM)*, and *recovery*.

Configurations: The Pentium II processor provides on-chip logic to support three different configurations: *uniprocessor (UP)*, *multiprocessor (MP)*, and *functional-redundancy-checking (FRC)*[1].

3.3 The CAA Anatomy

CAA-Related Signals: CAA-related signals implemented in the Pentium II processor are summarized in Tables 1 and 2. Some other interrupts and exceptions (e.g., divide-by-zero) are also defined and can be used to detect hardware faults [4]. Since they mostly detect software faults and our study is focused on direct protection against hardware faults, these mechanisms are not considered in evaluating the coverage.

The Machine Check Architecture (MCA) is a set of 64-bit registers to log all types of hardware errors. It consists of one set of global registers for logging configuration data, five sets of error-reporting registers for storing data on detected errors, and the logging logic. Each set

---

[1]The FRC has been deleted from the Pentium II specification in April 1998. See Section 3.3 for more details.

Signal	Description
AERR#	address parity error
BINIT#	bus initialization
BERR#	bus error
IERR#	internal error
FRCERR	FRC comparison error
THERMTRIP#	thermal overrun error

Table 1: The Pentium II Detection Signals

Signal	Description
RESET#	CPU reset
INIT#	initialization
BINIT#	bus initialization
FLUSH#	cache flush
SMI#	system management interrupt
NMI	non-maskable interrupt

Table 2: The Pentium II Recovery Signals

of error-reporting registers is associated with a specific on-chip hardware unit (or group of hardware units). If an error is detected, the machine-check exception is raised.

The CAA of the APIC (Advanced Programmable Interrupt Controller): Errors in the APIC are handled separately without involvement of the MCA. Error detection is done by modulo-3 checksum calculated in continuous cycles over its 2-bit data lines. Upon detection of an error, the corresponding bit in the *error status register* is set, followed by an automatic retry. In the meantime, an error interrupt is generated.

Thermal Monitoring: The processor protects itself from catastrophic overheating via an internal thermal sensor. If an abnormal condition is detected, it asserts the THERMTRIP# pin and then shuts down the processor.

The Built-In-Self-Test (BIST) Unit provides single stuck-at fault coverage of the microcode and large logic arrays, as well as testing of the L1/L2 caches, TLBs and other on-chip storage elements. Its details are not disclosed by Intel and thus its coverage cannot be decided.

The Test Access Port is an implementation of the IEEE 1149.1 JTAG Boundary Scan standard [13] and is used during off-line test mode.

The FRC Unit: The FRC configuration is an implementation of master/checker duplexing that aims to cover all other PDA/CAA elements not protected by the previous mechanisms. However, according to Intel [12], the FRCERR pin was removed from the specification in April 1998. Consequently, the protection provided by the FRC is not considered in evaluating the CAA coverage. The reason for its removal was not revealed in spite of our inquiries.

4 Case Study 2: IBM S/390 G5 Processor

The IBM S/390 G5/G6 microprocessors are the latest models that implement the ESA/390 instruction set architecture in CMOS technology. Both high performance and high confidence are considered as primary design objectives. Compared to G5, the G6 model offers additional performance improvement without much difference in architectural design. The single-chip G5 microprocessor is thus used for evaluation.

Because it is solely used in IBM's S/390 G5/G6 mainframe systems, it is short of public documentation on microprocessor specification details. As a result, in addition to using publicly available technical information [14–20], we have also received advice from one of chief designers [21].

4.1 The Fault Model

The fault model of the G5 consists of both *permanent faults* and *transient faults* [18]. The corresponding error model includes *hard (or solid) errors* and *soft errors* [19].

4.2 The System Model

The PDA/CAA Model: Figures 4 and 5 show the PDA and CAA model, respectively, for the G5 processor.

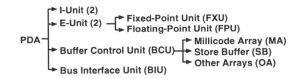

Figure 4: The G5 PDA

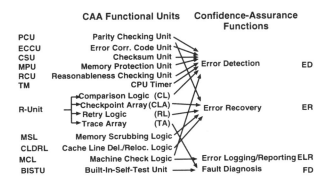

Figure 5: The G5 CAA

Operation Modes: Six modes are provided: *load*, *test*, *operating*, *recovery*, *stop*, and *check-stop*.

Configurations: Two major configurations are supported: *uniprocessor (UP), multiprocessor (MP)*. Each can be further divided into: UP (MP) with spare only, UP (MP) with service assist processor (SAP) only, and UP (MP) with both SAP and spare.

4.3 The CAA Anatomy

CAA-Related Signals: The G5 processor provides the instruction SIGNAL PROCESSOR that decodes and acts on a set of codes to control its operation and defines some CAA-related interruptions, summarized in Table 3.

Detection	Recovery
sense	start
emergency signal	stop
service signal	restart
check-stop signal	CPU reset
malfunction alert	initial CPU reset
machine-check interruption	subsystem reset
	clear reset
	power-on reset

Table 3: The S/390 G5 CAA-Related Signals

Duplicate-and-Compare of I- and E-unit. The G5 processor has duplicated I-units and E-units and compares the outputs in order to check control, arithmetic, and other logic functions in these PDA elements. The compare-and-detect cycle is completely overlapped in the instruction execution pipeline to minimize the performance overhead.

R-Unit. It is the recovery unit composed of an ECC-code protected checkpoint array, a trace array, the comparison logic and the retry logic. The checkpoint array consists of 256 registers and holds the entire CPU state, timing facility, and other state information during each cycle. At every clock cycle, the outputs from two I and E units are compared. If they are same, they are stored in the checkpoint array. Otherwise, an instruction retry is initiated that is transparent to the software. If the retry threshold is exceeded due to a permanent fault, the check-stop signal is raised and the processor enters the check-stop operation mode.

L1 Cache Protection. The L1 cache (called *buffer control element*) consists of store buffers, a millicode array, comparison logic, data arrays, cache directory, TLBs (Translation Lookaside Buffer), and address translation logic. Store buffers are protected by ECC-codes. The millicode array stores microcodes and is protected by CRCs. Comparison logic compares the outputs from two I- and E-units. All other L1 storage arrays are protected by parity. In addition, the G5 processor contains the logic that allows failed L1 cache lines to be logically deleted during its normal operation, leading to degradation instead of complete

loss of performance. To tolerate permanent faults, spare word lines are also included that replace the failed word lines diagnosed during BIST.

Memory Scrubbing Logic. To avoid the accummulation of soft errors in seldom-accessed memory locations, the memory-scrubbing function is implemented in millicode to "scrub" the whole memory continuously.

Machine Check Logic. It provides a machine-check interrupt to report hardware errors and supply information on extent of damage, the location, and the nature of the fault.

Concurrent Repair with Sparing. The G5 processor can be configured as a spare (called *integrated coupling facility*) to replace a failed processor due to permanent faults without any assistance from the operating system.

5 Results and Analysis

5.1 The Coverage Matrices

Based on the methodology of Section 2, the PDA coverage matrices for the Pentium II processor and the G5 processor are obtained as shown in Tables 4 and 5, respectively. "N" in the tables indicates the negative conclusion on presence of a CA function that is drawn from the assessment. It implies that the available documentation presents no evidence at all that the function exists in the corresponding PDA element. An entry other than "N" in a cell (such as *parity*) identifies the specific technique of a CA function.

Since the Pentium II CAA is **not covered at all** by any CA functions, and the only protected G5 CAA element is the checkpoint array in the R-unit (by ECC codes), their CAA coverage matrices are sparse and thus not shown.

PDA	CA Functions		
Elements	ED	ER	ELR
FDU	parity (only MIS)	N	MCA (only MIS)
DEU	N	N	N
RU	time-out	reset	MCA
L1C	parity	N	MCA
L2C	parity	N	MCA
BIU	parity	N	MCA
	ECC	correction	MCA
	protocol	retry	MCA
APIC	checksum	retry	Y
Temperature	sensor	reset	N

Table 4: The Pentium II PDA Coverage Matrix

PDA Elements	CA Functions			ELR
	ED	ER		
		TF	PF	
I-Unit	dup./comp.	retry	sparing	MCL
E-Unit	dup./comp.	retry	sparing	MCL
BCE MA	parity	retry	sparing	MCL
BCE SB	ECC	cor., retry	sparing	MCL
BCE OA	CRC	retry	del./rel.	MCL
BIU	ECC	cor., retry	sparing	MCL

Table 5: The G5 PDA Coverage Matrix

5.2 About the Coverage Provided by the CAA

1. Table 4 shows that the CAA in the Pentium II processor only provides protection for storage arrays and communication buses which are the "easy" parts to check; the more complex data and instruction processing logic (FDU, DEU, RU), and the control logic remain uncovered. In contrast, the G5 processor uses the duplicate-and-compare technique to check them in addition to using error codes for storage arrays as shown in Table 5, thus providing a far more complete coverage and containment.

2. It can be seen from Table 4 that while the Pentium II processor employs ECCs for single-bit error correction and the retry logic for an errorneous bus transaction, recovery from the majority of detected errors (e.g., a soft error in L1 cache) is still limited to the primitive form of restart since the CPU state is not available without additional assistance of software. Moreover, extensively logged error data by the MCA are at best used for later analysis with no help for timely recovery. While it has been recognized as a common practice for design of high-performance COTS processors, Table 5 shows an exception: the G5 processor implements a checkpoint array and instruction retry logic that allows complete and fast recovery from transient faults transparent to the system software.

3. The MCA is the "hardcore" of the Pentium II processor that contains critical data on detected errors in sets of registers (three 64-bit global control and status registers and fifteen 64-bit data reporting registers). These storage arrays themselves are also subject to soft errors yet are not protected at all. By comparison, the G5 processor's checkpoint array in the R-unit stores the entire CPU state and is protected with ECC-code.

4. The enabling of most CA functions (except BINIT# observation, AERR# observation, FRC configuration, and BIST) is made by system software and the critical

configuration information is simply stored in a register (EBL_CR_POWERON, aliased to MC0_CTL_MSR) without any storage protection. This poses the risk of both transient faults and malicious faults that can potentially compromise the CAA, especially by disabling some or all of the CA functions. In contrast, the G5 processor protects these sensitive data in its checkpoint array protected with ECC codes.

5.3 About the Technical Documentation

For a system designer who intends to use a COTS microprocessor, various forms of its technical documentation are primary sources for understanding components. In the Intel case, although it provides a comprehensive set of documentation that is made publicly accessible at its Web site [7–12], the specification of CAA has been poorly organized, and is incomplete, sketchy, and scattered all over the documentation. As in most such cases it is very difficult to extract useful information from it in order to evaluate its built-in CA functions, let alone to verify it.

For example, the defined MCA model-specific error codes are important in order to understand the coverage provided by the MCA. However, all mnemonics in the MM-MMM sub-fields [7] (vol. 3, p. 13-12) are not explained throughout the documentation.

In the IBM case, while the G5 processor designers have published an extensive set of papers that address its CAA design in an organized way [14–20], the complete technical documentation is not available to the general public and thus limits an outsider's ability to do an impartial and complete assessment of its CAA.

6 Conclusions

The case studies of the Intel Pentium II processor and the IBM S/390 G5 processor disclose two important issues in building high-confidence systems with contemporary high-performance COTS microprocessors:

1. The coverage provided by the built-in error detection and recovery logic of a COTS microprocessor needs to be carefully assessed. This study suggests that although they are comparable in terms of performance, the IBM S/390 G5 processor is expected to provide high confidence in the presence of faults (say, transient faults) while the Pentium II processor provides low confidence.

The characterics of a low-confidence COTS processor such as the Pentium II processor is that the CAA design falls far behind the PDA design. For instance, after the deletion of FRC configuration from their specifications, the Pentium II processor is left without any error detection coverage at all for major parts of the PDA and for all error detection and recovery architecture (the CAA). Error containment boundaries also have been eliminated for that logic. Therefore sufficient external error detection and recovery augmentations are required when such a low-confidence COTS component is used in high-confidence computing systems, with an approach such as presented in [22].

2. The poorly organized or non-disclosed CAA specification creates great difficulty in understanding and in turn assessing the "confidence" aspect of a COTS processor. The "open-source" may be a way to do it.

Acknowledgement

The authors wish to thank Mr. Timothy J. Slegel for his kindness and valuable advice on understanding the S/390 G5 processor. We also wish to thank Dr. Phil Koopman and anonymous reviewers for their constructive crititism and suggestions on improving the paper.

References

[1] P. Koopman et al. Comparing operating systems using robustness benchmarks. In *Proc. of 16th Symposium on Reliable Distributed Systems*, pages 72–79, 1997.

[2] F. Salles, M. Rodriguez, J.-C. Fabre, and J.-C. Fabre. MetaKernels and fault containment wrappers? In *Digest of FTCS-29*, pages 189–194, June 1999.

[3] D. T. Stott, M.-C. Hsueh, G. L. Ries, and R. K. Iyer. Dependability analysis of a commercial high-speed network. In *Digest of FTCS-27*, pages 248–258, 1997.

[4] H. Madeira and J. G. Silva. Experimental evaluation of the fail-silent behavior in computers without error masking. In *Digest of FTCS-24*, pages 350–359, June 1994.

[5] Y. He. *An Investigation of Commercial Off-The-Shelf (COTS) Based Fault Tolerance*. PhD thesis, Computer Science Department, UCLA, September 1999.

[6] W. G. Bouricius, W. C. Carter, and P. R. Schneider. Reliability modeling techniques for self-repairing computer systems. In *Proc. of 24th National Conference of ACM*, pages 295–309, 1969.

[7] Intel Corp. *Intel Architecture Software Developer's Manual, Vols. 1-3*, 1999. Order No. 243190-243192.

[8] Intel Corp. *Addendum - Intel Architecture Software Developer's Manual, Vols. 1-3*, 1997. Order No. 243689-001, 243690-001, 243691-001.

[9] Intel Corp. *P6 Family Of Processors Hardware Developer's Manual*, Sept. 1998. Order No. 244001-001.

[10] Intel Corp. *Pentium II Processor Developer's Manual*, October 1997. Order No. 243502-001.

[11] Intel Corp. *Datasheet - Pentium II Processor at 350 MHz, 400, and 450 MHz*, August 1998. Order No. 243657-003.

[12] Intel Corp. *Pentium II Processor Specification Update*, July 1999. Order No: 243337-028.

[13] IEEE Standard Board. *IEEE Standard Test Access Port and Boundary-Scan Architecture*. IEEE, 1993.

[14] IBM Corp. *ESA/390 Principles of Operation*, 1999. SA22-7201-06.

[15] T. J. Slegel et al. IBM's S/390 G5 microprocessor design. *IEEE Micro*, 19(2):12–23, March/April 1999.

[16] P. R. Turgeon et al. The S/390 G5/G6 binodal cache. *IBM Journal of Research and Development*, 43(5/6):661–670, Sept./Nov. 1999.

[17] M. A. Check and T. J. Slegel. Custom S/390 G5 and G6 microprocessors. *IBM Journal of Research and Development*, 43(5/6):671–680, Sept./Nov. 1999.

[18] L. Spainhower and T. A. Gregg. IBM S/390 parallel enterprise server G5 fault tolerance: A historical perspective. *IBM Journal of Research and Development*, 43(5/6):863–873, Sept./Nov. 1999.

[19] M. Mueller et al. RAS strategy for IBM S/390 G5 and G6. *IBM Journal of Research and Development*, 43(5/6):875–887, Sept./Nov. 1999.

[20] P. Song et al. S/390 G5 CMOS microprocessor diagnostics. *IBM Journal of Research and Development*, 43(5/6):899–913, Sept./Nov. 1999.

[21] T. J. Slegel. Personal communication, March 2000.

[22] A. Avižienis. A fault tolerance infrastructure for dependable computing with high-performance COTS components. In *Digest of ICDSN 2000*, June 2000.

Evaluating COTS Standards for Design of Dependable Systems *

C.J. Walter
WW Technology Group
Columbia, MD
cwalter@wwtechnology.com

N. Suri
Chalmers Univ.
Gothenburg, Sweden
suri@ce.chalmers.se

T. Monaghan
US Intl. Trade Org.
Washington, D.C

Abstract

This experience report presents a study on the fault tolerance (FT) support capabilities of various COTS standards prior to their inclusion in design of dependable systems. A standalone analysis and relative comparison of the FT attributes for SCI, ATM, Futurebus+ and Fiber Channel is presented.

1 Introduction & Objectives

Recent military programs specifically target reducing the cost of design, acquisition and upgrade of systems through the use of commercial off-the-shelf (COTS) and open source standards. In order to enable systems to take advantage of commercial interface standards, these programs are actively participating with industry organizations responsible for these standards, to include requirements critical to system performance such as real-time (RT) and fault tolerance (FT). This report provides an overview of work we have performed in support of these efforts in analyzing the suitability of selected standards to real systems and applications.

The increasing use of different standards in critical applications and necessity of correct and continuous operation of system services require an in-depth analysis and understanding of the dependability features of these standards. Thus, four specific communication standards were examined to disseminate their FT capabilities and features, in the context of application needs of backplane, processing and I/O. The standards discussed in this study are: Asynchronous Transfer Mode (ATM), Fiber Channel (FC), Scalable Coherent Interface (SCI), and Futurebus+ (FB+).

Within the scope of potential military applications, different domains warrant considerably different requirements of mission times, availability, reliability, maintainability, latency, size and environmental factors. This report focuses on air applications, and on

three distinct sub-categories for communications for avionics applications: backplane, extended interconnects, and sensor/video networks - their basic requirements are summarized in Table 1. The numbers in brackets indicate desired scalability ranges.

	Backplane (max)	Extended Interconnect	Senor/Video Network
# of nodes	30 (1000)	4-6 (30-40)	32(256)
Max. size	1m	30-50m	150m
Data Thruput	1.6-12 Gbs	1.6-8 Gbs	1.6-12 Gbs
FT	No SPF[a]	No SPF	No SPF
FDIR	Yes	Yes	Yes
Max. BER Bit Error Rate	10E-10 detected 10E-14 undetected	10E-10 detected	10E-10 detected

[a]Given design specs: No single point of failure shall bring down the entire box, cause dissemination of bad data, or cause loss of comm. between any two nodes.

Table 1: Summary of Avionics Requirements

2 Stand-alone Analysis of Standards

In this section, the fault handling capabilities of standards are assessed considering them as individual functional units, without reference to the overall system framework. In subsequent analysis, we address the role a specific standard is expected to perform within a systems context - these issues are deferred here on account of space constraints. The discussion in this section highlights the salient FT attributes of each standard as identified during extensive reviews.

An important *caveat* is a strongly expressed caution that appealing FT attributes (or lack of them) in any of the standards are very dependent on the functionality a standard actually performs within the context of a system. Also, the relative likelihood (and relative impact on system ops. for each application scenario) of each possible fault case in discrete standards must also be taken into consideration prior to ascertaining the overall dependability capability of each standard.

*Supported in part by NAWC N62269-95-C-0130 and NSF Career CCR 9896321

For each standard, we present (a) its functional attributes and (b) basic assessment of their FT support capabilities. Our review procedure is as follows:

1. Identify the operational/functional capabilities of each standard for covering varied fault behavior.
2. Identify weaknesses in each standard that are better handled by the other units of the system. (For example, if a standard is capable of supporting retry, but does not possess the capability of logging/storing the system state to recover from).
3. Perform relative classification of standards to identify strengths and weaknesses for FT support.

3 SCI – Capabilities & Perspectives

SCI consists of high-speed point-to-point unidirectional communication links between neighboring nodes that allow for higher bandwidths over greater distance between nodes than possible for standard high performance backplane buses. In order to provide bi-directional communications between SCI nodes, the nodes and the point-to-point unidirectional communication links must form a ring topology. Typically, the number of nodes on a ring is small and the sub-network is referred to as a ringlet. One node on each SCI ringlet is assigned housekeeping tasks (initialization, timer maintenance, discarding damaged packets) and termed as the *scrubber*. A register insertion technique allows multiple nodes to transmit simultaneously on the ring, increasing the performance as a factor of N, where N is the number of nodes on the ring. On account of the ring topology employed by SCI, the magnitude increase depends upon the specific data flow pattern of the particular application.

The approach for SCI is to define an interconnect system that scales well with increasing number of processors, provides a coherent memory system, and defines a simple interface between modules. Issues of average response time, average throughput, and fairness in order to provide the necessary features for time-shared applications are specifically part of the standard. SCI uses a packet switching protocol with a 64-bit addressing mechanism.

SCI is designed to support both message passing and shared memory paradigms. Message passing is supported without any special low level protocol support. Shared memory is supported via the cache coherency protocols and remote transaction protocols (which allow locked memory transactions to be efficiently supported with packet protocols). The coherence protocols are based on single responder directed transactions and distributed directories, where processors sharing cache lines are linked together by pointers.

The SCI/Real-Time Working Group has proposed features for priority-based preemptive arbitration and queuing protocols; support for both priority-based shared memory and message passing architectures; a standard global clock synchronization method; and a standard event notification method. In addition, FT features are provided for single-bit hard error detection and correction; and hardware sub-action fault-retry protocol support.

In the following section, we highlight possible FT strengths indicated by (+) and weaknesses (-) of the SCI standard. ± indicates attributes without a definitive perceived strength or weakness. **Note:** We utilize this nomenclature of +, - and ± across all standards.

3.1 Strengths

+ The use of ringlets provide (a) a compartmentalized fault containment regions for the system, and (b) fault isolation and associated distributed fault recovery capabilities. The basic ring configuration of SCI allows for flexibility of topologies (switches, meshes, processor grids, butterfly ringlets, redundant ringlets) - all of which facilitate scalability and FT reconfiguration. The usage of ring-wraps and ring-replace techniques can facilitate link fault recovery.

+ Fault traceability by explicit HW logging & replay mechanisms. The Command and Status Registers (CSRs) provide error logging counters.

+ Live insertion capability is a useful feature for introducing test conditions into the standard.

+ Distributed recovery list approach in the cache coherency protocol provides resiliency to any single memory fault effects.

+ SCI utilizes 16 bit polynomial CRC error check versus 32 bit CRC in ATM/FC. This may appear restrictive, however, when one considers the transfer of large contiguous data streams, the SCI mechanisms will use multiple blocks to facilitate this data transfer with 16 bit CRC coverage on *each* data block as compared to the ATM/FC use of a single 32 bit CRC on the entire data block.

3.2 Cautions

± The use of timeouts in the protocol can provide a useful detection mechanism. However, current SCI versions do not have mechanisms to support complete SW level end-to-end retry. HW retry is provided, though only at the ringlet level.

3.3 Concerns

- The priority and fairness access criteria can interfere with the correct operation of the system resulting in operational bottlenecks.

- The use of a single scrubber on each ringlet presents a risk of unit failure if the scrubber fails (The same risk applies to the of the master clock, clock and flag line). However, the RT extensions to SCI contain provisions for an alternate scrubber. Nevertheless, errors are restricted to SCI ringlets illustrating fault isolation features of SCI.
- To account for faulty CRC calculations on a receiver (as to a corrupted frame), the CRC stomp mechanism must be deferred, with stations marking the packets.
- Systems based on multiple ringlets will require and mechanisms not discussed in the standard. These must be analyzed to guarantee that recovery from failures does not result in blocking.
- The time-of-death mechanism to control packets is heavily based on the system time synchronization capabilities. Correspondingly, the CSR global time capabilities should be to determine its ability to tolerate errant clocks.
- The overall fault management, identified as a potential requirement, is not fully addressed within the standard, and would need to be provided as an additional processing layer. However, the operational protocols of the standard do represent the basic FT capabilities as well as provision for interface hooks to the higher system layers.

4 Fiber Channel (FC) – Perspectives

The ANSI FC standard is a universal interface for data channels which is optimized for the predictable transfer of large blocks of data such as those used in file transfers, disk and tape storage systems, communications, and imaging devices. FC provides bi-directional connections and support for connected and connectionless operations with separate fibers for each direction. FC is designed primarily to be a local area network; however, as it is switch based, it can also be used for networks ranging from backplane to wide area networks. The framing protocol supports variable-length frames; hardware disassembly/reassembly of sequences; and control of the fabric by delimiters. A small built-in command set provides configuration management and support for error recovery. Multiple classes of services are provided. Class 1 service offers dedicated connection between two ports with guaranteed ordered delivery. Class 2 service is frame switched with buffer-to-buffer flow control, guaranteed delivery, but order is not guaranteed. Class 3 service uses datagrams without guaranteed delivery or order of receipt. Class 4 provides extended link services that provide common functions for entity addressing, data specification, and generic status.

FC topologies can be point-to-point, cross-point switch, or arbitrated loop configurations. With point-to-point, fabric elements are not present and therefore fabric services are not available. When used in point-to-point applications, a data channel establishes a dedicated connection between two pieces of equipment. The standard does not define the implementation of the fabric but sets forth the following requirements. There must be: a single-level address domain; the number of ports are only restricted by the 24 bit ID field; heterogeneous fabric elements from multiple vendors should be supported FC is optimized for input and output as well as communications between nodes. FC can also provide processor-to-memory services even though it is not optimized for these services.

4.1 Strengths

+ As the fabric is not fixed, system re-configuration over errors can be tailored by the choice of topology. The fabric can be changed without requiring HW/SW changes to computers/controllers/peripherals.

+ Unlike "passive" interconnects between nodes in traditional networks, FC allows for an active fabric which can be self-managed for error recovery.

+ Can be configured to support either connection or connectionless services based on communication level error rates.

+ The 8B/10B code scheme provides stable dc signal balance (sends same number of 1s and 0s) for the receiver. This provides a good transition density for easier clock recovery and allows error checking for unrecognized codes.

4.2 Cautions

± Fault handling is highly dependent on the capabilities of the underlying fabric.

± The use of the "hunt" group can permit the fabric to select an alternate/idle port if the primary port is inaccessible/busy. However, this mechanism is unspecified in FC.

± FC error logs provided for at the adaptation layer could be useful in fault isolation, but may need to be augmented with additional system state information to be practically usable.

4.3 Concerns

- FC is geared towards transfer of large data blocks; consequently the impact of a fault may require re-transfer of an entire data block resulting in an inefficient fault recovery process and limited traceability.

- BER rate claimed "in the absence of faults" indicating a misunderstanding of fault definitions to include only permanent faults without consideration of the occurrence of transients.

5 Futurebus+ (FB+) – Perspectives

The FB+ standard defines a backplane bus that provides performance and scalability for single and multiple bus multiprocessor systems. Allocation of bus bandwidth to competing modules is provided by either centralized or distributed arbitration. Bus allocation rules are defined to address the needs of both RT (priority based), and fairness (equal opportunity access based) configurations. Two data transfer protocols are available: compelled or packet mode. The compelled mode relies on a master/slave handshake for every data beat; the packet mode uses a fixed length block of data with an embedded synchronization pulse. Bus, system and node management are done primarily via Control and Status Registers (CSRs) and a bus monarch. CSRs are areas of memory that contain information on a node's capability, configuration and operation. The bus monarch is a node that controls the configuration and initialization of the bus. The bus monarch is selected during bus initialization through a competition between capable nodes and performs a number of duties. These include: determining the node population, polling nodes for self-test status, deciding the arbitration type (central or distributed) and enabling nodes accordingly, programming arbitration priorities and propagation delays, setting parallel protocol configuration, enabling memory space, and performing extended diagnostics.

5.1 Strengths

+ The use of the geographical address parity bit and the alternating parity bit can aid the process of fault detection.

+ Most connections can be converted to split transactions in order to prevent long data latency and as alternate channels over errors.

+ The availability of the reflected field, error detection and correction for address/data lines, protocol violation monitors, and arbitration monitors can support FT services.

+ Live insertion allows on-line replacement of faulty components and supports high-availability goals.

5.2 Cautions

± CSR's present potential capabilities for error management. However, these features are not documented/formalized in the base standard.

± FB+ presents multiple profiles; designers need be careful of the capability actually available for a chosen profile.

5.3 Concerns

- The base standard has many signals not protected by fault detection mechanisms: status, capability, arbitration condition, geographical address, central arbitration, and reset lines.

- The multi-party asynchronous bus arbitration protocols present limited resolution in identifying faults within the interfaces. Furthermore, the reliance of data transfer on the centralized arbitration mechanism can result in high fault susceptibility. This aspect is typically handled by providing for a redundant arbiter; however, the functionality is still that of a centralized unit.

- The false detection of signaled acknowledgments can result in potential for faulty reads of capability modes or of transferred data. There also exists a potential for undetected bus errors, based on occurrence of transient control line errors with specific timing windows (cases of early release of bus during the time the slave is reading data). The use of a double-read of data or the longitudinal parity can possibly alleviate this problem.

6 ATM – Perspectives

ATM aims to provide a flexible facility for the transmission and switching of mixed media traffic comprising voice, video and data. It provides a multiplexing and switching method for Broadband Integrated services Digital Networks (B-ISDN) based on fixed size cells and header information which identifies explicit channel information. ATM provides high performance with low latency and high capacity based on a constant bit rate. Variable bit rate services can also be handled to allow for flexible allocation of bandwidth among users. ATM uses small packets that are transported over lightweight virtual circuits that are a fixed 53-bytes (48-byte payload, 5-byte header). This approach allows the protocol to be independent of the physical layer and application hardware. Connections can be established as either permanent or switched via these virtual circuits. Cell routing is based on a two-level addressing structure: the virtual path (VPI) and virtual channel (VCI) indicators. The end-to-end concatenation of VCIs is the virtual channel connection (VCC) which are uni-directional and do not provide for error recovery or flow control. The VPI identifies the physical path that is associated with a set of VCIs. All cells associated with a VCC are transported along the same route through the network and delivered with the cell sequence preserved.

6.1 Strengths

+ Capability for handling constant- rate, variable-rate, connectionless and connection-oriented framing, multiplexing, and transport services are useful over system re-configurations.

+ The generic flow control field defined at the user network interface is capable of implementing a modest level of congestion control.

+ Capability for negotiating quality of service parameters allows for efficient allocation of bandwidth and priority management over error handling. ATM cell related parameters include: error, loss and block ratios; mis-insertion rate, transfer delays and variations.

6.2 Cautions

± There is a high dependency (and deferred responsibility) for fault and FCR's error management on the ATM Switch Fabric, the ATM's AAL and other higher levels/controllers.

± ATM switching architectures have their own classification with related strengths and weaknesses.

6.3 Concerns

- As the ATM operates on a virtual cell/connection basis, it can be difficult to implement a fault retry capability. Also, as no error control is performed within the network, the future fault-tolerance capabilities are limited by the information encapsulation possible within the 5-byte block header.

- Similar latency/detection liabilities as FC due to the transfer of large data blocks.

- The data message header is provided with an 8-bit CRC for every 32-bits. However, data error checks occur only at the Adaptation Layer level and are handled solely by the use of a 32 bit CRC for the entire block. (See discussion of CRC use in the section on SCI)

- Limited capabilities for path re-establishment on the occurrence of faults in the initial message route. The corruption of the routing table can become a major hindrance to system operation.

- Cases with faults in the priority assignment and handling mechanism impact system performance.

- Limited fault detection and recovery capabilities based on the Alarm Indication Signals (AIS) and use of Far-End-Receive-Failure (FERF) signals; recovery limited to simple message re-transmittal.

7 Discussion & Comparative Analysis/Applications of the Standards

Based on the standalone properties of standards, Table 2 attempts to summarize the capabilities of each standard in different application scenarios. The various expected roles a standard is required to perform in a system are broadly classified in Table 2. A key basis for matching of standards and applications is the operational capabilities of the standards and the desired operational specifications. Unless this basic match is achieved, a match of a standard to any dependability attribute is of little value.

The initial intent of the analysis was to formulate a standard test-set of fault types and grade each individual standard accordingly with respect to their fault-handling capabilities. A proper comparison was impossible due to the lack of a common fault model across all the standards. It is perhaps more relevant to quantify the general number of fault scenarios possible in each standard and to document the nature of fault-tolerance capabilities or liabilities in each standard and use this for comparison across the standards.

At the design stage, the functional, performance and throughput aspects of these standards were the design drivers, and not the FT issues which only come to the fore when these standards are utilized to create dependable services. This situation results in many fault-tolerance attributes being introduced as add-on features. Thus, the basis of our evaluation of these standards is to consider:

- Which standard offers better possibilities for supporting additive fault-tolerance capabilities?
- Which standard can possibly be used without proving detrimental to the overall system level fault-tolerance capabilities (i.e., by providing hooks or the capability of deferring fault handling to a higher system layer).

The design trends appear to aim at providing a sufficient set of mechanisms so that a standard can be regarded as a "highly dependable" entity capable of performing the desired functions with a high degree of resilience to faults. This approach is acceptable, although one needs to be cautious that there is no guarantee that a dependable system will necessarily result. The dependability of a system is very much a function of the overall system paradigm, the operational structure of the system and the specific resource and redundancy management protocols used. It should be noted that the coverage of faults from a system level perspective may not directly reflect or relate to capabilities of fault coverage at the individual block level.

	Interconnects: Desired Attributes					Supported by:			
	IP^a	BP/IO	S/V	IB	MM	SCI	ATM	FC	FB+
BW Allocation	High	V.High	V.High	V.High	Mixed	Yes	Yes	Yes	Yes
Arbitration Resolution						No	Yes	Yes	Yes
Isochronous	No	No	Yes	No	No	Yes	Yes	Yes	Yes
RT Support	Yes	Yes	No	Yes	Yes	Yes	Yes	Yes	Yes
Block size	Small	Mixed	Large	Mixed	Mixed	Mixed	Large	Large	Mixed
Msg. passing	Yes	Yes	No	Yes	Yes	Yes	No	No	Yes
Synchronization	Yes	Yes	No	Yes	Yes	Yes	Y/N^b	Y/N	Yes
P→M transfer	Low	High	V.Low	High	V.High	Yes	Ltd.	Ltd.	Yes
Shared Memory	Yes	Yes	No	Yes	Yes	Yes	No	No	Yes
Cache Support	Yes	Yes	No	Yes	Yes	Yes	No	No	Yes
FT Mechanisms						CSR	Network	Network	CSR
Roll-forward Recovery	Yes	Yes	No	Yes	Yes	Yes	No	No	No
Roll-back Recovery	Yes	Yes	Yes	Yes	Yes	Yes	Yes	Yes	Yes
Reconfigurable	Yes	Yes	No	Yes	Yes	Yes	No	No	Yes
Latency (fault-free)	V.Low	V.Low	Low	Low	V.Low	10ns	.5ns	μs	ns
Topology	S/L^c	S/L	Star	Linear	S/L	Ring/Switch	Switch	Switch	Linear

Table 2: Applications & Relative Comparisons Across Standards

^{a}IP=Inter-Processor Comm., BP=Backplane Comm., SV=Sensor/Video, IB=Inter Block Comm., MM=Memory Mgmt.
^{b}Only for specific configs. and classes of service
^{c}Star/Linear

The "dependability" of a system is essentially a qualitative measure of a system's capability in being able to deliver the expected services with a desired or specified level of assurance. The aspects of functional behavior of the system and its dependability qualities are also strongly interlinked; thus, the continued emphasis on addressing the functional role of a standard from a system level perspective.

Our ongoing work addresses the issue: If the system is built using these standards, do these standards facilitate the system being able to achieve its desired or specified fault-tolerance and dependability goals? The method for achieving this goal consists of resolving a series of questions.

- What are the fault tolerance specifications of the entire system?
- What is the exact role/functionality the chosen standard provides in the system? Subsequent to this, what roles do individual standards perform best within the specified system framework?
- Considering the above mentioned aspects: Does the standard display sufficient:
  - current capability of supporting dependability requirements - can it provide a self contained fault-resilient block?
  - capability to support possible extensions which aid in better matching of the expected functionality and capabilities of the standard, and availability of interfaces to other system layers to defer error handling?

It is recommended that such a structured approach be used to determine if the standard's attributes match the requirements of the system framework. It has already been emphasized that the nature of the system model is crucial in determining the role the standard can be expected to perform.

Overall, we have analyzed and documented the capabilities of the various standards for their basic ability to support FT. We have deliberately refrained from suggesting the use of one standard over another, as only when the role of a specific standard is known within the context of a system, can objective comparisons be made across the standards.

References

[1] M. Richards et al., *Rapid Prototyping of Application Specific Signal Processors*, Kluwer, ISBN 0-7923-9871-8, 1997.

[2] Navy's Next Generation Computer Resources (NGCR) Program, 1994+, http://www.faqs.org/rfcs/rfc1679.html

[3] C. Walter, et al., "Dependability Issues in the Reuse of Standard Components in Open Architectures," *AIAA Computing in Aerospace 10*, pp. 443-453, 1994.

[4] C. Walter, et al., "Dependability Framework for Critical Military Systems Using Commercial Standards," *AIAA 14th Digital Avionics Systems Conf.*, pp. 184-192, 1995.

[5] *Scalable Coherent Interface*, IEEE Press, #1596, 1992.

[6] *Futurebus+ – Logical Protocol Specification*, ISO/IEC 10857:1994(E) (ANSI/IEEE 896.1), 27 April 1994.

[7] *ATM User-Network Interface Specification*, ISBN 0-13-225863-3, 10 September 1993, ATM Forum/Prentice Hall.

[8] *Fiber Channel Arbitrated Loop (FC-AL)*, ANSI draft standard, revision 4.2, 11 March 1994.

Session 4C

Student Forum

Session 5A

Measurement and Assessment

Whither Generic Recovery from Application Faults?
A Fault Study using Open-Source Software

Subhachandra Chandra and Peter M. Chen
Computer Science and Engineering Division
Department of Electrical Engineering and Computer Science
University of Michigan
{schandra,pmchen}@eecs.umich.edu
http://www.eecs.umich.edu/Rio

Abstract

This paper tests the hypothesis that generic recovery techniques, such as process pairs, can survive most application faults without using application-specific information. We examine in detail the faults that occur in three, large, open-source applications: the Apache web server, the GNOME desktop environment, and the MySQL database. Using information contained in the bug reports and source code, we classify faults based on how they depend on the operating environment. We find that 72-87% of the faults are independent of the operating environment and are hence deterministic (non-transient). Recovering from the failures caused by these faults requires the use of application-specific knowledge. Half of the remaining faults depend on a condition in the operating environment that is likely to persist on retry, and the failures caused by these faults are also likely to require application-specific recovery. Unfortunately, only 5-14% of the faults were triggered by transient conditions, such as timing and synchronization, that naturally fix themselves during recovery. Our results indicate that classical application-generic recovery techniques, such as process pairs, will not be sufficient to enable applications to survive most failures caused by application faults.

1. Introduction

As computers become an integral part of today's society, making them dependable becomes increasingly important. Field studies [Gray91] and everyday experience make it clear that the dominant cause of failures today is software faults, both in the application and system layers. Reducing the number of software faults and surviving the ones that remain is therefore an important challenge for the fault-tolerance community.

One key component of this quest to avoid and survive software faults is understanding what types of faults occur in released applications. This understanding can help us develop recovery techniques for surviving software faults and develop new languages and tools for avoiding software faults in the future. Unfortunately, most production software in the past was proprietary and therefore hard to analyze. In particular, most companies were understandably reluctant to release information on the exact failings of their software.

However, the recent trend toward open-source software may make this information available. There are now widely used, open-source programs of all types, including operating systems, databases, web servers, web browsers, word processors, spreadsheets, and a host of others. Open-source programs share a number of important characteristics. First, they are widely used and hence form a relevant base of software to study. For example, the Apache web server is used by 54% of all web sites [Netcraft99]. Second, their development process is open. Open development allows others to peruse the history of bugs and software revisions, information which is normally not public. Last, while there is little hard data comparing the quality of open-source with proprietary software, the rapid increase in the use of open source software like Apache and Linux indicates that the quality of open-source software is good enough for mainstream use. Both open-source and proprietary software are released quickly and with plentiful bugs, perhaps as a result of the current pace of innovation in the computer industry. We believe this trend toward open-source, open-development software presents a treasure-trove of information for research in software reliability.

In this paper, we use information in bug reports and source code to understand and classify faults that occur in three widely used, open-source programs. The goal of this paper is to provide information to guide research on how to survive application faults. In particular, we wish to test the hypothesis that generic (i.e. not application-specific) recovery techniques, such as process pairs, can survive a majority of application faults. Our methodology differs from that of prior studies [Lee93]. We reason from bug reports and source code as to whether a purely generic recovery system would have recovered from application faults, while past studies examine the field behavior of implemented, mostly generic recovery systems. This comparison is valuable because of our focus on purely generic recovery and because there is no data available on the effectiveness of recovery on widely used, open-software systems. For this software, we find that only a small fraction (5-14%) of faults are triggered by transient conditions (so-called Heisenbugs) which can be survived with generic recovery techniques such as rollback and retry.

2. Recovery from Software Faults

Faults may be classified into two categories: operational and design [Gray91]. Operational faults are caused by conditions such as wear-out and can be handled with simple replication. Faults caused by design bugs are much more difficult to handle, because simply replicating a buggy design often results in dependent failures in which all the replicas fail. Software faults are difficult to survive because they are all caused by design bugs.

Faults may occur in application or system software. In this paper, application software refers to any software that runs on top of the recovery system, that is, software for which the recovery system is responsible for recovering. System software refers to software that runs below the recovery system, that is, software that recovers itself. The scope of this paper is limited to faults that occur in application software and how often a recovery system can recover from these faults.

We categorize techniques for recovering from software faults as either application-specific recovery or application-generic recovery. Both styles of recovery involve redundancy. In application-specific recovery, a non-fault-tolerant design is made fault-tolerant by adding code that is specific to the application. This includes techniques where the programmer makes calls to fault-tolerance libraries or reconstructs part of the program state during recovery. An extreme example of application-specific recovery is N-version programming, which uses N independent implementations of the same program [Avizienis85]. Recovery blocks also use multiple implementations of a block of code, but use a passive-replication style with error-checking and rollback to avoid

running multiple versions at the same time [Randell75]. Application-specific recovery can be very effective, but is often prohibitively expensive to implement.

Because of the cost of implementing application-specific recovery for each application, researchers have suggested various application-generic ways to survive software faults. These techniques do not add redundant, specific code for each application (we do not consider error checking code as redundant, though technically most error checks are application-specific and redundant). As a result, application-generic techniques need no information about the application, nor do they require any assistance from the application programmer in the form of extra code. Instead, application-generic recovery typically relies on time redundancy. For example, process pairs [Gray86] are similar to recovery blocks, but instead of retrying the operation on a different implementation of the code block, process pairs retry the operation on the same code (possibly on a different computer). Process pairs, and rollback-recovery protocols in general [Elnozahy99, Huang93], survive a specific class of software faults known as "Heisenbugs" [Gray86]. Heisenbugs are transient, non-deterministic faults that disappear when the operation is retried, even if the same code is used. The transient nature of the fault arises because some factor external to the program has changed; for example, a different interleaving order of threads may occur during retry and so avoid a race condition. Note that a truly generic recovery mechanism must preserve all application state (e.g. by checkpointing or logging), because there is no application-specific code to reconstruct missing state. Hence only a change external to the application can allow the application to succeed on retry.

It has been hypothesized that most faults that occur in released applications are transient [Gray86]. The intuition for this hypothesis is that transient faults such as race conditions are more difficult to reproduce and hence debug than non-transient faults (so-called Bohrbugs), so transient faults are more likely to remain in released software. This is an important hypothesis for guiding research in how to recover from software faults, because it encourages work on application-generic recovery. The primary goal of this paper is to test this hypothesis by analyzing bug reports and bug fixes of several large, widely used, open-source programs.

3. Categorizing Software Faults

We classify software faults based on how they depend on the operating environment. By operating environment, we mean states or events that occur outside of the application being studied. The operating environment includes both software and hardware. Software examples of operating environment include other programs, such as the DNS name server and user-level applications, or the kernel, such as the number of available slots in the kernel's process table. Hardware examples include transient hardware conditions such as disk ECC errors and events such as clock interrupts to the thread scheduler. The operating environment also includes the timing of the workload requests to the program (e.g. the user's typing speed). However, we consider the sequence of workload requests made to the program as part of the program, rather than as part of the operating environment, because the sequence of requests is usually fixed for any given program task. That is, we assume the user is not willing to aid recovery by avoiding certain input sequences.

It is important to note that given a fixed operating environment, a set of concurrent, sequential processes is completely deterministic [Dijkstra72]. Non-deterministic execution is always due to a change in the operating environment. For example, a race condition is non-deterministic because of the different times a clock interrupt is delivered to the thread scheduler. This connection between changing operating environment and non-deterministic execution is why we classify faults based on their dependence on the operating environment.

We classify software faults into two main categories: environment-independent and environment-dependent.

Environment-independent faults occur independent of the operating environment. Given a specific workload (e.g. requested operations from the user), an environment-independent fault will always occur. As an example, one release of Apache had an environment-independent fault that caused it to fail whenever a browser submitted a long URL (Section 5.1). Because environment-independent faults do not depend on the operating environment, they are completely deterministic (non-transient). Hence application-generic recovery techniques will not survive these faults.

Environment-dependent faults depend on the operating environment. For these faults, the operating environment plays some role in triggering the design bug in the program. For example, the program may not deal gracefully with a slow network, a full disk, or an operating system that has run out of file descriptors. Because environment-dependent faults depend on the operating environment, the program may behave differently when the requested operation is retried. Hence, application-generic recovery techniques may survive these faults if the environment changes enough to avoid the fault when the operation is retried.

Environment-dependent faults can be further classified into transient and non-transient, depending on how likely it is for the operating environment to be fixed in the absence of application-specific recovery. In *environment-dependent-nontransient* faults, the environment is unlikely to be changed enough to avoid the bug during retry. For example, the program may fail if the disk is full. We consider this an environment-dependent-nontransient bug because most current systems do not fix this condition automatically. Of course, some systems may provide a way to automatically increase the disk capacity and hence avoid the bug during retry. If this becomes common, we would re-classify this as an environment-dependent-transient fault.

Like environment-dependent-nontransient faults, *environment-dependent-transient* faults depend on the environment. Unlike environment-dependent-nontransient faults, however, the environmental dependency is such that simply retrying the operation is likely to encounter a different environment and hence succeed. For example, a race condition will typically be triggered by a specific interleaving of threads by the thread scheduler. If the operation is retried, the environmental condition (the specific interleaving of threads) is likely to be different, and the operation may succeed. As another example of an environment-dependent-transient fault, a program may create child processes but not kill them. These programs typically fail when the operating system runs out of processes. A typical generic recovery system would kill all processes related to the application (thereby changing the operating environment), recover the program, and successfully continue.

4. Software and Faults Targeted

Every piece of software goes through a huge number of bugs over its lifetime of development and use. In this study we look at a subset of the faults that were detected by the users of released versions of the software. Fault-recovery techniques are generally directed at this subset of faults. Among this subset of faults we concentrate on high-impact faults, i.e. those that cause the software to crash, return an error condition, cause security problems, or stop responding. There are many other types of faults that we do not examine, such as those encountered during compilation and installation. These faults do not cause critical outages because they occur before the software is being used in a production setting. We assume that users test new versions of software before incorporating them into their production environment.

Our primary source of data for analyzing faults is the on-line bug reports that are maintained for open-source software. These bug reports contain information about each reported fault, including the symptoms accompanying the fault, the results of the fault, the operating environment and workload that induces the fault, and, in most cases, how the underlying bug was fixed. A key field in all the bug reports we study is the "How To Repeat" field. We use the information supplied in this field along with the comments entered by the developers of the software to decide which fault class the fault belonged to. The developers also provide information on how the bug was fixed and whether they could repeat the failure on their development machines.

We analyze three large, open-source applications: Apache, GNOME, and MySQL. Apache is a robust and commercially used open-source implementation of an HTTP (web) server. As of November 1998, Apache was being used by 36% of the 53,265 Internet domains owned by U.S businesses with annual revenue of $10 million or more [SiteMetrics98], and as of October 1999, Apache was being used as a web server by 54% of over 8 million sites polled in a survey [Netcraft99]. The Apache bug reports are available at http://bugs.apache.org. Of all the bugs reported, we consider bugs on production versions of the software that were categorized as severe or critical. The site has a total of 5220 bug reports listed, and in our study we narrow these to 50 unique bug reports meeting these criteria.

GNOME (GNU Network Object Model Environment) is an open-source desktop environment for users and a powerful application framework for software developers. GNOME, along with KDE, is included in most of the Linux distributions available today. GNOME is also used by users running other flavors of UNIX on their hardware. We use two sources of fault information for our survey. The first (http://bugs.gnome.org) provides us with bug reports and the second (http://cvs.gnome.org) provides us with information about how the bugs were fixed. The GNOME package comes with a set of core files and libraries and a number of applications. We look at faults in the core files and libraries and four commonly used GNOME applications: panel (a user customizable toolbar), gnome-pim (a personal information manager), gnumeric (a spreadsheet application), and gmc (a file management utility). We looked at about 500 bug reports and narrowed them to 45 unique bugs meeting our criteria.

MySQL is a multi-user, multi-threaded SQL database server designed for client-server implementations. It is a fast and robust server aimed at handling small to medium amounts of data. These features make it the database server of choice for web applications and ISP's offering database-hosting services. All the fault data used in our study was obtained from the archives of the mysql mailing list at http://www.geocrawler.com. There are about 44,000 messages archived at the website. In this study, we use all the messages from the archives that matched one of the following keywords: "crash", "segmentation", "race", and "died" (we looked at a few hundred messages and found that these keywords were the ones commonly used to describe serious bugs). We then narrowed these messages to 44 unique bugs.

5. Results

We categorize the faults for each of the three applications into the three classes discussed earlier and describe more fully the causes of all the environment-dependent faults. There are too many environment-independent faults to describe each one fully in the limited space available, so we give descriptions of several representative ones.

5.1. Apache

Table 1 contains the results of classifying 50 faults for Apache. The overwhelming majority of faults do not depend on the operating environment. These deterministic bugs are relatively easy to repeat, so it is perhaps surprising that Apache suffered from so many in released software. Even for deterministic faults, testing all the boundary conditions is notoriously difficult.

The following are some of the environment-independent bugs reported for Apache:

- dies with a segfault when the submitted URL is very long. This problem was a result of an overflow in the hash calculation.
- SIGHUP kills apache on Solaris and Unixware. Normally, this should gracefully restart/rejuvenate Apache.
- dumps core on Linux/PPC if handed a nonexistent URL. The problem is that ap_log_rerror() uses a va_list variable twice without an intervening va_end/va_start combination.
- this error occurs when directory listing is turned on and the directory has zero entries. The palloc() call used in index_directory() doesn't handle size zero properly.
- shared memory segment keeps growing and reaches sizes exceeding 100 Mbytes in less than 5 hours of operation. When a HUP signal is sent to rotate logs, Apaches freezes or dies. This is caused by memory leaks in the application.

Of the 14 faults that do depend on the operating environment, half are due to conditions that persist during recovery. The conditions of the operating environment that trigger the 7 environment-dependent-nontransient bugs are:

- high load leading to an unknown resource leak. Resource leaks in the application will persist during recovery, assuming a generic recovery mechanism that saves and recovers all application state.

Class	# Faults
environment-independent	36
environment-dependent-nontransient	7
environment-dependent-transient	7

Table 1: Classification of faults for Apache.
Environment-independent faults do not depend on the operating environment and are therefore deterministic. Environment-dependent-nontransient faults depend on the operating environment, and the environmental condition that triggers the fault is likely to persist during retry. Environment-dependent-transient faults depend on the operating environment, and the environmental condition that triggers the fault is likely to be fixed during retry.

- lack of file descriptors. As above, truly generic recovery mechanisms will recover all application resources such as file descriptors, so this condition will persist during recovery.
- disk cache used by the application gets full and the application cannot store any more temporary files.
- size of log file is greater than maximum allowed file size.
- full file system.
- unknown network resource.exhausted.
- removal of PCMCIA network card from the computer

The remaining faults are triggered by conditions in the operating environment that are likely to be fixed during recovery. The conditions of the operating environment that trigger the 7 environment-dependent-transient bugs are:

- call to Domain Name Service returns an error. This is likely to change when the DNS server is restarted.
- child processes hangs during peak load and consume all available slots in the process table. As part of automatic recovery, the recovery system is likely to kill all processes associated with the application.
- user presses stop on the browser in the midst of a page download. This fault depends on the exact timing of the requested workload, which is not likely to be repeated during recovery.
- hung child processes hang onto required network ports. These will likely be killed during recovery and the ports will be freed.
- slow Domain Name Service response. The cause of the slow DNS response will likely be fixed eventually without application-specific recovery, either by restarting DNS, or by fixing the network.

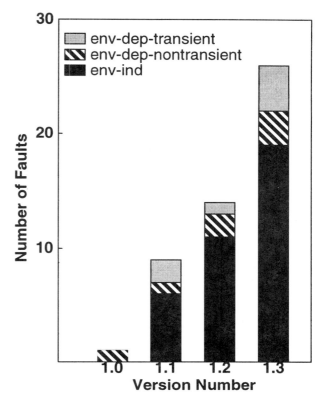

Figure 1: Distribution of faults for Apache over software releases.

- slow network connection. The network may be fixed by the time Apache recovers.
- lack of events to generate sufficient random numbers in /dev/random. During recovery, it is likely that more events will be generated for /dev/random.

Figure 1 shows the distribution of faults over releases of the Apache software. The fault distribution exhibits two distinct properties. First, the relative proportion of environment-independent bugs stays about the same even for new releases of the software. Second, the total number of bugs reported increases with newer releases of software. This is probably due to an increase in the number of users of the newer releases.

5.2. Gnome

Table 2 contains the results of classifying 45 faults for GNOME. As with Apache, the overwhelming majority of faults do not depend on the operating environment.

The following are some of the environment-independent bugs reported for Gnome:

- clicking on the "tasklist" tab in gnome-pager settings, causes the pager to die.

101

Class	# Faults
environment-independent	39
environment-dependent-nontransient	3
environment-dependent-transient	3

Table 2: Classification of faults for GNOME. Environment-independent faults do not depend on the operating environment and are therefore deterministic. Environment-dependent-nontransient faults depend on the operating environment, and the environmental condition that triggers the fault is likely to persist during retry. Environment-dependent-transient faults depend on the operating environment, and the environmental condition that triggers the fault is likely to be fixed during retry.

- clicking on the "prev" button in the "year" view of the gnome calendar application causes it to crash. This was due to assigning a value to a local copy of the variable instead of the global copy.

- the spreadsheet application "gnumeric" crashes if a tab is pressed in the "define name" dialog or in the "File/Summary" dialog. This was caused by initializing a variable to an incorrect value.

- double-clicking on a "tar.gz" file that is lying as an icon on the desktop crashes gmc, the gnome file manager. This was caused due to the declaration of a variable as "long" instead of "unsigned long".

- after clicking the main button once to pop up the main menu, a click again on the desktop in order to remove the menu freezes the desktop.

The conditions in the operating environment that trigger the 3 environment-dependent-nontransient bugs are:

- hostname of the machine was changed while the application was running.

- open sockets left around by sound utilities while exiting. Each open socket consumes a file descriptor and the application runs out of file descriptors.

- file has an illegal value in the owner field. Application crashes when trying to edit the file or its properties

The conditions in the operating environment that trigger the 3 environment-dependent-transient bugs are:

- unknown failure of application which works on a retry

- race condition between a image viewer and a property editor. Race conditions depend on the exact timing of thread scheduling events, and these are likely to change during retry.

- race condition between a request for action from an applet and its removal.

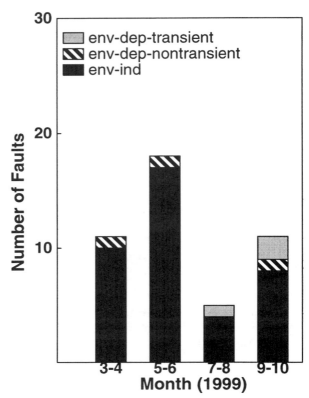

Figure 2: Distribution of faults for GNOME over time.

Figure 2 shows the distribution of faults reported over time. We used time as opposed to releases because of the nature of GNOME. GNOME is a collection of modules, each of which are released independently. There is an occasional major release of all the modules put together. But there was only one release over the period we performed the fault study. The distribution shows that the proportion of environment-independent bugs is very high over all periods. GNOME shows a decrease in the number of faults reported for a short interval before increasing again. This was probably a period of few changes in the software.

5.3. MySQL

Table 3 contains the results of classifying 44 faults for MySQL. As with the other two applications, the overwhelming majority of faults do not depend on the operating environment.

The following are some of the environment-independent bugs reported for MySQL:

- updating an index to a value that will be found later while scanning the index tree and hence creating duplicate values in the index will crash MySQL. This was solved by first scanning for all matching rows and then updating the found rows.

Class	# Faults
environment-independent	38
environment-dependent-nontransient	4
environment-dependent-transient	2

Table 3: Classification of faults for MySQL. Environment-independent faults do not depend on the operating environment and are therefore deterministic. Environment-dependent-nontransient faults depend on the operating environment, and the environmental condition that triggers the fault is likely to persist during retry. Environment-dependent-transient faults depend on the operating environment, and the environmental condition that triggers the fault is likely to be fixed during retry.

- a query which selects zero records and has an "order by" clause will cause the server to crash. This was due to some missing initialization statements.

- the use of a "count" clause on an empty table causes MySQL to crash. This was cause due to missing check for empty tables.

- an "OPTIMIZE TABLE" query crashes the server. This was caused by a missing initialization statement.

- a "FLUSH TABLES" command after a "LOCK TABLES" command crashes the server.

The conditions in the operating environment that trigger the 4 environment-dependent-nontransient bugs are:

- shortage of file descriptors due to competition between MySQL and a web server.

- server crashes when it receives a connection request from a remote machine if reverse DNS is not configured for the remote host.

- size of database file is greater than the maximum allowed file size.

- full file system prevents all operations on the database.

The conditions in the operating environment that trigger the 2 environment-dependent-transient bugs are:

- race condition between the masking of a signal and its arrival. race conditions depend on the exact timing of thread scheduling events, and these are likely to change during retry.

- race condition between a new user login and commands issued by the administrator.

Figure 3 shows the distribution of faults over releases of the MySQL software. The fault distribution exhibits two distinct properties similar to what Apache exhibits. One, the relative proportion of environment-independent bugs stays about the same even with new releases of the

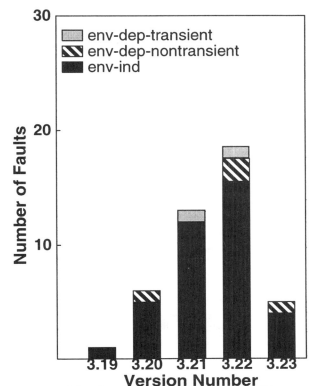

Figure 3: Distribution of faults for MySQL over software releases.

software. Two, the total number of bugs reported increases with newer releases of software. This is probably due to increase in the number of users of the newer releases. The last release has a substantially lower number of faults because the release is very new and hence very few users are using the software and reporting bugs.

5.4. Discussion

The distributions of faults for the three pieces of software we looked at show that there are very few environment-dependent faults. Of the 139 bugs we looked at, we found 14 (10%) environment-dependent-nontransient faults and 12 (9%) environment-dependent-transient faults. We acknowledge that classifying bugs between environment-dependent-transient and environment-dependent-nontransient classes is subjective and depends upon the recovery system in place. However, this does not affect the fact that the number of environment-independent faults is very high.

This result differs from the general perception that a majority of bugs in released software are Heisenbugs [Gray86]. According to this perception, most Bohrbugs are caught during development, or perhaps during early releases of the software. As these bugs are fixed and the software becomes more stable, the relative percentage of

Heisenbugs in the remaining bugs should increase. In today's software culture, however, new features and code are added very quickly, and this rapid rate of change may prevent the application from reaching stability.

Another possible explanation for why Heisenbugs are so rare is that they occur infrequently and so do not appear in bug reports. However, recovery efforts should be directed at the faults that occur most frequently in practice, and these appear to primarily consist of environment-independent Bohrbugs.

As with any case study based on reported data, a few limitations apply to our work. First, results may differ widely for other applications; for example, mission-critical applications undergo more rigorous testing than most software, and this may change the distribution of faults. Second, the reported data may be biased; for example, people may tend not to report faults they cannot duplicate. Third, we analyze the distribution of bugs, rather than the distribution of actual failures. Finally, we reason from bug reports about the ability for generic recovery mechanisms to recover from specific faults. An important avenue of future research is to implement generic recovery and verify its ability to survive a specific fault [Lee93]. This would serve as an end-to-end check on whether the bug report had a complete list of environmental dependencies for that fault.

6. Surviving Software Faults

In this section we look at various techniques to survive software faults belonging to different classes. Some of these techniques are well known, especially for environment-dependent-transient faults and some categories of environment-dependent-nontransient faults. For other categories of faults we suggest some techniques to survive them and refer to techniques suggested by researchers.

6.1. Environment-Independent Faults

Since environment-independent faults are guaranteed to reoccur given a specific workload there is no easy or general technique to recover applications after the fault has manifested itself. The best way to survive such faults is to prevent them from occurring in the first place. However, this is not always possible due to the difficulties associated with testing all of the boundary conditions the software may encounter in the field. Formal code inspections and thorough testing are highly effective to remove software faults before releasing software [Weller93].

There also exist languages and tools to help solve some of the problems in this category. Languages like Java, which are type-safe and allocate/deallocate memory auto-

matically, can be used solve problems like buffer overflows and memory leaks. Tools like Purify can also help find problems related to memory allocation and deallocation. Tools like Ballista [Kropp98] test functions for boundary conditions and place wrapper code around them to prevent failure. Using standard libraries like POSIX helps prevent problems related to inconsistent function behavior on different operating systems.

6.2. Environment-Dependent-Nontransient Faults

Most environment-dependent-nontransient faults are due to some resource being exhausted, such as file descriptors, sockets, or disk space. There are two general approaches for solving resource exhaustion. One way is to detect the problem and automatically increase the resources available to the application. For example, the operating system may be able to dynamically increase the number of file descriptors available to a process. This approach works when the application only temporarily exceeds the resources available (e.g. during a peak load).

The second approach is to try to automatically decrease the amount of resources used by the application. One way to do this is to use garbage collection techniques to discern which resources are no longer needed and reclaim these. For example, the system may monitor which file descriptors are used and automatically close the unused ones. Or the system may provide "virtual sockets" to an application by multiplexing the application's sockets onto the system's sockets.

Some applications implement application-specific solutions to prevent some environment-dependent-nontransient faults. One example is Apache, which can be rejuvenated by sending it a special signal. During rejuvenation, Apache kills all its child processes and thereby reclaims any process structures used up by zombie processes. This technique is widely used by web administrators to reduce failures in Apache. A more detailed discussion of this type of rejuvenation can be found in [Huang95].

6.3. Environment-Dependent-Transient Faults

Process pairs [Gray86] and rollback-recovery protocols [Elnozahy99, Huang93] in general solve faults in this class very well. Faults in this class are related to either time or to an environmental condition which is expected to change very frequently. So retrying the same operation at a later time will usually succeed. Some techniques have also been suggested to induce changes in the environment to increase the success of a retry without affecting the program correctness. One such technique changes the message ordering to simulate changes in the environment

[Wang93].

7. Related Work

Several prior studies have examined the faults that occur in released software. Most of these studies do not discuss the interaction between the faults and a recovery system. Because of this, their error descriptions are not sufficiently detailed to classify faults precisely into transient and non-transient faults. For comparison purposes, however, we can infer a rough classification based on the information they do provide. Our rough classification of faults studied in related papers supports our conclusion that most faults in released software are non-transient, and therefore, that application-specific recovery is needed to survive these faults.

Sullivan and Chillarege study faults in the MVS operating system and the DB2 and IMS database systems [Sullivan91, Sullivan92]. They categorize some errors as being timing or synchronization related, either in terms of the error type or the error trigger. These errors are likely to be environment-dependent-transient faults. They found that 5-13% of the faults were timing or synchronization related. Sullivan and Chillarege were surprised (as we were) that most faults were non-transient bugs (e.g. boundary conditions) that would have been relatively easy to catch during the testing phase.

Lee and Iyer study faults in the Tandem GUARDIAN operating system [Lee93]. They also have a category for errors related to timing and race conditions, which comprise 14% of the faults. Again, these results match ours conclusion that most faults do not depend on the operating environment and so are non-transient.

Lee and Iyer also examined how often the Tandem process-pair mechanism enabled the system to recover from a software fault. They found that 82% of the software faults could be recovered with process pairs. This is a much higher fraction than our estimates and requires some explanation. First, we are assuming a pure application-generic recovery system, and the Tandem operating system's process pair implementation uses some application-specific information. For example, Lee and Iyer report that many errors were recovered because the backup process did not start from the same state as the failed primary (this eliminates their "memory state" and "error latency" categories). Second, a large fraction of recovered faults were due to the backup not re-executing the requested task (perhaps because the task was directed at a specific processor rather than to the process-paired application). In our model, all requested tasks need to be executed; we do not assume a user will generously avoid the fault trigger, nor do we consider faults below the process-paired applica-

tion. Third, many recovered faults in [Lee93] only affected the backup process. This results from bugs introduced by the process-pair system. Lee and Iyer count these as transient bugs; we are only concerned with bugs in the application itself. After eliminating these sources of differences from consideration, only 29% of the software faults are transient bugs in the operating system. This is still somewhat higher than we found, and we conjecture that this is due to two reasons. First, Tandem software is probably tested more thoroughly than most current software, and this testing likely eliminates more non-transient faults than transient ones. Second, operating system software interacts more closely with the hardware than the application-level software we study. This interaction creates more dependencies on the environment, which increases the fraction of environment-dependent-nontransient and environment-dependent-transient faults.

Several schemes have been proposed to enable generic recovery to work for a larger class of faults. For example, some recovery techniques seek to increase the non-determinism in the application by re-ordering events such as message receives [Wang93]: these are basically techniques to induce change to the external environment. These do not transform environment-independent faults into environment-dependent faults. Rather, they increase the chance that a environment-dependent fault will experience a different operating environment (order of message receives, in this case) during recovery. A second technique that seeks to reduce the impact of software bugs is software rejuvenation [Huang95]. Software rejuvenation takes advantage of recovery code that is already present in the application, e.g. code to re-initialize the application's state. Software rejuvenation seeks to prevent failures by invoking this application-specific recovery code before the program crashes.

8. Conclusions and Future Work

In this paper, we have tested the hypothesis that generic recovery techniques, such as process pairs, can survive most software faults without using application-specific information. We examined in detail the faults that occurred in three, large, open-source applications: the Apache web server, the GNOME desktop environment, and the MySQL database. Using information contained in the bug reports and source code, we classified faults based on how they depended on the operating environment. We found that 72-87% of the faults were independent of the operating environment and were hence deterministic (non-transient). Recovering from these faults requires the use of application-specific knowledge. Half of the remaining faults depended on a condition in the operating environment that was likely to persist on retry. These faults are also likely to require application-specific recovery. Unfortunately, only 5-14% of the faults were caused by transient conditions, such as timing and synchronization, that would naturally fix themselves during recovery. Our data indicate that classical application-generic recovery techniques, such as process pairs, will not be sufficient to enable these applications to survive most software faults.

In the future, we hope to implement applications like Apache and MySQL using various fault-tolerant techniques and test how well they recover from the bugs reported in error logs. This will allow us to verify the conclusions we drew from information in the error logs; for example, it will allow us to verify that a fault did not depend on an unreported environmental condition.

9. Acknowledgments

We are grateful to the open-source community for providing useful, robust software and for providing a wealth of information to help make future programs even more useful and robust. We thank the program committee and reviewers, particularly Ravi Iyer and Chandra Kintala, for their insightful feedback.

This research was supported in part by NSF grant MIP-9521386, NSF CAREER Award MIP-9624869, IBM University Partnership Program #19981020024, Intel Technology for Education 2000, and AT&T Labs.

10. References

[Avizienis85]   Algirdas Avizienis. The N-Version Approach to Fault-Tolerant Software. *IEEE Transactions on Software Engineering*, SE-11(12):1491–1501, December 1985.

[Dijkstra72]   Edsger W. Dijkstra. Hierarchical Ordering of Sequential Processes. Technical report, Academic Press, 1972. In Operating Systems Techniques, Hoare and Perrott eds.,.

[Elnozahy99]   E.N. Elnozahy, L.Alvisi, Y.-M. Wang, and D. B. Johnson. A Survey of Rollback-Recovery Protocols in Message-Passing Systems. Technical Report CMU-CS-99-148, Carnegie Mellon University, June 1999.

[Gray86]   Jim Gray. Why do computers stop and what can be done about it? In *Proceedings of the 1986 Symposium on Reliability in Distributed Software and Database Systems*, pages 3–12, January 1986.

[Gray91]   Jim Gray and Daniel P. Siewiorek. High-Availability Computer Systems. *IEEE Computer*, 24(9):39–48, September 1991.

[Huang93]   Y. Huang and C. Kintala. Software Implemented Fault Tolerance: Technologies and Experience. In *Proceedings of the 1993 International Symposium on Fault-Tolerant Computing*, pages 2–9, June 1993.

[Huang95]   Y. Huang, C. Kintala, N. Kolettis, and N. Fulton. Software Rejuvenation: Analysis, Module and Applications. In *Proceedings of the 1995 International Symposium on Fault-Tolerant Computing*, pages 381–390, June 1995.

[Kropp98]   N. P. Kropp, P. J. Koopman, and D.P. Siewiorek. Automated Robustness Testing of Off-the_shelf Software Components. In *Proceedings of the 1998 International Symposium on Fault-Tolerant Computing*, pages 230–239, June 1998.

[Lee93]   I. Lee and R. Iyer. Faults, Symptoms, and Software Fault Tolerance in the Tandem GUARDIAN Operating System. In *International Symposium on Fault-Tolerant Computing (FTCS)*, pages 20–29, 1993.

[Netcraft99]   The Netcraft Web Server Survey. At http://www.netcraft.com/survey/

[Randell75]   Brian Randell. System Structure for Software Fault Tolerance. *IEEE Transactions on Software Engineering*, 1(2):220–232, June 1975.

[SiteMetrics98]   Internet Server Survey. At http://www.sitemetrics.com/serversurvey/ ss_98_q3/revseg.htm

[Sullivan91]   M. Sullivan and R. Chillarege. Software Defects and Their Impact on System Availability– A Study of Field Failures in Operating Systems. In *Proceedings of the 1991 International Symposium on Fault-Tolerant Computing*, June 1991.

[Sullivan92]   M. Sullivan and R. Chillarege. A Comparison of Software Defects in Database Management Systems an d Operating Systems. In *Proceedings of the 1992 International Symposium on Fault-Tolerant Computing*, pages 475–484, July 1992.

[Wang93]   Yi-Min Wang, W. Kent Fuchs, and Yennuan Huang. Progressive Retry for Software Error Recovery in Distributed Systems. In *Proceedings of the 1993 Symposium on Fault-Tolerant Computing*, June 1993.

[Weller93]   Edward F. Weller. Lessons from Three Years of Inspection Data. *IEEE Software*, 10(5):38–45, September 1993.

Software-Implemented Fault Detection for High-Performance Space Applications

Michael Turmon, Robert Granat, and Daniel S. Katz

M/S 126-347; Jet Propulsion Laboratory; Pasadena, CA 91109
{turmon,granat,daniel.s.katz}@jpl.nasa.gov

Abstract

We describe and test a software approach to overcoming radiation-induced errors in spaceborne applications running on commercial off-the-shelf components. The approach uses checksum methods to validate results returned by a numerical subroutine operating subject to unpredictable errors in data. We can treat subroutines that return results satisfying a necessary condition having a linear form; the checksum tests compliance with this condition. We discuss the theory and practice of setting numerical tolerances to separate errors caused by a fault from those inherent in finite-precision numerical calculations. We test both the general effectiveness of the linear fault tolerant schemes we propose, and the correct behavior of our parallel implementation of them.

1 Introduction

We first outline the general outlook and goals of the spaceborne computing effort motivating this work, and then we describe the detailed contents of this paper.

1.1 Supercomputing in Space

Within NASA's High Performance Computing and Communications Program, the Remote Exploration and Experimentation (REE) project [11] at the Jet Propulsion Laboratory will enable a new type of scientific investigation by bringing commercial supercomputing technology into space. Transferring such computational power to space will enable highly-autonomous, flexible missions with substantial on-board analysis capability, mitigating control latency issues due to fundamental light-time delays, as well as inevitable bandwidth limitations in the link between spacecraft and ground stations. To do this, REE does not need to develop a single computational platform, but rather to define and demonstrate a process for rapidly transferring commercial high-performance computing technology into ultra-low power, fault-tolerant architectures for space.

Traditionally, spacecraft components have been radiation-hardened to protect against faults caused by natural galactic cosmic rays and energetic protons. Such radiation-hardening lowers the clock speed and increases the required power of a component. Even worse, the time needed to radiation-harden a component guarantees both that it will be outdated when it is ready for use in space, and that it has a high cost which must be spread over a small number of customers. Typically, at any given time, radiation-hardened components have a power:performance ratio that is an order of magnitude lower, and a cost that is several orders of magnitude higher than contemporary commodity off-the-shelf (COTS) components. The REE project is therefore attempting to use COTS components in space, and handling the resulting faults in software. The project consists of three initiatives: applications, computing testbeds, and system software.

Under the applications initiative, five Science Application Teams (SATs) were chosen to develop scalable science applications, and to port them to REE testbeds running REE system software:

- The Gamma-ray Large Area Space Telescope (GLAST) identifies gamma rays in a sea of background cosmic rays and reconstructs the gamma ray trajectories.

- The Next Generation Space Telescope (NGST) processes images on-board to reduce the effect of the cosmic rays on the CCD cameras. Also, fully on-board tuning of a deformable mirror allows accurate focus.

- Mars Rover Science, which identifies various materials on Mars using texture analysis and image segmentation. Also, stereo image pairs are analyzed for use in autonomous navigation.

- The Orbiting Thermal Imaging Spectrometer uses hyperspectral images to obtain temperature and emissivity, performs spectral unmixing, and classifies images.

- The Solar Terrestrial Probe Project (STP) examines using fleets of spacecraft for radio astronomical imaging and plasma moment analysis.

The power:performance and raw compute speed offered by

REE allow these teams to develop new approaches to science data processing and autonomy. The applications mentioned above are generally MPI programs which are not replicated, and therefore can take full advantage of the computing power of the hardware. (REE also intends to support Triple Modular Redundancy in software for smaller applications that require high reliability, as opposed to high availability.)

Under the testbeds initiative, a system designed to deliver 30 MOPS/watt is currently being built, to be delivered in June 2000. This testbed consists of 40 COTS processors connected by a COTS network fabric. Through future RFPs, the project will obtain additional testbeds that perform faster while using less power. Criteria that are required of the testbeds are: consistency with rapid transfer (18 month or less) of new Earth-based technologies to space, no single point of failure, and graceful degradation in the event of permanent hardware failure.

The system software initiative will provide the services required to let the applications use the hardware reliably in space, as well as creating an easy-to-use development environment. The system software is also intended to use commercial components as much as possible. The major challenge for this initiative is to develop a middleware layer between the operating system and the applications which accepts that both permanent and transient faults will occur and provides for recovery from them.

1.2 Fault Tolerance via Software

Most of the transient faults will be single event upsets (SEUs); their presence requires that the applications be self-checking, or tolerant of errors, as the first layer of fault-tolerance. Additional software layers will protect against errors that are not caught by the application [5]. For example, one such layer would automatically restart programs which have crashed or hung. This works in conjunction with self-checking routines: if an error is detected, and the computation does not yield correct results after a set number of retries, the error handling scheme aborts the program so that it can be automatically restarted.

SEUs affecting data are particularly troublesome because they typically have fewer obvious consequences than an SEU to code — the latter would be expected to cause an exception. Note that since memory will be error-detecting and correcting, faults to memory will be largely screened; most data faults will therefore affect the microprocessor or its cache.

Due to the nature of scientific codes, much of their time is spent in certain common numerical subroutines — as much as 70% in one NGST application, for example. Protecting these subroutines from faults provides one ingredient in an overall software-implemented fault-tolerance scheme. It is in this context that we describe and test the mathematical background for using checksum methods to validate results returned by a numerical subroutine operating in an SEU-prone environment. Following the COTS philosophy laid out above, our general approach has been to wrap existing parallel numerical libraries (ScaLAPACK, FFTW) with fault-detecting middleware. We can treat subroutines that return results satisfying a necessary condition having a linear form; the checksum tests compliance with this necessary condition. Here we discuss the theory and practice of setting numerical tolerances to separate errors caused by a fault from those inherent in finite-precision numerical calculations.

To separate these two classes of errors, we employ well-known bounds on error-propagation within linear algebraic algorithms. These bounds provide a maximum error that is to be expected due to register effects; any error in excess of this is taken to be the product of a fault. Adapting these bounds to the fault tolerant software setting yields a series of tests having different efficiency and accuracy attributes. To better understand the characteristics of the tests we develop, we perform controlled numerical experiments using the tests, as well as experiments in an REE testbed environment, as described above, which supports software fault injection.

1.3 Notation

We close this introduction by introducing some useful notation. Matrices and vectors are written in uppercase and lowercase roman letters respectively; A^T is the transpose of the matrix A (conjugate transpose for complex matrices). Any identity matrix is always I; context provides its dimension. A is *orthogonal* if $AA^\mathsf{T} = I$. A square matrix is a *permutation* if it can be obtained by re-ordering the rows of I. The size of a vector v is measured by its *p-norm*, a non-negative real number $\|v\|_p$; similarly for matrices A. See [8] (hereafter abbreviated GVL), sections 2.2 and 2.3, for the definitions. The *submultiplicative property* of p-norms implies that $\|AB\|_p \le \|A\|_p \|B\|_p$ and similarly for vectors.

2 General Considerations

In this paper we are concerned with these operations:
- Product: find the product $AB = P$, given A and B.
- LU decomposition: factor A as $A = PLU$ with P a permutation, L unit lower-triangular, U upper-triangular.
- Singular value decomposition: factor A as $A = UDV^\mathsf{T}$, where D is diagonal and U, V are orthogonal matrices.
- System solution: solve for x in $Ax = b$ when given A and b
- Matrix inverse: given A, find B such that $AB = I$.
- Fourier transform: given x, find y such that $y = Wx$, where W is the matrix of Fourier bases.
- Inverse Fourier transform: given y, find x such that $x = W^\mathsf{T} y$.

Although standard numerical packages provide many other routines, the ones above were identified by science application teams as the being of the most interest, partly on the basis of amount of time spent within them.

Each of these operations has been written to emphasize that some linear relation holds among the subroutine inputs and its computed outputs; we call this the *postcondition*. For the product, system solution, inverse, and transforms, this postcondition is necessary and sufficient, and completely characterizes the subroutine's task. For the other two, the postcondition is only a necessary condition and valid results must enjoy other properties as well. In either case, identifying and checking the postcondition provides a powerful sanity check on the proper functioning of the subroutine.

Before proceeding to examine these operations in detail, we mention two points involved in designing fault tolerant techniques. Suppose for definiteness that we plan to check one $m \times n$ matrix. Any reasonable checksum scheme must depend on the content of each matrix entry, otherwise some entries would not be checked. This implies that simply computing a checksum requires $O(mn)$ operations. Checksum fault tolerance schemes thus lose their attractiveness for operations taking $O(mn)$ or fewer operations (e.g. trace, sum, and 1-norm) because it is simpler and more directly informative to achieve fault-tolerance by repeating the computation. The second general point is that, although the postconditions above are linearly-checkable equalities, they need not be. For example, the largest eigenvalue of A is bounded by functions of the 1-norm and the ∞-norm, both of which are easily computed but not linear. One could thus evaluate the sanity of a computation by checking postconditions that involve such inequalities. None of the operations we consider requires this level of generality.

The postconditions we consider generically involve comparing two linear maps, which are known in factorized form

$$L_1 L_2 \cdots L_p \overset{?}{=} R_1 R_2 \cdots R_q \quad . \tag{1}$$

This check can be done exhaustively via n linearly independent probes for an $n \times n$ system. Of course, exhaustive comparison would typically introduce about as much computation as would be required to recompute the answer from scratch. On the other hand, a typical fault to data fans out across the matrix outputs, and a single probe would be enough to catch most errors:

$$L_1 L_2 \cdots L_p w \overset{?}{=} R_1 R_2 \cdots R_q w \tag{2}$$

for some probe vector w. This approach, known as result-checking (RC), is recommended by Blum and Kannan [1] and, accessibly, Blum and Wasserman [3]. The idea is also the basis for the checksum-augmentation approach introduced earlier by Huang and Abraham [9] for systolic arrays, under the name algorithm-based fault tolerance (ABFT).

Both techniques have since been extended and refined by several researchers [4, 7, 10, 13, 14, 2, 6]; a comparison of RC and ABFT is in [12].

There are two designer-selectable choices controlling the numerical properties of this fault detection system: the checksum weights w and the comparison method indicated above by $\overset{?}{=}$. When no assumptions may be made about the operands, the first is relatively straightforward: the elements of w should not vary greatly in magnitude so that results figure essentially equally in the check. At the minimum, w must be everywhere nonzero; better still, each partial product $L_{p'} \cdots L_p w$ and $R_{q'} \cdots L_q w$ of (2) should not vary greatly in magnitude. For Fourier transforms, this yields a weak condition on w and its transform — we have chosen a slowly decaying exponential which satisfies the condition. For the matrix operations, little can be said in advance about the factors so we are content to let w be the vector of all ones. Our implementation allows an arbitrary w to be supplied by those users with more knowledge of expected factors.

3 Error Propagation

After the checksum vector, the second choice is the comparison method. As stated above, we perform comparisons using the corresponding postcondition for each operation. To develop a test that is roughly independent of the matrices at hand, we use the well-known bounds on error propagation in linear operations. In what follows, we develop a test for each operation of interest. For each operation, we first cite a result bounding the numerical error in the computation's output, and then we use this bound to develop a corollary defining a test which is roughly independent of the operands. Those less interested in this machinery might review the first two results and skip to section 4. Throughout, we use **u** to represent the numerical precision of the underlying hardware; it is the difference between unity and the next larger floating-point number.

It is important to understand that the error bounds given in the results are *qualitative* and determine the general characteristics of roundoff in an algorithm's implementation. The estimates we obtain in this section are bounds based on worst-case scenarios, and will typically predict roundoff error larger than practically observed. (See GVL, section 2.4.6, for more on this outlook.) In the fault tolerance context, using these bounds uncritically would mean setting thresholds too high and missing some fault-induced errors. Their value for us, and it is substantial, is to indicate how roundoff error scales with different inputs. This allows fault tolerant routines the opportunity to factor out the inputs, yielding performance that is more nearly input-independent. Of course, some problem-specific tuning will likely improve performance. One goal is to simplify this tuning process as much as possible.

Result 1 *Let* $\hat{P} = \texttt{mult}(A, B)$ *be computed using a dot-product, outer-product, or gaxpy-based algorithm. The error matrix* $E = \hat{P} - AB$ *satisfies*

$$\|E\|_\infty \leq n\|A\|_\infty\|B\|_\infty \mathbf{u} \tag{3}$$

Proof. See GVL, section 2.4.8. □

Corollary 2 *An input-independent checksum test for* $\texttt{mult}$ *is*

$$d = \hat{P}w - ABw \tag{4}$$

$$\|d\|_\infty/(\|A\|_\infty\|B\|_\infty\|w\|_\infty) \underset{<}{\overset{>}{\scriptstyle}} \tau\mathbf{u} \tag{5}$$

where τ *is an input-independent threshold.*

The test is expressed as a comparison (indicated by the $\underset{<}{\overset{>}{\scriptstyle}}$ relation) with a threshold; the latter is a scaled version of the floating-point accuracy. If the discrepancy is larger than $\tau\mathbf{u}$, a fault would be declared, otherwise the error is explainable by roundoff.

Proof. The difference $d = Ew$ so, by the submultiplicative property of norms and result 1,

$$\|d\|_\infty \leq \|E\|_\infty\|w\|_\infty \leq n\|A\|_\infty\|B\|_\infty\|w\|_\infty\mathbf{u}$$

and the dependence on A and B is removed by dividing by their norms. The factor of n is unimportant in this calculation, as noted in the remark beginning the section. □

For the remaining operations, we require the notion of a *numerically realistic* matrix. The reliance of numerical analysts on certain proven algorithms is based on the rarity of certain pathological matrices that cause, for example, pivot elements in decomposition algorithms to grow exponentially. Even algorithms regarded as stable and reliable can be made to misbehave when given such unlikely inputs. Because the underlying routines will fail under such pathological conditions, we may neglect them in designing an fault tolerant system; such a computation is doomed even without faults. Accordingly, the results below must assume that the inputs are numerically realistic to obtain usable error bounds.

Result 3 *Let* $(\hat{P}, \hat{L}, \hat{U}) = \texttt{lu}(A)$ *be computed using a standard LU decomposition algorithm with partial pivoting. The backward error matrix* E *defined by* $A + E = \hat{P}\hat{L}\hat{U}$ *satisfies*

$$\|E\|_\infty \leq 8n^3\rho\,\|A\|_\infty\mathbf{u} \tag{6}$$

where the growth factor ρ *depends on the size of certain partial results of the calculation, and is bounded by a small constant for numerically realistic matrices.*

Proof. See GVL, section 3.4.6. □

We note in passing that this is close to the best possible bound for the discrepancy, because the error in simply writing down the matrix A must be of order $\|A\|\mathbf{u}$.

Corollary 4 *An input-independent checksum test for* $\texttt{lu}$ *as applied to numerically realistic matrices is*

$$d = \hat{P}\hat{L}\hat{U}w - Aw \tag{7}$$

$$\|d\|_\infty/(\|A\|_\infty\|w\|_\infty) \underset{<}{\overset{>}{\scriptstyle}} \tau\mathbf{u} \tag{8}$$

where τ *is an input-independent threshold.*

Proof. We have $d = Ew$ so, by the submultiplicative property of norms and result 3,

$$\|d\|_\infty \leq \|E\|_\infty\|w\|_\infty \leq 8n^3\rho\,\|A\|_\infty\|w\|_\infty\mathbf{u} \quad .$$

As before, the factor of $8n^3$ is unimportant in this calculation. For numerically realistic matrices, the growth factor ρ is bounded by a constant, and the indicated test is recovered by dividing by the norm of A. □

Result 5 *Let* $(\hat{U}, \hat{D}, \hat{V}) = \texttt{svd}(A)$ *be computed using a standard singular value decomposition algorithm. The forward error matrix* E *defined by* $A + E = \hat{U}\hat{D}\hat{V}^\mathsf{T}$ *satisfies*

$$\|E\|_2 \leq \rho\,\|A\|_2\mathbf{u} \tag{9}$$

where ρ *is a constant not much larger than one for numerically realistic matrices* A.

Proof. See GVL, section 5.5.8. □

Corollary 6 *An input-independent checksum test for* $\texttt{svd}$ *as applied to numerically realistic matrices is*

$$d = \hat{U}\hat{D}\hat{V}^\mathsf{T}w - Aw \tag{10}$$

$$\|d\|_\infty/(\|A\|_\infty\|w\|_\infty) \underset{<}{\overset{>}{\scriptstyle}} \tau\mathbf{u} \tag{11}$$

where τ *is an input-independent threshold.*

Proof. See the appendix. □

The test for SVD has the same normalization as for LU decomposition.

Result 7 *Let* $\hat{B} = \texttt{inv}(A)$ *be computed using Gaussian elimination with partial pivoting. The backward error matrix* E *defined by* $(A + E)^{-1} = \hat{B}$ *satisfies*

$$\|E\|_\infty \leq 8n^3\rho\,\|A\|_\infty\mathbf{u} \tag{12}$$

with ρ *as in result 3.*

Proof. See GVL, section 3.4.6, which defines the backwards error for the linear system solution $Ax = b$. Since A^{-1} is calculated by solving the multiple right-hand-side problem $AA^{-1} = I$, the bound given there on $\|E\|_\infty$ applies here with the same growth factor ρ. (This growth factor depends only on the pivots in the LU factorization which underlies the inverse computation.) □

Algorithm	Δ	σ_1	σ_2	σ_3	Note
mult	$\hat{P} - AB$	$\|A\|\|B\|$	$\|\hat{P}\|$	$\|\hat{P}w\|$	—
lu	$\hat{P}\hat{L}\hat{U} - A$	$\|A\|$	$\|\hat{P}\hat{L}\hat{U}\|$	$\|Aw\|$	σ_1 easier than σ_2
svd	$\hat{U}\hat{D}\hat{V} - A$	$\|A\|$	$\|\hat{U}\hat{D}\hat{V}^{\mathsf{T}}\|$	$\|Aw\|$	σ_1 easier than σ_2
inv	$I - A\hat{B}$	$\|A\|\|A^{-1}\|$	$\|A\|\|\hat{B}\|$	$\|A\|\|\hat{B}w\|$	$\|A\hat{B}w\|$ useless
fft	$(\hat{y} - Wx)^{\mathsf{T}}$	$\|x\|$	—	—	result is a vector
ifft	$(\hat{x} - W^{\mathsf{T}}y)^{\mathsf{T}}$	$\|y\|$	—	—	result is a vector

Table 1. Algorithms and corresponding checksum tests.

Corollary 8 *An input-independent checksum test for* inv *as applied to numerically realistic matrices is*

$$d = w - A\hat{B}w \tag{13}$$

$$\|d\|_\infty / (\|A\|_\infty \|A^{-1}\|_\infty \|w\|_\infty) \gtrless \tau\mathbf{u} \tag{14}$$

where τ is an input-independent threshold.

Proof. See the appendix. □

We remark that this bound on discrepancy, larger than that for lu, is the reason matrix inverse is numerically unstable. We close this section with tests for Fourier transform operations. The $n \times n$ forward transform matrix W contains the Fourier basis functions, recall that $W/\sqrt{n}$ is unitary.

Result 9 *Let $\hat{y} = $* fft$(x)$ *be computed using a decimation-based fast Fourier transform algorithm; let $y = Wx$ be the infinite-precision Fourier transform. The error vector $e = \hat{y} - y$ satisfies*

$$\|e\|_\infty \leq n \log_2 n \|x\|_\infty \mathbf{u} \tag{15}$$

Proof. See the appendix. □

Corollary 10 *An input-independent checksum test for* fft *is*

$$d = (\hat{y} - Wx)^{\mathsf{T}} w \tag{16}$$

$$|d| / (\|x\|_\infty \|w\|_\infty) \gtrless \tau\mathbf{u} \tag{17}$$

where τ is an input-independent threshold.

Proof. This follows from result 9 after neglecting the leading constant. □

Corollary 11 *An input-independent checksum test for* ifft *is*

$$d = (\hat{x} - W^{\mathsf{T}}y)^{\mathsf{T}} w \tag{18}$$

$$|d| / (\|y\|_\infty \|w\|_\infty) \gtrless \tau\mathbf{u} \tag{19}$$

where τ is an input-independent threshold.

Proof. The proof, very similar to corollary 10, is omitted. □

4 Implementing the Tests

It is straightforward to transform these results into algorithms for error detection via checksums. The principal issue is computing the desired matrix norms efficiently from results needed in the root calculation. For example, in the matrix multiply, instead of computing $\|A\|\|B\|$, it is more efficient to compute $\|\hat{P}\|$ which equals $\|AB\|$ under fault-free conditions. By the submultiplicative property of norms, $\|AB\| \leq \|A\|\|B\|$, so this substitution always underestimates the upper bound on roundoff error, leading to false alarms. On the other hand, we must remember that the norm bounds are only general guides anyway. All that is needed is for $\|AB\|$ to scale as does $\|A\|\|B\|$; the unknown scale factor can be absorbed into τ.

Taking this one step farther, we might compute $\|\hat{P}w\|$ as a substitute for $\|A\|\|B\|\|w\|$. Here we run an even greater risk of underestimating the bound, especially if w is nearly orthogonal to the product, so it is wise to use instead $\lambda\|w\| + \|\hat{P}w\|$ for some problem-dependent λ. Extending this reasoning to the other operations yields the comparisons in table 1. The error criterion used there always proceeds from the number $\delta = \|\Delta w\|$ for the indicated difference matrix Δ; this matrix is of course never explicitly computed. In addition to the obvious

$$T0: \qquad \delta/\|w\| \gtrless \tau\mathbf{u} \quad \text{(trivial test)} \tag{20}$$

we provide three other comparison tests

$$T1: \qquad \delta/(\sigma_1\|w\|) \gtrless \tau\mathbf{u} \quad \text{(ideal test)} \tag{21}$$

$$T2: \qquad \delta/(\sigma_2\|w\|) \gtrless \tau\mathbf{u} \quad \text{(approx. matrix test)} \tag{22}$$

$$T3: \quad \delta/(\lambda\|w\| + \sigma_3) \gtrless \tau\mathbf{u} \quad \text{(approx. vector test)} \tag{23}$$

The *ideal test* is the one recommended by the theoretical error bounds, and is based on the supplied input arguments, but may not be computable (e.g., for inv). In contrast, both approximate tests are based on computed quantities, and may also be suggested by the reasoning above. The *matrix test*

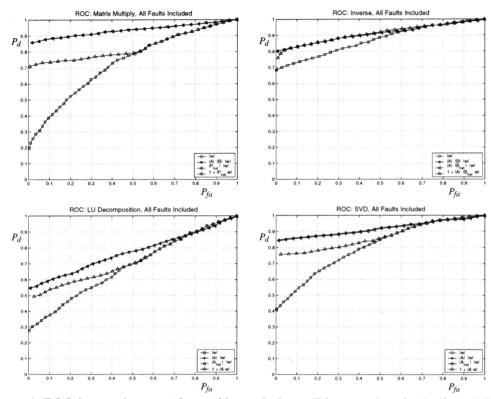

Figure 1. ROC for random matrices of bounded condition number, including all faults.

involves a matrix norm while the *vector test* involves a vector norm and is therefore more subject to false alarms. (Several variants of the matrix tests are available for these operations.) We note that the obvious vector test for `inv` uses $A\hat{B}w$, but since $\hat{B} = \mathtt{inv}(A)$, this test becomes almost equivalent to $T0$: so we suggest using the vector/matrix test shown in table 1. The ideal tests $T1$ for the Fourier transforms need only the norm of the input, which is readily calculated, so other test versions are omitted. Clearly the choice of which test to use is based on the interplay of computation time and fault-detection performance for a given population of input matrices. Because of the shortcomings of numerical analysis, we cannot predict definitively that one test will outperform another. The experimental results reported in the next section are one indicator of real performance, and may motivate more detailed analysis of test behavior.

5 Results: Simulated Fault Conditions

We first discuss Matlab simulations of the checksum tests for the operations `mult`, `lu`, `svd`, and `inv` under fault conditions. We then discuss the behavior of a fault tolerant

`fft` operation as implemented on a testbed environment, and tested using simulated fault injection.

5.1 Matlab Simulations

In this section we show results of Matlab simulations of the proposed checksum tests. These simulations are intended to verify the essential effectiveness of the checksum technique for fault tolerance, as well as to sketch the relative behaviors of the tests described above. Due to the special nature of the population of test matrices, and the shortcomings of the fault insertion scheme, these results should not be taken as anything but an estimate of relative performance, and a rough estimate of ultimate absolute performance.

We briefly describe the simulation setup. In essence a population of random matrices is used as input to a given computation; faults are injected in half these computations, and a checksum test is used to attempt to identify the affected computations. Random test matrices A of a given condition number κ are generated by the rule

$$A = 10^{\alpha}\, U D_{\kappa} V^{\mathsf{T}} \quad . \tag{24}$$

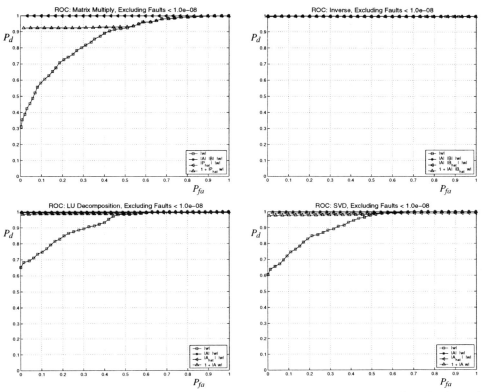

Figure 2. ROC for random matrices of bounded condition number, excluding faults of relative size less than 10^{-8}.

The random matrices U and V are the orthogonal factors in the QR factorization of two square matrices with normally distributed entries. The diagonal matrix D_κ is filled in by choosing random singular values, such that the largest singular value is unity and the smallest is $1/\kappa$. These matrices all have 2-norm equal to unity; the overall scale is set by α which is chosen uniformly at random between -8 and +8. A total of 2000 64×64 matrices (forty applications of the rule (24) for each κ in $\{2^1, ..., 2^{20}\}$) is processed.

Faults are injected in half of these runs (1000 of 2000) by first choosing a matrix to affect, and then flipping exactly one bit of its 64-bit representation. For example, if a call to If lu is to suffer a simulated fault, first one of A, L, or U is selected, and then one bit of the chosen matrix is toggled. If A was selected, one can expect the computed $\hat{L}$ and $\hat{U}$ to have many incorrect elements; if L was selected, only one element of the LU decomposition would be in error. This scheme is intended to simulate errors occurring at various times within the computation.

Characteristics of a given scheme are concisely expressed using the standard receiver operating characteristic (ROC)

curve. For a given error tolerance, a certain proportion of False Alarms (numerical errors tagged as data faults, P_{fa}) and Detections (data faults correctly identified, P_d) will be observed. The ROC plots these two proportions parametrically as the tolerance is varied; this describes the performance achievable by a certain detection scheme and provides a basis for choosing one scheme over others.

Each of the four tests described above is used to identify faults; for a fixed τ this implies observing a certain false alarm rate and fault-detection rate. The pair (P_{fa}, P_d) may be plotted parametrically, varying τ to obtain an ROC curve which illustrates the overall performance of the test. See figure 1. In these figures, $T0$ is the line with square markers and $T3$ is marked by upward pointing triangles; $T0$ lies below $T3$. $T2$ is shown with left pointing triangles, and $T1$, the optimal test, with asterisks; these two tests nearly coincide.

Of course, some missed fault detections are worse than others since many faults occur in the low-order bits of the mantissa and cause very minor changes in the matrix. Accordingly, a second set of ROCs is shown in figure 2. In

113

| | Average-Case | | Worst-Case | |
	All	Sig.	All	Sig.
mult	0.85	1.00	0.63	0.92
inv	0.80	1.00	0.32	0.50
lu	0.54	1.00	0.43	0.90
svd	0.84	1.00	0.60	0.87
Mean	0.74	1.00	0.50	0.80

Table 2. P^* for four sets of experiments.

this set, faults which cause such a minute perturbation are screened from the results entirely; the screen is placed at a fault size of one part in 10^{-8} and filters about 40% of all faults. This corresponds to the accuracy of single-precision floating point and is well beyond the precision of the science data being analyzed. These ROCs are more informative about fault-detection performance in an operating regime similar to that of our science applications.

We may make some general observations about the results. Clearly $T0$, the un-normalized test, fares poorly in all experiments. This illustrates the value of the results on error propagation that form the basis for the normalized tests. Generally speaking,

$$T0 \ll T3 < T2 \approx T1 \quad . \tag{25}$$

This confirms theory, in which $T1$ is the ideal test and the others approximate it. In particular, $T1$ and $T2$ are quite similar because generally only an enormous fault can change the norm of a matrix — these cases are easy to detect.

Further, we note that the most relevant part of the ROC curve is when $P_{fa} \approx 0$; we may in fact be interested in the value P^*, defined to be P_d when $P_{fa} = 0$. This value is summarized for these experiments in table 2. The first two columns of this table come from the data in figures 1 and 2. The other columns are from similar experiments using a worst-case matrix population taken from the Matlab "gallery" matrices; this is a worst-case population because it contains many members that are not "numerically realistic" in the sense of section 3. Under the average-case test conditions, essentially all faults could be detected with no false alarms; this level of performance is surely adequate for REE purposes. In worst-case — and no science application should be in this regime — effectiveness drops to about 80%. This gives an indication of the loss in fault-detection performance incurred by a numerically ill-posed application.

5.2 Testbed Simulations

Effectiveness of the fault tolerant `fft` routine, implemented in C, was carried out on the REE interim testbed, a parallel system running the Lynx OS. Fault injection software available on the testbed was used to simulate radiation-induced SEUs affecting memory, registers, code, and the

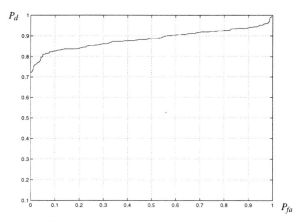

Figure 3. ROC for fault tolerant FFT.

stack. A population of uniformly scaled random matrices was used as the input to the `fft` routine. The test was conducted in the following manner: each calculation was performed twice — once without the use of fault injection, and once while under the influence of simulated fault injection, during which zero or more faults were induced in memory as the calculation was being performed. The result with and without fault simulation was compared for each matrix, in order to verify whether a fault had been injected. For purposes of characterizing the performance of the fault detection, differences between the two results were considered insignificant (not faulty) if the square error was less than 10^{-8}. We note that this is similar, but not identical to the manner in which significant faults were identified in the preceding section.

Figure 3 shows an ROC curve summarizing the result of the tests for 1000 input matrices. This curve is not directly comparable to those in figures 1 and 2; nevertheless we observe that the fault tolerant `fft` does detect over 70% of errors without risk of false alarms. Our explanation of this result is inhibited by the limitations of the instrumentation: the fault injection software currently does not record the times, locations, or magnitudes of injected faults. However, one possible explanation for some faults going undetected is that the testbed allows faults to be injected in the matrix after it has been used in calculation of the checksum. Improvements in instrumentation should allow a more thorough analysis of these results. With increased understanding we believe these results can be improved.

6 Parallel Implementation

In our parallel implementation of the checksum procedures we use the ScaLAPACK routines PDGEMM for `mult`, PDGETRF for `lu`, PDGETRI for `inv`, and PDGESVD for `svd`. For `mult`, we use the checksum test $T2$ for reasons of computational cost, as the test requires only the calculation of the norm of the resultant matrix product. For `lu` and `svd`, we employ the ideal checksum test $T1$, as in these cases the norm of the matrix can be calculated before the factorization is performed in place. Our choice of checksum test for `inv` is complicated by the fact that `PDGETRI` requires that the input matrix already be in its LU-factorized form. We therefore employ a modified version of the checksum test $T3$, in which $\sigma_3 = \|\hat{B}\| \|Aw\|$: $\hat{B}$ is readily available as the result of the computation, and Aw can be obtained by multiplying w successively by $\hat{U}$, $\hat{L}$, and $\hat{P}$.

In our implementation we consider the possibility that induced faults could affect the calculated norms, thereby compromising the validity of the checksum test. To prevent erroneously large norms from eliminating errors from detection, the routines compare the norms against the system dependent maximum double precision floating point value; detection of a norm that exceeds that value raises an error.

In order to address numerical issues concerning our implementation of the checksum procedures, we compared the results of our implementation with those generated by Matlab computations. We performed a series of tests using an assortment of randomly perturbed matrices from the Matlab gallery selection. These matrices are generally ill-conditioned or poorly scaled, but serve as a demanding test to check our routines against a known standard.

From our tests, we ascertained that there is excellent agreement between Matlab and the ScaLAPACK implementation of our routines. Indeed, when the matrix is badly scaled, ill-conditioned, or numerically unrealistic — causing ScaLAPACK and Matlab to differ according to the full answer — our ScaLAPACK implementation finds the error in the checksum calculation also. In essence, the message is: if the computation did not succeed, the checksum test discovers it.

7 Conclusions and Future Work

Theoretical results bounding the expected roundoff error in a given computation provide several types of input-independent threshold tests for checksum differences. The observed behavior of these tests is in good general agreement with theory, and readily computable tests are easy to define. All the linear algebra operations considered here (`mult`, `lu`, `inv`, and `svd`) admit tests that are effective in detecting faults at the 99% level on typical matrix inputs. Tests of the numerical characteristics of our parallel implementation of the fault detection schemes indicate excellent agreement with another numerical package for most operations, except in cases when the matrix is badly scaled, ill-conditioned, or numerically unrealistic. In those cases, the schemes detect an error in the checksum calculation.

Test programs calling our parallel implementations have been installed on the REE project testbed, where they can be tested under simulated fault conditions. Of the operations described here, `mult` and `fft` have both been tested not only under the protection of the fault tolerant schemes described here, but also under an additional layer of software fault tolerance as described in Section 1.2.

The fault tolerant `fft` routines have also been integrated into the image texture analysis and segmentation application which is part of the Mars Rover Science project. This application is being tested with simulated fault injections on the REE project testbed under the software framework described above, both with and without the fault tolerant routines. While conclusive results are not yet available, preliminary testing indicates that the checksum scheme effectively protects the Fourier transform operations within the application from SEUs.

We expect that continued integration of fault tolerant routines with the various science applications will lead to these applications being resistant to SEUs throughout large portions of the computation. Other common subroutines, such as those involving sorting, order statistics, and numerical integration, also require more than $O(n)$ time and are candidates for fault-hardened versions. The fault-hardening described here is just one of the protections that will be needed to use COTS computers in space, but it is an essential one.

Acknowledgment

This work was carried out by the Jet Propulsion Laboratory, California Institute of Technology, under contract with the National Aeronautics and Space Administration.

References

[1] M. Blum and S. Kannan. Designing programs that check their work. In *Proc. 21st Symp. Theor. Comput.*, pages 86–97, 1989.

[2] M. Blum, M. Luby, and R. Rubinfeld. Self-testing correcting with applications to numerical problems. *Journal of computer and system sciences*, 47(3):549–595, 1993.

[3] M. Blum and H. Wasserman. Reflections on the Pentium division bug. *IEEE Trans. Computing*, 45(4):385–393, 1996.

[4] D. L. Boley, R. P. Brent, G. H. Golub, and F. T. Luk. Algorithmic fault tolerance using the Lanczos method. *SIAM J. Matrix Anal. Appl.*, 13(1):312–332, 1992.

[5] F. Chen, L. Craymer, J. Deifik, A. J. Fogel, D. S. Katz, A. G. S. Jr., R. R. Some, S. A. Upchurch, and K. Whisnant. Demonstration of the REE fault-tolerant parallel-processing supercomputer for spacecraft onboard scientific data processing. In *Proc. ICDSN (FTCS-30 & DCCA-8)*, 2000.

[6] A.-R. Chowdhury and P. Banerjee. A new error analysis based method for tolerance computation for algorithm-based checks. *IEEE Trans. Computing*, 45(2), 1996.

[7] M. P. Connolly and P. Fitzpatrick. Fault-tolerent QRD recursive least squares. *IEE Proc. Comput. Digit. Tech.*, 143(2):137–144, 1996. (IEE, not IEEE).

[8]   G. H. Golub and C. F. V. Loan. *Matrix Computations*. Johns Hopkins Univ., Baltimore, second edition, 1989.

[9]   K.-H. Huang and J. A. Abraham. Algorithm-based fault tolerance for matrix operations. *IEEE Trans. Computing*, 33(6):518–528, 1984.

[10]   F. T. Luk and H. Park. An analysis of algorithm-based fault tolerance techniques. *Journal of Parallel and Distributed Computing*, 5:172–184, 1988.

[11]   REE project, March 1999. "Project Plan: Remote Exploration and Experimentation (REE) Project," available at www-ree.jpl.nasa.gov.

[12]   P. Prata and J. G. Silva. Algorithm-based fault tolerance versus result-checking for matrix computations. In *Proc. FTCS-29*, pages 4–11, 1999.

[13]   S. J. Wang and N. K. Jha. Algorithm-based fault tolerance for FFT networks. *IEEE Trans. Computing*, 43(7):849–854, 1994.

[14]   H. Wasserman and M. Blum. Software reliability via run-time result-checking. *Journal of the ACM*, 44(6):826–849, 1997.

Appendix

Proof of Corollary 6. Let $d = \hat{U}\hat{D}\hat{V}^\mathsf{T} w - Aw$; then $d = Ew$ where E is the error matrix bounded in result 5. We claim that an input-independent checksum test for svd is

$$\|d\|_2/(\|A\|_2\|w\|_2) \overset{>}{_{\sim}} \tau\mathbf{u} \quad . \tag{26}$$

Indeed, by the submultiplicative property and result 5,

$$\|d\|_2 \le \|E\|_2\|w\|_2 \le \rho\,\|A\|_2\|w\|_2\mathbf{u}$$

and the dependence on A is removed by dividing by its norm. The constant ρ is negligible for numerically realistic matrices, and the claim follows. To convert this test, which uses 2-norm, into one using the ∞-norm, we note that these two norms differ only by constant factors (see GVL sections 2.2.2 and 2.3.2) which may be absorbed into τ. $\square$

Proof of Corollary 8. Note that $d = \Delta w$ where $\Delta = I - A(A + E)^{-1}$. Some algebra is necessary to extract the error E from Δ. Using the Sherman-Morrison formula (GVL section 2.1.3) to rewrite the inverse of $A + E$ we obtain

$$\Delta = I - A[A^{-1} - A^{-1}(I + EA^{-1})^{-1}EA^{-1}]$$
$$= (I + EA^{-1})^{-1}EA^{-1} \tag{27}$$

For numerically realistic matrices, A dominates E and the first factor is negligible. Heuristically, this is because $E \ll A$ implies $EA^{-1} \ll AA^{-1} = I$, collapsing that factor to I. More formally, inverting a numerically realistic matrix produces an error matrix E such that for any vector v, $\|Ev\| \ll \|Av\|$ otherwise the backward error E would be comparable to A. Since v is arbitrary and A is invertible, we may let $v = A^{-1}u$, obtaining that $\|EA^{-1}u\| \ll \|u\| = \|Iu\|$, showing that the operator EA^{-1}

is dominated by I. Therefore we may neglect the first factor and the norm of the error is bounded by

$$\|d\|_\infty = \|\Delta w\|_\infty$$
$$\le \|E\|_\infty \|A^{-1}\|_\infty \|w\|_\infty$$
$$\le 8n^3\rho\,\|A\|_\infty \|A^{-1}\|_\infty \|w\|_\infty\mathbf{u} \tag{28}$$

using the submultiplicative property of norms. As before, the factor of $8n^3$ is unimportant in this calculation. Invoking the assumption that A is a numerically realistic matrix allows us to neglect the growth factor ρ, yielding the indicated test. $\square$

Proof of Result 9. Decimation algorithms are based on compact factorizations of the $n \times n$ unitary transform matrix W:

$$y = W_N W_{N-1} \cdots W_1 x$$

where $N = \log_2 n$, and each W_k performs one bank of $n/2$ "butterfly" operations. The infinite-precision computation may therefore be written as a recurrence

$$z_0 = x$$
$$z_{k+1} = W_{k+1} z_k \quad (k \ge 0) \tag{29}$$

where $y = z_N$. The finite-precision computation finds, in turn,

$$\hat{z}_0 = x$$
$$\hat{z}_{k+1} = \texttt{mult}(W_{k+1}, \hat{z}_k) \quad (k \ge 0) \tag{30}$$

and $\hat{y} = \hat{z}_N$. The proof proceeds by developing a recurrence for the size (always expressed in ∞-norm) of the error vector

$$e_{k+1} = z_{k+1} - \hat{z}_{k+1}$$
$$= W_{k+1} z_k - \texttt{mult}(W_{k+1}, \hat{z}_k)$$
$$= W_{k+1} z_k - (W_{k+1}\hat{z}_k + \tilde{e}_k)$$
$$= W_{k+1} e_k - \tilde{e}_k \tag{31}$$

where by Result 1, and the observation that exactly two entries of each row of W_k are nonzero, $\tilde{e}_k$ satisfies

$$\|\tilde{e}_k\| \le 2\,\|W_{k+1}\|\,\|\hat{z}_k\|\mathbf{u}$$
$$= 2\,\|z_k - e_k\|\mathbf{u}$$
$$\le 2(\|z_k\| + \|e_k\|)\mathbf{u} \quad . \tag{32}$$

Combining with (31) yields the bound

$$\|e_{k+1}\| \le \|W_{k+1}\|\,\|e_k\| + 2(\|z_k\| + \|e_k\|)\mathbf{u}$$
$$= (1 + 2\mathbf{u})\|e_k\| + 2\|z_k\|\mathbf{u} \quad . \tag{33}$$

Since $\|W_k\| = 2$, $\|z_k\| \le 2^k\|x\|$, and we obtain the recurrent upper bound

$$\|e_0\| = 0$$
$$\|e_{k+1}\| \le (1 + 2\mathbf{u})\|e_k\| + 2^{k+1}\|x\|\mathbf{u} \quad (k \geq 0) \tag{34}$$

For any reasonable floating-point system, $1 + 2\mathbf{u} \le 2$. Using this, it is easy to see $\|e_k\| \le k\,2^k\,\|x\|\mathbf{u}$, establishing the claim $\|e_N\| \le n\log n\,\|x\|\mathbf{u}$. $\square$

Session 5B

Practical Experience Reports III ♦ Validation and Evaluation

An Automatic SPIN Validation of a Safety Critical Railway Control System

S. Gnesi, G. Lenzini
IEI - CNR
Area della Ricerca di Pisa - S. Cataldo
Viale Alfieri 1 , 56010 Pisa, Italy
{gnesi, lenzini}@iei.pi.cnr.it

D. Latella
CNUCE - CNR
Area della Ricerca di Pisa - S. Cataldo
Viale Alfieri 1, 56010 Pisa, Italy
d.latella@cnuce.cnr.it

C. Abbaneo
Ansaldobreda Segnalamento Ferroviario (ASF)
Via dei Pescatori 35, Genova, Italy
cabbaneo@asf.ansaldo.it

A. Amendola, P. Marmo
Ansaldobreda Segnalamento Ferroviario (ASF)
Via Argine 425, Napoli, Italy
{amendola, marmo}@asf.ansaldo.it

Abstract

This paper describes an experiment in formal specification and validation performed in the context of an industrial joint project. The project involved an Italian company working in the field of railway engineering, Ansaldobreda Segnalamento Ferroviario, and the CNR Institutes IEI and CNUCE of Pisa. Within the project two formal models have been developed describing different aspects of a safety-critical system used in the management of medium-large railway networks. Validation of safety and liveness properties has been performed on both models. Safety properties have been checked primarily in presence of Byzantine faults as well as of silent faults embedded in the models themselves. Liveness properties have been more focused on a communication protocol used within the system. Properties have been specified by means of assertions or temporal logical formulae. We used PROMELA as specification language, while the verification was performed using the verification tool suite SPIN.

1 Introduction

The increasing request for safety and better performance in automatic management of modern railways has forced the introduction of sophisticated dependable, computer-based, control systems [3]. Such systems have an intrinsic degree of complexity and require innovative validation techniques during design and developing phases. Traditional methodologies, such as testing and simulation, could be insufficient when applied to this kind of systems. Exhaustive testing is usually impossible because of the high number of runs to be analyzed, while simulation can provide useful information only on a limited set of sequences. An alternative approach is the use of Formal Methods (FM) to deal with these problems.

In the last decade many industries, like Ansaldobreda Segnalamento Ferroviario (ASF), started pilot projects [11, 15, 16, 6] directed to evaluate the impact of FM on their production costs. As a result, positive experiences [4, 7] have shown how, for railway control systems, it has been possible to formalize significant models and to perform validation using model checking [8, 17, 9] approaches. In some cases industries developed their own validation environment, as the LIVE of ASF [1].

In this paper we describe the results of a real project jointly carried out by ASF and the CNR Institutes IEI and CNUCE, in the context of the Pisa Dependable Computer Center of Consorzio Pisa Ricerche. The project consisted of two distinct parts: (a) designing a formal model of a critical control system; (b) verifying specific *safety* properties under the hypothesis of Byzantine behavior [14] of one of the system components, and verifying *liveness* properties of a dependable communication protocol used within the system. In this paper we focus on the general structure of the formal validation effort, while particular modeling strategies can be found in [10]. Industrial choices internal to ASF induced us to use PROMELA [12] as formal language and and SPIN [13] as model checker. In fact, SPIN was already used within ASF in successfully verifying safety properties of different parts of the system [2].

The paper is organized as follows: in Section 2 we briefly and informally describe the system and all its component units; in Section 3 we introduce the framework of our formalization work; in Section 4 and Section 5 we explain the formal models used and the properties verified on them, and

119

we discuss some significant result; finally in Section 6 we critically summarize on the whole experience.

2 System Description

The railway system considered in this work is a programmable centralized control system developed by ASF, specifically designed to manage a medium/large railway network. The system is composed by some control posts, from which *critical* commands are composed, and by *Peripheral Control Units*(PCUs) which in turn execute them. These commands are critical because their execution affect machineries such as railway semaphores, rail points, or level crossings. For this reason particular attention has been reserved to guarantee the safety of the system in case of fault-silent and Byzantine faults in some of the system components.

A control hardware, called *Safety Nucleus* (SN) has been specifically designed for control and safety purposes. It monitors on the state of the system and tries to discover a faulty component. Its architecture is based on a triple modular redundant [18] configuration of computers running different versions of the same program. It has to face also with internal consensus problems, but hardware constraints make the implementation of the classical solution of consensus in distributed architecture problem (i.e. the Byzantine Generals Problem [14, 5]) impossible. So, SN guarantees system safety not by looking for consensus, but excluding a faulty component or forcing the whole system in a safe shutdown.

3 Formal Specification and Verification

We developed two PROMELA models, called respectively TMR and TMR-PCU, each of them describing different views of the SN-PCU system. In particular:

1. the TMR model describes in detail the triple modular configuration of SN. The TMR model has been developed to verify safety properties of the triple modular redundant mechanism of the SN in presence of Byzantine behavior of one of its components;

2. the TMR-PCU model describes in detail the SN-PCU communication protocol, and the PCU architecture. Aspects of the SN behavior not related to the communication protocol have been left out. The TMR-PCU model has been developed to verify liveness properties of the SN-PCU protocol, and safety properties when hardware silent faults in the communication occur in the communication media or in some of the PCUs.

4 The TMR model

The general architecture of TMR (Fig. 1) consists of: (1) three identical *central modules*, called A, B and C, implementing the triple modular redundancy; (2) a module called *exclusion logic*, devoted to check the consistency of the three modules; (3) the PCUs, composed by n control units (in our study we have considered $n = 2$); (4) communication *channels* between the modules (three symmetric channels), the modules and the exclusion logic (three symmetric channels), and the modules and the PCUs (a single bus); Our PROMELA model reflects quite faithfully this general

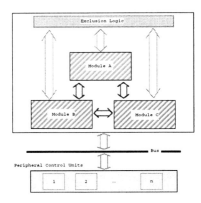

Figure 1. The TMR architecture

architecture.

The behavior of a module consists of a repeated sequence of *phases*. During each phase a central module runs local computations or communicates with other components of the system. In particular, in a *synchronization* phase each module sends to and receives from the other two modules, with time-out, a synchronization message. All of the communications in the ACC are synchronous with time-out: a time-out expiration is interpreted by the receiver as a sign of inactivity, while two time-outs force the receiver to a safe shut-down. In a *data exchange* phase each module broadcasts its local state, while in a *distributed voting* phase it votes on the information received. In a *communication with the exclusion logic*, the result of the voting is sent to the exclusion logic which can disconnect a module resulting in disagreement. Finally, in a *communication with the PCU*, a module communicates with the PCUs.

In developing the PROMELA code we had to solve the problem of simulating a time-out in the communications. In fact PROMELA does not deal with time. As a general solution we defined a particular EMPTY message, whose presence in a channel must be interpreted, by the receiver, as absence of any message it was waiting for. The *send* action changed too: it has been implemented as a non deterministic choice between either transmitting the "real" message or transmitting the EMPTY message. In the following we report a synthesis of the PROMELA code implementing the synchronization phase for the module C[1].

```
/***        in the global environment        ***/

#define EMPTY 0 // the empty message
#define SYNCH 1 // the synchronization message
[..]

activeA=1;   /* state of A, in C viewpoint   */
sentA = 0;   /* flag "sent" (to module A)     */
recvA = 0;   /* flag "received" (from module A)*/

do
/* communication with A */
 :: (!sentA) ->
     if
     // send the synch (if A is active)
     :: true -> outA!(SYNCH && activeA);
     // send the empty message
     :: true -> outA!(EMPTY);
     fi;
     sentA = 1;
 :: (!recvA && inA?[synA]) -> inA?synA;
       recvA = 1;
/* set the activity state of A */
     if
     :: synA == SYNCH -> activeA = 1;
     // time-out implies not activity
     :: else -> activeA = 0;
     fi;
/* communication with B */
 [ ... the same for B ... ]

 :: (sentA && sentB && recvA && recvB) -> break;
od;

/* eventually safe shutdown*/
if
/* if the other modules are not active */
:: !activeA && !activeB ->
       \\ global state of module C
       global_activeC = 0;
       goto SHUTDOWN
:: else -> skip
fi;
```

The PROMELA code implementing the other phases is similar to the one of synchronization, except for the type of messages involved or for some local computation.

More interesting is the implementation of a Byzantine behavior. In this context, Byzantine behavior is to be intended as in Lamport et al. [14]: a Byzantine module runs the same algorithm as a loyal module, but it can arbitrarily fail in executing it, and in particular it may send wrong messages, or send no message at all. In this interpretation all the communication phases have been realized also in a *Byzantine* version, where a communication error in sending a message may occur. In the following we report the PROMELA code corresponding to the implementation of a Byzantine communication in the synchronization phase of module C:

```
/* communication with A */
:: (!sentA) ->
    if
    /* send the synch (if A is active) */
    :: true -> outA!(SYNCH && activeA);
```

```
// send the wrong message */
:: true -> outA!(-SYNCH);
// send the empty message
:: true -> outA!(EMPTY);
fi;
sentA = 1;
```

4.1 Formal Verification TMR

In this section we list some of the properties verified on the TMR model and the related results. We used either LTL formulae, or PROMELA *assertions*[2]. We used assertions for those properties that could be expressed as an invariant on all the run sequences. In the following we assumed that only one module might show a Byzantine behavior.

(TMR1) *After a communication phase it is always true that if two modules do not receive any reply from the third module, this latter module will be eventually disconnected by the exclusion logic.*

(TMR2) *After a communication phase, it is always true that if one module does not receive any reply from the other two modules, it will switch eventually in a safe shut-down state.*

(TMR3) *After a distributed voting phase, it is always true that if two modules, in reciprocal agreement on the global state knowledge, recognize that a third module is not in agreement with them, this latter module will be eventually disconnected by the exclusion logic.*

All the previous informal properties have been formalized with different LTL formulas with the following common structure:

```
[] (p -> [] (q -> <> r) )
```

where p, q and r are formalized as predicate on variables.

(TMR4) *After a communication phase, every module has sent and received a message (eventually the empty message) from the other modules.*

```
assert{(recvB+recvC==2) && (sentB+sentC==2)}
```

The previous assertion has been placed after each communication phase.

(TMR5) *If a module is in safe shut-down state then necessarily the other two have caused a time-out in a previous communication phase.*

```
assert{activeB + activeC == 0}
```

---

[1]We have omitted all the atomic directives and other strictly implementation details.

[2]An assertion in PROMELA is a statement including a boolean expression, which is evaluated each time the statement is executed. If the expression evaluates to false a violation of the correctness requirement is reported.

The previous assertion has been placed after the SHUTDOWN entry label. The verification runs have been performed using the compiler options of SPIN: COLLAPSE (CO) to compress the state vector and MA to obtain a minimal automaton encoding. In Table 1 we report on the results of the verifications.

Table 1. Verification results on the TMR model.

property	state vector	depth	result
TMR1	192	5266	success
TMR2	192	5266	success
TMR3	196	45273	fail
TMR4	188	297515	success
TMR5	188	6808	success

4.2 Discussion

We briefly discuss the result about the property TMR3. In analyzing the counter example we noticed that the Byzantine module C caused one of the loyal module to be disconnected by the exclusion logic. In fact module C, not participating in a communication with one module, makes that module believe that module C is not active. Successively in the distributed voting the loyal module is found in disagreement, and then disconnected by the exclusion logic. This is a typical disagreement situation due to Byzantine behaviors. Discussing with ASF, we realized that in the real system there were further control mechanism (e.g. Control Redundant Check on all the messages) that guarantee anyway the safety in similar situation at a detail level not possible in our model.

5 The TMR-PCU model

The TMR-PCU describes in detail the SN-PCU communication protocol, and the PCU behavior. Target of the protocol is the delivery of critical commands also in presence of faults in the communication media. A scheme of TMR-PCU architecture is reported in Figure 2. We want to stress: (1) the three identical *central modules*, called *module A, B* and *C*, implementing part of the SN; (2) the PCUs composed by n control units (in our study we considered $n=2$), each constituted by two computers, we call A and B; (3) the *interconnections* among the modules (three symmetric channels), the ones between the modules and the PCUs (two busses). With the TMR-PCU model we were interested to verify:

1. *liveness properties* of SN-PCU communication protocol in an error-free environment hypothesis. This protocol is implemented as a distributed algorithm designed to assure a cyclic use of the busses and a cyclic

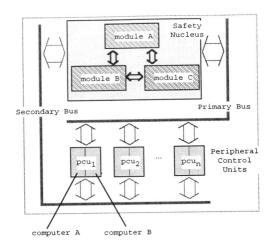

Figure 2. The TMR-PCU architecture

selection of two modules demanded to send the commands.

2. *safety properties* of SN-PCU communication protocol in case of some hardware faults. In particular we were interested in silent faults in the interconnection busses and in the computers A and B of a peripheral unit.

We now briefly describe the protocol run by a central module and the one run by a peripheral unit, giving the PROMELA code where significant.

5.1 A central module

Before communicating with the PCUs a module tries to infer information about the global state of the system. In particular, in a *synchronization* phase (the same of the TMR) a module tries to know the other modules activity state. This information is used in a distributed tournament procedure to decide which two modules have to be selected to send a message. In a *diagnostic* phase each module collects information about the global state of the PCU computers and of the busses. This information is used to decide which bus to use. Finally, in a *message elaboration* phase depending on the state of peripheral computers from a previous diagnostic, either the effective peripheral command, or a DIAGNOSTIC message is prepared.

5.2 A peripheral unit

In TMR-PCU the PCU model is realized in more detail. In the **decide the state** phase, a non-deterministic choice is made to decide on the functional state of the busses and of the computers A and B of the peripheral unit. In case of a state set to "fault" every communication resulted in a fault-silent behavior. Then each computer of each units waits for a message from one of the busses. Then it replies with an acknowledgment to all the modules. In the following we report a synthesis of the PROMELA code:

```
/* recvA1,recvB1: #messages via bus1 */
/* recvA2,recvB2: #messages via bus2 */
/* stateBUS1, stateBUS2: state of bus1, bus2 */
/* stateA, stateB: state of computer A,B */
/* loop */
do
::
/* decide the state */
    if
/* fault in the 1st computer */
    :: stateA = 0
/* 1st computer is ok */
    :: stateA = 1
/* fault in the 2nd computer */
    [... the same for stateB ... ]
/* fault in the 1st bus */
    :: stateBUS1 = 0
/* 1st bus is ok */
    :: stateBUS1 = 1
/* fault in the 2nd bus */
    [... the same for BUS2 ...]
/* no fault */
    :: else -> skip
    fi;
RECEIVING:skip;
    i = 0;
    /* Promela channels defined */
    /* A1, A2 : computer A-BUS1, A-BUS2 */
    /* B1, B2 : computer B-BUS1, B-BUS2 */
    do
/* computer A receives from bus1 */
    :: !DONE && A1in?[PCU1, senderA1, msg] ->
        A1in?PCU1, senderA1, msg;
        if
/* if it is a diagnostic message */
    ·   :: msg == DIAGNOSTIC -> skip;
/* if it is a command message */
        :: else -> msg[i] = msg; i++;
        fi;
/* acknowledgment to all the module */
        A1out!PCU1,A,(stateA && stateBUS1);
        A1out!PCU1,B,(stateA && stateBUS1);
        A1out!PCU1,C,(stateA && stateBUS1);
        recvA1++;
/* computer A receives from bus2 */
    [... the same using A2, stateBUS2,
            recvA2, senderA2 and stateA ..]
/* computer B receives from bus1 */
    [... the same using B1, stateBUS1,
            recvB1, senderB1 and stateB ..]
/* computer B receives from bus2 */
    [... the same using B1, stateBUS2,
            recvB2, senderB2 and stateB ..]
    :: DONE -> break;
    od;
RECEIVED: skip
/* endloop */
od;
```

5.3 Formal Verification on TMR-PCU

In this section we informally list some of the properties verified on the TMR-PCU model, and the most meaningful results.

(PCU1) *Correctness of the communication protocols, in absence of faults.*

We verified this properties checking for absence of deadlock. Here, with the term *correctness*, we mean correctness of the diagnostic test and of the tournament algorithm

run by a module. In this case we slightly modified the PROMELA code of the PCUs in such a way to force a peripheral unit to receive messages according to the right cyclic use of the busses. An incorrect use of it by one of the central module would have caused a deadlock.

The following properties have been verified in presence of faults.

(PCU2) *When two or more modules are active each peripheral unit eventually receives exactly two messages, in a single loop.*

(PCU2′) *In presence of Byzantine errors in one module, when two or more modules are active each peripheral unit eventually receives exactly two messages, in a single loop.*

(PCU3) *When two or more modules are active each peripheral unit eventually receives exactly two message via different busses, in a single loop.*

(PCU4) *When two or more modules are active each computer of every peripheral units receives exactly one message, in a single loop.*

All the previous properties have been formulated with different LTL formulas with the following common structure:

$$([]p) \rightarrow (([]<>q) \&\& [](q \rightarrow(<>r)))$$

where p, q and r are predicate on variables.

In the Table 2 we report some significant results.

Table 2. Verification results on the TMR-PCU model.

property	state vector	depth search	output
PCU1	352	44047	success
PCU2	284	25465	success
PCU2′	284	1295	fail
PCU3	284	25465	success
PCU4	284	405178	success

5.4 Discussion

We briefly discuss the result of property PCU2′. We wanted to prove safety properties of the tournament algorithm in the hypothetic situation of a persistent Byzantine module. We proved that a Byzantine behavior in the communication with the periphery phase, makes fail the tournament algorithm. Analyzing the counter-example, we noticed that three modules (and not two) send a message to the periphery. Indeed, in the real system the exclusion logic, which we have omitted in this model, should have been forced the system to a safe shutdown before entering in the communication with the periphery phase.Indeed this is what happens in reality, as proved by ASF on the real system. With this result we have underlined the critical role of safety logic: if it should fail in disconnecting a Byzantine module before it enters into the communication with the periphery phase the tournament algorithm might be wrongly executed.

6 Conclusions

The work described in this paper, related to a industrial project, consisted of the verification effort performed on a safety-critical system developed by ASF. During the formal verification we found some erroneous situations that underline potentially weaknesses in the system itself, successively corrected.

Although briefly described in this paper, many formalization problems has been faced during the modeling phase, primarily due to the lack of any concept of time in the PROMELA language, and secondly to an inappropriate (with respect to our needs) treatment of the termination of a processes in its run time support. This obliged us to follow modeling choices that have had a substantial impact in the formalization effort and, indirectly, in the state dimension of the model. To overcome this last problem we needed to design *ad hoc* abstraction strategies. All these formalization issues can be found in a companion paper [10].

7 Acknowledgment

This work was partly supported by the CNR/GMD co-operation project DECOR and by Progetto speciale CNR "Strumenti Automatici per la Verifica Formale nel Progetto di Sistemi Software ".

References

[1] A.Amendola, L. adn P.Marmo, and F.Poli. Experimental Evaluation of Computer-Based Railway Control Systems. In *Proc. of FTCS-27*, pages 380–384, 1997.

[2] A.Cimatti, F.Giuchiglia, G.Mongardi, D.Romano, F.Torielli, and P.Traverso. Model Checking Safety Critical Software with SPIN: an Application to a Railway Interlocking System. In *Proc. of 3rd SPIN*, 1997.

[3] A. Amendola. Dependability of Railway Control Systems. In *Proc. of FTCS-26 (Pannel)*, pages 150–155, 1996.

[4] C. Bernardeschi, A. Fantechi, S. Gnesi, S. Larosa, G. Mongardi, and D. Romano. A Formal Verification Environment for Railway Signaling System Design. *Formal Methods in System Design*, 2(12):139–161, 1998.

[5] W. Bevier and W. Young. Machine Checked Proofs of the Design and Implementation of a Fault-Tolerant Circuit. Technical Report NAS1-18878, NASA, 1990.

[6] A. Borälv. A Case Study: Formal Verification of a Computerized Railway Interlocking. *Formal Aspect of Computing*, 10(4):338–360, 1998.

[7] A. Cimatti, F. Giunchiglia, G. Mongardi, D. Romano, F. Torielli, and P. Traverso. Formal Verification of a Railway Interlocking System using Model Checking. *Formal Aspect of Computing*, 10(4):361–380, 1998.

[8] E. M. Clarke and E. A. Emerson. Design and Synthesis of Ssynchronization Skeletons using Branching Time Temporal Logic. In *Lecture Notes in Computer Science*, volume 131, pages 52–71. Springer-Verlag, 1981.

[9] E. M. Clarke, E. A. Emerson, and A. P. Sistla. Automatic Verification of Finite-State Concurrent Systems Using Temporal Logic Specification. *ACM Transaction on Programming Languages and Systems*, 8(2):244–263, 1986.

[10] S. Gnesi, D. Latella, G. Lenzini, C. Abbaneo, A. Amendola, and P. Marmo. A Formal Specification and Validation of a Critical System in Presence of Byzantine Errors. *Lecture Notes in Computer Science*, 1785:535–549, 2000. Proc. of TACAS 2000.

[11] J. F. Groote, S. F. M. van Vlijemn, and J. W. C. Koorn. The Safety Guaranteeing System at Station Hoorn-Kersenboogerd in Propositional Logic. In *Proc. of 10th Annual Conference on Computer Assurance (COMPASS'95)*, pages 57–68, 1995.

[12] G. J. Holzmann. *Design and Validation of Computer Protocols*. Prentise Hall, 1991.

[13] G. J. Holzmann. The Model Checker SPIN. *IEEE Transaction on Software Engineering*, 5(23):279–295, 1997.

[14] L. Lamport, R. Shostak, and M. Pease. The Byzantine Generals Problem. *ACM Transaction on Programming Languages and Systems*, 4(3):382–401, 1982.

[15] P. G. Larsen, J. Fitzgerald, and T. Brookers. Applying Formal Specification in Industry. *IEEE Software*, 13(7):48–56, 1996.

[16] M. J. Morely. Safety-Level Communication in Railway Interlockings. *Science of Communication*, 29:147–170, 1997.

[17] J. P. Queille and J. Sifakis. Specification and verification of concurrent systems in CESAR. *Lecture Notes in Computer Science*, 137:337–371, 1982. Proc. 5th International Symposium on Programming.

[18] N. Storey. *Safety Critical Computer Systems*. Addison-Wesley, 1996.

Sensitivity Analysis on Dependencies in Dynamic Availability Models for Large Systems

Meng-Lai Yin   *Craig L. Hyde*   *Rafael R. Arellano*

Fullerton, California, Raytheon[†]

Email: mlyin@west.raytheon.com

Abstract

Assumptions about independence are made when modeling the availability and reliability of large systems. The challenge, then, is to show that the loss of fidelity due to the independence assumptions is not significant. A sensitivity analysis that can cover all the situations for a dynamic system is the focus of this study. We attack this problem by conducting a series of sensitivity analyses on the dependencies identified in the system hierarchy. By showing the importance of the dependencies that have been modeled and the insignificance of the differences caused by the independence assumptions, the appropriateness of the modeling approach is demonstrated. This sensitivity analysis thus earns the analysts confidence in the model.

1. Introduction

The purpose of this study is to evaluate the independence assumptions made in modeling the availability of a dynamic large system, where computational efficiency is a main concern. Computational efficiency is mainly due to the largeness problem in the modeling field. Considerable research has been studied in dealing with this problem [3], such as recognizing the symmetries in the system [5] and the hierarchical decomposition method [4]. A technique that is commonly used when dealing with large system models is the statistical independence (s-independence) assumption. This assumption states that the status (for example, failed or operational) of a component is statistically independent with the status of other components. Furthermore, the operational requirements on one subsystem are assumed to be independent of the state of other subsystems.

By making this independence assumption, a large model can be reduced. Unfortunately, the fidelity of the model is also decreased. Sensitivity analyses are usually suggested to demonstrate the appropriateness of the independence assumptions made. However, for dynamic systems, a single sensitivity analysis that covers all the situations is impossible because of the inefficiency.

The motivation of this study is to efficiently show the propriety of a model, where independence assumptions have been made. Usually, a large system would contain several dependence situations. These dependencies can be classified into "critical" or "non-critical" in terms of the overall assessment. Due to the computational complexity, only the "critical" dependencies will be modeled, while independence assumptions are made to those "non-critical" dependencies. How to ensure the propriety of the classification is the topic discussed here.

2. Preliminary

2.1 A space-based augmentation system

The example system considered in this paper is a Spaces Based Augmentation System (SBAS) [2]. The basic idea of this system is to use the Global Positioning System (GPS) for navigation operations. Integrity, reliability, availability and accuracy are of significant concern for such a safety-critical system.

Conceptually, the system can be divided into two segments: the space segment and the ground segment. The space segment consists of GPS (Global Positioning System) satellites and GEO (Geostationary Earth Orbit) satellites. The ground segment develops the integrity and correction data to be broadcast (through GEO satellites) to the users. According to the functionality, 4 subsystems are identified in the ground segment: the reference subsystem, the central processing subsystem, the network subsystem, and the broadcasting subsystem. A 4-level system hierarchy is illustrated in Figure 1. The four levels are the system level, the segment level, the

---

[†] This paper is approved by the Raytheon Company's paper clearance process.

subsystem level and the component level. Dependencies are also shown in the figure by the solid and dashed rectangles across different modules in one level. The solid rectangles represent the critical dependencies that have been modeled, while the dashed rectangles represent the non-critical dependencies where the independence assumptions have been made.

2.2 Dependencies and the Modeling Approach

As shown in Figure 1, on the component level, the dependency among GPS, GEO and the reference stations are classified as critical. The dependency among the ground components are treated as non-critical. This relationship is propagated to the upper levels in the system hierarchy. When the segment level is encountered, the dependency between the space segment and the ground segment is partially critical, meaning that the dependency is not completely modeled. From this, we can see that the model is actually performed at the lower levels, i.e. the component and subsystem levels, as will be explained next.

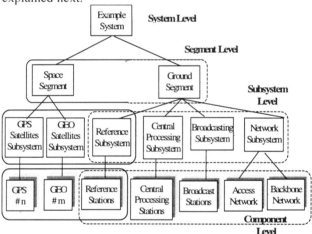

Figure 1. The System Hierarchy and the Dependencies

On the component level, all the GPS satellites are dependent because they share the same repair facilities; so are the GEO satellites. This dependency has been characterized in the model. Moreover, the dependency between the satellites and the reference stations exists due to the geometric relationship. In particular, the geometry of a satellite determines which reference stations can receive its signal. Note that this relationship is dynamic, because the satellites and the earth are moving over time. In other words, the models for different users at different locations are different. Therefore, the model is dynamic, i.e., time and location dependent. To capture the dynamic feature of the system, a tool was developed, which divides the continuous time into discrete time steps, and divides the continuous covered area into discrete grid points. At each time step and grid point, a model is constructed that addresses the situation for that particular time and location.

The above description highlights the complexity of this assessment process. Because of the largeness problem, methods that can reduce the computation time are needed. In particular, the hierarchical decomposition method and utilization of the symmetries that exist in the system are applied. The hierarchical decomposition method is applied, as shown in Figure 2. The system is decomposed into two parts: part 1 is with the satellites and the "critical" reference stations, part 2 includes the rest of the system. Note that only the reference stations that can see the in-view satellites are included in the model. Stations that are required to perform the navigation function are called the "critical" stations. The "non-critical" reference stations can also view the in-view satellites, but are used as backups.

A state diagram model is used to describe the situations of the in-view satellites and the critical reference stations (part 1). Because of the dynamic nature of the system, the state diagram model must be on the component level where individual satellites and reference stations can be identified. On the other hand, a block diagram model is applied to part 2, which includes the non-critical reference stations. The hierarchical decomposition method is again applied in the block diagram model. Each subsystem is decomposed into several components and the estimations on the component level are summarized in the sub-system level. Furthermore, symmetries are recognized in the block diagram model. In particular, if component failure behaviors are the same, symmetries are used to reduce the model. For example, the "n-1 of n working" combination is symmetric and only one computation is required. Note that if the symmetry were not used, n computations would be necessary. The symmetry is also applied when the dynamic feature of the network was modeled, as presented in [6].

From the above description, we can see that this modeling approach emphasizes the dependency between the satellites and the critical reference stations, while leave the dependency among the ground components not modeled. In other words, this modeling approach assumes that the satellites' and critical reference stations' dependence is more important than the dependence caused by the network. How to justify this modeling approach is the purpose of the sensitivity analysis.

3. The sensitivity analysis

3.1 The approach

A static model that captures the details of the dependencies among the ground components, especially the network dependencies, was developed. The high fidelity of this static model makes it a candidate for performing the sensitivity analysis. This model consists of both the space segment and the ground segment. However, unlike the dynamic model, time and location are determined when this model is constructed. In other words, the static model can only cover a specific area and time, while it is important to show the appropriateness of the model for the entire service volume.

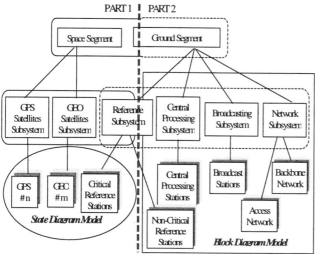

Figure 2. The Modeling Approach

The idea to handle this problem is to identify the situations where the independence assumption can have significant impacts, then apply the static model to the identified cases. The static model result is compared to that of the full dynamic model in order to see the effect of the independence assumption. This leads to a series of sensitivity analyses, as will be discussed in the next few sections. The method for conducting the series of analyses is from the highest possible level in the system hierarchy to the lowest one.

For example, on the segment level shown in Figure 2, the dependency is between the space segment and the ground segment. Although the dividing line is not an absolute between the two segments, in general, independence is assumed between the two segments at this level. Thus, the segment level sensitivity analysis will be conducted for the space/ground dependency. The knowledge gained from the segment-level sensitivity analysis will be used as the basis for the following sensitivity analyses. This will be described in Section 3.2.

The next sensitivity analysis is performed at the subsystem level. At this level, the dependency between the satellites and the ground subsystems will be analyzed first because it is considered the critical dependency and is assumed to be more important than the network dependency. This will be discussed in Section 3.3.

The subsystem-level space/ground dependency study identifies the situations where the network dependency can be important. The network dependency is than

examined for the identified situations at the subsystem level. Note that the static model is constructed at the component level, where the network dependency and other dependencies are detailed. This analysis will be presented in Section 3.4.

Thus, the approach is to narrow down the sensitivity analysis to the most critical areas. The results from each step can be used to justify the modeling approach and check the results from the dynamic model.

3.2 Segment-level analysis on the space/ground dependency

The space and the ground segments are dependent. For the particular operation mode considered here, the performance of the space segment determines the requirements applied to the ground segment. The performance of the space segment is degradable. As shown in Figure 3, when the geometry of all the available in-view satellites can provide full performance, there is no need for the ground segment to provide support. In other words, when the space segment itself can provide the required integrity, availability and accuracy, the ground segment is not required.

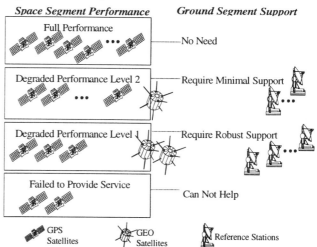

Figure 3. Dependency between the Space Segment and the Ground Segment

The performance of the space segment can be degraded due to geometry and/or satellite failures. When this happens, the space segment alone cannot provide the required robustness for navigation. Hence, the ground segment has to be used in conjunction with the satellites. Under this situation, the requirements on the ground segment depend on the status of the space segment. For the purpose of determining the ground segment requirements, two degraded levels are identified. Degraded level 2 has a better space segment performance than degraded level 1 has. Consequently, the ground segment is required to perform better during degraded level 1 than in degraded level 2. Note that the ground segment by itself cannot provide navigation service; it always has to utilize signals sent from the satellites. If there are insufficient space assets to even provide a position solution, then the ground segment cannot help.

Thus, the system is considered "available" when the following three situations exist:

(1) The space segment has full performance. In this case the ground segment is not required to contribute to the system availability.

(2) The space segment is in degraded level 2, and the ground segment provides the required minimal support.

(3) The space segment is in degraded level 1, and the ground segment provides the required robust support.

For a specific user, use $P(c,n,g)$ to denote the probability that g out of the n satellites in view, on a c satellites constellation, are working with a shared repair queue. The computation of this probability can be found in [1]. Then, the availability of the system under the operation mode for a specific user can be described by the following formula:

$$A(c,n,A_m,A_r) = \sum_{i=f}^{n} P(c,n,i) + (\sum_{j=r}^{f-1} P(c,n,j)) \bullet A_m + (\sum_{k=a}^{r-1} P(c,n,k)) \bullet A_r$$

(1)

where f is the number of satellites required to have full performance, r is the number of satellites required to be in degraded performance level 2, and a is the number of satellites required to be in degraded performance level 1. A_m is the probability that the ground segment can meet the minimal requirement and A_r is the probability that the ground segment can satisfy the robust requirement.

From the above formula, an upper-bound availability and a lower-bound availability for a specific user can be derived. For a given space segment situation and the user's location and time, the upper bound happens when the ground segment is perfect, meaning the availability from the ground segment is 1. In other words, the upper bound is

$$A_{upper} = \sum_{i=f}^{n} P(c,n,i) + \sum_{j=r}^{f-1} P(c,n,j) + \sum_{k=a}^{r-1} P(c,n,k) \cdot$$

This can be further reduced to

$$A_{upper} = \sum_{i=a}^{n} P(c,n,i) \cdot$$

Note that when the ground segment is perfect, the upper bound is not dependent on the number of satellites required to satisfy full performance and degraded performance level 2, i.e. f and r in the formula. As long as the number of satellites in view can provide a position solution, the system is available.

On the other hand, when the ground segment is totally failed, meaning the probability for both A_m and A_r are 0, the system availability for a particular user is

$$A_{lower} = \sum_{i=f}^{n} P(c,n,i) \cdot$$

Thus, the upper and lower bounds of the availability are determined by the space segment performance alone. Moreover, the lower bound availability is determined by the required number of satellites to have full performance (f). The upper bound availability is determined by the required number of satellites to provide performance for degraded level 2, i.e. a.

Theoretically, when there are 4 in-view satellites, a position solution can be obtained. Therefore, the value of a in this sensitivity analysis is chosen to be 4. When full performance is required, more stringent requirements on the space segment is applied. The requirement for f depends on the geometry of the satellites when the assessment is made. In this study, a range from 6 to 10 is used for the value of f. The upper bound availability (where the ground is perfect) and the lower bound availability (where the ground is totally failed) with different required numbers of satellites for full performance (different value of f are displayed in Figure 4.)

Sensitivity on Space/Ground Segment Dependency

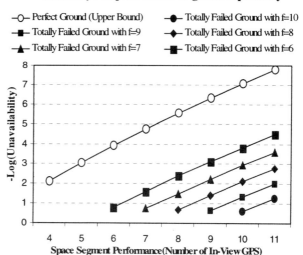

Figure 4. Segment-Level Sensitivity Analysis on the Space/Ground Dependency

This chart presents the effects of the dependency between the space segment and the ground segment. The upper bound and the lower bounds are shown. These curves address situations having different geometry where the number of satellites required to provide full performance varies from 6 to 10. In the next section, the subsystem-level sensitivity analysis that provides more details on the effects caused by imperfect ground segment is discussed.

3.3 Subsystem-level sensitivity analysis on the space/ground dependency

When the segment level analysis is discussed, the ground segment is either working perfectly (the upper bound) or failed completely (the lower bound). The ground segment is performance degradable, just like the space segment, and is characterized in formula (1) by the probability A_m and A_r. The effect of imperfect ground segment is pursued here. Note that the values of A_m and A_r are the modeling results based on the status of the subsystems in the ground segment. Moreover, the models are different when different times and locations are considered. Therefore, different sets of A_m and A_r are examined.

Figure 5 shows the effects of various ground conditions on the overall availability, where the number of satellites required for full performance is 10 based on the geometry. A series of sensitivity analyses have been conducted based on different A_m and A_r. A_m ranges from 0.99999 to 0.99, and A_r varies from 0.9999 to 0.9, assuming that A_m and A_r are having one order of magnitude difference. In Figure 6, the cases where 6 satellites are required to provide full performance according to the geometry are shown, with the same set of A_m and A_r.

Sensitivity Analyses on Ground Robustness

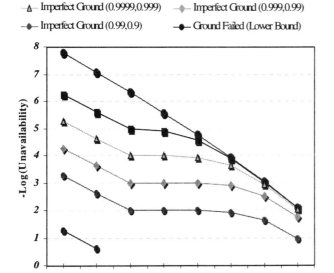

Figure 5. Subsystem-Level Space/Ground Dependency Sensitivity Analysis (10 GPS are Required to Provide Full Performance)

From this study, we learned that the sensitivity of the ground subsystem is related to the space segment performance. In other words, the effect of imperfect ground subsystems is more substantial when the space segment performance is more critical. For example, the space segment performance in Figure 5 is more critical than the situations in Figure 6, because higher number of satellites is required to have full performance. When comparing Figure 5 to Figure 6, the changes on the ground in Figure 5 have more significant effects on the overall availability than the effects in Figure 6, particularly with a large number of satellites in view.

3.4 Subsystem-level sensitivity analyses on the network dependency

The above analyses highlight the areas where the network dependency can be important. For example, consider the situations in Figure 6, where the number of satellites required for full performance is 6, and the requirement for the overall system availability is 0.999. The critical situations are identified using the following logic. When the number of in-view satellites is 7, the availability for the situation where A_m=0.99 and A_r=0.9 is higher than 0.999, as shown in the figure. However, the values of A_m and A_r are sensitive to the network dependency. In other words, when the ground model which assumes independence among the subsystems results in A_m=0.99 and A_r=0.9, the network dependency might have significant effects on the overall system availability which cause the requirement to not be met. The static model that can capture the details of the network dependency is then constructed addressing this particular situation.

The result from the static model was used as the baseline for this subsystem-level sensitivity analysis. Different sets of parameters for components MTBF (Mean Time Between Failures) and MDT (Mean Down Time) that are applied to the block diagram model were examined. These input parameters vary because of different philosophies in handling the ground subsystem's dependencies when block diagram model is applied. The purpose of this study is to select the most realistic input parameters for the block diagram model during dynamic assessment.

Figure 7 shows the availability results for many different sets of input parameters to model the dependencies of the ground segment in a simplified way. Each set matches a specifically colored bar in the graph. The first bar in each cluster represents the results of the detailed static model, which accounts for all the ground segment dependencies. As expected, the result shows that the impact of the network dependency is not as significant as that of the space/ground dependency.

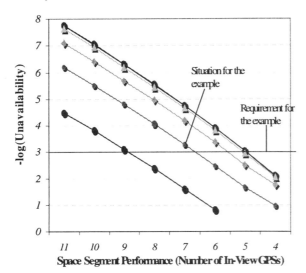

Sensitivity Analysis on Space/Ground Dependency

— ● — Perfect Ground(Upper Bound)   — ■ — Imperfect Ground (0.99999,0.9999)

···▲··· Imperfect Ground(0.9999,0.999)   ··· ◆ ··· Imperfect Ground (0.999,0.99)

— ◆ — Imperfect Ground(0.99,0.9)   — ● — Ground Failed (lower bound)

Figure 6. Subsystem-Level Space/Ground Dependency Sensitivity Analysis (6 GPS are Required to Provide Full Performance)

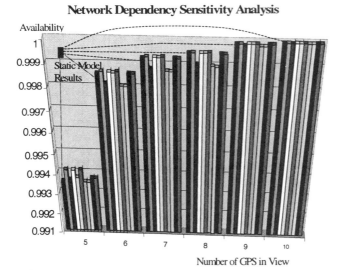

Network Dependency Sensitivity Analysis

Figure 7. The Impacts of Network Dependency

4. Conclusion and future research

In this paper, an approach to pursue a sensitivity study on the dependencies for a large system's dynamic availability estimation is discussed. A case study that applies this method to a space based augmentation system is presented. The sensitivity analysis justifies the propriety of the modeling approach used to mitigate the largeness problem.

There is always a tradeoff between the modeling fidelity and computational efficiency. Dependency is usually a focal point when an argument occurs between the two. Understanding each dependency situation should be the first step taken, not only when constructing the model, but also when conducting a sensitivity study. The modeling approach of how the dependencies were dealt with was explored. In this example, the space/ground dependency is considered more important than the network dependency. This sensitivity analysis shows the appropriateness of this modeling philosophy.

To justify the modeling approach and earn the confidence of the model is as important as constructing the model and obtaining results. Just like constructing and solving a large system's model, the sensitivity analysis faces the same challenge of the largeness problem. This paper presents a method to efficiently conduct the sensitivity analysis so that dynamic modeling results can be verified. This method can be used to identify which dependencies in a large system are critical so that a simplified model that focuses only on the critical dependencies can be constructed and validated.

In this example, the static model that handles the network dependency is still manageable. If the model to handle dependencies caused by all the independence assumptions involves a large number of components, the largeness problem would occur. How to deal with the integrated dependencies caused by several independence assumptions is a research area to be pursued.

5. References

[1] C. Shively, Closed Form Unavailability Approximations for GNSS Satellite Navigation and RAIM Functions," *Proceedings of the Institute of Navigation National Technical Meeting*, Jan 1993.

[2] *Global Positioning System: Theory and Applications,* edited by Bradford W. Parkinson and James J. Spilker Jr., American Institute of Aeronautics and Astronautics, Inc., 1996.

[3] J.F. Meyer, "Performability: a retrospective and some pointers to the future," Performace Evaluation 14(1992), pp. 139-156.

[4] R.A. Sahner and K.S. Trivedi, "A Hierarchical, Combinatorial-Markov Method of Solving Complex Reliability Models," *Proceedings of the 1986 Fall Joint Computer Conference, AFIPS*, pp. 817-825.

[5] W.H. Sanders, "Reduced Based Model Construction Methods for Stochastic Activity Networks," *IEEE journal on Selected Areas in Communications,* Vol.9, No.1, Jan. 1991, pp. 25-36.

[6] M.L. Yin, L.E. James, R.R. Arellano, R. Hettwer, "Real Time Estimation for Location-Dependent Reliability on a Dual-Backbone Network Subsystem," Proceeding of the FTCS, 1999, pp. 340-343.

Session 5C

Student Forum

Session 6A

Mobile Agents

Fault-Tolerant Execution of Mobile Agents

Luís Moura Silva   Victor Batista   João Gabriel Silva

Departamento Engenharia Informática
Universidade de Coimbra - POLO II
Vila Franca - 3030 Coimbra
PORTUGAL
Email: luis@dei.uc.pt

Abstract: In this paper, we will address the list of problems that have to be solved in mobile agent systems and we will present a set of fault-tolerance techniques that can increase the robustness of agent-based applications without introducing a high performance overhead. The framework includes a set of schemes for failure detection, checkpointing and restart, software rejuvenation, a resource-aware atomic migration protocol, a reconfigurable itinerary, a protocol that avoids agents to get caught in node failures and a simple scheme to deal with network partitions. At the end, we will present some performance results that show the effectiveness of these fault-tolerance techniques.

1.Introduction

Mobile agents are an emerging technology that is gaining momentum in the field of distributed computing. It has being exploited in several applications domains, like Electronic Commerce, Information Retrieval, Network Management and Telecommunications, Workflow Management and Internet Computing [1]. However, it is already understood that mobile agent technology will only be used in real applications if some important problems (like security and fault-tolerance) can be solved in an effective way.

Several commercial mobile agent implementations have already been presented in the market, including Aglets from IBM [2], Concordia from Mitsubishi [3], Odyssey from General Magic [4], Voyager from ObjectSpace [5], Jumping Beans from AdAstra [6] and Grasshopper from IKV [7]. Current mobile agent platforms still lack proper support for fault-tolerance mechanisms. Only a few systems provide some partial solutions to the problem.

Our main interest is to use the mobile agent technology in telecommunication systems and network management. In these field of applications the support for fault-tolerance is of paramount importance. Thereby, we realized there was a need to develop a general framework of fault-tolerance mechanisms for platforms of mobile agents, being able to provide a

high level of dependability at the lowest cost as possible. We have implemented a set of fault-tolerance mechanisms that improve the reliability of the middleware and the agent-based applications. Traditional techniques like failure detection, checkpointing, replication and software rejuvenation have been integrated in the middleware of the platform. Together with these mechanisms we have also implemented a set of schemes to provide fault-tolerant execution of mobile agents. These fault-tolerant mechanisms have been implemented in the JAMES platform [8], a Java-based mobile agent infrastructure that has been developed on behalf of a Eureka Project (Σ!1921). This project has three partners: University of Coimbra (Portugal), Siemens SA (Portugal) and Siemens AG (Germany). Although we have been using this paltform all the mechanisms that will be presented in this paper are general-purpose enough and can be ported to other existing agent platforms.

The rest of the paper is organized as follows: section 2 presents some related work that has been published in the literature. Section 3 presents and overview of the JAMES platform. Section 4 describes the protocols and mechanisms that we have implemented to improve the reliability of the platform and the mobile agents. Section 5 presents some performance results that were collected in a real implementation. Section 6 concludes the paper.

2. Related Work

The Concordia system includes a transactional queuing mechanism and a two-phase commit protocol to ensure the atomic migration of agents [9].

In [10] was presented a protocol that provides the *exactly-once* property in the migration of mobile agents. Every time an agent wants to migrate it is replicated to a set of nodes. In every group of replicas there is one worker node, which is responsible for the execution of the agent. The other replica nodes receive a copy of the agent and act as observers of the worker node. When the worker fails the observers will detect it and will elect a new worker by running an election protocol. The elected worker will try to provide the same service or, if not possible, will execute an exception handling mechanism.

In [11] was presented a variation of this protocol. The proposed scheme includes the distributed storage of recovery information and it used a three-phase commit protocol. However, the execution of a 3PC protocol is more expensive and introduces a higher latency.

In [12] is presented a theoretical algorithm to deal with malicious faulty processors that may corrupt the agent code and data. The algorithm makes use of replication and voting to mask the effects of malicious faulty processors. This approach can be too costly for some agent-based applications.

In [13] another fault-tolerance mechanism was presented. In this scheme, there is a checkpoint manager (CM) that monitors all the agents inside a cluster of machines. The CM, which is assumed to be very reliable, is responsible to keep track of the agents and to restart the agents when there is a node failure. The main problem is the fact that the CM is a single point of failure.

In [14] was presented a scheme to achieve *exactly-once* semantics by executing the migration of agents between hosts in a distributed transaction.

In the Tacoma system [15] there is also some support for reliability. The authors explain there is a notion of a rear guard agent associated to each agent. That rear guard is responsible for launching a new agent should a failure cause the agent to vanish.

All these papers present some partial contributions to the issue of fault-tolerance in mobile agent systems. However, in our opinion there are still some problems that need to be addressed and some of the fault-tolerance techniques have to be adapted to the characteristics of mobile agent systems.

In the JAMES project we have been working deeply in this issue of fault-tolerance and we have implemented a set of schemes to increase the reliability of agent-based applications. In the next section we will present a brief overview of the JAMES platform. The interested reader can get more details about the platform in another paper [8].

3. Overview of the JAMES Platform

In the JAMES project we have developed a Java-based infrastructure of mobile agents with enhanced support for network management. Our industrial partners (Siemens) are now developing two software products for telecommunications that use the platform. Both applications have requirements for high-dependability. These requirements have driven our efforts to develop a set of effective fault-tolerance mechanisms that can be used in practice without degrading too much the performance of the applications.

The JAMES platform provides the running environment for mobile agents. In every host of the

network there should be an agency of the JAMES platform. These agencies provide the necessary mechanisms for agent migration. There should be also one or more Agent Managers: these nodes are seen as the "entry" points of the system, allowing the launching of agent-based applications to the network and providing all the management and monitoring of the running agents. Figure 1 shows a global snapshot of the system, with two Agent Managers, four Agencies and two mobile agents. We can have more than one Agent Manager in order to enhance the availability of that part of the system.

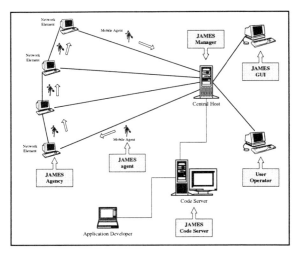

Figure 1: An Overview of the JAMES Platform.

The programmer writes the applications that are based on a set of mobile agents. These applications are written in Java and should use the JAMES API for the control of mobility. After writing an application the programmer should create a jar file that should be placed in the Code Server. The host machines that execute the JAMES manager provide a Graphical User Interface for the remote control and monitoring of agents, agencies and applications. With this interface, the user can manage all the Agents and Agencies in the system, being able to observe their execution status, to start up, shut down or to install new agents and Agencies.

The JAMES platform has been built from scratch with fault-tolerance and robustness in mind. The mechanisms will be explained in the next section.

4. Fault-Tolerance Mechanisms for Mobile Agent Systems

Mobile agents are inherently more robust than RPC systems, since they are not so dependent on the availability of the network and when the agent migrates to a server machine it is not affected by a temporary failure of the client or the network. However, the paradigm of mobile agents has some important differences that have a relevant impact in the way the fault-tolerance mechanisms should be designed. We have identified seven main differences that have some impact in the fault-tolerance mechanisms:

(i) **autonomy**: the execution of mobile agents requires some degree of autonomy. When the agent is sent to the network the end-user may have no control over its execution but expects the agent to safely finish within the temporal limits of the applications. The effective tracking of agents plays an important role in a mobile agent system.

(ii) **asynchronous interaction**: in RPC systems the client and the server are involved in a synchronous interaction and can easily detect the failures of each other. In a mobile agent system the detection of failures is much more complicated and requires some special support from the underlying platform.

(iii) **disconnected computing**: the mechanism of failure detection should also deal with the situation of disconnected computing and network partitioning.

(iv) **resource control**: when we send a particular piece of code to be executed in a remote server we have to take care to see if there are enough system resources to allow its execution. Thereby, the system should provide some support for resource control.

(v) **weak and strong migration**: for portability reasons most of the Java-based mobile agent platforms only provide a weak migration of the agents, i.e. they do not migrate the execution context of the agent. This issue may have some impact in the structure of the code and in the way some primitives like checkpoint and failure recovery can be used by the applications.

(vi) **transactional support**: when a mobile agent interacts with a remote server it may execute some operations that affect the state of the server and modify the state of the agent itself. In order to tolerate the occurrence of failures it is necessary to apply some transaction processing techniques to the server's resource manager that should taken into account the mobility of client object.

(vii) **adaptive computing**: this paradigm of mobile agents deals more easily with changes in the network environment than monolithic client/server solutions. Thereby, the fault-tolerance mechanisms play an important role in this issue since they should provide the necessary support for on-the-fly upgrading, failure reconfiguration and adaptive computing.

For all these reasons it is necessary to re-think some of the mechanisms of fault-tolerance that have been used in traditional solutions and to devise some new techniques to solve the particular problems of this paradigm. In the next sub-sections we will present some mechanisms that have been implemented in the

three main parts of a mobile agent system: Agent Manager, Platform Agencies and the Mobile Agents.

4.1 Fault-Tolerance for the Manager

The Agent Manager is the "entry point" of the applications and is responsible for the high-level management of the platform. In order to increase the reliability and the scalability of this part of the system there should be more than one Agent Manager in the network. When the system runs with a set of Managers it is necessary to include some fault-tolerance schemes for failure detection, data persistency, failure recovery and reconfiguration.

4.1.1 Persistency of the Manager Data

Every Agent Manager maintains in stable storage the critical information about the running applications, including the identification of the mobile agents, their jar files and their itinerary.

4.1.2 Failure Detection

Failure detection is achieved by a simple diagnosis protocol: the Agent Managers act as observers of all the others and they exchange *alive* messages between them. If there is a failure in one Manager it should be detected by the majority of the others.

4.1.3 Failure Recovery and Reconfiguration

Within a specific, but customizable, amount of time the system should try to restart the failed Manager. During this time the other Managers do not execute any recovery action. If the failed Manager is able to recover it will resume its execution by reading the log from stable storage. It will get the necessary information about the applications it is responsible for and will inform the other Managers and the Agencies in the network that it is alive. Next, it will get the current status of the mobile agents of those particular applications.

If the failed machine is not able to recover then the user should select a new one, or alternatively, the system should execute an election protocol to select one of them. The election protocol is quite simple since we associate a different sequence number to every Agent Manager. The elected Manager should take the role of the failed one and will be responsible for the management of its applications and mobile agents. It will inform all the Agencies of the network about this change. The Agencies should then reconfigure their internal tables and their communication channels towards this new Manager.

4.2 Fault-Tolerance for the Agencies

While in the case of the Agent Manager we have used a passive replication scheme in the Agencies of the network we decided to use a simple failure detection and recovery. This approach introduces a much lower overhead than replication but still achieves a high-level of dependability.

4.2.1 Failure Detection

Failure detection is the first step of fault-tolerance. We assume the occurrence of fail-stop and omission failures. Byzantine and malicious failures are out-of-scope of our mechanisms[1]. In our model, failed nodes can recover or not and the system can be affected by network partitioning. The protocols should deal with these situations.

In our protocol every Agency maintains a Network Status Table with the updated status of every node in the system and a watchdog process. Failure detection is achieved by *alive* messages. Every *alive* message piggybacks some information about the mobile agents that are currently executing in every Agency of the network. Each node can be in four different status: running, unknown, short-term failed and long-term failed. When the node responds properly to the diagnosis protocol it is in the running status. When a node cannot be contacted its status is changed to unknown. In this case, the diagnosis algorithm will execute a consensus protocol to determine if the Agency is really unavailable or not. If the node is determined to be unavailable it is set to short-term failed. If after some amount of time the node does not recover it is considered long-term failed. This distinction between short and long term failures is useful for the recovery algorithm. The algorithm is robust against out-of-order messages, duplicates and false alarms.

4.2.2 Checkpointing

Periodically, every Agency of the system takes an internal checkpoint of its internal state to its local stable storage. This operation involves some thread synchronization and makes use of Java object serialization to save the critical data of the Agency.

4.2.3 Failure Recovery

It is necessary to distinguish between two failure scenarios: the Agency is unavailable because the underlying machine just crashed or the Agency crashed but the node is up and running. In the first case the Agency will have to wait for the node to recover. In the second case, the node will try to restart the Agency automatically.

When the Agency recovers from a crash it will inspect its local stable storage and will reconstruct its internal state from the previous checkpoint. Communication channels to the other Agencies and the Agent Managers are also established and the Manager will be contacted to get the current status of the executing mobile agents. This Agency may have some Agents in stable storage that should be recovered locally if they are still to be restarted. However, if these agents have been already recovered in some other node, they will be simply discarded from stable storage.

4.2.4 Resource Control

Together with fault-tolerance another important feature in a platform of mobile agents is a good set of mechanisms for resource control. In our platform we have included some schemes to control the use of some important resources of the underlying operating system, namely: the use of threads, sockets, memory, disk space and CPU load. These mechanisms have been glued with the atomic migration protocol (presented in section 4.3.2) to prevent the crash of Agencies when they receive an incoming agents that require more system resources than those that are available.

4.2.5 System Monitoring

The information from the resource control module is merged with the diagnosis protocol and is provided to the end-user of the application. The most relevant information is presented in the Graphical User Interface. This way the system manager may have some feedback from the network environment and will be able to take some preventive actions in the Agencies of the platform.

4.2.6 On-the-Fly Upgrading

Our platform provides a flexible mechanism for the remote upgrading of mobile agents as well as Agencies. The JAMES Agency is divided in two modules: a small jrexec daemon and the Agency itself. The jrexec daemon is a static piece of software that is proprietary to the platform: once installed it does not need to be constantly upgraded. It implements an instance of the *Class Loader* and receives some network commands regarding the installation of the JAMES Agency. The jrexec daemon will be instantiated every time the machine is booted. The daemon can receive a jar file containing a JAMES Agency and it will perform its local installation. Through this daemon the Agency can be upgraded on-the-fly without killing the other applications that are executing in the platform.

4.2.7 Software Rejuvenation

When the Agent Manager or the user-operator realizes that a particular Agency is running low with system resources (memory, sockets or threads) then there is a possibility to refresh the state of that Agency. This technique is called software rejuvenation [16] and has been proved to be a very effective technique to prevent the occurrence of failures. The Agent Manager can send some remote commands to the jrexec daemon to refresh the local memory by calling the local Java garbage collector; to kill or to reboot the local Agency; or to install a new version of the Agency.

4.3 Fault-Tolerance for the Agents

Providing fault-tolerance for the mobile agents is a quite demanding task since they are moving entities in a network environment. We have implemented a set of

---

[1] The interested reader can see [12] for a mechanism that tolerates byzantine failures.

techniques, including agent failure detection, an atomic migration protocol, a reconfigurable itinerary, a recovery protocol, a scheme to avoid the blocking of agents in failed Agencies, a mechanism to deal with network partitions and the integration of mobile agents with a transactional service. These techniques are described in the next sub-sections.

4.3.1 Failure Detection

The detection of failures is provided by the underlying platform. The diagnosis protocol referred in section 4.2.1 is responsible for the detection of failures at the middleware level. The *alive* messages that are exchanged by the Agencies also carry some information about the agents that are running on the local nodes. In the system there is a set of surveillance nodes[2] that maintain an Agent Lookup Directory with the current status of the running agents. This directory is used for agent tracking purposes but is also useful to determine the agents that have been caught in a node failure or a network partition. If an Agency is not able to contact any surveillance node then it keeps all the status information in a local cache that can be flushed to stable storage. Later on, when the Agency reconnects to the network it will send its local information to the surveillance node.

Every entry in the agent status directory is composed by the following tuple:

```
<agent_id; status; failure_counter; migration_counter;
current_node; previous node; probable_next_node>
```

The Lookup Directory is maintained in stable storage and is replicated by the surveillance nodes to increase its availability. The agent_id is established by the underlying platform when the agent is created and is guaranteed to be a unique value. The agent can have five different status: executing, finished, failed, restarting and sleeping. This last case represents the case when an agent is stored in persistent storage waiting for some trigger to start its execution. The other three cases are self-explanatory. The two next counters of the tuple (failure_counter, migration_counter) are incremented every time the agent fails and migrates to a different node, respectively. The three last counters are mainly used for agent tracking but also to determine the agents that have been caught in a node failure.

Basically, an agent can fail in four different scenarios:

(i)   it may fail when it is migrating between nodes. This solution is presented in section 4.3.2;

(ii)   it may fail when the local Agency crashes. The solution is described in section 4.3.6;

(iii)   the agent can be caught in a network partition. In this case the agent is allowed to continue with its execution and there will be a separate

mechanism to cope with agent duplication due to network partitioning. The solution to this problem is also explained in section 4.3.6;

(iv)   it may hang-up in a running Agency due to a software bug. This case is usually hard to determine. The Agency will try to monitor the execution of the agent and if it detects any anomaly it will try to restart the failed agent. However, in some cases it is not possible to distinguish an agent that has hang-up or is taking too long to execute. For this reason we have introduced the notion of max-time-to-execute (mtte). In every Agency the mtte can have a different value. We understand that specifying a mtte is not an easy task for any application programmer but it is the only practical way to detect agent hang-ups. When a particular agent exceeds this limit of time it is killed and will execute some recovery code that should be provided by the application programmer.

4.3.2 Atomic Migration Protocol

The protocol to migrate the agents between Agencies has been made atomic to failures, that is, it assures that a mobile agent is completely migrated to a remote server, or not at all. If there is a failure during the process of migration the agent will not be lost and will be restarted in the previous server. The atomic property is achieved through a two-phase commit protocol that has been enhanced with support for resource-awareness.

The protocol makes use of log files that are maintained in stable storage. If there is a failure during the agent transfer, the log files will be used to determine where the agent should be restarted. The sender Agency starts the transaction by saving in stable storage the serialized state of the mobile agent. Every migration has a transaction_id that is associated with each event that is logged in stable storage. Before sending the agent to the other Agency it firstly send a message ("*Can I Send the Agent?*") that carries the size of the agent and some related information. The receiver Agency makes use of the resource control module to determine if it is feasible or not to execute the agent. The remote Agency can reply with three possible responses: *Yes, Wait* or *No*. In the first case it is clear that there are enough resources to execute the agent. In the second case it means the Agency is overloaded at the moment and the sender Agency should wait some time to retry the migration of the agent. The third case represents a case where the remote Agency refuses the incoming agent, mainly for security reasons.

When the remote Agency receives the agent it is saved in the stable storage. Then it sends an acknowledge message to the sender Agency. This machine logs this information but the transaction is not yet committed. The remote Agency will try to execute the agent. If it succeeds it sends a commit message to the sender Agency. This machine logs this information in its log and the transaction is completed. The state of the agent is not discarded from stable storage since it can be

---

[2] In the current version, the surveillance nodes correspond to the Agent Managers.

useful for a future recovery operation. It will be only deleted when the agent has finished its global execution and the platform executes a distributed garbage collection algorithm. If there was any problem to start the agent in the remote server the transaction is aborted and the agent should be restarted at the sender Agency. The same happens if the remote Agency crashes and is not able to send the `abort` message. The failure is detected by the diagnosis protocol and the agent is also restarted from the sender Agency.

This atomic migration protocol departs from previous work [9-10] since it is resource-aware. The transaction is only committed if there are enough resources at the remote Agency and if it was able to start the agent without crashing or running out-of-memory. This scheme has proved to be very effective when we were doing stress testing of the platform. Some results of these tests have been presented in [17]. We have executed some applications with thousands of agents and the platform did never crash. We conducted the same tests in other existing platforms and they ran out of system resources.

The support for resource control is a very important issue if we want to use mobile agents in production codes.

4.3.3 Explicit Checkpointing
In some applications it is possible that a mobile agent takes a long time to execute in some Agency. If there is a failure an important amount of computation can be lost. To avoid restarting the agent from scratch in that Agency it could be important to save its internal state periodically in stable storage, in the form of a checkpoint. The platform offers two methods to save and retrieve the state of the agent, namely: `checkpoint()` and `restart()`. The use of these routines is from the responsibility of programmer. Since we only provide weak migration the `checkpoint()` primitive has to be used with some care. This primitive should only be called in the places of the code where the agent can be restarted without loading the execution context and the stack of the threads. With these two primitives a failed agent can restart its execution from its last checkpoint, instead of its initial state when it arrived to the Agency.

4.3.4 Reconfigurable Itinerary
In order to adapt the execution of a migratory agent to the occurrence of failures it is necessary to provide a reconfigurable itinerary. When there is a failure in the next Agency of the itinerary the agent receives a specific exception. The application programmer should provide an exception handler where she specifies the action that should be taken. Basically, there is a list of five alternatives:
(i) The programmer can add dynamically a new node to the itinerary
(ii) The agent just dies and notifies the monitoring system;

(iii)　The agent can jump to the next available Agency in the itinerary;
(iv) The agent can go back to the Agent Manager;
(v) Or finally, the agent just waits until the destination Agency is up and running.

When the programmer chooses the last option, where the agent keeps polling the next Agency, it is also necessary to specify the maximum time the agent should wait for the restart of the next Agency. When that waiting time expires the agent is sent back home. If the programmer does not specify any exception handler the system takes this last option by default. The creation of dynamic itineraries is also allowed even without the occurrence of failures, since the agent is allowed to create its own itinerary besides from reacting to failures in the network.

4.3.5 Disconnected Computing
When there is a failure or a disconnect operation of some Agency in the network the platform provides a shield to the other Agencies and to the executing agents. All the exceptions generated by the communication sub-system are masked and properly handled by the platform. By using the features of the reconfigurable itinerary and a set of persistent output queues the system is able to cope with situations of disconnected computing. When the Agency is connected again the communication channels will be re-established, the protocols will be resumed and all the partial results and agents that were kept in the output queues will be sent to and from the Agency.

4.3.6 Failure Recovery
Failure recovery should be applied in two main cases: when the agent is migrating and when it is executing code in some Agency.
A- Failure Recovery in the Migration Protocol
If the agent fails in the migration process it will be restarted in the sender Agency after inspecting the logs associated with the atomic migration protocol. If the failed Agency is able to recover the migration is retried once more. But, if the Agency does not recover the agent may have to run some recovery code or may have to reconfigure its itinerary, as explained in section 4.3.4.

B- Failure Recovery for an Executing Agent
If the agent fails but the Agency is not affected by this failure, the agent will be locally restarted from the previous checkpoint that is available in stable storage. If the agent fails due to a failure in the Agency two things may happen:
(1) if the Agency recovers the failed agent is restarted (at least) from the initial checkpoint that was saved when the agent arrived to that Agency.
(2) if the Agency is not able to recover the agent will be caught by this failure and it could be potentially lost if the Agency never recovers. It is then necessary to execute another recovery protocol that is explained next. This protocol

avoids the blocking of agents and is able to cope with network partitions.

Recovering Agents that are caught in Agency Failures

This protocol relies on the information that is collected by the failure detection sub-system and is stored in the Agent Lookup Directory. This directory is maintained by every surveillance node in the network. One of these nodes is elected to run the recovery protocol for a particular failed agent or a set of failed agents. When an Agency fails the system will try to restart that server through the functionality provided by the remote `jrexec` daemon. If it recovers all the recovery code will be executed in that machine and all the failed agents will be restarted from stable storage. If the machine does not recover after a certain amount of tries it will be declared failed and another node of the network will have to restart the blocked agents of that Agency.

In this point, we depart from previous approaches that make use of Agency replication to avoid the blocking of failed agents [10]. Instead, we will make use of the checkpoint trail that was left in the stable storage of previous machines visited by the failed agent. As the reader may have noticed we do not discard the serialized state of the agents from stable storage when a migration is successfully committed since these checkpoints can be used to solve this recovery problem.

The agent is then restarted from a previous Agency and no additional overhead is imposed to the system. It is not guaranteed that the recovering Agency will be the previous one since it can also have failed. The surveillance node will execute an election protocol to determine which Agency has got the most up-to-date state of a failed agent. In practice, the Agency that responds with the higher `migration_counter` will be one selected to restart that failed agent. The restart procedure may involve the execution of some recovery code or may require some reconfiguration in the agent's itinerary.

This recovery procedure tolerates any number of failures with a minimum overhead: only the storage overhead to maintain the checkpoints in the local stable storage devices while the agent has not finished its execution. Moreover, this protocol was made robust against recovering Agencies and network partitions.

In the first case, suppose that a failed Agency recovers after some time and the surveillance node already elected another Agency where the failed agent has been restarted. The restarting Agency will inspect the Lookup Directory: if the agent status is set to `finished` and/or `restarting` and the `failure_counter` is higher than the local value then the agent is not restarted in that Agency. The

application will make use of the restarted agent. Otherwise, it will take the active role and avoid the agent restarting from a previous Agency.

Recovering Agents that are caught in Network Partitions

The protocol takes a different approach in the case of network partitions. If the unavailable Agency has not actually failed but is instead in a different network partition then the agent will try to continue with its normal execution. In this situation, the recovery protocol will elect another Agency to restart the agent and we can have duplicated agents in the network, although in different partitions. However, we have solved this situation in a very pragmatic way: in some cases, agents can execute in duplicate and the application at the Agent Manager will determine which result should be used.

In practice, we have to distinguish the recovery actions according to the semantics of the application. For the time being, we have adopted two relevant semantics for the execution of the agent itinerary: *best-effort* and *atomic*. In the first case, the agent will try to execute in the maximum number of nodes in the itinerary, while in the second case the agent has to execute a task in exactly all the nodes. The tasks that are executed by the agent are also classified in two possible semantics: *at-most-once* and *at-least-once*. These notions are inherited from the RPC systems. The applications should be classified according to these semantics.

When there is a network partition some of the nodes can be not available to the corresponding Agent Manager. To facilitate the explanation of the algorithm we will use the following notation:
- the original agent that is caught in a network partition is called Ag;
- the agent that is restarted by the recovery protocol in the other partition is called Ag';
- the mobile agent has a maximum time to perform the whole itinerary (mtwi);
- the agent maintains an history about the nodes that have been visited and the tasks that have been executed.

In the occurrence of a network partition the recovery sub-system will start a new agent (Ag') in a previous Agency of the itinerary. This agent is a duplicated instance of agent Ag. The normal agent (Ag) will continue its normal execution by the available nodes of its partition or it will have to wait until the network is connected. The recovering agent (Ag') will check the semantics of the application: if the execution of the itinerary should be *atomic* the agent retries the migration to the nodes of the other partition. The operation is repeated during a particular amount of time; if unsuccessful the agent goes back to the Agent Manager. If the semantics is *best-effort* the agent reconfigures its itinerary and will try to execute in some other nodes of its partition.

If the task semantics is *at-most-once* we have to avoid the repeated execution of non-idempotent tasks. For this purpose, the agent will inspect in every Agency if the other instance of agent has already executed there. If not, it will execute its local tasks and will leave a flag indicating it has visited that node. If the flag is already active the agent will not execute its task on that node and it will have two alternatives: go back to the Manager if the itinerary should be executed in an *atomic* way, or instead, go to the next available node if the semantics is *best-effort*.

If the user has specified a finite value for mtwi, then the application may wait during that amount of time for the arrival of both agents (Ag and Ag') and any other instance that may have resulted from any other failure. If both agents arrive at the final destination this means the network partition has been merged within that time interval. The application will inspect the results of the duplicated agents and use the semantics of the application. If the semantics associated with the itinerary is *best-effort* the application will use the results from the agent that has visited more nodes. If the semantics is *atomic* the application will use the results of an agent that has executed all the tasks in all the nodes of the itinerary; otherwise, all the partial results will be discarded to ensure the "all-or-nothing" property. In this later case, the application may retry that network operation by launching a new instance of the agent, with a different identifier.

If the mtwi value has not been specified the Manager will work with the first arriving result (either from Ag or Ag'). If the agent should have executed in all the nodes of the itinerary and this was not done the Manager will discard the results of that agent (most probably Ag'). In any case the status of that agent will be set to finished. If a duplicated agent arrives after the agent status is set to finished it will be simply discarded.

This algorithm follows a pragmatic approach to deal with network partitions. We are now integrating the algorithm with a garbage collection protocol for discarding duplicated agents and we are also working on the support for distributed transactions.

5. Performance Results

In this section we present some performance results that measure the overhead introduced by the fault-tolerance techniques in the execution of a simple application in a closed network of machines. The JAMES platform supports two different kinds of agents: the simple agent and the FT-Agent. This latter one uses the support for fault-tolerance. We have measured the execution time of both classes of agents in the same application to evaluate the overhead

introduced by the FT-Agent. However, we have also done a partial implementation of another fault-tolerance protocol presented in [10]. That scheme relies in the replicated execution of mobile agents to avoid the blocking of agents in the case of failure.

All the measurements were taken in a cluster of Pentium II 300MHz PCs running Windows NT4.0. The machines were connected through a dedicated 10Mbit/sec switched Ethernet. The JAMES platform was running under the JDK1.2 Virtual Machine. There was one machine running the JAMES Manager and five running JAMES Agencies. All the results were repeated at least four times and the standard deviation was below 5% the average values. In our tests we have changed the size of the agent to better understand its impact in the performance degradation caused by the fault-tolerance protocols. In the first set of experiments, we used a very simple mobile agent that had to visit all the Agencies of that cluster and collect some data about the memory usage of each Agency. This agent has really a small computation to do in every machine of the system. The tests were made using the simple agent, the FT-Agent and Rothermel's protocol (RP) that is based on agent replication. The number of additional replicas was changed between 1 and 4. It is worth to note that in Rothermel's protocol to tolerate two failures it is necessary to have a minimum of five agent replicas. The execution times of the six different versions are presented in Figure 2.

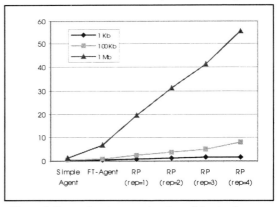

Figure 2: Comparing the execution time of the simple agent, the FT-Agent and the Replication of agents.

When the agent size is small (~1kb) the FT-Agent introduces a performance overhead of about 20% when compared in the execution time of the simple agent, without fault-tolerance. With the same agent the RP protocol with 2 additional replicas (rep=2) introduced a performance overhead of 300%. With four additional replicas (rep=4) the overhead was around 576%. These two versions of that RP protocol are able to tolerate one and two replica failures, respectively, while our FT-Agent is able to cope with any number of failures with a much lower cost. When we increase the size of the agent up to 1Mbytes we increase obviously the performance overhead. In this case, the simple agent took 1.4 seconds, the FT-Agent took 6.6 seconds, while the agent that used the RP protocol (rep=4) took 55 seconds to execute. This difference in the execution time clearly shows the benefits of using a failure-recovery scheme instead of a replication protocol.

This simple application is in the fact the worst scenario for performance of the fault-tolerance schemes since the mobile agent performs a very small amount of computation. In the second set of experiments we have introduced a working time of 1 second in every task of the agent itinerary. In Figure 3 we present the performance overhead of the two fault-tolerance schemes against the execution of the normal agent.

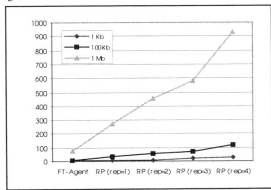

Figure 3: Performance overhead of the fault-tolerance schemes (working time = 1sec).

Our fault-tolerance scheme (FT-Agent) presents a performance overhead of 1%, 6.41% and 74.72% when we changed the size of the agent between 1Kb, 100Kb and 1Mb. For the same sizes the overhead of the RP protocol with four replicas was 27.2%, 119.5% and 926.9%. The difference is significant. Some more results have been collected but the conclusions are basically the same.

6. Conclusions
The Mobile Agents paradigm offers a new possibility for the development of applications in distributed systems. However, this technology can only be effectively deployed in real applications if the agent middleware provides a systematic support for fault-tolerance.

This paper presents a framework of fault-tolerant mechanisms that increase the dependability of the mobile agent platforms and the applications. The proposed mechanisms have been implemented in a particular platform (JAMES) but are general purpose enough to be ported to other similar agent platforms. The main goal of our work was to achieve a high level of dependability with low-cost techniques. We presented some performance results that were taken in a real implementation. These results show that the proposed techniques are quite promising.

Acknowledgements
This work was partially supported by the Portuguese *Ministério da Ciência e Tecnologia*, the European Union through the R&D Unit 326/94 (CISUC) and the project JAMES (Eureka Σ!1921).

References
[1] V.Pham and A.Karmouch. "Mobile Software Agents: An Overview", IEEE Communications Magazine, 26:37, July 1998
[2] IBM Aglets , http://www.trl.ibm.co.jp/aglets/
[3] Concordia, http://www.meitca.com/HSL
[4] Odyssey, http://www.genmagic.com/agents/
[5] Voyager, http://www.objectspace.com/voyager/
[6] Jumping Beans, http://www.JumpingBeans.com
[7] Grasshopper Platform, http://www.ikv.de
[8] L.M.Silva, P. Simões, G.Soares, P. Martins, V. Batista, C. Renato, L. Almeida, N. Stohr. "JAMES: A Platform of Mobile Agents for the Management of Telecommunication Networks", Proc. of IATA '99, Stockholm, Sweden, August 1999, http://james.dei.uc.pt
[9] T. Walsh, N. Paciorek, D. Wong. "Security and Reliability in Concordia", 31st Annual Hawaii Int. Conference on System Sciences, HCISS31, January 1998
[10] K. Rothermel, M. Strasser. "A Fault-Tolerant Protocol for Providing the Exactly-Once Property of Mobile Agents", Proc. of the 17th IEEE Symposium on Reliable Distributed Systems, SRDS'98, 100:108, October 1998
[11] F.Assis Silva, R.Popescu-Zeletin. "An Approach for Providing Mobile Agent Fault-Tolerance", Proc. 2nd Int. Workshop on Mobile Agents, MA'98, Stuttgart, Germany, September 1998
[12] F. Schneider. "Towards Fault-Tolerant and Secure Agentry", Proc. of the 11th Int. Workshop on Distributed Algorithms, 1997.
[13] M. Dalmeijer, E. Rietjens, D. Hammer, A. Aerts, M. Schoede. "A Reliable Mobile Agents Architecture", Proceedings of ISORC98, 1998
[14] H. Vogler, T. Kunkelmann, M. Moschgath. "Distributed Transaction Processing as a Reliability Concept for Mobile Agents", Proc. 6th IEEE Workshop on Future Trends of Distributed Computing Systems, FTDCS'97, 1997
[15] D.Johansen, R.van Renesse, F.Schneider. "Operating System Support for Mobile Agents", Proc. 5th IEEE Workshop on Hot Topics in Operating Systems, IEEE, 1995
[16] Y.Huan, C.Kintala. "Software Implemented Fault-Tolerance: Technologies and Experience", Proc. 23rd Fault-Tolerant Computing Symposium, FTCS-23, pp. 2-9, 1993
[17] L.M.Silva, G.Soares, P.Martins, V.Batista, L.Santos. "The Performance of Mobile Agent Platforms", Proc. ASA/MA'99, Palm Springs California, October 1999

Exploiting non-determinism for reliability of mobile agent systems

Ajay Mohindra, Apratim Purakayastha
IBM Thomas J. Watson Research Center
P. O. Box 218
Yorktown Heights, NY 10598
{ajaym,apu}@us.ibm.com

Prasannaa Thati
Department of Computer Science
University of Illinois
Urbana, IL 61801
thati@cs.uiuc.edu

Abstract

An important technical hurdle blocking the adoption of mobile agent technology is the lack of reliability. Designing a reliable mobile agent system is especially challenging since a mobile agent is potentially affected by failure of any host that it visits, or failure of any communication link that it needs to traverse. Previous work in this domain has attempted techniques such as periodic checkpointing of mobile agent state and restarting upon machine or communication recovery. Such approaches render an agent unavailable until a machine or a communication link itself recovers. In this paper, we take an alternate approach based on the premise that a mobile agent can often complete its task in more than one way. We capture such redundancy in non-deterministic constructs in the agent language and maintain state about an agent's actual computational path in its possible computational tree. We design and implement a distributed recovery scheme that detects a failure, rolls back an agent's computation, and restarts the agent from a previous point in its computational tree down a different but equivalent computational path without waiting for the actual failure itself to be repaired.

1 Introduction

Mobile agents are useful for certain tasks such as searching and filtering information, and monitoring remote events. They are also appropriate for networks with low bandwidth, high latency, and intermittent connectivity. Although numerous mobile agent systems have been proposed [2, 4, 7, 12, 14, 15], they have not been widely used in practice. One significant technical concern regarding mobile agent systems is their lack of reliability. In this paper, we focus on the reliability aspects of mobile agent systems. We formulate, design, and implement a mobile agent system that exploits non-determinism in the agent code to achieve greater reliability.

A mobile agent potentially executes on a number of different hosts migrating from one to the other. Building a reliable mobile agent system is especially difficult since failure of any one of the hosts or failure of communication between any two hosts may adversely affect the mobile agent. A few systems (see Section 2), have proposed periodic checkpointing of mobile agent state and restoration of the agent upon recovery of the failed host. In such systems, the mobile agent cannot proceed until the failed host has recovered. Other systems have proposed using message queuing for reliable agent migration. In such systems, the agent cannot proceed if the queue manager fails or loses communication.

Our approach is based on the assertion that a mobile agent can often perform its task in more than one way. For example, a search agent can retrieve pertinent information by using one information source or another. In this model, a mobile agent makes *choices* as it proceeds with its computation. If a failure occurs after making a certain choice, our system detects the failure and restarts the mobile agent with a different choice. This approach allows the mobile agent to proceed with its computation by routing the agent around failures in contrast with previous approaches where the mobile agent has to wait for the failures themselves to be repaired. We design and implement the reliability mechanisms in the context of *NetPebbles* [9], a mobile agent system that allows scripting with network components. The agent language in NetPebbles has non-deterministic constructs which we exploit for the purposes of reliability.

The rest of the paper is organized as follows. Section 2 discusses related work and identifies the key differences in our approach from other approaches. Section 3 outlines the NetPebbles programming model, introduces its non-deterministic constructs, and illustrates how such non-determinism can be exploited for greater reliability. Section 4 describes our distributed recovery scheme consisting of failure detection, rollback, and garbage collection mechanisms. Section 5 presents implementation and a preliminary evaluation of our system. Finally, Section 6 concludes and outlines future work.

2 Related Work

A number of mobile agent systems have explored reliability issues. The Tacoma [12] and the Ara [11] systems counter processor failures by providing checkpointing primitives whereby an agent can save its state. The Voyager [4] and Concordia [15] systems also provide checkpointing facilities to deal with processor failures. In these systems, a mobile agent cannot proceed with its computation until the failed host recovers and restores the state of the mobile agent from persistent storage. Moreover, these systems also require frequent checkpointing at all hosts that the mobile agent visits. In Concordia, reliable agent migration is realized using a message queuing system for communication. If the queue manager fails or loses communication, the agent is delayed until the queue manager recovers. In contrast with the above, our system can recover and restart a mobile agent from a previous execution context, independent of the recovery of a failed host or a communication link. In the context of computer-aided manufacturing, Wolfson *et al* propose "intelligent routers" that are similar to mobile agents [17]. They use the ISIS [1] distributed programming environment for fault tolerance of intelligent routers in a local area network. In [5], Johansen *et. al* propose a detection and recovery protocol for implementing fault-tolerant itinerant computations. Mobile agent systems can be deployed on ISIS-like distributed programming environments, but it is not clear how such systems scale beyond local area networks.

Strasser *et al* [13, 14] discuss two approaches for improving reliability in agent systems. The first approach allows an agent to specify a flexible *itinerary* with the possibility to defer the visit to currently unavailable machines or to select alternate machines in case of machine failures. The second approach uses a fault-tolerant protocol to implement *exactly-once* execution property for agents using formation of explicit *stages* of computation and results in a constrained lock-step manner of execution. Such execution constraints, although useful for certain classes of applications, are not desirable in general. In [16], Wang *et al* describe a method of bypassing software faults by exploiting available non-determinism in message deliveries at runtime.

In contrast, our approach exploits component and task level redundancies to bypass faults.

Using non-determinism to improve reliability of mobile agents is certainly inspired by well-known fault tolerance techniques that use temporal redundancy of software modules [10]. The domain of mobile agents, however, introduces some unique challenges which must be addressed. First, the migratory nature of mobile agents makes it difficult to ascertain faults and initiate recovery. Second, the process of recovery not only includes starting the agent from a checkpoint at some previous host, but may also include garbage collecting the residual state of the mobile agent that persists at other hosts visited by the agent after the checkpoint operation.

```
dim fundYield[5]
fund = "GROWTH"
a = createComponent("IMutualFund","name = "+fund)
fundYield = a.getAvgAnnualReturn(fund, 5)
c = createComponent("IDisplay") at "mypc.com"
c.plot(fund, fundYield)
exit
```

Figure 1. An example script that locates a Mutual Fund data component to determine the average annual rate of return for the last five years for a specific fund. NetPebbles's constructs are shown in **boldface**.

3 NetPebbles Programming Model

The NetPebbles environment offers a component-based programming model. A NetPebbles programmer writes a script by first selecting required interfaces from a catalog and then invoking interface methods as if the components implementing the interfaces are local. An end user simply starts a script and thereafter the NetPebbles runtime dynamically determines the component sites and transparently moves the state of the script to the component sites as necessary. When the script execution completes, the script returns to the starting site with the results. For a comprehensive discussion of the NetPebbles programming model, please refer to [9].

3.1 An Example script

We illustrate the NetPebbles programming model using an example script. Figure 1 shows a script that determines the average annual return for a mutual fund for the last five years. At the time of writing the script, the programmer knows that the script needs to use two interfaces, namely, "IMutualFund", and "IDisplay". The "IMutualFund" interface implements a method that provides the average annual return for a mutual fund. Each component that implements this interface may only provide data for a selected set of funds. The "IDisplay" interface provides methods to plot the results. For brevity, we ignore error conditions in the script.

In the first `createComponent()` call, the runtime attempts to create a component that implements the "IMutualFund" interface and supports the specified fund. The runtime uses the component catalog to determine the location of the appropriate component and migrates the script to that location. The runtime at the new location instantiates the component and invokes the "getAvgAnnualReturn()" method on the component instance with the fund name and number of years as arguments. The results from the method invocation are stored in the array variable "fundYield". The script then uses the component catalog to determine the location of the component that implements the "IDisplay" interface. When a component is found, the runtime migrates the script to the location specified by the **at** construct ("mypc.com") and downloads the component to that location. The runtime at the new location creates an instance of the component and displays the results by invoking the "plot()" method. Finally, with the **exit** statement, the script completes execution, and the runtime initiates garbage collection of all component instances.

3.2 Non-determinism in NetPebbles

The NetPebbles programming model is based on the premise that there is more than one way to arrive at the correct result. To explore this premise, we added two programming constructs that exploit non-determinism. The two constructs are "`createComponent`" (as described in Section 3.1) and "`any`". We briefly describe each of these constructs below. The list is not exhaustive, and based on our experience with these two constructs, we plan to add more constructs, such as `asmanyas` and `atleast(N)`, in the future. Note that the focus of our work is *not* to explore novel language constructs but the underlying fault-tolerance mechanisms (see Section 4) to support such constructs.

createComponent construct: In NetPebbles, more than one component may be available that implements the same interface, i.e., provides semantically equivalent function. When the NetPebbles runtime, say at L_1, resolves an interface name from the com-

ponent catalog, the catalog may return more than one location where the desired component is available. The runtime makes a non-deterministic *choice*, selects one location, say L_2, from the list and tries to migrate the script to L_2. The runtime at L_1 may be unable to migrate the script due to the failure of host L_2 or failure of the communication link between L_1 and L_2. Even after successful migration to L_2, a failure may still occur during component instantiation or method execution. When such a failure is detected by L_1, the runtime makes another selection from the list of component locations and restarts the script. Figure 1 shows an example script that uses the `createComponent` construct.

Any construct: While the `createComponent` construct provides component-level redundancy in NetPebbles, the **any** construct provides task-level redundancy. The **any** construct is similar to the ALT construct in Occam [6]. It consists of a set of *tasks* enclosed by boolean *guards*. The **any** construct allows the script to proceed with the computation as soon as any one of the guards evaluates to "true". If more than one guard evaluate "true" then the runtime makes a non-deterministic *choice* and executes the statements contained in any one of the guard blocks. If during the execution of these statements, the script encounters a failure, the NetPebbles runtime rolls back the script and chooses another task whose guard evaluates to "true". If there is no such task, then the **any** construct fails. Figure 2 shows an example that uses the **any** construct. In the example, the script computes the average annual return for a mutual fund for last five years, and compares the result with the returns for the market, using either the Russell2000 index or the S&P500 index. In the example, both the guards evaluate to "true" and the runtime makes a *choice* between the two possibilities. After obtaining the returns for an index, the script displays the comparison at machine "mypc.com".

In this paper, we discuss the use of non-determinism in the context of NetPebbles. The non-deterministic constructs that we use, however, are generic in nature and can easily be applied to other mobile agent systems. The `createComponent` construct essentially enables an agent to choose a host among several hosts that offer the same function. In other systems such as Aglets [7] or Agent-Tcl [2], an explicit migration step such as a `dispatch` method or an `agent_jump` command is used to migrate an agent from one site to another. In these systems, it is straightforward to augment these instructions with a multiple destination site names such that the agent can choose to migrate to any of these sites to accomplish its goal. Our approach can then be applied by non-deterministically

```
dim fundYield[5]
fund = "GROWTH"
a = createComponent("IMutualFund","name="+fund)
fundYield = a.getAvgAnnualReturn(fund, 5)
dim  indexYield[5]
any
  case (true)
    index = "Russell2000"
    b = createComponent("IMarketIndex","name="+index)
    indexYield = b.getAvgAnnualReturn(index,5)
  endcase
  case (true)
    index = "S&P500"
    b = createComponent("IMarketIndex","name="+index)
    indexYield = b.getAvgAnnualReturn(index,5)
  endcase
endany
c = createComponent("IDisplay") at "mypc.com"
c.plot(fund, fundYield, index, indexYield)
exit
```

Figure 2. A script that uses the **any** construct to compare the average annual return of a mutual fund to that of Russell 2000 index or the S&P500 index. NetPebbles's constructs are shown in **boldface**.

choosing from the list of specified hosts, and recovering and retrying another host upon detecting a failure. The task level non-deterministic constructs which we explore are equally applicable to any other mobile agent system. For example, a group of Agent-Tcl commands can be placed under the **any** construct if such a construct were to be added to the Agent-Tcl vocabulary. Our system can then non-deterministically choose to evaluate any task block in the same manner as in NetPebbles.

4 The Distributed Recovery Scheme

In the NetPebbles system a script migrates from one machine to another during its execution. During its lifetime, a script can encounter a variety of failures such as node failures, communication-link failures, and component failures. The effect of any such failure is the same – the script cannot continue its execution. To handle failures, the NetPebbles runtime uses non-determinism to route around failures instead of waiting for failures themselves to heal.

While executing a non-deterministic construct in a script, the runtime makes a *random choice* from a set of viable alternatives. The choice can either be a component-level choice as made by the **createComponent** construct or a task-level choice as made by the **any** construct. We refer to the script state when a choice is made as a *choice point*, and the cur-rent host as the *choice host* for that choice point. Each possible choice at a choice point is assigned a unique identifier known as the *choice id*. The ordered collection of all past *choice points* in a script's lifetime is its *choice history*. A script's choice history is abstractly represented as a vector of choice ids that identify the choices the script has made so far. Similarly, a choice point is abstractly represented as a vector of choice ids that identify the choices until and including the one at the choice point. A script carries its choice history and the vector of corresponding choice hosts along with it.

The recovery strategy of NetPebbles is to find a fault-free path in a script's computation tree. Figure 3 illustrates this concept. Points marked by A, A', and A'' correspond to *choice points*, and each outgoing edge at these nodes represents a choice. When a failure, denoted by a cross (X in Figure 3a), is detected by the runtime, the script is rolled back to the most recent *choice point A'*, and an alternate choice is made (Figure 3b). If the new choice also leads to a failure, the current choice at A is declared faulty and the script is rolled back and restarted with a different choice at A (Figure 3c).

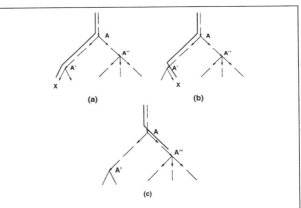

Figure 3. The figure illustrates the NetPebbles recovery scheme. The computation path of the script is marked by a solid black line. The choicepoints are marked by A, A' and A". Failures are indicated by a cross (X). When a failure is detected, the computation is rolled back and restarted from the most recent choice point with an available choice.

The distributed recovery scheme uses three underlying services at each node in the system: failure detection, rollback, and garbage collection. The failure detection service monitors scripts that have made a choice at the local node and detects failed choices. The rollback service saves a script's state at the local node before every choice made by the script, and when notified of a failed choice, it restores the appropriate state and restarts the script with a different choice. The garbage collection service actively tracks a migrating script and initiates garbage collection at all appropriate hosts when informed of a failed choice.

4.1 Failure Detection

In our failure detection scheme, a script is monitored at every choice point in its choice history by the corresponding choice hosts to detect any failed choices. A script's choice at a choice point is declared failed if all the choice points it leads to and the script have failed. A choice point fails if the corresponding choice host fails, or all choices at the choice point have failed. The script fails if its current host fails, or it is unable to migrate because of a network partition, or one of its components at the current host has failed.

Given the fact that exact failure detection in an asynchronous system with arbitrary host and communication failures is impossible [8], our aim is to approximate this scheme as accurately and efficiently as possible. In particular, our specific design goals are to recover from multiple faults and network partitions, minimize message complexity, minimize time to initiate recovery, and minimize false failure detection (declaring a fault when there is none).

There are several approaches for failure detection. In the simplest approach, every choice point (the corresponding choice host) and the script's current host send periodic heartbeats to all predecessor choice points in the script's choice history. A choice point declares its current choice as failed if it does not receive any heartbeat during a pre-configured time interval. This naive approach has a prohibitive $O(n^2)$ message complexity, where n is the number of choice points in a script's choice history.

Our current approach is a simple modification of the above scheme. A choice point and the script send regular heartbeats only to its immediately preceding choice point in the script's choice history. For choice points that are further up in the choice history, heartbeats are sent with decreasing probability. More precisely, assuming n choice points $CP_1, \cdots, CP_n$ in a script's choice history, CP_i sends periodic heartbeats to CP_j for $1 \le j < i$ with probability r^{i-j-1}, where $0 \le r \le 1$. The script sends heartbeats to each CP_i for $1 \le i \le n$ with probability r^{n-i}. As before, a choice host initiates recovery if and only if it does not receive any heartbeat in a pre-specified period. Figure 4 illustrates this scheme.

This probabilistic scheme has a tunable message

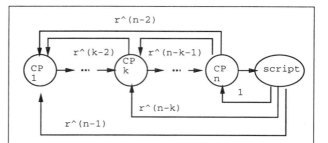

Figure 4. This figure illustrates the flow of heartbeats between a script and the choice points in the script's choice history. The script and its choice points send heartbeats to each previous choice point in the script's choice history with geometrically decreasing probability. Here r is the probability of sending a heartbeat and n is the number of choice points in a script's choice history.

complexity and accuracy. In fact, the naive approach is a special case of this scheme with $r = 1$. For false failure detection to occur, a choice point has to miss heartbeats from all the successor choice points and the script's current host. Therefore, the probability of such a false failure detection at CP_i is

$$\prod_{i<j\le n+1} [(1 - r^{(j-i-1)}) + pr^{(j-i-1)}]$$

assuming p is the probability of a message loss. Since $p \le 1$, smaller the r, higher the probability of false failure detection. For $r < 1$, the expected number of messages sent per period is $\sum_{i=1}^{n+1} \sum_{j=1}^{i-1} r^{i-j-1}$ which evaluates to

$$\frac{n + 1 - \sum_{i=1}^{n+1} r^{i-1}}{1 - r}$$

Thus message complexity varies from $O(n)$, when $r = 0$, to $O(n^2)$, when $r = 1$.

4.2 Checkpointing and Rollback

The rollback service at a node maintains in a table an association between the choice histories of the script that it has observed in the past and the script's local state. When notified of a script's failed choice, the rollback service uses the information to reset the script's local state to what it was just before the choice was made.

The table is initially empty and is modified on two occasions. First, when a local script executes a nondeterministic construct, a new choice id is generated for the new choice and is appended to the script's choice history. Information associating the new choice history and the execution state of the script and its local components is added to the table. Second, when a node receives a script with a previously unobserved choice history, the state of the script's local components is checkpointed. The state is then associated with the received choice history and this information is added to the table.

When notified of a failed choice, the rollback service searches the table for the choice history that has the failed choice point as a prefix and is minimal according to the prefix relation, and restores the state associated with the choice history. The rollback service also notifies the local components to undo any changes that need special handling. Further, if the failed choice was made locally then restoring the local state automatically resumes execution of the script from the nondeterministic statement that made the choice. The stored information about the failed choice is used to make a different choice.

The use of a rollback scheme for recovery has implications on the types of components that a script can use. The state of each component needs to be *rollbackable*, that is, either the component supports methods that are idempotent or the component supports additional methods that would allow the effects of non-idempotent methods to be undone. On surface, such requirements may seem to be too constraining for component developers, but in reality many components already exhibit such properties. For example in the system administration domain, components that read system state are idempotent in nature, and components that update system state also support actions that undo the changes. Examples of the latter include components that *install/un-install* software, *start/kill* daemons, and *enable/disable* file permissions.

4.3 Garbage Collection

When a script completes execution, it returns to its starting host. The garbage collection service at the starting host initiates a clean up of the script's distributed state by informing all the nodes visited by the script. A script carries along with it a list of nodes that it has visited. This list is updated as the script migrates in the network.

The garbage collection service also helps rollback the distributed state of a script when one of its choices fail. When notified of a failed choice by the local failure detection service, the garbage collection service notifies the rollback service at all the nodes that the script visited after the choice. This notification effectively

resets the script's state at all nodes to what it was before the choice. Identifying the nodes which need to be notified requires explicit tracking of the script. Note that when a choice fails, the script need not be present at the corresponding choice host. In order to track scripts, when a script migrates to a remote node, the local garbage collection service saves the script's choice history and remote node address in a persistent store.

Network partitions may delay garbage collection indefinitely. To alleviate this problem, the garbage collection service may use a policy of automatically garbage collecting the local script state after a certain period of inactivity.

4.4 False Failure Detection and Multiple Script Incarnations

The failure detection service may declare a choice to have failed even if it hasn't. Such false detections are possible because of arbitrary communication delays and loses. As a result, multiple incarnations of the same script may execute simultaneously in the system. Multiple incarnations may not always affect program correctness, although they waste system resources. A script whose execution has no side effects, the results returned by all but one of the incarnations can simply be ignored. A script that only performs idempotent operations over the network is an example of a script with no side effects. On the other hand, multiple incarnations of scripts that cause side effects can affect program correctness if they are not handled appropriately. A system administration script that modifies the machine state is an example of a script with side effects.

Multiple script incarnations are handled in the Net-Pebbles system as follows. Since the garbage collection service actively tracks a script, the cleanup messages sent by it after a false rollback eventually catch up with the obsolete incarnation. When a rollback service is informed of a failed choice of a script, and it finds a local incarnation of the script with the failed choice id in its choice history, the garbage collection service kills the obsolete incarnation.

The cleanup messages sent by the garbage collection service after a false rollback may take considerable time to catch up with obsolete incarnations. Meanwhile, obsolete incarnations should not interfere with the execution of the latest incarnation. The NetPebbles system ensures this non-interference as follows. All script related messages such as migration or garbage collection messages contain the script's choice history. When a node receives a message, it checks if the received choice history is obsolete by comparing the choice history with

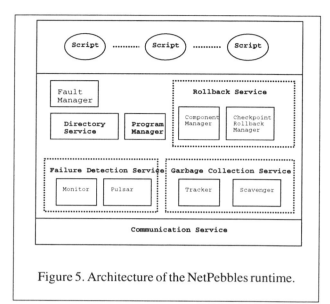

Figure 5. Architecture of the NetPebbles runtime.

the script's latest choice history known to the node. When a node receives a message with an obsolete choice history, it simply discards the message. In particular, when a node receives an obsolete incarnation (a migration message), it does not entertain the incarnation. This effectively kills the obsolete incarnation.

5 Implementation and Preliminary Evaluation

In this section, we first describe the implementation of NetPebbles, with emphasis on its distributed recovery scheme; we then present preliminary experimental results and discuss the performance and scalability of the implementation.

5.1 Implementation Overview

Figure 5 shows the architecture of the NetPebbles runtime. The NetPebbles runtime has been implemented in Java. It consists of a Program Manager, a Fault Manager, a Directory Service, a Rollback Service, a Failure Detection Service, a Garbage Collection Service, and a Communication Service.

When a NetPebbles runtime is first started, it initiates a scheduler that performs pre-emptive round-robin scheduling of all threads in the system. The scheduler is necessary to ensure fair thread scheduling in the heavily threaded NetPebbles runtime[1]. The system then starts the threads related to the program manager, failure detection, garbage collection and rollback

---

[1]Thread scheduling in some JVMs can be unfair and may cause starvation.

services. We now describe each of the components and the interactions between them.

Program Manager: This module includes an interpreter for executing scripts, and maintains the execution context of scripts that have visited the local node. It also generates globally unique identifiers for scripts launched at the local node. When a program manager receives a script, it modifies the script's list of visited nodes, associates an existing execution context with the script (if the script is revisiting the node) or creates a new one (for a new script), and inserts a program thread into the scheduler's queue. The program thread is an interpreter which repetitively extracts the next element from a script's statement stack and executes it. The statement stack essentially plays the role of program counter and is modified appropriately by the execution of the topmost statement. The interpreter informs the fault manager about executing a non-deterministic statement. The fault manager then extends the script's choice history and checkpoints the script along with the script's stack, data, and local components. Execution of a statement may also result in script migrations; for example, when a script uses a component located at a remote node, or when a `createComponent` call creates a component at a remote node. During migration, the script's stack and data is serialized along with other system level information such as the script's choice history and list of visited nodes, and sent to the intended host. When a script completes execution, it is sent back to its starting host. The program manager also informs the fault manager about arrivals and departures of all scripts.

Directory Service: This service provides an interface to a component catalog for resolving component creation requests from scripts. The component catalog has been implemented using the LDAP [3] distributed directory services.

Fault Manager: This module coordinates all fault-tolerance related activities. When a script arrives at a node, the fault manager checks to see if the script incarnation is obsolete (see Section 4.4). If the script incarnation is obsolete, the fault manager informs the program manager to discard the incarnation.

With the help of the rollback service, the fault manager maintains for each script, an association between the script's observed choice histories and the script's local state (see Section 4.2). When a script arrives at the local node, the fault manager informs the failure detection service to send heartbeats (see Section 4.1) to all choice points in the script's choice history. These heartbeats are cancelled when the script departs. Further, when a script executes a non-deterministic construct, the fault manager informs the failure detection service to monitor the new choice. When informed of a failed choice, the fault manager uses the garbage collection service to restore the script's distributed state to what it was just before the choice was made.

Failure Detection Service: This service consists of a pulsar thread and a monitor thread that continuously process requests in their respective queues. A request in the pulsar's queue specifies a heartbeat targeted at a particular choice point of a script. The request specifies the target, probability and scheduled time for a heartbeat. The target is a triplet of choice host address, script id, and choice point. A request in monitor's queue specifies the time by which the next heartbeat for a particular choice point is to be received. The monitor sleeps until it is interrupted by a broken deadline or the receipt of a heartbeat. If the monitor misses a heartbeat, it signals a failure to the fault manager. Since heartbeats are periodic, both the pulsar and monitor reschedule a request after sending or receiving a heartbeat.

Rollback Service: This service consists of a component instance manager, and a checkpoint and a rollback manager. The former maintains associations between scripts and components created by the scripts at the local host. It also generates global names that are used to refer to components uniformly across different nodes. The checkpoint and rollback manager is used by the fault manager to store and retrieve a script's local state (see Section 4.2).

Garbage Collection Service: This service consists of two threads: a tracker and a scavenger. The tracker maintains information in a persistent store to track scripts that migrated away from the local node. The scavenger processes "cleanup" requests received from other hosts. If the request is in response to the completion of a script then the scavenger cleans up all script related information at the local node. If the request is in response to a failed choice, the scavenger informs the fault manager to rollback the script's local state to the appropriate choice point. The garbage collection service propagates the cleanup message to remote nodes using information maintained by the tracker.

5.2 Preliminary Experimental Results

In this section, we present the performance results of our distributed recovery scheme. We perform two sets of experiments. The first set measures "null overhead" of the system, where we estimate the overhead of simply running the fault tolerance machinery even if there are no actual failures in the system. The second set measures the recovery time of our system when

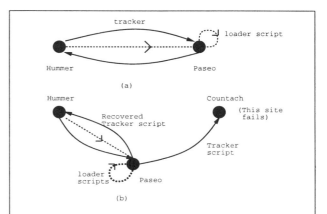

Figure 6. (a) shows the experimental configuration for measuring the null overhead of the fault tolerance mechanism. (b) shows the experimental configuration to determine the overhead associated with recovery processing.

failures actually happen.

Experimental configuration: We use three machines for the different experiments conducted: an IBM ThinkPad running Windows 98 ("hummer"), and two IBM PCs running Windows NT ("paseo" and "countach"). The machines are Pentium II class machines connected via a 16MB/sec token ring network. Figure 6a shows the experimental configuration for the first set of experiments. We use a number of "loader" scripts that start from the machine "hummer", migrate to the machine "paseo", executing an infinite *while loop* with alternate sleep and wakeup times. Increasing the number of such loader scripts simulates increasing *load* on the system. When fault tolerance is enabled, loading the system in such a fashion results in monitors being scheduled on "hummer", and heartbeats being scheduled on "paseo" that are to be sent to "hummer". When a system is loaded by a certain number of loader scripts, a "tracker" script is sent from "hummer" to "paseo", and returned immediately back to "hummer", where we measure the *roundtrip time* for the tracker script. We measure the roundtrip time under various load conditions with and without enabling fault tolerance and thereby measure the overhead of fault tolerance under various load conditions. Note that the measurements report the elapsed "wall-clock" time.

Figure 6b shows the experimental configuration for the second set of experiments. We used the loader scripts exactly in the same manner as in the first set of experiments. However, in this case, the "tracker" script is first sent from "paseo" to "countach". When the tracker script reaches "countach", a failure is simulated on "countach" by aborting the runtime. The monitor for the tracker script on "paseo" eventually detects the failure and starts the recovery process for the script. Upon recovery, another choice in the tracker script gets activated and the script migrates to "hummer" and returns immediately to "paseo" to complete execution. In this experiment, we measure the *recovery time* on "paseo". The recovery time is the time between the detection of the failure by the monitor thread and scheduling of the rolled back script for execution.

We use heartbeat probability of 1.0 for both sets of experiments to fully expose the overheads related to fault tolerance. The experimental load was varied from 0 to 100 loader scripts in steps of 20. Although we ran tests with up to 200 loader scripts, the NetPebbles runtime occasionally ran out of memory for loads higher than 100. We are confident that for load values of up to 100, the system is not affected by extraneous factors. We conducted 9 trials for each data point on the result graphs. For each data point, we discarded the two highest and the two lowest values to eliminate outliers, and computed the arithmetic average of the remaining 5 values. The coefficient of variations for measured data points was less than 0.05 in most cases, [2] giving us relatively high confidence in the computed averages.

Results: Figure 7 shows the overhead of our fault tolerance machinery for different system loads. For low system load (up to 20 loader scripts), the overhead of fault tolerance is less than 30%. For moderate loads (up to 40 loader scripts), the overhead of fault tolerance is roughly 60%. For heavy loads (up to 60 and higher loader scripts), the overhead of fault tolerance is roughly 100%. For heavy load cases, the processors are at their maximum utilization and there is heavy contention between concurrent threads (program threads, pulsar thread, monitor thread). The initial results from our implementation are not discouraging as we have increased the load by a factor of 5 (from 20 to 100) and the overhead has only increased up to a factor of 2.

Figure 8 shows the recovery time for a script with increasing system load. The recovery time is relatively low (a few tens of milliseconds) when the system is loaded lightly to moderately (up to 40 loader scripts). However, with loads of 60 or higher, the processors again reach maximum utilization and concur-

---

[2] In cases with low load since there was no competition for the processor, the execution times varied only a little. In cases with high load, since the processor was fully utilized, tracker threads always had to wait, and hence execution times varied only a little. In cases of moderate load, however, the execution time varied more as sometimes the tracker threads "got lucky" and were scheduled quickly while most loader threads were sleeping, and at other times they had to wait appreciably.

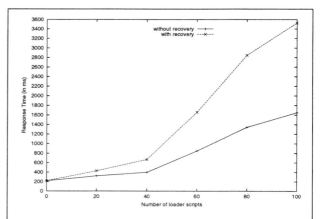

Figure 7. The graph shows the "null overhead" of our recovery scheme. The y-axis shows the roundtrip time of the tracker script. The x-axis shows the number of loader scripts in the system. The overhead of the recovery scheme is minimal for light to moderate loads (for up to 40 loader scripts). For higher loads, the recovery scheme results in appreciable overhead.

rent threads face tremendous contention. The recovery time increases roughly by a factor of 20 when the load increases from 40 to 100.

The initial performance results indicate that high system load must be managed carefully in our system. To expose all the overheads in our system, we fixed the heartbeat probabilities in our system at 1.0. Decreasing the heartbeat probability, and increasing monitoring timeout will likely make the system scale better. Techniques such as grouping heartbeats together will also likely improve system performance. To keep the initial implementation clean, we have also used Java language threads quite liberally in our system. Streamlining the usage of threads in our system, and possibly using native thread packages will likely improve system performance appreciably.

6 Conclusions and Future Work

In this paper, we describe a scheme that exploits non-determinism to address the issues of reliability and fault tolerance for mobile agents. First, we describe the non-deterministic constructs of the NetPebbles programming model and illustrate how mobile agents can use these constructs. Next, we describe a distributed recovery scheme that exploits non-determinism to provide fault tolerance. We present the design and implementation of the rollback scheme in context of the

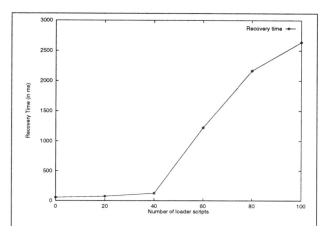

Figure 8. The graph shows the recovery time of the tracker script when a failure occurs. The y-axis shows the recovery time on the choice point host. The x-axis shows the number of loader scripts on the choice point host. The recovery time is minimal for light to moderate loads (for up to 40 loader scripts). For higher loads, the recovery time increases appreciably.

NetPebbles system along with some preliminary performance measurements. Our initial performance results are promising but indicate that high system load must be managed carefully.

In the future, we plan to investigate additional constructs for providing non-determinism in the programming model. We also plan to implement more sophisticated failure detection schemes such as ones that use voting. We plan to fine tune the implementation by making judicious use of Java language threads and possibly using native thread packages. We also plan to study the effects of decreasing the pulse probability, and increasing monitoring timeout on the overall system performance and scalability. Techniques such as grouping pulses together will also likely improve system performance.

Acknowledgments

We would like to thank Murthy Devarakonda and Yuanyuan Zhou for their valuable input on reliability and fault tolerance aspects of NetPebbles.

References

[1] K. P. Birman and T. A. Joseph. Reliable Communications in the Presence of Failures. *ACM Transactions on Computer Systems*, 5(1):47–76, 1987.

[2] R. S. Gray. Agent Tcl: A Transportable Agent System. *Workshop of Intelligent Information Agents in Fourth International Conference on Information and Knowledge Management*, December 1998.

[3] T. Howes and M. Smith. A Scalable Deployable Directory Service for the Internet. In *Proceedings of INET 95*, 1995.

[4] Objectspace Inc. Voyager. *http://www.objectspace.com/products/voyager*, 1998.

[5] D. Johansen, K. Marzullo, F. B. Schneider, K. Jacobsen, and D. Zagorodnov. NAP: Practical Fault-Tolerance for Itinerant Computations. Technical report, Cornell University, 1998.

[6] G. Jones. *Programming in Occam*. Prentice Hall International, 1987.

[7] D. Lange, M. Oshima, and O. Mitsuru *Programming and Deploying Java Mobile Agents with Aglets*. Addison-Wesley Publishing Co, 1998.

[8] N. Lynch. *Distributed Algorithms*. Morgan Kauffman Publishers, 1996.

[9] A. Mohindra, A. Purakayastha, D. Zukowski, and M. Devarakonda. Programming Network Components using NetPebbles: An Early Report. In *Fourth Annual Usenix Conference on Object Oriented Technologies and Systems*, April 1998.

[10] V. P. Nelson and B. Carroll. *Fault Tolerant Computing*. IEEE Computer Society Press, 1987.

[11] H. Peine and T. Stolpmann. The Architecture of the Ara Platform for Mobile Agents. In *Proceedings of the First International Workshop on Mobile Agents*, 1997.

[12] F. B. Schneider. Towards Fault tolerant and Secure Agents. *11th International Workshop on Distributed Algorithms*, Germany, September, 1997.

[13] M. Strasser and K. Rothermel. Reliability Concepts for Mobile Agents. *International Journal of Cooperative Information Systems*, 7(4), 1998.

[14] M. Strasser, K. Rothermel, and C. Maihofer. Providing Reliable Agents for Electronic Commerce. *IEEE*, 1998.

[15] T. Walsh, N. Paciorek, and D. Wong. Security and Reliability in Concordia. In *Hawaii International Conference on System Sciences*, June 1998.

[16] Y.-M. Wang, Y. Huang, and W. K. Fuchs. Progressive Retry for Software Error Recovery in Distributed Systems. In *Proceedings of the International Symposium on Fault Tolerant Computing*, 1993.

[17] C. D. Wolfson, E. M. Voorhees, and M. M. Flatley. Intelligent Routers. In *9th International Conference on Distributed Systems*, June 1989.

Session 6B

Practical Experience Reports IV ◆ System Architecture

A New Rolling Stock Architecture Using Safety Computers and Networks

Jean-Baptiste Boullié and Michel Brun

Technicatome, B.P. 34000,13791 Aix-en-Provence Cedex 3 – France

E-mail: {jboullie,mbrun}@tecatom.fr

Abstract

Many embedded systems carrying out safety functions in railway applications are still operated with conventional relay-based systems, at the expense of kilometers of wiring in each train. To cope with this issue, Technicatome has developed a demonstrator for RATP (the Paris subway company) to assess pros and cons of alternative architectures based on interconnected digital systems. This demonstrator is currently in operation on an MF 88 train set. The paper summarizes the main features of this experiment.

1 Introduction

In order to satisfy the ever increasing requirements of customers, the number of functions performed by the successive generations of control systems embedded in rolling stock has increased continuously, together with their complexity.

Sticking to the classical technology, this would undoubtedly lead to a reduction of reliability and therefore availability, and an increase in both the complexity of maintenance actions and of the procurement and maintenance costs.

To tackle this issue, the RATP has introduced new process control architectures based on computer networks in its latest generation of rolling stock.

The RATP is seeking to assess the advantages, constraints (in terms of installation, development methods, etc.) and performance (availability, costs, etc) implied by this new technology.

The use of computers guarantees the handling of the various complex functions with a high degree of adaptability and flexibility, and the use of networks leads to the simplification of wiring and a reduction in the number of connection points. Moreover, the use of digital interconnected systems facilitates the introduction of redundancy to support safety and availability, thus leading to the global enhancement of dependability. Finally, maintenance is made easier and improved by means of all the diagnostic aids that can be provided by the computers.

It is worth noting that currently, these technological upgrades are restricted to "safety-related" functions. Safety-critical functions (emergency braking devices, traction circuit breakers, door-opening systems, etc.) still use a more conventional technology (i.e., train lines and safety relays). This conservative attitude is quite common in the railway domain and it is based on the following: the introduction of a new technology (especially, digital technology) is necessarily a slow process, performed step by step and continuously supported by field experience.

RATP has chosen the rolling stock *door process control system* as a demonstrator, because of its complexity and the fact that there is no natural safe-state for such function. Indeed, two opposed safety objectives will be handled:

- *S1-Spurious door opening*: the probability of the occurrence of this first catastrophic event — opening of one door while the train is moving — should be less than 10^{-9} per hour of operation,

- *S2-Doors kept closed*: the probability of occurrence of this second catastrophic event — failure of more than one door opening when the train comes to a stop at a station platform — should be less than 10^{-8} per hour of operation.

The specifications for this second function also include an availability objective, which is consistent with the current availability results of the RATP system:

- *A1*: The global unavailability of the system should be better than 9 failures to open a door per day over the whole set of RATP trains.

The sequel of the paper is divided into five sections. After a short description of the targeted application, the paper presents the safety principles used at system level to cope with the conflicting dependability objectives. Then, it addresses the safety principles used at the computer level. In turn, some aspects of the dependability assessment are presented and discussed. A few remarks are made concerning the certification of a part of the system according to the new European standards EN 50126, EN 50128 and EN 50129. Finally, a conclusion is drawn.

2 Safety principles

2.1 Safe state

It is worth pointing out that a door-opening system cannot rely on a natural safe state, as does, for example, a braking system.

The search for a safe configuration for a door that is taking into account the structure of a subway train facing the various undesirable events has led to define the *safe state of a door as "a door configured as closed".*

In each coach, at least 3 doors are present to allow the stream of passengers to flow through. Hence, this redundancy can be used to cope with the opposed safety objectives, which results in the following mitigated operational objective:

- *O1*: One door kept closed for a limited period of time (1 hour) is tolerable, if and only if, no other door of the same coach is kept closed.

The counter part of the choice of such a safe state for a door has led to a necessary availability requirement, in order to avoid the failure of two doors in the same coach.

This way, the train can operate normally with a door configured as close, but still enabling the stream of passengers to flow through the other doors.

2.2 System architecture

Figure 1 depicts the architecture of the door control system; it involves three main components: the cab computers, the local computers and the networks.

The basic functional break down and mapping can be described as follows. The cab computers carry out the main acquisition and control processing tasks: they generate the "open" and "close" commands for each door; these commands are transmitted via a field bus network and are received by the local computers actually controlling the doors. These three components are briefly described in the sequel. More architectural details can be found in Section 3.

2.2.1 The cab computers. They are located in each driver's cab and are Triple Modular Redundant (TMR) systems based on fail-safe units. Such a high level of redundancy is required as the failure of a cab computer may affect every door (these computers control elaboration of the "open" and "close" commands for all the doors of the train). Thanks to the low demand on input consolidation (in particular, the cab computer has only a few discrete I/Os), the three units of the TMR can be kept asynchronous. This solution reduces the amount of hardware and software dedicated to the inter-unit communication. It is worth noting that, while the use of fail-safe units (see Section 3) is not mandatory to satisfy the dependability requirements of the cab computers.

Nevertheless this allows for a significant simplification of off-line testing and diagnosis, so an unsafe failure detection of cab computer not only relies on 2/3-discrepancy detection, but also on intrinsic failure detection of each unit.

2.2.2 Local computers. According to dependability allocation, the local computer is only related to the safety objective of one door. Unlike the cab computer, this computer has to cope with several I/O, and moreover the cost of these interfaces is proportional to the number of doors. It is thus important to reduce the hardware devoted to each door. Accordingly, the most suitable solution is a non-redundant architecture using a fail-safe computer for each of the 18 doors of the MF 88 train set. Furthermore, this allows decentralized processing of local door management functions, local consolidation of the commands received from the cab computers (the 2/3 vote is processed by local software, thus preventing the use of any hard-wired logic). Moreover, this architecture allows for a modular design (one computer for each door), thus facilitating deployment and maintenance.

2.2.3 The networks. The network layers are not directly in charge of the safety, but the network is a bottleneck for the availability of the system. The architecture uses a double medium FIP (Factory Industry Protocol) trackside network to connect all the cab and local computers.

3 Computer architecture

3.1 Objectives

The TMR units and the local computers are safety computers built around a safety-oriented processing board (the CSG board for *"Carte Sécuritaire de Gestion"*) designed by Technicatome.

The CSG board is meant to meet major safety requirements pertaining to embedded railway applications. The main objectives are:

- Very high level of safety: namely, SIL4 according to IEC 61508;
- High reliability: approximately 50,000 hours in severe environmental conditions;
- High computing power: more than 2 MIPS in safety conditions.

More strict safety and availability requirements may be fulfilled via redundancy, thanks to the modularity of the architecture.

These safety computers are also being used for the control/monitoring of nuclear submarine reactors, as well as space and other military and industrial applications [1]. They have been used in operational systems for more than 10 years.

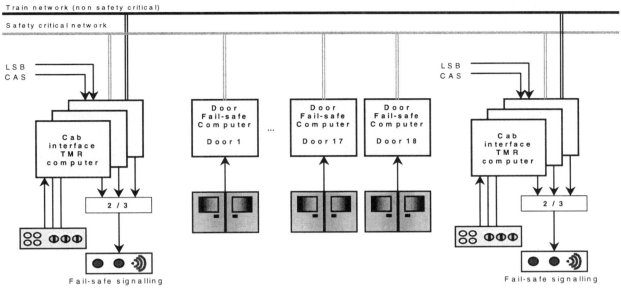

Legend: L S B = Lower Speed Bound, C A S: = Check of Alarm Signal, T M R = Triple Modular Redundant

Figure 1: Architecture of the door control system

3.2 The processing unit

3.2.1 Principles. The CSG board is built on standard components, and is based on a few basic architectural principles:

- No redundancy at the hardware level (i.e., single CPU),
- Redundancy in the time and space domains at the software level, with on-line monitoring and hardware voting of results,
- Cyclic software executive,
- Design principles minimizing detection latency.

The consistent application of theses architectural choices allows the safety objective of rate of 10^{-9} unsafe failures per hour.

The main advantage of such architectural choices is that they do not significantly compromise the usual performance of the processing unit. The extra cost for the hardware (reliability, size, consumption) is limited to 15% compared to a non safety-oriented unit. The processing unit performance is 50% of that of a non safety-oriented unit. Moreover, the use of standard components makes it possible to reach the industrial long-term perennially objectives pertaining to these fields of application.

3.2.2 "Dual time" structure. Concerning the effect of hardware faults, error detection essentially relies on space and time redundancy of the application software executed on a unique CPU. Specific design and coding

rules are applied to differentiate the redundant executions of software: duplication of memory resources associated with vital functions, logical segregation of resources through the addressing systems and control of access, use of specific structures for simplex resources such as interruptions or data acquired by network. During the design phase, each software component is either of twin-check or dissymmetrical type, depending on the safety objectives. The alternative is chosen according to application requirements (mainly, the safety objective to be achieved).

3.2.3 Control flow monitoring. The proper execution of software is checked on-line by the monitoring of the elementary procedures sequencing. This monitoring is considered with special attention during software and hardware design: systematic data updating at each cycle, monitoring of software operation during elementary procedure chaining, development of a cyclic software and specific management of interruptions, use of two clocks and safety watchdogs. Appropriate means (e.g., dynamic watchdog) are deployed to ensure their operation.

3.2.4 Voter. A hardware device, independent of the microprocessor, is used to vote safety-critical information. According to the needs, it consists of a transformer based fail-safe logic hardware fail-safe or a digital hardware voter including a sequence checker (acting on computer outputs) and applied to intermediate and final data.

3.2.5 Low error detection latency. All hardware-monitoring devices necessary to implement the principles described earlier are either fail-safe or periodically checked. Special care is taken during design to ensure that this periodic test cannot lead to an unsafe situation. In particular, a specific processor check is used to reduce the presence of dormant faults in the computation functions. This check uses the independent hardware voter as result checker, as it is not possible to trust the processor to check itself.

In addition, all major components (ROM, RAM, etc.) are periodically tested to activate dormant faults in parts of the hardware that are not frequently activated. Moreover, instruction checks are implemented via coding (Hamming code).

3.3 Hardware architecture

3.3.1 General layout. The safety-oriented computer is a single mono-processor board (**Figure 2**). All processing resources (CPU, memory) are located on the board and outside communications are achieved by asynchronous serial links, and interface cards, connected to the CSG board via a "serial safety-oriented bus" which provides a secured communication medium.

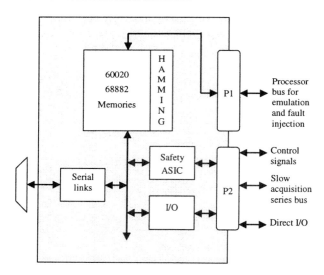

Figure 2: Functional layout of the CPU board (Double Europe card version)

This bus gives access to secured I/Os, as well as non safety-oriented utilities (e.g., displays).

3.3.2 Basic resources. In its standard version, the board includes the following resources:
- 68020-68882 at 20 MHz,
- PROM (up to 256 KB),
- Interface with external world:
  - Serial links RS232 (up to 6),

- One safety serial bus to access safety input/output boards,
- One available M-Module connection for open extension (e.g. for network links).

3.3.3 Safety ASIC. Most hardware error detection mechanisms (dynamic watchdogs, address decoding, bus access control circuits, voter, etc.) as well as some utilities (timers, etc.) of the processing unit card are grouped into an ASIC-type component. Thus, the reliability of the processing unit board is considerably enhanced.

3.4 Safety of the network

One key requirement of the demonstrator was to use a standard industrial network. As no widely available network is currently certified for high safety requirements, we decided to use a standard FIP field bus [2] for simplicity, low cost and basic determinism feature.

The architecture relies on the intrinsic redundancy capabilities of this field bus to achieve the targeted availability objectives. However, despite the protection provided by the communication protocol, safety is achieved by the introduction of additional protection mechanisms (e.g., CRC coding, time stamping of messages) independent from the communication device. This relieves the necessity to demonstrate the dependability of these components, and ensures a high level of independence with respect to the choice of the communication network.

3.5 Key features of the development process

At application level, the design life cycle is classical, based on more than 10 years of continuous improvement. For the development of safety-oriented application software, we use a methodology that is backed by the maximum use of standard tools and methods (Teamwork, Keyone, CMF, etc.). This toolset covers all the software development phases from specification to validation and configuration management.

All real time management and safety functions of the CSG board forms a "basic function library" linked with the application software via automatic tools. This library is not specific to an application and benefits from improvements to all applications.

The usual software life cycle is as follows:
- Graphical and textual specification,
- Manual coding using a subset of C language,
- Integration and validation based on a scenario that can be automatically replayed.

160

It is worth noting that, for such a "classical" design process to achieve cost-effectively a high safety level, on e has to ensure that:

- Great care is taken to constrain the application complexity,
- There is a clear strategy for multi-application reuse,
- Long term methodology / tools improvement strategy exists that is relying on actual field experience analysis [3].

On this last item, new methodologies and tools exist that are supposed to allow a dramatic improvement in safety-critical software development. Our strategy is to introduce a methodology or tool only if it offers an improvement opportunity to cope with problems that are clearly identified from feedback experience of hundreds of safety-critical software versions.

4 Dependability assessment

4.1 Functional compliance

To achieve and demonstrate functional compliance, we use state-of-the-art design organization and methods as required by recent safety standards (e.g., EN 50126). The key points of this methodology are as follows: i) implementation of the quality plan in compliance with usual critical application standards, ii) implementation of a software workbench supporting this methodology, iii) automatic testing and replay of the various tests conducted, and iv) implementation of an independent structure to carry out functional acceptances.

4.2 Processing unit's failure rate

The dependability evaluation relies on two complementary approaches:

- Analytical evaluation based on a functional failure model,
- Experimental evaluation by means of fault injection.

4.2.1 Analytical evaluation. Safety evaluation includes both a generic part and an applicative part. The generic part has been carried out once for every CSG-based application. This generic analysis is based on a functional failure model of the components and on a functional model of the safety mechanisms implemented by the CSG board.

This generic safety evaluation shows that each application based on CSG safety mechanisms will achieve safety objectives assuming the application uses in a convenient way the generic safety principles.

The applicative part is carried out for each application. This specific evaluation is meant to:

- Ensure that the safety rules are respected by the application; it is supported by means of a conformity matrix and an optional fault injection campaign.
- Analyze any specific interface board, and its link with the overall system objectives.

Two main types of modeling activities can be distinguished at component level and at board level (including the role of the fault tolerance mechanisms).

a) Component-level analysis: The random failures of the components are the main source of potential unsafe state, for which the techniques aimed at directing the failures have been defined and validated.

For the safety demonstration, two failure models are taken into account:

1) *Discrete hardware components*: Basic data used to build standardized fault models are preferably extracted from the EN50129 standard (Appendix C) or from the UTE 80-810 standard.

2) *Integrated hardware components*: The analysis is carried out on the basis of the functional model of the components (processor, memory unit, I/O components,...); at this abstraction level, the failure model is built according to the expected services for each component. This functional model does not aim at reflecting the structure of the components, but, rather at describing what the component is meant to do (or not to do, in the case of a failure) according to his user's manual. This approach can be summarized as follows (e.g., see [4]). "Do not mind why a failure occurs, but define rather how the component might fail". Such a model is compliant with the EN50129 recommended failure model.

b) Board-level analysis: An application based on CSG is supposed to use the different fault tolerance mechanisms described in Section 3.2 (e.g., to use a redundant application software).

Each of these mechanisms has been designed to cope with one (or several) functional component failure. It is thus possible to build a model of how each mechanism works, and then to analyze the effects of a given component failure on the application.

It is then possible to use classical techniques like functional FMECA and Petri nets to evaluate the consequences of component failures at board level.

4.2.2 Fault injection. This now widely recognized principle of fault injection-based analysis (e.g., see [5, 6]) has been used by Technicatome since 1984 to complement the dependability evaluation process.

The technique being used is a software-implemented fault injection (SWIFI) technique; it is based on the simulation of hardware failures on a CPU operating, in real time, the actual application software [7]. The behavior of the computer is observed while running in the presence of injected faults. Such a fault injection testing campaign is intended to verify, on the actual final application, that the global unsafe failure rate (percentage of failures resulting in a potentially dangerous action of the computer) is compliant with what is expected for a CSG-based application. A significant discrepancy may show that, despite the different controls used in development process (coverage matrix), a safety mechanism has not been correctly used by the application.

The injection of faults is controlled automatically during test campaigns carried out over several weeks that allow the studying of several million faults on a CPU. This procedure has been used for more than 15 years now, applying a specific methodology and supported by tools so as to run the testing campaigns, About 14,000,000 faults have been injected in various computers. For the RATP application considered in this paper, about 500,000 faults were injected.

5 Third-party certification

Even if the conduct of such an experiment does not require a formal certification process, all the necessary justifications and analyses have been carried out during design and validation process.

To go even further, we decided to involve a third-party certification for a core sub-system: the cab compute. For that process, although the original developments were based on specific RATP standards, it was decided to adopt the new European standards (EN 50126, EN 50128 and EN 50129).

In fact, we decided to implement this certification process, because, according to the new standards, it is now required that a third party certifies any safety critical equipment.

The cab computer was evaluated in 1999 and the certificate was delivered, on October 27 1999, with minor restrictions due to the experimental nature of this application.

Even if the initial development was started in reference to another standardization framework, still, no major problem was raised during the certification process. This shows that the basic requirements of these various standards are quite similar.

However, much effort was necessary to explicitly relate the requirement expressed in these standards: in particular, some of the tasks had to be reorganized or reformulated to conform to the new standards. So, even if no fundamental technical difference exists between these standards, it ended up in a rather costly exercise, that shows that the way justification has to be provided, directly affects the global cost.

6 Conclusion

The paper has summarized the main architectural features of a new computerized rolling stock system. It also provided insights about the lessons learnt during this study, both from the validation and certification aspects, in particular for what concerns the cost impact resulting from the consideration of the emerging European standards.

The described experimental platform is installed on an MF 88 train on Line 7 of the Paris metro. It came into service in 1999, in parallel with the existing door management system to enable a comparison to be made between the operations of the two systems.

Acknowledgement. The authors would like to thank the anonymous referees for their constructive comments. Jean Arlat provided useful guidance for the elaboration of the final version of this paper.

References

[1] P. Stéphan and O. Dieudonné, "ASTREE - Odometric Safety Control Unit", in Proc. IFAC SAFECOMP' 92, Zurich, Switzerland, 1992, pp. 153-158 (Pergamon Press).

[2] CENELEC EN 50170 "General Purpose Field Communication System", December 1996.

[3] J.-C. Laplace and M. Brun, "Critical Software for Nuclear Reactors: 11 Years of Field Experience Analysis", *Proc ISSRE'98*, Paderborn, Germany, 1998, pp. 364-368 (IEEE CS Press).

[4] J. A. Abraham and W. K. Fuchs, "Fault and Error Models for VLSI", *Proc. of the IEEE*, vol. 74, pp. 639-654, May 1986.

[5] J. Arlat, . Costes, Y. Crouzet, J. -C. Laprie and D. Powell, "Fault Injection and Dependability Evaluation of Fault-Tolerant Systems", *IEEE Trans. on Computers*, vol. 42, pp. 913-923, August 1993.

[6] J. V. Carreira, D. Costa and J. G. Silva, "Fault Injection Spot-checks Computer System Dependability", *IEEE Spectrum*, vol. 36, pp. 50-55, August 1999.

[7] M. Brun, "The Fault Injection Technique", *IEEE Int. Workshop on Fault and Error Injection for Dependability Validation of Computer Systems*, Gothenburg, Sweden, 1993 (Chalmers Univ. of Technology).

Reliability-Availability-Serviceability Characteristics of a Compressed-Memory System

Jim Chen[Ψ], David Har, Ken Mak, Charles Schulz, Brett Tremaine, Mike Wazlowski[γ]

[Ψ]IBM S390 Global Hardware Development Division
2455 South Road
Poughkeepsie, NY 12601

IBM T. J. Watson Research Center
P.O. Box 218
Yorktown, NY 10598

[γ]Email: mew@us.ibm.com
FAX: 914-945-2141

Abstract

New compression innovations and high-density silicon technology enable us to introduce main-memory compression. This technology is able to achieve, in most cases, 2:1 or better compression without impacting performance. It provides an enormous cost/perfomrance advantage, given the cost content of memory in modern enterprise servers. The complex and highly parallel data manipulations central to this compression implementation would, if unprotected by extensive error detection and error correction techniques, offer several potential data integrity exposures. This paper describes the memory subsystem of an enterprise class server with a compressed mainstore and the methods which have been employed to guarantee the integrity of the compressed data. These methods consist of a novel ECC algorithm which includes address information in the code words, the use of CRC codes for compressed data blocks, and various consistency checks on the memory management structures used in the management of a compressed mainstore.

1.0   Introduction

Corporate buyers of server-class computers demand the highest level of reliability, availability, and serviceability (RAS) for their servers. This demand is driven by the fact that when a corporation's web site or intranet is down, they lose the ability to make money. Accordingly, corporations strive to minimize the downtime of their servers. Server makers understand the needs of the corporate customer and attempt to differentiate themselves from the competition by offering higher levels of RAS. Traditionally this has meant that servers be equipped with redundant power supplies, RAID disk arrays, and ECC protected memory. Fault-tolerant servers[1] are also available for mission-critical applications.

The advent of 0.25um silicon technology and new compression algorithms[2] have made main-memory compression possible without adversely impacting the performance of enterprise servers. The system described in this paper, shown in Figure 1, is an Intel-based 4-way symmetric multiprocessor (SMP) whose processor bus speed is 100MHz[3]. The system has a 32MB shared L3 cache with a 1KB line size and 4-way set-associativity. The L3 cache contains uncompressed data and serves to hide the longer latency required to access compressed main memory.

We are investigating ways of attaining RAS specific to compressed-memory servers. Traditional methods of RAS are generally applicable to compressed-memory systems as well, but ways to enhance the RAS characteristics of the new compression logic require our investigation. To that end, the flow of the rest of the paper is as follows. Section 2 describes the compressed memory system and its RAS features. Section 3 discusses the ECC used to protect physical memory.

2.0 Main-Memory Compression

Conventional computer systems have *virtual* memory and *real* memory. Virtual memory allows each operating system process to have identical views of "memory". The processor , via page tables, translates virtual addresses to the real addresses the memory controller observes on the system bus. A system with main-memory compression stores data in memory in a variable-length compressed format which therefore requires the introduction of another level of address indirection. The memory controller still observes real addresses on the processor bus, but after the data is compressed, it is tightly packed into *physical* memory using physical addresses. The additional address translation from real memory to physical memory is performed by the compression translation table (CTT) as shown in Figure 2.

2.1 Basic Flow for Compressed Data

Data is compressed when an L3 writeback is required and it is uncompressed upon an L3 miss. For an L3 writeback, data is taken from the cache, compressed, and then stored in physical memory. The CTT entry corresponding to the L3 line just compressed is updated with the information needed to find the compressed data at a later time. For an L3 miss, the CTT entry for the L3 line is read to obtain the pointers to the compressed data. The compressed data is then read from memory, decompressed, and put on the processor bus as well as written into the L3 cache.

The large number of gates in the compression/decompression logic increases the probability of having a faulty gate or a design error which can corrupt the data. Hence, an additional method for verifying the integrity of the compressed data is needed. While it is true that the complexity of the coded format of the compressed data provides some degree of fault detection, there are a number of faults that cannot be detected by format errors. An example of this would be a compressed code which indicates the letter 'a' should be repeated four times. This code could erroneously be replaced with the letter 'b' repeated four times instead. The compressed code would be valid but the data certainly would not. Another example is an error in the repetition count. It is clear that we cannot rely on the compressed data coding alone to detect faults.

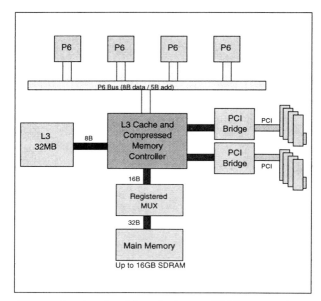

Figure 1: An Intel-based 4-way SMP enterprise server with main-memory compression.

2.2 CRC

The compression and decompression of L3 cache lines is performed by dedicated logic on the memory controller which consists of between 1 to 2 million gates. The complex nature of the compression transformation renders inadequate common main memory error detection and correction schemes such as ECC for the detection of errors introduced during either the compression or the decompression process. What is needed is a mechanism to determine if the data which exits from the decompressor is exactly the same as the data which had earlier entered the compressor, as shown in Figure 3.

A standard method for insuring the integrity of delivered data over communication lines is the cyclic-redundancy-check (CRC) code. In some sense, compressed memory can be viewed as a communications channel, where the compressor is the modulator, the physical memory is the channel or network, and the decompressor is the demodulator. CRC can achieve error detection for main memory compression just as it does for a communications channel. In this scheme, a simple recursive mathematical operation is performed on each word of a data block to yield a codeword. The codeword is attached to the compressed version of the data block for storage in physical memory. During decompression, the same CRC function is performed on the output of the decompressor. Finally the saved codeword is compared with the newly generated codeword. If there is a mismatch between the stored codeword and the newly generated codeword, then an error has occurred which has caused the output data to differ from the data before the compression.

Figure 4 shows the compression and decompression processes with the CRC mechanism attached. Input words from the L3 cache are presented to the compressor logic and the CRC generator. When the compression is complete, the CRC code word is appended to the compressed block and the combination is stored in physical memory. When that data is again requested, the compressed block and codeword are fetched from physical memory. The compressed block is passed to the decompressor. As data words emerge from the decompressor, they are passed to another CRC generator circuit. At the completion of the decompression operation, the codewords are compared, and if there is a difference an interrupt is generated..

Error coverage with this scheme is very complete. All errors in the compressor and decompressor logic are covered since the CRC is generated on the data before encoding it, and checked on the data after decoding. In addition many errors associated with the storage and management of the data in physical memory are also covered with this scheme. Errors in the storage and management of the compressed data which cause some of the bits in a compressed block or even an entire sector to get substituted, will cause the CRC to flag an error.

The compression logic uses a code based on the CRC-32 code as described in Tsai[5]. This code was originally developed for other purposes but it is well suited to the compression application. It is important the CRC algorithm be chosen so the implementation

has a bandwidth equivalent to the bandwidths of the compressor and decompressor. The compressors currently in use compress 4 bytes per clock cycle. The CRC-32 algorithm exactly matches this bandwidth.

2.3 Compression Translation Table

The compression translation table (CTT) contains the information necessary to retrieve the compressed data from physical memory. This information includes the addresses of 256B blocks of compressed data and other attributes. Each 1KB block of real memory is direct-mapped to a single entry in the CTT, as shown in Figure 2. Because the CTT is stored in physical memory, it is possible for a CTT entry to be corrupted by either a memory chip failure or a memory controller failure which results in an errant write to the CTT. The former type of failure will be discussed in the section on ECC. The type of failure characterized by an errant write to the CTT would require a great deal of time and resources to debug in the lab as the machine might continue to function for quite some time after the failure occurred. It was deemed necessary that we find a way to mitigate this exposure which did not require a large investment in terms of logic or storage. A solution is to include an even parity bit in each CTT. The parity bit achieves a 50% error detection rate for a single CTT. Since the width of main memory is 32B, or two CTT entries, the error detection rate goes up to $1-(0.5 *0.5)=75\%$ when two consecutive CTT entries are read. In general, the error detection rate grows upward as $1-0.5^n$, where n is the number of distinct CTT entries read from the contaminated region.

The parity bit is calculated by performing the exclusive-or of all the bits in the CTT entry with the exception of the parity bit itself. The calculated value is stored in the CTT after a compression operation. It should be pointed out that this is the only time a CTT entry is modified. The CTT parity bit is checked each time the CTT entry is read just before the decompression operation begins. An interrupt is issued if a CTT parity error is detected.

2.4 Free-list

A data structure called the free-list is used to hold pointers to the 256B blocks of physical memory that are currently not in use by the system. During a compression operation, 256B blocks of physical memory are allocated from the free-list to satisfy the storage requirements of the compressed data. Conversely, if the size of the compressed data has decreased since the previous compression operation, 256B blocks of data will be put back on the free-list.

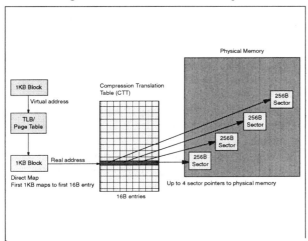

Figure 2: Address translation from a real address to a physical address is accomplished via a direct-mapped compression translation table.

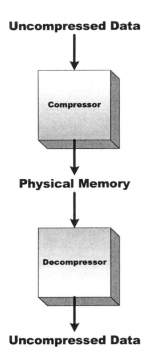

Figure 3:Compress/Decompress Flow

As shown in Figure 5, the free-list is implemented as a linked-list. Each node of the list contains pointers to sixty-three free 256B blocks and one pointer to the next 256B block in the free-list. The node is itself a free 256B block which means the free-list requires no additional storage.

Since the free-list is stored in memory, the same contamination issues previously discussed for the CTT apply to the free-list as well. To solve the problem of errant writes to a free-list block, a parity bit has been added to each 16B entry of the 256B blocks on the free-list. The parity is calculated by taking the exclusive-or of the bits in the block pointers of each 16B of a block. This method provides even parity for each 16B datum. The parity bits are checked when a node is taken off the free-list and an interrupt is issued if an error is detected. An interrupt is also issued if the free-list is empty and the allocation of a block is attempted.

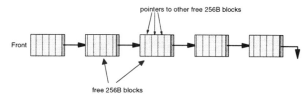

pointers to other free 256B blocks

Front

free 256B blocks

Figure 5: The free-list data structure is composed of free 256B blocks which contain pointers to other free 256B blocks.

2.5 Free Block Checks

In addition to the possibility of the free-list becoming corrupted while it resides in main memory, it is also possible for the free-list to become corrupted by logic errors in the free-list logic itself. This type of error results in a bad 256B block address being written to the free-list. The free-list parity bit offers no protection against this type of failure since the bad address will be included in the parity calculation.

Some protection against the bad block address failure can be achieved by detecting the error when the bad address is about to be allocated. Whenever a block is allocated from the free-list, its address is checked to ensure that it is within the known acceptable range of free blocks. The acceptable range of free blocks is determined at boot time and stored in registers. While this may seem like a coarse check, it has proved to be quite valuable for detecting invalid block addresses such as 0x0 in chip simulation.

Unfortunately, this type of error checking does not guard against an equally deadly failure where the same address is put on the free-list twice. It is simple to perform a duplicate check on a small locality of the free-list but it is impractical to perform this type of check globally across the entire free-list. We currently have no means to check for duplicate addresses.

3.0   Error-Correcting Code

Error-correcting codes (ECC) are used to detect and correct bit-errors when transmitting and receiving data. ECC is used on processor buses as well as in memory systems[5]. When used in memory systems, the ECC code word is stored with the data in memory. When the data is read back from memory, a new ECC code word is calculated based on the data just read. This code word is compared to the code word read from memory. If there is no difference between the newly generated code word and the code word read from memory, it is highly likely that no error has occurred. We say highly likely because there is a small probability that multiple errors could occur which result in a valid code word. If there are differences then the data may either be corrected or an error may be flagged based on the specific ECC code in use. These ECC codes try to ensure that the data stored is the data retrieved but they solely protect the data lines. There is no guarantee that when reading address 0x0 you get the data from address 0x0. In the scheme described above, it is possible to get valid ECC data but have read the data from address 0x2 when trying to read from address 0x0 due to some kind of address

Uncompressed Data

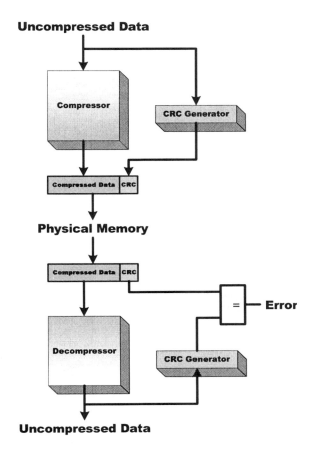

Figure 4: Compress/Decompress with CRC Checking

error. The ECC data would show that no error has occurred but the data was read from the wrong address.

We have implemented an ECC scheme which greatly reduces the exposure to this kind of addressing error. Address information is used when generating the ECC code word which makes the code word specific to that address.

3.1 ECC Calculation

The ECC provides data protection against memory failures at the chip-level when using 4-bit wide memory devices. For a memory array configured in m-bit-per-chip, the proper ECC to use should be capable of correcting all single-symbol errors and detecting all double-symbol errors, where a symbol error is any one of the $2^m - 1$ error patterns generated from a failure of a memory chip. Using this single-symbol correcting double-symbol detecting (SSC-DSD) code, the memory may continue to

function as long as there is no more than one chip failure in the group of array chips covered by the same ECC word[6]. All errors generated from a single chip failure are automatically corrected by the ECC, regardless of the failure mode of the chip. Sometime later when a second chip in the same chip group fails, a double symbol error will be generated in the same ECC word from the two failing chips. The double symbol error would be detected but not corrected by the ECC. To prevent data loss in this case, a proper maintenance procedure should be followed so the number of symbol errors would not accumulate beyond two in any ECC word.

The ECC described here is a (146,130) SSC-DSD code with m = 4[7]. An ECC word consists of 128 data bits, 2 parity bits calculated from the memory address of the data bits, and 16 check bits. In addition, every 146-bit ECC word is divided into 36 4-bit symbols corresponding to the data and check bits, and two 1-bit symbols corresponding to the memory address parity bits. The 36 4-bit symbols of an ECC word are stored in 36 different memory chips. The memory address parity bits are not stored in the memory. The single-symbol error correcting and double-symbol error detecting capability of the ECC applies to the data symbols, the check symbols, and the address parity symbols.

A parity check matrix is used to generate check bits from data bits and address parity bits in a memory store operation. Each of the 16 ECC check bits is generated by exclusive-or circuits that take as inputs a subset of the 128 data bits and two address parity bits as indicated by the ones in each row of the parity check matrix. The parity check matrix used has been optimized to reduce the circuitry in generating check bits and in detecting and correcting symbol errors[8]. When the data is fetched from memory, the syndrome is generated from the 144-bit fetched data word according to the parity check equations specified by the parity check matrix. There are 16 syndrome bits. If the syndrome is all zero, no error has occurred. Otherwise the syndrome is used to correct a single-symbol error or detect a double-symbol error.

3.2 Handling m=8 Chip Failures

The ECC code described above works well for 4-bit wide memory chips. However, the trend in the SDRAM device market is towards wider memory chips. Indeed, the standard SDRAM device at the time of this writing is 8 bits wide. This trend leads us to the problem of trying to protect 8-bit wide SDRAM devices with our current ECC.

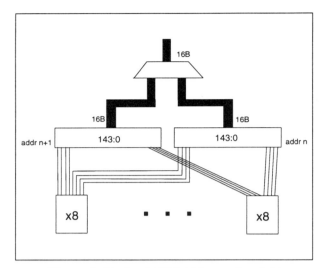

Figure 6: Each x8 SDRAM supplies 4 bits to consecutive 16B words enabling the use of an m=4 ECC which protects against x8 chip failures.

The solution turns out to be fairly straightforward. The current ECC has a symbol width of m=4 and we need to extend that to m=8. The ECC corrects 4-bit symbols from a 144-bit data word. If we extend the data word width to 288 bits, we can correct two 4-bit symbols by using the same ECC circuitry twice. All that remains now is to wire the SDRAMs in such a way that the 4-bit symbols from each 144-bit data word come from the same 8-bit wide SDRAM device, as shown in Figure 6. An alternative solution is to design an SSC-DSD code with m=8 [6]. For example, a (280, 256) code may be used. The number of check bits required is 24.

Doubling the width of the main-memory may not be possible in all cases due to pin limitations on the memory controller chip. However, if the data is registered by a set of flip-flops going-to as well as coming-from the SDRAM devices, then it is possible to double the memory width, without doubling the memory controller data bus width, by adding a multiplexer. For our case, these flip-flops were already necessary in order to accommodate the late arrival of data from the SDRAM chips.

4.0   Conclusion

The importance customers place on the RAS characteristics of server-class computers compels server manufacturers to attain the highest RAS possible. New technologies such as main-memory compression create new components of the data path whose reliability needs to be addressed. Through the use of a minimal amount of additional circuitry, this

paper has shown how to achieve desirable RAS characteristics for an enterprise server with main-memory compression. The ECC algorithm presented incorporates address information into the ECC code word which allows it to detect both data and address errors.

References

[1] M. Abbott, D. Har, L. Herger, M. Kauffmann, K. Mak, J. Murdock, C. Schulz, T. B. Smith, B. Tremaine, D. Yeh, L. Wong *Durable Memory RS/6000 System Design*, Digest of Papers, The Twenty-Fourth Annual International Symposium on Fault-Tolerant Computing, Austin, Texas June 15-17, pp. 414-423, 1994.

[2] P. A. Franaszek, J. Robinson, J. Thomas, Parallel compression with cooperative dictionary construction. In *Proceedings DCC '96 Data Compression Conference*, pp. 200-209, IEEE, 1996

[3] C. Schulz, B. Tremaine, P. Coteus, D. Poff; "High Performance Intel Server with Compressed Main Memory"; presented at 1999 PSI Symposium, IBM Research Triangle, Raleigh, NC October 25-26, 1999.

[4] Tu-Chih Tsai, Parallel CRC Generation and Verification, Research Report RC 17830(78492)26MAR1992, IBM Research, March 1992.

[5] C. L. Chen and M. Y. Hsiao, "Error-Correcting codes for Semiconductor Memory Applications," IBM Journal of Research and Development, pp.124-134, March 1984.

[6] C. L. Chen, "Error-Correcting Codes for Byte-Organized Memory Systems," *IEEE Transactions on Information Theory*, pp. 181-185, March 1986.

[7] C. L. Chen, B. Tremaine, M. Wazlowski, "A (146,130) Error-Correction Code Utilizing Address Information", IBM Patent Application Docket Number YO899-0400, 1999.

[8] C. L. Chen, "Symbol Error Correcting Codes for Memory Applications," Proceedings of the twenty-sixth International Symposium on Fault-Tolerant Computing, pp. 200-207, June 1996.

A Fault Tolerant Signal Processing Computer

Kenneth Prager, Michael Vahey, William Farwell, James Whitney, and Jon Lieb

Raytheon Company
P.O. Box 902
El Segundo, CA 90245
{keprager, mdvahey, wdfarwell, jtwhitney, jklieb}@west.raytheon.com

Abstract

A fault tolerant computer has been designed for radiation environments which employs COTS components. The use of radiation-tolerant but not fully hardened COTS devices provides significantly higher performance than specialty, fully hardened parts.

The computer architecture consists of multiple, redundant processing nodes, each containing levels of internal redundancy, and multiple point-to-point communication ports on a crossbar switch. The nodes are linked together via ports to form a distributed crossbar network with inherent fault tolerance.

A key attribute of the architecture is the provision for selectable levels of error detection and recovery. The trade-offs between performance and degree of fault tolerance can be dynamically adjusted to meet specific system needs and parts selection at any particular time.

Keywords—Fault detection, fault recovery, configurable computing, single event upset, distributed crossbar, voting

Submission Category—Practical Experience Report

1. Introduction

The High Performance Processing System (HPPS) has been designed to meet very high performance/throughput signal processing needs while operating reliably in a radiation environment. The target throughput for HPPS, by the year 2005, is 1 tera-operations per second, with storage requirements of 20 giga-bytes of random access memory. Data input rates up to 10 giga-samples per second are anticipated.

Two approaches are employed to achieve these goals:

1) A multi-processing node architecture with multiple levels of fault tolerance enables the use of commercial integrated circuits. This is viable for many radiation environments [1]-[3]. The technology employed can thus be near the leading edge of Moore's Law of increasing performance.

2) Configurable computing is employed within nodes to provide both higher performance/power ratios than other types of processors and for enhanced node reliability. Alternative configurations with varying degrees of redundancy provide on-chip management of both soft and hard failures [4]-[6].

The fault-tolerance features of the HPPS are described in this paper. A prototype is currently in operation to demonstrate the architecture and to quantify the effectiveness of the associated fault recovery algorithms.

2. Architecture

The HPPS architecture employs multiple computation nodes interconnected with a distributed network. A number of programmably selectable fault tolerance features are built into both the nodes and the network allowing the degree of fault tolerance to be tailored depending on system requirements and the failure rates of the specific devices used.

2.1. Distributed node architecture

A distributed node architecture is particularly well suited for a highly fault-tolerant system [7]. It is defined here as a plurality of independent processing nodes on a common interconnection network. We have focused on crossbar-based networks, for greatest flexibility in configuration and ease of node-level-redundant fault tolerance implementation.

A distributed crossbar offers the advantages of scalability of network size, flexibility of network topology, and fault tolerant design. A distributed crossbar consists of non-blocking crossbar switches at each node, whereby all nodes are connected directly via point-to-point physical links. For example, Figure 1 shows 12 fully connected nodes. Each link is an independent, point-to-point physical path providing simultaneous half-duplex communication at a rate per link of 2.125 GBytes/sec using 2001 technology.

For fault tolerance, the nodes are fully independent—each includes it's own power supply and clock generation circuitry. Additionally, each node contains a voting circuit capable of checking any 2 or voting any 3 of the 12 input ports. As a result—since the network switching, power supply, clocking, and voting are fully distributed—there are no single point failure mechanisms. The system is fully isotropic, with all node and interconnect failures correctable by m of n node sparing and use of alternative multiple-link paths between nodes. Fault tolerance mechanisms also exist

169

within each node allowing a multilevel hierarchy of fault tolerance. Finally, the interconnect-rich architecture enables node-level voting in any possible configuration of participating nodes.

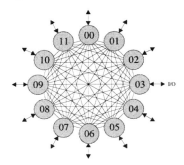

Figure 1. Fully connected network of 12 nodes

The distributed crossbar network offers considerable flexibility for both performance and fault tolerance. The following features can be configured, and dynamically reconfigured on an as-needed basis:

1) Data flow between nodes can be set to match the particular algorithm flow diagram.
2) The link bandwidth between nodes may be increased by using multiple, alternative paths simultaneously.
3) Selection can be made among multiple spare links to map around failed links or nodes.

Another feature of a "crossbar at each node" approach is that a multiplicity of different network architectures may be constructed from common node building blocks. Obviously, any network employing ≤12 ports/node may be assembled; this would include 2-D and 3-D meshes and rings. An interesting possibility is a hierarchical network, where clusters of fully connected nodes are themselves interconnected into a larger network. This provides local regions with high connectivity within a larger, scalable network. Figure 2 gives three examples: a ring, mesh, and cluster of clusters, where each circle represents an autonomous processing node.

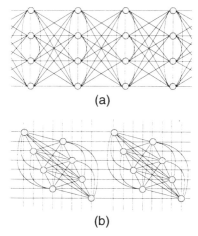

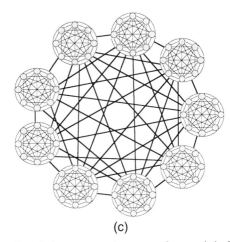

(c)

Figure 2. Interconnect examples. (a) Ring of clusters: chain of overlapping clusters of 8 fully connected nodes, which may be closed into a ring; (b) Mesh of clusters; (c) Cluster of clusters. Also, each node has at least one additional I/O port.

During operation, each node initializes independently, either on power up or on receipt of a global start signal. Initialization includes built-in self test, general purpose (GP) computer program loading, configurable computer compilation, and external I/O crossbar configuration. At the end of this setup period, status checking is performed between each node and every other node to which it should be connected. This assures that the nodes and the links between them are operational. If a plurality of nodes indicate a bad node or link, then a re-mapping is performed by each node, with preloaded mapping tables or algorithms which engage spare nodes and alternate links.

The entire system configuration—or set of configurations if multiple configurations are used—is stored in a distributed manner in the non-volatile memory of each node. Similarly, the system wide fault detection and correction processes are stored in a distributed manner in each node. Thus the system as a whole is immune to multiple failures—up to the number of spares for full performance—and beyond that with predetermined levels of reduced performance.

2.2. Processing nodes and switch fabric

As depicted in Figure 3, the processing node has five subsystems:

1) A network interface called the Fault-Tolerant Interface Core (FTIC).
2) A configurable compute engine.
3) An industry-standard, commercial-off-the-shelf GP or DSP chip.
4) Memory, both dynamic RAM (DRAM) and non-volatile memory (NVM).

5) A DC-to-DC converter, directly transforming system-provided power to the power forms used by the node devices.

6) Local clock oscillators.

The core of the architecture is the FTIC, whose block diagram is shown in Figure 3. This custom-designed circuit enables a wide variety of processor devices to be used in the distributed node architecture. There are 12 bi-directional, duplex ports, each at 2.125 GBytes/sec (17 Gbps) in 2001. The relative allocation of the available bandwidth between duplex send and receive paths is programmable for each port, in 0.125 GByte (1 Gbit) increments. This enables an optimum communication setup for each application.

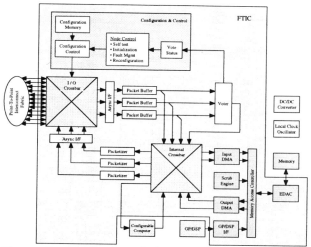

Figure 3. Node description with additional Fault-Tolerant Interface Core (FTIC) details.

Each port routes at high speed through the non-blocking crossbar switch, which is set by configuration control logic. Internal connections to the crossbar go to driver/receiver and buffering circuits, which execute standard, asynchronous handshaking protocol. For voting, a multiple handshake algorithm is used, where the flow from each of the three sending (i.e., voted) nodes is limited to the rate of the slowest of either the slowest input being voted or the voting node. This allows each node to have its own internal clock, and the data flow rate among the nodes during algorithm execution is automatically throttled to the rate of the slowest node in the set of nodes participating.

The FTIC also handles communication between internal node components:

1) Crossbar to memory, to configurable computer, and to the GP computer.

2) GP computer to memory and to configurable computer

3) Configurable computer to memory

The memory interface includes real-time error detection and correction (EDAC), a scrub engine to implement a programmed optimum read-correct-write cycle time for all DRAM locations, and a re-map circuit for permanent (hard) bit-errors.

Finally, the FTIC contains circuitry to support health status monitoring, initialization, inter-node configuration, and fault management. It is expected that most of the control of these functions is via software in the GP computer.

3. Fault management strategies

A number of capabilities provide for the management of all categories of faults—random single-event upsets (soft failures), recurring intermittent failures, and permanent (hard) failures.

The approach is to employ multiple levels of fault management. At the first level (level 1), faults are detected and corrected within each processing node. At the second level (level 2), nodes cooperate in fault detection, but correction is done within an identified bad node (typically, by re-initialization). At the third level (level 3), detection and correction are done at the network level, by node comparison or voting, and mapping around of bad nodes and links.

The specific strategies employed are described in the following sections.

3.1. Real-time correction (transparent)

3.1.1. Within nodes (level 1). EDAC with scrubbing is a key tool for memory. A wide variety of EDAC choices are available [8]; our initial application uses a double-error correction, triple-error detection algorithm. A key feature is scrubbing that is programmable both in scrub rate and in the region of memory to be scrubbed (so that non-critical regions may be omitted).

To mitigate logic failures, the configurable computer may be set to perform its algorithms in triplicate and vote internally, on an application-by-application basis.

Finally, there may be acceptable transient errors in the node output data (e.g., a corrupted data point), which can be tolerable in many applications; these cases of acceptable transients may be considered "correct-by-default."

3.1.2. Multi-node transparent correction (level 3).
This uses network voting capability, where three nodes perform the identical operation and the outputs voted in one or multiple nodes. Output data are voted when three output messages are at the voter node or when two have arrived and the voter-timeout signal is active. Node failure status is continuously monitored, and error detection messages are sent to the processors that generated the data. Recovery of a faulty processor is initiated at the earliest time consistent with system operation.

If one of the three nodes exhibits a transient failure that subsequently recovers, no other remedial action is needed. On the other hand, if a node becomes continuously bad (e.g., program corruption), or shows a high frequency of intermittent failure, then a recovery action is required.

The overall mean-time-to-upset (MTTU), or time to a failure which the voter cannot correct, depends on time of operation on two nodes after a non-transient failure, before an upset node is recovered, as well as on the inherent upset rate of the individual nodes. Figure 4 plots voting MTTU versus node upset rate for various recovery times.

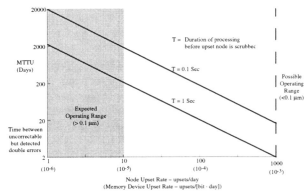

Figure 4. Mean-time-to-upset for two of three voting.

3.2. Periodic correction

3.2.1. Within nodes (level 1).
The configurable computing devices are periodically re-programmed to clear any upsets in the programming registers within these parts. The overhead time depends on the device design. Checksums of programming states are also taken for recurring (hard) failure detections. Also, the GP computing device may be periodically re-booted to correct undetected upsets. Finally, memory scrubbing with EDAC is also a periodic correction activity, with programmable parameters.

3.3. Checking without real-time correction

3.3.1. Within nodes (level 1).
Checking processes are employed to determine that programs continue to execute properly. These include a) watch dog timers, b) memory bounds checking, c) periodic self tests or health status checks interspersed with application programming. An example health status check is to process a set of stored test data, checksum the result, and compare to a stored checksum.

Hardware checksums are also included in the packets of data transmitted on inter-node ports. These are checked on receipt. This class of checking is performed autonomously at every node. Failures in this case indicate potential inter-node faults.

Error detection flags indicate that data output during the period of time since the previous check is suspect.

Recovery is initiated and a failure detection message is propagated. Processing results are suspended during the recovery and input data will not be processed until the next independent input data frame. Note that some failures (e.g., a completely non-operating processor) cannot be found by this method; some level 2 or 3 support is also necessary.

3.3.2. Multi-node Detection (level 2).
Here, multiple nodes perform the same program, but on different data, and periodically share status (e.g., point in program execution). A discrepancy indicates a node upset.

3.3.3. Multi-node Detection (level 3).
Here, two nodes perform the same processing on the same data, with outputs continuously compared using the voter circuit, in a "compare 2" mode. Since this is a real-time process, all data processed up to the point of detection are assured to be good.

Any mismatch will initiate a recovery and a failure detection message. Processing results are suspended during the recovery and input data will not be processed until the next independent input data frame. The robustness of the recovery is programmer specified. For periodic data, it may be sufficient to not process that frame of data and just propagate the failure detected message and no output data. Alternately, the processing will be restarted from a roll-back data set, such that no processed data is lost, but is delayed.

3.4. Recovery of hard failures

These are defined as permanent failures of a device or interconnect between devices. Also included are recurring intermittent failures or areas of excessive SEU rate. The remedial actions available are to map around the failure, using redundant, spare resources, or to disable the affected area and continue processing with reduced performance.

In either approach, there are two methods of management, depending on whether a node or device completely fails (gross failure) or whether there is only a localized failure.

3.4.1. Localized failure management within nodes (level 1).
Memory Re-map: redundant memory addresses are reserved in each DRAM or NVM device. If there is a permanently killed bit or address, a mapping table reroutes that address to a redundant address. For DRAMs, redundancy may be desirable at the row or row-segment level, to allow high-speed block accesses (which must be in contiguous address sequences within a row segment). If the redundancy is exhausted, then blocks of memory are disabled, resulting in a smaller but still usable device for reduced performance. Failed addresses are identified by EDAC; control logic then assesses the frequency of failures to determine if a map-around is necessary. The address re-mapping can

optionally be done in the GP processor or in special hardware in the FTSF.

For NVMs, the correct data must be reloaded into the mapped-in, redundant address. For single bit failures, the existing EDAC can provide the data to be entered. A complete address failure requires an external source of reprogramming information. If there is sufficient NVM size, the unique information for all nodes might be stored in the NVM space of each node. This not only supports NVM recovery, but simplifies the configuration of spare nodes for node-level redundancy.

Logic Re-map: configurable computing devices are compiled as specific interconnections of common internal elements to perform various algorithms. It is possible to carry extra, spare elements so that a modified interconnection compilation could replace a failed element with the most accessible spare. Failure is detected by the means in place for soft failures, with recurring failures causing the initiation of an off-line built-in self-test (BIST) routine, which provides effective diagnosis for configurable devices. A subsequent re-routing of the configurable computing devices occurs off-line, using specialized software.

3.4.2. Global failure management among nodes (level 3).
If a device or interconnect within a node exhibits an unrecoverable hard failure (i.e., no viable alternate function mapping), then that node is no longer functional. A defective node or interconnection between nodes must be corrected at the processor network level, by re-mapping the network to use a spare node or interconnect. Detection, as for other hard errors, utilizes the soft error detection mechanisms, with filters to identify recurring errors as hard.

Re-mapping depends on the network topology. The simplest case is the fully connected network. For example, Figure 1 illustrates such a network with 10 active and 2 spare nodes. Note that any two failures (whether nodes or interconnects) are easily corrected by simply engaging a spare node. This is sufficiently straightforward that a re-mapping table for any combination of two failures can be stored in each node. In most cases, many more than two interconnect failures can be corrected, since not all interconnects are used; this involves invoking alternative paths of two or more links using the nonblocking crossbars at appropriate intermediate nodes. The exact amount of fault tolerance depends on the specific link usage.

If the network is not fully connected, then the process of allocating spare locations/links, and the re-mapping process, are more constrained. In the case of general "networks of fully connected clusters" (see Section 2.2.1), allocating one or more spare nodes per cluster is effective. Networks that are configured uniquely to an application will need a uniquely-designed sparing concept.

3.4.3. Global failure isolation and recovery algorithm using fault hypotheses.
The primary mechanism for detecting and recovering from errors across a collection of nodes is the voting of messages which these nodes exchange. A given node may both send and receive voted messages. Messages which that node receives for voting may allow errors to be detected within the nodes which sent those messages, as well as within the node performing the vote. Messages which the node sends to be voted by others allow detection of errors within itself and within the nodes which vote its messages. These two processes together are the principal sources of information for generating fault hypotheses when vote failures occur.

Because single event upsets (SEUs) are the most common cause of failures, many faults are transient in nature. Consequently vote results are filtered before being passed on to the fault hypothesis generator.

The output of the vote results filter may suggest both the location of the fault and its cause. Vote errors are due to either a disagreement in the data sent by redundant nodes or to the failure of a redundant message to arrive within its expected time window. For example, a node operating in triplex may receive two of three required messages on time, and fail to receive the third. This suggests that a possible location of the fault is the redundant node that failed to send the message. A possible cause is the node's control software, since the message was not sent, rather than its data generation software as would be suspected if the message were sent but contained incorrect data.

Filtered vote results from both the sender and receiver of messages are used to generate fault hypotheses associated with a given node and the nodes with which it communicates. Associated with each hypothesis is a degree of belief given the observed vote results. More than one fault hypothesis may be instantiated for a single vote result, with differing degrees of belief.

A collection of diagnostic routines is available for collecting additional evidence to support or refute instantiated fault hypotheses. For example, if a communication link fault is suspected, a packet echo diagnostic might be run. Failure of this test supports the communications link fault hypothesis, while success provides disconfirming evidence. Evidence from different sources is combined using the Dempster-Shafer theory of evidence [9].

A set of recovery actions exists to deal with detected faults. Each recovery action applies to one or more faults, and will be executed if the belief in that fault hypothesis exceeds a threshold for the given recovery action. The recovery may or may not be successful, and this provides additional evidence for this and other fault hypotheses. For example, a redundant communications channel may be used if a communications fault is suspected. If this does not solve the problem, belief in the communications link fault hypothesis is reduced, and the belief in other hypotheses such as a program fault may be increased.

Correction of fault conditions may require multiple processing cycles. In particular, if a node is determined to have a program fault it must be reset by its communication partners. This may require many processing cycles for the faulted node to recover and resynchronize with its peers. In the interim, its vote partners must operate in a reduced fault tolerance capacity.

4. Model-year 2000 demonstration system

4.1. Hardware design

We have built a four node system to test our fault detection and recovery algorithm concepts. The prototype system hardware are housed in a VME chassis. Each node consists of a Motorola MVME2400 processor board, which includes a 350 MHz 750 PowerPC GP processor. Each node also has a PMC mezzanine card containing three Xilinx Virtex-1000 FPGAs; which are used to emulate the FTIC and configurable computer.

Table 1. Summary of HPPS architecture programmability.

• Distributed crossbar with redundant links
– Selection of active/redundant links is fully programmable
– Number of spare links is programmable
– Links may be combined on command for higher bandwidth
– Relative bandwidth of duplex send/receive channels can be set for each port
• Real-time fault tolerance
– Selectable asynchronous voting at each node, including no vote, comparison of 2, vote of 3
– Memory EDAC with programmable scrub rate
– CRC codes on network links
• Programmable periodic fault tolerance
– Memory scrub rate
– Configurable computer: test and scrub configuration
– GP computer: wellness checks and reboot
– Processing applications can be handed off to spare nodes in a round-robin fashion to allow periodic activities to be transparent
• Hard failure reconfiguration
– On-node: memory map and configurable computer re-mapping using spare circuitry
– Multi-node: reconfiguration of distributed crossbar to utilize spare nodes

4.2. Initial demonstration

The fault management strategies described in Section 3 are currently being tested and analyzed. The software redundancy modes are selected by the operator using the a GUI setup control panel. System status is logged and displayed on the Operator Status Display.

For evaluation of fault detection and recovery algorithms, each node executes at least two threads (one to simulate the node generating data and another one for the voting node). A variety of failure scenarios are being simulated by forcing both random and pre-determined faults. This is done using both hardware fault injection points and software intervention.

5. Conclusion

The HPPS processing system has been designed to provide high throughput at low power while operating in a fault tolerant manner. This is due to the use of both configurable computing elements and COTS components. As summarized in Table 1, the system supports multiple methods for detecting and correcting transient and permanent faults. To maximize performance efficiency, the programmer selects the method(s) most appropriate for each function. This allows very high dependability computing where required, albeit at a performance or power penalty, or very efficient computing with lower dependability.

References

[1] Daily, W., "Parts Issues in High Volume Satellite Productions and Deployment," *Proceedings of Workshop on Electronic Components for the Commercialization of Military and Space Systems*, 1998.

[2] Fox, A. , et al, "Suitability of COTS IBM 64 M DRAM in Space," *IEEE Trans on Nuc. Sci.* 1998.

[3] Shaw, D.C., et al; "Radiation Evaluation of an Advanced 64 Mb 3.3 V DRAM", *IEEE Trans. on Nuc. Sci., Vol. 42, No. 6*, Dec. 1995.

[4] "Pleiades: Ultra-Low-Power Hybrid and Configurable Computing," DARPA ITO Sponsored Research: 1998 Project Summary, University of California, Berkeley, <http://www.darpa.mil/ito/psum1998/E266-0.html>

[5] Villasenor, J., and Hutchings, B., "The Flexibility of Configurable Computing," *IEEE Signal Processing Magazine*, September 1999.

[6] Villasenor, J., and Mangione-Smith, W. H., "Configurable Computing," *Scientific American*, June 1997.

[7] Pradhan, D. K., *Fault Tolerant Computer System Design*, Prentice Hall, 1996.

[8] Lin, S. and Costello, D., *Error Control Coding*, Prentice Hall, 1982.

[9] Gordon, J. and Shortliffe, E, H., "The Dempster-Shafer Theory of Evidence," in *Rule-Based Expert Systems*, edited by Buchanan, B. G. and Shortliffe, E. H., Addison Wesley Publishing Company, Inc., pp. 272-292, 1984.

Session 6C

Student Forum

Session 7

Day 2 ♦ Opening Session

Session 8A

Analysis and Evaluation

Performability of Algorithms for Connection Admission Control*

John F. Meyer
Department of Electrical Engineering and Computer Science
The University of Michigan
Ann Arbor, Michigan 48109 USA
jfm@eecs.umich.edu

Abstract

Connection admission control (CAC) in broadband, ATM-based telecommunication networks is a problem of recognized importance. We consider algorithms for this purpose that accommodate variable bit rate (VBR) connections and are based on effective bandwidth computations. Arriving VBR traffic streams are assumed to be leaky-bucket regulated and are represented by worst-case, periodic, on-off, fluid sources that are randomly phased. Moreover, certain traffic classes may benefit from statistical multiplexing (S-VBR) while others may not (NS-VBR). We then evaluate the ability of such CAC algorithms to perform in the presence of fluctuating channel capacity, where the performability variable Y_T is the fraction of some specified busy period T during which the quality of service requirement is violated. A general base model that supports Y_T is then formulated and instances of the resulting performability model are constructed and solved using UltraSAN.

1. Introduction

Regarding methods of connection admission control (CAC) in ATM-based telecommunication networks, techniques that employ effective bandwidth computations have dealt primarily with congestion at the burst level. Moreover, two basic approaches have been generally recognized for this purpose (see [7], for example). The first is suited to *burst scale delay* systems which employ large buffers to accommodate burst congestion. The principal quality of service (QOS) measure in this case is the probability of buffer overflow and, with regard to burst admission, a multiplexed load is acceptable if this probability is less than or equal to a very small number (typically 10^{-9}). Alternatively, one

can consider *burst scale loss* systems which employ smaller buffers, provided they are large enough to guarantee loss QOS at the ATM-cell level. In this case, the principal QOS measure is the probability of saturation, i.e., the probability P_{sat} that the aggregate bit arrival rate exceeds capacity, thus causing bursts to be lost. Here, a multiplexed load is regarded as being acceptable if P_{sat} is no greater than some very small value (again typically 10^{-9}).

The investigation that follows considers CAC algorithms for the second scenario where, historically, an important set of initial results were those obtained by Hui [2]. The model used by Hui to evaluate the burst scale loss probability P_{sat} presumes unbuffered resources; hence, it initially appeared to have limited applicability in an ATM setting. Since then, however, a number of studies have shown how Hui's approach can be extended to buffered resources. Effort in this direction was led by Kelly [3] who derived several alternative formulations of buffer-related effective bandwidths (EBs) according to the nature of the QOS requirement. More recently, Ewalid, Mitra, and Wentworth [1] have exploited Hui's results via an innovative transformation of a two-resource (buffer-channel) problem into one involving a single resource (buffer or channel). This is done by imposing a reasonable constraint on how both resources are allocated relative to a specified traffic class. Moreover, by focusing the analysis on the buffer output (channel input), the "bufferless results" of Hui can then be applied.

Extending the analysis of [1], which uses the the basic Chernov bound to estimate P_{sat}, we have been able to formulate improved EBs using the modified Chernov bound [6]. This patent application also describes a Table-Based CAC algorithm which circumvents known difficulties associated with controlling the admission of mixed statistically multiplexable (S-VBR) and nonstatistically multiplexable (NS-VBR) sources. Relevant material from both [1] and [6] is reviewed in Section 2.

In particular, the Table-Based algorithm just cited relies

---

*This work was supported by the Italtel Central Research Laboratories, Milan, Italy.

on an ordering of classes according to their "relative multiplexabilities" and a table of precomputed EBs for incremental values of residual capacity. The latter suggests that the evaluation of such algorithms can be extended quite naturally to channels with fluctuating capacity. For example, such capacity variations could result from link faults and subsequent recovery actions, a setting that is well suited to performability modeling (as surveyed in [4, 5], for example). A general performability model for this purpose is introduced in Section 3, followed by the formulation of a performability variable Y_T that quantifies the extent to which the QOS requirement is violated during a specified busy period T. Section 4 describes the model's construction and solution (with respect the prescribed measure) using Ultra-SAN[1] and Section 5 presents the results of an initial evaluation study. Finally, the model has features that permit extensions in several directions. These are summarized in Section 6 along with a number of suggestions for further research.

2. Background

2.1. Traffic Assumptions

As in [1], traffic sources are represented by worst-case, regulated rate processes. Specifically, given a leaky bucket characterized by parameters r (the token rate, which regulates the mean input rate), B_T (the token buffer capacity, which bounds the burst size), and P (the peak rate permitted, where $r \leq P$), these are deterministic sources that behave as follows. If $r < P$ then the worst-case arrival process (when so regulated) is a deterministic, on-off, periodic rate process. The duration of an on period is $T_{\text{on}} = B_T/(P - r)$, during which the rate is equal to the peak rate P. The source is then off (rate = 0) for a duration $T_{\text{off}} = B_T/r$. Accordingly, the source is able to transmit the maximum amount of information (burst size) permitted by the leaky bucket, namely $Q = B_T P/(P - r)$; the mean rate is likewise maximized ($= r$) with respect to the period $T_{\text{on}} + T_{\text{off}}$. Individual sources are therefore identical except for their phases, where the latter are assumed to be statistically independent random variables uniformly distributed over the period $T_{\text{on}} + T_{\text{off}}$. If $r = P$ then the periodicity disappears, i.e., the output of the regulator becomes a constant bit rate (CBR) source with rate r. Heterogeneity is introduced by considering a set $\mathcal{J} = \{1, 2, \ldots, J\}$ of J traffic classes that are distinguished by leaky buckets with differing parameter values, i.e., for each $j \in \mathcal{J}$, source class j is characterized by the parameter triple $(r_j, B_{T,j}, P_j)$.

[1] UltraSAN is a software package for model-based performability evaluation of systems represented by stochastic activity networks (SANs); see [8], for example.

2.2. Resource Allocation

With these input assumptions, the analysis in [1] concerns the probabilistic behavior of channel (trunk) utilization at the output of a buffer with capacity B. At this point, such behavior can be viewed as the input to a bufferless resource, thus permitting application of some important results described in [2]. Quantifying loss at the burst level, the *saturation probability* P_{sat} is the probability that the total instantaneous demand S (aggregate burst rate) exceeds the channel capacity C, i.e.,

$$P_{\text{sat}} = \Pr[S > C]. \tag{1}$$

The QOS requirement places an upper bound on P_{sat}, i.e., for some specified positive real γ,

$$P_{\text{sat}} \leq e^{-\gamma}. \tag{2}$$

This allowed burst-loss probability is assumed to be very small, e.g., 10^{-9}, in which case $\gamma \approx 20.72$.

To reduce the allocation problem to a single resource (either the buffer or the channel), it is assumed that buffer/bandwidth allocations for a class-j connection are such that both resources are exhausted simultaneously. This permits the formulation of the *no-saturation effective bandwidth* (NEB) $e_{0,j}$ of a class-j source, where this terminology is justified by the fact that a connection vector $n = (n_1, n_2, \ldots, n_J)$, where n_j is the number of sources in class j, is admissible with no saturation ($P_{\text{sat}} = 0$) if and only if

$$\sum_{j=1}^{J} n_j e_{0,j} \leq C. \tag{3}$$

Further, letting w_j denote the fraction of time that the channel is utilized by a class-j source, the product $w_j e_{0,j}$ is equal to the mean rate r_j permitted by the regulator, whence

$$w_j = \frac{r_j}{e_{0,j}}. \tag{4}$$

For the purposes that follow, the quantities $e_{0,j}$ and w_j serve to fully characterize traffic class j.

2.3. Chernov Bounds

As in [1], but conforming more closely with the notation of [3], let

X_{ji}: Load due to the ith class-j source.

$W_j(x)$: Probability distribution function (PDF) of X_{ji} (sources in given class are the same except for random phasing).

$M_j(s) = \log E[e^{sX_{ji}}] = \log \int_0^\infty e^{sx} dW_j(x)$: Logarithmic moment generating function (LMGF) of X_{ji}.

$S = \sum_{j=1}^{J} \sum_{i=1}^{n_j} X_{ji}$: Aggregate load for connection vector n.

$M_S(s) = \sum_{j=1}^{J} n_j M_j(s)$: LMGF of S.

Then, given that saturation is possible, Chernov's bound applies to the random variable $S - C$, yielding

$$P_{\text{sat}} \leq e^{-F_n(s^*)}, \qquad (5)$$

where $F_n(s) = sC - M_S(s)$ and s^* is the unique value of s that maximizes $F_n(s)$, i.e.,

$$F_n(s^*) = \sup_{s \geq 0} F_n(s).$$

The multiplexability distinctions and subsequent analysis of [1] are based on the basic Chernov bound (BCB) given by (5). An improved bound, first considered by [2] in this context, is the modified Chernov bound (MCB)

$$P_{\text{sat}} \leq \frac{e^{-F_n(s^*)}}{s^* \sqrt{2\pi \sigma_n^2(s^*)}}, \qquad (6)$$

where

$$\sigma_n^2(s) = \frac{\partial^2}{\partial s^2} M_S(s) = \sum_{j=1}^{J} n_j M_j''(s).$$

Although the use of (6) results in analytic complications (due to the nature of the denominator) that do not exist for the basic bound (5), we have shown that they can be dealt with effectively [6].

Letting $K_n(s^*) = s^* \sqrt{2\pi \sigma_n^2(s^*)}$ and assuming that saturation is possible, by taking logarithms on both sides of the MCB, the QOS requirement will be satisfied by connection vector n if $-F_n(s^*) - \log K_n(s^*) \leq -\gamma$. Equivalently, letting

$$G_n(s^*) = F_n(s^*) + \log K_n(s^*), \qquad (7)$$

the admission criterion is simply

$$G_n(s^*) \geq \gamma. \qquad (8)$$

When compared with the BCB-based criterion $F_n(s^*) \geq \gamma$, this is more liberal since, except for extreme values of n, $\log K_n(s^*) > 0$.

2.4. Multiplexability

If bandwidth is allocated to class-j VBR sources in isolation then class j is *statistically multiplexable* (S-VBR) if the maximum number of admissible sources exceeds the maximum $n_{0,j} = C/e_{0,j}$ permitted with no saturation; otherwise it is *nonstatistically multiplexable* (NS-VBR). With a slight abuse of notation, let n_j denote the connection vector consisting of n_j class-j sources only, i.e.,

$n_j = (0, 0, \ldots, 0, n_j, 0, \ldots, 0)$. Then, ignoring the QOS requirement, saturation occurs in the interval

$$N_j = \{ n_j \mid n_{0,j} < n_j \leq n_{0,j}/w_j \}, \qquad (9)$$

where the upper bound insures stability. Note that if $w_j = 1$ then the interval N_j is empty and nothing more needs to be done. This is consistent with the definition (4) of w_j, where its value is 1 if class j is bandwidth limited, including the CBR extreme where $e_{0,j} = P_j = r_j$.

If we now impose the QOS constraint then, by the MCB-based admission criterion (8), source class j is S-VBR if, for some $n_j \in N_j$, $G_{n_j}(s^*) \geq \gamma$; otherwise it is NS-VBR. Formulating the summands of (7) in terms of n_j, $n_{0,j} = C/e_{0,j}$ and the class-j utilization fraction w_j, it can be shown [6] that

$$F_{n_j}(s^*) = n_{0,j} \left[\log \left(\frac{n_{0,j}}{n_j w_j} \right) \right.$$
$$\left. + \left(\frac{n_j}{n_{0,j}} - 1 \right) \log \left(\frac{n_j - n_{0,j}}{n_j(1 - w_j)} \right) \right] \qquad (10)$$

and

$$\log K_{n_j}(s^*) = \frac{1}{2} \log \left(\frac{2\pi n_{0,j} (n_j - n_{0,j})}{n_j} \right)$$
$$+ \log \left(\log \left(\frac{n_{0,j} (1 - w_j)}{(n_j - n_{0,j}) w_j} \right) \right), \qquad (11)$$

thus providing a closed-form solution of $G_{n_j}(s^*)$ for isolated class j. In the limit as n_j approaches either its lower bound $n_{0,j}$ or upper bound $n_{0,j}/w_j$, $G_{n_j}(s^*) \to -\infty$. However, with the exception of values very near these extremes (which will not arise in practice), $G_{n_j}(s^*)$ is a nicely behaved function of n_j over the interval N_j. Specifically, it has a maximum value which occurs when n_j is quite close to $n_{0,j}$; beyond this point, $G_{n_j}(s^*)$ decreases montonically with increasing n_j and remains larger than $F_{n_j}(s^*)$ until n_j is very close to $n_{0,j}/w_j$.

2.5. Characterization of S-VBR Classes; EB Computations

In view of the above, whether a traffic class can profit from statistical multiplexing can be decided as follows. Let $m_j(C)$ denote the maximum value of $G_{n_j}(s^*)$, i.e.,

$$m_j(C) = \max_{n_j \in N_j} G_{n_j}(s^*). \qquad (12)$$

Then, in terms of (12) and the value of the QOS exponent γ, it can be shown [6] that

class j is S-VBR for capacity C iff $m_j(C) \geq \gamma$. (13)

Although this characterization is similar to that of [1], it differs quantitatively, thereby altering the S-VBR/NS-VBR dichotomy. In particular, a class that is NS-VBR according to the BCB-based definition may be S-VBR according to (13).

As in the BCB-based analysis of [1] but in terms of our modified S-VBR criterion, the problem of computing effective bandwidths (EBs) differs considerably according to the following three cases.

Case 1: $\max_{j \in \mathcal{J}} m_j(C) < \gamma$. Here, by (13), no class is S-VBR (all are NS-VBR).

Case 2: $\min_{j \in \mathcal{J}} m_j(C) \geq \gamma$. Again, by (13), this says that all source classes are S-VBR.

Case 3: Neither of the above, i.e., there is a proper mix of S-VBR and NS-VBR classes.

In Case 1, nothing can be gained by statistical multiplexing since all classes are NS-VBR; hence the EBs are just the NEBs $e_{0,j}$ for all $j \in \mathcal{J}$. In Case 2, the boundary of the set of admissible connection vectors can be characterized strictly in terms of the modified Chernov bound. Moreover, as described in [6], the EBs can be computed via an approximating hyperplane that accurately (and conservatively) bounds the admissible set.

By its definition, Case 3 involves a proper mix of S-VBR and NS-VBR classes, resulting in an admission boundary that gets distorted by the influence of the NS-VBR classes. As demonstrated in [1] and emphasized in their concluding remarks, this interaction can preclude an accurate linear approximation of the admissible set. Indeed, this was the challenge that motivated our development of the Table-Based CAC algorithm [6]. In particular, this algorithm relies on precomputed EBs for various values of residual channel capacity, suggesting an extension to channels whose capacities fluctuate randomly for certain reasons.

3. CAC Performability

3.1. Fluctuating Capacity

In what follows, we assume that capacity fluctuations are due to link faults and subsequent fault recovery actions. However, other interpretations can likewise be considered, either by adjusting certain parameter values in the capacity submodel or perhaps altering this submodel to fit the needs of a given interpretation. More formally, we consider a channel whose physical capacity ranges over a set $\mathcal{C}$ of $K + 1$ equally spaced values

$$\mathcal{C} = \left\{ \frac{kC}{K} \mid k = 0, 1, \dots, K \right\},$$

where, here, C denotes the fault-free capacity. In turn, we let

$$Z = \{Z_t \mid t \in [0, \infty)\} \tag{14}$$

be a stochastic process that represents how capacity varies as a function of continuous time, where the random variables Z_t take values in the state space $\mathcal{C}$. In the presence of such fluctuations, we need to address issues concerning both how connections are admitted (e.g., to what extent is the admission algorithm aware of the actual capacity Z_t) and how such connections are affected by capacity changes once they have been admitted.

3.2. A Performability Model

The above suggests a variety of possible studies concerning the ability of a CAC algorithm to perform in the presence of fluctuating capacity. As noted at the outset, we assume that connection admissions are decided according to the criteria and EB computations developed for the Table-based CAC algorithm. However, to simplify things for this initial investigation, we suppose that the traffic is homogeneous, i.e., there is but one traffic class ($J = 1$). Accordingly, the possibility of mixed S-VBR/NS-VBR traffic (Case 3; see Section 2.5) is excluded. This implies that the EB e_1^m of a class-1 connection (the superscript m indicates computation relative to the modified Chernov bound) is either its NEB $e_{0,1}$ (Case 1) or is determined by Case 2 computations. Moreover, since there is only one traffic class, the hyperplane construction for Case 2 reduces to determining a single point, namely the maximum number $n_{\max,1}$ of class-1 sources that can be connected without exceeding the QOS bound $e^{-\gamma}$ on P_{sat}.

In either case, this EB depends the total amount of bandwidth (channel capacity) that is assumed to be available for allocation. For the study that follows (and again in the interest of simplifying things initially), we suppose that the CAC algorithm has no knowledge of fault-caused fluctuations in the channel's capacity. In other words, we are assuming that EB computations for the purpose deciding admissibility are based on the fault-free capacity C. Hence, in Case 1, the maximum number of connections that can be admitted is $n_{0,1} = C/e_{0,1}$. In Case 2 (recalling the definition (12) of $m_j(C)$ and applying it to class 1), from the development in [6] it follows that $n_{\max,1}$ is either the value of n_1 for which $G_{n_1}(s^*) = m_1(C)$ (if $m_1(C) = \gamma$) or the larger of the two values of n_1 that satisfy $G_{n_1}(s^*) = \gamma$ (if $m_1(C) > \gamma$).

Accordingly, let

$$A = \{A_t \mid t \in [0, \infty)\} \tag{15}$$

be a stochastic process representing the dynamics of connection admission control, i.e., A_t is the number of (class-1) sources connected to the channel at time t. Then, under the above assumptions,

$$A_t \leq \begin{cases} n_{\max,1} & \text{if class 1 is S-VBR} \\ & \text{(as judged by the CAC algorithm)} \\ n_{0,1} & \text{else} \end{cases}$$

At first glance, consideration of an NS-VBR class (the 'else' case) appears uninteresting since its NEB is allocated to each connection and, hence, saturation is not possible with respect to the fault-free capacity C. Moreover, since the class is NS-VBR for capacity C it must be NS-VBR for any capacity $Z_t < C$. However, such a reduction in capacity may cause saturation and, as soon as this occurs, the QOS requirement is violated. Indeed, if the NS-VBR class is bandwidth limited ($w_1 = 1$, which is true in particular for any CBR class) then the conditions that characterize saturation, a QOS violation, and instability (the negation of condition (17) given below) are all equivalent.

Generally, saturation will be possible at time t if the number A_t of connections at time t exceeds the no-saturation maximum with respect to the actual capacity Z_t, i.e.,

$$A_t > Z_t/e_{0,1} . \tag{16}$$

If (16) holds and, moreover, the system is stable in the sense that the mean aggregate load does not exceed the capacity (as required in order to formulate the MCB; see (9)), i.e.,

$$A_t w_1 \leq Z_t/e_{0,1} \tag{17}$$

then using the MCB to approximate P_{sat} at time t,

$$P_{\text{sat}}(t) \approx e^{-G_{A_t}(s^*)} ; \text{ else } P_{\text{sat}}(t) = 0 . \tag{18}$$

Further, specializing equations (10) and (11) to class 1 and capacity Z_t, the variables n_1 and $n_{0,1}$ can then be expressed terms of the random variables A_t and Z_t, namely, $n_1 = A_t$ and $n_{0,1} = Z_t/e_{0,1}$. Making these substitutions in the equations just referred to, the random variable $G_{A_t}(s^*)$ (which depends on Z_t as well as A_t) is given by the sum

$$G_{A_t}(s^*) = F_{A_t}(s^*) + \log K_{A_t}(s^*) , \tag{19}$$

where

$$F_{A_t}(s^*) = \frac{Z_t}{e_{0,1}} \left[\log \left(\frac{Z_t e_{0,1}}{A_t w_1} \right) \right.$$
$$\left. + \left(\frac{A_t e_{0,1}}{Z_t} - 1 \right) \log \left(\frac{A_t - Z_t/e_{0,1}}{A_t (1 - w_1)} \right) \right] \tag{20}$$

and

$$\log K_{A_t}(s^*) = \frac{1}{2} \log \left(\frac{2\pi Z_t (A_t - Z_t/e_{0,1})}{A_t e_{0,1}} \right)$$
$$+ \log \left(\log \left(\frac{Z_t (1 - w_1)}{(A_t e_{0,1} - Z_t) w_1} \right) \right) . \tag{21}$$

These formulas imply that the base model

$$(A, Z) = \{(A_t, Z_t) \mid t \in [0, \infty)\} \tag{22}$$

suffices to describe the behavior of $G_{A_t}(s^*)$ and hence, by (18), how the saturation probability $P_{\text{sat}}(t)$ varies randomly as a function of time. In turn, this permits a number of QOS-related performability measures to be supported by the base model (22), where an interesting example is the following.

Let $T = [u, v]$ denote a specified busy period ($u < v$) and let Y_T denote the fraction of period T during which the QOS requirement is violated (not satisfied). By definition (2), such a violation occurs at time t if

$$P_{\text{sat}}(t) > e^{-\gamma} . \tag{23}$$

Moreover, (23) will occur if and only if either

1) the system is stable (17), saturation is possible (16), and (assuming (18) to be exact) $G_{A_t}(s^*) < \gamma$, or

2) the system is unstable due to a mean aggregate load at time t that exceeds Z_t.

Then to formulate Y_T in terms of the base model, it suffices to consider a binary-valued reward variable whose defining predicate captures the above conditions, i.e., the variable

$$V_t = \begin{cases} 1 & \text{if } (A_t e_{0,1} > Z_t \geq A_t w_1 e_{0,1} \text{ and} \\ & G_{A_t}(s^*) < \gamma) \text{ or } A_t w_1 e_{0,1} > Z_t \\ 0 & \text{else} \end{cases} \tag{24}$$

The first half of the predicate (to the left of 'or') states condition 1); the second half is just the negation of (17), thereby formalizing condition 2). Hence, $V_t = 1$ if and only if the QOS requirement is violated according to (23). In turn, the performability variable in question can be expressed as

$$Y_T = \frac{\int_u^v V_t \, dt}{v - u} , \tag{25}$$

permitting the evaluation of various measures of Y_T such as its mean and, if feasible, selected points of its probability distribution function.

4. Model Construction and Solution

Using stochastic activity networks (SANs) and Ultra-SAN (see footnote 1), instances of the performability model just described can be constructed and solved as follows. Throughout, we assume a fixed QOS requirement for the admitted connections, namely $P_{\text{sat}} \leq 10^{-9}$, implying a value of $\gamma = 20.72$ for the QOS exponent. We also assume that the fault-free capacity of the channel is fixed at $C = 150$ Mbps. If desired, however, the model can be easily modified so as to incorporate both γ and C as parameters. The quantization factor K is likewise fixed, where we let $K = 15$. (A larger value of K can be considered by expanding the capacity submodel accordingly.) Hence, fluctuations in capacity range over $K + 1 = 16$ equally spaced levels, namely the (Mbps) values in the set

$$\mathcal{C} = \{0, 10, 20, \ldots, 150\}.$$

All other numerical choices are parameterized, permitting a great deal of flexibility in experimenting with various instances of the resulting base model.

4.1. Admissions Submodel

By our general definition (15) of the process A that represents the admitted connections, the maximum value of A_t depends on whether the traffic class is S-VBR or NS-VBR with respect to capacity C. To decide this, the (single) traffic class in question is described by the two parameters whose values fully characterize the class with respect to its EB computation. Specifically, since there is but one traffic class, we simplify notation by letting $e_0 = e_{0,1}$ $w = w_1$. Given the values of these parameters, we decide whether the class is S-VBR or NS-VBR and, in turn, determine the maximum number of connections that can be admitted according to its EB (see Section 3.2). For convenience, we introduce this as an additional parameter, denoted $n_{\max}$, where

$$n_{\max} \leq \begin{cases} \lfloor n_{\max,1} \rfloor & \text{if the traffic class is S-VBR} \\ \lfloor C/e_0 \rfloor & \text{else} \end{cases}$$

($\lfloor x \rfloor$ denotes the *floor of* x), permitting the quantity $n_{\max,1} = C/e_1^m$ to be computed off-line in case the class is S-VBR.

To complete the submodel's formulation, we assume that connection admission requests arrive as a Poisson process with rate *ad_rate* (connections/hr) and that the holding time of a connection is exponentially distributed with mean $1/rel\_rate$ (minutes). Moreover, as just discussed, A_t is bounded according to EB-based admission control, i.e., a connection request at time t is denied (blocked) if $A_t = n_{\max}$. Accordingly, the admissions submodel corresponds to an M/M/$n_{\max}$/$n_{\max}$ queue and is easily specified by a single-place SAN with two exponentially distributed timed activities. The marking of this place at time t is A_t, where a parameter, denoted n_{init}, permits specification of the initial marking (whence $\Pr[A_0 = n_{\text{init}}] = 1$). One of the two timed activities represents the admission of a connection (when the activity completes); the other represents the release of a connection.

4.2. Capacity Submodel

Given that the fault-free capacity is $C = 150$ Mbs, we assume that losses of channel capacity are caused by four

different types of faults, denoted f_0, f_1, f_2, and f_3. Each fault type results in a different capacity reduction, where the loss caused by type f_{i+1} is twice that of f_i. More precisely, so as to conform with our earlier choice of $K + 1 = 16$ capacity levels, for $0 \leq i \leq 3$ we suppose that an occurrence of fault-type i results in a capacity loss of $10 * 2^i$ Mbps. Thus, for example, if fault type f_0 occurs at time t then the capacity Z_t is 10 Mbps less than it was just before the fault occurred; if type f_1 occurs, the reduction is 20Mbps, etc. Once a fault of a given type occurs, a recovery action is initiated and, during the recovery phase, we assume that no other faults of that type occur. However, faults of different types are presumed to occur independently. Hence, it is possible for all four types to be in effect simultaneously (prior to a recovery from any of them), in which case the total capacity reduction is $\sum_{i=0}^{3} 10 * 2^i = 150$ Mbps. In other words, this state of Z corresponds to a complete loss of the channel.

Probabilistically, we make some choices which insure that Z is a time-homogeneous Markov process. Specifically, we assume that, for $0 \leq i \leq 3$, fault-type f_i arrives as a Poisson process with rate a_i (faults/hour) and that its recovery phase has an exponentially distributed duration with mean $1/r_i$ (minutes). If all of these parameters have positive values, the result is a 16-state Markov process. Moreover, Z can be conveniently specified by a SAN with four places (corresponding to the four fault types). Associated with each place are two exponentially distributed timed activities whose completions represent a fault arrival and a fault recovery, respectively. Assuming that the channel is initially fault-free ($\Pr[Z_0 = C] = 1$), the initial marking of each place is 1, signifying the absence all fault types at time $t = 0$.

4.3. Performability Variable Specification and Solution

When the two SANs just described for A and Z are composed (placed side by side), the resulting SAN specifies the product base model (A, Z). As so specified, the latter is a time-homogeneous Markov process with $(n_{\max} + 1) * 16$ states. Although its nature is simple enough to permit manual specification of its generator matrix, as $n_{\max}$ gets larger (e.g., $n_{\max} = 90$ implies 1456 states), this can be a time-consuming task. Using UltraSAN, this matrix is constructed automatically (and almost instantaneously) by invoking the tool's *reduced base model generator*.

However, a much more beneficial advantage of SAN specification is the variety of solution algorithms provided by UltraSAN, particularly the kind of reward model solvers that are suited to performability evaluation. Generally, using UltraSAN's *performability variable editor*, a reward variable is specified by

i) a predicate (stated in terms of place markings and model parameters) which, if true, results in the reward rate given by ii) (if false, the reward rate is 0), and

ii) a function of place markings and parameters that specifies the reward rate, per se.

Specifically, for the reward variable V_t defined by (24), part i) is obtained by expressing the random variables of the predicate

$$(A_t e_0 > Z_t \geq A_t w e_0 \text{ and } G_{A_t}(s^*) < 20.72)$$
$$\text{or } A_t w e_0 > Z_t \tag{26}$$

in terms of place markings and the model's parameters. In particular, A_t is just the marking of the single place of the admissions SAN and Z_t is the weighted sum

$$\sum_{i=0}^{3} 10 * 2^i * MARK(fi),$$

where place fi represents fault-type f_i in the capacity SAN. As already shown, the random variable $G_{A_t}(s^*)$ can be expressed in terms of A_t and Z_t as the sum of (20) and (21); hence, this part of the predicate is similarly accounted for. As for the reward-rate function (part ii)), by the definition of V_t, this rate is always 1 (whenever the predicate holds); hence, this is specified simply as a constant having value 1.

Finally, regarding the performability variable Y_T, the definition given by (25) is generally referred to as *time-averaged accumulated reward* with respect to the reward variable V_t. Using UltraSAN, the expected value of Y_T (the performability measure) can be obtained via the tool's *accumulated reward solver*, where time interval $[u, v]$ is specified in the solver's control panel. In addition, UltraSAN's *pdf solver* can be used to evaluate selected points on the PDF of Y_T, i.e., probabilities of the form $\Pr[Y_T \leq y]$ for selected values of y.

5. Evaluation Results and Their Implications

Using the model just described, the following summarizes the results of several evaluation experiments distinguished by different choices of parameter values for the base model (A, Z). Among other things, the results indicate that the model is indeed valid with respect to known theoretical properties that distinguish various traffic class types (S-VBR, NS-VBR, and bandwidth limited NS-VBR). Indeed, checks against such properties were very helpful in debugging the model's specification. Moreover, the results themselves are interesting since they illustrate how QOS degradation differs according to the multiplexability of the traffic class.

All of the experiments assume the following choices of parameter values for the capacity submodel Z_t, where MTTR denotes the *mean time to recover* from the corresponding fault type.

Fault type f_i	Arrival rate a_i (faults/hour)	MTTR $1/r_i$ (minutes)
f_0	1	2
f_1	0.5	5
f_2	0.25	10
f_3	0.1	60

There is no real justification for these choices; they simply provide what appears to be reasonable example of random channel capacity fluctuations due to faults of the indicated types. Given these parameter values, the steady-state probability distribution of Z_t has a mean value of 137.34 Mbps and a standard deviation of approximately 26 Mbps. A complete loss of capacity occurs very rarely, i.e., in steady state, $\Pr[Z_t = 0] \approx 4*10^{-5}$.

Regarding the admissions submodel A, the connection admission rate is taken to be

$$ad\_rate = 27 \text{ connections/hour}$$

and the mean holding time is

$$1/rel\_rate = 2 \text{ minutes},$$

resulting in an offered load of 0.9 Erlangs. At time $t = 0$, we suppose that there are no admitted connections, i.e., we let $n_{\text{init}} = 0$ and, hence, $\Pr[A_0 = 0] = 1$. However, in view of the above parameter values, this process is in a steady-state condition after a relatively short period of time. The remaining parameters of this submodel characterize the traffic class, per se, where six classes are considered in the six experiments that follow (one class per experiment). These are distinguished by the parameter values indicated in Table 1. The NEB e_0 of a class is specified in Mbps. For the

Exp.	e_0	w	n_{max}	Comments
1	5	0.1	90	S-VBR; SMG ≈ 3.0
2	30	0.01	7	S-VBR; SMG ≈ 1.4
3	5	0.35	35	S-VBR; SMG ≈ 1.2
4	7.5	0.5	20	NS-VBR; not BL
5	10	0.3	15	NS-VBR; not BL
6	15	1.0	10	NS-VBR; BL

Table 1. Traffic classes for the experiments.

S-VBR classes, SMG refers to the *statistical multiplexing gain* of the class, i.e., the ratio of its NEB to its EB. For the NS-VBR classes, BL abbreviates "bandwidth limited" ($w = 1.0$).

Experiment	$E[Y_T]$	$E[Y_{1,T}]$	$E[Y_{2,T}]$	$E[Y_{3,T}]$
1	$1.787506e-05$	$1.682160e-36$	$1.787507e-05$	$7.649926e-06$
2	$3.832134e-03$	$3.124129e-04$	$4.346339e-03$	$7.649901e-06$
3	$1.787507e-05$	$1.682160e-36$	$1.787507e-05$	$7.703254e-06$
4	$5.779344e-05$	$0.000000e+00$	$5.779344e-05$	$1.747107e-05$
5	$8.060584e-05$	$0.000000e+00$	$8.060584e-05$	$9.747280e-06$
6	$3.727401e-04$	$0.000000e+00$	$3.727401e-04$	$3.727401e-04$

Table 2. Evaluation results for busy period $T = [0, 1]$.

Experiment	$E[Y_T]$	$E[Y_{1,T}]$	$E[Y_{2,T}]$	$E[Y_{3,T}]$
1	$5.718949e-05$	$1.940929e-36$	$5.718951e-05$	$2.455540e-05$
2	$9.268044e-03$	$3.386793e-04$	$9.800601e-03$	$2.455532e-05$
3	$5.718951e-05$	$1.940929e-36$	$5.718951e-05$	$2.472596e-05$
4	$1.831420e-04$	$0.000000e+00$	$1.831420e-04$	$5.594009e-05$
5	$2.527479e-04$	$0.000000e+00$	$2.527479e-04$	$3.125983e-05$
6	$1.100605e-03$	$0.000000e+00$	$1.100605e-03$	$1.100605e-03$

Table 3. Evaluation results for busy period $T = [100, 101]$.

The results obtained for each experiment are summarized in Tables 2 and 3 corresponding to two choices of the busy period $T = [u, v]$, both having a 1-hour duration. The first is $T = [0, 1]$, saying (since $Z_0 = 1$ with probability 1) that the channel is fault-free just prior to its use. The busy period assumed for Table 3 is $T = [100, 101]$, at which time the capacity fluctuations have settled into a steady-state condition. (The behavior of the admissions submodel is essentially steady-state during either period.) In addition to the performability variable Y_T in question (25), three other variables are evaluated in order to better understand how admission-capacity differences affect the value of Y_T. The latter are likewise defined in terms of reward variables, namely

$$V_{1,t} = \begin{cases} 1 & \text{if } A_t e_0 > C \\ 0 & \text{else} \end{cases} \quad (27)$$

$$V_{2,t} = \begin{cases} 1 & \text{if } A_t e_0 > Z_t \\ 0 & \text{else} \end{cases} \quad (28)$$

$$V_{3,t} = \begin{cases} 1 & \text{if } A_t w e_0 > Z_t \\ 0 & \text{else} \end{cases} \quad (29)$$

and are averaged over the same time interval $T = [u, v]$. Accordingly, the variable

$$Y_{1,T} = \frac{\int_u^v V_{1,t} dt}{v - u} \quad (30)$$

expresses the fraction of busy period T during which saturation would occur with respect to the CAC-assumed capacity

C. The lower-level performability variable

$$Y_{2,T} = \frac{\int_u^v V_{2,t} dt}{v - u} \quad (31)$$

is the fraction of T during which saturation actually occurs and

$$Y_{3,T} = \frac{\int_u^v V_{3,t} dt}{v - u} \quad (32)$$

is the fraction of T during which the mean aggregate load exceeds the actual capacity. The measures tabulated for each experiment are the expected values of these variables.

5.1. Evidence of Model Correctness

We note first that these results satisfy certain conditions that must hold if the base model and performability variables have been correctly specified. For example, saturation at time t is necessary for a QOS violation at time t and, hence, in terms of the reward variables (24) and (28), $\forall t \in T, V_t = 1 \Rightarrow V_{2,t} = 1$. Therefore, by (25) and (31) and for any $y \geq 0$, $\Pr[Y_T \leq y] \geq \Pr[Y_{2,T} \leq y]$, implying (by a well known characterization of expectation) that $E[Y_T] \leq E[Y_{2,T}]$. In the other direction, instability at time t is sufficient for a QOS violation at time t, which in terms of (24) and (29) says that, $\forall t \in T, V_{3,t} = 1 \Rightarrow V_t = 1$. Reasoning as above, it follows that $E[Y_{3,T}] \leq E[Y_T]$. Hence, if the model is correct, the results obtained for these measures should satisfy both these inequalities, i.e.,

$$E[Y_{3,T}] \leq E[Y_T] \leq E[Y_{2,T}]. \quad (33)$$

An inspection of Tables 2 and 3 confirms that (33) indeed holds for each of the six experiments.

In the case of NS-VBR classes, some additional conditions can likewise be used to check the model's validity. For example, the CAC algorithm will not admit an NS-VBR connection that causes saturation with respect to the assumed capacity C. This is borne out by the $E[Y_{1,T}] = 0$ outcomes for Experiments 4-6. Further, a QOS violation at time t coincides with actual channel saturation at time t; hence, equality must hold on the right side of (33). Comparing the values of measures $E[Y_T]$ and $E[Y_{2,T}]$ for each of Experiments 4-6, we see that they are indeed identical. Moreover, if the class is bandwidth limited ($w = 1$) then the conditions for saturation (16) and instability (17) are the same. This implies that equality holds on both sides of (33), i.e., all three of these measures should have identical values. The results of Experiment 6 demonstrate that the model is valid in this sense.

5.2. Dependence on Initial Conditions

Since the two busy periods considered ($T = [0, 1]$ and $T = [100, 101]$) have the same duration (both represent a busy hour), what distinguishes them is knowledge of the state Z_u of the channel at the time u when the period initiates. (There is also a distinction with respect to the initial state A_u of the admitted connections, but this turns out to be negligible for the parameter values considered.) As noted earlier, since the channel is assumed to be fault-free at time 0, the busy hour for Table 2 begins at a time when the channel is known to have its full capacity of 150 Mbps. On the other hand, the busy hour for Table 3 initiates when the capacity fluctuations are in a steady-state condition.

As one might expect, the mean amount of QOS loss, per the performability measure $E[Y_T]$, is worse for the steady-state busy hour. Specifically, examining the ratio

$$\frac{E[Y_{[100,101]}]}{E[Y_{[0,1]}]}$$

that compares a Table-3 entry with its corresponding entry in Table 2, this ratio ranges from 2.4 (Experiments 2 and 3) to 3.2 (Experiment 1). In other words, the extent of the QOS loss is approximately 2.5 to 3 times the amount experienced when the busy hour begins with a fault-free channel. This is an important observation since it says that even a small amount of added knowledge about the channel's status (namely that it is fully available when use begins) can improve a CAC algorithm's ability to perform in the presence of fluctuating capacity. In particular, this is encouraging for future work which, with various extensions of the admissions submodel, can examine more realistic scenarios regarding the extent of such knowledge. Such comparisons also demonstrate the importance of transient performability

solutions since, without it, the evaluation data for Table 2 could not be obtained.

5.3. Dependence on the Traffic Class

S-VBR Classes

As for differnces in the performability $E[Y_T]$ that exist for a given choice of T, among the S-VBR classes considered (Experiments 1-3), performability is the worst ($E[Y_T]$ is the largest) for Experiment 2. This is likely due to the fact that each connection in this case (see Table 1) requires a considerable allocation of bandwidth (30 Mbps for no saturation) and yet, due to extreme burstiness ($w = 0.01$), this class is S-VBR with respect to the fault-free capacity C. In particular, its SMG permits the CAC algorithm to admit $n_{max} = 7$ connections, i.e., 2 more than the no-saturation maximum of 150/30 = 5 connections. Generally, it can be shown that, under steady-state conditions, the measure $E[Y_{1,T}]$ expresses the steady-state probability of exceeding the no-saturation maximum, i.e., from definitions (27) and (30) it follows that

$$E[Y_{1,T}] = \Pr[A_t > C/e_0]. \qquad (34)$$

Hence, for Experiment 2, this probability (as given by Table 3) is relatively high, i.e., $3.3868*10^{-4}$. By contrast, we see that such probabilities for Experiments 1 and 3 are in the order of 10^{-36}. As a consequence, the class assumed for Experiment 2 is considerably more sensitive to QOS losses caused by capacity reductions.

For S-VBR classes in general, a tempting conjecture is that the value of the performability measure $E[Y_T]$ should vary inversely with SMG. This is based on the intuitive feeling that a traffic class which benefits from the statistical nature of its bit rate is less likely to be affected by random fluctuations in capacity. However, the SMG is determined by the maximum number of connections that can be admitted without compromising the QOS requirement. This ignores other factors, notably the probabilities of experiencing connection demands that are near or equal to this maximum number. Since these probabilities are bounded from above by the probability $\Pr[A_t > C/e_0]$, by (34), the measure $E[Y_{T,1}]$ is indicative of their values. In particular, comparing Experiments 2 and 3, although the class assumed in Experiment 2 has a higher SMG, as noted in the previous paragraph, the value of $E[Y_{1,T}]$ is much, much larger than that of Experiment 3. This appears to explain a resulting performability $E[Y_T]$ that, in comparison with Experiment 3, is worse by two orders of magnitude.

NS-VBR classes

Regarding the three NS-VBR classes (Experiments 4-6), for either choice of T we see that the performability $E[Y_T]$

is worst for the BL class (Experiment 6). Indeed, comparing the values of $E[Y_T]$ for all six experiments in either Table 2 or Table 3, this class results in the greatest amount of QOS loss. However, this is not due to its BL nature. Generally, as we noted earlier (see the last paragraph of Section 5.1), NS-VBR connections experience a QOS violation whenever saturation occurs, i.e., the total allocated bandwidth exceeds the current capacity Z_t. Accordingly, the performability of the CAC algorithm is not affected by the fact that an NS-VBR class is BL. Indeed, given two NS-VBR classes having the same NEB, where one is BL ($w = 1$) and the other it not ($w < 1$), the only difference (all other things being equal) is the extent to which saturation is due to instability. In other words, the values of measure $E[Y_{3,T}]$ can differ but the values of $E[Y_T] = E[Y_{2,T}]$ must be the same for both classes. Although this fact is not illustrated by the experiments of Tables 2 and 3, it has been observed by comparing the classes of Experiments 4 and 5 with their bandwidth limited counterparts.

6. Summary and Suggestions for Future Work

The research presented above is very encouraging in several respects. First of all, it demonstrates that CAC algorithm performability in the presence of fluctuating channel capacity can indeed be evaluated with respect to an appropriately specified base model. Further, the results of a handful of evaluation experiments have already provided valuable insight into how such performability, as quantified by $E[Y_T]$, varies according to the nature of the traffic class. And perhaps most importantly, the base model described in Section 3 provides a framework for a number of worthwhile extensions. Specifically, some interesting possibilities in this regard are the following.

1) Generalize the admissions submodel A so as to represent the control of non-homogeneous traffic ($J > 1$).

2) Extend the base model (A, Z) to permit the admissions submodel to have additional knowledge about the state of the capacity submodel Z. For example, this could represent information passed on by the network management system concerning its estimate of available capacity.

3) Replace the exponential distributions assumed in the current Markov model (those associated with connection arrivals, holding times, fault arrivals, and recovery times) with distributions that conform more closely to what is experienced in actual networks. Assuming that mean values of the old and new distributions coincide, estimations of $E[Y_T]$ obtained by simulation (using UltraSAN) can then be compared with numerical values derived from the Markov model.

4) Alter the capacity submodel so as to represent less severe but more frequent changes in capacity due, say, to transient faults or phenomena such as interfering connection demands (other than those being controlled by the admission algorithm).

5) Replace the channel interpretation of the capacity submodel with that of another resource. For example, Z_t could represent the buffer space in a network node that is available for VBR traffic allocation at time t, where its random nature results from buffer-sharing with uncontrolled sources such as available bit rate (ABR) traffic.

Finally, the performability variable Y_T considered in this study is an instance of a general class of variables which can be defined and evaluated in the same manner. Accordingly, with respect to either the current model or any of the extensions suggested above, other aspects of how CAC is affected by a randomly varying resource can likewise be investigated.

References

[1] A. I. Ewalid, D. Mitra, and R. H. Wentworth. A new approach for allocating buffers and bandwidth to heterogeneous, regulated traffic in an ATM node. *IEEEJSAC*, pages 1115–1127, August 1995.

[2] J. Y. Hui. Resource allocation for broadband networks. *IEEE-JSAC*, pages 1598–1608, June 1988.

[3] F. P. Kelly. Effective bandwidth at multi-class queues. *Queueing Systems*, pages 5–16, September 1991.

[4] J. F. Meyer. Performability: A retrospective and some pointers to the future. *Performance Evaluation*, 14(3-4):139–156, February 1992.

[5] J. F. Meyer. Performability evaluation: Where it is and what lies ahead. In *Proc. 1995 IEEE Int'l Computer Performance and Dependability Symposium*, pages 334–343, Erlangen, Germany, April 1995.

[6] J. F. Meyer, S. Montagna, R. Paglino, and A. Puglisi. Admission control of mixed VBR sources in broadband networks. International patent application no. PCT/IT 98/00373, 1998.

[7] J. W. Roberts, editor. *Performance Evaluation and Design of Multiservice Networks, Final Report of the COST 224 Project*. Commission of the European Communities, Luxembourg, 1992.

[8] W. H. Sanders et al. The UltraSAN modeling environment. *Performance Evaluation*, 24(1):89–115, October-November 1995.

On the Quality of Service of Failure Detectors*

Wei Chen
Oracle Corporation
One Oracle Drive, Nashua, NH 03062, USA
weichen@us.oracle.com

Sam Toueg
DIX Departement d'Informatique
Ecole Polytechnique
91128 Palaiseau Cedex, France
sam@dix.polytechnique.fr

Marcos Kawazoe Aguilera
Department of Computer Science
Cornell University
Ithaca, NY 14853-7501, USA
aguilera@cs.cornell.edu

Abstract

We study the quality of service (QoS) of failure detectors. By QoS, we mean a specification that quantifies (a) how fast the failure detector detects actual failures, and (b) how well it avoids false detections. We first propose a set of QoS metrics to specify failure detectors for systems with probabilistic behaviors, i.e., for systems where message delays and message losses follow some probability distributions. We then give a new failure detector algorithm and analyze its QoS in terms of the proposed metrics. We show that, among a large class of failure detectors, the new algorithm is optimal with respect to some of these QoS metrics. Given a set of failure detector QoS requirements, we show how to compute the parameters of our algorithm so that it satisfies these requirements, and we show how this can be done even if the probabilistic behavior of the system is not known. Finally, we briefly explain how to make our failure detector adaptive, so that it automatically reconfigures itself when there is a change in the probabilistic behavior of the network.

1. Introduction

Fault-tolerant distributed systems are designed to provide reliable and continuous service despite the failures of some of their components. A basic building block of such systems is the *failure detector*. Failure detectors are used in a wide variety of settings, such as network communi- cation protocols [8], computer cluster management [18], group membership protocols [5, 7, 21, 17, 16], etc.

Roughly speaking, a failure detector provides some information on which processes have crashed. This information, typically given in the form of a list of *suspects*, is not always up-to-date or correct: a failure detector may take a long time to start suspecting a process that has crashed, and it may erroneously suspect a process that has not crashed (in practice this can be due to message losses and delays).

Chandra and Toueg [9] provide the first formal specification of *unreliable failure detectors* and show that they can be used to solve some fundamental problems in distributed computing, namely, *consensus* and *atomic broadcast*. This approach was later used and generalized in other works, e.g., [15, 13, 1, 3, 2].

In all of the above works, failure detectors are specified in terms of their *eventual* behavior (e.g., a process that crashes is eventually suspected). Such specifications are appropriate for asynchronous systems, in which there is no timing assumption whatsoever.[1] Many applications, however, have some timing constraints, and for such applications, failure detectors with eventual guarantees are not sufficient. For example, a failure detector that starts suspecting a process one hour after it crashed can be used to solve asynchronous consensus, but it is useless to an application that needs to solve many instances of consensus per minute. Applications that have timing constraints require failure detectors that provide a *quality of service (QoS)* with some quantitative timeliness guarantees.

In this paper, we study the QoS of failure detectors in

---

*Research partially supported by NSF grant CCR-9711403 and an Olin Fellowship.

[1]Even though the *fail-aware* failure detector of [13] is implemented in the "timed asynchronous" model, its specification is for the asynchronous model.

191

systems where message delays and message losses follow some probability distributions. We first propose a set of metrics that can be used to specify the QoS of a failure detector; these QoS metrics quantify (a) how *fast* it detects actual failures, and (b) how *well* it avoids false detections. We then give a new failure detector algorithm and analyze its QoS in terms of the proposed metrics. We show that, among a large class of failure detectors, the new algorithm is optimal with respect to some of these QoS metrics. Given a set of failure detector QoS requirements, we show how to compute the parameters of our algorithm so that it satisfies these requirements, and we show how this can be done even if the probabilistic behavior of the system is not known. The QoS specification and the analysis of our failure detector algorithm is based on the theory of stochastic processes. To the best of our knowledge, this work is the first comprehensive and systematic study of the QoS of failure detectors using probability theory.

1.1. On the QoS Specification of Failure Detectors

We consider message-passing distributed systems in which processes may fail by crashing, and messages may be delayed or dropped by communication links.[2] A failure detector can be *slow*, i.e., it may take a long time to suspect a process that has crashed, and it can make *mistakes*, i.e., it may erroneously suspect some processes that are actually up (such a mistake is not necessarily permanent: the failure detector may later stop suspecting this process). To be useful, a failure detector has to be reasonably fast and accurate.

In this paper, we propose a set of metrics for the QoS specification of failure detectors. In general, these QoS metrics should be able to describe the failure detector's *speed* (how fast it detects crashes) and its *accuracy* (how well it avoids mistakes). Note that speed is with respect to processes that crash, while accuracy is with respect to processes that do not crash.

A failure detector's speed is easy to measure: this is simply the time that elapses from the moment when a process p crashes to the time when the failure detector starts suspecting p permanently. This QoS metric, called *detection time*, is illustrated in Fig. 1.

How do we measure a failure detector's accuracy? It turns out that determining a good set of accuracy metrics is a delicate task. To illustrate some of the subtleties involved, consider a system of two processes p and q connected by a lossy communication link, and suppose that the failure detector at q monitors process p. The output of the failure detector at q is either "I suspect that p has crashed" or "I trust that p is up", and it may alternate between these two outputs from time to time. For the purpose of measuring the

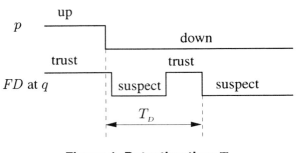

Figure 1. Detection time T_D

accuracy of the failure detector at q, suppose that p does not crash.

Consider an application that queries q's failure detector at random times. For such an application, a natural measure of accuracy is the probability that, *when queried at a random time*, the failure detector at q indicates correctly that p is up. This QoS metric is the *query accuracy probability*. For example, in Fig. 2, the query accuracy probability of FD_1 at q is $12/(12 + 4) = .75$.

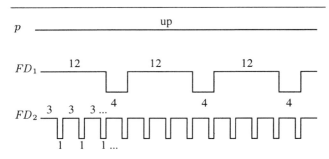

Figure 2. FD_1 and FD_2 have the same query accuracy probability of .75, but the mistake rate of FD_2 is four times that of FD_1

The query accuracy probability, however, is not sufficient to fully describe the accuracy of a failure detector. To see this, we show in Fig. 2 two failure detectors FD_1 and FD_2 such that (a) they have the same query accuracy probability, but (b) FD_2 makes mistakes more frequently than FD_1.[3] In some applications, every mistake causes a costly interrupt, and for such applications the *mistake rate* is an important accuracy metric.

Note, however, that the mistake rate alone is not sufficient to characterize accuracy: as shown in Fig. 3, two failure detectors can have the same mistake rate, but different query accuracy probabilities.

---

[2]We assume that process crashes are permanent, or, equivalently, that a process that recovers from a crash assumes a new identity.

[3]The failure detector *makes a mistake* each time its output changes from "trust" to "suspect" while p is actually up.

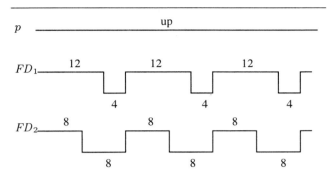

Figure 3. FD_1 and FD_2 **have the same mistake rate** $1/16$, **but the query accuracy probabilities of** FD_1 **and** FD_2 **are** .75 **and** .50, **respectively**

Even when used together, the above two accuracy metrics are still not sufficient. In fact, it is easy to find two failure detectors FD_1 and FD_2, such that (a) FD_1 is better than FD_2 in both measures (i.e., it has a higher query accuracy probability *and* a lower mistake rate), but (b) FD_2 is better than FD_1 in another respect: specifically, whenever FD_2 makes a mistake, it corrects this mistake faster than FD_1; in other words, the *mistake durations* in FD_2 are smaller than in FD_1. Having small mistake durations may be important to some applications.

As it can be seen from the above, there are several different aspects of accuracy that may be important to different applications, and each aspect has a corresponding accuracy metric.

In this paper, we identify six accuracy metrics (since the behavior of a failure detector is probabilistic, most of these metrics are random variables). We then use the theory of stochastic processes to quantify the relation between these metrics. This analysis allows us to select two accuracy metrics as the *primary* ones in the sense that: (a) they are not redundant (one cannot be derived from the other), and (b) together, they can be used to derive the other four accuracy metrics.

In summary, we show that the QoS specification of failure detectors can be given in terms of three basic metrics, namely, the detection time and the two primary accuracy metrics that we identified. Taken together, these metrics can be used to characterize and compare the QoS of failure detectors.

1.2. The Design and Analysis of a New Failure Detector Algorithm

In this paper, we consider a simple system of two processes p and q, connected through a communication link. Process p may fail by crashing, and the link between p and

q may delay or drop messages. Message delays and message losses follow some probabilistic distributions. Process q has a failure detector that monitors p and outputs either "I suspect that p has crashed" or "I trust that p is up" ("suspect p" and "trust p" in short, respectively).

A Common Failure Detection Algorithm and its Drawbacks. A simple failure detection algorithm, commonly used in practice, works as follows: at regular time intervals, process p sends a heartbeat message to q; when q receives a heartbeat message, it trusts p and starts a timer with a fixed timeout value TO; if the timer expires before q receives a newer heartbeat message from p, then q starts suspecting p.

This algorithm has two undesirable characteristics; one regards its accuracy and the other its detection time, as we now explain. Consider the i-th heartbeat message m_i. Intuitively, the probability of a *premature timeout* on m_i should depend solely on m_i, and in particular on m_i's delay. With the simple algorithm, however, the probability of a premature timeout on m_i also depends on the heartbeat m_{i-1} that precedes m_i! In fact, the timer for m_i is started upon the receipt of m_{i-1}, and so if m_{i-1} is "fast", the timer for m_i starts early and this increases the probability of a premature timeout on m_i. This dependency on past heartbeats is undesirable.

To see the second problem, suppose p sends a heartbeat just before it crashes, and let d be the delay of this last heartbeat. In the simple algorithm, q would permanently suspect p only $d + TO$ time units after p crashes. Thus, the worst-case detection time for this algorithm is the *maximum* message delay plus TO. This is impractical because in many systems the maximum message delay is orders of magnitude larger than the average message delay.

The source of the above problems is that even though the heartbeats are sent at regular intervals, the timers to "catch" them expire at irregular times, namely the receipt times of the heartbeats plus a fixed TO. The algorithm that we propose eliminates this problem. As a result, the probability of a premature timeout on heartbeat m_i does *not* depend on the behavior of the heartbeats that precede m_i, and the detection time does *not* depend on the maximum message delay.

A New Algorithm and its QoS Analysis. In the new algorithm, process p sends heartbeat messages $m_1, m_2, \ldots$ to q periodically every η time units (just as in the simple algorithm). To determine whether to suspect p, q uses a sequence $\tau_1, \tau_2, \ldots$ of fixed time points, called *freshness points*, obtained by shifting the sending time of the heartbeat messages by a fixed parameter δ. More precisely, $\tau_i = \sigma_i + \delta$, where σ_i is the time when m_i is sent. For any time t, let i be so that $t \in [\tau_i, \tau_{i+1})$; then q trusts p at time t if and only if q has received heartbeat m_i or higher.

Given the probabilistic behavior of the system (i.e., the probability of message losses and the distribution of message delays), and the parameters η and δ of the algorithm, we determine the QoS of the new algorithm using the theory of stochastic processes. Simulation results given in [10] are consistent with our QoS analysis, and they show that the new algorithm performs better than the common one.

In contrast to the common algorithm, the new algorithm guarantees an upper bound on the detection time, and this bound depends only on the parameters η and δ of the algorithm — not on the probabilistic behavior of the heartbeats.

Moreover, the new algorithm is optimal in the sense that it has the best possible query accuracy probability with respect to any given bound on the detection time. More precisely, we show that among all failure detectors that send heartbeats at the same rate (they use the same network bandwidth) and satisfy the same upper bound on the detection time, the new algorithm has the best query accuracy probability.

The algorithm that we give here assumes that p and q have synchronized clocks. This assumption is not unrealistic, even in large networks. For example, GPS and Cesium clocks are becoming accessible, and they can provide clocks that are very closely synchronized (see, e.g., [23]). In [10], we show how to modify this algorithm so that it works even when synchronized clocks are not available.

Configuring our Algorithm to Meet the Failure Detector Requirements of an Application. Given a set of failure detector QoS requirements (provided by an application), we show how to compute the parameters of our algorithm to achieve these requirements. We first do so assuming that one knows the probabilistic behavior of the system (i.e., the probability distributions of message delays and message losses). We then drop this assumption, and show how to configure the failure detector to meet the QoS requirements of an application even when the probabilistic behavior of the system is not known.

1.3. Related Work

In [14], Gouda and McGuire measure the performance of some failure detector protocols under the assumption that the protocol stops as soon as some process is suspected to have crashed (even if this suspicion is a mistake). This class of failure detectors is less general than the one that we studied here: in our work, a failure detector can alternate between suspicion and trust many times.

In [22], van Renesse *et. al.* propose a scalable gossip-style randomized failure detector protocol. They measure the accuracy of this protocol in terms of the *probability of premature timeouts*.[4] The probability of premature timeouts, however, is not an appropriate metric for the specification of failure detectors in general: it is implementation-

specific and it cannot be used to compare failure detectors that use timeouts in different ways.

In [19], Raynal and Tronel present an algorithm that detects member failures in a group: if some process detects a failure in the group (perhaps a false detection), then all processes report a group failure and the protocol terminates. The algorithm uses heartbeat-style protocol, and its timeout mechanism is the same as the simple algorithm that we described in Section 1.2.

In [23], Veríssimo and Raynal study *QoS failure detectors* — these are detectors that indicate when a service does not meet its quality-of-service requirements. In contrast, this paper studies the QoS *of* failure detectors, i.e., how well a failure detector works.

The probabilistic network model used in this paper is similar to the ones used in [11, 6] for probabilistic clock synchronization.

All proofs and many technical details are omitted here, and they can be found in [10].

2. On the QoS Specification of Failure Detectors

We consider a system of two processes p and q. We assume that the failure detector at q monitors p, and that q does not crash. Henceforth, real time is continuous and ranges from 0 to ∞.

2.1. The Failure Detector Model

The output of the failure detector at q at time t is either S or T, which means that q suspects or trusts p at time t, respectively. A *transition* occurs when the output of the failure detector at q changes: An *S-transition* occurs when the output at q changes from T to S; a *T-transition* occurs when the output at q changes from S to T. We assume that there are only a finite number of transitions during any finite time interval.

Since the behavior of the system is probabilistic, the precise definition of our model and of our QoS metrics uses the theory of stochastic processes. In particular, most of the metrics we proposed are random variables. To keep our presentation at an intuitive level, we omit the technical details related to this theory (they can be found in [10]).

2.2. Primary Metrics

We propose three primary metrics for the QoS specification of failure detectors. The first one measures the speed of a failure detector. It is defined with respect to the runs in which p crashes.

---

[4]This is called "the probability of mistakes" in [22].

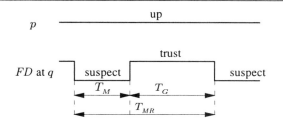

Figure 4. Mistake duration T_M, good period duration T_G, and mistake recurrence time T_{MR}

Detection time (T_D): Informally, T_D is the time that elapses from p's crash to the time when q starts suspecting p permanently. More precisely, T_D is a random variable representing the time that elapses from the time that p crashes to the time when the final S-transition (of the failure detector at q) occurs and there are no transitions afterwards (Fig. 1).[5]

We next define some metrics that are used to specify the accuracy of a failure-detector. Throughout the paper, all accuracy metrics are defined with respect to *failure-free* runs, i.e., runs in which p does not crash.[6] There are two primary accuracy metrics:

Mistake recurrence time (T_{MR}): this measures the time between two consecutive mistakes. More precisely, T_{MR} is a random variable representing the time that elapses from an S-transition to the next one (Fig. 4).

Mistake duration (T_M): this measures the time it takes the failure detector to correct a mistake. More precisely, T_M is a random variable representing the time that elapses from an S-transition to the next T-transition (Fig. 4).

As we discussed in the introduction, there are many aspects of failure detector accuracy that may be important to applications. Thus, in addition to T_{MR} and T_M, we propose four other accuracy metrics in the next section. We selected T_{MR} and T_M as the primary metrics because given these two, one can compute the other four (this will be shown in Section 2.4).

2.3. Derived Metrics

We propose four additional accuracy metrics:

Average mistake rate (λ_M): this measures the rate at which a failure detector make mistakes, i.e., it is the average number of S-transitions per time unit. This metric is important

to long-lived applications where each failure detector mistake (each S-transition) results in a costly interrupt. This is the case for applications such as group membership and cluster management.

Query accuracy probability (P_A): this is the probability that the failure detector's output is correct at a random time. This metric is important to applications that interact with the failure detector by querying it at random times.

Many applications can make progress only during *good periods* — periods in which the failure detector makes no mistakes. This observation leads to the following two metrics.

Good period duration (T_G): this measures the length of a good period. More precisely, T_G is a random variable representing the time that elapses from a T-transition to the next S-transition (Fig. 4).

For short-lived applications, however, a closely related metric may be more relevant. Suppose that an application is started at a random time in a good period. If the *remaining part* of the good period is long enough, the short-lived application will be able to complete its task. The metric that measures the remaining part of the good period is:

Forward good period duration (T_{FG}): this is a random variable representing the time that elapses from a random time at which q trusts p, to the time of the next S-transition.

At first sight, it may seem that, on the average, T_{FG} is just half of T_G (the length of a good period). But this is incorrect, and in Section 2.4 we give the actual relation between T_{FG} and T_G.

2.4. How the Accuracy Metrics are Related

Theorem 1 below explains how our six accuracy metrics are related. We then use this theorem to justify our choice of the primary accuracy metrics. Henceforth, $Pr(A)$ denotes the probability of event A; $E(X)$, $E(X^k)$, and $V(X)$ denote the expected value (or mean), the k-th moment, and the variance of random variable X, respectively.

Parts (2) and (3) of Theorem 1 assume that in failure-free runs, the probabilistic distribution of failure detector histories is *ergodic*. Roughly speaking, this means that in failure-free runs, the failure detector slowly "forgets" its past history: from any given time on, its future behavior may depend only on its recent behavior. We call failure detectors satisfying this ergodicity condition *ergodic failure detectors*. Ergodicity is a basic concept in the theory of stochastic processes [20], but the technical details are substantial and outside the scope of this paper.

Theorem 1 *For any ergodic failure detector, the following results hold: (1)* $T_G = T_{MR} - T_M$. *(2) If* $0 < E(T_{MR}) < \infty$, *then* $\lambda_M = 1/E(T_{MR})$, *and* $P_A = E(T_G)/E(T_{MR})$. *(3) If* $0 < E(T_{MR}) < \infty$ *and* $E(T_G) = 0$, *then* T_{FG} *is always 0.*

---

[5]If there is no such final S-transition, then $T_D = \infty$; if such an S-transition occurs before p crashes, then $T_D = 0$. We henceforth omit the boundary cases of other metrics since they can be similarly defined.

[6]As explained in [10], these metrics are also meaningful for runs in which p crashes.

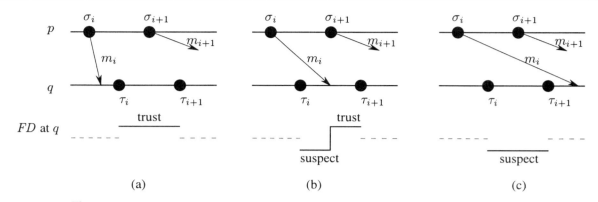

Figure 5. Three scenarios of the failure detector output in one interval $[\tau_i, \tau_{i+1})$

If $0 < E(T_{MR}) < \infty$ and $E(T_G) \neq 0$, then (3a) for all $x \in [0, \infty)$, $Pr(T_{FG} \leq x) = \int_0^x Pr(T_G > y)dy/E(T_G)$, (3b) $E(T_{FG}^k) = E(T_G^{k+1})/[(k+1)E(T_G)]$. In particular, (3c) $E(T_{FG}) = [1 + V(T_G)/E(T_G)^2]E(T_G)/2$.

The fact that $T_G = T_{MR} - T_M$ holds is immediate by definition. The proofs of parts (2) and (3) use the theory of stochastic processes. Part (2) is intuitive, while part (3), which relates T_G and T_{FG}, is more complex. In particular, part (3c) is counter-intuitive: one may think that $E(T_{FG}) = E(T_G)/2$, but part (3c) says that $E(T_{FG})$ is in general larger than $E(T_G)/2$ (this is a version of the "waiting time paradox" in the theory of stochastic processes [4]).

We now explain how Theorem 1 guided our selection of the primary accuracy metrics. Parts (2) and (3) show that λ_M, P_A and T_{FG} can be derived from T_{MR}, T_M and T_G. This suggests that the primary metrics should be selected among T_{MR}, T_M and T_G. Moreover, since $T_G = T_{MR} - T_M$, it is clear that given the joint distribution of any two of them, one can derive the remaining one. Thus, two of T_{MR}, T_M and T_G should be selected as the primary metrics, but which two? By choosing T_{MR} and T_M as our primary metrics, we get the following convenient property that helps to compare failure detectors: if FD_1 is better than FD_2 in terms of both $E(T_{MR})$ and $E(T_M)$ (the expected values of the primary metrics) then we can be sure that FD_1 is also better than FD_2 in terms of $E(T_G)$ (the expected values of the other metric). We would not get this useful property if T_G were selected as one of the primary metrics.

3. The Design and QoS Analysis of a New Failure Detector Algorithm

3.1. The Probabilistic Network Model

We assume that processes p and q are connected by a link that does not create or duplicate messages, but may delay or drop messages. Processes p and q have access to synchronized clocks (the case where synchronized clocks are not available is treated in [10]).

We assume that the message loss and message delay behavior of any message sent through the link is probabilistic, and is characterized by the following two parameters: (a) *message loss probability* p_L, which is the probability that a message is dropped by the link; and (b) *message delay* D, which is a random variable with range $(0, \infty)$ representing the delay from the time a message is sent to the time it is received, under the condition that the message is not dropped by the link. We assume that the expected value $E(D)$ and the variance $V(D)$ of D are finite. Note that our model does not assume that the message delay time D follows any particular distribution, and thus it is applicable to many practical systems.

For simplicity we assume that the probabilistic behavior of the network does not change over time. In Section 6, we explain how to modify the algorithm so that it dynamically adapts to changes in the probabilistic behavior of the system.

3.2. The Algorithm

The new algorithm works as follows. The monitored process p periodically sends heartbeat messages $m_1, m_2, m_3, \ldots$ to q every η time units, where η is a parameter of the algorithm. Every heartbeat message m_i is tagged with its sequence number i. Henceforth, σ_i denotes the sending time of message m_i. The monitoring process q shifts the σ_i's forward by δ — the other parameter of the algorithm — to obtain the sequence of times $\tau_1 < \tau_2 < \tau_3 < \ldots$, where $\tau_i = \sigma_i + \delta$. Process q uses the τ_i's and the times it receives heartbeat messages, to determine whether to trust or suspect p, as follows. Consider time period $[\tau_i, \tau_{i+1})$. At time τ_i, q checks whether it has received some message m_j with $j \geq i$. If so, q trusts

Process p:

1   for all $i \geq 1$, at time $\sigma_i = i \cdot \eta$, send heartbeat m_i to q

Process q:

2   Initialization: $output = S$;   {suspect p initially}

3   for all $i \geq 1$, at time $\tau_i = \sigma_i + \delta$:

4   **if** did not receive m_j with $j \geq i$ **then** $output \leftarrow S$;
           {suspect p if no fresh message is received}

5   upon receive message m_j at time $t \in [\tau_i, \tau_{i+1})$:

6   **if** $j \geq i$ **then** $output \leftarrow T$;
           {trust p when some fresh message is received}

Figure 6. Failure detector algorithm NFD-S with parameters η and δ

---

p during the entire period $[\tau_i, \tau_{i+1})$ (Fig. 5 (a)). If not, q starts suspecting p. If at some time before τ_{i+1}, q receives some message m_j with $j \geq i$ then q starts trusting p from that time until τ_{i+1}. (Fig. 5 (b)). If by time τ_{i+1}, q has not received any message m_j with $j \geq i$, then q suspects p during the entire period $[\tau_i, \tau_{i+1})$ (Fig. 5 (c)). This procedure is repeated for every time period. The detailed algorithm with parameters η and δ is denoted by NFD-S, and is given in Fig. 6.[7]

Note that from time τ_i to τ_{i+1}, only messages m_j with $j \geq i$ can affect the output of the failure detector. For this reason, τ_i is called a *freshness point*: from time τ_i to τ_{i+1}, messages m_j with $j \geq i$ are *still fresh* (useful). With this algorithm, q trusts p at time t if and only if q received a message that is still fresh at time t.

3.3. The QoS Analysis of the Algorithm

We now give the QoS of the algorithm (for a detailed analysis see [10]). We assume that the link from p to q satisfies the following *message independence* property: (a) the message loss and message delay behavior of any message sent by p is independent of whether or when p crashes; and (b) the behaviors of any two heartbeat messages sent by p are independent.[8] Henceforth, let $\tau_0 \stackrel{\text{def}}{=} 0$, and $\tau_i = \sigma_i + \delta$ for $i \geq 1$ (as in line 3 of the algorithm).

We first formalize the intuition behind freshness points and fresh messages:

---

[7] This version of the algorithm is convenient for illustrating the main idea and for performing the analysis. We have omitted some obvious optimizations.

[8] In practice, this holds only if consecutive heartbeats are sent more than some Δ time units apart, where Δ depends on the system. So assuming that the behavior of heartbeats are independent is equivalent to assuming that $\eta > \Delta$.

Lemma 2 *For all $i \geq 0$ and all time $t \in [\tau_i, \tau_{i+1})$, q trusts p at time t if and only if q has received some message m_j with $j \geq i$ by time t.*

The following definitions are for runs where p does not crashes.

Definition 1

(1) For any $i \geq 1$, let k be the smallest integer such that for all $j \geq i + k$, m_j is sent at or after time τ_i.

(2) For any $i \geq 1$, let $p_j(x)$ be the probability that q does not receive message m_{i+j} by time $\tau_i + x$, for every $j \geq 0$ and every $x \geq 0$; let $p_0 = p_0(0)$.

(3) For any $i \geq 2$, let q_0 be the probability that q receives message m_{i-1} before time τ_i.

(4) For any $i \geq 1$, let $u(x)$ be the probability that q suspects p at time $\tau_i + x$, for every $x \in [0, \eta)$.

(5) For any $i \geq 2$, let p_S be the probability that an S-transition occurs at time τ_i.

The above definitions are given in terms of i, a positive integer. Proposition 3, however, shows that they are actually independent of i.

Proposition 3 *(1) $k = \lceil \delta / \eta \rceil$. (2) For all $j \geq 0$ and for all $x \geq 0$, $p_j(x) = p_L + (1 - p_L) Pr(D > \delta + x - j\eta)$. (3) $q_0 = (1 - p_L) Pr(D < \delta + \eta)$. (4) For all $x \in [0, \eta)$, $u(x) = \prod_{j=0}^{k} p_j(x)$. (5) $p_S = q_0 \cdot u(0)$.*

By definition, if $p_0 = 0$ then for every $i \geq 1$, the probability that q receives m_i by time τ_i is 1. Thus, if $p_0 = 0$ then, with probability one, q trusts p forever after time τ_1. Similarly, it is easy to see that if $q_0 = 0$ then, with probability one, q suspects p forever. So $p_0 = 0$ and $q_0 = 0$ are degenerated cases of no interest. We henceforth assume that $p_0 > 0$ and $q_0 > 0$.

The following theorem summarizes our QoS analysis of the new failure detector algorithm.

Theorem 4 *Consider a system with synchronized clocks, where the probability of message losses is p_L, and the distribution of message delays is $P(D \leq x)$. The failure detector NFD-S of Fig. 6 with parameters η and δ has the following properties.*

(1) The detection time is bounded:

$$T_D \leq \delta + \eta. \tag{3.1}$$

(2) The average mistake recurrence time is:

$$E(T_{MR}) = \frac{\eta}{p_S}. \tag{3.2}$$

(3) The average mistake duration is:

$$E(T_M) = \frac{\int_0^{\eta} u(x) \, dx}{p_S}. \tag{3.3}$$

From $E(T_{MR})$ and $E(T_M)$ given in the theorem above, we can easily derive the other accuracy measures using Theorem 1. For example, we can get the query accuracy probability $P_A = 1 - E(T_M)/E(T_{MR}) = 1 - 1/\eta \cdot \int_0^\eta u(x)\,dx$.

Theorem 4 (1) shows an important property of the algorithm: the detection time is bounded, and the bound does not depend on the behavior of message delays and losses.

In Section 4, we show how to use Theorem 4 to compute the failure detector parameters, so that the failure detector satisfies some QoS requirements (given by an application).

3.4. An Optimality Result

Among all failure detectors that send heartbeats at the same rate and satisfy the same upper bound on the detection time, the new algorithm provides the best query accuracy probability. More precisely, let $\mathcal{C}$ be the class of failure detector algorithms A such that in every run of A, process p sends heartbeats to q every η time units and A satisfies $T_D \leq T_D^U$ for some constant T_D^U. Let A^* be the instance of the new failure detector algorithm NFD-S with parameters η and $\delta = T_D^U - \eta$. By part (1) of Theorem 4, we know that $A^* \in \mathcal{C}$. We can show that

Theorem 5 *For any $A \in \mathcal{C}$, let P_A be the query accuracy probability of A. Let P_A^* be the query accuracy probability of A^*. Then $P_A^* \geq P_A$.*

4. Configuring the Failure Detector to Satisfy QoS Requirements

Suppose we are given a set of failure detector QoS requirements (the QoS requirements could be given by the application that uses this failure detector). We now show how to compute the parameters η and δ of our failure detector algorithm, so that these requirements are satisfied. We assume that (a) the local clocks of processes are synchronized, and (b) one knows the probabilistic behavior of the messages, i.e., the message loss probability p_L and the distribution of message delays $Pr(D \leq x)$. In Section 5, we consider the case when (b) does not hold, and in [10] we treat the case when both (a) and (b) do not hold.

We assume that the QoS requirements are expressed using the primary metrics. More precisely, a set of QoS requirements is a tuple (T_D^U, T_{MR}^L, T_M^U), where T_D^U is an upper bound on the detection time, T_{MR}^L is a lower bound on the average mistake recurrence time, and T_M^U is an upper bound on the average mistake duration. In other words, the

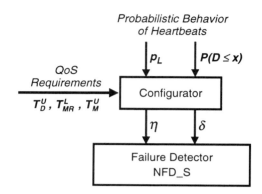

Figure 7. Meeting QoS requirements with NFD-S. The probabilistic behavior of heartbeats is given

requirements are that:[9]

$$T_D \leq T_D^U, \quad E(T_{MR}) \geq T_{MR}^L, \quad E(T_M) \leq T_M^U. \qquad (4.4)$$

Our goal, illustrated in Fig. 7, is to find a configuration procedure that takes as inputs (a) the QoS requirements, namely T_D^U, T_{MR}^L, T_M^U, and (b) the probabilistic behavior of the heartbeat messages, namely p_L and $Pr(D \leq x)$, and outputs the failure detector parameters η and δ so that the failure detector satisfies the QoS requirements in (4.4). Furthermore, to minimize the network bandwidth taken by the failure detector, we want a configuration procedure that finds the largest intersending interval η that satisfy these QoS requirements.

Using Theorem 4, our goal can be stated as a mathematical programming problem:

$$\begin{aligned} \text{maximize} \quad & \eta \\ \text{subject to} \quad & \delta + \eta \leq T_D^U \qquad (4.5) \\ & \frac{\eta}{p_S} \geq T_{MR}^L \qquad (4.6) \\ & \frac{\int_0^\eta u(x)\,dx}{p_S} \leq T_M^U \qquad (4.7) \end{aligned}$$

where the values of $u(x)$ and p_S are given by Proposition 3. Solving this problem is hard, so instead we show how to find some η and δ that satisfy (4.5)–(4.7) (but the η that we find may not be the largest possible). To do so, we replace (4.7) with a simpler and stronger constraint, and then compute

---

[9]Note that the bounds on the primary metrics $E(T_{MR})$ and $E(T_M)$ also impose bounds on the derived metrics, according to Theorem 1. More precisely, we have $\lambda_M \leq 1/T_{MR}^L$, $P_A \geq (T_{MR}^L - T_M^U)/T_{MR}^L$, $E(T_G) \geq T_{MR}^L - T_M^U$, and $E(T_{FG}) \geq (T_{MR}^L - T_M^U)/2$.

the optimal solution of this modified problem (see [10] for more details). We obtain the following procedure to find η and δ:

- *Step 1*: Compute $q_0' = (1 - p_L)Pr(D < T_D^U)$, and let $\eta_{\max} = q_0'T_M^U$.

- *Step 2*: Let $f(\eta) =$

$$\frac{\eta}{q_0' \prod_{j=1}^{\lceil T_D^U/\eta \rceil - 1} [p_L + (1 - p_L)Pr(D > T_D^U - j\eta)]}.$$
(4.8)

Find the largest $\eta \leq \eta_{\max}$ such that $f(\eta) \geq T_{MR}^L$. To find such an η, we can use a simple numerical method, such as binary search (this works because when η decreases, $f(\eta)$ increases exponentially fast).

- *Step 3*: Set $\delta = T_D^U - \eta$.

Theorem 6 *Consider a system with synchronized clocks. With the parameters η and δ obtained by the above procedure, the failure detector algorithm NFD-S of Fig. 6 satisfies the QoS requirements given in (4.4).*

As an example of the configuration procedure of the failure detector, suppose we have the following QoS requirements: (a) a crash failure is detected within 30 seconds, i.e., $T_D^U = 30\,s$; (b) on average, the failure detector makes at most one mistake per month, i.e., $T_{MR}^L = 30$ days $= 2\,592\,000\,s$; (c) on average, the failure detector corrects its mistakes within one minute, i.e. $T_M^U = 60\,s$. Assume that the message loss probability is $p_L = 0.01$, the distribution of message delay D is exponential, and the average message delay $E(D)$ is $0.02\,s$. By inputting these numbers into the configuration procedure, we get $\delta = 20.03\,s$ and $\eta = 9.97\,s$. With these parameters, our failure detector satisfies the given QoS requirements.

5. Dealing with Unknown Message Behavior

In Section 4, our procedure to compute the parameters η and δ of NFD-S to meet some QoS requirements assumed that one knows the probability p_L of message loss and the distribution $Pr(D \leq x)$ of message delays. This assumption is not unrealistic, but in some systems the probabilistic behavior of messages may not be known. In that case, it is still possible to compute η and δ, as we now explain. We proceed in two steps: (1) we first show how to compute η and δ using only p_L, $E(D)$ and $V(D)$ (recall that $E(D)$ and $V(D)$ are the expected value and variance of message delays, respectively); (2) we then show how to estimate p_L, $E(D)$ and $V(D)$.

Computing Failure Detector Parameters η and δ Using p_L, $E(D)$ and $V(D)$. With $E(D)$ and $V(D)$, we can bound $Pr(D > t)$ using the following *One-Sided Inequality* of probability theory (e.g., see [4], p.79): For any random variable D with a finite expected value and a finite variance,

$$Pr(D > t) \leq \frac{V(D)}{V(D) + (t - E(D))^2}, \text{ for all } t > E(D).$$
(5.9)

With this, we can derive the following bounds on the QoS metrics of algorithm NFD-S.

Theorem 7 *Consider a system with synchronized clocks and assume $\delta > E(D)$. For algorithm NFD-S, we have $E(T_{MR}) \geq \eta/\beta$, $E(T_M) \leq \eta/\gamma$, $P_A \geq 1 - \beta$, $E(T_G) \geq (1 - \beta)\eta/\beta$, and $E(T_{FG}) \geq (1 - \beta)\eta/(2\beta)$, where*

$$\beta = \prod_{j=0}^{k_0} \frac{V(D) + p_L(\delta - E(D) - j\eta)^2}{V(D) + (\delta - E(D) - j\eta)^2},$$

$$k_0 = \lceil (\delta - E(D))/\eta \rceil - 1,$$

and

$$\gamma = \frac{(1 - p_L)(\delta - E(D) + \eta)^2}{V(D) + (\delta - E(D) + \eta)^2}.$$

Theorem 7 can be used to compute the parameters η and δ of the failure detector NFD-S, so that it satisfies the QoS requirements given in (4.4). The configuration procedure is given below. This procedure assumes that $T_D^U > E(D)$, i.e., the required detection time is greater than the average message delay (a reasonable assumption).

- *Step 1*: Compute $\gamma' = (1 - p_L)(T_D^U - E(D))^2/(V(D) + (T_D^U - E(D))^2)$ and let $\eta_{\max} = \min(\gamma' T_M^U, T_D^U - E(D))$.

- *Step 2*: Let $f(\eta) =$

$$\eta \cdot \prod_{j=1}^{\lceil (T_D^U - E(D))/\eta \rceil - 1} \frac{V(D) + (T_D^U - E(D) - j\eta)^2}{V(D) + p_L(T_D^U - E(D) - j\eta)^2}.$$
(5.10)

Find the largest $\eta \leq \eta_{\max}$ such that $f(\eta) \geq T_{MR}^L$.

- *Step 3*: Set $\delta = T_D^U - \eta$.

Notice that the above procedure does not use the distribution $Pr(D \leq x)$ of message delays; it only uses p_L, $E(D)$ and $V(D)$.

Theorem 8 *Consider a system with synchronized clocks. With parameters η and δ computed by the above procedure, the failure detector algorithm NFD-S of Fig. 6 satisfies the QoS requirements given in (4.4), provided that $T_D^U > E(D)$.*

Estimating p_L, $E(D)$ and $V(D)$. It is easy to estimate p_L, $E(D)$ and $V(D)$ using heartbeat messages. For example, to estimate p_L, one can use the sequence numbers of the heartbeat messages to count the number of "missing" heartbeats, and then divide this count by the highest sequence number received so far. To estimate $E(D)$ and $V(D)$, we use the synchronized clocks as follows: When p sends a heartbeat m, p timestamps m with the sending time S, and when q receives m, q records the receipt time A. In this way, $A - S$ is the delay of m. We then compute the average and variance of $A - S$ for multiple past heartbeat messages, and thus obtain accurate estimates for $E(D)$ and $V(D)$.

6. Concluding Remarks

An Adaptive Failure Detector. In this paper, we assumed that the probabilistic behavior of heartbeat messages does not change. In some networks, this may not be the case. For instance, a corporate network may have one behavior during working hours (when the message traffic is high), and a completely different behavior during lunch time or at night (when the system is mostly idle): During peak hours, the heartbeat messages may have a higher loss rate, a higher expected delay, and a higher variance of delay, than during off-peak hours. Such networks require a failure detector that *adapts* to the changing conditions, i.e., it dynamically reconfigures itself to meet some given QoS requirements.

It turns out that we can use the configuration procedure given in Section 5 to make our failure detector adaptive. The idea is to periodically estimate the *current* values of p_L, $E(D)$ and $V(D)$ using the n most recent heartbeats. These estimates are then fed into the configuration procedure to recompute new failure detector parameters η and δ.

The above adaptive algorithm forms the core of a failure detection service that is currently being implemented and evaluated [12]. This service is intended to be shared among many different concurrent applications, each with a different set of QoS requirements. The failure detector in this architecture dynamically adapts itself not only to changes in the network condition, but also to changes in the current set of QoS demands (as new applications are started and old ones terminate).

References

[1] M. K. Aguilera, W. Chen, and S. Toueg. On quiescent reliable communication. *SIAM Journal on Computing*. To appear.

[2] M. K. Aguilera, W. Chen, and S. Toueg. Using the heartbeat failure detector for quiescent reliable communication and consensus in partitionable networks. *Theoretical Computer Science*, 220(1):3–30, June 1999.

[3] M. K. Aguilera, W. Chen, and S. Toueg. Failure detection and consensus in the crash-recovery model. *Distributed Computing*, 2000. To appear.

[4] A. O. Allen. *Probability, Statistics, and Queueing Theory with Computer Science Applications*. Academic Press, 2nd edition, 1990.

[5] Y. Amir, D. Dolev, S. Kramer, and D. Malkhi. Transis: a communication sub-system for high availability. In *Proceedings of the 22nd Annual International Symposium on Fault-Tolerant Computing*, pages 76–84, Boston, July 1992.

[6] K. Arvind. Probabilistic clock synchronization in distributed systems. *IEEE Transactions on Parallel and Distributed Systems*, 5(5):475–487, May 1994.

[7] O. Babaoğlu, R. Davoli, L.-A. Giachini, and M. G. Baker. Relacs: a communications infrastructure for constructing reliable applications in large-scale distributed systems, 1994. BROADCAST Project deliverable report, Department of Computing Science, University of Newcastle upon Tyne, UK.

[8] R. Braden, editor. *Requirements for Internet Hosts-Communication Layers*. RFC 1122, Oct. 1989.

[9] T. D. Chandra and S. Toueg. Unreliable failure detectors for reliable distributed systems. *Journal of the ACM*, 43(2):225–267, Mar. 1996.

[10] W. Chen. *On the Quality of Service of Failure Detectors*. PhD thesis, Cornell University, May 2000.

[11] F. Cristian. Probabilistic clock synchronization. *Distributed Computing*, 3(3):146–158, 1989.

[12] B. Deianov and S. Toueg. Personal communication, 2000.

[13] C. Fetzer and F. Cristian. Fail-aware failure detectors. In *Proceedings of the 15th Symposium on Reliable Distributed Systems*, pages 200–209, Oct. 1996.

[14] M. G. Gouda and T. M. McGuire. Accelerated heartbeat protocols. In *Proceedings of the 18th International Conference on Distributed Computing Systems*, May 1998.

[15] R. Guerraoui, M. Larrea, and A. Schiper. Non blocking atomic commitment with an unreliable failure detector. In *Proceedings of the 14th IEEE Symposium on Reliable Distributed Systems*, pages 41–50, Sept. 1995.

[16] M. G. Hayden. *The Ensemble System*. PhD thesis, Department of Computer Science, Cornell University, Jan. 1998.

[17] L. E. Moser, P. M. Melliar-Smith, D. A. Argarwal, R. K. Budhia, and C. A. Lingley-Papadopoulos. Totem: A fault-tolerant multicast group communication system. *Commun. ACM*, 39(4):54–63, Apr. 1996.

[18] G. F. Pfister. *In Search of Clusters*. Prentice-Hall, Inc., 2nd edition, 1998.

[19] M. Raynal and F. Tronel. Group membership failure detection: a simple protocol and its probabilistic analysis. *Distributed Systems Engineering Journal*, 6(3):95–102, 1999.

[20] K. Sigman. *Stationary Marked Point Processes, an Intuitive Approach*. Chapman & Hall, 1995.

[21] R. van Renesse, K. P. Birman, and S. Maffeis. Horus: a flexible group communication system. *Commun. ACM*, 39(4):76–83, Apr. 1996.

[22] R. van Renesse, Y. Minsky, and M. Hayden. A gossip-style failure detection service. In *Proceedings of Middleware '98*, Sept. 1998.

[23] P. Veríssimo and M. Raynal. Time, clocks and temporal order. In S. Krakowiak and S. K. Shrivastava, editors, *Recent Advances in Distributed Systems*, chapter 1. Springer-Verlag, 2000. to appear.

Session 8B

Theory

Fault-Secure Scheduling of Arbitrary Task Graphs to Multiprocessor Systems

Koji Hashimoto
Hitachi Research Laboratory
Hitachi, Ltd.
Hitachi-city, Ibaraki 319-1292, Japan
khasimo@gm.hrl.hitachi.co.jp

Tatsuhiro Tsuchiya   Tohru Kikuno
Department of Informatics and Mathematical Science
Osaka University
Toyonaka-city, Osaka 560-8531, Japan
{t-tutiya, kikuno}@ics.es.osaka-u.ac.jp

Abstract

In this paper, we propose new scheduling algorithms to achieve fault security in multiprocessor systems. We consider scheduling of parallel programs represented by directed acyclic graphs with arbitrary computation and communication costs. A schedule is said to be 1-fault-secure if the system either produces correct output for a parallel program or it detects the presence of any single fault in the system. Although several 1-fault-secure scheduling algorithms have been proposed so far, they can all only be applied to a class of tree-structured task graphs with a uniform computation cost. In contrast, the proposed algorithms can generate a 1-fault-secure schedule for any given task graph with arbitrary computation costs. Applying the new algorithms to two kinds of practical task graphs (Gaussian elimination and LU-decomposition), we conduct simulations. Experimental results show that the proposed algorithms achieves 1-fault security at the cost of small increase in schedule length.

1. Introduction

In recent years, much research has been conducted on methods for high reliability multiprocessor scheduling under various system models (e.g., [8, 13]). This paper focuses on fault-secure multiprocessor scheduling. The goal of fault-secure scheduling is to detect errors in computation of parallel programs carried out on multiprocessor systems. The basic approach to achieving fault security is to duplicate every task of a program and compare outputs of copies to ensure that either the output of the program is correct or at least one of the comparisons reports the existence of errors.

The concept of fault security was originally introduced in logic circuit design [7]. A circuit is *fault-secure* if for any single fault within the circuit, the circuit either produces correct output or produces a non-codeword. Banerjee and Abraham [1] first applied this concept to multiproces-

sor scheduling. Gu et al. [3] have investigated the formal characterization of fault-secure multiprocessor schedules by introducing the concept of *k-fault-secure scheduling*. In a *k*-fault-secure schedule, the output of a system is guaranteed to be either correct or tagged as incorrect for up to *k* processor faults. In their model, a parallel program is composed of a set of tasks and represented by a directed acyclic graph, and the number of processors is unlimited. Some scheduling algorithms have been proposed to achieve 1-fault security in [3]. More recently, Wu et al. [14] proposed an optimal fault-secure scheduling algorithm. Given the number of processors, the algorithm generates a 1-fault-secure schedule with the minimum schedule length.

However, the algorithms proposed in [3] and [14] assume that communication costs are negligible and all tasks have a uniform unit execution time. Moreover, these algorithms can only be applied to a class of tree-structured task graphs.

In this paper, we propose a new scheduling algorithm for achieving 1-fault security in multiprocessor systems with a distributed memory architecture, in which processors communicate with each other solely by message-passing. For comparison purposes, we also present a straightforward algorithm. We consider parallel programs represented by directed acyclic graphs with arbitrary computation and communication costs. Multiprocessor scheduling for most precedence-constrained task graphs is an NP-complete problem in its general form [2]. The algorithms we propose in this paper are heuristic; that is, schedules they produce are not necessarily optimal.

It is well known that inter-processor communication has serious effects on the performance of parallel processing. *Task duplication* [9] is an effective technique for improving the performance by reducing overheads of the communication. This technique eliminates communication delays by duplicating tasks among PEs. The technique thus improves the start times of tasks that need to wait for their preceding tasks, and also improves the finish time of the given program consequently.

In our approach to achieving 1-fault security, every task

in the given task graph is replicated, and equality tests are carried out between the copies. The proposed algorithms schedule copies of tasks based on the task duplication technique to achieve better performance while maintaining 1-fault-secure properties.

2. Preliminaries

2.1. System and Task Model

We consider a multiprocessor system that consists of n identical processing elements (PEs) and that runs one application program at a time. All PEs are fully connected with each other via a reliable network. A PE can execute tasks and communicate with another PE at the same time. This is typical with dedicated I/O processors and direct memory access.

A parallel program is represented by a weighted directed acyclic graph (DAG) $G = (V, E, w, c)$, where V is the set of nodes and E is the set of edges. Each node represents a task v, and is assigned a computation cost $w(v)$, which indicates the task execution time. Each edge $< v, v' > \in E$ from v to v' corresponds to the precedence constraint that task v' cannot start its execution before receiving all necessary data from task v. Given an edge $< v, v' >$, v is called an *immediate predecessor* of v', while v' is called an *immediate successor* of v. If there exists a path from v' to v, v' is called a *predecessor* of v. A task that has no immediate successors is called an *output task*. Each edge is assigned a communication cost $c(v, v')$, which indicates the time required for transferring necessary data between different PEs. If the data transfer is done within the same PE, the communication cost is zero. In the following, we call such a weighted DAG a *task graph*. Various applications are known to be represented by weighted DAGs (e.g., [12]). Figure 1 shows examples of task graphs. In the figure, the number adjacent to each node represents the execution time of the task represented by the node, and the number on each edge is the communication cost for data transfer.

We introduce some definitions and terminology as in [6]. For a path in a task graph, its *length* is defined as the summation of task execution times along the path excluding communication delays. The *level* of a task is defined as the length of the longest path from the node representing the task to a node that has no successor nodes. In Figure 1(a), for example, the levels of v_6 and v_7 are 9 and 2, respectively. Finally, the *height* of a task is defined as

$$height(v) = \begin{cases} 0, & U = \emptyset, \\ 1 + \max_{u \in U} height(u), & U \neq \emptyset, \end{cases}$$

where U is a set of immediate successors of v. In Figure 1(a), for example, the heights of v_6 and v_7 are 3 and 0, respectively.

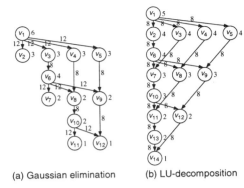

(a) Gaussian elimination   (b) LU-decomposition

Figure 1. Task graphs.

2.2. Scheduling

In general, multiprocessor scheduling refers to the process in which tasks in a given task graph are assigned to PEs and the time slots in which the tasks are executed are determined. When more than one copy of each task is allowed to be scheduled, it is also necessary to specify from which copies to which copies data are transferred.

To distinguish between a task $v \in V$ and its scheduled copies, we call the latter the *instances* of v. We represent by $D(s) = (\alpha_1, \alpha_2, \cdots, \alpha_r)$ the fact that the instance s of v receives necessary data from $\alpha_1, \alpha_2, \cdots, \alpha_r$ which are instances of the immediate predecessors of v. By definition, r is equal to the number of the immediate predecessors. We always write α_i's in ascending order of the indices of the corresponding tasks.

Fault-secure scheduling, as discussed here, refers to producing a schedule with which even if any single fault occurs, the system can either produce the correct result for a given program or detect the fault. We call such a schedule a *1-fault-secure schedule* [3]. The goal of our research is to minimize the schedule length while achieving 1-fault security.

In our approach to achieving the 1-fault security property, every task $v \in V$ is replicated to produce at least two copies of its output and equality tests are carried out between different copies of some tasks. To do so, we need to allocate *tests* to PEs, in addition to the normal tasks of V. A test reports either "*equal*" or "*not equal*" according to the equality of the outputs of the copies compared. A fault is detected when some test reports "*not equal*". We assume that the outcome of a test carried out on a fault-free PE is always correct.

We use the notation $\tau(\alpha_1, \alpha_2, \cdots, \alpha_m)$ to indicate a test that compares the outputs of instances $\alpha_1, \alpha_2, \cdots, \alpha_m$ of the same task. Each test requires time for execution, and receiving data for comparison also incurs a communication delay. However the computation and communication costs of tests do not have any effect on the correctness of the proposed algorithms. Thus we do not introduce notations to represent these costs in this paper.

2.3. Fault Model and 1-Fault-Secure Schedule

We assume that a fault in a PE can result in errors in the outputs of an arbitrary set of instances of tasks and tests allocated to the PE. We call such a set a *fault pattern* if it is not empty, that is, a fault pattern is a non-empty subset of instances of tasks and tests that consists of all the instances whose outputs can be made erroneous directly by a fault in the system.

If a task receives erroneous outputs of other tasks, then the task itself may or may not become erroneous. We assume that an error in an instance of task causes a (possibly empty) subset of instances that receive data from that instance to be erroneous [4].

As in [3, 4], we introduce the notion of *interpretation*, which represents a possible error scenario.

Definition 1 (Interpretation) Given a schedule S, an *interpretation* I for S is a set $\sum = \{c, e, n, \mu_1, \mu_2, \cdots\}$ of *labels*, with distinguished labels "c", "e", "n", together with an assignment of a label to each instance of S such that:

1. each instance of a task is assigned a label from $\sum - \{e, n\}$, and

2. each instance of a test is labeled either "e" or "n".

In the definition, "c" means "*correct*", whereas μ_i represents an erroneous value of an output. Therefore, an instance of a task labeled "c' produces a correct output value, while an instance assigned a label μ_i outputs an erroneous value. The labels "e" and "n" represent the two possible outcomes of a test, "*equal*" and "*not equal*" respectively. In the following, we use $Label_I(s)$ as the label assigned by an interpretation I to an instance s of S.

The next definition gives the rule of producing scenarios for a given fault pattern.

Definition 2 (Consistency of Interpretation)
Given a schedule S and a fault pattern P', an interpretation I of S is *consistent* with P' if and only if the following conditions are satisfied.

(A) for an instance s of a task, if $Label_I(s) \neq$ "c", then either $s \in P'$ or there is at least one instance α in $D(s)$ such that $Label_I(\alpha) \neq$ "c".

(B) for an instance t of a test $\tau(\alpha_1, \alpha_2, \cdots, \alpha_m)$, if $Label_I(t) =$ "e", then either $t \in P'$ or $Label_I(\alpha_1) = Label_I(\alpha_2) = \cdots = Label_I(\alpha_m)$.

(C) for an instance t of a test $\tau(\alpha_1, \alpha_2, \cdots, \alpha_m)$, if $Label_I(t) =$ "n", then either $t \in P'$ or $Label_I(\alpha_i) \neq Label_I(\alpha_j)$ for some α_i and α_j ($i \neq j, 1 \leq i, j \leq m$).

(D) for two instances, s and s', of a task, with $D(s) = (\alpha_1, \alpha_2, \cdots, \alpha_r)$ and $D(s') = (\alpha_1', \alpha_2', \cdots, \alpha_r')$, if $s, s' \notin P'$ and $Label_I(\alpha_q) = Label_I(\alpha_q')$ for all q ($1 \leq q \leq r$), then $Label_I(s) = Label_I(s')$.

(E) for two instances, s and s', of a task, with $D(s) = (\alpha_1, \alpha_2, \cdots, \alpha_r)$ and $D(s') = (\alpha_1', \alpha_2', \cdots, \alpha_r')$, if $s, s' \notin P'$ and there exists at least one α_q ($1 \leq q \leq r$) such that $Label_I(\alpha_q) \neq Label_I(\alpha_q')$, then $Label_I(s) \neq Label_I(s')$.

Condition (A) implies that in any valid scenario for a fault pattern P', the output of s can be erroneous only if either s is computed on the faulty PE or one of the instances of the immediate predecessors of v is erroneous. Conditions (B) and (C) indicate that the outcome of a test carried out on a non-faulty PE is determined by the labels of instances participating in the test, while a valid scenario may assign "e" or "n" arbitrarily to tests carried out on the faulty PE. Condition (D) states that different instances of a task computed on non-faulty PEs with identical input values must have the same output value. Condition (E) is the assumption that instances of a task computed on non-faulty PEs with different input values from each other must have different output values.

Based on the concept of interpretation, we define a 1-fault-secure schedule as follows.

Definition 3 (1-Fault-Secure schedule) A schedule S is 1-fault-secure if and only if for every fault pattern P' and for every interpretation I that is consistent with P', $Label_I(s) =$ "c" for every instance s of every output task, or there exists at least one instance t of a test such that $Label_I(t) =$ "n".

3. 1-Fault-Secure Scheduling Algorithms

In this section, we present two scheduling algorithms STR and $TDFS$ to achieve the 1-fault security property. Both algorithms tag each instance with "0" or "1", which we call the *version number*.

3.1. Straightforward Algorithm

A simple way of achieving 1-fault security is to simply duplicate a non-fault-secure schedule. We refer to this algorithm as STR. Algorithm STR produces the non-fault-secure schedule by applying DSH, which is a (non-fault-secure) scheduling algorithm proposed by Kruatrachue [9]. Figure 2 shows an example of applying STR. In the figure,

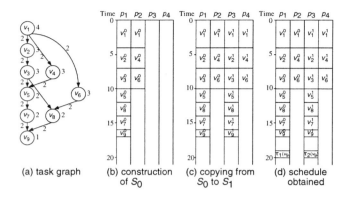

Time	p_1	p_2	p_3	p_4
0	v_1^0	v_1^0		
5	v_2^0	v_4^0		
	v_3^0	v_6^0		
10	v_5^0			
	v_8^0			
15	v_7^0			
	v_9^0			
20				

(b) construction of S_0

Time	p_1	p_2	p_3	p_4
0	v_1^0	v_1^0	v_1^1	v_1^1
5	v_2^0	v_4^0	v_2^1	v_4^1
	v_3^0	v_6^0	v_3^1	v_6^1
10	v_5^0		v_5^1	
	v_8^0		v_8^1	
15	v_7^0		v_7^1	
	v_9^0		v_9^1	
20				

(c) copying from S_0 to S_1

Time	p_1	p_2	p_3	p_4
0	v_1^0	v_1^0	v_1^1	v_1^1
5	v_2^0	v_4^0	v_2^1	v_4^1
	v_3^0	v_6^0	v_3^1	v_6^1
10	v_5^0		v_5^1	
	v_8^0		v_8^1	
15	v_7^0		v_7^1	
	v_9^0		v_9^1	
20	$\tau_1(v_9)$		$\tau_2(v_9)$	

(d) schedule obtained

(a) task graph

Figure 2. Illustrative example of Algorithm STR.

v^i denotes an instance of v tagged with "i", and $\tau(v)$ denotes a test in which all instances of v participate. S_0 and S_1 are non-fault-secure schedules generated by DSH.

In a schedule generated by STR, every instance tagged with "0" exchanges necessary data only with other instances within S_0, while every instance tagged with "1" does so with other instances within S_1. In other words, each instance tagged with "0" never receive any data from instances tagged with "1", and vice versa. Clearly, therefore, the system needs to compare only the results of the output tasks. The method of scheduling tests is explained in the following subsection because it is common to Algorithm $TDFS$.

The time complexity of DSH is known to be $O(|V|^4)$ [9], where $|V|$ denotes the number of tasks in the task graph. As explained in Section 3.3, the complexity of scheduling one test is $(O(|V|^2)$. Therefore, the complexity of STR is $O(|V|^4)$.

3.2. Task Duplication Based Algorithm

In this section, we propose a new 1-fault-secure scheduling algorithm, which we refer to as $TDFS$. Algorithm $TDFS$ schedules each task based on *task duplication* [9], which can improve performance. $TDFS$ also tags every instance with either "0" or "1", and allocates tests by using this information. Unlike STR, however, $TDFS$ allows tasks with different version numbers to be allocated to the same PE. In addition to output tasks, therefore, it may be necessary to test other tasks. $TDFS$ examines whether a test is needed or not when each instance is scheduled. Tests are scheduled after all the instances of tasks have been scheduled. The outline of $TDFS$ is described below.

Algorithm $TDFS$
Input: G, a task graph; P, a set of PEs $\{p_1, p_2, \cdots, p_n\}$ $(n \geq 2)$

Output: S, a 1-fault-secure schedule
Begin
  $S :=$ empty; $TQ :=$ empty
  /*TQ is a set of tasks that need to be tested.*/
  Partitioning:
    Partition the set of tasks in G into task groups $G_1, \cdots, G_m$
    according to height.
    /*Task groups are arranged in descending order of height.*/
  Apply Basic algorithm BA to each task group:
    For $i = 1$ to m do
      $S := BA(G_i, TQ, S)$
    End_For
    Put all output tasks into TQ
  Schedule tests for tasks in TQ:
    $S := TST(TQ, S)$
End

3.2.1 Partitioning

In $TDFS$, a given set of tasks is first partitioned into subsets according to their heights in such a way that all tasks with the same height will belong to one subset. We call each subset a *task group*. For example, consider the task graph in Figure 1(a). The set of all tasks is partitioned into five task groups as follows.

$$G_1 : \quad v_1 \qquad G_2 : \quad v_3 \qquad G_3 : \quad v_3, v_6$$
$$G_4 : \quad v_5, v_8 \quad G_5 : \quad v_9, v_{10} \quad G_6 : \quad v_2, v_7, v_{11}, v_{12}$$

3.2.2 Basic Algorithm

Once the program has been partitioned into task groups, the Basic algorithm described in this section is applied to each task group. This algorithm consists of two steps.

In Step 1, all tasks in the given task group are scheduled and tagged with "0". The tasks are scheduled one by one according to their priorities (the task with the highest priority is scheduled first). Priorities are assigned in descending order of level. Tasks at the same level are prioritized according to the number of immediate successors (the task with the greatest number of immediate successors is given the highest priority).

Now suppose that $v \in G_i$ is the task to be scheduled. Note that all tasks in G_1, G_2, $\cdots$, G_{i-1} have already been scheduled, i.e., a partial schedule S' already exists. In Step 1, v is scheduled to one of the n PEs by adding its instance, say s. All instances scheduled in Step 1, including s, are tagged with "0", The PE on which s will be placed is determined by repeating the following process for every PE.

First, the earliest start time of s is computed, given that s is scheduled on the PE. This can be done by calling Procedure TDP [9]. Once the start time of s on that PE has been obtained, instances from which s receives data are determined. According to the concept of task duplication, TDP may duplicate predecessors of v in order to improve the start time of s. Therefore, for each immediate predecessor ip of v, there often exists more than one instance of ip that can send data to s so that s can receive data before the designated start time. For each ip, the algorithm checks whether or not an instance of ip exists that is tagged with "0" and can deliver data to s before the start time. If there is such an instance, it is chosen; otherwise, another instance of ip which is tagged with "1" is chosen.

If predecessors of v are duplicated by TDP, instances which provide data to those predecessor instances are also determined as described above. Scheduling the new instance may necessitate testing some other tasks. Based on the state of data exchanges between instances, the algorithm determines which tasks, if any, need to be tested. Such tasks are put into a queue TQ called a *test queue*. The details of how these tasks are determined are shown later.

After repeating this process for all PEs, the task is scheduled to the PE that can execute it earliest among all the PEs. If there is more than one such PE, then a PE is chosen such that the tasks needed to be tested is minimized.

In Step 2, all tasks in the task group are duplicated and tagged with "1". The newly duplicated copies are scheduled in the same order as in Step 1. The PE to each is scheduled is determined in the same way as in Step 1, except that (1) an instance is never scheduled to the same PE where its corresponding task was scheduled in Step 1, and (2) instances tagged with "1" rather than "0" are chosen first as instances for receiving data. Consequently, every task is allocated to at least two different PEs.

The tasks to be tested are determined as follows. Suppose that an instance s of v is scheduled on a PE p. Let i be the version number of s ($i = 0, 1$). Then we test every predecessor a of v that satisfies one of the following two conditions.

1. a is an immediate predecessor of v and s receives data from an instance of a that is tagged with "$1 - i$", or

2. a is a predecessor of v and an instance of a that is tagged with "$1 - i$" is already assigned to p.

The pseudo-code of the Basic algorithm is given below.

Basic algorithm BA
Input: G_i, a task group; TQ, a test queue; S', a partial schedule
Output: S, a partial schedule
Begin
    Arrange tasks in G_i according to their priorities
    Step 1:
        For each task v in G_i do
            For each PE p in P do
                $DTlst[p] :=$ NULL
                /*$DTlst$ is a list containing duplicated predecessors of v.*/
                $TTlst[p] :=$ NULL
                /*$TTlst$ is a list containing tasks that need to be tested.*/

                $ST[p] := TDP(v, p, DTlst[p])$
                /*$ST[p]$ is the earliest start time of v on p.*/
                $TTlst[p] := CKT(v, p, DTlst[p], S')$
                /*Put tasks that need to be tested into $TTlst[p]$.*/
            End_For
            $p_t :=$ the PE whose $ST[p_t]$ is the smallest
            Schedule v^0 with $DTlst[p_t]$ to p_t at time $ST[p_t]$
            Put tasks in $TTlst[p_t]$ into TQ.
        End_For
    Step 2:
        For each task v in G_i do
            $p_a :=$ the PE to which v has been scheduled in Step 1
            For each PE p in $P - \{p_a\}$ do
                $DTlst[p] :=$ NULL; $TTlst[p] :=$ NULL
                $ST[p] := TDP(v, p, DTlst[p])$
                $TTlst[p] := CKT(v, p, DTlst[p], S')$
            End_For
            $p_t :=$ the PE where $ST[p_t]$ is the smallest
            Schedule v^1 with $DTlst[p_t]$ to p_t at time $ST[p_t]$
            Put tasks in $TTlst[p_t]$ into TQ.
        End_For
End

Algorithm for checking whether test is needed CKT
Input: v_a, an assigned task; p_a, assigned PE candidate;
       $DTlst[p_a]$, a list of tasks duplicated; S', a partial schedule
Output: $TTlst[p_a]$, list of tasks needed to be tested;
Begin
    For each instance v in $DTlst[p_a] \cup \{v_a\}$ do
        For each immediate predecessor α of v do
            flag $:= NECESSARY$
            If α is in $DTlst[p_a]$ Then flag $:= UNNECESSARY$
            Else
                For each instance α_i of α in S' do
                    If (the arrival time of data from α_i to v
                        $\leq$ the start time of v on p_a) and
                    (the version number of $\alpha_i =$ that of v) Then
                      flag $:= UNNECESSARY$; Break
                    End_If
                End_For
            End_If
            If (flag $= NECESSARY$) Then put v into $TTlst[p_a]$
        End_For
        For each predecessor x of v do
            If (x is on p_a) and (the version number of $x \neq$ that of v)
                Then put x into $TTlst[p_a]$
        End_For
    End_For
End

3.2.3 Scheduling of Tests

After the instances of all tasks have been scheduled, tests for the tasks in TQ are scheduled. A test for a task v is assigned to a PE p where neither instances of v nor instances of its predecessors are assigned. If there is more than one

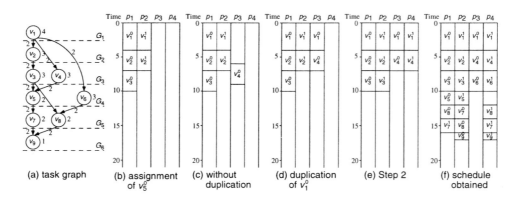

Figure 3. Illustrative example of Basic algorithm.

qualifying PE, the one on which the test can be executed earliest is selected.

If there is no such PE, the test is duplicated and scheduled in such a way that each of the two copies is executed on a different PE from each other.

All the instances of v in S participate in the test. Note that there may be more than two instances of v in S, because v may be duplicated by Procedure TDP as successors of v are scheduled. Therefore, tests are not necessarily binary equality checks, unlike in [3, 4, 14].

Scheduling Algorithm for Tests TST
Input: TQ, a test queue; S', a partial schedule
Output: S, a 1-fault-secure schedule
Begin
  For each task v in TQ do
    Find PEs to which no instances of v or its predecessors are assigned, and put them into AP.
    If ($AP \neq$ NULL) Then
      For each PE p in AP do
        $ST[p]$:= the earliest start time of the test τ on p.
      p_t := the PE where $ST[p_t]$ is the smallest
      Schedule τ to p_t at time $ST[p_t]$
    Else
      For each PE p in P do
        $ST[p]$:= the earliest start time of the test τ_1 on p.
      p_{t_1} := the PE whose $ST[p_{t_1}]$ is the smallest
      Schedule τ_1 to p_{t_1} at time $ST[p_{t_1}]$
      For each PE p in $P - \{p_{t_1}\}$ do
        $ST[p]$:= the earliest start time of the test τ_2 on p.
      p_{t_2} := the PE whose $ST[p_{t_2}]$ is the smallest
      Schedule τ_2 to p_{t_2} at time $ST[p_{t_2}]$
    End_If
  End_For
End

3.2.4 Time complexity

The complexity of task level and height calculation is $O(|E|)$, where $|E|$ denotes the number of edges in the task graph. Each instance of a task is scheduled by applying Procedure TDP to n PEs both in Step 1 and in Step 2 of the Basic algorithm. The computational complexity of Procedure TDP is known to be $O(|V|^3)$ [9], where $|V|$ denotes the number of tasks in the task graph. Therefore, the complexity of scheduling of one instance is $O(n|V|^3)$. When calculating the start time of an instance on each PE, $TDFS$ checks whether its predecessors need to be tested or not. The complexity of this check is $O(n|V|^2)$. Also, the computational complexity of scheduling one test is $O(|V|^2)$. Since $|E| < |V|^2$ and the number of task is $|V|$, the complexity of $TDFS$ is $O(|V|^4)$, given that n is fixed.

3.2.5 Illustrative Example

Figures 3 and 4 illustrate how Algorithm $TDFS$ works. In this example, we assume that the number of PEs, n, is four and that the task graph shown in Figure 3(a) is given. The set of tasks is partitioned into six task groups G_1, G_2, $\cdots$, G_6. Tasks in each task group are ordered according to their priorities as follows.

$$G_1: \quad v_1 \qquad G_2: \quad v_2 \qquad G_3: \quad v_3, v_4$$
$$G_4: \quad v_5, v_6 \qquad G_5: \quad v_7, v_8 \qquad G_6: \quad v_9$$

These task groups are ordered according to their heights. Then the Basic algorithm is applied to each task group in order. The task group whose height is the largest is selected first.

Now suppose that task groups G_1 and G_2 have been scheduled. Then the Basic algorithm is applied to G_3. In Step 1, each task in G_3 is scheduled, and its instance is tagged with "0". This is done by applying Procedure TDP to each PE. For example, an instance of v, which is indicated by v_4^0 in Figure 3, is scheduled as follows. As shown in Figure 3(b), an instance of v_3 (indicated by v_3^0) has already been assigned to p_0. It can be seen that the start times of v_4^0 on p_1 and on p_2 are 10 and 7, respectively. The start time of v_4^0

208

would be 6 on p_3 if no instances were duplicated, as shown in Figure 3(c). (Note that v_4 must receive necessary data from v_1.) In order to improve the start time of v_4^0, TDP applies *task duplication*. Figures 3(c) and (d) illustrate the concept of task duplication. In this case, TDP duplicates v_1 and schedules another instance to p_3 at time 0. (All instances generated in Step 1 are tagged with "0".) As a result of this duplication, v_4^0 can receive necessary data directly from v_1 without any communication delay, and the start time of v_4^0 on p_3 becomes 4. As a result, p_3 can start execution of v_4^0 earlier than p_1 and p_2. Therefore, v_4^0 is scheduled to p_3 as shown in Figure 3(d).

In Step 2, each task in G_3 is duplicated and scheduled to one of the n PEs other than the PE to which its instance is already scheduled. For example, since an instance of v_4 (v_4^0) is already scheduled to p_3 in Step 1, TDP is applied to p_1, p_2, and p_4. As a result, an instance tagged with "1" (v_4^1) is scheduled to p_4. (All instances generated in Step 2 are tagged with "1".) Similarly, each remaining task is scheduled so as to be executed on two different PEs as shown in Figure 3(e).

The Basic algorithm is applied to the remaining task groups G_4, G_5 and G_6. As a result, a schedule is obtained as shown in Figure 3(f).

When TDP calculates the start time of an instance on a PE, $TDFS$ also checks whether the predecessors of the instance need to be tested or not. For example, when an instance of v_7 with version number "0" (v_7^0) is scheduled to p_2, the algorithm decides to test four tasks; namely, v_1, v_2, v_3 and v_5, because v_7^0 receives data directly from v_5^1, and for v_1, v_2, v_3, which are all predecessors of v_7, their instances tagged with "1" are already assigned to p_2 (v_1^1, v_2^1, v_3^1).

Finally, TQ becomes $\{v_1, v_2, v_3, v_5, v_9\}$, and tests for these tasks are scheduled. In this example, since v_1, which is a common predecessor to the tasks in TQ, is assigned to all PEs, every test is duplicated and assigned to two distinct PEs. As a result, a 1-fault-secure schedule is obtained as shown in Figure 4(b).

4. Correctness Proof of Proposed Algorithms

In this section, we present a sketch of the correctness proof of Algorithm $TDFS$. For complete proofs of Algorithms STR and $TDFS$, readers are referred to [5].

In the following proofs, we let S denote a schedule generated by $TDFS$. As in [3, 4], we introduce an MVC_DAG $G' = (V', E')$ for S, where V' is the set of nodes and E' is the set of edges. G' represents the state of data exchanges between instances in S, i.e., G' is unique to S. Each node represents an instance of a task in S. If an instance s' receives necessary data from another instance s, then there is an edge from s to s'. If there exists a path from s' to s, we call s' an *ancestor* of s. Figure 4(c) shows an example of an

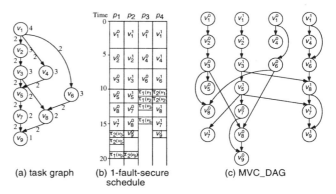

Figure 4. Example of MVC_DAG.

MVC_DAG for the schedule in Figure 4(b).

Lemma 1 For every fault pattern P' and for every interpretation I consistent with P', if a task v is tested in S, then the following conditions hold.
[Case 1:] If there exists only one instance t of the test in S, the following two conditions hold for every pair of instances, s and s', of v, where s and s' have different version numbers.

1. if $Label_I(s) \neq Label_I(s')$, then the test reliably reports "*not equal*", i.e., $Label_I(t) = $ "n".

2. if the outcome of the test is unreliable, then $Label_I(s) = Label_I(s') = $ "c".

[Case 2:] If there are two instances of the test in S, the following condition holds for every pair of instances, s and s', of v, where s and s' have different version numbers.

1. if $Label_I(s) \neq Label_I(s')$, then one of the two instances of the test, t_1 or t_2 reliably reports "*not equal*", i.e., $Label_I(t_1) = $ "n" or $Label_I(t_2) = $ "n".

Proof: If $Label_I(s) \neq Label_I(s')$, then there exists at least one ancestor of s or s', say x, in P'. In Case 1, the algorithm never assigns the test to PEs where s, s', or their ancestors have been scheduled. Therefore, $t \notin P'$, that is, the outcome of t is reliable. Consequently, t reliably reports "*not equal*". If t is not reliable, i.e., $t \in P'$, then for the same reason mentioned above, the labels of all the instances of v and its ancestors must be "c". That is, $Label_I(s) = Label_I(s') = $ "c".

In Case 2, there are two instances of the test in S. Each of them has been assigned to a different PE. Since only one PE is assumed to be faulty, it is obvious that either $t_1 \notin P'$ or $t_2 \notin P'$. Therefore, if $Label_I(s) \neq Label_I(s')$, then either t_1 or t_2 reliably reports "*not equal*". □

Lemma 2 Let s and s' be two instances of a task v, each with a different version number, and let $D(s) = (\alpha_1, \alpha_2, \cdots, \alpha_r)$ and $D(s') = (\alpha_1', \alpha_2', \cdots, \alpha_r')$. For every fault pattern

P' and for every interpretation I consistent with P', if $Label_I(s) = Label_I(s') \neq$ "c", then the following conditions hold.

[Case 1:] If $s \notin P'$ and $s' \notin P'$, then $Label_I(\alpha_q) = Label_I(\alpha'_q)$ for all q $(1 \leq q \leq r)$ and there exists at least one p $(1 \leq p \leq r)$ such that $Label_I(\alpha_p) = Label_I(\alpha'_p) \neq$ "c".

[Case 2:] If $s \in P'$ and $s' \notin P'$, then $Label_I(\alpha'_p) \neq$ "c" holds for some p $(1 \leq p \leq r)$.

Proof: In Case 1, from conditions (A), (D) and (E) in Definition 2, it is clear that $Label_I(s) = Label_I(s') \neq$ "c" if and only if the condition described above holds. In Case 2, it is clear from condition (A) in Definition 2 that if $Label_I(s') \neq$ "c", then $Label_I(\alpha'_p) \neq$ "c" for some p $(1 \leq p \leq r)$. (Note that $s \in P'$ and $s' \in P'$ never hold simultaneously.) □

Lemma 3 Let s and s' be two instances of a task v, each with a different version number. For every fault pattern P' and for every interpretation I consistent with P', if $Label_I(s) = Label_I(s') \neq$ "c", then there exists an instance t of some test in S such that $Label_I(t) =$ "n".

Proof: We prove this by induction.

[Base Step] From the definition of height, no tasks in the task group G_1 have immediate predecessors. Therefore, if $v \in G_1$, then $Label_I(s) = Label_I(s') =$ "c" or $Label_I(s) \neq Label_I(s')$ holds. Next, suppose $v \in G_2$ and $Label_I(s) = Label_I(s') \neq$ "c". When $s, s' \notin P'$, by Lemma 2, there is an instance α such that $Label(\alpha) \neq c$ and α is both in $D(s)$ and in $D(s')$. In this case, whichever version number α is tagged with, $TDFS$ guarantees that the task corresponding to α is tested. Lemma 1 also ensures that the test for α reliably reports "*not equal*". When $s \in P'$ and $s' \notin P'$, s' receives data from an instance assigned to the same PE as s. Due to the rule of assigning tests, a test is assigned for this instance, and by Lemma 1 it reliably reports "*not equal*".

[Induction Step] Assume that the lemma holds if $v \in G_1 \cup G_2 \cup \cdots \cup G_k (k \geq 2)$. Now suppose $v \in G_{k+1}$ and $Label_I(s) = Label_I(s') \neq$ "c". Then two cases must be considered, namely, [Case 1:] $s \notin P'$ and $s' \notin P'$, and [Case 2:] $s \in P'$ and $s' \notin P'$. For Case 1, we can prove that there is a test that reports "not equal" by Lemma 1 and Lemma 2. For Case 2, we can prove this by Lemma 1. Thus the lemma follows. (For a complete proof, see [5].) □

Theorem 1 $TDFS$ generates 1-fault-secure schedules.

Proof: Suppose that an instance of an output task v is labelled with an erroneous value. Then, by Lemma 3, there is a test that reports "not equal", or there is another instance of v that is labelled with "c". Also in the latter case, there

is a test that reliably reports "*not equal*" by Lemma 1, since all output tasks are tested. Thus the theorem follows from the definition of a 1-fault-secure schedule. □

5. Experimental Evaluation

5.1. Simulation Environment

Using a large number of task graphs as a workload, we performed simulations for comparison studies of Algorithms STR and $TDFS$. In the simulations, we used task graphs for two practical parallel computations: Gaussian elimination [10] and LU-decomposition [11]. These task graphs can be characterized by the size of the input matrix because the numbers of tasks and edges in the task graph depends on the size. For example, the task graph for Gaussian elimination shown in Figure 1(a) is for a matrix of size 3. The number of nodes in these task graphs is roughly $O(N^2)$, where N is the size of matrix. In the simulation, we varied the matrix sizes so that the graph sizes ranged from about 100 to 400 nodes. For each task graph size, we generated six different graphs for ccr values of 0.1, 0.5, 1.0, 2.0, 5.0 and 10.0 by varying communication delays. The *communication-to-computation ratio* (ccr) is defined as follows [10].

$$ccr = \frac{\text{average communication delay between tasks}}{\text{average execution time of tasks}}$$

In the simulation, for each task graph, the execution time of a test is set to the smallest execution time of tasks, and the communication cost between a test and tasks is set to the average communication delay between tasks.

As a baseline, we used the finish time of a (non-fault-secure) schedule generated by DSH. All results presented in this section are normalized to this length. In the studies, we considered two cases: the number of PEs $n = 8$, and $n = 16$.

5.2. Evaluation Results

Figures 5 and 6 show the simulation results for Gaussian elimination and LU-decomposition task graphs, respectively. The value of ccr is fixed to 5, and the matrix size is varied so that the number of tasks in the corresponding task graph ranges from 100 to 400. The results show that $TDFS$ outperforms STR. As the matrix size increases, the difference between the performance of $TDFS$ and that of STR increases. The following reason is conjectured. In general, as the size of the task graph increases, its parallelism also increases (here, parallelism means the maximum number of tasks that can be executed in parallel at a time). We can take advantage of the parallelism only if we have a sufficient number of PEs. In this simulation, the number of PEs n is fixed regardless of the size of task graph. Therefore, as the matrix size increases, $TDFS$ can extract more parallelism than STR because STR can essentially use only $n/2$ PEs.

Figures 7 and 8 show the simulation results when the matrix size is 24. In this simulation, we varied the value of ccr from 0.1 to 10.0. In both kinds of task graphs, when the value of ccr is small, e.g., $ccr < 1.0$, STR shows better performance than $TDFS$. In most cases, the number of tests in a schedule obtained by STR is smaller than $TDFS$ because STR requires tests for the output tasks only. Note that as communication delays decrease, the amount of idle time between tasks, which is available for scheduling tests by $TDFS$, decreases. As a result, $TDFS$ has worse performance than STR. On the other hand, when $ccr \geq 1.0$, $TDFS$ shows better performance than STR.

Compared with the non-fault-secure scheduling algorithm DSH, $TDFS$ achieved 1-fault security at the cost of a small increase in schedule length. For example, in the case where $n = 16$ and $ccr \geq 1$, $TDFS$ achieved 1-fault security with less than 20% overhead. (Note that each result is normalized to the schedule length of DSH.)

6. Conclusions

In this paper, we proposed two multiprocessor scheduling algorithms, STR and $TDFS$, to achieve 1-fault security. We showed that the time complexity of these algorithms is $O(|V|^4)$, where $|V|$ is the number of tasks in the given task graph.

We performed simulation studies using two kinds of task graphs for practical parallel computation; namely, Gaussian elimination and LU-decomposition. As a result, it was found that $TDFS$ outperforms STR especially when the value of ccr is large ($ccr \geq 1.0$).

A drawback of $TDFS$ is its running time. For example, for a Gaussian elimination task graph with matrix size = 24 (the number of tasks is 297), it took 8391 seconds to produce a 1-fault-secure schedule. (We conducted the simulations on a COMPAQ XP1000 workstation.) We consider improving the running time as future work.

References

[1] P. Banerjee and J. A. Abraham, "Fault-secure algorithms for multiple processor systems," Proc. of *11th Int'l Symp. on Computer Architecture*, pp. 270-287, 1984.

[2] H. El-Rewini, H. H. Ali, and T. Lewis, "Task scheduling in multiprocessing systems," *IEEE Computer*, vol. 28, no. 12, pp. 27-37, 1995.

[3] D. Gu, D. J. Rosenkrantz, and S. S. Ravi, "Construction and analysis of fault-secure multiprocessor schedules," Proc. of *21th IEEE Int'l Symp. on Fault-Tolerant Computing*, pp. 120-127, 1991.

[4] D. Gu, D. J. Rosenkrantz, and S. S. Ravi, "Fault/error models and their impact on reliable multiprocessor schedules," Proc. of *IEEE Workshop on Fault-Tolerant Parallel and Distributed Systems*, pp. 176-184, 1992.

[5] K. Hashimoto, "Multiprocessor scheduling algorithms for high reliability," PhD dissertation, Dept. of Informatics and Mathematical Science, Osaka University, 2000.

[6] K. Hashimoto, T. Tsuchiya, and T. Kikuno, "A multiprocessor scheduling algorithm for low overhead fault-tolerance," Proc. of *17th IEEE Int'l Symp. on Reliable Distributed Systems*, pp. 186-194, 1998.

[7] B. W. Johnson, "Design and Analysis of Fault-Tolerant Digital Systems," Addison-Wesley, 1989.

[8] S. Kartik and C. Siva Ram Murthy, "Task allocation algorithms for maximizing reliability of distributed computing systems," *IEEE Trans. Computers*, vol. 46, no. 6, pp. 719-724, 1997.

[9] B. Kruatrachue, "Static task scheduling and grain packing in parallel processing systems," PhD dissertation, Electrical and Computer Eng. Dept., Oregon State Univ., Corvallis, 1987.

[10] Y.-K. Kwok and I. Ahmad, "Dynamic critical-path scheduling: an effective technique for allocating task graphs to multiprocessors," *IEEE Trans. Parallel and Distributed Systems*, vol. 7, no. 5, pp. 506-521, 1996.

[11] R. E. Lord, J. S. Kowalik, and S. P. Kumar, "Solving linear algebraic equations on an MIMD computer," *J. ACM*, vol. 30, no. 1, pp. 103-117, 1983.

[12] K. R. Pattipati, T. Kurien, R. -T. Lee, and P. B. Luh, "On mapping a tracking algorithm onto parallel processors," *IEEE Trans. Aerospace and Electronic Systems*, vol. 26, no. 5, pp. 774-791, 1990.

[13] S. Tridandapani, A. K. Somani, and U. R. Sandadi, "Low overhead multiprocessor allocation strategies exploiting system spare capacity for fault-detection and location," *IEEE Trans. Computers*, vol. 44, no. 7, pp. 865-877, 1995.

[14] J. Wu, E. B. Fernandez, and D. Dai, "Optimal fault-secure scheduling," *Computer Journal*, vol. 41, no. 4, pp. 208-222, 1998.

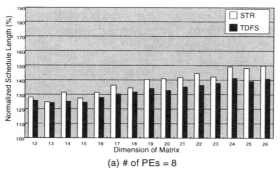

(a) # of PEs = 8

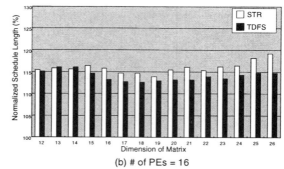

(b) # of PEs = 16

Figure 5. Results for Gaussian elimination task graphs.

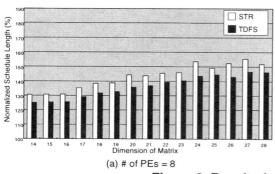

(a) # of PEs = 8

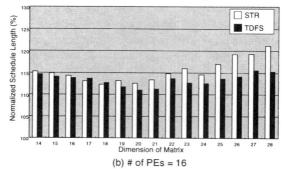

(b) # of PEs = 16

Figure 6. Results for LU-decomposition task graphs.

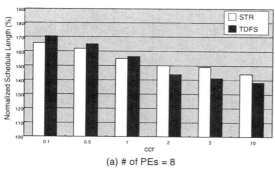

(a) # of PEs = 8

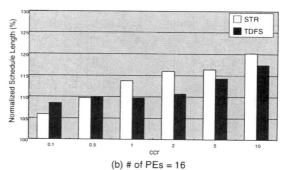

(b) # of PEs = 16

Figure 7. Results for Gaussian elimination task graphs.

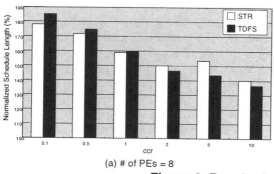

(a) # of PEs = 8

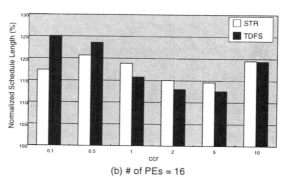

(b) # of PEs = 16

Figure 8. Results for LU-decomposition task graphs.

Diagnosis of Regular Structures

Antonio Caruso[2], Stefano Chessa[1], Piero Maestrini[1,2], Paolo Santi[1,2].

[1] *Istituto di Elaborazione dell'Informazione, Area della Ricerca del CNR di Pisa – S. Cataldo, 56100 Pisa, Italy.*
[2] *Dipartimento di Informatica, University of Pisa, Corso Italia 40, 56125 Pisa, Italy.*

Abstract

This paper introduces an efficient diagnosis algorithm for regular structures (EDARS). The algorithm provides a diagnosis which is correct, but possibly incomplete, if the cardinality of the actual fault set is below a "syndrome-dependent bound", asserted by the algorithm itself. The time complexity of EDARS is $O(nt)$ when executed on t-regular structures of size n.

The correctness and the completeness degree of EDARS, were evaluated by means of simulation. Grids, hypercubes and Cube-Connected Cycles (CCC) structures were considered. Simulation results with grid structures showed a strong influence of structure degree over diagnosis performance. Furthermore, comparisons of simulation results obtained with hypercubes, CCCs, and grids of same size and degree, showed that diameter and bisection width also appear to influence the performance of EDARS, particularly with respect to diagnosis completeness.

1 Introduction

System-level diagnosis, which was introduced by Preparata, Metze and Chien [1], aims at diagnosing systems composed by units (usually processors) connected by point-to-point bidirectional links. A system S is represented by the *system graph* $G=(N,E)$, an undirected graph where node set N represents the units and edge set E represents the links. Edge (u,v) exists if and only if units u and v are interconnected. The cardinality[1] $n=\#N$ is called the size of the system. If edge (u,v) exists, units u and v are said to be *adjacent*, denoted $u \leftrightarrow v$.

Diagnosis is based on tests between units. The *testing* unit u provides a test sequence as input to the *tested* unit v, which returns an output sequence to u. The testing unit compares the actual and the expected output sequences and provides a binary test outcome (0 if the actual and the expected results match, 1 otherwise).

The PMC model assumes that tests of faulty units performed by non-faulty units always return 1 (that is, the test has perfect coverage), while the test outcome of the tests performed by faulty units is arbitrary. This invalidation rule is shown in Table 1. Similar diagnostic models assume different invalidation rule [2] or are based on comparisons between units [3]. In the PMC model, every test requires a bidirectional link between the testing and the tested unit. In this paper it is assumed that tests are reciprocal and that any two units u,v with $(u,v) \in E$ test each other.

In the following, notation $u \xrightarrow{\gamma} v$ denotes the test of unit v performed by unit u with outcome $\gamma \in \{0,1\}$. Notation $u \xleftrightarrow{\delta \quad \gamma} v$ denotes both the test of unit v performed by u with outcome γ and the test of unit u performed by unit v with outcome δ. Given a set N_f of faulty units (*actual fault set*), the set of all test outcomes is called *syndrome*, denoted σ.

The syndrome is collected by an external, reliable diagnoser and it is decoded by a *diagnosis algorithm*. This algorithm provides a *diagnosis* of the system by partitioning set N into subsets F of units declared faulty, subset K of units declared non-faulty, and subset S of *suspect* units. Given a syndrome σ, the diagnosis is said to be *correct* if $F \subseteq N_f$ and $K \subseteq N–N_f$. The diagnosis is said to be *complete* if $S=\varnothing$.

A system is said *one-step t_0-diagnosable* if correct and complete diagnosis is always possible for all fault sets N_f with $\#N_f \le t_0$. The value of t_0, called the *diagnosability* of the system, is limited above by the minimum number of the tests undergone by units in the system. Under the hypothesis of reciprocal tests, this equals the minimum of the node degrees in G [1,4]. A general one-step diagnosis algorithm is reported in [5].

As an alternative to the preceding "deterministic" approach, Scheinerman [6] considered random graphs (i.e., graphs in which every test link exists with probability p) and showed that correct and complete diagnosis can be obtained with probability approaching 1 as $n \to \infty$ if the average number of links per unit is slightly above $\log(n)$.

Table 1. Invalidation rule of the PMC model.

Testing unit	Tested unit	Test outcome
Fault-free	Fault-free	0
Fault-free	Faulty	1
Faulty	Fault-free	0 or 1
Faulty	Faulty	0 or 1

---

[1] Throughout this paper $\#X$ denotes the cardinality of set X, for any X.

Blough et al. [7] reinforced this result by proving that $\log(n+c)$ test links per unit, where c is a small constant, are necessary and sufficient to achieve asymptotically correct diagnosis.

The preceding results are of relatively little value in the perspective applications of this theory, i. e. the diagnosis of massive parallel processing systems and the "wafer-scale" VLSI testing [8]. In both applications the system graph is t-regular (i.e. every unit has the same degree t), and the node degree is (or it is upper-bounded by) a small constant, with the exception of some massive parallel systems where the interconnection structure is a hypercube.

Increasing the degree, i. e. the number of links, would imply increasing costs and, in the case of application to wafer-scale VLSI testing, would also conflict with technological constraints. For this reason, the theory of system-level diagnosis should pursue the best possible trade-off between diagnosis performance and cost of the interconnection structure.

Along this trend of research, Somani and Agarwal [9], LaForge et al. [10], and Huang et al. [11] presented probabilistic algorithms which apply to regular or quasi-regular systems. The proposed algorithms provide diagnoses which are complete but possibly incorrect, although the probability of incorrect diagnosis, which was studied analytically and/or by means of simulation, is relatively small.

Another approach [12] is based on algorithms which provide correct, although possibly incomplete, diagnosis. Diagnosis correctness is guaranteed by a deterministic bound or it is asserted by the diagnosis algorithm itself [13,14,15].

The diagnosis algorithm for regular structures presented and evaluated in this paper, is a further development of the latter approach. The algorithm has time complexity $O(nt)$ when executed on t-regular structures of size n. The performance of the algorithm, in terms of diagnosis correctness and completeness, was evaluated by means of simulation over two-dimensional grids, hypercubes and Cube-Connected Cycles (CCC). Simulation studies showed that the performance of the algorithm is sensible to the degree of the structure. They also provided evidence that the diagnosis completeness is affected by other structure parameters [16] such as diameter (defined as the maximum of the minimum distances between nodes) and bisection width (defined as the cardinality of the minimum number of links, whose removal partitions a graph into two subgraphs with equal cardinality). As far as the authors know, the influence of diameter and bisection width on diagnosis completeness was never measured before.

The grids, hypercubes and CCCs structures are defined as follows.

A grid structure of size $n=L^2$, where L is a positive, even integer, is composed by n units arranged in L columns and L rows. Each unit is indexed by a pair (x,y) of

integers, with $x=0...L-1$ and $y=0...L-1$. Hereafter unit indexed by (x,y) will be denoted u_{xy}. Units are connected to a constant number of neighbors, according to the rules specified below. Depending on the number of neighbors (3, 4, 6 or 8), grids considered in this paper will be called *triangular*, *square*, *hexagonal* or *octagonal*. The units are connected according to the following rules:

- In triangular *grids*, denoted G_3, unit u_{xy} is connected to units indexed by:

  o $(x,(y\pm1)\,mod\,L)$;

  o $((x+1)\,mod\,L, y)$ if x and y are both even or both odd, and to $((x-1)\,mod\,L, y)$ otherwise.

- In *square grids*, denoted G_4, unit u_{xy} is connected to units indexed by $(x,(y\pm1)\,mod\,L)$ and $((x\pm1)\,mod\,L, y)$.

- In *hexagonal grids*, denoted G_6, unit u_{xy} is connected to units indexed by:

  o $(x, (y\pm1)\,mod\,L)$ and $((x\pm1)\,mod\,L, y)$;

  o $((x\pm1)\,mod\,L, (y+1)\,mod\,L)$ if x is even, and to $((x\pm1)\,mod\,L, (y-1)\,mod\,L)$ otherwise.

- In *octagonal grids*, denoted G_8, unit u_{xy} is connected to units indexed by $(x,(y\pm1)\,mod\,L)$, $((x\pm1)\,mod\,L,y)$ and $((x\pm1)\,mod\,L, (y\pm1)\,mod\,L)$;

Grids G_3, G_4, G_6 and G_8 are 3, 4, 6 and 8-regular structures, due to the wrap-around links crossing the border: for this reason they are also called toroidal grids. Examples of grids of size 16 are shown in Figure 1.

Non-toroidal grids NG_3, NG_4, NG_6 and NG_8 of size n may be derived from G_3, G_4, G_6 and G_8 of the same size by removing the wrap-around links crossing the border. This implies that the degree of units lying on the border is smaller than the degree of internal units: hence, non-toroidal grids are quasi-regular structures. In this paper,

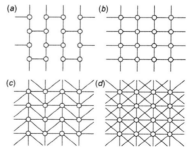

Figure 1. Grids G_3 (a), G_4 (b), G_6 (c), and G_8 (d) with L=4.

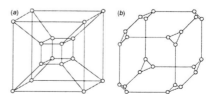

Figure 2. Hypercube with d=4 (a), and CCC with d=3 (b).

consideration will be limited to toroidal grids.

An hypercube of dimension d, denoted H_d, is composed by $n=2^d$ units. Every unit u is labeled with a d-digits binary number denoted $lab(u)$. Units are connected based on the Hamming distance of their labels, denoted d_H: edge (u,v) exists if and only if $d_H(lab(u),lab(v))=1$. The hypercube of dimension $d=4$ is shown in Figure 2 (*a*). It is immediate that hypercubes are d-regular structures, and the degree $d=log\ n$ increases with the size.

A Cube-Connected Cycles (*CCC*) structure of dimension d, denoted CCC_d, is composed by 2^d cycles of units, each comprising d units. Each unit is labeled with a pair (c,l), $0 \le c < 2^d$ and $0 \le l < d$, where c is a d-digits binary number identifying a cycle and l is an integer identifying a unit within the cycle. Unit (c,l) is connected to units $(c,l\pm1$ mod $d)$ and to unit $(c \oplus 2^l, l)$, where $\oplus$ denotes the bitwise exclusive-or operator. Every unit in the *CCC* has degree 3, hence the *CCC* is a 3-regular structure. CCC_3 is depicted in Figure 2 (*b*).

The rest of the paper is organized as follow. The EDARS algorithm is introduced in Section 2. The syndrome-dependent and the syndrome-independent bounds are introduced in Sections 3 and 4, respectively, and the issues related to the completeness of the diagnosis are discussed in Section 5. Section 6 presents the simulation experiments. Conclusions are drawn in Section 7.

2 An Efficient Diagnosis Algorithm for Regular Structures

In this section we introduce the diagnosis algorithm EDARS (Efficient Diagnosis Algorithm for Regular Structures), based on the PMC model. The following definitions are exploited in the description of the algorithm.

Given any syndrome σ, an *aggregate* A is a connected component of the system graph of node set $A \subseteq N$. The cardinality of A, denoted $\#A$, is called the *area* of A. The set $B(A)=\{u \notin A \mid \exists\ v \in A,\ u \leftrightarrow v\}$ is called the boundary of A. Hereafter we will use the word aggregate to mean both a connected subgrid A and its node set A. An aggregate A is a Z-aggregate if $u \xleftrightarrow{0\quad 0} v$ for every pair u,v with $u,v \in A$, $u \leftrightarrow v$.

From the invalidation rule of the PMC model, the following properties are immediate:

(a) if $u \xleftrightarrow{1\quad 0} v$, then u is faulty;

(b) if u is known to be faulty, then any unit $v \in A_0(u)$ is also faulty;

(c) if $u \xleftrightarrow{1\quad 1} v$, then at least one unit between u and v is faulty;

(d) if $u \xleftrightarrow{0\quad 0} v$, then u and v are both faulty or both non-faulty.

The following definitions have been introduced in [5]:

A directed path from u to v consisting of 0-labeled edges, is denoted by $u \Rightarrow_0 v$. Given a syndrome σ, any unit $u \in N$, and any subset $X \subseteq N$, sets $\Delta_1(u)$, $\Delta_1(X)$, $D_0(u)$, $D_0(X)$, $A_0(u)$, $A_0(X)$ and $L(u)$ are defined as follows:

- $\Delta_1(u) = \{v \in N: u \xrightarrow{1} v \text{ or } v \xrightarrow{1} u\}$,
  $\Delta_1(X) = \bigcup_{u \in X} \Delta_1(u)$ are the disagreement sets of u and X, respectively;

- $D_0(u) = \{v \in N: u \Rightarrow_0 v\} \cup \{u\}$, $D_0(X) = \bigcup_{u \in X} D_0(u)$ are the *zero descendant sets* of u and X, respectively;

- $A_0(u) = \{v \in N: v \Rightarrow_0 u\}$, $A_0(X) = \bigcup_{u \in X} A_0(u)$ are the *zero ancestor sets* of u and X, respectively;

- $L(u) = \Delta_1(D_0(u)) \cup A_0(\Delta_1(D_0(u)))$ is the *implied faulty set* of u.

Informally, the implied faulty set of a unit u is defined as the set of units that must be faulty under the assumption that u is non-faulty.

Given a syndrome σ, EDARS is divided into three subsequent steps.

The first step (*Local Diagnosis*) performs a preliminary classification of units, partitioning N into sets F, D and Z. Set F contains faulty units identified by exploiting properties (a) and (b). Units in set D (*dual units*) are defined in disjoint pairs with the property that, for every pair, each unit accuses the other of being faulty. From Property (c), at least one unit in every pair must be faulty. The remaining units are assigned to set Z (*zero-units*). Adjacent zero-units must test each other with outcome 0, since otherwise the units should have been put into set F or D. By Property (d), they must be in the same state.

The second step (*Fault-Free Core Identification*) partitions the subgraph Z, of node set Z, into Z-aggregates. It is immediate that all units in a Z-aggregate are in the same state. The *Fault-Free Core* (*FFC*) is defined as the union set of the Z-aggregates of maximum cardinality. Under the hypotheses stated in Theorem 1, the *FFC* is non-empty and actually fault-free. In this step, the algorithm also asserts the syndrome–dependent bound T_σ, with the property that the diagnosis returned by EDARS is correct if the actual number of faulty units is less than T_σ.

In Step 3 (*Augmentation*) the *FFC* is recursively augmented with units in $D_0(FFC)$, which are non-faulty under the invalidation rule of Table 1. Similarly, set F constructed in Step 1 is augmented with units belonging to $\Delta_1(FFC)$ and to $A_0(FFC)$, which must be faulty under the rules of Table 1.

As shown in [15], the time complexity of EDARS is $O(nt)$. The algorithm is reported in Table 2.

It should be observed that the cardinality of set F constructed in Step 1 could be increased by determining the implied faulty set of every unit and by declaring faulty those units which are in their own implied faulty set. It is easily seen that set F constructed by the algorithm of Table 2 is a subset of the set which would result from the preceding rule. Similarly, it should be observed that the rule used in Table 2 to construct set D is a matching on the subgraph induced by units which test each other with outcome 1, and that $\#D$ could be maximized (at the expense of the Z-aggregates cardinalities) by using a maximum matching algorithm. However, this would increase the time complexity of the algorithm and, as evidenced by simulation experiments, the advantages, if any, would be negligible [15].

3 Diagnosis Correctness: the Syndrome-Dependent Bound

Given any syndrome σ, the diagnosis is correct if there exists at least one Z-aggregate (that is $\alpha > 0$) and every Z-aggregate of area α is fault-free. Under these conditions the FFC defined in Step 2 is non-empty and actually fault-free. Under the same conditions, Step 3 augments set FFC with units which are actually non-faulty and set F with units which are actually faulty.

Given any syndrome σ, the following theorem relates the diagnosis correctness to the *syndrome-dependent bound* T_σ asserted by the diagnosis algorithm in Step 2:

Theorem 1. *Given syndrome σ, the diagnosis returned by EDARS is correct provided $\alpha > 0$ and $\#N_f < T_\sigma$.*

Proof. Recalling that set D is constructed by addition of disjoint pairs of units and that at least one unit in every pair must be faulty, the number of faults in the system is at least $\#F + \#D/2$ (where F is the set of faulty units constructed in the first step). If some Z-aggregate of area α, where α is the maximum of the Z-aggregate cardinalities, is not fault-free, this implies that the Fault-Free Core contains α faulty units, and the diagnosis is incorrect. However, this also implies that $\#N_f \geq \alpha + \#F + \#D/2 = T_\sigma$, thus contradicting the hypothesis $\#N_f < T_\sigma$. □

Given some (unknown) fault set N_f and syndromes σ arising from N_f, assume that F is the set of units declared faulty by EDARS and that T_σ is the syndrome-dependent bound asserted by the algorithm itself. If the diagnosis is correct, must be $F \subseteq N_f$. From Theorem 1, the response of the algorithm can be relied upon as a correct diagnosis if $\#F < T_\sigma$ and it is firmly expected that the maximum cardinality of N_f be less than T_σ.

It should be kept in mind that bound T_σ depends on the cardinalities of sets constructed in steps 1 and 2 of EDARS (namely, $\#F$, $\#D$, and α). Such cardinalities are dependent on the current syndrome σ, which, in turn, depends on the actual fault set. Simulations experiments reported in Section 6 showed that the diagnosis validation based on T_σ is quite reliable, since the average of T_σ always resulted above $\#N_f$ as long as $\#N_f$ did not exceed $n/2$ (with the exception of some CCC structure). In most cases the difference between the average of T_σ and $\#N_f$ was comfortably large and the standard deviation was quite small.

Table 2. **The EDARS algorithm.**

```
{initialization: sets F, D, and Z are empty}
    F:= ∅; D:= ∅; Z:= ∅;
{Step one: Local Diagnosis}
    {identification of faulty units}
    While ∃u∈N–F,∃v∈N:u ←1 0→ v Do
        F:=F∪{u}
    EndWhile {u is faulty by Property (a)}
    {F is augmented according to Property(b)}
    F:=F∪ A₀(F)
    {identification of dual units}
    While ∃u,v∈N–(F∪D):u ←1 1→ v Do
        D:=D∪{u,v}
    EndWhile
    {identification of set Z of zero-units}
    Z:=N–(D∪F);
{Step Two: Fault-Free Core Identification}
    Q:=EmptyQueue; h:=1; {Z-aggregate count}
    While ∃u∈Z do
        Z:=Z–{u}; Zₕ:={u}; h:=h+1; insert(u,Q);
        While NonEmpty(Q) Do
            u:=remove(Q);
            for each u∈Z:u↔v Do
                Z:=Z–{v}; Zₕ:=Zₕ∪{v}; insert(v,Q)
            EndDo
        EndWhile
    EndWhile;
    α:= Max(#Z₁,...,#Zₕ);
    FFC := ⋃_{#Zᵢ=α} Zᵢ {set FFC is the Fault-Free Core}
    Tσ:= α +#F+#D/2;  {syndrome-dependent bound}
Assertion: the diagnosis is correct if
        α>0 and #Nf<Tσ;
{Step Three: Augmentation}
{the zero descendants of the FFC are non faulty}
    FFC:=FFC∪D₀(FFC);
{disagreement set of the FFC are faulty}
    F:=F∪Δ₁(FFC);
{zero ancestors of faulty units are faulty}
    F:=F∪A₀(F);
{Diagnosis and Validation}
    S:=N–(FFC∪F); {S is the set of suspect units}
    return(FFC,F,S,Tσ);
```

4 Diagnosis Correctness: the Syndrome-Independent Bound

The *syndrome-independent bound*, denoted T, is defined as the minimum of T_σ over set Σ of all syndromes which give rise to at least one Z-aggregate. Contrary to T_σ, bound T ensures correct diagnosis whenever the cardinality of the actual fault set is less than T, independently of the actual syndrome. Under this hypothesis, letting σ be any admissible syndrome of N_f, the correctness of the diagnosis is ensured by Theorem 1, since $T_\sigma \geq T$.

The syndrome-independent bounds for square grids, denoted T_4, and for non-toroidal square grids, denoted

Table 3. Values of T_4, NT_4, NT_6 and NT_8 for some grid sizes.

n	T_4	NT_4	NT_6	NT_8
64	16	10	16	18
1024	128	101	129	145
16384	885	762	937	1044

NT_4, were derived by a worst case analysis in [13] and [14]. The syndrome-independent bound for non-toroidal hexagonal and octagonal grids, denoted NT_6 and NT_8, respectively, was derived by a similar analysis in [15]. The syndrome-independent bounds NT_6 and NT_8 may be taken as approximations (from below) of the bounds for G_6 and G_8.

These bounds could not be expressed analytically; however, they could be limited by tight lower and upper bounds, from which it is seen that all bounds are $\Theta(n^{2/3})$. Some values of T_4, NT_4, NT_6 and NT_8 for grids of different degrees and sizes are reported in Table 3.

5 Diagnosis Completeness

Given any syndrome σ and the partition of set N into subsets FFC, F and S provided by EDARS, the diagnosis is incomplete if $S \neq \emptyset$. Assume $S \neq \emptyset$ and consider the subgraph of G induced by S: it is immediate that $S \cap \Delta_1(FFC) = \emptyset$, $S \cap D_0(FFC) = \emptyset$, and $S \cap A_0(F) = \emptyset$. Let $S_1, \ldots, S_h$, of node sets $S_1, \ldots, S_h$, be the connected components of S, and consider the boundaries $B_1, \ldots, B_h$ of aggregates $S_1, \ldots, S_h$. It is immediate that, for every B_i, $i=1, \ldots, h$, must be $B_i \cap FFC = \emptyset$, since otherwise would be $S \cap \Delta_1(FFC) \neq \emptyset$ or $S \cap D_0(FFC) \neq \emptyset$. Thus, all the units in B_i must be faulty. This means that $\#\bigcup_{i=1,\ldots,h} B_i$ provides a lower bound to the number of faults needed to produce incomplete diagnosis with the given syndrome. A syndrome-independent lower bound could be found by taking the minimum of $\#\bigcup_{i=1,\ldots,h} B_i$ over the set of all possible syndromes.

Given an arbitrary aggregate S of area β, lower bounds to the cardinality of its boundary were given in [13] for square grids and in [15] for hexagonal and octagonal grids. These bounds are as follows:

- $f_1(\beta) = 2 + 2\sqrt{2\beta - 1}$ in square grids;

- $f_2(\beta) = 3 + \sqrt{12\beta - 3}$ in hexagonal grids;

- $f_3(\beta) = 4 + 4\sqrt{\beta}$ in octagonal grids.

Since f_1, f_2 and f_3 are increasing functions of β, the minimum of $\#\bigcup_{i=1,\ldots,h} B_i$ occurs when $h=1$ and $\#S=1$, that is, there exists a unique S_i of area $\beta=1$. This means that the diagnosis provided by EDARS may be incomplete only if the number of faults is at least $f_1(1)=4$ in square grids, at least $f_2(1)=6$ in hexagonal grids and at least $f_3(1)=8$ in oc-

tagonal grids. Observe that these values coincide with the degrees t of the respective grids, which are also known to be upper bounds to the one-step diagnosability. Assuming at most t faults, EDARS could be trivially extended to diagnose as non-faulty the (unique) unit in S. This means that EDARS may also be regarded as an efficient algorithm for one-step diagnosis of grids.

The preceding worst case analysis is very pessimistic. In fact, the probability that $\#N_f$ faults distributed over set N yield at least one boundary of faulty units circumscribing a non-empty aggregate may be very small. An evaluation of such probability, which required meticulous analysis of the interconnection structure, was provided in [12] and [10] for the case of square grids. Extending this analysis to other regular structures could prove to be very difficult while providing limited results. The research reported in this paper used simulation to estimate the probability of incomplete diagnoses and the degree of incompleteness for a wide range of regular structures. One important goal of simulation was to gain an insight of the parameters of the interconnection structure which influence diagnosis completeness. One such parameter is clearly the degree; however, simple reasoning suggests that diameter and bisection width may also play some role.

Consider an arbitrary unit u not yet diagnosed as either non-faulty or faulty as the second step of EDARS is completed. This unit may be diagnosed during the Augmentation step, provided it is reached by either a chain of 0-descendants of the FFC or a chain of 0-ancestors of set F. With uniform distribution of faults, the probability of such chains decreases with their lengths. A small diameter of the interconnection structure appears to indicate that the chains connecting unit u to the FFC or to set F tend to be relatively short and, thus, relatively likely to occur. On the other hand, the probability of diagnosing u is also related to the number of distinct paths between u and units belonging to either FFC or F. In turn, this number is somehow related to the bisection width of the structure, and a larger bisection width could decrease the probability that the state of units remains unidentified.

As it will be reported in Section 6, the simulation results yielded by EDARS with structures of same degree but different diameter and/or bisection width, closely agree with the preceding conjecture.

As an example, Table 4 displays some output data reported by simulation experiments with some structures of size $n=64$, namely G_3, G_4, G_6 and G_8, hypercube H_6 and CCC_4. For every structure, fault sets of cardinalities ranging from $0.1n$ to $0.5n$ were distributed uniformly over the node set, and the syndromes were generated assuming probabilities $p=0.5$ and $q=0.5$. The table reports the output parameters *%incomplete*, $E(\#N_d)$, and $E(T_\sigma)$. Parameter *%correct* is not reported since all diagnoses resulted correct.

Table 4. Simulation results for structures of size n=64.

	#N_f	.1n	.3n	.5n
G_3	%incomplete	3.53	82.51	100.00
	$E(\#N_d)$	1.11	4.78	21.08
	$E(T_\sigma)$	63.18	56.71	42.53
G_4	%incomplete	0.20	22.81	96.90
	$E(\#N_d)$	1	1.44	9.33
	$E(T_\sigma)$	63.67	62.35	52.41
G_6	%incomplete	0.00	1.07	32.30
	$E(\#N_d)$	0	1.1	1.71
	$E(T_\sigma)$	63.94	63.68	62.99
G_8	%incomplete	0.00	0.03	9.15
	$E(\#N_d)$	0	0	1.49
	$E(T_\sigma)$	63.98	63.88	63.7
H_6	%incomplete	0.00	1.47	32.90
	$E(\#N_d)$	0	1	1.42
	$E(T_\sigma)$	63.94	63.68	63.03
CCC_4	%incomplete	3.37	88.97	100.00
	$E(\#N_d)$	1.22	6.33	22.07
	$E(T_\sigma)$	63.18	54.37	41.78

6 Simulation Experiments

Extensive simulation experiments were conducted to the purpose of evaluating the performance of EDARS with the regular structures defined in Section 1. For every simulation experiment, parameters defining the structure and its size, the fault distribution and its parameters, and the number of faults to be distributed are given. Fault distribution may be uniform, in which the same failure probability is assigned to every unit, or multivariate, in which a random number of faults are distributed uniformly around some "seeds", also distributed uniformly. For the sake of brevity, all results reported in this paper refer to uniform distribution.

Once the faults have been distributed over the structure, the syndrome is generated according to the invalidation rule of the PMC model described in Table 1. The outcomes of tests performed by faulty units are determined randomly, assuming probability p, or q, for test outcome 1 if the tested unit is non-faulty, or faulty, respectively. Probabilities p and q are input parameters of the simulator.

Every simulation experiment consists of executing EDARS over a number of fault sets (sample), chosen to guarantee a target confidence interval[1] for all the output

---

[1] The confidence interval [17], calculated with precision r, is defined as the number i such that the probability $P(\,|E(T_\sigma)\text{-}\mu(T_\sigma)|\leq i)$ is greater than or equal to r, where $\mu(T_\sigma)$ is the average of T_σ calculated over the universe of all possible fault sets of given cardinality. In all the experiments performed r was set to 0.98.

data of the experiment. The size of the sample was always at least 250, unless a larger size was required to achieve the target confidence interval with output data which were to be averaged over a subset of the sample (e.g., those fault sets which led to incomplete diagnosis).

The main data reported for every simulation experiment are:

- *%correct*: the percentage of fault sets which led to correct diagnosis;

- $E(T_\sigma)$: the average of the syndrome-dependent bound;

- *%incomplete*: the percentage of fault sets which led to incomplete diagnosis;

- $E(\#N_d)$: the average number of units left unidentified by EDARS, considering only those fault sets which led to incomplete diagnosis;

- *%suspect*: the percentage of units left unidentified by EDARS considering the entire sample.

Additional parameters reported by the simulator are the average cardinalities of sets F and D constructed in the first step of EDARS, the average cardinality of the *FFC* constructed in the second step of EDARS, and the average numbers of non-faulty and faulty units left undiagnosed by EDARS, when diagnosis resulted incomplete.

6.1 Evaluation of EDARS with grids

Simulation experiments with grids covered sizes ranging from 64 to 16384, fault sets cardinalities ranging from $0.1n$ to $0.5n$, uniform and multivariate distributions, probabilities p and q ranging from 0.25 to 0.75 in steps of 0.25. Results are summarized in Figures 3 to 7 which, for the sake of brevity, report only results obtained with uniform distribution and with probabilities $p=q=0.5$. Results obtained with multivariate distribution and with different values of p and q were quite similar. Complete simulation results are reported in [15].

Referring to grids of size 64 and 1024, Figures 3 and 4 report $E(T_\sigma)$ as percentage of the grid sizes (denoted *%SDB*). It is seen that $E(T_\sigma)$ is above (in the cases G_6 and G_8, far above) the cardinality of the actual fault set in the entire cardinality range covered by simulation. This means that the diagnosis of grids returned by EDARS is quite reliable if the expected number of faulty units is below $0.5n$. One interesting result displayed in the figures is that *%SDB* decreases as the size of the grid increases, indicating that the diagnosis does not converge toward asymptotic correctness.

Both the percentage of incomplete diagnoses and $E(\#N_d)$ increase as the cardinality of the actual fault set increases. The combined effect of such facts is responsible for the behavior shown in Figures 5 and 6, which report *%Suspect*, considering grids with $n=64$ and $n=1024$. *%Suspect* increases with the fault set cardinality, and the rate of increase is more sensible for large grids, indicating that the diagnosis does not converge toward asymptotic completeness.

The comparison of the performance of EDARS with grids of different degrees confirms the expected dependency of diagnosis correctness and completeness from the degree of the structure. This property is further evidenced in Figure 7, which plots the percentage of units which the algorithm is unable to diagnose as a function of the grid degree, considering fault sets of cardinalities ranging from $0.1n$, to $0.5n$. From the figure it is seen that the gain in diagnosis completeness due to the increased degree of the structure is more perceivable with large cardinalities of the fault set. For example, while grid G_3 is sufficient, on the average, to ensure almost complete diagnosis if the number of faults is $0.1n$, the degree of the grid should be at least 4 when this number is $0.3n$, and at least 6 with fault sets of cardinality $0.5n$.

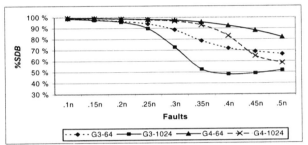

Figure 3. **Triangular and square grids:** $E(T_\sigma)$ **expressed as percentage of the grid size for** n=64 **and 1024.**

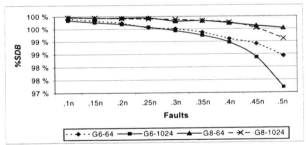

Figure 4. **Hexagonal and octagonal grids** $E(T_\sigma)$ **expressed as percentage of the grid size for** n=64 **and 1024.**

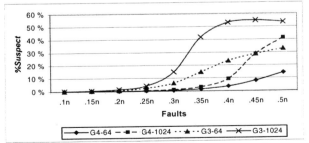

Figure 5. **Triangular and square grids: percentage of suspect units for** n=64 **and 1024.**

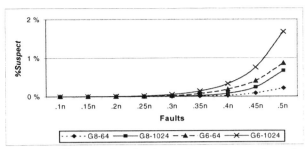

Figure 6. **Hexagonal and octagonal grids: percentage of suspect units for** n=64 **and 1024.**

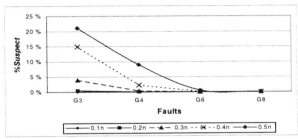

Figure 7. **Percentage of suspect units for grids with** n=256 **and** $\#N_f$ = 0.1n, 0.2n, 0.3n, 0.4n **and 0.5n.**

6.2   Evaluation of EDARS with hypercubes

The most notable result of simulation experiments with hypercubes is the average of the syndrome-dependent bound T_σ, which is very close to n in the full range of simulation experiments, where fault set cardinalities ranged from $0.1n$ to $0.5n$. This means that the diagnosis returned by EDARS is almost certainly correct in all cases. Figure 8 displays $E(T_\sigma)$ as percentage of the hypercube size (denoted %SDB) for hypercubes H_6, H_{10} and H_{14}. Contrary to the case of grids, this percentage tends to increase as the size of the structure increases, indicating that the diagnosis tends to converge toward asymptotic correctness.

For all the sizes considered, the diagnosis of hypercubes resulted always complete with fault sets of cardinality $0.1n$. Above this cardinality, simulation experiments reported a percentage of incomplete diagnoses which increase as fault sets become larger. However, the percentage of incomplete diagnoses was always below 40%, even with fault set of cardinality $0.5n$. When the diagnosis is incomplete, the average number of suspect units exceeded 1 only slightly, independently of the size of the hypercube. This means that, contrary to the case of grids, the percentage of suspect units in hypercubes tends to decrease as the size of the structure increases, i.e. the diagnosis tends to converge toward completeness as n tends to infinite. This behavior, displayed in Figure 9, is compared to the corresponding behavior of grids in Figure 10, assuming fault sets of cardinality $0.5n$. The fact that diagnosis provided by EDARS with hypercubes is asymptotically correct and complete agrees with the theoretical studies by [6] and [7], according to which a degree slightly above *log n* is necessary and sufficient to achieve asymptotically correct and complete diagnosis. Thus, EDARS may be regarded as a well-performing diagnosis algorithm for hypercubes and, reasonably, for regular structures in general.

6.3 Evaluation of EDARS with *CCC*s

The performance of EDARS with *CCC* structures was evaluated to the purpose of gaining insight on the influence of parameters of the interconnection structure, other than the degree, on diagnosis correctness and completeness. In fact, *CCC* structures have the same constant degree as triangular grids, but the diameter and the bisection width are sensibly different, and the differences may vary considerably with the size of the structure.

Simulation experiments considered *CCC*s of dimensions $d=4$, $d=7$ and $d=11$, corresponding to sizes $n=64$, $n=896$ and $n=22528$. Figure 11 reports $E(T_\sigma)$ as percentage of the *CCC* size (denoted %SDB). It is seen that $E(T_\sigma)$ is above $\#N_f$ in the entire range assumed for its cardinality, for sizes $n=64$ and 896. For size $n=22528$, $E(T_\sigma)$ was slightly less than $\#N_f$ when $\#N_f$ was $0.5n$, meaning that in this case the correctness of diagnosis cannot be guaranteed. However, simulation results showed that even in this case the diagnosis returned by EDARS was always correct. Contrary to the case of grids, %SDB increases as n increases as long as the cardinality of the fault sets is at most $0.4n$. The situation is reversed for fault sets of cardinality $0.5n$. The same behavior is displayed by %Suspect (Figure 12), thus showing that the performance of EDARS with *CCC*s scales, to a certain extent, with the size of the structure.

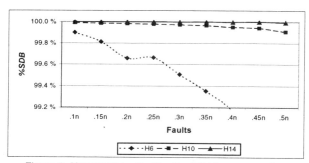

Figure 8. Hypercubes H_6, H_{10}, H_{14}: $E(T_\sigma)$ expressed as percentage of the hypercube size.

Table 5. Degree, diameter and bisection width of hypercubes and grids G_6 and G_8 for some structure sizes.

	CCC_4, $n=64$	G_3, $n=64$	CCC_7, $n=896$	G_3, $n=900$	CCC_{11}, $n=22528$	G_3, $n=22500$
degree	3	3	3	3	3	3
diameter	9	8	16	30	26	150
bisection width	8	8	64	30	1024	150

Table 6. Degree, diameter and bisection width of *CCC*s and grid G_3 for some structure sizes.

	H_6	G_6, $n=64$	H_8	G_8, $n=256$
degree	6	6	8	8
diameter	6	6	8	8
bisection width	32	24	128	64

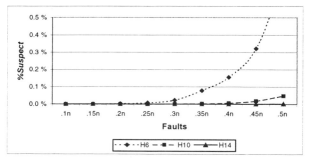

Figure 9. Hypercubes H_6, H_{10}, H_{14}: percentage of suspect units.

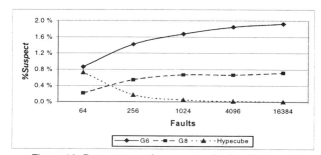

Figure 10. Percentage of suspect units for G_6, G_8 and hypercubes with $\#N_f=0.5$.

6.4 Comparison of different structures

The influence of structure parameters other than degree over diagnosis correctness and completeness is enlightened by comparison of simulation results yielded by EDARS with structures of different diameter and/or bisection width. Figure 13 compares hypercube H_6 with grid G_6 of size $n=64$, and hypercube H_8 with grid G_8 of size $n=256$. As shown in Table 5, the degree and the diameter are the same for H_6 and G_6 and for H_8 and G_8, while bisection widths are different, more noticeably in the case of G_8 and H_8. Figure 13 plots the average number of suspect units, expressed as a percentage of the size. In G_6 and H_6 this percentage is essentially the same, except for a slightly superior performance of the hypercube when the cardinality of the fault set is relatively large. Comparing the same percentages obtained with structures of size 256, it is seen that H_8 tends to outperform G_8 as the cardinality of the actual fault set increases.

The different performances of EDARS with grids and hypercubes of the same size, degree and diameter, and the circumstance that diagnosis completeness increases more perceivably in the case of H_8 and G_8, where the difference of bisection widths is larger, support the conjecture that bisection width plays a role in determining the degree of diagnosis completeness.

This thesis is confirmed by comparing the simulation results obtained with grids G_3 and CCCs of approximately the same size, namely G_3 with n=64 and 900, and CCC_4 (n=64) and CCC_7 (n=896). In this case, the degree is 3 for both grids and CCCs, but diameters and bisection widths are different, as seen from Table 6. As reported in Figures 14 and 15, CCC_7 outperforms grid G_3 of size n=900 in terms of diagnosis correctness and, more remarkably, in terms of diagnosis completeness. The advantage of CCC structure over G_3 increases with the increase of the fault set cardinality, although the results tend to converge as this cardinality approaches $0.5n$. The preceding results agree with the circumstance that the diameter is smaller and the bisection width is larger than in the case of CCCs than in the case of G_3.

The comparison of CCC_4 with G_3 of size n=64 deserves special attention, because both structures have the same bisection width but, contrary to the situation occurring with larger sizes, the diameter of the grid is smaller than the diameter of the CCC. The expectation that EDARS performs better with G_3 than with CCC_4 is confirmed by simulation experiments. As seen from Figures 14 and 15, the performance with G_3 is slightly better than with CCC_4 in term of both diagnosis correctness and diagnosis completeness. The advantage of G_3, is more noticeable in diagnosis completeness and it increases with the increase of the fault set cardinality.

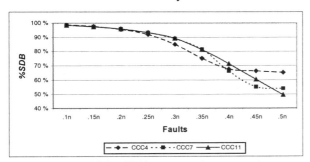

Figure 11. **CCCs: $E(T_\sigma)$ expressed as percentage of the CCC size.**

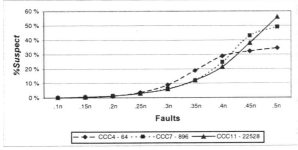

Figure 12. **CCCs: percentage of suspect units.**

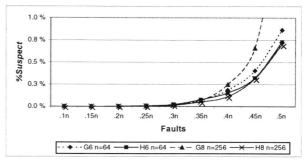

Figure 13. **Percentage of suspect units for G_6 (n=64), H_6, G_8 (n=256) and H_8.**

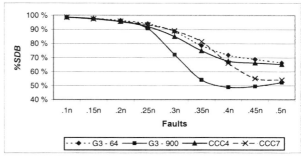

Figure 14. **CCCs and triangular grids: $E(T_\sigma)$ expressed as percentage of the size of the structure.**

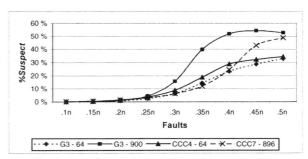

Figure 15. **CCCs and triangular grids: percentage of suspect units.**

7   Conclusion

An O(nt) algorithm for the diagnosis of regular structures (EDARS) has been introduced. Given a syndrome σ, EDARS returns, along with the diagnosis, a syndrome-dependent bound T_σ. The diagnosis provided by EDARS is correct, but possibly incomplete, if the cardinality of the actual fault set is less than T_σ

The performance of EDARS when applied to regular structures of different degrees, diameters and bisection widths has been evaluated by means of simulation.

The comparison between grids of different degrees, whose results are reported in Section 6.1, underlines the influence of degree over diagnosis correctness and completeness. From simulation experiments it is also seen that, regardless of the degree of the grid, the percentage of units that EDARS is unable to diagnose increases with the cardinality of the fault set, and that for given grid degree and fault set cardinality, this percentage increases as the size of the grid increases.

Comparisons of simulation results yielded by grids of selected sizes and degrees and by comparable hypercubes and *CCC*s, showed that, beside degree, diameter and bisection width also appear to influence the performance of EDARS, particularly with respect to diagnosis completeness.

The evidence that the degree of diagnosis completeness is notably influenced by some parameters of the interconnection structures other than the degree, is a relevant result, particularly in view of the application to wafer-scale testing, where almost complete diagnosis is a crucial goal. If this goal could only be achieved by a relatively large degree, the cost of the interconnection structure to be embedded on the wafer would be negatively affected. The same goal could perhaps be achieved with reduced cost as a combined effect of multiple parameters. For this reason the extent to which diameter and bisection width influence the cost of the interconnection structure in a wafer environment deserves a deeper investigation. This way, cost/performance tradeoffs based on different choices of degree, diameter and bisection width could be evidenced and exploited in the identification of "good" interconnection structures for the purpose of wafer-scale testing.

References

[1]   F.P. Preparata, G. Metze, and R.T. Chien, "On the Connection Assignment Problem of Diagnosable Systems". *IEEE Trans. on Comp.*, vol. EC-16, pp. 848 - 854, Dec. 1967.

[2]   F. Barsi, F. Grandoni, and P. Maestrini, "A theory of diagnosability of digital systems". *IEEE Trans. on Comp.*, vol. C-25, pp. 585 - 593, June 1976.

[3]   J. Maeng and M. Malek, "A Comparison Connection Assignment for Self-Diagnosis of Multicomputer Systems". *Proc. FTCS-11*, IEEE Comput. Soc. Publ., pp. 173 - 175, June 1981.

[4]   S.L. Hakimi and S. L. Amin, "Characterization of Connection Assignment of Diagnosable Systems". *IEEE Trans. on Comp.*, vol. C-23, pp. 86 - 88, Jan. 1974.

[5]   A.T. Dahbura and G.M. Masson, "An $O(n^{2.5})$ Fault Identification Algorithm for Diagnosable Systems", *IEEE Trans. on Comp.*, vol. c-33 n. 6, pp. 486 - 492, June 1984.

[6]   E.R. Scheinerman, "Almost Sure Fault Tolerance in Random Graphs", *SIAM J. on Computing*, vol. 16 n. 6, pp. 1124 - 1134, December 1987.

[7]   D. Blough, G. Sullivan, and G.M. Masson, "Efficient Diagnosis of Multiprocessor System Under Probabilistic Models", *IEEE Trans. on Comp.*, Vol. 41, No. 9, pp. 1126 - 1136, September 1992.

[8]   S. Rangarajan, D.,Fussel, and M. Malek, "Built-in Testing of Integrated Circuit Wafers", *IEEE Trans. on Comp.*, vol. 39 n. 2, pp. 195 - 205, February 1990.

[9]   A. K. Somani and V. K. Agarwal, "Distributed Diagnosis Algorithm for Regular Interconnected Systems", *IEEE Trans. on Parallel and Dist. Syst.* vol. 41 n. 7, pp. 899 - 906, July 1992.

[10]   L.E. LaForge, K. Huang, and V.K. Agarwal, "Almost Sure Diagnosis of Almost Every Good Element", *IEEE Trans. on Comp.*, vol. 43 n. 3, pp. 295 - 305, March 1994.

[11]   K. Huang, V.K. Agarwal, L. LaForge, and K. Thulasiraman, "A Diagnosis Algorithm for Constant Degree Structures and Its Application to VLSI Circuit Testing", *IEEE Trans. on Parallel and Dist. Syst.* vol. 44 n.4, pp.363 - 372, April 1995.

[12]   P. Maestrini and P. Santi, "Self-Diagnosis of Processor Arrays Using a Comparison Model", *Proc. 14th SRDS-Symp. on Reliable and Distributed Syst.*, Bad Neuenahr, Germany, pp. 218 - 228, September 1995.

[13]   S. Chessa, *Self-Diagnosis of Grid-Interconnected Systems With Applications to Self-Test of VLSI Wafers*, PhD Thesis TD–2/99, University of Pisa, Italy, Department of Computer Science, March 1999.

[14]   S. Chessa, P. Maestrini, "Correct and Almost Complete Diagnosis of Processor Grids", Technical Report IEI B4 – 13-05-99, Istituto di Elaborazione dell'Informazione, Pisa, Italy, pp. 30, May 1999.

[15]   P. Santi, *Evaluation of a Self-Diagnosis Algorithm for Regular Structures*, PhD Thesis, University of Pisa, Italy, Department of Computer Science, November 1999.

[16]   A. Varma and C. S. Raghavendra, *Interconnection Networks for Multiprocessors and Multicomputers: Theory and Practice*, IEEE Computer Society Press, Los Alamitos, 1994.

[17]   A.M. Law and W.D. Kelton, *Simulation Modeling and Analysis*, McGraw-Hill, New York, 1982.

Session 8C

Software Demonstrations

OFTT: A Fault Tolerance Middleware Toolkit for Process Monitoring and Control Windows NT Applications

Myron Hecht, Xuegao An, Bing Zhang, Yutao He
SoHaR Incorporated
8421 Wilshire Blvd. Suite 201
Beverly Hills, CA, 90211
{myron,xuegao,bzhang,yutao}@sohar.com

Abstract

This paper describes the OFTT (OLE Fault Tolerance Technology), a fault tolerance middleware toolkit running on the Microsoft Windows NT operating system that provides required fault tolerance for networked PCs in the context of industrial process monitoring and control applications. It is based on the Microsoft Component Object Model (COM) and consists of components that performs checkpoint-saving, failure detection, recovery, and other fault tolerance functions. The ease with which this technology can be incorporated into one application represents the primary innovation. It is hoped that by making fault tolerance more compatible with standard software architectures, more reliable PC-based monitoring and control systems can be built conveniently.

1. Introduction

Windows NT-based PCs have become popular platforms in industrial process monitoring and control applications such as SCADA (Supervisory Control And Data Acquisition) [1]. A typical configuration in this context is a PC in the control room connected to a number of Programmable Logic Controllers (PLCs) on the plant floor via an industrial automation network. A PLC interfaces with various types of input/output devices (such as sensors, valves), reads inputs, processes data, and generates corresponding control outputs. In the meantime, data are sent to the PC where they will be further processed, stored, and made available for other applications [2]. Historically, hardware vendors define proprietary data formats in developing device drivers. An application that needs to access these data has to resolve the format inconsistency by itself independently. As a result, development and maintenance of application software is a difficult and time-consuming task. To solve the problem, a standard software architecture, *OLE for Process Control* (OPC) [3] has been developed by the industrial process control community. OPC is based on Microsoft's OLE/COM [4] technology and specifies a unified interface for accessing different types of data. A hardware vendor encapsulates details of the device driver into a COM object (called *OPC server*) that provides standard interfaces (called *OPC interfaces*) to any application (called an *OPC client*) in a consistent manner.

The OPC standard does not address redundancy. Redundancy is necessary because PCs are becoming increasingly integrated into industrial automation processes and manufacturing execution systems. Failures can have significant financial consequences - even though the Windows NT based PCs are not being used for direct control in hazardous or tight deadline closed loop applications. Although many researchers have investigated developing highly available Windows NT applications [5-9], none has addressed the issue in the context of process monitoring and control applications and the fault tolerance for distributed objects like DCOM. It is the design objective of the OFTT to provide application developers with a reusable, easily-integrated, OPC-33compliant middleware toolkit such that applications can be made fault tolerant with minimal modifications.

The remainder of the paper is organized as follows. Section 2 describes the design of the OFTT software architecture and its fault tolerance techniques. Section 3 presents the implementation experiences. An example is given in Section 4 to illustrate the application of the OFTT toolkit. Section 5 draws the conclusion.

2. OFTT Description

This section provides a top level description of the OFTT technology. The first subsection describes reference system configurations; the second identifies the software architecture and major components.

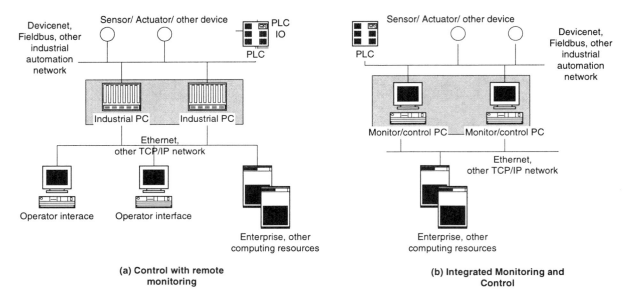

Figure 1. Reference System Configurations

2.1 System Configuration

OFTT is based on the *primary/backup approach*. As shown in Figure 1, two redundant computers are paired up via one or dual Ethernet networks and form a single logic execution unit. One is the *primary* node and the other the *backup* node. The same copy of an application (either an OPC server, or an OPC client, or both) resides on each node.

During normal operation, only the copy on the primary node is executed. In the meantime, its state is checkpointed and sent to the backup node periodically. In case of the primary fails due to either node failures, NT crashes, or application failures, the copy on the backup node will start running with the latest checkpoint.

2.2 Software Architecture

The basic design philosophy of the OFTT toolkit is to minimize the interference caused by adding fault tolerance on the normal application development process. A developer who has the domain-specific expertise yet has little background in fault tolerance can just focus on performance and functionality optimization in the design and implementation. If fault tolerance is also required, the application may simply add the services provided by the OFTT

toolkit. This can be done at different levels of transparency, either by including a header file, inserting a single line in the application source code, or more sophisticated usage of the OFTT toolkit.

The OFTT toolkit is built on top of the Microsoft COM component architecture. Fault tolerance functions such as state checkpointing, failure detection and recovery are implemented as COM objects. Its top-level software architecture is shown in Figure 2. It consists of *OFTT engine, fault tolerance interface module (FTIM), message diverter,* and *system monitor*. Details of each component are discussed in the following sections.

2.2.1 OFTT Engine

The OFTT engine is the core of the OFTT toolkit and controls all aspects of fault tolerance. In particular, it performs the follow functions:

- **Role management**: it determines the role of a node in the primary/backup pair (i.e., whether it is the primary or the backup) during the startup and switchover by negotiating with the peer node.

- **Failure detection**: it monitors the status of all software components that are linked with the fault tolerance interface module on the same node and the status of the peer node by checking the heartbeat messages from each monitored component. If it does not receive the message after the pre-specified timeout, it considers the component fails and initiates a recovery provision. Failure detection for itself is done by the OFTT engine on the peer node. It simply sends out the heartbeat message periodically.

- **Recovery management**: How to recovery from a detected failure is controlled by the *recovery rule* that specifies whether to initiate a local recovery (e.g., a transient fault), or to transfer control to the backup node (e.g., a permanent fault). An application that uses the OFTT can explicitly specify the recovery rule either statically at compilation time or dynamically at run-time. The current implementation only supports static decision.

- **Status reporting**: it reports and updates the status of each monitored component to the system monitor.

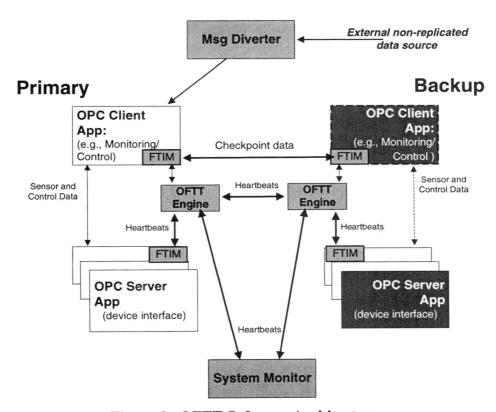

Figure 2. OFTT Software Architecture

OFTT engine is implemented as a client-side COM server and runs as a separate process started by the application.

2.2.2 Fault Tolerance Interface Module (FTIM)

Fault tolerance interface modules are responsible for checkpointing the application state, monitoring the status of the application, and communicating with the OFTT engine. It is implemented as a client-side COM server in the form of dynamic link library

(DLL) and is linked to an application that wants to use OFTT services at the compilation time.

As mentioned previously, the OPC specification identifies two different types of applications, OPC server and OPC client. An OPC server is simply responsible for converting data from different types of I/O devices into the standard format. In this aspect, it is *stateless*. In contrast, an OPC client usually performs more sophisticated functions and uses data from many OPC servers. As a result, to reduce the overhead incurred by checkpointing the state, two different types of fault tolerance interface module are provided: *OPC client FTIM* and *OPC server FTIM*. The difference between these two is that OPC client FTIM takes checkpoints while OPC server FTIM does not.

State Checkpointing. In the OFTT design, the application and the FTIM run as two separate threads within the same address space. The main application thread performs the task and may contain multiple threads. On the other hand, the FTIM thread, incorporated as a DLL, is responsible for taking checkpoint (for OPC clients), sending the heartbeat messages to the OFTT engine, and receiving the control from the OFTT engine. For statically generated kernel-objects such as threads, its context can be easily obtained using the standard Win32 API (*GetThreadContext ()*) and a memory walkthrough will extract the relevant data such as stack, global variables. For some dynamically generated kernel-objects such as a thread generated dynamically by the main application thread (by using *CreateThread()*), its handle (the starting address) can not be accessed directly through the standard Win32 APIs. In this case, a mechanism that manipulates the IAT (Import Address Table) and intercepts corresponding Win32 APIs has been developed to obtain the information.

Application Programming Interfaces (APIs). As stated before, the OFTT toolkit provides the application with a set of APIs in order for it to add fault tolerance. As a result, it is not totally transparent compared to the method in [9]. However, as has been shown in [10,11], in some cases, user directed checkpointing mechanism can improve the performance. Moreover, some event-based checkpointing is necessary. As a result, the OFTT has developed a set of APIs that allows the application to use the fault tolerance in different levels of transparency. The following basic set of APIs has been provided:

- *OFTTInitialize()*: the application requires the OFTT services. At the minimum, it is the only API an application needs to add in order to use the OFTT services.
- *OFTTSelSave()*: Checkpoint variable designation. It identifies specific variables that need to be checkpointed.
- *OFTTSave()*: Checkpoint save. Copy the address space (or the selected subset) and the stack to the peer node immediately, without waiting for a checkpoint period.
- *OFTTGetMyRole()*: Identify role (primary or backup) of a node
- *OFTTWatchdogCreate(), OFTTWatchdogSet(), OFTTWatchdogReset(),OFTTWatchdogDelete()*:

Used to manage a reliable watchdog timer object.
- *OFTTDistress()*: Report a significant problem in the application to the OFTT engine and request a switchover (if application on the peer node is functional).

2.2.3 Message Diverter

The Message Diverter allows the primary/backup nodes to be a consistent logic unit that interacts with other applications and handles all I/O messages to and from applications, and diverts messages to the correct node. The current implementation uses Microsoft Message Queue. In particular, the message queue will store and transmit messages to the primary copy of the application. If a message is sent during a switchover, the message non-delivery is detected and retried.

2.2.4 System Monitor

The System Monitor displays the status of the components in a process monitoring and control system including hardware, operating system, OFTT components, and applications. Although necessary for system test, evaluation, and maintenance purposes, it does not need to be present for the operation of the OFTT fault tolerance provisions.

3. Implementation Experience

The work presented in the paper has shown that component-based software architecture such as COM is a viable means to support fault tolerance in the development of industrial process monitoring and control applications. In the meantime, the following development experience has been observed.

3.1. Access Information of Kernel-Related Objects

While Windows NT provides a rich set of Win32 APIs and libraries, it also complicates the programming effort, especially those related to kernels. The information on dynamically created kernels such as threads is not directly accessible via standard APIs. This creates difficulties in implementing checkpointing and recovery mechanisms as stated before. In addition, there exist a significant amount of functions and features that are documented little or none at all. As an example, the performance monitor is claimed to be a powerful utility to access the NT kernels. However, it is not completely specified and in some cases is just misleading. For instance, the thread start address in the performance counter is always the pointer to a routine in NTDLL.DLL [12] and thus can not be used as the start address of a thread created dynamically.

3.2. Non-determinism of Windows NT

The lack of determinism in Windows NT start-up and thread dispatching did result in a number of design changes in the checkpointing and recovery scheme. For instance, the start-up logic was originally designed as follows: when a node starts up, it is in backup role and waits for a periodic time stamp from its peer node. It will shut down itself if it does not receive the message after a time-out period. This logic was used to minimize the impact of network failures (i.e., both nodes becomes the primary). However, because of the lack of predictability in the start-up time, the first node that starts up would

frequently shut down since the second node may not start operation of the OFTT middleware before the time-out period elapsed. As a result, additional logic was added to initiate retries several times before it shuts down. It effectively solves the original problem.

3.3. DCOM Issues

While DCOM is powerful, it does have several limitations that have hindered the development of the OFTT toolkit. First of all, the DCOM does not have a well-defined built-in fault tolerance infrastructure. For example, its RPC service does not behave well in the presence of failures, and additional design efforts have to be made in order to compensate for the deficiency. Second, generation and installation of the DCOM server object proxy and stub increase extra development and configuration management effort. Some bugs encountered were due to the complexity.

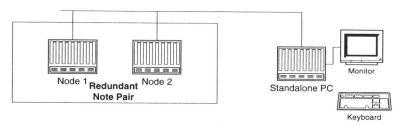

Figure 3. Demonstration Configuration

4. An Application Example

We have developed one application to demonstrate how the OFTT toolkit can be integrated to support the required fault tolerance. The application keeps track of the usage of a simulated small office telephone system that consists of 5 telephone lines and 10 callers. Numbers of busy lines are displayed in the histogram. The application is preferred to be fault tolerant since it records the past and present states of the system.

Figure 3 shows the hardware configuration. It consists of 3 PCs connected via an Ethernet. Two nodes are the primary/backup pair and run the application that has been added with the fault tolerance capability by the OFTT toolkit. The third PC acts as the user interface and test computer. The software configuration is shown in Table 1.

We will demonstrate the ability of the system to continue operating in the presence of the following failures:

a. node failure,
b. NT crash (blue screen of death),
c. application software failure,
d. OFTT Middleware failure.

Table 1. Software Configuration

Node	Software Element
Primary	OFTT Engine
	Call Track application (linked to OFTT Client FTIM)
Backup	OFTT Engine
	Call Track application (linked to OFTT Client FTIM)
Test and Interface	OFTT System Monitor
	Telephone System Simulator Calling History generator

5. Conclusion

OFTT is a middleware toolkit based on the COM architecture that can be easily integrated to process monitoring and control Windows NT applications where high-availability is of primary importance. It is also suitable for the large installed base of monitoring and control software running on Windows NT PCs. In addition to industrial applications, the OFTT toolkit can be used in other environments where high availability is a benefit. These include continuous environmental monitoring, laboratory automation, and multiparameter patient monitoring.

6. Acknowledgement

This work was sponsored in part by the NASA under the Small Business Innovative Research Program, Contract NAS 8 97037. Dr. Eltefaat Shokri's effort in the project is greatly appreciated. The authors also wish to thank anonymous reviewers for their inspiring comments and helpful suggestions.

References

[1] I. Breskin, "SCADA Takes the Factory Floor", *Managing Automation*, April, 2000. http://www.managingautomation.com.

[2] R. Daly, "Process Control and Execution", *Managing Automation*, June, 1999, pp. 34-36.

[3] OPC Foundation, "*OPC Overview*", v1.0, http://www.opcfoundation.org, Oct. 1998.

[4] Microsoft Corp. and DEC., "*The Component Object Model Specification*", Redmond, WA, 1995.

[5] W. Vogels, D. Dumitriu, K. Birman, R. Gamache, M. Massa, R. Short, J. Vert, J. Barrera, and J. Gray, "The Design and Architecture of the Microsoft Cluster Service", *Digest of FTCS-28*, pp. 422-431, June 1998.

[6] H. Abdel-Shafi E. Speight, and J. K. Bennett, "Efficient User-Level Thread Migration and Checkpointing on Windows NT Clusters", *Proc. Of the 3rd USENIX NT Symposium*, Seattle, Washington, July, 1999.

[7] J. Srouji, P. Schuster, M. Bach, and Y. Kuzmin, "A Transparent Checkpoint Facility On NT", *Proc. Of the 2nd UNENIX NT Symposium*, Seattle, Washington, pp. 77-85, August, 1998.

[8] Y. Huang, P. E. Chung, C. Kintala, C.-Y. Wang, and D.-R. Liang, "NT-SwiFT: Software Implemented Fault Tolerance on Windows NT", *Proc. Of 2nd USENIX Windows NT Symposium*, pp. 47-54. Seattle, Washington, August, 1998.

[9] P. E. Chung, W.-J. Lee, Y. Huang, D.-R. Liang, and C.-Y. Wang, "Winckp: a Transparent Checkpointing and Rollback Recovery Tool for Windows NT Applications", *Digest Of FTCS-29*, June, 1999.

[10] J. S. Plank, M. Beck, G. Kingsley, and K. Li, "Libckpt: Transparent Checkpointing under Unix", *Proc. Of USENIX Winter Technical Conference*, New Orleans, LA, pp. 213-223, January, 1995.

[11] Y. Huang and C. Kintala, "Software Fault Tolerance in the Application Layer". In M. Lyu, editor, *Software Fault Tolerance*, pp. 231-248. John Wiley & Sons, 1995.

[12] M. Pietrek, private communication, August, 1999.

DEEM: a Tool for the Dependability Modeling and Evaluation of Multiple Phased Systems

A. Bondavalli[1], I. Mura[2], S.Chiaradonna[3], R. Filippini[3], S.Poli[3], F. Sandrini[3]

[1] DIS, University of Florence, Via Lombroso 6/17 I-50134 Firenze, Italy {a.bondavalli@dsi.unifi.it}
[2] Motorola Technology Center, Via P.C. Boggio 65/A,10139 Torino, Italy
{Ivan_Mura@email.mot.com}
[3] CNUCE Istituto del CNR, Via Vittorio Alfieri 1, 56010 Ghezzano (Pisa) ITALY,

Abstract

Multiple-Phased Systems, whose operational life can be partitioned in a set of disjoint periods, called "phases", include several classes of systems such as Phased Mission Systems and Scheduled Maintenance Systems. Because of their deployment in critical applications, the dependability modeling and analysis of Multiple-Phased Systems is a task of primary relevance. However, the phased behavior makes the analysis of Multiple-Phased Systems extremely complex.. This paper is centered on the description and application of DEEM, a dependability modeling and evaluation tool for Multiple Phased Systems. DEEM supports a powerful and efficient methodology for the analytical dependability modeling and evaluation of Multiple Phased Systems, based on Deterministic and Stochastic Petri Nets and on Markov Regenerative Processes.

1 Introduction

Many systems devoted to the control and management of critical activities have to perform a series of tasks that must be accomplished in sequence. Their operational life consists of a sequence of non-overlapping periods, called *phases*. These systems are often called Multiple-Phased Systems (MPS). They include several classes of systems that have been object of active research during the last decades, such as those known as Phased Mission Systems (PMS) and Scheduled Maintenance Systems (SMS). MPS are very general, since their phases can be distinguished along a wide variety of differentiating features.

(1) During a specific phase, an MPS is devoted to the execution of a particular set of tasks, which may be different from the activities performed within other phases.

(2) The performance and dependability requirements of an MPS can be completely different from one phase to another.

(3) During some phases the system may be subject to a particularly stressing environment, thus experiencing dramatic increases in the failure rate of its components.

(4) In order to accomplish its mission, a MPS may need to change its configuration over time, to adopt the most suitable one with respect to the performance and dependability requirements of the phase being currently executed, or simply to be more resilient to an hazardous external environment.

(5) The successful completion of a phase, as well as the activities performed therein, may bring a different benefit to the MPS with respect to that obtained with other phases.

Many examples of MPS can be found in various application domains. For instance, systems for the aided-guide of aircraft, whose mission-time is divided into several phases such as take-off, cruise, landing, with completely different requirements. A very important sub-class of MPS is represented by the so-called Scheduled Maintenance Systems encountered in almost all the application domains where an artefact is to be used for long time and is periodically subject to maintenance actions. An SMS is easily formulated as a MPS considering that the system is run for a number of operational phases, and then undergoes a maintenance phase.

This paper describes DEEM (DEpendability Evaluation of Multiple-phased systems), the dependability modeling and evaluation tool specifically tailored for MPS, being currently developed by the University of Florence and CNUCE-CNR. DEEM supports the methodology proposed in [10] for the dependability modeling and evaluation of MPS. This methodology relies upon Deterministic and Stochastic Petri Nets (DSPN) as a modeling tool and on Markov Regenerative Processes (MRGP) for the model

231

solution. Due to their high expressiveness, DSPN models are able to cope with the dynamic structure of MPS, and allow defining very concise models. DEEM models are solved with a very simple and computationally efficient analytical solution technique based on the separation of the MRGP underlying the DSPN of a MPS.

The paper is organized as follows. Section 2 describes the modeling features of DEEM and its Graphical User Interface, giving an overview of our DSPN approach. Section 3 describes the specialized solution algorithm implemented by DEEM, highlighting the advantages over previous general MRGP solutions. Then, Section 4 describes how DEEM works. Finally, our concluding remarks are given in Section 5, where we also discuss some possible extensions of the DSPN modeling methodology and the issues related to their inclusion in the DEEM solution technique.

2 The DEEM approach to model MPS

DEEM employs the DSPN formalism [1] for the modeling of MPS. DSPN models extend Generalized Stochastic Petri Nets and Stochastic Reward Nets, allowing for the exact modeling of events having deterministic occurrence times. A DEEM model may include immediate

transitions, represented by a thin line, transitions with exponentially distributed firing times, represented by empty rectangles, and transitions with deterministic firing times, represented by filled rectangles.

Besides the introduction of deterministic transitions, DEEM makes available a set of modeling features that significantly improve DSPN expressiveness:

- firing rates of timed transitions may specified through arbitrary functions of the marking;
- arbitrary functions of the marking may be employed to include additional enabling conditions, named guards, to the specification of the transitions;
- rewards can be defined as arbitrary functions of the model marking;
- arc cardinalities may be expressed through marking-dependent functions.

This rich set of modeling features, accessible through a Graphical User Interface, provides DEEM with a general modeling scheme in which two logically separate parts are used to represent MPS models. One is the System Net (SN), which represents the failure/repair behavior of system components, and the other is the Phase Net (PhN), which represents the execution of the various phases, as described in Figure 1.

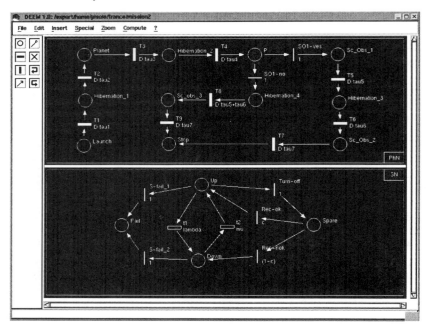

Figure 1: DEEM Interface and the DSPN model of the MPS in [10]

SN contains only exponentially distributed and immediate transitions, whereas the PhN contains all the deterministic transitions of the overall DSPN model and may

as well contain immediate transitions. A token in a place of the PhN model represents a phase being executed, and the firing of a deterministic transition models a phase change.

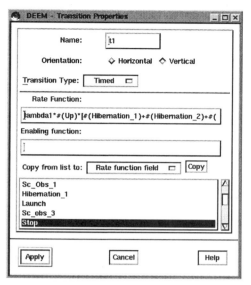

Figure 2: Property windows associated to Transition t1

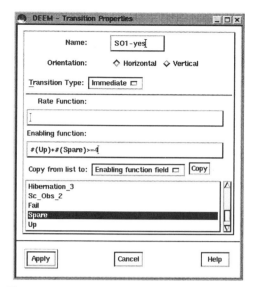

Figure 3: Property windows associated to TransitionSO1-yes

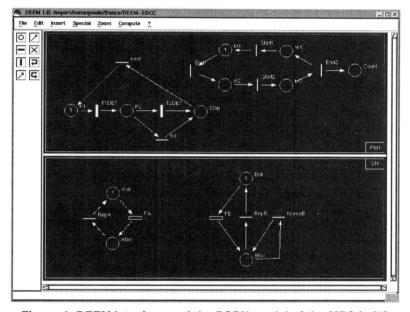

Figure 4: DEEM Interface and the DSPN model of the MPS in [5]

Each net is made dependent on the other one by marking-dependent predicates which modify transition rates, enabling conditions, reward rates, etc., to model the specific MPS features. Marking dependent attributes of the various objects (arcs, places and transitions) can be defined through the DEEM property window associated to each object.

Figure 2 shows the window associated to transition T1 of the SN of Figure 1, while Figure 3 shows that associated to transition SO1-yes of the PhN.

Phase-triggered reconfigurations, which add a significant complexity to the treatment of dependencies among phases, are easily handled by DEEM through the implicit mapping which is embedded in the model (as in [2; 4; 7; 12]). Any structure of the SN sub-model can be considered, whereas the DSPN of the PhN must possess distinct markings corresponding to different phases. This limitation is introduced because the DEEM solution algorithm focuses on the time-dependent evolution of the MPS, and thus requires to distinguish the sequence of phases performed during the MPS history. DEEM is able to automatically recognize MPS models that are amenable to analytical solution from those that violate the required assumptions. The transient solution allows to evaluate the dependability related measures at specific time instants, thus providing a means to estimate the probability of successful mission completion, the relative impact of each single phase on the overall dependability figures, etc.

Notice that the constraint on the PhN still allows for quite general structures of the sub-model. In particular, the PhN is not limited to have a linear structure, but it may take a tree structure with a dynamic choice of the next phase to perform (using enabling guards) to model a dynamic profile of the mission. It may have a cyclic structure as well, provided that the marking includes enough information to distinguish phases performed within a cycle from those executed within another one, as exemplified in Figure 4.

3 The DEEM specialized analytical solution

DEEM provides a specific and efficient analytical solution for MPS models. We briefly recall the background mathematics and then describe the solution algorithm.

3.1 The analytical technique

The specialized solution finds its ground by observing that the only deterministic transitions in a DSPN model of a MPS are the phase duration, and that these transitions are enabled one at the time. Thus, the marking process $\{M(t), t \geq 0\}$ of the DSPN is a Markov Regenerative Process (MRGP) [6] for which the firing times of the deterministic transitions are indeed regeneration points. Moreover, the following property holds of the DSPN model of a MPS:

Property 1: in every non-absorbing marking of the DSPN there is always one deterministic transition enabled, which corresponds to the phase being currently executed.

The general solution method for MRGP processes considers computing matrix $V(t)$, whose entry $\overset{\perp}{m}, \overset{\perp}{m}{}'$ is the occupation probability of marking $\overset{\perp}{m}{}'$ at time $t \geq 0$ given the initial marking $\overset{\perp}{m}$. Matrix $V(t)$ is the solution to the generalized Markov renewal equation $V(t) = E(t) + K(t) * V(t)$, where $K(t)$ and $E(t)$ are the global and local kernel matrices [6] and '*' is the

convolution operator. Instead of directly attacking the solution of the generalized Markov renewal equation by numerical algorithms or Laplace-Stiltjes transform, DEEM computes matrix $V(t)$ according to the following analytical method, proposed in [10].

Let S denote the state space of the MRGP process, let $1, 2, K, n$ be the set of phases the MPS can perform, and finally let τ_i denote the duration of phase i, $i = 1, 2, K, n$. Consider the following subsets of S:

$$S_i = \{\overset{\perp}{m} \in S \mid phase\ i\ is\ being\ performed,\ i = 1, 2, K, n\}$$

$$S_{n+1} = \{\overset{\perp}{m} \in S \mid no\ phase\ is\ being\ performed\}$$

Owing to **Property 1**, and because different phases correspond to distinct markings of the DSPN model, sets S_i, $i = 1, 2, K, n+1$, are a partition of the marking space S. The stochastic process $\{M_i(t), t \geq 0\}$, defined as the restriction of the MRGP within the execution of phase i, is a continuous-time Markov chain with state space S_i, $i = 1, 2, K, n$. Denote with Q_i the transition rate matrix of $\{M_i(t), t \geq 0\}$, $i = 1, 2, K, n$. The transient analysis of the MRGP is carried out by separately considering the evolution of the processes $\{M_i(t), t \geq 0\}$.

Consider the block structure that is induced on matrix $V(t)$ as a result of the marking space partitioning. Each block $V_{i,j}(t)$ is separately computed as follows. Consider the unique path $p(i, j)$ that links phase i to phase j according to the structure of the PhN. This path is a set of phases $p(i, j) = \{p_1, p_2, K, p_r\}$, with $p_1 = i$, and $p_r = j$. Block $V_{i,j}(t)$ is given by:

$$V_{i,j}(t) = \left(\prod_{h=1}^{r-1} e^{Q_{p_h} \tau_{p_h}} \Delta_{p_h, p_{h+1}} \right) e^{Q_j \delta} \quad (1)$$

where $\delta = t - \sum_{h=1}^{r-1} \tau_{p_h}$, and $\Delta_{p_h, p_{h+1}}$, $h = 1, 2, K, r-1$ is the branching probability matrix, whose entry $\Delta_{m,m'}^{p_h, p_{h+1}}$ is defined as the probability that $\overset{\smallsmile}{m}{}'$ is the initial marking of phase p_{h+1}, given that $\overset{\perp}{m}$ is the marking at the end of phase p_h.

3.2 The solution algorithm

Equation (1) allows to evaluate $V(t)$ through the separate analysis of the various alternative paths which compose the mission, and only requires the derivation of matrix exponentials $e^{Q_i t}$, and branching probability matrices $\Delta_{i,j}$, $i, j = 1, 2, \text{K}, n$, which can be automatically obtained when the reachability graph is generated. The solution of the DSPN model is thus reduced to the cheaper problem of solving a set of homogeneous, time-continuous smaller Markov chains.

To compute a block $V_{i,j}(t)$ and then the dependability figures of the system, the solution engine of DEEM takes as input the DSPN model and its initial probability vector, and performs the following steps:

1) Builds RGP, the reachability graph of the PhN submodel. This graph has exactly one stable marking $\overset{\perp}{m}_i$ for each phase i the MPS may perform.

2) For each stable marking $\overset{\perp}{m}_i$ in RGP, builds the reachability graph RGS($\overset{\perp}{m}_i$) of the whole DSPN model when marking $\overset{\perp}{m}_i$ is the only one permitted for the PhN. From RGS($\overset{\perp}{m}_i$) obtains the transition rate matrix Q_i of the continuous-time Markov chain describing the evolution of the DSPN during the execution of phase i.

3) For each pair of stable marking $\overset{\perp}{m}_i$ and $\overset{\perp}{m}_j$ in RGP, such that marking $\overset{\perp}{m}_j$ is reachable from $\overset{\perp}{m}_i$ through the single firing of some deterministic transition $t_{i,j}^{Det}$, builds the reachability graph RGS($\overset{\perp}{m}_i, \overset{\perp}{m}_j$) of the whole DSPN model, when the initial marking of the PhN is $\overset{\perp}{m}_i$, and transition $t_{i,j}^{Det}$ is the only one allowed to fire. From RGS($\overset{\perp}{m}_i, \overset{\perp}{m}_j$) obtains the branching probability matrix $\Delta_{i,j}$ for the transition from phase i to phase j.

4) Multiplies the matrix exponentials and the branching probability matrices, according to the order given by Equation (1), to obtain matrix $V_{i,j}(t)$.

5) Evaluates the specific dependability measure of interest for the MPS from the initial probability vector and $V_{i,j}(t)$, according to the standard computation algorithms.

4 DEEM at work

As already described in Section 2, DEEM possesses a GUI inspired by [3] and realized using an X11 installation with Motif runtime Libraries which the user employs to define his model of a MPS. We remark that while building the models, the attributes of the model objects, like rates or probabilities, can be expressed through parameters rather than numerical values directly. Therefore, prior to proceed to the model evaluation ('Transient Analysis' in the 'Compute' Menu), the user has to assign values to the parameters. DEEM automatically builds a parameter table collecting all the symbols defined in the model. This table is made accessible through the command 'Parameters' in the 'Compute' Menu, as described in Figure 5.

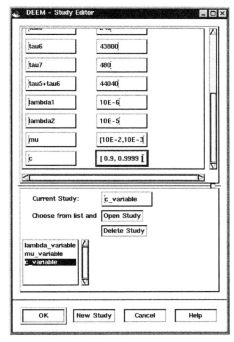

Figure 5: Parameters window with one study for the example in Figure 1.

Many studies can be defined, each represented by a column in the table. In each study one parameter is allowed to take a range of values and another parameter to take a set, this way a family of curves can be obtained by the evaluation of a single study. The specific dependability measure of interest for the MPS evaluation is defined through the general mechanism of marking-dependent reward functions ('Set Reward Function' in the 'Compute Menu').

Then the evaluation can be launched (on the selected study) and the algorithm described in Section 3 is executed. Values are returned in a file which can be further elaborated for producing plots or tables of the dependability measures.

The main computational cost of the DEEM solution algorithm is that required for the transient solutions and the multiplications in step 4) of the algorithm sketched in the previous section. Notice that the DEEM approach to generate the required matrices ever requires to handle the entire state space of the MRGP process. Thus, DEEM is able to deal with all the scenarios of MPS that have been analytically treated in the literature, at a cost which is comparable with that of the cheapest ones [9; 11; 13], completely solving the issues posed by the phased-behavior of MPS.

It is worthwhile remarking the advantages DEEM offers for the modeling and evaluation of MPS when compared to general-purpose DSPN tools (such as DSPNexpress 2.000 [8]). On the modeling side, the tool GUI allows defining the PhN and SN sub-models to neatly model the phase-dependent behaviors of MPS. On the evaluation side, the specialized separate algorithm implemented by DEEM results in a relevant reduction of the MPS model solution time.

5 Concluding remarks

This paper focused on the description of DEEM, the dependability modeling and evaluation tool specifically tailored for Multiple Phased Systems, being currently developed by the University of Florence and CNUCE-CNR. DEEM supports the methodology proposed in [10] for the dependability modeling and evaluation of MPS. Modeling is based on Deterministic and Stochastic Petri Nets, able to cope with the dynamic structure of MPS, and on a set of modeling features that significantly improve the expressiveness allowing for the definintion of very concise models. DEEM models are then solved with a very simple and computationally efficient analytical solution technique based on the separation of the MRGP underlying the DSPN of a MPS. DEEM deals with all the scenarios of MPS that have been analytically treated in the literature, at a cost that is comparable with the cheapest ones, completely solving the issues posed by the phased-behavior of MPS.

We intend to extend DEEM capabilities for analyzing a wider class of Systems. The first step will consist in moving from DSPN to Markov Regenerative Stochastic Petri Net (MRSPN). MRSPN models, characterized by having a Markov Regenerative Process as their underlying stochastic marking process, allow the tractability of MPS having random (instead of constant) phase duration. The modeling of non-exponential intra-phase activities will be the next step. To deal efficiently with intra-phase models other than time-homogeneous Markov chains, we are developing a specialization of the Markov Regenerative Process (MRGP) theory driven by the peculiar characteristics of MPS.

DEEM will be made available soon to the academic world, for information see http://bonda.cnuce.cnr.it.

References

[1] M. Ajmone Marsan and G. Chiola, "On Petri nets with deterministic and exponentially distributed firing times," in "Lecture Notes in Computer Science 266", Ed., Springer-Verlag, 1987, pp. 132-145.

[2] M. Alam and U. M. Al-Saggaf, "Quantitative Reliability Evaluation of Reparaible Phased-Mission Systems Using Markov Approach," IEEE Transactions on Reliability, Vol. R-35, pp. 498-503, 1986.

[3] S. Allmaier and S. Dalibor, "PANDA - Petri net analysis and design assistant," in Proc. Performance TOOLS'97, Saint Malo, France, 1997.

[4] B.E. Aupperle, J.F. Meyer and L. Wei, "Evaluation of fault-tolerant systems with non-homogeneous workloads," in Proc. IEEE FTCS-19 Fault Tolerant Computing Symposium, 1989, pp. 159-166.

[5] A. Bondavalli, I. Mura and K. S. Trivedi, "Dependability Modelling and Sensitivity Analysis of Scheduled Maintenance Systems," in Proc. EDCC-3 European Dependable Computing Conference, September 15-17,Prague, Czech Republic, 1999, pp. 7 – 23 (also Lecture Notes in Computer Science N. 1667)

[6] H. Choi, V.G. Kulkarni and K.S. Trivedi, "Transient analysis of deterministic and stochastic Petri nets.," in Proc. 14th International Conference on Application and Theory of Petri Nets, Chicago Illinois, USA, 1993, pp. 166-185.

[7] J. B. Dugan, "Automated Analysis of Phased-Mission Reliability," IEEE Transaction on Reliability, Vol. 40, pp. 45-52, 1991.

[8] C. Lindemann, A. Reuys and A. Thummler, "DSPNexpress 2.000 Performance and Dependability Modeling Environment," in Proc. IEEE FTCS-29 Fault-Tolerant Computing Symposium, June 15-18, Madison, Wisconsin, USA, 1999, pp. 228-231.

[9] J.F. Meyer, D.G. Furchgott and L.T. Wu, "Performability Evaluation of the SIFT Computer," in Proc. IEEE FTCS'79 Fault-Tolerant Computing Symposium, June 20-22, Madison, Wisconsin, USA, 1979, pp. 43-50.

[10] I. Mura, A. Bondavalli, X. Zang and K. S. Trivedi, "Dependability Modeling and Evaluation of Phased Mission Systems: a DSPN Approach," in Proc. DCCA-7 Dependable Computing for Critical Applications, San Jose CA, 1999, pp. 319—337.

[11] I. Mura and A. Bondavalli, "Hierarchical Modelling and Evaluation of Phased-Mission Systems," to appear in IEEE Transactions on Reliability, Vol. 48, December 1999.

[12] M. Smotherman and K. Zemoudeh, "A Non-Homogeneous Markov Model for Phased-Mission Reliability Analysis," IEEE Transactions on Reliability, Vol. 38, pp. 585-590, 1989.

[13] A. K. Somani, J. A. Ritcey and S. H. L. Au, "Computationally-Efficent Phased-Mission Reliability Analysis for Systems with Variable Configurations," IEEE Transactions on Reliability, Vol. 41, pp. 504-511, 1992

Loki: A State-Driven Fault Injector for Distributed Systems *

Ramesh Chandra, Ryan M. Lefever, Michel Cukier, and William H. Sanders
Center for Reliable and High-Performance Computing
Coordinated Science Laboratory and Department of Electrical and Computer Engineering
University of Illinois at Urbana-Champaign, Urbana, Illinois 61801
{ramesh, lefever, cukier, whs}@crhc.uiuc.edu

Abstract

Distributed applications can fail in subtle ways that depend on the state of multiple parts of a system. This complicates the validation of such systems via fault injection, since it suggests that faults should be injected based on the global state of the system. In Loki, fault injection is performed based on a partial view of the global state of a distributed system, i.e., faults injected in one node of the system can depend on the state of other nodes. Once faults are injected, a post-runtime analysis, using off-line clock synchronization, is used to place events and injections on a single global timeline and to determine whether the intended faults were properly injected. Finally, experiments containing successful fault injections are used to estimate the specified measures. In addition to reviewing briefly the concepts behind Loki and its organization, we detail Loki's user interface. In particular, we describe the graphical user interfaces for specifying state machines and faults, for executing a campaign, and for verifying whether the faults were properly injected.

Keywords : *Distributed system validation, Experimental evaluation, Fault injection, State-driven fault injection.*

1. Introduction

The increasing use of distributed systems to build critical applications motivates the development of techniques to validate their dependability. Fault injection is an important and effective way to validate such systems. However, fault injection of distributed systems is a difficult and challenging task. The reasons for this are as follows. The behavior of a distributed system depends on the state changes and events occurring in the system's different processes. Thus, the

faults occurring in such a system can depend on its global state. This necessitates that, while injecting faults in a system, the fault injector keep track of its global state to inject realistic faults and/or errors. One approach would be to synchronize at all state changes in the system, but this would be far too intrusive, and might affect the behavior of the system in unacceptable ways. The alternative to synchronization is to use state change notifications to keep track of the global state. Though these notifications are less intrusive than synchronization, fault injections based on notifications could occur in improper states, since the system could change state between notifications. Measurements based on such improper injections are not valid.

A fault injector for distributed systems should thus be able to inject faults based on the global state of the system, and at the same time not be too intrusive to the system under study. It should also be able to determine whether a particular set of faults were injected as intended, so measures can be calculated using only the intended injections. With these issues in mind, we have developed a global state-driven fault injector, called *Loki*, for distributed systems. Loki injects faults in a distributed system based on a partial view of its global state obtained using notifications, and can determine, using a post-analysis, whether each fault was injected as intended. In this paper, we describe the features of the Loki fault injector and how to use it for conducting a fault injection campaign. We also provide an overview of Loki concepts and the Loki runtime architecture.

Other fault injection and measurement tools, including EFA [6], Orchestra [5], SPI [2], NFTAPE [8], DOCTOR [7], and CESIUM [1], have also focused on distributed systems. These tools work well for their intended purposes. However, Loki is unique in that it supports fault injections based on the global state of the system combined with a powerful language for defining measures. For a comparison of these tools with Loki, see [4].

The remainder of the paper is organized as follows. Section 2 presents a brief description of the concepts underlying Loki, namely, partial view of the global state, and off-line

---

*This research has been supported by DARPA Contract F30602-96-C-0315.

clock synchronization. Section 3 provides an overview of the Loki runtime architecture. Sections 4, 5, and 6 illustrate the use of Loki for performing a fault injection campaign. In particular, Section 4 describes the specification of a campaign using the Loki interface; Section 5 details the execution of a campaign using the Loki interface; and Section 6 explains off-line analysis of the execution results and how to obtain the required measures from them. Finally, Section 7 presents our conclusions.

2. Review of Loki concepts

In this section, we briefly review the basic concepts of Loki, namely, the partial view of the global state and off-line clock synchronization. Additionally, we introduce various terms that are used in the rest of the paper. More details of what is presented here can be found in [4].

The concept of *state* is fundamental to Loki. We assume that at the desired level of abstraction (for fault injection), the execution of a component of the distributed system under study can be specified as a state machine. The global state of the system is the vector of the local states of all of its components. During the fault injection process, it may be necessary to inject faults in a component based on the state of other components of the system. It can be seen that to do this, it is not necessary to keep track of the complete global state of the system at all times; instead, it is sufficient to track an "interesting" portion of the global state that is necessary for the injection of the required faults. This interesting portion is called the *partial view of the global state*, and its selection depends on the particular system under study and the faults to be injected.

In Loki, the distributed system (under study) is divided into basic units (i.e., processes) from each of which state information is collected and into each of which faults are injected. Such a basic unit of the distributed system along with the Loki runtime attached to it is called a *node*. The Loki runtime maintains the partial view of the global state for each of these nodes and injects faults in them when necessary. It also records state changes and fault injections along with their occurrence times. The runtime only uses the necessary *state change notifications* between nodes to keep track of the partial view of the global state. Also, to be as non-intrusive to the system as possible, the runtime does not block the system while these notifications are in transit. This means that the system could change state while the notification is in transit, implying that the partial view could sometimes be out-of-date. This could lead to incorrect fault injections and hence incorrect measures.

To avoid such errors, Loki performs a post-runtime check on every fault injection to determine whether it has indeed been performed in the desired state (an off-line check is used to avoid the expense and intrusiveness of an

on-line check). Only the correct fault injections are then used in computing the measures. The post-runtime check involves placing the local times from each of the nodes into a single global timeline and then determining whether the fault was injected in the right state. Loki uses an *off-line clock synchronization* algorithm to translate the local times to a global timeline. Synchronization messages, which are used by this algorithm, are generated by the runtime before and after the application execution. These messages are non-intrusive, since they are generated when the application is not executing. This algorithm assumes that the drifts of the system clocks are linear. A more detailed explanation of the algorithm, along with its use in Loki, can be found in [4].

3. Overview of Loki runtime architecture

In this section, we provide a short overview of the Loki runtime architecture. The runtime executes along with the distributed system and maintains the partial view of the global state necessary for fault injections. It also performs fault injections when the system transitions to the desired states and collects information regarding state changes, fault injections, and their occurrence times.

As shown in Figure 1, there is a Loki runtime for each of the nodes in the distributed system. The runtime can be divided into two main parts: one that is independent of the system under study and one that is dependent on it. The *state machine, state machine transport, fault parser,* and *recorder* constitute the system-independent part, while the *probe* is the system-dependent part. The state machine keeps track of the partial view of the global state necessary for its node. It receives local state change notifications from the probe, and state change notifications of remote nodes from remote state machines. The state machines of different nodes send state change notifications to each other using the state machine transport. The recorder records the state changes and fault injections along with their times of occurrence. Boolean fault expressions are used to trigger fault injections. The fault parser parses these fault expressions on every state change and instructs the probe to inject the corresponding fault when an expression is satisfied. The probe in Loki has to be implemented by the system designer. The designer can either select a probe among the pre-implemented probes in Loki, or develop his/her own probe. Therefore, the designer will have considerable freedom in selecting the type of faults to inject into the system. The probe monitors the local node for state transitions and notifies the state machine of them. Also, it is the probe that performs the actual fault injections when the fault parser instructs it to do so. For more details regarding the runtime, its components, and their functions, refer to [4].

The evaluation of a system using Loki can be divided

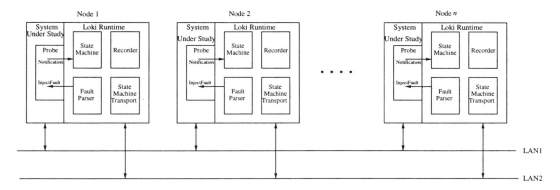

Figure 1. Loki runtime architecture

into five main phases, namely,

1. An initial synchronization-message-passing phase,

2. A fault injection and observation collection phase,

3. A second synchronization-message-passing phase,

4. Determination of experiments with properly injected faults, and

5. Computation of measures using these experiments.

In the remainder of this paper, we show how a system designer can use Loki to evaluate a system, by providing information about the five phases of evaluation in Loki. More specifically, we describe specification and execution of fault injection campaigns and off-line processing using the Loki graphical user interface.

4. Campaign specification

Loki is based on the concept of a *fault injection campaign*. A fault injection campaign for a distributed system is made up of one or more *studies*. At the study level, the system is described using state machines, which are defined by a state machine specification and a fault specification. Each study consists of a set of *experiments*, each of which is one run of the distributed application along with the fault injections corresponding to the study. Campaigns can be defined using Loki's graphical user interface, the *Loki interface*.

The Loki Manager, shown in Figure 2, controls the main functionality of the Loki interface. The panel of buttons along the bottom of the Loki Manager allows a campaign to be imported, exported, created, deleted, or copied. After a campaign is created, it can be specified with the "Edit Campaign" button. This launches a Campaign Manager window, which is similar to the Loki Manager, using which studies for the selected campaign can be created, deleted, copied, or edited. If a study is edited, a Study Manager is launched, which is also similar to the Loki Manager. Three parameters

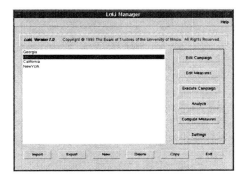

Figure 2. The Loki manager

of the study must be specified in the Study Manager: the number of experiments in the study, the time between experiments, and the application timeout. The Study Manager also allows state machines to be created, deleted, copied, and edited. After the state machines for a study have been created, each state machine must be defined with a state machine specification and a fault specification, and the distributed system must be instrumented for the study.

4.1. State machine specification

State machine specification is done using the State Machine Editor which can be seen in Figure 3, and is launched from the Study Manager. The State Machine Editor's "File" menu allows the user to save and close the editor. The "Edit" menu provides undo functionality for the state machine canvas and the ability to set the state machine's properties. The third menu item is the "Panel" menu; and it determines the control mode to be used when editing on the state machine canvas. The last menu item is the "Panel Size" menu, which allows the size of the canvas to be increased or decreased.

The three basic components that can be placed on the state machine canvas are states, event-triggered state transi-

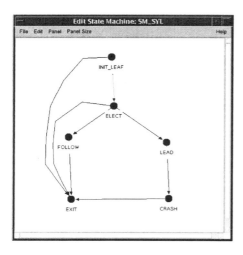

Figure 3. The state machine editor

tions, and comment boxes. States are represented on the canvas by named nodes. The state transitions are represented by connection lines between two states. The connection lines are associated with events that trigger the transitions. The comment boxes are text areas that can be used to note additional information about the state machine. The type of components that are placed on the canvas is determined by the control mode that is selected from the "Panel" menu, e.g., in the "State" mode, states can be placed on the canvas. When a state is created, it is given a name, and a list is designated of state machines that should be notified when the state machine enters the state. This list helps the state machines to maintain the partial view of the global state. When a state transition is created, the event that triggers the transition must also be provided by the user.

4.2. Fault specification

After the state machines have been specified, the fault specifications should be defined. The Fault Specification Editor is launched from the Study Manager at the same time as the State Machine Editor. It shows a listing of all the faults that should be injected into the state machine's corresponding application. The fault specification of each fault consists of three parameters. They are the fault name, a fault expression that determines when the fault should be injected, and an indication of whether the fault should be injected only the first time that the expression is true, or every time that the expression becomes true. As described earlier, the actual fault injection code is called a "probe." The method for specifying a probe is given in Section 4.3.

The main part of the fault specification is the fault expression that triggers the fault. The expression represents some partial view of the global state in the distributed system. The variables in the fault expression are (state

machine:state) pairs. The expressions make use of '&' for an AND, '|' for an OR, and '~' for a NOT. An example expression is:

```
((StateMachine1:State5)&(~(StateMachine3:
State3)))
```
This indicates that a fault should be injected when StateMachine1 is in State5 and StateMachine3 is not in State3.

4.3. Instrumenting the distributed system

After the state machine and fault specifications in a study have been defined, the application corresponding to each state machine must be instrumented. The Loki runtime is implemented in C++; therefore, the instrumented portion must also be programmed in C++. There are three steps to instrument an application:

- Probe Implementation

- Event Notification

- Use of `appMain()`

A probe must be defined for the application, and its `injectFault()` function must be implemented. This function takes in a fault name (which corresponds to the name given in the fault specification), implements injection of the fault, and returns the time when the fault is actually injected. By having the Loki user write the `injectFault()` code, Loki is capable of providing a high degree of freedom in the types of faults injected. The probe should also indicate to the state machine the occurrence of events that were specified in the state machine specification. This is done using the `notifyEvent()` method of the state machine and passing the event name and the time at which the event occurred as parameters. Another requirement is that `appMain()`, instead of `main()` must be used to start the application.

The instrumentation can be performed both when the application's source code is available and when it is not. If it is available, then the probe can be integrated into the application code. `notifyEvent()` and `injectFault()` can directly be a part of the application's source code. For this to be done, the application's `main()` function should be renamed to `appMain()`. If the source code is not available, the probe can be used as a monitor for the application. The probe's `appMain()` function is used to start the application, and it can monitor the application's input and output for events. These events are then communicated to the state machine using the `notifyEvent()` method. The `injectFault()` method can inject faults from outside the application. The first approach provides more accurate event notification and fault injection, but it is more intrusive than the second approach.

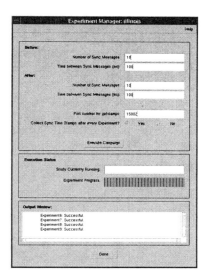

Figure 4. The experiment manager

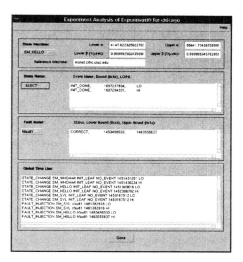

Figure 5. Analysis window for an experiment

5. Campaign execution

After a campaign is fully specified, it can be executed. To do this, the Experiment Manager, shown in Figure 4, is launched from the Loki Manager. There are six parameters in the top panel of the Experiment Manager that must be set before a campaign is executed. The Loki runtime passes synchronization messages for the off-line clock synchronization as discussed in Section 2. These messages are passed between all the hosts in the distributed system. The first two parameters represent the number of synchronization messages that should be passed before each experiment, and the delay between those messages. The next two parameters are similar, but correspond to synchronization messages that are passed after experiments. The fifth parameter indicates the port number that the synchronization messages should be passed on. The last parameter specifies whether the synchronization messages are to be passed after each experiment, or after each study.

Once all the parameters are set, the campaign can be executed with the "Execute Campaign" button. It executes each study one after another. Within each study it executes the specified number of experiments, passing synchronization messages as indicated above. During execution, the middle panel of the Experiment Manager indicates the current study and displays the experiment's progress. The bottom panel indicates whether studies and experiments were successfully executed.

6. Off-line processing

Off-line processing consists of two steps: campaign analysis and measure estimation. The campaign analysis creates global timelines for the different experiments, and determines whether the faults were properly injected. Measure estimation in Loki uses the results of these proper fault injections to calculate statistically representative measures.

6.1. Campaign analysis

Two windows are used during campaign analysis: "Analysis," which performs analysis computations for a campaign and displays preliminary results for a study, and "Experiment Analysis," which shows the details for a particular experiment. The conversion to global timeline is done only once for each study. When the analysis is run for the first time, the "Analysis" window is disabled, and a dialog box shows the progress of the conversion to a global timeline. If the conversion to the global timeline has already been performed, the "Analysis" window allows the user to select a study in order to obtain a report of how many faults were correctly injected, incorrectly injected, and not injected at all for each state machine in the study. The user can also focus on one particular experiment of the study by clicking the "Examine Analysis" button.

The "Experiment Analysis" window, shown in Figure 5, presents detailed information on each experiment. The top part of the window gives the clock synchronization results for the different machines. For the meaning of these results, refer to [4]. The second part of the window shows information on each state of the selected state machine. Each entry consists of the event name, the time in clock ticks, and an indication of whether the time is an upper or lower bound of the event. Note that a time instant on a local timeline, when projected to the global timeline, becomes a time interval defined by a lower and upper bound. Hence, there are two entries for each event. The third part of the window shows all the occurrences of a fault in the selected state machine. For each fault occurrence, there is an indication of whether the fault was injected properly, not injected properly, or not injected at all. The two bounds related to each fault are also shown. The last part of the window shows the global timeline for the given experiment. The first column indicates the event type (state transition or fault injection). The second column shows the state machine in which the event occurred. If the event is a state transition, the third column indicates the ending state of the state change, and the fourth column indicates the event that triggered the transition. If a fault was injected, the third column contains the fault name. For both cases, the next column shows the time in clock ticks, and the last column indicates whether the time shown is a lower or upper bound.

6.2. Measure estimation

The goal of measure estimation in Loki is to provide a mechanism to obtain statistically representative measures which are interesting to the user. Loki uses a flexible language to describe these measures. The definition of measures is done at two levels, namely, at the study level and at the campaign level.

Each of the measures specified at the study level consists of an ordered sequence of (subset selection, predicate, observation function) triples, and is defined for a particular study. The *subset selection* is used to select a subset of experiments based on the observation function outcomes of the previous triple. Note that the subset selection of the first triple would select all the experiments of the study. The *predicate* is a Boolean expression containing queries of the form (state machine, state, time), and (state machine, start state, event, time), combined with AND, OR, and NOT. The outcome of the predicate applied to the global timeline of an experiment is called the *predicate value timeline* and is a combination of impulses and steps. The *observation function* is defined on the predicate value timeline and its outcome is called the *observation value*. The above triples are applied, in the specified order, to each of the global timelines in the study to obtain the corresponding final observation values.

Measures at the campaign level are obtained by collating the final observation values of different experiments. Depending on the method of collation, and the observations used during collation, statistically significant results such as the first four moments, and percentiles for various α-levels can be computed for these measures.

7. Conclusions

This paper describes Loki, a state-based fault injector for distributed systems. Loki is unique in its ability to inject faults based on a partial view of the global state of a distributed system and its ability to check afterwards whether the faults were correctly injected. Moreover, Loki provides a powerful language to define sophisticated measures. We have shown in this paper how a user can, by using the Loki interface, specify the fault injection campaign and the faults to be injected, execute a campaign, and analyze the obtained results to verify whether the faults were properly injected. Preliminary performance results using a simple example [4] showed that, depending on the application and the OS, high probabilities of correct fault injection can be expected for states in which the application will remain for at least several OS time-slices.

References

[1] G. Alvarez and F. Cristian. Centralized failure injection for distributed, fault-tolerant protocol testing. In *Proceedings of the 17th IEEE International Conference on Distributed Computing Systems (ICDCS'97)*, pages 78–85, May 1997.

[2] D. Bhatt, R. Jha, T. Steeves, R. Bhatt, and D. Wills. SPI: An instrumentation development environment for parallel/distributed systems. In *Proceedings of the 9th International Parallel Processing Symposium*, pages 494–501, 1995.

[3] R. Chandra, R. M. Lefever, M. Cukier, and W. H. Sanders. *Loki User's Manual – version 1.0*. Coordinated Science Laboratory, University of Illinois at Urbana-Champaign, Illinois 61801, August 1999.

[4] M. Cukier, R. Chandra, D. Henke, J. Pistole, and W. H. Sanders. Fault injection based on the partial global state of a distributed system. In *Proceedings of the 18th IEEE Symposium on Reliable Distributed Systems*, pages 168–177, October 1999.

[5] S. Dawson, F. Jahanian, T. Mitton, and T. L. Tung. Testing of fault-tolerant and real-time distributed systems via protocol fault injection. In *Proceedings of the 26th International Symposium on Fault-Tolerant Computing (FTCS-26)*, pages 404–414, June 1996.

[6] K. Echtle and M. Leu. The EFA fault injector for fault-tolerant distributed system testing. In *Proceedings of the IEEE Workshop on Fault-Tolerant Parallel and Distributed Systems*, pages 28–35, 1992.

[7] S. Han, K. G. Shin, and H. A. Rosenberg. DOCTOR: An integrated software fault injection environment for distributed real-time systems. In *Proceedings of the International Computer Performance and Dependability Symposium*, pages 204–213, 1995.

[8] D. T. Stott, Z. Kalbarczyk, and R. K. Iyer. Using NFTAPE for rapid development of automated fault injection experiments. In *Digest of FastAbstracts of the 29th Annual International Symposium on Fault-Tolerant Computing (FTCS-29)*, pages 39–40, June 1999.

Sensitivity Analysis for System Design Improvement

Sergio Contini, Stefan Scheer, Marc Wilikens
Joint Research Centre, Institute for Systems, Informatics and Safety
T.P. 210, I-21020 Ispra (VA), Italy, name.surname@jrc.it

Abstract

In order to help identifying suitable design modifications for complex systems, there is a need to 1) determine the weakest elements of the system, 2) identify a better design alternative, and 3) evaluate the effect of the adopted solution on system safety / availability. This is a well-known procedure applied to a single system failure mode. In reality, several undesired system states have to be checked for. On the other side, systems grow in complexity, and components are often multi-functional so that they could affect several system states concurrently and even in conflicting terms. This paper presents the sensitivity analysis module of the ASTRA package, based on component importance analysis techniques to be applied to all system failure states concurrently. The technique employs fault-tree analysis and Markovian processes as basic probabilistic models.

1. Introduction

Dependability analysis of systems becomes increasingly important the more complex these systems are evolving, and the more crucial aspects of modern society are involved; the range lasts from severe financial losses to loss of human life. The analysis is performed by means of a set of probabilistic models aiming at supporting the design process in order to ensure, with reasonable confidence, a future behavior close to specifications.

A complex system may present one or more failure modes. To each System Failure Mode (SFM) a probabilistic model is applied to quantify the probabilistic parameters of interest. The need to improve the system design calls for tools to support the designer in identifying the weakest parts of the system, i.e. where design improvement is more effective. Consequently, different design solutions may be defined, evaluated and compared from the dependability viewpoint. In trying to improve the system design from e.g. the safety viewpoint, taking into account other constraints such as costs, weight etc., it is important to consider also the effects of changes on other performance measures

such as, for instance, system availability. In fact, an increase of safety generally implies a reduction of availability and vice-versa, i.e. trade-off has to be made by the designer [1].

Among the available quantitative analysis techniques the Fault Tree Analysis (FTA) can be considered as the fundamental one for modeling complex systems failure logic [2]. It presents several advantages, i.e. applicability to systems made up by any number of components, highly systematic construction procedure, calculation of Minimal Cut Sets, components importance, unavailability, failure frequency, etc. FTA's main limitation concerns the independence of component failure and repair processes. For this reason, Markovian Processes (MP) are applied to complement FTA in order to correctly model dependent failures. Due to the high importance of fault trees and Markovian Processes, a lot of software tools are available, based on different approaches, and efforts are being made to define more efficient methods able to analyze systems of growing complexity. Concerning FTA, the Binary Decision Diagrams (BDD) approach proved to be much more powerful than any other analysis method previously developed. Some software packages developed based on BDD [3, 4, 5] allow to completely quantify, in few seconds, fault trees which had not been possible to quantify before without adopting approximations.

The availability of these powerful methods opens the possibility to develop new interactive support tools for dependability studies. One of these is the Sensitivity Analysis Module (SAM) of the ASTRA tool set (Advanced Software Tools for Reliability Analysis).

This paper, after a brief introduction of the ASTRA architecture, will present the analysis procedure implemented in SAM in order to support the designer in improving a complex system taking into account conflicting requirements on safety and availability.

2. Sensitivity Analysis

Sensitivity Analysis (SA) is a technique applied to investigate the relative importance of input model parameters in determining the value of an assigned output variable. Several methods are currently used in Sensitivity Analysis studies [6, 7].

In system dependability analysis the input parameters are the failure probability at component level, and the output variable is the occurrence probability of one of the system failure modes. The currently applied SA procedure is based on three main steps:

- Ranking of components according to their importance to system failure.
- Definition of an improving design alternative.
- Assessment of the effects of the adopted design solution to system failure probability.

Step 1. Components Ranking

One of the most useful results in system analysis is the component importance index, which represents a measure of the relative contribution to system failure probability, i.e. the occurrence of a given SFM, due to component failure. Thus, components can be ranked according to their importance in the system. Consequently, the weakest system points, to be considered for subsequent design improvement, can easily be identified on a rational and objective basis: they are made up of components whose failure modes present the highest importance index.

Several importance measures for components have been developed in the past [8] and are being used especially in fault tree analysis, among those, two will be presented.

The *importance index for unavailability,* due to Fussell-Vesely, $I_j^{FV}(t)$, is expressed by:

$$I_j^{FV}(t) = I_j^B(t) * q_j(t) / Qs(t) \qquad (1)$$

where $q_j(t)$ and $Qs(t)$ are respectively the component and system SFM unavailability. $I_j^{FV}(t)$ represents the contribution to SFM occurrence probability due to the j-th component failure.

The importance index for safety, based on failure frequency, is due to Barlow-Proschan:

$$I_j^{BP}(t) = \int_0^t I_j^B(x) * \omega_j(x) \, dx / Ws(t) \qquad (2)$$

where $\omega_j(x)$ and $Ws(t)$ are respectively the unconditional failure frequency of the j-th component and the SFM expected number of failures (upper bound for the unreliability). $I_j^{BP}(t)$ represents the frequency of SFM occurrence caused by the failure of the j-th component expressed by its unconditional failure intensity $\omega(t)$.

In equations (1) and (2)

$$I_j^B(t) = \delta Qs(t) / \delta q_j(t) \qquad 3)$$

represents the probability that the j-th component is in a critical state.

Step 2. Design Modification

Having identified the weakest system points, the design can be improved by identifying and implementing more reliable solutions. Following the design modification the system model is updated.

Step 3. Re-analysis of the Model

The modified model is then re-analyzed to assess the improvements made.

In case that the solution is not yet acceptable, the three steps of the procedure are re-applied.

This analysis procedure has been implemented in an interactive module of ISPRA-FTA [9] and is being offered by several other fault tree analysis tools. All these tools allow the user to apply SA to a single SFM and to modify only the reliability parameters of a selected component.

3. The ASTRA Tool Set

Within its activities on dependability and reactor safety, the authors have been working on a new set of tools for complex systems reliability analysis. The result is ASTRA [10], which integrates, in a user-friendly environment, several modules supporting reliability studies during the different design phases. ASTRA, whose structure is sketched in Figure 1 (see below), works on PC under Windows 95/98/NT operating systems.

ASTRA is composed of several modules: The Fault Tree Analysis module (FTA), including the Time-Dependent Probabilistic Analysis and the Online Editor; the Event-Tree Analysis module (ETA) supporting the generation of event-trees through the use of functional dependency rules; the SAM module, which is the subject of this paper, and the Reliability Database module embedding a library of component failure models. Markovian Analysis and the Uncertainty Analysis modules are planned to be developed in the near future. Finally, with the Software Failure Analysis module (SFA, under development), it will possible to automatically generate fault trees of systems with embedded software components starting from system specification. Each module has its own user interface, graphical representation of results, and a report writer. All modules are driven by the Project Management Interface, which allows the user to manage the data generated during the different phases of the design process.

4. Sensitivity Analysis within ASTRA

The main features of ASTRA-SAM [11] are briefly listed below:

1) SAM uses Fault tree and Markovian processes as basic probabilistic models. Each SFM is analyzed by means of the fault tree technique. Markovian processes are used for modeling subsystem failures.

2) Sensitivity Analysis is performed on the system as a whole. Thus, as many fault trees as the number of SFM are concurrently analyzed.

3) The possibility to assign target values to the occurrence probability of each SFM. Thus, a risk matrix can be defined to describe the relationships between consequence and probability for each SFM.

4) In examining the weakest part of the system, different design solutions can be considered, such as:
   - Use of a component of better quality or of higher maintainability. This means a change of reliability parameters, thus resulting in higher reliability/availability values. Changes may affect failure rates, repair time, on-demand unavailability, and test intervals depending on the component type (not repairable, on-line maintained, acting on demand or tested/inspected);
   - Use of a redundant subsystem, thus increasing the reliability/availability of the component's function. A library of pre-analyzed redundant configurations is available, comprising (a) K/N majority voting for active components or tested components with given testing policy, (b) parallel configuration, (c) stand-by configuration, (d) more complex user-defined configurations. Common Cause Failures (CCF) and dependency on repair processes can also be introduced in these configurations, since they are quantified by means of Markovian processes.
   - A change of the system failure logic which leads to the fault tree logic modification.

5) Following any system modification, all fault trees are quantified all together and results are graphically displayed. A *step-gain* value is calculated to allow the user to appreciate the goodness of the modification just adopted.

6) The user can manage a decision tree containing all modifications made. A *path-gain* value is calculated to allow him to compare different design alternatives.

The ASTRA-SAM Analysis Procedure

The analysis procedure implemented in SAM allows the concurrent analysis of all fault trees associated to system failure modes.

For a given system, let N be the number of SFM, considered important for design improvement, and $\{f_1, f_2, ..., f_i, ..., f_N\}$ the corresponding set of fault trees. The analysis of these trees delivers the set of Top Events' occurrence probabilities, representing the initial situation: $\{P_{01}, P_{02}, ..., P_{0k}, .., P_{0N}\}$. P_{0k} represents the occurrence probability of the k-th SFM. For each Top Event, the set of components importance values $\{I_{1k}, I_{2k}, ..., I_{jk}, ..., I_{Mk}\}$, can consequently be calculated, where I_{jk} represents the importance of the j-th component belonging to the k-th fault tree. Furthermore, a set of goals to be achieved during the analysis for each fault trees is required. Let $\{P_{gk}, k = 1, 2, ...N\}$ be a set of goals; P_{gk} represents the goal associated with the k-th fault tree, i.e. k-th SFM.

From the sake of simplicity the dependence from the mission time t of probabilities and importance measures will not be represented.

In order to perform sensitivity analysis it is necessary to determine the Global Importance Index of each basic event in the whole system. This can be calculated by combining the importance of this event in all trees it belongs to with a criticality index, say d, representing the cost of the consequences of the occurrence of the SFM. Therefore, let $\{d_k, k = 1, 2, ..., N\}$ be the set of criticality indices of SFM.

d_k and P_{gk} are determined as follows. In many industrial fields SFM are categorized as e.g. catastrophic, critical, marginal, and negligible. Each category is also associated with a probabilistic threshold (P_g) representing the target to be achieved during the design development phases. A risk table is generally used to represent the relationships between category and probability.

In ASTRA-SAM d can be calculated as

$$d = - A \, Log \, [\, P_g / (P_{gM} - P_{gm})] \qquad (4)$$

where P_{gM} and P_{gm} are respectively the maximum and minimum values of P_g in the risk matrix, and A (A > 1) is a constant coefficient, or, alternatively, as a step function representing the index d as a function of the risk category.

The assignment of d is an important issue, since it affects the design improvement strategy. d is used as a weight to determine the global importance of basic events in the whole system. For this reason the analyst should define d in a way considered suitable for the objectives of the analysis. Obviously, if all SFM have the same importance, e.g. they belong to the same category, then $d = 1$ for all of them.

The three steps of the basic analysis procedure described above have been implemented in ASTRA-SAM as follows.

Step 1. Components Ranking

System components may belong to one or more fault trees. Let C_{jk} be the j-th component belonging to the k-th fault tree. For each component a Global Criticality Index, G_j (j=1,2, ..., nc), is calculated as follows:

$$G_j = \sum_{k=1}^{N} I_{jk}\, \alpha_k\, d_k \qquad (5)$$

where:
- I_{jk} is the importance index of the j-th component in the k-th fault tree;
- α_k takes the value 0 (1) if C_j does not (does) belong to the k-th fault tree;
- d_k is the criticality index of the k-th fault tree.

nc is the total number of different components failure modes belonging to all fault trees.

Components are ranked according to their global importance value G_j under the hypotheses adopted for calculating d_k.

Step 2. Design Modification

Having identified the weakest system points on the basis of G_j, the system design is improved by identifying and implementing more reliable solutions. ASTRA-SAM allows studying different solutions, i.e. changing component parameters, applying the redundancy concept through the selection from the library of one out of the available configurations, or changing the system architecture.

Step 3. Re-analysis of the Model

All fault trees containing the adopted design modifications are analyzed. For each defined design alternative the step gain is calculated, giving a measure of the effectiveness of the adopted design solution, i.e. the reduction of the occurrence probability of each SFM from step i-1 to step i (see Appendix).

The path gain represents a cumulative measure of the effectiveness of all the adopted modifications made from the initial situation (step 0) up to step i. For the generic k-th fault tree, the h-th path gain at the i-th step can be calculated as:

$$\Delta_{pkh}^{(i)} = 100\,[P_{0k} - P_{fkh}^{(i)}] / S \qquad (6)$$

with

$$S = \sum_{k}^{N} (P_{0k} - P_{gk}) \qquad (7)$$

being S a normalizing factor.

The total system gain at step i and for the h-th alternative (i.e. path in the decision tree) can be obtained as a simple sum of the total gains obtained for each fault tree:

$$\Delta_{Th}^{i} = \sum_{k}^{N} \Delta_{phk}^{i} \qquad (8)$$

The total gain corresponding to all system design alternatives, i.e. paths of the decision tree, are displayed as it is shown in Figure 2 (see below). Graphical results are also given at fault tree level for different analysis steps.

With the re-analysis of all fault trees, new SFM probabilities as well as new global importance indexes are obtained. If all targets are reached or if the analyst considers the results to be sufficient, the analysis ends; otherwise the three steps are applied again.

Decision Tree Handling

In SAM the way of approaching the final system design configuration is done in a highly interactive way: all system modifications and subsequent adopted improvements are kept in a decision tree.

Each node keeps information about the step and the path gains as well as all the results of the analysis of all fault trees. The generic path from the root of the tree to the i-th node describes one of the potential solutions, made up by modifications associated with nodes on the path. Horizontally, the decision tree is growing when different design alternatives are adopted for the same weak point. Vertically, the tree is growing any time the three steps of the analysis procedure are re-executed.

When a given potential alternative can a-posteriori be considered not significant, it can be deleted to avoid developing a branch that cannot give any acceptable solution. Given two or more potential solutions, i.e. paths at comparable total gain, the choice of the best one may need some additional considerations on constraints such as costs or weight.

Figure 3 (see below) shows the user interface managing the decision tree. The corresponding path gains are shown on the right side of the screen.

6. Conclusions and Further Developments

In the paper the main aspects of the system design improvement method implemented in the ASTRA tool set have been described. This method is also applicable to complex event trees of nuclear plants. The event tree model is applied to describe the possible consequences of the occurrence of a pre-defined initiating event in case of partial or complete failure of safety related systems modeled by fault trees.

Furthermore, the system improvement method implemented in SAM may advantageously be integrated in online monitoring tools to support maintenance activities [12].

For the current implementation of SFA [13], it is under investigation to exchange the extensive use of FTA with sensitivity analysis techniques, which would allow covering a wider range of dependability aspects.

Promising results in applying ASTRA-SAM have been obtained from the analysis of control systems of chemical plants and of a turbine-driven electrical power system [14].

Concerning future activities, the developments of ASTRA-MKA (Markovian Analysis module) and its integration with FTA will allow substituting the library with a tool allowing the use of more complex configurations.

Another important aspect to be developed in the near future is the introduction of the uncertainty in reliability data at component level; this means that the selection of the most critical component will be based not only on the mean values, but also on the dispersion around the mean.

Appendix

Gain Value Calculation

Let P_{0k} be the occurrence probability of the k-th fault tree representing the failure model of the k-th SFM at step 0. Let P_{gk} be the assigned goal to be achieved. Starting from P_{0k} ($P_{0k} > P_{gk}$), the goal P_{gk} is reached in one or more steps, where at each step a system modification is made on the selected component. At a given step i, the SFM probability, say P_{fk}, changes from $P_{fk}^{(i-1)}$ to $P_{fk}^{(i)}$. When $P_{fk}^{(i-1)} < P_{fk}^{(i)}$ the modification made has worsened the system. Independently of the path, on a scale 0-100, the gain at the i-th step, referred to as *step-gain*, is represented as $\Delta_{sk}^{(i)}$ and is given by:

$$\Delta_{sk}^{(i)} = 100 \, [P_{fk}^{(i-1)} - P_{fk}^{(i)}] \, / \, [P_{fk}^{(i-1)} - P_{gk}]$$

It can easily be seen that:

If $P_{fk}^{(i)} = P_{fk}^{(i-1)}$ then $\Delta_{sk}^{(i)} = 0$ (no improvement)

If $P_{fk}^{(i)} \leq P_{gk}$ then $\Delta_{sk}^{(i)} \geq 100$ (goal satisfied)

If $P_{fk}^{(i-1)} < P_{fk}^{(i)}$ then $\Delta_{sk}^{(i)} < 0$ (system worsened)

At the i-th step the higher is $\Delta_{sk}^{(i)}$, the more effective are the modifications made to the system. Consequently, the "effort" still to be done to reach the goal for a given fault tree is given by $P_{fk}^{(i)} - P_{gk}$.

References

[1] Geervliet, S. M., Bolt, R.: Design Optimisation with Conflicting Requirements. Safety and Reliability, Lydersen, Hansen & Sandtorv (eds). Balkema, Rotterdam, 1998.

[2] Vesely, W. E., et. al.: Fault Tree Handbook, NUREG-0492, US-NRC, Washington DC, 1981.

[3] Coudert, O., Madre, J. C.: Metaprime: An Interactive Fault Tree Analyser with Binary Decision Diagrams. IEEE Transactions on Reliability, Vol. 43, 1994.

[4] Aralia Group: Computation of Prime Implicant of a Fault Tree within Aralia. Proceeding of the European Safety and Reliability Association, ESREL '95, Bournemouth, England, 1995.

[5] Contini, S.: ASTRA-FTA: Logical and Probabilistic Analysis Modules. EUR 18727 EN, 1999.

[6] Homma, T., Saltelli, A.: Importance Measures in Global Sensitivity Analysis of Nonlinear Models. Reliability Engineering & System Safety. Vol 52, N. 1, 1996.

[7] Marseguerra, M. et al.: Sensitivity Analysis of a Nonlinear Reliability Model. Safety and Reliability, Lydersen, Hansen & Sandtorv (eds). Balkema, Rotterdam, 1998.

[8] Henley, E. J., Kumamoto, H.: Reliability Engineering and Risk Assessment, Prentice-Hall, 1981.

[9] Contini, S.: ISPRA-FTA: Interactive Software Package for Reliability Analysis. Fault Tree Analysis Tool for Personal Computers. EUR 13997 EN, 1991.

[10] Contini, S., Scheer, S., Wilikens, M., de Cola, G., Cojazzi, G.: ASTRA: An Integrated Tool Set for Complex Systems Dependability Studies. Tool Support for System Specification, Development and Verification, Berghammer, R., Lakhnech Y. (eds.), Advances in Computing Science, Springer, 1999.

[11] Contini, S.: ASTRA-SAM: Sensitivity Analysis Module, Knowledge Handbook, EUR 18728 EN, 1999.

[12] Contini, S., Wilikens, M., Masera, M.: The Use of RAMS for On-line Maintenance and Decision Support. International Conference on Probabilistic Assessment and Management, Crete, Greece, 1996.

[13] Mauri, G., McDermid, J. A., Papadopoulos, Y.: Extension of Hazard and Safety Analysis Techniques to Address Problems of Hierarchical Scale, IEE Colloquium on Systems Engineering of Aerospace Projects, London, IEEE Digest No: 98/249, pp. 41-46, IEEE, 1998.

[14] Baietto, A.: The Role of Sensitivity Analysis to Integrate Safety Specifications in Control System Design for Energetic Applications (in Italian). Polytechnic of Turin, 1997.

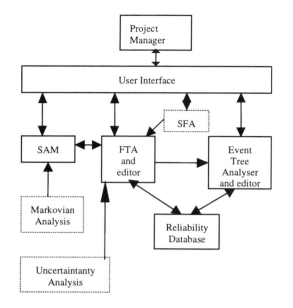

Figure 1:

The basic ASTRA architecture with SFA (Software Failure Analysis), Markovian Analysis, and Uncertainty Analysis to be under development.

The Sensitivity Analysis module fundamentally makes use of the Fault Tree Analyser.

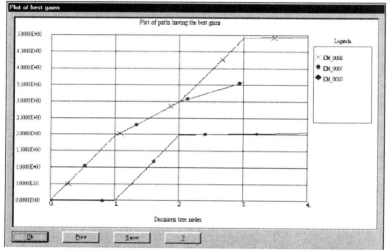

Figure 2: Plot of gains.

This summary of plots shows the calculated gain values for three paths that have been followed until now. The x-ed path, for example, has reached a gain value of 5 after four modifications to the system have taken place.

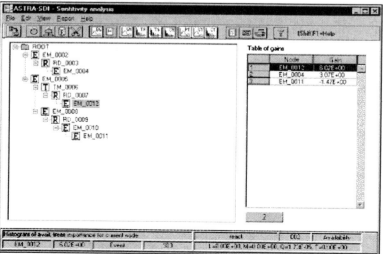

Figure 3: Decision tree.

This tree, for example, contains two main branches starting from the root node; the second main branch itself consists of two major sub-branches. "E" stands for "event modification", "T" for "tree modification", and "R" for "applying redundancy". On the right side it can be seen that the calculated gain value at node "EM_0012" is 6.

Session 9A

Testing of COTS Systems

Joint Evaluation of Performance and Robustness of a COTS DBMS through Fault-Injection*

Diamantino Costa[1], Tiago Rilho and Henrique Madeira

CISUC – Centre for Informatics and Systems of the University of Coimbra

http://cisuc.dei.uc.pt, Polo II, Pinhal de Marrocos, Coimbra P3030, Portugal

{dino,henrique}@dei.uc.pt, rilho@student.dei.uc.pt

Abstract

This paper presents and discusses observed failure modes of a common-off-the-shelf (COTS) Database Management System (DBMS) under the presence of transient operational faults induced by SWIFI. The standard Transaction Processing Performance Council (TPC) TPC-C benchmark and associated environment is used here together with fault-injection technology, building a framework that discloses both dependability and performance figures. Over 1600 faults were injected in the database server of a Client/Server computing environment built upon Oracle 8.1.5 database engine and Windows NT running on COTS machines with Intel Pentium processors. A macroscopic view on the impact of faults revealed that: 1) A large majority of the faults caused no observable abnormal impact in the database server; In 96% of hardware faults and 80% of software faults the database server behaved normally. 2) Software faults are more prone to let the database server hanging or cause abnormal terminations. 3) Up to 51% of software faults lead to observable failures in the client processes.

1. Introduction

The joint evaluation of performance and dependability of common off-the-shelf (COTS) systems is a manifold motivation research. There is an increasing trend today for using COTS technology in mission critical and business critical systems. Systems designers see COTS components as an opportunity to cut development costs and minimize the risk of infant defects. However, this attitude puts a tremendous demand on COTS behavior, since they are not designed with the harsh requirements of critical systems in mind. *Do COTS savings necessarily mean less robustness?* A bit of common sense and also some field findings lead us to an affirmative answer. But another question remains -

How less dependable can a COTS system be? This question is relevant since many applications can tolerate a system with reduced dependability requirements, provided that there is an estimation of how less dependable the system can be.

The lack of practical dependability metrics is one factor commonly pointed out by the industry and end buyers for disregarding dependability issues in either COTS product design or purchase decision. Typically, buying dependability is an all or nothing decision (and sometimes a question of faith). For instance, it is very difficult (or even impossible) to bind a COTS computing platform to a given availability class without having representative data on the way the system behaves in the field. We advocate that dependability metrics should learn from (and walk side by side with) established performance metrics. First, this will favor its acceptance by the vendors, since lots of previous investments may be reused. Second, performance losses, even minimal ones, are often the "Achilles heel" of several dependability improvement techniques, and represents the main reason why they are not adopted by the vendor industry. By giving a sharp image of the system performance/dependability figures, we will unveil designs that "sell" only raw performance but actually behave poorly in presence of (unavoidable) faults. Thus, the joint measurement of performance and dependability figures will enable us to tune the systems/designs for different tradeoffs between dependability requirements and performance rates.

Software faults are recognized as the major cause of system outages. Existing studies show a clear predominance of software faults [1][2][3][4]. Given the huge complexity of today's software, the weight of software faults tends to increase, making clear that the evaluation of the dependability of COTS systems must take into account software faults.

Fault injection has become an established approach of validating specific fault handling mechanisms and assessing the impact of faults in actual systems, allowing the

---

*Work supported by the Portuguese Foundation for Science and Technology (FCT), Program Praxis XXI, grant No. 2/2.1/TIT/1570/95.

[1]Presently at CISUC, on leave from Critical Software Lda.,www.criticalsoftware.com; Research supported by FCT, PRAXIS XXI, grant No. BD/5636/95.

251

estimation of fault-tolerant system measures such as fault coverage and error latency [5]. Given the increasing relevance of software faults it is clear that fault injection technologies should be extended to the injection of this kind of faults.

In spite of having good indications that the erroneous system behavior induced by hardware faults with SWIFI techniques also emulate (some) software faults, the fact is that the accurate emulation of software faults through SWIFI is still an open issue. Recent efforts towards this end [6][7] suggest that current SWIFI technology can model the errors induced by software faults to some extent, but there is not an established way to emulate general classes of software faults by SWIFI tools yet. Nevertheless, SWIFI seems to be the most effective method to assess the dependability of COTS systems. In this study we use the XceptionNT fault injection tool, which is a version of Xception [8] for the Windows NT operating system. XceptionNT has been enhanced with new features to support emulation of software faults. One distinctive advantage of the Xception family of tools is its capability to perform fault-injection without need for source code. This is a sound advantage to perform the evaluation of COTS systems.

In this experimental study we focus on a commercial DBMS as a case study for establishing an environment for the joint evaluation of performance and dependability of COTS. Multiple factors can be found for this specific research:

1. Database applications have traditionally been an area with fault-tolerance needs, concerning both data integrity and availability. Several mechanisms and techniques needed to achieve fault-tolerance, such as transactions, checkpointing, logging, and replica control management born from the research in the database area.

2. COTS DBMS are core components of enterprise information systems (EIS), ranging from LAN based two-tier client/server systems to WAN based three-tier systems. Assuring DBMS dependability is of utmost importance, not only because they represent the reliable storage of organizations critical data, but also because its failure can adversely impact distributed enterprise applications.

3. DBMS industry holds a reputed infrastructure for performance evaluation. The set of benchmarks managed by the TPC are recognized to be among the most successful benchmark initiatives of the overall computer industry. The addition of dependability clauses to the TPC benchmarks specifications, as suggested and partly experimented in our own study, was first claimed in the TPC milieu.

This paper presents and discusses observed failure modes of a strict COTS DBMS system under the presence of transient operational faults induced by SWIFI. The impact of faults is assessed at different abstraction levels, ranging from monitoring of machine exceptions at the operating system level to trace and log files and a consistency-checking tool at the DBMS level. Consistency

tests performed at the database application level have also been performed. Database integrity is measured using the set of semantic rules and associated consistency tests ("business logic") defined in [9]. The MTTR of observed crashes is also calculated. To summarize, this paper gives the following contributions:

- First, and to the best of our knowledge, it is the first experimental fault-and-error-injection (FEI) study conducted over a strict COTS DBMS system.

- Second, it gives insight on the failure modes of a COTS DBMS due to transient hardware faults and software faults (bugs).

- Last, but not the least, it leverages the reputed infrastructure of TPC performance benchmarks, adding up a fault load and fault impact measurements, thus enabling joint evaluation of performance and dependability figures.

The paper is organized as follows: the next section describes the related work. Section 3 surveys COTS failures in general (and specific data on COTS DBMS failures) setting the ground for the fault model herein used and elaborates on the specific issues of emulation software faults with SWIFI technology. Section 4 details the testbed, including the target system, the workload, the set of faults and the set of measurements observed. It also describes experiment setup and execution. Section 5 presents and discusses the experimental results and Section 6 concludes the paper, outlining the most significant results and summing up the main contributions.

2. Related work

The only work found in the literature so far that specifically cross relates experimental evaluation of both performance and dependability is [10]. This study addresses the evaluation of fault-tolerant systems and used synthetic workloads to exercise the available fault-tolerant mechanisms.

In [11] a simulation study was performed to assess formal figures for availability, reliability and mean transaction time for repairable database configurations. In [2] a study on failure data collected in a WindowsNT LAN is presented. A comprehensive survey on field outages and their root software errors in two COTS DBMS products with large distribution (IMS and DB2) is presented in [12].

A substantial research work cross relating fault injection and databases has been done in the RIO project at the University of Michigan. The project pursues the thesis that non-volatile memory (NVRAM) could be as reliable as disk on application and OS failures. In [13], a study focused on the evaluation of main memory resistance to operating system software crashes estimated that only around 2% of the injected faults lead to data corruption in the file cache. In [14], a simulation study was made to measure the contribution of transactions to the fail-stop behavior of a POSTGRES database. This work, which shares almost the same test bed with [13], concluded that 7% of the faults caused fail-stop violations (in the sense that faulty data was written to stable storage) without transactional support. When transactions were added this figure dropped to 2%.

In [15] another fault injection study focused on a database buffer cache corruption is presented. This study provides valuable feedback to improve the design of the evaluated DMBS (a database mainly targeted to telecommunication applications) and presents measurements of performance degradation in presence of faults.

In [16] a comprehensive robustness benchmarking study of 15 POSIX compliant COTS OS is carried out. Combinations of exceptional and valid input parameters are passed to OS system calls and C library routines. System behavior is monitored to collect error notifications and failure symptoms. The most pertinent conclusion to our own study is a revealed rate of 6% to 19% of *silent failures* per single OS, i.e., situations where "an OS returns no indication of error on an experimental operation which clearly cannot be performed". While *abort failures* were prevalent, this clearly indicates that one should not rely exclusively on crash failures when modeling COTS software faulty behavior.

From all the referenced work, the work done at University of Michigan and the study in [15] hold the closest relationship to the work presented here. However, these evaluation studies were motivated by different goals. In [15] the focus is the evaluation of the system behavior in the presence of data buffer corruption with the goal of improving the error detection mechanisms of the target system. Because of this, the errors injected were very specific, which somehow limit the applicability of the results to other systems and evaluation objectives. Ng and Chen [13] evaluated the relative reliability/robustness of main memory and disk in the presence of OS crashes. In this work, runs that did not quickly lead to OS crashes were intentionally discarded from the set of analyzed faults. Furthermore, with the purpose of accelerating the rate of activated faults, multiple faults were injected in a single run (for instance, in [24] 10 faults per run were injected). This setup is perfectly acceptable if the goal is to cause OS crashes but is somehow less accurate if we are running after other failure modes.

In our study, more than stimulating the SUT to fail quickly in order to evaluate recovery code performance and availability, we are interested in making it fail in more subtle ways. These "subtle" failure modes are a paramount means for assessing the integrity of the SUT. In fact, field studies revealed that failures with higher impact on system availability are less likely to affect system integrity [4]. Last but not least, we stick here to the single-fault model in order to be able to do root failure analysis.

3. Dependability evaluation of COTS systems

This section starts with surveying field data on COTS failures followed by a discussion on the specific issues of emulation software faults with SWIFI technology. Our main purpose here is to settle the ground for understanding both the fault model and the relevant measurements made in this experimental evaluation.

3.1 Fault model

The experimental evaluation of COTS dependability requires the fault models used in the experiments to be representative of actual faults. In other words, it means that the injected faults/errors must induce erroneous system behavior similar to the one caused by real faults.

Table 1 summarizes available results characterizing operational failures and its main underlying causes. The rightmost column represents failures whose root causes could not be found, failures due to environmental reasons or other minor causes. We include the evaluation works done by Gray [1] and Lee [4] despite the fact that the systems assessed do not qualify as COTS systems. This was done mainly because as far as we know similar studies on plain COTS do not exist yet. The same reason, i.e., lack of suitable data, justifies the inclusion of outcomes from [17].

While cross comparison between the different studies should be made very carefully, one clear pattern emerging from the data in Table 1 is the predominance of software

Table 1. Observed field failures by root cause

Study	Hardware	Software	Operations	Unknown/ Other
[1] Fault-tolerant Tandem product line;	7%	62%	15%	16%
[4] Tandem GUARDIAN90 OS;	4%	77%	5%	14%
[17] Survey based on input from system administrators of Windows NT servers;	20%	42%	10%	28%
[2] 70 Windows NT based mail servers;	9%	18%	22%	29%

faults. The share of operation faults (mainly due to end user or system administrator) causing system failures is also increasing. The gap between software and other causes is particularly evident in the two fault-tolerant systems [1][4]. This feature was somehow expected since these systems were specially built to address hardware faults. As a conclusion (for this subsection), the experimental evaluation of COTS dependability should rely on a mix of all these classes of faults, but with a clear predominance of software faults and operation faults.

3.2 Software fault injection in COTS

Typical software faults found in the field are originated in the design/coding phases and remain undetected throughout the testing procedures thus affecting the operational phase of a software product life cycle. This class of faults has been characterized in several studies [3][4][18].

The adoption of SWIFI techniques for fault forecast and robustness evaluation of computer systems in presence of software faults is emerging. Two basic approaches can be

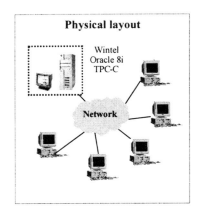

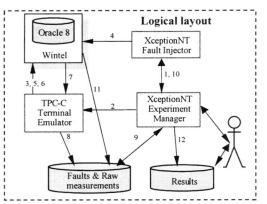

1. Fault parameters
2. Start workload
3. Database instance "fresh" install
4. Fault Injection
5. Database instance shutdown
6. Database instance startup
7. Fault impact "probes" & measures
8. Raw data from TPC-C and DBMS
9. Raw data and faults
10. Fault impact readouts
11. Database log and trace activity
12. Processed results

Figure 1. Testbed layout

used: run-time software implemented fault-injection (RTSWIFI) or compile time instrumentation (CTSWIFI).

Techniques based on compile time instrumentation (CTSWIFI) can only be used when the target system source code is available, which is a major drawback as the source code is not available for most COTS systems. Even a successful open source component such as Linux is clearly being powered by the increasing availability of traditional (non open source) software products running on top of this operating system.

The second approach (RTSWIFI) is basically the extension of low-intrusive SWIFI tools to the injection of software faults. This method can be used even when the source code is not available and has less setup and execution costs than compile-time instrumented fault injection. However, as the faults/errors are injected at very low level (assembly code level; processor register and memory), the mapping between the induced low level errors and the software faults defined at higher levels is not clear. Nevertheless, a recent study [6] comparing the cost and accuracy of CTSWIFI and RTSWIFI show that RTSWIFI is up to 4 times less expensive in terms of execution time while the accuracy of both techniques is almost the same (RTSWIFI is slightly less accurate).

The approach used in this work is RTSWIFI. The enhancements introduced in the XceptionNT tool to accommodate the injection of software faults consist basically of new fault triggers and fault types (see used fault sets in the next section). A new fault trigger technique using on-the-fly instruction decoding coupled to simple temporal or spatial triggers was introduced. This technique significantly reduces the setup cost by choosing the actual fault location and fault type at run-time.

4. Experiment definition and setup

Figure 1 shows the testbed layout used in these experiments. The key components such as the target system, workload, set of faults and the set of measurements are described in the following subsections. The fault-injection tool is XceptionNT, a port of Xception [8] to the WindowsNT/Pentium platform. Since Xception has already

been used extensively in the past, no dedicated section is used to describe the intricacies of the Xception fault-injection process [19].

4.1 Target system

Oracle™ was chosen as target DBMS because it is widely used and it represents quite well a typical (and very sophisticated) DBMS. The same reasons apply to the choice of a *Wintel* based platform. Table 2 details the target system configuration, together with data on OS and hardware infrastructure.

4.2 Workload

TPC-C is the standard benchmark of the Transaction Processing Performance Council for the evaluation and comparison of the performance and the price/performance in database systems due to OLTP loads. This benchmark models a typical business environment where a large number of users are submitting light to medium-weight business transactions against a database system. The company illustrated by TPC-C is a wholesale supplier with a number of geographically distributed sales districts and associated warehouses. Several transaction types are modeled, ranging from stock level checking, to placement of new orders of assets, delivery, tracking and payment of orders. A detailed description of the implementation of TPC-C is out of the scope of this paper and it can be found in [9]. The implementation used in this work is a standard

Table 2. Target System Configuration

Server	*Hardware Platform*	Intel Pentium II processor based machines with 128 MB RAM
	Operating System	Windows NT 4.0 Server build 1381 with SP3
	DBMS	Oracle 8 Server Release 8.1.5.0.0 Oracle Net Server 8.1 Dedicated server session (TP-lite)
Client		Intel Pentium based machine with 64 MB RAM WindowsNT 4.0 Workstation with SP3 Oracle Net Client 8.1
Network		10 Mbit Ethernet with TCP/IP

Table 3. Hardware faults model

Location	Type	Trigger	Duration
CPU registers; {EAX,...,EDX, EBP; ESP, EFlags, EIP, CS, DS, ES, FS, GS, ESI, EDI}	Bit-flip. One bit at a time.	[1..60] seconds. Start of time is first instruction of DBMS process	1 CPU instruction

implementation derived from best practices found in recent full disclosure reports available at the TPC web site. Five concurrent clients were used to submit transactions during one minute per injection run. According to TPC-C rules one checkpoint was made per injection run (here at 30 seconds from workload start time).

4.3 Faults

4.3.1 Hardware transient faults. Hardware transient faults are emulated by injecting bit flip errors in the processor registers. Bit flip faults have been injected at random concerning both fault locations and fault triggers. At first sight, relying exclusively in the register model may seem too much restrictive. However, it should be stressed that the Pentium processor is far from the RISC "load store" memory access model. In fact, the Intel x86 architecture is rich in instructions with mixed memory and register operands (and compilers use it a lot). This way, it is possible to interfere with memory operands and memory access (address generation included) by manipulating register contents. Table 3 summarizes the hardware fault parameters used in this experimental work. A total of 1078 hardware faults were injected.

4.3.2 Software faults. Software faults are injected at run-time via on-the-fly instruction decode. The trigger process works in a similar way to hardware faults but the context corruption procedure is different. Instead of performing a previously defined (at setup time) context corruption, the fault is mimicked according to the target instruction type. A total of 555 software faults were injected. See Table 4 for details (including fault distributions).

Assign faults are injected when the target instruction is a

Table 4. Software fault and error types

Fault Type	Target instruction (assembly level)	Error type	Assembly level
Assign	Mov mem imm Mov reg. imm	Missing/ wrong initialization	NOP (50%) Corrupt source operand (50%)
Check	All conditional branch instructions.	Missing check. Off-By-One Negation.	NOP (25%) Off-by-one (50%) Negation (25%)
Overlay	Repeat store string instructions	"Overlay"	ECX corrupted: - Add one (80%) - 2-12 bytes (10%) - 4186 (10%)
Pointer	All load and store instructions.	Corrupt target/ source address	Same as in Assign fault type

Table 5. *Assign* and *pointer arithmetic* faults (error types)

Operand Corruption type	Distribution	High level error mimicked
Boundary	70%	Add or subtract one
Change-to-zero	10%	Supports NULL pointers (wrong/missing initialization; wrong pointer arithmetic)
Change-to-one	10%	Forces a TRUE condition; wrong/missing initialization and wrong pointer arithmetic
Random	10%	Wrong/missing initialization

move operation from an immediate operand to either a memory or register operand (mimics most of the high level initializations, e.g,, the C language construct *int i=0*). The assignment operation is faulted by either replacing the instruction with a NOP, which mimics missing initialization, or by corrupting the source operand (wrong initialization value). The source operand is corrupted with the error "type" distribution shown in Table 5.

Checking and string overlay faults are injected in a similar way to the one described for the assignment faults. The main difference is that the target instructions are instructions related to checking instructions and store string instructions. The distributions for the corruption types are described above in Table 4.

4.4 Readouts, errors and failures

Table 6 summarizes the measurements along with its classification in terms of two main criteria: level of abstraction and if they were built-in or developed on-purpose.

Possible machine level exceptions rose within the Oracle process as well as exit code values were saved for each injection run. The exit code is used to conclude whether Oracle had terminated normally or abnormally. By default, on the Win32 platform certain kinds of exceptions (memory access violations and illegal instructions for instance) force the termination of the issuing threads, which in turn might cause the owner process to terminate.

DBVERIFY is described as a database administrator (DBA) helper tool capable of pinpointing database data file corruption [20]. It performs a physical data structure integrity check on an offline data file. Its primary use is

Table 6 – Error, failure and monitoring techniques

Name	Abstraction level	Built-In ?
Exception handling	OS	Yes
Exit code	OS	Yes
Oracle internal checks	DBMS	Yes
DBVERIFY	DBMS	Yes
OdBit	DBMS	No
Gold database	DBMS/Application	No
TPC-C consistency tests	Application	No

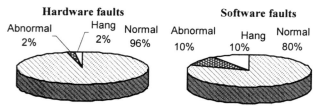

Figure 2. Impact of faults in the Oracle server process

when you need to insure that a backup database (or a data file) is valid before it is restored or as a diagnostic aid when you have encountered data corruption problems. We have used it here to assess if database files (both data and log files) got corrupted.

Oracle performs an extensive logging and error reporting activity [21]. This activity is materialized in several kinds of trace files per database instance. The *alert* file records information about internal errors and administrative activities, such as database instance startup, shutdown, recovery and backups. Oracle also writes additional information about internal errors to the alert file, such as the location and name of any additional trace files generated because of the error. A suite of Perl scripts was developed to scan the trace files and summarize the relevant data for this experimental work. It should be stressed that no special configuration was used for benefit of error logging. While a more detailed time scale would be very convenient to measure internal error detection latency (and Oracle gives that under a special configuration) we decided to keep up with the default configuration in order to avoid interference with typical Oracle execution.

OdBit [22], which stands for *Oracle DataBase Integrity Testing*, performs consistency and integrity checking at the database instance level. The metadata held in a relational DBMS such as Oracle is rich in rules describing the relations between data objects such as tables, views or even PL/SQL procedures [23]. Those rules are maintained by the core database engine to enforce referential integrity and consistency. OdBit extracts those rules from the Oracle data dictionary and checks them against the stored data. For the readers familiar with database technology, data objects checked include synonyms, dependencies, clusters or tables. With some checks, we are simply verifying that a particular

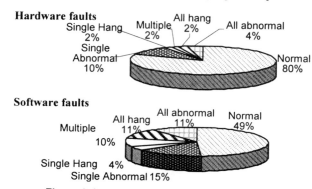

Figure 3. Impact of faults in the TPC-C client

object exists. For instance, if we have a synonym, then the object the synonym refers to must exist. Checking table integrity is a little bit more complex. When addressing a table, several rules are verified, such as check constraints, primary keys, foreign keys or unique constraints.

A *gold database* was also used to support error detection. The *remote terminal emulator* (RTE), part of the TPC-C benchmark, was slightly modified to submit the random transactions to a *gold* database instance as well. This gold database instance was located in a separate machine and, for each injection run, it was kept in the same initial state as the target database. At the end of an injection run the target and the gold databases were compared for mismatches. The comparison is made through the SQL SELECT MINUS construct that is able to pinpoint differences per table and on a record basis.

Last but not least, all consistency tests recommended in the TPC-C specification were implemented. These tests reflect the so-called "business logic", i.e., rules involving data and business processes that typically are difficult to model in terms of relational constraints. For instance, one of such consistency conditions states that the year-to-date sales volume of orders in a warehouse must be equal to the sum of year-to-date volume values per district.

5. Results

We start by presenting and discussing the "broad picture" results. The observations made mimic the ones that are (or might be) made by typical users or system/database administrators when something goes wrong with its applications or systems. Next, it is presented a model of error, failure and recovery in our SUT. The wealth of information available from several sources (Oracle logs, OS logs and Xception database) is condensed in several models by abstraction level and fault type. This perspective on the impact of faults is more useful to give feedback to system designers, since it provides quantitative insights on first errors, how they propagate and what failure types they cause.

We end up by presenting and discussing dependability metrics that can be drawn from this experimental framework and how they can be improved (both of them) to be a component of a dependability benchmark environment.

5.1 First insights: a macroscopic vision

Figures 2 and 3 show the macroscopic view of the impact of faults in the Oracle server process and TPC-C workload client processes, respectively. The impact of faults is evaluated through process failure modes, considering normal termination, abnormal termination, and process hang. For the TPC-C client processes, single hang and single abnormal conditions refer to failure modes of a single client process. All abnormal and all hang are limit conditions where all five client processes terminate abnormally or enter in a frozen state. Runs classified as *multiple* experienced other combinations of hanged and aborted clients.

The first evident result is that the software faults have a more severe impact in the system than hardware faults. Another interesting (and surprising) result is that in the large majority of injected hardware faults – 96% of the faults – the Oracle server (apparently) behaves normally. It is worth noting that the platform is a regular Wintel machine with very few error handling mechanisms. A noticeable difference between hardware and software faults is that the latter set is more prone to cause *hang* and *abnormal* failures (10% each class) than the hardware faults (2% each class). Observable impact in the client processes follows the same basic trend observed for the Oracle server process but with some noticeable deviations. The *normal* condition is also dominant but the percentages observed for normal process termination are not so high as for the faults injected in the server process. An interesting observation is that the percentage of Oracle server hangs is basically the same as *all hangs* observed for the clients (i.e., all client processes hang as the consequence of the server failure). However, the same is not true for abnormal termination, as the percentage of *all abnormal* failures observed in the clients is larger than the percentage of abnormal terminations in server.

Figure 4 shows the impact of the faults with the SUT running both TPC-C and the test suite for database error detection (the error detection issue is analyzed in the next section; here we are interested in the global behavior of the system). The test suite includes the data consistency tests specified in the TPC-C benchmark, Oracle internal assertions, execution of the DBVERIFY command, and the execution of the OdBit tool to check the consistency of the data in the TPC-C tables. One interesting (and unexpected) side effect of running this test suite is that the observable behavior changed significantly. In fact, the extra test execution step at the end of the benchmark activated latent errors leading to a substantial increase in the amount of hangs observed, that otherwise would appear as normal termination. In some sense, the test suite represents a second workload. Considering that a typical database server executes SQL commands from different applications (each one is a workload) then the results observed with consistency tests may be more representative of real cases. However, this "workload" is more a stress test since it is particularly targeted at error detection as it scans database structures for inconsistency detection.

5.2 Error, Recovery and Failures

The percentages of errors detected by Oracle assertions are shown in Figure 5. For the large majority of faults, the errors remained undetected for the observed period. Several possible circumstances account for this: the error(s) stayed latent, their effects were overwritten or tolerated by normal system execution, or the induced error(s) could not be detected by the available means. The single and multiple error detection patterns for hardware and software faults are quite different. The more aggressive effects of the software

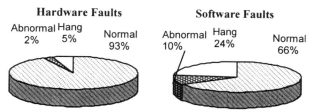

Figure 4. Impact of faults with the test suite

faults result in an higher coverage of multiple errors when compared to the same figure for hardware faults.

One unexpected outcome was the coverage obtained by the running Oracle DBVERIFY utility (see section 4 for details on DBVERIFY). Not a single database corruption was detected for the overall set of injections! This outcome was really surprising because we observed Oracle error messages alerting for data file corruption in nine injection runs and in none of these cases the DBVERIFY detected any error (We checked the effectiveness of the tool by doing direct corruption in the data files and in all cases the tool detected). We see three scenarios that might explain this apparent inconsistency: 1) data file corruption was detected in the in-memory image of the file and its propagation to the disk file was avoided. 2) Oracle incorrectly signaled an error that never really happened, i.e., the fault effects may have changed an error status variable or a checking instruction was affected. 3) The algorithm used by the online corruption checking is different from the offline (DBVERIFY) version. Part of our skepticism on accepting zero detection of data file structural corruption was motivated by common feelings that wild memory access due to pointer/addressing errors might cause such a corruption. Previous work in the RIO project [24] concluded that OS file cache corruption leads to disk file corruption for a significant number of times. However, differences in Oracle managed file cache may justify this behavior.

One very important result is that the execution of the OdBit utility to detect data inconsistencies in the data stored in the TPC-C tables has never detected any error. This means that none of the injected faults (in a total of 526 injected against a SUT with the test suite) caused a committed transaction to produce data that violated the relational constraints in presence. In other words, faults may cause the lost of some uncommitted transactions but all the committed transactions behave according to the transaction model. We have observed that the execution of OdBit often leads to a database hang or internal error detection (and subsequent abnormal termination). This can be seen as

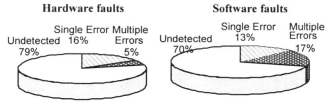

Figure 5. Coverage of Oracle internal consistency checks

OdBit's contribution to the "error activation" behavior already presented in section 5.1.

For 6.4% of injection runs (in a set of 526 runs with the test suite), TPC-C consistency tests were able to detect discrepancies in the database, i.e., the stored data did not verify (at least one of) the consistency clauses. Moreover, TPC-C consistency tests "detected" 0.95% of faults that were not "detected" by any other of the remaining error detection "mechanisms". This is a very interesting figure since it clearly indicates that "business logic" inconsistencies might show up as a result of transient hardware faults or software faults. Furthermore, in around 1% of the cases those inconsistencies might remain unnoticed unless dedicated auditing is performed. Most of the inconsistencies detected seemed to be due to "lost" *payment* transactions. This is reasonable since payment transactions account for nearly 50% of all transactions submitted.

The comparison between the target and gold databases revealed that in 28.3% of injection runs there was a discrepancy. However only in 4.9 % of runs was a discrepancy observed without any other detection from other error detection mechanisms. These discrepancies reflect the cases where one (or more) transaction(s) are submitted to both the target and gold databases but, due to the fault impact, are only completed in the gold database.

Figure 6 shows detailed error propagation for hardware and software faults, respectively. Rounded-corner rectangle shapes represent states, arrows are transitions between states and the number next to each arrow is the observed probability for that transaction to occur. Memory access violation is (by a great distance) the dominant error trace observed at the operating system level. Only few of unhanded exceptions of types *STATUS PRIVILEGED INSTRUCTION* and *STATUS INTEGER DIVIDE BY ZERO* were found. These are unsuccessful status codes signaled by the OS kernel that translates the analogous low-level hardware exceptions. This is true for both hardware and software faults.

Surprisingly, the majority of memory access violation conditions did not lead to a premature termination or caused the Oracle to hang. While there is no available data that would easily contest or confirm it, we draw the following hypothetical scenario: First, most of OS exceptions might happen to be well handled internally by Oracle, which would assert a high robustness of the DBMS code. Second, the exceptions might have been rose (eventually) in Oracle server threads that act as application (user) peer entities. Oracle is designed to tolerate user or server thread failures [23]. A background thread, PMON, resolves the failure by rolling back the current transaction of the aborted thread and releasing any resources that this thread was using. Recovery of the failed user or server thread is automatic. However, if the aborted thread is a background thread, the database instance cannot usually continue delivering proper service.

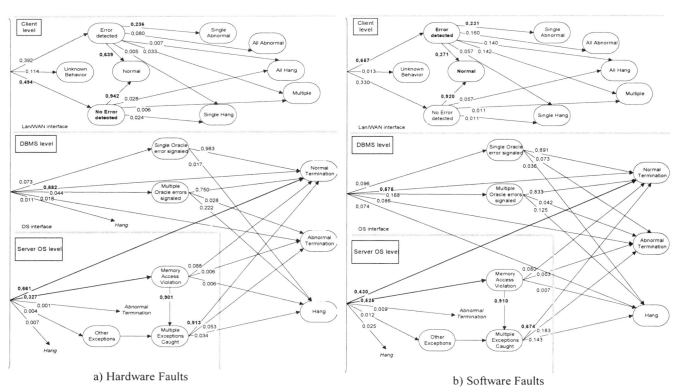

a) Hardware Faults

b) Software Faults

Figure 6. Error propagation model

It is worth mentioning that, concerning memory access violations, software faults behaved in a significantly different way: about one third (32.6%) of the runs with multiple exceptions caught lead to either abnormal or hang behavior while the analogous figure for hardware faults is only around 9%.

5.3 Performance degradation and recovery cost

The evaluation of the recovery mechanisms concerning performance should take into account two figures of merit: 1) performance degradation in normal operation due to the presence of the recovery mechanisms and 2) recovery cost, measured as the time needed to recover after a fault. These recovery measures are common ground in the database community. For example, TPC benchmarks include specific clauses to state that the performance measures must be taken with the overhead of the recovery mechanisms (but TPC do not consider benchmarking in the presence of faults yet). However, many DBMS allow a wide range of tuning configurations, affecting both performance in normal operation and the recovery cost. The experiments to assess the recovery measures (and dependability measures) in a wide range of configurations of the setup used in this work are under way (they will take several months). In this section we present the results corresponding to the two configurations evaluated so far: database with the archive log OFF and with the archive log ON.

Table 7. Performance loss with archiving enabled

No archive	Archiving log	Average performance loss
378 Tpm	293 Tpm	22.5%

The performance achieved in both configurations (see Table 7) is just the transactions per minute with raw tuning (i.e., we haven't tried to improve speed by doing specific tuning). The performance overhead due to the archive log is 22.5%. Naturally, this figure depends on the speed of the tertiary disk in which the archives are stored (there are several ways to tune the archiving mechanism to reduce this overhead).

The gains in availability due to the archive log cannot be meaningfully measured by injection of transient faults. In fact, the archive log just stores the content of the on-line redo log files in a permanent way. Having the archive log ON is possible to recover the database from any point in the past (since all the redo log entries are preserved) or to recover from total lost of the data files (together with data file backup).

The percentage of injected faults that cause the activation of the recovery mechanisms was 29.5%. The cost of recovery measured in time and number of Oracle data blocks (the size of each block is 8Kbytes) read and written from/to disk are represented in Table 8. As faults in a real environment are rare events, the recovery cost is really non-significant. However, the performance degradation in

normal operation due to the necessary recovery mechanisms is very important.

6. Conclusions and Future work

A joint evaluation of performance and dependability in a COTS DBMS done through fault-injection was presented. Errors that emulate transient hardware faults as well as software faults were injected. The system did run with a TPC-C compliant workload that mimics on-line transaction processing requirements available in today client/server computing environments. The impact of faults in the system was evaluated at several abstraction levels.

A macroscopic observation based on the termination of the server and client processes revealed that:

1) A large majority of the faults caused no observable abnormal impact in the DBMS. In 96% of hardware faults and 80% of software faults the database server terminated normally after workload execution.

2) Software faults are more prone to let the database server hanging or cause abnormal terminations.

3) The impact of faults in the TPC-C clients follows the same relative trends observed in the server but malevolent

Table 8 – Recovery cost

Recovery time (seconds)		Count of blocks read and written during recovery	
Mean recovery time	7.1	Average blocks read	235
Standard deviation	2.4	Maximum blocks read	878
Maximum recovery time	13.0	Minimum blocks read	1
Minimum recovery time	4.0	Average blocks written	195
Percentage of faults that caused Oracle recovery	29.5%	Maximum blocks written	821
		Minimum blocks written	1

effects are more noticeable; up to 51% of software faults lead to observable failures in the client processes.

4) The insertion of a test suite that executed after the TPC-C workload significantly modified the observable impact. For software faults, the hang failures raised from 10% to 24% while the normal figure dropped from 80% to 66%. This behavior agrees with the well-known workload effect in experimental evaluation, since the test suite can be seen as another (albeit special) workload. The test suite awaked latent errors that otherwise would remain hidden.

A detailed analysis conducted over several sources, ranging from machine level exception handling to business logic in the TPC-C environment, further lead to the following results:

1) Memory access violations are the dominant error trace observed at the operating system level, detecting 52.5% and 32.7% of the injected software and hardware faults (respectively).

2) Oracle does a good job on recovering from failures due *to invalid memory access* conditions. The majority of errors found were tolerated and ultimately led to normal termination.

3) Oracle internal checks detected errors, due to hardware and software faults, in 21% and 30% of injection runs, respectively. These figures show that by carefully monitoring database trace files, DBAs can achieve a wider understanding on failure status than would be attained by simply monitoring processes up/down state.

4) No (durable) database corruption was detected. Despite the fact that in some injection runs Oracle internal checks signaled data file corruption, off-line tests performed on all data files did not detect any corruption.

5) The relational constraints as well as the internal consistency of the metadata that Oracle uses to describe user data were not affected by the faults injected. In other words, all the committed transactions behaved according to the transaction model.

6) Transient hardware and software faults might however cause errors that are only detected at the "business logic" level, i.e., by inspecting a set of rules that reflect data consistency at an higher abstraction model than the relational one. In 0.95% of injection runs, the induced errors were only detected by the TPC-C consistency tests. This shows that periodic inspection of a COTS DBMS should be made in order to certify its integrity, since apparent "failure" free behavior is not enough to reach a confident judgment.

The tradeoff in terms of performance loss in normal operation to enable no-loss recovery in presence of media faults (archive log ON) was found to be 22.5%. We foresee that this figure might be improved with dedicated database tuning. A significant number of injected faults – 29.5 % - triggered the database recovery mechanism. The MTTR was found to be 7.1 seconds. While this MTTR seems inadequate to fulfill requirements of telecommunications database, for instance, it seems to fit less stringent application areas.

Reasoning on all the results presented, the usage of a COTS DBMS like Oracle seems to be an effective way to benefit from COTS components economics while holding a fair confidence on service reliability. However, in certain business areas where data integrity is a must, customized "business logic" checking should be implemented. In fact, the experimental work here described shows that, due to transient hardware or software faults, there is a chance that data gets corrupted in a very subtle way, so that detection by built-in checking techniques was not possible.

Future work will leverage the evaluation framework to address dependability benchmarking of COTS DBMS. This includes support for new fault models (notably operations faults) and emulation of specific failures that are hard to trigger by fault/error injection, new system workloads and configurations (TPC-D, distributed database, primary and standby database, etc) as well as migrate the evaluation building blocks to other platforms.

12. References

[1] J. Gray, "A Census of Tandem Systems Availability Between 1985 and 1990," IEEE Trans. on Reliability, Vol.39, No.4, pp.409-418, Oct., 1990.

[2] M. Kalyanakrishnam, Z. Kalbarczyk, R. Iyer, "Failure Data Analysis of a LAN of Windows NT Based Computers", Proceedings of SRDS'18, October, Switzerland, pp. 178-187, 1999.

[3] M. Sullivan and R. Chillarege, "Comparison of Software Defects in Database Management Systems and Operating Systems", Proceedings of FTCS-22, pp. 475-484, July 1992.

[4] I. Lee and R. K. Iyer, "Software Dependability in the Tandem GUARDIAN System", IEEE Transactions on Software Engineering, Vol. 21, No. 5, pp. 455-467, May 1995.

[5] J. Arlat et al, "Fault Injection and Dependability Evaluation of Fault Tolerant Systems", IEEE Transactions on Computers, Vol. 42, No. 8, pp. 919-923, August 1993.

[6] J. Christmansson, M. Hiller, and M. Rimén, "An Experimental comparison of Fault and Error Injection", Proceedings of ISSRE'98, pp. 369-378, USA, 1998.

[7] H. Madeira, M. Vieira and D. Costa, "On the Emulation of Software Faults by Software Fault Injection," Proc. of Intl. Conference on Dependable Systems and Networks, June 25-28, New York, USA, 2000.

[8] J.Carreira, H.Madeira, J.Silva, "Xception: A technique for the evaluation of dependability in modern Computers", IEEE Transactions on Software Engineering, Vol.24, No.2, pp. 125-136, February 1998.

[9] Transaction Processing Performance Council, "TPC Benchmark C, Standard Specification, Revision 3.3," 1998.

[10] T. Tsai and R. K. Iyer, "An Approach to Benchmarking of Fault-Tolerant Commercial Systems", Proc. of the 26th IEEE Fault Tolerant Computing Symposium, FTCS-26, Sendai, Japan, pp. 314-323, June 1996.

[11] T.J. Teorey and W.T.Ng, "Dependability and Performance Measures for the Database Practitioner", IEEE Transactions on Knowledge and Data Engineering, Vol.10, No. 3, May/June, 1998, pp.499-503.

[12] M. P. Sullivan, "System Support for Software Fault Tolerance in Highly Available Database Management Systems," Ph.D. Thesis, 1992.

[13] W.T. Ng and P. M. Chen, "Integrating Reliable Memory in Databases", In Proceedings of VLDB 1997, pages 76-85, August 1997.

[14] S. Chandra and Peter M.Chen, "How Fail-Stop are Faulty Programs?", FTCS'28, Munich, Germany,1998, pp. 240-249.

[15] M. Sabaratnam et al., "Evaluating the Effectiveness of Fault Tolerance in Replicated Database Management Systems", Proceedings of FTCS'29, June 15-18, Madison, Wisconsin, 1999, pp. 306-313.

[16] P. Koopman and J. deVale, "Comparing the robustness of POSIX Operating Systems", Proceedings of FTCS'29, June 15-18, Madison, Wisconsin, 1999, pp. 22-29.

[17] Sunbelt International, "NT Reliability Survey Results", http://www.sunbelt-software.com/ntrelres3.htm, published March, 23, 1999.

[18] J. Christmansson and R. Chillarege, "Generation of an Error Set that Emulates Software Faults Based on Field Data," presented at FTCS'26, Sendai, Japan, 1996, pp. 304-313.

[19] D. Costa and H. Madeira, "Experimental Assessment of COTS DBMS Robustness under Transient Faults", Proc. of the Pacific Rim Dependable Computing Symposium, 17-18 December, HongKong, China, 1999.

[20] Oracle Corporation, "Oracle8i Utilities Release 8.1.5", Part no. A67792-01, February, 1999.

[21] Oracle Corporation, "Oracle8i Error Messages Release 8.1.5", Part no. A67785-01, February, 1999.

[22] T.R. Silva, D. Costa, H. Madeira, "OdBit: A Tool for Oracle Databases Integrity Testing", Technical Report, CISUC, University of Coimbra, 1998.

[23] Oracle Corporation, "Oracle 8i Server Concepts Manual", 1999.

[24] W. T. Ng and P. M. Chen, "The Systematic Improvement of Fault Tolerance in the Rio File Cache", Proc. of FTCS'29, June 15-18, Madison, Wisconsin, 1999, pp. 306-313.

Robustness Testing of the Microsoft Win32 API

Charles P. Shelton
ECE Department & ICES
Carnegie Mellon University
Pittsburgh, PA, USA
cshelton@cmu.edu

Philip Koopman
ECE Department & ICES
Carnegie Mellon University
Pittsburgh, PA, USA
koopman@cmu.edu

Kobey Devale
ECE Department & ICES
Carnegie Mellon University
Pittsburgh, PA, USA
kdevale@ece.cmu.edu

Abstract

Although Microsoft Windows is being deployed in mission-critical applications, little quantitative data has been published about its robustness. We present the results of executing over two million Ballista-generated exception handling tests across 237 functions and system calls involving six Windows variants, as well as similar tests conducted on the Linux operating system. Windows 95, Windows 98, and Windows CE were found to be vulnerable to complete system crashes caused by very simple C programs for several different functions. No system crashes were observed on Windows NT, Windows 2000, and Linux. Linux was significantly more graceful at handling exceptions from system calls in a program-recoverable manner than Windows NT and Windows 2000, but those Windows variants were more robust than Linux (with glibc) at handling C library exceptions. While the choice of operating systems cannot be made solely on the basis of one set of tests, it is hoped that such results will form a starting point for comparing dependability across heterogeneous platforms.

1. Introduction

Different versions of the Microsoft Windows operating system (OS) are becoming popular for mission- and safety-critical applications. The Windows 95/98 OS family is the dominant OS used in personal computer systems, and Windows NT 4.0 has become increasingly popular in business applications. The United States Navy has adopted Windows NT as the official OS to be incorporated into onboard computer systems [15]. Windows CE and Windows NT Embedded are new alternatives for embedded operating systems. Thus, there is considerable market and economic pressure to adopt Windows systems for critical applications.

Unfortunately, Windows operating systems have acquired a general reputation of being less dependable than Unix-based operating systems. In particular, the infamous "Blue Screen Of Death" that is displayed as a result of Windows system crashes is perceived by many as being far more prevalent than the equivalent kernel panics of Unix operating systems. Additionally, it is a common (although

meagerly documented) experience that Windows systems need to be rebooted more often than Unix systems. However, there is little if any quantitative data published on the dependability of Windows, and no objective way to predict whether the impending move to Windows 2000 will actually improve dependability over either Windows 98 or Windows NT.

Beyond the dependability of Windows itself, the comparative dependability of Windows and Unix-based systems such as Linux has become a recurring theme of discussion in the media and Internet forums. While the most that can usually be quantified is mean time between reboots (anecdotally, Unix systems are generally said to operate longer between reboots than Windows NT), issues such as system administration, machine usage, the behavior of application programs, and even the stability of underlying hardware typically make such comparisons problematic. It would be useful to have a comparison of reliability between Windows and Unix systems based on direct, reproducible measurements on a reasonably level playing field.

The success of many critical systems requires dependable operation, and a significant component of system dependability can be a robust operating system. (Robustness is formally defined as the degree to which a software component functions correctly in the presence of exceptional inputs or stressful environmental conditions [6].) Of particular concern is the behavior of the system when confronted with exceptional operating conditions and consequent exceptional data values. Because these instances are by definition not within the scope of designed operation, it is crucial that the system as a whole, and the OS in particular, react gracefully to prevent compromising critical operating requirements. (Some systems, such as clustered web servers, can be architected to withstand single-node failures; however there are many critical systems in the embedded computing world and mission-critical systems on desktops which cannot afford such redundancy, and which require highly dependable individual nodes.)

This paper presents a quantitative comparison of the vulnerability of six different versions of the Windows Win32 Application Programming Interface (API) to robustness failures caused by exceptional function or system call parameter values. These results are compared to the results of similarly testing Linux for exception handling robustness.

Exception handling tests are performed using the Ballista robustness testing harness [1] for both Windows and Linux. In order to perform a reasonable Windows-to-Linux comparison, 237 calls were selected for testing from the Win32 API, and matched with 183 calls of comparable functionality from the Linux API. Of these calls, 94 were C library functions that were tested with identical test cases in both APIs, with the balance of calls being system calls. Beyond C library functions, the calls selected for testing were common services used by many application programs such as memory management, file and directory system management, input/output (I/O), and process execution/control. The results are reported in groups rather than as individual functions to provide a reasonable basis for comparison in those areas where the APIs differ in the number and type of calls provided.

2. Background

The Ballista software testing methodology has been described in detail elsewhere [3], [9] and is publicly available as an Internet-based testing service [1] involving a central testing server and a portable testing client that was ported to Windows NT and Windows CE for this research. Thus, only a brief summary of Ballista testing operation will be given.

The Ballista testing methodology is a combination of software testing and fault injection approaches. Specifically selected exceptional values (selected via typical software testing strategies) are used to inject faults into a system via an API. For testing an OS, this involves selecting a set of functions and system calls to test, with each such Module under Test (MuT) being exercised in turn until a desired portion of the API is tested. Parameter test values are distinct values for a parameter of a certain data type that are randomly drawn from pools of predefined tests, with a separate pool defined for each data type being tested. These pools of values contain exceptional as well as non-exceptional cases to avoid successful exception handling on one parameter from masking the potential effects of unsuccessful exception handling on some other parameter value. Each test case (the execution of a single MuT with a single test value selected for each required parameter in the call) is executed as a separate task to minimize the occurrence of cross-test interference. A single Ballista test case involves selecting a set of test values, executing constructors associated with those test values to initialize essential system state, executing a call to the MuT with the selected test values in its parameter list, measuring whether the MuT behaves in a robust manner in that situation, and cleaning up any lingering system state in preparation for the next test (including freeing memory and deleting temporary files).

Ballista testing looks only for non-robust responses from software, and does not test for correct functionality. This, combined with a data type-based testing strategy, rather than a functional testing strategy, results in a highly scalable testing approach in which the effort spent on test development tends to grow sub-linearly with the number of MuTs to be tested. An additional property of Ballista testing results is that in practice they have proven to be highly repeatable. Virtually all test results reproduce the same robustness problems every time a brief single-test program representing a single test case is executed.

Ballista uses the CRASH scale [9] to measure robust or non-robust responses from MuTs. CRASH is an acronym for the different robustness failures that can occur. In Catastrophic failures, the most severe robustness failure type, the application causes a complete system crash that requires an OS reboot for recovery. In Restart failures, the application enters a state where it "hangs" and will not continue normal operation, requiring an application restart for recovery. Abort failures are an abnormal termination of an application task as the result of a signal or thrown exception that is not specific enough to constitute a recoverable error condition unless the task elects (or is forced by default) to terminate and restart. Silent failures occur when a function or call is performed with invalid parameter values, but the system reports that it was completed successfully instead of returning an error indication. Finally, Hindering failures report an incorrect error indication such as the wrong error reporting code. Ballista can automatically detect Catastrophic, Restart, and Abort failures; Silent failures and Hindering failures currently can be detected in only some situations, and require manual analysis.

Earlier Ballista publications (e.g., [3], [8], [9]) describe the software testing and fault injection heritage of this approach. Ballista can be thought of as using software testing principles to perform fault injection at the API level instead of the source code or object code level. The most closely related current research effort is the work done at Reliable Software Technologies on testing Windows NT [4], [5] in light of Ballista results on Unix systems. That work focuses on a broad coverage of functions for a single OS version with relatively simple testing values. Nonetheless, their results found many Abort-type failures in Windows NT, and a few Catastrophic failures that were caused by very complex execution sequences that could not be isolated for bug-reporting purposes. Other recent related work is the Fuzz project at the University of Wisconsin [12], [13], which has concentrated on Unix systems. There does not appear to be any previously published work that performs testing-oriented dependability comparisons of multiple Windows versions, nor comparisons of Windows to Unix robustness.

3. Implementation

The existing Ballista testing system ran only on Unix systems. Thus, testing Windows required porting the client-side testing harness to Windows as well as creating Windows-specific test values and an inter-API comparison methodology.

3.1. Porting to Windows Desktop Systems

Porting the Ballista testing client software to the Windows platform faced many difficulties, chief among them the fact that Windows has no simple analog to the fork() system call implemented on POSIX systems (POSIX [7] is the standard for Unix). Thus it is more difficult to spawn a child process for each test case being executed. To overcome this, the Windows version of the Ballista test harness creates a memory-mapped file for each test case, writes data for that particular test case's parameters to this file, and then spawns the testing process. The testing process retrieves the data for the current test case from the memory location created by the calling process, and reports results for the test to that same memory location.

The Win32 API uses a thrown-exception error reporting model in addition to the error return code model (using the POSIX "errno" variable or the Win32 GetLastError() function) used by the POSIX API. While on POSIX systems Abort failures can be detected by simply monitoring the system for the occurrence of signals (most often SIGSEGV or SIGBUS), in Windows systems there are both legitimate and non-robust occurrences of thrown error reporting conditions. The Win32 API documentation [11], [14] does not provide sufficient information to make a per-function list of permissible and non-permissible thrown exceptions. For Windows testing, the Ballista test harness intercepted all integer and string exception values, and to be more than fair in evaluation, assumed that all such exceptions were valid and recoverable. In normal operation, any unrecoverable exceptions trigger the Windows top-level exception filter and display an "Application Error" message window before terminating the program. We disabled this exception filter and replaced it with code that would record such an unrecoverable exception as an Abort failure. (This technique could in fact be used to improve the robustness of an application program, but only by restarting abnormally terminated tasks. That approach might be sufficiently robust for many users, but is considered to be non-robust at the application level by most of the critical-system designers we have had discussions with.)

There were additional challenges involved in porting the Ballista testing client to a Windows environment, such as obtaining a remote procedure call (RPC) package that was compatible with the Unix-based Ballista testing server's RPC implementation. Most UNIX systems use ONC RPC, but Windows only supports DCE RPC, so a third party ONC RPC Windows client had to be used. Most porting issues were related to differing OS interface architectures, and were not fundamental to the Ballista approach.

Because many Win32 calls have four or more parameters, a very large number of test cases could be generated without exhausting all potential combinations of test values for a single MuT. Therefore, testing was capped at 5000 randomly selected test cases per MuT. 72 Windows MuTs and 34 POSIX MuTs were capped at 5000 tests each (per OS) in this manner. All other MuTs performed exhaustive testing of all combinations with fewer than 5000 tests. In order to fairly compare the desktop Windows variants, the same pseudorandom sampling of test cases was performed in the same order for each system call or C function tested across the different Windows variants. Previous findings have indicated that this random sampling gives accurate results when compared to exhaustive testing of all combinations [9].

The Win32 and POSIX APIs use different data types. However, most of the Windows data types required were minor specializations of fairly generic C data types. In those cases, the same test values used in POSIX were simply used for testing Windows. The only major data type for which new test values had to be created for testing Windows was the HANDLE type. The tests for this type were largely created by inheriting tests from existing types and adding test cases in the same general vein as existing data type tests. Overall, the data values used for testing were selected based on experience with previous Ballista testing and a general background knowledge from the software testing literature [2].

3.2. Porting to Windows CE

The Ballista client for Windows NT does not work on the Windows CE platform because Windows CE is designed to be an embedded operating system that runs on specialized hardware for consumer electronics and mission-critical systems. These systems have tighter memory constraints than a normal desktop PC. Also, Windows CE programs must be compiled and linked for specific hardware using tools that run on Windows NT, and then downloaded to the Windows CE device.

To overcome this problem, the Ballista client was split into two components: the test generation and reporting functions that run on a Windows NT PC, and the test execution and control functions that run on the target Windows

Table 1. Robustness Failure rates by Module under Test (MuT) for Windows versions and Linux.

	System Calls Tested	System Calls with Catastrophic Failures	System Calls with Calculated Failure Rates	System Percent Restart Failures by Call	System Percent Abort Failures by Call	C Library Functions Tested	C Library Functions with Catastrophic Failures	C Library Functions with Calculated Failure Rates	C Library Percent Restart Failures by Function	C Library Percent Abort Failures by Function
Linux	91	0	91	0.2%	7.1%	94	0	94	0.8%	34.9%
Windows 95	133	7	126	0.1%	11.6%	94	1	93	0.02%	24.7%
Windows 98	143	5	138	0.1%	13.3%	94	2	92	0.0%	24.6%
Windows 98 SE	143	6	137	0.1%	12.9%	94	1	93	0.0%	25.0%
Windows NT	143	0	143	0.3%	23.5%	94	0	94	0.01%	24.6%
Windows 2000	143	0	143	0.4%	22.7%	94	0	94	0.05%	24.1%
Windows CE	71	10	61	0.1%	13.3%	82 (108)	18 (27)	64	0.0%	14.0%

	Total MuTs (Functions + Calls) Tested	Overall MuTs with Catastrophic Failures	Overall MuTs with Calculated Failure Rates	Overall Percent Restart Failures by MuT	Overall Percent Abort Failures by MuT
Linux	183	0	183	0.5%	21.9%
Windows 95	227	8	219	0.08%	17.2%
Windows 98	237	7	230	0.06%	17.8%
Windows 98 SE	237	7	230	0.06%	17.8%
Windows NT	237	0	237	0.20%	23.9%
Windows 2000	237	0	237	0.23%	23.3%
Windows CE	153 (179)	28 (37)	125	0.04%	13.7%

CE target using file I/O and process creation, but does not provide mechanisms for process synchronization or control. Therefore, the test execution component running on the target must create another process that actually runs the test and records the result in the target's file system. The NT process must remain idle and wait for this file to appear on the target to get the results of the current test case and report them. Unfortunately this means tests are several orders of magnitude slower than tests run on the other Windows OS versions, taking five to ten seconds per test case.

Error classification was also a problem on Windows CE. Windows CE does not support the normal C++ `try/catch` exception handling scheme, so we had to use the Win32 structured exception handling constructs, `__try/__except` and `__try/__finally`. We did not use these on the other Windows platforms because the Microsoft documentation [11] recommends using C++ `try/catch` whenever possible, and states that the two exception handling methods are mutually exclusive.

The exceptions that we observed on Windows CE appeared to be analogous to the signals thrown in POSIX systems. For example, the exception `EXCEPTION_ACCESS_VIOLATION` thrown in Windows CE is comparable to a `SIGSEGV` signal thrown in UNIX. Therefore, we classified these exceptions as abort failures. The only exceptions observed were `EXCEPTION_ACCESS_VIOLATION`, `EXCEPTION_DATATYPE_MISALIGNMENT`, and `EXCEPTION_STACK_OVERFLOW`.

3.3. Comparison methodology

Perhaps the greatest challenge in testing Windows systems and then comparing results to Linux was creating a reasonable comparison methodology. While C library functions are identical on both systems, the system calls have different functionality, different numbers of parameters, and somewhat different data types. However, the Bal-

CE platform. For each system call or function tested, the test execution and control portion is compiled on the PC and downloaded to the Windows CE machine via a serial port connection. The test generation component running on the PC initiates each test case by starting the test execution process on the target and passing the parameter list via the command line arguments.

Windows CE provides a remote API that allows Windows NT applications to communicate with the Windows lista techniques of basing tests on data types and of normalized failure rate reporting were used to create an arguably fair comparison of exception handling test results.

Basing tests on data types rather than MuT functionality permits comparing APIs with similar functionality but different interfaces. Because the data type test definitions are nearly identical for both Windows and Linux, the same general tests in the same general proportions are being run regardless of functionality. Of course there is always the possibility of accidental bias. But, because the tests were originally developed specifically to find problems with POSIX systems by students who had no Windows programming experience, if anything the tests would be biased toward finding problems on the previous testing target of POSIX rather than specifically stressing Windows features.

Normalized failure rate data was used to permit comparison among different interfaces to similar functionality between Windows and Linux. Normalization is performed by computing the robustness failure rate on a per-MuT basis (number of test cases failed divided by number of test cases executed for each individual MuT). Then, the MuTs are grouped into comparable classes by functionality, such as all MuTs that perform memory management. The individual failure rates within each such group are averaged with uniform weights to provide a group failure rate, permitting relative comparisons among groups for all OS implementations. As an example, the I/O Primitives group consists of `{close dup dup2 fcntl fdatasync fsync lseek pipe read write}` for POSIX and `{AttachThreadInput CloseHandle DuplicateHandle FlushFileBuffers GetStdHandle LockFile LockFileEx ReadFile ReadFileEx SetFilePointer SetStdHandle UnlockFile UnlockFileEx WriteFile WriteFileEx}` for Win32. Robustness failure rates for the I/O Primitives group are computed by averaging the 10 individual failure rates for the POSIX calls, and comparing against the averaged result for the 15 individual Win32 call failure rates for some particular Windows implementation. While even this level of comparison obviously is not perfect, it has the virtue of encompassing the same set of higher-level functionality across two different APIs. For the purposes of achieving generic-level functionality comparisons, calls that did not have an obvious grouping counterpart for both POSIX and Windows were discarded.

In all, 3,430 distinct test values incorporated into 37 data types were available for testing POSIX, and 1,073 distinct test values incorporated into 43 data types were available for testing Windows. Given the cap of 5000 tests per MuT, a total of over 148,000 tests were run on each implementation of the C library, plus an additional 380,000 tests on each implementation of the Win32 API compared to 210,000 tests on the Linux system calls.

We did not test any functions in the Graphical Device Interface (GDI) or any Windows device driver specific code. Similarly, although we did not detect any obvious resource "leakage" during testing, we did not specifically target that type of failure mode for testing, nor did we test the systems under heavy loading conditions. While these are clearly potential sources of robustness problems, we elected to limit testing to comparable situations between Windows and Linux, and to restrict results to include only highly repeatable situations to lend confidence to the accuracy of the conclusions.

4. Experimental Results

Ballista robustness testing was performed on the following operating systems on comparable Pentium-class computers with at least 64 megabytes of RAM:

- Windows 95 revision B
- Windows 98 with Service Pack 1 installed
- Windows 98 Second Edition (SE)/Service Pack 1
- Windows NT 4.0 Workstation/Service Pack 5
- Windows 2000 Professional Beta 3 (Build 2031)
- Windows CE 2.11 running on a Hewlett Packard Jornada 820 Handheld PC
- RedHat Linux 6.0 (Kernel version 2.2.5)

The Microsoft Visual C++ compiler (version 6.0) was used for all Windows systems, and the GNU C compiler (version 2.91.66) was used for the Linux system. (Technically the results for C library testing are the result of the GNU development team and not Linux developers, but they are so prevalently used as a pair to implement POSIX functionality with the C binding that this seems a reasonable approach.)

In all, 91 POSIX system calls, 143 Win32 system calls, and 94 C library functions were tested on all desktop operating systems. (10 Win32 system calls were not supported by Windows 95, but were tested on the other desktop Windows platforms.) Because it implements a subset of the Win32 API, only 71 Win32 system calls and 82 C library functions were tested on Windows CE. Table 1 shows the results of robustness testing. The percentages of failures are uniformly weighted averages across all functions tested for that OS. Functions with Catastrophic failures are excluded because the system crash interrupts the testing process, and the set of test cases run for that function is incomplete.

Windows CE gives preferred support to the UNICODE 16-bit character set as opposed to the ASCII 8-bit character set that is used on both UNIX and other Windows platforms. There were 26 C functions that had both an ASCII and a UNICODE implementation. The failure rates for both versions were comparable with the exception of

Table 2. Overall robustness failure rates by functional category. Catastrophic failure rates are excluded from numbers, but their presence is indicated by a "*".

	System Calls					C Library							
	Memory Management	File/Directory Access	I/O Primitives	Process Primitives	Process Environment	C char	C file I/O management	C memory	C I/O stream	C string	C time	C math
Linux	0.08%	8.8%	0.4%	6.6%	9.1%	30.4%	73.5%	27.8%	80.4%	28.0%	13.2%	2.6%
Windows 95	*3.0%	*17.3%	*11.6%	*10.2%	*19.6%	0.0%	33.9%	2.7%	*33.2%	54.4%	53.2%	7.1%
Windows 98	3.1%	*17.3%	*12.5%	*12.4%	*23.1%	0.0%	33.3%	2.7%	*38.6%	*52.1%	52.0%	7.1%
Windows 98 SE	3.1%	*17.3%	*11.9%	*11.9%	*22.0%	0.0%	33.3%	2.7%	39.9%	*52.2%	52.0%	14.8%
Windows NT	13.9%	36.1%	23.0%	24.8%	17.4%	0.0%	32.9%	13.5%	38.7%	51.3%	43.8%	6.2%
Windows 2000	13.9%	34.7%	22.4%	25.3%	13.8%	0.0%	34.0%	7.4%	39.0%	48.9%	40.3%	9.0%
Windows CE	*6.7%	22.0%	17.5%	*5.0%	*16.1%	0.0%	*	8.2%	*	*33.4%	N/A	6.9%

strncpy, which had a Catastrophic failure in the UNICODE version but not in the ASCII version. Since Windows CE uses the UNICODE character set as a default, we only report the failure rates for the UNICODE versions of these C functions. The numbers in parentheses in the Windows CE rows in Table 1 represent the number of functions tested when counting both ASCII and UNICODE functions separately.

In order to compare Windows results to Linux results, the different calls and functions were divided into twelve groupings as shown in Table 2 and Figure 1. These groupings not only serve to permit comparing failure rates across different APIs, but also give a summary of failures for different types of functions. Each failure rate is a uniformly weighted average across all functions tested for that particular OS; the total failure rates give each group's failure rate an even weighting to compensate for the effects caused by different APIs having different numbers of functions to implement each function category. Again, functions with Catastrophic failures are excluded from this calculation. Functions tested on Windows CE in the C file I/O management and the C stream I/O groups had too many functions with Catastrophic failures to report accurate group failure rates; 6 out of 10 in the former and 11 out of 14 in the latter. Windows CE does not support functions in the C time group, so no results for that group are reported.

Table 2 and Figure 1 show that there are significant differences in the robustness failure rates of Linux and Windows, as well as between the Windows 95/98 family and the Windows NT/2000 family of operating systems. Windows CE was unlike either family of desktop Windows variants. (It should be noted that the dominant source of robustness failures is Abort failures, so these results should be interpreted in light of the degree to which those failures affect any particular application.)

Windows 95, Windows 98, and Windows 98 SE exhibited similar failure rates, including a number of functions that caused repeatable Catastrophic system crash failures. Five of the Win32 API system calls: DuplicateHandle(), GetFileInformationByHandle(), GetThreadContext(), MsgWaitForMultipleObjects(), and MsgWaitForMultipleObjectsEx(), plus two C library functions, fwrite() and strncpy(), caused Catastrophic failures for certain test cases in Windows 98. Listing 1 shows a representative test case that has crashed Windows 98 every time it has been run on two different desktop machines, a Windows 95 machine, a Windows 98 laptop computer, and our Windows CE device.

Windows 98 SE had Catastrophic failures in the same five Win32 API system calls as Windows 98, plus another in the CreateThread() call, but eliminated the Catastrophic failure in the C library function fwrite(). Windows 95 had all the Catastrophic failures of Windows 98 except for MsgWaitForMultipleObjectsEx(), which was not implemented in Windows 95. Windows 95 also did not exhibit Catastrophic failures in the C library function strncpy(). Windows 95 did, however, have three additional calls with Catastrophic failures: FileTimeToSystemTime(), HeapCreate(), and ReadProcessMemory().

Windows CE had abort failure rates that did not correspond to either the Windows 95/98 family, or the Windows NT/2000 family, and had significantly more functions with Catastrophic failures than any other OS tested, especially in the C library functions. Windows CE had Catastrophic failures in ten Win32 system calls: CreateThread(), GetThreadContext(), InterlockedDecrement(), InterlockedExchange(), InterlockedIncrement(),

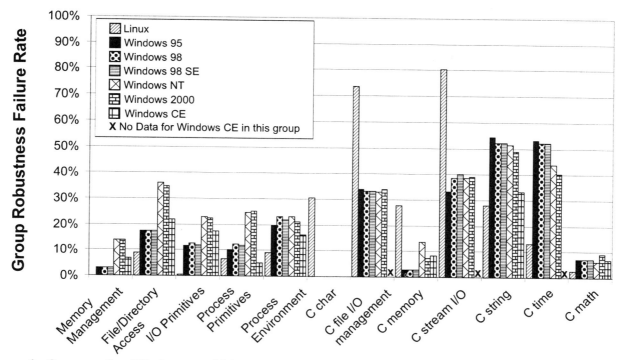

Figure 1. Comparative Windows and Linux robustness failure rates by functional category.

MsgWaitForMultipleObjects(), MsgWaitForMultipleObjectsEx(), ReadProcessMemory(), SetThreadContext(), and VirtualAlloc(). Windows CE also had 18 C library functions with Catastrophic failures (27 counting ASCII and UNICODE functions separately), 17 of which failed due to the same invalid C file pointer as a parameter.

For several of the functions with Catastrophic failures we could not isolate the system crash to a single test case. We could repeatedly crash the system by running the entire test harness for these functions, but could not reproduce it when running the test cases independently. These system crashes were probably due to inter-test interference, which indicates that system state was not properly cleaned between test cases, even though each test is run in a separate process to minimize this effect. All system calls and functions with Catastrophic failures across all OS's are listed in Table 3 by function group.

Windows NT, Windows 2000, and Linux exhibited no Catastrophic failures during this testing. This is certainly not to say that they cannot be made to crash, but rather that they have reached a different plateau of overall robustness - it is, at a minimum, difficult to find a simple C program that crashes them when run as a single task in user mode. Thus,

Listing 1. A line of code that produces Catastrophic failures on Windows 95, Windows 98 and Windows CE

```
GetThreadContext(GetCurrentThread(),
                 NULL);
```

one can consider that there is some merit to Microsoft's claim that Windows NT is more reliable than Windows 98 (as, for example, stated on their Web site [10]).

Restart failures were relatively rare for all the OS implementations tested. However, they might be a critical problem for any system that assumes fail-fast semantics, including clustered servers that otherwise do not require ultra-high dependability hardware nodes. In, general Restart failures were too infrequent for comparisons to be meaningful.

The classification of Aborts as failures is controversial. In systems in which task termination is acceptable (systems requiring fail-fast operation that can withstand the latency of task restarts), or desirable (debugging scenarios), they may not be considered a problem. However, in some critical and embedded systems that either do not have time to accomplish a task restart or cannot withstand the loss of state information accompanying a task restart, Abort failures can be a significant problem. Our experience in talking with companies that require high levels of field reliability is that Aborts are indeed considered failures for those applications. For other applications that do not share the same philosophy, Abort numbers may not have significant meaning

Given that Abort failures are relevant for some applications, Figure 1 shows that there are striking differences in Abort failure rates across operating systems and functional groupings. For example, Linux has more than a 30% Abort failure rate for C character operations, whereas all the Win-

Table 3. Functions that exhibited Catastrophic failures by OS and function group. A "*" indicates that the failure could not be reproduced outside of the test harness.

	Windows 95	Windows 98	Windows 98 SE	Windows CE
Memory Management				
HeapCreate	X			
VirtualAlloc				X
File/Directory Access				
FileTimeToSystemTime	X			
GetFileInformationByHandle	X	X	X	
Process Primitives				
MsgWaitForMultipleObjects	X	X	X	X
*MsgWaitForMultipleObjectsEx		X	X	X
*ReadProcessMemory	X			X
*CreateThread			X	X
Process Environment				
GetThreadContext	X	X	X	X
*InterlockedDecrement, *InterlockedExchange				X
*InterlockedIncrement, SetThreadContext				X
I/O Primitives				
*DuplicateHandle	X	X	X	
C file I/O management				
clearerr, fclose, fflush				X
_wfreopen, fseek, ftell				X
C I/O stream				
*fwrite	X	X		X
*fread				X
(UNICODE and ASCII) fgetc, *fgets, fprintf,				X
(UNICODE and ASCII) fputc, fputs, fscanf,				X
(UNICODE and ASCII) getc, putc, ungetc				X
C string				
*strncpy		X	X	
(UNICODE) *_tcsncpy				X

dows systems have zero percent failure rates (this difference is presumably because Windows does boundary checking on character table-lookup operations). Linux also has higher failure rates on C file I/O management, C stream I/O, and C memory operations. For other groupings Linux has a much lower Abort failure rate. It is interesting to note that the similar code bases for the Windows 95/98 pairing and the Windows NT/2000 pairing show up in relatively similar Abort failure rates. Windows CE generally has lower abort failure rates than Windows NT and Windows 2000, but the significant number of functions that can cause complete system crashes indicates that despite this, Windows CE is less stable than Windows NT/2000.

The issue of Silent failures is a potentially thorny one. Silent failures cannot be measured directly by Ballista because they involve situations in which there is no observable indication of a failure. (Note: this is not to say they are non-observable in the usual sense of non-activated injected faults that do not affect results. The problem is that there is an exceptional condition that ought to generate observable results to attain robust operation, but does not. As an example, a Silent failure might be a call that reads data from a non-existent file, but returns seemingly valid data bytes with no error indication.)

It is impractical to annotate millions of tests to identify Silent failures. However, we can estimate silent failure rates by voting results across different versions of the same API. Based on previous experience with POSIX [8], we would expect there to be approximately a 10% pass-with-non-exceptional test rate (but, this is a very gross approximation), with the rest of the test cases with a pass with no error reported being Silent failures. If one presumes that the Win32 API is supposed to be identical in exception handling as well as functionality across implementations, if one system reports a pass with no error reported for one particular test case and another system reports a pass with an error or a failure for that identical test case, then we can declare the system that reported no error as having a Silent failure. We wrote a script to automatically vote across identical test cases for each system to generate estimated Silent failure rates. (Note: this analysis does not apply to Linux because it is not an identical API.) Windows CE is not included in this analysis because although the API is similar, it is not identical. Some parameters are not used in Windows CE, and over half of the functions tested on the other Win32 platforms were not supported. Therefore, silent failure rates cannot be reported accurately for Windows CE.

Based on the estimated Silent failures, it seems that the Win32 calls for Windows 95/98/98 SE have a significantly higher Silent failure rate than Windows NT/2000. C library functions vary, with Windows 95/98/98 SE having both higher and lower Silent failure rates than Windows NT/2000 depending on the functional category. Figure 2

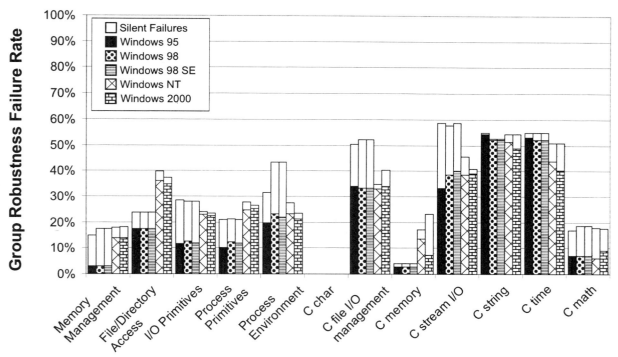

Figure 2. Abort, Restart, and estimated Silent failure rates for Windows desktop operating systems.

shows the overall robustness failure rates for the different Windows variants tested, including these estimated Silent failure rates. Based on these results, it appears that Windows NT and Windows 2000 suffer fewer robustness failures overall than Windows 95/98/98 SE. The only significant exceptions are for the File and Directory Access category as well as the C memory management category, which both suffer from higher Abort failure rates on Windows NT and Windows 2000. (A possible limitation of this approach is that it cannot find instances in which all versions of Windows suffer a Silent failure. This hidden Silent failure rate may be significant, but quantification is not practical.)

5. Conclusions and Future Work

This work demonstrates that it is possible to compare the robustness of different OS APIs on a relatively level playing field. The use of data type-based testing techniques and normalization of test results by functional groupings enables a detailed comparison of APIs having generally similar capabilities but different interfaces.

Applying the Ballista testing methodology to several Microsoft Windows operating systems revealed a variety of robustness failures. The Windows CE OS and the Windows 95/98/98 SE family of operating systems were clearly vulnerable to robustness failures induced by exceptional parameter values, and could be crashed via a variety of

functions. Additionally, the Windows 95/98/98 SE systems had a significant level of Silent failure rates in which exceptional operating situations produced neither abnormal termination nor any other indication of an exception when such an indication was demonstrated possible by other Windows variants. Windows NT and Windows 2000 proved as resistant to system crashes as Linux under these testing conditions, and in most cases had fewer Silent failures than the Windows 95/98/98 SE family (although only a relative comparison was possible; the absolute level of Silent failures is more difficult to determine).

An examination of Abort failures (exceptions too non-specific to be recoverable) and Restart failures (task "hangs") showed differences among the Windows variants and between Windows and Linux. Linux had a significantly lower Abort failure rate in eight out of twelve functional groupings, but was significantly higher in the remaining four. The four groupings for which Linux Abort failures are higher are entirely within the C library, for which the POSIX and Win32 APIs are identical.

Windows CE has abort failure rates comparable to Windows NT and Windows 2000, but has several functions that cause complete system crashes. This makes Windows CE a less attractive alternative for embedded systems, where dependability and reliability are of much higher importance than in desktop PC applications. While abort failures may be recoverable by task restarts, a complete OS crash will more than likely cause complete system failure. It should be noted that many of the catastrophic failures found in Windows CE were traceable to incorrect handling of a single bad parameter value, namely an invalid C file pointer (the actual parameter was a string buffer typecast to a file pointer). It could be argued that since we can trace problem to one underlying cause that we should not penalize Windows CE for seventeen functions that happen to take the same parameter. However, developers who wish to use Windows CE in their systems would have to generate software wrappers for each of the seventeen functions they use to protect against a system crash because they only have access to the interface, not the underlying implementation.

It is also interesting to note that several of the Win32 system calls that crashed on Windows CE also crashed on Windows 95/98/98 SE (some with the exact same parameter values, as in Listing 1), despite the fact that they were developed by different teams within Microsoft and have different code bases. One can speculate that this indicates the underlying causes of these errors may be in the specification rather than the implementation; however the problem may simply be that different programmers tend to make the same sorts of mistakes in similar situations.

While it is not appropriate to make sweeping claims about the dependability of Windows or Linux from these test results alone, a few observations seem warranted by the data presented. The marked difference in finding catastrophic failures in Windows CE and the Windows 95/98/98 SE family compared to the other OS families lends credibility to Microsoft's statement that the Windows NT/2000 systems are more reliable overall. A relative assessment of Linux vs. Windows NT reliability is less clear-cut. Linux seems more robust on system calls, but more susceptible to Abort failures on C library calls (which are actually part of the GNU C compiler suite for Linux) compared to Windows NT.

Future work on Windows testing will include looking for dependability problems caused by heavy load conditions, as well as state- and sequence-dependent failures. In particular, we will attempt to find ways to reproduce the elusive crashes that we have observed to occur in both Windows and Linux outside of the current robustness testing framework.

6. Acknowledgements

This work was supported by Emerson Electric, Lucent Technologies, Asea Brown Boveri (ABB), and Darpa (contract DABT63-96-C-0064). Equipment support was provided by Intel, Compaq and Microsoft. Thanks to Jiantao Pan and Meredith Beveridge for their assistance.

7. References

[1] Ballista Robustness Testing Service, http://www.cs.cmu.edu/~koopman/ballista/index.html, November 1999.

[2] Beizer, Boris, *Black Box Testing: Techniques for Functional Testing of Software Systems*. John Wiley & Sons, Inc., New York, 1995.

[3] DeVale, J., Koopman, P., Guttendorf, D., "The Ballista Software Robustness Testing Service," Testing Computer Software Conference, 1999.

[4] Ghosh, A., Schmid, M., Hill, F., "Wrapping Windows NT Software For Robustness," 29th Fault Tolerant Computing Symposium, June 15-18, 1999.

[5] Ghosh, A., Schmid, M., "An Approach to Testing COTS Software for Robustness to Operating System Exceptions and Errors," 10th International Symposium on Software Reliability Engineering, November 1-4, 1999.

[6] IEEE Standard Glossary of Software Engineering Terminology (IEEE Std610.12-1990), IEEE Computer Soc., Dec. 10, 1990.

[7] IEEE Standard for Information Technology - Portable Operating System Interface (POSIX) Part 1: System Application Program Interface (API) Amendment 1: Realtime Extension [C Language], IEEE Std 1003.1b-1993, 1994.

[8] Koopman, P., DeVale, J., "Comparing the Robustness of POSIX Operating Systems," 29th Fault Tolerant Computing Symposium, June 15-18, 1999.

[9] Kropp, N., Koopman, P. & Siewiorek, D., "Automated Robustness Testing of Off-the_Shelf Software Components," 28th Fault Tolerant Computing Symposium, June 23-25, 1998.

[10] Microsoft Corp., Choosing the Best Windows Desktop Platform For Large and Medium-Sized Businesses and Organizations, white paper, June 1998, http://www.microsoft.com/windows/platform/info/how2choose-mb.htm, November 1999.

[11] Microsoft Corp., Microsoft Platform Software Development Kit Documentation, 1999.

[12] Miller, B.P., Fredriksen, L. & So, B., "An empirical study of the reliability of Unix utilities," Communications of the ACM, 33(12): 32-43, December 1990.

[13] Miller, B.P., D. Koski, C. Pheow Lee, V. Maganty, R. Murthy, A. Natarajan & J. Steidl, "Fuzz Revisited: A Re-examination of the Reliability of UNIX Utilities and Services," University of Wisconsin, CS-TR-95-1268, April 1995.

[14] Simon, R., *Windows NT Win32 API SuperBible*. Waite Group Press, Corte Modera, CA, 1997.

[15] Slabodkin, Gregory, "Software glitches leave Navy Smart Ship dead in the water," Government Computer News, http://www.gcn.com/archives/gcn/1998/july13/cov2.htm, July 13, 1998.

Session 9B

Byzantine Faults

From Crash Fault-Tolerance to Arbitrary-Fault Tolerance: Towards a Modular Approach

Roberto BALDONI*   Jean-Michel HELARY†   Michel RAYNAL†

Abstract

This paper presents a generic methodology to transform a protocol resilient to process crashes into one resilient to arbitrary failures in the case where processes run the same text and regularly exchange messages (i.e., the case of round-based protocols). The methodology follows a modular approach encapsulating the detection of arbitrary failures in specific modules. This can be the starting point for designing tools that allow automatic transformation. We show an application of this methodology to the case of consensus.

1 Introduction

Providing specifications and designing solutions for distributed algorithms in an environment where processes can exhibit arbitrary behavior (*e.g.*, omit to execute a statement or corrupt the value of a local variable) is notably more difficult than in a crash context. Additionally, most of the time both specifications used in the crash model are inadequate because if a process shows an arbitrary faulty behavior from the beginning of its execution, it is impossible for others to detect it. Solutions used in the crash model become inadequate because a malicious process can exhibit failures more subtle than crashes and these failures can lead to the violation of the correctness criteria of the algorithm.

Our goal is to propose a methodology to transform distributed algorithms resilient to process crashes into algorithms resilient to arbitrary failures. This method relies on a modular approach that aims to "encapsulate" each type of failure in a specific module[1]. Because of the semantic nature of arbitrary failures, the actual design of some of these modules cannot be performed independently of the algorithm that will use them. However, our aim is to propose a

design *method* that is independent of a particular algorithm. In that sense, this paper contributes to a better understanding of the tools that can be used to produce algorithms resilient to arbitrary failures. To illustrate this methodology, we show how it works in the case of consensus.

Consensus: a Case Study. Consensus is a fundamental paradigm for fault-tolerant distributed systems. Each process proposes a value to the others. All correct processes have to agree (Termination) on the same value (Agreement) which must be one of the initially proposed values (Validity). Solving consensus in asynchronous distributed systems where processes can crash is a well-known difficult task: Fischer, Lynch and Paterson have proved an impossibility result [7] stating that *there is no deterministic solution to the consensus problem in the presence of even a single process crash*. A way to circumvent this impossibility result is to use the concept of unreliable failure detectors introduced by Chandra and Toueg [3]. Each process is equipped with a failure detector module that provides it with a list of processes it currently suspects to have crashed. A failure detector module can make mistakes by not suspecting a crashed process or by erroneously suspecting a correct one. Formally, a failure detector module is defined by two properties: completeness (a property on the actual detection of process crashes), and accuracy (a property that restricts the mistakes on erroneous suspicions). In a context where processes encounter arbitrary failures, the specifications and solutions used in the crash model are inadequate, as discussed hereafter.

Specification issues. The traditional Validity property is not adequate to define the consensus problem in an arbitrary failure setting. A faulty process can initially propose an irrelevant value (i.e., a value different from the one it should propose) and then behave correctly. There is no way for the other processes to detect this failure. Consequently, the set of correct processes could agree on an irrelevant value v proposed by a process. An advance has been done by Doudou and Schiper [5] to circumvent this drawback: they have introduced a new Validity property, namely the *Vector Validity* property. This property requires that the decision value is a vector containing a certain number (at least one)

*Università "La Sapienza", Roma, Italy. baldoni@dis.uniroma1.it.
† IRISA, Campus de Beaulieu, Université Rennes1, Rennes, France. {helary,raynal}@irisa.fr.

[1]Previous alternative approaches by different authors are summarized in the Chapter 12 of [1]. In the asynchronous case, they provide only a masking of arbitrary faulty messages by *identical* faulty messages and thus, do not address all types of arbitrary failures.

of initial values of correct processes. So, processes have first to construct vectors (from processes initial values) and then to agree on one of these vectors (*Vector Consensus*). One interesting feature of this construction is the following: if a process falsifies an entry from a process, it will be detected as faulty by correct processes. In a sense, this allows to "certify" initial values of correct processes.

Solution issues. Malkhi and Reiter [10] have been the first to propose an extension of failure detectors able to cope with other types of failures. They have introduced a failure detector class $\Diamond S(bz)$ based on the notion of a *quiet* process. A process p is quiet if there exists a time after which some correct process does not receive anymore messages from p. (Note that a crashed process is a quiet process). More recently, Doudou et al. [6] have pointed out that, in presence of arbitrary failures, it is no longer possible to define failure detection modules independently of the protocols that rely on them: unlike process crashes, other types of failure are not context-free. In particular, the notion of quiet process is not an extension of the notion of crashed process: a process can be quiet (or mute) to some processes with respect to a given protocol, without being crashed. To cope with this notion, the authors have introduced the notion of *muteness detectors*, and particularly the class $\Diamond M_{\mathcal{A}}$, where $\mathcal{A}$ denotes a particular protocol. It can be seen as an instantiation of a generic class of omission failure detectors, introduced by Dolev et al. [4]. Moreover, the specification of this failure detector makes sense only in the context of regular round-based distributed algorithms (a precise definition of this class of algorithms is provided in [6]).

Faulty processes are prone to all kinds of non-muteness failures, (*e.g.* corrupting the content of a message). Kihlstrom, Moser and Melliar-Smith [9] have pointed out that messages need to be *signed* as well as *certified*. The signature allows a receiver to authenticate the sender, while the certificate is a well-defined amount of redundant information carried by messages that allows a receiver to check if the content of a message is valid and if the sending of the message was done "at the right time". In other words, a certificate allows a receiver to "look into the sender process" in order to see if the actions that produced the sending were correct. Using these tools, several consensus protocols have been proposed for the arbitrary failure context ([5],[9],[10]). All these solutions use unreliable failure detectors to detect muteness failures, but leave the detection of other types of failure to the protocols themselves.

Results of the Paper. In the methodology proposed in this paper, each type of failure exhibited by a faulty process is detected by a specific module. We make two assumptions on the class of protocols to which the proposed approach applies. First, to meet the requirement of muteness failure detectors, we consider only regular round-based protocols (as in [6]). Roughly speaking, we require from such protocols that they have a regular communication pattern (asynchronous rounds), i.e., that each correct process communicates regularly with others (note that this does *not* assume synchronous systems). Second, we assume that each process "knows" the program of every other process participating in the algorithm (this is satisfied when all processes are assumed to follow the same program). From the application of the methodology it follows that each process has to be actually composed of five modules: (i) a round-based protocol module which executes the algorithm; (ii) a muteness failure detection module which detects permanent omission failures; (iii) a non-muteness failure detection module which reveals other types of failures; (iv) a signature module which filters out messages in which the sender must be identified; (v) a certification module which manages certificates to be associated with messages. It is important to assume that certificates themselves cannot be corrupted. We will explain how this assumption can be enforced.

This methodology is then applied to the transformation of the Hurfin and Raynal Consensus protocol [8] designed for the crash model, into a Consensus protocol resilient to arbitrary failures. The complete process structure of the resulting protocol is shown. We use a muteness failure detector of the class $\Diamond M$, whose implementation has been discussed in [6]. The design of uncorruptible certificates and a reliable implementation of the non-muteness failure detection module are described in detail, according to the general methodology. As far as we know, such an issue had never been addressed before.

The resulting protocol assumes a maximum number of non-correct processes $F \leq \min(\lfloor (n-1)/2 \rfloor, C)$ where C is the maximum number of faulty processes that the underlying certification service used by the protocol can cope with [2]. The protocol satisfies Agreement, Termination and Vector Validity with at least $\alpha = n - 2F$ entries from correct processes (note that, due to definition of F, we have $\alpha \geq 1$).

The paper is made of five sections. Section 2 presents the asynchronous model with arbitrary failures. Section 3 addresses the general methodology to transform process crash resilient protocols into arbitrary failure resilient ones. The case study of consensus is presented in Sections 4 (protocol in the crash model) and 5 (transformed protocol).

2 The Model

A Distributed Computation. We consider a system consisting of $n > 1$ processes $\Pi = \{p_1, p_2, \ldots, p_n\}$ executing the *same* program text. In the following, a *correct* process

---

[2]Usual certification mechanisms require $C = \lfloor (n-1)/3 \rfloor$.

274

is a non-faulty process, as explained below. Every pair of processes is connected by a *reliable* channel. We also assume that channels are FIFO (this simplifies the solution when addressing arbitrary failures) and that each process p possesses a private key and a public key. The private key is used by p to sign, in an unforgeable way, outgoing messages. There is no assumption about the relative speed of processes or the message transfer delays.

Faulty Process. The very concept of arbitrary failures is intended to englobe any possible behavior as seen from outside the process [12]. However, the design of tools for detecting such faulty behaviors rests upon a careful analysis of their cause. This analysis leads to classify failures into two different types: (1) *Muteness failures* (Permanent Message Omission.) The process stops sending messages it is supposed to send. This includes, but is not limited to, *the process crash*, where the process stops executing statements of its program and halts. (2) *Non-Muteness Failures*, including: corruption of a variable value, transient omissions of statements, duplication of a statement, execution of a spurious statement, misevaluation of an expression, etc.[3]

Note that a process may behave correctly with respect to some process, but exhibit a faulty behavior with respect to some other process. However, by definition, a process that makes even a single fault with respect to only one process is a faulty process.

3   Detecting Arbitrary Behaviors

In this section, we consider generic methods to design failure detection tools. Here, genericity means that methods themselves are independent of the protocols using the detection tools, even if detection tools are actually designed to be used by particular protocols (and sometimes mixed with them). The situation is similar to the one encountered when, *e.g.*, designing loops for sequential programs: the design method (based on invariants, stop conditions, etc.) is independent of particular programs, whereas each loop is actually designed in the context of a particular program.

Manifestation of Non-Muteness Failures. In an asynchronous distributed computation, failures experienced by a process cannot be revealed to other processes unless the faulty process has to communicate with others (according to the program specification), via *protocol messages*[4]. As a consequence, detection of failures is closely related to the *receipt of protocol messages*. Then, the key idea is: *each process has to check whether the right message has been sent by the right process at the right time with the right arguments*.

---

[3]A more detailed analysis can be found in the full version [2].

[4]If a process must not send any message (according to the program specification), its behavior can be considered as non-relevant since it has no effect on the other processes.

Since the detection of (i) permanent omission failures (muteness) (ii) processes falsifying their identity (i.e., wrong sender) has been extensively addressed in [6] and [9] respectively, we will concentrate on the detection of other failures. These failures can be revealed to other processes via messages. We have identified two kinds of "externally" visible wrong messages:

1. Out-of-order messages (i.e., wrong time), revealing either a *non-permanent sending omission* or a *sending duplication*. This case includes a message that does not belong to the set of messages that can be generated by the text of the program.

2. Wrong Expected Messages (i.e., right time, but wrong message or wrong content). This case includes messages sent after misevaluation of a condition statement (substituted messages), or messages whose content is syntactically or semantically incorrect.

Tools for Detection of Non-Muteness Failures. These tools are based, on the one hand, on certification mechanisms, and, on the other hand, on state machines built from the text of the protocol.

Certificates. A certificate is a piece of redundant information, including a part of the process history. This history includes internal, send and receipt events. The certificate is appended to the message sent, and is used by the receiver to check if the content of the message is consistent with the sender's history (no semantically incorrect message). It also allows the receiver to check that the decision to send this message (and not another one, in case of choice) is the correct one (no substituted message).

Consider a message m from p to q, containing a value v. This value has been updated by p according to its own history. Similarly, the sending event of m is a consequence of the receipt of other messages, and is enabled by a set of conditions involving local variables of p. The certificate appended to m must contain proper information able to witness: the value v, the fact that the required receipt events have been correctly taken into account, and the values of p's local variables involved in the enabling condition.

Let us remark that we have to assume that certificates themselves cannot be corrupted, since a corrupted certifying information could be consistent with a corrupted information to certify. The concept of *reliable Certification Module* encapsulates this assumption. Technically, it can be enforced by the very composition of certificates: they are composed of a set of signed messages, *e.g.* messages whose receipt is the cause of the sending of m, or whose content has influenced the update of a local variable whose value is involved in m. Reliability results from the fact that no process can falsify the content of a signed message without being detected as faulty by a correct receiver, and from the cardinality of the set of signed messages allowing majority tests to be performed. The correctness of a certificate can thus be verified at the recipient side, by a *certificate analyzer* (implemented by a state machine, as explained below).

We will say that a certificate attached to m is *well-formed with respect to a value v* if it has been analyzed as correct and if the receiver can extract information consistent with the value of v and with the action to send m.

The design of certificates depends on the protocol to transform. The previous principles constitute a "guideline" for this design. If the protocol has been proved correct in the crash model, it remains only to prove that certificates are well-formed with respect to (1) values carried by messages and (2) to decisions enabling their send event.

State machines. Under the assumption that every process knows the program text of the other processes, every process can build an ad-hoc state machine (*e.g.*, a finite state automaton) modeling the expected behavior of another process. Let $\mathcal{SM}_p(q)$ be the state machine modeling the behavior of process q with respect to process p. In this state machine, transitions are triggered when p receives a message from q. In every state, a set of receipt events are enabled. *Out-of-order messages* are those whose receipt events are not enabled. *Wrong Expected messages* are either (i) those whose receipt event is enabled, but whose syntactic composition is not consistent with the one of the corresponding expected message or (ii) those whose receipt event is enabled, but whose certificate is not well formed with respect to either its arguments or the action to send that particular message. When such events occur, they trigger a transition to a particular terminal state, called *faulty state*. The actual design of a particular state machine has to be done in the particular context of the protocol to transform.

Handling local variables. Each local variable is a way that a faulty process can use to "attack" correct processes by corrupting its value. This may happen when the value of a local variable is initialized, or updated independently of the receipt of messages. As a consequence, expressions involving local variables should be, as much as possible, replaced with expressions involving only values of certificates, because certificates cannot be corrupted. Moreover, it can happen – from the definition of the protocol – that some variables cannot be certified. In order to secure an update, the transformed protocol must generate an exchange of messages between all processes. After this exchange, each process has a *vector of values*, ensuring that a given number α (at least one) of entries are correct. An entry is correct if 1) it is the value of a correct process, and 2) if a process falsifies this entry, it will be detected as faulty by correct processes. In other words, this vector is certified by messages exchanged to build it. Such a technique is called *Vector certification.*

General Methodology for Protocol Transformation. A process of the transformed protocol consists of five modules whose role has been presented in the introduction. More precisely, the structure of a process p_i is given in Figure 1. The same figure also shows the path followed by a message m (resp. m') received (resp. sent) by p_i.

Signature module. Each message arriving at p_i is first processed by this module which verifies the signature of the sender (by using its public key). If the signature of the message is inconsistent with the identity field contained in the message, the message is discarded and its sender identity (known thanks to the unforgeable signature), is passed to the non-muteness failure detection module to be added to a set $faulty_i$. Otherwise, the message is passed to the muteness failure detection module. Also, each message sent by p_i is signed by the signature module just before leaving the process. This module is generic, in the sense that it can be implemented independently of the protocols using it [13].

Muteness failure detection module. This module is devoted to the detection of mute processes [6]. It manages a set $suspected_i$ of processes suspected to be mute to p_i. The receipt of a message will be taken into account by this detector, that will remove the sender from the set $suspected_i$ (if necessary). Then, the message is passed to p_i's non-muteness failure detection module.

Non-muteness failure detection module. This module receives messages from the muteness failure detection module and checks if they are properly formed and follow the program specification of the sender (i.e., it actually implements the state machine described above). In the affirmative, it passes the message to p_i's certification module. This module maintains a set ($faulty_i$) of processes it detected to experience one of the manifestations of non-muteness failure. We say "process p_i declares p_j to be faulty" at some time, if, at that time, $p_j \in faulty_i$. We assume that that this module is reliable, i.e., if p_i is correct and $p_j \in faulty_i$, then p_j has experienced an incorrect behavior detected by the non-muteness failure detection module of p_i. Finally, as for the set $suspected_i$, p_i's round-based protocol module can only read $faulty_i$ (note that, if p_i is faulty, it can misevaluate an expression involving $faulty_i$).

Reliable Certification Module. This module is responsible, upon the receipt of a message from the non-muteness failure detection module, for updating the corresponding certificate local variable. It is also in charge of appending properly formed certificates to the messages that are sent by p_i.

Round-based Protocol Module. This module is the one that executes the protocol and it is generated by the transformation of the round-based protocol in the crash model by applying the rules defined above in this Section.

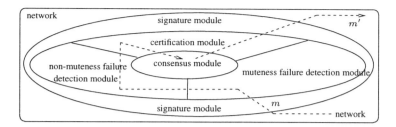

Figure 1. Structure of a process p_i.

4 Hurfin-Raynal's Consensus Protocol

This section provides a brief description of a version of Hurfin-Raynal's protocol [8] that assumes FIFO channels (this constraint is not required by the original protocol). It will be used as an example to show the transformation methodology. As other crash-resilient consensus protocols, it assumes a majority of correct (i.e., non-crashed) processes and uses a failure detector of the class $\Diamond\mathcal{S}$ (Strong Completeness and Eventual Weak Accuracy). It proceeds in successive asynchronous rounds, using the rotating coordinator paradigm. During a round, a predetermined process (the round coordinator) tries to impose a value as the decision value. To attain this goal, each process votes: either (vote CURRENT) in favor of the value proposed by the round coordinator (when it has received one), or (vote NEXT) to proceed to the next round and benefit from a new coordinator (when it suspects the current coordinator).

During each round, the behavior of each process p_i is determined by a finite state automaton. This automaton is composed of 3 states. The local variable $state_i$ will denote the automaton state in which p_i currently is. During a round, the states of the automaton have the following meaning:

- $state_i = q_0$: p_i has not yet voted (q_0 is the automaton initial state).
- $state_i = q_1$: p_i has voted CURRENT and has not changed its mind (p_i moves from q_0 to q_1).
- $state_i = q_2$: p_i has voted NEXT.

The protocol manages the progression of each process p_i within its automaton, according to the following rules. At the beginning of round r, $state_i = q_0$. Then, during r, the transitions are:

- *Transition $q_0 \rightarrow q_1$ (p_i first votes CURRENT).* This transition occurs when p_i receives a CURRENT vote (line 7), and is in the initial state q_0 (line 10). This means that p_i is the round coordinator, or has not previously suspected the round coordinator. Moreover, when p_i moves to q_1 and is not the current coordinator, it broadcasts a CURRENT vote (line 10).
- *Transition $q_0 \rightarrow q_2$ (p_i first votes NEXT).* This transition occurs when p_i, while in the initial state q_0, suspects

the current coordinator (line 13). This means that p_i has not previously received a CURRENT vote. Moreover, when p_i moves to q_2, it broadcasts a NEXT vote (line 13).

- *Transition $q_1 \rightarrow q_2$ (p_i changes its mind).* This transition (executed by statements at line 15) is used to prevent a possible deadlock. A process p_i that has issued a CURRENT vote is allowed to change its mind if p_i has received a (CURRENT or NEXT) vote from a majority of processes but has received neither a majority of CURRENT votes (so it cannot decide), nor a majority of NEXT votes (so it cannot progress to the next round). Then p_i changes its mind in order to make the protocol progress: it broadcasts a NEXT vote to favor the transition to the next round (line 15). In the text, the abbreviation $change\_mind$ means $(state_i = q_1) \wedge (\mid rec\_from_i \mid > n/2)$.

Protocol Description. In addition to the local variable $state_i$, process p_i manages the following four local variables:

- r_i defines the current round number.
- est_i contains the current estimation by p_i of the decision value.
- $nb\_current_i$ (resp. nb_next_i) counts the number of CURRENT (resp. NEXT) votes received by p_i during the current round.
- rec_from_i is a set composed of the process identities from which p_i has received a (CURRENT or NEXT) vote during the current round.

Finally, $suspected_i$ is a set managed by the associated failure detector module; p_i can only read this set.

Function consensus() consists of two concurrent tasks. The first task handles the receipt of a DECIDE message (line 2); it ensures that if a process p_i decides (line 2 or line 12), then all correct processes will also receive a DECIDE message. The second task (lines 3-18) describes a round: it consists of a loop that constitutes the core of the protocol. Each (CURRENT or NEXT) vote is labeled with its round number[5].

---

[5]In any round r_i, only votes related to round r_i can be received. A vote from p_k related to a past round is discarded and a vote related to a future round r_k (with $r_k > r_i$) is buffered and delivered when $r_i = r_k$.

```
function consensus($v_i$)

(1) $r_i \leftarrow 0$; $est_i \leftarrow v_i$;
    cobegin
(2)  || upon receipt of DECIDE($p_k, est_k$) send DECIDE($p_i, est_k$) to $\Pi$; return($est_k$)

(3)  || loop % on a sequence of asynchronous rounds %
(4)     $c \leftarrow (r_i \bmod n) + 1$; $r_i \leftarrow r_i + 1$; $state_i \leftarrow q_0$; $rec\_from_i \leftarrow \emptyset$; $nb\_next_i \leftarrow 0$; $nb\_current_i \leftarrow 0$;
(5)     if $(i = c)$ then send CURRENT($p_i, r_i, est_i$) to $\Pi$ endif;

(6)     while $(nb\_next_i \leq n/2)$ do % wait until a branch can be selected, and then execute it %
(7)        upon receipt of CURRENT($p_k, r_i, est_k$)
(8)           $nb\_current_i \leftarrow nb\_current_i + 1$; $rec\_from_i \leftarrow rec\_from_i \cup \{p_k\}$;
(9)           if $(nb\_current_i = 1)$ then $est_i \leftarrow est_k$ endif;
(10)          if $(state_i = q_0)$ then $state_i \leftarrow q_1$ ; if $i \neq c$ then send CURRENT($p_i, r_i, est_i$) to $\Pi$   endif;
(11)       endif;
(12)          if $(nb\_current_i > n/2)$ then send DECIDE($p_i, est_i$) to $\Pi$; return($est_i$) endif

(13)       upon $(p_c \in suspected_i)$ if $(state_i = q_0)$ then $state_i \leftarrow q_2$; send NEXT($p_i, r_i$) to $\Pi$ endif

(14)       upon receipt of NEXT($p_k, r_i$) $nb\_next_i \leftarrow nb\_next_i + 1$; $rec\_from_i \leftarrow rec\_from_i \cup \{p_k\}$

(15)       upon $(change\_mind)$ $state_i \leftarrow q_2$; send NEXT($p_i, r_i$) to $\Pi$
(16)    endwhile

(17)    if $(state_i \neq q_2)$ then $state_i \leftarrow q_2$; send NEXT($p_i, r_i$) to $\Pi$ endif
(18) endloop
     coend
```

Figure 2. Hurfin-Raynal's $\diamond S$-based Consensus Protocol (adapted to FIFO channels)

• At the beginning of a round r, the current coordinator p_c proposes its estimate v_c to become the decision value by broadcasting a CURRENT vote carrying this value (line 5).

• Each time a process p_i receives a (CURRENT or NEXT) vote, it updates the corresponding counter and the set rec_from_i (lines 8 and 14).

• When a process receives a CURRENT vote for the first time, namely, CURRENT(p_k,r,est_k), it adopts est_k as its current estimate est_i (line 9). If, in addition, it is in state q_0, it moves to state q_1 (line 10).

• A process p_i decides on an estimate proposed by the current coordinator as soon as it has received a majority of CURRENT votes, i.e., a majority of votes that agree to conclude during the current round (line 12).

• When a process progresses from round r to round $r+1$ it issues a NEXT (line 17) if it did not do it in the **while** loop. These NEXT votes are used to prevent other processes from remaining blocked in round r (line 6).

The complete analysis and proof of this protocol can be found in [8].

5 Making the Protocol Resilient to Arbitrary Failures

In this section, we concentrate on the certification, the non-muteness failure detection and the resulting consensus modules (muteness failure detection is ensured by a module of class $\diamond \mathcal{M}$ [6], and signature module is independent of the protocol).

5.1 Designing Certificates

Certificates must witness values of the local variables, and correct evaluation of conditions enabling the sending events, as described in Section 3, in order to allow a receiver to detect a sender failure by using a non-muteness failure detection module (i.e., a state machine).

Initial values. Values v_i proposed by the processes cannot be certified, because they are initial values. So, it is necessary to apply the Vector Certification technique. In the context of consensus, this leads to the Vector Consensus problem[6], specified by the classical Agreement and Termination properties and the following Vector Validity property [5].

Every process decides on a vector $vect$ of size n:

• For every process p_i: if p_i is correct, then either $vect[i] = v_i$ or $vect[i] = null$, and

• At least $\alpha \geq 1$ elements of $vect$ are initial values of correct processes.

---

[6]The *Vector Consensus* notion has first been proposed in synchronous systems where it is called *Interactive Consistency* problem [11].

278

The transformation that must be applied to the original protocol is standard. It consists in a preliminary phase during which every process sends its proposition to every other process. Thus, each process constructs a vector whose j-th entry is the value received from process p_j. For each process p_i, the problem lies in obtaining a vector of proposed values certifying initial values of correct processes (certified vector). This certified vector will then be used as the value proposed by p_i to the consensus protocol.

Let INIT denote the messages used in this preliminary phase. Each message INIT sent by p_i carries its proposed value v_i. Messages INIT have an empty certificate. However, they are signed. This allows the vector built by a process p_i to be certified, in the following way: each time p_i receives $\langle \text{INIT}(p_j, v_j), cert_j \rangle$ (here, $cert_j = \emptyset$) from p_j, its certification module adds this signed message to the certificate est_init_i.

The text of this procedure for process p_i is described in Figure 3, lines 4-9.

Each process initially broadcasts its value v_i and then waits for $(n - F)$ values from other processes. Each time p_i receives a value, the message is added to est_cert_i.

Exiting from the initial while loop (lines 6-9) we say that "est_cert_i is well-formed with respect to a value est_vect_i" if the following conditions are satisfied:

- $|est\_cert_i| = (n - F)$, and
- The value est_vect_i is correct with respect to the $(n - F)$ INIT messages contained in est_cert_i (intuitively, this means that those $(n - F)$ messages "witness" that est_vect_i is a correct value, because $n - F \geq n - C$).

We have the following results:

Proposition 1 *Eventually, every correct process builds a vector est_vect_i such that $est\_vect_i[i] = v_i$ and $\forall k \neq i$: $est\_vect_i[k] = v_k$ or $est\_vect_i[k] = null$, and est_cert_i is well-formed with respect to est_vect_i.*

Proposition 2 *No process can build two different initial certified vectors.*

Due to space limitations, the proof of these propositions is omitted[7].

Certifying values carried by the other messages. Apart from INIT messages, three types of messages are exchanged in the original protocol, namely, CURRENT, NEXT and DE-CIDE. These messages carry the identity of their sender, the round number where they have been sent, and (except NEXT), the current estimation of the sender.

Identity of the sender. This value is certified by the signature of the message, as explained in Section 3.

Estimate value. In the transformed protocol, estimate values are vectors. The current estimate value of p_i will be denoted est_vect_i. The initial value of est_vect_i is certified

by est_cert_i, as explained above. This variable can then take successive values: it can be updated at most once per round due to the delivery of the first CURRENT message received during this round. When this occurs, the certificate est_cert_i is also updated, with the certificate of the CURRENT message. Since this message is properly formed, its certificate $cert_k$ contains a correct certificate est_cert_k (i.e., a certificate well-formed with respect to the value est_vect_k contained in the CURRENT message). During a round, est_cert_i is said to be "*well-formed with respect to est_vect_i*" if the value est_vect_i is the value included in the $(n - F)$ messages contained in est_cert_k. Otherwise, it means that process p_i has either omitted to execute the update of est_vect_i, or corrupted its value.

Similarly, a process decides a value est_vect_c at round r either when it has received $(n - F)$ valid CURRENT messages (lines 20-21) or when it receives a valid DECIDE message from another process (lines 2-3). In the first case the process authenticates its decision by using a certificate $current\_cert_i$ made of the set of the $(n - F)$ signed CURRENT messages (line 21), in the second case the message DECIDE (with the same certificate) is relayed to the other processes (line 3).

We say that $current\_cert_i$ is well formed with respect to r and est_vect if the following conditions are satisfied:

- $|current\_cert_i| = (n - F)$ (otherwise process p_i misevaluated the condition of line 20).
- the certificate of each message in $current\_cert_i$ contains a est_cert_c well formed with respect to est_vect.
- the certificate of each message in $current\_cert_i$ contains a $next\_cert$ well formed with respect to r.

Round number. A process progress from round $r - 1$ to round r ($r > 1$) when it has received enough NEXT messages (i.e., at least $\lceil \frac{n}{2} \rceil$ in the original protocol, at least $(n - F)$ in the transformed protocol). So, the new value of r (resulting from the assignment $r \leftarrow r + 1$ performed at the beginning of the new round) is certified by the signed messages NEXT whose reception has triggered the start of the new round. This set of signed messages constitute the certificate $next\_cert_i$. This certificate is reset to the empty set at the beginning of each round. When a new round r ($r > 1$) starts (before resetting $next\_cert_i$), we say that $next\_cert_i$ is well-formed with respect to $r - 1$ if the following two conditions are satisfied:

- $|next\_cert_i| = (n - F)$ (otherwise process p_i has misevaluated the condition allowing to start a new round, line 14 in the text).
- The value $r - 1$ is consistent with respect to the information in the $(n - F)$ NEXT messages contained in est_cert_i (i.e., all messages refer to round $r - 1$). Otherwise process p_i has corrupted the value of r at the beginning of the round, line 11 in the text).

As far as round 1 is concerned, this value cannot be cer-

---

[7]It can be found in the full paper [2].

279

tified by NEXT messages. Since $next\_cert_i$ is initialized to the empty set, we will say that $next\_cert_i$ *is well-formed (with respect to round 0)* if $next\_cert_i = \emptyset$ (Otherwise either p_i has corrupted r or c at the beginning of the round 1 (line 11) or has misevaluated the condition $i = c$ (line 12).

Certifying sending events of messages.

Messages CURRENT.

- At the beginning of a round r, the current coordinator p_c proposes its estimate est_vect_c to become the decision value by broadcasting a CURRENT message carrying this value (line 12). This message is certified by $est\_cert_c \cup next\_cert_c$. est_cert_c is used to certify the value proposed by the coordinator est_vect_c, that is, est_cert_c must be well formed with respect to est_vect_c. $next\_cert_c$ is used to certify the value of the current round r (i.e., $next\_cert_c$ must be well formed with respect to $r - 1$).

- When p_i receives the first CURRENT valid message while in state q_0 (line 18), it relays a CURRENT message (line 19) by using the signed valid message CURRENT just received as a certificate. This certificate contains $est\_cert_c \cup next\_cert_c$ used to certify r and est_vect_c (as above).

Messages NEXT.

- If, while it is in the initial state q_0, p_i suspects the current coordinator, it broadcasts a NEXT message (line 24) and moves to q_2. This message is certified by $est\_cert_i \cup current\_cert_i \cup next\_cert_i$. Those certificates ($current\_cert_i$ and $next\_cert_i$) will be used by the non-muteness failure detection module of the receiver to decide whether p_i has misevaluated or not the sending condition (at line 23). Moreover, as NEXT messages can also be sent at lines 28 and 31, est_cert_i is used to allow the receiver to determine the condition that has triggered the NEXT message it receives.

- When the predicate at line 28 becomes true, in order to avoid a deadlock, process p_i broadcasts a NEXT message to favor the transition to the next round (line 29). This message is certified by $current\_cert_i \cup next\_cert_i$. $current\_cert_i$ and $next\_cert_i$ are used to certify the non-misevaluation of the predicate *change_mind*.

- When a process progresses from round r to round $r+1$ it issues a NEXT message if it did not do so in the **while** loop. These NEXT messages are used to prevent other processes from remaining blocked in round r (line 31). This message is certified by $next\_cert_i$ which will allow a receiver to check the correct evaluation of the condition at line 14 by verifying if $next\_cert_i$ is well formed with respect to r.

Messages DECIDE. We have discussed above the use of certificates $current\_cert$ to authenticate the decision to send those messages.

Certifying other local variables. Apart from the local variables r, est_vect, and c (which depends directly on r), certified as explained above, the protocol manages other local

variables that are not transmitted in messages, but are nevertheless involved in some evaluations. These variables are $nb\_current$, nb_next, rec_from and $state$. Hence, these local variables must be certified. A way to do this is to replace them by expressions obtained from certificates. In the original protocol augmented with the certificates designed above, we will obtain:

- $nb\_current_i$ (resp. nb_next_i) can be replaced by using the cardinality of the certificate $current\_cert_i$ (resp. $next\_cert_i$).

- $state_i$ can assume three values (q_0, q_1, q_2). Each state can be identified (when necessary) by using certificates in the following way:

  - $state_i = q_0$: no CURRENT message has been received by p_i and p_i has not sent a NEXT message, that is, $(|current\_cert_i| = 0) \wedge \langle \text{NEXT}(p_i, r_i), cert \rangle_i \notin next\_cert_i$.

  - $state_i = q_1$: a CURRENT message has been received by p_i and p_i has not sent a NEXT message: $(|current\_cert_i| \geq 1) \wedge \langle \text{NEXT}(p_i, r_i), cert \rangle_i \notin next\_cert_i$.

  - $state_i = q_2$: p_i has sent a NEXT message: $\langle \text{NEXT}(p_i, r_i), cert \rangle_i \in next\_cert_i$.

- rec_from_i can be replaced by the variable REC_FROM_i using certificates in the following way:
$REC\_FROM_i \equiv \{p_\ell | \langle \text{NEXT}(p_\ell, r_\ell), cert \rangle_\ell \in next\_cert_i \vee \langle \text{CURRENT}(p_\ell, est\_vect_\ell, r_\ell), cert \rangle_\ell \in current\_cert_i \}$. *The predicate change_mind.* It follows that the predicate $change\_mind \equiv (state_i = q_1) \wedge (| rec\_from_i | > (n - F))$ is now expressed in terms of certificates:

$$(|current\_cert_i| \geq 1) \wedge \langle \text{NEXT}(p_i, r_i), cert \rangle_i \notin next\_cert_i \wedge |REC\_FROM_i| \geq (n - F))$$

5.2 Consensus and Certification Module

The text of the protocol executed by these two modules is presented in Figure 3. To facilitate the comparison with the original protocol described Figure 2, the new parts are presented in gray . For better reading, assignments performed by the reliable certification module (update of certificates) are displayed | inside a box |.

5.3 Non-Muteness Failure Detection Module

The non-muteness failure detection module of process p_i is composed of a set of finite state automata, one for each process. The module associated with p_i is depicted in Figure 4. It represents the view p_i has, during the current round r_i, on the behavior of p_k with respect to its automaton during the same round.

Automaton States. The automaton of process p_i related to a process p_k is composed of 6 states. Three are

function consensus(v_i)

(1) $\boxed{next\_cert_i \leftarrow \emptyset}$; $\boxed{est\_cert_i \leftarrow \emptyset}$; $r_i \leftarrow 0$;
   cobegin

(2) || **upon receipt of a properly signed and formed** $\langle \text{DECIDE}(p_k, est\_vect_k),\ cert_k\ \rangle_k$

(3)   **send** $\langle\ \text{DECIDE}(p_i, est\_vect_k),\ cert_k\ \rangle_i$ **to** Π; **return**(est_vect_k)

(4) || **for** $k \leftarrow 1$ **to** n **do** $est\_vect_i[k] \leftarrow null$ **endfor**;

(5)   **send** $\langle\ \text{INIT}(p_i, v_i), \emptyset\rangle_i$ **to** Π;

(6)   **while** $|est\_cert_i| \neq (n - F)$ **do**

(7)   **wait receipt of** $\langle\ \text{INIT}(p_k, v_k), cert_k\rangle_k$;

(8) $\boxed{est\_cert_i \leftarrow est\_cert_i \cup \langle\ \text{INIT}(p_k, v_k), cert_k\rangle_k}$; $est\_vect_i[k] \leftarrow v_k$

(9)   **end while**

(10)   **loop** % on a sequence of asynchronous rounds %
(11) $c \leftarrow (r_i \bmod n) + 1$; $r_i \leftarrow r_i + 1$;
(12)   **if** $(i = c)$ **then send** $\langle\ \text{CURRENT}(p_i, r_i, est\_vect_i),\ est\_cert_i \cup next\_cert_i\ \rangle_i$ **to** Π **endif**; % $q_0 \rightarrow q_1$ for $i = c$ %
(13) $\boxed{next\_cert_i \leftarrow \emptyset}$; $\boxed{current\_cert_i \leftarrow \emptyset}$;
(14)   **while** $(|next\_cert_i| \leq (n - F))$ **do**
(15)   **upon receipt of a properly signed and formed** $\langle\ \text{CURRENT}(p_k, r_i, est\_vect_k),\ cert_k\ \rangle_k$
(16) $\boxed{current\_cert_i \leftarrow current\_cert_i \cup \langle\ \text{CURRENT}(p_k, r_i, est\_vect_k), cert_k\rangle_k}$;
(17)   **if** $(|current\_cert_i| = 1)$ **then** $\boxed{est\_cert_i \leftarrow cert_k}$; $est\_vect_i \leftarrow est\_vect_k$ **endif**;
(18)   **if** $(|current\_cert_i| = 1) \wedge (\langle\ \text{NEXT}(p_i, r_i), cert_i\rangle_i \notin next\_cert_i) \wedge (i \neq c)$ % $q_0 \rightarrow q_1$ for $i \neq c$ %
(19)   **then send** $\langle\ \text{CURRENT}(p_i, r_i, est\_vect_i),\ current\_cert_i\ \rangle_i$ **to** Π **endif**;
(20)   **if** $(|current\_cert_i| = (n - F))$ **then**
(21)   **send** $\langle\text{DECIDE}(p_i, est\_vect_i),\ est\_cert_i\ \rangle_i$ **to** Π; **return**(est_vect_i) **endif**

(22)   **upon** $(p_c \in (suspected_i \vee faulty_i))$
(23)   **if** $((|current\_cert_i| = 0) \wedge \langle\ \text{NEXT}(p_i, r_i), cert_i\rangle_i \notin next\_cert_i)$
(24)   **then send** $\langle\ \text{NEXT}(p_i, r_i),\ current\_cert_i \cup next\_cert_i \cup est\_cert_i\ \rangle_i$ **to** Π % $q_0 \rightarrow q_2$ %
(25)   **endif**

(26)   **upon receipt of a properly signed and formed** $\langle\ \text{NEXT}(p_k, r_i),\ cert_k\ \rangle_k$
(27) $\boxed{next\_cert_i \leftarrow next\_cert_i \cup \langle\ \text{NEXT}(p_k, r_i), cert_k\rangle_k}$

(28)   **upon** ($change\_mind$) % $q_1 \rightarrow q2$ %
(29)   **send** $\langle\ \text{NEXT}(p_i, r_i),\ current\_cert_i \cup next\_cert_i\ \rangle_i$ **to** Π
(30)   **endwhile**

(31)   **if** $(\langle\ \text{NEXT}(p_i, r_i), cert_i\rangle_i \notin next\_cert_i)$ **then send** $\langle\ \text{NEXT}(p_i, r_i),\ next\_cert_i\ \rangle_i$ **to** Π **endif** % $q_0/q_1 \rightarrow q_2$ %
(32)   **endloop**
   coend

Figure 3. Merging of the Consensus and $\boxed{\text{Certification}}$ **Modules of Process** p_i

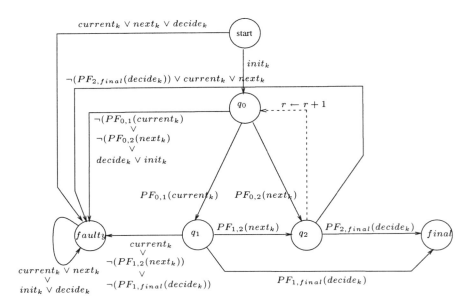

$current_k \vee next_k \vee decide_k$

$init_k$

$\neg(PF_{2,final}(decide_k)) \vee current_k \vee next_k$

$\neg(PF_{0,1}(current_k))$
$\vee$
$\neg(PF_{0,2}(next_k))$
$\vee$
$decide_k \vee init_k$

$r \leftarrow r+1$

$PF_{0,1}(current_k)$ $PF_{0,2}(next_k)$

$PF_{1,2}(next_k)$ $PF_{2,final}(decide_k)$

$current_k$
$\vee$
$\neg(PF_{1,2}(next_k))$
$\vee$
$\neg(PF_{1,final}(decide_k))$

$current_k \vee next_k$
$\vee$
$init_k \vee decide_k$

$PF_{1,final}(decide_k)$

Figure 4. Automaton of the p_i's non-muteness failure detection module to monitor process p_k.

related to a single round (as the ones described in Section 4: q_0, q_1, q_2), one is the initial state $(start)$, one is the final state $(final)$ and one is the state declaring p_k is faulty $(faulty)$.

Automaton Transitions. A transition is triggered each time a message arrives form p_k. More precisely, a condition is evaluated and, according to the result of this evaluation, the automaton moves from its current state a to another state b. In particular, if the condition is evaluated to false, the automaton moves from the current state to the sate $faulty$. The condition is composed of the following predicates.

- The predicate $type\_of\_message_k$ is true if the message of that type is not an Out-of-order message and is syntactically correct.

- $PF_{a,b}(type\_of\_message)$ returns true if $type\_of\_message_k$ is true, and if the message is not a Wrong Expected Message. Thus, the set of predicates PF implements the certificate analyzer (see section 3). Due to space limitations, the detailed explanation of transitions (depicted on Figure 4) is omitted (see [2]).

References

[1] Attiya H. and Welch J., *Distributed Computing*, Mac Graw Hill, 1998.

[2] Baldoni R., Helary J.M., and Raynal M., From Crash Fault-Tolerance to Arbitrary Fault-Tolerance: Towards a Modular Approach, http://www.irisa.fr/EXTERNE/bibli/pi/1307/1307.html.

[3] Chandra T. and Toueg S., Unreliable Failure Detectors for Reliable Distributed Systems. *JACM*, 34(1):225–267, 1996.

[4] Dolev D., Friedman R., Keidar I. and Malkhi D., Failure Detectors in Omission Failure Environments, *Brief announcement in Proc. 16th ACM Symposium on PODC*, p.286, 1997.

[5] Doudou A. and Schiper A., Muteness Failure Detectors for Consensus with Byzantine Processes, *Brief announcement in Proc. 17th ACM Symposium on PODC*, p. 315, 1998.

[6] Doudou A., Garbinato B., Guerraoui R. and Schiper A., Muteness Failure Detectors: Specification and Implementation. *Proc. Third EDCC*, LNCS 1667, pp. 71-87, 1999.

[7] Fischer M.J., Lynch N. and Paterson M.S., Impossibility of Distributed Consensus with One Faulty Process. *JACM*, 32(2):374–382, April 1985.

[8] Hurfin M. and Raynal M., A Simple and Fast Asynchronous Consensus Protocol Based on a Weak Failure Detector, *Distributed Computing*, 12(4):209-233, 1999.

[9] Kihlstrom K.P., Moser L.E. and Melliar-Smith P.M., Solving Consensus in a Byzantine Environment Using an Unreliable Fault Detector. *OPODIS'97*, Chantilly, pp. 61-76, 1997.

[10] Malkhi D. and Reiter M., Unreliable Intrusion Detection in Distributed Computations. In *Proc. of the 10th IEEE CSFW*, pp. 116–124, Rockport (MA), 1997.

[11] Pease L., Shostak R. and Lamport L., Reaching Agreement in Presence of Faults. *JACM*, 27(2):228-234, 1980.

[12] Powell D., Failure Mode Assumptions and Assumption Coverage, in *Proc. of the 22nd Int. Symp. on Fault-Tolerant Computing (FTCS-22)*, Boston, MA, pp.386-95, 1992.

[13] Rivest, R. L., Shamir, A. and Adleman, L., A Method for Obtaining Digital Signatures and Public-key Cryptosystems, *CACM*, 21(2):120-126, 1978.

Dynamic Byzantine Quorum Systems

Lorenzo Alvisi*   Dahlia Malkhi†   Evelyn Pierce‡   Michael K. Reiter§   Rebecca N. Wright¶

Abstract

Byzantine quorum systems [13] enhance the availability and efficiency of fault-tolerant replicated services when servers may suffer Byzantine failures. An important limitation of Byzantine quorum systems is their dependence on a static threshold limit on the number of server faults. The correctness of the system is only guaranteed if the actual number of faults is lower than the the threshold at all times. However, a threshold chosen for the worst case wastes expensive replication in the common situation where the number of faults averages well below the worst case.

In this paper, we present protocols for dynamically raising and lowering the resilience threshold of a quorum-based Byzantine fault-tolerant data service in response to current information on the number of server failures. Using such protocols, a system can operate in an efficient low-threshold mode with relatively small quorums in the absence of faults, increasing and decreasing the quorum size (and thus the tolerance) as faults appear and are dealt with, respectively.

1 Introduction

Quorum systems are valuable tools for implementing highly available distributed shared memory. Mathematically, a quorum system is simply a set of sets (called *quorums*), each pair of which intersect. The principle behind their use in distributed data services is that, if a shared variable is stored at a set of servers, read and write operations need be performed only at a quorum of those servers. The intersection property of quorums ensures that each read has access to the most recently written value of the variable.

Traditionally, quorum systems have been used for *benign fault tolerance*, i.e., maintaining data availability in the presence of unresponsive servers (*crashes*). Recently, Byzantine quorum systems have been introduced to provide data availability even in the presence of arbitrary (*Byzantine*) faults [13]. The Byzantine fault model is attractively powerful in that it can be used to analyze a wide variety of faulty behaviors; for example, it has been proposed as a framework for modeling security problems such as intrusions and sabotage.

One important limitation of standard Byzantine fault-tolerance techniques, quorum-based or otherwise, is their dependence on a static, pessimistically defined *resilience threshold*, which limits the number of faults.[1] The designer must decide in advance what maximum number of simultaneous failures the system will tolerate and build the system to tolerate that number of faults, at the expense of keeping an appropriate number of separate up-to-date copies of each data item for this worst-case failure assumption. If the chosen threshold is higher than necessary, the excess replication is wasted, so that the system is unnecessarily inefficient and unwieldy. On the other hand, if the threshold is chosen too low, the correctness guarantees of the system are nullified. Furthermore, even if a threshold is appropriately positioned for the worst case failure scenario, this scenario will usually be relatively rare; the degree of replication required will be wasted in the average case.

In this paper, we present a method of dynamically raising and lowering the resilience threshold of a quorum-based Byzantine fault-tolerant data service in response to estimates of the number of server failures. ([1] presents failure detection methods that might be used to obtain these estimates for such services.) The goal of our work is to design protocols that allow a quorum system to respond *at run time* to the presence or absence of detected faults. This flexibil-

---

*Department of Computer Sciences, University of Texas at Austin, USA. Email: lorenzo@cs.utexas.edu.

†School of Computer Science and Engineering, The Hebrew University of Jerusalem, Israel. Email: dalia@cs.huji.ac.il.

‡Department of Computer Sciences, University of Texas at Austin, USA. Email: tumlin@cs.utexas.edu.

§Bell Labs, Lucent Technologies, Murray Hill, NJ, USA. Email: reiter@research.bell-labs.com.

¶AT&T Labs–Research, Florham Park, NJ, USA. Email: rwright@research.att.com.

This document describes work partially supported by NSF CAREER award CCR-9734185, DARPA/SPAWAR grant N66001-98-8911, NSF CISE grant CDA-9624082, and United States Air Force contract F30602-99-C-0165. Any opinions, findings, conclusions or recommendations expressed in this document are those of the author(s) and do not necessarily reflect the views of any of these sponsoring organizations.

---

[1]Papers such as [13] consider generalized fault structures, offering a more general way of characterizing fault tolerance than a threshold. However, such structures remain static, and therefore necessarily worst-case.

ity comes at a cost: tolerating a given maximum number of faults requires more servers in our approach than in a static system. However, with a fixed number of servers, our protocols allow a system to operate in low-threshold mode with smaller quorums than a static approach would require for the same worst-case threshold. A natural way of using a dynamic quorum system is to increase the threshold when faults are detected, and decrease it again when the failures have been dealt with. The threshold could also be raised or lowered based on external evidence that the threat of an attack has increased or decreased, such as information in server logs or new information about the value of the data being stored.

The difficulty in dynamically adjusting Byzantine quorum systems can be exemplified as follows. Consider a threshold *masking quorum system* [13] of $n = 9$ replicated servers with quorums consisting of all sets of 6 servers. This guarantees that every pair of quorums intersect in 3 servers or more, and can tolerate a threshold $b = 1$ of Byzantine server failures while still guaranteeing that the majority of every quorum intersection is correct. Now, suppose that some client, detecting a possible failure in the system, wishes to reconfigure the quorum system to raise the resilience threshold to $b = 2$. This can be accomplished by making every set of 7 servers a quorum, thereby guaranteeing that every pair of new quorums intersect in at least 5 servers, a majority of which are correct. However, if the client informs an old quorum of 6 servers about the new configuration (Figure 1), or even a newly adjusted quorum of 7 servers (dashed line), then there is no guarantee that the intersection with the *old* quorum will contain a majority of correct servers. As a result, another client, which still uses a quorum of size 6, may obtain conflicting information by a collusion of 2 faulty servers.

Our methods address this very problem. We describe protocols that guarantee *safe* shared variable semantics [8] in the face of repeated configuration changes, and despite the use of arbitrarily stale quorum configurations by clients. Our work is the first of which we are aware that provides data replication with safe variable semantics in the face of a varying resilience threshold in a Byzantine environment, with no reliance on any concurrency control mechanism (e.g., no locking).

Our approach makes use of a *threshold variable* $\mathcal{B}$ which is coupled with the ordinary replicated variables that our system maintains, and is designated to maintain the current resilience threshold b. We show how to implement such a threshold variable with stronger semantics than safety in order to maintain the safety of the ordinary variables. Updates to $\mathcal{B}$ are made to *announce sets*, which are generally larger than ordinary quorums and are guaranteed to be observed by clients who may be using arbitrarily old thresholds. Ordinary variable operations are accordingly modified to take

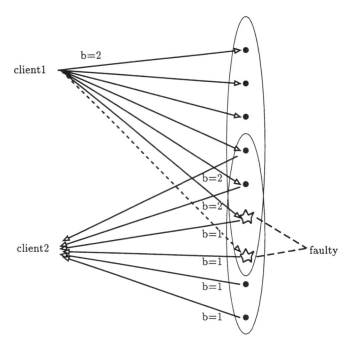

Figure 1. Byzantine failures in quorum threshold adjustment.

$\mathcal{B}$ into account. Maintaining safety of variables is complicated by the fact that we allow reads and writes to occur simultaneously with adjustments to $\mathcal{B}$. The challenge is to guarantee sufficient intersection of new quorums with previously written quorums (of unknown thresholds) without accessing too many servers in the normal case.

The structure of the remainder of the paper is as follows. We discuss related work in Section 1.1. In Section 2, we give our system model and preliminary definitions. In Section 3 we introduce the threshold adjustment framework and its requirements. In Section 4, we present the protocols for reading and modifying a dynamic threshold in threshold masking quorum systems. In Section 5, we present the enhanced protocols for reading and writing shared variables using the dynamic threshold. Section 6 generalizes some of the concepts of dynamic threshold adjustments to topographically defined quorum systems. We discuss performance and optimizations in Section 7 and conclude in Section 8.

1.1 Related Work

Our work builds on a substantial body of knowledge on quorum systems and their uses, which was initiated in [6, 16]; for a survey of quorum systems work, see [12]. More specifically, our methods are designed for Byzantine quorum-based replication, which was introduced in [13]

and further investigated in various works [3, 15, 14].

Our consideration of Byzantine faults makes our treatment fundamentally different from most prior works on dynamic quorum reconfiguration with benign failures only. In [5, Ch. 8, *missing writes* protocol] and [7, 10], a quorum system is reconfigured by forming a write-quorum in such a way that following readers learn about the reconfiguration in the course of the normal read protocol. Byzantine faults complicate this scheme in that (undetectably) faulty servers might misinform a reader. As discussed earlier, this is especially significant when increasing the resilience threshold, since the reader, which may be using an out-of-date quorum system, could be misled by a new threshold of colluding Byzantine faulty servers.

Quorum *adaptation* for crash failures is discussed in [4]. In their approach, if a server u fails while u is the only server contained in the intersection of two quorums Q_i and Q_j, then the intersection property is maintained by removing u from Q_i and Q_j and by substituting another correct server. Our work differs from [4] in two significant ways. First, the fact that we treat Byzantine failures means that we must enable on-the-fly changes not only to the set of quorums, but also to the very intersection property that defines those quorums. Second, our clients (which we assume to be potentially numerous and transient) do not communicate between themselves and cannot inform one another of changes. Our work differs from [4, 9] as well, in that our protocols can take hints on the possible level of failures in the system in order to adjust the resilience threshold, rather than rely on specific detection of server failures.

Some work in Byzantine agreement considers dynamic threshold changes during the run of the protocol. For example, Bar-Noy et al [2] present an optimal-round agreement protocol that lowers its operating threshold midway through the protocol in order to improve efficiency while still maintaining overall the resilience of the original threshold. Our work differs from theirs by considering general replicated data rather than agreement protocols, but more fundamentally in that our protocols allow the fault threshold to be raised or lowered as fault-tolerance needs change. In particular, they take a detected fault as a sign that therefore there are fewer remaining faults in the system, while we may take it as a sign that the initial threshold was too optimistic and should be increased.

2 Preliminaries

Our system consists of a set U of data servers such that the number $n = |U|$ of servers is fixed. During an execution of the system, a server receives input messages and responds to each with a (non-null) output message. The *correct response* of a server for each input message is defined by a function F that maps the preceding history of all inputs that server received since the beginning of time to an output message. A server that receives the sequence of inputs $m_1, \ldots, m_k$ should respond to m_k with $F(m_1, \ldots, m_k)$, the correct response. At any given moment a server may be either *correct* or *faulty*. A correct server responds to any request with the correct response. We allow Byzantine failures: a faulty server may respond with an arbitrary response (including no response). However, note that a correct response is defined irrespective of a server's prior faulty output behavior (or state modifications). In practice, since servers usually have a state that does not include the entire history, this means that for a once-failed server to be considered correct, it must be recovered to the state that it would have held if it had never failed.

The set of clients of the service is disjoint from U. Each client is assumed to have a FIFO channel to each server. In our system, clients may be numerous and transient. In particular, clients are not aware of each other, nor do they necessarily have the ability to communicate with one another. We restrict our attention in this work to server failures; clients and channels are assumed to be reliable.

We use a replicated data service model based on *quorum systems*, which are defined as follows:

Definition: A *quorum system* on a set U is a set $\mathcal{Q} \subseteq 2^U$ such that $\forall Q_1, Q_2 \in \mathcal{Q}, Q_1 \cap Q_2 \neq \emptyset$. Elements of $\mathcal{Q}$ are called *quorums*. ∎

In such a service, clients perform read and write operations on a variable by reading or writing its value at a quorum of servers. The intersection property ensures that any read operation observes the value of the most recent write operation; timestamps can be used to distinguish this value from older ones.

A useful type of quorum system for Byzantine fault tolerance is the *b-masking quorum system*:

Definition: A *b-masking quorum system* is a quorum system $\mathcal{Q}$ such that $\forall Q_1, Q_2 \in \mathcal{Q}, |Q_1 \cap Q_2| \geq 2b + 1$. ∎

This additional intersection property ensures that in spite of up to b faults in the system, any two quorums intersect in at least $b + 1$ correct servers. This enables clients to determine the correct variable value using an algorithm that combines voting and timestamps. A b-masking quorum system is thus designed to tolerate failures in a system with a static resilience threshold b.

For the greater part of this paper we focus our attention on a particular type of b-masking system called a *threshold* quorum system. Threshold systems are defined as follows:

Definition: A *threshold* masking quorum system is a quorum system $\mathcal{Q}$ such that $\forall Q \in \mathcal{Q}, |Q| = \lceil (n + 2b + 1)/2 \rceil$. ∎

For simplicity, we assume hereafter that n is odd, so that we can eliminate the ceiling operator from our calculations.

Ordinary (i.e., static) b-masking quorum systems support replicated variables in a Byzantine environment as follows. To emulate a shared variable V, each server u stores a "copy" V_u of V along with a timestamp variable $T_{V,u}$. A timestamp is assigned by a client to $T_{V,u}$ when the client writes V_u. Our protocols require that different clients choose different timestamps, and thus each client c chooses its timestamps from some set $\mathcal{T}_c$ that does not intersect $\mathcal{T}_{c'}$ for any other client c'. The timestamps in $\mathcal{T}_c$ can be formed, e.g., as integers appended with the name of c in the low-order bits. Note that faulty servers may return arbitrary values both for variables and for timestamps. The read and write operations are implemented as follows.

Write: For a client to write the value v to variable V, it queries servers in some quorum Q to obtain the timestamp t_u from $T_{V,u}$ at each $u \in Q$. The client then chooses a timestamp $t \in \mathcal{T}_c$ greater than the highest timestamp value in $\{t_u\}_{u \in Q}$ and greater than any timestamp it has chosen in the past, and updates V_u and $T_{V,u}$ at each server u in some quorum Q' to v and t, respectively.

Read: For a client to read a variable V, it queries servers in some quorum Q to obtain values v_u, t_u from variables $V_u, T_{V,u}$ at each $u \in Q$. From among all $\langle v_u, t_u \rangle$ pairs returned by at least $b + 1$ servers in Q, the client chooses the pair $\langle v, t \rangle$ with the highest timestamp t, and then returns v as the result of the read operation. If there is no pair returned by at least $b + 1$ servers, the result of the read operation is $\perp$ (a null value).

A server u that receives an update $\langle v, t \rangle$ during a write operation updates $V_u, T_{V,u}$ to $\langle v, t \rangle$, respectively, iff $t > T_{V,u}$. This pair of protocols guarantees *safe* [8] variable semantics, i.e., a read operation that does not overlap a write operation returns the value of the most recent write (the proof of this assertion can be found in [13]).

3 Threshold Adjustment

The read/write protocols above provide safe variable emulation in a Byzantine environment with a static resilience threshold. The goal of this work is to extend these protocols so as to allow dynamic adaptations of quorum systems to varying resilience thresholds. The challenge is to maintain safety of any replicated variable in the system while dynamically performing such changes, without stopping the normal operation of the system.

To accommodate changes in the threshold setting, we introduce a new replicated variable $\mathcal{B}$ that contains the current

threshold setting. The variable $\mathcal{B}$ can be written with integral values in the range $[b_{min}, b_{max}]$. The threshold variable has an associated timestamp $T_\mathcal{B}$ that follows the same rules as the timestamps of other variables: every update to the variable is stamped with a unique timestamp that is greater than any timestamp used in a previously completed operation.

A client that wishes to change the resilience threshold for the system must first write the up-to-date threshold into $\mathcal{B}$, and then continue performing operations with the new resilience threshold accounted for. Intuitively, a client can update $\mathcal{B}$ in much the same way that it updates any other shared variable. There is one significant complication, however: because the threshold is dynamic, different clients may have different memories of its value depending on how recently they have accessed the quorum system. It is therefore necessary that new threshold values be written to a set of servers whose intersection with *all possible quorums* (i.e., defined by any $b \in [b_{min}, b_{max}]$) is sufficiently large to allow clients to determine unambiguously the correct current threshold during any given operation; the client can then continue or restart the operation accordingly. Hence, in a *threshold write* operation, $\mathcal{B}$ is updated at all servers in an *announce set*. A few issues need to be addressed in order to specify threshold adjustment fully. First, we need to specify the intersection requirement between the announce set and all ordinary quorums in such a way that threshold adjustments will be noticed by all potential clients. Second, we need to specify threshold write and read protocols. Third, we need to modify our read/write protocols to account for threshold adjustments. These will be the topic of discussion in the remainder of this paper.

Since the system for which we design our protocols has a dynamically changing resilience threshold, a standard threshold constraint, e.g., "the number of faulty servers in the system at any given time does not exceed b," does not suffice for our purposes. Rather, in order to guarantee correctness, we need a statement that the dynamically written threshold values are correct. To this end, we adopt the following assumption for the remainder of the paper.

Assumption 1 *Let o be any operation, i.e., a threshold read, threshold write, variable read, or variable write. Let b be the minimum among (i) the value written in the last write to $\mathcal{B}$ preceding o (in some serialization of all preceding writes) and (ii) the values written to $\mathcal{B}$ in any threshold writes that are concurrent with o. Then, no quorum access issued within o returns more than b faulty responses (i.e., no more than b servers are "currently" faulty).*

In practice, Assumption 1 amounts to requiring that the threshold should be changed proactively and at a reasonable rate.

The goal of our threshold adjustment protocols is to maintain safety of all replicated variables despite possible modifications to the resilience threshold. For the purpose of safety, we treat the associated threshold variable $\mathcal{B}$ as an integral part of any variable V. Accordingly, the modified safety condition that our protocols will satisfy is the following.

Safety: A read operation on V that overlaps no writes to V or threshold write operations to $\mathcal{B}$ returns the value of the most recent write to V that precedes this read, in some serialization of all write operations preceding it.

4 Quorum Adjustment in Threshold Systems

In this section we present and discuss protocols that allow clients to read and adjust the fault tolerance of a threshold masking quorum system. An important property of our protocols is that they require no direct interaction among clients; all information is passed through shared variables.

4.1 Basic Protocol

We wish to design protocols in which the resilience threshold of the underlying quorum system can be dynamically adjusted to any value within some range $[b_{min}, b_{max}]$. The simplest way to ensure that clients always use the correct threshold is to require clients to read the threshold before any read or write, and to adopt a threshold value only if at least $b_{max} + 1$ servers in a quorum agree on this threshold and its associated timestamp. By Assumption 1 and the definition of b_{max}, no more than b_{max} responses to any query will be faulty. Therefore, if the announce set for a threshold change intersects every possible quorum (i.e., every set of size $(n + 2b + 1)/2$ for $b_{min} \leq b \leq b_{max}$), in at least $2b_{max} + 1$ servers, it follows that the response to any query will include at least $b_{max} + 1$ notifications of the change. (One advantage of this approach is that clients need not maintain their own copy of the current value of the threshold b. In particular, new clients can join without having to initialize a copy of the threshold.)

We take as announce sets all sets of size $n - b_{max}$, i.e., the largest number of servers guaranteed to be available under any threshold setting. This value will be sufficient provided that the intersection between any quorum and any announce set is of size at least $2b_{max} + 1$. That is, we need:

$$2b_{max} + 1 \leq ((n + 2b_{min} + 1)/2) + (n - b_{max}) - n$$

It follows that $n \geq 6b_{max} - 2b_{min} + 1$, and thus we need at least $6b_{max} - 2b_{min} + 1$ servers to provide a dynamic threshold quorum system whose threshold ranges from b_{min} to b_{max}. We take this as an assumption for the remainder of the paper.

Assumption 2 $n \geq 6b_{max} - 2b_{min} + 1$.

Note that Assumption 2 is a generalization of the $4b + 1$ servers required by a static threshold system, i.e., one where $b_{min} = b_{max}$ [13].

The protocol for raising or lowering the threshold using an announce set of size $n - b_{max}$ is as follows:

Threshold write: For a client to set $\mathcal{B}$ to a new threshold value b, it queries servers in some announce set A (of size $n - b_{max}$) to obtain values b_u, t_u from variables $\mathcal{B}_u, T_{\mathcal{B},u}$ at each $u \in A$. It then chooses a timestamp $t \in \mathcal{T}_c$ greater than the largest timestamp in $\{t_u\}_{u \in Q}$, and greater than any timestamp it has chosen in the past. Finally, at each server u in some announce set A', it updates $\mathcal{B}_u$ and $T_{\mathcal{B},u}$ to b and t, respectively. (Note that this is exactly the static variable write protocol except that an announce set is used instead of a standard quorum.)

Threshold read: For a client to read the current threshold value b from $\mathcal{B}$, it queries servers in some quorum Q of size $(n + 2b_{min} + 1)/2$ to obtain values b_u, t_u from variables $\mathcal{B}_u, T_{\mathcal{B},u}$ at each $u \in Q$. Of the $\langle b_u, t_u \rangle$ pairs returned by at least $b_{max} + 1$ servers in Q, it selects the pair $\langle b, t \rangle$ with the highest timestamp t, provided that it is not *countermanded* as defined below. If there is no such pair, or if $\langle b, t \rangle$ is countermanded, then it sets b to $\perp$ (undefined).

Definition: A threshold/timestamp pair $\langle b, t \rangle$ is *countermanded* in a given query if at least $b_{max} + 1$ servers return threshold timestamps (not necessarily identical) greater than t. A threshold value b is countermanded if all the pairs it appears in are countermanded. ∎

The purpose of this definition is made clear by the following theorem:

Theorem 1 *If b is older than the most recently completed threshold write at the time of a threshold read, then it will be countermanded in that read.*

Proof: If no threshold write operations are taking place concurrently with the threshold read, then the result follows immediately from Assumption 1, the intersection property between announce sets and quorums, and the fact that $b_{max} \geq b$. Furthermore, for any b, the number of correct servers whose threshold timestamp exceeds that of b is monotonically nondecreasing over the course of a threshold write. Therefore the result holds during threshold writes as well. ∎

4.1.1 Correctness

The correctness of the threshold variable follows from the following theorem and subsequent corollary to Theorem 1.

Theorem 2 *In any threshold read that does not overlap a threshold write, the most recently written threshold value (in the serialization consistent with timestamp order of the writes) is returned.*

This theorem is easily seen to be implied by the following two lemmas:

Lemma 1 *For any such threshold read, the most recently written threshold/timestamp pair is returned by at least $b_{max} + 1$ servers.*

Proof: Let b be the most recently written threshold value. The announce set for this threshold intersects all possible quorums in at least $2b_{max} + 1$ servers by Assumption 2. Because b was set in the most recent threshold write, and the current threshold read does not overlap any threshold writes, the variable $\mathcal{B}$ has not been overwritten at any correct servers in this set. By Assumption 1 and the fact that $b \leq b_{max}$, at least $b_{max} + 1$ servers in any possible quorum will return the threshold b along with the most recent timestamp. ∎

Lemma 2 *For any such threshold read, the most recently written threshold is not countermanded.*

Proof: The most recently written threshold has the highest (nonforged) timestamp. Therefore if the correct threshold is b, then by Assumption 1, no more than b servers may forge higher timestamps in their response to the query. Since $b < b_{max} + 1$, the value b is not countermanded. ∎

Corollary 1 *A threshold read that overlaps one or more threshold writes will not return a threshold older than the value in the most recently completed threshold write.*

Proof: This follows from Theorem 1 and the fact that the read does not return a countermanded value. ∎

Remark: A consequence of this theorem and corollary is that the protocol given above implements a weakened version of *regular* variable semantics [8] for the threshold variable; i.e., a query that overlaps one or more writes will return either the value of the most recently completed write, the value of one of the writes which it overlaps, or $\perp$. This is a stronger guarantee than that provided by safe semantics.

5 Variables Implemented with Dynamic Threshold Systems

In a quorum system whose resilience threshold is dynamic, a change to the quorum structure may require some attention to the variables that make use of that threshold. Specifically, an increase in the threshold may compromise the integrity of previously written variables unless some specific corrective action is taken.

Suppose, for example, that the threshold of a system is increased from b to $b + 3$. Once this operation is complete, clients performing read and write operations will learn of the new threshold and perform those operations on quorums of the new size. Unfortunately, values that have been written under the previous threshold will appear only at an *old* quorum of servers. The intersection between an old quorum and a new one is only guaranteed to be $2b+4$, not the $2b+7$ required for tolerating an additional 3 faults.

More generally, the main difficulty is that if a variable was last written when the threshold was smaller than the current threshold b, then reading from a quorum of size $(n + 2b + 1)/2$ does not suffice to ensure that $b+1$ correct servers will respond with the latest value. Rather, to ensure that $b + 1$ correct servers will respond with the latest value, it may be necessary to increase the quorum used during a read operation to $(n + 2b + 1)/2 + b - b_{min}$.

A similar problem occurs when a writer accesses a quorum of servers in order to determine a timestamp for the write. The writer needs to access a quorum that guarantees intersection in one correct server with the most recently written quorum. The difficulty is that the latter could have a quorum size that corresponds to an arbitrarily old threshold. If the current threshold b can be determined, then a quorum of size $(n + 2b + 1)/2 - b_{min}$ suffices to intersect in $b + 1$ with any other quorum, and hence, in at least one correct server. However, if the threshold cannot be determined, which can happen when a write operation overlaps a threshold-write operation, then a (potentially larger) quorum of size $(n + 2b_{max} + 1)/2 - b_{min}$ needs to be accessed in order to determine a correct timestamp for the write operation.

We address these issues in the protocol below.

5.1 The Protocol

The protocol for reading and writing a variable V using dynamic thresholds is as follows:

Read: For a client to read variable V, it performs the following steps:

1. Perform a threshold read using the protocol in Section 4 to obtain current threshold b. If $b = \perp$, return $\perp$ as the result of the read.

2. Query servers in a quorum Q of size $(n + 2b + 1)/2$ to obtain values v_u, t_u from variables $V_u, T_{V,u}$ at each $u \in Q$.

3. Of the $\langle v_u, t_u \rangle$ pairs returned by at least $b_{min} + 1$ servers in Q, consider the pair $\langle v, t \rangle$ with the highest value of t. If no such pair exists, return $\perp$ as the

result of the read. If $\langle v, t \rangle$ appears in $b + 1$ identical responses, return v as the result of the read.

4. Otherwise (i.e., $\langle v, t \rangle$ appears at least $b_{min} + 1$ times but fewer than $b + 1$), query servers in an additional set C of size $b - b_{min}$, to obtain values v_u, t_u from variables $V_u, T_{V,u}$ at each $u \in Q'$, where $Q' = Q \cup C$ contains $(n + 2b + 1)/2 + b - b_{min}$ servers.

5. Of the $\langle v_u, t_u \rangle$ pairs that appear in at least $b + 1$ responses from Q', select the pair $\langle v', t' \rangle$ with the highest value of t' and return v' as the result of the read. If no such pair exists, return $\perp$ as the result of the read.

Write: For a client to write value v to variable V, it performs the following steps:

1. Perform threshold read using the protocol in Section 4 to obtain the current threshold b. If $b = \perp$, then use $b = b_{max}$.

2. Query servers in a quorum Q of size $(n + 2b + 1)/2 - b_{min}$ to obtain timestamp t_u from $T_{V,u}$ at each $u \in Q$.

3. Create a new timestamp $t \in \mathcal{T}_c$ such that t is larger than any timestamp in $\{t_u\}_{u \in Q}$ and any timestamp used before by this client.

4. Write v and t to V_u and $T_{V,u}$, respectively, at each server u in a quorum of size $(n + 2b + 1)/2$.

Note that in a steady system state, when reads and writes obtain the up-to-date threshold b, they perform operations simply by accessing ordinary b-masking quorums, i.e., of size $(n + 2b + 1)/2$. Following adjustments to the threshold, though, operations may incur the higher costs of accessing larger quorums.

5.1.1 Correctness

The following theorem proves the correctness of the above protocol—namely, that it maintains safety of the variable V:

Theorem 3 *A read operation that overlaps no write operations to V or threshold write operations to $\mathcal{B}$ returns the value of the most recent write to V that precedes this read, in some serialization of all write operations preceding it.*

Proof: Let W denote the set of all write operations preceding the read. By Theorem 2, Step 1 of the read operation obtains the most recently written threshold b or a concurrently written one. Therefore, by Assumption 1, any quorum of responses obtained in the read contains at most b faulty responses. Consider the write operation in W with the highest

timestamp. Since this write completed at $(n + 2b_{min} + 1)/2$ or more servers, its value and timestamp appear in at least $b_{min} + 1$ of the responses returned in Step 2 of the read protocol. It is then returned in Step 3 if it appeared in $b + 1$ of the responses from Step 2, or otherwise will be returned in Step 5 since reading from $(n + 2b + 1)/2 + b - b_{min}$ (Step 4) intersects any previous write quorum in at least $2b + 1$ servers.

It is left to show that there is a serialization of the writes in W in which the write with the highest timestamp is last, i.e., that a write operation w_2 that follows a write operation w_1 uses a higher timestamp. This follows from the facts that if w_2 uses the threshold b', then at most b' faulty responses to its query in Step 2 are returned, and that $(n + 2b' + 1)/2 - b_{min}$ servers must intersect the quorum written in w_1 in $b' + 1$ servers (and thus at least one correct server). ∎

6 Other b-Masking Quorum Systems

In this section, we briefly discuss how to employ two additional b-masking quorum systems in an environment with a dynamically varying resilience threshold, and how to set an appropriate announce set for changing the threshold value. Thus, the utility of our methods is not limited to the threshold construction.

6.1 BoostFPP quorum system

BoostFPP masking quorum systems [15] are constructed as a composition of two quorum systems. The first is a quorum system based on a finite projective plane (FPP), suggested originally by [11]. In the FPP quorum system, there are $q^2 + q + 1$ elements and quorums of size $q + 1$ (corresponding to the hyperplanes of the FPP), where $q = p^r \geq 2$ for some prime p and integer r. Each pair of distinct quorums in FPP intersect in exactly one element. The second quorum system is a threshold b-masking quorum system with some system size $s \geq 4b + 1$. The composition of the two systems is made by replacing each element of the FPP with a distinct copy of a threshold system. That is, the universe for a boostFPP system is $U = \bigcup_{i=1}^{q^2+q+1} U_i$ where each U_i is a set of s servers, and $U_i \cap U_j = \emptyset$ for any $i \neq j$. Each U_i is called a "super element". A quorum is selected by first selecting a quorum of super elements in the FPP, say $U_{i_1}, \ldots, U_{i_{q+1}}$, and then selecting $\lceil (s + 2b + 1)/2 \rceil$ servers from each U_{i_j}. A boostFPP is a b-masking quorum system since every pair of quorums of super elements intersect in at least one super element, say U_i, while the selection of threshold quorums within U_i guarantees intersection of $2b + 1$ elements.

To employ boostFPP with a variable resilience threshold $b_{min} \leq b \leq b_{max}$, we leave the FPP construction of super elements unmodified, and change only the selection of servers within each super-element. That is, we require that $s \geq 6b_{max} - 2b_{min} + 1$ and for each U_i and any threshold b, we select quorums in U_i as in the threshold system, e.g., an ordinary quorum has $\lceil (s + 2b + 1)/2 \rceil$ servers in each U_i, and an announce set comprises of $s - b_{max}$ servers from each such U_i.

It is easily seen that such selections guarantee the required intersection size between announce sets and ordinary quorums, as well as between read and write quorums and pairs of write quorums, as in the threshold system case.

6.2 M-grid quorum system

An M-Grid masking quorum system is described in [15]. For any resilience threshold b, where $b \leq (\sqrt{n} - 1)/2$, M-Grid is constructed as follows: The universe of n servers is arranged as a $\sqrt{n} \times \sqrt{n}$ grid. A quorum in an M-Grid consists of any choice of $\sqrt{b+1}$ rows and $\sqrt{b+1}$ columns. Formally, denote the rows and columns of the grid by R_i and C_i, respectively, where $1 \leq i \leq \sqrt{n}$. Then, the quorum system is

$$\text{M-Grid}(b) =$$

$$\left\{ \bigcup_{j \in J} C_j \cup \bigcup_{i \in I} R_i : J, I \subseteq \{1 \ldots \sqrt{n}\}, |J| = |I| = \sqrt{b+1} \right\}$$

M-Grid maintains the requirement of b-masking quorum systems as follows: If a pair of quorums overlap in a full row or column, then there are $\sqrt{n} \geq 2b + 1$ elements in their intersection. Otherwise, their intersection contains the crossing points of all rows of one quorum with columns of the other, and vice versa, and hence contains at least $2\sqrt{b+1}\sqrt{b+1} > 2b + 1$ elements.

To make use of M-Grid quorum systems with a variable resilience threshold $b_{min} \leq b \leq b_{max}$, we need to require that $b_{max} \leq (\sqrt{n} - 1)/2$. The grid arrangement remains static for all quorum systems, but the number of rows/columns in each quorum will depend on b, the current resilience threshold. For the purpose of setting the threshold variable $\mathcal{B}$, we use announce sets comprising of $\left\lceil \frac{(b_{max}+1)}{\sqrt{b_{min}+1}} \right\rceil$ rows and $\left\lceil \frac{(b_{max}+1)}{\sqrt{b_{min}+1}} \right\rceil$ columns, which guarantees that they intersect any quorum ever used in $2b_{max} + 1$ servers. With these announce sets, we use the same threshold write and threshold read protocols as for the threshold b-masking system. Unfortunately, the read and write protocols cannot use ordinary size quorums, since in general, quorums in M-Grid(b) may not intersect quorums in M-Grid(b') in $b + b_{min} + 1$ elements as required. Hence, for Step 2 of the read protocol, we need to use quorums comprising of $\max\{\sqrt{b+1}, \frac{b+b_{min}+1}{2\sqrt{b_{min}+1}}\}$ rows and columns to guarantee intersection of $b_{min} + 1$ correct servers with any previously written quorum, and intersection of $2b + 1$

with other quorums using the b threshold (the normal case). In Step 4 of the read protocol, we use enlarged quorums of $\frac{b+1}{\sqrt{b_{min}+1}}$ rows and $\frac{b+1}{\sqrt{b_{min}+1}}$ columns, guaranteeing intersection in $b + 1$ correct servers. For Step 2 of the write protocol, a quorum comprising of $\frac{b+1}{2\sqrt{b_{min}+1}}$ rows and $\frac{b+1}{2\sqrt{b_{min}+1}}$ columns is queried for timestamps, guaranteeing intersection in $b + 1$ servers (and hence, one correct) with any previously written quorum. Finally, it suffices to send updates to ordinary b-quorums containing $\sqrt{b+1}$ rows and $\sqrt{b+1}$ columns.

The proof of correctness is essentially identical to the threshold system case, simply making use of the intersection size statements for this construction.

7 Discussion

7.1 Comparison to static quorums

When deploying a system in practice, the maximum anticipated number of failures b_{max} is typically calculated as a function of the total number of servers n, e.g., based on an analysis of the probability of each individual server failing. A disadvantage of the approach in this paper, as compared to a static quorum system deployment, is that it can accommodate fewer values of b_{max} for a given n: ours requires $n \geq 6b_{max} - 2b_{min} + 1$ servers, as opposed to only $n \geq 4b_{max} + 1$ in the static case. However, for those configurations of n and b_{max} where our dynamic approach is possible, our approach performs better than a static quorum system in the common case, where there are no Byzantine failures and the system runs with a threshold of (or close to) b_{min}.

More specifically, the measure of efficiency that we consider is quorum size, since this determines the number of servers a client must access in order to perform an operation. Let $Q(b)$ denote the quorum size for a static quorum system with threshold b; e.g., in the threshold system, $Q(b) = (n + 2b + 1)/2$. For all of the quorum constructions we have described—threshold, boostFPP, and M-Grid—variable read and write operations access quorums of only size $Q(b_{min})$ while the system runs with a threshold of b_{min} and there are no threshold write operations. This compares favorably to the $Q(b_{max})$-sized quorums that a static system would use.

That said, when the threshold is raised to some $b > b_{min}$, penalties can be experienced that exceed the costs of accessing a static system. For example, in the threshold quorum construction, the threshold write itself accesses $n - b_{max}$ servers; variable read operations may access quorums of size $Q(2b - b_{min})$; and variable writes may access quorums of size $Q(b_{max})$ when concurrent with threshold write operations. Similarly, our variable read and write protocols for M-Grid employ quorums comprised of $O(b)$ rows and columns, so their cost is on the order of $Q(b^2)$. Also, because read operations return $\perp$ if the threshold read does, the likelihood that a read operation returns $\perp$ is increased.

In the performance discussion above, we have ignored the number of communication rounds performed by our protocols, and indeed, have not attempted to optimize for it. An obvious direction for optimization is to couple together the threshold reading with the value or timestamp reading at the beginning of variable read or write operations. For brevity, we do not include these in the exposition here.

7.2 An alternative approach

One of the strongest restrictions on the work we have presented here is that of Assumption 1. At the cost of making writes pessimistically static (and thus more expensive) we can weaken this restriction while still maintaining safety. Specifically, we can replace it with:

Assumption 3 *Any operation that is concurrent with no threshold writes receives no more than b faulty responses in any quorum access, where b is the current value of $\mathcal{B}$. In addition, no quorum access in any operation (even one concurrent with threshold writes) returns more than b_{max} faulty responses.*

A consequence of the second half of this assumption is that a write quorum performs correctly if it intersects all other write quorums in at least $b_{max} + 1$ servers. This is accomplished by any write quorum size between $(n + b_{max} + 1)/2$ and $n - b_{max}$. However, there remains the requirement of ensuring that every read quorum intersects every write quorum in at least $2b + 1$ servers, where b is the current threshold during the read.[2] If we use a write quorum of the smallest size, reads are *more* expensive than in the static case for values of b that are sufficiently close to b_{max}. If, on the other hand, we use write quorums of size $n - b_{max}$, it becomes unnecessary for read operations to be aware of the current threshold at all; we have shown above that a read quorum based on b_{min} intersects such a write quorum in at least $2b_{max} + 1$ servers. This is a potentially useful trade-off for systems in which reads are much more frequent than writes. It is, however, a static system and as such is uninteresting from the point of view of this work.

A more interesting approach is to set the write quorum to the same size as in a static b_{max} system, i.e. $(n + 2b_{max} + 1)/2$. In this case, a read quorum can be sure of a sufficient intersection with the previous write quorum if it is of size $(n + 4b - 2b_{max} + 1)$, where b is the current threshold. If $b = b_{max}$, then this is exactly the same as a static b_{max} read quorum; if $b < b_{max}$ it is an improvement even over a static read quorum for b, let alone b_{max}. For systems in which

write operations are sufficiently less frequent than read operations, this alternative way of using a varying threshold may be attractive.

8 Conclusion

In this paper, we have presented protocols for reading and adjusting the Byzantine fault tolerance level of a threshold masking quorum system, and shown how these protocols can be extended to other types of b-masking quorum systems, specifically M-Grid and boostFPP systems. In doing so, we have preserved the safe variable semantics provided by such systems.

References

[1] L. Alvisi, D. Malkhi, E. Pierce, and M. Reiter. Fault detection for Byzantine quorum systems. In *Proceedings of the 7th International Working Conference on Dependable Computing for Critical Applications*, pages 357–372, January 1999.

[2] A. Bar-Noy, D. Dolev, C. Dwork, and R. Strong. Shifting gears: Changing algorithms on the fly to expedite Byzantine agreement. *Information and Computation*, 97(2):205–233, 1992.

[3] R. A. Bazzi. Synchronous Byzantine quorum systems. In *Proceedings of the 16th ACM Symposium on Principles of Distributed Computing*, pages 259–266, August 1997.

[4] M. Bearden and R. Bianchini. A fault-tolerant algorithm for decentralized online quorum adaptation. In *Proceedings of the 28th International Symposium on Fault-Tolerant Computing (FTCS 98)*, pages 262–271, June 1998.

[5] P. A. Bernstein, V. Hadzilacos, and N. Goodman. *Concurrency control and recovery in database systems*. Addison-Wesley, 1987.

[6] D. K. Gifford. Weighted voting for replicated data. In *Proceedings of the 7th Symposium on Operating Systems Principles*, pages 150–162, 1979.

[7] M. Herlihy. Dynamic quorum adjustment for partitioned data. *ACM Transactions on Database Systems*, 12(2), June 1987.

[8] L. Lamport. On interprocess communications (part ii: algorithms). *Distributed Computing*, 1:86–101, 1986.

[9] E. Lotem, I. Keidar, and D. Dolev. Dynamic voting for consistent primary components. In *Proceedings of the 16th ACM Symposium on Principles of Distributed Computing (PODC)*, August 1997.

[10] N. Lynch and A. Shvartsman. Robust emulation of shared memory using dynamic quorum-acknowledged broadcasts. In *Proceedings of the 20th Annual International Symposium on Fault-Tolerant Computing (FTCS'97)*, June 1997. Seattle, Washington.

[11] M. Maekawa. A $\sqrt{n}$ algorithm for mutual exclusion in decentralized systems. *ACM Transactions on Computer Systems*, 3(2):145–159, 1985.

---

[2]Since the safety property applies to reads that do not overlap threshold adjustment operations, b is well defined.

[12] D. Malkhi. *Quorum Systems.* in *The Encyclopedia of Distributed Computing.* Joseph Urban and Partha Dasgupta editors, Kluwer Academic Publishers, To be published.

[13] D. Malkhi and M. Reiter. Byzantine quorum systems. *Distributed Computing*, 11(4):203–213, 1998.

[14] D. Malkhi, M. Reiter, A. Wool, and R. N. Wright. Probabilistic Byzantine quorum systems. Technical Report 98.7, AT&T Research, 1998.

[15] D. Malkhi, M. K. Reiter, and A. Wool. The load and availability of Byzantine quorum systems. In *Proceedings 16th ACM Symposium on Principles of Distributed Computing (PODC)*, pages 249–257, August 1997. To appear in Siam Journal of Computing.

[16] R. H. Thomas. A majority consensus approach to concurrency control for multiple copy databases. *ACM Transactions on Database Systems*, 4(2):180–209, 1979.

Session 10A

Analysis and Verification

A Tool Suite for Diagnosis and Testing of Software Design Specifications

J. Jenny Li and J. Robert Horgan
Telcordia Technologies (formerly Bellcore)
445 South St.
Morristown NJ 07960-6438
(973)829-4753
{jjli | jrh}@research.telcordia.com

Abstract

Available statistical data shows that the cost of finding and repairing software rises dramatically in later development stages. Much research has been done using verification and validation techniques to prove correctness in terms of certain properties. Such approaches and the approach of software testing are complementary. Testing reveals some errors that cannot be easily identified through verification, and vice versa. The new technology of generating implementation code from design specifications if based on highly reliable designs is another approach to reliable software.

This paper presents a dynamic slicing technology and an accompanying tool suite for understanding, diagnosis and testing of software design specifications. We apply state-of-the-art technology in coverage testing, diagnosis and understanding of software source code to those of software designs. We use a simulation of the specifications to collect the execution trace for computing the coverage and slicing data. Our technology first generates a flow diagram from a specification and then automatically analyses the coverage features of the diagram. It collects the corresponding flow data during simulation to be mapped to the flow diagram. The coverage information for the original specification is then obtained from the coverage information of the flow diagram. This technology has been used for C, C++, and Java, and has proven effective [1].

Keywords:

Software design specification, coverage testing, software engineering tool, χSuds, and Specification and Description Language (SDL[2]).

1 Introduction

As software becomes more complex and distributed, structural issues become as important as issues of data structure and algorithms. Software programming is moving towards high-level design, which raises new research issues. Software source-code level programming often utilizes many tools such as debuggers, purifiers, testers, etc. As programming moves up to the level of software design specification, a set of new tools on the design specification level will be required. Without proper engineering tools, direct code generation can only be used once with the first version. Figure 1 illustrates the situation.

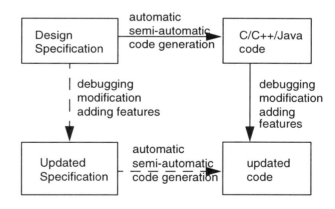

FIGURE 1 . A Software Development Paradigm [3]

Figure 1 shows that without proper tools, modifications to the software have to be done on the generated source-code level. The automatic or semi-automatic code generation can only be used once for the first version of the system. The debugging and enhancement have to be done on the generated source code level, because design level analysis is not possible without tool support. The current situation recalls the early history of Fortran where people sometimes wrote programs in Fortran but directly modified the generated assembly codes. Our set of software tools is intended to allow the development process to move along the dashed lines instead of the solid lines in Figure 1. This also promises a more reliable and up-to-date software design specification.

Our software systems are characterized by their huge size (typically well over a million lines of code) and complexity. These systems are composed of interdependent distributed components, some developed in-house, some commercially available, and others developed by the customer. The system configuration, that is, the components comprising the system, typically varies for each customer. Each configuration is given in one design specification. We use the Specification and Description Language (SDL)[2] specification of a software design as our concrete example to demonstrate our underlying technology and the application of our tools.

Most research on software specifications uses verification and validation techniques to prove correctness in terms of certain properties. A prominent approach of this category is model checking [4], which searches through all reachable states. We believe such an approach is similar to exhaustion testing. It is sometimes impossible to do an exhaustion test under market time pressure, which often requires 100% reachable state coverage. Not much research has addressed the issue of specification understanding, diagnosis and profiling, which are useful for coding on the design level.

This paper describes technologies underlying the tool suite we have developed for design specification understanding, debugging, and testing. The χSuds toolsuite contains the tools: χATAC, χVue, χSlice, χRegress and χProf. χVue and χSlice are specification understanding and diagnosis tools. χProgress and χATAC are two testing tools. χProf is a performance profiling tool. The underlying technique is to create a flow graph of the specification, thus laying out its execution structure. Then the simulator is instrumented to collect execution traces. The trace file records how many times a given part of the specification, such as a process, a transition, a decision, a state inputs, or a data flow, has been exercised in each simulation of the specification. The coverage data are then used to analyze the design.

The remainder of the paper is organized as follows.

Section two illustrates the underlying theory of our approach through an SDL example. Section three describes the χSUDS-SDL tool suite that implements our method and presents some experimental results. Section four concludes with discussions of the strength and limitations of our technology.

2 The Underlying Technology

Different test coverage tools use different coverage criteria. Some of the well-known criteria used in χSuds-SDL include: *function*, *basic transition*, *decision*, and *dataflow* coverage. Function coverage simply checks that each process or procedure of the SDL has been executed at least once. A basic transition is simply a statement sequence of the specification that is always executed sequentially, including states and decision constructs (it has no internal branching constructs). Basic transition coverage checks that each basic transition has been executed at least once, which implies that each statement has been executed at least once. Decisions are conditional branches from one basic transition to another. They could be states or decision constructs. Decision coverage checks that each such condition, decision matching or input mapping, has been executed, so that all true and false paths have been taken as well as all input alternatives and decision alternatives. Dataflow coverage counts the times variables are used subsequent to their definitions.

Our coverage-based approach includes three steps: 1) specification instrumentation for trace collection and specification prioritizing for test case generation (χAtac); 2) simulation and execution trace recording; and 3) trace analysis for specification understanding (χVue), diagnosis (χSlice), test case reduction (χRegress), and performance profiling (χProf). Each step is built on the previous step.

We use an SDL specification of a simple example application to illustrate these concepts and our approach. SDL is based on a model of communicating extended finite state machines (CEFSMs[5]). It provides hierarchical abstraction of a system structure. The top level is a system level specification. Each system includes some blocks. Each block can include either blocks or processes. Blocks communicate through channels. Each channel can be either delaying or non-delaying. Each process of a block is defined by an extended finite state machine. They communicate through signal routes. Signal routes have no delay. In general, SDL specification provides a process view of a system's software design. Figure 2 is the system and block level diagram of the design specification of a small telecom system.

Figure 2 shows that the system Li_TELECOM includes two distributed blocks: CallHandler and ResourceMgr. CallHandler controls call processing and ResourceMgr involves inventory control and remote database access. The channel between CallHandler and ResourceMgr is a delaying one, which indicates that the two blocks can be implemented on different CPUs with a non-negligible delay. This reflects the reality that database information can be stored remotely. CallHandler includes two processes: Caller and Callee. ResourceMgr has two processes: TMgr and CMgr. The process view of the software design is quite clear. The Caller process interacts with the call originator party. Callee handles the terminator party. And TMgr and CMgr control two kinds of resources. A partial specification for one of the processes, Caller, is given in Figure 3.

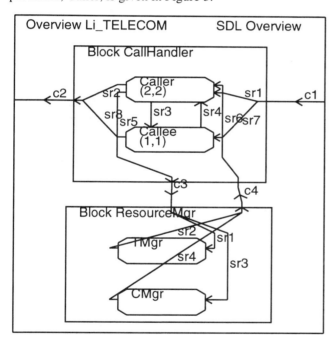

FIGURE 2 . System and Block Level Specification of a Simple Telecom System

We need to record the execution count of each statement during simulation. Our approach is to inject a single probe inside each basic transition. All the other coverage data can be deduced from the counts for basic transitions. Figure 3 shows that the partial Caller has 18 basic transitions.

We derived a flow diagram for each process, where each node is a basic transition and each edge is at least one possible execution sequence between them. Each process

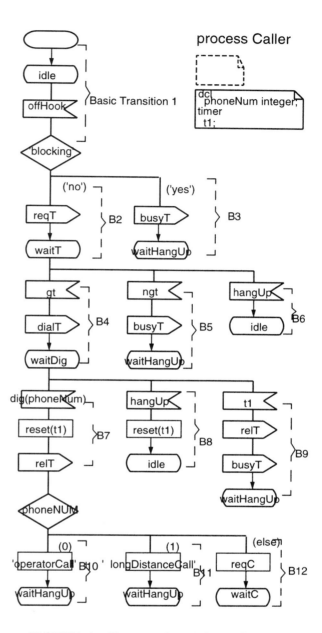

FIGURE 3 . Process Level Specification, Partial Caller

corresponds to one flow diagram. A flow diagram for partial Caller is given in Figure 4.

Each node of the diagram is either a full transition of an EFSM or a part of a transition (as defined as basic transitions previously). The branching of the nodes is caused either by the state transitions due to different inputs or by decision matching. For example, following state "waitT" are three branches corresponding to input "gt", "ngt" and "handUp", and following decision "phoneNum" are three branches corresponding to the matching value of the decision: "0", "1", or "else". The dashed lines connect the partial flow graph to the rest of the graph. The loops are given implicitly by reusing the name of a basic transition. For example, transition 6 goes back to transition 1 is a loop.

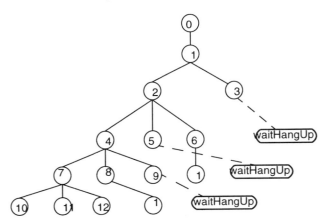

FIGURE 4 . Flow Diagram of Partial Process Caller

In summary, the instrumentation step injects probe into each node of the flow diagram. The instrumented specification will then be simulated. In order for the dynamic slicing working for design specifications, two major obstacles must be overcome.

One obstacle results from the difference between an actual program and a design specification. It is that specifications allow informal text such as "blocking?" in Figure 3. We treat informal text as a regular statement to be counted during simulation. The only effect of the informal text is that we cannot use the actual execution of a fully programmed transition, but must rely on simulation. We have developed our own specification simulation tool, which is compatible with existing commercial tools such as Telelogic SDT[7] and Verilog Geobe[8]. Each test case in this context is a single simulation or execution of the specification.

The other obstacle is that the probes themselves must also be a design specification so that they are consistent with the format of the specification for simulation. The resultant instrumented design specification of Figure 3 is given in Figure 5.

Each basic transition in Figure 5 includes one probe given in the specification format, an SDL task in this example. SDL specifications require tasks to follow

inputs. Probes must be placed at syntactically legitimate locations inside each basic transition. For example, it must be placed after the input signal "offhook" in the first basic transition. The parameters to the probes indicate to which basic transitions they belong.

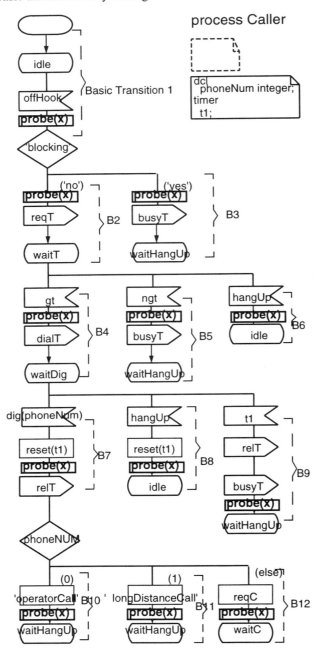

FIGURE 5 . Instrumented Process Level Specification, Partial Caller

Probes provide hooks for dynamic slicing. The

following section will discuss how the specification dynamic slicing technique can be used in a tool suite, χSuds, to guide the generation of simulation test cases. After the simulation, the trace data are used to analyze and test the specification.

3 χSUDS-SDL Implementation and Usage

Our tools use the instrumented specification and its simulation to analyze various properties of a specification. Although our tools have been used in large industrial systems, the design of a small telecom system of Figure 2 is discussed in this paper. Our tools analyze and display the textual representation of the system which includes 300 lines of SDL code derived from the four components of Figure 2.

We follow the following scenario. First we are given an unfamiliar specification in SDL (the 300 lines of SDL code) and asked to add new features. We used χVue to identify where each feature (e.g. "offhook") is implemented. We accidentally ran into a native error in the design. We used χSlice to locate and repair the bug quickly. Then we attempted to determine the performance bottlenecks of the design. This was done using χProf profiling tool. Lastly, we validated the design from a set of regression tests. We were able to prioritize the tests and remove redundant tests. After regression testing which showed that the design conformed to the tests, we noticed that the coverage of the design was less than 95%. We were able to use χAtac to improve the coverage. Experiments like this show the usefulness of our tools.

3.1 Feature Identification and Debugging Tools

Both χVue and χSlice use the concept of an *execution slice* of a specification, which is the part of the specification executed by a particular test case. The difference between slices can be used to identify features or bugs in a specification.

- ## Tool 1: χVue

When a developer decides to modify a feature of the system, he/she must first locate and understand the specification for the feature to be modified. Suppose, for example in our experiment, that we are to add a call-forwarding feature to the system Li_TELECOM. We have to find out where in the Caller specification the call request to the Callee is implemented and then add the actual Callee identification task before it. We created a

first simulation test where the Caller sends a call request to a Callee and a second case that is as similar as possible to the first one, except that the caller does not send a call request. The χVue tool now marks the occurrence-specific parts of the specification. Several heuristics are available, but the simplest and often the most effective is to look for parts of the specification that are executed in the first case but not in the second. In this example, the difference of the components covered by the two test cases is where the call request is made.

The tool interface helps users to focus on key parts of a large specification. An initial display lists all the processes in the specification and displays the number of marked transitions in each one. In this case, χVue points the developer to 10 transitions in the Caller. It shows that the process Caller is the major module to be considered when adding a new feature, call-forwarding, to the system.

From this first display, the user can click on one process to display the specification with the marked transitions (Figure 6). The scroll bar on the left has red

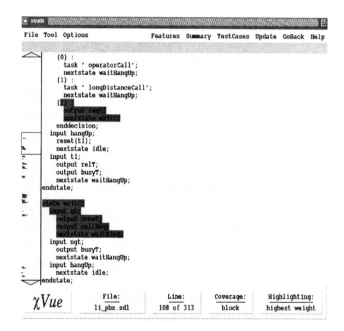

FIGURE 6 . Locating the Specification for Call-Forwarding Feature

(darker) pixels indicating where in the process the marked transition is located. The user can click on these red (darker) spots and the display scrolls until the marked transition appears in the main window. The second highlighted transition on the screen turns out to be involved in the sending of call requests. Addition of call forwarding feature would require a Callee identification task in this basic transition.

Case studies such as this have shown that a tool like χVue provides "good places to start looking". The tool may not identify exactly the code that needs to be changed, but its heuristics are very good at focusing attention on important areas. Since the whole specification consists of 67 basic transitions and 4 processes, it is obviously very useful to be able to narrow down quickly and focus on just a few transitions in just one of these processes. This case study uses a very small example. For larger specifications, such as Signaling System 7 (SS7), consisting of tens of thousands of transitions, our tool will be even more useful. Our tool does scale to these larger systems, based on our experimental results.

- Tool 2: χ**Slice**

Debugging tools for software specifications are rare. Checking specification correctness is often done using verification techniques such as model checking, which searches through all reachable states. We believe such an approach is similar to exhaustion testing. Due to market time pressure, sometimes it is impossible to do an exhaustion test, which often requires 100% of the reachable state coverage. Moreover, even if the time allows for verification, none of these techniques locate the bugs automatically as we have done using our tools.

We assume that the parts covered by successful test cases are bug-free and the bugs are residing in the parts of the specifications that are covered by the failed test cases. Therefore, finding the common parts of the failed test cases and subtracting the parts in the succeeded test cases will help the users to identify the bugs. In our experiment, the χSlice tool helps us identify an unexpected native bug in the specification. In this scenarios, the simulation has worked successfully for some time, so several bug-free test cases are available. Then a problem is reported with a test case that exhibits errors: test9. The tool automatically identifies in which part of the specification the fault is probably located. It turns out to be a native bug that has been overlook previously. Figure 7 shows the GUI of the χSlice tool, which displays the test cases that have been executed. The result of the tests can be input manually as passed, failed or disabled (thus not taking the test into account).

In Figure 7, all the test cases are listed, and the user marks boxes with a check indicate which tests passed and an X marks the test that failed. In this example the case highlighted in red (or darker in monochrome graph), has

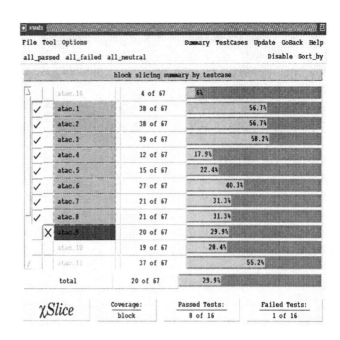

FIGURE 7 . Displaying Failed and Succeeded Tests

been flagged as showing the bug while eight earlier tests, highlighted in green (or lighter), do not.

Then the χSlice bug finding engine displays the offending design specification as given in Figure 8. The error found in this example is that the resource was not

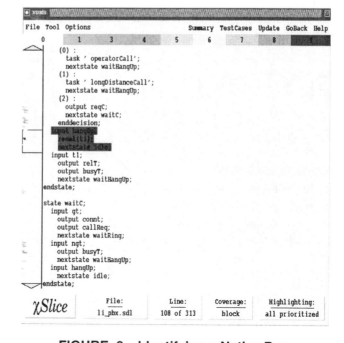

FIGURE 8 . Identifying a Native Bug

released properly after time-out.

3.2 χProf Performance Profiling Tool

It is important to identify performance bottlenecks of software specifications to guide the redesign of the system when the specification is a design document. Designers intended to have optimal performance can be stressed by larger and larger data sets until performance bounds are encountered. Execution profiles, showing how much time is spent in each function or subroutine, are the common ways of understanding such performance limitations.

The χProf tool leverages the coverage data already collected in χSuds to provide a simple kind of profiling that counts the number of times each transition is executed. While transitions may differ in their execution times, especially for time-consuming system calls, transition counting tends to be a reliable guide to system performance stress points. Execution time profiling is usually done at the process level to keep down the overhead of processing system times. Execution time in SDL states could include waiting time for system user inputs, which can be very large when the user is taking a break. It does not make sense to consider this delay as system performance bottleneck. Transition counting can point more directly to the exact point in the specification that most impacts performance. The tool shows the performance problem on the process level. For example, the process Caller takes up most of the execution steps: 55.6% (308/554).

A user might need to know where in the process Caller the specification simulation spends most of its effort as the number of calls grows larger. χProf provides a convenient interface for exploring this kind of question. Figure 9 shows the actual specification of the process Caller, with color highlighting to indicate the transitions most frequently executed. The color coding, shown near the top of the window, gives ranges of transition counts for each color. Red (darker) pixels in the scroll bar allow the developer to locate critical specification point quickly. Commonly, only a few transitions are executed a large number of times; these transitions provide opportunities for optimization. In this example, the most execution is on the state "idle". Reducing the number of times the process enters the "idle" state will improve the performance of the entire system.

Note that we treat states as basic transitions because we define a basic transition as a node in a flow graph of a process. A state is represented as a node in the flow

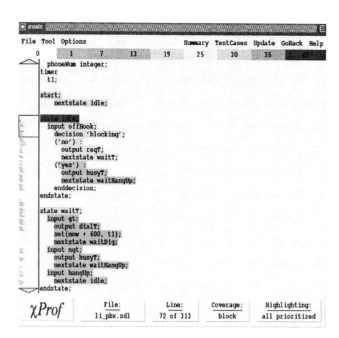

FIGURE 9 . Identifying the Most Frequently Executed Transitions

diagram because it does not represent a branching.

3.3 Design Validation Tools

Software designs are frequently modified to either fix a problem or implement a new feature, even in the coding stage. Testing is required to ensure that the new feature works and the old ones still work. In our experiments, we identified four possible situations: 1) running tests to cover only the modified parts; 2) running tests to cover the entire specification; 3) testing the entire specification under time constrain; 4) designing new tests to achieve maximum coverage.

*   Case 1: Partial Testing

It is not economical to re-run all the tests from the previous version after each small change. In most cases, the change may amount to less than 10% of the specification. Designers need to focus on the part of the specification they have, in fact, changed and then develop or re-use tests that cover these parts as quickly as possible. The question of how to select a set of tests to be re-run and in what order arises. χRegress can determine which cases do not cover any of the modified design. These test cases do not need to be rerun because the change does not affect them. For example, suppose a bug in the design has been found by the χSlice tool. A fixing effort is to add the release of resource "T" after handing up at the "waitDig" state. The red point of the Figure 8 highlights the place to be changed.

χRegress identifies the tests that do not simulate the transition of "input handUp; reset(t1);" at the state of "waitDig". It turns out in this case that only test case "atac.9" covers this transition. Therefore, we need only to rerun this test after the modification. We do not have to rerun the entire set of tests, 15 of them. We have cut cost by 14/15(93.3%).

- `Case 2: Full Testing`

After some major changes, users might want to retest the entire specification. Regression test set is often very large or very long running, because it grows as the design evolves. Old tests are rarely discarded because it is hard to tell if they are redundant by looking only at the description of the tests. χRegress help with this process by ranking the test cases in order of increasing coverage on the modified part of the design. The tool can also consider the cost of running each test.

Figure 10 shows how it ranks the 15 existing tests based on both basic transition coverage and a decision coverage, for a small telecom system. χRegress selects atac.1 as the first test case because it gives the maximum coverage with respect to block and decision coverage per unit cost. It lists subsequent tests according to their additional coverage per unit.

The tester can use Figure 10 to choose a reduced set of tests that will be permanently retained. In this case, test case "atac.11" can be discarded because it does not increase the total coverage of the test set. Note that it does not mean that it covers the same transitions as the test "atac.10" does.

The ranking of the test is not unique. In fact, in this example, the tests can be ranked differently to achieve the same coverage and cost efficiency. This order is called optimal order, which always provides the optimal answer. In this order, test case "atac.11" again does not contribute to the increase of coverage. It confirms that this test can be discarded. The new ranking is given in Figure 11.

- `Case 3: Testing Under Constraints`

Alternatively, χRegress can also be used to find a subset of the original tests that provides a desired level of coverage at minimal cost. In some situation, under the time-to-market pressure, the testers are not able to run all the tests. Previous experience shows that up to some level of testing, the efficiency of finding bugs decreases. In our example, coverage does not change much after running the first 7 tests. We achieve an acceptable coverage while cut the cost in half.

Running a small set of test cases dose not guarantee finding bugs that could have been detected by the full set of tests (excluding the redundant ones). Since the saving is dramatic, sometimes it is worth the risk. A reduced set of tests selected by χRegress is more likely to detect faults

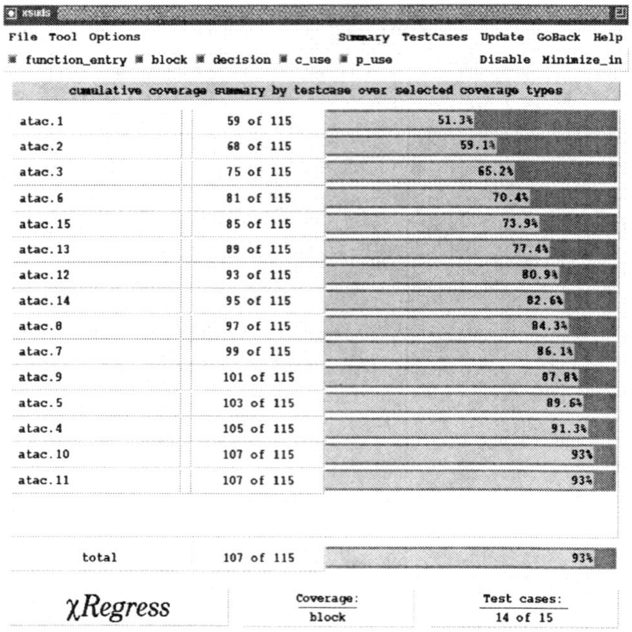

atac.1	59 of 115	51.3%
atac.2	68 of 115	59.1%
atac.3	75 of 115	65.2%
atac.6	81 of 115	70.4%
atac.15	85 of 115	73.9%
atac.13	89 of 115	77.4%
atac.12	93 of 115	80.9%
atac.14	95 of 115	82.6%
atac.8	97 of 115	84.3%
atac.7	99 of 115	86.1%
atac.9	101 of 115	87.8%
atac.5	103 of 115	89.6%
atac.4	105 of 115	91.3%
atac.10	107 of 115	93%
atac.11	107 of 115	93%
total	107 of 115	93%

FIGURE 10. Ranking of 15 Tests

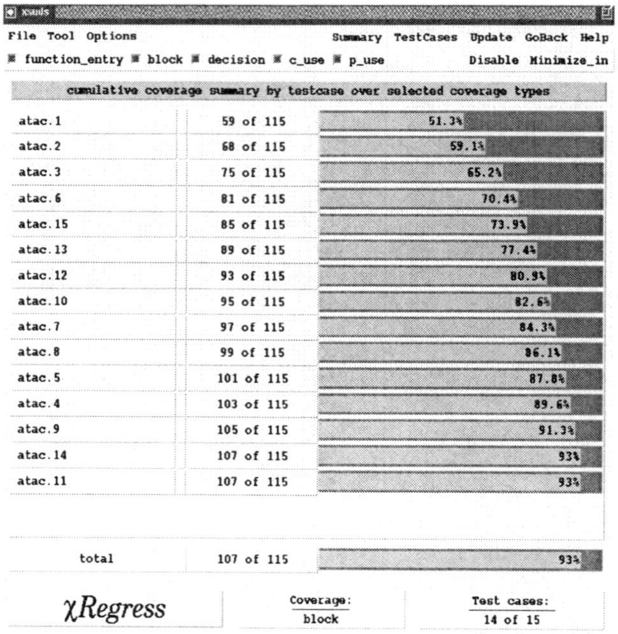

atac.1	59 of 115	51.3%
atac.2	68 of 115	59.1%
atac.3	75 of 115	65.2%
atac.6	81 of 115	70.4%
atac.15	85 of 115	73.9%
atac.13	89 of 115	77.4%
atac.12	93 of 115	80.9%
atac.10	95 of 115	82.6%
atac.7	97 of 115	84.3%
atac.8	99 of 115	86.1%
atac.5	101 of 115	87.8%
atac.4	103 of 115	89.6%
atac.9	105 of 115	91.3%
atac.14	107 of 115	93%
atac.11	107 of 115	93%
total	107 of 115	93%

FIGURE 11. Another Ranking of 15 Tests

not detected by a manually selected subset of the same size. It is more likely to detect faults not detected by a randomly or arbitrarily selected reduced set of the same size.

- Case 4: Coverage Testing

In our experiment, regression tests give a 93% basic transition coverage. If the target system is a safety-critical system, it is desirable to achieve 100% coverage. χAtac can prioritize the rest of design specification to be tested. The priority is based on the coverage information. Whichever basic transition (or decisions, or c-use, or p-use) that can achieve the highest coverage has the highest priority. Some transitions or states dominate others in the same process in that, if the dominating one is covered by a test, then many others must also be covered. The dominating ones are found by analyzing the flow diagram of the specification process. The dominating ones with the most dominated have the highest priority and are good places for the users to start in writing test cases; if they are covered then coverage of the specification can be greatly increased with just a few test cases[6]. The dominator concept has great potential for organizing testing task systematically and efficiently. For instance, arriving at node 12 in Figure 4 requires the execution also goes through node 1, 2, 4, and 7. It will cover at least 5 basic transitions. Node 18 dominates node 1, 2, 4, and 7. Arriving at node 6 requires only going through node 1 and 2, i.e. node 6 dominates node 1 and 2. It covers 3 basic transitions. Node 12 should obviously have higher priority than node 6.

After each test simulation, the priorities should be changed. For example, after running the simulation that goes through node 1, 2, 4, 7 and 12, the coverage of node 6 from node 1 and 2 only increases the count by one because the node 1 and 2 are already covered. In this situation, the node 6 and node 3 have the same priority, while they do not (node 6, 3; and node 3, 2) before the simulation.

The χAtac component of χSuds tool implements this technology of prioritizing specification transitions, states, decisions, c-use and p-use. Figure 12 shows how χAtac displays the priorities before any test cases have been run. In fact, this is the start-up screen of the tool.

In Figure 12, the color scale at the top of the window indicates that, if any one of the basic transitions highlighted in red (darkest in monochrome graph) is tested, at least 31 basic transitions will be covered. It dominates 30 other transitions. The developer can concentrate on these in writing his/her first test case. After

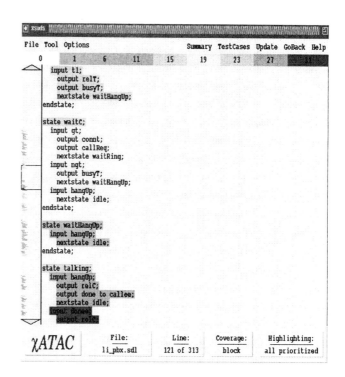

FIGURE 12. Identifying Coverage Testing Priorities

this case has been run, the updated χAtac display will prioritize just those transitions that remain uncovered to help in creating the next test case. For example, in this case, we design a first test case "atac.1" to cover the red transition of "input donee; output relC". Running of this first test will cause an update to the display.

Figure 12 shows basic transition coverage concept. We can also prioritize the specification based on decision coverage.

χAtac is most useful in achieving 100% coverage, which is very difficult to achieve without the aid of a tool.

4. Conclusions

The use of traces or execution histories as an aid to testing and analysis is a well established technique for programming languages like C and C++. It includes some very sophisticated tools such as PROVIDE that store traces and allow the programmer to replay execution and query the trace to show data values, data flows, program source, and so on during testing and debugging sessions [9]. But testing and analysis are rarely mentioned in the field of software specification for designs even though early fault detection can cut cost. Our χSuds-C/C++ tool suite is capable of prioritizing the transitions and test cases for testing, feature identification, debugging and performance profiling. We extended this technology to the software design specification level to allow more efficient specification validation and maintenance.

χSuds techniques mostly use dynamic analysis, which uses simulation traces to relate design specification components to specific simulations, a semantic relationship that is extremely difficult to discover statically. However one must always keep in mind that the results of dynamic analysis depend on the simulations used. If the simulation set is limited, important specification behavior may be missed. Furthermore, the probes injected to the specification might affect some time-sensitive simulation behavior.

We have implemented these techniques in a tool suite called χSuds-SDL to demonstrate the usefulness of the techniques. Our experimental results show the benefits of the tools. It helps users to quickly grasp and understand the design specification, to debug an unfamiliar specification, to identify performance bottleneck and to validate the design efficiently, i.e. with highest testing coverage and lowest cost. χVue helps user identify features and understand the specification. χSlice finds bugs quickly. χRegress reduces the size of test cases and thus testing effort. χProf identifies performance bottlenecks. Guided testing execution-path creation (χAtac) based on the basic transition dominator concept can help a designer create efficient test cases quickly. It can also help verification and validation cover most of the reachable states. All these tools are combined into one environment with a consistent GUI interface and a robust underlying design.

Another advantage of our tool is its user-friendly GUI. This is important since the volume of information from a large system design specification can easily overwhelm the designer. Our GUI organizes the information in a comprehensible way. More details on the usage of the tool can be found in [10].

Testing, diagnosis, debugging and profiling software design specifications will become the biggest cost drivers in the software industry as the software development moves up to the specification level and code is automatically generated. Dynamic analysis techniques, based on simulation and using tools like χSuds, offer great potential for keeping these costs under control and automating code generation, i.e., making coding on the specification level more reliable and efficient. χSuds-SDL continues to evolve, it promises a better graphical SDL

representation interface. Some internal and external organizations have expressed their interest in using the tool suite. Due to space limitation, this paper showed only the experiments on a small system. We have also applied our tools to a very large and complex system with over 300 pages of SDL specification.

Besides extending the techniques to the validation of design specification, we have also extended it to other research area such as reliability and performance prediction. When each component of the specification is a network component, we can also applied this tool suite to the validation of network configuration and automatic configuration generation. We are investigating this new potential application of our techniques. We hope that the tool suite will make a significant contribution to improve reliability and efficiency of software design specification development, especially programming on the design level in the telecommunications industry.

References

[1] Agrawal, H., Alberi, J., Li, J. J. and et al., "Mining System Tests to Aid Software Maintenance", IEEE Computer, July 1998, pp64-73.

[2] International Telegraph and Telephone Consultative Committee, "SDL User Guidelines," Blue book: IXth Plenary Assembly, Melbourne, 14-25 Nov. 1988, Geneva: International Telecommunication Union, 1989.

[3] Li, J. J. and Horgan, J.R., "To Maintain a Reliable Software Specification", ISSRE98, pp59-69.

[4] Atlee, J. M., and Gannon, J., "State-based Model Checking of Event-Driven System Requirements", IEEE Trans. Software Engineering, Vol. 19, No.1, Jan. 1993, pp24-40.

[5] Brand, D. and Zafiropulo, P., "On Communicating Finite-State Machines", Journal of ACM, Vol. 30, No. 2, April, 1983, pp. 323-342.

[6] Agrawal, H., "Dominators, Super Blocks, and Program Coverage" *Conference Record of the 21st Annual ACM SIGPLAN-SIGACT Symposium on Principles of Programming Languages (POPL'94)*, Portland, Oregon, January 1994, pp. 25-34

[7] www.telelogic.com

[8] www.verilog.com

[9] Moher, T., PROVIDE: A Process Visualization and Debugging Environment, IEEE Transactions on Software Engineering, Vol. 14, No. 6, June 1988.

[10] www.xsuds.com or xsuds.argreenhouse.com

Enabling Automated Analysis Through the Formalization of Object-Oriented Modeling Diagrams*

Betty H.C. Cheng[†] and Laura A. Campbell
Michigan State University
3115 Engineering Building
East Lansing, MI 48824
E-mail: {chengb,campb222}@cse.msu.edu

Enoch Y. Wang
Lucent Technologies
Intelligent Network Unit
6200 East Broad Street
Columbus, OH 63213
E-mail: ewang@lucent.com

Abstract

As the impact of and demand for software increases, there is greater need for rigorous software development techniques that can be used by a typical software engineer. In order to integrate informal and formal approaches to software development, we added formal syntax and semantics definitions to existing object-oriented modeling notations. This formalization enables developers to construct object-oriented models of requirements and designs and then automatically generate formal specifications for the diagrams. This paper describes how the resulting diagrams via their specifications can be analyzed using automated techniques to validate behavior through simulation or to check for numerous properties of the diagrams, including inter- and intramodel consistency.

1. Introduction

It is clearly evident that the role of software is significantly increasing. Accordingly, the need to have high assurance in software's correctness increases for systems where correct operation is imperative. Recent studies have shown that the software quality problem is greatest during the early lifecycle phases of requirements and design, which can have a lasting impact on the reliability, cost, and safety of a system [8]. Also, requirements errors are between 10 and 100 times more costly to correct at later phases of the software lifecycle than at the requirements phase itself [8].

One approach to this problem is to document software requirements and design using a formal language; such a doc-

ument is called a *formal specification*. This approach is one of the basic elements of the software engineering disciplines referred to as *formal methods*. The advantages to using formal methods are significant, including the use of notations that are precise, verifiable, and facilitate automated processing. A formal specification can be rigorously manipulated to allow the designer to assess the consistency, completeness, and robustness of a design before it is implemented. Other approaches to requirements analysis and design include numerous object-oriented techniques. These "informal" methods enable the rapid construction of a system model using intuitive graphics and user-friendly languages. While such techniques have proved to be useful tools, the graphical notations used with these methods are often ambiguous, resulting in diagrams that are easily misinterpreted.

One object-oriented development approach, the *Object Modeling Technique* (OMT) [14], a precursor to the Unified Modeling Language (UML) [13], uses three types of models to express important domain-related concepts: object models, dynamic models, and functional models. Each model contributes to the understanding of a system, but the object model is of central importance. Those elements of a system that define its static structure are given by an *object model*. The *dynamic model* describes the behavior of the system through a state transition diagram. And the data and the services of a system are captured by the *functional model*. The main attractive feature of the OMT approach is that by using these three notations in a complementary manner, the system developer can express and refine (evolve) system requirements into a design and implementation. However, the lack of precise definitions for the notations makes it difficult to combine this approach with rigorous, systematic software development methods. In addition, the lack of a systematic process further hinders the effective use of the modeling notation.

This paper describes the types of automated analysis

---

*This work is supported in part by NSF grants CDA-9700732, CDA-9617310, CCR-9633391, CCR-9901017, and DARPA grant No. F30602-96-1-0298, managed by Air Force's Rome Laboratories, and Eaton Corporation.

[†]Please contact this author for all correspondences.

techniques that may be applied to diagrams when the syntax and semantics of the diagram notation have been formalized. We specifically use OMT to systematically model a real distributed multimedia application [18]. The diagrams are then used to generate formal specifications, expressed in terms of LOTOS (Language of Temporal Ordering Specification) [12] specifications, based on formalization rules that we have previously developed for the OMT notation [1, 17, 19]. These formal specifications enable the diagrams to be analyzed by a number of existing automated reasoning utilities, including behavior simulators, model checkers, and rewriting systems. It is noted that the OMT notation plays a large role in the Unified Modeling Language (UML) notation. Therefore, the formalizations that we have developed for OMT are being reused for the key UML diagrams, that is, the object and the dynamic models. Similarly, the analysis techniques that we are able to apply to the specifications for the OMT diagrams can also be applied to the UML diagrams. An overarching goal of this project is to facilitate technology transfer and exchange by integrating commonly used informal development techniques where there is good tool support for analyzing and manipulating the formal specifications.

Other projects have explored the addition of formal syntax and/or semantics to informal modeling techniques [6, 7, 10, 15]. But none of these techniques consider all three modeling perspectives and fully address the automated analysis capabilities afforded by the formalization. The remainder of this paper is organized as follows. Section 2 gives background material including an overview of the formalization process and specification analysis tools. Section 3 presents the results of the analysis of the formal specifications of the graphical models for the distributed multimedia system. Section 4 compares the specification analysis tools. Section 5 gives a summary and discusses future investigations.

2. Background

This section overviews the notation that is used for the formal specifications of the diagrams. We also give a brief overview of the process that has been developed to support a systematic development of the object-oriented models from requirements to design [18]. Finally we briefly describe the two suites of specification analysis tools that are applied to the diagram specifications.

2.1. Generation of formal specifications

Figure 1 contains a high-level overview of the object-oriented diagrams and their corresponding formal specifications. We have formalized the object-oriented models in terms of full LOTOS syntax that allows the information

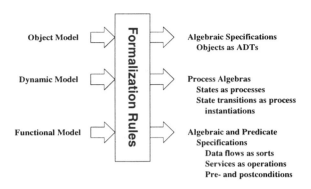

Figure 1. Overview of formalization rules

expressed in the graphical object, dynamic, and functional models to be captured in algebraic specifications and process algebras [1, 17, 19]. The commonalities between the ACT ONE algebraic specifications and the basic LOTOS process algebras induced by the formalization rules make it possible to integrate the object, dynamic, and functional models into a full integrated LOTOS specification. This specification can then be subjected to a variety of analyses, both static and dynamic, using available LOTOS tool suites that are described later. We have developed a prototype system, VISUALSPECS [4], that supports the graphical construction of object-oriented models and the automated generation of formal specifications according to our formalization rules.

Overview of the design process. We developed a systematic design process for constructing and refining the object-oriented models. The process explicitly addresses the consistency between the formal specifications of two adjacent levels of abstraction thus enabling stepwise refinement and consistency checking [16].

The proposed design paradigm focuses on the process in order to facilitate a stepwise refinement of designs. The design process contains iterations of model development. For each step of model development during a given iteration, corresponding formal specifications are derived or refined (see Figure 2(a)). In the design process, Steps 1-3 focus on creating system-level versions of object, dynamic, and functional models, respectively. Steps 4-7 are refinements and decompositions of the models from Steps 1-3. An object functional model (OFM) in Step 5 is a variation of dataflow diagrams, and it depicts visible services offered by the object. A service refinement functional model (SRFM) in Step 6b is also a variation of dataflow diagrams, depicting a system/object service in terms of the services provided by the aggregate objects of the system/object. Step 8 composes the dynamic models for all aggregate objects to depict the overall system behavior. The formal specifications of the diagrams enable automated analysis to check that the diagram and specification refinements are consistent with earlier versions of diagrams and specifications.

We have developed an analysis process to be used in tandem with the above mentioned design process. For each design iteration, both static and dynamic analyses are supported (Figure 2(b)). Syntax and semantics checking must be successfully completed before other types of analyses are possible with the available tools. Then simulation and state-based exploration are enabled for validating requirements and finding design flaws, where there is special emphasis placed on concurrency analysis, such as deadlock detection and safety.

2.2. Analysis tools

TOPO[1] [11] (Toolset to support product realization from LOTOS specifications) is a LOTOS tool suite developed by the University of Madrid that offers syntax and semantics checking. LOLA is a transformational and state exploration tool built atop TOPO that provides several types of expansion (state space generation), interactive simulation, and test composition. TOPO can handle "incomplete" specifications; that is, not every operation needs to be fully defined with algebraic equations.

CADP[2] [5] (Caesar/Aldebaran Development Package), developed by INRIA and Verimag, also offers syntax and semantics checking of LOTOS specifications, as well as interactive simulation and test composition. However, its additional features for viewing, manipulating, and comparing Labeled Transition Systems (LTSs) did not have a counterpart in TOPO/LOLA. We were especially interested in automating the comparison of the LTSs that represent a design before and after refinement, the generation of counterexamples for deadlock cases, and the verification of temporal logic properties against LTSs.

3. Formalization/analysis process

In order to gain empirical experience with our formalization techniques and process model, we applied the formalization and integration rules and design process to an industrial project, the *Environmental Information System* (ENFORMS) [3], a multimedia distributed decision support system, developed over a three year period involving 15 software developers with support from NASA, EPA, and USDA. ENFORMS has been developed to facilitate the access, integration, and analysis of environmental science data relevant to a regional study that has local and global impacts. The objective of ENFORMS is to provide users with

[1]Information about TOPO is available at http://selva.dit.upm.es/~lotos/tools/topo.html
[2]Information about CADP is available at http://www.inrialpes.fr/vasy/cadp.html

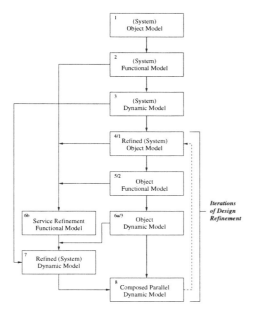

(a) Design process

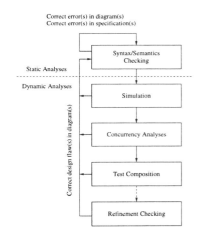

(b) Analysis process

Figure 2. Iterative design process and tandem analysis process

convenient access to and manipulation of large amounts of multimedia information that may be distributed across many sites.

By applying the formalization rules and the analysis techniques to the ENFORMS system, we determined that:

- The formalization and integration rules for OMT models can help designers to derive more precise and integrated descriptions of design information.

- Our design process facilitates the refinement of design.

- Based on the formal specifications derived from OMT models, automated analysis can be performed to check design consistency and to facilitate understanding and communication about the design.

The remainder of this section describes automated analysis results obtained from requirements analysis and design models, respectively.

3.1. Requirements modeling: analysis results

ENFORMS is intended to offer convenient access to a large volume of widely diverse and distributed earth science data. The main requirements of the system are twofold. First, because the archive contains a potentially large volume of data, a selective browsing mechanism is necessary to help users navigate the archive. Second, the distributed nature of the stored items should be transparent to the user with respect to the browser.

3.1.1. Models and specifications.
At the most abstract level, the system should allow a user to browse a set of indices regarding the data, retrieve desired data, and perform analysis on the retrieved data. Based on the requirements analysis, the system level object model, object functional model (OFM), and dynamic model shown in Figure 3 depict the ENFORMS system at a high level of abstraction. The "ground wire" in the OFM represents access to internal data items, bubbles represent processes, and arrows represent data flows. At the most abstract level, ENFORMS essentially waits for the user to format a request. Afterwards, the user may continue to browse and formulate requests, or may transmit the request for data. If the data is found, then it becomes available for analysis. Otherwise, the user must format a new request.

The LOTOS specification shown in Figure 4 was produced automatically from the models in Figure 3 according to our formalization rules. Sorts and operations (lines 13-41) are derived from the object and object functional models, while processes (lines 44-81) reflect the behavior described in the dynamic model.

3.1.2. Automated analysis.
At this stage, although no algebraic equations regarding the service operations have yet been introduced, the specification may be subjected to syntax and semantics analysis and also interactive simulation.

Syntax and semantics checking. While the parts of LOTOS specifications that are automatically generated should be syntactically correct, the specifier may introduce syntax errors when adding algebraic equations or additional operations at the specification level, for example

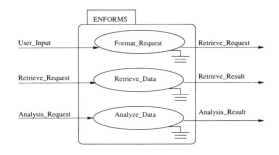

(a) System level
object model

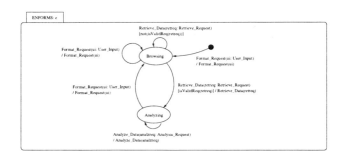

(b) System level object functional model

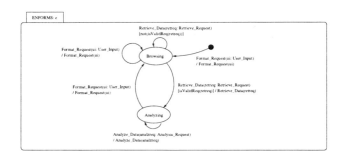

(c) System level dynamic model

Figure 3. Object-oriented models of ENFORMS

when defining services precisely in order to perform more detailed simulations. Thus syntax checking should not be omitted. Semantics checking can be used to show inter-model consistency; that is, the data sorts and service operations used in the dynamic model of an object should be those depicted in the corresponding object model and object functional model.

Simulation. Using interactive simulation, the specifier can "execute" the behavior described by the diagrams via the specifications in a stepwise fashion. The trace shown in Figure 5 confirms the requirement that retrieval of data must be preceded by formatting a request, and analysis of data must be preceded by its retrieval. Simulation can be used to validate requirements, to increase confidence that

```
1    specification ENFORMS [Format_Request, Retrieve_Data,
2                          Analyze_Data] (e : ENFORMS) : noexit
3
4        (* Format_Request : ui: User_Input -> Retrieve_Request *)
5        (* Retrieve_Data  : rr: Retrieve_Request -> Retrieve_Result *)
6        (* Analyze_Data    : ar: Analysis_Request -> Analysis_Result *)
7
8        library
9            BOOLEAN
10       endlib
11
12       type ENFORMS is Boolean
13           sorts
14               Data_Archives, Data_Indices, User_Input,
15               Retrieve_Request, Retrieve_Result,
16               Analysis_Request, Analysis_Result, ENFORMS
17           opns
18               undef_Data_Archives : -> Data_Archives
19               _eq_ : Data_Archives, Data_Archives -> Bool
20               undef_Data_Indices : -> Data_Indices
21               _eq_ : Data_Indices, Data_Indices -> Bool
22               undef_User_Input : -> User_Input
23               _eq_ : User_Input, User_Input -> Bool
24               undef_Retrieve_Request : -> Retrieve_Request
25               _eq_ : Retrieve_Request, Retrieve_Request -> Bool
26               undef_Retrieve_Result : -> Retrieve_Result
27               _eq_ : Retrieve_Result, Retrieve_Result -> Bool
28               undef_Analysis_Request : -> Analysis_Request
29               _eq_ : Analysis_Request, Analysis_Request -> Bool
30               undef_Analysis_Result : -> Analysis_Result
31               _eq_ : Analysis_Result, Analysis_Result -> Bool
32               undef_ENFORMS : -> ENFORMS
33               _eq_ : ENFORMS, ENFORMS -> Bool
34               Format_Request : User_Input -> Retrieve_Request
35               Retrieve_Data : Retrieve_Request -> Retrieve_Result
36               Analyze_Data : Analysis_Request -> Analysis_Result
37               isValidReq : Retrieve_Request -> Bool
38               isValidRes : Retrieve_Result -> Bool
39               make_ENFORMS : Data_Archives, Data_Indices -> ENFORMS
40               getArchives : ENFORMS -> Data_Archives
41               getIndices : ENFORMS -> Data_Indices
42       endtype
43
44   behavior
45
46       Format_Request ? ui : User_Input;
47           Format_Request ! Format_Request (ui);
48               Browsing [Format_Request, Retrieve_Data, Analyze_Data] (e)
49   where
50       process Browsing [Format_Request, Retrieve_Data,
51                         Analyze_Data] (e : ENFORMS) : noexit :=
52           Format_Request ? ui : User_Input;
53               Format_Request ! Format_Request (ui);
54                   Browsing [Format_Request, Retrieve_Data,
55                             Analyze_Data] (e)
56               []
57           Retrieve_Data ? retreq : Retrieve_Request;
58               (
59                   [isValidReq (retreq)] ->
60                       Retrieve_Data ! Retrieve_Data (retreq);
61                           Analyzing [Format_Request, Retrieve_Data,
62                                      Analyze_Data] (e)
63                   []
64                   [not (isValidReq (retreq))] ->
65                       Browsing [Format_Request, Retrieve_Data,
66                                 Analyze_Data] (e)
67               )
68       endproc
69
70       process Analyzing [Format_Request, Retrieve_Data,
71                          Analyze_Data] (e : ENFORMS) : noexit :=
72           Format_Request ? ui : User_Input;
73               Format_Request ! Format_Request (ui);
74                   Browsing [Format_Request, Retrieve_Data,
75                             Analyze_Data] (e)
76               []
77           Analyze_Data ? analyzreq : Analysis_Request;
78               Analyze_Data ! Analyze_Data (analyzreq);
79                   Analyzing [Format_Request, Retrieve_Data,
80                              Analyze_Data] (e)
81       endproc
82
83   endspec
```

Figure 4. Automatically generated specifications

the system or object in question behaves as desired, or to debug erroneous behavior.

State exploration-based analysis. The automatically generated specification provides a framework into which de-

```
<n>,Undo,Menu,Refused,Sync,Print,Trace,Exit,?> t

[   1] - format_request    ? ui_2:user_input;
[   1] - format_request    ! format_request(ui_2);
[   2] - retrieve_data     ? retreq_10:retrieve_request;
[   1] - [isvalidreq(retreq_10) = true] ->
         retrieve_data     ! retrieve_data(retreq_10);
[   2] - analyze_data      ? analyzreq_14:analysis_request;
[   1] - analyze_data      ! analyze_data(analyzreq_14);
```

Figure 5. LOLA simulation trace

signers may add additional detail. For example, the specifier may introduce some constants and algebraic equations (Figure 6, lines 24-32 and lines 33-57) to further define the *Retrieve Data* service. The refined specification as shown also contains pre- and postconditions (lines 4-8) for the *Format Request* and *Retrieve Data* services. After performing syntax and semantics checking as well as interactive simulation, LOTOS specifications can be composed with a "test" process (in this case, the specification under test is the specification of the ENFORMS system). The simple test process asks whether two consecutive successful query formulations and data retrievals are possible.

The results of the test depend on the reachability of a "success" event in the composed behavior. TOPO/LOLA describes the outcome in terms of "must pass" (all execution paths lead to success), "may pass" (some execution paths lead to success), or "reject" (no paths lead to success). TOPO/LOLA also indicates how many paths are explored, how many paths lead to success, and how many paths do not terminate with success. The same type of analysis can be applied using CADP, where CADP's results can be shown in a more intuitive text-based representation of an LTS graph, Figure 7. Or this graph can be drawn with tools included in the CADP toolset.

In either case, the results of the test indicate that such a pattern of behavior is possible with the current design. They do not mean that we can say the design is correct or the specification is correct, only that we are likely to get a result back when we make a retrieval request.

3.2. Design modeling: analysis results

The object-oriented models for the high level ENFORMS system were next refined to include more design information (Figure 2(a), Step 4). The system design presented in the refinement of the ENFORMS system is based on the design presented in the project documentation [2]. ENFORMS is a distributed system that realizes its functionality through a collection of communicating software components. The distributed operation is supported by a *client-server* architecture, so the main components of interest examined in the refinement are a Client, two different types of servers, an Archive Server and a Name Server, and a Channel. Archive Servers

```
1   specification ENFORMS [Format_Request, Retrieve_Data,
2                    Analyze_Data] (e : ENFORMS) : noexit
3
4   (* Format_Request : ui: User_Input -> Retrieve_Request *)
5   (*   ensures  result = Format_Request (ui, getIndices(e)) *)
6   (* Retrieve_Data : rr: Retrieve_Request -> Retrieve_Result *)
7   (*   requires isValidReq (rr) *)
8   (*   ensures  result = Retrieve_Data (rr, getArchives(e)) *)
9   (* Analyze_Data   : ar: Analysis_Request -> Analysis_Result *)
10
11  library
12     BOOLEAN
13  endlib
14
15  type ENFORMS is Boolean
16    sorts
17        Data_Archives, Data_Indices, User_Input,
18        Retrieve_Request, Retrieve_Result,
19        Analysis_Request, Analysis_Result, ENFORMS
20    opns
21        ......
22        ......
23        ......
24        dataArchives : -> Data_Archives
25        dataIndices : -> Data_Indices
26        valid_User_Input : -> User_Input
27        valid_Retrieve_Request : -> Retrieve_Request
28        valid_Retrieve_Result : -> Retrieve_Result
29        Format_Request : User_Input, Data_Indices ->
30                          Retrieve_Request
31        Retrieve_Data : Retrieve_Request, Data_Archives ->
32                          Retrieve_Result
33    eqns
34      forall da : Data_Archives,
35             rq, rqx, rqy : Retrieve_Request,
36             rs, rsx, rsy : Retrieve_Result
37    ofsort Bool
38        undef_Retrieve_Request eq
39            undef_Retrieve_Request = True;
40        valid_Retrieve_Request eq
41            valid_Retrieve_Request = True;
42        undef_Retrieve_Request eq
43            valid_Retrieve_Request = False;
44        rqx eq rqy = rqy eq rqx;
45        undef_Retrieve_Result eq undef_Retrieve_Result = True;
46        valid_Retrieve_Result eq valid_Retrieve_Result = True;
47        undef_Retrieve_Result eq valid_Retrieve_Result = False;
48        rsx eq rsy = rsy eq rsx;
49        isValidReq (valid_Retrieve_Request) = True;
50        isValidReq (undef_Retrieve_Request) = False;
51        isValidRes (valid_Retrieve_Result) = True;
52        isValidRes (undef_Retrieve_Result) = False;
53    ofsort Retrieve_Result
54        isValidReq (rq) =>
55            Retrieve_Data (rq, da) = valid_Retrieve_Result;
56        not (isValidReq (rq)) =>
57            Retrieve_Data (rq, da) = undef_Retrieve_Result;
58  endtype
59
60  behavior
61     ......
62     ......
63     ......
64  endspec
```

Figure 6. Enhanced formal specification

```
des (0, 9, 10)
(0, "FORMAT_REQUEST !VALID_USER_INPUT", 1)
(1, "FORMAT_REQUEST !VALID_RETRIEVE_REQUEST", 2)
(2, "RETRIEVE_DATA !VALID_RETRIEVE_REQUEST", 3)
(3, "RETRIEVE_DATA !VALID_RETRIEVE_RESULT", 4)
(4, "FORMAT_REQUEST !VALID_USER_INPUT", 5)
(5, "FORMAT_REQUEST !VALID_RETRIEVE_REQUEST", 6)
(6, "RETRIEVE_DATA !VALID_RETRIEVE_REQUEST", 7)
(7, "RETRIEVE_DATA !VALID_RETRIEVE_RESULT", 8)
(8, SUCCESS, 9)
```

Figure 7. CADP output in textual format

handle requests for data issued by Clients, while the Name Server is responsible for maintaining a table of active Archive Servers and handling Client requests for copies of this server table. The Channel represents the connection between the Client and either of the Archive Servers.

3.2.1. Models and specifications.

The system level object model for the ENFORMS system is refined to include the new objects as shown in Figure 8, where the diamond indicates aggregation, a filled circle indicates the "zero or more" relationship, and the double lines indicate that the attributes are omitted for this discussion. Object-oriented models for all four of these aggregate objects, the Client, Archive Server, Name Server, and Channel, are developed, and LOTOS specifications are derived for all four of the objects in the same manner in which specifications were derived for the high-level ENFORMS system.

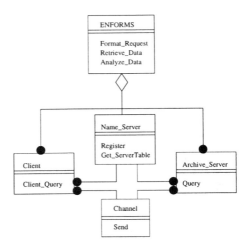

Figure 8. Refined object model

Service refinement. The refinement of ENFORMS into aggregate objects Client, Archive Server, Name Server, and Channel now allows us to refine the high level *Retrieve Data* service in the ENFORMS class into a composition of services offered by the aggregates. ENFORMS uses the Client's *Client Query* service to implement the high-level *Retrieve Data* service. Thus the client-server architecture suggests a refinement of the dynamic model of the ENFORMS system (Figure 9) to depict the *Retrieve Data* service being handled by the Client's *Client Query* service. The modified parts of the model (indicated by shaded states or transition text outlined by dotted rectangles) specify that:

1. When a request for the high-level *Retrieve Data* service occurs, the input argument Retrieve Request is decomposed into Data Archive Name and Query Request.

2. The Query Request is redirected to a Client object for a *Client Query* service.

3. The ENFORMS system enters the WaitQuery state to await a Query Result from the Client.

4. When a Query Result is received from the Client, ENFORMS converts the Query Result to a Retrieve Result and delivers it to the user.

As indicated in Step 8 of the design process (Figure 2(a)), the dynamic models of instantiations of all the aggregate objects and the ENFORMS object are composed concurrently (Figure 10), and the refined object-oriented models are again translated to LOTOS to create the refined specification.

3.2.2. Automated analysis. Now that the objects have been composed concurrently, we can subject the entire design, or individual pieces of it, to syntax and semantics checking, interactive simulation, and different concurrency analyses.

Syntax and semantics checking. The individual specifications or the specification for the entire refined ENFORMS system (composed of the individual objects) can each be syntax and semantics checked for inter- and intramodel consistency; that is, the diagrams associated with each object are consistent among each other, and between objects in the system.

Simulation. The Client and Archive Server may be interactively simulated with either TOPO/LOLA or CADP, where CADP tools can also be used to draw the graph of the corresponding LTS. Our initial analysis results indicate that the Name Server presents a problem. While it can be simulated in TOPO/LOLA, expansion must be limited to an explicit depth because in isolation it becomes an infinite behavior of handling potential Archive Server registrations or Client requests. On the other hand, CADP must generate a *finite* graph, so it cannot be used to its full potential with the *isolated* Name Server (although graph generation may be arbitrarily stopped by the user in order to view the different labels on transitions that have been created thus far). These analysis results help us to realize that the current Name Server design does not distinguish multiple registrations of the same Archive Server, handle deletions of entries from the server table, enforce an upper bound on the number of table entries, nor recognize a bad registration entry such as one containing an invalid address.

However, we note that when *composed* with the current design of the Name Server, an Archive Server only registers with the Name Server once and uses its own address, which is presumably valid. In reality, we can only model a finite number of Archive Servers, so there will be some upper bound on the number of server table entries. The location of the Name Server is already known to the Archive Server, the communication medium between them is assumed to be reliable (we are modeling the registration as a synchronization on LOTOS gates), and there is no provision

made in the current design for an Archive Server to go offline once it has registered with the Name Server. Given these project constraints, we decide that no change in the designs of the aggregate objects is required at this time.

State exploration-based analysis. Next, the specification of the entire system is subjected to *expansion* with TOPO/LOLA to exhaustively generate all possible execution paths. Expansion may be limited to an explicit depth (which would be necessary in the case of infinite behavior), but here we ask TOPO/LOLA to generate all possible paths of this finite behavior. Any deadlocks found at this stage probably indicate synchronization problems among the objects. TOPO/LOLA finds four deadlocks that, after we examine the log file, are attributed to the Client being unable to submit a query with an undefined address. After adding a guarding condition to the dynamic model of the Client to check for undefined Archive Server addresses, the expansion has no deadlocks.

Next, the specification of the entire system is composed with a revised test process updated to reflect constants PCS and STORET denoting specific Archive Server instantiations as shown in Figure 10. The two valid_Retrieve_Request constants are replaced with tuples Retrieve_Request(PCS, valid_Query_Request) and Retrieve_Request(STORET, valid_Query_Request), introduced during refinement of the high-level ENFORMS *Retrieve Data* service (Figure 9). If all paths lead to success, then we can say that the original high-level specification and the more detailed refinement are testing equivalent (with respect to this simple test).

However, the initial results from TOPO/LOLA are discouraging, with 30 deadlocks and no successes. By examining the log file, these results seem to be due to the incompleteness of the specification. New operations introduced during the service refinement design step (Figure 2(a), Step 6b) were not further defined with equations, which caused deadlocks. After these equations are introduced, the results are slightly improved with 2 successes, but unfortunately we now have 80 deadlocks as more paths have been explored. After examining the log file, unraveling paths to deadlock, and performing interactive simulation, some deadlocks are determined to be caused by the Client having an outdated copy of the server table. In the current design, the Client acquires a copy of the server table only during initialization. Thus, if it acquires a copy of the server table prior to the registration of any Archive Server, then the Client must return an undefined query result because, to its knowledge, there is no available Archive Server. The simple solution adopted in this case study is to let the Client obtain an up-to-date copy of the server table before any at-

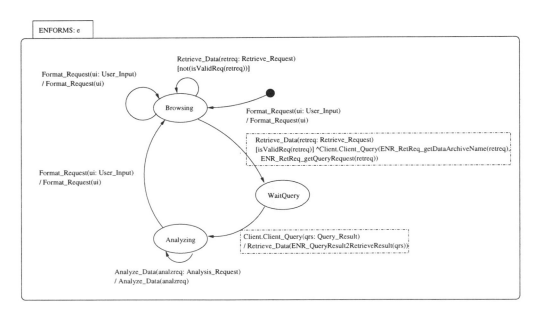

Figure 9. Dynamic model for refined ENFORMS system

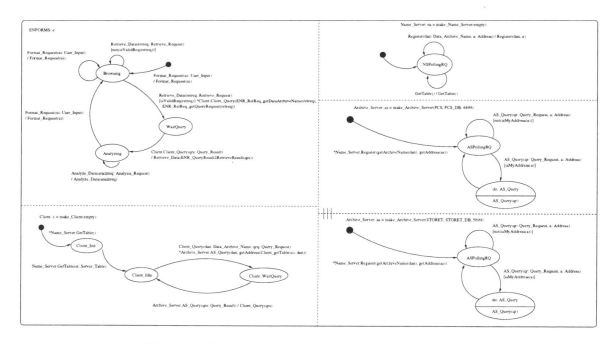

Figure 10. Dynamic models composed concurrently

tempt to retrieve data from an **Archive Server**. The revised dynamic model for the **Client** is shown in Figure 11, where revisions are indicated by shaded states or dotted rectangles outlining transition text.

After revising the **Client** design, the test expansion is repeated. This time, among the 160 execution paths explored with TOPO/LOLA 112 reach *success* while 48 lead the test process into deadlock. Further investigation shows that all 48 deadlocks can be attributed to the abstraction of internal computations. That is, if the **Client** attempts to query an **Archive Server** before that **Archive Server** has registered, then the **Client** will not be able to make the connection and must return an undefined query result. In this context, the client-server design of the refined ENFORMS system realizes the *Retrieve Data* service over distributed archives transparently.

4. Analysis discussion

During the requirements phase, TOPO and LOLA were useful for syntax and semantics checking and interactively simulating even very abstract or "incomplete" specifications. CADP was most useful at the end of the requirements phase to obtain a picture (literally) of the system's behavior, but at the cost of requiring more details in the specifications, such as explicitly denoting which operators are constructors.

During the design phase, again TOPO and LOLA proved useful at the beginning, when ideas were preliminary and many details were omitted. CADP was most useful at the intermediate stage, when individual objects were fairly well-defined and were ready for composition into the larger system, and towards the end of the study, when we examined the refined ENFORMS system under test.

From our experiences, TOPO and LOLA were most useful at the earlier stages of both phases of model development, when specifications are more abstract with less detail. As a phase moves forward, gradually more detail becomes available as decisions are made based on simulation results or new requirements or domain information. CADP needed more details up front than TOPO and LOLA, making it more suitable to use towards the end of a phase, which in this investigation meant (1) the end of the requirements phase, (2) the end of describing individual aggregate objects prior to their composition, and (3) the end of composing the aggregate objects concurrently.

Finally, we found the LTS minimization and graphing capability of CADP to be quite useful in obtaining a visual overview of the system, a feature that is not available in TOPO. Additionally, CADP provides counterexamples for deadlock, the ability to search for patterns of events in an LTS, and the potential for checking temporal logic properties against an LTS.

We found that while the tools do have some feature overlap, largely they offer tradeoffs in the way that they accomplish the overlapped tasks. Additionally, they each have some features not found in the other, so, in general, they can be effectively used in a complementary fashion.

5. Conclusions

This paper described a number of automated analyses that can be applied to object-oriented diagrams whose syntax and semantics have been formalized [1, 17, 19]. A specific process [18] is described to construct and refine the object-oriented diagrams. The formalization rules for the diagrams enable the diagrams to be analyzed via their corresponding formal specifications using a number of automated techniques, including behavior simulation and state-based model exploration. An overarching goal of the project is to enlarge the user community for the resulting software development technique. As a result, a commonly used object-oriented language was selected as the target of the formalization process, and commonly used specification languages whose semantics matched the intent of the informal models were selected. The formal specification languages also had to have automated tool support. The paper focused on the different analysis techniques that are applicable to the specifications of the diagrams that facilitate diagram checking and refinement. Behavior simulation is also enabled through the formalization rules, thereby also facilitating requirements capture.

Current and future investigations are focused on exploring additional analysis techniques that can be applied to the formalized diagrams, with a particular emphasis on design refinement capabilities and code generation. We are also exploring the remainder of the UML notation, where our presumption is that different application domains will require different process models for using the UML notation [9]. We are also continuing to refine our prototype framework [4] that supports the graphical construction of the object-oriented models and generates the corresponding formal specifications according to our formalization rules. In particular, we are exploring how the results from the analysis tools can be automatically processed to provide further feedback for refining and correcting the diagrams.

References

[1] R. H. Bourdeau and B. H. C. Cheng. A formal semantics of object models. *IEEE Trans. on Software Engineering*, 21(10):799–821, October 1995.
[2] R. H. Bourdeau, B. H. C. Cheng, and G. C. Gannod. A requirements analysis report for a regional decision support system. Technical Report MSU-CPS-94-70, Michigan State University, Department of Computer Science, A714 Wells Hall, East Lansing, 48824, November 1994.

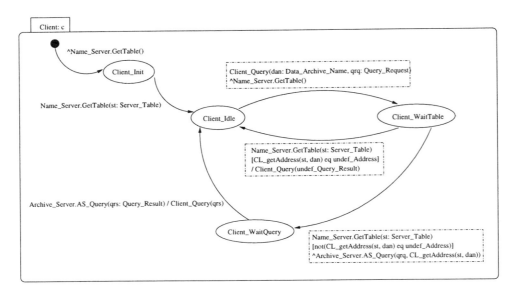

Figure 11. Modified Client model (shading/dotted lines indicate revisions)

[3] R. H. Bourdeau, B. H. C. Cheng, and B. Pijanowski. A regional information system for environmental data analysis. *Photogrammetric Engineering & Remote Sensing*, 62(7), July 1996. Special issue on "Remote Sensing and Global Environmental Change".

[4] B. H. C. Cheng, E. Y. Wang, and R. H. Bourdeau. A graphical environment for formally developing object-oriented software. In *Proc. of IEEE 6th International Conference on Tools with Artificial Intelligence*, November 1994.

[5] J.-C. Fernandez, H. Garavel, A. Kerbrat, R. Mateescu, L. Mounier, and M. Sighireanu. Cadp (cæsar/aldebaran development package): A protocol validation and verification toolbox. In R. Alur and T. A. Henzinger, editors, *Proceedings of the 8th Conference on Computer-Aided Verification (New Brunswick, New Jersey, USA)*, volume 1102, pages 437–440, Aug. 1996.

[6] T. C. Hartrum and P. D. Bailor. Teaching formal extensions of informal-based object-oriented analysis methodologies. In *Proc. of Computer Science Education*, pages 389–409, 1994.

[7] F. Hayes and D. Coleman. Coherent models for object-oriented analysis. In *Proceedings of OOPSLA '91*, pages 171–183, 1991.

[8] R. R. Lutz. Targeting safety-related errors during software requirements analysis. In *SIGSOFT'93 Symposium on the Foundations of Software Engineering*, 1993.

[9] W. E. McUmber and B. H. Cheng. UML-based analysis of embedded systems using a mapping to VHDL. In *Proc. of IEEE High Assurance Software Engineering (HASE99)*, Washington, DC, November 1999.

[10] A. M. D. Moreira and R. G. Clark. Adding rigour to object-oriented analysis. *Software Engineering Journal*, 11(5):270–280, 1996.

[11] S. Pavon and M. Llamas. The testing functionalities of LOLA. In J. Quemada, J. A. Manas, and E. Vazquez, editors, *Formal Description Techniques*, volume III, pages 559–562. IFIP, Elsevier Science B.V. (North-Holland)., 1991.

[12] J. Quemada, S. Pavon, and A. Fernandez. State exploration by transformation with LOLA. In *Workshop on Automatic Verification Methods for Finite State Systems*, Grenoble, June 1989.

[13] Rational Software Corporation, Santa Clara, CA 95051-0951. *UML Notation Guide*, 1.0 edition, January 1997.

[14] J. Rumbaugh, M. Blaha, W. Premerlani, F. Eddy, and W. Lorensen. *Object-Oriented Modeling and Design*. Prentice Hall, Englewood Cliffs, New Jersey, 1991.

[15] M. Shroff and R. B. France. Towards a Formalization of UML Class Structures in Z. In *Proceedings Twenty-First Annual International Computer Software and Applications Conference (COMPSAC'97)*, pages 646–651. IEEE Comput. Soc, Los Alamitos, CA, USA, aug 1997.

[16] E. Y. Wang. *Integrating Informal and Formal Approaches to Object-Oriented Analysis and Design*. PhD thesis, Michigan State University, Department of Computer Science, March 1998. Also available as Department of Computer Science, Michigan State University Technical Report, MSU-CPS-98-44.

[17] E. Y. Wang and B. H. C. Cheng. Formalizing and integrating the functional model into object-oriented design. In *Proc. of International Conference on Software Engineering and Knowledge Engineering*, June 1998. Nominated for Best Paper.

[18] E. Y. Wang and B. H. C. Cheng. A rigorous object-oriented design process. In *Proc. of International Conference on Software Process*, Naperville, Illinois, June 1998.

[19] E. Y. Wang, H. A. Richter, and B. H. C. Cheng. Formalizing and integrating the dynamic model within OMT. In *IEEE Proceedings of the 19th International Conference on Software Engineering*, pages 45–55, Boston, MA, May 1997. IEEE.

Deadlock Detection of EFSMs Using Simultaneous Reachability Analysis *

Bengi Karaçalı[†], Kuo-Chung Tai, Mladen A. Vouk
Department of Computer Science
North Carolina State University, Box 7534
Raleigh, NC 27695-7534 USA
{bkaraca,kct,vouk}@eos.ncsu.edu

Abstract

Simultaneous reachability analysis (SRA) is a recently proposed technique to alleviate the state space explosion problem in reachability analysis of concurrent systems. Its goal is to reduce the number of generated states while guaranteeing the detection of certain types of faults in the system such as deadlock and unexecutable transitions. The main idea of SRA is to allow a global transition in a reachability graph to contain a set of local transitions (i.e. transitions of individual processes) such that the state reached by the global transition is independent of the execution order of the associated local transitions. In this paper, we show how to apply the SRA approach to systems modeled as extended finite state machines (EFSMs) with multiple ports. Empirical results from applying our SRA algorithm to the dining philosophers problem indicate that our algorithm reduces the number of generated states and the computation time by about 90%.

1. Introduction

Reachability analysis has been a successful approach to verification and testing of communication protocols [10]. It involves systematically generating reachable states of a specified system. Various properties of a system can be verified using reachability analysis. Unfortunately the state explosion problem restricts the scalability of reachability analysis since in the worst case the number of generated states grows roughly exponentially with the number of processes in the system [10].

In order to scale reachability analysis, various relief strategies have been proposed. Some of these strategies are based on making restrictive assumptions about the structure

or the topology of the system as described in [9] and references therein. Other methods simplify the model while preserving certain properties [3]. Compositional methods apply reachability analysis in a modular fashion [8].

In recent years, two major approaches, partial-order reduction and simultaneous reachability analysis, have been investigated for alleviating the state explosion problem. The goal of these approaches is to reduce the number of states generated during reachability analysis while guaranteeing the detection of certain types of faults in the system.

Partial order methods exploit parallelism in a system [5], [12]. The basic idea of partial-order reduction can be explained by the following example. Consider a global state G =$(s_1, s_2, ..., s_n)$ of an n-process concurrent system, where s_i, $1 \leq i \leq n$, is a local state of process P_i. Assume that each s_i, $1 \leq i \leq n$, has exactly one local transition to another local state s_i' of P_i and that these n local transitions are enabled (i.e., eligible for execution) and independent from each other (i.e., the result of executing these transitions is independent of execution order). The traditional reachability analysis generates $n!$ different interleavings of these n transitions from G to $G'=(s_1', s_2', ..., s_n')$. According to partial-order reduction, only one of these $n!$ sequences of n transitions is generated from G to G'.

Simultaneous reachability analysis (SRA) differs from partial-order reduction in that the former allows a global transition in a reachability graph to contain a set of independent local transitions. Consider the example mentioned earlier. According to SRA, only one global transition is generated from G to G', with the global transition being the set of these n local transitions. Ozdemir and Ural developed an SRA-based reachability graph generation algorithm for the communicating finite state machine (CFSM) model [9]. Later Schoot and Ural improved the earlier algorithm [14] and showed that combining their new algorithm with partial order reduction techniques improves the performance of partial-order reduction for the verification of CFSM-based concurrent systems [13].

In this paper, we apply the SRA approach to a concurrent

---

*This work was supported in part by an IBM fellowship and NSF grants CCR-9320992 and CCR-9901004
[†] Corresponding author

system modeled as a set of multi-port extended finite state machines (EFSMs). An EFSM is an augmentation of a regular finite state machine with local variables. In our multi-port EFSM model, each EFSM contains a set of ports for receiving different types of messages. The concept of multiple ports is used in distributed programming languages like Ada and specification languages like Lotos and Estelle [1], [11]. Software for client/server computing and internet computing is often designed with multiple ports [1]. Our multi-port EFSM model is more expressive than the CFSM model and facilitates the specification of complex concurrent programs.

SRA for EFSMs is more difficult than that for CFSMs due to the existence of race conditions between processes sending messages to the same port. In this paper we show an SRA-based reachability graph generation algorithm for a system of EFSMs and prove that the generated reachability graph, called simultaneous reachability graph (SRG), contains the same set of deadlock states as the traditional reachability graph for the same system.

In Section 2, we present the background information, namely the multi-port EFSM model and reachability analysis definitions. In Section 3, we define the dependency relation for the multi-port EFSM model. In Section 4, we present our algorithm for generating the SRG for a system of EFSMs and show theoretical properties of this algorithm. In Section 5, we provide the empirical results of applying our SRA-based algorithm to the dining philosophers problem. Finally we present our conclusions in Section 6.

2. Preliminaries

2.1. Multi-Port EFSM Model

An extended finite state machine (EFSM) is a finite state machine in which each transition is associated with a predicate defined over a set of variables. We consider a set of EFSMs that communicate with each other by sending and receiving messages, where each EFSM contains a set of ports for receiving different types of messages. We refer to this EFSM model as the multi-port EFSM model. Compared to the EFSM models in [7],[2], the multi-port EFSM model has more expressive power.

Our multi-port EFSM model assumes asynchronous message passing, which involves nonblocking send and blocking receive. A port of an EFSM can receive messages from one or more other EFSMs. Messages that arrive at a port are received in FIFO order. Each port has a bounded queue. The message delivery scheme between EFSMs is assumed to be causal-ordering, meaning that if a message is sent before another message (from the same or different EFSMs) to the same port of an EFSM, then the former arrives at the port before the latter [1].

Formally, a multi-port EFSM P is defined as an 8-tuple $P = < Q, q_0, V, T, I, O, F, \delta >$, where

1. Q: Set of states of P
2. q_0: Initial state of P
3. V: Set of local variables of P
4. T: Set of port names of P
5. I: Set of input messages for all ports of P
6. O: Set of output messages of P
7. F: Set of final states of P, $F \subset Q$
8. δ: Set of transitions of P

Each transition $t \in \delta$ contains the following information:

- head(t): the start state of t, head(t)$\in Q$.
- tail(t): the end state of t, tail(t)$\in Q$.
- t_{pred}: a predicate involving variables in V, constants, and arithmetic/relational/boolean operations.
- t_{comp}: a computation block, which is a sequence of computational statements (assignment, loop, etc) involving the received message, variables in V, and constants.
- ?$pn.m$: receive operation, where $pn \in T$ is a port name in P and m an input message in I. in_port(t)={pn} and in_msg(t)={m}.
- !$pn.m$: send operation, where $pn \in T$ is a port name of another EFSM and m an output message in O. out_port(t)={pn} and out_msg(t)={m}.

Determining whether transition t of process P is executable (or enabled) when head(t) is the current state of P involves evaluating t_{pred} and checking the queue for port in_port(t). If t_{pred} is true and the queue is not empty, then t is said to be executable or enabled, meaning that t is eligible for being selected for execution. Otherwise, t is said to be disabled. If t is selected for execution, the first message in the queue for in_port(t) is removed, t_{comp} is executed, the send operation associated with t is performed, and tail(t) becomes the current state of P. Figure 1 illustrates a transition t with in_port(t)={r1} and out_port(t)={r2}. Note that at most three of the following parts may be missing in a transition: the predicate, receive operation, computational block and send operation. If both the predicate and the receive operation are missing, the transition is said to be a spontaneous transition.

Figure 1. General Format of a Transition

In this paper, we analyze a system of multi-port EFSMs $P_1, P_2, \ldots P_n$, with each P_i, $1 \leq i \leq n$ denoted by $< Q_i, q_{i,0}, V_i, T_i, I_i, O_i, F_i, \delta_i >$. Each EFSM P_i is also referred to as a process. $q_{i,0}$ denotes the initial state of P_i and $q_{i,j}$ the jth state of P_i. $T_{i,j}$ refers to the jth port of P_i. For a transition t, proc(t) is the process that contains transition t.

A transition sequence of a system of multi-port EFSMs is composed of zero or more transitions of these EFSMs. Length of a transition sequence ω, denoted by $|\omega|$, is the number of transitions in ω. For example, $\omega = t_1 t_2 \ldots t_n$ has $|\omega| = n$. For any two transition sequences σ and ω, $\sigma\omega$ denotes the concatenation of the two sequences. For a transition sequence $\omega = t_1 t_2 \ldots t_k$ and for any $i, 0 \leq i \leq k$, $t_1 \ldots t_i$ is called a prefix of ω. A permutation of a set of transitions is a sequence of these transitions in arbitrary order. For a set T of transitions, perm(T)={ all permutations of transitions in T }. $|T|$ denotes the cardinality of T. If $|T| = n$, then $|$perm(T)$|=n!$.

2.2. Reachability Analysis

Reachability analysis of a system of multi-port EFMSs involves systematic enumeration of all reachable global states from the initial global state of the system. The analysis produces a reachability graph whose states are checked for different types of faults.

```
Generate_RG(M: A set of multi-port EFSMs)
RG: Reachability graph, RG = (V, E), V: nodes, E: edges
open: Set of unexplored nodes of RG
V ← ∅, E ← ∅
Generate the initial global state and put it in open
while open ≠ ∅
    G ← the most recently added global state in open
    remove G from open
    if G is a deadlock state, report deadlock
    else if G is a nonprogress state, report nonprogress
    else G_edges ← Generate_RGEdges(G)
        for each e ∈ G_edges
            determine successor G' of G along edge e
            if G' ∉ V
                V ← V ∪ {G'} and open ← open ∪ {G'}
            E ← E ∪ {e}
return RG
```

Figure 2. Algorithm Generate_RG

Definition 2.1 *A global state G of a system M of multi-port EFSMs contains the local state, the values of local variables and the contents of port queues for each process in M. The initial global state of M, denoted as G_0, contains the initial local states, initial local variable values and empty port queues for all processes in M. A final global state of M contains a final local state and empty port queues for each process in M.*

Definition 2.2 *Let G be a global state in the reachability graph of a system M of multi-port EFSMs. G' is an immediate sequential successor of G, denoted by $G \xrightarrow{t}_M G'$, if t is an enabled transition of G and G' is the state reached by t from G. $G \xrightarrow{t}_M G'$ is denoted by $G \xrightarrow{t} G'$, if M is implied.*

Definition 2.3 *A sequential successor G' of G, reached by a transition sequence ω, is denoted by $G \xrightarrow{\omega} *G'$.*

Definition 2.4 *The reachability graph (RG) of a system of multi-port EFSMs is the set of all global states sequentially reachable from the initial global state of the system.*

Definition 2.5 *A non-final state G in the RG of a system of multi-port EFSMs is said to be a nonprogress state if G has no executable transitions. G is said to be a deadlock state if it is a nonprogress state and all port queues for all processes are empty.*

Algorithm Generate_RG shown in Figure 2 constructs the reachability graph for a set of EFSMs in depth first fashion and performs on-the-fly analysis for detecting deadlock and nonprogress states. Global states that are discovered and not yet expanded are maintained in a set called *open*. The initial global state is placed in *open* at the beginning of the algorithm. At each step, the last global state added to *open* is expanded, unless it is a deadlock or nonprogress state; in which case, the encountered fault is reported. Expanding a state G involves generating the edges and successors of G. Function Generate_RGEdges(G) returns a set of edges where each edge corresponds to an enabled transition of G. The algorithm stops when all reachable states are expanded.

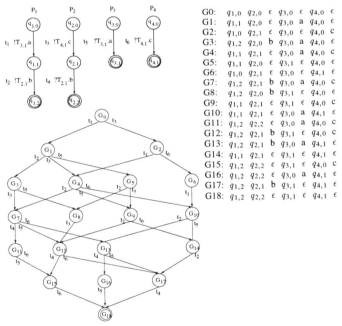

G0:	$q_{1,0}$ $q_{2,0}$ ϵ $q_{3,0}$ ϵ $q_{4,0}$ ϵ
G1:	$q_{1,1}$ $q_{2,0}$ ϵ $q_{3,0}$ a $q_{4,0}$ ϵ
G2:	$q_{1,0}$ $q_{2,1}$ ϵ $q_{3,0}$ ϵ $q_{4,0}$ c
G3:	$q_{1,2}$ $q_{2,0}$ b $q_{3,0}$ a $q_{4,0}$ ϵ
G4:	$q_{1,1}$ $q_{2,1}$ ϵ $q_{3,0}$ a $q_{4,0}$ c
G5:	$q_{1,1}$ $q_{2,0}$ ϵ $q_{3,1}$ ϵ $q_{4,0}$ ϵ
G6:	$q_{1,0}$ $q_{2,1}$ ϵ $q_{3,0}$ ϵ $q_{4,1}$ ϵ
G7:	$q_{1,2}$ $q_{2,1}$ b $q_{3,0}$ a $q_{4,0}$ c
G8:	$q_{1,2}$ $q_{2,0}$ b $q_{3,1}$ ϵ $q_{4,0}$ ϵ
G9:	$q_{1,1}$ $q_{2,1}$ ϵ $q_{3,1}$ ϵ $q_{4,0}$ c
G10:	$q_{1,1}$ $q_{2,1}$ ϵ $q_{3,0}$ ϵ $q_{4,1}$ ϵ
G11:	$q_{1,2}$ $q_{2,2}$ ϵ $q_{3,0}$ a $q_{4,0}$ c
G12:	$q_{1,2}$ $q_{2,1}$ b $q_{3,1}$ ϵ $q_{4,0}$ c
G13:	$q_{1,2}$ $q_{2,1}$ b $q_{3,0}$ a $q_{4,1}$ ϵ
G14:	$q_{1,1}$ $q_{2,1}$ ϵ $q_{3,1}$ ϵ $q_{4,1}$ ϵ
G15:	$q_{1,2}$ $q_{2,2}$ ϵ $q_{3,1}$ ϵ $q_{4,0}$ c
G16:	$q_{1,2}$ $q_{2,2}$ ϵ $q_{3,0}$ a $q_{4,1}$ ϵ
G17:	$q_{1,2}$ $q_{2,1}$ b $q_{3,1}$ ϵ $q_{4,1}$ ϵ
G18:	$q_{1,2}$ $q_{2,2}$ ϵ $q_{3,1}$ ϵ $q_{4,1}$ ϵ

Figure 3. Example 1

An example system of processes P_1, P_2, P_3, and P_4 is shown in Figure 3. The transitions are labeled with numbers for ease of reference. Final states are designated with double circles. For simplicity, each process $P_i, 1 \leq i \leq 4$, has no local variables and its transitions contain only send and receive operations. The RG of the example system and the details of all global states are also in the figure. The format of a global state in this example is <local state of P_1, local state of P_2, queue contents for $T_{2,1}$, local state of P_3, queue contents for $T_{3,1}$, local state of P_4, queue contents for $T_{4,1}$>.

3. Dependency Relation

Dependency between transitions is a fundamental concept in partial-order reduction. According to [4], a valid dependency relation involves two transitions, while a valid conditional dependency relation involves a global state and two transitions. For the multi-port EFSM model, below we define a valid conditional dependency relation.

Definition 3.1 *Let G be a global state of a system M of EFSMs. Two transitions t_1 and t_2 of M are said to be independent wrt G if:*

1.t_1 and t_2 are enabled transitions of G
2.proc(t_1)$\neq$proc(t_2) and
3.either out_port(t_1)$\neq$out_port(t_2) or out_port(t_1)=out_port(t_2)= ϵ

t_1 and t_2 are said to be dependent wrt G otherwise. If t_1 and t_2 do not satisfy condition (2), they are said to be process-dependent. If t_1 and t_2 do not satisfy condition (3), they are said to be race-dependent.

Let S be a set of enabled transitions at a global state G of a system of EFSMs. If no two transitions of S are process-dependent (race-dependent), then S is said to be process-independent (race-independent) at G. S is said to be an independent transition set at G, if it is process-independent and race-independent at G. S is said to be a maximal independent transition set at G, if G has no enabled transition t, $t \notin S$ such that $S \cup \{t\}$ is an independent transition set at G. In the remainder of this paper, when we mention independent transitions wrt a global state, we often omit *"wrt a global state"* if this global state is implied.

Assume that transitions t_1 and t_2 are independent wrt global state G. If $G \xrightarrow{t_1 t_2} *G'$, then $G \xrightarrow{t_2 t_1} *G'$. Thus, the execution of t_1 at G cannot disable t_2 and vice versa. This property can be generalized to three or more independent transitions wrt a global state, as shown below.

Lemma 3.1 *Let G be a global state of a system M of EFSMs. Let T be an independent set at G. Let σ and ω be two permutations of T. If $G \xrightarrow{\sigma} *G'$, then $G \xrightarrow{\omega} *G'$.*

Definition 3.2 *Let G be a global state of a system M of EFSMs. Let t be a transition of M and let $\omega = t_1 t_2 \ldots t_k$ be a transition sequence of M, where $G_1 \xrightarrow{t_1} G_2 \ldots G_k \xrightarrow{t_k} G'$ and $G = G_1$. t and ω are said to be independent wrt G if t and t_i, $1 \leq i \leq k$ are independent wrt G_i.*

Lemma 3.2 *Let G be a global state of a system M of EFSMs. Let t be a transition of M and ω be a transition sequence of M. If $G \xrightarrow{\omega t} *G'$ and t and ω are independent wrt G, then $G \xrightarrow{t\omega} *G'$.*

Lemma 3.3 *Let G be a global state of a system M of EFSMs. Let σ and ω be transition sequences of M. If $G \xrightarrow{\omega\sigma} *G'$ and $\forall t$ in σ, t and ω are independent wrt G, then $G \xrightarrow{\sigma\omega} *G'$.*

The race set of a transition t is defined as the set of transitions that send a message to the same port as t. Formally, $race(t) = \{t' | out\_port(t') = out\_port(t), t \neq t'$, and t and t' are transitions of different processes$\}$. A transition is referred to as a *racing transition* if its race set is not empty. A port is said to be a race port if two or more EFSMs have transitions with this port as out_port. Thus, for a racing transition t, $out\_port(t)$ is a race port. Let t be a racing transition at a global state G. Since the definition of race(t) is coarse, t does not necessarily have a race with each transition in race(t) at G or at any other state reachable from G. In order to make the set of possible racing transitions more precise, it is necessary to apply some program analysis techniques.

4. Simultaneous Reachability Analysis of EFSMs

In this section we present the simultaneous reachability analysis of multi-port EFSMs. Simultaneous reachability analysis is conducted on a reduced reachability graph referred to as simultaneous reachability graph (SRG). Any global state of SRG is also a global state of RG. The initial state of SRG is that of RG, namely G_0.

Definition 4.1 *An immediate simultaneous successor G' of G reached by an independent transition set T at G, is denoted by $G \xrightarrow{T} G'$, where $G \xrightarrow{\omega} *G'$ and $\omega \in perm(T)$.*

Definition 4.2 *A simultaneous successor G' of G reached by a sequence of transition sets $T_1 T_2 \ldots T_l$ is denoted by $G \xrightarrow{T_1 T_2 \ldots T_l} *G'$.*

An edge of an SRG state G corresponds to a set of transitions independent wrt G. G_{edges} denotes the set of edges of G. G_{trans} denotes the set of transitions of processes at G. Enabled and disabled transitions of G are referred to as $G_{enabled}$ and $G_{disabled}$, respectively.

4.1. Basic Approach to SRG Generation

The construction of a simultaneous reachability graph is similar to that of a traditional reachability graph except for the way edges are generated and incorporated into the graph. Figure 2 shows an algorithm for constructing the RG of a finite system of multi-port EFSMs. This algorithm is used for SRG generation with the following two modifications. First, Generate_RGEdges(G) is replaced with algorithm Generate_SRGEdges(G), which returns a set of SRG edges of G. Second, determining the successor G' along edge e involves executing transitions in e simultaneously. The transitions in e can be executed in any order to obtain G' since they are pairwise independent wrt G.

The simultaneous reachability graph for Example 1 of Figure 3 is shown in Figure 4.

Figure 4. SRG for Example 1

The main idea of edge generation for an SRG state G is assigning independent subsets of $G_{enabled}$ to G_{edges}. In order to reach optimal reduction in reachability graph size, our basic approach is to select as large independent sets as possible from subsets of $G_{enabled}$. Following this approach maximal independent subsets of $G_{enabled}$ are constructed in two steps.

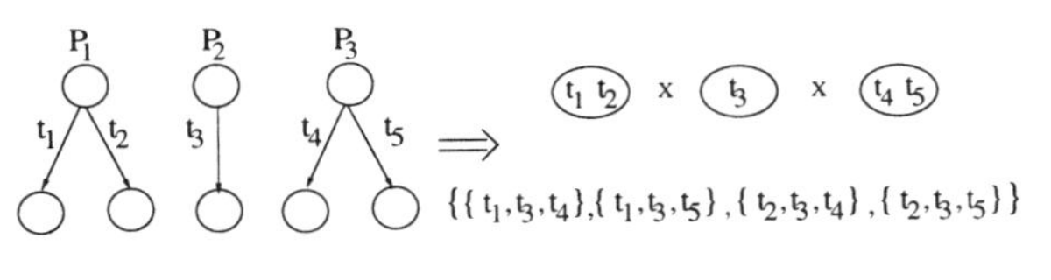

![Figure 5 diagram]

Figure 5. Example 2

In step 1, transitions of $G_{enabled}$ are grouped into sets such that each set is composed of pairwise process-dependent transitions. Thus, each such set is the set of enabled transitions of a process at G. The Cartesian product of the sets of pairwise process-dependent transitions yields maximal process-independent sets. Figure 5 illustrates this computation for the three processes of Example 2.

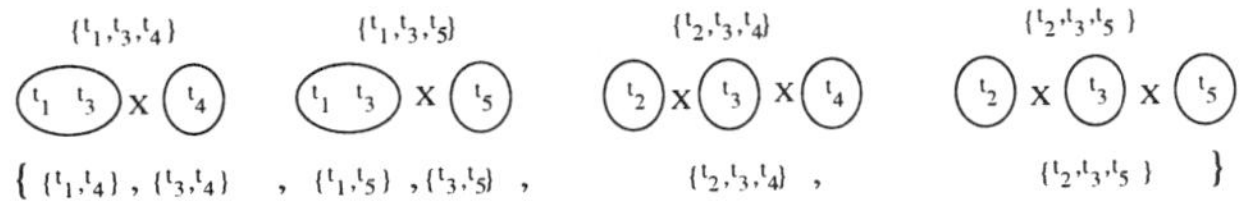

![Figure 6 diagram]

Figure 6. Maximal Independent Sets for Ex. 2

Since maximal process-independent sets at a global state G may contain race-dependent transitions, each set S produced in step 1 is further processed in step 2. This processing involves first grouping transitions in S into sets such that each set is composed of transitions with the same out_port.

The Cartesian product of these sets yields the maximal independent subsets of S. The union of the sets produced in step 2 for each set produced in step 1 for G yields G_{edges}. Figure 6 illustrates step 2 of maximal independent set computation for the processes in Example 2. We assume that transitions in Example 2 have different out_ports except t_1 and t_3.

The above approach to generating G_{edges} from maximal independent subsets of $G_{enabled}$ is incomplete due to the existence of so called potentially executable transitions and racing transitions of successor states. Below we discuss these two types of transitions and show how to modify our basic approach accordingly. Then we present the complete algorithm Generate_SRGEdges.

4.2. Potentially Executable Transitions

A disabled transition t of process P_i at a global state G is said to be a potentially executable transition if P_i has at least one enabled transition at G and t_{pred}=true. According to the basic approach described in Section 4.1, every transition set produced by step 1 contains one enabled transition of P_i. This creates a problem if transition t needs to be executed in order to detect some types of faults. To solve this problem, we need to delay execution of P_i until t becomes enabled. This can be accomplished as follows. For every transition set S, produced by step 1, that contains an enabled transition t' of P_i, then $S \setminus \{t'\}$ is also produced by step 1.

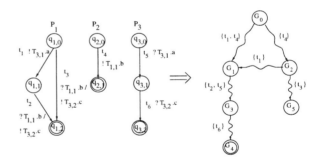

Figure 7. Example 3

The term *"potentially executable transitions"* was defined in [9]. In [5] the presence of potentially executable transitions is referred to as confusion. Example 3 in Figure 7 illustrates potentially executable transitions. At G_0, transitions t_1 and t_4 are enabled and t_3 is a potentially executable transition of P_1. So G_0 has 2 global edges $\{t_1, t_4\}$ and $\{t_4\}$. The latter edge ensures that there is a path from G_0 in which P_1 does not make any progress. Note that G_5 is a nonprogress state. If G_0 did not have edge $\{t_4\}$, state G_5 would not be generated.

In order to generate extra edges that delay the execution of processes with potentially executable transitions we modify step 1 of maximal independent set computation for

G, described in Section 4.1, as follows: After grouping the enabled transitions of G into sets of pairwise process-dependent transitions, we add a special transition, t_{null}, to the sets formed by enabled transitions of a process with a potentially executable transition. After this modification, the Cartesian product of these sets may produce transition sets containing t_{null}. If a transition set in the Cartesian product contains only t_{null}, then we ignore this transition set. This situation occurs only if each process at G having enabled transitions also has potentially executable transitions. If a transition set in the Cartesian product contains t_{null} as well as other transitions, then we delete t_{null} from this set. This situation occurs when there exists at least one process at G that has both enabled and potentially executable transitions. According to this modified step 1, if a generated transition set S has t from a process with a potentially executable transition, then $S \setminus \{t\}$ is also generated by step 1. Note that the use of t_{null} is to simplify the construction of extra edges due to potentially executable transitions.

In Example 3, shown in Figure 7, G_0 has $\{t_1\}$ and $\{t_4\}$ as process-independent sets. $\{t_1\}$ becomes $\{t_1, t_{null}\}$ due to the existence of a potentially executable transition t_3. Computation of $\{t_1, t_{null}\} \times \{t_4\}$ yields $\{\{t_1, t_4\}, \{t_{null}, t_4\}\}$. After the removal of t_{null}, step 1 produces $\{\{t_1, t_4\}, \{t_4\}\}$.

4.3. Racing Transitions of Successor States

An enabled transition t of process P_i at a global state G may have a race with a transition t' of process P_j, $j \neq i$, at a global state G' such that G' is reachable from G. According to step 2 of the basic edge generation approach described in Section 4.1, t' is not taken into consideration in the construction of G_{edges}. As a result, the generated transition sequences from G do not explore the situation where t' occurs before t. Thus, the basic approach fails to detect faults that happen in transition sequences from G in which t' occurs before t. t' is referred to as a racing transition of successor states of G.

Consider Example 4 shown in Figure 8. Transitions t_1 and t_4 have a race since they send messages to port $T_{3,1}$. We need to generate paths in which t_1 occurs before t_4 and vice versa. However, t_1 is executable at G_0 while t_4 is not even a transition of some process at G_0. In order to construct the path on which t_4 happens before t_1, we need an edge in which t_1 is not executed. In Example 4, the enabled transitions of G_0 are t_1 and t_3. Since t_1 is a racing transition, we select sets $\{t_1, t_3\}$ and $\{t_3\}$. Global state G_2 has enabled transitions t_1 and t_4, which have race-dependency. Hence, these transitions are selected on separate edges.

In order to handle racing transitions of successor states, the entire system needs to be considered to identify race ports. At a global state G if there exists an enabled transition t with out_port(t) being a race port, there may be

transition seqences from G_0 in which a transition racing with t occurs before t. In order to guarantee the generation of such sequences from G, we need to generate edges of G that do not contain t. Hence, for each set S generated in step 2 that contains t, we also generate $S \setminus \{t\}$.

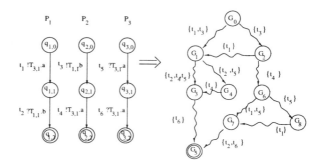

Figure 8. Example 4

In order to generate the extra edges to handle race transitions of successor states, we modify step 2 of maximal independent set computation for a global state G. Recall that, step 1 generates maximal process-independent sets wrt G, which are further processed in step 2 to eliminate race-dependency. When the transitions of each S from step 1 are grouped according to their out_ports, we add t_{null} to each set that corresponds to a race port. After this modification, the Cartesian product of these sets may produce transition sets containing t_{null}. If a transition set in the Cartesian product contains only t_{null}, then we ignore this transition set. This situation occurs only if each transition in S is a racing transition. If a transition set in the Cartesian product contains t_{null} as well as other transitions, then we delete t_{null} from this set. This situation occurs when there exists at least one racing transition. According to this modified step 2, if a generated transition set E has a racing transition t, then $E \setminus \{t\}$ is also generated by step 2.

In Example 4, shown in Figure 8, G_0 has $\{t_1, t_3\}$ as the maximal process-independent set. Grouping of the transitions in this set according to ports yields $\{t_1\}$ for port $T_{3,1}$ and $\{t_3\}$ for port $T_{1,1}$. Since t_3 is a racing transition, the set for port $T_{3,1}$ is modified to $\{t_1, t_{null}\}$. $\{t_3\} \times \{t_1, t_{null}\}$ yields $\{\{t_1, t_3\}, \{t_{null}, t_3\}\}$. After the removal of t_{null}, G_0 has edges $\{t_1, t_3\}$ and $\{t_3\}$ as shown in Figure 8.

4.4. Algorithm Generate_SRGEdges

Our SRA-based edge generation algorithm for a global state G, called Generate_SRGEdges, is shown in Figure 9. We use set notation throughout the algorithm. Capital letters denote sets and bold face capital letters denote sets of sets. Symbols $\setminus$, $\cup$, and $\cap$ denote set minus, union and intersection, respectively. We refer to elements in a set A as A_i, $1 \leq i \leq |A|$.

Algorithm Generate_SRGEdges(G) returns a set of independent transition sets wrt G. We assume i, $1 \leq i \leq n$, is an index to processes, where n is the number of processes in the system. We assume j, $1 \leq j \leq |T|$, is an index to ports, where $|T|$ is the number of ports in the system. The algorithm consists of 2 steps. In step 1 we form a set **PD** that contains sets of enabled transitions at G that are pairwise process-dependent wrt G. In order to form **PD**, we consider each process that has enabled transitions. A_i contains enabled transition of P_i. If P_i has a potentially executable transition, then we add $A_i \cup \{t_{null}\}$ to **PD**. Otherwise we add $\{A_i\}$ to **PD**. **CP1** stores the Cartesian product of member sets of **PD**. Each set of **CP1** that is non-empty after removing t_{null} is added to **Sets1**.

In step 2, race-dependency is eliminated from each set E in **Sets1**. In this step, we form a set **RD** for each E that contains the sets of transitions of E that are pairwise race-dependent wrt G. We consider each port that appears in the out_ports of transitions of E. B_j contains transitions of E whose out_ports are T_j. If T_j is a race port, we add $B_j \cup \{t_{null}\}$ to **RD**. Otherwise, we add B_j to **RD**. **CP2** stores the Cartesian product of member sets of **RD**. Each set of **CP2** that is non-empty after removing t_{null} is added to G_{edges}.

```
Generate_SRGEdges(G:GlobalState)
 i : Index to processes in the system, 1 ≤ i ≤ n, where n is the number of processes
 j : Index to ports in the system, 1 ≤ j ≤ |T̄|, where |T| is the number of ports
 G_edges ← ∅, PD ← ∅, RD ← ∅
 // Step 1: Generate transition sets that are process-independent
 For 1 ≤ i ≤ n
     A_i ← { enabled transitions of P_i at G }                    // Process-dependency
     if A_i ≠ ∅
         if P_i has a transition t such that t ∈ G_disabled and t_pred=true
             PD ← PD ∪ {A_i ∪ {t_null}}                            // Potentially Executable Transition
         else
             PD ← PD ∪ {A_i}
 CP1 ← PD_1 × PD_2 × PD_3 × ... × PD_|PD|
 for each E ∈ CP1
     E ← E \ {t_null}
     if E ≠ ∅, Sets1 ← Sets1 ∪ {E}
 // Step 2: For each set in Sets1, generate subsets that are race-independent
 for each E ∈ Sets1
     For 1 ≤ j ≤ |T|
         B_j ← { transitions in E whose out_port is T_j }          // Race-dependency
         if B_j ≠ ∅
             if T_j is a race port
                 RD ← RD ∪ {B_j ∪ {t_null}}                        // Racing transition of successors
             else
                 RD ← RD ∪ {B_j}
     CP2 ← RD_1 × RD_2 × RD_3 × ... × RD_|RD|
     for each D ∈ CP2
         D ← D \ {t_null}
         if D ≠ ∅, G_edges ← G_edges ∪ {D}
 return G_edges
```

Figure 9. Algorithm Generate_SRGEdges

In the following discussion, **CP2(E)** and **RD(E)** denotes **CP2** and **RD**, respectively, for a transition set E as used in step 2 of algorithm Generate_SRGEdges.

Lemma 4.1 *If t is a racing transition at global state G*

and G_{edges} is produced by Generate_SRGEdges(G), then $S \in G_{edges}$, where $t \in S$, implies $S \setminus \{t\} \in G_{edges}$.

Proof: Since $S \in G_{edges}$, $\exists E \in$ **Sets1** at the end of step 1 such that $S \subseteq E$. Let $RD(E)_u \in$ **RD(E)** be the set for transitions of E whose out_port is out_port(t). Since t is a racing transition, $\{t, t_{null}\} \subseteq RD(E)_u$.

Case 1: $S \in$ **CP2(E)**. Then $S' = S \setminus \{t\} \cup \{t_{null}\} \in$ **CP2(E)**. When t_{null} is removed from S', $S' \in G_{edges}$.

Case 2: $S \cup \{t_{null}\} \in$ **CP2(E)**. Then $S' = S \cup \{t_{null}\} \setminus \{t\} \cup \{t_{null}\} \in$ **CP2(E)**. When t_{null} is removed from S', $S' = S \setminus \{t\} \in G_{edges}$.

Lemma 4.2 *Let P be a process with a potentially executable transition at global state G. Let G_{edges} be the set of edges produced by Generate_SRGEdges(G). If $S \in G_{edges}$ contains a transition t of P, then $S \setminus \{t\} \in G_{edges}$.*

Proof: *Case 1:* t is a racing transition. By Lemma 4.1, $S \setminus \{t\} \in G_{edges}$.

Case 2: t is not a racing transition. Since $S \in G_{edges}$, $\exists D \in$ **CP1** such that $S \subseteq D$. Since t is from a process with a potentially executable transition, $\exists D' = D \setminus \{t\} \cup \{t_{null}\} \in$ **CP1**. Let $E = D \setminus \{t_{null}\}$ and $E' = D' \setminus \{t_{null}\}$. Then $E' = E \setminus \{t\}$ and $\{E, E'\} \subseteq$ **Sets1**. We consider **CP2(E)** and **CP2(E')**. Since t is not racing, $\forall R \in$ **CP2(E)**, $R \setminus \{t\} \in$ **CP2(E')**. Since $S \in G_{edges}$, $S' = S \setminus \{t\} \in G_{edges}$.

Lemma 4.3 *Let M be a system of multi-port EFSMs. If G is a reachable global state in the SRG of M then G is also a reachable global state in the RG of M.*

Proof: The initial state of both RG and SRG is G_0. Let $T_1 T_2 \ldots T_k$ be the simultaneous path to G from G_0 on SRG. Let $\sigma =$ perm(T_1)perm(T_2) $\ldots$ perm(T_k). Then $G_0 \xrightarrow{\sigma} *G$.

Lemma 4.4 *Let G be a global state of a system M of EFSMs. If $G \xrightarrow{\sigma} *G'$, then $\exists (T, G'', G''', \omega, \alpha)$ such that T is a set produced by Generate_SRGEdges(G), $G \xrightarrow{T} G'' \xrightarrow{\alpha} *G'''$, $G' \xrightarrow{\omega} *G'''$, and $|\alpha| \leq |\sigma|$.*

See Appendix A for the proof of Lemma 4.4.

Lemma 4.5 *Let G be a global state of a system M of EFSMs. If $G \xrightarrow{\sigma} *G'$, then $\exists (G'', \omega, \beta)$ such that $\beta = T_1 \ldots T_k$ where T_i, $1 \leq i \leq k$, is a set produced by Generate_SRGEdges(G), $G \xrightarrow{\beta} *G''$, and $G' \xrightarrow{\omega} *G''$.*

Proof: At G, by Lemma 4.4, $\exists (T_1, G_1, G_1', \omega_1, \alpha_1)$ such that T_1 is a transition set produced by Generate_SRGEdges(G), $G \xrightarrow{T_1} G_1 \xrightarrow{\alpha_1} *G_1'$, and $G' \xrightarrow{\omega_1} *G_1'$. Note that G_1 is also an RG state by Lemma 4.3. By Lemma 4.4 at G_1 a simultaneous successor of G that uses transitions of α_1, which is a subsequence of σ, exists. By repeatedly applying Lemma 4.4 (at most $|\sigma|$ times) until α becomes empty, we can find

321

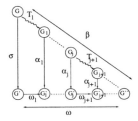

Figure 10. Illustration for Lemma 4.5

an SRG path to a state G''. Let k be the length of the SRG path, $T_1 T_2 \ldots T_k$, from G to G''. We refer to the SRG nodes on this path as $G_1, G_2 \ldots G_k$ where G_1 is reached from G by T_1, G_2 is reached from G_1 by T_2, etc.

By induction on j, the number of SRG edges from G to G'', $1 \le j \le k$, we show below that if $G \xrightarrow{\sigma} *G'$ and $G \overset{\beta}{\rightsquigarrow} *G''$ then there exists ω such that $G \xrightarrow{\sigma} *G' \xrightarrow{\omega} *G''$.

Basis: $j = 1$. By Lemma 4.4, $\exists (T_1, G_1, G_1', \omega_1, \alpha_1)$, such that T_1 is a set produced by Generate_SRGEdges(G), $G \overset{T_1}{\rightsquigarrow} G_1 \xrightarrow{\alpha_1} *G_1'$, and $G' \xrightarrow{\omega_1} *G_1'$. Since $j = 1$, $\beta = T_1$, $\alpha_1 = \epsilon$ and $G_1 = G_1'$. Then $G \overset{\beta}{\rightsquigarrow} *G''$ and $\omega = \omega_1$, where $G \xrightarrow{\sigma} *G' \xrightarrow{\omega} *G''$.

Induction: By induction hypothesis, $G \overset{T_1, T_2, \ldots T_j}{\rightsquigarrow} *G_j$ and $\exists (\alpha_j, \omega_j)$ such that $G_j \xrightarrow{\alpha_j} *G_j'$ and $G' \xrightarrow{\omega_1 \ldots \omega_j} *G_j'$. By Lemma 4.4, there exists $T_{j+1}, G_{j+1}, G_{j+1}', \omega_{j+1}, \alpha_{j+1}$ such that T_{j+1} is a set produced by Generate_SRGEdges(G), $G_{j+1} \xrightarrow{\alpha_{j+1}} *G_{j+1}'$, and $G_j' \xrightarrow{\omega_{j+1}} *G_{j+1}'$.

When $j = k$, $\beta = T_1 T_2 \ldots T_k$ and $\alpha_k = \epsilon$. Then $G'' = G_k$ and $G \overset{\beta}{\rightsquigarrow} *G''$. By induction, $\omega = \omega_1 \omega_2 \ldots \omega_k$, where $\omega_k = \epsilon$ and $G \xrightarrow{\sigma} *G' \xrightarrow{\omega} *G''$.

The theorem below shows that every deadlock state in a traditional reachability graph exists in the corresponding simultaneous reachability graph and vice versa.

Theorem 4.1 *Let M be a system of multi-port EFSMs. G is a global deadlock state in the RG of M iff G is a global deadlock state in the SRG of M.*

Proof: If Part: If G is a deadlock state in SRG then G is a deadlock state in RG. By Lemma 4.3, every global state in SRG is also a global state in RG. So the deadlock state G of SRG is also a deadlock state in RG.
Only If Part: If G is a deadlock state in RG then G is a deadlock state in SRG. Since G is reachable from G_0, by Lemma 4.5, there exists an SRG state G'' simultaneously reachable from G_0 such that $G \xrightarrow{\omega} *G''$. Since G is a deadlock state, ω must be empty. So $G = G''$.

5. Empirical Study

Our empirical study compares the cost of building the simultaneous reachability graph versus the traditional reacha-

bility graph for different versions of the the dining philosophers problem. We measure cost in terms of the graph size -global states and edges- and the graph construction time. The purpose of presenting the time figures is to show that the overhead of our algorithm is not significant. We also report the static SRA overhead which is the time required to analyze the specification and identify dependent transitions.

The EFSM specifications of the versions considered focus only on the communication events between distinct processes. Since the goal of the study is deadlock detection, we have decided to focus on interprocess communication. Consequently, all of the specified EFSMs consist of transitions with non empty in_ports and/or nonempty out_ports, where each transition represents a synchronization event.

The experiments were conducted on a SUN Ultra 5 workstation with 360Mhz and 64M memory. The modules for generating traditional and simultaneous reachability graphs were implemented in java (JDK 1.2). The EFSM specifications of the problems were provided manually.

The dining philosophers problem [3] consists of philosophers sitting at a round table. Each philosopher eats and sleeps in an alternating fashion. There is a fork between two neighboring philosophers. In order to eat, a philosopher must acquire its left and right forks. Once eating is complete, he releases both of the forks. The port names for the forks are AF(Ask_Fork) and RF(Release_Fork). AFr(Ask_Fork_Response) is used for the philosophers.

We have considered 3 versions of this problem with varying number of philosopher and fork instances. In the deadlocking version, DFD, each philosopher first picks up his left fork and then his right fork. The situation where each philosopher has acquired only his left fork constitutes a circular deadlock; none of the philosophers can continue unless the right neighbor releases the right fork. In this version, we let each philosopher eat once and then exit. The non-deadlocking version forces any two neighboring philosophers to pick their forks in reverse order. We have considered 2 non-deadlocking versions, DF and DFC. In DF, the philosophers perform exactly one eating task. In DFC, they continue the eating and sleeping cycle.

Table 1 shows the empirical results for 3 different versions of the dining philosophers problem. First column identifies the problem size in terms of the number of philosophers and the forks. The cost details of DF, DFD, and DFC are presented in the following columns. For each version, first the traditional graph (RG) size (states V, and edges E) and construction time is reported. Then the simultaneous reachability graph (SRG) size, SRA overhead and SRG construction time is reported. The last column indicates the SRA improvement, calculated as $1 - (SRG$ States$/RG$ states). We have reported only the cases for which we could build the traditional reachability graph without running out of computational resources.

Prob.Size [Phil.,Fork]	RG V	E	T (ms)	SRG V	E	O (ms)	T (ms)	%V Red.
DFD								
[2,2]	68	104	117	9	11	69	125	87%
[3,3]	679	1533	692	21	37	71	142	97%
[4,4]	6284	18820	10949	49	113	76	174	99%
[5,5]	56749	212125	159771	113	321	67	245	100%
DF								
[2,2]	65	100	110	20	25	67	120	69%
[3,3]	665	1496	651	72	144	64	191	89%
[4,4]	6011	17832	11869	680	1999	75	1039	89%
[5,5]	54429	202188	140274	2405	9745	59	3311	96%
DFC								
[2,2]	99	190	152	22	28	69	134	78%
[3,3]	1635	4922	4095	162	345	71	313	90%
[4,4]	23023	91424	214871	1127	3495	79	2386	95%

Table 1. Results for Dining Philosophers

6. Conclusion

Simultaneous reachability analysis (SRA) is a recently proposed approach to alleviating the state explosion problem in the generation of a reachability graph (RG). In this paper, we have applied the SRA approach to concurrent systems specified in the multi-port EFSM model. We have defined a dependency relation for transitions in a system of EFSMs. We have developed an SRA-based RG generation algorithm, which guarantees the detection of all deadlock states in a system of EFSMs. Also we have implemented this algorithm and carried out several empirical studies. Due to space limitations, only a small portion of our empirical results were reported in Section 5. Our empirical results indicate that the SRA approach provides significant saving in time and space in reachability analysis. It is easy to extend our SRA-based RG generation algorithm to construct RG generation tools for port-based distributed languages such as Ada, Estelle and SDL.

We are investigating possible improvements of our work on SRA for the multi-port EFSM model. One consideration is to refine the dependency relation for transitions. The motivation is that increasing the number of independent transitions allows more transitions to be included in edges for concurrent execution. This idea of refinement of dependency relation has been shown to be useful in the context of partial-order reduction [4]. Another consideration is to modify our SRA-based RG generation algorithm to eliminate unnecessary edges. In order to do so, we need to apply program analysis techniques to obtain more precise information about possible race conditions between transitions.

We will apply the SRA approach to the mailbox-based message passing model, which is more complicated than the port-based message passing model considered in this paper. The language Promela allows use of mailboxes and shared variables, and the SPIN tool has been constructed for verifying Promela programs [6]. We plan to implement an SRA-based RG generation tool for Promela.

As mentioned in the introduction section, both SRA and partial-order reduction can be used to alleviate the state explosion problem. One major advantage of the SRA approach over the partial-order reduction approach is that the former can be used with compositional techniques while the latter cannot. Compositional techniques build reachability graphs in modular fashion, reducing graphs before using them for composing larger ones. Since it is not known a priori which interleavings of transitions maybe needed in later composition steps, information on all interleavings should be retained. Given n independent transitions at a global state, partial order reduction techniques select only one of the $n!$ interleavings. While this approach is sufficient for analyzing the particular version of a concurrent program under consideration, loss of information on other possible interleavings prohibits using the generated reachability graph for compositional purpose. The SRA approach, on the other hand, maintains information on all interleavings by containing independent transitions of a global state in one edge. This property permits combining SRA with compositional methods.

A. Appendix

Figure 11. Illustration for Lemma 4.4

Proof: Given $G \xrightarrow{\sigma} *G'$. The lemma is illustrated in Figure 11. Let $\sigma = t_1 t_2 \ldots t_k$. We select a subset I of $G_{enabled}$ as follows: We start with $I = \emptyset$. We consider each t in $G_{enabled}$ such that t is in σ. Let j be the index of t in σ. If t is the first transition of a process in σ and there are no transitions racing with t in the subsequence $t_1 \ldots t_{j-1}$, $G_1 \xrightarrow{t_1} G_2 \ldots G_{j-1} \xrightarrow{t_{j-1}} G_j$ and $G = G_1$, then add t to I; t is independent with all transitions $t_i, 1 \leq i \leq j-1$ wrt G_i. Note that $|I| > 0$ since $t_1 \in I$.

When construction of I is complete, transform σ into σ' as follows: For $1 \leq i \leq |I|$, let t be the ith transition considered in I. Let j be the index of t in σ. Swap t with the transitions in the subsequence $t_1 \ldots t_{j-1}$. Let the sequence formed be σ_i. By Lemma 3.2, $G \xrightarrow{\sigma_i} G'$. Let $\sigma' = \sigma_{|I|} = \sigma_1' \sigma_2'$ where σ_1' contains transitions of I. Note that $G \xrightarrow{\sigma'} G'$.

The argument below shows that there is at least one set produced by Generate_SRGEdges that contains I. By construction, $I \subseteq G_{enabled}$ and I is an independent set wrt G. This means the transitions in I belong to different processes and hence appear in different member sets of **PD** at step 1 of algorithm Generate_SRGEdges. Then there exists at least one set in **Sets1** at the end of step 1, that contains I. Let E be that set. Since I is an independent set, no two transitions of I are race-dependent. Hence transitions of I appear in different member sets of **RD(E)** at step 2 and at least one set in **CP2(E)** contains I. Since $t_{null} \notin I$, at least one set in G_{edges} contains I. Then there exist a set T, produced by Generate_SRGEdges such that $T = I$ or $T \supset I$.

Case 1: $T = I$. Let $\omega = \epsilon$ and $G \xrightarrow{\sigma'\omega} *G'''$. Let $\alpha=\sigma'_2$. Note $|\alpha| \leq |\sigma|$. Let ρ be a permutation of T where $\rho = \sigma'_1$. Since $G \xrightarrow{T} G''$, by Lemma 3.1, $G \xrightarrow{\rho} *G''$. Since $\sigma'\omega=\rho\alpha$, $G \xrightarrow{T} G'' \xrightarrow{\alpha} *G'''$.

Case 2: $T \supset I$. This implies $\exists t$, $t \in T \setminus I$. Let T be a set generated by Generate_SRGEdges such that $T \setminus I$ is minimal. (This means $\nexists T'$ produced by the algorithm such that $|T' \setminus I| < |T \setminus I|$.) In the rest of the proof we will use contradiction on the minimality of T to show that $\forall t \in T \setminus I$, t is independent with σ' wrt G. Assume $T \setminus I$ has a transition t of process P such that t is dependent with t_i in σ' wrt G_i, where $\sigma'=t_1 \ldots t_k$, $G_1 \xrightarrow{t_1} \ldots G_i \xrightarrow{t_i} G_{i+1} \ldots G'$, $G = G_1$.

Case 2.1: σ' has no transition of P. Then t and t_i cannot be process-dependent wrt G_i; they must be race dependent wrt G_i. Then t must be a racing transition. By Lemma 4.1, $T \setminus \{t\}$ is also generated. This contradicts minimality of T.

Case 2.2: σ' has a transition of P. Let t' be the first transition of P in σ'.

Case 2.2.1: $t' \in G_{disabled}$. Then t' is a potentially executable transition. (t'_{pred}=true at G, since it is the first transition of P in σ'.) By Lemma 4.2, $T \setminus \{t\} \in G_{edges}$. This contradicts minimality of T.

Case 2.2.2: $t' \in G_{enabled}$. Let j be the index of t' in σ. Since t' is the first transition of P in σ and $t' \notin I$, during construction of I, there must be a transition t_l in σ, such that l is the index of t_l in σ, $l < j$ and t' must be dependent with t_l wrt G_l, where $t_1 \ldots t_{l-1}$ is a prefix of σ and $G \xrightarrow{t_1 \ldots t_{l-1}} *G_l$. Then t' is a race transition.

Case 2.2.2.1: t is a racing transition. By Lemma 4.1, $T \setminus \{t\} \in G_{edges}$ which contradicts minimality of T.

Case 2.2.2.2: t is not a racing transition. Let D be a set in **CP1** where $T \subseteq D$. Since t and t' are the enabled transitions of P, if $D \in$ **CP1** so is D' where $D' = D \setminus \{t\} \cup \{t'\}$. Let $E = D \setminus \{t_{null}\}$ and $E' = D' \setminus \{t_{null}\}$. At the end of step 1, $\{E, E'\} \subseteq$ **Sets1**, where $E' = E \setminus \{t\} \cup \{t'\}$. Let $RD(E)_u$ be the set in **RD(E)** that contains transitions of E with out_port out_port(t). Let $RD(E)_v$ be the set in **RD(E)** that contains transitions of E with out_port out_port(t'). Let $RD(E')_u$ and $RD(E')_v$ be the corresponding sets for E'.

If there is a set of transitions B_j in E that are racing with t' then **RD(E)**$\setminus RD(E)_u \setminus RD(E)_v \cup \{RD(E)_v \cup \{t'\}\}$=**RD(E')** where $RD(E)_u = \{t\}$ and $RD(E)_v = B_j \cup \{t_{null}\}$. If $T \in$**CP2(E)** then $T' = T \setminus \{t\} \cup \{t_{null}\} \in$**CP2(E')**. After t_{null} is removed from both T and T', $T' \in G_{edges}$. This contradicts minimality of T.

If no transition of E is racing with t', **RD(E)**$\setminus RD(E)_u =$ **RD(E')**$\setminus RD(E')_v$ where $RD(E)_u = \{t\}$ and $RD(E')_v = \{t', t_{null}\}$. If $T \in$**CP2(E)**, then $T' = T \setminus \{t\} \cup \{t_{null}\} \in$**CP2(E')**. After t_{null} is removed from both T and T', $T' \in G_{edges}$. This contradicts minimality of T.

Since in every case we have reached a contradiction, we conclude $\forall t \in T \setminus I, t$ is independent with σ' wrt G. Let ω be a permutation of $T \setminus I$ and $G \xrightarrow{\sigma'\omega} *G'''$. By Lemma 3.3, $G \xrightarrow{\omega\sigma'} *G'''$. Let ρ be a permutation of T where $\rho = \omega\sigma'_1$. Since $G \xrightarrow{T} G''$, by Lemma 3.1, $G \xrightarrow{\rho} *G''$. Let $\alpha=\sigma'_2$. Note $|\alpha| \leq |\sigma|$. Since $\omega\sigma'=\rho\alpha$, $G \xrightarrow{T} *G'' \xrightarrow{\alpha} *G'''$.

References

[1] G. R. Andrews. *Foundations of Multithreaded Parallel and Distributed Programming*. Addison-Wesley, 2000.

[2] P.-Y. M. Chu and M. T. Liu. Global state graph reduction techniques for protocol validation. In *Proc. IEEE 8th Intl. Phoenix Conf. on Computers and Comm.*, Mar. 1989.

[3] S. Duri, U. Buy, R. Devarapalli, and S. Shatz. Using state space reduction methods for deadlock analysis in ada tasking. In *Proceedings of the Intl. Symposium on Software Testing and Analysis*, pages 51–60, June 1993.

[4] P. Godefroid and D. Pirottin. Refining dependencies improves partial-order verification methods. In *Proc. (CAV'93)*, volume 697 of *LNCS*, pages 438–449, 1993.

[5] P. Godefroid and P. Wolper. Using partial orders for the efficient verification of deadlock freedom and safety properties. In *Proc. (CAV'91)*, volume 575 of *LNCS*, pages 332–342. Springer, 1992.

[6] G. J. Holzmann. The model checker SPIN. *IEEE Transactions on Software Engineering*, 23(5):279–295, May 1997.

[7] C.-M. Huang, Y.-C. Lin, and M.-J. Jang. An executable protocol test sequence generation method for EFSM-specified protocols. In *Protocol Test Systems VIII, Proc. 8th Intl. Workshop on Protocol Test Systems*, pages 20–35. Chapman & Hall, 1995.

[8] W. JenYeh and M. Young. Compositional reachability analysis using process algebra. In *Proceedings of the Symposium on Testing, Analysis, and Verification*, pages 49–59, 1991.

[9] K. Ozdemir and H. Ural. Protocol validation by simultaneous reachability analysis. *Computer Communications*, 20:772–788, 1997.

[10] M. Pezzè, R. N. Taylor, and M. Young. Graph models for reachability of concurrent programs. *ACM Trans. on Software Engineering and Methodology*, 4(2):171–213, 1995.

[11] K. Turner. *Using Formal Description Techniques*. John Wiley Sons Ltd., Amsterdam, 1993.

[12] A. Valmari. A stubborn attack on state explosion. In *Proc. (CAV'90)*, volume 531 of *LNCS*, pages 156–165, 1991.

[13] H. van der Schoot and H. Ural. An improvement of partial-order verification. *Software Testing, Verification and Reliability*, 8:83–102, 1998.

[14] H. van der Schoot and H. Ural. On improving reachability analysis for verifying progress properties of networks of CFSMs. In *Proc. 18th Intl. Distributed Computing Systems*, pages 130–137, 1998.

Session 10B

Group Communication

A Low Latency, Loss Tolerant Architecture and Protocol for Wide Area Group Communication*

Yair Amir, Claudiu Danilov, Jonathan Stanton
Department of Computer Science
The Johns Hopkins University
Baltimore, Maryland 21218 USA
{yairamir, claudiu, jonathan}@cs.jhu.edu

Abstract

Group communication systems are proven tools upon which to build fault-tolerant systems. As the demands for fault-tolerance increase and more applications require reliable distributed computing over wide area networks, wide area group communication systems are becoming very useful. However, building a wide area group communication system is a challenge. This paper presents the design of the transport protocols of the Spread wide area group communication system. We focus on two aspects of the system. First, the value of using overlay networks for application level group communication services. Second, the requirements and design of effective low latency link protocols used to construct wide area group communication. We support our claims with the results of live experiments conducted over the Internet.

Keywords—**Group Communication, Overlay Networks, Reliable Multicast, Wide Area Networks, TCP/IP.**

1 Introduction

There exist some fundamental difficulties with high-performance group communication over wide-area networks. These difficulties include:

- The characteristics (loss rates, amount of buffering) and performance (latency, bandwidth) vary widely in different parts of the network.

- The packet loss rates and latencies are significantly higher and more variable than on local area networks.

- It is not as easy to implement efficient reliability and ordering on top of the available wide area multicast mechanisms as it is on top of local area hardware broadcast and multicast. Moreover, the available best effort wide area multicast mechanisms come with significant limitations.

Group communication has been used for many years in high-availability application domains such as stock markets and command and control systems. A more recent area of interest in group communications involves wide-area applications. These include distributed simulation and distributed object applications with a large number of active objects, as well as database replication, network and service monitoring, and collaborative design and interaction.

We create a group communication service, called Spread, which provides high performance in both local area and wide area networks. Spread provides all the services of traditional group communication systems, including unreliable and reliable delivery, FIFO, causal, and total ordering, and membership services with strong semantics. Two advances allow this: the incorporation of an overlay network architecture in the group communication system, and the development of a new point-to-point protocol for the wide area network, tailored to that architecture.

Spread creates an overlay network that can impose any arbitrary network configuration including for example, point-to-multi-point, trees, rings, trees-with-subgroups and any combinations of them to adapt the system to different networking environments. Coupled with that, a new point-to-point protocol for the wide area network, the Hop protocol, is designed for this environment. The Spread architecture allows multiple protocols to be used on links between sites and within a site. To validate the usefulness of the Hop protocol for this environment, we compare it with using TCP on the wide area links between sites.

Spread is very useful for applications that need the traditional group communication services such as causal and

---
*This work was supported in part by grants from the National Security Agency (NSA) and the Defense Advanced Research Projects Agency (DARPA).

total ordering, and membership and delivery guarantees, but also need to run over wide area networks. In fact, it is the first available group communication system to fully support strong semantics across wide area networks as far as we know. In addition, other applications may find Spread a better fit compared with the different reliable IP-Multicast schemes because of several technical differences:

- *Scalability with the number of collaboration sessions.* IP-Multicast is very good at supporting a small number of sessions, each broadcast to a large number of clients. Spread, on the other hand, can support a large number of different collaboration sessions, each of which spans the Internet but has only a small number of participants. The reason is that Spread utilizes *unicast* messages on the wide area network, routing them between Spread nodes on the overlay network. Therefore, IP-Multicast related resources are not required on the network routers.

- *Scalability with the number of groups.* Spread can scale well with the number of groups used by the application without imposing any overhead on network routers. Group naming and addressing is no longer a shared resource (the IP address for multicast) but rather a large space of strings which is unique per collaboration session.

- *Routing.* All of the current IP-Multicast routing methods build routing trees in an incremental way. This is very good for being able to scale to millions of users on a session. However, since Spread has to maintain membership, it requires little additional work to reconstruct routing trees every time the membership changes. This provides Spread with the ability to construct optimal routing trees. Note that these trees are on the overlay network and not on the physical network. Both IP-Multicast and Spread support pruning.

The Spread toolkit is available publicly. More details on the Spread system can be found at http://www.spread.org/.

2 An Overlay Network Architecture for Wide Area Group Communication

Our goal for a multicast architecture is to facilitate efficient group communication services for local and wide area networks. These services include unreliable and reliable dissemination of messages to process groups, ordering guarantees on messages, and membership services. These services usually adhere to strict semantics such as Virtual Synchrony[5] and its flavors[14, 7]. This range of services can be used to more easily develop, or make fault-tolerant,

applications ranging from replicated database servers to group collaboration tools to streaming multimedia.

The Spread system uses generally long-running daemons to establish the basic message dissemination network and provide basic membership and ordering services, while user applications link with a small client library, can reside anywhere in the network, and will connect to the closest daemon to gain access to the group communication services. There is a small cost to using a daemon-client architecture, which is extra context-switches and inter-process communication, however, on modern systems this cost is minimal in comparison with wide-area latencies.

A "site" in Spread consists of a collection of daemons which can all communicate over a broadcast or multicast domain. This is usually limited to a local area network. We will use the term "site" to refer to this collection of locally connected daemons as a whole. Each site selects one daemon, based on the current membership, that acts as gateway, connecting all the members of the site to other sites.

The Spread architecture solves five main problems: end-to-end reliability, configuration of an overlay network, low-latency forwarding over high-latency links, the high cost of membership changes, and scalability.

2.1 End-to-End Reliability

Guaranteed end-to-end reliability is a result of the properties of two separate protocols in Spread. First, each link guarantees that all packets sent on it will eventually be reliably received on the other side as long as there is not a membership change. Second, the membership protocols detect lost links, crashed daemons, and network partitions and then recover the necessary state to continue making progress and to report to the application if any messages were not able to be reliably delivered because of crashes or partitions. The three possible cases are:

- *No failures, no slow receivers.* Here the eventual reliability of each link is sufficient to result in all messages getting to all recipients reliably.

- *No failures, slow receivers.* Here we impose a global window of outstanding messages which will limit the speed at which new messages are generated to the rate the slowest receiver can handle. Combined with link reliability, this produces end-to-end reliability.

- *Failures.* Here the membership protocol takes over and recovers the system state, resends messages as needed, and informs the application of which messages have guaranteed reliability according to the semantics defined by Extended Virtual Synchrony Model [14].

In general, Spread decouples the dissemination and local reliability mechanisms from the global ordering and stability protocols. This decoupling allows messages to be forwarded on the network immediately despite losses or ordering requirements. The only place where messages are delayed by Spread is just before delivering them to the clients, to preserve the semantic guarantees. Decoupling local and global protocols also permits pruning, where data messages are only sent to the minimal necessary set of network components, without compromising the strong semantic guarantees.

2.2 Overlay Networks

We define "overlay network" as a virtual network constructed such that each link connects two edge nodes in an underlying physical network, such as the Internet. Each virtual link in the overlay network can translate into several hops in the underlying network, and the cost attached to a virtual link is some aggregated cost of the underlying network links over which it travels.

Spread constructs an overlay network between all the sites that have currently active daemons. This network is constructed based on information contained in the static configuration file given to Spread, the current daemon membership list, and any available network cost information. These sources produce a network that dynamically changes as daemons are started or crash, and as partitions and merges occur. The configuration file provides information about all potential machines in the Spread system, but does not constrain which members are currently running.

The overlay network is used to calculate source based optimal routing paths from each source site to every other site. Source based routing over the shortest path[15] produces the best routes when it is feasible to do. For the application domain Spread is targeted at, the calculations associated with source based routing are feasible. After a membership change a new overlay network is constructed and the routing trees are recalculated based on the new network.

The membership service provides each daemon with an identical view of the current global membership and the link weights of the current overlay network. Then, each Spread daemon independently calculates a shortest path multicast tree from each site to every other currently connected site. Since each daemon uses identical weights and an identical graph they are guaranteed to compute the same routing trees.

Figure 1 presents a sample set of sites located around the United States and the overlay networks that were constructed between them based on different needs. Each site may contain several tens of daemons, each of them serving many clients. The figure shows the real network used for the experiments reported in Section 4. The overlay network labeled "Multicast Tree Network" shows a shared tree

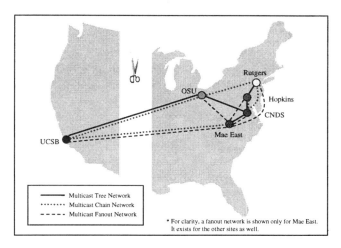

Figure 1. Network Testbed

network where the tree rooted at each site is the same. The network labeled "Multicast Fanout Network" shows a point-to-multipoint multicast network where each site has direct connections to all other sites.

The major cost of using an overlay network is that since the overlay is constructed only between end nodes in the underlying network, inefficiencies exist in the routing paths. However, this disadvantage is outweighed by several key benefits the overlay architecture provides: First, the algorithms used in the overlay network can be easily changed and do not require changes to basic network infrastructure (e.g. routers). Second, routers can be made simpler and faster, while complex protocols and processing can occur on end nodes where more abundant resources exist. For example, as a result of the difficulties encounterd while deploying and upgrading IP-Multicast in routers, most of the work on high level multicast services, such as reliability, has used an overlay network approach.

2.3 Low-latency Forwarding

Group communication applications are often very latency sensitive, both the low-level membership and ordering protocols themselves, and the high-level applications built on top of a group communication toolkit. Spread uses two approaches to solve this problem. First, the global ordering protocols used in Spread were designed to be latency-insensitive as much as possible. Second as many sources of added latency in the dissemination path (for both data messages and control messages) were removed.

The most significant change was to design a point-to-point reliability protocol which did not delay packets until they were in order, but rather could forward them out of order and let a higher level protocol deal with delivering them to the application in order. In this way, messages are delayed only at the receiver and not while in transit. Therefore, no latency is added because of reliability and routing. Latency is incurred only due to flow control on the network and to preserve semantics on the receiver. This protocol is discussed in Section 3.2.

2.4 Membership Costs

Spread uses a daemon-client architecture. This architecture has many benefits, the most important for the wide-area setting being the resultant ability to pay the minimum necessary price for different causes of group membership changes. Simple joins and leaves of processes translate into a single message. A daemon disconnection or connection does not pay the heavy cost involved in changing wide area routes. Only network partitions between different local area components of the network require the heavy cost of a full-fledged membership change. Luckily, there is a strong inverse relationship between the frequency of these events and their cost in a practical system. The process and daemon membership correspond to the more common model of "Lightweight Groups" and "Heavyweight Groups"[10].

Although, a wide area membership service is operational in Spread (which is available for download), the details of a wide area membership service is beyond the scope of this paper.

2.5 Scalability

A group communication system always involves trade-offs in performance, scalability, and services. As mentioned above, Spread supports a very large number of groups active at any time(such as several thousand), and a very large number of active Spread configurations at any time (essentially unlimited). Spread also uses a hierarchal architecture to scale the number of daemons and users into the tens to hundreds of daemons and thousands of users. The hierarchy Spread uses consists of three levels:

- *Sites.* There are between 1 and 100 sites. Each site is connected to some of the others through point-to-point WAN links forming a multicast forest (optimal source-based trees).

- *Daemons.* Each site can contain between 1 and 50 daemons. The site uses a ring based protocol to provide ordering, reliability, and flow control amoung the daemons.

- *Users.* Each daemon can support (in theory) between 1 and a few thousand users connected at once (in practice we have tested upto a couple hundred). The daemon accepts TCP or Unix Domain Socket connections from client applications.

3 Wide Area Link Protocols

Given the framework above, each link between two daemons that are directly connected on the overlay network, can be formed by one of several protocols. In this section we discuss the requirements for a wide area link protocol and describe the Hop protocol that addresses these requirements.

Before we dive into wide area protocols, it is worthwhile to explain what protocol is used within each 'site'. Within a site, the Spread daemons use the Ring protocol to provide data dissemination, reliability, and flow control. The Ring protocol uses the unreliable multicast service provided by IP, and is based on the same ideas as the Totem[3] system and achieves similar performance.

Spread couples these rings with a wide area protocol such as the Hop protocol in order to create a complete optimized network connecting a set of local area networks.

3.1 Requirements for Wide Area Link Protocols

For wide-area links, two protocols are discussed in this paper: TCP and the Hop protocol. Here we will compare TCP as the link protocol in a Spread created multicast tree, with the use of the Hop protocol in a Spread multicast tree. We will call these two protocol choices: TCP based multicast, and Hop based multicast. To provide the global group communication services, the link protocols must provide eventually reliable transport and link-level flow control.

TCP is a very mature protocol that provides both reliable transport and flow control. However, TCP also provides other guarantees, in particular FIFO ordering. TCP will not deliver any data out of order, which can cause problems when multiple TCP connections are chained to create our overlay network. Specifically, since messages are delayed until they can be delivered in order, losses will cause delays in forwarding the data to the next link down the tree. Furthermore, when the data is finally recovered, a burst of buffered data is then immediately forwarded down the tree. These micro-delays and micro-bursts cause end-to-end latency increases and an increased burstiness on the network which itself causes degraded performance.

These issues call for a design of a protocol which better fits the requirements of a wide area link protocol in our overlay architecture.

The Hop protocol is designed to provide only the required services, specifically reliability and flow control. The Hop protocol forwards packets as soon as they are received even if prior packets are missing. The Spread system provides all the standard group communication orderings at a higher level, where messages are only delayed just before being delivered to the application.

Both the TCP based multicast and Hop based multicast protocols have several advantages over emulated multicast, where end-to-end links are used between all the application instances. Not only can they utilize multicast trees to avoid sending N copies of the data across the sender's network, but they can also achieve localized recovery of lost packets without requiring the original sender to re-send the data. Localized recovery is crucial for high latency multicast networks, not only for large[11], but also for small groups where the members are widely dispersed in the network. Each unicast link in the Spread multicast tree has buffers on the sending side to store data until it has successfully reached the other end of the link.

Most current reliable multicast protocols have some form of localized recovery, such as creating virtual local subgroups along the tree[11], or using nack avoidance algorithms and expanding ring nacks[8]. All of these techniques create an approximation of recovering the missing data from the closest node. Spread has an accurate knowledge of the current membership and the structure of the overlay network. As discussed in Section 2.1 we do not have one protocol provide end-to-end reliability directly. Instead, we rely on link reliability, liveness and global flow control to guarantee end-to-end reliability. Each link is guaranteed to eventually transfer each packet to the other side. Failure recovery and liveness is guaranteed by Spread's membership protocols.

Before we discuss the Hop protocol, we mention that as a global optimization to allow packing of small messages and fragmentation of large messages, all of the network protocols used by Spread (Ring, Hop, TCP) actually operate on packets constructed of one or more data fragments and control messages. All control information used by the protocols is piggybacked on data packets when possible. If no data is available, control messages are sent as separate packets.

3.2 The Hop Protocol

The Hop protocol operates over an unreliable datagram service such as UDP/IP. The core goal of the Hop protocol is to provide the lowest latency and highest throughput possible when transferring packets across wide-area networks. The key elements of the Hop protocol are:

- *Non-Blocking:* packets are forwarded despite the loss of packets ordered earlier.

- *Lazy-Selective-Retransmits:* nacks are sent for specific lost packets after a short delay to avoid requesting data which was not lost but merely arrived out of order or is sequenced after lost data.

- *Rate-based flow control:* a rate based flow regulator provides explicit support for high delay-bandwidth

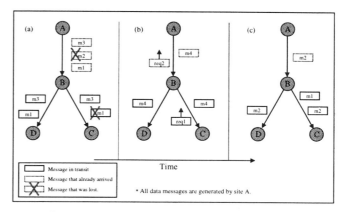

Figure 2. Hop Protocol Forwarding Scenario

networks. In addition, the rate based regulator can utilize bandwidth reservations services if such exist in the physical network.

The Hop protocol establishes a bidirectional connection between every two daemons that are directly connected on the overlay network. These two daemons maintain a list of counters and a table of open packets which have not yet been acknowledged. To establish reliable transmission in the presence of losses, Hop uses selective nacks where the receiver requests specific data packets (identified by their sequence number) when loss is detected. The receiver continues to request lost packets until they are recovered. If a lost packet has not been received after N nacks, the Hop protocol declares the link failed and the membership protocol reconfigures the system. This is necessary to eliminate the "failure to receive" problem that can occur either because of a networking fault that deletes certain packets or a malicious attacker who keeps removing one particular packet from the network.

All details of the Hop protocol have been ommitted because of space limitations. They can be found in the Tech Report version at http://www.cnds.jhu.edu/.

Figure 2 presents a case with three hop links where data flows from site A to sites B, C, and D. Messages are assigned different sequence numbers on different links according to their arrival at the parent node. The message labels m1-m4 represent the message identifier and not the sequence number assigned on each link. Suppose, as shown in Figure 2.(a), that packet m2 is lost on the link between sites A and B and subsequently packet m1 is lost on the link between B and C. Note that the loss of packet m2 does not preclude B from forwarding packet m3. Figure 2.(b) shows the nacks for messages m1 and m2 and the concurrent forwarding of m4. In Figure 2.(c) message m2 is recovered by B and immediately forwarded to C and D. Then message m1 is retransmitted to C. Note, that to allow this aggressive behavior, the order for the sequence numbers between sites

B and C were as follows: m1 got link sequence 1, m3 got link sequence 2, m4 got link sequence 3, and m2 got link sequence 4. This is the reason a request for m2 was not triggered by site C.

In Section 4 we evaluate both the Hop protocol and TCP for their usefulness in providing a link protocol for the Spread group communication system.

4   Performance and Results

We conducted experiments over the Internet to test the correctness of the implementation and to measure the performance of the different protocols. Figure 1 shows the layout of our testbed which consisted of six sites:

- Hopkins - at the Computer Science department at Johns Hopkins University, Maryland.

- CNDS - our lab at the Center for Networking and Distributed Systems at Johns Hopkins.

- UCSB - at the ECE department at the University of California, Santa Barbara.

- Mae East - on AboveNet Communications network at one of the Internet main connecting hubs, Virginia.

- OSU - at the math department at Ohio State University.

- Rutgers - at the Center for Information Management, Integration and Connectivity at Rutgers University, New Jersey.

Since the focus of this paper is architectural support and protocols for the wide area setting, only one computer from each site participated in the experiments. The computers involved ranged from Sparc-5 to Ultra-5 workstations running Solaris, and Pentium II workstations running Linux. During the tests the computers were also under normal user load, and no changes were made to their operating system. Since none of the Spread protocols use wall clock time, no effort was made to synchronize the system clocks of the machines.

The network characteristics of any particular connection over the Internet may vary significantly depending on the time of day, other users, news events, etc. To minimize the effects of these variations on our experiments, each experiment was conducted a number of times (between 30 to 200 times depending on the specific experiment). Each set of measurements for one experiment was run at approximately the same time (within a few minutes of each other). Separate experiments (reported in separate graphs or tables) were run at different times and so comparing results between tables might not be highly accurate. Because of these variances, any one data point may vary over time, however we believe the aggregate trends of the graphs and results are valid.

4.1   Overlay Networks

For this experiment we created two different overlay networks between the above six sites by adjusting the weights of the links in the configuration of Spread. A Fanout network contains a direct link between each two sites so that every source sends directly to every other site. This was created by assigning equal weights to every link. A shared-tree multicast network was created as shown in Figure 1. This tree was constructed based on measurements of network latency. The experiment shown in Table 1 was conducted using TCP as the link protocol in Spread.

Table 1. Throughput using TCP and several network configurations.

Sending Site	Fanout	Tree
Mae East (Kbits/sec)	487.32	559.79
CNDS (Kbits/sec)	666.94	560.71
Rutgers (Kbits/sec)	184.99	568.34
UCSB (Kbits/sec)	328.81	578.84

In tests run on each of the two networks (Fanout and Tree), for every test, one of the four sites (Mae East, CNDS, Rutgers, UCSB) was a source of a stream of 10000 reliable messages of 1024 bytes. The sending application on that site always made messages available to Spread. The remaining five sites were running a receiving application that computed the running time of the test at that site. The numbers in Table 1 represent the throughput of the slowest receiving site measured in kilobits per second. The difference between the fastest and slowest receiver in most of the tests was negligible. As in any reliable multicast system, the maximum sustained throughput is limited to the throughput of the slowest link.

Table 1 shows how both fanout and multicast tree overlay networks are each better than the other for different source sites. When the CNDS site is the source, the fanout network provides better throughput. This is probably because CNDS has extremely high throughput connectivity to the Internet and thus the first few hops do not form a bottleneck. However, when Rutgers or UCSB are multicasting, the multicast tree network yields much better throughput. Even though the Mae East site is located very close to a major Internet backbone peering point, providing better connectivity then almost any typical server, the multicast tree network was still 15 percent better then the fanout network.

This experiment validates the usefulness, described in Section 2, of source based routing using the overlay networks. For example, while messages generated by CNDS can be sent through a fanout configuration, messages sent by UCSB will be sent using a tree configuration.

4.2 Link Protocols

Here we evaluate the tradeoffs of using the Hop protocol versus using a TCP based link protocol. We started by evaluating the overhead latency associated with each protocol on one link. Then, the latency on a multi-link network was evaluated with regards to number of links, the size of the packets, and the load on the network. Finally, the throughput of a link and a full network were evaluated under varying levels of additional packet loss.

All latency tests were done by an application level program which multicasts a reliable Spread message to a group, and then listens for a response message. A second application runs on the other site and acts as an echo-response server, sending anything it receives immediately back to the sender through Spread. The sender application calculates round-trip latency times by taking the difference between the time it received the echo-response and the time it sent the original message. These latency tests are repeated 30 times back to back and the minimum, average, and maximum are reported. All results are reported as round-trip times, which include time transferring the message from the client to the Spread daemon, processing time in the daemon, network transfer time, the receiving daemon's processing time and the transfer to the receiving application, and a similar reverse path back to the sender. For the tables and figures reporting 'ping' results, the standard 'ping' program was run from between the daemons using 1024 byte packets. We believe the ping latencies provide us with an effective lower bound.

Table 2. Link Latency (Mae East to UCSB).

	ping	tcp	hop
min (ms)	103.3	108.946	107.798
average (ms)	104.1	136.277	108.493
max (ms)	106.8	311.649	110.944

Table 2 shows the single link latency for a link between Mae East and UCSB for 1024 byte messages. Clearly the ping latency is the best, however both the TCP link protocol and the Hop link protocol have minimum times very close to ping. The Hop protocol also is very stable across all the tests, with a variance of only 3 milliseconds, the same as ping, while TCP produced a large variance of over 200 milliseconds between the minimum and maximum latency.

To more realistically evaluate latency over a wide-area network, we also constructed an overlay network consisting of six sites in a chain. This chain is shown in Figure 1,

as running from Mae East to UCSB to OSU to Rutgers to CNDS to Hopkins. Note, we realize this is not a practical setup, or even an efficient chain. However, using this chain demonstrates how the protocols interact when packets must be forwarded many times, and how the performance of the protocols scales with the diameter of the multicast network.

Table 3. Link Throughput under loss.

Add Loss Rate	0%	5%	10%	20%
Mbits/Sec	1.38	1.27	1.11	0.995
Percentage	100	92	81	72

Table 4. Network Throughput under loss.

Add Loss Rate	0%	5%	10%	20%
Mbits/Sec	2.20	2.09	1.81	1.39
Percentage	100	95	82	63

The experiments reported in Figure 3 and Figure 5 use the chain network. The sender application is always run from one of the ends of the chain. The receiver application is placed on each of the other sites, and 30 to 200 latency tests each using a 1024 byte reliable message are run. The results of the tests are averaged and graphed. The ping line on the graph was calculated by adding the individual ping times from site to site along the chain.

The results in Figure 3 show how the Hop latency stays close to the ping latency as the number of hops and distance traveled increases, while the TCP latency is significantly higher. This is made more clear in Figure 4 which graphs the percentage overhead of TCP and Hop in comparison with ping times. TCP has an overhead of between 38 and 66 percent on all number of links, while Hop has an overhead of at most 18 percent and as little as 5 percent.

Figure 5 shows the same chain network with the sender placed at Hopkins instead of Mae East. Here the improved end-to-end latency of Hop over TCP as the network latency increases becomes clearer. When the network ping latency increases significantly after OSU, the TCP latency increases even more, while Hop latency stays within a small percentage of ping latency. Figure 6 shows how the percentage overhead of Hop decreases substantially as the network latency increases. When the network latency is small, for example on the local area networks connecting CNDS and Hopkins, the application and IPC overhead of Spread become comparable with the actual network latency. In a working Spread configuration, these local area, low latency networks would use the Ring protocol instead of TCP or

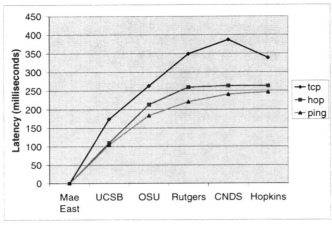

Figure 3. Chain Latency (Mae East)

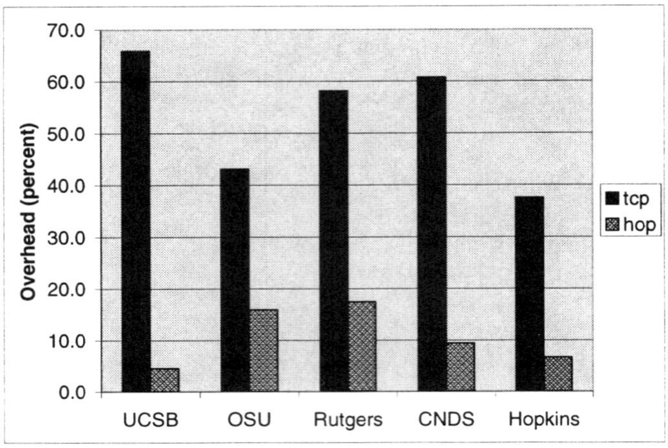

Figure 4. Protocol Latency Overhead (Mae East)

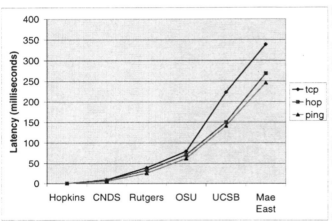

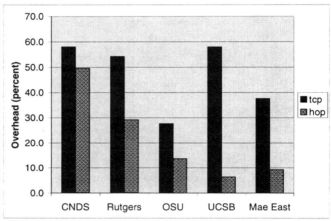

Figure 5. Chain Latency (Hopkins)

Figure 6. Protocol Latency Overhead (Hopkins)

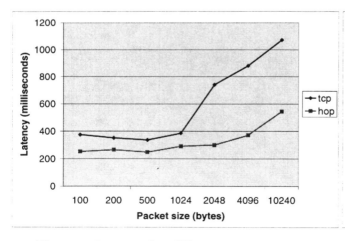

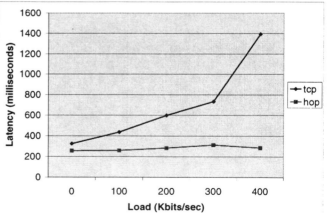

Figure 7. Latency for different size of packets

Figure 8. Latency under Load

Hop. The Ring protocol is designed for local area networks and has excellent performance.

Next, we evaluate the latency for various packet sizes. The results presented in Figure 7 use the same chain network. In this test, reliable messages of varying sizes were sent by the application. The larger message sizes are actually sent as several packets on the physical network, however since each message was only sent after the previous one was received this does not become a throughput test. The Hop protocol does not have a large increase in latency beyond what can be attributed to the size of the message in comparison with TCP, which has a significant increase in latency for packets above 1024 byte.

Next, we evaluate the latency under load. The results presented in Figure 8 use the same chain network. In this test a load application using Spread was flooding the network from Mae East with a controlled level of messages per second. Concurrently, the latency test application measured reliable, 1024 byte message latency between Mae East and Hopkins. The Hop protocol has almost constant latency as the background load increases from 0 to 400 kilobits per second. The stability under load is attributed to the Hop protocol's forwarding policy, which does not delay packets even when there is loss or other application traffic. TCP latency shows a steady increase as the background load increases with a jump between 300 and 400 kilobits per second where the latency grows to almost a second and a half.

Finally, we evaluated the Hop protocol's behavior under various levels of packet loss. These tests were done on both a single link between Mae East and UCSB, which are shown in Table 3, and on the multicast tree shown in Figure 1, whose results are reported in Table 4. These tests were done by dropping packets randomly based on a uniform distribution on each side of every link. These losses were in addition to any actual packet loss which occurred on the network. All tests were done with a stream of 10000 reliable Spread messages of 1024 bytes by the same testing application as was used in Section 4.1.

In the link experiment, the throughput decreases at 3 to 10 percent more then the actual loss rate. This seems to us quite reasonable. In the network experiment using 6 sites and 5 links the system still maintained a 63 percent throughput even with 20 percent loss on every link. Overall, the degradation on the whole network is less then double the loss rate on a single link.

We believe that the performance demonstrated by the above experiments validate the viability and usefulness of the Hop protocol in real-life system settings.

5   Related Work

Group communication systems in the LAN environment have a well developed history beginning with ISIS [6], and more recent systems such as Transis [2], Horus [16], Totem [3], and RMP [18]. These systems explored several different models of Group Communication such as Virtual Synchrony [5] and Extended Virtual Synchrony [14]. Newer work in this area focuses on scaling group membership to wide-area networks [4].

A few of these systems have added some type of support for either wide-area group communication or multi-LAN group communication. The Hybrid paper [17] discusses the difficulties of extending LAN oriented protocols to the more dynamic and costly wide-area setting. The Hybrid system has each group communication application switch between a token based and symmetric vector based ordering algorithm depending on the communication latency between the applications. While their system provides a total order using whichever protocol is more efficient for each participant, Hybrid does not handle partitions in the network, or provide support for orderings other then total.

The Multiple-Ring Totem protocol [1] allows several rings to be interconnected by gateway nodes that forward packets to other rings. This system provides a substantial performance boost compared to a single-ring on large LAN environments, but keeps the assumptions of low loss rates and latency and a fairly similar bandwidth between all nodes that limit its applicability to wide-area networks.

The Transis wide-area protocols Pivots and Xports by Nabil Huleihel [12] provide ordering and delivery guarantees in a partitionable environment. Both protocols are based on a hierarchical model of the network, where each level of the hierarchy is partitioned into small sets of nearby processes, and each set has a static representative who is also a member of the next higher level of the hierarchy. The Congress work [4] approaches the problem of providing wide-area membership services separately from actual multicast and ordering services, and provides a general membership service that can provide different semantic guarantees.

IP-Multicast is actively developed to support Internet wide unreliable multicasting and to scale to millions of users. Many reliable multicast protocols which use IP-multicast have been developed, such as SRM [8], RMTP [13], Local Group Concept (LGC) [11], and HRMP [9].

The development of reliable protocols over IP-Multicast has focused on solving scalability problems such as Ack or Nack implosion and bandwidth limits, and providing useful reliability services for multimedia and other isochronous applications. Several of these protocols have developed localized loss recovery protocols. SRM has enhancements to localize the recovery by using the TTL field of IP-Multicast to request a lost packet from nearer nodes first, and then expand the request if no one close has it. Several other variations in localized recovery are discussed in [8].

Other reliable multicast protocols like LGC use the distribution tree to localize retransmits to a local group leader who is the root of some subtree. RMTP also uses "Designated Receivers" (DR) who act as the head of a virtual subtree to localize recovery of lost packets and provides reliable transport of a file from one sender to multiple receivers located around the world. RMTP is based on the IP-Multicast model, but created user-level multicast through UDP and modified *mrouted* software. RMTP did not examine the tradeoffs in link protocols discussed in this paper because it handles reliability over the entire tree, with the DR's only acting as aggregators of global protocol information.

HRMP [9] is a reliable multicast protocol which provides a efficient local reliability based on a ring, while using standard tree-based protocols such as ack trees to provide reliability between rings. This work theoretically analyzes the predicted performance of such a protocol and shows it to be better then protocols utilizing only a ring or a tree.

6 Conclusion

We presented an architecture for wide area group communications that was implemented in the Spread system. This architecture takes advantage of the ability to construct user level overlay networks to efficiently disseminate reliable messages to process groups.

We described Hop, an efficient point-to-point reliable transport protocol for connecting sites on a wide area multicast tree. Experiments conducted over the Internet validated the low latency and high stability of the Hop protocol under various load and loss conditions.

Acknowledgements

We thank Michal Miskin-Amir, one of the creators of Spread. We thank Jithesh Parameswaran for programming the optimal routing computations in Spread. We also wish to thank Nabil Adam, Richard Holowczak, Michael Melliar-Smith, Louise Moser, Alec Peterson, and Robert Stanton for allowing us to use their systems in our testings.

References

[1] D. Agarwal, L. E. Moser, P. M. Melliar-Smith, and R. K. Budhia. The totem multiple-ring ordering and topology maintenance protocol. *ACM Transactions on Computer Systems*, 16(2):93–132, May 1998.

[2] Y. Amir, D. Dolev, S. Kramer, and D. Malki. Transis: A communication subsystem for high-availability. In *Digest of Papers, The 22nd International Symposium on Fault-Tolerant Computing Systems*, pages 76–84, 1992.

[3] Y. Amir, L. E. Moser, P. M. Melliar-Smith, D. Agarwal, and P. Ciarfella. The totem single-ring ordering and membership protocol. *ACM Transactions on Computer Systems*, 13(4):311–342, November 1995.

[4] T. Anker, G. V. Chockler, D. Dolev, and I. Keidar. Scalable group membership services for novel applications. In M. Mavronicolas, M. Merritt, and N. Shavit, editors, *Proceedings of the workshop on Networks in Distributed Computing*, DIMACS Series in Discrete Mathematics and Theoretical Computer Science, 1998.

[5] K. P. Birman and T. Joseph. Exploiting virtual synchrony in distributed systems. In *11th Annual Symposium on Operating Systems Principles*, pages 123–138, November 1987.

[6] K. P. Birman and R. V. Renesse. *Reliable Distributed Computing with the Isis Toolkit*. IEEE Computer Society Press, March 1994.

[7] A. Fekete, N. Lynch, and A. Shvartsman. Specifying and using a partionable group communication service. In *Proceedings of the 16th annual ACM Symposium on Principles of Distributed Computing*, pages 53–62, August 1997.

[8] S. Floyd, V. Jacobson, C. Liu, S. McCanne, and L. Zhang. A reliable multicast framework for light-weight sessions and application level framing. *IEEE/ACM Transactions on Networking*, 5(6):784–803, December 1997.

[9] L. Gu and J. Garcia-Luna-Aceves. New error recovery structures for reliable networking. In *Proceedings of the Sixth International Conference on Computer Communications and Networking*, September 1997.

[10] K. Guo and L. Rodrigues. Dynamic light-weight groups. In *Proceedings of 17th International Conference on Distributed Computing Systems*, pages 33–42, May 1997.

[11] M. Hofmann. A generic concept for large-scale multicast. In B. Plattner, editor, *International Zurich Seminar on Digital Communications*, number 1044 in Lecture Notes in Computer Science, pages 95–106, Februrary 1996.

[12] N. Huleihel. Efficient ordering of messages in wide area networks. Master's thesis, Institute of Computer Science, The Hebrew University of Jerusalem, Jerusalem, Israel, 1996.

[13] J. Lin and S. Paul. Rmtp: A reliable multicast transport protocol. In *Proceedings of IEEE Infocom*, pages 1414–1424, March 1996.

[14] L. E. Moser, Y. Amir, P. M. Melliar-Smith, and D. A. Agarwal. Extended virtual synchrony. In *Proceedings of the IEEE 14th International Conference on Distributed Computing Systems*, pages 56–65, June 1994.

[15] J. Nonnenmacher and E. W. Biersack. Performance modelling of reliable multicast transmission. In *Proceedings of INFOCOM 97*, April 1997.

[16] R. V. Renesse, K. Birman, and S. Maffeis. Horus: A flexible group communication system. *Communications of the ACM*, 39(4):76–83, April 1996.

[17] L. E. Rodrigues, H. Fonseca, and P. Verissimo. A synamic hybrid protocol for total order in large-scale systems. In *Proceedings of the 16th International Conference on Distributed Computing Systems*, May 1996. Selected portions published in.

[18] B. Whetten, T. Montgomery, and S. Kaplan. A high performance totally ordered multicast protocol. In *Theory and Practice in Distributed Systems, International Workshop*, LNCS, page 938, September 1994.

A Reliable Many-to-Many Multicast Protocol for Group Communication over ATM Networks

R. R. Koch, L. E. Moser, P. M. Melliar-Smith
Department of Electrical and Computer Engineering
University of California, Santa Barbara, CA 93106
{ruppert, moser, pmms}@alpha.ece.ucsb.edu

Abstract

Reliable many-to-many multicasting of messages is an integral part of group communication systems. Such systems typically employ a reliable multicast protocol that operates below the causal or total ordering layer of the protocol stack. In this paper, we present ARMP, a reliable many-to-many multicast protocol for group communication over wide-area ATM networks. We describe how the ATM environment affects the design of ARMP, which differs significantly from the design of reliable multicast protocols intended for other environments.

1. Introduction

Group communication systems [1, 2, 3, 4, 5] simplify the design of fault-tolerant distributed systems by providing services such as causal or total ordering of messages, membership services, and virtual or extended virtual synchrony. Reliable message delivery is an essential part of any group communication system, which must contain a protocol that provides reliable many-to-many multicasting of messages.

While several protocols have been developed that multicast data efficiently and reliably over the Internet [6, 7], most of those protocols support a single sender node (or a small number of sender nodes) and a large number of receiver nodes. System topology and congestion control, as well as positive acknowledgment (ACK) and negative acknowledgment (NAK) implosion are major issues. Buffer management, although sometimes excluded [8], is typically also an integral part of a reliable multicast protocol.

In this paper, we describe ARMP, a reliable many-to-many multicast protocol that we have developed for the Atomic Group System, a wide-area group communication

system for Asynchronous Transfer Mode (ATM) networks. ARMP, the lower layer of the Atomic Group System, provides a many-to-many multicast service to the upper layer ordering protocol, which imposes a causal and total order on messages delivered by ARMP.

The wide-area ATM network environment for which ARMP is intended has a large impact on the design of the ARMP protocol. The strategies that are appropriate for ATM networks differ significantly from those of reliable multicast protocols developed for other types of networks.

Other researchers have attempted to augment the unreliable point-to-point connections of the ATM standard [9] with reliability. Most of them have incorporated reliability into the ATM infrastructure [10, 11]. Those approaches require significant modifications of the ATM specifications. None of the proposed extensions has been implemented in commercially available products. A many-to-many multicast framework for ATM networks is described in [12], but its main focus is routing and security; it does not address reliable message delivery.

2. Overview of the Atomic Group System

Atomic Group is a group communication system that we have developed for wide-area ATM networks. It provides totally (and causally) ordered delivery of multicast messages. Such a delivery guarantee is also known as an atomic multicast, from which the Atomic Group System derives its name.

Atomic Group is intended to handle a large number of processes, distributed over a wide area. However, very few messages need to be multicast to all of the processes. Rather, messages are delivered to only those processes that require them. Consequently, processes are structured into many small- or medium-sized process groups containing a few, or a few tens, of processes. A process can join or leave a process group at any time, and can be a member of multiple process groups at the same time. All members of a

This research was supported by DARPA and the Office of Naval Research under contract N00174-95-K-0083, and by DARPA and the Air Force Research Laboratory, Rome, under contract F30601-97-1-0284.

process group are peers. Every member is both a sender and a receiver. All messages sent by any one member of the group must be received reliably by all of the members of the group. Consequently, a node receives N times as many messages from a group as it sends to the group, if there are N members in the group.

Instead of being addressed to specific individual processes, messages are addressed to the group as a whole, which is designated by a unique process group name. Every process that is a current member of the group receives messages addressed to the group in exactly the same order. In addition to reliable and ordered delivery of messages, Atomic Group also provides a membership service. If a process crashes or cannot be reached due to loss of communication, the membership algorithm excludes the faulty process and notifies all remaining members of the membership change. Thus, every process knows the members of all groups of which it is a member at all times.

To achieve high throughput, Atomic Group follows the *participant minimality* concept [13]. This concept states that the sender and the receivers of a message should be the only processes involved in the multicasting of a message. Atomic Group also has the property of *message size minimality* [14], which requires that the length of a message should not be a function of the total number of processes in the system but rather a function of the number of processes that should receive the message. Atomic Group does even better: the message size is independent of the number of recipients of a message, as well as of the overall system size. The message size overhead of ARMP ranges from 2–3% for 1kB messages under moderate and heavy loads.

In addition to high throughput, Atomic Group delivers messages with low latency. The total ordering protocol of the Atomic Group System is based on timestamps derived from physical clocks. Details about the ordering protocol and the clock synchronization algorithm are given in [15].

Following the participant minimality concept, ARMP creates a many-to-many multicast domain for each process group. It delivers messages from all senders to the upper layer of the Atomic Group protocol stack in source order.

3. Atomic Group Reliable Multicast Protocol

The lowest layer of the Atomic Group protocol stack is the Atomic Group Reliable Multicast protocol, which provides reliable many-to-many multicast services to the ordering and membership protocols. It also provides buffer management as well as flow and congestion control.

Because ATM provides one-to-many multicasts but not many-to-many multicasts, ARMP must fabricate the many-to-many multicast domains that it requires. Because routing is not a part of ARMP, only two out of several approaches are feasible and efficient: a single core-based tree and mul-

tiple source trees. With N processes in a group and a single core node, the core-based tree consists of $N - 1$ point-to-point connections and one 1-to-N multicast connection, with each message transmitted twice. The multiple source tree approach uses N distinct 1-to-N multicast connections, with each message transmitted only once. The multiple source tree approach consumes less bandwidth and provides lower transmission latency, with no single point of failure. These advantages led us to choose multiple source tree routing for ARMP.

When forming a new group, ARMP can choose between two strategies for setting the quality of service (QoS) parameters. Traffic is unspecified (Available Bit Rate (ABR), Unspecified Bit Rate (UBR)) or specified (Constant Bit Rate (CBR), Variable Bit Rate (VBR)). Not specifying a sender's data traffic pattern makes the system more flexible. If a receiver has allocated all of its available bandwidth, no additional senders can connect to it unless some of the established connections are torn down and reestablished with a reduced traffic rate — a rather expensive procedure. On the downside, unspecified ATM traffic suffers from message loss in the same way as Internet traffic due to statistical multiplexing if the backbone is congested. In contrast to Internet traffic, unspecified ATM traffic is not prone to latency jitter due to congestion because the buffers in ATM switches are smaller than those used in IP routers. The choice of the appropriate traffic type not only influences the design of ARMP's congestion control, but also the expected message loss rates. Designed to be a low-latency protocol, ARMP sets up connections as VBR connections.

Group communication systems that provide virtual synchrony [1] require the system to be able to retransmit a message from a faulty sender if any non-faulty member of the group has received that message. Thus, all group members, rather than only the sender of a message, must buffer the message until the message becomes stable. A message is stable if every non-faulty member of the group has received a copy of the message. Correspondingly, each member of the group must send acknowledgments to the entire group, not only to the sender of the message, so that the other members of the group can remove stable messages from their buffers. This is the first major difference of ARMP compared to most Internet-based reliable multicast protocols.

ARMP uses sequence numbers to implement reliable source-ordered message delivery. Gaps in the sequence numbers indicate missing messages. To achieve low message delivery latency, ARMP is designed as a receiver-initiated protocol, with explicit retransmission request messages (NAKs), together with positive acknowledgments piggybacked on messages for buffer management. To minimize the cost of positive acknowledgments and to avoid ACK implosion, ARMP uses timestamps as positive acknowledgments. Compared to traditional positive acknowledgment schemes for multicast messages, timestamp acknowledgments require less bandwidth and less processing [16], at the expense of some increase in buffer utilization. Timestamp acknowledgments require each sender to know the set of receivers.

Congestion and flow control are central issues in the design of ARMP. Whereas flow control deals with the availability of buffer space at the receivers, congestion control regulates the traffic that enters the network. Network congestion is unlikely to occur when using a networking service that provides quality of service. As shown in Section 9, ARMP's congestion control significantly differs from algorithms used for TCP/IP [17] and TCP/IP-friendly multicast protocols.

4. Message Types in ARMP

ARMP employs four types of messages: regular messages, heartbeat messages, retransmissions, and retransmission requests, which are depicted in Figure 1. No special messages are necessary for either buffer management or congestion control.

When sending a regular message to a process group, the sender increments the sequence number of the last regular message it sent to that group, and attaches the new sequence number to the message, together with the sender's current timestamp and acknowledgment timestamp. ARMP uses 32-bit sequence numbers and 64-bit timestamps.

Heartbeat messages assure group members that a sender is still alive even if it does not send regular messages, and provide the group members with the sender's current timestamp, which the ordering protocol needs. The ordering protocol generates heartbeat messages within a specified interval if no useful data needs to be sent. Heartbeat messages are handled differently from regular messages for efficiency reasons. No delivery guarantee is provided for heartbeat messages. By the time that a retransmitted heartbeat could reach a receiver, its information would have become obsolete. The sender tags heartbeat messages with the sequence number of the last regular message it sent, and the sender's current timestamp and acknowledgment timestamp.

A retransmission request for a set of messages contains two sequence numbers, req_{from} and req_{upto}, and the process identifier of the creator of the messages. The retransmission request message requests retransmission of all messages with sequence numbers between req_{from} and req_{upto} inclusive. Retransmission requests do not carry a sequence number, current timestamp, or acknowledgment timestamp.

A retransmitted message carries the same sequence number, the same current timestamp, the same acknowledgment timestamp, and the same payload as the original message. It does, however, carry an additional ID field that contains the process ID of the creator of the message. In ATM networks,

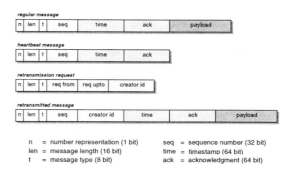

Figure 1. Format of messages used by ARMP.

messages do not need to be tagged with sender IDs, because the virtual channels specify the sender. If the node other than the originator of a message retransmits the message, the creator ID allows the receiver to identify the originator. The creator ID field is used so that ARMP can distinguish between regular messages and retransmitted messages.

5. Detecting Missing Messages in ARMP

For each connection, the receiver accepts messages from the sender for that connection, and delivers them in source order to the upper layer. The state of a receiver's connection is described by two variables, *largestseq* and *delivered*, and one queue. The variable *largestseq* holds the largest sequence number that the connection has received thus far, whereas the variable *delivered* holds the sequence number of the last message delivered to the upper layer of the protocol stack. Both values increase monotonically. The value of *largestseq* is always greater than or equal to the value of *delivered*.

We say that the protocol is in *up-to-date* mode when *largestseq* equals *delivered*. Inequality between these two values indicates that the connection has detected a gap in the sequence numbers and is waiting for the retransmission of messages. If a regular message is received and $seq > largestseq$, the receiver updates *largestseq* and compares the sequence number of the message with the value of *delivered*. If $seq = delivered + 1$, the message is delivered to the upper layer and *delivered* is incremented. If not, the message is queued. Figure 2 shows the action that ARMP takes when it receives messages for the various combinations of *largestseq* and *delivered*.

The receiver's queue holds messages that ARMP has received but has not yet delivered, both regular and heartbeat messages. Messages are queued in order of their sequence number. Because heartbeat messages distribute the current clock reading of the sender, a new heartbeat message renders all previous heartbeat messages obsolete. ARMP stores

message	< del	= del	= del+1	> del+1
< lseq − 1	D		E	F
= lseq				
= lseq + 1			A	
> lseq + 1				B

heartbeat	< del	= del	= del+1	> del+1
< lseq − 1	D		G	
= lseq		A		
= lseq + 1			C	
> lseq + 1				

A : deliver message, set $largestseq = delivered = seq$

B : queue message, issue request for $[largestseq + 1|seq)$, set $largestseq = seq$

C : queue heartbeat, issue request for $[largestseq + 1|seq]$, set $largestseq = seq$

D : ignore message

E : deliver message, try to deliver enqueued messages, set *delivered* to largest sequence number delivered

F : queue message without issuing a retransmission request

G : queue heartbeat without issuing a retransmission request

Figure 2. State table of ARMP.

the most recent heartbeat message for each sequence number, $seq \in (delivered|largestseq]$, for which the regular message with that sequence number has not yet been received by all processes in the group.

When ARMP receives a regular message, either it delivers the message immediately, followed by a heartbeat message with the same sequence number if ARMP has already queued such a heartbeat message or, alternatively, it queues the received message. When ARMP receives a heartbeat message, if $seq = delivered$, it delivers the heartbeat message; otherwise, it queues that message, possibly overwriting a heartbeat message that it previously queued. The value of *delivered* is not affected by heartbeat messages. Queuing heartbeats increases the efficiency of the total ordering protocol. Delivery of a heartbeat message, carrying the same sequence number as the most recently delivered regular message, provides the total ordering layer with a more recent timestamp from the source of that regular message and accelerates the ordering of messages from other sources.

6. Retransmission of Messages in ARMP

Retransmission of messages is one of the primary responsibilities of any reliable multicast protocol. The retransmission mechanism must be efficient in its use of bandwidth and must have low latency. These two requirements contradict each other. The protocol must be designed so that it has acceptable performance for both criteria. The ATM

environment, for which ARMP was designed, will lead to a design that differs from most Internet multicast protocols.

Any retransmission protocol consists of five basic steps: detecting the need to request a retransmission, requesting the retransmission, retransmitting requested messages, receiving and delivering retransmitted messages, and repeating a request if the retransmission was not received successfully. The second and fifth steps are similar, but many protocols use different mechanisms to trigger those steps (e.g., gaps in the sequence numbers vs. timeouts).

In contrast to most reliable multicast protocols, an ARMP sender is not responsible for buffering the messages it has sent. Instead, the receivers store messages until they become stable. Each sender reliably receives its own messages.

6.1. Requesting Missing Messages

If a receiver receives a regular message with a sequence number greater than $largestseq + 1$ or a heartbeat message with a sequence number greater than $largestseq$, it must have missed at least one regular message. It then sends a retransmission request asking for all regular messages with numbers $seq \in [largestseq + 1|seq)$ in case of a regular message or $seq \in [largestseq + 1|seq]$ in case of a heartbeat message. The variable $largestseq$ is then set to the sequence number of the message that triggered the retransmission, and a retransmission request timer is started.

Retransmission requests are multicast to all members of a group for three reasons. First, ARMP need not set up special retransmit connections for each pair of nodes, which would add another $(N - 1)^2$ connections for a group of N nodes. Second, knowing about previous requests allows ARMP to suppress retransmissions under certain conditions, as shown in Section 6.2. Third, retransmission requests are used to adjust congestion control parameters.

Retransmission requests are independent of each other. If ARMP detects a second gap in the sequence numbers before it has closed the first gap, it sends a new request message asking for only the messages needed to close the second gap. ARMP does not request messages from the first gap in the new request.

Pingali *et al* [18] have compared several retransmission strategies for multicast protocols. They have concluded that receiver-initiated reliable multicast protocols, such as ARMP, achieve a significantly higher throughput than sender-initiated protocols because the receiver-initiated approach avoids ACK implosion. The more processes that participate in a multicast, the larger the performance gap becomes. They have also demonstrated that randomly delayed NAKs improve the performance even further, because such randomization prevents NAK implosion. NAK implosion occurs when many receivers miss the

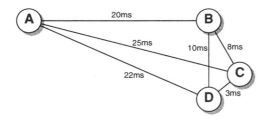

Figure 3. Group topology that leads to the failure of the distance approximation algorithm.

same message and flood the network with retransmission requests. Delaying the retransmission request, by a short random interval, allows a receiver to cancel its retransmission request if it receives a retransmission request from another receiver requesting the same message. For this technique to be effective, the mean delay must be greater than the channel latency.

The technique of delaying retransmission requests is not used in ARMP because it increases the retransmission latency. Delaying NAKs works well if many processes request the same message. If the number of requesting receivers is large then, due to randomization, some receivers should incur only a small delay. However, randomly delayed NAKs increase delivery latency significantly when only a small number of processes request a specific message. ARMP is tailored for relatively small process groups, for which NAK implosion is not as critical as for large groups. Furthermore, the use of VBR connections minimizes the probability of loosing messages in the ATM backbone. Because message loss in the receiver's input buffers is not highly correlated between processes, this source of message loss cannot cause NAK implosion. Delaying retransmission requests increases retransmission latency significantly but provides only a marginal benefit.

6.2. Multicasting Retransmitted Messages

Because message loss is caused by congestion most of the time, retransmission algorithms must not contribute to further congestion. Ideally, only the closest neighbor of the requesting node should retransmit the message. Although a process might know the mean latency of its own incoming channels, it typically has no knowledge of the entire set of N^2 latencies between all of the members of the group. Thus, a process cannot easily determine that it is the process closest to the process requesting the retransmission. It is possible to estimate that process A is the process closest to the requesting process B if B is the process closest to A. This approximation may be inaccurate, as shown in the example of Figure 3, where process A regards itself as being

closest to the requesting process B when it is actually the most distant. In contrast, the other two processes, C and D, do not regard themselves as being the processes closest to B, although C is indeed the process closest to B.

Although the approximation does not work for all topologies, it is a good heuristic for many topologies. No deterioration of the retransmission algorithm results if the set of retransmitting processes that was chosen at random is augmented by one or more processes that regard themselves as being close to a process requesting a retransmission. If the K $(1 \leq K \ll N)$ presumably-closest processes retransmit the messages, the probability that the actual closest process is among those K processes increases as K increases. However, as K increases, more processes incorrectly assume that they are among the processes closest to the process requesting the retransmission. Increased overhead, and network and buffer overloads, are the direct consequence. Therefore, ARMP sets $K = 1$.

In addition to the presumably-closest process, the originator of a requested message always retransmits the requested messages because it is the only process in the group that is guaranteed to hold the messages in its buffer. Consequently, two processes retransmit a requested message most of the time. None of the retransmissions is artificially delayed. Delayed retransmissions have the same disadvantages as delayed retransmission requests. For the same reasons, we reject delayed retransmissions in ARMP.

However, ARMP does disregard retransmission requests for a message if another process has recently requested retransmission of that message. If a process receives a request for messages m_1, m_2, and m_3, but another process has already requested m_1 and m_2, the process retransmits only message m_3 if it is among the processes selected to retransmit the message and the first request was sent less than half the retransmission timeout interval ago.

6.3. Reception of Retransmitted Messages

A retransmitted message is transmitted with its original header information, but it includes the process identifier of the originator of the message. When a process receives the retransmitted message, it handles the message as a regular message that had been transmitted by the process that originated it. Message retransmission might result in a message being received multiple times.

When ARMP receives a regular or retransmitted message, if the sequence number of the message is less than or equal to *delivered*, it ignores the message. If the message is already queued, ARMP also ignores it. If $seq = largestseq + 1$, ARMP queues the message and takes no special action. If ARMP receives a retransmitted message with $seq > largestseq + 1$, it does not know if the original messages are still en route or if they were lost. Although un-

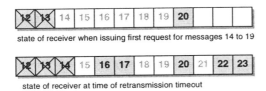

state of receiver when issuing first request for messages 14 to 19

state of receiver at time of retransmission timeout

Figure 4. Request scenario. Received messages are depicted shaded, missing messages unshaded. Messages delivered to the upper layer are crossed out.

likely for ATM networks, which exhibits a small variance in propagation delay, the immediate sending of a retransmission request might add unnecessary overhead. Therefore, ARMP enqueues the message and sets the retransmission timeout.

6.4. Retransmission Request Timeout

When issuing a retransmission request, a process starts a timeout. On expiration of this timeout, the process determines whether it has received all of the messages it requested. It generates a new retransmission request for any messages that are still missing. Figure 4 at the top illustrates a scenario in which a process requests messages 14 to 19 after having received message 20. At that time, the process has delivered messages up to 13 to the upper layers of the protocol stack. During the retransmission timeout, it has received missing messages 14, 16, and 17 as well as the new messages 22 and 23, and has delivered message 14. On expiration of the timeout, ARMP issues two new retransmission requests: one for message 15 and one for messages 18 and 19. It has already requested retransmission of message 21 when it received message 22, and set another timeout for message 21.

Currently, a node sets the retransmission request timeout to 2.5 times the propagation delay to its closest neighbor. This value has been determined empirically.

6.5. Initialization

The initialization of ARMP is straightforward. On the sender side of a connection, no initialization is required and a new sender starts transmissions with sequence number one. New receiver connections must synchronize to the existing senders by copying the sequence number of the first message received into *largestseq* and *delivered*. Because *largestseq* = *delivered*, the first message can be delivered immediately. If the first message received is either a retransmitted message or a retransmission request message,

the message is ignored and the synchronization is postponed until a regular message is received.

This initialization scheme bears the risk that a newly connected process will lose one or more of the first messages that it should have received. This behavior is acceptable if the receivers eventually synchronize. The upper layers of the Atomic Group system require all receivers to synchronize at the same point in the message sequence. The Atomic Group membership protocol contains mechanisms to ensure this.

7. Buffer Management

Buffer management in ARMP is based on timestamps. The protocol acknowledges messages from multiple senders with a single timestamp value [2]. This significantly reduces the bandwidth consumed by positive acknowledgments. The protocol requires that each sender includes a copy of its local clock in each message it sends. The timestamp acknowledgment algorithm can be based either on physical clocks or on Lamport clocks. Physical clocks, as used in ARMP, yield better performance [16].

When sending an acknowledgment, which it piggybacks onto either regular or heartbeat messages, a receiver acknowledges all messages from all senders that carry a timestamp less than or equal to the acknowledgment timestamp.

A node can delete all messages that carry a timestamp less than or equal to the smallest of all of the last acknowledgment timestamps that it has received from each of the receivers.

Both senders and receivers are required to send messages and acknowledgments at a minimum rate to keep the protocol alive. Furthermore, the senders must know about all of the receivers and the receivers must know about all of the senders. ARMP satisfies these requirements. All nodes send messages with piggybacked acknowledgments on a regular basis to keep the ordering protocol alive. Membership information is available through the membership protocol that runs above ARMP. Note that this does not introduce a direct circular dependence because obsolete membership information leads either to advanced (in case of increasing membership) or delayed (in case of decreasing membership) buffer clearance, but does not affect the delivery of messages to the upper layers. However, advanced deletion of messages might cause problems in case some receivers are still missing messages. This is remedied by defining a single point in virtual time at which a process becomes a member. Details are given in [15].

8. Flow Control for ARMP

Almost all group communication systems implement some form of flow control. Flow control ensures that receivers have sufficient buffer space available to hold all messages sent. This is done by limiting the number of unstable messages in the system.

Flow control algorithms can be divided into two classes: conservative and optimistic [19]. Conservative schemes divide the available buffer space among all senders in advance. If a sender uses its share, it stops sending — even if other senders do not use all of their shares. Optimistic algorithms don't reserve buffer space. Instead, they distribute the knowledge of the current buffer utilization to all senders. Because this knowledge cannot be transferred instantaneously, most optimistic flow control schemes are not resilient against buffer overflow (an exception is [4]).

For wide-area protocols, for which the information about available buffer space takes a significant amount of time to reach the senders, a conservative flow control scheme is appropriate. In ARMP, each process allocates buffer space of size b when a new process joins the group. If one of the existing group members is not able to allocate the buffers, the new process is not allowed to join the group.

Depending on the number of buffers reserved, network bandwidth, and link latency, either flow control or congestion control controls the messages a process can send. If $b \leq 2TB$ (where T is the link latency and B is the bandwidth of the sender-receiver link), availability of buffer space is the limiting factor. As stated in [16], timestamp-based acknowledgments schemes require more buffer space than sequence number-based algorithms.

In ARMP different message types are treated differently by the flow control algorithm. Regular messages are subject to flow control. If the number of unstable messages exceeds the limit, regular messages are stored in a queue.

Flow control need not impose restrictions on retransmitted messages because the original messages have been accounted for already in the number of unstable messages.

Retransmission requests are acted upon by the receiver immediately after reception. Therefore, they do not consume buffer space. Accordingly, ARMP's flow control does not restrain retransmission requests.

Although heartbeat messages consume buffer space at the receiver if they cannot be delivered because preceding messages are still outstanding, they must not be delayed by flow control. Heartbeats are small and are sent only sporadically during low traffic situations. Moreover, heartbeat messages are needed to break deadlocks.

In general, flow control algorithms are prone to deadlock. If a sender has a quota of m messages and all of them are lost, the receiver neither acknowledges any of the messages, nor sends a retransmission request (because it cannot detect a gap in sequence numbers). Most protocols use timers that trigger the retransmission of a message if the message has not been acknowledged after a certain time. ARMP uses the heartbeat messages that the upper layer of

Atomic Group generates. Because heartbeat messages carry the sequence number of the last message sent, a receiver becomes aware of message loss as soon as it successfully receives the heartbeat message.

9. Congestion Control for ARMP

Because ARMP exploits the quality of service guarantees offered by ATM, preventing congestion in the underlying network is not a primary concern. In ARMP the focus shifts from network congestion towards receiver input buffer overflow, the probability of which increases with an increasing number of senders. Although the issue of input buffer overflow arises for any multicast protocol that employs multiple senders, the problem usually is overshadowed by network congestion.

Congestion control algorithms can be divided into two classes: window-based and rate-based. Window-based algorithms adapt quicker to changes in the environment, but require a higher overhead for multicast protocols [20]. In particular, a sender must maintain a different window for each receiver in the group to avoid limiting the throughput below the throughput of the bottleneck connection. Moreover, window-based congestion control schemes do not work well with timestamp-based acknowledgments because receivers do not acknowledge messages immediately. The time it takes for a sender s to receive an acknowledgment for its message from a receiver r is larger than the round-trip time between s and r. Thus, a window-based congestion control restricts the message flow more than necessary. We have therefore developed a Rate-based Congestion Control algorithm (RCC).

The basic functionality of RCC resembles TCP. A sender's transmission rate is increased by a value inversely proportional to the current transmission rate every time a sender's message becomes stable. In case of transmission errors, the rate is reset to a minimum value, and a slow-start algorithm brings the rate up to half of the sender's rate before failure.

A number of reliable multicast protocols have adopted a similar approach, but they either allow only a single sender [21], lack robustness [22], or lack fairness [23].

RCC ensures fairness for ARMP processes and, in addition, provides TCP-fairness [20]. Although it is designed to run over CBR or VBR ATM channels, ARMP cooperates with IP-over-ATM traffic when used over networks, such as ABR and UBR ATM channels, that do not provide quality of service.

9.1. Round-Trip Time Estimation

An important parameter of any congestion control algorithm is the Round-Trip Time (RTT). Since ATM networks

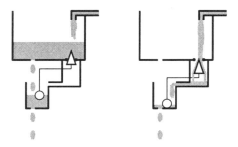

Figure 5. Design of a smart leaky bucket.

```
do_not_send_before = last_msg_sent_at
    + size_of_last_msg / allowed_rate;
if (do_not_send_before > Get_current_time())
    enqueue(message);
else
    if (do_not_send_before > Get_time()
                    - bucket_memory)
        last_msg_sent_at = do_not_send_before;
    else
        last_msg_sent_at = Get_current_time()
                    - bucket_memory;
    size_of_last_msg = message.len;
    send(message);
```

Figure 6. Pseudocode for the smart leaky bucket algorithm.

exhibit low jitter, ARMP does not need to incorporate the variance of RTT into their algorithms.

Letting a sender derive RTT directly from latency measurements and then pick the maximum value for all receivers leads to unfairness. Senders on the periphery of the network would see RTT values twice as large as senders in the center of the network. Therefore, we set RTT to $2T$, with T being the maximum channel latency for any sender-receiver pair. Atomic Group's clock synchronization algorithm [15] provides the value of T.

9.2. Sending a Message

Every time Atomic Group wants to send a message, the Rate-based Congestion Control algorithm checks if the node's transmission rate exceeds the currently allowed transmission rate. The rate comparison is done by using a variation of a leaky bucket algorithm, which we call the *smart leaky bucket* (Figure 5). The smart leaky bucket gives limited credit for periods during which the bucket is empty. The float-controlled bypass valve allows the fluid to make up for times during which the main container is empty. If the lower container is empty, the valve opens and a limited amount of fluid can exit at an increased rate. A message is sent as soon as all of its bits have percolated through the large bucket. Figure 6 shows the smart leaky bucket pseudocode. The `allowed_rate` is given in bytes/s, and the `bucket_memory` is given in units of time. In our experiments we obtained the best results by setting the value of `bucket_memory` to 50 ms.

If RCC does permit ARMP to send a message, ARMP enqueues the message in a send queue (the same queue that is used by flow control). If the upper protocol layers transmit too many messages, the send queue fills up and ARMP notifies the upper layer to stop the transmission of new messages temporarily.

In addition to the regular send queue, which holds regular messages, ARMP uses a high-priority send queue to store retransmitted messages. Messages are taken out of the regular queue only if the high-priority queue is empty.

To reduce message delivery latency, all entries in the high-priority queue are sorted by timestamps.

9.3. Increasing the Allowed Transmission Rate

As stated in [17], multiplicative increase policies lead to network instabilities. When it is not in slow-start mode, RCC increases the allowed transmission rate λ of a sender according to

$$\lambda = \lambda + \frac{\text{MTU}\, len}{\text{RTT}^2\, \lambda} \qquad (1)$$

every time some of the sender's messages become stable, where len is the number of bytes of the acknowledged messages. MTU determines the gradient of the rate increase. To obtain growth-rates similar to TCP, we set MTU equal to 576, the smallest maximum transmission unit size allowed for IP. Indeed, equation (1) translates into the formula used in the TCP Reno algorithm if λ is substituted with window-size/RTT. λ increases by MTU/RTT every RTT time units, which is equivalent to increasing the window size by MTU bytes every RTT time units.

When increasing the send rate, RCC must make sure that a sender's transmission credit given by the smart leaky bucket remains unchanged. We therefore have to increase `do_not_send_before` by

$$\text{size\_of\_last\_msg} \left(\frac{1}{\lambda_{old}} - \frac{1}{\lambda_{new}} \right)$$

every time the allowed transmission rate is increased.

Being a rate-based congestion control algorithm, RCC must take measures to prevent a *rapid start up*. Unlike window-based schemes that start increasing a sender's window by receiving the acknowledgment of the first message sent after the window was reset, rate-based schemes react to acknowledgments initiated by messages that were sent before the allowed transmission rate is reset. In wide-area networks the number of acknowledgments can be significant. The congestion control algorithm therefore must ignore acknowledgments that arrive within the round-trip time between the sender and the creator of the acknowledgment. For timestamp-based acknowledgments, the delay must be significantly larger. We set this time to RTT.

9.4. Decreasing the Allowed Transmission Rate

Every time a transmission is unsuccessful, RCC resets the sender's allowed transmission rate. A sender learns about a transmission failure when it receives a retransmission request. Retransmission requests are broadcast to all senders. A sender does not distinguish whether it is the creator of the missing message — it reacts to all incoming requests in the same way.

When receiving a retransmission request, RCC resets the allowed transmission rate to λ_{init} =MTU/RTT, which corresponds to a window size of one. Furthermore, it calculates a threshold thr as half of the previous value of the allowed transmission rate. Before it enters slow-start mode, RCC destroys any credit given by the smart leaky bucket algorithm.

In slow-start mode, RCC increases the allowed transmission rate by

$$\lambda = \lambda + \frac{len}{\text{RTT}}$$

every time a sender's message of length len becomes stable. As soon as $\lambda > thr$, RCC leaves the slow-start mode.

To prevent RCC from setting thr to half of λ_{init}, no new threshold is calculated if a node receives another request for the same messages from a different node. As long as the new request contains a sequence number that has been requested already, RCC ignores the new request. Even if the requested sequence numbers do not overlap, RCC ignores all requests if they arrive within RTT time units after it has received the first request. This prevents RCC from setting the threshold to $\lambda_{init}/2$ in case a burst of messages is lost. This measure does not suppress a necessary reduction of λ because $\lambda = \lambda_{init}$ as long as RCC ignores all incoming acknowledgments.

Unlike TCP, which increases a sender's window every time a transmission is successful, RCC increases a sender's allowed transmission rate only if the sender transmits messages as fast as it is allowed. In case a sender sends with a rate $< \lambda$, RCC reduces the sender's allowed transmission rate. These two measures smoothen the burstiness of the traffic — which is necessary to prevent input buffer overflow when multiple senders are active.

9.5. Input Buffer Management

As stated previously, the likelihood of input buffer overflow increases with an increasing number of senders. Because most operating systems do not allow a user process to determine the current utilization of the network interface's input buffer, ARMP implements its own input buffer. It uses the asynchronous socket interface to retrieve incoming messages as soon as they are received and stores them in its own input buffer, which is implemented as a FIFO queue. Because the signal handler has a higher priority than an ARMP process, any buffer overflow that occurs will occur in ARMP's input buffer.

To signal a transmission failure ARMP does not wait until the buffer overflows. Instead, it monitors the buffer constantly and sends a message as soon as the buffer usage exceeds a limit L. This way ARMP forces all senders to reduce their send rates. ARMP uses a retransmission request message containing an empty request list. A sender does not distinguish between a retransmission request for a regular message and an empty retransmission request: it resets its allowed transmission rate and enters the slow-start mode.

To estimate L, we assume that none of the nodes currently is in slow-start mode and that the receiver purges messages from its input buffer at a constant rate λ_{out}. We let the sum of all of the sender's transmission rates reach λ_{out} at time $t_0 = 0$, and assume that N senders are arranged in the worst-case network topology (i.e., the channel latency from all senders to the receiver equals $\frac{1}{2}$RTT). If all senders increase their allowed transmission rate according to equation (1), the senders have generated

$$n = N \int_0^t \frac{\text{MTU}}{\text{RTT}^2} \tau \, d\tau = N \frac{\text{MTU} \, t^2}{2 \, \text{RTT}^2} \qquad (2)$$

more bytes then the receiver can handle at time t. Buffer overflow will occur if n exceeds b_{in}, the capacity of the receiver's buffer. By setting $n = b_{in}$ and $t = t_{crit}$ in equation (2) and solving for t_{crit}, we obtain

$$t_{crit} = \text{RTT} \sqrt{\frac{2b_{in}}{N \, \text{MTU}}}$$

The variable t_{crit} denotes the time at which all senders together have generated b_{in} more bytes than the receiver's input buffer can hold. The receiver's empty request must not arrive later than t_{crit} at all senders if buffer overflow is to be prevented. Because it takes $\frac{1}{2}$RTT for the empty request to travel to the senders, and another $\frac{1}{2}$RTT for messages to reach the receiver, the receiver must send the request when its buffer load exceeds

$$L = N \int_0^{t_{crit} - \text{RTT}} \frac{\text{MTU}}{\text{RTT}^2} \tau \, d\tau = \frac{N \, \text{MTU}}{2} \left(\sqrt{\frac{2b_{in}}{\text{MTU}}} - 1 \right)^2$$

$$= b_{in} - \sqrt{2N \, b_{in} \, \text{MTU}} + \frac{1}{2} N \, \text{MTU}$$

345

For $N = 40$ senders, MTU=576 bytes, and a buffer size of 100kB, we obtain $L = 43.64$kB.

10. Conclusion

We have presented ARMP, the reliable many-to-many multicast protocol of the Atomic Group system. The ATM environment, for which ARMP is designed, has lead to design choices that differ significantly from reliable multicast protocols developed for the Internet. Key differences are:

- Multicasting ACKs
- Simplified RTT measurement
- No ACK or NAK suppression
- No ACK or NAK delay
- Rate-based congestion control.

We have described the rationale behind our design choices, have discussed aspects of the implementation of the protocol, and have presented simulations of its behavior.

References

[1] K. P. Birman and R. van Renesse. *Reliable Distributed Computing with the Isis Toolkit.* IEEE Computer Society Press, Los Alamitos, CA, 1994.

[2] P. Ezhilchelvan, R. Macedo, S. Shrivastava. Newtop: A fault-tolerant group communication protocol. *Proceedings of the 15th IEEE International Conference on Distributed Computer Systems*, 296-306, Vancouver, Canada, May 1995.

[3] W. Jia, J. Cao, E. Nett and J. Kaiser. A high performance reliable atomic group protocol. *Proceedings of the IEEE International Conference on Parallel and Distributed Systems 1996*, 378–385, Tokyo, Japan, June 1996.

[4] L. E. Moser, P. M. Melliar-Smith, D. A. Agarwal, R. K. Budhia and C. A. Lingley-Papadopoulos. Totem: A fault-tolerant multicast group communication system *Communications of the ACM*, 39(4):54–63, April 1996.

[5] R. van Renesse, K. Birman, M. Hayden, A. Vaysburd and D. Karr. Building adaptive systems using Ensemble. *Software — Practice and Experience*, 28(9):963-979, July 1998.

[6] S. Floyd, V. Jacobson, C. G. Lui, S. McCanne, and L. Zhang. A reliable multicast framework for light-weight sessions and application level framing. *IEEE/ACM Transactions on Networking*, 5(6):784–803, December 1997.

[7] B. Whetten, T, Montgomery and S. Kaplan. A high performance totally ordered multicast protocol. *Proceedings of the International Workshop of Theory and Practice in Distributed Systems*, 33-57, Dagstuhl Castle, Germany, September 1994.

[8] B. N. Levine, and J. J. Garcia-Luna-Aceves. A comparison of known classes of reliable multicast protocols. *Proceedings of the IEEE International Conference on Network Protocols*, 112–121, Columbus, OH, November 1996.

[9] The ATM Forum. ATM user-network interface signaling specification, version 4.0. *af-sig 0061-000*, July 1996.

[10] G. Carle. Adaption layer and group communication server for reliable multipoint services in ATM networks. *Proceedings of the International Workshop on Multimedia: Advanced Teleservices and High-Speed Communication*, 128–138, Heidelberg, Germany, September 1994.

[11] G. Carle. Reliable group communication in ATM networks. *Proceedings of the Twelfth Annual Conference of the European Fibre Optic Communications and Networks*, 30–34, Heidelberg, Germany, June 1994.

[12] S. C. Chuang. A flexible and secure multicast architecture for ATM networks. *IEEE Globecom*, 701–707, Singapore, November 1995.

[13] R. Guerraoui and A. Schiper. Total order multicast to multiple groups. *Proceedings of the 17th IEEE International Conference on Distributed Computing Systems*, 578–585, Baltimore, MD, May 1997.

[14] L. Rodrigues, R. Guerraoui and A. Schiper. Scalable atomic multicast. *Proceedings of the 7th IEEE International Conference on Computer Communications and Networks*, 12–15, Lafayette, LA, October 1998.

[15] R. R. Koch. The Atomic Group Protocols: Reliable Ordered Message Delivery for ATM Networks. Ph.D. Thesis, Department of Electrical and Computer Engineering, University of California, Santa Barbara, CA, June 2000.

[16] K. Berket, R. Koch, L. E. Moser, and P. M. Melliar-Smith. Timestamp acknowledgment for determining message stability. *Proceedings of the International Conference on Parallel and Distributed Computing and Networking*, 1–8, Brisbane, Australia, December 1998.

[17] V. Jacobson. Congestion avoidance and control. *Proceedings of the ACM Symposium on Communications Architectures and Protocols*, 314–329, Stanford, CA, August 1988.

[18] S. Pingali, D. Towsley and J. F. Kurose. A comparison of sender-initiated and receiver-initiated reliable multicast protocols. *Performance Evaluation Review, Proceedings of the ACM SIGMETRICS Conference on Measurement and Modeling Computer Systems*, 22(1):221–230, May 1994.

[19] S. Mishra and L. Wu. An evaluation of flow control in group communication. *IEEE/ACM Transactions on Networking*, 6(5):571–587, October 1998.

[20] J. Golestani. Fundamental observations on multicast congestion control in the Internet. *Proceedings of the Conference on Conputer Communication (INFOCOM)*, 990–1000, New York, NY, March 1999.

[21] J. R. Cooperstock and S. Kotsopoulos. Exploiting group communication for reliable high volume data distribution. *Proceedings of the IEEE Pacific Rim Conference on Communications, Computers and Signal Processing*, 558–561, Victoria, Canada, May 1995.

[22] J. C. Bolot, T. Turletti, and I. Wakeman. Scalable feedback control for multicast video distribution in the Internet. *Proceedings of the ACM Symposium on Communications Architectures, Protocols and Applications*, 24(4):58–67, October 1994.

[23] A. Koifman and S. Zabele. RAMP: A reliable adaptive multicast protocol. *Proceedings of the 15th IEEE Conference on Computer Communications*, 1442–1451, San Francisco, CA, March 1996.

A Gossip-based Reliable Multicast for Large-scale High-throughput Applications

Qixiang Sun
Department of EECS
M.I.T.
qsun@mit.edu

Daniel C. Sturman
IBM T. J. Watson Research Center
30 Saw Mill River Road
Hawthorne, NY 10532 - USA
sturman@us.ibm.com

Abstract

Group-based reliable multicast is an important building block for distributed applications. For large systems, however, traditional approaches do not scale well due to centralized recovery mechanisms and excessive message overhead. In this paper, we present a reliable probabilistic multicast, rpbcast, that is a hybrid of the centralized and gossip-based approaches. In particular, rpbcast extends previous work by supporting high packet rates and many active senders. Rpbcast uses gossip as the primary retransmission mechanism and only contacts loggers if gossips fail. Large groups of active senders are supported using negative gossip *that specifies those messages a receiver is missing instead of those messages it received. Moreover, we show that negative gossip allows* pull *based recovery and converges faster than* push *based recovery. Rpbcast also applies hashing techniques to reduce message overhead and approximate group membership for garbage collection. We describe the key features of* rpbcast *and present simulation results.*

1 Introduction

Reliable multicast has many uses in distributed applications. For instance, group communication services often require a reliable broadcast/multicast channel to collaborate on a task. Reliable multicast is also important in more generic applications that simply need to disseminate information reliably to multiple receivers. Replicated database services and stock quote distribution are two examples. One generalization of these information distribution services is the publish/subscribe paradigm. In pub-lish/subscribe, information flows from publishers to subscribers via mass distribution services such as reliable multicast. Typically, there are large numbers of publishers (senders) and subscribers (receivers).

Many multicast protocols have been proposed in the research literature. However, most do not scale well to large numbers of senders and receivers in widely distributed applications. Aside from group size, high transmission rates within a multicast group are also problematic because more dropped packets will overload retransmission sources faster and result in higher delivery latency.

In this paper, we propose a hybrid approach for building a reliable multicast that handles high transmission rates and many senders. We merge the reliability guarantee of a centralized logging approach and the high performance aspects of a gossip-based approach. In section 2, we survey some previous work. Section 3 describes the key features of our hybrid protocol. Section 4 presents simulated results of our protocol comparing to Log-based Receiver-reliable Multicast (*LBRM*) [6] and Bimodal Multicast (*pbcast*) [1]. We conclude in section 5 and briefly discuss some future work.

2 Previous Work

Two general approaches exist for building reliable multicast. The first approach uses *loggers*: centralized servers with stable storage that archive packets and handle retransmission requests. The scalability of this approach depends on the availability of logger resources such as logger processing speed and network link bandwidth. With large groups or high traffic multicast groups, logger resources are easily exhausted.

One example of the centralized approach is

Log-Based Receiver-reliable Multicast (*LBRM*) [6]. *LBRM* is *receiver-reliable* because individual receivers are responsible for detecting missing packets and requesting the appropriate retransmissions from dedicated loggers. In order to detect missing packets, senders include a sequence number in each packet. Hence any gap in the sequence number implies that there are missing packets. However, during idle periods, a receiver may not realize that it is missing the latest packet. Thus receiver-reliable multicast also requires senders to periodically send *heartbeat* messages to notify receivers of the latest sequence number. *LBRM* uses a variable heartbeat scheme to reduce heartbeat overhead.

An alternative to receiver-reliable protocols are *sender-reliable* protocols where senders require packet arrival acknowledgments (ACK) from each receiver and retransmit any unacknowledged packets. Reliable Multicast Transport Protocol (*RMTP*) [7] is a sender-reliable protocol. One drawback in sender-reliable multicast is the ACK implosion problem, which occurs when many ACK messages converge on the sender site. *RMTP* uses a hierarchical structure to reduce the number of ACKs at the sender site. For large groups, receiver-reliable protocols introduce less network and processing overhead than sender-reliable protocols. Furthermore, receiver-reliable protocols are ideal for enforcing application-level end-to-end reliability.

A second reliable multicast approach relies on peer-based recovery mechanisms. Instead of dedicated loggers, peer-based mechanisms use all members in a multicast group, both senders and receivers, as retransmission sources. When a particular receiver is missing a packet, any group member may process and service retransmission requests. An example of the peer-based approach is Scalable Reliable Multicast (*SRM*) [3]. Servicing rate is no longer a constraining factor in *SRM* because any member may handle a retransmission request. However, the message overhead introduced by peer-based requests and repairs is substantial. In *SRM*, requests and repairs are multicast, making the protocol less scalable from a network bandwidth perspective. Moreover, a retransmission request in *SRM* may cause redundant retransmissions from different members. *SRM* resolves this problem by randomizing the delays in retransmissions and suppressing retransmissions when other members have already serviced them.

A more scalable peer-based protocol is Bimodal multicast (*pbcast*) [1]. *Pbcast* uses point-to-point

gossip to reduce excessive message traffic. In *pbcast*, each member in the multicast group periodically gossips to other members. During each gossip round, each receiver selects a random target in the multicast group and sends a digest of the current buffer to the gossip target. Upon receiving the digest, the target receiver can determine if the gossiper has a packet which the target does not and request retransmission via point-to-point channels. This approach avoids *SRM*'s redundant retransmission problem. Thus, *pbcast* is more stable than *SRM* in terms of throughput under varying network conditions [9]. Other gossip style protocols include replicated database maintenance [2], group membership [4], resource discovery [5], and failure detector [11].

Without loggers to archive old packets, peer-based approaches usually do not guarantee reliable delivery. For example, suppose some members disconnect for a long period. Then the entire multicast group has to stall progress when each member's message buffer is full, or exclude disconnected members from the multicast group in order to release buffer space. In large-scale information dissemination applications, neither stalling nor excluding members is desirable. Ozkasap et al. [8] proposes selectively archiving a packet for a longer duration than the garbage collection limit. However, this approach does not fully guarantee reliable delivery either since network congestion may cause a packet to be dropped before arriving at designated archiving sites, even after many rounds of gossip.

3   Reliable   Probabilistic   Multicast (rpbcast)

To provide a stronger reliability guarantee without explicit acknowledgments from all receivers, we extend *pbcast* by introducing loggers with stable storage. In our reliable probabilistic multicast (*rpbcast*), we guarantee that if a sender does not crash before its message arrives at a logger, then all receivers will eventually receive the message. More formally, *rpbcast*'s fault tolerance model assumes transient crashes and link failures, ie. members in the multicast group will eventually recover. Thus *rpbcast* guarantees message delivery if each member eventually reaches an always up state. If a sender also has first logging capability, then as long as the sender recovers *rpbcast* also guarantees message delivery to all members.

Reliable multicast in *rpbcast* is divided into three phases. The first phase distributes a packet *en mass*

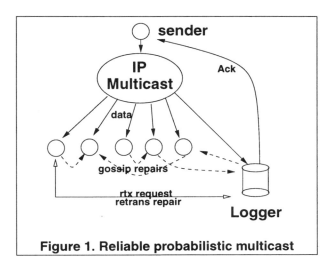

Figure 1. Reliable probabilistic multicast

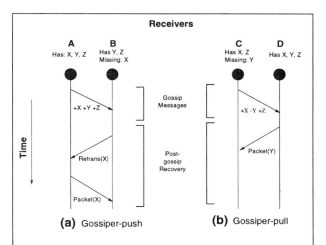

(a) Gossiper-push   **(b)** Gossiper-pull

Figure 2. Gossip recovery examples: In (a), gossiper A pushes out a missing packet X to B. In (b), gossiper C pulls in a missing packet Y from D.

to all receivers through an unreliable channel such as IP multicast. The second phase repairs lost packets in a distributed manner using periodic gossips. If the previous two phases fail, then the last phase utilizes loggers for retransmission. Figure 1 illustrates these interactions.

Rpbcast is a receiver-reliable [10] protocol. Each multicast packet in *rpbcast* includes a sender-based sequence number. After receiving a packet, each receiver independently determines which packets are missing and whether to solicit retransmissions. *Rpbcast* relies on *application layer feedback* to decide whether the protocol should try to recover a missing packet. This approach allows individual applications to define their own reliability criteria. Once an application decides to ask for retransmissions, the receiver will request packet retransmission in successive gossip rounds.

In designing our hybrid gossip and log-based multicast protocol, we emphasize

- guaranteeing reliable packet delivery to all receivers

- maintaining low delivery latency,

- balancing retransmission service load,

- and reducing network traffic, both per link and per node.

The following sections detail various aspects of *rpbcast* and how they contribute to our overall design objectives. Section 3.1 describes the gossip recovery phase of the protocol. Section 3.2 discusses using negative gossips and hashing heartbeats in the gossip phase. Section 3.3 outlines the logger

recovery phase. Section 3.4 deals with garbage collection mechanisms in the protocol. And section 3.5 presents an approximate membership used in garbage collection.

3.1 Gossip Recovery Phase

Gossip recovery is the primary retransmission mechanism in *rpbcast*. In a single gossip round, a receiver randomly selects a gossip target and sends a unicast gossip message to the target. This message reflects the sender's current message buffer, including missing packets. Upon receiving a gossip message, the target may retransmit any missing packets to the gossiper (gossiper-pull), may ask the gossiper for retransmissions (gossiper-push), or both. Figure 2 illustrates the two forms of gossip initiated retransmissions.

Rpbcast uses gossiper-pull recovery because of faster convergence and lower latency. Demers et al in [2] gave an intuitive reason for why gossiper-pull converges faster in database replication. In reliable multicast, the same observation holds because gossiper-pull is more effective than gossiper-push when a majority of the group members have a message.

To illustrate the difference in convergence rate, suppose we have 100 receivers and that gossip targets are selected uniformly. Now consider the scenario where a multicast packet is only received by a fraction of all receivers. Figure 3 shows the num-

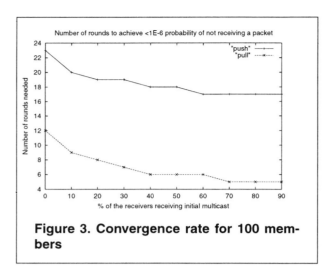

Figure 3. Convergence rate for 100 members

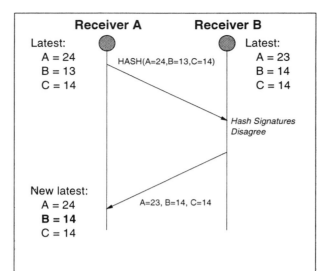

Figure 4. Hashing and merging heartbeat information

ber of rounds before the probability of at least one receiver not receiving the packet is less than 10^{-6}.

Under normal conditions, where a multicast reaches most receivers, gossiper-pull will have a lower expected delivery latency than gossiper-push. Gossiper-pull also allows a receiver to request retransmission immediately after detecting a missing packet instead of waiting until the next gossip cycle, thus further improving packet delivery latency. In comparison, our hybrid protocol *rpbcast* uses only gossiper-pull while *pbcast* uses gossiper-push.

3.2 Negative Gossip and Hashing Heartbeats

One potential drawback of the gossip approach is the network overhead introduced by the period gossip messages. In this section, we describe two optimizations for reducing this overhead.

The first optimization is the use of *negative gossip*. A negative gossip is analogous to NACKs in other transfer protocols. Instead of describing a member's message buffer content in the gossip messages (*positive gossip*), a member in *rpbcast* explicitly lists all currently missing messages. Note that listing missing messages will usually be smaller than describing the entire message buffer, especially under high send rates. Since our protocol uses the gossiper-pull mechanism, this optimization does not effect the performance of the gossip phase. A second benefit of using *negative gossip* is the ability of a responder to quickly inform the gossiper that a message can no longer be recovered through gossips. This second benefit is highly desirable in our hybrid approach because it serves as a notification for the gossiper to fall back on using loggers immediately. Positive

gossips are insufficient for this task because a responder cannot distinguish between the cases that the gossiper is missing a message and that the gossiper has received and garbage collected a message. Section 3.3 will go into more detail of using this notification in the logger recovery phase.

The second optimization for gossip messages involves distribution of latest sequence numbers, commonly known as *heartbeats*. Heartbeats are necessary in receiver-reliable protocols to facilitate detection of lost messages, especially if a member is missing the latest message. A simple and relatively efficient solution is using *LBRM*'s variable heartbeat scheme. However, this scheme will induce considerable overhead if the number of idle senders is large. Alternatively, we can also propagate heartbeats through gossip messages.

Consider a naive alternative approach that includes all the latest sequence numbers from each sender in every gossip message. Note that combining the latest sequence numbers and negative gossip in each gossip message is equivalent to positive gossip, ie. listing all previously received messages. Thus we lose the reduced message size benefit from negative gossips. To improve upon the naive approach, we take advantage of that fact that we have N heartbeats in one gossip message as opposed to N separate heartbeat multicast messages in *LBRM*'s variable heartbeats scheme.

We realize this advantage by "compressing" N heartbeats into something smaller to reduce heartbeats overhead, which is not possible if each heartbeat is in a different message. More specifically, *Rpbcast* compresses the heartbeats through hashing. Let HB_i be the last known sequence number from idle sender i, then *rpbcast* computes $hsig = HASH(\cup_i HB_i)$ using some collision-free hash function $HASH$. Instead of gossiping all N heartbeats, *rpbcast* gossips the hash signature $hsig$. If the gossip target has the same signature, ie. they agree on the latest sequence numbers, then no further information exchange is necessary. On the other hand, if signatures differ, then the target will respond with a list of its heartbeats and let the gossiper merge the difference. Figure 4 demonstrates the interaction. Note that sending a hash signature and then merging the difference is essentially a gossiper-pull mechanism for finding out the latest sequence numbers. One optimization is for the gossiper to also update the target if the target is behind in some heartbeat values. This optimization is equivalent to having both pull and push in one gossip round.

Gossip with hashing as described above does not function well as the main heartbeat distribution mechanism: when a new heartbeat value appears at a particular sender, every member will see a different signature and cause a mass exchange of heartbeat values. To avoid this problem, *rpbcast* requires each sender to initially multicast its heartbeat value before entering an idle period. This initial multicast mass-distributes the new heartbeat value. Consequently, the hashing optimization will only handle minor corrections. Thus the periodic heartbeat is replaced by one multicast and gossips. Another optimization is to use a variable gossip rate for hash signatures. This optimization reduces message traffic and thus lowers overhead.

The effectiveness of gossip with hashing for distributing heartbeat information depends on how often hash signatures disagree. Since a heartbeat value is unchanged during a particular idle period, disagreements can only occur immediately following a sender's transition from active to idle. If this active-to-idle transition and loss rate on the initial heartbeat multicast are high, then the hashing scheme will behave like the naive approach because disagreements result in a full exchange of heartbeat values. On the other hand, if these rates are low compared to the gossip period and that the number of idle senders is reasonably large, then the hashing optimization will result in significantly lower overhead than that incurred by *LBRM*'s variable heartbeats.

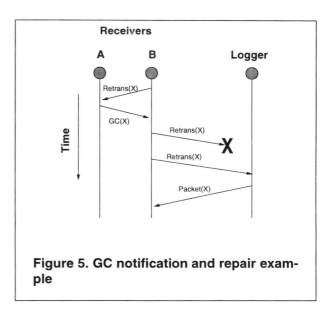

Figure 5. GC notification and repair example

3.3 Logger Recovery Phase

As noted earlier, a member may fail to recover a missing message through gossiping due to message buffer garbage collection. Under this circumstance, the member needs to be notified of contacting a logger for future retransmission requests. In *rpbcast*, when member A requests retransmission for a message that has already been garbage collected at member B, B will send a *garbage collected notification* to A. This notification will alert A to stop gossiping about the missing message and send all future requests directly to a logger. A member can determine that a message has been garbage collected locally if (1) the requested message is not in its message buffer and (2) the member is not currently missing the requested message. Figure 5 illustrates the use of garbage collected notification.

Note that loggers in *rpbcast* are similar in function to the logging servers in *LBRM*. However, *rpbcast* uses loggers strictly as backup to gossip-based retransmissions while *LBRM* relies on loggers to handle all retransmissions. This difference allows *rpbcast* to spread most of the retransmission work load across all members instead of the few dedicated servers. Furthermore, all loggers in *rpbcast* are identical and equal in function while *LBRM* imposes an hierarchy on participating loggers. If a logger in *rpbcast* leaves or crashes, there is no need to run leader election or other protocols to redistribute work load among the remaining loggers. Moreover, we can add more loggers to the system to increase logger availability, hence improve reliability and fault tolerance against logger failures.

3.4 Garbage Collection

There are three places in *rpbcast* that need garbage collection (GC): at receivers, at loggers, and at senders. Since *rpbcast* is a hybrid protocol, its garbage collection scheme is also a hybrid. *Rpbcast* enforces stability oriented GC for loggers, ACK based GC for senders, and no GC restrictions for receivers.

Garbage collection at receivers is not restricted. However we typically use either age-oriented or buffer-oriented GC. In an age-oriented approach, a message is garbage collected after a fixed amount of time. The buffer-oriented approach simply removes the oldest message in the buffer when space is needed. *Rpbcast* currently uses the age-oriented approach. For very high send rates, the age-oriented approach may be infeasible due to large memory requirements.

Garbage collection at loggers is stability oriented. To simplify the discussion, assume, for the moment, that we have a membership from which a logger can determine which members are required to acknowledge a message. Section 3.5 presents more details of this membership protocol. With the membership information, loggers only need to wait for acknowledgments before garbage collection. Explicit ACKs from each receiver are impractical for a large group due to the ACK implosion problem. In *rpbcast*, we exploit the information contained in gossip messages to derive these acknowledgments.

Recall that a gossip message contains a hash signature of heartbeats (latest sequence numbers) and a list of missing messages. Therefore, messages with ids smaller than the heartbeat values and are not in the missing message list must have been received by the gossiper earlier. Hence gossips also contain implicity acknowledgments which loggers can use. These derived ACKs are the mechanism for garbage collection at loggers. In the event of a receiver crashing and never recovering, loggers may garbage collection a message after a long period of time, for example several days.

Garbage collection at sender requires acknowledgments from a logger. Consequently, loggers in *rpbcast* must explicitly send an ACK to the sender. As a backup in the case of logger's acknowledgments are lost, senders can also infer ACKs from a logger's gossip message similar to the derived ACKs described above. This requirement is necessary to ensure a message will reach some logger.

3.5 Approximate Membership

Membership information is used in *rpbcast* for two purposes: selecting a gossip target and maintaining stability oriented garbage collection at loggers. For selecting a gossip target, we do not need a precise and up-to-date membership all the time. As long as membership changes are eventually propagated to every member, *rpbcast* will function correctly. This observation suggests that gossip is an appropriate tool for distributing membership. In fact, *rpbcast* distributes membership information in the same manner as heartbeats. Current membership information is hashed and sent with each gossip message. When disagreements occur with hashed signatures, the full membership information is exchanged.

This lazy approach to membership is not sufficient for loggers because they need to know precisely when a new member has joined or left the group. A simple solution is to let loggers handle all membership joins and leaves. As long as one logger knows about a join or a leave, the gossips will take care of the propagation. Again, an initial multicast of join and leave events will improve protocol's efficiency.

A weaker version of joins and leaves is also possible, partially based on [4]. In this weaker version, a new member multicasts a join message to the group until it receives k distinct gossip replies, ie. k sponsors. Note that each gossip reply signifies that a member has accepted the join and began propagating that information. Once a new member has received k gossips, the precise moment of its joining is determined by the maximum sequence numbers from all k replies. For example, sponsor 1 may reply sequence numbers $\{15, 6\}$ while sponsor 2 replies sequence numbers $\{12, 8\}$. Then the moment of joining is when the sequence numbers are $\{15, 8\}$.

This join mechanism is correct because garbage collection of any message sent after a sponsor's acceptance of the new member will first require that sponsor's acknowledgment. Since acknowledgments are derived from the sponsor's gossips to the loggers, the loggers will learn about the new member's existence before garbage collecting and act accordingly. Therefore, no messages after the moment of joining will be garbage collected without the new member's acknowledgments.

Note that loggers may keep more messages than strictly necessary under this weak membership, especially if a join attempt failed to secure k sponsors. However, loggers can treat a failed join as a member

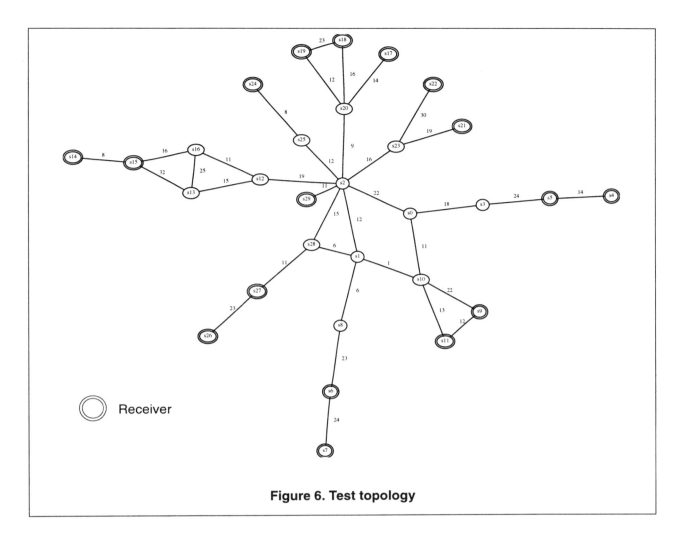

Figure 6. Test topology

crash and wait for that member to rejoin. Another minor detail is distinguishing between multiple join attempts from the same member. We solve that problem by attaching a unique and strictly increasing id, such as the local time, to each join attempt. The reason we take the maximum of all the sequence numbers is to ensure that if some of the sponsors fail before propagating their membership information to a logger, we still have the correct behaviors. Obviously, requiring k sponsors tolerates $k - 1$ failures. Leave operation is identical to the join operation.

3.6 Other Parameters

Three other parameters will effect *rpbcast*. Selecting who to gossip to is central to the protocol's performance. Several options exists: uniform gossip, linear bias toward near neighbors, or other biasing schemes. Our experimental results in the next section suggest linear biasing is a good candidate.

A second parameter is how often to gossip. Our current protocol has a fixed gossip period. An alternative to the fixed period scheme is randomized gossip delays or hot/cold rumor spreading as proposed in [2]. We have not experiemented with these alternatives.

The last parameter is when to multicast retransmissions. *LBRM* uses a statistical acknowledgments approach for determine when to multicast retransmissions. A similar scheme might work in *rpbcast*. However, it is unclear how to incorporate this approach without introducing excessive network overhead.

4 Results

Our experiments focus on comparisons between gossip-based *pbcast*, log-based *LBRM*, and our hybrid protocol *rpbcast*. We implemented these three protocols as agents in UC Berkeley's Network Simu-

Table 1. Protocol specific parameters		
Parameter	Value	Protocols
Gossip period	0.25 sec	[r]pbcast
GC limit	10 rounds	[r]pbcast
Gossip selection	linear bias	[r]pbcast
Min heartbeat rate	0.25 sec	lbrm
Max heartbeat rate	32 sec	lbrm
Back off factor	2	lbrm
Retransmission rate	0.25 sec	lbrm

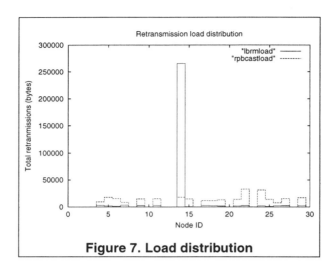

Figure 7. Load distribution

lator NS2 using C++ and conducted test runs using NS2.

4.1 Experimental setup

Our test topology is a thirty node tier-hierarchy topology generated by Georgia Tech's Internetwork Topology Models (GT-ITM). Figure 6 shows the topology layout. The numbers on each link are the latencies for those links.

Of the thirty nodes, eighteen fringe nodes participate in our multicast experiments. Moreover, each receiver can also be a sender in our experiment. Node 14 on the far left side of network is the designated logger for both *LBRM* and *rpbcast*. Each link in the network is a 100Mb/sec bidirectional link.

Unfortunately, NS2 does not simulate packet servicing time at individual nodes. We approximate request service time by imposing a fixed limit on how many recovery requests a node can process in a second. In our experiments, we do not count multicast data packets toward this service limit because we are only interested in bounding overhead processing time. The default service limit is 1000 repair retransmissions per second. We also set the router queue limit to be 50 packets. In our test runs, we did not observe any packet loss due to queue overflow. Other protocol specific parameters are summarized in table 1.

In our experiments, each test run consists of 10 seconds of multicast traffic plus some additional lingering time to reliably deliver packets to every receiver. During this 10 seconds, each sender independently generates 1 kilobyte packets, with Poisson arrival rates. When we vary multicast rates in our experiments, we vary the expected number of packets generated by each sender. Since neither *pbcast* nor *LBRM* has any implicit membership controls, we maintain a constant membership throughout the test runs.

4.2 Retransmission load distribution and link utilization

The key advantage of gossip-based multicast over log-based multicast is balanced distribution of retransmission requests among all receivers. Figure 7 illustrates typical load distribution for *LBRM* and *rpbcast* when the network is not congested. This particular load distribution is for 18 senders with 1% packet loss and 360 packets per second overall.

As expected, the logger in *LBRM*, node 14, has significantly more retransmissions than any receivers in *rpbcast*. The retransmission traffic from non-logger nodes in *LBRM* are packets that did not reach the logger during the initial multicast, and are therefore retransmitted by the sender. *Rpbcast*'s balanced load distribution also results in better link utilization. Figure 8 shows the overall traffic per link. Notice the four peaks in the figure for *LBRM*. These four links are the bottleneck links from the logger to the hub in the center of the network. In practice, we expect large link bandwidth between a logger and the network backbone, thus higher link usage may not be as significant as logger service rate.

Balanced load distribution in *rpbcast* is not free. In order for every receiver to act as a retransmission source, each receiver has to buffer a packet for some time. Thus a receiver in *rpbcast* has higher memory requirements than *LBRM*. For our experiments, we buffer each packet for 10 gossip rounds. Thus each node buffers all packets that arrived in the past 2.5 seconds. In practice, we suggest a fixed buffer size and garbage collecting oldest packets when space is needed. This approach will effect convergence time. However, under average network conditions,

354

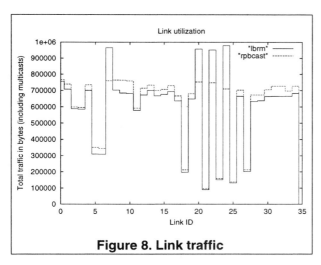

Figure 8. Link traffic

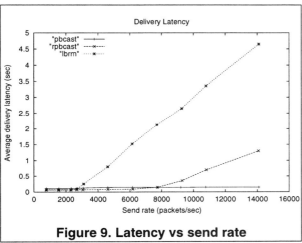

Figure 9. Latency vs send rate

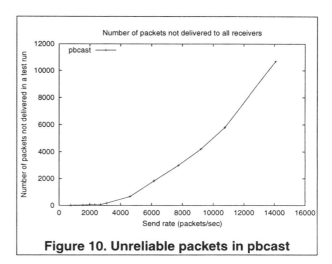

Figure 10. Unreliable packets in pbcast

two or three rounds of gossiping is usually sufficient for delivering a packet to all receivers. In the worse case, receivers will resort back to contacting the logger. In particular *rpbcast* has the same behavior as *LBRM* when the network saturates due to an extended period of external noise.

4.3 Delivery Latency

The motivation for distributing retransmission requests among all receivers is to maintain low delivery latency under high send rates. We define delivery latency as the time between a sender multicasting a packet and all receivers receiving the packet. With high send rates, the number of missing packets will also increase, thus overloading dedicated loggers and introducing higher latency. Figure 9 illustrates this behavior.

In this experiment, we set packet size to 1 kilobyte, loss rate at 1%, and maximum retransmission

limit at 1000 requests per second. The most interesting aspect of the latency figure is the crossover point between *LBRM* and *rpbcast*. Before the cross-over, the logger in *LBRM* is not overloaded. Hence *LBRM* is able to provide timely retransmissions, whereas *rpbcast* is randomly selecting retransmission sources, some of which do not succeed. After the cross-over point, the logger at node 14 can not keep up with retransmission requests, resulting in higher latency. This bottleneck does not exist in *rpbcast* until a much higher send rate, when gossips fail to service all retransmissions before garbage collection. If we stretch the plot farther out to the point where the network saturates, both *LBRM* and *rpbcast* will have large latencies. These latency results suggest that a further optimization would be to use *LBRM* for low send rate and switch to *rpbcast* after detecting logger congestion.

One may also notice that *rpbcast* has lower latency than *pbcast*. This result supports our claim that pull-based recovery exhibits lower latency than push-based recovery. Another point to mention is that, although *pbcast* has constant latency, it does not deliver packets to all receivers at high send rates. Figure 10 shows the number of packets not received by all receivers.

4.4 Non-repair related overhead

Another important scalability factor is message overhead. Since each protocol must repair roughly equal number of packets, we separate retransmission packets from other protocol-specific overhead. In non-repair related overhead, we measure the amount of non-multicast and non-repair packets. This overhead for *pbcast* includes gossip messages

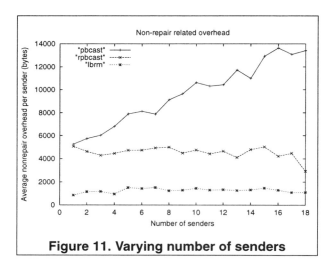

Figure 11. Varying number of senders

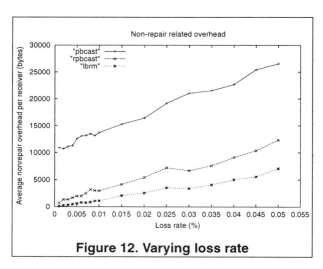

Figure 12. Varying loss rate

and retransmission requests. In our implementation of *pbcast*, we use an interval representation for gossiping buffer content instead of listing each packet in the buffer. We chose the interval representation because high multicast rates will result in very large gossip messages if we simply list individual packets. In the worst case where we miss every other packet, an interval representation is twice as large as explicitly listing packets. For *LBRM*, the overhead messages consist of acknowledgments, periodic heartbeats, and retransmission requests. *Rpbcast* overhead consists of gossips, garbage collected notifications, and acknowledgments.

Three variables contribute to the variations in protocol overhead: number of senders, packet loss rate, and multicast rate. We present two sets of overhead measurements by varying the number of senders and the packet loss rate. Since a higher multicast rate simply results in more dropped packets, we omit that measurement here. Figure 11 shows changes in protocol overhead as we vary the number of senders from a single sender to all 18 senders. In these test runs, the loss rate is 1%, and multicast traffic rate is fixed at approximately 360 total packets per second.

Note that because of the positive gossips, overhead for *pbcast* is approximately linear with the number of senders. On the other hand, *LBRM* and our *rpbcast* are insensitive to the number of senders. The constant difference in overhead between *rpbcast* and *LBRM* is due to additional information in *rpbcast*'s gossip messages, such as hashing signatures. If an application also requires membership information, then overhead for *LBRM* will increase due to an additional membership protocol while *rpbcast* overhead already includes membership over-

Table 2. Delivery latency

Distribution	Average latency	Std. Dev.
uniform	0.069361	0.162196
linear	0.082338	0.187496
quadratic	0.135950	0.439507

head. Observe that when every node is sending packets (18 senders), no idle heartbeats are generated. Consequently, *rpbcast* overhead decreases by half because hash signatures for heartbeats are no longer needed.

A similar experiment was conducted with loss rates ranging from 0.1% to 5%. Figure 12 shows the increase in protocol overhead as loss rate increases. The growth in overhead in all three protocols is dominated by more retransmission requests. *Pbcast* has more overhead than the other two because of the positive gossips. Again the difference between *LBRM* and *rpbcast* is the hash signature information in gossip messages.

4.5 Effects of different gossip selection distribution

In these test runs, we use linear biasing based on estimated round trip time in *rpbcast* for selecting gossip target. We also explored using uniform selection and quadratic biasing where the selection probability decreases quadratically with respect to the increase in round trip time. Figure 13 and table 2 summaries link utilization and latency for each of the three distributions. The experiments have 1% loss rate and approximately 360 packets per second.

Uniform selection has the lowest delivery latency. However, uniform gossips result in higher network

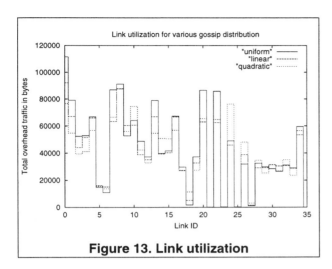

Figure 13. Link utilization

traffic than biased distributions. Since the difference in network traffic is insignificant between linear and quadratic biasing, we chose linear biasing in the test runs because of the better latency.

5   Conclusion

In this paper we have described our hybrid protocol *rpbcast* for high send rates and many active senders. We preserved performance advantages of gossip-based multicast while adding packet reliability guarantees using loggers. Three other contributions of the protocol are:

- Negative gossip messages that describe what a receiver does not have. This change allows efficient pull-based recovery which converges faster. Negative gossips also reduce gossip overhead in environments with large numbers of senders. A secondary benefit is a simple detection and notification mechanism for garbage collected packets.

- Gossiping and hashing heartbeat and membership information to reduce overhead in environments with large sender population. Without hashing, gossiping heartbeats neutralizes advantages of negative gossips. Also, overhead of continuously gossiping membership will be much higher without hashing.

- Approximate membership for the purpose of gossiping and garbage collection. The weak membership presented in section 3.5 also exploits the flexiblity in the garbage collection criteria to avoid expensive join/leave operations.

Our performance results demonstrate that *rpbcast* improves upon previous work in situations with high send rate and many senders. We recognize that our protocol is not an ideal solution for low send rates or few senders. In those cases, *LBRM* certainly out-performs *rpbcast*. We emphasize applications of our protocol in large scale information distribution services, such as publish/subscribe systems. For future work, we intend to move from simulated results to real world application. We also intend to explore the integration of variable gossip rates to reduce overhead, sampling negative gossips for multicasting retransmissions, and dynamically switching between *LBRM* and *rpbcast* based on logger congestion.

Acknowledgments

We would like to thank Idit Keider, Mark Astley, and Nancy Lynch for their input on the design and testing of our hybrid protocol. Discussions with these three individuals were very helpful in the development of the protocol. We would also like to thank Ken Birman and Oznur Ozkasap for their assistance in understanding *pbcast*.

References

[1] K. P. Birman, M. Hayden, O. Ozkasap, Z. Xiao, M. Budiu, and Y. Minsky. Bimodal multicast. *ACM Transactions on Computer Systems*, 17(2):41–88, May 1999.

[2] A. J. Demers, D. H. Greene, C. Hauser, W. Irish, and J. Larson. Epidemic algorithms for replicated database maintenance. In *Proceedings of the Sixth Annual ACM Symposium on Principles of Distributed Computing*, pages 1–12, Vancouver, British Columbia, Canada, August 1987.

[3] S. Floyd, V. Jacobson, C.G. Liu, S. McCanne, and L. Zhang. A reliable multicast framework for light-weight sessions and application level framing. *IEEE/ACM Transactions on Networking*, pages 784–803, December 1997.

[4] R. Golding and K. Taylor. Group membership in the epidemic style. Technical Report UCSC-CRL-92-13, UC Santa Cruz, Dept. of Computer Science, 1992.

[5] M. Harchol-Balter, T. Leighton, and D. Lewin. Resource discovery in distributed networks. In

18th Annual ACM-SIGACT/SIGOPS Symposium on Principles of Distributed Computing, Atlanta, May 1999.

[6] H. Holbrook, S. Singhal, and D. Cheriton. Log-based receiver-reliable multicast for distributed interactive simulation. In *Proceedings of ACM SIGCOMM '95*, 1995.

[7] J.C. Lin and S. Paul. A reliable multicast transport protocol. In *Proc. of IEEE INFOCOM'96*, pages 1414–1424, March 1996.

[8] O. Ozkasap, R. van Renesse, K. Birman, and Z. Xiao. Efficient buffering in reliable multicast protocols. In *First International Workshop on Networked Group Communication*, Pisa, November 1999.

[9] O. Ozkasap, Z. Xiao, and K. P. Birman. Scalability of two reliable multicast protocols. Technical report, Cornell University, Dept. of Computer Science, 1999.

[10] S. Pingali, D. Towsley, and J. Kurose. A comparison of sender-initiated and receiver-initiated reliable multicast protocols. *IEEE JSAC*, 15, April 1991.

[11] R. van Renesse, Y. Minsky, and M. Hayden. A gossip-style failure detection service. In *Proc. of Middleware '98*, pages 55–70, September 1998.

Session 10C

System Demonstrations

Fault-Tolerant Ethernet for IP-Based Process Control: A Demonstration

S. Song‡, J. Huang‡, P. Kappler‡, R. Freimark†, J. Gustin†, and T. Kozlik†

‡Honeywell Technology Center, MN   †Honeywell Industrial Automation and Control, AZ
{Sejun.Song}@honeywell.com

Abstract

We present an efficient middleware-based fault-tolerant Ethernet (FTE) prototype developed for process control networks. This unique approach requires no change of commercial-off-the-shelf (COTS) hardware (switch, hub, Ethernet physical link and Network Interface Card (NIC)) and software (Ethernet driver and protocol), yet it is transparent to application software. The FTE performs failure detection and recovery for handling multiple points of network failures and supports communications with non FTE-native devices. In this demonstration, we focus on presenting the failure detection and recovery behavior under various failure modes and scenarios. Further, multiple failure handling, node departure and non FTE-native node and FTE node communication scenarios will be presented. The FTE protocol status will be displayed using an FTE User Interface on a COTS-based network system.

1 Introduction

Network fault tolerance has been one of the most important system capabilities required by mission-critical network systems such as process control applications. Various proprietary fault-tolerant network solutions have been researched and manufactured targeting at specific product lines [1]. Today, distributed control systems are being developed using commercial-off-the-shelf (COTS) network products to reduce product development cycle time and cost and achieve system interoperability. In the process control industry, Ethernet is becoming a de facto choice for open control network strategies [2, 3, 4]. *Ethernet*, however, was not originally designed to handle network faults. Therefore, various research, development, and standardization efforts are under way to add fault-tolerance capabilities to Ethernet-based mission-critical networks.

In recent years, several traditional PC and network equipment suppliers, including 3Com, Adaptec, Compaq, Znyx, and Intel, recently rolled out dual-NIC-based redundant Ethernet products for mission-critical information systems. However, these products may not be suitable for the distributed control system (DCS) environment, as the products are designed based on a client-server model instead of an end-to-end LAN redundancy model.

In this paper, we present a COTS-based fault-tolerant Ethernet (FTE) [5, 6] middleware solution. Our work is unique in that it uses COTS products and provides end-to-end fault-tolerant network communication between peer nodes rather than end server nodes. Furthermore, the FTE handles multiple faults as well as supports non FTE-native nodes without performance degradation. The FTE has been developed to address the following requirements:

- Multiple faults must be detected. In the presence of multiple faults, any peer nodes should be able to communicate as long as a healthy link exists between them.
- Domain-wide failover time must be less than 2 sec.
- Nodes that do not run the FTE middleware must be able to communicate with FTE nodes as long as a physical link exists between them.
- The applied multi-fault detection and recovery protocol and algorithms must support TCP/IP, UDP/IP, and IP multicast traffic with no application-notable degradation.
- Performance scalability should be considered to support larger network systems, which may have hundreds of nodes.
- The fault-tolerant Ethernet must be compatible with, and capable of using, COTS Ethernet hubs and switches.

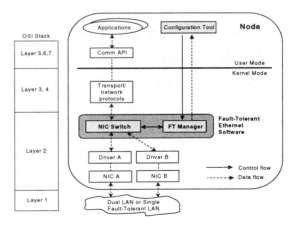

Figure 1-1. Fault-Tolerant *Ethernet* Architecture

Our FTE design and prototype are based on several guiding principles:

(1) *No change to COTS products*—Commodity hardware and software have become basic building blocks of control systems and networks. Ideally, fault-tolerant Ethernet shall be capable of being built and run with any vendor products (i.e., COTS hubs, switches, NICs, and drivers) in a "plug-and-play" fashion. To support such flexibility and interoperability, we employed a middleware approach. As shown in Figure 1-1, a piece of FTE software is sliced into the network communications stack, between the network data link layer and the transport and network protocol layers.

(2) *Separation of mechanisms from algorithms*—The FTE may evolve in terms of its failure detection and recovery capabilities and network management functions. To maintain the algorithm evolvability and configurability, we separate the FTE's data transmission and failure detection and recovery mechanisms from its failure detection and recovery algorithms. As a result, the FTE consists of two functional components, NIC Switch and Fault-Tolerant Manager (see Figure 1-1), the former implementing the mechanisms and the latter configurable for various algorithms.

(3) *Simplicity*—In accordance with the universal principle of keeping a design simple, we emphasize the FTE's functional simplicity to ensure that it can be easily validated, applied, and maintained in practice.

(4) *Transparency*—The fault-tolerant Ethernet must be transparent to applications using protocol standards or common APIs (e.g., sockets connected to applications should not need to be torn down and reestablished). Further, applications use only one IP address to communicate with multi-homed devices.

The FTE addressed the following challenging technical issues:

- *Channel health-based multi-fault detection and recovery*—to detect multiple faults, we employ a decentralized derivation approach to let each node obtain the state information of the entire network.

- *MAC address management*—for the IP-MAC address resolution, we maintain a MAC address resolution table (MART). For good performance, we employ a hashing function technique for the table lookup.

- *Support for non FTE-native nodes*—the implications of IP and ARP is addressed.

We prototyped the FTE design and experimented the performance in various ways. Our work is being adopted in part by the Fieldbus Foundation as a standardization effort.

In the demonstration, we focus on presenting the correctness of the detection and recovery behavior with various failure situations. First, we demonstrate the basic failure detection and recovery such as LAN mode handling, Heartbeat stop and node departure case, partial failure, crossed cable, and switch failure. Second, several failure scenarios are presented such as supporting non-FTE and handling multiple faults. The correctness of the protocol for each case is demonstrated with network monitoring tools as well as FTE user interface. We also present the performance evaluation result from the demonstration.

2 Demonstration System Settings

Our COTS-based demonstration network system setting is described in Figure 2-1. The network system is configured with 4 NT PC-based FTE nodes, 2 NT PC-based non FTE-native nodes or Internet connection, and redundant Fast Ethernet switches (100Base-TX).

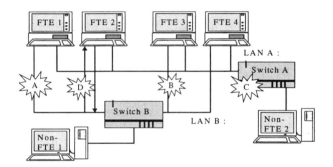

Figure 2-1. FTE Demonstration Network

3 Demonstration Scenarios

3.1 FTE User Interface Features

Using the FTE user interface shown in Figure 3-1, we can update various parameter settings as well as display the current network status.

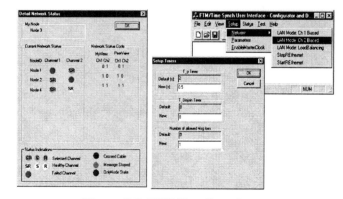

Figure 3-1. FTE User Interface

The network status is displayed by using different colors and characters. A green light indicates that the LAN is active; a yellow light shows that the LAN is healthy but not active. The letters (SR, S, R) describe potential partial failure status. SR indicates that data can be both sent and received by the LAN. S indicates that data only can be sent but not received by the LAN. R indicates that data only can be received but not sent by the LAN. A red light indicates that the LAN failed. A blue light warns the physical cable is configured wrong. A purple light indicates the node stopped sending out heartbeat. A black light shows that there are no other FTE nodes in the network system. We can also update the system parameter settings such as the biased LAN mode, heartbeat timer (Tp), MaxMsgLossAllowed, and disjoin timer (Td), where:

- *Tp*—a "heartbeat" time interval (in seconds) specifying how often a node needs to send out a pair of "I_AM_ALIVE" messages on its two channels.
- *MaxMsgLossAllowed*—the maximum number of consecutive MsgPair messages lost on one channel that is tolerable by the MsgPair protocol.
- *The biased LAN mode*—select the default active LAN.
- *Td*—if the heartbeat message of an FTE node is not received before the timer expires, the node entry will be removed from the FTE node list.

3.2 Failure Scenarios

The failure condition is demonstrated based on the following scenarios. Initially, there is no network failure and LAN mode is channel 1 biased.

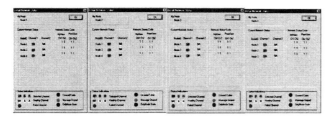

Figure 3-2. Initial Condition

Cable failure (Complete failure (B)):

- *Failure condition:* Node 1's channel 1 cable failed.
- *Assertion:* Node 1 communicates to all the other nodes via channel 2. All the other nodes communicate to node 1 via channel 2. Nodes 2 ~ 4 continue to use channel 1.

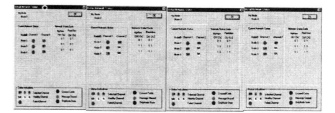

Figure 3-3. Cable Failure

Switch failure (Complete failure (C)):

- *Failure condition:* Switch A on channel 1 failed.
- *Assertion:* All the nodes swap to channel 2 and indicate channel 1 failed.

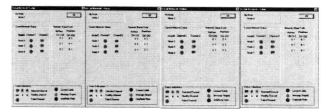

Figure 3-4. Switch Failure

Crossed cable: Node i's LAN A is connected to Node j's LAN B, or vice versa.

- *Failure condition:* Plug off node 2's both cables. Plug channel 1 cable in switch B and channel 2 cable in switch A.
- *Assertion:* nodes 1, 3, and 4 indicate that the node 2's cable is configured wrongly.

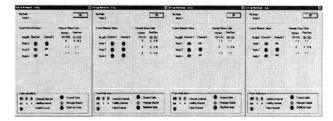

Figure 3-5. Crossed Cable

Heartbeat stop and node departure:

- *Failure condition:* Node 2 stops sending its heartbeat message.
- *Assertion:* After the disjoin timer expires, the other nodes remove the node 2 entry from their FTE node list. Node 2 keeps receiving messages from the other nodes, but the other nodes indicate that node 2 is no longer an FTE node.

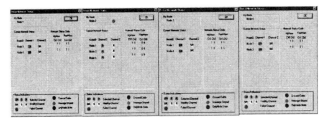

Figure 3-6. Heartbeat Stop and Node Departure

LAN mode handling:
- *Failure condition:* Change the LAN mode to channel 2.
- *Assertion:* All the nodes swap their selected channel to channel 2.

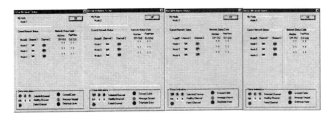

Figure 3-7. LAN Mode Handling

Partial failure (D): A component may fail partially; for example, part of an 8-wire Category 5 cable may be cut. Such a fault results in loss of network transmission in one direction but not the other or in transmission of garbled bytes. Another example is that a NIC can transmit but it cannot receive.
- *Precondition:* The LAN mode is channel 2 biased. Node3's channel 2 cable already failed.
- *Failure condition:* Node 2's channel 2 receiving part of the cable further failed.
- *Assertion:* Nodes 1 and 4 continue to use channel 2. The other communications uses channel 1. Node 2 indicates that its channel 2 can only send but cannot receive.

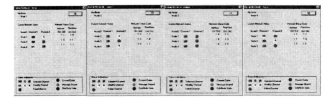

Figure 3-8. Partial Failure

Multiple failure handling: Multiple faults may happen before the first fault is fully recovered.
- *Precondition:* The LAN mode is channel 1 biased.
- *Failure condition:* Node 1's channel 1 and node 2's channel 2 failed.

- *Assertion:* Node 1 and 2 can not see each other. Node 1 communicates to nodes 3 and 4 via channel 2. Node 2 communicates to nodes 3 and 4 via channel 1. Nodes 3 and 4 communicate via channel 1.
- *Test:* Node 3 sends unicast packets to nodes 1 and 2.
- *Result:* Node 1 receives the packet via channel 2. Node 2 receives the packet via channel 1. The data traffic is checked using a network sniffer monitor.

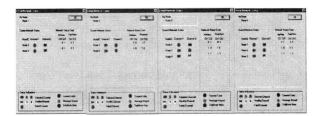

Figure 3-9. Multiple Failure Handling

3.3 Support for Non-FTE Nodes

- *Precondition and test:* The LAN mode is channel 1 biased. Start communications from non-FTE node 2 on channel 1 to FTE node 1.
- *Failure condition:* Change the LAN mode to channel 2 biased.
- *Assertion:* the communication continues without any message loss or stop.
- *Result:* Communication between non-FTE and FTE nodes are not affected by any FTE protocol.

4 Experimental Data Posted at the Demo Booth

The experimental evaluation was conducted with the actual FTE prototype on a small-scale system testbed. Below we present our results on efficiency and effectiveness of the FTE software.

4.1 Performance Evaluation
We define several metrics for quantitatively measuring the run-time performance of the FTE software and protocol:
- *Failover time (seconds)*—the time elapsed from when a LAN failure occurs to the time the related nodes have switched from their active channels to standby channels. The metric measures the total time it takes the FTE software to detect a failure and recover from it.
- *End-to-end swap time (milliseconds)*—the time interval between the time the first node started its

channel swap operation to the time the last node completed its channel swap operation.

The experimentation results are provided in Figure 4-1 and Figure 4-2.

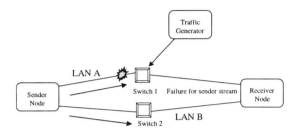

Figure 4-1. Measurement of LAN Failover Time

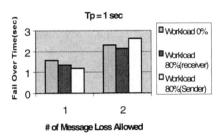

Figure 4-2. LAN Failover Time vs. MaxMsgLossAllowed

4.2 Hashing Effectiveness and Execution Time

We investigated the effectiveness of the hashing function in terms of "collision ratio" and "entry chain length" for a given set of MAC addresses following certain distributions. The results are compared in terms of collision ratio and collision chain length under the different settings of number of nodes, MAC address patterns, and load factor parameters.

Figure 4-3 and Figure 4-4 illustrate the different results of using the following MAC address distribution patterns.

- Pattern 1: all NICs from one manufacture.
- Pattern 2: NICs from different manufactures

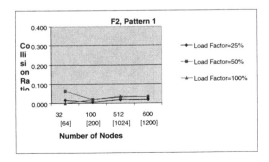

Figure 4-3. Collision ratio with Pattern 1

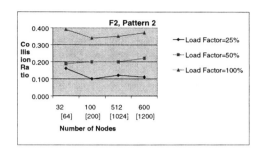

Figure 4-4. Collision Ratio with Pattern 2

We also performed hashing execution time experiments to evaluate the run-time overhead of the hashing operations. First, we compared the hashing with the sequential search approach to quantify the amount of overhead reduced by the hashing approach (Figure 4-5). Second, we measured the hashing execution time with and without the memory caching to quantify the caching effect on the hashing (Figure 4-6).

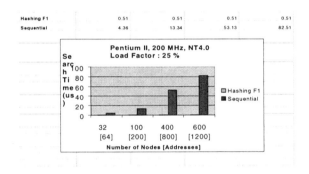

Figure 4-5. Hashing vs. Sequential Search

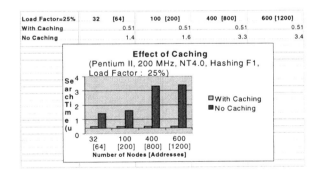

Figure 4-6. Effect of Caching on a Slow Node

5 Summary and Lessons Learned

The FTE is an open fault-tolerant network solution being developed in Honeywell for process control networks. It differs from the existing fault-tolerant networks deployed in the process control industry in that it builds on the Ethernet standard and COTS products with no change to hardware and software (hubs/switches, NICs, and drivers). It is also unique compared with the dual-NIC products being developed by network and PC vendors, in which the FTE provides end-to-end LAN redundancy support for all the nodes on the network, whereas the network fault-tolerance capabilities offered by the dual-NIC products are limited to information server nodes and small-scale systems with limited number of devices. The FTE is capable of handling multiple faults, supporting non-FTE nodes regardless of the FTE protocol, and providing efficient support for larger network systems with hundreds of nodes.

The following failure modes and scenarios were demonstrated on a FTE-based network system:

- Complete failure such as switch failure, NIC failure, and cable failure
- Partial failure
- Crossed cable fault
- Heartbeat stop and node departure scenario
- Multiple failure handling scenario
- Non FTE-native node and FTE node communication scenario

During the FTE design and prototyping, we learned several important lessons. First, our middleware approach provides good performance with fast and deterministic response time as well as application transparency dealing with one IP address only. The kernel-level implementation not only has little effect on the protocol performance with concurrent workload, but also has less chance of message loss compared with the upper layer solutions.

Second, supporting different MAC addresses, we can use heterogeneous NICs without any modification. The MAC address management overhead is reduced using our software hashing. It is proven to be effective and efficient for the middleware-based FTE.

Third, we found that adhering to *"separation of mechanisms from algorithms"* principle allows us to meet various changing requirements. For example, FTE was first developed to handle a single fault and then to deal with multiple faults. With the principle enforced, we were able to encapsulate the algorithm changes within individual software modules without affecting existing APIs.

Finally, we learned much about the implications of supporting IP protocols such as ARP and internet-control message protocol (ICMP). Manipulation of MAC addresses is required. The impact of these implications on simple network-management protocol (SNMP)-based network management tools is yet to be investigated.

References

[1] C. Edmonds, "Programmable Controller Networking—Dual Cable, Redundancy, Multiple Networks and Application," *ISA'92 Advances in Instrumentation and Control,* Vol. 47, Part 2, October 1992.

[2] Automation Research Corporation, "Worldwide Plant Automation Systems Outlook—Market Analysis and Forecast Through 2002," *ARC,* Three Allied Drive, Dedham, MA 02026, July 1998.

[3] Automation Research Corporation, "Ethernet-Based Control Network Strategies," *Automation Strategies Report, Automation ARC,* Three Allied Drive, Dedham, MA 02026, October 1997.

[4] D. Loy and R. Schmalek, "Thoughts About Redundancy in Fieldbus Systems Anchored in OSI Layer-4 and Applied to the Lontalk Protocol on Neuron-Based Network Nodes," *Proceedings of the IEEE International Workshop on Factory Communication Systems,* October 1995.

[5] J. Huang, S. Song, L. Li, P. Kappler, R. Freimark, J. Gustin, and T. Kozlik, "An Open Solution to Fault-Tolerant Ethernet: Design, Prototyping, and Evaluation" Invited Paper, *Proceeding of the 18th IEEE International Performance, Computing, and Communications Conference,* Phoenix, February 1999.

[6] S. Song, J. Huang, P. Kappler, R. Freimark, J. Gustin, and T. Kozlik, "Fault-Tolerant Ethernet for IP-Based Process Control" *Technical Report ISS_R00_001,* Honeywell Technology Center.

Demonstration of the Remote Exploration and Experimentation (REE) Fault-Tolerant Parallel-Processing Supercomputer for Spacecraft Onboard Scientific Data Processing

Fannie Chen
Jet Propulsion Laboratory
Fannie.Chen@jpl.nasa.gov

Loring Craymer
Jet Propulsion Laboratory
Loring.Craymer@jpl.nasa.gov

Jeff Deifik
Jet Propulsion Laboratory
Jeff.Deifik@jpl.nasa.gov

Alvin J. Fogel
Jet Propulsion Laboratory
Alvin.J.Fogel@jpl.nasa.gov

Daniel S. Katz
Jet Propulsion Laboratory
Daniel.S.Katz@jpl.nasa.gov

Alfred G. Silliman, Jr.
Jet Propulsion Laboratory
Alfred.G.Silliman@jpl.nasa.gov

Raphael R. Some
Jet Propulsion Laboratory
Raphael.R.Some@jpl.nasa.gov

Sean A. Upchurch
Jet Propulsion Laboratory
sau@alumni.caltech.edu

Keith Whisnant
University of Illinois
kwhisnan@uiuc.edu

Abstract

This paper is the written explanation for a demonstration of the REE Project's work to-date. The demonstration is intended to simulate an REE system that might exist on a Mars Rover, consisting of multiple COTS processors, a COTS network, a COTS node-level operating system, REE middleware, and an REE application. The specific application performs texture processing of images. It was chosen as a building block of automated geological processing that will eventually be used for both navigation and data processing. Because the COTS hardware is not radiation hardened, SEU-induced soft errors will occur. These errors are simulated in the demonstration by use of a software-implemented fault-injector, and are injected at a rate much higher than is realistic for the sake of viewer interest. Both the application and the middleware contain mechanisms for both detection of and recovery from these faults, and these mechanisms are tested by this very high fault-rate. The consequence of the REE system being able to tolerate this fault rate while continuing to process data is that the system will easily be able to handle the true fault rate.

1. Introduction

The goal of the Remote Exploration and Experimentation (REE) Project [1] is to move supercomputing into space in a cost effective manner and to allow the use of inexpensive, state of the art, commercial-off-the-shelf (COTS) components and subsystems in these space-based supercomputers. The motivation for the project is the lack of bandwidth and long round trip communication delays which severely constrain current space science missions. Unlike typical radiation-hardened space-based systems, the use of COTS hardware will require the REE system to withstand relatively high rates of single event upset (SEU) induced errors. Depending on mission environments and component technologies, an REE system will be required to withstand average fault rates of between 1 and 100 SEU-induced soft errors per CPU-MB-day with occasional peaks of up to 1000 soft errors per CPU-MB-day[2]. Unlike traditional fault tolerant computer systems, however, the REE computer need not provide 100% reliability, but is instead, as with many sampled data or convergent-computation systems, allowed to occasionally fail in a computation. Periodic resets to flush latent errors, and other techniques which provide less than 100% availability, are also permissible. Further, the REE computer need not support hard real time or mission critical computation, as these tasks can be off-loaded to the spacecraft control computer.

The flexibility afforded by the above requirements allows the system to be optimized for high-performance, low-power, supercomputing rather than for "hard" fault tolerance. Thus, REE seeks to maximize simplex operation and minimize resource replication, redundant executions and other high-overhead strategies. (We should note that software-implemented triple-modular redundancy (TMR) and other high-overhead techniques will be developed and integrated into a suite of operational options for flexible fault tolerance, but it is expected that these will not be the primary operating modes of the system. It is, however, expected that a small subset of nodes may be called upon, from time to time, to operate in a highly reliable and real time manner.)

Another project goal is to allow scientists to develop science applications in their laboratories and to easily port the resulting software to the REE computer with minimal or no re-engineering for fault tolerance or for the spacecraft computing environment. In addition to COTS hardware, the project thus seeks to utilize a commercial operating system and to support standard commercial application development tools (compilers, debuggers, etc.) and methods to the maximum extent practical.

The REE computer architecture is a Beowulf-type[1] [3] parallel processing supercomputer comprising a multiplicity of processing nodes interconnected by a high speed, multiply redundant communication fabric. In the current instantiation of the system, dual Power PC 750 based computational nodes containing 128MB of main memory and dual redundant Myrinet [4] interfaces are interconnected via a redundant Myrinet fabric. The node level operating system is Lynx [5] Operating System (OS), to which multiple versions of MPI [6] have been ported. The current system may contain up to 20 nodes (40 processors) and is extensible to at least 50 nodes with a power:performance of better than 30MOPS/Watt. The applications are written so that they may be automatically configured to execute on up to 50 processors with the system being informed, by the application, of the optimal number of processors for maximum throughput and the system assigning the number of processors available based on system status and operational constraints such as available power, spares availability and mission phase.

There are currently 5 science teams writing applications for potential future NASA missions which may incorporate the REE computer. To aid application developers, a library of fault-detection-enabled scientific subroutines for linear algebra and Fast-Fourier Transform (FFT) routines has been developed. Work is ongoing to determine the utility of an error-correction-enabled library. In addition, continued analysis of application fault tolerance requirements and determination of the applications' native error tolerance is ongoing, as is the development of a generalized taxonomy of scientific software structure and the applicability (and overhead costs) of various software-implemented fault-tolerance (SIFT) mechanisms to these constructs.

---

[1] Beowulf-class computers were originally defined as parallel clusters of commodity hardware and open-source operating systems and tools. This definition has grown to include most clusters composed of personal computer central processing units (CPUs) and commodity operating systems and tools.

While we are currently in the process of expanding and documenting guidelines for application software developers, and while some of the SIFT strategy is the responsibility of the applications themselves, three system software layers have thus far been defined to aid in achieving the required fault tolerance:

> A middleware layer which, conceptually, resides between the OS and the application,
> a reliable communications layer which ensures that all system level communications are either error free or error-noted and which, conceptually, is viewed as a series of driver level enhancements to the node OS, and
> A global coordination system which manages the overall system.

The combination of node operating system, reliable communications software, middleware, and global coordination layers are simply referred to as the REE System Software. Some of the responsibilities of the REE system software include:

1. Managing system resources (maintaining state information about each node and about the global system, performing system resource diagnostics, etc.).
2. Job scheduling (globally scheduling jobs across the system, local job scheduling within the node, allocation of resources to jobs, etc.).
3. Managing the scientific applications (launching the applications, monitoring the applications for failure, initiating recovery for applications, etc.)

The key components of the REE systems software are shown in Figure 1.

The immediate concern of the Applications Manager is to oversee the execution of the scientific applications. As the applications represent the ultimate "customer" of the REE environment, efficiently supporting their required dependability level is paramount. The Applications Manager monitors the science application for externally visible signs of faulty behavior as well as for messages generated internally by the applications requesting fault tolerance services.

Fault tolerance concerns for the REE System Software must also be addressed since these components ultimately ensure the correct operation of the REE environment. Several of its operations, such as scheduling and resource allocation are considered to be critical and therefore must be protected at all costs. We currently envision that these operations will therefore be run under the software-implemented TMR system previously discussed. Another module which must be protected is the Applications Manager. This software module, which is resident on each node engaged in applications processing, must be

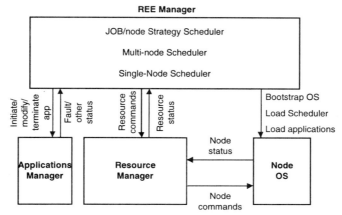

Figure 1. REE system software block diagram

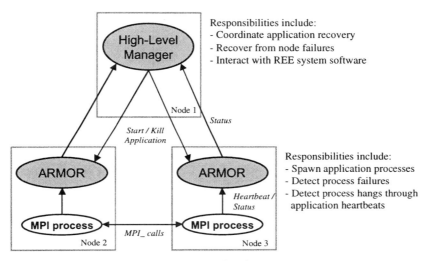

Responsibilities include:
- Coordinate application recovery
- Recover from node failures
- Interact with REE system software

Responsibilities include:
- Spawn application processes
- Detect process failures
- Detect process hangs through application heartbeats

Figure 2. MPI application manager

self-checking to ensure correct operation of this "middleware" layer.

This demonstration will show one of REE's scientific applications executing under the Applications Manager. Faults will be injected into the nodes executing the application by a software implemented fault injector, and the cooperative interactions between the application, the Applications Manager and the COTS node operating system to protect the integrity of the computation will be shown.

2. Application Manager

The scientific applications executing on an REE platform are programmed using MPI [6], a standardized messaging interface used to implement parallel applications. These are typically computationally intensive programs that perform such actions as on-board image filtering and signal processing.

Core routines within each application, such as matrix multiplication, employ algorithm-based fault tolerance (ABFT) to help protect against data faults. Internal ABFT techniques, however, do not mitigate the need for an external entity controlling the applications. Capabilities such as launching application processes, terminating rogue application processes, detecting failures in application processes, and migrating failed processes to functioning nodes are some responsibilities that must be relegated to an external controlling entity. The Application Manager fulfills this role. REE currently uses the Chameleon application manager written by Prof. Ravi Iyer et. al at the University of Illinois [7] [8].

The Application Manager provides its fault tolerance services to the scientific MPI applications through ARMOR processes (Adaptive Reliable Mobile Objects of Reliability). ARMORs are built from a library of reusable components that implement specific services and techniques for providing fault tolerance. An overriding

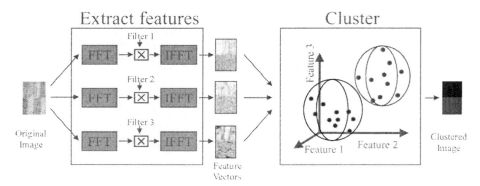

Frequency and orientation tuned
filters convolved with image to
produce Feature Vectors

Vectors for each pixel near each other
in feature space are grouped together
into the same cluster.

Figure 3. Rover texture analysis application

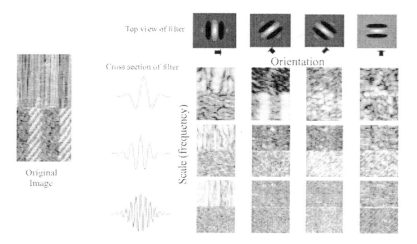

Figure 4. Image response to several filters

goal of the ARMOR concept is to have a uniform architecture through which customized levels of fault tolerance can be achieved. For REE, the ARMORs have been customized to provide oversight to MPI applications.

Because the target MPI applications often consist of several processes and because these applications cannot sacrifice performance, replication is not viewed as an acceptable approach for ensuring fault tolerance in an environment with constrained processing resources. Effective reporting and detection of errors is considered most important, as the target MPI applications can tolerate occasional restarts and rollbacks to previous checkpoints.

A challenge to the applications manager is to provide these error detection and recovery services to the target applications as transparently as possible. For the most part, the Applications Manager treats the MPI application as a black box entity. Each MPI process is directly

overseen by an ARMOR executing on the same node, as shown in Figure 2. Failures in the application are detected by the ARMOR and communicated to a high-level ARMOR that coordinates recovery.

For tolerating non-crash failures, the overseeing ARMOR exposes a non-intrusive API (application programming interface) to the MPI application. Non-intrusive mean that the MPI application only need be lightly instrumented with API calls; no fundamental redesign of the application is necessary. Through this interface, the application can communicate vital information to the overseer ARMOR process so that the Application Manager can better gauge the health of the application. Examples include the reporting of correctable and uncorrectable ABFT errors directly detected by the application, as well as periodic updates to the ARMOR concerning the application's progress. Also

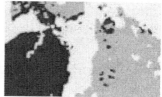

Figure 5. Example of texture segmentation input and output

currently being investigated is applying some of the error detection techniques found within ARMOR processes to the MPI applications as well [7]. (These include such things as control flow signature checking on the process's execution.) The ultimate goal of these techniques is to improve a process's self-checking capabilities, and the MPI applications outfitted with these techniques would work in tandem with the overseeing ARMOR to accomplish this goal.

Recovery of an MPI application is complicated by the fact that current MPI implementations do not allow single MPI processes to be restarted; instead, all processes must be launched again to restart the application. For this reason, there exists a single high-level ARMOR named the Fault Tolerance Manager (FTM) that coordinates the actions among all other ARMORs (the ARMORs that directly oversee each MPI process). The FTM is also responsible for handling node failures that affect one or more MPI applications. Whenever the FTM detects a node failure through its heart-beating mechanism, it must migrate all affected processes to another node. Selecting a spare node is done with the assistance of Resource Manager, an REE System Software component that is external to the Applications Manager. Again, the MPI applications themselves are oblivious to the exact recovery actions taken by the FTM and other ARMORs.

3. REE Application Demonstration

We will demonstrate one of the REE Science Applications, the Texture Analysis application developed by the Rover Science Team [9]. This parallel (MPI) application segments images according to texture information. This is one of the methods that a Mars Rover would use to determine rock types. The application can process any number of images. The processing steps for each image are shown in Figure 3. First, a number of filters are applied to the image. Each filter is a combination of a frequency and an orientation, as shown in Figure 4. The results of each filter are a feature vector. The feature vector measures the response of each pixel in the original image to the filter. After completing the filtering, clusters are segmented in the feature vector space. Then, each pixel is painted to show the cluster to which it belongs, as seen in Figure 5.

In order to test this application, two levels of fault-protection have been applied. The first level is Chameleon, used as the application manager. Once the application starts successfully, Chameleon ensures that it continues running until it has completed. The application has been slightly modified to make heartbeat calls to the Chameleon ARMORs, and Chameleon is aware of how often these heartbeats should occur. If one fails to occur within the response window, Chameleon assumes that the application has hung, or is stuck in a loop, and restarts it. The application also writes out its status to a log file. It can then read this file when it is started or restarted to know what images and filters have already been processed, so that it can start on the first image or filter that has not yet been completed. This "checkpointing" could be done at a finer level such as each FFT, but this current level is sufficient for testing and demonstration.

The second level of fault-protection is inside the application, though the application code itself is not modified. Instead, an ABFT [10] version of the FFT library is used. The ABFT versions of the FFT routines have the same calling sequences as the basic routines, but they check to see if the FFT was completed successfully before returning. If the FFT was not successful, they retry once. If this retry is also unsuccessful, the ABFT version of the FFT calls exit, which essentially promotes the problem to Chameleon to deal with by restarting the application on the current rock or filter. A flowchart of the ABFT operation is shown in Figure 6.

The demonstration to be shown will use the application running on an embedded system at the Jet Propulsion Laboratory (JPL). Through a series of scripts, output files will be transferred to the demonstration machine and displayed. An application-based fault injector named SWIFI (developed at JPL) will be used to insert random SEUs into memory and registers at 10 to 100 times the expected fault rate on the Martian Surface [2], which will exercise the two existing levels of fault protection. The demonstration machine will compare the application outputs from the code running with random fault injection to outputs previously generated from an unfaulted application. This will show the effects and overhead of the fault-protection layers.

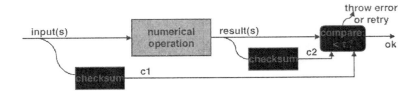

Figure 6. ABFT flowchart

4. Conclusions

The REE project requires that dependability be provided through software. Extensive error detection and recovery services are provided to the target applications through a variety of mechanisms including checkpointing, TMR, and ABFT-enabled scientific subroutine libraries. The applications are built and tested without fault-tolerance features, and then modified to use substantially off-the-shelf fault-tolerance components. The initial application manager being used by REE is built from a series of ARMORs, and is controlled by the prototype REE system software. Through the application manager and system software, the application is able to tolerate process failures, process hangs, and node failures. The ABFT-enabled libraries are essentially transparent to the application and provide high fault coverage of the mathematical routines themselves, though not of logical or arithmetic codes outside the library routines. Additional fault detection strategies will be required to protect the remainder of the application codes, the node operating system and system software.

It is possible that, in addition to having ARMOR technology protect the application manager, comparable error detection and recovery techniques can be extended to the REE system software as well. Because the REE system software does not have the strict requirement of being completely off-the-shelf, additional customizations can be made to the REE processes that allow them to take advantage of ARMOR technology. Specifically, the underlying ARMOR architecture can be embedded into the REE processes, allowing REE system software to take advantage of the reconfigurable error detection and recovery services currently found in standalone ARMORs. It is the intent of the REE project that the integration of the REE system software into the overall SIFT layer will result in a unified approach toward providing dependability to all facets of the REE software, including the target scientific applications.

Over the next 18 months, the REE project will continue the development of SIFT approaches for space-based parallel COTS supercomputing. The Project will culminate in the development of a final flight-capable prototype hardware/software system during the 2003-2004 time frame.

5. Acknowledgements

The work described in this publication was carried out at the Jet Propulsion Laboratory (JPL), California Institute of Technology under a contract with the National Aeronautics and Space Administration (NASA).

6. References

[1] R. Ferraro, "NASA Remote Exploration and Experimentation Project," http://www-ree.jpl.nasa.gov/

[2] R. Ferraro, R. R. Some, J. Beahan, A. Johnston, and D S. Katz, "Detailed Radiation Fault Modeling of the REE First Generation Testbed Architecture," to appear in Proceedings of *2000 IEEE Aerospace Conference.*

[3] T. Sterling, J. Salmon, D. Becker, D. Savarese, *How to Build a Beowulf*, The MIT Press, 1999.

[4] Myrinet is a class of products of Myricom, Inc. (http://www.myricom.com/).

[5] Lynx OS is a product of Lynx Real Time Systems, Inc. (http://www.lynx.com/)

[6] M. Snir, S. W. Otto, S. Huss-Lederman, D. W. Walker, J. Dongarra, *MPI: The Complete Reference*, The MIT Press, 1996.

[7] S. Bagchi, B. Srinivasan, K. Whisnant, Z. Kalbarczyk, R. Iyer, "Hierarchical Error Detection in a Software Implemented Fault Tolerance (SIFT) Environment," to appear in *IEEE Transactions on Knowledge and Data Engineering*, March 2000.

[8] Z. Kalbarczyk, S. Bagchi, K. Whisnant, R. Iyer, "Chameleon: A Software Infrastructure for Adaptive Fault Tolerance," *IEEE Transactions on Parallel and Distributed Computing*, June 1999.

[9] R. Castaño, T. Mann and E. Mjolsness, "Texture Analysis for Mars Rover Images," *Applications of Digital Image Processing XXII*, Proc. of SPIE, Vol. 3808, Denver, July, 1999.

[10] M. Turmon, R. Granat, "Algorithm-Based Fault Tolerance for Spaceborne Computing: Basis and Implementations," to appear in Proceedings of *2000 IEEE Aerospace Conference.*

Session 11A

Testing and Applications of Coding

Test-Point Insertion to Enhance Test Compaction for Scan Designs[+]

Irith Pomeranz and Sudhakar M. Reddy
Electrical and Computer Engineering Department
University of Iowa
Iowa City, IA 52242, U.S.A.

Abstract

Test compaction procedures to reduce the test application time for scan designs terminate when they cannot reduce the test application time without reducing the fault coverage. We propose a procedure for placing observation points that allows higher levels of compaction to be achieved without loss of fault coverage. The observation point values are read only at the last time unit of every test, and therefore, they can be scanned-out at the same time as the next-state values.

1. Introduction

Test compaction procedures for scan designs were described in [1]-[4]. In general, test compaction is important in reducing test application time and test storage requirements. In the compaction procedures of [1]-[4], the goal is to minimize the test application time by finding an appropriate balance between the number of test vectors applied consecutively using the circuit clock (without using the scan chain), and the number of scan operations. For a circuit with N_{SV} state variables, and assuming that the scan clock and the circuit clock have the same cycle time, a scan-in/out operation can be replaced by N_{SV} test vectors applied using the circuit clock, without increasing the test application time. Whenever it is possible to propagate fault effects and set the circuit state using fewer than N_{SV} test vectors, scan operations to achieve these goals can be avoided, and the test application time can be reduced.

Although the procedures of [1]-[4] typically produce significant reductions in test application time, they may fail to reduce the test application time for some circuits. In addition, it may sometimes be necessary to further reduce the test application time without compromising the fault coverage. For such applications, we propose

in this work a procedure for test-point insertion that allows the test application time to be reduced below the levels possible without test-points. Clearly, there is an area overhead associated with the insertion of observation points. This overhead must be justified by the need to reduce the test application time.

Test-point insertion is done here in conjunction with the static compaction procedure of [4]. Only observation points are considered in this work. The values on the observation points are used only in time units that are followed by a scan-out operation. This implies that values of observation points can be scanned-out at the same time as values of next-state variables. In a symmetric way, control points can be inserted and used only in the first time unit after a scan-in operation, implying that the values of the control points can be scanned-in at the same time as present-state variable values. Next, we provide more details of the procedure of [4] and the observation point insertion procedure.

The static compaction procedure of [4] is based on the operation of *combining* tests. A test is represented as $\tau_i = (L_i, T_i, U_i)$, where L_i is a scan-in vector to be applied at the beginning of the test, T_i is a sequence of test vectors to be applied using the circuit clock after L_i is scanned-in, and U_i is the expected fault-free scan-out vector. Combining two tests τ_i and τ_j consists of removing the scan vectors U_i and L_j, and concatenating T_i and T_j to obtain the sequence T_iT_j. The resulting test is $\tau_{i,j} = (L_i, T_iT_j, U_{i,j})$, where $U_{i,j}$ is the fault-free scan-out vector expected after L_i is scanned-in, and the sequences of test vectors T_i and T_j are applied. The procedure of [4] attempts to combine as many test pairs as possible in order to remove scan operations, thus reducing the test application time. The combination of two tests is accepted only if it does not reduce the fault coverage. The procedure stops when no additional test pairs can be combined without reducing the fault coverage. In the procedure proposed here, observation point insertion is used after the procedure of [4] terminates to allow additional test pairs to be combined without reducing the fault coverage. Using observation points,

+ Research supported in part by NSF Grant No. MIP-9725053, and in part by SRC Grant No. 98-TJ-645.

it is possible to combine tests that cannot be combined otherwise, thus achieving further reductions in test application time.

Although the procedure of [4] is applicable to full or partial scan circuits, we consider only full scan circuits in this work. The paper is organized as follows. In Section 2, we describe the procedure from [4] and extend it to accommodate the presence of observation points. In Section 3, we describe a procedure for observation point insertion, and two variations aimed at reducing the computational complexity. Experimental results are presented in Section 4. Section 5 concludes the paper.

2. Preliminaries

In this section, we describe the compaction procedure from [4], and extend it to the case where observation points are present in the circuit.

The procedure of [4] starts from an *initial test set*. For full scan circuits considered in this work, the initial test set T is computed based on a combinational test set T_C (i.e., T_C is computed assuming that all the present-state variables are primary inputs, and all the next-state variables are primary outputs). For every vector $c_i \in T_C$, T includes a test $\tau_i = (L_i, T_i, U_i)$ defined as follows. We partition c_i into c_{iS} which is the sub-vector of c_i applied to the present-state variables, and c_{iI} which is the sub-vector of c_i applied to the primary inputs. We set $L_i = c_{iS}$, and $T_i = (c_{iI})$. If z_i is the response of the combinational circuit to c_i, then $U_i = z_{iS}$, where z_{iS} is the sub-vector of z_i corresponding to the next-state variables.

The basic compaction procedure from [4] considers pairs of tests (τ_i, τ_j) such that τ_i and τ_j are in T, and attempts to combine them. It is successful when τ_i and τ_j can be combined without reducing the fault coverage. If τ_i and τ_j can be combined, they are replaced in T by the combined test $\tau_{i,j}$. The procedure terminates when no additional test pairs can be combined without reducing the fault coverage.

The test pairs (τ_i, τ_j) are considered by increasing distance between U_i and L_j. The distance between L_i and U_j is the number of bits where U_i and L_j differ (in full scan circuits, U_i and L_j are fully specified; an extension of this definition to partial scan circuits can be found in [4]). The rationale behind this order is as follows. The sequence T_j contained in τ_j is designed to be applied starting from state L_j. After combining τ_i and τ_j, T_j is applied starting from state U_i obtained at the end of T_i (U_i is obtained in the fault free circuit; here, we consider faults that result in the same state U_i at the end of T_i). If $U_i = L_j$, then in the combined test, T_j is applied starting

from the state for which it was designed. In this case, all the faults detected by T_j starting from state L_j will be detected by the combined test. As a heuristic, we assume that the smaller the distance between U_i and L_j, the more likely it is that T_j in the combined test will continue to detect the same faults. Therefore, the combination is more likely to be successful.

The procedure from [4] is given next.

Procedure 1: The basic compaction procedure [4]

(1) Let $T = \langle \tau_1, \tau_2, \cdots, \tau_m \rangle$ be the initial test set. Fault simulate T with fault dropping. During simulation, each test is started from its scan vector. Let the set of faults detected by T be F_D.

(2) Set $S = \phi$ (S is the set of test pairs already considered).

(3) Select a test pair (τ_i, τ_j) such that $\tau_i, \tau_j \in T$, $(\tau_i, \tau_j) \notin S$, and the distance between U_i and L_j is the minimum of all the pairs not in S. If no pair can be selected, stop.

(4) Add (τ_i, τ_j) to S.

(5) Remove τ_i and τ_j from T, and add $\tau_{i,j}$ to T. Resimulate T (only faults that were previously detected by τ_i or τ_j need to be resimulated; additional faults may be avoided as discussed in [4]).

(6) If all the faults in F_D are detected, go to Step 2 (in this case, $\tau_{i,j}$ is accepted and it replaces τ_i and τ_j in T).

(7) Reintroduce τ_i and τ_j into T, and remove $\tau_{i,j}$ from T. Go to Step 3 (in this case, $\tau_{i,j}$ cannot replace τ_i and τ_j since the fault coverage goes down, and they are reintroduced into T).

We use Procedure 1 both before and after the insertion of observation points into the circuit. This requires us to change the simulation procedure embedded in Procedure 1. When observation points exist, a fault f is detected by a test $\tau_i = (L_i, T_i, U_i)$ if one of the following conditions is satisfied. (1) f is propagated by T_i to a primary output. (2) f is propagated by T_i to a next-state variable at the last time unit of T_i. In this case, f will be detected when the values of the next-state variables are scanned out. (3) f is propagated by T_i to an observation point at the last time unit of T_i. In this case, f will be detected when the values of the observation points are scanned out. The first two conditions are also used when no observation points exist in the circuit. The third condition is added to accommodate detections on observation points.

376

3. The proposed procedures

In this section, we demonstrate the effects of observation point insertion on the ability to combine additional tests. We describe a compaction procedure that inserts observation points to enhance compaction, and then describe two variations of this procedure aimed at reducing the computational complexity.

For illustration, we consider a circuit with three primary inputs and four state variables. A combinational test set for the circuit is shown in Table 1. The primary input values appear first, followed by the values of the present-state variables. The initial test set obtained from the combinational test set of Table 1 is shown in Table 2.

Table 1: A combinational test set

i	c_{il}	c_{iS}
0	0000	011
1	1001	010
2	0100	110
3	0111	001
4	1101	011
5	1010	000

Table 2: Initial test set

i	L_i	T_i	U_i
0	011	0000	011
1	010	1001	010
2	110	0100	001
3	001	0111	000
4	011	1101	101
5	000	1010	100

After applying Procedure 1, we obtain the test set shown in Table 3. No observation points were inserted into the circuit so far. All the faults detected by the combinational test set of Table 1 are detected by the test sets of Tables 2 and 3.

Table 3: Compacted test set w/o observation points

i	L_i	T_i	U_i
0	011	0000	011
1	011	1101	101
2	000	1010	100
3	110	0100,0111,1001	010

Next, we attempt to combine τ_0 and τ_1 of Table 3. We omit τ_0 and τ_1, add $\tau_{0,1}$ at the end of the test set, and renumber the tests to obtain the test set shown in Table 4. Simulating all the faults under the test set of Table 4, we find the one fault, f_1, remains undetected. However, when we consider the last time unit under T_2, we find that there is a line g_1 that carries different values in the fault free

and faulty circuit in the presence of f_1. Consequently, by placing an observation point on line g_1, it is possible to detect f_1. We place an observation point on line g_1, and accept the test set of Table 4 as the new test set T.

Table 4: Combining τ_0 and τ_1 of Table 3

i	L_i	T_i	U_i
0	000	1010	100
1	110	0100,0111,1001	010
2	011	0000,1101	101

Next, we attempt to combine τ_1 and τ_0 of Table 4. We omit τ_1 and τ_0, add $\tau_{1,0}$ at the end of the test set, and renumber the tests to obtain the test set of Table 5. Simulating the test set of Table 5, we find that f_1 is detected by τ_0 on the observation point g_1 we added before. There is another fault, f_2, which is detected by τ_1 on the observation point g_1. We also find that two faults, f_3 and f_4, remain undetected. Considering the last time unit under T_1, we find that f_3 results in different fault free and faulty values on a line g_2. Considering the last time unit under T_0 and T_1, we find that f_4 results in different fault free and faulty values on a line g_3. We place observation points on lines g_2 and g_3, and accept the test set of Table 5 as the new test set T.

Table 5: Combining τ_0 and τ_1 of Table 4

i	L_i	T_i	U_i
0	011	0000,1101	101
1	110	0100,0111,1001,1010	100

When we try to combine τ_0 and τ_1 of Table 5 in any order, we find that in every case, at least one undetected fault remains, that does not result in different fault free and faulty values on any line in the last time unit of the combined test. Consequently, insertion of observation points cannot help to detect the fault, and the combination is not accepted. The test set of Table 5 is the final test set for this circuit. The test set of Table 5 requires three scan operations instead of five scan operations required for the test set of Table 3.

Next, we describe a compaction procedure that inserts observation points to improve the levels of compaction that can be achieved.

The procedure first calls Procedure 1 to compact the initial test set as much as possible without inserting observation points. It then considers pairs of tests similar to the way Procedure 1 does, however, it also inserts observation points to enable combinations that were not possible without observation point insertion. This is done as follows.

After combining a pair of tests τ_i and τ_j to obtain a test set T containing $\tau_{i,j}$ instead of τ_i and τ_j, we have a set of faults F that were detected by the initial test set, and are not detected by T. For every fault $f \in F$, we find a set of candidate observation points $OP(f)$. The set $OP(f)$ is computed as follows. For every test $\tau_i \in T$, we simulate f under τ_i. Considering only the last time unit of T_i, we find every line g whose fault free and faulty values differ, and we add g to $OP(f)$. The set $OP(f)$ has the property that if an observation point is added on any line $g \in OP(f)$, f will be detected by at least one test in T.

If $OP(f) = \phi$ for any $f \in F$, $\tau_{i,j}$ is rejected, and τ_i and τ_j are reintroduced into the test set. Otherwise, we use a covering procedure to find a minimal set of observation points for all the faults in F. The selected observation points are added to a set OP that contains all the observation points inserted so far.

The procedure described above is given next. In the procedure, we impose an upper bound N_{OP} on the number of observation points inserted into the circuit. If the combination of a pair of tests requires the number of observation points to exceed N_{OP}, we do not combine this test pair.

Procedure 2: Compaction with observation point insertion (I)

(1) Construct the initial test set T. Set $OP = \phi$ (OP is the set of observation points).

(2) Compact T as much as possible without inserting new observation points by calling Procedure 1.

(3) Set $S = \phi$ (S is the set of test pairs already tried).

(4) Select a pair of tests (τ_i, τ_j) such that $\tau_i, \tau_j \in T$, $(\tau_i, \tau_j) \notin S$, and the distance between U_i and L_j is the minimum of all the pairs not in S. If no pair can be selected, stop.

(5) Add (τ_i, τ_j) to S.

(6) Remove τ_i and τ_j from T, and add $\tau_{i,j}$ to T. Resimulate T. Let F be the set of faults that remain undetected.

(7) For every $f \in F$, find the set $OP(f)$ of all the observation points on which f can be detected by T.

(8) If $OP(f) = \phi$ for any $f \in F$, remove $\tau_{i,j}$ from T, restore τ_i and τ_j, and go to Step 4.

(9) Select a minimal subset $OP(F)$ that covers $OP(f)$ for every $f \in F$. If $|OP \cup OP(F)|$ exceeds a preselected constant N_{OP}, remove $\tau_{i,j}$ from T, restore τ_i and τ_j, and go to Step 4.

(10) Add $OP(F)$ to OP, and go to Step 2.

In Step 10 of Procedure 2, after adding observation points to the circuit, Procedure 2 goes to Step 2 where it calls Procedure 1 to try and compact T as much as possible without inserting any additional observation points. In this way, Procedure 2 takes maximum advantage of every

observation point. However, calling Procedure 1 repeatedly may be time consuming. In addition, we found experimentally that very few test pairs require the same observation points, and therefore, the benefit of calling Procedure 1 after the insertion of every subset of observation points is not high. Therefore, we define Procedure 3 which is similar to Procedure 2, except that in Procedure 3, we continue to allow new observation points to be inserted without ever calling Procedure 1 again. This is achieved by going back to Step 3 from Step 10 of Procedure 3, instead of going back to Step 2 as in Procedure 2. From Step 3, Procedure 3 continues to consider additional test pairs while adding new observation points if necessary.

To compare the complexities of Procedures 1, 2 and 3, we assume that Procedures 1, 2 and 3 consider the same worst-case number of test pairs, denoted by N_1. For each test pair, we denote the number of operations performed by Procedures 1, 2 and 3 by c_1 (this excludes the calls to Procedure 1 performed by Procedure 2 when it goes back to Step 2). Although this results in a rough estimate of complexity that neglects the contribution of the observation point insertion step, it is sufficient for our purposes. Using the values defined above, the complexity of Procedure 1 is $C_1 = N_1 c_1$. Procedure 3 calls Procedure 1, and then goes through a computation that considers pairs of tests, similar to Procedure 1. According to our assumptions, Procedure 3 considers N_1 test pairs and performs c_1 operations for each pair. Consequently, we obtain $2C_1$ for its overall complexity. Procedure 2 also considers N_1 test pairs. However, in addition to the c_1 operations it performs for a test pair, it may also call Procedure 1. We obtain $C_1 + N_1(c_1 + C_1) \approx N_1 C_1$ for its complexity. This is significantly higher than the complexity of Procedure 3. Although this is a rough estimate, it reflects the fact that Procedure 2 calls Procedure 1 repeatedly. Thus, Procedure 3 is expected to be significantly faster than Procedure 2.

To further reduce the complexity of the compaction procedure, we make the following modification to Procedure 3. During Procedure 1, we record the maximum distance between the vectors U_i and L_j of any pair of tests (τ_i, τ_j) that was combined successfully. We denote this distance by D_{MAX}. Initially, before calling Procedure 1, we set $D_{MAX} = 0$. Every time Procedure 1 combines a pair of tests (τ_i, τ_j) successfully, if the distance $D_{i,j}$ between U_i and L_j is larger than D_{MAX}, we update D_{MAX} to be equal to $D_{i,j}$. During observation point insertion, we consider a pair of tests (τ_i, τ_j) only if the distance between U_i and L_j does not exceed D_{MAX}. This reduces the value of N_1 in the computation above, thus reducing the complexity of the procedure. We refer to the modified procedure as Procedure 4. In cases where Procedure 1 cannot combine any tests, we set D_{MAX} equal to the number of state variables in order to allow any test pair to be combined during observation point insertion.

To determine the bound N_{OP} on the number of observation points, we assume that the observation points are connected to a separate scan chain that will be shifted out at the same time as the scan chain to which the circuit flip-flops are connected. Thus, as long as the number of observation points does not exceed the number of state variables of the circuit, the test application time does not increase because of the need to read observation point values. We return to this assumption at the end of Section 4.

4. Experimental results

In this section, we report the results obtained by applying Procedures 2, 3 and 4 to benchmark circuits.

Circuit parameters are shown in Table 6. After the circuit name, we show the number of primary inputs, the number of primary outputs, the number of state variables, and the number of combinational tests used for constructing the initial test set. We used the combinational test sets of [5], which are highly compacted, and result in initial test sets that are already compact.

Table 6: Circuit parameters

circuit	inp	out	s.v	tests
s208	11	2	8	27
s298	3	6	14	24
s344	9	11	15	15
s382	3	6	21	25
s386	7	7	6	70
s400	3	6	21	24
s420	19	2	16	43
s510	19	7	6	54
s526	3	6	21	50
s641	35	24	19	22
s820	18	19	5	94
s953	16	23	29	76
s1196	14	14	18	118
s1423	17	5	74	26
s1488	8	19	6	101
s5378	35	49	179	100

For one circuit, s382, we show in Table 7 a comparison of Procedures 2, 3 and 4 described in the previous section. For each procedure, we have in Table 7 a row for every number of observation points. The first column for every procedure shows the number of observation points. In this column, I stands for the initial test set, and 0 corresponds to compaction without inserting observation points. Since the results of all the procedures in these two

rows are the same, they appear only in the left part of the table. The three procedures may differ for higher numbers of observation points. Following the number of observation points, we show the number of tests in the compacted test set T, and the total length of all the tests (the length of a test τ_i is the length of the sequence T_i included in it, e.g., in Table 5, the length of τ_0 is two and the length of τ_1 is four). Next, we show the total number of clock cycles required for application of the compacted test set T, and the percentage of clock cycles out of the number of cycles required to apply the initial test set before compaction. The number of clock cycles is computed as follows. We denote the number of tests by N_T, the number of flip-flops by N_{SV}, and the total length of all the tests by Δ. The number of clock cycles required for test application is equal to $(N_T + 1)N_{SV} + \Delta$. The first term corresponds to scan in/out operations for N_T tests. The second term corresponds to the test vectors applied without scan. This equation assumes that the same clock speed is used during scan, and during the application of primary input vectors. We return to this assumption later on.

Table 7: Results for s382

	Procedure 2					Procedure 3					Procedure 4			
			cycles					cycles					cycles	
ops	tst	len	tot	%	ops	tst	len	tot	%	ops	tst	len	tot	%
I	25	25	571	100.00										
0	23	25	529	92.64										
2	21	25	487	85.29	2	22	25	508	88.97	2	22	25	508	88.97
3	20	25	466	81.61	3	21	25	487	85.29	3	21	25	487	85.29
5	19	25	445	77.93	5	20	25	466	81.61	5	20	25	466	81.61
6	17	25	403	70.58	6	19	25	445	77.93	6	19	25	445	77.93
10	16	25	382	66.90	10	18	25	424	74.26	10	18	25	424	74.26
15	15	25	361	63.22	16	17	25	403	70.58	16	17	25	403	70.58
18	14	25	340	59.54	19	16	25	382	66.90	19	16	25	382	66.90
21	13	25	319	55.87	21	14	25	340	59.54	21	15	25	361	63.22

It can be seen that all the procedures reduce the test application time compared to the case where no observation points are added. Procedure 4 achieves lower levels of compaction than Procedure 3, which achieves lower levels of compaction than Procedure 2. However, the differences are justified by the reduced computational complexity. Similar results were observed for other circuits we considered.

To report the results for additional circuits, we select a single number, i, of observation points for every circuit, and report the results of Procedure 4 when it inserts i observation points. The value of i never exceeds the number of state variables of the circuit, N_{sv}. We use $i < N_{SV}$ if inserting $i + 1, \cdots, N_{SV}$ observation points does not help reduce the test application time. The results are shown in Table 8. Under column *initial*, we show the information for the initial test set. Under column *0 ops*, we show the results of Procedure 1 that does not insert observation points. Under column *i ops* we show the results obtained by Procedure 4 with *i* observation points. In every case, we show the number of tests in the test set T, and the total length of all the tests. We then show the total number of clock cycles required for application of the test set T, and the percentage of clock cycles out of the number of cycles required to apply the initial test set before compaction. The percentage is omitted for the initial test set, since it is always 100%. For the case where *i* observation points are inserted, we show the value of *i* under the corresponding column.

Table 8: Results of Procedure 4

| | initial | | | 0 ops | | | | *i* ops | | | |
| | | | | | | cycles | | | | | cycles | |
circuit	tst	len	cycles	tst	len	tot	%	*i*	tst	len	tot	%
s208	27	27	251	23	27	219	87.25	8	16	27	163	64.94
s298	24	24	374	20	24	318	85.03	14	17	24	276	73.80
s344	15	15	255	11	15	195	76.47	11	9	15	165	64.71
s382	25	25	571	23	25	529	92.64	21	15	25	361	63.22
s386	70	70	496	42	70	328	66.13	6	36	67	289	58.27
s400	24	24	549	20	24	465	84.70	20	13	24	318	57.92
s420	43	43	747	40	43	699	93.57	16	31	43	555	74.30
s526	50	50	1121	44	50	995	88.76	21	32	50	743	66.28
s641	22	22	459	15	22	326	71.02	19	8	22	193	42.05
s820	94	94	569	42	94	309	54.31	5	37	94	284	49.91
s953	76	76	2309	19	76	656	28.41	26	7	76	308	13.34
s1196	113	113	2165	25	113	581	26.84	18	15	113	401	18.52
s1423	26	26	2024	26	26	2024	100.00	74	14	26	1136	56.13
s1488	101	101	713	38	101	335	46.98	1	37	101	329	46.14
s5378	100	100	18179	100	100	18179	100.00	71	77	98	14060	77.34

It can be seen that Procedure 4 reduces the test application time for all the circuits considered. It is also important to note that for *s*1423, Procedure 1 cannot reduce the test application time of the initial test set at all. This is partly due to the fact that the combinational test set from which the initial test set was constructed is highly compacted. The insertion of observation points allows the test application time to be reduced to 56.13% of its initial value. A similar situation occurs for *s*5378.

It is possible to insert fewer observation points than those resported in Table 8. In Table 9, we report the results obtained for *s*1423 by inserting various numbers of observation points.

In computing the number of clock cycles required for test application, we assumed that the scan clock and the circuit clock have the same cycle time, and that the observation points are connected to a separate scan chain.

Table 9: Results for *s*1423

Procedure 4

			cycles	
ops	tst	len	tot	%
I	26	26	2024	100.00
0	26	26	2024	100.00
3	25	26	1960	96.34
6	24	26	1876	92.69
9	23	26	1802	89.03
20	22	26	1728	85.38
22	21	26	1654	81.72
28	20	26	1580	78.06
36	19	26	1506	74.41
41	18	26	1432	70.75
54	17	26	1358	67.09
60	16	26	1284	63.44
68	15	26	1210	59.78
74	14	26	1136	56.13

Next, we study the effects of these assumptions by considering the results reported in Table 8.

The number of clock cycles required for test application was computed above as $(N_T + 1)N_{SV} + \Delta$ assuming that the cycle times of the scan clock and the circuit clock are the same. Let us assume that the cycle time of the scan clock is A times larger than the cycle time of the circuit clock, where $A > 1$ is a constant. The number of circuit clock cycles required for test application becomes $(N_T + 1)N_{SV}A + \Delta$. From Table 8, Δ is approximately the same before and after compaction. In addition, N_{SV} and A are constants. Consequently, the reduction in the number of clock cycles due to compaction is determined by N_T. For all the circuits reported in Table 8, N_T is reduced (Δ is sometimes reduced as well, but only marginally). We conclude that the test application time is reduced independent of A. In fact, the absolute reduction is higher when A is larger.

Until now, we assumed that the observation point values are read through a separate scan chain. Alternatively, it is possible to multiplex the observation points with the primary outputs of the circuit. In both of these solutions, reading the observation point values does not increase the test application time. Another alternative is to connect the observation points to the same scan chain connecting the circuit flip-flops. In this case, the number of clock cycles required for test application becomes $(N_T + 1)(N_{SV} + N_{OPS}) + \Delta$, where N_{OPS} is the number of observation points. Thus, the test application time increases with the number of observation points. This increase must be compensated for by the reduction in the number of tests due to compaction.

It is important to note that Procedure 4 was designed based on the assumption that the observation points are connected to a separate scan chain. Consequently, an observation point was added if it reduced the number of tests by any amount. This strategy may not be effective if the length of the scan chain is increased by the addition of an observation point. In this case, it may be necessary to modify Procedure 4 so as to make a different assumption. Specifically, an observation point must reduce the number of tests sufficiently to compensate for the increase in the length of the scan chain. An observation point that does not achieve sufficient compaction should not be added.

Nevertheless, when Procedure 4 reduces the number of tests sufficiently, a reduction in test application time is achieved even without targeting a single scan chain directly. In Table 10, we show the numbers of clock cycles for such circuits, using the equation $(N_T + 1)(N_{SV} + N_{OPS}) + \Delta$ for computing the number of clock cycles.

Table 10: Clock cycles for a single scan chain

| circuit | initial | | i ops | | |
	tot	%	i	tot	%
s641	459	100.00	19	364	79.30
s820	569	100.00	5	474	83.30
s953	2309	100.00	26	516	22.35
s1196	2165	100.00	18	689	31.82
s1488	713	100.00	1	367	51.47

5. Concluding remarks

We proposed three procedures for placing observation points in full scan circuits to improve the levels of compaction that can be achieved without loss of fault coverage. The compaction procedures were based on the operation of combining test pairs. The combination of two tests resulted in the removal of the scan operation at the end of the first test and at the beginning of the second test, thus reducing the test application time.

All three procedures first combined as many test pairs as possible without inserting observation points. When the combination of any two tests left some faults undetected, observation points were added to allow these faults to be detected, if possible, thus allowing the test pair to be combined. The procedures differed in the effort expended, e.g., in trying to maximize the utilization of every test-point, and in the expected levels of compaction. In our implementation, observation point values were read only at the last time unit of every test. Thus, observation point values could be scanned-out at the same time as the next-state values.

References

[1] D. K. Pradhan and J. Saxena, "A Design for Testability Scheme to Reduce Test Application Time in Full Scan", in Proc. 10th VLSI Test Symp., April 1992, pp. 55-60.

[2] S. Y. Lee and K. K. Saluja, "An Algorithm to Reduce Test Application Time in Full Scan Designs", in Proc. 1992 Intl. Conf. on Computer-Aided Design, Nov. 1992, pp. 17-20.

[3] S. Y. Lee and K. K. Saluja, "Test Application Time Reduction for Sequential Circuits with Scan", IEEE Trans. on Computer-Aided Design, Sept. 1995, pp. 1128-1140.

[4] I. Pomeranz and S. M. Reddy, "Static Test Compaction for Scan-Based Designs to Reduce Test Application Time", in Proc. 7th Asian Test Symp., Dec. 1998, pp. 198-203.

[5] S. Kajihara, I. Pomeranz, K. Kinoshita and S. M. Reddy, "Cost-Effective Generation of Minimal Test Sets for Stuck-at Faults in Combinational Logic Circuits", IEEE Trans. on Computer-Aided Design, Dec. 1995, pp. 1496-1504.

Method to Recover Internet Packet Losses Using
(*n*, *n* − 1, *m*) Convolutional Codes

Masayuki Arai   Anna Yamaguchi   Kazuhiko Iwasaki

Graduate School of Engineering, Tokyo Metropolitan University

1-2 Minami Ohsawa, Hachioji, 192-0397 Tokyo, Japan

e-mail: (arai@info.,anna@info.,iwasaki@)eei.metro-u.ac.jp

Abstract

A new method to recover packet losses using (n, n − 1, m) convolutional codes is proposed. The method is used to encode and decode packets transmitted over the Internet. An independent erasure channel is assumed for packets transmission. We then theoretically analyze the method ability to recover packet losses. The sufficient conditions are derived for packet losses that can be recovered. We evaluate the method using computer simulations, supplemented by comparisons with a simple parity method, which has the same redundancy. The results show that the proposed method has a superior performance.

1   Introduction

With the advancement of the Internet, techniques for dependable networking have become important. The traffic congestion causes not only poor performance, but also poor dependability. In the Internet, the traffic congestion occurs when routers receive more packets than their capacity. The packets that overflow the queue of the routers are just thrown away. This is considered to be a main cause of packet losses. Therefore, it is important to recover packet losses efficiently for dependable networks.

In the Internet, there are many routers on the paths, and the packet-loss probabilities vary with time and location [1-3]. Various measurements between 37 Internet sites were reported [1]. Packet loss ratios were measured for Europe and the US [2], and for Japan [3].

Many techniques have been proposed to recover packet losses. One is automatic repeat request (ARQ) [4] that is used in the TCP/IP. In the ARQ, receivers send back information that either they have received a packet, that is positive acknowledgement (ACK), or they have not received the packet, that is negative acknowledgement (NACK). The sender retransmits the packets that have not reached to receivers. Other techniques for recovering packet losses are forward error correction (FEC) and hybrid ARQ [5]-[7].

In the FEC, redundant packets are sent with information packets and the receiver reconstructs the lost information packets using these redundant packets. The receiver cannot always recover all of the lost packets, even if the FEC is applied. The limits are specified by the coding methods. In the hybrid ARQ, redundant packets are sent in a similar way to the FEC. If receivers cannot recover any packets, they send back ACK or NACK similar to ARQ, and the lost packets are retransmitted. For example of the FEC and the hybrid ARQ, the Reed-Solomon (RS) codes are applied for an erasure channel [6], and multicast transmissions [7].

Each technique has advantages and the selection which method should be adopted depends on the characteristics of the network performance and the transmitted information such as multimedia data, file data, and others.

In this manuscript, we propose a coding method for packet-loss recovery using convolutional codes. We theoretically analyze the ability to recover lost packets for our method. An independent erasure channel is assumed for the Internet transmission. The numerical results using computer simulation are also shown.

This manuscript is organized as follows. In chapter 2, we show transmission model, the encoding scheme, and decoding method. In chapter 3, theoretical analyses for packet loss recovering are presented. In chapter 4, we will show simulation of our method and compare it with the simple parity technique. Chapter 5 is the conclusion.

2   Preliminaries

2.1   Transmission model

Figure 1 shows the transmission model that we consider in this manuscript.

Let $\mathbf{u}_i = [u_{i1}, u_{i2}, \ldots, u_{ik}]$ denote k information packets [8], where u_{ij} expresses a packet of fixed length l. In other words, we consider $u_{ij} \in GF(2^l)$. The sets of packets $\mathbf{u}_i = [u_{i1}, u_{i2}, \ldots, u_{ik}]$ then enter into the encoder and redundant packets $[p_{i1}, \ldots, p_{i(n-k)}]$ are generated. We call a set of k information packets and $(n - k)$ redundant packets a code group, that is $\mathbf{v}_i = [v_{i1}, v_{i2}, \ldots, v_{in}]$. In this manuscript, we will consider systematic convolutional codes, therefore the following equation holds:

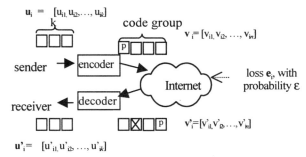

Fig.1. Transmission model.

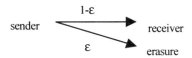

Fig. 2. Independent erasure channel.

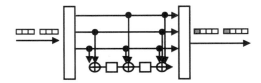

Fig. 3. Encoder for (4, 3, 2) convolutional code.

$$v_{ij} = \begin{cases} u_{ij} & (1 \le j \le k) \\ p_{i(j-k)} & (k+1 \le j \le n) \end{cases}.$$

The code groups generated by the encoder are sent to the receiver over the Internet. Each packet may be lost due to such as router buffer overflows in the Internet. In this manuscript, we assume there is an independent erasure channel as shown in Fig. 2. A packet is successfully received by the receiver with probability $(1 - \varepsilon)$ independently of transmission time, where packet loss probability ε is a constant.

The packets that reached to the receiver, $v'_i = [v'_{i1}, v'_{i2}, \ldots, v'_{in}]$ are decoded. Let the packet losses be denoted by $e_i = [e_{i1}, e_{i2}, \ldots, e_{il}]$. We assume that received packets are uncorrupted. If packet v_{ij} is received, then $v'_{ij} = v_{ij}$. If packet v_{ij} is lost, then v'_{ij} is unknown. The positions of lost packets in e_i are located by the method such as sequence numbers that each packet includes [9],[10].

2.2 Encoding

In our method, we apply $(n, n - 1, m)$ convolutional codes [8],[11],[12]. Our method extends use of convolutional codes over $GF(2^l)$, where l is the number of bits in a packet.

For every $k = n - 1$ information packets $u_i = [u_{i1}, u_{i2}, \ldots, u_{ik}]$, the set of n output packets $v_i = [v_{i1}, v_{i2}, \ldots, v_{i(k+1)}]$, called a code group, is generated by the following equation:

$$v_i = u_i \, G_i(D),$$

where D means delay operator, $G_i(D)$ is the generator matrix. Matrix $G_i(D)$ is expressed as

$$G_i(D) = \begin{bmatrix} I_k & g(D) \end{bmatrix} = \begin{bmatrix} I_k & \begin{matrix} g_1(D) \\ \vdots \\ g_k(D) \end{matrix} \end{bmatrix}.$$

Matrix I_k expresses a $k \times k$ identity matrix. Each of $g_1(D), \ldots, g_k(D)$ is a polynomial with a degree that is at most m as shown below:

$$g_1(D) = g_{11} + g_{12}D + \ldots + g_{1(m+1)}D^m$$
$$\vdots$$
$$g_k(D) = g_{k1} + g_{k2}D + \ldots + g_{k(m+1)}D^m$$

where $g_{ij} = 0$ or 1 $(1 \le i \le k, 1 \le j \le m + 1)$. $g(D)$ is used to generate a redundant packet. The generator matrix for redundant packet p_i is also expressed as a binary $k \times (m + 1)$ matrix as follows:

$$G_i = \begin{bmatrix} I_k & g \end{bmatrix}, \quad g = \begin{bmatrix} g_{11} & \cdots & g_{1(m+1)} \\ \vdots & \ddots & \vdots \\ g_{k1} & \cdots & g_{k(m+1)} \end{bmatrix}.$$

Parameter m denotes constraint length that shows how many previous code groups affect one redundant packet [8]. To generate parity packet p_i for code group v_i, not only information block u_i, but also blocks $u_{i-1}, \ldots, u_{i-m}$ are needed. That is, the following equation holds for p_i and $u_{ij} \in GF(2^l)$:

$$\begin{aligned} p_i = &\; g_{11}u_{i1} + g_{12}u_{(i-1)1} + \ldots + g_{1(m+1)}u_{(i-m)1} \\ &+ g_{21}u_{i2} + g_{22}u_{(i-1)2} + \ldots + g_{2(m+1)}u_{(i-m)2} \\ &\ldots\ldots\ldots \\ &+ g_{k1}u_{ik} + g_{k2}u_{(i-1)k} + \ldots + g_{k(m+1)}u_{(i-m)k}, \end{aligned} \quad (1)$$

where symbol "+" means addition over $GF(2^l)$, that is a bit-wise exclusive-or calculation for each packet. The term $g_{ij}u_{i'j'}$ expresses logical product of g_{ij} and $u_{i'j'}$. That means

$$g_{ij}u_{i'j'} = \begin{cases} 0 & (g_{ij} = 0), \\ u_{i'j'} & (g_{ij} = 1). \end{cases}$$

For example, consider the (4, 3, 2) convolutional code shown in Figure 3, where $G_i(D)$ is expressed as

$$G_i(D) = \begin{bmatrix} I_3 & \begin{matrix} 1 + D \\ 1 + D^2 \\ 1 + D + D^2 \end{matrix} \end{bmatrix}.$$

The matrix g is expressed as

$$g = \begin{bmatrix} 1 & 1 & 0 \\ 1 & 0 & 1 \\ 1 & 1 & 1 \end{bmatrix}.$$

Figure 4 shows an example of encoding using the encoder shown in Fig. 3. The information packets $u_{11}, u_{12}, \ldots,$ are input into the encoder and redundant packets are generated. Packet p_1 is expressed as

$$p_1 = u_{11} + u_{12} + u_{13}.$$

The preceding packets are considered as zeros. Similarly, p_2

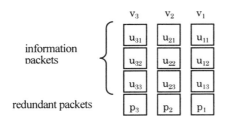

Fig. 4. An example of encoding for the (4, 3, 2) convolutional code.

and p_3 are

$$p_2 = u_{21} + u_{22} + u_{23} + u_{11} + u_{13},$$
$$p_3 = u_{31} + u_{32} + u_{33} + u_{21} + u_{23} + u_{12} + u_{13}.$$

2.3 Decoding

Traditionally, convolutional codes are mainly used for error detection and correction for the datalink layer such as radio and mobile communications [5],[11]. In such cases, positions of erasures cannot always be recognized and decoding methods for an erasure channel are not well investigated. In this manuscript, a decoding method for an erasure channel shown in Fig. 2 is presented.

When continuous s code groups $\mathbf{v'}_i$, $\mathbf{v'}_{i+1}$,..., $\mathbf{v'}_{i+s}$ arrived, some packets $\mathbf{e} = [\mathbf{e}_i\ \mathbf{e}_{i+1}, ..., \mathbf{e}_{i+s}]$ may be lost. Positions of erasures $\mathbf{e}$ can be located by the receiver. The following equation based on Eq. (1) holds for the packets in code group $\mathbf{v'}_i$ and m preceding blocks $\mathbf{v'}_{i-1}, \mathbf{v'}_{i-2}, ..., \mathbf{v'}_{i-m}$:

$$
\begin{aligned}
&g_{11}\mathbf{v'}_{i1} + g_{12}\mathbf{v'}_{(i-1)1} + ... + g_{1(m+1)}\mathbf{v'}_{(i-m)1} \\
&+ g_{21}\mathbf{v'}_{i2} + g_{22}\mathbf{v'}_{(i-1)2} + ... + g_{2(m+1)}\mathbf{v'}_{(i-m)2} \qquad , (2) \\
&\quad \cdots\cdots \\
&+ g_{k1}\mathbf{v'}_{ik} + g_{k2}\mathbf{v'}_{(i-1)k} + ... + g_{k(m+1)}\mathbf{v'}_{(i-m)k} + \mathbf{v'}_{i(k+1)} = 0
\end{aligned}
$$

where $\mathbf{v'}_{i(k+1)}$ is the redundant packet received. The lost packets in the equation that are regarded as unknown quantities. From Eq. (2), the $(s + m)$ equations system

$$
\begin{cases}
g_{11}\mathbf{v'}_{i1} + g_{12}\mathbf{v'}_{(i-1)1} + ... + g_{1(m+1)}\mathbf{v'}_{(i-m)1} \\
+ g_{21}\mathbf{v'}_{i12} + g_{22}\mathbf{v'}_{(i-1)2} + ... + g_{2(m+1)}\mathbf{v'}_{(i-m)2} \\
\quad \cdots\cdots\cdots \\
+ g_{k1}\mathbf{v'}_{ik} + g_{k2}\mathbf{v'}_{(i-1)k} + ... + g_{k(m+1)}\mathbf{v'}_{(i-m)k} + \mathbf{v'}_{i(k+1)} = 0 \\
\qquad\qquad\qquad \vdots \\
g_{11}\mathbf{v'}_{(i+s+m)1} + g_{12}\mathbf{v'}_{(i+s+m-1)1} + ... + g_{1(m+1)}\mathbf{v'}_{(i+s)1} \\
+ g_{21}\mathbf{v'}_{(i+s+m)2} + g_{22}\mathbf{v'}_{(i+s+m-1)2} + ... + g_{2(m+1)}\mathbf{v'}_{(i+s)2} \\
\quad \cdots\cdots \\
+ g_{k1}\mathbf{v'}_{(i+s+m)k} + g_{k2}\mathbf{v'}_{(i+s+m-1)k} + ... + g_{k(m+1)}\mathbf{v'}_{(i+s)k} + \mathbf{v'}_{(i+s+m)(k+1)} = 0
\end{cases}
\quad (3)
$$

holds for continuous $(s + 2m)$ code groups $\mathbf{v'}_{i-m}, \mathbf{v'}_{i-m+1}, ..., \mathbf{v'}_i$. $\mathbf{v'}_{i+1}, ..., \mathbf{v'}_{i+s+m}$, where these equations contain t unknown quantities. If the Eqs. (3) have a unique solution, the lost packets can be reconstructed.

3 Ability to recover packet losses with $(n, n - 1, m)$ convolutional codes

3.1 All the parity packets are erasure-free

In this section it is assumed that redundant packets are erasure-free. Under this assumption we analyze the ability to recover lost packets using $(n, n - 1, m)$ convolutional codes. Let the m code groups immediately preceding and m immediately succeeding the code group $\mathbf{v'}_i$ be received correctly (or already recovered). This condition is known as the guard space requirement.

[*Lemma 1*] Suppose that in a code group $\mathbf{v'}_i$, t information packets are lost and redundant packet $p_i = v_{i(k+1)}$ is received, and there is a guard-space for $\mathbf{v'}_i$. If t rows in the generator matrix $\mathbf{g}(D)$

$$
\mathbf{g}(D) = \begin{bmatrix} g_1(D) \\ \vdots \\ g_k(D) \end{bmatrix}
$$

are linearly independent, packet losses can be recovered.
[proof]

From Eq. (1) the following equation holds for redundant packet p_i.

$$
\begin{aligned}
p_i &= g_{11}u_{i1} + g_{12}u_{(i-1)1} + ... + g_{1(m+1)}u_{(i-m)1} \\
&+ g_{21}u_{i2} + g_{22}u_{(i-1)2} + ... + g_{2(m+1)}u_{(i-m)2} \\
&\quad \cdots\cdots\cdots \\
&+ g_{k1}u_{ik} + g_{k2}u_{(i-1)k} + ... + g_{k(m+1)}u_{(i-m)k} \quad .
\end{aligned}
$$

Let $\mathbf{e} = [e_{ij1} ... e_{ijt}] = [\mathbf{v'}_{ij1} ... \mathbf{v'}_{ijt}]$ denote lost packets. Since it is assumed that m preceding code groups are erasure-free, the following packets are erasure-free: $\mathbf{v'}_{(i-1)1}, ... , \mathbf{v'}_{(i-1)k}, \mathbf{v'}_{(i-2)2}, ... , \mathbf{v'}_{(i-m)1}, ... , \mathbf{v'}_{(i-m)k}$. Since the receiver according to the assumption receives p_i correctly, thus the above equation can be written as

$$
\begin{aligned}
&g_{11}\mathbf{v'}_{i1} + g_{12}\mathbf{v'}_{(i-1)1} + ... + g_{1(m+1)}\mathbf{v'}_{(i-m)1} \\
&+ ... + g_{k1}\mathbf{v'}_{ik} + ... + g_{k(m+1)}\mathbf{v'}_{(i-m)k} = \textit{known value}.
\end{aligned}
$$

Among $\mathbf{v'}_{i1}, ... , \mathbf{v'}_{ik}$ packets $e_{ij1}, ... , e_{ijt}$ are unknown and the others are known. The above equation is further rewritten as

$$g_{j11}e_{ij1} + g_{j21}e_{ij2} + ... + g_{jt1}e_{ijt} = F_i,$$
$$F_i = p_i + \sum_{\substack{\text{received packets} \\ 1 \le x \le k,\ 1 \le y \le m+1}} g_{xy}\mathbf{v'}_{(i-y+1)x} \ .$$

Similarly, the following equation holds

$$g_{j12}e_{ij1} + g_{j22}e_{ij2} + ... + g_{jt2}e_{ijt} = F_{i+1},$$
$$F_{i+1} = p_{i+1} + \sum_{\substack{\text{received packets} \\ 1 \le x \le k,\ 1 \le y \le m+1}} g_{xy}\mathbf{v'}_{(i-y+2)x} \ .$$

Finally, the following equation system holds

$$[e_{i\,j1} \cdots e_{i\,jt}] \begin{bmatrix} g_{j11} & \cdots & g_{j1(m+1)} \\ \vdots & \ddots & \vdots \\ g_{jt1} & \cdots & g_{jt(m+1)} \end{bmatrix} = [F_i \cdots F_{i+m}].$$

That is

$$\mathbf{e} \cdot \mathbf{g}_{subt} = [F_i \cdots F_{i+m}].$$

Matrix $\mathbf{g}_{subt}$ is a $t \times (m+1)$ sub-matrix of generator matrix $\mathbf{g}$. For having unique solution for the above equation, it is the necessary and sufficient condition that there exists a $t \times t$ sub-matrix $\mathbf{g}_{subtt}$ of matrix $\mathbf{g}_{subt}$, where determinant $|\mathbf{g}_{subtt}| \neq 0$. By reference [13], the following three conditions are equivalent: $|\mathbf{g}_{subtt}| \neq 0$, all rows of $\mathbf{g}_{subtt}$ are linearly independent, and all columns of $\mathbf{g}_{subtt}$ are linearly independent. If these conditions hold, t rows of $\mathbf{g}_{subt}$ are linearly independent. If t rows of $\mathbf{g}$ are linearly independent, the above condition holds for every $\mathbf{g}_{subt}$ of size $t \times (m+1)$.
[Q.E.D.]

In Fig. 5, three lost packets in i-th code group, which are shaded, are recovered by the equations from i-th, (i + 1)-th, and (i + 2)-th code groups. For these code groups, the simultaneous equations hold:

$$[e_{i1} \ e_{i2} \ e_{i3}] \begin{bmatrix} 1 & 1 & 0 \\ 1 & 0 & 1 \\ 1 & 1 & 1 \end{bmatrix} = [F_i \ F_{i+1} \ F_{i+2}],$$

where $[e_{i1} \ e_{i2} \ e_{i3}] = [v'_{i1} \ v'_{i2} \ v'_{i3}]$. Three rows in the above matrix are linearly independent. Then, the lost packets can be recovered.

[*Corollary 1*] If continuous t row vectors of the generator matrix $\mathbf{g}(D)$ are linearly independent and there is a guard space for a code group, burst packet losses of length t within the code group can be recovered.

[*Theorem 1*] Suppose that for code groups $\mathbf{v'}_i, \ldots, \mathbf{v'}_{i+s}$ t information packets

$$\mathbf{e} = [\mathbf{e}_i \ \cdots \ \mathbf{e}_{i+s}] = [e_{i1\,j1} \ e_{i2\,j2} \ \cdots \ e_{it\,jt}] = [v'_{i1\,j1} \ \cdots \ v'_{it\,jt}]$$

are lost, all the redundant packets $p_{i1}, p_{i+1}, \ldots, p_{i+s}$ are received, and there is a guard-space for $[\mathbf{v'}_i \ldots \mathbf{v'}_{i+s}]$. If rows of the following matrix $\mathbf{g}^*_{subt}(D)$

v'$_{i+2}$ v'$_{i+1}$ v'$_i$ v'$_{i-1}$ v'$_{i-2}$

Fig.5 An example of packet-loss pattern which can be recovered.

$$g^*_{subt}(D) = \begin{bmatrix} D^{i1-i} \cdot g_{j1}(D) \\ \vdots \\ D^{it-i} \cdot g_{jt}(D) \end{bmatrix}$$

are linearly independent, packet losses $\mathbf{e} = [e_{i1j1} \ e_{i2j2} \ldots \ e_{itjt}]$ can be recovered.
[proof]

Without loss of generality we can suppose that $i = i1 \leq i2 \leq \ldots \leq it = i + s$. From Eq. (1) for code groups $\mathbf{v'}_i, \ldots, \mathbf{v'}_{i+s}$ the following simultaneous equations hold:

$$\begin{cases} g_{11}v'_{i1} + g_{12}v'_{(i-1)1} + \ldots + g_{1(m+1)}v'_{(i-m)1} \\ \quad + \ldots + g_{k1}v'_{ik} + \ldots + g_{k(m+1)}v'_{(i-m)k} + v'_{i(k+1)} = 0 \\ \qquad\qquad \vdots \\ g_{11}v'_{(i+s+m)1} + g_{12}v'_{(i+s+m-1)1} + \ldots + g_{1(m+1)}v'_{(i+s)1} \\ \quad + \ldots + g_{k1}v'_{(i+s+m)k} + \ldots + g_{k(m+1)}v'_{(i+s)k} + v'_{(i+s+m)(k+1)} = 0 \end{cases}$$

In these equations the variable $\mathbf{e} = [e_{i1j1}, \ldots, e_{itjt}] = [v'_{i1j1}, \ldots, v'_{itjt}]$ are unknown and the others are known. The unknown values in code group $\mathbf{v'}_i$ appear in $(m + 1)$ equations, that is for i-th, (i + 1)-th, ... , and (i + m)-th code groups. The unknown value e_{ixjx} appears in the equations for ix-th, (ix + 1)-th, ... , (ix + m)-th code groups as $g_{jx1}e_{ixjx}$, $g_{jx12}e_{ixjx}, \cdots, g_{jx(m+1)}e_{ixjx}$, and e_{ixjx} does not appear in the equations for i-th, ...,(ix - 1)-th, and (ix + m + 1)-th, ... , (i + s + m)-th code groups. Then, above simultaneous equations can be rewritten as:

$$[e_{i1j1} \ \cdots \ e_{itjt}] \begin{bmatrix} g_{j11} & \cdots & & g_{j1(m+1)} & 0 & \cdots & 0 \\ & \vdots & & & & & \\ 0 & \cdots & 0 & g_{jx1} & \cdots & g_{jx(m+1)} & 0 & \cdots & 0 \\ & & & & \vdots & & & \\ 0 & \cdots & 0 & & & g_{jt1} & \cdots & g_{jt(m+1)} \end{bmatrix} = [F_i \ \cdots \ F_{i+s+m}],$$

that is

$$\mathbf{e} \cdot \mathbf{g}^*_{subt}(D) = [F_i \ldots F_{i+s+m}],$$

where $\mathbf{g}^*_{subt}$ is $t \times (s + m)$ matrix. The values $F_i, \ldots, F_{i+s+m}$ are sum of the known variables in each equation. The necessary and sufficient condition for these equations to have a unique solution is that there exists a $t \times t$ sub-matrix $\mathbf{g}^*_{subtt}$ of matrix $\mathbf{g}^*_{subt}$ whose determinant $\det|\mathbf{g}^*_{subtt}| \neq 0$.
[Q.E.D.]

In Fig. 6 four packets shaded are lost. The following simultaneous equations holds:

$$[e_{i2} \ e_{i3} \ e_{(i+1)3} \ e_{(i+2)3}] \begin{bmatrix} 1 & 0 & 1 & 0 & 0 \\ 1 & 1 & 1 & 0 & 0 \\ 0 & 1 & 1 & 1 & 0 \\ 0 & 0 & 1 & 1 & 1 \end{bmatrix} = [F_i \ F_{i+1} \ F_{i+2} \ F_{i+3} \ F_{i+4}].$$

Four rows in matrix are linearly independent. The lost packets can be recovered.
[*Corollary 2*] The lost packets $\mathbf{e} = [v'_{i\,j1}, \ldots, v'_{i\,jt}]$ can be recovered with t ($t \leq m$) equations that hold for i-th, (i + 1)-th, ...,(i + t - 1)-th code groups, if the $t \times t$ sub-matrix $\mathbf{g}_{subtt}$ of

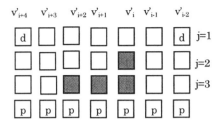

Fig. 6. An example of packet-loss pattern which can be recovered.

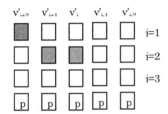

Fig. 7. An example of packet-loss patterns which can be recovered

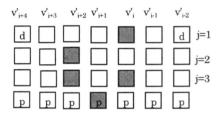

Fig. 8. An example of packet-loss pattern which can be recovered.

generator matrix **g**,

$$\mathbf{g}_{subtt} = \begin{bmatrix} g_{j1\,1} & \cdots & g_{j1\,t} \\ \vdots & \ddots & \vdots \\ g_{jt\,1} & \cdots & g_{jt\,t} \end{bmatrix}$$

satisfies the condition that all rows are linearly independent and there is a guard space for the code group $\mathbf{v'}_i$. This implies that t loss-packets can be recovered before $(i + m)$-th code group arrives.

[*Lemma 2*] If there is a guard space, it is possible to design such $(n, n - 1, m)$ convolutional codes that can always recover one packet loss in a code group using only one equation.

[proof]

Consider the codes with generator matrix **g**(D) that each g_i(D) contains a constant term, that is,

$$g_{j1} = 1 \quad (1 \le j \le k).$$

This code can recover one packet loss. Since the following equation for the given code group

$$\mathbf{v'}_{i1} + \mathbf{v'}_{i2} + \ldots + \mathbf{v'}_{ik} + g_{12}\mathbf{v'}_{(i-1)1} + \ldots + g_{k2}\mathbf{v'}_{(i-1)k}$$
$$+ \ldots + g_{k(m+1)}\mathbf{v}_{(i-m)k} + \mathbf{v'}_{i\,k+1} = 0$$

contains only one unknown quantity $\mathbf{v'}_{i\,j1}$, it can be reconstructed by this equation.
[Q.E.D.]

Based on *Lemma 2*, the (4, 3, 2) convolutional code shown in Fig. 3 can recover one packet loss in a code group as soon as the code group arrives, and this packet loss does not affect recovering losses in the succeeding code groups. Such loss patterns as shown in Fig. 7 can always be recovered. In Fig.7, at first, the following equation holds for $\mathbf{v'}_i$

$$\mathbf{v'}_{i2} = F_i$$

Then, the unknown packet $\mathbf{v'}_{i2}$ is recovered. Similarly, for code groups $\mathbf{v'}_{(i+1)}$, $\mathbf{v'}_{(i+2)}$, the following equations hold:

$$\mathbf{v'}_{(i+1)2} = F_{i+1},$$
$$\mathbf{v'}_{(i+2)1} = F_{i+2}.$$

The unknown packets $\mathbf{v'}_{(i+1)2}$, $\mathbf{v'}_{(i+2)1}$ are also recovered, unknown quantities in the previous code groups are recovered and can be regarded as received correctly.

3.2 Some redundant packets are lost

In this section we assume that $(t + y)$ packet losses **e** $= [\mathbf{v'}_{i1\,j1},\ldots,\mathbf{v'}_{ir\,jt}, p_{i(t+1)}, \ldots, p_{i(t+y)}]$ occur in code groups from i-th to $(i + s)$-th, including t information packets and y redundant packets. Again let $\mathbf{g^*}_{subt}$ be a $t \times (s + m)$ matrix shown below:

$$\mathbf{g^*}_{subt} = \begin{bmatrix} g_{j11} & \cdots & g_{j1(m+1)} & & 0 & \cdots & 0 \\ & & & \vdots & & & \\ 0 & \cdots & 0 & g_{jx1} & \cdots & g_{jx(m+1)} & 0 & \cdots & 0 \\ & & & \vdots & & & \\ 0 & \cdots & 0 & & & g_{jt1} & \cdots & g_{jt(m+1)} \end{bmatrix}.$$

The $t \times (s + m - y)$ matrix $\mathbf{g^*}_{subt-y}$ is constructed from the above $\mathbf{g^*}_{subt}$ by removing $\{i(t + 1)\}$-th, ... , $\{i(t+y)\}$-th columns.

[*Theorem 2*] Suppose that $(t + y)$ packet losses **e** $= [\mathbf{v'}_{i1\,j1},\ldots,\mathbf{v'}_{ir\,jt}, p_{i(t+1)}, \ldots, p_{i(t+y)}]$ occur in code groups from i-th to $(i + s)$-th, including t information packets and y redundant packets. If all row vectors of the matrix $\mathbf{g^*}_{subt-y}$ are linearly independent and there is a guard space for $[\mathbf{v}_i \ldots \mathbf{v}_{i+s}]$, the lost information packets $\mathbf{e'} = [\mathbf{v'}_{i1\,j1},\ldots,\mathbf{v'}_{ir\,jt}]$ are recovered.
[proof]

First, we will assume that all the lost redundant packets $[p_{i(t+1)}, \ldots, p_{i(t+y)}]$ are received. The $(s + m)$ simultaneous equations hold from *Theorem 1*:

$$[e_{i1\,j1} \cdots e_{ir\,jt}] \begin{bmatrix} g_{j11} & \cdots & g_{j1(m+1)} & & 0 & \cdots & 0 \\ & & & \vdots & & & \\ 0 & \cdots & 0 & g_{jx1} & \cdots & g_{jx(m+1)} & 0 & \cdots & 0 \\ & & & \vdots & & & \\ 0 & \cdots & 0 & & & g_{jt1} & \cdots & g_{jt(m+1)} \end{bmatrix} = [F_i \cdots F_{i+s+m}].$$

That is,

$$\mathbf{e}' \cdot \mathbf{g} *_{subt} = [F_i \dots F_{i+s+m}] .$$

Since $F_{i(t+1)}$, ..., $F_{i(t+y)}$ actually contain unknown variables, y equations are useless. Therefore, the above equation can be rewritten as

$$\mathbf{e}' \cdot \mathbf{g} *_{subt-y} = \mathbf{F}',$$

where $\mathbf{F}'$ is consisting of $[F_i, ..., F_{i+s+m}]$ except for $F_{i(t+1)}$, ..., $F_{i(t+y)}$. Then, a sufficient condition for recovering lost information packets $\mathbf{e}'$ is that above simultaneous equations have unique solution.
[Q.E.D.]

In Fig. 8 five packets including redundant packet p_{i+1} are lost. If we assume p_{i+1} is received, the following simultaneous equations hold:

$$\begin{bmatrix} e_{i2} & e_{i3} & e_{(i+2)2} & e_{(i+2)3} \end{bmatrix} \begin{bmatrix} 1 & 1 & 0 & 0 & 0 \\ 1 & 1 & 1 & 0 & 0 \\ 0 & 0 & 1 & 0 & 1 \\ 0 & 0 & 1 & 1 & 1 \end{bmatrix} = \begin{bmatrix} F_i & F_{i+1} & F_{i+2} & F_{i+3} & F_{i+4} \end{bmatrix}.$$

Until F_{i+1} contains the unknown variable p_{i+1}, the second left column is useless. The rows of the following sub-matrix $\mathbf{g} *_{subt-y}$

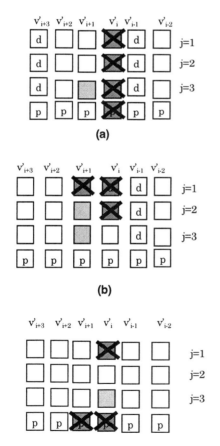

(a)

(b)

(c)

Fig. 9. Examples of packet-loss pattern which cannot be recovered.

$$\mathbf{g} *_{subt-y} = \begin{bmatrix} 1 & 0 & 0 & 0 \\ 1 & 1 & 0 & 0 \\ 0 & 1 & 0 & 1 \\ 0 & 1 & 1 & 1 \end{bmatrix}$$

are linearly independent. Therefore, the packet losses shown in Fig. 8 can be recovered.

[*Corollary 3*] Packet losses $\mathbf{e} = [e_{ij1}, ..., e_{ijt}]$ which contain a redundant packet p_i can be recovered if the following sub-matrix $\mathbf{g}_{sub1}$

$$\mathbf{g}_{sub1} = \begin{bmatrix} g_{j12} & \cdots & g_{j1(m+1)} \\ \vdots & \ddots & \vdots \\ g_{j(t-1)2} & \cdots & g_{j(t-1)(m+1)} \end{bmatrix}$$

satisfies the condition that all rows are linearly independent and there is a guard space for the code group $\mathbf{v}'_i$.

[*Corollary 4*] If more than $(m + 1)$ packets in one code group or more than $(s + m)$ packets in continuous s code groups are lost, they cannot be recovered.

This is because at most $(m + 1)$ equations hold for packets in one code group $\mathbf{v}'_i$, and at most $(s + m)$ equations hold for continuous s code groups.

Figure 9 illustrates examples of packet losses that cannot be recovered with the (4, 3, 2) convolutional code. The packets that are shaded can be recovered. Those marked by "×" cannot be recovered even if the shaded packets are correctly received. In Fig. 9(a) the simultaneous equations hold:

$$\begin{bmatrix} e_{i1} & e_{i2} & e_{i3} & e_{(i+1)3} \end{bmatrix} \begin{bmatrix} 1 & 0 & 0 \\ 0 & 1 & 0 \\ 1 & 1 & 0 \\ 1 & 1 & 1 \end{bmatrix} = \begin{bmatrix} F_{i+1} & F_{i+2} & F_{i+3} \end{bmatrix}.$$

From the equations, $\mathbf{v}'_{(i+1)3}$ can be recovered, but others cannot. In Fig. 9(b) the following simultaneous equations hold:

$$\begin{bmatrix} e_{i1} & e_{i2} & e_{(i+1)1} & e_{(i+1)3} & e_{(i+1)3} \end{bmatrix} \begin{bmatrix} 1 & 1 & 0 & 0 \\ 1 & 0 & 1 & 0 \\ 0 & 1 & 1 & 0 \\ 0 & 1 & 0 & 1 \\ 0 & 1 & 1 & 1 \end{bmatrix} = \begin{bmatrix} F_i & F_{i+1} & F_{i+2} & F_{i+3} \end{bmatrix}.$$

From this equations, lost packets $\mathbf{v}'_{(i+1)2}$ and $\mathbf{v}'_{(i+1)3}$ are recovered. In Fig. 9(c) only the following equation holds for $(i + 2)$-th code group:

$$e_{i3} = F_{i+2} .$$

The equations for i-th, and $(i + 1)$-th code groups are not derived because redundant packets are lost. From this equation, lost information packet $\mathbf{v}'_{i1}$ cannot be recovered.

3.3 (n, k, m) convolutional codes, $k < n - 1$

In the previous sections, we analyzed the ability to recover packet losses for $(n, n - 1, m)$ convolutional codes. This is considered as the special case of (n, k, m) convolutional codes. With (n, k, m) convolutional codes, redundant packets p_i^1, p_i^2, ..., p_i^{n-k} are generated by generator matrices G_i^1, G_i^2, ..., G_i^{n-k}. Therefore, more than one equation may hold for each code group. We can recover lost packets using these equations similarly to the case of $k = n - 1$. That is, recovery of lost packets is possible if all rows in the matrix $\mathbf{g}_{sub**}$ are linearly independent. The matrix $\mathbf{g}_{sub**}$ is shown as

$$\mathbf{g}_{sub**} = \begin{bmatrix} \mathbf{g}^1{}_{sub**} & \mathbf{g}^2{}_{sub**} & \cdots & \mathbf{g}^{n-k}{}_{sub**} \end{bmatrix},$$

where $\mathbf{g}^x{}_{sub**}$ is the sub-matrix for x-th redundant packet.

All of above theorems, lemmas, and corollaries are extendable for the cases of (n, k, m) convolutional codes by conversion of the sub-matrix.

4 Estimated success for recoverability

In this section we evaluate the ability to recover lost packets using the proposed method with computer simulation and compare the codes with simple parity that have the same redundancy.

Figure 10 indicates a result of simulation for the (4, 3, 2) convolutional code with generator matrix in section 2.2. The result for the (4, 3) simple parity is also indicated. The X-axis represents packet-loss probability and the Y-axis is the ratio of correctly received or recovered packets to the amount of sent packets. As shown in Fig. 10, when packet loss probability ε is lower than 0.25, that is equal to the redundancy of the codes, our method can reconstruct more packets than that with simple parity. This is because the proposed method can recover two or three packet losses in a code group that cannot be recovered with the (4, 3) simple parity.

On the other hand, if a packet loss probability increases, $\varepsilon > 0.25$, the performance of the proposed method gets worse. This is due to many packet losses that occurred in a code group affect the following code groups and disturb recovering. The method with simple parity, however ineffective when the amount of lost packets within a code group is more than one, but can always reconstruct a single loss.

Consider the generator matrix $\mathbf{g}$ for the (8, 7, 3) convolutional code shown below:

$$\mathbf{g} = \begin{bmatrix} 1 & 0 & 0 & 1 \\ 1 & 0 & 1 & 0 \\ 1 & 1 & 0 & 0 \\ 1 & 0 & 1 & 1 \\ 1 & 1 & 0 & 1 \\ 1 & 1 & 1 & 0 \\ 1 & 1 & 1 & 1 \end{bmatrix}$$

Three rows in the above matrix are linearly independent, but four rows are not always linearly independent. Continuous

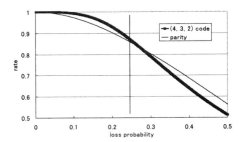

Fig.10. Simulation for the (4, 3, 2) convolutional code.

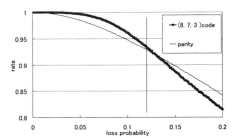

Fig. 11. Simulation with the (8, 7, 3) convolutional code.

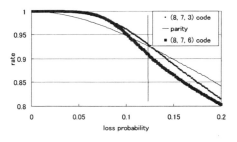

Fig. 12. Simulation with the (8, 7, m) convolutional code, where m=3 or 6.

Table 1. Simulation with the (8, 7, m) convolutional code, where m = 3 or 6.

loss prob.	before recovery	simple parity	(8, 7, 3) conv.	(8, 7, 6) conv.
0	0	0	0	0
0.005	3575	118	0	0
0.01	7046	534	7	2
0.015	10551	1201	28	5
0.02	13946	1944	117	30
0.025	17395	2825	196	57
0.03	21262	4193	420	85
0.035	24611	5415	619	259
0.04	27991	6746	1031	411
0.045	31499	8819	1643	595
0.05	34791	10399	2262	1095

four rows are also linearly independent. From *Lemma 1*, the code with the above **g** can recover such packet losses that three packet losses in a code group, and four burst packet losses within a code group.

Figure 11 shows a result for the (8, 7, 3) convolutional code with generator matrix shown above and results for the (8, 7) simple parity. Fig. 11 shows a similar tendency to the case of the (4, 3, 2) convolutional code. The ability to recover lost packets is higher when packet-loss ratio is lower than 0.125, that is the redundancy of the codes.

Figure 12 shows a result for (8, 7, m) convolutional codes, where m = 3, and 6. The generator matrix of (8, 7, 6) convolutional code is shown below

$$\mathbf{g} = \begin{bmatrix} 1 & 1 & 0 & 0 & 1 & 1 & 0 \\ 1 & 0 & 1 & 1 & 0 & 1 & 1 \\ 1 & 0 & 0 & 1 & 1 & 1 & 1 \\ 1 & 1 & 1 & 0 & 0 & 0 & 1 \\ 1 & 1 & 0 & 1 & 0 & 0 & 1 \\ 1 & 0 & 1 & 0 & 1 & 0 & 1 \\ 1 & 0 & 1 & 1 & 1 & 1 & 1 \end{bmatrix}$$

where five rows are linearly independent. Our methods again show a better performance compared with the method of (n, $n - 1$) simple parity, when packet-loss ratio is less than code redundancy.

In Fig. 12, the (8, 7, 6) convolutional code seems to be inferior to the (8, 7, 3) convolutional code. When packet-loss ratio is low, the abilities seem to be similar, and as packet loss-ratio increases, the ability of the (8, 7, 6) convolutional code gets worse rapidly. Table 1 is a part of the numerical results of Fig. 13. In the table, each value shows how many packets are lost or unrecovered in sent 700,000 (7 x 100 code groups x 1000 times) information packets. As shown in the table, when packet-loss ratio is very low, such as less than 0.03, the (8, 7, 6) convolutional code performs better than the (8, 7, 3) convolutional code.

Constraint length m improves the ability of recovering for lower packet-loss probability. It is possible that the number of linearly independent row vectors in generator matrix increase for larger m. But large m affects badly the ability when packet-loss ratio is high.

Even for the same value of m, there are many variations of (n, $n - 1$, m) convolutional codes to design generator matrix. For larger k ($k = n - 1$) and m, the number of possible generator matrix extremely increases, and it becomes more difficult to find an optimum generator matrix.

Based on the measurements of packet losses in the Internet [3], the average packet-loss probability is low even when the network is performing well. It is observed that burst packet losses increase occur when congestion occurs. In a burst erasure channel, the proposed method will have a better performance than the simple parity method.

5 Conclusions

We proposed a method for packet-loss recovery using (n, $n - 1$, m) convolutional codes. We theoretically analyzed the method ability to recover packet losses. Theorems and Lemmas were developed to show the sufficient conditions to recover packet losses for such conditions that information and redundant packets were lost. The numerical results were shown for the proposed method and a simple parity method that has the same redundancy. The comparison showed that the proposed method had a better ability to recover packet losses than the simple parity method. This is because the proposed method can recover the loss patterns such as multiple packet losses in a code group. We also showed that larger constraint length improved the recovery ability for low packet loss probabilities.

Acknowledgement

We deeply appreciate Dr. Yoshihisa Desaki for his helpful discussions. This work was supported in part by Grant-in-Aid for Science Research (number 09680429) from the Ministry of Education, Science, and Culture, in Japan.

References

[1] V. Paxon, "End-to-End Routing Behavior in the Internet," *SIGCOMM'96*, pp. 25-38, Aug. 1996.

[2] M. Yajnik, J. Kurose, and D. Towsley, "Packet Loss Correlation in the Mbone Multicast Network," *IEEE GLOBECOM*, pp. 94-99, Nov. 1996.

[3] M. Arai, A. Chiba, and K. Iwasaki, "The Measurement and Modeling of Burst Packet Losses in Internet End-to-End Communications," proceedings of Pacific Rim International Symposium On Dependable Computing, pp. 260-267, Dec. 1999.

[4] A. S. Tanenbaum, *Computer Networks 3rd Edition*, Prentice Hall, 1996.

[5] H. Liu, H. Ma, M. E. Zarki, and S. Gupta, "Error Control Schemes for Networks: An Overview," *ACM Mobile Networks & Applications*, No. 2, pp. 167-182. 1997.

[6] L. Rizzo, "Effective Erasure Codes for Reliable Computer Communication Protocols," *Computer Communication Review*, Vol. 27, No. 2, pp. 24-36. Apr. 1997

[7] J. Nonnenmacher, E. Biersack, and D. Towsley, "Parity-Based Loss Rrecovery for Reliable Multicast Transmission," *IEEE Trans. Networking*, Vol. 6, No. 4, pp. 349-361. Aug. 1998.

[8] S. Lin, D. J. Costello Jr. , *Error Control Coding: Fundamentals and Applications*, Prentice-Hall, 1983.

[9] H. Balakrishnan, H. S. Rahul, and S. Seshan, "An Integrated Congestion Management Architecture for Internet Hosts," *Computer Comunication Review*, Vol. 29 No. 4, pp. 175-186, Oct., 1999.

[10] J. Kato, A. Shimizu, S. Goto, "End-to-End Delay Distribution on the Internet," *IEICE Trans. Inf.&Syst.*, Vol. E82-D, No. 4, pp. 762-767, Apr. 1999.

[11] I. S. Reed, and X. Chen, *Error-Control Coding For Data Networks*, Kluwer Academic Publishers, 1999.

[12] W. W. Peterson, and E. J. Weldon Jr, *Error-Correcting Codes* 2nd edition, The MIT Press, 1972.

[13] G. Birkhoff, and S. Maclane, *A Study Of Modern Algebra*, The Cacmillan Company, 1965.

One-Shot Reed-Solomon Decoding
for High-Performance Dependable Systems

Yasunao Katayama and Sumio Morioka

IBM Research, Tokyo Research Laboratory
1623-14 Shimotsuruma, Yamato, Kanagawa 242-8502 Japan
{yasunaok, E02716}@jp.ibm.com

Abstract

This paper presents a scheme of ultra-fast one-shot Reed-Solomon decoding (prototyped (40-34,32,8) soft-IP demonstrating over 7Gb/s using 0.35 um ASIC technology) and discusses its application to future dependable computer systems, taking a redundant array memory system as an example. We compare different memory configurations and identify improved fault-tolerance to single-bit failures as well as chip and card failures for smaller system overheads when random quad-byte one-shot Reed-Solomon decoding is used. We also discuss an alternative use of the powerful coding gain, i.e., an application to the dynamic refresh interval control of DRAMs, in order to optimize the refresh overheads in performance and power consumption. We believe that the one-shot Reed-Solomon decoding offers an advanced error correction capability for various parts of future high-performance computer systems, where system-level reliability can suffer because of rapidly increasing data size and speed.

1. Introduction

As a growing number of businesses start to choose servers for mission-critical applications, their reliability is receiving significant attention. The trend is expected to be further expedited in the future. This is because, driven by the application factors such as the wide spread of the Internet e-business, and deep computing, and by the technology factors such as the rapid advance of semiconductor and optical communication technologies, the amount of data processed by a computer is increasing at an accelerated pace, and consequently the reliability of the processing for each data item must improve at least proportionally just in order to maintain overall system-level reliability at today's level. In this context, research on advanced error detection and correction schemes at ultra-high-speed is becoming extremely important as one of the indispensable techniques

for future dependable computer systems to increase reliability, reduce service costs, and maintain data integrity.

Among various existing error control techniques, those using Reed-Solomon (RS) codes [1-3] are well known for their advanced multi-symbol error correction capability and are widely used in various systems such as storage and communication systems. On the other hand, because of their advanced error correction capability, the decoding of RS codes takes a longer time than, for example, that of much simpler Hamming codes. When the number of maximum correctable symbols $t > 1$, estimation of errors in RS codes needs extensive computation including a number of nonlinear operations such as multiplication and divisions as opposed to the case of Hamming codes, where the decoding can be performed in far fewer operations. In addition, since existing RS decoding algorithms such as algebraic decoding or transform decoding [1,2] assume implementation using sequential circuit and decoder implementation work mostly deals with optimization within a given algorithm framework, existing schemes are not very suitable for parallel combinational logic representations. Global optimization for combinational logic representation across algorithms, VLSI architectures and Boolean logic levels has not been worked out systematically. As a result, decoder hardware using existing algorithms is too slow when implemented in sequential circuits, and too large when implemented in combinational circuits.

Indeed, existing RS decoder designs using algebraic decoding, have been based on the premise of implementation using sequential circuits with serial I/O configurations [4-8], and the performance is so far limited to around 1Gb/s even with highly pipelined architecture and custom design. In addition, the latency of the circuit is quite high (> 1 ms) because of the serial decoder designs. There is a decoder design with parallel I/O configurations using the transform decoding algorithm [9], but since the internal data processing needs to be arranged in a cascaded manner, the latency is still quite high (approx. 1.8 ms).

As a result, even though the reliability of relatively slower I/O subsystems can be improved by using powerful

390

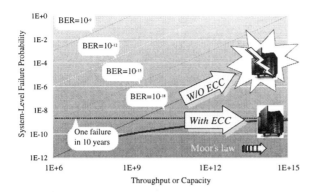

Figure 1. Illustrating system-level failure rate as a function of rapidly increasing data throughput and capacity. Beyond the gigabit generations, error detection and correction schemes using advanced ECC (error control code) can be important even for systems with low BER (Bit Error Rate).

RS codes, error correction techniques for improved reliability of higher performance subsystems, such as the memory subsystem, are rather limited. At most, the use of SSC-DSD code (Single Symbol error Correction with Double Symbol error Detection) [10,11] has recently been proposed and used for durable memory system designs [12] for correcting both single-bit and chip failures, or SSC-SED (Single Symbol error Correction with additional Single bit Error Detection) capability [13] is used for main frames [14]. Otherwise SEC-DED (Single bit Error Correction with Double bit Error Detection) codes with burst error detection capability [3] are commonly used. DEC (Double bit Error Correction) codes [15] or DSC (Double Symbol Correction) codes for memory systems [16,17] are found in the literature, but the decoding overhead of these powerful error correction codes has to be kept small for the present high-performance memory subsystems.

Even though the memory reliability may not immediately require an advanced error correction capability, it can become a serious problem as the statistical variation becomes larger due to the increasing memory capacity and fabrication process complexity (see Fig. 1). In addition, as fault-tolerant techniques shift toward more software solutions, the CPU and memory subsystem need to be extremely reliable. Furthermore, even the conventional RS code applications existing in the I/O subsystems are requiring higher processing speed (a good example is an optical communications) as the whole system runs faster.

Considering the situation above, we here present our recent result on a ultra-fast one-shot RS encoder/decoder design and address its importance in future computer systems from two different perspectives, taking the memory subsystem as an example.

2. One-Shot Reed-Solomon Decoding

Here, we present our results in designing n ultra-fast RS decoder with block erasure decoding and error calculation bypassing.

2.1. Decoding Reed-Solomon Codes

The decoding problem of a systematic (n, k, m) RS code $(t = [(n - k)/2])$, defined over a Galois field $GF(2^m)$, starts with calculating the syndrome, for example, defined as $S_i = Y(a^i)$, $i = 0, 1, \ldots, 2t - 1$, from the received word $Y(x)$. Here, n is the code word length, k is the information word length, m is the number of bits per symbol, and a is a primitive element of $GF(2^m)$. When $e \leq t$, where e is the actual number of errors in $Y(x)$, the location of errors i_k, $k = 0, 1, \ldots, e - 1$ and error values E_{i_k} can be estimated by various techniques.

Among those, algebraic decoding [1,2] is the most popular decoding algorithm and translates the error value estimation problem into an algebraic problem of solving the following two sets of matrix equations. The first one is to identify the locations of errors i_k:

$$\begin{pmatrix} S_0 & S_1 & \cdots & S_{e-1} \\ S_1 & S_2 & \cdots & S_e \\ \vdots & & \ddots & \vdots \\ S_{e-1} & S & \cdots & S_{2e-2} \end{pmatrix} \begin{pmatrix} \Lambda_e^{(e)} \\ \Lambda_{e-1}^{(e)} \\ \vdots \\ \Lambda_1^{(e)} \end{pmatrix} = \begin{pmatrix} S_e \\ S_{e+1} \\ \vdots \\ S_{2e-1} \end{pmatrix} \quad (1)$$

where $\Lambda^{(e)}(x) = \prod_{k=0}^{e-1}(1 + xa^{i_k})$ is the error-locator polynomial, and the second one is to calculate the actual error values E_{i_k}:

$$\begin{pmatrix} 1 & 1 & \cdots & 1 \\ a^{i_0} & a^{i_1} & \cdots & a^{i_{e-1}} \\ \vdots & & \ddots & \vdots \\ a^{i_0(e-1)} & a^{i_1(e-1)} \cdots a^{i_{e-1}(e-1)} \end{pmatrix} \begin{pmatrix} E_{i_0} \\ E_{i_1} \\ \vdots \\ E_{i_{e-1}} \end{pmatrix} = \begin{pmatrix} S_0 \\ S_1 \\ \vdots \\ S_{e-1} \end{pmatrix} \quad (2)$$

By utilizing the regular structures of the above matrices (the first one called Toeplitz matrix, the second one Vandermonde matrix), many good iterative algorithms suitable for ALU-based or sequential circuit implementations are known, including the Berlekamp-Massey, Euclid, and Forney algorithms [1,2]. However, efficient parallel decoding is difficult to achieve by using these known algorithms [18].

2.2. New Error Evaluation Algorithm

In order to solve these equations in a symbol-parallel manner efficiently, our main idea involves the use of a new error evaluation algorithm with the following features [19]:

(1) The algorithm uses only one polynomial $Er(x)$, for symbol-parallel, direct linear error evaluation (instead of using two polynomials with costly divisions as is the case for the Forney algorithm [1,2])

(2) $Er^{(e)}(x)$ is a polynomial of degree $e-1$ (not $n-1$ as is the case for the transform decoding [1,2]).

(3) Error polynomials for various numbers of errors, $e = 1, 2, ..., t$, are combined to reduce the total number of multipliers.

The new error polynomial is derived by first constructing a polynomial of degree t-1 that satisfies $E_{i_k} = Er^{(e)}(a^{i_k})$, $k = 0, 1, 2, ..., e-$ in terms of error values E_{i_k} and a^{i_k}, and then converting these unknown values into the predetermined $\Lambda_i^{(e)}$ and S_i:

$$Er^{(e)}(x)$$

$$= \frac{\sum\limits_{k=0}^{e-1} E_{i_k} \prod\limits_{j \neq k}(x+a^{i_j}) \prod\limits_{m, l \neq k, m>l}(a^{i_m}+a^{i_l})}{\prod\limits_{m>l}(a^{i_m}+a^{i_l})}$$

$$= \frac{\sum\limits_{k=0}^{e-1} E_{i_k}(\sum\limits_{j=0}^{e-1} x^j \Lambda_{e-j-1\,i_k}^{(e)})f^{(e-1)}(\Lambda_{1i_k}^{(e)}, \Lambda_{2i_k}^{(e)}, ..., \Lambda_{e-1\,i_k}^{(e)})}{f^{(e)}(\Lambda_1^{(e)}, \Lambda_2^{(e)}, ..., \Lambda_e^{(e)})}$$

$$= \frac{\sum\limits_{k,j,m=0}^{e-1} E_{i_k}a^{i_k m} x^j Er_{jm}^{(e)}(\Lambda_1^{(e)}, \Lambda_2^{(e)}, ..., \Lambda_e^{(e)})}{f^{(e)}(\Lambda_1^{(e)}, \Lambda_2^{(e)}, ..., \Lambda_e^{(e)})}$$

$$= \frac{\sum\limits_{j,m=0}^{e-1} S_m x^j Er_{jm}^{(e)}(\Lambda_1^{(e)}, \Lambda_2^{(e)}, ..., \Lambda_e^{(e)})}{f^{(e)}(\Lambda_1^{(e)}, \Lambda_2^{(e)}, ..., \Lambda_e^{(e)})}. \qquad (3)$$

Note that $\Lambda_j^{(e)}$ is equal to the elementary symmetric function of degree j consisting of all a^{i_l}, $l = 0, 1, 2, ..., e-1$. Similarly, $\Lambda_{j\,i_k}^{(e)}$ is equal to the elementary symmetric function of degree j consisting of all a^{i_l}, $l = 0, 1, 2, ..., e-1$, except a^{i_k}. They are related by $\Lambda_{j\,i_k}^{(e)} = \Lambda_j^{(e)} + a^{i_k}\Lambda_{j-1\,i_k}^{(e)}$.

The general form of $f^{(e)}$ (the determinant of a Vandermonde matrix) in $GF(2^m)$ can be given as follows: By using the relation between the Schur function $s_\lambda = \det[(a^{i_k})^{\lambda_j}]_{0 \leq k, j \leq e-1}$, with the partition $\lambda = (\lambda_0, \lambda_1, \lambda_2, ..., \lambda_{e-1})$ (the conjugate given by $\lambda' = (\lambda_0', \lambda_1', \lambda_2', ..., \lambda_{e-1}')$), and the elementary symmetric functions e_{λ_i}, given by $s_\lambda = \det[e_{\lambda_i'-i+j}]_{0 \leq i, j \leq e-1}$ [21], and the commutative relation in the square operation and addition in $GF(2^m)$, we see that $f^{(e)}$ can be written in the following form [18,19]:

$$f^{(e)} = \prod\limits_{m>l}(a^{i_m}+a^{i_l})$$

$$= \begin{vmatrix} \Lambda_1^{(e)}\Lambda_3^{(e)} & & \cdots & & 0 \\ 1 & \Lambda_2^{(e)}\Lambda_4^{(e)} & & \ddots & \vdots \\ 0 & \Lambda_1^{(e)}\Lambda_3^{(e)} & & \ddots & \\ & & \ddots & & \\ \vdots & & \ddots & \Lambda_{e-2}^{(e)} & \Lambda_e^{(e)} \\ 0 & & \cdots & \Lambda_{e-3}^{(e)} & \Lambda_{e-1}^{(e)} \end{vmatrix}. \qquad (4)$$

Since $f^{(e)}$ is constant for each received word, the error evaluation can be done without division, once $1/f^{(e)}$ is calculated. Please note that since the determinant for $f^{(t)}$ contains all the necessary calculations for $f^{(e)}$, $e = 1, 2, ..., t-1$ as submatrices, multiplier circuits for calculating all $f^{(e)}$ can be efficiently combined.

In order to get a similar combined formula, $\Lambda_i^{(e)}$ is calculated directly using Peterson-like formulation, instead of expanding iterative algorithms like the Berlekamp-Massey or Euclid algorithms:

$$\Lambda_i^{(e)} = \frac{\tilde{\Lambda}_i^{(e)}}{\tilde{\Lambda}_0^{(e)}},$$

$$\tilde{\Lambda}_i^{(e)} = \begin{vmatrix} S_0 & S_1 & \cdots & S_{e-1} \\ S_1 & S_2 & \cdots & S_e \\ \vdots & & \ddots & \vdots \\ S_{e-i-1} & S_{e-i} & \cdots & S_{2e-i-2} \\ S_{e-i+1} & S_{e-i+2} & \cdots & S_{2e-i} \\ \vdots & & \ddots & \vdots \\ S_e & S_{e+1} & \cdots & S_{2e-1} \end{vmatrix}, \quad i = 0, 1, ..., e. \qquad (5)$$

The division by $\widetilde{\Lambda}_0^{(e)}$ in Eq. (5) can be eliminated if both the numerator and denominator of Eq. (3) are multiplied by an appropriate power of $\widetilde{\Lambda}_0^{(e)}$. A different sharing formula has been obtained for high-performance serial decoders [4].

Here we show some formula for $f^{(e)}$, $Er_{jm}^{(e)}$ and $\widetilde{\Lambda}_i^{(e)}$ up to $e = 4$ ($Er_{jm}^{(e)}$ not listed are zero).

$$f^{(2)} = \Lambda_1^{(2)}$$

$$f^{(3)} = \Lambda_1^{(3)}\Lambda_2^{(3)} + \Lambda_3^{(3)} = f^{(2)}(\Lambda_1^{(3)})\Lambda_2^{(3)} + \Lambda_3^{(3)}$$

$$f^{(4)} = \Lambda_1^{(4)}\Lambda_2^{(4)}\Lambda_3^{(4)} + \Lambda_3^{(4)2} + \Lambda_4^{(4)}\Lambda_1^{(4)2}$$

$$= f^{(3)}(\Lambda_1^{(4)}, \Lambda_2^{(4)}, \Lambda_3^{(4)})\Lambda_3^{(4)} + \Lambda_4^{(4)}\Lambda_1^{(4)2}. \qquad (6)$$

$$Er_{10}^{(2)} = 1$$

$$Er_{01}^{(2)} = 1$$

$$Er_{00}^{(2)} = \Lambda_1^{(2)}$$

$$Er_{21}^{(3)} = 1$$

$$Er_{20}^{(3)} = \Lambda_1^{(3)}$$

$$Er_{12}^{(3)} = 1$$

$$Er_{10}^{(3)} = \Lambda_1^{(3)2}$$

$$Er_{03}^{(3)} = 1$$

$$Er_{01}^{(3)} = \Lambda_1^{(3)2} + \Lambda_2^{(3)}$$

$$Er_{00}^{(3)} = \Lambda_1^{(3)} \Lambda_2^{(3)}$$

$$Er_{32}^{(4)} = \Lambda_1^{(4)}$$

$$Er_{31}^{(4)} = \Lambda_1^{(4)2}$$

$$Er_{30}^{(4)} = \Lambda_1^{(4)} \Lambda_2^{(4)} + \Lambda_3^{(4)}$$

$$Er_{23}^{(4)} = \Lambda_1^{(4)}$$

$$Er_{21}^{(4)} = \Lambda_1^{(4)} \Lambda_2^{(4)} + \Lambda_3^{(4)} + \Lambda_1^{(4)3}$$

$$Er_{20}^{(4)} = \Lambda_1^{(4)} (\Lambda_1^{(4)} \Lambda_2^{(4)} + \Lambda_3^{(4)})$$

$$Er_{14}^{(4)} = \Lambda_1^{(4)}$$

$$Er_{12}^{(4)} = \Lambda_3^{(4)} + \Lambda_1^{(4)3}$$

$$Er_{11}^{(4)} = \Lambda_1^{(4)} \Lambda_3^{(4)}$$

$$Er_{10}^{(4)} = \Lambda_2^{(4)} (\Lambda_1^{(4)} \Lambda_2^{(4)} + \Lambda_3^{(4)})$$

$$Er_{05}^{(4)} = \Lambda_1^{(4)}$$

$$Er_{03}^{(4)} = \Lambda_3^{(4)} + \Lambda_1^{(4)3}$$

$$Er_{01}^{(4)} = \Lambda_2^{(4)} (\Lambda_1^{(4)} \Lambda_2^{(4)} + \Lambda_3^{(4)}) + \Lambda_1^{(4)2} \Lambda_3^{(4)}$$

$$Er_{00}^{(4)} = \Lambda_3^{(4)} (\Lambda_1^{(4)} \Lambda_2^{(4)} + \Lambda_3^{(4)}) . \tag{7}$$

$$\tilde{\Lambda}_1^{(1)} = S_1$$

$$\tilde{\Lambda}_0^{(1)} = S_0$$

$$\tilde{\Lambda}_2^{(2)} = \tilde{\Lambda}_1^{(1)} S_3 + S_2^2$$

$$\tilde{\Lambda}_1^{(2)} = \tilde{\Lambda}_0^{(1)} S_3 + \tilde{\Lambda}_1^{(1)} S_2$$

$$\tilde{\Lambda}_0^{(2)} = \tilde{\Lambda}_0^{(1)} S_2 + \tilde{\Lambda}_1^{(1)} S_1$$

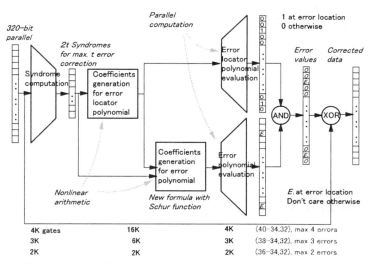

Figure 2. Soft IP core design example for one-shot Reed-Solomon encoder/decoder. After mapping into a 0.35-um ASIC technology, the delay for $t = 4$ is 45 ns, resulting in over 7-Gb/s random quad-byte decoding throughput. The gate sizes shown below the diagram are before the technology mapping counted in a unit of 2-input XOR and AND gates.

$$\tilde{\Lambda}_3^{(3)} = \tilde{\Lambda}_2^{(2)} S_5 + S_1 S_4^2 + S_3^3$$

$$\tilde{\Lambda}_2^{(3)} = \tilde{\Lambda}_1^{(2)} S_5 + \tilde{\Lambda}_2^{(2)} S_4 + S_0 S_4^2 + S_2 S_3^2$$

$$\tilde{\Lambda}_1^{(3)} = \tilde{\Lambda}_0^{(2)} S_5 + \tilde{\Lambda}_1^{(2)} S_4 + \tilde{\Lambda}_2^{(2)} S_3$$

$$\tilde{\Lambda}_0^{(3)} = \tilde{\Lambda}_0^{(2)} S_4 + \tilde{\Lambda}_1^{(2)} S_3 + \tilde{\Lambda}_2^{(2)} S_2$$

$$\tilde{\Lambda}_4^{(4)} = \tilde{\Lambda}_3^{(3)} S_7 + \tilde{\Lambda}_2^{(2)} S_6^2 + S_4^4 + S_3 S_4^2 S_5 + S_3^2 S_5^2 + S_1 S_5^3$$

$$\tilde{\Lambda}_3^{(4)} = \tilde{\Lambda}_2^{(3)} S_7 + \tilde{\Lambda}_3^{(3)} S_6 + \tilde{\Lambda}_1^{(2)} S_6^2 + S_3 S_4^3 + S_2 S_4^2 S_5 + S_1 S_4 S_5^2 + S_0 S_5^3$$

$$\tilde{\Lambda}_2^{(4)} = \tilde{\Lambda}_1^{(3)} S_7 + \tilde{\Lambda}_2^{(3)} S_6 + \tilde{\Lambda}_3^{(3)} S_5 + \tilde{\Lambda}_0^{(2)} S_6^2 + S_3^2 S_4^2 + S_2 S_4^3 + S_2^2 S_5^2 + S_0 S_4 S_5^2$$

$$\tilde{\Lambda}_1^{(4)} = \tilde{\Lambda}_0^{(3)} S_7 + \tilde{\Lambda}_1^{(3)} S_6 + \tilde{\Lambda}_2^{(3)} S_5 + \tilde{\Lambda}_3^{(3)} S_4$$

$$\tilde{\Lambda}_0^{(4)} = \tilde{\Lambda}_0^{(3)} S_6 + \tilde{\Lambda}_1^{(3)} S_5 + \tilde{\Lambda}_2^{(3)} S_4 + \tilde{\Lambda}_3^{(3)} S_3 . \tag{8}$$

2.3. Soft-IP Design

Figure 2 shows the gate size and delay of the prototyped soft-IP macro. By using the proposed new decoding algorithm optimized for one-shot decoding of RS codes, the entire decoding can be performed by means of parallel combinational circuits. A soft-IP design implemented with a 0.35-um ASIC technology achieved 45-ns decoding latency for random quad-byte corrections (worst case; 3.0 V, 95 °C) for (40-34,32,8) code configuration [20]. This corresponds to more than 7-Gb/s decoding performance through non-pipelined parallel processing of a 320-bit-long sequence of data, far outperforming the existing designs [5-9]. When used with more advanced ASIC technology of 0.25 um and beyond, and with pipeline processing, the algorithm is expected to provide a throughput that is up to 10 times faster still. Our decoder design can achieve one-shot data-path arithmetic, matching the data-rate of the memory subsystem, for significant performance improvements over those premised on the sequential circuit representation, without increasing the gate count much.

The sizes of the circuits have been further reduced, thanks to the use of a new logic optimization algorithm for highly parallel combinational circuits [20]. The soft-IP macro has about 24K primitive gates before technology mapping, and is about 90K cells (1 XOR = 3 cells, 1 AND = 2 cells) after that, including the driver gates. The logic optimization program also helps in maintaining the small the fanout by sharing gates. In addition to processing at a very high speed, this advanced error correction circuit, since it consists of only combinational circuits (i.e., not clock circuits or registers), can maintain power consumption at an acceptable level (below 2 W with continuous quad-byte corrections at peak performance).

Being fast and small, our decoder design can be used at various places in the system design, where reliability is an issue. Also, from the reliability point of view, our design will add no additional soft errors since there are no registers involved.

2.4. Block Erasure Decoding Algorithm

During the design of our soft-IP, we also defined a new encoding algorithm [20] to reduce the encoder/decoder circuit size. Here, it will be extended to a new block erasure decoding algorithm suitable for correcting errors due to card failure. The parity $R(x)$ is usually calculated from the information word $M(x)$ and the generator polynomial of the code $G(x)$ as

$$R(x) = M(x)x^{2t} \mod G(x) . \quad (9)$$

Let $R_0, R_1, .., R_{2t-1}$ be coefficients of the polynomial $R(x)$, i.e., parity values. The following relation always holds from the definition of the syndrome:

$$\begin{pmatrix} a^0 & a^0 & \cdots & a^0 \\ a^0 & a^1 & \cdots & a^{2t-1} \\ \vdots & & \ddots & \vdots \\ a^0 & a^{2t-1} & \cdots & a^{(2t-1)(2t-1)} \end{pmatrix} \begin{pmatrix} R_0 \\ R_1 \\ \vdots \\ R_{2t-1} \end{pmatrix} = \begin{pmatrix} R(a^0) \\ R(a^1) \\ \vdots \\ R(a^{2t-1}) \end{pmatrix} . (10)$$

Therefore, parity values are obtained from the output from the syndrome generator $R(a^0), R(a^1), ..., R(a^{2t-1})$ using $M(x)x^{2t}$ as an input. This multiplication requires an additional matrix operation of size $(2t \times 2t)$, but, the extra circuit size is much smaller than the original encoder size

$(k \times 2t)$.

This encoding method can be considered as an erasure decoding for the parity symbols. Once a series of symbol failure is detected, and if it is identified as a card failure, we can perform block erasure correction to correct the card failure. In other words, we can calculate erasure values for a series of bytes at known locations by using a linear transform of the syndromes.

Let us assume the case where a received word contains a series of t symbol erasures starting from the location number a^{i_0}. As long as the Forney syndrome for the received word

$$S_i' = \sum_{j=0}^{t} \Psi_j S_{i+t-j} , \quad (11)$$

where the erasure-locator polynomial is given by

$$\Psi(x) = \sum_{j=0}^{t-1} (1 + a^{i_0+j}x) , \quad (12)$$

is zero, the received word requires only the block erasure correction. In this case, the erasure error values $E_{i_0}, E_{i_0+1}, ..., E_{i_0+t-1}$ can be calculated from the syndromes, using linear matrix operations by solving

$$\begin{pmatrix} S_0 \\ S_1 \\ \vdots \\ S_{t-1} \end{pmatrix} = \begin{pmatrix} 1 & 1 & \cdots & 1 \\ a^{i_0} & a^{i_0+1} & \cdots & a^{i_0+t-1} \\ & & \vdots & \\ a^{(t-1)i_0} & a^{(t-1)(i_0+1)} & \cdots & a^{(t-1)(i_0+t-1)} \end{pmatrix} \begin{pmatrix} E_{i_0} \\ E_{i_0+1} \\ \vdots \\ E_{i_0+t-1} \end{pmatrix} . \quad (13)$$

Please note that when no other error exists (i.e., the Forney syndromes are all zero), the erasure correction can be nearly as fast as syndrome checking, since the inverse of the matrix in Eq. (13) can be hardwired for each potential block erasure location, just like the encoding circuit.

2.5. Bypassing Unnecessary Error Calculation Steps

It is noteworthy that when the actual number of error e is smaller than the maximum t, the correct values for the word containing errors can be determined much earlier thanks to the combinational one-shot decoder design. When errors are found. our $t = 4$ decoder can calculate errors at a comparable speed to a $t = 1$ decoder when $e = 1$ by selecting the $t = 1$ decoding path as a default path, and determining by whether or not $e = 1$ or not in parallel. This can be done using the relation

$$S_0S_7 = S_1S_6 = S_2S_5 = S_3S_4 . \quad (14)$$

The delay when $e = 2, 3$ could be improved using a

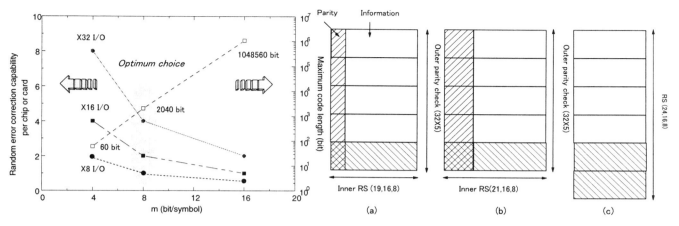

Figure 3. The maximum number of correctable random-bit errors (for ×8, ×16, and ×32 I/O, respectively) and maximum code block length of RS codes as a function of bit per symbol m. It shows that $m = 8$ offers the optimum choice.

Figure 4. Three redundant memory array system configurations to be investigated. (a) Configuration with a conventional SSD-DSD RS code and a striped parity check code; (b) With a more powerful DSC-TSD RS code and a striped parity check code; (c) With a $t = 4$ (quad-symbol error correction) RS code. $m = 8$ is assumed for all.

similar technique as well. When no error occurs, the syndrome calculation for error checking requires a delay for the syndrome calculation of log(mn), which depends little on whether the code is Hamming or RS, but mostly depends on the code length.

3. Application to Redundant Memory Array Systems

The present ultra-high-performance RS decoder can offer an advanced error correcting capability for various parts of future computer systems in order to achieve improved reliability. We show here a case study, by taking the memory subsystem as an example, since we believe that this can be one of the places where high-performance error correction will be strongly required in future high-performance dependable computing.

3.1. Code Word Configurations

An appropriate choice of an error correction code is very important to offer maximum correction capability with minimum parity overhead. For the present purpose, since we need to correct both single-bit failures, which are random failures and chip or card failures, which are block failures.

RS codes offers a powerful correction capability for these failures if we chose m correctly. Figure 3 shows the number of correctable random-bit failure and maximum code block length against bit per symbol m. By choosing $m = 4$, it offers the most flexible single-bit failure correction, but the maximum code length is too small for memory subsystems. Also, it requires too many symbol corrections for chip or card failures since the I/O width tends to be larger. On the other hand, if we take $m = 16$, even though

Table 1. Comparison among three configurations (a)-(c). Configuration (c) offers the best error correction capability in spite of small overheads in memory granularity, access latency, and parity.

	(a)	(b)	(c)
Inner code length	152 b (SSC-DSD)	168 b (DSC-TSD)	None
Outer code length	160 b	160 b	192 b (QSC)
Code block size	760 b	840 b	192 b
Parity overhead	48 %	64 %	50 %
Memory granularity (256Mb ×8 I/O)	2048 MB	2048 MB	512 MB
Latency (no error)	2 clk	2 clk	1 clk
Latency (one error)	3 clk	3 clk	2 clk
Maximum correctable single-bit errors or chip failures	2	3	4
Maximum correctable single-bit errors or chip failures with known 1 card failure	1	2	2
2 card failure recovery	No	No	Possible

the maximum code length is more than enough, it offers only limited single-bit failure corrections for a given number of parity bits, in particular for ×8 or ×16 I/O configurations per chip or card. Therefore, $m = 8$ seems the optimum choice.

3.2. Memory Array Configurations

We discuss the advantage of one-shot RS decoding in constructing a better redundant memory array system. We assume the following three redundant memory array systems shown in Fig. 4 under the following assumptions:

(1) We use 256-Mb, 8-bit I/O DRAM chips.
(2) Each card performs 32-bit I/O.
(3) The system has a 128-bit memory bus.

Configuration (a) is a typical case with conventional SSC-SSD code as an inner code and striped parity check code as an outer code. Configuration (b) assumes a more powerful DSC-TSD (double-symbol error correction, triple-symbol error detection) code. The outer code is striped parity check code similar to (a). Configuration (c) assumes a simpler 1-dimensional arrangement using a $t = 4$ (quad-symbol error correction) RS-code. In every case, we assume $m = 8$ for efficient single-bit and chip failure protection.

3.3. Comparison: More Reliability for Smaller Overheads

Table 1 compares the three memory configurations in terms of overheads in parity, memory granularity, and access latency with respect to error-correction capability. We think that the configuration (c) offers the best configuration in terms of the tradeoff between error correction capability and error-correction overheads to the system. Let us explain one by one.

Since (a) and (b) are two-dimensional product code configurations, the total number of bits accessed for (a) and (b) is much larger than a typical cache line size. Not only does this simultaneous access to a large number of bits cause power supply line noise, but also most of the accessed bits could be wasted, since they are used only for error correction. This two-dimensional code arrangement also causes larger memory granularity. Thus, the memory update needs to occur in a much larger unit. Furthermore, since error checking is required for both inner and outer codes in every access, the latency becomes higher.

On the other hand, since configuration (c) is a simple one-dimensional code structure, the power, granularity, and latency overheads are smaller. The parity overhead is comparable to case (a) and is much better than case (b).

In addition to these advantages in terms of the overheads associated with the error correction, configuration (c) offers much better error correction capability for single-bit

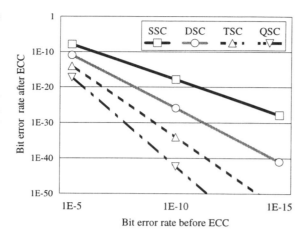

Figure 5. Bit error rate after RS error correction (BER_t) as a function of bit error rate before error correction (BER_0). for different t=1-4. $m = 8$ is assumed.

failure, chip failure, and card failure situations, as is shown in Table 1. When no card failure is detected, configuration (c) can offer recovery from up to four symbol failures arising from either single-bit or chip failures. On the other hand, the configuration (a) and (b) cannot correct 2 or 3 errors, respectively, in the same code block even with the outer parity check code. Moreover, it is noteworthy that, in configuration (c), there still is significant error correction capability even when a card failure occurs (as strong as (b), but with a similar parity overhead). Furthermore, (a) and (b) can only handle 1 card failure, but (c) can handle up to 2 card failures, when no other failure coexists.

3.4. Coding Gain Analysis

The advantage of symbol-based RS codes over bit-based ECC codes in case of chip or card failure is clear [11]. If powerful multiple-byte RS codes are used, their capability of correcting random bit errors is also satisfactory.

If we assume that the errors are distributed randomly over the address space, the bit error rate of a memory chip or system before error-correction is given by

$$BER_0 = N_{error} / N_{total}, \qquad (15)$$

where N_{error} is the total number of errors and N_{total} is the total number of bits in the memory system. Assuming $BER_0 \ll 1$ and that single bit failure is the dominant symbol failure mode, the effective bit error rate of (n, k, m) RS code applied is given by

$$BER_t \simeq (BER_0)^{t+1} {}_{mn-1}C_t . \qquad (16)$$

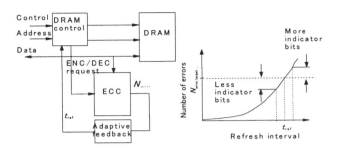

Figure 6. Block diagram of proposed system. The dynamic control of the refresh interval, is achieved by monitoring the number of refresh errors in the memory subsystem.

Figure 5 plots BER_t as a function of t for different BER_0. BER_t at $t = 4$ for $BER_0 = 10^{-10}$ is comparable to BER_t at $t = 2$ for $BER_0 = 10^{-15}$.

4. Application to Dynamic Refresh Interval Control of DRAMs

In addition to the improved reliability, the present one-shot RS decoding offers an alternative use of its powerful coding gain for overall average performance improvement, by adaptively saving the worst case conditions within a system [22]. Here, we discuss this aspect by applying the one-shot RS decoding to control of the DRAM dynamic refresh interval. The primary purpose is to optimize the refresh overheads in performance and power consumption without losing reliability.

4.1. Main Idea

Roughly speaking, DRAM retention time is doubling in every generation [23]. This relation has two aspects: the system side and the technology side. The former is driven by the requirement of maintaining the refresh overhead in memory access below a few percent. The latter comes from the tradeoff between refresh power and cell leakage current [23]. However, it is possible that this trend may not continue because of larger statistical variations arising from more complex processes and higher density of gigabit DRAM generations. In that case, the use of the error correction codes can become an attractive technique for maintain the 2X retention time trend within reasonable economic constraints (yield, etc.).

Therefore, we propose dynamic control of the refresh interval by monitoring the number of soft-failures in the memory subsystem, for an optimum tradeoff between reliability, performance, and refresh power consumption as is shown in Fig. 6. For example, a refresh rate higher than

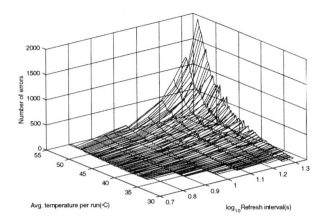

Figure 7. Number of refresh failures versus refresh interval and temperature.

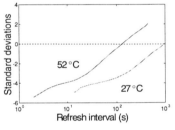

Figure 8. N_{error} in a normal plot. y=0 corresponds to where the half of all of the cells fail.

the specification may be required when the temperature exceeds the specifications because of sudden cooling fan malfunction or unexpected radioactive exposure. On the other hand, when a power line failure occurs, or during low-battery condition with battery operated pervasive devices, it is nice to increase the refresh interval to reduce the data retention power, if the data reliability can be maintained at an acceptable level.

In addressing the task of maintaining robustness while using dynamic refresh interval control, it is important to first examine how various perturbations affect the bit error rate characteristics of a DRAM. In particular, we will discuss how sensitive parameters such as temperature T and the refresh interval t_{ref} affect the number of errors N_{error} in the DRAM. Figure 7 shows a 3-dimensional plot of N_{error} as a function of t_{ref} and T for a commercially available DRAM. N_{error} increases significantly as t_{ref} increases. N_{error} versus t_{ref}, is typically divided into two regions: the main distribution and the tail distribution [24-26]. See Fig. 8 for a normal plot of N_{error}/N_{total} versus log t_{ref}. In our work, we consistently observed a third distinct section below both the main and tail distributions. Since the inverse of the slope of the lines measures the fluctuation of the time to data failure, it can be seen that the tail distribution has a larger spread and a slower increase in the number of errors, which can work as a buffer region for the adaptive refresh control scheme. Additionally, an increase in T will also lead to an exponential increase in N_{error}. It is interesting to note that in the region of interest, the relationship between $\log t_{ref}$ and T when N_{error} is fixed is a straight line whose slope is constant regardless of N_{error}. This means that the amount of change in $\log t_{ref}$ to compensate for a given change in T to maintain a certain N_{error} is constant.

Figures 7 and 8 give us an idea of how to achieve fault-tolerant feedback control of the DRAM refresh interval without relying a specific functional dependency of N_{error} on T. In order to keep the system reliability constant, the refresh interval controller should dynamically adjust t_{ref} to compensate for changes in N_{error} to maintain

$$N_{error} \simeq N_{error\_target}. \qquad (17)$$

where N_{error_target} is given by

$$N_{error\_target} = (BER_t \, / \, _{mn-1}C_t)^{1/(t+1)} N_{total} . \qquad (18)$$

Since

$$\Delta N_{error} = (dN_{error}/ dt_{ref})\Delta t_{ref} + (dN_{error} / dT)\Delta T, \qquad (19)$$

and

$$(dN_{error} / dT)\Delta T \sim N_{error} - N_{target}. \qquad (20)$$

The system converges to $\Delta N_{error} \sim 0$ as long as

$$\Delta t_{ref} \simeq \gamma (N_{error} - N_{target}) / (dN_{error}/ dt_{ref}), \qquad (21)$$

where $\gamma \sim 1$ controls the feedback. Please note that we can estimate ΔN_{error} using selected indicator bits (i.e., weak cells) in order to keep the power consumption associated with the error correction low. dN_{error}/dt_{ref} can be dynamically estimated while controlling the feedback.

The proposed adaptive feedback control method using N_{error} is better than the method of adjusting t_{ref} by using more indirect information (such as T) since there always remain uncertainties and variations in the exact functional dependence of N_{error}. In other words, it is unlikely that every DRAM retention failure is explained by a single failure mechanism especially for weak cells. Tracking N_{error} will give a more accurate description of the state of the system and how t_{ref} should be changed.

4.2. Experimental Results

The system described above was implemented in two different experimental test systems. The first one consists of a (36, 32, 8) RS encoder/decoder, an adaptive refresh

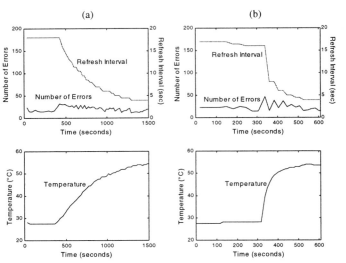

Figure 9. Data showing robustness against temperature changes. (a) moderate increase 0.06 °C/s (left). (b) rapid increase at 0.61 °C/s (right).

rate controller implemented using an Altera 10K100 FPGA, and a commercially available 16 Mb DRAM. The second one consists of a (40-34,32,8) RS encoder/decoder in ASIC [20] with two commercially available 64 Mb DRAMs. In order to also demonstrate the data retention power advantage, we choose low-standby DRAM parts.

Figures 9 (a) and (b) show experimental data showing robustness against T changes for the first test system. The experiment starts after finding an appropriate t_{ref} at a low T which then increases. The starting t_{ref} is 18 seconds in both cases, which is more than two orders of magnitude longer than the specification. As T is increased, t_{ref} becomes smaller, but N_{error} stays near $N_{error\_target} = 25$. We intentionally made *the* N_{error_target} a little higher (10^{-15} error rate is given when $N_{error\_target} \simeq 5$ when memory desnsity is 16 Mb) to make sure the system still worked. Since N_{error} is kept low, the reliability of the DRAM is maintained as T changes. In Fig. 9 (b), T increases much more quickly than in Fig. 9 (a), with a maximum gradient of 0.61 °C/s. Still, the refresh interval controller can make adjustments and keep N_{error} to an acceptable level. The refresh interval at room temperature is > 15 seconds, more than 100 times larger than the specification value of 128 ms. Therefore, the refresh overheads in both memory bandwidth and refresh power are reduced by that factor. Though we consider that this is rather an extreme limit, still no uncorrectable errors were found.

The power consumption to check and correct only selected indicator bits adds negligible power consumption, since the duty ratio of the DRAM active data transfer is greatly reduced. Indeed, the second test system with the ASIC error correction circuit implementation shows that the power associated with error correction is indeed negligible when around 10 indicator bits are monitored every 10 seconds. In this case, the required ECC throughput for (36,32,8) RS code is only 288 b/s, so the ECC power consumtion is reduced accordingly.

5. Conclusion

This paper presents the algorithm and soft-IP design of an ultra-fast one-shot RS decoding scheme and identifies its advantage for the future computer systems, where maintaining system-level reliability is expected to suffer because of increasing data size and speed. By taking a redundant array memory system as an example, we show that the present one-shot RS decoding with the block erasure decoding and speculative error calculation can offer a simpler arrangement with improved reliability and smaller error correction overheads. In addition, we show an alternative use of the powerful coding gain for optimizing the refresh overheads in performance and power consumption by dynamically controlling the DRAM dynamic refresh interval with direct feedback from the error information in the system. We acknowledge technical help from Z. Wu and E. J. Stuckey, and discussions with T. B. Smith, M. Auslander, R. H. Dennard, C. L. Chen, D. L. Cohn, M. Blaum, S. S. Lavenberg, K. Iwano, and S. Shimizu.

6. References

[1] R. E. Blahut, *Theory and Practice of Error Control Codes*, Addison-Wesley, 1984.

[2] S. B. Wicker and V. K.Bhargava (eds.), *Reed-Solomon Codes and Their Applications*, IEEE Press, 1994.

[3] T. R. N. Rao and E. Fujiwara, *Error-Control Coding for Computer Systems*, Prentice Hall, 1989.

[4] A. M. Patel, "On-the-fly decoder for multiple byte errors," *IBM J. Res. Develop.*, vol. 30, pp. 259-269, May 1986.

[5] W. Wilhelm, "A New Scaleable VLSI Architecture for Reed-Solomon Decoders," *IEEE J. Solid-state Circuits*, vol. 34, No.3, pp. 388-396, 1999.

[6] S. Kwon and H. Shin, "An Area Efficient VLSI Architecture of a Reed-Solomon Decoder/Encoder for Digital VCRs," *IEEE Trans. Consumer Electronics*, vol. 43, pp. 1019-1027, 1997.

[7] G. Lee, B. Kwuan, S. Lee, J. Jung, S. Nam, Y. Chun, D. Han, K. Park, Y. Choi, D. Cho and J. Lee, "A VLSI Design of RS Codec for Digital Data Recorder," *Proc. ASIC Design Workshop*, pp. 115-124, 1996.

[8] T. Iwaki, T. Tanaka, E. Yamada, T. Okuda and T. Sasada, "Architecture of High Speed Reed-Solomon Decoder," *IEEE Trans. Consumer Electronics*, vol. 40, pp. 75-81, 1994.

[9] M. A. Neifeld and J. D. Hayes, "Error-correction schemes for volume optical memories," *Applied Optics*, vol. 35, pp. 8183-8191, Dec. 1995.

[10] C. L. Chen and L. E. Grosbach, "Fault-Tolerant Memory Design in the IBM Application System/400 ™ ," *Proc. the 21st International Symposium on Fault-Tolerant Computing*, pp. 393-400, June 1991.

[11] C. L. Chen, "Symbol Error Correcting Codes for Memory Applications," *Proc. the 26th International Conference on Fault-Tolerant Computing*, pp. 200-207, June 1996.

[12] M. Abbott, et al., "Durable Memory RS/6000™ System Design," *Proc. the 26th International Symposium on Fault-Tolerant Computing*, pp. 414-423, June 1994.

[13] E. Fujiwara and M. Hamada, "Single b-bit Byte Error Correcting and Double Bit Error Detecting Codes for High-Speed Memory Systems," *Proc. the 22nd International Symposium on Fault-Tolerant Computing*, pp. 494-501, June 1992.

[14] L.Spainhower and T. A. Gregg, "G4: A fault-Tolerant CMOS Mainframe," *Proc. the 28th International Symposium on Fault-Tolerant Computing*, pp. 432-440, June 1998.

[15] H. Imai and Y. Kamiyanagi, "A Construction Method for Double-Error Correcting Codes for Application to Main Memories, " (in Japanese) *Trans. IEICE Japan*, J60-D, pp. 861-868, Sep. 1977.

[16] G.-L. Feng, X. Wu, and T. R. N. Rao, "New Double-Byte Error-Correcting Codes for Memory Systems," *IEEE Trans. Inform. Theory,* vol. 44, pp. 1152-1163, 1998.

[17] I. I. Drummer, "Nonbinary double-error-correcting codes designed by means of algebraic varieties," *IEEE Trans. Inform. Theory,* vol. 41, pp. 1657-1666, 1995.

[18] Y. Katayama, and S. Morioka, "One-shot Reed Solomon Decoder," *Proc. the 33rd Annual Conference on Information Sciences and Systems (CISS)*, March 1999.

[19] Y. Katayama, and S. Morioka, "Error Evaluation Algorithm for One-shot Reed-Solomon Decoder," *Proc. IEEE Information Theory Workshop*, June 1999.

[20] S. Morioka, and Y. Katayama, "Design Methodology of One-shot Reed-Solomon Encoder and Decoder," *Proc. IEEE International Conference on Computer Design*, Oct. 1999.

[21] I. G. Macdonald, *Symmetric Functions and Orthogonal Polynomials*, American Mathematical Society, 1998.

[22] Y. Katayama, E. J. Stuckey, S. Morioka, and Z. Wu, "Fault-Tolerant Refresh Power Reduction of DRAMs for Quasi-Nonvolatile Data Retention," *Proc. IEEE International Symposium on Design and Fault Tolerance in VLSI Systems,* Nov. 1999.

[23] K. Itoh, Y. Nakagome, S. Kimura, and T. Watanabe, "Limitations and Challenges of Multi-Gigabit DRAM circuits, " *Symposium on VLSI circuits Dig. Tech. Papers*, pp. 2-7, June 1996.

[24] S. Uno, T. Yamashita, H. Oda, S. Komori, Y. Inoue, and T. Nishimura, "Leakage Current Observation on Irregular Local PN Junctions Forming the Tail Distribution of DRAM Retention Characteristics, with new Test Structure," *Proc. IEEE International Electron Device Meeting Tech. Dig.*, 6.6.1, Dec. 1998.

[25] K. Saino, K. Okonogi, S. Horiba, M. Sakao, and M. Komuro, "Control of Trench Sidewall in Bias ECR-CVD Oxide-Filled STI for Enhanced DRAM Retention Time," *IEEE International Electron Device Meeting Tech. Dig.*, 6.5.1, Dec. 1998.

[26] A. Hiraiwa, M. Ogasawara, N. Natsuaki, Y. Itoh, and H. Iwai, "Local-Field-Enhancement Model of DRAM Retention Failure," *IEEE International Electron Device Meeting Tech. Dig.*, 6.7.1, Dec. 1998.

Session 11B

Panel

Session 12

Panel

Session 13A

Software Fault Injection

A Fault Injection Approach Based on Reflective Programming

Eliane Martins, Amanda C.A.Rosa[*]
Institute of Computing – Unicamp
{eliane, amandapo}@dcc.unicamp.br

Abstract

This paper presents an approach for the validation of OO applications by software-implemented fault injection (SWIFI) that is based on computational reflection. The primary motivation for the use of reflection is that it allows a clear separation between functional aspects and non-functional aspects, the later being related to instrumentation necessary for fault injection and monitoring. Besides separation of concerns, the use of OO programming and reflection is also intended to provide more flexibility, extensibility, portability and reusability for the instrumentation features. Ease of use, not only to the instrumentation programmer but also to the user, is also a goal. This paper presents FIRE, a prototyping tool that supports the proposed approach. FIRE was implemented using OpenC++1.2, and it's aimed to validate C++ applications. Preliminary results on the use of FIRE are also presented.

1 Introduction

Fault injection is the deliberate introduction of faults into a system to observe its behavior [1]. By accelerating the occurrence of errors and failures, it is a valuable approach to validate the dependability properties of a system. In this text we use the terminology introduced in [16], in which: a failure occurs when the service provided by the system doesn't conforms to its specification. A failure can occur because of the presence of errors in the system. A fault is the cause of an error. Dependability is a quality that can be characterized by a set of factors: reliability, availability, security and safety.

Fault injection can take various forms according to the abstraction used to represent the system and to the type of faults considered. In *Software-implemented fault injection* (SWIFI), faults are injected at the actual software of a computing system by corrupting code or data. SWIFI, as other fault injection techniques, is thus a valuable complement to other validation techniques in that it can

supply important parameters for analytical modeling, for example. It allows data about errors and failures to be obtained in shorter period of time than measurement of field data. Or else, it complements traditional white-box or black-box testing methods in that it goes beyond assessing software reliability, allowing to answer questions such as [31]: what is the probability that the software will fail in a way that will result in a loss? Or what is the effectiveness of fault-tolerance mechanisms?

This paper presents an approach for testing OO applications by SWIFI. This approach is based on the use of computational reflection (or simply, reflection) to introduce the instrumentation required to inject faults and monitoring its effects.

Reflection allows a system the ability to reason about itself [20, 28]. With reflection, a system can contain a representation of its own behavior, which can be examined and changed. This representation is causally connected to the behavior it describes, that is, if one of them changes, this leads to a corresponding effect on the other. Reflection can thus be a suitable mechanism to implement SWIFI, in that it can be used to inspect the internal behavior of a system (useful for monitoring purposes) and to change this behavior (useful for injection purposes).

Reflection introduces a new architectural model, in that there is a meta-level and a base level. The base level is used in this study to implement the target system objects. The meta-level allows programmers to observe and manipulate data structures and/or actions performed at the base level, and thus, is used here to implement fault injection and monitoring features.

A number of researches nowadays are using reflection in a variety of areas, such as middleware platforms in distributed systems [22, 3], fault-tolerant applications [9, 10, 17] and testing [23], only to mention a few examples. Fault injection and monitoring facilities can thus be provided with functional independence from the target application, thus reducing changes in its structure and

---

[*] Now in CPqD Foundation: amanda@cpqd.com.br.

also allowing such features to be reused in multiple applications.

The use of OO programming and reflection is aimed at providing a technique that possesses the following properties: *ease of use* not only for tool users but also for tool developers and maintainers; *separation of concerns*, in that there is independence between the target system and the instrumentation features necessary for injection and monitoring, and also between the instrumentation mechanisms with respect to each other; *extensibility*, in that new classes of faults can be added without further difficulties; *portability* among various applications and platforms, and *reusability* of existing instrumentation features to derive new ones.

A prototype software architecture, FIRE, was built in support to the proposed approach, to demonstrate its usefulness.

This paper is organized as follows: Section 2 provides some aspects of software-implemented fault injection, presenting some related studies; Section 3 contains a brief overview of reflective programming, focusing mainly on the reflective programming language Open C++ 1.2, used in this study; Section 4 gives a brief presentation of FIRE. Section 5 presents some results of the application of FIRE to the validation of a distributed fault-tolerant application. Finally, a summary and some concluding remarks given in Section 6 conclude the paper.

2 Software-implemented fault injection approaches

Software implemented fault injection (SWIFI) can be used on a software system to simulate both software faults and the failures of systems external to the software, but connected to it through interfaces [32, 1.4.4]. Software faults represent design and implementation faults, such as variables/parameters that are wrong or not initialized, incorrect assignments or incorrect condition checks. External system failures represent all external factors that are not related to faults in the code but that alter the software state [32, 3.2]. Most commonly used in SWIFI tools are the consequences of hardware failures. As failures on hardware components are viewed, by the software components interacting with them, as faults, hardware failures will be referred as hardware faults in what follows. In this way, hardware faults can be represented by [14]: storage data corruption (alteration of general or special registers, modification of memory space) or communication data corruption (alteration of messages transferred through a communication medium).

Another dimension for the characterization of faults, specially those representing hardware faults, is on the basis of the repetition pattern: faults can be transient (never repeated), intermittent (periodically repeated) and permanent (always repeated).

Many tools have been developed to support software fault injection, and they use different approaches to instrument the target system. In what follows we present a sample of such tools, only to illustrate these approaches.

One of the first tools, FIAT [29], adds fault injection and monitoring capabilities into the application code and operating system. It can inject memory faults at runtime; faults are triggered when target system execution reaches some specified locations (spatial triggering). FTAPE [30], also inserts code at the operating system level to activate faults; faults can be activated based on event occurrences (timeout or access to a specified address) or on the amount of activity performed by the system. This tool can inject processor, memory and I/O faults. For the later, routines are inserted at the disk driver, generating exceptions that simulate device faults.

SFI [27] and its successor, Doctor [12], use different approaches to inject different types of faults. Code alteration is used to inject processor faults: to simulate faults in functional units, instructions using that unit are altered at source code level; then the program is compiled with the altered components. Fault activation occurs when the program executes the erroneous component. To inject communication faults, library routines are altered so as to provide erroneous communication services. For memory faults they use a high priority process (called memory fault injection process), running concurrently with the target application This process injects faults at selected addresses by reading, altering and then writing back the contents of a specified location. These faults are activated in a temporal basis, that is, once a fault has been injected, the memory fault injection process will pause itself for a time period, determined during the experiment set-up phase. This will repeat until the experiment is completed.

Another tool based on the use of an external process is SOFIT [2], aimed at testing applications running under Unix or other operating systems providing virtual image of a process. This virtual image is examined or modified by a process having privilege to do so - in this case, its parent process. The target process execution must be stopped, in order that its virtual image could be examined or modified for testing purposes. This tool that way can inject various types of faults.

In ProFi [19] fault injection uses the trace-mode of a processor. When trace-mode is active, a trace routine is executed before each instruction of the target application. The trace routine runs in supervisor mode and has access to the whole system memory and all programmer-visible registers. The trace routine is thus used to inject processor faults.

FERRARI [15] uses software traps to inject processor and bus faults. Software traps are triggered either by the program counter or by a timer. When the traps are triggered, the injector, located at the trap handling routine, injects faults at specified locations, by changing the content of selected registers or memory location. The faults can be transient or permanent, and they emulate errors in address line, data line and condition code flags.

Xception [3] uses performance monitoring and debugging features included in many recent processors to inject faults and monitoring a target system. Processor's built-in hardware exceptions are used to trigger instrumentation functions. Faults can be triggered not only after a specified time has elapsed, but also when an instruction in a specified location is fetched or else when data stored in a specified location is accessed. Trace mode can also be used when it is required to execute some instructions step-by-step, but this is not a main feature of the tool.

EFA [8] and Orchestra [7] are examples of tools that use a middleware-based approach, in which injection code is inserted in an intermediate layer between the application and the operating system. These tools are aimed at validating communication systems so they corrupt communication data.

Higher level fault models are considered in a fault injection tool based on a technique designated as *extended propagation analysis* (EPA), presented in [32, 6.4], which inserts instrumentation at some locations into the source code to perform fault injection. When an instrumented location is executed, the current values at that location are overwritten by newly selected values.

The tool presented in this paper, FIRE, was developed for the testing of O-O applications. FIRE does not need any particular monitoring and debugging features offered by the hardware or by a debugger. Nor either is it necessary to run the injector/monitor in a privileged mode. FIRE inserts code into pre-specified locations of the source code to perform injection and monitoring such as the EPA-based tool, but FIRE uses computational reflection for that purpose. As SOFIT, FIRE is also developed using OO paradigm to improve reusability, but FIRE does not use any specific operating system feature. Like the middleware-based approach, FIRE can also intercept and corrupt communication systems data. In addition, FIRE has also access to a high-level application internal information, which is usually not possible with the aforementioned approach.

Besides interference in application's execution speed, which is hard to avoid when using software-based instrumentation, another limitation of the approach proposed here is the need of the source code. Hence, it is suitable for use by software developers during the testing phase.

3 Reflective programming and OO

3.1 Reflection in OO languages

Computational reflection (from here on called just *reflection*) is the capability of a computational system to reason about or act upon itself [20]. Conventional systems manipulate data that represents entities that are external to the system. A reflective system, in addition to that, contains data that represents structural and behavioral aspects of the system itself (*meta-information*). This meta-information must be causally connected to the actual behavior of the system, such that changes in system behavior lead to changes in its meta-information and vice-versa.

Reflection is achieved by subdividing a system into two levels: *functional* (or *base-*) level, in which the application's functionality is implemented, and *non-functional* (or *meta-*) level, which performs observation and manipulation of the base-level structure or behavior.

In object orientation Patti Maes [20] introduced the *metaobject approach* to implement reflection. An object x can be associated with a metaobject ^x that represents the meta-information of x.

A metaobject is an object; thus, it can be manipulated in the same manner as a base-level object. Therefore, metaobjects can have one or more other metaobjects associated to them. In its concept, it would be possible to build an infinite hierarchy of meta-levels in which metaobjects in a given layer control the ones in a layer bellow. However, [18] presents the results of a study in which it is recommended that the number of layers of such a hierarchy may not exceed 3, for complexity and performance concerns.

Reflection presents several advantages for software-implemented fault injection. First, the separation in base level and meta-level allows the independence of injection/monitoring features from the application's functions. Second, implementing injection and monitoring features at the meta-level enhances modularity and reusability once these features can be developed independently of the target application, and can be incorporated and removed whenever necessary. And third, the use of metaobjects allows the customization of instrumentation features in an object-by-object basis.

3.2 The OpenC++

OpenC++ 1.2 [5], an extension of the C++ that supports reflection, is being used in this study. Its main features are [5, 18]:
- Objects in base-level can be reflective or normal (non-reflective). Reflective objects have an associated metaobject, which controls its behavior. A non-reflective objective is a standard C++ object.

- Each base-level reflective object can be associated with only one metaobject. Furthermore, metaobjects cannot be shared.
- Metaobjects can control method invocation and attribute access of its base-level object.
- A metaobject is an instantiation of a meta-level class. Meta-level classes are associated with base-level classes at compile-time.
- Meta-level classes inherit from the predefined *MetaObj* class. The subclasses of *MetaObj* can redefine its methods. Such methods allow a metaobject to control method calls, and read or write access to attributes at the base level, among others.

A program in OpenC++1.2 is a C++ program that contains clauses to declare classes, methods, and attributes as reflective. These clauses are embedded as C++ comments that start with //MOP. To declare methods and attributes as reflective, one must precede them with the clause: //MOP reflect. To associate a base-level class with a meta-level class, the clause //MOP reflect class must be used.

A category_name can be associated with reflective methods and attributes; that way, a metaobject recognizes that the reflective method or attribute has a category and changes method invocations and attribute access accordingly. These features will be clarified with the example in section 5.1.

4 FIRE: a reflective fault injection tool

FIRE, which stands for Fault Injection using a REflective Architecture, was developed using the C++ language and the pre-processor OpenC++1.2. Reflection was used to implement an injection and monitoring library, which is linked to the target application. The items that follow describe this tool.

4.1 The architecture

The reflective architecture proposed in this study is shown in **Figure 4.1**. Its main components are: a target *application*, a *meta-level library*, and a *controller*. The target application should be written in C++, so aspects of concurrency have not been considered.

The *meta-level library* contains metaobjects called *schedulers* each composed of an *injector* and a *sensor*. An *injector* is responsible for the introduction of pre-specified faults into a reflective object, and a *sensor* is responsible for readout collection. As a metaobject, a *scheduler* is created when its associated reflective object is instantiated. Its function will be further explained in 5.1. The *scheduler* is a composite object created because of a limitation of OpenC++1.2: each base-level object can be associated with one and only one meta-object, but we need to guarantee separation of concerns between instrumentation functions.

The *controller* controls the experiments: it starts the application, controls *injectors* and *sensors* and stores results. The *controller* is composed of three objects: the *injection manager*, the *monitor* and *user interface*. The *injection manager* reads the pre-specified faults from a *Fault* file and transfers them to *schedulers*, which transfer them to *injectors* at injection time. The *monitor* receives and stores the collected data in the *History* file. The *user interface* helps users to observe and control the execution of experiments at runtime.

4.2 Fault model

As initially SWIFI researchers were mainly interested in observe the effect of hardware faults into software systems, their focus was mainly on low level software more than on applications. So the fault models are meant to emulate the consequences of faults into processor functional units or memory. Whereas our focus is on high-level software, composed of a set of objects interacting by exchanging messages.

From the point of view of an object, we can state that FIRE is able to inject internal or external faults. Internal faults affect protected features of an object (the OpenC++ MOP does not allow private features of an object to be reflected). Whereas external faults affect the object's interface. That way we can emulate the effect of faults either of an object's internal components, as well as those of component external to the object but interacting with it.

An important problem in SWIFI approaches is relative to whether the fault model represents actual fault manifestation. Studies such as [26] and [11, cap.7] concludes that bit-flip faults in microprocessor can be emulated by software, producing a similar error set as the HWIFI techniques. And also, [6] shows that transient gate level faults can be emulated by software. So, hardware fault models such as bit-flips, stuck-at or bridging are used for many SWIFI tools that focus on software at the assembly level [4, 11, and 19]. However the effect of software faults is hard to implement with such tools.

In our approach, as fault injection is applied at source code level, the effect of software, as well as hardware faults can be modeled as erroneous data coming into or out the target software.

Finally it is worth mentioning an experimental study that was carried out by C. C. Michael whose results, presented in [32, cap.3.2.1], could be useful for SWIFI researches. The study was relative to error propagation in software; the obtained results suggest that software seems to present fairly consistent propagation behaviors once an error affecting its state is activated. Therefore, even if a fault injector fails to mimic real faults, the results obtained are still meaningful to predict software behavior in the presence of faults.

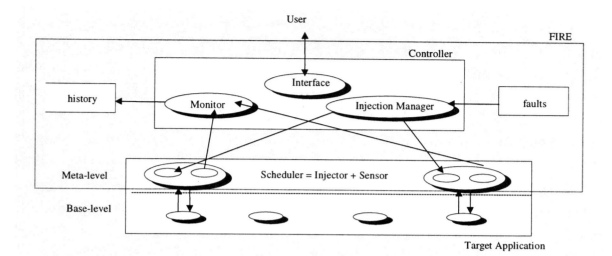

Figure 4-1. FIRE's architecture.

4.3 Triggering mechanism

FIRE injects faults during runtime, by altering the state of the injectable object (s), which are instances of reflective classes. A triggering mechanism is thus necessary, i.e., a condition or external event that leads to the injection of faults [4]. For that purpose FIRE uses the invocation trap facility offered by the OpenC++ 1.2 MOP . Invocation traps occur either when a reflective method is called or when a reflective attribute is accessed. For illustration, suppose an *injectable object* and its corresponding *scheduler* metaobject. As Figure **4-2** shows, if another base-level object sends a **request** message to the injectable object, the *scheduler* intercepts the **request** message and takes over the execution. Later the *scheduler* returns the execution to the *injectable object* that returns a **response** message to its client. From the point of view of the client object, reflection is transparent, that is, it sends a message requesting a service and receives the response with no knowledge that the message has been intercepted and manipulated in the meta-level.

Therefore the number of *scheduler'* invocations is used for establish injection start and repetition pattern. Fault injection begins after a pre-specified number of *scheduler's* invocations occur. Permanent faults are emulated by introducing a fault at each invocation; an intermittent fault corresponds to repeatedly introducing a fault at user-specified number of invocations; and transient faults are introduced in one unique invocation.

Since an invocation trap occurs each time a reflective feature is accessed, permanent faults can be emulated as easy as transient faults; moreover, the overhead to inject permanent or temporary faults is quite the same.

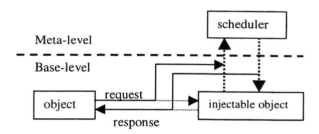

Figure 4-2. The invocation trap mechanism.

4.4 Monitoring

FIRE can collect several data concerning the behaviour of the target system. Data collection for monitoring purposes can be done: i) after the injection of each fault, in which case data are sent to the *monitor* by the *injectors*; ii) each time an attribute or method of a reflective object is accessed, in which case, data are sent to the *monitor* by the *sensors*. In the second case monitoring is performed on objects selected for that purpose. The user can thus indicate whether instances of a class may be injected, monitored or both.

A *scheduler* invokes sensors in the same way as *injectors*. *Sensors,* as well as *injectors,* can be turned on/off during runtime, which provides the user the ability to tune monitoring/injection according to system activity. This can be useful, for example, if the user desires to inject/monitor according to system state.

411

4.5 Multi-level architecture

FIRE allows reflective applications to be injected and monitored. When the application is structured using several levels, the following situations can be envisaged:

a. Injecting (or monitoring) base-level objects that are instances of non-reflective classes: in such case we have the same situation as in single level applications, so the non-reflective class can be instrumented to become reflective so that a scheduler meta-object can be associated with its instances.

b. Injecting (or monitoring) objects of the last meta-level: this situation is similar to the previous one; the difference is that a scheduler is associated with a meta-object, instead of a base-level object.

c. Injecting (or monitoring) intermediate level objects: in such case we consider as intermediate level an object that already has a meta-object. As in OpenC++ 1.2 an object can be associated with only one meta-object, injection (and monitoring) features should be introduced at higher levels. **Figure 4-3** illustrates the case in which it is required to inject faults into a base level object that already has a meta-object. Data from the base level is reified together with data from the meta-level to the meta-meta-level. So, in principle it would be possible to corrupt base level data but it is not guaranteed that the intermediate meta-level will propagate the corrupted data down to the base level. This is because in OpenC++ 1.2 reification occurs before a reflective method is executed, so the corrupted data could be processed or overwritten by the meta-level.

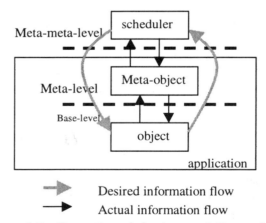

Desired information flow
Actual information flow

Figure 4-3. Example of instrumentation of a multi-level application.

5 Using FIRE

In FIRE's approach the fault injection process comprises the following steps: 1. preparation of the target application; 2. Definition of faults; 3. Experiments execution; 4. Results analysis. Currently, FIRE gives support to steps 2 and 3.

We next briefly describe the first three phases. Then, initial results obtained with the use of FIRE are presented, followed by a discussion about the usefulness of the approach, based on the experience we had using it.

5.1 Preparation of the target application

This phase, although not yet supported by FIRE, is easy to perform manually. It consists in the instrumentation of the target application, in which the user indicates: the class(es) to be injected (and/or monitored), the reflective features (attributes or methods) and which objects of the reflective class (es) will be injected. This is illustrated by the example shown in **Figure 5-1** where text in bold indicates the clauses that should be introduced by the user, as indicated in 3.2.

```
1.    # include "scheduler.h"
2.    class Example {
3.    public:
4.        Example( );
5.        . . .
6.        // MOP reflect (injection):
7.        int var_ex;
8.        . . .
9.    }
10.   // MOP reflect class Example: SchedulerMetaObj
11.   main ( ) {
12.   Example e1;
13.   refl_Example e2;
14.   x = e2.var_ex;
15.   y = e1.var_ex;
16.   ...
17.   }
```

Figure 5-1. Inclusion of clauses to generate reflective classes and objects

Line 1 contains the inclusion of the metaobject library that contains the *scheduler* class. In line 6, a public attribute of the class *Example* is declared as being reflective by using the clause: *//MOP reflect (injection). Injection* is the *category name* (see 3.2), which, associated with the attribute, indicates to the *scheduler* that a fault has to be injected when this attribute is accessed. Other possible *category names* are *monitoring*, to indicate methods/attributes to be monitored, or *both*, in which case, injection and monitoring are to be performed.

The use of the clause *//MOP reflect class* in line 10 indicates that objects of the class *Example* can be reflective and the associated metaobject are instances of the class *SchedulerMetaObj*. In fact, when the OpenC++ pre-processor finds this clause in the source code, it creates a new subclass for *Example*, named *refl_Example*, which is reflective. Therefore, normal objects (i.e., non-reflective objects) are instances of class *Example* (line 12) and injectable objects are instances of the class *refl_Example* (line 13). Given that *var_ex* is declared as reflective, and *e2* is a reflective object, when executing the instruction in line 14 the access to *var_ex* is intercepted. As *e1* is a normal (non-reflective) object, the access to *var_ex* in line 15 is performed as usual.

Now to clarify how the interception to the meta-level occurs, we present the *scheduler* in Figure 5-2. For the sake of conciseness only the aspects of interest for the current example are presented here.

```
1.   Class SchedulerMetaObj: public MetaObj {
2.   public:
3.     void Meta_Read (Id var_id, ID category, ArgPac& value) {
4.       ...
5.       if ((category == injection || category == both) &&
6.           (injector-> Is_On ( )) && Injection_time ( ))
7.         {
8.   // code to invoke the injector and perform data corruption
9.                              ...
10.                Meta_HandleRead (var_id, value) ;
11.        }
12.    ...
13.  }
```

Figure 5-2. Definition of the *scheduler* metaobject.

In OpenC++, all metaobject classes inherit from the pre-defined class MetaObj that offers methods that can be redefined by its subclasses. Examples of such methods are Meta_Read and Meta_HandleRead, shown in the figure. Meta_Read is called when an attribute identified by var_id is read. This method is redefined, as shown in lines 3 to 11, so that the *injector* is called to corrupt the attribute at the appropriate moment. Note that before calling the *injector*, the scheduler must check the category to determine what action it should undertake. The value parameter is a reference to a location at which the result of the read access is to be stored. ArgPac is a class provided by OpenC++ that implements a stack of objects of various types, including ArgPac objects. This structure is used to store data reified to the meta-level. The method Meta_HandleRead executes the actual read access after fault injection. In this way, when *e2.var_ex* is accessed in the example in Figure 5-1, the *injector* may corrupt its value, when Meta_Read is invoked. Afterwards its value is read (by the method Meta_HandleRead) and assigned to *x*.

After instrumentation the application should be submitted to OCC, the OpenC++ pre-processor and then compiled and linked with FIRE's meta-object library. The user can declare various classes and reflective objects, in that ways allowing various objects to be injected without the need of further recompilations. Although this allows a gain in productivity it is not recommended because of the impact on the application's execution speed.

5.2 Fault generation

In this step the user should generate the *Faults* file used during experiments execution. Each fault in this file is an instance of a class of the metaobject library and is characterised by the following attributes:

- Level, that indicates to the *scheduler* whether the data to be corrupted is in the base level or in a meta-level.
- Target class, which indicates the class whose instances are to be injected.
- Selection mode, which indicates whether the arguments of a reflective method are user-specified or chosen at random for injection.
- Operation, which indicates the operation to be used to corrupt a target value using the operators provided by C/C++ language. They comprise: assignment of a wrong value, bitwise or logical operations, shift and complement.
- Mask, that is used by the operations to corrupt a value.
- Repetition pattern, that indicates whether faults are transient, intermittent or permanent. For intermittent faults, it indicates also the repetition period.
- Start, that indicates the time of application of the fault with respect to the beginning of the experiment.

Fault generation can be done manually by the user or with the aid of the *fault generator* provided by FIRE.

5.3 Experiments execution and data collection

After preparing the target application and define the faults to be injected the user can begin the execution. The name of the target application executable code, as well as those of the *Faults* and *History* files should be given. Afterwards:

1. The *Injection Manager* reads a fault instance from the *Faults* file and stores it into a buffer that is accessible to all *scheduler* objects created during the application's execution.
2. The application is started. Each time a reflective object is created, its corresponding *scheduler* is also created. Once created the *scheduler* checks, by consulting the buffer, whether its corresponding object is an instance of the target class for the current run. If so, the *injector* is "turned on". As indicated in Figure 5-2, the *scheduler* checks if the *injector* is "on" before calling it. The sensors are created in a similar manner. When a reflective object is deleted the *scheduler* associated with it is also destroyed.
3. Faults are injected by corrupting the values of attributes, arguments or return values of methods.

Those values are available at the meta-level through ArgPac objects, which represent a stack (see 5.1). The pointer to the stack top is passed from the stack to the injector, which then chooses the item to inject according to the options made by the user at fault generation phase. The mask and the operation specified in the fault instance are then applied to the item to be corrupted.

4. Steps 1 to 3 are repeated until the *Faults* file is empty.

During execution, all data collected by the *injectors* or by the *sensors* are sent to the monitor and stored in the *History* file. Collected data consist in the fault attributes, as well as the outputs produced by the application: results or error messages generated by the error detection mechanisms. Information collected by the sensors is relative to the values of each attribute or method's arguments. The application's exit code, returned by the *exit( )* call, is also stored.

5.4 Preliminary results

FIRE has been implemented in Sun workstations running the SunOS 4.1 (a variant of Unix) operating system. To demonstrate its applicability and the usefulness of the reflective approach for fault injection, some experiments were ran using as target a distributed object-oriented application that implements a fault-tolerant stack, *RobustStack* [8]. This application uses two optional mechanisms to tolerate software faults: recovery blocks (RB) and N-version programming (NVP). Three variants of stack are used. The application has a client-server architecture. The client contains the user program that uses the stack services and the servers, in number of 3, each containing one of the aforementioned variants. The communication between the client and the server machines was via TCP/IP sockets. We present in the following a summary of the experiments undertaken and the main results obtained. Further details can be found on [25].

Experiment 1. This experiment consisted in injecting the method *push(item)* of an instance of the class RobustStack, in the client site. For each run, the insertion of 100 items was performed; only permanent faults were considered. The experiment consisted of two runs, one for testing each fault tolerance mechanism. In this way we observe the behavior of RB and NVP mechanisms when all versions received the same corrupted input data. In this case, no failure was observed, in that a failure is considered here as the insertion of a corrupted item into the stack. Since the item was corrupted prior to the invocation of the fault-tolerance mechanisms, each version received the same corrupted item, which did not

satisfy the class invariant[1], and the versions reported no success. At the end, the item was not inserted and an exception was signaled, as expected. Even the NVP approach did not present a failure, since voting was performed on the result of the class invariant performed by each server object.

Experiments 2 and 3. These experiments were intended to show how easy it was to adapt FIRE to a distributed configuration. Here again faults consisted in corrupting the argument of the method *push(item)*, but this time, in one or two variants. Therefore, we had a *scheduler* running in each server machine and another running on the client, for monitoring purposes, together with the other FIRE components. For each run, the client requested to push 10 items into the stack. This time, transient, permanent and intermittent faults were introduced. An erroneous behavior was observed when injecting temporary faults for the RB mechanism: all variants returned no success in pushing the requested item onto the stack, even when no faults were injected for a given invocation. This also occurred when injecting permanent faults starting at some moment after the first invocation of the *push( )* method. Hence, a fault in state restoration implementation for the recovery block mechanism was revealed. Moreover, an implementation fault in the second variant was also revealed.

Performance issues. We compared the reflective approach used by FIRE with another approach based on source code alteration, i.e., faults were introduced before compile-time, as in mutation testing, so no need of metaobjects were necessary at runtime to inject faults. This comparison was intended mainly to obtain a preliminary evaluation of the impact of reflection in application's execution.

We measured the time taken to insert 200 items into a fault-tolerant stack in the following situations: i) faults were introduced into the first variant and ii) faults were introduced into two variants. In both cases, only the recovery block mechanism was observed. In order that injections performed by FIRE could mimic injections made by source code alteration, only permanent faults starting with the first activation of the injected method were considered. In the first case the overhead introduced by the reflective approach was of 7,7% and in the second case there was a 3% overhead in execution time. Of course we need further performance measurement experiments to corroborate such results but it seems that the overhead introduced by reflection becomes less important when compared with time taken for network communication and disk accesses. [9] presents some

---

[1] The class invariant is a predicate stating that the top stack item must correspond to the number of elements into the stack. For example, item 4 could only be pushed onto the stack if it already contained 3 elements.

measurements taken in an environment that is quite the same used here. They observed that for an invocation of 1Kb of parameters the time for trapping an invocation is about 0.1 ms, in which 80% of this time is used for packing the parameters in an ArgPac object. Of course this could not be negligible for centralized applications that do not use resources such as disks, but more important than to calculate the performance overhead, our aim in future works is to determine whether this overhead is predictable, which could be useful when testing real-time applications.

Another important result concerning the two techniques is that the source code alteration did not detect the faults revealed by FIRE.

5.5 Discussion

The initial results obtained when using FIRE point that the proposed approach fulfilled the expected properties. The current approach is extensible by simply adding other classes to the metaobject library or by specializing the current available classes (fault, scheduler, injector and sensor) by using current object-oriented techniques. Moreover, it is easy to customize faults according to the base class. For example, disk or communication faults can be injected into objects that deal with disk or network I/O. FIRE can be ported to different platforms, depending only on the availability of the current pre-processor used to generate reflective classes in the new platforms. Separation of concerns is another property, in that any metaobject class can be substituted without affecting the other classes; moreover, they are completely independent of the target application. FIRE is easy to use, in that applications instrumentation is simple, the user should only introduce some clauses, without being aware of the way metaobjects were implemented, or where they will reside. The use of a system to automate instrumentation is being envisaged to enhance the tool's usability. Finally, the metaobject library can be reused in the development of other tools. The uniform interface between metaobjects and objects provided by the OpenC++ MOP contributes to simplify reuse.

We also came across with some limitations due mainly to the metaobject protocol that was used. One of the main drawbacks is the static binding of objects to metaobjects. If there are many objects to inject into an application, the only options are: i) to re-instrument and recompile the application each time a different class that is to be considered; or ii) to create all metaobjects at once. Option causes an increase in the overhead since invocation traps occur even for all reflective objects.

Another important drawback is the limited amount of meta-information available at the meta-level, which prevented FIRE to inject into objects private features. It was also not possible to inject or monitoring non-reflective attributes because this would require the introduction of extra code into the application. For the same reason, injection and monitoring could not address non-scalar data types.

Finally, when reflective applications are under test, we could not guarantee that fault injection and monitoring features will be adequately performed for a base level object that is already associated with a metaobject.

Other limitations are: i) the need of a source code and ii) the dependency on the metaobject protocol. The change to a more appropriate metaobject protocol is being undertaken.

6 Conclusion

In this paper we have presented FIRE, a fault injection tool using a reflective architecture, that can be used to validate OO applications written in C++. The use of the reflection mechanism allows instrumentation facilities for fault injection and monitoring to be separated in a meta-level, while application objects are in the base level. A first prototype of this tool was developed for a Unix platform (Sun OS) and is based on OpenC++1.2 metaobject protocol. Preliminary experiments have shown the usefulness of the approach for fault injection tools development, in that it provides ease of use, extensibility, flexibility, separation of concerns, portability and reusability of the instrumentation features implemented as metaobjects.

Up to now, FIRE can inject faults in methods, through the corruption of values of arguments and in attributes, altering values during the reading or writing.

One limitation of FIRE is that its features are strongly dependent on the metaobject protocol used, that is, the one of OpenC++1.2, which imposed several restrictions, among others already discussed in this text, portability to other Unix or non-Unix platforms is limited. For that reason one of our ongoing work is the porting of FIRE to OpenC++2.5, which is available for Unix variants (Solaris, Linux) and Windows. The difficulty was that the metaobject protocol is totally different. However, the metaobject library was not affected by such modifications, which shows once more the tool's portability.

Another ongoing research is relative to the use of design patterns to model fault injection and monitoring features, thus extending reusability to the design level.

Acknowledgments

We thank the Brazilian financial agencies FAPESP and CNPq for their support to the development of this work. Thanks also to the referees whose comments allowed us to improve this text.

References

[1] Arlat, J.; M. Aguera; L. Amat; Y. Crouzet; J.-C. Fabre; J.-C. Laprie; E. Martins; D. Powell. "Fault injection for dependability

validation - a methodology and some applications". *IEEE Trans. on Softw. Eng.*, vol. 16, n. 2, Feb. 1990, pp. 166-182.

[2] Avresky, D.R.; P.K. Tapadiya. *A Method for Developing a Software-Based Fault Injection Tool*. Technical Report, Departement of Computer Science, Texas A&M University n° 95-021, 1995.

[3] Blair, G.; M. Papathomas. "The Case for Reflective Middleware". Obtained vai Internet, Mar/2000, on site: www.newcastle.research.ec.org/cabernetworkshops/3rd-plenary-papers/36-blair.html.

[4] Carreira, J.; H. Madeira,; J.G. Silva. "Xception: a software fault injection and monitoring in processor functional units". *5th IFIP International Working Conference on Dependable Computing for Critical Applications*, Urbana-Champaign, Illinois, USA, 1995, pp. 135 -149.

[5] Chiba S., *Open-C++ Release 1.2 Programmer's Guide*, Technical Report n° 93-3, Dept. Information Science, University of Tokyo, 1993.

[6] Czeck, E. "Estimates of the abilities of software-implemented fault injection to represent gate-level faults". *Int. Workshop on Fault and Error Injection for Dependability Validation of Computer Systems*, Gothemburg, Sweden, 1993.

[7] Dawson, S.; F. Jahanian,; T. Mitton. *ORCHESTRA: a Fault Injection Environment for Distributed Systems*. Available on site: www.ecs.umich.edu.

[8] Echtle, K.; M. Leu. "The EFA Fault Injector for Fault-Tolerant Distributed System Testing". *Proc. Workshop on Fault-Tolerant Parallel and Distributed Systems*, Amherst, USA, 1992.

[9] Fabre, J.-C.; T. Pérennou. "FRIENDS: A Flexible Architecture for Implementing Fault Tolerant and Secure Distributed Applications". In *Proc. of EDCC-2*, Italy, 1996, pp 4-20.

[10] Ferreira, L.L.; C.M.F. Rubira. "Reflective Design Patterns to Implement Fault Tolerance". In *Proc. of the Workshop on Reflective Programming in C++ and Java*. Canada, Oct/1998, pp81-85.

[11] Fuchs, E. *Software Implemented Fault Injection*. PhD dissertation, Technical University of Vien, April/1996.

[12] Han, S.; H.A. Rosenberg,; K.G.Shin. *DOCTOR: an Integrated Software Fault Injection Environment*. Technical Report, University of Michigan n° CSE-TR-192-93, 1993.

[13] Hoffman D., "Hardware Testing and Software IC's", *Proc. Pacific NW Software Quality Conference*. Portland, Oregon, Sept. 1989.

[14] Hsueh, M.C.; T.K. Tsai; R.K. Iyer. "Fault Injection Techniques and Tools". *IEEE Computer*, Apr/1997, pp. 75-82.

[15] Kanawati, N.; G. Kanawati,; J. Abraham. "FERRARI: A Tool for the Validation of System Dependability Properties". *Proc. FTCS-22*, IEEE CS Press, Los Alamitos, Calif., 1992, pp. 336-344.

[16] Laprie, J-C. "Dependability – Its Attributes, Impairments and Means". *Predictability Dependable Computing Systems (B. Randell, J.-C. Laprie, H. Kopetz, B. Littlewood, eds)*. Springer, Berlin, Germany, 1995, pages 3-18.

[17] Lisboa, M.L.B. "A New Trend on the Development of Fault Tolerant Applications: Software Meta-Level Architectures". In *Proc. of DCIA'98*, South Africa, Jan/1998, pp 148-157.

[18] Lisboa, M.L.B. *Computational Reflection in the Object Model*. Tutorial presented at II Brazilian Symposium of Programming Languages, Campinas, SP, Brazil, 1997, 53 pages. (in Portuguese)

[19] Lovric, T.; K. Echtle. "ProFI: a Processor Fault Injection for Dependability Validation". *IEEE International Workshop on Fault and Error Injection for Dependability Validation*, Gothenburg, Sweden, Jun 1993.

[20] Maes, P., "Concepts and Experiments in Computational Reflection". In *Proc. OOPSLA'87*, 1987, p.147-155.

[21] Michael, C.C. "On the Uniformity of Error Propagation in Software". *Proc. of the 12th. Annual Conference on Computer Assurance (COMPASS'97)*, USA, 1997, apud [Voas97].

[22] Oliva, A.; L.E. Buzato. "Composition of Meta-Objects in Guarana". In *Proc. of the Workshop on Reflective Programming in C++ and Java*. Canada, Oct/1998, pp 86-90.

[23] Pinto, I.V.; A.M.A. Price. "A System to Support OO Programs Testing using a Reflective Approach". In *Proc. of XII Brazilian Symposium on Software Engineering*, Parana, Brazil, Oct/1998, pp87-103. (in Portuguese)

[24] Prado, D.P. "*Fault-tolerant System Implementation Using Object-Oriented Programming*". Master Thesis, Institute of Computer Science, State University of Campinas (Unicamp), Campinas, Brazil, Jan/1998. (in Portuguese).

[25] Rosa, Amanda. *A Reflective Architecture for Fault Injection into Object Oriented Applications*. Master Thesis, UNICAMP, Campinas, Brazil, 1998. (in Portuguese)

[26] Rimen, M.; I. Ohlsson, ; J. Torin. "On Microprocessor Error Behavior Modeling". In *Proc. of FTCS-24*, Austin, Texas, USA, 1994, pp 76-85.

[27] H.A.Rosenberg, K.G.Shin. "Software Fault Injection and its Application in Distributed Systems". In *Proc. FTCS-23*, Toulouse, França, 1993.

[28] Smith, B.C. *Procedural Reflection in Programming Languages*. PhD Thesis, MIT. Available as Technical Report of MIT Computer Science Laboratory, nr.272, 1982. (apud [20])

[29] Segall, Z.; D.Vrsalovic; D.P.Siewiorek; D.Yaskin; J.Kownacki; J.Barton; R.Dancey; A.Robinson; T.Lin. "FIAT-Fault Injection Based Automated Testing Environment". In *Proc. FTCS-18*, Tokyo, Japan, 1988, pp102-107.

[30] Tsai, T.K; R.K Iyer. "FTAPE: a Fault Injection Tool to Measure Fault Tolerance". In *Proc of AIAA Computing in Aerospace 10*, San Antonio, Texas, USA, 1992, pp.339-346.

[31] Voas, J.; McGraw, G.; L. Kassab,; L. A. Voas. " 'Crystal Ball' for Software Liability". *IEEE Computer*, June/1997, pp.29-36.

[32] Voas, J.M.; G. McGraw. *Software Fault Injection. Inoculating Programs Against Errors*. John Wiley & Sons, 1998

On the Emulation of Software Faults by Software Fault Injection

Henrique Madeira, Diamantino Costa
Centro de Informática e Sistemas
University of Coimbra - Portugal
[henrique, dino]@dei.uc.pt

Marco Vieira
Instituto Superior de Engenharia de Coimbra
Coimbra - Portugal
mvieira@isec.pt

Abstract

This paper presents an experimental study on the emulation of software faults by fault injection. In a first experiment, a set of real software faults has been compared with faults injected by a SWIFI tool (Xception) to evaluate the accuracy of the injected faults. Results revealed the limitations of Xception (and other SWIFI tools) in the emulation of different classes of software faults (about 44% of the software faults cannot be emulated). The use of field data about real faults was discussed and software metrics were suggested as an alternative to guide the injection process when field data is not available. In a second experiment, a set of rules for the injection of errors meant to emulate classes of software faults was evaluated. The fault triggers used seem to be the cause for the observed strong impact of the faults in the target system and in the program results. The results also show the influence in the fault emulation of aspects such as code size, complexity of data structures, and recursive versus sequential execution

1. Introduction

Fault injection has been extensively used in the last decade to evaluate fault tolerance mechanisms and to assess the impact of faults in systems [1, 2]. A major issue is to assure that the injected faults are representative of actual faults, as this is a necessary condition to obtain meaningful results. It is widely accepted that existing fault injection technologies can emulate hardware faults, either transient or permanent. However, the emulation of software faults is still a rather obscure step.

Software faults are recognized as the major cause of system outages. Existing studies show a clear predominance of software faults [3, 4], and given the huge complexity of today's software the weight of software faults tends to increase, which makes clear the relevance of extending the fault injection technologies to the

[1] Work partially supported by FCT, Praxis XXI, contract No. 2/2.1/TIT/1570/95 and grant No. BD/5636/95.

injection of this kind of faults. Among the different techniques, Software Implemented Fault Injection (SWIFI) is clearly the fault injection technique most used today, which makes it the logical choice for this work.

The possible emulation of software faults by fault injection greatly increases the relevance and usefulness of fault injection in the validation of fault tolerance mechanisms and in the evaluation of the dependability features of computer systems. Furthermore, having accurate ways to emulate software faults it is possible to assess the consequences of hidden bugs in a system (experimental risk assessment). This aspect is particularly relevant as it is well known that even the most comprehensive testing process cannot assure that the complex software products are free of bugs.

Fault injection literature is rich in works aiming to study hardware faults. However, only few studies have addressed the problem of injection of software faults. This can be explained by the fact that the knowledge on the software faults experienced by systems in the field is very limited, which makes the definition of meaningful sets of faults (or errors) to inject rather difficult.

The key issue surrounding the injection of software faults is the accuracy of the emulation of this class of faults. Recent studies [5, 6] have proposed the use of field data on discovered software faults to devise a set of rules to generate errors that once injected in a system emulate different types of software faults. However, the accuracy of the errors injected according to these rules has never been evaluated in practice.

To the best of our knowledge, no previous work has evaluated the accuracy of injected faults/errors against actual software faults. Thus we decided to undertake this step and compare the effects of the real software faults with the faults/errors injected by a SWIFI tool (the Xception). In short, the contributions of this study are:

- Evaluation of the capabilities of SWIFI tools in what regards the demands of the emulation of software faults. This has been done by evaluating the use of a typical fault injection tool in two different ways:

  a) Emulation of specific (and real) software faults found in programs. In this case the accuracy of the emulated faults is evaluated against a set of real software faults obtained from a large set of program implementations developed independently by participants in a programming contest;

b) Injection of faults generated by rules similar to the ones proposed in [5].

- Evaluation of the influence in the software fault emulation of aspects such as code size, complexity of data structures, and recursive versus sequential code;

- Proposal of the use of software metrics to guide the fault injection process when field data on actual software faults is not available.

The next section presents related research. Section 3 presents a general discussion of the problem of software faults emulation. The setup used in this study is presented in section 4. Section 5 presents the results of emulation of a set of real software faults by fault injection, and in section 6 the emulation of general classes of software faults is evaluated and discussed. Section 7 concludes the paper.

2. Related Work

The study of software faults has been mainly related to the software development phase, as the software faults are originated during the different steps of this phase (requirement definition, specification, design, coding, testing, etc). This is an important area of software engineering and many studies have contributed to the improvement of the software development methodologies, with particular emphasis on software testing, software reliability modeling and software reliability risk analysis [7, 8].

The fault history during the development phase, the operational profile, and other process measures have been used in software reliability models to estimate the reliability of software and to predict software faults for risk assessment [8, 9, 10].

The study of the software reliability during the operational phase is substantially different from the software under development. The operational environment and the software maturity are different during the operational phase, and the software reliability should be studied in the context of the whole system. The difficulties are not only in the instrumentation required to collect data on software faults but also in the fact that the software faults must be analyzed taking into account the system architecture and not only software modules. Maybe these difficulties account for the fact that the number of works on software faults during the operational phase is lower than the studies available for the development phase. Nevertheless, the study of the effects of actual software faults in the field is of utmost importance for our work, as this is just the kind of faults we want to emulate by fault injection.

The software dependability of Tandem systems are studied in [3, 4] and the impact of software defects on the availability of a large IBM system is presented in [11].

An important contribution to promote the collection and study of observed faults is the Orthogonal Defect Classification (ODC) [12]. ODC is a classification schema for software faults (i.e., defects) in which defects are classified into non-overlapping attributes and used as a source of information to understand and improve the software product and the software development process.

Several fault injection techniques have been proposed [13] and many fault injection studies have been published. However, only few studies have addressed the problem of injection of software faults [14, 15]. In spite of the fact that the issue of how accurately the injected faults emulate real software faults remains largely unknown, fault injection has been used with success in several research works where software faults are the most relevant class of faults. Examples of software weaknesses revealed by faults injected at random can be found in [16, 17].

Mutation testing is a specific form of fault injection that consists of creating different versions of a program by making small syntactic changes [18]. Mutation can be considered as a static fault injection technique, as the source code is changed instead of the program/system's state, as happens in classical fault injection. Mutation has been largely used for software testing. An experimental comparison of the errors and failure modes generated by actual software faults and mutations is presented in [19].

In [20] software faults such as corruption of instructions at machine code-level and specific programming errors have been inserted at random in the code to improve the design of a reliable write-back file cache.

To the best of our knowledge, only three studies focus on the specific problem of the accurate emulation of software faults by fault injection so far [5, 6, 21]. The first two studies propose the same basic set of rules for the generation of errors that emulate software faults. These rules are obtained from the analysis of field data about discovered software faults that have been classified using ODC. In [21] an experimental comparison between fault and error injection is presented and the evaluation is mainly directed towards the comparison of the costs of each approach. These papers are seminal papers somehow, as they give a contribution to the solution of the problem of emulation of software faults by fault injection, but they raise several open questions at the same time:

- If the errors generated by using the proposed rules were injected in a real system would they really emulate the expected software faults?

- Are existing SWIFI tools appropriate to inject the errors for the emulation of software faults? If not, is it possible to enhance these tools to achieve this goal?

- Is the correct emulation of software faults dependent on specific features of the code such as code size, complexity of data structures, recursive versus sequential code, and other features?

- Is there any possibility of turning away the need for field data on actual software faults to generate representative sets of faults?

Answering the above questions is the motivation behind the present work. Although the definite answers to some of those questions clearly need more comprehensive studies, the results presented in this paper reveal significant aspects of the problem.

3. Software fault emulation using SWIFI

The definition of software faults requires the notion of correctness of software. In a broad view, the correctness of software should be measured taking into account the end user/customer needs. However, the needs and degree of satisfaction of the user are too vague to be useful for our purposes. Typically, the development of a software product comprises the requirements, specification, design, code development, test, and product deployment. For the purpose of this work, it is assumed that the requirements and specification are correct (but the code is not correct).

A software fault can be characterized by the change in the code that is necessary to correct it. This is the notion of defect proposed in ODC [22]. In ODC a trigger and a type characterize a defect (fault). The trigger describes the general conditions that make the fault to be exposed and the type represents the fault in the source code. The following fault types in ODC are directly related to the code:

Assignment - values assigned incorrectly or not assigned;

Checking - missing or incorrect validation of data or incorrect loop or conditional statements;

Interface - errors in the interaction among components, modules, device drivers, call statements, etc;

Timing/serialization – missing or incorrect serialization of shared resources;

Algorithm - incorrect or missing implementation that can be fixed by (re)implementing an algorithm or data structure without the need for a design change;

Function - incorrect or missing implementation of a capability that affects a substantial amount of code and requires a formal design change to be corrected.

The classes of triggers defined in ODC are associated to common activities of the development process: review/inspection, function test, and system test. Only the system test class of triggers is relevant for our study, as it represents the broad environmental conditions when the faults are exposed during the operational use in the field. These general conditions (triggers) are startup/restart, workload volume/stress, recovery/exception, hardware/software configuration, and normal mode. The normal mode category means that the software fault has been exposed when everything was supposed to work normally. This is the trigger category relevant for our study as all the

experiments have been done with the target system working in normal conditions (i.e., it was not at startup, etc).

As mentioned above, a software fault is characterized by the necessary change in the source code to correct it. As the source code is normally written in a high-level language and the typical SWIFI tools inject faults at the machine code-level, it means that the fault classification and the fault emulation by fault injection are done at different abstraction levels (see figure 1).

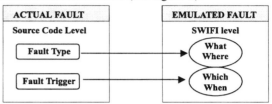

Figure 1 – Fault classification at source code level and fault emulation at SWIFI level.

In a typical SWIFI tool faults are defined according to three main classes of parameters: what (what should be changed/corrupted), where (where, in the code, should the change be applied), when (when, during the program execution, should the change be inserted). The traditional When parameter should, in our opinion, be decomposed in which (which instruction or event acts as fault trigger) and when (when, during the various executions of the trigger instruction or trigger event is the fault injected).

ODC fault types have a clear translation into the what and where fault injection parameters. However, ODC fault triggers cannot be used to define the SWIFI fault triggers because ODC triggers just represent general environmental conditions in which the faults should be injected.

The probability of a software fault resulting into a failure is heavily dependent on the operational profile. Assuming a fault exists, the probability of the faulty code to be executed is p1 (see figure 2). If the faulty code is executed, the probability of error generation is p2. If errors are generated, the probability of these errors resulting into a failure is p3. Thus, the probability of a software fault resulting into a failure is the product of p1, p2, and p3.

Figure 2 – Probability of a software fault exposure.

Ideally, the fault trigger should reproduce the chain reaction in figure 2. However, the need of accelerating the process suggests that errors should be injected instead of faults (p1 = p2 = 1) which leads us to the paramount question of the representativeness of the injected errors.

The error representativeness can be regarded in two different perspectives:

- *Representativeness concerning fault type:* The injected errors are considered software errors if they could have been caused by a real software fault of any type. That is, what is required is to avoid the injection of errors specific of other kinds of faults such as hardware faults.

- *Representativeness concerning fault trigger:* The injected errors should emulate the errors that would have been caused if the faulty code had been executed with the input data required to generate errors.

Software faults are then emulated by injecting errors (using SWIFI tools) defined in terms of the parameters that describe the What, Where, Which, and When attributes. The exact parameters depend on the SWIFI tool and the target system. As a general indication, the fault type is described by the attributes What and Where and the fault trigger is described by Which and When.

4. Experimental setup

4.1. Target system and the Xception fault injector

The target system is a Parsytec PowerXplorer with four PowerPC 601 processors running under the Parix, which a Unix like operating system for parallel machines. The system has no special fault tolerance mechanisms and is relatively simple, which makes it a good choice for the present experiments. The version of Xception used is targeted for the PowerPC 601, and the experiments are controlled by a host computer (a Sun/Solaris machine).

The Xception is described in detail in [23]. However, a very brief description is provided here to facilitate the discussion on the software fault emulation in the next sections. Xception uses the debugging and performance monitoring features existing in most of the modern processors to inject faults by software and to monitor the activation of the faults and their impact on the target system behavior. Faults are injected with minimum interference for the target application. The target application is not modified, no software traps are inserted, and it is not necessary to execute the target application in trace mode.

Xception provides a comprehensive set of fault triggers, including spatial and temporal fault triggers, and triggers related to the manipulation of data in memory. Faults injected by Xception can affect any process running on the target system and it is possible to inject faults in applications for which the source code is not available.

Xception also includes the Experiment Management software, which runs in the host system and is responsible for the fault definition, experiment execution control, outcome collection, and some preliminary results analysis (detailed analysis is performed off-line using MS Excel).

4.2. Sample programs

The programs used in this study are of two different types: several implementations of two programs resulting from the International Olympiads in Informatics (IOI) from ACM International Collegiate Programming Contest [24] and a program actually used in real life. The two contest programs are Camelot and JamesB and the other program is SOR. These programs represent different degrees of program complexity and different size and all of them are written in C.

Camelot – This program computes the minimum number of moves required to gather all the pieces of a chessboard in the same square. Only two kinds of pieces are considered: one king and a variable number of knights ranging from 0 to 63 knights. The size of the different versions of this program (made by the different teams) ranges from 200 to 360 lines of code.

JamesB – This program codifies strings according to a specific algorithm. A seed received as a parameter with each string determines the actual codification. The result is the coded version of the original string. The size of the available versions of this program is about 100 code lines.

SOR – This program is an implementation of a parallel algorithm to solve the Laplace equation over a grid. The algorithm is based on the over-relaxation scheme with red-black ordering. This program has near 2400 lines of code. The result is given in the form of a matrix.

5. Emulation of actual software faults

The goal of this section is to evaluate the possibilities of a SWIFI tool (the Xception) to emulate real software faults. To do that we need to have access to programs with known real software faults. The programs resulting from the IOI programming contest provide an easy source of software faults. Several factors make these programs an interesting source of software faults for this research:

- All the programs are written according to a formal, clear, and correct problem specification;
- The programs were written by skilled programmers;
- The contest gives us rapid access to several implementations from the same specification (237 teams in the IOI 98 contest). These alternative programs normally use different design strategies and algorithms, which makes it possible to compare the influence of different program control and data structures in the failure modes caused by the software faults;
- There is a test case (i.e., a set of data inputs and correct results) associated to each problem specification, which works as an acceptance criteria for correct programs from the contest judges' point of view. Only bugs found in programs that passed in the test cases were considered as representative of real faults.

The search for software faults among the programs produced in the contest was done following these steps:

1. The programs considered correct in the contest were selected (these programs passed the contest test case);

2. Selected programs were intensively tested by using a very thorough test case. This was achieved by running the programs a huge number of times with random input data sets. These tests may run for hours. Programs failing this intensive test have software faults;

Program	% Wrong results	% Correct results
C.team1	7.3%	92.7%
C.team2	16.9%	83.1%
C.team3	1.0%	99.0%
C.team4	30.8%	69.2%
C.team5	2.9%	97.1%
JB.team6	0.05%	99.95%
JB.team7	1.8%	98.2%

Table 1 – Failure symptoms of the real software faults.

3. Programs with software faults were then analyzed in detail to identify the fault. The input data that exposed the fault was used to help the bug identification.

Seven software faults have been identified in seven different programs. Five software faults were in the implementations of Camelot and two faults in the JamesB. The software faults have been analyzed and classified according to the following fault types (to simplify the identification Camelot programs are named as C.team# and JamesB named as JB.team#):

Assignment – 2 faults (JB.team6, C.team4);

Checking – 1 fault (C.team1);

Algorithm – 4 faults (JB.team7, C.team2, C.team3, C.team5).

The failure symptoms due to the software faults observed in the programs are presented in table 1. These results were obtained from the intensive tests and correspond to more than 10.000 runs for each program. Other failure modes such as program hangs or system crashes have not been observed in any of the programs.

One first comment is that the test case used in the programming contest is not very effective, as C.team2 and C.team4 failed quite often

and that was not detected by the contest test case. Nevertheless, from more than one hundred of correct (according to the contest test case) programs submitted to the intensive test, only the seven programs above failed.

To evaluate the possibility of accurate emulation of the actual software faults by using the Xception each fault was analyzed in order to determine the adequate Xception fault trigger and fault models. For the algorithm faults we concluded that the accurate emulation by the Xception (or any other machine code-level SWIFI tool) is simply not possible (this will be discussed further on). However, assignment and checking faults could in fact be emulated. In general, one fault can be emulated in several ways, using different possibilities of fault trigger and fault models.

To compare the fault emulation done by Xception with the actual faults, the correct version of each program (i.e. the version obtained after removing the bug) was executed

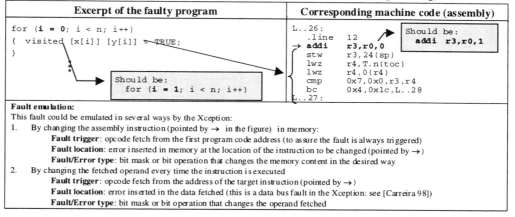

Figure 3 – Example of an assignment fault in the program C.team4.

with the same test case used in the faulty version. However, a fault was injected in each run to emulate the effects of the bug. If the results are the same in both runs it means Xception do emulate the fault accurately.

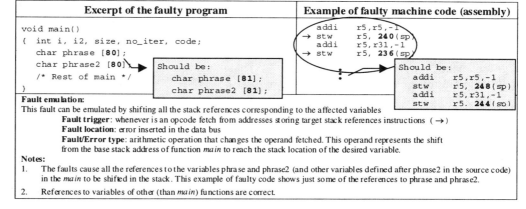

Figure 4 – Example of an assignment fault in the program JB.team6.

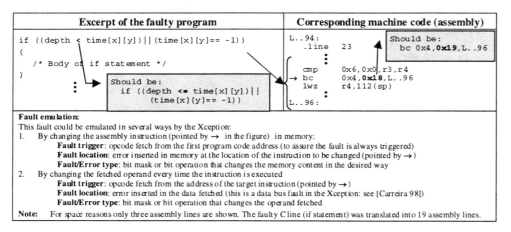

Excerpt of the faulty program	Corresponding machine code (assembly)

`if ((depth < time[x][y])||(time[x][y]== -1))`
`{`
`    /* Body of if statement */`
`}`
 	
Should be:
`    if ((depth <= time[x][y])||`
`              (time[x][y]== -1))`
	`L..94:`
	`    .line    23`
	
	`    cmp    0x6,0x0,r3,r4`
	`→   bc     0x4,0x18,L..96`
	`    lwz    r4,112(sp)`
	`L..96:`
	
	Should be:
	`    bc 0x4,0x19,L..96`

Fault emulation:
This fault could be emulated in several ways by the Xception:
1. By changing the assembly instruction (pointed by → in the figure) in memory:
    Fault trigger: opcode fetch from the first program code address (to assure the fault is always triggered)
    Fault location: error inserted in memory at the location of the instruction to be changed (pointed by →)
    Fault/Error type: bit mask or bit operation that changes the memory content in the desired way
2. By changing the fetched operand every time the instruction is executed
    Fault trigger: opcode fetch from the address of the target instruction (pointed by →)
    Fault location: error inserted in the data fetched (this is a data bus fault in the Xception: see [Carreira 98])
    Fault/Error type: bit mask or bit operation that changes the operand fetched
Note: For space reasons only three assembly lines are shown. The faulty C line (if statement) was translated into 19 assembly lines.

Figure 5 – Example of a checking fault in the program
C.team1.

For a better understanding of the way the discovered software faults have been emulated let us examine some of these faults in detail (see figures 3, 4, 5, and 6).

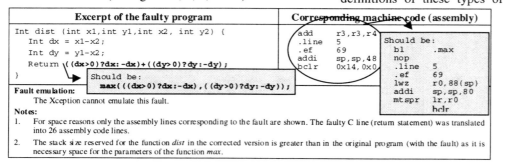

Excerpt of the faulty program	Corresponding machine code (assembly)

`Int dist (int x1,int y1,int x2, int y2) {`
`    Int dx = x1-x2;`
`    Int dy = y1-x2;`
`    Return ((dx>0)?dx:-dx)+((dy>0)?dy:-dy);`
`}`
 	
Should be:
`    max(((dx>0)?dx:-dx),((dy>0)?dy:-dy));`
	`add    r3,r3,r4`
	`.line    5`
	`.ef      69`
	`addi     sp,sp,48`
	`bclr     0x14,0x0`
	
	Should be:
	`bl       .max`
	`nop`
	`.line    5`
	`.ef      69`
	`lwz      r0,88(sp)`
	`addi     sp,sp,80`
	`mtspr    lr,r0`
	`bclr`

Fault emulation: The Xception cannot emulate this fault. **Notes:** 1. For space reasons only the assembly lines corresponding to the fault are shown. The faulty C line (return statement) was translated into 26 assembly code lines. 2. The stack size reserved for the function *dist* in the corrected version is greater than in the original program (with the fault) as it is necessary space for the parameters of the function *max*.

Figure 6 – Example of an algorithm fault in the program
C.team5.

The emulation of specific faults by the Xception requires manual intervention for determining specific locations in memory to set fault triggers or to insert errors. The loader provides this information. Another manual task is the definition of the right mask and bit level operation to insert the desired error.

The Xception could not entirely emulate the assignment fault shown in figure 4. The reason is in the fact that the fault trigger used (opcode fetch from a specified address) is implemented by using the processor breakpoint registers, which are only two in the PowerPC. Using the traditional SWIFI approach of inserting trap instructions to trigger the faults could solve this, but this technique is very intrusive. Another relevant aspect concerning the emulation of this fault is that it requires large manual intervention. Extra software tools to assist the definition of this kind of faults (assignment faults causing shifts in the stack) are required to make the process usable.

Figure 6 shows an example of an algorithm fault. In general algorithm faults cause considerable changes at the machine code-level and cannot be emulated by SWIFI tools. In some cases, algorithm faults can be decomposed in assignment and/or checking faults. For example, the fault in figure 6 corresponds to an incorrect assignment to the return parameter of function dist (it is assigned the sum of two values instead of the larger value). However, the emulation of algorithm faults by "equivalent" assignment/checking faults is very doubtful.

The ODC types function, interface, and timing/ serialization were not analyzed, as we didn't find software faults of these types in the used programs. However, considering the definitions of these types of faults we would say that function faults suffer the same problems as algorithm faults and cannot be accurately emulated by SWIFI tools. Interface faults are somehow similar to assignment faults (wrong assignments at the modules and function interface) and some of them can be emulated. The accurate emulation of timing/serialization faults is heavily dependent on the specific fault.

The results of this experiment can be summarized as follows:

A. Assignment and checking faults can (in general) be accurately emulated by Xception (or SWIFI tools);

B. The present version of Xception cannot emulate some assignment faults (faults affecting stack shifts) or the emulation requires high manual intervention. However, it is possible to define new Xception features to facilitate the accurate emulating of this set of faults (tools for assisting the fault definition, new fault triggers, and fault types);

C. A third set of faults cannot be emulated by the Xception and their emulation by SWIFI tools doesn't seem feasible. Algorithm faults and function faults fall in this category. This set of faults represents the limits of the Xception model (and SWIFI tools models) in emulating real software faults. Considered the field data results published in [5] these kind of faults (algorithm and function) accounts for nearly 44% of the software faults.

6. Emulation of classes of software faults

Much more important than the emulation of a specific software fault by fault injection is the emulation of faults of the same class. This goal requires two steps:

1. Definition of a set of rules for the generation of errors that emulate an entire class of faults (instead of a specific fault as in section 5);

2. Validation and tuning of these rules by comparing the impact of the errors injected using the rules with available data on the impact (failure modes) of real faults of the same class. Additionally, if the injected errors emulate the same class of software faults it is expected (at least as a hypothesis) to identify some patterns in terms of impact in the target system.

The rules proposed in [5] were used starting point for the experiments in this section and the experimental setup is basically the same as described in section 4.

6.1. What can be done with no field data

Even more ambitious than the injection of classes of software faults is the objective of injecting faults/errors that emulate the classes of faults most likely to affect a given program. The use of field data to guide the injection process presumes that it is possible to emulate classes of software faults by fault injection, which is not obvious. Furthermore, the need of having field data on previous faults to emulate software faults represents a strong limitation. This is due to the following reasons:

- Field data on previous software faults is not available in most cases;

- Field data is specific of the application/system in which it has been produced;

- When available it means that the product has already been delivered and has been being used for a long time, which means that the relevance of injecting faults for fault removal or fault forecast in that particular product is doubtful;

- Normally a software fault is registered only one time (when the fault is corrected), no matter the number of users that have experienced a failure due to that particular defect. This means that relevant information about the frequency of failures caused by a defect is normally not registered.

These limitations show the interest of investigating the possibilities of emulating software faults without relying on field data. The analysis of how the field data is used in [5] shows that field data is only used for two purposes: a) to distribute the injected errors by the software components and b) to choose the most common type of errors. All the other parameters are generated at random.

Existing studies [10, 9, 25] indicate that fault probability correlates with the software module complexity. This suggests that existing metrics (and tools) to predict the probability of a given module having software faults could be used when field data is not available. These metrics are based on static or dynamical aspects of the code and, in some cases, the metrics also include information from the development process. Software metrics can be used to choose the modules to inject faults or to decide on the number of faults to inject in each module. Obviously, the number of faults to inject in each module and the type of error can also be chosen at random, which means that all the possible software faults and locations are equally likely.

6.2. Programs, data sets, and result collection

A large set of programs has been used to evaluate the influence of aspects such as different algorithms for the same problem, code size, complexity of data structures, recursive versus non-recursive execution, and parallel versus sequential execution. Naturally, the programs used in section 5 in which we found real software faults of type assignment and checking were selected. The following table shows all the programs and the main reasons (features) why they have been selected.

Programs	Features
C.team1, C.team10	Recursive algorithms, about 280 lines, 1 real faults (corrected)
C.team2, C.team8	Non-recursive algorithms, about 250 lines
C.team9	Non-recursive algorithm, use many dynamic structures, about 250 lines
JB.team6	Non-recursive algorithms, 1 real fault (corrected), about 100 lines
JB.team11	Non-recursive algorithms (≠ from JB.team6), about 100 lines
SOR	Parallel program, real life program, larger size: 2400 lines

Table 2 – Target programs and main features.

A test case composed by 300 input data sets randomly generated has been used for all the programs of the same kind. That is, all the injections in all the Camelot (C.team#) programs, for example, used the same test case. In this way it is possible to compare the results of all the injections in the same program and the results of all the injections in different programs of the same type. Each test case corresponds to 300 runs of the program (each specific input data set) and one fault and the target system is rebooted between injections to assure a clean state.

The results collected are the failure modes (symptoms). The following failure modes are considered:

Correct results – Program terminated normally and the output is correct;

Incorrect results – Program terminated normally but the output is incorrect;

Program hang – The program hangs (possibly went into a dead loop) and was terminated by the experiment manager software after a timeout;

Program crash – The program terminated abnormally and generated errors detected by the system (incorrect instructions, etc).

6.3. The parameters what, where, which, when

The sets of errors to inject are described in terms of the parameters what, where, when, and which. These errors are injected at machine code-level (Xception level) and represent the actual data or instruction corruption injected. Obviously, we need to define a subset of error types to make the experiments tractable, as otherwise the number of faults to inject would be nearly infinite. Table 3 describes the error types in high-level language terms.

Type of fault	Correct	Change	Correct	Change	Correc	Changed	Correct	Change
Checking	>=	>	=	≠	[i]	[i-1]	[i]	[i+1]
	>	>=	≠	≠	Only for checking over arrays			
	<=	<	=	>=	<	<=	and	or
	true	false	false	true	=	<=	or	and
Assignment	value	value+	value	value-1	value	unassigned	value	random

Table 3 – Subset of injected error types.

Once the list of used error type is selected, the error parameters are generated in the following way, for each class of faults:

1. All possible fault locations were identified. This was done manually at the assembly level. To assist this process, the assignment and checking statements in the source code were first identified and the compiler facilities in terms of symbol tables and labels were used to help the identification of the assembly instructions corresponding to the assignment and checking statements;

2. Some fault locations were chosen at random from the list of all possible fault locations. These were the locations where the errors were injected (**where** parameter);

3. For each location all possible error types (among the subset previously defined) that can be applied were selected (**what** parameter). For example, in an assignment location four different faults are generated, one for each error type (The number of error types from table 3 that can be applied to each fault location depends on the actual instruction. This is particularly true for the checking error types);

4. The instructions selected to work as trigger for the injection were the same instructions selected as location to inject the fault (**which** parameter);

5. The fault was inserted every time the trigger instruction was executed (when parameter).

Table 4 shows the result of applying the above criteria to the used programs. A total number of 108.600 faults were injected. Each program run corresponds to one fault, no matter the number of times the fault is triggered during the program run.

6.4. Results and discussion

The failure mode results (total faults) are presented in figure 7 and figure 8 for assignment and checking faults respectively. Several aspects should be noted:

- The injected faults have a much stronger impact than typical software faults (only a relatively small percentage of the faults stay dormant and have not affected the system);

- One aspect not represented in the charts (figures 7 and 9) is that when the result of the programs is correct the faulty code (i.e., code affected by the error injected) has been executed. Thus, the reasons why the error generated did not affect the results are related to the input data sets;

- There are no clear patterns in the failure mode results when all the faults of the same type are considered

Program	Assignment			Checking		
	Possible locations	Chosen locations	Injected faults (all error types)	Possible locations	Chosen locations	Injected faults (all error types)
C.team1	92	8	9600	49	8	4800
C.team2	63	5	6000	45	6	7800
C.team8	84	8	9300	31	9	3300
C.team9	87	9	10800	53	9	3300
C.team10	88	9	10800	43	8	4200
JB.team6	29	5	6000	10	5	3300
JB.team11	21	5	5700	11	5	2100
SOR	363	12	14400	195	12	7200

Table 4 – Injected faults.

- The influence of specific features of the programs (code size, algorithm, recursive, etc) is not evident in the global results. However, for the assignment faults

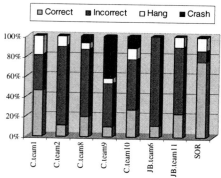

Figure 7 – Failure modes observed in each program for assignment faults.

injected in recursive programs (C.team1 and C.team10) and in the large SOR program a higher percentage of correct results was obtained;

- The program C.team9, which intensively uses dynamic structures (i.e., structures such as linked lists that use intensively memory allocation/free functions), has a high percentage of crashes;

- The SOR program, which is a parallel program, seems to be quite sensitive to checking faults, as a large percentage caused crashes have been observed.

- The percentages of crashes and program hangs observed for the JamesB programs are very low. A possible explanation is in the fact that these programs are small (around 100 C code lines) and very simple, when compared to the other programs.

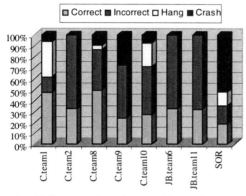

Figure 8 – Failure modes observed in each program for checking faults.

Figure 9 and figure 10 show the failure modes for each error type (What parameter). In figure 10 the error types are represented by a pair of symbols in which the first represents the correct checking and the second the result of the corruption (e.g., <= < means that the error caused a <= checking to be changed into a <). While the results for each error type for the emulation of assignment faults are relatively similar, the same does not apply to the error types used to emulate checking faults. The percentage of correct results in some error types is very low or even null. For example, when the checking assignment is changed from != to = or from true to false the percentage of correct values is very low. On the other hand, when the error injected turns a < into a <= the percentage of correct values is much higher.

Although the results presented in figure 10 are expected, we cannot immediately conclude that some of

the error types do not emulate software errors. We should remember that the other parameters (where, which, and when) play an important role as they represent the fault locations and the fault triggers.

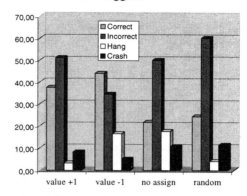

Figure 9 – Failure modes observed for assignment faults (all faults).

The accuracy of the injections should be analyzed in the two perspectives discussed in section 3: fault type and fault trigger. It is easy to understand that random fault triggers (which and when) are not representative of real software faults. Faults injected in this way represent naïve software faults similar to the ones easily found in ad-hoc testing. A central question seems to be the independent evaluation of the accuracy of the fault types (what; where) and the fault triggers (which; when).

Another interesting aspect is that the injected errors also emulate hardware faults, which might explain the general small percentage of correct results. In fact, as mentioned in section 3, it is very difficult or even impossible to prevent injected errors from emulating software and hardware faults at the same time. The random fault trigger used is also typical from hardware faults. Thus, the failure modes observed have the contribution of the hardware faults that are also emulated by the injected errors. In fact, previous experiments using Xception [23] or using hardware (pin-level) fault injectors [26] shown that hardware faults can cause failure modes with a large percentage of incorrect results and system crashes.

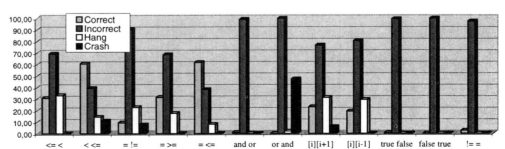

Figure 10 – Failure modes observed for checking faults (all faults).

425

7. Conclusions

This paper presents an experimental study on the emulation of software faults by fault injection. A set of real software faults found in different programs has been compared with faults injected by the Xception to evaluate the accuracy of the injected faults. The results of this experiment revealed three different kinds of software faults: i) faults that can be accurately emulated by the Xception; ii) faults that could be emulated if Xception was improved with extra fault triggers, fault models, and tools to avoid the need of manual fault definition iii) faults that could never be emulated by Xception (or any other SWIFI tool).

A second issue investigated was the possibility of emulation of all the faults of the same class. The use of field data about real faults was discussed and software metrics were suggested as an alternative to guide the injection process when field data was not available. A set of rules for the injection of errors meant to emulate software faults were evaluated. For each studied class of faults a large number of faults (more than 100.000) were injected according to the set of rules. The impact these faults has been studied in detail and the results obtained with the faults injected to emulate faults of the same class were compared. Results show that the injected faults have a much stronger impact than typical software faults, as only a small percentage of the faults stay dormant and have not affected the system. Another result is that there are no clear patterns in the failure mode results when all the faults of the same type are considered. The analysis of the results obtained for each error type injected reveled significant differences. However, the random fault triggers used seem to be the cause of the strong impact of the faults in the target system and in the program results. The presented results also show the influence in the fault emulation of aspects such as code size, complexity of data structures, and recursive versus sequential execution.

Further research is needed to understand the fault triggers required for the emulation of subtle software faults such as the ones that escape comprehensive test procedures. A promising approach seems to be devising ways to perform an independent evaluation of the accuracy of the fault types and the fault triggers.

8. References

[1] J. Arlat et al, "Fault Injection and Dependability Evaluation of Fault Tolerant Systems", IEEE Transactions on Computers, vol. 42, no. 8, pp. 919-923, Aug. 1993.

[2] R. K. Iyer, "Experimental Evaluation", Special Issue FTCS-25 Silver Jubilee, 25th IEEE Symp. on Fault Tolerant Computing, FTCS-25, pp. 115-132, Jun. 1995.

[3] J. Gray, "A Census of Tandem Systems Availability Between 1985 and 1990", IEEE Transactions on Reliability, vol. 39, no. 4, pp. 409-418, Oct. 1990.

[4] I. Lee and R. K. Iyer, "Software Dependability in the Tandem GUARDIAN System", IEEE Transactions on Software Engineering, vol. 21, no. 5, pp. 455-467, May 1995.

[5] J. Christmansson and R. Chillarege, "Generation of an Error Set that Emulates Software Faults", Proc. 26th Fault Tolerant Comp. Symp., FTCS-26, Sendai, Japan, pp. 304-313, Jun. 1996.

[6] J. Christmansson and P. Santhanam, "Error Injection Aimed at Fault Removal in Fault Tolerance Mechanisms – Criteria for Error Selection using Field Data on Software Faults", Proc. of the 7th IEEE Int. Symp. on Software Reliability Engineering, ISSRE'96, Oct. 30 to Nov. 2, 1996, New York, USA, 1996.

[7] M. R. Lyu, "Handbook of Software Reliability Engineering", IEEE Comp. Society Press, McGraw-Hill, 1996.

[8] J. Musa, "Software Reliability Engineering", McGraw-Hill, 1996.

[9] T. Khoshgoftaar et. al., "Process Measures for Predicting Software Quality", High Assurance Systems Engineering Workshop, HASE'97, Washington D.C., USA, IEEE CS Press, HASE'97, 1997.

[10] J. P. Hudepohl et. al., "EMERALD: A Case Study in Enhancing Software Reliability"" Proc. of IEEE 8th Int. Symp. Soft. Reliability Engineering, ISSRE'98, pp. 85-91, Nov. 1998.

[11] M. Sullivan and R. Chillarege, "Software defects and their impact on systems availability – A study of field failures on operating systems", Proc. 21st Fault Tolerant Comp. Symp., FTCS-21, pp. 2-9, Jun. 1991.

[12] R. Chillarege, I. S. Bhandari, J. K. Chaar, M. J. Halliday, D. Moebus, B. Ray, M. Wong, "Orthogonal Defect Classification – A Concept for In-Process Measurement", IEEE Trans. Soft. Eng., vol. 18, no. 11, pp. 943-956, Nov. 1992.

[13] Mei-Chen Hsueh, T. Tsai, R. K. Iyer, "Fault Injection Techniques and Tools", IEEE Computer, vol. 30, no. 4, pp. 75-82, Apr. 1997.

[14] J. Hudak, B. Suth, D. Siewiorek, and Z. Segall, "Evaluation and Comparison of Fault-Tolerant Software Techniques", IEEE Trans. on Reliability, vol. 42, no. 2, pp. 190-204, Jun. 1993.

[15] W. Kao, "Experimental Study of Software Dependability", Ph.D. Thesis, Technical Report CRHC-94-16, Department of Computer Science, Univ. of Illinois at Urbana-Champaign, Illinois, USA, 1994.

[16] J. Voas, et al, "Predicting how Badly 'Good' Software can Behave", IEEE Software, 1997.

[17] D. Blough and T. Torii, "Fault-Injection-Based Testing of Fault-Tolerant Algorithms in Message-Passing Parallel Computers", 27th IEEE Fault Tolerant Computing Symp., FTCS-27, Seattle, USA, pp. 258-267, Jun. 1997.

[18] R. DeMillo et al, "An Extended Overview of the Mothra Software Testing Environment", Proc. ACM SIGSOFT/IEEE 2nd Workshop on Soft. Testing, Verification, and Analysis, pp. 142-151, Jul. 1988.

[19] M. Daran and P. Thévenod-Fosse, "Software Error Analysis: A Real Case Study Involving Real Faults and Mutations", Proc. of 3rd Symp. on Software Testing and Analysis, ISSTA-3, San Diego, USA, pp. 158-171, Jan. 1996.

[20] Wee T. Ng, Peter M. Chen, "Systematic improvement of fault tolerance in the RIO file cache", Proc. 30th Fault Tolerant Computing Symp., FTCS-29, Madison, WI, USA, Jun. 1999.

[21] J. Christmansson, M. Hiller, and M. Rimén, "An Experimental comparison of Fault and Error Injection", Proc. 9th IEEE Int. Symp. on Software Reliability Engineering, ISSRE'98, pp. 369-378, USA, 1996.

[22] R. Chillarege, "Orthogonal Defect Classification", Chapter 9 of "Handbook of Software Reliability Engineering", Michael R. Lyu Ed., IEEE Computer Society Press, McGrow-Hill, 1995

[23] J. Carreira, H. Madeira, and J. G. Silva, "Xception: Software Fault Injection and Monitoring in Processor Functional Units", IEEE Transactions on Software Engineering, vol. 24, no. 2, Feb. 1998.

[24] Int. Olympiads Informatics, http://olympiads.win.tue.nl/ioi/

[25] S. Benlarbi, K. eman, N. Goel, "Issues in Validating Object-Oriented Metrics for Early Risk Prediction", Dig. Fast Abst, 10th Int. Symp. on Software Reliability Engineering, ISSRE'99, Boca Raton, Florida, USA, pp. 17-18, Nov. 1999.

[26] H. Madeira and J. G. Silva, "Experimental evaluation of the fail-silent behavior in computers without error masking", Proc. 24th Fault Tolerant Comp. Symp., FTCS 24, Austin, USA, Jun. 1994, pp. 350-359.

Reliability Testing of Applications on Windows NT

Timothy Tsai
Reliable Software Technologies*
21351 Ridgetop Circle, Suite 400
Dulles, VA 20166 USA
ttsai@rstcorp.com

Navjot Singh
Bell Labs Research, Lucent Technologies
600 Mountain Ave, Rm. 2B-413
Murray Hill, NJ 07974 USA
singh@research.bell-labs.com

Abstract

The DTS (Dependability Test Suite) fault injection tool can be used to (1) obtain fault injection-based evaluation of system reliability, (2) compare the reliability of different applications, fault tolerance middleware, and platforms, and (3) provide feedback to improve the reliability of the target applications, fault tolerance middleware, and platforms. This paper describes the architecture of the tool as well as the procedure for using the tool. Data from experiments with the DTS tool used on the Apache web server, the Microsoft IIS web server, and the Microsoft SQL Server, along with the Microsoft Cluster Server (MSCS) and Bell Labs watchd *(part of NT-SwiFT) fault tolerance packages is presented to demonstrate the utility of the tool. The observations drawn from the data also illustrate the strengths and weaknesses of the tested applications and fault tolerance packages with respect to their reliability.*

1. Introduction

Microsoft Windows NT is becoming a platform of choice for many applications, including services with dependability requirements. While the advantages of NT include decreased cost and leveraging of commercial development, testing, and support, the dependability of NT is a concern, especially compared to Unix systems that have traditionally formed the foundation for many high dependability products. In order to address this concern, several vendors, including Microsoft [10] and Bell Labs [13], have produced high availability software solutions that mostly depend on resource and process monitoring coupled with application restarts to handle error conditions.

The available commercial solutions all claim to increase availability by tolerating a variety of faults. However, these claims are usually not substantiated by rigorous testing but rather are based on a combination of analytical modeling, simulation, component analysis, and experience.

One significant obstacle to the task of systematic testing of system dependability, in terms of either availability or another quantity, is the lack of easy-to-use fault injection tools. Fault injection is a necessity when testing the robustness of a system to unintended or unexpected events, because such events are often difficult to produce through traditional testing methods. This work addresses the need for an easy-to-use fault injection tool that can be used for a variety of software projects based on Windows NT.

The Dependability Test Suite (DTS) is a tool for testing the error and failure detection and recovery functionality of a server application. Most of the code for the tool has been written in Java to produce a simple, yet practical graphical interface and to facilitate portability among different applications.

This paper describes the DTS fault injection tool and illustrates its use with actual applications. The DTS tool is described in Section 3. Section 4 gives the results of experiments to illustrate the use of the DTS tool in (1) comparing the reliability of fault tolerance middleware, (2) comparing the reliability of applications with similar functionality, and (3) providing useful feedback to improve the target system. A summary and ideas for future work are given in Section 5.

2. Related Work

The current state of the art in fault injection includes many fault injection mechanisms and tools. Iyer [6] and Voas [17] provide good summaries of many techniques and tools, as well as background and further references.

DTS depends on a method of fault injection called *software-implemented fault injection* (SWIFI). Instead of using hardware fault injectors or simulation environments, SWIFI tools use software code to emulate the effects of hardware and software faults on a real system. Such tools include FIAT [1], FERRARI [7], FINE [8], FTAPE [15],

---

*This work was performed while the author was with Bell Labs Research, Lucent Technologies, Murray Hill, NJ, USA.

427

DOCTOR [5], Xception [2], and MAFALDA [12]. These tools have been implemented for a variety of operating systems, including many Unix variants and real-time operating systems. In contrast to DTS, none of these tools were implemented on Windows NT, although the architectures of these tools do not preclude such an implementation. Rather, interest in Windows NT and its reliability have recently begun to increase. Also, many of these tools focus on the reliability of the operating system or the platform rather than the reliability of applications. Fuzz [11] is one fault injection tool that tested the reliability of Unix utilities, applications, and services.

The basic DTS architecture is not dependent on a particular fault injection mechanism. However, the initial DTS tool implementation is based on the interception of library calls and corruption of library call parameters. This method of fault injection is not unique. The Ballista [9] tool uses a similar technique to test the robustness of operating systems by fault injecting a set of common system calls used to access the file system. The Ballista work was performed on machines running Mach and various flavors of Unix. Ghosh [4] presents a tool for testing the reliability and robustness of Windows NT software applications. It should be noted that this fault injection technique injects faults during the execution of the target programs and therefore is very different from mutation testing [3], which injects faults into source code before compilation.

None of these tools or studies injects faults into high availability systems. Thus, the focus of the testing is mostly on the target applications or the OS, in the case of Ballista. In addition, most of the tools were developed specifically for the types of fault injection performed, rather than being modular to be compatible with a variety of fault models and target programs.

3. DTS

The main goals in designing the DTS fault injection tool were ease of use, automation, extensibility, portability, and most importantly, the ability to produce useful results. These considerations were important in determining the architecture, coding language, and user interface.

The tool is distributed with the management and user interface software residing on the control machine and the fault injection mechanism, workload generator, and data collector present on a separate target machine. This separation of the control and target machines is necessary if there is a possibility of a machine crash caused by an injected fault. Otherwise, a machine crash would require human intervention to restart the testing process. In addition, a distributed design allows for testing of distributed systems, especially if failover may occur or if correlated faults on multiple machines are to be injected. Nonetheless, although the tool is distributed in nature, it may be used with all components on a single machine if none of the above issues is pertinent.

The majority of the DTS code is written in Java. The Java language includes many features that facilitate fast code development. These features include socket creation and use, thread management, object-oriented software reuse, convenient graphical libraries, and portability. The small portion of the code that could not be implemented in Java uses the Java Native Interface (JNI) and C. The JNI-implemented code is used for process control and other system-dependent tasks such as Windows NT event log access. For portability reasons, Java does not support a notion of process identifiers (PID's), which is needed to properly terminate processes, especially those that have been fault injected and therefore may not be responding to normal termination messages.

DTS is controlled via a graphical interface and a set of configuration files. One main configuration file is used to specify test parameters such as timeout periods, a fault list file name, and workload parameters. The fault list file contains a list of faults to be injected. Workloads are specified by creating parameter files with names of applications or services to execute or by creating Java classes that are used by the DTS workload generator. More details on the DTS architecture are contained in [14]. The user's manual [16] contains detailed information about the steps needed to configure and to use the tool.

The DTS tool injects faults by corrupting the input parameters to library calls. The resulting errors emulate the effects of several different types of faults, including application design and coding defects and unintended interactions of the application with the environment and nonstandard input. For the results in Section 4, the main goals of the experiments are to compare different applications and fault tolerance middleware. Thus, the main considerations for selecting faults are the ability to trigger error detection and recovery, the ability to discover failure coverage holes, and reproducibility. Other experiments that aim to produce a characterization of a single system's reliability (e.g., in terms of a reliability or availability estimate) will require a real-world profile of the faults being modeled.

The *workload* is the combined system resource usage (e.g., usage of operating system data structures, communication ports, etc.) caused by the execution of the application programs, the fault tolerance middleware, and the operating system. A *workload generator* is a set of programs that initiates the programs and creates the program inputs and environments in a controlled and reproducible manner to generate a particular workload. DTS assume that the workload is created by a client-server set of programs. This assumption is valid for many applications of interest because reliability concerns are particularly important for server programs. The server program is also referred to as the "target program" because the focus of the fault injections is to evaluate the reliability of the server program, in the context of the operating system, fault tolerance middleware, and the client program. Note that the client program affects the overall reliability of the client-server system because client-initiated actions, such as client request retires, may be required for correct operation in the presence of faults. Non client-server types of workload scenarios are also supported by DTS, including applications with direct user interaction. However, some additional coding of Java classes may be necessary.

The DTS data collector presents results that include the following:

- Outcome: The outcome for each injected fault is one of the following:
  1. Normal success: The server was able to provide correct responses to all requests without any server restarts or request retransmissions.
  2. Server restart with success: After a restart of the server, the server provided a correct response.
  3. Server restart and client request retry with success: After a restart of the server and the retransmission of at least one client request, the server provided a correct response.
  4. Client request retry with success: After at least one client request was retransmitted, the server provided a correct response.
  5. Failure: At least one of the client requests did not succeed, either because no response was received or an incorrect response was received. This means that the server has failed, and the fault tolerance middleware, if present, has not prevented the failure of the server.

- Response time: The total time for the client and server programs to complete.
- Detailed results: The specific response to each individual request.

Most of the results are client-oriented, which means that most of the results can be determined by examining the client program behavior. Usually the client program is a synthetic program that is specifically written for DTS. Some results, such as whether the server program has been restarted, cannot be determined from examining the client program output. The determination of server program restarts is dependent on the middleware used to perform the restart. Some middleware, such as Microsoft Cluster Server [10], write output to the Windows NT event log. Other middleware, such as NT-SwiFT [13], create a separate log file.

Figure 1 shows the sequence of actions performed by the DTS tool for an experiment. An experiment consists of a series of workload sets (e.g., all faults for Apache, for IIS, and for SQL Server). Each workload set consists of a set of fault injection runs. A fault injection run includes the actions associated with the injection of a single fault. For each workload (W), a set of faults is injected. The set of faults depends on the set of functions to inject (F), the number of parameters for a particular function (P), the number of iterations to inject per function (I), and the number of fault types (T). This means that for a fault injection run, the workload programs are started, one fault is injected, and the workload programs are terminated. The fault injection run is repeated until all parameters of all functions have been injected with all fault types (actually, some faults are skipped if DTS determines that the fault will probably not be activated).

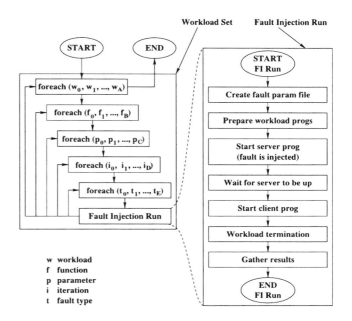

Figure 1. Experiment flow chart

4. Experimental results

To demonstrate the utility of the DTS tool, several experiments were performed. The server programs studied were (1) Apache web server version 1.3.3 for Win32, (2) Microsoft Internet Information Server (IIS) version 3.0, and (3) Microsoft SQL Server version 7. Although IIS can serve as an HTTP server, an FTP server, and a gopher server, only the HTTP functionality was tested in these experiments.

The first three programs were executed as NT services in three different configurations: (1) as a stand-alone service, (2) with Microsoft Cluster Server (MSCS), and (3) with the watchd component of NT-SwiFT. All experiments were conducted on the same machines. The hardware platform was a 100 MHz Pentium PC with 48 MB of memory running Windows NT Enterprise Server 4.0 with Service Pack 4. Additional experiments were conducted on a faster 400

MHz Pentium II PC with 128 MB of memory running Windows NT Enterprise Server 4.0 with Service Pack 4. Only the results for the slower 100 MHz Pentium machine are presented here because the faster machine was not yet equipped with MSCS in our lab. However, on the faster machine, the results for Apache, IIS, and SQL Server as stand-alone services and with watchd were essentially identical to those on the slower machine.

For each server program, a simple client program was created to send requests to the server program. For the Apache and IIS web servers, the HttpClient program sends two types of requests: (1) an HTTP request for a 115 kB static HTML file and (2) an HTTP request for a 1 kB static HTML file via the Common Gateway Interface (CGI). For the SQL Server, the SqlClient program sends an SQL select request based on a single table. Both HttpClient and SqlClient check the correctness of the server reply. If the reply is incorrect or if the reply is not received within a timeout period (a default of 15 seconds), the request is retried. A second retry is attempted if necessary. Each client program waits 15 seconds before attempting a retry. After a correct reply is received or the third attempt fails, the client program outputs information about the success or failure of the requests and the number of retries attempted.

For the NT programs, faults were injected by intercepting all calls to the functions in KERNEL32.dll. On our machine, KERNEL32.dll contains 681 functions. Of those 681 functions, 130 functions had no parameters and thus were not candidates for function parameter corruption. The remaining 551 functions were injected. To decrease the total time for the experiments, only the first invocation of the each function was injected (i.e., the CreateEventA() function is injected the first time it is called, but not the second or subsequent times). Further invocations can also be injected, but preliminary experiments showed that such injections produced similar results. For each function, each function parameter was injected with three types of faults: (1) reset all bits to zero, (2) set all bits to one, and (3) flip all bits (i.e., one's complement for the parameter value). Each parameter of every function is injected with these three types of faults. Thus, for functions with two parameters, 6 different faults will be injected (2 parameters with 3 fault types for each parameter). Only one fault is injected for each execution of the server program. Although these types of corruption may seem simplistic, they were already effective in differentiating among different workloads (e.g., MSCS vs. watchd) and in helping to discover bugs that lead to failure scenarios. It may be interesting to introduce additional types of corruption based on data types (e.g., treating pointers and Boolean variables differently). However, this requires symbolic information and is compiler dependent, thus affecting the portability of the fault injection method.

Three server programs were studied in the experiments: the Apache web server, the Microsoft IIS web server, and the Microsoft SQL Server. Each was executed as an NT service (1) with no fault-tolerance middleware, (2) with MSCS, and (3) with watchd. It should be noted that the outcome of these experiments is dependent on the workload (especially the requests issued by the client and the configuration of the application) and the specific faults that are injected.

A particular server program will not necessarily call all functions in a DLL. In fact, the majority of functions in KERNEL32.dll are not called. Table 1 shows the number of activated functions for each workload. See Section 4.1 for an explanation of Apache1 and Apache2. To shorten the total time for the experiments, if an injected function is not called, all other injections for that function will be skipped because it is assumed that the function will also not be called if the server program is rerun for the next fault.

Table 1. Number of called KERNEL32.dll **functions per workload**

Server Program	Fault-Tolerance Middleware		
	None	MSCS	watchd
Apache1	13	17	13
Apache2	22	24	22
IIS	76	76	70
SQL	71	74	70

4.1. Comparison of fault tolerance middleware packages

Figure 2 shows NT results for comparisons of the Apache web server, the IIS web server, and the SQL Server as stand-alone NT services, with MSCS, and with watchd. For the Apache web server, the NT service consists of multiple processes. The Apache web server was specifically configured to start only two processes for the purposes of these experiments. The first process is a management process that spawns child processes that actually service requests. By default, Apache spawns multiple child processes. Since the tool only targets one process for injection, if one of the other child processes picks up the request, then injected faults may not be activated in a reproducible manner. Configuring Apache for only one child process guarantees that the same child process will pick up the request each time, thus ensuring reproducible results. Two sets of results are given for injections into the Apache web server, one set for injections into the first process (labeled as "Apache1" in this paper) and a second set for injection into the child process (labeled

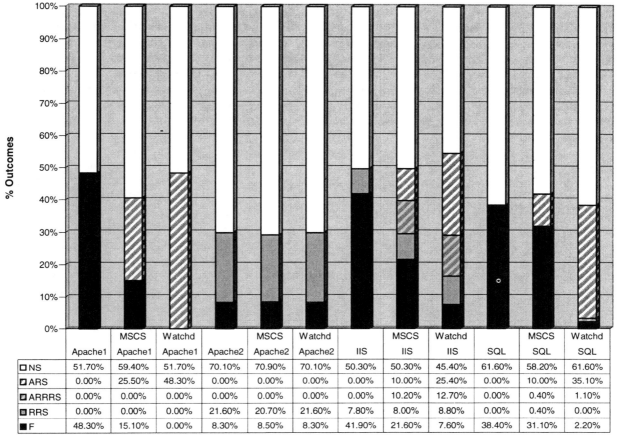

		MSCS	Watchd		MSCS	Watchd		MSCS	Watchd		MSCS	Watchd
	Apache1	Apache1	Apache1	Apache2	Apache2	Apache2	IIS	IIS	IIS	SQL	SQL	SQL
☐ NS	51.70%	59.40%	51.70%	70.10%	70.90%	70.10%	50.30%	50.30%	45.40%	61.60%	58.20%	61.60%
▨ ARS	0.00%	25.50%	48.30%	0.00%	0.00%	0.00%	0.00%	10.00%	25.40%	0.00%	10.00%	35.10%
▨ ARRRS	0.00%	0.00%	0.00%	0.00%	0.00%	0.00%	0.00%	10.20%	12.70%	0.00%	0.40%	1.10%
▥ RRS	0.00%	0.00%	0.00%	21.60%	20.70%	21.60%	7.80%	8.00%	8.80%	0.00%	0.40%	0.00%
■ F	48.30%	15.10%	0.00%	8.30%	8.50%	8.30%	41.90%	21.60%	7.60%	38.40%	31.10%	2.20%

FT Middleware/Server Program

NS = Normal Success
ARS = Application Restart with Success
ARRRS = Appication Restart and Request Retry with Success

RRS = Request Retry with Success
F = Failure

Figure 2. Standalone/MSCS/watchd comparisons for Windows NT

as "Apache2"). IIS and SQL server both consist of a single process and are labeled as "IIS" and "SQL" respectively.

Figure 2 shows NT results respectively for Apache1, Apache2, IIS, and SQL. Each figure shows the results for one workload as a stand-alone service, with MSCS, and with watchd. The normalized outcomes of the workload sets are displayed graphically in the charts and numerically below the charts. The possible outcomes are the five outcomes described in Section 3. Each outcome is given as a percentage of the total number of activated faults for that particular workload set. It should be noted that different workload sets, even for the same server program can produce a different number of activated faults, due to the effect of the fault tolerance middleware and the influence of non-determinism inherent in the server programs. However, these effects do not change the conclusions that can be drawn from the data. The faults injected into the extra functions that are called by each server program due to the fault tolerance middleware all result in normal success outcomes,

and only one function exhibited non-deterministic behavior: zeroing out all bits in the nNumberOfBytesToRead parameter for ReadFileEx() for SQL Server with the original version of watchd sometimes caused a detected error and sometimes caused a successful restart.

Several interesting observations can be made from Figure 2. First, perhaps the most important and obvious observation is that both MSCS and watchd are effective in increasing the reliability of all three server programs. The solid black portions of the figures represent the fault injection runs that resulted in failures, i.e., cases where the server program was not able to produce the correct response even after repeated client request retries. The failure percentages for all server programs decreased markedly when MSCS or watchd was used. In fact, for Apache1, all failure outcomes were eliminated using watchd.

The effectiveness of MSCS and watchd in reducing the number of failures is attributable to their ability to detect situations in which the monitored server program is malfunctioning and then to initiate a recovery action, which entails a server program restart for these experiments. Discounting the effects of non-determinism and additional activated faults caused by using MSCS and watchd, the number of normal success and request retry with success remain essentially the same for each server program. The difference is reflected in the portion of failure outcomes that become success with restart outcomes due to the MSCS and watchd restart mechanisms.

Figure 2 also reveals the effectiveness of the Apache architecture in handling faults. The Apache web server consists of multiple processes. The first process (Apache1) functions as a management process. Its duties include spawning the additional processes (Apache2) that actually service incoming web requests. The first process does not service any web requests itself. If one of the Apache2 processes dies, the Apache1 process will spawn another Apache2 process. This failure detection and restart mechanism within Apache is similar to that for MSCS and watchd. For this reason, MSCS and watchd, are effective with the Apache1 process but have no effect on the Apache2 process. The reason for this lack of efficacy is that both MSCS and watchd only monitor the first process that is started for any application. Thus, the child processes that are spawned by the first process are not monitored. Because the Apache1 process does not service any web requests, request retries produce no additional success outcomes, as seen in Figure 2. In addition, because the Apache2 process is not monitored by MSCS or watchd, no restarts initiated by MSCS or watchd occur. However, restarts of the Apache2 process by the Apache1 process do occur and are manifested as normal success and request retry with success outcomes.

Figure 2 shows that while both MSCS and watchd decrease the number of failure outcomes, watchd does a much better job for the fault set used. In fairness to MSCS, only the generic service resource monitor is used. A custom service resource monitor that is specially tailored to interact with and monitor all aspects of the IIS and SQL Server programs would probably improve the MSCS results. However, Microsoft only provides an API for creating the custom resource monitors and not the actual custom resource monitors. Thus, the comparison between MSCS and watchd is based on the default MSCS and watchd packages.

4.2. Comparison of applications with similar functionality

From the experimental data, some interesting observations about the relative reliability and performance characteristics of Apache and IIS can be made. Figure 3 shows the outcomes of the fault injection runs for Apache and IIS as stand-alone services, with MSCS, and with watchd. The Apache results are a combination of the Apache1 and Apache2 results because both Apache processes must be considered in a comparison to IIS, which includes its total functionality in a single process. The Apache1 and Apache2 results are weighted based on the relative number of activated faults for each process. Figure 3 shows that the Apache web server exhibits a lower percentage of failure outcomes than IIS as a stand-alone service, with MSCS, and with watchd. As a stand-alone service and with MSCS, the occurrence of failure outcomes for IIS is twice that for Apache. However, if watchd is used, then the difference is not as great (7.60% vs. 5.80%) because far fewer faults result in failure with watchd.

Table 1 shows that many more functions are activated for IIS than for Apache. To view Apache and IIS on a more common basis, Table 2 compares Apache to IIS counting only faults that were activated for both programs. Fewer faults were activated for the Apache1 process because the Apache2 process provides most of the web serving functionality. The third row of data shows the Apache1 and Apache2 outcomes added together. As with Figure 3, Apache exhibits fewer failures than IIS as a stand-alone service, with MSCS, and with watchd. However, the difference is even more pronounced (e.g., 5.7% vs. 26.0% failures for Apache vs. IIS as stand-alone services compared to 20.58% vs. 41.90% in Figure 3).

It is often useful to consider performance in the presence of faults. Figure 4 shows the average response times for Apache and IIS as stand-alone services, with MSCS, and with watchd. The response times are grouped based on the outcomes of the fault injection runs. The outcome types are the same those as in Figures 2 and 3 with one exception. Failure outcomes are further subdivided into two outcomes: (1) Failures where a response is received from the server program, but the response is incorrect and (2) failures where no response is received. Obviously, if no response is received, the response time will be infinite, and therefore these faults are omitted from Figure 4. No occurrences of a particular outcome exist in some cases. The response times are in seconds and are given with corresponding 95% confidence intervals (shown as error bars in the figure).

Some observations about the relative performance of Apache and IIS can be draw from Figure 4. First, there is no appreciable difference in the performance overhead due to the use of MSCS or watchd in either application. Second, for faults that result in normal success outcomes, Apache is faster, especially when MSCS is used. The normal success outcome average response times for Apache and IIS as stand-alone services (14.21 vs. 18.94 seconds) are essentially the same as the corresponding average response times for Apache and IIS when no faults are injected. Third, the average response times associated with applica-

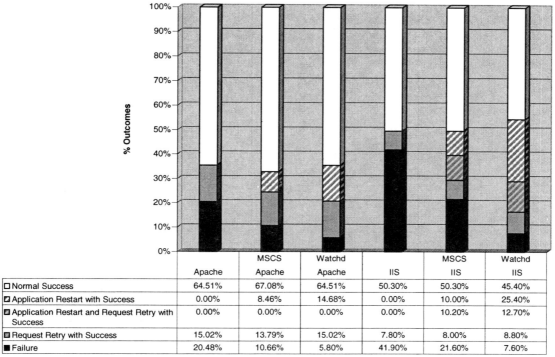

	Apache	MSCS Apache	Watchd Apache	IIS	MSCS IIS	Watchd IIS
☐ Normal Success	64.51%	67.08%	64.51%	50.30%	50.30%	45.40%
◩ Application Restart with Success	0.00%	8.46%	14.68%	0.00%	10.00%	25.40%
◪ Application Restart and Request Retry with Success	0.00%	0.00%	0.00%	0.00%	10.20%	12.70%
▥ Request Retry with Success	15.02%	13.79%	15.02%	7.80%	8.00%	8.80%
■ Failure	20.48%	10.66%	5.80%	41.90%	21.60%	7.60%

FT Middleware/Server Program

Figure 3. Comparison of Apache to IIS

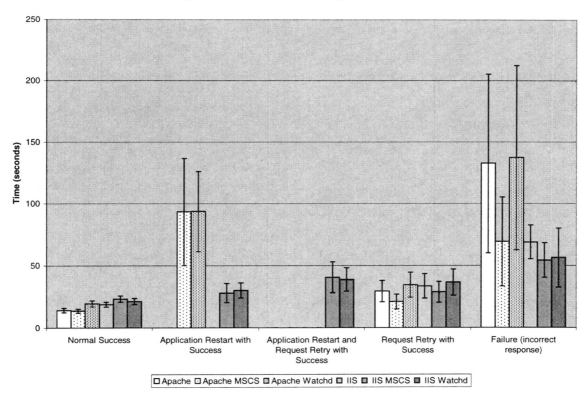

☐ Apache ☐ Apache MSCS ▦ Apache Watchd ◫ IIS ▩ IIS MSCS ▦ IIS Watchd

Figure 4. Average response times for Apache and IIS (with 95% confidence intervals)

Table 2. Comparison of Apache to IIS counting only common faults

| Server Program | Fault-Tolerance Middleware | | | | | | | | | | | |
| | Stand-alone service | | | | With MSCS | | | | With watchd | | | |
	Activated	Failure	Restart	Retry	Activated	Failure	Restart	Retry	Activated	Failure	Restart	Retry
Apache1	30	20.0%	0%	0%	36	8.3%	8.3%	0%	30	0%	20.0%	0%
Apache2	111	1.8%	0%	33.3%	120	2.5%	0%	30.8%	111	1.8%	0%	33.3%
Apache1+Apache 2	141	5.7%	0%	26.2%	156	3.8%	1.9%	23.7%	141	1.4%	0%	26.2%
IIS	123	26.0%	0%	33.3%	135	9.6%	11.1%	40.0%	123	12.2%	22.0%	43.1%

tion restarts are lower for IIS than for Apache. Much of this discrepancy is due to the way that Apache seems to handle some problems during service startup. For some faults, the Apache1 process dies immediately after being started by the Windows NT Service Control Manager (SCM). However, the SCM assumes that the service is in the "Start Pending" state. When any service is in a pending state, the SCM locks its database, which causes any state change requests to the SCM to be denied. Thus, both MSCS and watchd must wait until the "Start Pending" state times out before initiating a restart of the service. Although both Apache and IIS experience this scenario, for Apache the number of occurrences is greater and the wait time for each occurrence before the pending state ends is greater.

The main lessons drawn from Figure 4 are (1) both MSCS and watchd are comparable in impacting performance and (2) the application being monitored can affect how quickly the fault tolerance middleware is able to recover from detected problems.

4.3. Fault tolerance middleware improvements

In addition to comparing fault tolerance middleware, the DTS tool also plays an important role in the identification of fault tolerance middleware weaknesses by suggesting ways in which the failure coverage of the fault tolerance middleware can be improved. All outcomes for individual fault injection runs are recorded. Thus, the specific faults that result in failure can be studied to determine the reason for the hole in the failure coverage. This testing and debugging procedure is much more effective with the use of the DTS fault injection tool. Fault injection is necessary to produce the more esoteric problems caused by the combination of faults with such factors as unexpected input or interactions between threads or processes or with the environment. These problems can be especially potent during non-steady state periods of operation, such as process initialization or termination or during periods of stress.

The results from the initial experiment involving

watchd were studied to improve the original version of watchd (Watchd1) and to create an improved version (Watchd2). Watchd1 starts monitored processes by calling a startService() function that communicates with the SCM to start the service process. In order to monitor the newly created process, watchd obtains the handle of the new process by calling the getServiceInfo() function. For operation in the absence of faults, calling start-Service() followed by getServiceInfo() worked well. However, some faults caused the service process to fail after startService() was called and before get-ServiceInfo() was called. This small window of opportunity was sufficient to prevent watchd from correctly obtaining the necessary process handle, and therefore the failed process could not be monitored and restarted. The Watchd2 version merged the functionality of getServi-ceInfo() into startService().

Figure 5 shows the results of using Watchd1 and Watchd2 with Apache1, IIS, and SQL. The results for Apache2 are not shown because watchd has no effect on the outcomes for Apache2, as discussed earlier in Section 4.1. As seen in Figure 5, the Watchd2 improvements had mixed success. The failure outcomes for Apache1 actually increased, while no change was seen for SQL. Only IIS with Watchd2 showed an improvement in the results, with a dramatic decrease in the percentage of failure outcomes.

A second iteration of studying the Watchd2 data resulted in the creation of another improved version (Watchd3). The Watchd2 version combined the tasks of starting the service process and obtaining a process handle to the new process in a single startService() function. This decreased the time window of opportunity for the new process to fail in between the two tasks. However, the opportunity for the new process to fail still existed. To address this problem, the Watchd3 version explicitly checks for a valid process handle before returning from the startService() function. If the process handle is not valid, then a new attempt to start the service process occurs. The check for the valid process handle is further augmented by commu-

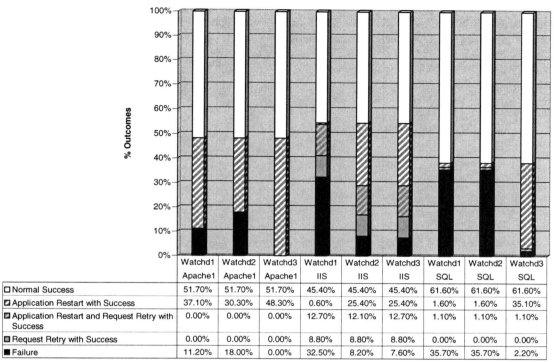

	Watchd1	Watchd2	Watchd3	Watchd1	Watchd2	Watchd3	Watchd1	Watchd2	Watchd3
	Apache1	Apache1	Apache1	IIS	IIS	IIS	SQL	SQL	SQL
☐ Normal Success	51.70%	51.70%	51.70%	45.40%	45.40%	45.40%	61.60%	61.60%	61.60%
▨ Application Restart with Success	37.10%	30.30%	48.30%	0.60%	25.40%	25.40%	1.60%	1.60%	35.10%
▨ Application Restart and Request Retry with Success	0.00%	0.00%	0.00%	12.70%	12.10%	12.70%	1.10%	1.10%	1.10%
▨ Request Retry with Success	0.00%	0.00%	0.00%	8.80%	8.80%	8.80%	0.00%	0.00%	0.00%
■ Failure	11.20%	18.00%	0.00%	32.50%	8.20%	7.60%	35.70%	35.70%	2.20%

FT Middleware/Server Program

Figure 5. Comparison of original to improved `watchd`

nication with the SCM to ensure that the service is properly started. These improvements dramatically improved the results for Apache1 and SQL, as shown in Figure 5. The results for IIS were unchanged compared to the results with Watchd2. However, a dramatic improvement had already been obtained with the Watchd2 improvements.

It should be noted that the chart in Figure 2 includes the results using Watchd3. For Apache1, IIS, and SQL, the results with Watchd1 were all slightly worse than with MSCS. However, the results with Watchd3 were all much better than with MSCS. The conclusion that can be drawn is that the iterative improvements using the DTS tool helped `watchd` in a significant way.

5. Conclusion

This paper described the architecture and use of the DTS fault injection tool. Experiments with the tool demonstrated the usefulness of the tool in several ways.

First, the most practical use of the tool is in the system validation phase of testing. Individual fault injection runs can be used to provide reproducible feedback for improving the target system. The improvement may target the server program, the fault tolerance middleware, or the operating system. The DTS architecture facilitates the testing of different applications, middleware, and systems. This paper

showed the dramatic fault coverage improvement gained for the `watchd` middleware. Similar improvements are also possible for other fault tolerance middleware, such as MSCS, or for server programs or the operating system. The essential contribution of fault injection is the triggering of scenarios that would not normally be encountered in the course of conventional functional testing.

Second, the results of DTS experiments can be used as a starting point for comparing the reliability of applications on Windows NT. Certainly, attention has to be given to the selection of the experimental fault and workload sets. Nonetheless, the DTS tool is useful as a test bed for performing fault injection-based evaluation of specific systems, although care has to be taken in generalizing conclusions about the intrinsic reliability of a particular application, operating system, or fault tolerance middleware.

Several experiments using the DTS tool with several server programs and fault tolerance middleware packages on a Windows NT platform were performed. The results indicate that both MSCS and `watchd` are useful for increasing the failure coverage of the system (as represented by unity minus the percentage of failure outcomes). In particular, the improved `watchd` exhibited high failure coverage (greater than 90%) for all tested server programs. The `watchd` failure coverage was higher than for MSCS. The Apache and IIS server programs were both targeted for testing to demonstrate the use of the DTS tool in comparing server programs with similar functionality. Both reliability and performance results were obtained. The Apache web server exhibited greater reliability and better performance for situations where no application restart or client request retry was required. However, when restart was necessary, IIS was much faster.

The current work has been performed on a Windows NT platform. The DTS tool has already been ported to the Linux platform with minimal effort. Only system-dependent Java Native Interface components needed to be rewritten. Testing Apache on Linux with and without watchd has obtained preliminary results. Work is ongoing to determine appropriate fault and workload sets that will allow the Linux results to be compared to the Windows NT results. The fault and workload sets must be described in a system-independent way that can be applied to both types of systems. The DTS architecture has been designed to support Java plugin classes to support different fault injection mechanisms, workloads, and data collection strategies. See the user's manual [16] for implementation details.

Another possible interesting application of DTS is availability modeling. Most commercial systems that are concerned with reliability are described using availability numbers. Usually availability is expressed in orders of magnitude (i.e., number of nine's of availability). This lack of precision is a result of the lack of tools to measure directly the availability of a system. The state of the art is to combine human experience with analytical models to yield estimates of availability. The DTS tool may play a role in providing testing-based parameters as input to analytical models that would then be able to yield estimates that are more precise. This might provide the basis for work in developing availability benchmarks.

The DTS tool is available for download at http://www.bell-labs.com/projects/swift/ntdts.

6. Acknowledgments

The authors gratefully acknowledge the design and development effort of Chris Dingman and Michael Vogel, as well as suggestions and feedback from Chandra Kintala. The authors also recognize the role of the reviewers of this paper in providing invaluable comments and suggestions.

References

[1] J. H. Barton et al. Fault injection experiments using FIAT. *IEEE Transactions on Computers*, 39(4):575–582, Apr. 1990.

[2] J. Carreira, H. Madeira, and J. G. Silva. Xception: Software fault injection and monitoring in processor functional units. In *Proceedings 5th International Working Conference on Dependable Computing for Critical Applications*, pages 135–149, Urbana, IL, Sept. 1995.

[3] R. A. DeMillo, D. S. Guindi, K. N. King, W. M. McCracken, and A. J. Offutt. An extended overview of the Mothra software testing environment. In *Proceedings of the 2nd Workshop on Software Testing, Verification, and Analysis*, pages 142–151, Banff, Alberta, July 1988.

[4] A. K. Ghosh and M. Schmid. Wrapping Windows NT binary executables for failure simulation. In *Proceedings Fast Abstracts and Industrial Practices 9th International Symposium on Software Reliability Engineering (ISSRE'98)*, pages 7–8, Paderborn, Germany, Nov. 1998.

[5] S. Han, K. G. Shin, and H. A. Rosenberg. DOCTOR: An integrated software fault injection environment for distributed real-time systems. In *International Computer Performance and Dependability Symposium*, pages 204–213, Apr. 1995.

[6] R. K. Iyer and D. Tang. Experimental analysis of computer system dependability. In D. K. Pradhan, editor, *Fault-Tolerant Computer System Design*, chapter 5, pages 282–392. Prentice Hall PTR, Upper Saddle River, NJ, 1996.

[7] G. A. Kanawati, N. A. Kanawati, and J. A. Abraham. FERRARI: A tool for the validation of system dependability properties. In *Proceedings 22nd International Symposium on Fault-Tolerant Computing*, pages 336–344, Boston, Massachusets, July 1992.

[8] W.-L. Kao and R. K. Iyer. Define: A distributed fault injection and monitoring environment. In *Proceedings of IEEE Workshop on Fault-Tolerant Parallel and Distributed Systems*, June 1994.

[9] N. P. Kropp, P. J. Koopman, and D. P. Siewiorek. Automated robustness testing of off-the-shelf software components. In *Proceedings 28th International Symposium on Fault-Tolerant Computing (FTCS-28)*, pages 231–239, Munich, Germany, June 1998.

[10] Microsoft Windows NT clusters. White Paper, 1997. Microsoft Corporation.

[11] B. P. Miller, D. Koski, C. P. Lee, V. Maganty, R. Murthy, A. Natarajan, and J. Steidl. Fuzz revisited: A re-examination of the reliability of UNIX utilities and services. Technical Report CS-TR-1995-1268, University of Wisconsin, Madison, Apr. 1995.

[12] M. Rodríguez, F. Salles, J. C. Fabre, and J. Arlat. MAFALDA: Microkernel assessment by fault injection and design aid. In *Proceedings 3rd European Dependable Computing Conference (EDCC-3)*, pages 143–160, Prague, Czech Republic, June 1999. Springer. LNCS 1667.

[13] SwiFT: Software implemented fault tolerance for Windows NT. http://www.bell-labs.com/projects/swift.

[14] T. Tsai and N. Singh. Reliability testing of applications on Windows NT. Technical memorandum, Lucent Technologies, Bell Labs, Murray Hill, NJ, USA, May 1999.

[15] T. K. Tsai and R. K. Iyer. An approach to benchmarking of fault-tolerant commercial systems. In *Proceedings 26th International Symposium on Fault-Tolerant Computing*, pages 314–323, Sendai, Japan, June 1996.

[16] T. K. Tsai and N. Singh. *ntDTS User's Manual*. Lucent Technologies, Bell Labs, Murray Hill, NJ, USA, 2000. http://www.bell-labs.com/project/swift/ntdts.

[17] J. M. Voas and G. McGraw. *Software Fault Injection: Inoculating Programs Against Errors*. John Wiley & Sons, Inc., New York, 1998.

Session 13B

Replication

Implementing Flexible Object Group Invocation in Networked Systems

G. Morgan and S.K. Shrivastava
Department of Computing Science, Newcastle University,
Newcastle upon Tyne, NE1 7RU, England.

Abstract

Distributed applications should be able to make use of an object group service in a number of application specific ways. Three main modes of interactions can be identified: (i) request-reply: a client issues a request to multiple servers and waits for their replies; this represents a commonly occurring scenario when a service is replicated; (ii) group-to-group request-reply: a generalisation of the previous case, where clients are themselves groups; and (iii) Peer Participation: here all the members are regularly multicasting messages (asynchronous invocation); this represents a commonly occurring scenario when the purpose of an application is to share information between members, (e.g., a teleconferencing application). Customisation within each class of interaction is frequently required for obtaining better performance. This paper describes the design and implementation of a flexible CORBA object group service that supports the three types of interactions and enables application specific customisation. Performance figures collected over low latency LAN and high latency WAN are presented to support the case for flexibility.

1. Introduction

Distributed applications are increasingly being designed and implemented using CORBA middleware services. In the context of fault tolerant systems, the provision of an object group service is considered highly desirable, as many fault-tolerant distributed applications can be structured as one or more groups of objects that cooperate by multicasting invocations on member objects. A group is defined as a collection of distributed entities (objects, processes) in which a member entity communicates with other members by multicasting to the full membership of the group. The building of group based applications is considerably simplified if the members of a group can multicast reliably and have a mutually consistent view of the order in which events (such as invocations, membership changes) have taken place. In particular, we require the property that a given multicast be atomic: either all the functioning members are delivered the message or none; an additional property

of interest is guaranteeing total order: all the functioning members are delivered messages in causality preserving identical order. Management of replicated data for high availability is a good example of the application of groups; here each member process manages a copy of the data, and given atomic delivery and order, it is relatively easy to ensure that copies of data do not diverge. Another example is a collaborative application (e.g., a conference) where members of the group (conference participants) require delivery of messages in causality preserving identical order. Design and development of process groups with the accompanying membership service has been an active area of research [e.g., 1-6]. In the world of distributed objects, process group ideas can be mapped to object groups, and there have been many recent research efforts to enrich CORBA with an object group service [7-14].

Distributed applications should be able to make use of an object group service in a number of application specific ways. Three main modes of interactions can be identified: (i) request-reply: a client issues a request to multiple servers and waits for their replies; this represents a commonly occurring scenario when a service is replicated, fig. 1(i); (ii) group-to-group request-reply: a generalisation of the previous case, where clients are themselves groups; and (iii) Peer Participation: here all the members are regularly multicasting messages (asynchronous invocation); this represents a commonly occurring scenario when the purpose of an application is to share information between members, (e.g., a teleconferencing application), fig.1(ii).

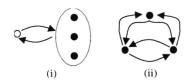

Figure 1: Request/Reply and peer participation

Customisation within each class of interaction is frequently required for obtaining better performance. Consider request-reply interaction between a client and an actively replicated service (in active replication all correctly functioning replicas perform processing). If the client and servers are all connected by high-speed, low latency network, then an efficient way of invoking the replicas would be for the client to multicast to the replicas directly using the underlying total order multicast service (in effect, the client acts as a member of the server group). On the other hand, if the client is separated from servers by a high latency communication path (e.g., WAN, Internet), then this method would be unattractive, and an alternative method that enabled a client to avoid directly multicasting to the replicas would be desirable. Different kinds of customisation might be needed for invoking passively replicated services (in passive replication, a single copy, the primary, performs processing, the remaining members act as backups). Another aspect of customisation is choice of the total order protocol. There are basically two ways of enforcing total order. In the asymmetric version, one of the members of the group assumes the responsibility for the ordering of messages within the group. Such a member is commonly termed a sequencer. In the symmetric version, all the members use a deterministic algorithm for message ordering: this requires the members to exchange, periodically, protocol specific messages amongst themselves to enable message ordering. It has been shown that symmetric protocols tend to be more attractive in situations where all the members are lively, and multicasting regularly (e.g., a conferencing application), so the need for periodically exchanging protocol specific messages just for ordering is eliminated, whereas asymmetric protocols are better in other situations [15]. An application should therefore be able to choose between the two.

In this paper we describe the design and implementation of a CORBA object group service that enables distributed applications to deploy and make use of object groups in a flexible manner as hinted above. We present performance figures collected over low latency LAN and high latency WAN to support the case for flexibility. We have taken a modular approach in the design of the service called the NewTop object group service. First we have implemented a CORBA group communication service that supports overlapping groups (objects can simultaneously belong to many groups) and symmetric and asymmetric total order protocols [13]. Then we have implemented an object invocation layer that uses the multicast service to provide the three specific ways of interacting with object groups mentioned above, together with application specific customisation. As we argue in the next section (related work), existing CORBA object group services do not support all of the functionality or the flexibility provided by our system. In this respect our system represents an advance.

In the next section we describe our layered design and relate our work to existing work on object groups. Section three presents the overview of the NewTop

service. Section four describes the design of the invocation layer. Performance figures of our system taken in LAN and Internet settings are presented in section five; these figures illustrate the need for the type of functionality and customisation supported by our system.

2. Approach and Related Work

2.1. Approach

The architecture of our system is depicted in fig. 2. The function of the invocation layer is to use the group communication service to support the three types of object group interactions, namely, request-reply, group-to-group request-reply and peer participation, each one of which can be customised in a specific manner for better performance as indicated earlier and to be discussed further here. The fig. shows how a request-reply interaction between a client and a server group is handled (only a single server is shown). The client application makes its request to the NewTop service; internal to the service, the request is handled by the invocation layer which then uses the group communication service to send NewTop specific message to servers; the message then travels up and down the protocol stack on the server side. The invocation layer employs open and closed groups (see below) to implement request-reply and group-to-group request-reply interactions to enable clients to obtain good performance in high latency as well as low latency networks.

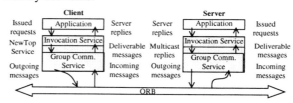

Figure 2: System architecture

Closed group - A client is considered a member of the server group and multicasts requests to each member of the server group directly. Closed groups are appropriate when clients and servers are connected by low latency communication paths (e.g., a LAN).

Open group - A client is not considered a member of the server group and issues requests to just a single member of the server group (that then multicasts the request within the group). Unlike the closed group, clients do not participate in group communication protocols as members of the server group. This makes the open group approach more suitable for use in cases where clients are separated from servers by high latency networks (e.g., a WAN).

The invocation layer achieves open and closed group approaches to client/server group interactions via overlapping of groups. A single group containing members that support some service is identified as a

440

server group. Clients wishing to access the service provided by a server group create a group containing themselves that overlaps with (shares membership of) the server group. A group that contains clients and servers is termed a client/server group. To satisfy open and closed groups, the overlapping of client/server and server groups may be achieved thus: closed group - client/server group contains the client and all the members of the server group (fig. 3 (i)); open group - client/server group contains the client and only one member of the server group (fig.3(ii)).

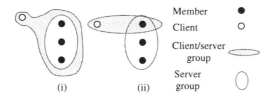

Member	●
Client	○
Client/server group	⬭
Server group	◯

(i)   (ii)

Figure 3: Achieving closed and open groups

Note that in the open group approach, a failure of the server within a client/server group (or the server's disconnection from the client due to some communication failure) will cause the binding between the client and the server to be broken, with the client/server group disbanded. A client can then rebind to some other server within the server group, by creating a new client/server group. In our current design, such actions are handled at the application level in some application specific manner. For example, a client application can be provided with a 'smart proxy' for the server that automatically does the rebinding as suggested here. Rebinding can also be performed at the ORB level, as discussed in section 2.2. In contrast, in the closed group approach, server failures can be automatically masked, without any need for rebinding; this is of course the advantage of making a client and all the servers members of a group.

There is no limit to the number of client/server groups a client may form. Nor is there any limit to the number of client/server groups the members of a server group may participate in. A given group can be configured to use either symmetric or asymmetric total ordering protocol. Furthermore, the open and closed group approaches may be used simultaneously by both clients and members of a server group. This permits implementation of group-to-group request-reply invocations (this will be discussed in a subsequent section).

In contrast to request-reply interactions, peer participation interaction is straightforward to implement (no overlapping groups are required); here the invocation layer simply provides 'one way send' invocation facility. In all, the invocation layer supports the following types of invocation primitives:

One way send - A request requires no reply. The issuer of such a request does not wait for replies and may continue processing;

Wait for first - Only wait for a reply from a single member of the server group;

Wait for majority - Wait for replies from a majority of the server group;

Wait for all - Wait for replies from all members of the server group.

Replies generated from a request are sent to the client directly (closed group approach) or indirectly via a member of the server group (open group approach).

The underlying group communication service has been designed to be suitable for a wide variety of group based applications; objects can simultaneously belong to many groups, group size could be large, and objects could be geographically widely separated. The service can provide causality preserving total order delivery to members of a group, ensuring that total order delivery is preserved even for multi-group objects. Both symmetric and asymmetric total order protocols are supported, permitting a member to use say symmetric version in one group and asymmetric version in another group simultaneously [5].

2.2. Related Work

Enriching CORBA with an object group service has been an active area of research [7-14]. Three ways of incorporating object groups in CORBA have been identified [7,8]. The integration approach takes an existing group communication system and replaces the transport service of the ORB by the group service [9]. Although this is a very efficient way of incorporating group functionality in an ORB, this approach is not CORBA compliant, lacking in interoperability.

The second approach called the interceptor approach also makes use of an existing group communication system; here messages issued by an ORB are intercepted and mapped on to calls of the group communication system. Well known examples of this approach are the Eternal [10,11] and AQuA [12] systems; Eternal uses the Totem group communication system [6], whereas AQuA uses the Ensemble group communication system [3]. Both Eternal and AQuA make use of group communication for supporting object replication only (and not for other uses of group communication, such as collaborative applications). They do so by using the closed group approach, and have been engineered for use in high speed LAN environments, rather than over the Internet. Ignoring for the moment that our system does not use the interception approach (it uses the service approach discussed below), the architecture of our system is different: rather than providing an integrated set of mechanisms for implementing a specific system function suitable in a specific setting (e.g., replication within LAN environments), we have enriched the group communication service with a set of high level invocation and group management primitives that can be used for supporting a wide variety of group based applications, with scope for optimisation based on knowledge of application behaviour and network latency. Naturally, our object group service will need to be used in conjunction with additional subsystems that provide specific functions; for example, in order to support passive replication, some form of state transfer facility would have to be implemented. We have shown elsewhere how a subsystem for replication of transactional objects (that itself uses the CORBA transaction service) can make use of the object group service [16].

The third approach is the service approach: it does not make use of any existing group communication system; rather the group communication system is implemented as a CORBA service from scratch. In addition to being CORBA compliant, the advantage here is that the service is directly available to application builders so can be used for a variety of purposes. This approach was first developed in the Object Group Service (OGS) [7,8], and has been taken in the NewTop service. The NewTop service offers a more comprehensive set of group management facilities than OGS. In particular, OGS does not support overlapping groups or group to group invocations.

NewTop can be adapted to exploit forthcoming enhancements to ORBs. As part of the ongoing development of CORBA, the OMG have recently adopted interceptors, messaging, and fault-tolerance specifications. Availability of ORBs with interceptors will enable the use of NewTop as a multicast transport service as demonstrated by the Eternal system. Exploitation of the messaging service will enable more efficient implementation of multicasting than is possible now. Since at present ORBs only provide one to one communication, multicasting has been implemented by making synchronous invocations in turn to all the members. Multiple threads of execution are used to obtain parallelism and prevent client blocking. Such a measure to prevent blocking will not be required if the ORB supported asynchronous invocation provided by the messaging service.

The forthcoming fault tolerance standard extends the Interoperable Object Reference (IOR) to handle object groups (IOGR - Interoperable Object Group Reference). This is achieved by embedding the IORs of group members within a single IOGR. NewTop can exploit this feature in a number of ways: in open groups, if the client ORB is unable to invoke one of the members of the object group (one IOR is identified as primary and will be chosen first by the ORB), an attempt may be made to invoke another member that is present in the IOGR. As this is executed at the ORB level (possibly with the aid of interceptors), the process is transparent to the client. In a closed group, a multicast may be initiated by the client ORB, sending an invocation to all members present in the IOGR.

Although not a CORBA service, the system described in [17] is worth mentioning. The paper describes a client access protocol for invoking object replicas, without the need for the client to use multicasts. We obtain the same functionality by making use of open groups.

3. Overview of the NewTop Object Group Service

The failure assumptions made by the NewTop service are the same as made in other group services referred to in this paper. It is assumed that processes/objects fail only by crashing, i.e., by stopping to function. The communication environment is modelled as asynchronous, where message transmission times cannot be accurately estimated, and the underlying network may well get partitioned, preventing functioning members from communicating with each other. The actual protocols used in the NewTop service will not be described here, as these details are not directly relevant to this paper; the interested reader is referred to [5].

The NewTop service is a distributed service and achieves distribution with the aid of the NewTop service object (NSO). In the following description, a group member will also be referred to as a client of the NewTop service. Each client is allocated an NSO. Group related communication required by a client is handled by its NSO. Referring to fig. 2 of section 2, the shaded box is an NSO. Only one NSO is required by a client, irrespective of how many groups the client participates in. Communication between a client and its NSO is handled by the ORB. Therefore, the NSO may reside within the same address space, in a different address space, or on a different node in the network to the group member associated with it. The most efficient configuration would be the client and its NSO within the same address space.

Internally, the NewTop service itself has been composed of a group communication subsystem that handles membership and reliable multicasts and the invocation subsystem. The group communication system provides clients with create, delete and leave group operations and causal and total order multicasts. In addition, it maintains the membership information (group view) and ensures that this information is kept mutually consistent at each member. This is achieved with the help of a failure suspector that initiates membership agreement as soon as a member is suspected to have failed. The client can obtain the current membership information by invoking 'groupDetails' operation. View updates are atomic with respect to message deliveries, as in virtually synchronous communication [2]. Message delivery is atomic with two types of ordering guarantees (causal and causality preserving total order) and in case of total order, two types of ordering techniques, symmetric and asymmetric, are supported. In the asymmetric version, one of the members of the group assumes the responsibility for the ordering of messages within the group. Such a member is commonly termed a sequencer. Electing a new sequencer, in case the original one departs from the group, is straightforward as the underlying membership service maintains consistent group views; so any deterministic algorithm can be used. In the symmetric version, all the members use a deterministic algorithm for message ordering.

In a group communication system a member is often required to stay lively within a group to avoid being suspected by other members. This usually takes the form of a member periodically sending "I am alive" or "NULL" messages during periods it has no application level messages to send. In NewTop, after a member has neglected to send a message for a period of time, the NewTop time-silence mechanism will send a "I am alive" message. A client of the NewTop service creating a group may decide if the group is to be lively or event driven:

· *Lively* – time-silence mechanism and failure suspicion is active throughout the lifetime of a group; the duration of the time-silence period is specified at the creation time. Such a configuration would be most appropriate in peer group settings.

· *Event* – The time-silence mechanism is only active when application dependent messages exist within the NewTop service environment. Once all these messages are delivered to group members the failure suspicion and time-silence mechanisms are shutdown. The appearance of further application dependent messages wakes up these mechanisms. Such a configuration would be most appropriate in request-reply group settings.

4. Flexible Object Group Invocation

In this section we describe how the invocation layer implements one way send, wait for first, wait for majority, and wait for all for a client invoking a group of servers. Replies generated from servers are sent to a client directly (closed group approach) or indirectly via a member of a server group (open group approach). Implementation using the closed group approach (fig. 3(i)) is relatively straightforward and will not be described here. Instead we will concentrate on the implementation using the open group approach; for a more detailed description, see [18].

4.1. Open group approach

The client forms a client/server group containing itself and only one member of the server group. As client requests are directed at only a single server, a mechanism that will propagate such messages

throughout the server group and collect replies ready for returning to the client is necessary. This mechanism is described, with reference to fig. 4, where all the requests/replies are causality preserving total order multicasts.

(i) *Receiving client request* - A request sent within a client/server group is received by the server. This server is considered to be the request manager for this particular client (fig. 4(i)).

(ii) *Distributing client request* - The request manager multicasts the request within the server group (fig. 4(ii)). This is achieved by the request manager acting as a client and issuing the incoming invocation as a new invocation (of the same type, e.g., wait for first, wait for all).

(iii) *Receiving server replies* - Each member of the server group multicasts replies within the group (fig. 4(iii)). This would be the case when each member is generating replies, as in active replication. A variation on this behaviour is when only one member generates the reply; this will be discussed in the next subsection.

(iv) *Returning server replies to client* - Server replies are gathered by the request manager (one, majority or all) and returned to the client (fig. 4(iv)). No reply is sent when the client invocation is of type one way.

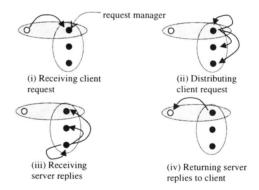

Figure 4: Client invocations in open groups

As observed earlier, a failure of the request manager will cause the binding between the client and the server to be broken, with the client/server group disbanded. A client can rebind to some other server within the server group, by creating a new client/server group. Consider this scenario further. Assume that the request manager fails as the servers are multicasting their replies (during the stage depicted in fig. 4(iii)). The server group will be reformed with the request manager removed, and no reply will be sent to the client. Client retries can be handled by the new request manager without causing re-execution, provided retries contain the same call number as the original call and servers retain the data of the last reply message (enabling the request manager to resend the reply). These are 'standard' techniques used in any RPC implementation. Logic for this can be provided either in the invocation layer or at the application level (in client and server stubs): in the current design, we have chosen the latter option. Note that client retries can be handled transparently using the IOGR feature of ORBs as discussed in section 2.2.

4.2. Optimisations

In the above scheme, clients can select any member of the server group for forming a client/server group (fig. 5(i)); total ordering of forwarded requests ensures that all the servers are delivered requests in identical causality preserving order. However, a request received by a request manager becomes deliverable only after it has been delivered through a multicast; this delay can be eliminated at the request manager if only a single request manager is used by all the clients (fig. 5(ii)). This optimisation will be termed restricted group optimisation.

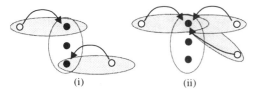

Figure 5: Single request manager optimisation

Further optimisation to the restricted group is possible, termed asynchronous message forwarding, when the client is expecting a reply from a single server (wait for first). The request manager, rather than making 'wait for first' calls on the servers (step (ii) of the previous section) makes 'one way send' invocation and simply returns a single reply itself. Combining the restricted open group and asynchronous message forwarding approaches as discussed here is particularly attractive for supporting passive replication. The request manager may assume the role of the primary; receiving, processing and replying to client requests. The remainder of the server group are passive members, receiving (but not necessarily acting upon) client requests. The asymmetric ordering protocol would be most suitable in this setting, with the role of the sequencer, request manager and primary all undertaken by the same group member.

4.3. Group to Group Invocations

The open group approach presented earlier provides an economic way of extension to group to group invocations. One scheme is illustrated in fig. 6; here a client invokes group gx; members of gx make another call to gy. Each member of the client group (gx in this case) uses the open group approach to invoke the server group (gy), using the same request manager. Another group, termed a client monitor group, containing gx and the request manager is created. The request manager expects the call request to come from all the members of gz (except itself), and filters them out,

except one, and forwards it to members of gy. Each member of gy multicasts its reply within gy. The request manager returns the replies to all the members of gx by multicasting within gz.

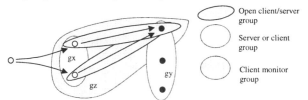

Figure 6: Implementing group to group invocations

The scheme described above is one of several ways of implementing group to group invocations. Another way would be to use request managers at each group to perform message distribution. In the design presented here, the aim has been to minimise inter-group (between gx and gy) multicasts. The only such multicast is from the request manger to members of gz; this is necessary to ensure atomic delivery to all the functioning members of gx.

4.4. On the use of Overlapping Groups

Isis system was first to use overlapping groups [2]; it supported closed groups for client-server interactions. We have taken this approach a step further and described the use of overlapping groups for supporting closed groups, open groups and for supporting group to group invocations. The AQuA system [12] also uses overlapping groups in a variety of ways for replica management. The group communication protocols used in NewTop have been designed to cope with overlapping groups in an efficient manner [5]. In the open group approach, we have relied on the use of a client/server group for invoking a single server. Since no multicasting is involved, a client can in principle invoke the server directly, without using the group system. Although this is possible (and used in [17]), we have chosen the former approach because it has the power of preserving causality (if any) between multiple client requests. This is illustrated with the help of fig. 7.

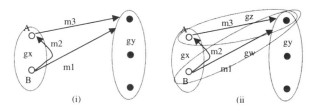

Figure 7: Ordering of related client requests

A group gx consists of two members (A and B). B issues an open group request to gy (m1). B then sends a message in gx (m2). During the processing of m2, A issues an open group request to gy (m3). We want to ensure that request m1 is serviced at gy before m3. This will be the case if requests m1 and m3 are sent using client/server groups (fig. 7(ii)).

5. Performance Evaluation

This section describes the experiments carried out to assess the benefits of customisation facilities made available to application developers. That is, we assess the advantages of being able to select between closed and open groups as well as two ways of enforcing total order (asymmetric or symmetric) for a given group. Two classes of experiments were carried out:

Request-Reply - A client issues a request to multiple servers and waits for their replies, fig. 1(i). Inter-server as well as client-server communication could be via a high speed LAN (local distribution) or Internet (wide area distribution). Performance of closed and open group approaches (figs. 8(i) and (ii) respectively), and the restricted group with asynchronous message forwarding optimisation (discussed in section 4.2) depicted here in fig. 8(iii)) have been evaluated under the two classes of ordering protocols.

Peer Participation - All the members are regularly multicasting by using the asynchronous method invocation operation, fig. 1(ii). Performance of locally distributed and widely distributed groups under the two classes of ordering protocols have been evaluated.

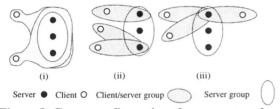

Server ●   Client ○   Client/server group ⬭   Server group ⬯

Figure 8: Group configurations for request-reply interactions

The two network environments used in the experiments were: (i) LAN: Pentium Linux machines connected by 100 Mbits fast Ethernet; and (ii) WAN: Pentium Linux machines were geographically separated by large distances, communicating via the Internet; the machines were located in Newcastle (United Kingdom), London (United Kingdom) and Pisa (Italy). The ORB used in these experiments was omniORB2 [19]. In all the experiments, group members reside in the same address space as their NSOs.

5.1. Request Reply Interactions

Two performance metrics are of interests: for a client we wish to know the RPC time for invoking a service, whereas for a server we wish to know the throughput (number of requests serviced per second). To measure server throughput, clients were configured to issue requests as frequently as possible: as soon as a reply is received, another request is issued. The server

used in this experiment is a CORBA object that simply returns a pseudo random number when requested to do so by a client. Client numbers were increased gradually from one to twenty. At each of these increments each participating client is timed for 1000 requests, and the average is taken.

Given the above scenario and assuming negligible computation time for a service (as is the case here), we would expect servers to become saturated (reach maximum throughput) with only small number of clients if the clients are connected by a low latency path to the servers; at the same time, RPC times would increase as the client numbers increased. On the other hand, if the clients are connected by a high latency path to the servers, then we would expect the server throughput to increase as the number of clients increased, and the RPC times would not be affected that much.

The server group consisted of three members in all these experiments with all groups designated as event driven; the following client/server group configurations were used:

(i) *Low latency*: clients and servers were all on the same LAN;

(ii) *Low and high latency*: servers were located on the same LAN in Newcastle; clients were equally distributed between London and Pisa; and,

(iii) *High latency*: servers and clients were geographically separated between Newcastle, London and Pisa.

5.1.1 Non-replicated service

To enable comparative analysis of the performance figures, CORBA RPC times without the use of the NewTop Object Group Service were first obtained. The figures obtained are shown in table 1.

The experiment was repeated, however, communication was achieved via the group service. Performance figures within the LAN environment are shown in graphs 1 and 2 and those over the Internet in graphs 3 and 4.

CORBA RPC	Timed request (milliseconds)	Throughput (requests per second)
Client and server on distinct nodes in LAN	0.9	1111.11
Client in Pisa and server in Newcastle	78.0	12.82
Client in London and server in Newcastle	81.0	12.34
Client in Pisa and server in London	86.0	11.62

Table 1: Performance of CORBA RPC

The first observation to be made is that the RPC time of a single client making a call via the NewTop service (2.5 msec, LAN and 209 msec, Internet) is around two and half times the performance of a single client making an RPC without the NewTop service. This drop in performance is inevitable and may be explained by the manner with which messages are handled; this message passing process is shown in fig. 9.

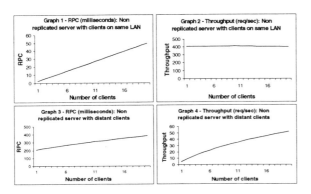

A request by a client for a pseudo random number is received by the client's NSO (m1). The client's NSO then multicasts this message to the replica group (m2). The server's NSO receives this message and queues this message as pending. Messages in the pending queue that satisfy ordering and delivery guarantees are then delivered to the NSO's associated application object (pseudo random number generator object) (m3). This delivery takes the form of an invocation. Results from the invocation are then queued by the server's NSO in the multicast pending list (m4). A thread is then created which handles the multicasting of messages held in this list. Finally, the client's NSO receives this return message (m5) and queues it in the messages pending list, awaiting delivery back to the client object of the NSO (m6). Assuming the client (server) NSO to be in the same address space as the client (server), request-reply message pairs m1-m6, m3-m4 will not generate any network traffic. On the other hand, message m2 as well as message m5 are each a CORBA RPC. As we have remarked earlier (section 2.2) expected availability of asynchronous messaging (and multicast services) in next generation ORBs will remove the main source of the inefficiency.

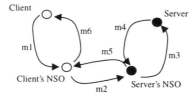

Figure 9: Message passing between NSOs and application objects

As the number of clients is increased, the behaviour obtained is consistent with the explanation of expected behaviour given earlier; so in the LAN environment, a single client is able to saturate the server, whereas the throughput of the server in the Internet environment increases with the number of clients.

5.1.2. Optimised group invocation

We first consider the group invocation requiring a reply from a single server (wait for first) and present the performance of the scheme depicted in fig. 8(iii) incorporating the restricted open group with asynchronous message forwarding optimisation that is ideal for passive replication. This will enable us to directly compare performance of group invocation with that of non-replicated invocation discussed in the previous subsection: in both the cases, the client invokes a single server; the only additional work required for group invocation is that the request manager is required to forward the request to all the members. Since this is performed asynchronously, we would expect the performance of optimised group invocation to closely match that of the non-replicated invocation. This is indeed the case when the asymmetric ordering protocol is used, with the role of the sequencer, request manager and primary all undertaken by the same group member.

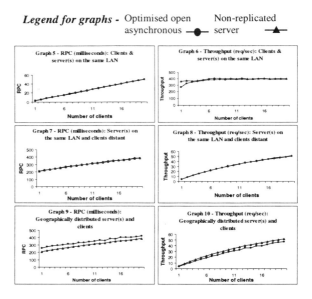

The performance figures (including those of non-replicated server obtained earlier) are presented in graphs 5 through to 10 for the optimised asynchronous open group combination.

5.1.3. Closed and open group invocations

We next compare the performance of request reply interactions using closed groups and open groups. In the closed group approach, a server failure is automatically masked, whereas in the open group approach, clients bound to that server are required to rebind. In the absence of failures, the open group approach is expected to perform better than the closed group approach, although within low latency networks, the difference between the two is not expected to be significant. The performance figures, for the case of the server group using asymmetric ordering protocol and clients invoking 'wait for all' are shown in graphs 11 through to 16. We note that when clients are separated from servers by high latency paths, the open group approach is most attractive.

Figures obtained for the case of the groups using the symmetric ordering protocols have been omitted here to save space, but we can make two observations: (i) the closed group approach does not perform well, because it gives rise to extensive protocol related multicast traffic amongst all the members for ensuring order; and (ii) under the open group approach, there is little to chose between the two; this is because message ordering is performed within one group only, and it does not matter which technique is used.

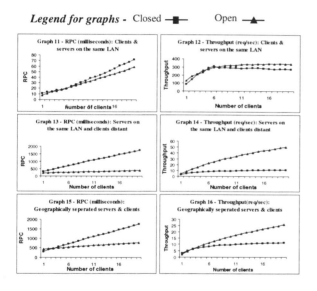

Legend for graphs - Closed —■— Open —▲—

5.2. Peer to Peer Interactions

The peer participation scenario is commonly associated with applications wishing to share information across a number of participants. GroupWare applications are typical examples of such applications (e.g., teleconferencing, shared whiteboards, Internet Relay Chat (IRC)). Members simply distribute messages (via multicast) throughout the group using one way send; the body of the message consists of a CORBA string type of 100 characters in length. All members issue multicasts as frequently as possible. Performance is measured by assessing how long a multicast takes to become deliverable at all members within a group from the time of the multicast's issue. The time taken for 1000 multicasts from each member to become deliverable at every

other member of the group is measured. This results in a figure per client (as all clients are multicasting). Each of these figures are then divided by a 1000 to gain a figure for the time taken for a single multicast. The resultant figures are then summed to allow a throughput figure for the group to be gained.

The group was designated as lively; two group configurations were used:

(i) *Low latency*: members were distributed over the same LAN; and,

(ii) *High latency*: members were distributed between Newcastle, London and Pisa.

The symmetric ordering scheme is superior to the asymmetric ordering scheme in peer to peer interactions. In the LAN environment the volume of messages that result from persistently sending asynchronous multicasts has resulted in a deterioration of performance in both the symmetric and asymmetric protocols as group membership rises. This deterioration is more extreme in the asymmetric protocol than the symmetric protocol. This indicates that the sequencer is receiving more messages than it can handle. The sequencer is a bottleneck. This bottleneck effect explains why the asymmetric performance deteriorates significantly as group membership rises. This deterioration is not evident in the symmetric scenario as the handling of messages and multicasting is more evenly spread throughout the group. In the Internet scenario, due to the large message transit times involved, the sequencer does not present a bottleneck. However, the cost of redirection is evident; the performance of the asymmetric protocol is approximately half that of the symmetric protocol.

Legend for graphs - Symmetric —■— Asymmetric —◆—

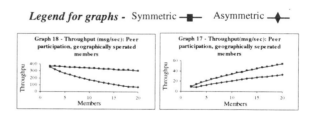

6. Concluding Remarks

We have taken a modular approach in the design of the NewTop object group service described here. First we have implemented a CORBA group communication service that supports overlapping groups (objects can simultaneously belong to many groups) and symmetric and asymmetric total order protocols. Then we have enriched the group communication service with a set of high level invocation and group management primitives that can be used for supporting a wide variety of group based applications, with scope for optimisation based on knowledge of application behaviour and network latency. For the case of request-reply interactions, we have implemented open and closed group approaches.

The closed group approach works well within low latency networks but does not scale to high latency networks (wide area distribution), where the open group approach is most suitable. The optimised version of the open group approach works well in all the settings and almost matches the performance of its non-replicated counterpart. Finally, experiments indicate that the asymmetric ordering protocol is more appropriate for groups that are used in request/reply mode, whereas the symmetric protocol is more suitable in peer to peer interactions.

Acknowledgements

G. Morgan was supported by EPSRC CASE PhD studentship with industrial sponsorship from HP Laboratories, Bristol.

References

[1] Amir, Y., et al, "Transis: A Communication Subsystem for High Availability", Digest of Papers, FTCS-22, Boston, July 1992, pp. 76-84.

[2] K. Birman , "The process group approach to reliable computing", CACM , 36, 12, pp. 37-53, December 1993.

[3] M. Hayden, "The Ensemble system", PhD thesis, Dept. of Computer Science, Cornell University, 1998.

[4] D. Dolev and D. Malki, "The Transis approach to high availability cluster communication", CACM, 39 (4), April 1996, pp. 64-70.

[5] P. Ezhilchelvan, R. Macedo and S. K. Shrivastava, "NewTop: a fault-tolerant group communication protocol", 15th IEEE Intl. Conf. on Distributed Computing Systems, Vancouver, May 1995, pp. 296-306.

[6] L.E. Moser, P.M. Melliar-Smith et al, "Totem: a Fault-tolerant multicast group communication system", CACM, 39 (4), April 1996, pp. 54-63.

[7] P. Felber, R. Guerraoui and A. Schiper, "The implementation of a CORBA object group service", Theory and Practice of Object Systems, 4(2), 1998, pp. 93-105.

[8] P. Felber, "The CORBA Object Group Service: a Service Approach to Object Groups in CORBA", PhD thesis, Ecole Polytechnique Federale de Lausanne, 1998.

[9] S. Maffeis, "Run-time support for object-oriented distributed programming", PhD thesis, University of Zurich, February 1995.

[10] P. Narasimhan, L, E. Moser and P. M. Melliar-Smith, "Replica consistency of CORBA objects in partitionable distributed systems", Distributed Systems Eng., 4, 1997, pp. 139-150.

[11] L.E. Moser, P.M. Melliar-Smith and P. Narasimhan, "A Fault tolerance framework for COBRA", Proc. of 29th Symp. On Fault Tolerant Computing, FTCS-29, Madison, June 1999.

[12] M. Cukier et al., "AQuA: an adaptive architecture that provides dependable distributed objects", Proc. of 17th IEEE Symp. on Reliable Distributred Computing (SRDS'98), West Lafayette, October 1998, pp. 245-253.

[13] G. Morgan, S.K. Shrivastava, P.D. Ezhilchelvan and M.C. Little, "Design and Implementation of a CORBA Fault-tolerant Object Group Service", Distributed Applications and Interoperable Systems, Ed. Lea Kutvonen, Hartmut Konig, Martti Tienari, Kluwer Academic Publishers, 1999, ISBN 0-7923-8527-6, pp. 361-374.

[14] S. Misra, Lan Fei, and Guming Xing, "Design, Implementation and Performance Evaluation of a CORBA Group Communication Service", Proc. of 29th Symp. On Fault Tolerant Computing, FTCS-29, Madison, June 1999.

[15] L. Rodriguez, H. Fonseca and P. Verissimo, "Totally ordered multicasts in large scale systems", 16th IEEE Intl. Conf. on Distributed Computing Systems, Hong Kong, May 1996, pp. 503-510.

[16] M.C. Little and S K Shrivastava, "Implementing high availability CORBA applications with Java", Proc. of IEEE Workshop on Internet Applications, WIAPP'99, San Jose, July 1999.

[17] C. T. Karamanolis and J.N. Magee, "Client access protocols for replicated services", IEEE Transactions on Software Engineering, Vol. 25, No. 1, 1999, pp. 3-22.

[18] G. Morgan, "A middleware service for fault tolerant group communications", Phd thesis, Dept. of Computing Science, University of Newcastle upon Tyne, September 1999.

[19] www.uk.research.att.com/omniORB/omniOB.html

Implementing e-Transactions with Asynchronous Replication

Svend Frølund[1]   Rachid Guerraoui[2]

[1] Hewlett-Packard Laboratories, Palo Alto, CA 94304

[2] Swiss Federal Institute of Technology, CH 1015, Lausanne

Abstract

An e-Transaction *is one that executes* exactly-once *despite failures. This paper describes a distributed protocol that implements the abstraction of* e-Transaction *in* three-tier architectures. *Three-tier architectures are typically Internet-oriented architectures, where the end-user interacts with front-end clients (e.g., browsers) that invoke middle-tier application servers (e.g., web servers) to access back-end databases. We implement the* e-Transaction *abstraction using an* asynchronous *replication scheme that preserves the three-tier nature of the architecture and introduces a very acceptable overhead with respect to unreliable solutions.*

1 Introduction

Until very recently, three-tier architectures were at the leading edge of development. Only a few tools supported them, and only a small number of production-level applications implemented them. Three-tier applications are now becoming mainstream. They match the logical decomposition of applications (presentation, logic, and data) with their software and hardware structuring (PCs, workstations, and clusters). Clients are diskless (e.g., browsers), application servers are stateless, but contain the core logic of the application (e.g., web servers), and back-end databases contain the state of the applications. A client submits a request to some application server, on behalf of an end-user; the application server processes the client's request, stores the resulting state in a backend database, and returns a result to the client. This simple interaction scheme is at the heart of the so-called *e-Business* game today.

Motivation. The partitioning of an application into several tiers provides for better modularity and scalability. However, the multiplicity of the components and their interdependencies make it harder to achieve any meaningful form of reliability. Current reliability solutions in three-tier architectures are typically *transactional* [1, 2]. They ensure *at-most-once* request processing through some form of "all-or-nothing" guarantee. The major limitation of those solutions is precisely the impossibility for the client-side software to accurately distinguish the "all" from the "nothing" scenario. If a failure occurs at the middle or backend tier during request processing, or a timeout period expires at the client side, the end-user typically receives an exception notification. This does not convey what actually happened, and whether the actual request was indeed performed.[1] In practice, end-users typically retry the transaction, with the risk of executing it several times, e.g., having the user charged twice. In short, current transactional technology typically ensures *at-most-once* request processing and, by retrying transactions, end-users typically obtain *at-least-once* guarantees. Ensuring *exactly-once* transaction processing is very desirable but also very challenging. Basically, some transaction outcome information should be made highly available, but it is not clear exactly *which* information should be preserved, *where* it should be stored, and for *how long*.

The motivation of our work is to define and implement the abstraction of *exactly-once Transaction (e-Transaction)* in a three-tier architecture. Intuitively, this abstraction masks (physical) transaction aborts, adds a liveness dimension to transactional systems that also includes the client side, and frees the end-user from the burden of having to resubmit transactions.

---

[1]The transactional guarantee ensures that if the request was indeed performed, all its effects are made durable ("all" scenario), and otherwise, all its effects are discarded ("nothing" scenario) [3].

Protocol. This paper presents a distributed protocol that implements the *e-Transaction* abstraction. We integrate a replication scheme that guarantees the *e-Transaction* liveness property with a transactional scheme that ensures the traditional safety counterpart. This integration involves the client, the application servers, and the database servers. To deal with the inherent non-determinism of the interaction with third-party databases, we make use of *write-once registers (wo-register)*. These are consensus-like abstractions that capture the nice intuition of *CD-ROMs* (they can be written once but read several times). Building on such abstractions leads to a modular protocol, and enables us to reuse existing results on the solvability of consensus in distributed systems, e.g., [4].[2] Indirectly, we contribute to better understand how the safety aspect of transactions can be practically mixed with the liveness feature of replication, and how a consensus abstraction can help achieve that mix.

Related work. Considerable work has been devoted to transaction execution on replicated data [3]. However, we know of no approach to replicate the actual "transaction processing-state" in order to ensure the fault-tolerance of the transaction itself, i.e., that it eventually commits *exactly-once*. Traditionally, it is assumed that a transaction that cannot access "enough" replicas is aborted [3], but the issue of how to reliably determine the transaction's outcome, and possibly retry it, is not addressed. In fact, addressing this issue requires a careful use of some form of non-blocking transaction processing, with some highly-available *recovery information* that reflects the "transaction-processing state". In [6], the problem of *exactly-once* message delivery was addressed for communication channels. The author pointed out the importance of reliably storing some "message recovery information". In the context of *exactly-once* transaction processing, this recovery information should represent the transaction-processing state. Several approaches were proposed in the literature to store that state for recovery purposes, e.g., [7, 8, 9]. Nevertheless, those approaches do not guarantee the high-availability of that state. Furthermore, they rely on disk storage at the client or at some application server. Relying on the client's disk is problematic if the client is a Java applet that does not have the right to access the disk. Solutions based on disk storage at a specific application server would make that server host dependent, and three-tier architectures are considered scalable precisely because they prevent any form of host dependence at the

---
[2]A wo-register can also be viewed as a distributed form of *software counter* [5].

middle-tier [10]. Our *e-Transaction* protocol uses the very same replication scheme, both as a highly available storage for the "transaction-processing state", and as an effective way to retry transactions behind the scenes. In contrast to most replication schemes we know about [11, 12, 13], we assume stateless servers that interact with third-party databases. Replication schemes have usually been designed in a client-server context: servers are stateful but do not interact with third-party entities. Having stateless application servers is an important aspect of three-tier applications. Stateless servers do not have host affinity, which means that we can freely migrate them. Moreover, fail-over is fast because we do not have to wait for a server to recover its state. Another characteristic of our replication scheme is its *asynchronous* nature: it tolerates unreliable failure detection and may vary, at run-time, between some form of primary-backup [12] and some form of active replication [11, 14].

Practical considerations. Our *e-Transaction* protocol was designed with a very practical objective in mind. In particular, we assume that the functionality of a database server is given: it is a stateful, autonomous resource that runs the XA interface [15] (the X/Open standard that database vendors are supposed to comply with in distributed transaction-processing applications). We preserve the three-tier nature of the applications by not relying on any disk access at the client site, or any application server site. We do not make any assumption on the failure detection scheme used by the client-side software to detect the crash of application servers, and we tolerate failure suspicion mistakes among application servers. The overhead of our *e-Transaction* protocol is very acceptable in a practical setting where application servers are run by the Orbix 2.3 Object Request Broker [16], and database servers by the Oracle 8.0.3 database management system [17]. In terms of the latency, as viewed by a client, our protocol introduces an overhead of about 16% over a baseline protocol that does not offer any reliability guarantee.

Roadmap. The rest of the paper is organized as follows. Section 2 defines our system model. Section 3 describes the *e-Transaction* problem. Section 4 describes the protocol. For space limitation, we only give here an intuitive idea of the protocol. More details can be found in [18]. Section 5 gives the performance of our protocol implementation. Finally, Section 6 puts our contribution in perspective through some final remarks.

2 A Three-Tier Model

We consider a distributed system with a finite set of processes that communicate by message passing. Processes fail by crashing. At any point in time, a process is either *up* or *down*. A crash causes a transition from up to down, and a recovery causes the transition from down to up. The crash of a process has no impact on its stable storage. When it is up, a process behaves according to the algorithm that was assigned to it: processes do not behave maliciously.

In the following, we outline our representation of the three types of processes in a three-tier application: clients, application servers, and database servers.

Clients

Client processes are denoted by $c_1, c_2, \ldots, c_k$ ($c_i \in$ *Client*). We assume a domain, "Request", of request values, and we describe how requests in this domain are submitted to application servers. Clients have an operation *issue()*, which is invoked with a request as parameter (e.g., on behalf of an *end-user*). We say that the client *issues* a request when the operation *issue()* is invoked. The *issue()* primitive is supposed to *return* a result value from the domain "Result". When it does so, we say that the client *delivers* the result (e.g., to the *end-user*). A result is a value in the "Result" domain, and it represents information computed by the business logic, such as reservation number and hotel name, that must be returned to the user. In practice, the request can be a vector of values. In the case of a travel application for instance, the request typically indicates a travel destination, the travel dates, together with some information about hotel category, the size of a car to rent, etc. A corresponding result typically contains information about a flight reservation, a hotel name and address, the name of a car company, etc.

After being issued by a client, a request is processed without further input from the client. Furthermore, the client issues requests one-at-a-time and, although issued by the same client, two consecutive requests are considered to be unrelated. Clients cannot communicate directly with databases, only through application servers.

We assume that each request and each result are uniquely identified. Furthermore, we assume that every result is uniquely associated with a transaction. When we say that a result is committed (resp. aborted), we actually mean that the corresponding transaction is committed (resp. aborted). For presentation simplicity we assume that a result and the corresponding transaction have the same identifier, and we simply represent such indentifiers using integers.

Application Servers

Application server processes are denoted by $a_1, a_2, \ldots, a_m$ ($a_i \in$ *AppServer*). Application servers are *stateless* in the sense that they do not maintain states accross request invocations: requests do not have side-effects on the state of application servers, only on the database state. Thus, a request cannot make any assumption about previous requests in terms of application-server state changes. Having stateless application servers is an important aspect of three-tier applications. Stateless servers do not have host affinity, which means that we can freely migrate them. Moreover, fail-over is fast because we do not have to wait for a server to recover its state. We do not model the chained invocation of application servers. In our model, a client invokes a single application server, and this server does not invoke other application servers. Chained invocation does not present additional challenges from a reliability standpoint because application servers are stateless. We ignore this aspect in our model to simplify the discussion.

Application servers interact with the databases through transactions. For presentation simplicity, we only explicitly model the commitment processing, not the business logic or SQL queries performed by application servers. We use a function, called *compute()*, to abstract over the (transient) database manipulations performed by the business logic. In a travel example, *compute()* would query the database to determine flight and car availabilities, and perform the appropriate bookings. However, the *compute()* function does not commit the changes made to the database. It simply returns a result. Since the commitment processing can fail, we may call *compute()* multiple times for the same request. However, *compute()* is non-deterministic because its result depends on the database state. We assume that each result returned by *compute()* is non-nil. In particular, we model user-level aborts as regular result values. A user-level abort is a logical error condition that occurs during the business logic processing, for example if there are no more seats on a requested flight. Rather than model user-level aborts as special error values returned by *compute()*, we model them as regular result values that the databases then can refuse to commit.

Every application server has access to a local failure detector module which provides it with information about the crash of other application servers. Let a_1 and a_2 be any two application servers. We say that server a_2 *suspects* server a_1 if the failure detector module of a_2 suspects a_1 to have crashed. We abstract the suspicion information through a predicate *suspect()*. Let a_1 and a_2 be any two application servers. The execution of *suspect*(a_1) by server a_2 at t returns true if and only if a_2 suspects a_1 at time t.

Database Servers

Database server processes are denoted by $s_1, s_2, \ldots, s_n$ ($s_i \in Server$). Since we want our approach to apply to off-the-shelf database systems, we view a database server as an XA [15] engine. In particular, a database server is a "pure" server: it does not invoke other servers, it only responds to invocations. We do not represent full XA functionality, we only represent the transaction commitment aspects of XA (*prepare()* and *commit()*). We use two primitives, *vote()* and *decide()*, to represent the transaction commitment functionality. The *vote*() primitive takes as a parameter a result identifier, and returns a vote in the domain Vote = {yes, no}. Roughly speaking, a yes vote means that the database server is able to commit the result (i.e., the corresponding transaction). The *decide*() primitive takes two parameters: a result identifier and an outcome in the domain Outcome = {commit, abort}. The *decide*() primitive returns an outcome value such that: (a) if the input value is abort, then the returned value is also abort; and (b) if the database server has voted yes for that result, and the input value is commit, then the returned value is also commit.

3 The Exactly-Once Transaction Problem

Roughly speaking, providing the *e-Transaction* (*exactly-once Transaction*) abstraction comes down to ensuring that, whenever a client issues a request, then unless the client crashes, there is a corresponding result computed by an application server, the result is committed at every database server, and then eventually delivered by the client. The servers might go through a sequence of aborted intermediate results until one commits and the client delivers the corresponding result. Ensuring database consistency requires that all database servers agree on the outcome of every result (abort or commit). Client-side consistency requires that only a committed result is returned to the end-user.

In the following, we state the specification of the *e-Transaction* problem. More details on the underlying intuition and the rationale behind the problem specification are given in [19]. For the sake of presentation simplicity, but without loss of generality, we consider here only *one* client, and assume that the client issues only *one* request. We omit explicit identifiers to distinguish different clients and different requests, together with identifiers that relate different results to the same request.

We define the *e-Transaction* problem with three categories of properties: *termination*, *agreement*, and *validity*. Termination captures liveness guarantees by preventing blocking situations. Agreement captures safety guarantees by ensuring the consistency of the client and the databases. Validity restricts the space of possible results to exclude meaningless ones.

- **Termination.**

   (T.1) If the client issues a request, then unless it crashes, the client eventually delivers a result;
   (T.2) If any database server s_i votes for a result, then s_i eventually commits or aborts the result.

- **Agreement.**

   (A.1) No result is delivered by the client unless the result is committed by all database servers;
   (A.2) No database server commits two different results;
   (A.3) No two database servers decide differently on the same result.

- **Validity.**

   (V.1) If the client delivers a result, then the result must have been computed by an application server with, as a parameter, a request issued by the client;
   (V.2) No database server commits a result unless all database servers have voted yes for that result.

Termination ensures that a client does not remain indefinitely blocked (T.1). Intuitively, this property provides *at-least-once* request processing guarantee to the end-user, and frees her from the burden of having to retry requests. Termination also ensures that no database server remains blocked forever waiting for the outcome of a result (T.2), i.e., no matter what happens to the client. This *non-blocking* property is important because a database server that has voted yes for a result might have locked some resources. These remain inaccessible until the result is committed or aborted [3]. Agreement ensures the consistency of the result (A.1) and the databases (A.3). Agreement also guarantees *at most-once* request processing

(A.2). The first part of Validity (V.1) excludes trivial solutions to the problem where the client *invents* a result, or delivers a result without having issued any request. The second part (V.2) conveys the classical constraint of transactional systems: no result can be committed if at least some database server "refuses" to do so. Basically, and as we point out in Section 6, the *e-Transaction* specification adds to the traditional termination properties of distributed databases, properties that bridge the gap between databases and clients on one hand, and between *at-least-once* and *exactly-once* on the other hand.

4 An Exactly-Once Transaction Protocol

Our *e-Transaction* protocol consists of several parts. One is executed at the client, one is executed at the application servers, and one at the database servers. The interaction schemes between the client, the application servers and the database servers is depicted on Figure 1. The client interacts with the application servers, which themselves interact with database servers. The horizontal boxes in the figure illustrate synchronization points through our *write-once* registers.

We give below an intuitive idea of the various components of our distributed *e-Transaction* protocol. More details can be found in the full paper [18].

Client Protocol

The client part of the protocol is encapsulated within the implementation of an *issue()* primitive. This primitive is typically invoked by the end-user of an e-transactional system. The primitive is invoked with a request as an input parameter and is supposed to eventually return a result. In the following, when we talk about the client executing a given step, we actually mean the *issue()* primitive is executing a given step. Our *e-Transaction* protocol is actually transparent to the client.

Basically, the client keeps retransmitting the request to the application servers, until it receives back a committed result. For a given request, the client might need to go through several tries (intermediate results) before it gets a committed result. Each try (result) corresponds to an individual transaction and several transactions might be triggered before one of them commits. The client does not initiate a new transaction unless the clients gets the confirmation that the previous transaction was aborted.

To optimize the failure-free scenario, the client does not initially send the request to all application servers unless it does not receive a result after a back-off period. After this period, the client sends the request to all application servers.

Application Server Protocol

Application servers execute what we call an *asynchronous replication* protocol [18]. In a "nice" run, where no process crashes or is suspected to have crashed, the protocol goes as follows. There is a default primary application server that is supposed to initially receive the client's request. The primary application server computes a result for the client's request, and orchestrates a distributed atomic commitment protocol among the database servers to commit or abort that result. The result corresponds to a unique transaction. Then the application server informs the client of the outcome of the result, i.e., of the corresponding transaction. The outcome might be commit or abort, according to the votes of the databases.

Any application server that suspects the crash of the primary becomes itself a primary and tries to terminate the result. If the result was already committed, the new primary finishes the commitment of that result and sends back the decision to the client. Otherwise, the new primary aborts the result, and informs the client about the abort decision.

Write-Once Registers

Some form of synchronization is needed among application servers because (1) the result computation is non-deterministic and (2) several primaries might be active at the same time - we do not assume reliable failure detection. We need to ensure that the application servers agree on the outcome of every result. We factor out the synchronization complexity through a consensus abstraction, which we call *write-once registers* (or simply *wo-registers*). A wo-register has two operations: *read()* and *write()*. Roughly speaking, if several processes try to write a value in the register, only one value is written, and once it is written, no other value can be written. A process can read that value by invoking the operation *read()*. More precisely:

- *Write()* takes a parameter *input* and returns a parameter *output*. The returned parameter is either *input* (the process has indeed written its value) or some other value already written in the register.

- *Read()* returns a value written in the register or the initial value $\perp$. If a value v was written in the register, then, if a process keeps invoking the *read()* operation, then unless the process crashes, eventually the value returned is the value v.

Intuitively, the semantics of a wo-register looks very much like that of a CD-ROM. In fact, a wo-register is a simple extension of a *consensus* object [20]. We simply assume here the existence of *wait-free* wo-registers [20]. It is easy to see how one could obtain a wait-free implementation of a wo-register from a consensus protocol executed among the application servers (e.g., [4]): every application server would have a copy of the register. Basically, writing a value in the wo-register comes down to *proposing* that value for the consensus protocol. To read a value, a process simply returns the decision value received from the consensus protocol, if any, and returns $\perp$ if no consensus has been triggered.

Of course, the existence of a shared wo-register implies the existence of a consensus protocol among application servers. Given our assumption of a majority of correct application servers, reliable channels, and an *eventually perfect failure detector* (see above), we can implement a consensus protocol that is even quite efficient in "nice" runs [21] (where no process has crashed or is suspected to have crashed).

Database Server Protocol

A database server is a pure server (not a client of other servers): it waits for messages from application servers to either vote or decide on results. The database server returns its vote (for a given result, i.e., transaction) when it is asked to do so, and commits a transaction when it is asked to do so. The database server protocol has a parameter that indicates whether the protocol is called initially or during recovery. During recovery, a database server informs the application servers about its "coming back".

Correctness Assumptions

We first give here the assumptions underlying the correctness of our protocol. We will discuss the practicality of these assumptions in Section 6.

We assume that a majority of application servers are *correct*: they are always up. The failure detector among application servers is supposed to be *eventually perfect* in the sense of [4]. In other words, we assume that the following properties are satisfied: (*completeness*) if any application server crashes at time t, then

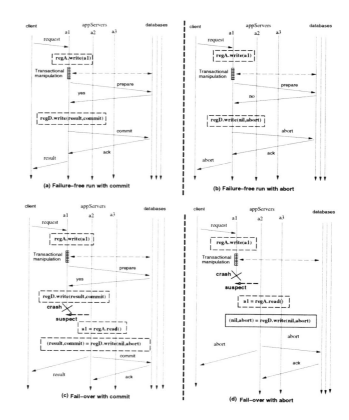

Figure 1: Communication steps in various executions

there is a time $t' > t$ after which it is permanently suspected by every application server; (*accuracy*) there is a time after which no correct application server is ever suspected by any application server. We also assume that all database servers are *good*: (1) they always recover after crashes, and eventually stop crashing, and (2) if an application server keeps computing results, a result eventually commits.[3]

We assume that clients, application servers, and database servers, are all connected through reliable channels. The guarantees provided by the reliable channel abstraction are captured by the following properties: (*termination*) if a process p_i *sends* message m to process p_j, then unless p_i or p_j crash, p_j eventually *receives* m; (*integrity*) every process *receives* a message at most once, and only if the message was previously *sent* by some process (messages are supposed to be uniquely identified).

---

[3]The assumption that results *eventually commit* does not mean that there will eventually be a seat on a full flight. It means that an application server will eventually stop trying to book a seat on a full flight, and instead compute a result that can actually run to completion, for example a result that informs the user of the booking problem.

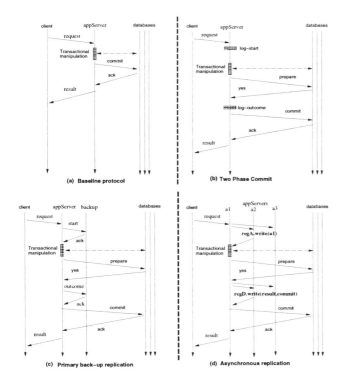

Figure 2: Communication steps in failure-free executions

5 Performance Measures

In the following, we contrast the performance of our protocol with that of alternative approaches that address similar issues.

Overview

Basically, we compare the performance of our protocol (Figure 2d) with those of a baseline protocol where no reliability is ensured (Figure 2a), a traditional 2PC protocol that ensures at-most-once request processing (Figure 2b), and a primary-backup replication scheme we adapted in [19] to implement *e-Transactions* (Figure 2c). The primary-backup scheme requires a perfect failure detection mechanism among the application servers (a false suspicion might lead to an inconsistency).

We focus here simply on "nice" runs where no process crashes or is suspected to have crashed. In particular, our performance measures takes into account the number of messages exchanged in a "nice" run of a *wo-register* implementation.

In terms of latency, we show that our protocol introduces an overhead of about 16% over the baseline unreliable protocol (that does not offer any guarantee).

This overhead is actually lower than the overhead of a 2PC protocol, which we show is around 23% in our environment. This might look surprising at first glance because our protocol also ensures a non-blocking property of databases besides the *exactly-once* guarantee (2PC is blocking [3], and ensures only *at-most-once* request delivery). However, in contrast to 2PC, our protocol does not induce any forced disk IO. We use the same replication scheme to ensure client's outcome determination as we use to guarantee non-blocking.

Analytic Measures

Figure 2 depicts the communication steps of the various protocols. Since our protocol requires a majority of correct application processes, we consider here the case where a single application server crash is tolerated. In that case, three application servers are required. In our primary-backup scheme, a single backup is enough.

We assume here an implementation of a *wo-register* using an optimized consensus protocol along the lines of [4]. Basically, in a "nice" run, it takes only a round trip message for the first primary to *write* into the register (the first consensus coordinator is the default primary application server).

In terms of the latency, as viewed by the client, our protocol introduces the same number of communication steps than a primary-backup scheme, but more than a 2PC protocol or an unreliable baseline protocol. The 2PC introduces however eager disk accesses.

Experimental Measures

We quantify here the performance of our protocol in a practical setting. Our implementation uses off-the-shelf middleware components: Orbix 2.3 Object Request Broker [16] and Oracle 8.0.3 [17].

The actual data manipulation by the application server is the same in all protocols: the application server executes some SQL statements to update a bank account on a single database, and ends the transaction. The client and servers execute on HP C180 PA-RISC workstations, running HP-UX 10.20. The machines are connected by a 10 Mbit/Sec. production ethernet, but we obtained the measurements in the late evening when it is lightly loaded. We measured the end-to-end latency as seen by clients. For each protocol, we executed multiple identical transactions to quantify the variation in response time. We computed the 90% confidence interval for the mean response time. In all cases, the width of this interval was found to be less than 10 %. In this test, a single back-end database (running on a cluster) is involved.

protocol	baseline	AR	2PC
start	3.4	3.5	3.5
end	3.4	3.5	3.4
commit	18.6	18.8	17.5
prepare	0	19.0	21.2
SQL	187.0	193.2	190.6
log-start	0	4.5	12.5
log-outcome	0	4.7	12.7
other	5.0	5.1	5.1
total	217.4	252.3	266.5
cost of reliability	0%	+16%	+23%

Figure 3: Comparing the latency of the protocols (milliseconds)

This configuration is, we believe, representative of current three-tier architectures where a single database is typically involved.

To implement the 2PC, we used the local disk file of the coordinator application server, which is the traditional approach taken by most transaction processing monitors. The application server logs information about the transaction before it is started and after the outcome has been determined. Logging is a synchronous operation, the application server waits for the logging operation to complete before it continues the protocol execution.

The resulting measurements are summarized in Figure 3. We measured the response time for three protocols. We did not measure the response time for the primary-backup scheme, (Figure 2c) because the response-time components are the same as our protocol (Figure 2a). In addition to the client-side elapsed time, we also allocated portions of this time to specific software components that service requests. Our implementation of 2PC is based here on the presumed abort optimization [22].

The "other" category in Figure 3 is the amount of time which is unaccounted for after allocating the response time to the listed components. Since the listed component times are all measured at the application server, the "other" category includes the communication cost of the client-server interaction. A round-trip Orbix RPC without parameters takes about 3-5 milliseconds in our environment, so the client-server communication accounts for most of the time in the "other" category.

The numbers in Figure 3 show that we save about 25 milliseconds by eliminating the forced-log IOs of a 2PC. In the 2PC, to maintain the log, the application server writes a start record before sending out pre-pare messages (this is based on a "presumed nothing" two-phase commit). When it knows the outcome, and the outcome is commit, it will write a commit record. Writing the start and commit records are eager IO operations.

6 Concluding Remarks

On the specification of e-Transactions. Intuitively, the *e-Transaction* abstraction is very desirable. If a client issues a request "within" an *e-Transaction*, then, unless it crashes, the request is executed *exactly-once*, and the client eventually delivers the corresponding result. If the client crashes, the request is executed *at-most-once* and the database resources are eventually released. As conveyed by our specification in Section 3, the properties underlying *e-Transactions* encompass all players in a three-tier architecture: the client, the application servers, and the databases. Not surprisingly, some of the properties are similar to those of *non-blocking transaction termination* [3]. In some sense, those properties ensure *non-blocking at-most-once*. Basically, the specification of *e-Transactions* extend them to bridge the gap between *at-most-once* and *exactly-once* semantics.

On the asynchrony of the replication scheme. The heart of our *e-Transaction* protocol is the *asynchronous* replication scheme performed among the application servers. Roughly speaking, with a "patient" client and a reliable failure detector, our replication scheme tends to be similar to a primary backup scheme [12]: there is only one active primary at a time. With an "impatient" client, or an unreliable failure detector, we may easily end up in the situation where all application servers try to concurrently commit or abort a result. In this case, like in an *active replication* scheme [11], there is no single primary and all application servers have equal rights. One of the characteristics of our replication protocol is precisely that it may vary, at run-time, between those two extreme schemes.

On the practicality of our protocol. Many of the assumptions we made are "only" needed to ensure the termination properties of our protocol. These include the assumption of a majority of correct application servers, the assumption of an eventually perfect failure detector among application servers, the assumption that every database server being eventually always up, and the liveness properties of wo-registers and communication channels. In other words, if any of these properties is violated, the protocol might block, but would not violate any agreement nor validity property of our specification. In practice, these termination-related assumptions need only hold during the processing of a request. For example, we only need to assume that, for each request, a majority of application servers remain up, and every database server will eventually stay up long enough to successfully commit the result of that request.[4] Furthermore, the assumption of a majority of correct processes is only needed to keep the protocol simple: we do not explicitly deal with application server recovery. Without the assumption of a majority of correct processes, one might still ensure termination properties by making use of underlying building blocks that explicitly handle recovery, as in [25, 21]. The assumption of reliable channels do not exclude link failures, as long as we can assume that any link failure is eventually repaired. In practice, the abstraction of reliable channels is implemented by re-transmitting messages and tracking duplicates.

Finally, to simplify the presentation of our protocol, we did not consider garbage collection issues. For example, we did not address the issue of cleanning the wo-register arrays. To integrate a garbage collector task, one needs to state that the *at-most-once* guarantee is only ensured if the client does not retransmit requests after some known period of time. Being able to state this kind of guarantees would require a timed model, e.g., along the lines of [26].

On the failure detection schemes. It is important to notice that our protocol makes use of *three* failure detection schemes in our architecture, and this is actually not surprising given the nature of *three-tier* systems. (1) Among application servers, we assume a failure detector that is eventually perfect in the sense of [4]. As we pointed out, false failure detections do however not lead to any inconsistency. (2) The application servers rely on a simple notification scheme to tell when a database server has crashed and recovered. In practice, application servers would detect database crashes because the database connection breaks when the database server crashes. Application servers would receive an exception (or error status) when trying to manipulate the database. This can be

---

[4]Ensuring the recovery of every database server (within a reasonable time delay) is typically achieved by running databases in clusters of machines [23, 24]. With a cluster, we can ensure that databases always recover within a reasonable delay, but we must still assume that the system reaches a "steady state" where database servers stay up *long enough* so that we can guarantee the progress of the request processing. In an asynchronous system however, with no explicit notion of time, the notion of *long enough* is impossible to characterize, and is simply replaced with the term *always*.

implemented without requiring the database servers to know the identity of the application servers. (3) Clients use a simple timeout mechanisms to re-submit requests. This design decision reflects our expectation that clients can communicate with servers across the Internet, which basically gives rise to unpredictable failure detection.

On the practicality of our implementation. Our current implementation was built using off-the-shelf technologies: the Orbix 2.3 Object Request Broker [16] and the Oracle 8.0.3 database management system [17]. Our prototype was however aimed exclusively at testing purposes. In terms of the latency, as viewed by a client, our protocol introduces an overhead of about 16% over a baseline protocol that does not offer any reliability guarantee. This overhead corresponds to the steady-state, failure and suspicion free executions. These are the executions that are the most likely to occur in practice, and for which protocols are usually optimized. Nevertheless, for a complete evaluation of the practicality of our protocol, one obviously needs to consider the actual response-time of the protocol in the case of various failure alternatives. This should go through the use of underlying consensus protocols that are also optimized in the case of failures and failure suspicions, e.g., [27, 21].

Acknowledgements

We are very grateful to to Meichun Hsu for her helpful comments about the structure of our protocol, and to Jim Gray for sharing with us his views about the meaning of reliability in three-tier architectures.

References

[1] D. Chappell, "How microsoft transaction server changes the com programming model," *Microsoft Systems Journal*, January 1998.

[2] Object Management Group, *CORBA Services—Transaction Service*, 1.1 ed., November 1997.

[3] P. A. Bernstein, V. Hadzilacos, and N. Goodman, *Concurrency Control and Recovery in Database Systems*. Reading, Mass.: Addison-Wesley, 1987.

[4] T. Chandra and S. Toueg, "Unreliable failure detectors for reliable distributed systems," *Journal of the ACM*, vol. 43, no. 2, pp. 225–267, 1996.

[5] J. H. Slye and E. N. Elnozahy, "Supporting nondeterministic execution in fault-tolerant systems," in *Proceedings of the IEEE International Symposium on Fault-Tolerant Computing*, June 1996.

[6] B. W. Lampson, "Reliable messages and connection establishment," in *Distributed Systems* (S. Mullender, ed.), Addison-Wesley, 1993.

[7] P. Bernstein, M. Hsu, and B. Mann, "Implementing recoverable requests using queues," in *Proceedings of the 1990 ACM SIGMOD International Conference on Management of Data*, May 1990.

[8] D. Lomet and G. Weikum, "Efficient transparent application recovery in client-server information systems," in *Proceedings of SIGMOD'98*, 1998.

[9] M. C. Little and S. K. Shrivastava, "Integrating the object transaction service with the web," in *Proceedings of the Second International Workshop on Enterprise Distributed Object Computing (EDOC)*, IEEE, 1998.

[10] S. Frølund and R. Guerraoui, "Corba fault-tolerance: why it does not add up," in *Proceedings of the IEEE Workshop on Future Trends of Distributed Systems*, December 1999.

[11] F. B. Schneider, "Replication management using the state machine approach," in *Distributed Systems* (S. Mullender, ed.), Addison-Wesley, 1993.

[12] N. Budhiraja, K. Marzullo, F. B. Schneider, and S. Toueg, "The primary-backup approach," in *Distributed Systems* (S. Mullender, ed.), Addison-Wesley, 1993.

[13] D. Powell, D. Seaton, G. Bonn, P. Verissimo, and F. Waeselynk, "The delta-4 approach to dependability in open distributed computing systems," in *International Symposium on Fault-Tolerant Computing Systems*, IEEE, June 1988.

[14] S. Frølund and R. Guerraoui, "X-ability: a theory of replication," in *Proceedings of the ACM Symposium on Principles of Distributed Computing (PODC)*, July 2000.

[15] x/Open Company Ltd, *Distributed Transaction Processing: The XA Specification*, 1991. XO/SNAP/91/050.

[16] IONA Technologies Ltd, *Orbix 2.2 Programming Guide*, 1997.

[17] Oracle Corporation, *Oracle8 Application Developer's Guide*. Chapter 18, Oracle XA, Relase 8.0, A58241-01.

[18] S. Frølund and R. Guerraoui, "Implementing e-transactions with asynchronous replication," Tech. Rep. HPL-2000-46, Hewlett-Packard Laboratories, April 1999.

[19] S. Frølund and R. Guerraoui, "Exactly-once-transactions," Tech. Rep. HPL-1999-105, Hewlett-Packard Laboratories, September 1999.

[20] M. Herlihy, "Wait-free synchronization," *ACM Transactions on Programming Languages and Systems*, vol. 13, pp. 123–149, January 1991.

[21] R. Boichat, S. Frølund, and R. Guerraoui, "Making consensus practical," Tech. Rep. DSC-2000-018, Swiss Federal Institute of Technology, Communication Systems Department, April 2000.

[22] J. Gray and A. Reuter, *Transaction Processing: Concepts and Techniques*. Morgan Kaufmann, 1993.

[23] P. S. Weygant, *Clusters for High-Availability: A Primer of HP-UX Solutions*. Prentice-Hall, Hewlett-Packard Professional Books., 1996.

[24] W. Vogels, D. Dumitriu, K. Birman, R. Gamache, M. Massa, R. Short, J. Vert, J. Barrera, and J. Gray, "The design and architecture of the microsoft cluster service—a practical approach to high-availability and scalability," in *Proceedings of the International Symposium on Fault-Tolerant Computing Systems*, June 1998.

[25] M. Aguilera, W. Chen, and S. Toueg, "Failure detection and consensus in the crash-recovery model," in *Proceedings of the International Workshop on Distributed Algorithms, Springer-Verlag (LNCS)*, April 1998.

[26] C. Fetzer and F. Cristian, "The timed asynchronous model," Tech. Rep. CS97-519, UCSD, September 1997.

[27] M. Hurfin and M. Raynal, "A simple and fast asynchronous consensus protocol based on a weak failure detector," *Distributed Computing*, vol. 12, no. 4, 1999.

Data Replication Strategies for Fault Tolerance and Availability on Commodity Clusters

Cristiana Amza, Alan L. Cox, and Willy Zwaenepoel
Department of Computer Science
Rice University
{amza, alc, willy}@cs.rice.edu

Abstract

Recent work has shown the advantages of using persistent memory for transaction processing. In particular, the Vista transaction system uses recoverable memory to avoid disk I/O, thus improving performance by several orders of magnitude. In such a system, however, the data is safe when a node fails, but unavailable until it recovers, because the data is kept in only one memory.

In contrast, our work uses data replication to provide both reliability and data availability while still maintaining very high transaction throughput. We investigate four possible designs for a primary-backup system, using a cluster of commodity servers connected by a write-through capable system area network (SAN). We show that logging approaches outperform mirroring approaches, even when communicating more data, because of their better locality. Finally, we show that the best logging approach also scales well to small shared-memory multiprocessors.

1 Introduction

We address the problem of building a reliable transaction server using a cluster of commodity computers, i.e., standard servers and system area networks (SAN). We use the Vista system as the transaction server [5]. Vista is a very high-performance transaction system. It relies on recoverable memory [2] to avoid disk I/O, thereby achieving its very high throughput. Because Vista does not store its data on disk, but rather keeps it in reliable memory, the data remains safe when the machine fails, but it is unavailable until the machine recovers.

In contrast, our work uses data replication to provide both reliability and data availability. We consider a primary-backup solution in a cluster of computers, in which a primary normally executes the transactions. The data is replicated on the backup, which takes over when the primary fails. We focus on the problem of maintaining good transaction throughput in spite of having to update the backup. We do not address other cluster issues such as crash detection and group view management, for which well-known solutions are available [12].

Recent work has suggested that such clusters can be built in a fairly transparent manner, taking a high-performance single-processor transaction system and simply extending it to mirror its execution or its data on the backup machine using write through [15]. Our experience is different: we found that with current machines and SANs, the performance of such a straightforward implementation is disappointing. We attribute this different outcome to the fact that, in our environment, the processor speed is much higher than in the experiments reported in Zhou et al. [15], while the network speed is approximately the same. Based on this observation, we investigate ways to restructure the single-processor transaction system to achieve better performance. We develop and compare four protocols to communicate the modifications made by the transactions from the primary to the backup.

From an architectural viewpoint, we also investigate whether there is any gain to be had from actively involving the processor on the backup machine during the normal operation (i.e., when the primary is functioning and processing transactions), or whether it suffices for the backup to be passive and simply function as a mirror site. This issue has implications for the extent to which the backup can or should be used to execute transactions itself, in a more full-fledged cluster, not restricted to a simple primary-backup configuration.

In our experiments, we use a 600Mhz Compaq Alpha 21164A (EV5.6) processor as both the primary and the backup, and a second-generation Memory Channel as the SAN. The Memory Channel is an instance of a network with "write through" capability, i.e., a memory region on one node can be mapped to a memory region of another node, and writes by the first node to that memory region are written through to the second node. Such capabilities are also available in the VIA standard [3]. We believe the chosen environment — processor, network, and transaction processing system — reflects state-of-the-art hardware and software.

Our conclusion is that log-based approaches with a log designed for good locality of access lead to the highest transaction throughput. The advantages of spatial locality of access in the logging approaches are two-fold. First, locality in the memory accesses, means better cache utilization on the primary. Second, locality in the I/O space accesses, offers better opportunities for data aggregation and thus optimal bandwidth utilization on the SAN between the primary and backup.

In the environment we are using, the difference between an active and a passive backup is moderate (14% to 29%). It is essential, however, that the log be designed with locality and reduced communication to the backup in mind, because of bandwidth limitations in current SANs, relative to current processor speeds. This is especially true when executing multiple transaction streams on a multiprocessor primary as this puts increased stress on the SAN.

We have also developed mirroring approaches, which have the lowest data communication requirements among the passive backup versions, but their performance is inferior to logging, because of their lesser locality.

These results reflect commonly held wisdom in disk-based transaction processing systems, where sequential disk access resulting from using logs leads to better performance than mirroring approaches [4]. Somewhat surprisingly, this wisdom appears to apply to memory-based systems as well, because of the importance of locality and the limited bandwidth of SANs relative to processor speeds and memory bandwidths.

The remainder of this paper is structured as follows. Section 2 provides the necessary background for our work. Section 3 evaluates the straightforward implementation of Vista on our platform. Section 4 describes how we restructure Vista for improved standalone performance. In Section 5 we report the performance of these restructured versions using a passive backup. A comparison to using an active backup is presented in Section 6. We discuss scaling to larger databases in Section 7. We investigate how the use of a small shared-memory multiprocessor as a primary affects the results in Section 8. Section 9 discusses related work. Section 10 concludes the paper.

2   Background

This section describes the transaction API, the implementation of that API in (single-node) Vista, the relevant characteristics and performance of the hardware on which we did the experiments, and the benchmarks used.

2.1   API

We support a very simple API, first introduced by RVM [8] and later implemented by a variety of systems, including Vista [5]. The transaction data is mapped into the virtual address space of the server. The API contains the following routines:

```
begin_transaction()
set_range()
commit_transaction()
abort_transaction()
```

begin_transaction, commit_transaction, and abort_transaction implement the customary transaction semantics [4]. The set_range operation takes as its argument a contiguous region of virtual memory. It indicates to the system that the transaction may modify some or all of the data in this region.

As in Zhou et al. [15], our primary-backup implements a 1-safe commit mechanism [4]. In a 1-safe design, the primary returns successfully from a commit as soon as the commit is complete on the primary. It does not wait for the commit flag to be written through to the backup. This leaves a very short window of vulnerability (a few microseconds) during which a failure may cause the loss of a committed transaction.

The API contains no provisions for expressing concurrency control. It is assumed that concurrency control is implemented by a separate layer of software.

2.2   Vista

We use Vista because it is, to the best of our knowledge, the fastest open-source transaction system available. As such, it provides a good "stress test" for a cluster-based server.

Vista achieves high performance by avoiding disk I/O. Instead, it relies on the Rio reliable memory system [2] to achieve persistence. Rio protects main memory against its two common causes of failure, namely power failures and operating system crashes. An un-interruptible power supply guards against power failures. Guarding against operating system crashes is done by protecting the memory during a crash and restoring it during reboot. Extensive tests have shown that very high levels of reliability can be achieved by these methods (see Chen et al. for detailed measurement results [2]).

Besides avoiding disk I/O, the presence of a reliable memory underneath allows considerable simplification in the implementation of transaction semantics [5]. Vista stores the database proper and all of its data structures, including an undo log, in Rio reliable memory. On a set_range it copies the current contents of the specified region to the undo log. Modifications to the database are then made in-place. In the case of an abort or a crash before the transaction completes, the data from the undo log is re-installed in the database during abort handling or during recovery. In the case of a commit, the undo log entry is simply deleted. No redo log is necessary, because the updates are already made in-place.

2.3 Hardware Environment

Compaq's Memory Channel network enables a processor within one machine to write directly into the physical memory of another machine without software intervention. In reality, a processor writes to an I/O space address that is backed by its local Memory Channel interface. That interface transmits the written value to the remote machine's interface, which then performs a DMA operation to deposit the value into physical memory. Thus, the remote processor is not involved in the transfer, but the normal cache coherence mechanism ensures that it sees the new value promptly. The kernel (software) and the remote processor are only involved at initialization time, when a mapping is created between the I/O space on the sending machine and the physical memory on the receiving one.

Only remote writes are supported; remote reads are not. This asymmetry gives rise to the double mapping of shared data: one (I/O space) mapping is used to write the data and another (ordinary) mapping is used to read the local copy of the data in physical memory. When the Memory Channel interface is configured in "loopback" mode, it applies any changes to the local copy in addition to transmitting them over the network. Loopback is not, however, instantaneous. There is a substantial delay between the write to I/O space and the change appearing in the local copy. This presents a problem, because a processor may not see its own last written value on a subsequent read. Consequently, the most practical method for implementing shared data is to disable loopback and perform "write doubling". In other words, the same write is performed on the local copy and the I/O space.

In our experiments, we use AlphaServer 4100 5/600 machines, each with 4 600 MHz 21164A processors and 2 GBytes of memory. Each AlphaServer runs Digital Unix 4.0F, with TruCluster 1.6 (Memory Channel) extensions. Each processor has three levels of cache, two levels of on-chip cache and an 8 Mbyte, direct-mapped, board-level cache with a 64-byte line size.

The servers are connected with a Memory Channel II network. We measured the network latency and bandwidth characteristics by a simple ping-pong test sending increasing size "packets" over the Memory Channel (we write contiguous chunks of memory of the "packet" size to simulate this). Uncontended latency for a 4 byte write is 3.3 microseconds. When one processor writes to another pro-

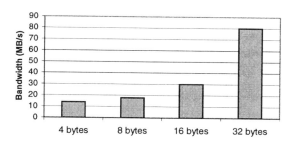

Figure 1. Effective Bandwidth (in Mbytes/sec) with Different Packet Sizes

cessor and the network is otherwise idle, we measured a maximum bandwidth of 80 Mbytes per second (for 1 Mbyte "packet" sizes).

Secondly, we used a test program to approximate the bandwidth variation of the system with the Memory Channel packet size. The Alpha chip has 6 32-byte write buffers. Contiguous stores share a write buffer and are flushed to the system bus together. The Memory Channel interface simply converts the PCI write to a similar-size Memory Channel packet. The current design does not aggregate multiple PCI write transactions into a single Memory Channel packet, so the maximum packet size supported by the system as a whole is 32 bytes. We measured the bandwidth variation by writing large regions with varying strides (a stride of one would create 32-byte packets, a stride of two, 16-byte packets and so on). Figure 1 shows the measured process-to-process bandwidths for 4 to 32-byte packets.

2.4 Benchmarks

We use the Debit-Credit and Order-Entry benchmarks provided with Vista [5]. These benchmarks are variants of the widely used TPC-B and TPC-C benchmarks.

TPC-B models banking transactions [10]. The database consists of a number of branches, tellers, and accounts. Each transaction updates the balance in a random account and the balances in the corresponding branch and teller. Each transaction also appends a history record to an audit trail. The Debit-Credit benchmark differs from TPC-B primarily in that it stores the audit trail in a 2 Mbytes circular buffer in order to keep it in memory.

TPC-C models the activities of a wholesale supplier who receives orders, payments, and deliveries [11]. The database consists of a number of warehouses, districts, customers, orders, and items. Order-Entry uses the three transaction types specified in TPC-C that update the database.

In both Debit-Credit and Order-Entry we issue transactions sequentially and as fast as possible. They do not perform any terminal I/O in order to isolate the performance of the underlying transaction system.

	Debit-Credit	Order-Entry
Single machine	218627	73748
Primary-backup	38735	27035

Table 1. Transaction Throughput for Straightforward Implementation (in transactions per second)

	Debit-Credit	Order-Entry
Modified data	140.8	38.9
Undo log	323.2	199.8
Meta-data	6708.4	433.6
Total data	7172.4	672.3

Table 2. Data Communicated to the Backup in the Straightforward Implementation (in MB)

The size of the database is 50 Mbytes, unless we explicitly say otherwise. This is the largest possible size for which we can do the appropriate mapping to the Memory Channel for all versions and configurations. We have also experimented with other database sizes (up to 1 Gbyte) and we show the results in section 7. For the experiments in section 8, where we run multiple transaction streams within a node, we use a 10 Mbyte database per transaction stream.

3 Straightforward Cluster Implementation

In an environment with a write-through network, the most straightforward extension of Vista to a primary-backup system is to simply map all of Vista's data — the database, the undo log, and the internal data structures — on to the backup node using the Memory Channel. Double writes are used to propagate writes to the backup. Other than inserting the double writes, this extension is completely transparent. On a failure, the backup simply takes over using its data structures, invoking the recovery procedure to undo any uncommitted transactions.

Table 1 presents the results for this implementation.

In short, throughput drops by a factor of 5.6 for Debit-Credit and by a factor of 2.7 for Order-Entry. This large drop in throughput is explained by the large amount of data that needs to be sent to the backup in this implementation, 7172 Mbytes for Debit-Credit and 672 Mbytes for Order-Entry. This communication and the implied extra local memory accesses necessary for the write-doubling adds 104.9 seconds to the 22.8 seconds single-machine execution time for Debit-Credit, resulting in a 5.6-fold decrease in throughput. Similarly, for Order-Entry, 672 Mbytes of data increase the execution time from 6.2 seconds to 17.1 seconds, or a 2.7-fold decrease in throughput. Closer inspection reveals that a very large percentage of the data communicated is meta-data, and only a small percentage reflects data modified by the transaction (see Table 2).

These numbers clearly indicate room for significant improvement by restructuring the software to use and communicate less meta-data. First, we discuss how we re-structure the standalone copy of the Vista library. Several versions are presented, reflecting further optimizations (see Section 4). While this re-structuring is obviously done with the intent of achieving better performance in a primary-backup configu-

ration, it turns out that it improves standalone performance as well. Second, we show how to adapt those versions for primary-backup execution in which the backup remains a passive entity (see Section 5). We mean by this that the CPU on the backup is not used. All data travels from the primary to the backup by virtue of a double write on the primary's data structures. Third, we present primary-backup versions in which the backup takes an active role (see Section 6). In other words, the data is communicated from the primary to the backup by message passing, not by write through. The backup CPU polls for incoming messages, and executes the commands in those messages.

4 Restructuring the Standalone System

4.1 Version 0: The Vista Library

A `set_range` call results in an undo log record being allocated in the heap and put in the undo log, which is implemented as a linked list. The base address and the length of the range are entered in the appropriate fields of this record. A second area of memory is allocated from the heap to hold the current version of the data, a pointer to that memory area is entered in the log record, and a `bcopy` is performed from the range in the database to this area. Database writes are in-place. On commit, a commit flag is set, the undo log record and the memory area holding the old data are freed.

4.2 Version 1: Mirroring by Copying

This version avoids the dynamic allocations and linked list manipulations of version 0. First, the linked list structure of the undo log is replaced by an array from which consecutive records are allocated by simply incrementing the array index. On a `set_range`, we only update this array to record the `set_range` coordinates. Second, a "mirror" copy of the database is introduced. The mirror copy is initialized to the same values as in the database. Writes to the database are then done in-place. On commit, a commit flag is set and for each `set_range` record, the corresponding range in the database is copied into the mirror. The undo log records are de-allocated by simply moving the array index back to its original location.

4.3 Version 2: Mirroring by Diffing

The mirror copy can also be maintained in a different fashion. As in Version 1, we maintain an array to record the areas on which a set_range has been performed, and we maintain a mirror copy of the database. As before, writes to the databases are done in-place. On a commit, however, for each set_range performed during the transaction, we compare the database copy and the mirror copy of the corresponding areas, and we update the mirror copy if necessary.

Version 2 has fewer writes than Version 1, because it only writes the modifications to the mirror, while in Version 1 the entire set_range area is written to the mirror. Version 2 does, however, incur the cost of the comparisons, while Version 1 performs a straight copy.

4.4 Version 3: Improved Logging

This version avoids the dynamic allocations and linked list manipulations, as do Versions 1 and 2. In addition, rather than using a mirror to keep the data for an undo, this data is kept in-line in the undo log. Specifically, rather than using a log record with a pointer to an area holding the old data as in Vista, we use a log record that includes the data. On a set_range we allocate such a log record by simply advancing a pointer in memory (rather than by incrementing an array index), and writing to this area the offset and the length of the set_range area followed by the data in it. Database writes continue to be done in-place. On a commit the corresponding undo log records are de-allocated by moving the log pointer back over the appropriate amount.

Version 3 has the same write traffic as Version 1. Its writes are, however, more localized than Versions 1 or 2. Version 3 only writes to the database and the undo log, while in Versions 1 and 2, the mirror copy is also written.

4.5 Performance

Table 3 reports the performance for the two benchmarks for each of the four versions. Although done with the intention of improving primary-backup performance by reducing the amount of data written to the backup, all the restructured versions improve the standalone performance of the transaction server. The improvement in Versions 1 and 2 is mainly a result of avoiding linked list manipulations and dynamic memory allocations. Comparing these two versions, we see that the cost of performing the comparison between the database and its mirror over the set_range areas in Version 2 outweighs the gains achieved by performing fewer writes.

	Debit-Credit	Order-Entry
Version 0 (Vista)	218627	73748
Version 1 (Mirror by Copy)	310077	81340
Version 2 (Mirror by Diff)	266922	74544
Version 3 (Improved Log)	372692	95809

Table 3. Standalone Transaction Throughput of the Re-structured Versions (in transactions per second)

More importantly, the additional substantial improvement in Version 3 results from the increased locality in the memory access patterns of the server. Accesses are strictly localized to the database and the undo log, while Versions 1 and 2 also access the mirror copy, which is much larger than the undo log.

5 Primary-Backup with Passive Backup

5.1 Implementation

For each of the Versions 0 through 3, we can define an equivalent primary-backup version by simply mapping a second copy of the data structures in Memory Channel space, and double writing any updates to those data structures. The primary-backup Version 0 is what we used for the experiments in Section 3.

A slight modification allows primary-backup implementations of Versions 1 and 2 that are more efficient during failure-free operation, at the expense of a longer recovery time. When mirroring is used, we maintain the undo log on the primary, but we do not write it through to the backup. This reduces the amount of communication that has to take place. On recovery, the backup will have to copy the entire database from the mirror, but since failure is the uncommon case, this is a profitable tradeoff. The primary-backup results for these Versions reflect this optimization.

5.2 Performance

Table 4 presents the results for Versions 0 through 3 using a passive backup strategy. In addition, Table 5 shows the data transmitted over the network for each version, broken down into modified transaction data, undo data, and metadata.

Several conclusions may be drawn from these results. First, and most important, Version 3, with its improved logging, continues to outperform all other versions by a substantial margin, and this regardless of the fact that it writes much more data to the backup than Version 2, mirroring by diffing. Better locality in its writes, translates to better coalescing in the processor's write buffers with larger Memory

Benchmark	Version	Modified Data	Undo Data	Meta-data	Total Data
Debit-Credit	Version 0 (Vista)	140.8	323.2	6708.4	7172.4
	Version 1 (Mirror by Copy)	140.8	323.2	40.4	504.4
	Version 2 (Mirror by Diff)	140.8	140.8	40.4	322.1
	Version 3 (Improved Log)	140.8	323.2	141.4	605.4
Order-Entry	Version 0 (Vista)	38.9	199.8	433.6	672.3
	Version 1 (Mirror by Copy)	38.9	199.8	3.7	242.4
	Version 2 (Mirror by Diff)	38.9	38.9	3.7	81.5
	Version 3 (Improved Log)	38.9	199.8	14.5	253.2

Table 5. Data transferred to Passive Backup for Different Versions (in MB)

	Debit-Credit	Order-Entry
Version 0 (Vista)	38735	27035
Version 1 (Mirror by Copy)	119494	49072
Version 2 (Mirror by Diff)	131574	51219
Version 3 (Improved Log)	275512	56248

Table 4. Primary-Backup Throughput (in transactions per second)

Channel packet sizes as a result. Thus, even if the total data communicated is higher, Version 3 makes much better use of the available Memory Channel bandwidth. Second, the differences between the mirroring versions are small, with Version 2 better than Version 1 (unlike in the standalone configuration). The overhead of the extra writes in Version 1 becomes more important as these writes now have to travel through the Memory Channel to the backup. All modified versions are better than Version 0 (Vista), by 210% to 610% for Debit Credit and 80% to 110% for Order-Entry.

6 Primary-Backup with Active Backup

6.1 Implementation

Unlike the versions described in Section 5, in which the CPU on the backup node is idle, in active backup schemes the backup CPU is actively involved. With an active backup, the primary processor communicates the committed changes in the form of a *redo* log. It is then the backup processor's responsibility to apply these changes to its copy of the data. Since this is the backup processor's only responsibility, it can easily keep up with the primary processor. If the log were to fill up, the primary processor must block.

We only consider active backup approaches based on a redo log. The reason is that they always communicate less data. The redo log-based approaches do not have to communicate the undo log or mirror, only the changed data.

The redo log is implemented as a circular buffer with two pointers: one pointer is maintained by the primary (i.e., the producer) and the other pointer is maintained by the backup

(i.e., the consumer). Quite simply, the backup processor busy waits for the primary's pointer to advance. This indicates committed data for the backup to consume. At commit, the primary writes through the redo log and only *after* all of the entries are written, does it advance the end of buffer pointer (the producer's pointer). Strictly speaking, the primary must also ensure that it does not overtake the backup, however unlikely that event may be. To avoid this possibility, the backup processor needs to write through its pointer back to the primary after each transaction is applied to its copy.

With active backup, although it is unnecessary for the primary to communicate mirror or undo log data to the backup, it must still maintain such information locally. We use the best local scheme, i.e., Version 3, to do this.

6.2 Performance

Table 6 compares the results for the best passive strategy to the active strategy. In addition, Table 7 shows the data transmitted over the network for these strategies, broken down in modified transaction data, undo log data, and meta-data.

The Active backup outperforms the Passive backup, by 14% for Debit-Credit and 29% for Order-Entry. The gains of the Active backup over the Passive backup for the Debit-Credit benchmark are comparatively smaller than the gains of either logging version over mirroring (14% versus 100%). We attribute this result to the significant reductions in communication overheads (PCI bus transactions and Memory Channel packets) due to coalescing already achieved by the best passive backup scheme. Compared to Debit-Credit, the throughput improvement of the Active backup over Passive backup is relatively higher in Order-Entry. The increased locality in the Active backup logging and further reduced communication overheads have more impact as the difference between the data transferred by the two versions is larger for this benchmark.

From Table 7, we see that the active approach tends to produce more meta-data to be sent to the backup. In the passive approach, the undo log carries some meta-data, but since the undo log is created as a result of set_range operations, a single piece of meta-data describes a whole

	Debit-Credit	Order-Entry
Best Passive (Version 3)	275512	56248
Active	314861	73940

Table 6. Passive vs. Active Throughput (in transactions per second)

contiguous region corresponding to the set_range arguments. In the active approach, in contrast, the meta-data describes modified data, which tends to be more spread out over non-contiguous regions of memory and therefore requires more meta-data entries. On the other hand, the set_range data is usually much larger than the actual data modified which results in a factor of 2 and 4 respectively decrease for the total data communicated.

7 Scaling to Larger Database Sizes

The Active backup is the only version where we are not limited by the Memory Channel space available and we can scale to any database size.

Table 8 presents the throughput variation of the Active backup version when increasing the database size. We see a graceful degradation in performance (by 13% and 22% respectively with a 1 Gbyte database). This is mainly due to the reduced locality of the database writes which results in more cache misses.

	Database sizes		
Benchmark	10 MB	100 MB	1GB
Debit-credit	322102	301604	280646
Order-entry	76726	69496	59989

Table 8. Throughput for Active Backup (in transactions per second) for Increasing Database Sizes

8 Using a Multiprocessor Primary

Parallel processing can increase the transaction throughput by the server. For throughput increases by a small factor, on the order of 2 to 4, such parallel processing can most economically/easily be done on commodity shared memory multiprocessors by a comparable number of processors. If the transaction streams are independent, or at least relatively independent, throughput increases should be near-linear. Synchronization between the different streams on an SMP is relatively inexpensive, and memory bandwidth appears to be sufficient to sustain multiple streams. When operating in a primary-backup configuration, this increase

in throughput, however, puts increased stress on the SAN between the primary and the backup. We would therefore expect the use of an SMP as a primary to favor those solutions that reduce bandwidth usage to the backup.

To validate this hypothesis, we carried out the following experiment. We used a 4-processor SMP as the primary, and executed a primary transaction server on each processor. The data accessed by the stream fed to different servers has no overlap, so the servers can proceed without synchronization, thus maximizing the possible transaction rates and exposing to the fullest extent possible any bottlenecks in the SAN.

The results are shown in Figure 2 for the Debit-Credit benchmark and in Figure 3 for the Order-Entry benchmark. We see that the Active logging version, shows a nearly linear increase in the aggregate throughput, while all the other versions do not scale well. The better scalability of the logging versions compared to the mirroring versions is again due to the fact that their accesses to I/O space memory show more locality with better opportunities for coalescing into larger I/O writes. This results in fewer transactions on the I/O bus and fewer Memory Channel packets sent, hence, lower communication overheads even when the total data communicated is higher.

The two benchmarks modify data mostly in small size chunks in random locations of the database with a large fraction of writes in 4-byte chunks (especially in Debit-Credit). With 32-byte packets, the process-to-process effective bandwidth of the system is 80 Mbytes/sec, while for 4-byte packets, the effective bandwidth is only about 14 Mbytes/sec (Figure 1). The Active logging version sends 32-byte packets, and thus takes advantage of the full 80 Mbytes/sec bandwidth and does not become bandwidth limited for either benchmark. The Passive logging version produces mixed packets (32-byte packets for the undo data and small packets for the modified data). Furthermore it sends more total data than the Active logging and becomes bandwidth limited at 2 processors. The two mirroring protocols do not benefit at all from data aggregation between consecutive writes and see an effective bandwidth below 20 Mbytes/sec with practically no increase in aggregate throughput with more processors.

9 Related Work

Clusters have been the focus of much research and several commercial products are available. Older commercial systems, such as Tandem [1] and Stratus [9], use custom-designed hardware. More recent efforts, such as Microsoft Cluster Service [12] and Compaq's TruCluster [13], use commodity parts.

Zhou et al. [15] address the more general problem of transparent process primary-backup systems, using check-

Benchmark	Version	Modified Data	Undo Data	Meta-data	Total Data
Debit-Credit	Best Passive (Version 3)	140.8	323.2	141.4	605.4
	Active	140.8	0	141.4	282.2
Order-Entry	Best Passive (Version 3)	38.9	199.8	14.5	253.2
	Active	38.9	0	24.7	63.6

Table 7. Data transferred to Active Backup vs. Passive Backup (in MB)

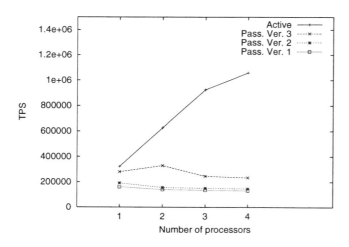

Figure 2. Transaction Throughput Using an SMP as the Primary (Debit-Credit Bench mark, in transactions per second)

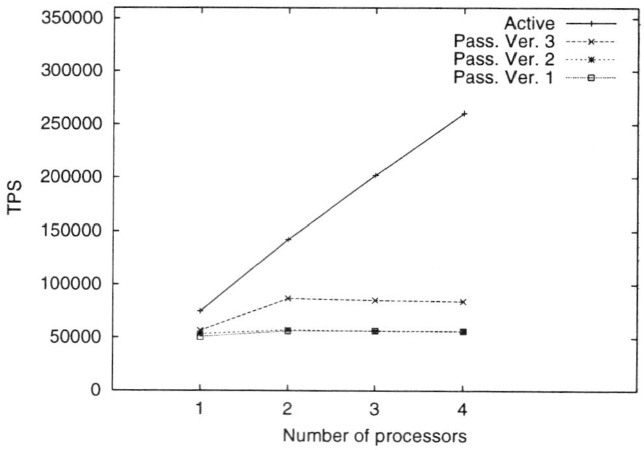

Figure 3. Transaction Throughput Using an SMP as the Primary (Order-Entry Benchm ark, in transactions per second)

pointing and rollback, while our work focuses exclusively on transaction processing. They do, however, use the Vista transaction processing system as an example application of their system. Their reported results were measured on a Shrimp network [6] connecting 66Mhz Pentiums. They came to the conclusion that transparent write through, with some optimizations, leads to acceptable performance in their environment. By virtue of doing solely transaction processing, our straightforward Vista implementation (Version 0) implements essentially the same optimizations, but performance remains disappointing. We attribute the difference in outcome to their use of a much slower processor (66Mhz Pentium vs. 600Mhz Alpha), while the networks are comparable in bandwidth. Shrimp also snoops on the memory bus, and therefore does not require double writing, which may be another factor affecting the results.

Papathanasiou and Markatos [7] study the use of remote memory to backup transaction processing. Although they do not use Vista, their standalone implementation appears similar, and the primary-backup implementation uses write through of the data structures of the primary. Their implementation uses 133Mhz Pentium processors running Windows NT and connected by a SCI ring network. They also use the Vista benchmarks to measure the performance of

their system. Their results are difficult to calibrate because they only provide primary-backup performance results, and no indication of standalone performance.

We use the same API as RVM [8] does to implement recoverable virtual memory, but the RVM system is based on disk logging. All disk-based systems, even optimized to write to a sequential log on disk, are ultimately limited by disk bandwidth. Vista used the RVM API to implement transactions based on reliable memory [5], thereby considerably improving its performance, but data availability is reduced because all data remains in memory. Our system overcomes Vista's main limitation, limited data availability, in an efficient way. Similar limitations exist in other systems based on reliable memory, e.g. Wu and Zwaenepoel [14].

10 Conclusions

Primary-backup services are essential in clusters attempting to provide high-availability data services. In this paper we have focused on transaction processing systems. We started from a standalone high-performance transaction processing system, Vista, that relies on reliable memory to achieve high transaction throughput. Although Vista would seem a prime candidate for conversion to a primary-backup system using the write through capabilities of modern system area networks, we found that such an implementation leads to transaction throughput much below that of a standalone server. Significant restructuring of the server was needed to achieve good performance. In particular, versions of the server that use logging optimized for locality in local and I/O space memory access were found to offer much better primary-backup performance than the original Vista system (by up to 710%) or systems that use mirroring (by up to 160%). Moreover, this result was found to be true not only for primary-backup configurations, but also for standalone servers. The primary-backup configuration with the best locality had both the best throughput and scaled well to small shared-memory multiprocessors.

Acknowledgments

This work was supported in part by NSF Grants CCR-9457770 and MIP-9521386 and by the Texas TATP program under Grant TATP-003604-0009-1997. We would also like to thank the anonymous reviewers for their comments, and Sandhya Dwarkadas, Robert Stets and Umit Rencuzogullari for their help and advice during our work on this paper.

References

[1] J. F. Bartlett. A Non Stop kernel. In *Proceedings of the 8th ACM Symposium on Operating Systems Principles*, pages 22–29, Dec. 1981.

[2] P. Chen, W. Ng, S. Chandra, C. Aycock, G. Rajamani, and D. Lowell. The Rio file cache: Surviving operating system crashes. In *Proceedings of the 7th Symposium on Architectural Support for Programming Languages and Operating Systems*, pages 74–83, Oct. 1996.

[3] Compaq, Intel and Microsoft Corporations. Virtual interface architecture specification, Version 1.0, Dec. 1997.

[4] J. Gray and A. Reuter. *Transaction Processing: Concepts and Techniques*. Morgan Kaufmann, 1992.

[5] D. Lowell and P. Chen. Free transactions with Rio Vista. In *Proceedings of the 16th ACM Symposium on Operating Systems Principles*, Oct. 1997.

[6] M. Blumrich et al. Design choices in the SHRIMP system: An empirical study. In *Proceedings of the 25th Annual International Symposium on Computer Architecture*, 1998.

[7] A. Papathanasiou and E. Markatos. Lightweight transactions on networks of workstations. In *Proceedings of the 18th International Conference on Distributed Computing Systems*, 1998.

[8] M. Satyanarayanan, H. Mashburn, P. Kumar, and J. Kistler. Lightweight recoverable virtual memory. In *Proceedings of the 14th ACM Symposium on Operating Systems Principles*, pages 146–160, Dec. 1993.

[9] D. Siewiorek and R. Swarz. *Reliable Computer System Design and Evaluation*. Digital Press, 1992.

[10] Transaction Processing Performance Council. TPC benchmark B standard specification, Aug. 1990.

[11] Transaction Processing Performance Council. TPC benchmark C standard specification, revision 3.2, Aug. 1996.

[12] W. Vogels and et al. The design and architecture of the microsoft cluster service. In *Proceedings of the 1998 Fault Tolerant Computing Symposium*, 1998.

[13] W.M. Cardoza et al. Design of the TruCluster multicomputer system for the digital unix environment. *Digital Equipment Corporation Technical Systems Journal*, 8(1), may 1996.

[14] M. Wu and W. Zwaenepoel. eNVy: A non-volatile main memory storage system. In *Proceedings of the 6th Symposium on Architectural Support for Programming Languages and Operating Systems*, pages 86–97, Oct. 1994.

[15] Y. Zhou, P. Chen, and K. Li. Fast cluster failover using virtual memory-mapped communication. In *Proceedings of the 1999 International Conference on Supercomputing*, June 1999.

Session 13C

Fast Abstracts

Session 14A

High Performance Architecture

Designing High-Performance & Reliable Superscalar Architectures
The Out of Order Reliable Superscalar (O3RS) Approach[1]

Avi Mendelson
Microprocessor Research Lab,
Intel Corporation, Israel
Avi.Mendelson@intel.com

Neeraj Suri
Dept. of Computer Engg.,
Chalmers University, Sweden
suri@ce.chalmers.se

Abstract

As VLSI geometry continues to shrink and the level of integration increases, it is expected that the probability of faults, particularly transient faults, will increase in future microprocessors. So far, fault tolerance has chiefly been considered for special purpose or safety critical systems, but future technology will likely require integrating fault tolerance techniques into commercial systems. Such systems require low cost solutions that are transparent to the system operation and do not degrade overall performance. This paper introduces a new superscalar architecture, termed as O3RS that aims to incorporate such simple fault tolerance mechanisms as part of the basic architecture.

Keywords: Superscalar architectures, Pipelines, Transient Errors/Recovery

1 Introduction

In order to achieve high integration and low power consumption, the trend in VLSI technology has been to shrink the geometry paralleling Moore's law of doubling device density every 18-24 months. Several companies [1] are currently fabricating chips using 0.18-micron technology, and it is expected that in 3-5 years the technology will reach the 0.1-micron limit. Such advanced technologies present some new challenges and concerns that are not apparent for current technology [6]. Among these new challenges is the need to protect the system from the disruptive effect of transient faults by integrating simple, low-cost fault tolerance mechanisms as part of the basic design for future commercial micro-architectures.

The need to protect against transients by integrating fault tolerance mechanisms arises from varied considerations such as (a) At 0.1 micron technology, the dv/dt ratio and expected transistor's threshold level indicates the growing occurrence of transient faults. A ballpark number is of 1-3 transients/day for an average application operating continuously, (b) It is expected that more and more asynchronous designs and dynamic logic circuits will be used, which are particularly prone to timing and transient faults. Thus, we can expect transients or "infrequent" faults (faults that appears only in small subsets of operational modes) will become part of future processor/computational models.

Traditionally, fault tolerance techniques are designed to protect safety critical systems such as aerospace, nuclear and similar control systems. Such systems often can trade performance and costs for dependability. Providing similar fault coverage to commodity processors is not a simple issue. Here, on one hand, both cost and high performance are essential, and on the other hand, the level of fault-coverage is important as well given their growing and pervasive role in embedded systems.

At the processor/architectural level, a variety of space/time redundancy techniques currently exist for integrating fault tolerance techniques. Though our interest in this paper is on time redundancy, for completeness, we briefly outline other commonly used time and space redundant fault tolerant techniques, namely:

- Error detection/error correction codes (ECC) used widely for protecting memory cells [7].

- Spatial redundancy techniques entailing physically duplicating the system (or specific functional units) so that the same program will be executed by different pieces of hardware in parallel and their execution results could be compared to verify the correctness of the execution. [8]. Such systems are relatively expensive and can be used for custom designs, but not for high performance commodity systems. An alternative to duplicating the entire system was proposed in [9], where instructions that reach the "instruction window", get duplicated and get sent to two independent execution-units. In this

---

[1] Work supported in part by NSF CAREER Grant CCR-9896321

technique, only the ALU part is duplicated.

- Temporal redundancy techniques propose re-executing each program (or fragments) and to test/compare their outcomes. The potential drawback of this scheme is that it might significantly reduce the overall performance. Recently, [5] proposes a new temporal redundancy based scheme termed AR-SMT that aims to limit the performance loss.

Our focus is on temporal redundancy approaches, and this paper aims to present a new architectural approach that addresses the processes of detection and recovery from transient errors in the logic of the computer, i.e., in the computational elements such as ALU, FPU, and address generation units. Towards these objectives, this paper is organized as follows. Section 2 presents the general structure of current superscalar architectures prior to addressing fault tolerance aspects in them. Section 3 reviews contemporary architectural schemes utilizing temporal redundancy. After introducing our proposed out of order reliable (O3RS) superscalar architectural approach in Section 4, Sections 5 and 6 develop the error recovery approaches. First, we present an approach to basic support for transient fault detection and recovery. Next, enhanced approaches to address transient recovery are developed. Section 7 outlines the performance results for the proposed approaches.

2 Superscalar Processors: Basics

In this section we present the structure of a typical superscalar architecture [2] similar to the Pentium-II family [3]. This section primarily establishes the conceptual structure and superscalar related terminology we will use throughout this paper.

Figure 2.1 depicts the basic structure of the execution pipeline of a general purpose, out-of-order superscalar processor with a reservation station(s). Instructions are fetched from the main memory or from the instruction cache in the program order into the decode unit. The decode unit is responsible for registering the instructions in the ROB (re-order buffer), for renaming their registers (from the user view registers into the the architectural registers) and for sending the instructions to the reservation tables that are associated with each of the execution units. Note that in the case of Pentium II, the X86 based instruction set is translated into microoperations, which are fixed length instructions. Thus, the internal execution model of the processor can be significantly different from the external (user) view.

Instructions in the reservation can be executed "out of order" as long as they preserve the semantics of the program. Thus, each instruction can be either in "*ready*" state (i.e., all their inputs are "ready") or in "*wait*" state. Whenever an execution unit is ready to execute a new operation, it fetches a "ready" operation from its local

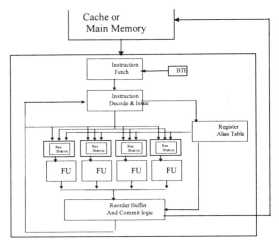

Figure 2.1 – Basic Architecture of Superscalar Out Of Order Processor

queue. No order is imposed between "*ready*" instructions.

When instructions are logged in the ROB, the Register Alias Table (RAT) determines if their source operands should be taken from the architectural register file or from the ROB. Each ROB entry keeps track of the program counter associated with its instruction and has a place to hold the execution result. The issue logic monitors the buses to detect writes to the ROB entries matching source operands of the waiting instructions.

The last pipeline stage in an out-of-order processor is instruction commit (retirement). Most current superscalar architectures ensure that the instructions modify the system resources, such as architectural registers (as opposed to renaming registers), caches, etc. in the same order as appears in the program or as generated by the compiler. Inside the micro-architecture, the instructions can be executed out of order, though the instructions need complete their executions in the program order.

In order to enhance performance, modern computer architectures use speculative execution which is based on different predictors (such as branch prediction). When the predictor fails, the retirement mechanism is also used for rolling back from exception or executing the wrong path. In such cases, the system needs to complete the execution of all the instructions prior to the roll-back point and to discard all results after that point.

3 Prior Approaches in Temporal Redundancy

The main goal of this paper is to develop low-cost, high performance support to timed redundancy techniques. In order to objectively evaluate the proposed techniques, we first discuss two existing architectural techniques for timed redundancy. For this discussion, we restrict this to pipelined, multi-threaded and superscalar models which are currently the most commonly used architectural paradigms.

3.1 The Instruction Duplication Technique

A simple technique to increase the fault toletance coverage at run time was proposed in [9]. Here an instruction sent from the instruction decoder to the instruction window allocates two entries in the ROB table, and is consequently sent out twice for execution. At commit time, the results of the two operations are compared and "retired" from the system only if both operation obtained the same result, i.e., fault-free situations.

3.2 The AR-SMT Technique

An alternate approach to time redundancy was recently proposed in [5] and termed as AR-SMT (Active-stream/Redundant-stream Simultaneous Multi Threading). This architecture extends existing SMT [10,11] machines that can execute two threads in parallel. In SMT, instructions are fetched from two independent streams of instructions (threads) and these share the system resources. In traditional SMT machines, the results are written back to their ROB, and each thread retires its instructions independently.

The AR-SMT suggests executing each program twice, by using two threads; one that is considered as the primary and the other as secondary. These threads are not symmetric in their priority and in their execution-mechanisms. The primary thread runs as before but writes its results to a special hardware mechanism termed "*Delay Buffer*". This buffer is used to ensure that both threads run in a lock-step manner (with a delay of at most the size of the delay buffer), and that the results produced by both threads are identical.

In order to reduce the overhead incurred by the use of SMT architecture, the author suggests improvements over the traditional SMT architectures, such as: (1) In order to sustain instruction bandwidth, a Trace Cache for each thread is proposed. Trace Caches keep the information in decoded form and do not need to perform bus accesses as long as a hit is achieved in the Trace Cache, (2) Use of aggressive prediction mechanisms to predict branches [13] as well as values [14,15]. (3) Allows the second thread to use values produced by the first thread. Thus, the second thread can take advantage of the maximum parallelism available by the machine. The uniqueness of the AR-SMT approach is its observation that the first thread can be used as a perfect predictor to the secondary thread. Thus, the second thread can utilize the maximum parallelism on the machine and re-execute operations as soon as their inputs are in the Delay Buffer.

The AR-SMT paper indicates that by using all these optimization techniques, the overhead of using AR-SMT machine is relatively small compared to the use of other temporal redundancy techniques. Although [5] provides simulation results to indicate the AR-SMT performance enhancement over SMT etc., a closer look at the potential implementations of the AR-SMT machine reveals that it can suffer from several limitations that may result in significant overhead and loss in performance. Specifically, these include:

- The use of multi-threaded technology invariably suffers from reduced instruction bandwidth that limits its performance. Adding Trace Caches can ease the problem for those applications that can fit into the Trace Cache. But, Trace Caches are inherently large (since they keep the instructions in their decoded form), so on one hand increasing the size of the Trace Cache can result in an unacceptable increase in the die size; on the other hand, splitting the Trace Cache between the threads increases memory traffic in the machine and consequently limits its performance.

- An efficient use of the Delay Buffer as an accelerator for the second thread forces a feedback loop to the ROB (and the instruction scheduler). In machines that run at a very high clock rate (and utilize super-pipelines to achieve it), such feedback will cause a major delay between the two threads. It may cause a performance loss and force the use of large Delay Buffers as well.

- The use of the Delay Buffer suffers from a major performance loss whenever the system is required to rollback, such as in the case of branch mis-prediction, exception handling and transients.

These limitations can either increase the cost of the AR-SMT solution and/or restrict its performance significantly. On this review of existing temporal redundancy approaches, the current paper targets developing an alternate cost-effective, low-overhead temporal redundancy approach. We emphasize that reducing the performance overhead in fault-free scenarios has more real impact on system performance than the performance loss reduction in the presence of faults.

3.3 The Diva Approach

Recently, [20] presented a new concept in designing complex superscalar systems. The new architecture calls to replace the traditional retirement mechanism of out-of-order machines, with a "checker" that re-executes the instructions. This checker, on one hand, can be simple since it uses the data produced by the fast and complex machine, and on the other hand can run with a slower clock rate, since it can save the need to execute speculative operations.

A DIVA based processor could handle transients as

well, but it necessitates major architecture enhancements which are not cost/performance effective and beyond the scope of our discussion here.

4 The Out Of Order *Reliable* Superscalar (O3RS) Architecture

We now introduce facets of the proposed O3RS architecture that aims to achieve maximal fault tolerance coverage at a minimal cost to either the die area or the fault-free performance of the machine. The basic approach utilizes time redundancy to enable recovery from transient/soft errors. In order to minimize the extra cost in area and performance, we suggest enhancing an existing superscalar mechanism only if it cannot guarantee fault-free execution by using traditional techniques such as adding ECC circuits.

4.1 At What Level Should New FT Techniques be Integrated?

It is clear that in order to guarantee the overall correctness of the system the entire system should be protected by both error detection and recovery (or error correction) mechanisms. However, we argue that it does not mean that the same mechanism should be used throughout in order to protect the system. Since most advanced memory systems integrate Error Correction Codes (ECC) techniques as part of the structure of the memory, registers and internal buses, we would like to integrate these techniques as part of our solution. Thus, unlike other papers such as [8,9] that execute the entire program twice (temporal redundancy), we argue that it is sufficient to enhance the protection mechanism for those parts of the system that cannot be protected by existing/alternate techniques.

In this section we examine each stage of the execution pipe to determine if additional fault tolerance mechanisms are warranted for adding to them:

Fetching: The fetching mechanisms chiefly use memory and bus technologies. Thus, no extra mechanisms are needed to guarantee the correctness of the data and instruction that are fetched.

Instruction decoder: If the instruction decoder works as a table look-up (as in many RISC architectures), we do not foresee the need to add any redundancy. But, if the instruction decoder is more complex (like many of the X86 architectures) we consider duplicating the control logic.

RAT and ROB: Since the ROB is a cyclic buffer; we assume it to be protected using conventional mechanisms such as ECC. In order to protect the RAT we may need to duplicate its control (sharing the same data).

In order to add our new mechanisms, we will have to modify the structure of the ROB (this will be discussed later in Sections 5 & 6)

Execution units: We do not assume any modification of the execution mechanism (one may consider to add more execution units as explained later in Sections 5 & 6)

Retirement mechanism: We need to design a new retirement mechanism and to incorporate the "voting mechanism" between the pair of operations in order to guarantee their proper execution.

Write-back: As long as the write-back is controlled by the ECC, we do not need to modify it.

This stage-by-stage pipeline analysis indicates two issues, namely:

- We can maintain a superscalar (transient) fault-free system without the use of expensive multi-threaded technology.

- From the complexity and performance point of view, the efficient design of the execution pipeline is a primary design driver given that this aspect cannot be efficiently addressed by existing time-redundancy based approaches.

5 A Basic Description of the Error Recovery Mechanism

In this section we start introducing the proposed architectural mechanisms. These mechanisms are based on temporal redundancy; i.e., execute each instruction twice, and incorporate specific recovery mechanisms in case of branch mis-prediction or in the case of transients. The primary design driver is reducing overheads.

In order to achieve this goal we propose the following modifications to the "traditional superscalar structures presented in Sec. 3. Here we outline the O3RS modifications and detail them further in Sec. 6. The basic O3RS modifications include:

- Modify the ROB table so that each operation, which is not LOAD or STORE, will be executed twice. In order to achieve this, we propose to add status bit to each ROB entry that indicates if the instruction is being executed for its first time or for a second time. Note that we do not care if an instruction will be executed twice on the same functional unit or on a different functional units since we assume transient/soft errors; i.e., the probability of an error to appear in a functional unit does not depend on its history of errors.

- Although we execute each instruction twice, we do not require two entries in the ROB and we do not impose any implicit order between the executions of the two instances.

- The results of the two independent executions of the

same operation will be retired iff: (a) The two executions agree on the results. (b) All previous results were committed.

If an operation cannot be committed, we need to distinguish between two cases: (a) both computations produced different results, so we need to re-execute the instruction until its result will be verified. (b) the execution was speculative, and the speculation was found to be false. In this case, the system should be rolled back to the last committed point.

If an execution unit is repeatedly found to encounter errors, the system can take it out of the active list (if enough execution units are available)

In order to describe the operations in the proposed method, we present the following example:

a.	ld R0,x	// load memory to R0
b.	cmp R0,$10	// compare R0 with 10
c.	jz l1	// jump if zero
d.	inc R0	// if R0 != 10 increment it
e.	l1: dec R0	// else decrement it

As these instructions depend on each other, they must be executed sequentially even on an out of order execution machine. Let us assume that x contains 10, so the execution pipe of our machine will look as in Fig. 5.

Fig. 5 presents four steps of the execution pipe of the new architectural technique (a simplification of its operation). Each column in the figure represents the "stream of operations" (as is fetched into the instruction

pipe), specifically the operations at the execution stage and the retirement stream. In this example, we assume no faults to occur.

Figure 5-A represents the start of the execution step; i.e., the first instruction (LD) is brought into the execution stage. Since load operation (LD) does not need to be verified via time redundancy mechanisms (as was explained in the previous section) we can move it immediately to the retirement stage (Figure 5-B), assuming a single cycle for load. At that point, the first instance of the compare instruction is forwarded to the execution phase.

Just after the first instance of the compare instruction is executed, the machine can now start its "second" execution in parallel with the first execution of the JZ operation (Figure 5-C). The first execution of the JZ indicates if the branch should be taken or not (in pipeline machine the branch prediction predicts the right direction before the JZ complete its operation). Since the first execution of the CMP indicates that the branch will be taken, it forwards the DEC instruction to the execution phase rather then the INC one. At that point (Figure 5-D), the JZ is being executed for the second time, and the DEC operation is being executed speculatively.

Note that during the second time an operation is executed, all of its inputs are known, so that it can start its execution immediately (assuming we have resource for that). If the system finds that the right answer to the compare instruction should be not-taken rather than taken, the system should roll-back (undo the DEC) and re-start the execution along the right path.

6 Hardware Enhancements For O3RS

In this section we provide a detailed description of the new hardware modifications needed to accomplish the proposed recovery mechanism. The goal of our proposed enhancements is to implement the new recovery mechanisms so it will result in minimal extra hardware that provides minimal overhead when no fault occurs. We will also show that the proposed recovery mechanism imposes low recovery overhead when the system needs to recover from either a transient/soft-error or from a branch mis-prediction, exception handling etc.

The implementation of the new algorithms utilizes the same basic superscalar structure used in previous sections. The instructions are fetched in a sequential order from the memory and are decoded in parallel. Each operation gets an entry in the ROB structure. As we have mentioned earlier, the ROB status bits are critical data and are protected extensively by ECC checks. The entries in the ROB are ordered in respect to their control dependencies. Each entry in the ROB contains in part information on the type of operation, what are the inputs (and if they are available) and a space to keep the

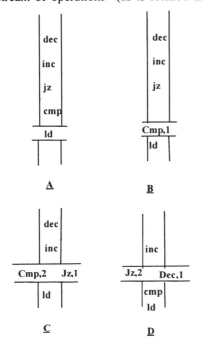

Figures 5A-D: Basic O3RS Operations

outcome of the operation. Each ROB entry contains also status bits that usually indicate:

E (Empty): The ROB entry is not attached to any operation.

W (Wait): The instruction is in the reservation station, and is waiting for inputs.

R (READY): The instruction is ready to be executed. (Moved to the reservation station)

D (Done): The operation is ready to be committed.

In order to incorporate the fault tolerant mechanisms, we suggest the following enhancements:

R: Indicates that the instruction is ready to be executed for the first time.

S: The instruction is ready to be executed for the second time.

D: The result of the two instances of the operation has been confirmed, and the operation is ready to be committed.

Note: (1) We ignore these extra bits if the instruction is LOAD or STORE. (2) Instructions do not need to check their dependencies when in S state. We could require that the second execution will start only if its sources are in D state. This might simplify the recovery mechanism but consequently reduce the overall performance due to the dependency resolutions. In the AR-SMT mechanism, it was suggested to use the delay buffer as a predictor for execution of the second thread. This mechanism complicates the hardware and may limit the frequency due to internal feedback loops. The O3RS mechanism achieves the same goal more efficiently and with simpler hardware.

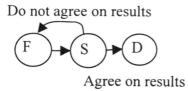

Do not agree on results

Agree on results

Figure 6.1 State transition of the ROB status

When the two executions of the same instruction do not agree upon the result, we suggest re-executing the instruction. A simple mechanism (as illustrated in the above state diagram: Fig. 6.1) calls to re-execute the instruction twice. A more sophisticated mechanism can either keep 2 output buffers and compare the third execution with both, or to copy the result of the second execution to the result buffer (in the ROB entry) and issue the instruction again in S state. As long as the error rate remains relatively low, we do not recommend complicating the hardware and believe that these simple mechanisms suffice. As mentioned earlier, it is more

important to facilitate low performance overhead from the incorporated fault-tolerance mechanisms during *fault-free* operations than the overhead issues while handling errors.

When the system needs to change its control flow (as a result of error, mis-prediction, etc.) the operation of the system is very similar to the regular operation of any superscalar machine. The system needs to flush all the entries in the ROB that are below the mis-prediction point, regardless if they are being executed for the first time or for the second time. The system also needs to complete the execution of any instruction that is not in the D state and located above the mis-speculated point.

The retirement mechanism in O3RS remains the same as before; i.e., it "retire sequence" of instructions as long as all of them are in D state.

7   Performance Issues

At this stage we have described the basic functionality of the proposed O3RS approach. Prior to addressing the achievable performance issues, we again emphasize that although the transient rates, even at 0.1 micron process, are expected to be in order of a fault/day two points are worth noting, namely (a) it is unacceptable not to protect the machines against such faults (b) for systems that contain several processors the probability for error increases significantly. Thus, from the performance perspective, it is more important to make sure that the fault detection mechanisms do not cause a performance lost, than to optimize the performance of the recovery mechanism. With this background, the set of performance figures in this section will be focused on demonstrating fault-free overhead cases.

In order to evaluate the new system, we use a modified version of the SimpleScalar simulator [17] developed at the University of Wisconsin, and run our proposed techniques on different applications, using different set of inputs for each. The main performance measurement we were looking for was the utilization of the execution units. A utilization of 0.5 means that on average, all the resources were utilized half of the time. A utilization greater than 1 indicates that the new approach

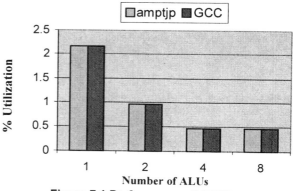

Figure 7.1 Performance of O3RS

slows down the system. Note that when a "regular" program is executed, the utilization corresponds to the CPI (Cycles Per Instruction) divided by the number of ALU's in the system. If the utilization is greater than 1, it means that the system was slowed down because of internal dependencies or due to system limitations.

Figure 7.1 presents the ALU utilization of the O3RS system running GCC compiler with 2 different inputs: GCC compiler (the compiler compiles itself) and AMPTJP program (both from INT SPEC 95). The Y-axis indicates the processor utilization and the X-axis (top row) indicates the number of ALU units. Each test runs for 100,000,000 simulated instructions. We can observe that (a) both inputs provide similar utilization numbers (b) if 2 ALUs (or more) are provided, the utilization is less then 1, meaning that there is no performance loss when applying the new technique. One can explain these numbers with the fact that the "second executed" instructions do not have to wait for inputs and so can be executed promptly, taking advantage of the relatively low ILP (Instruction Level Parallelism) of the GCC program.

Figure 7.2 presents the same utilization numbers for IJPEG program using 2 different inputs (Penguin and Vigo) taken from the SPEC 95 as well. The results presented here are similar to the result presented for the GCC run. The main difference is that in the IJPEG case, the system can well utilize up to 2 ALUs and only when four ALUs or more are used, that the extra cost for the new technique is diminished.

So far we mainly discussed the overall performance of the O3RS system and showed that it can take advantage of the current limitation in the available parallelism to execute the extra operations almost free of charge. Now we extend the discussion to other performance-related parameters of the system, such as instruction window, and fetch bandwidth.

From a performance viewpoint, one of the noticeable

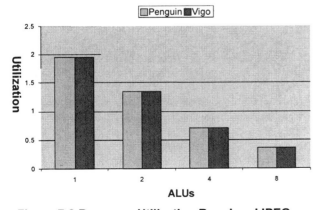

Figure 7.2 Resource Utilization Running IJPEG

disadvantages of the AR-SMT solution is that the implementation cost of an SMT machine is much higher, assuming the same level of performance. For example, in [5] it was assumed that each PE could fetch and decode up to 4 instructions each cycle. An implementation of such an instruction bandwidth is very difficult to achieve. On the other hand, limiting the instruction bandwidth can dramatically limit the overall performance of the system.

The [5,9] papers assume that each of the PE has its own trace cache and the number of the entries in the ROB for each thread remains the same regardless of the number of ALU's in the system. A more realistic assumption should be that the instruction window is split between the two threads in the system. Figure 7.3 shows the impact of the instruction window size (number of pending instructions) on the achievable ILP in the system. The X-axis measures the window size (8,16,32,64,128) for pending instructions, Y-axis measures ILP. The rows marked "MP3D" [solid line, bootm], "Walter" [dotted

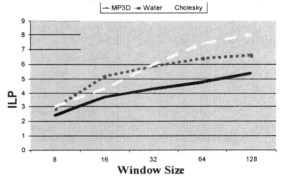

Figure 7.3: Impact of Instruction Window Size

line, middle] and "Cholesky" [dashed line] numerically represent the ILP values for these different applications.

Figure 7.3 demonstrates that by reducing the instruction window size from 64 ROB for a program to 32 entries for each thread, the system will lose about 15% of its performance (on average) for any SMT based approach. On the other hand, our proposed O3RS technique uses the same number of ROB entries as in "regular" superscalar. Consequently, it does not suffer from that performance degradation

The last chart we present (Figure 7.4) shows the slowdown of a single thread (out of 2 threads), assuming that the instruction window is split among them. In this experiment we assume 8% branch mis-prediction, and 5 cycles penalty for a branch miss. We also assume an 8 instruction fetch bandwidth.

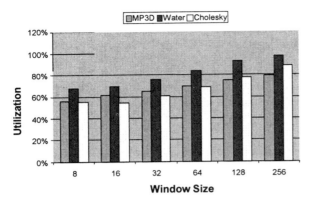

Figure 7.4: Utilization of a Single Thread

The chart indicates that on one hand, when the window size is relative small, the application is mainly limited by the instruction window size available for each thread. On the other hand, when the instruction window is large enough, the performance is limited by the instruction bandwidth and so the size of the window is less important.

8 Discussion & Conclusion

Overall, we have examined two basic time redundancy approaches of duplication and voting, and the associated integration of the fault-tolerance mechanisms within the structure of the superscalar architecture. An enhanced version of the recovery procedure that alleviates any performance loss over error recovery is also detailed.

Duplication of systems is the simplest implementation that may provide for good performance assuming that we can synchronize the duplicated instructions to occur in a lock-step manner. The drawback of this approach was identified to be the external addition of recovery mechanism, and the significant latency overhead. The duplication solution may also be costly in terms of hardware as we need to duplicate the entire system and the additional cost of voting and recovery.

The O3RS system approach presents a different outlook by integrating the fault tolerance capabilities as part of the internal structure of the superscalar architecture. The advantage of this approach is in enabling fast recovery mechanisms. The drawback is in flushing the execution pipe on error occurrences.

Looking at the ILP numbers, we can observe that computer architectures, such as the Pentium-II, generally have an average ILP of 1. Since such a machine is entitled to execute 2-3 ALU and address calculations per cycle, the average utilization of these units is less than half. Our proposal takes advantage of that and allows the second execution to use these free resources. Thus, in most cases the new O3RS mechanism will cause only minor performance slow down, if any at all.

When comparing the new O3RS system with similar techniques such as AR-SMT, the proposed O3RS technique presents a much simpler architectural and operational design that minimally impacts both the design effort and the performance. For example, the O3RS architecture does not use any Delay Buffers as was essentially required in the AR-SMT approach. The Delay Buffer can slow down the system in different ways one of which involves flushing the instructions from ROB and delay buffer. If such a flush operation is needed only for recovering from faults, we could use it as long as the probability for faults is low enough. Unfortunately, such operations are needed whenever branch a mis-prediction occurs and when the system experiences exceptions such as interrupts. Such operations occur often enough that they cannot be ignored.

Last, but not least, in this paper we assumed that transient errors are relatively infrequent thus leading to the application of basic time redundancy. However, if the soft-error rate increases, we will be able to incorporate more sophisticated recovery mechanisms such as the use of Roll-Forward recovery blocks [4] within O3RS. The roll-forward mechanism provides for sustained execution of dependent instructions as long as the inconsistency across replicates is not determined. When an error occurs, we save both replicate values and re-execute the operation again. If the new result commit with the first execution, the error was in the second execution, thus we can continue our normal execution assuming the original value was correct. If the new execution does not agree with the first execution, we need to roll back since there may be other operations in the execution pipe that based their uncommitted operation on a wrong result. We defer the details of the roll-forward blocks to a later document.

8.1 Conclusion

In this paper we have presented a novel approach for integrating fault tolerance capabilities within the structure of future microprocessor architectures. The basic driver is in providing for simple, low-cost mechanisms that provide coverage to transient faults which are likely to increase in occurrence as the device geometry shrinks and the level of device integration increases. Focussing on temporal redundancy techniques, our basic approach has been to look at various design alternatives in superscalar architectures such that the error recovery can be provided with minimal, if any, performance, design or operational overheads, and also with minimal modifications to the basic superscalar operations.

9 References

1. Diefendoff, K., "The Race to Point One Eight", *Microprocessor Report*, Vol. 12, # 12, pp. 10-22, Sept, 1998.

2. Johnson, M., "Superscalar Microprocessor Design", Prentice Hall, 1990.

3. Pentium II: Intel Architecture Manual, Intel Corp., 1997.

4. Mendelson, A. and Suri, N., "Cache Based Fault Recovery in Distributed Systems," *Proc. ICECCS*, pp. 19-129, 1997.

5. Rotenberg, E., "AR-SMT: A Microarchitecture Approach to Fault Tolerance in Microprocessors", Proc. FTCS-29, pp. 84-91, 1999.

6. Rubinfeld, P., "Virtual Roundtable on the Challenges and Trends in Processor Design: Managing Problems at High Speeds", *IEEE Computer*, 3(1):47-48, Jan 1998

7. Pradhan, D., "Fault Tolerant Computer System", *Prentice Hall*, 1998.

8. IBM 390x2 IBM System Journal, IBM Corp. 1996.

9. Sohi, G., Franklin, M. and Saluja, K., "A Study of Time-Redundant Fault Tolerant Techniques in High Performance Pipelined Computers", *Proc. FTCS-19*, pp. 436-443, 1989.

10. Tullsen, D., Eggers, S. and Levy, H. "Simultaneous Multithreading: Maximizing Chip Parallelism", *Proc. 22nd Intl. Symp. On Computer Architecture*, pp 392-403, 1995.

11. Tullsen, D., Eggers, S., Emer, J., Levy, H., Lo, J. and Stamm, R., "Exploiting Choice: Instruction Fetch and Issue on an Implementable Simultaneous Multithreading Processor" *Proc. 23rd Intl. Symp. on Computer Architecture*, pp 191 – 202, 1996.

12. Rotenberg, E., Jacobson, Q., Sazeides, Y. and Smith, J., "Trace Processors", *Proc. 30th Intl. Symp. on Microarchitecture*, Dec 1997.

13. Yeh, T. and Patt, Y., "Alternative Implementations of Two-Level Adaptive Branch Prediction", *Proc. 19th Intl. Symp. on Computer Architecture*, pp. 124-134, 1992.

14. Gabbay, F. and Mendelson, A., "Characterization of Value Prediction and its Impact on Modern Computer Architectures", *ACM Transaction on Computer Systems*, Vol 16, No 3, Sept 1998.

15. Lipasti, M., "Value Locality and Speculative Execution", PhD Thesis, Carnegie Mellon University, April 1997.

16. Anglada, R. and Rubio, A., "An Approach to Crosstalk Effect Analysis and Avoidance Techniques in Digital CMOS VLSI circuits", *International Journal of Electronics*, 6(5):9–17, 1988.

17. Burger, D. and Austin, T., "The Simplescalar Toolset, Version 2.0", Technical Report CS-TR-97-1342, University of Wisconsin, Madison, June 1997.

18. Spainhower, L. and Gregg, T., "G4: A Fault-Tolerant CMOS Mainframe", Proc. *FTCS-28*, pp. 432-440, 1998.

19. Tamir, Y. and Tremblay, M., "High-Performance Fault Tolerant VLSI Systems Using Micro Rollback", *IEEE Transactions on Computers*, 39(4): pp. 548-553, April 1990

20. Austin, T., "DIVA: A Reliable Substrate for Deep Submicron Microarchitecture Design", *Proc. MICRO-32*, pp.196-207, 1999

Fault Tolerance Through Re-execution in Multiscalar Architecture

Faisal Rashid   Kewal K. Saluja   Parameswaran Ramanathan

University of Wisconsin-Madison

1415 Engineering Drive

Madison WI 53706

{frashid,saluja,parmesh}@ece.wisc.edu

Abstract

Multi-threading and *multiscaling* are two fundamental microarchitecture approaches that are expected to stay on the existing performance gain curve. Both of these approaches assume that integrated circuits with over billion transistors will become available in the near future. Such large integrated circuits imply reduced design tolerances and hence increased failure probability. Conventional hardware redundancy techniques for desired reliability in computation may severely limit the performance of such high performance processors. Hence we need to study novel methods to exploit the inherent redundancy of the microarchitectures, without unduly affecting the performance, to provide correct program execution and/or detect failures (permanent or transient) that can occur in the hardware.

This paper proposes a time redundancy technique suitable for multiscalar architectures. In the multiscalar architecture, there are usually several processing units to exploit the instruction level parallelism that exists in a given program. The technique in this paper uses a majority of the processing units for executing the program as in the traditional multiscalar paradigm while using the remainder of the processing units for re-executing the committed instructions. By comparing the results from the two program executions, errors caused by permanent or transient faults in the processing units can be detected. Simulation results presented in this paper demonstrate that this can be achieved with about 5-15% performance degradation.

Key Words: Dynamic configuration, Fault-tolerance, Multiscalar architecture, Re-execution, Static configuration, Time redundancy

1 Introduction

High performance processor architectures are being driven by technological advances that are likely to provide billion-transistor integrated circuits in very near future. This can not be achieved without reducing and compromising design tolerances and working with reduced signal integrity. Clearly, such designs will be more susceptible to failures and circumventing the occurrence of transient and permanent faults that can occur in such high performance processors is important if they are to continue to provide correct results. This paper investigates methods of achieving fault tolerance in such state-of-the-art high performance processors without compromising the performance.

The focus of this paper is a technique to implement fault tolerance in a current state-of-the-art microarchitecture, namely multiscalar architecture [9] . Our goal is to provide fault-tolerance at low cost (low hardware overhead), low performance degradation, and low error latency with high fault coverage. Our technique exploits the architectural features of a multiscalar high performance processor to implement time redundant fault tolerance in the form of code re-execution [3]. Our method does not use traditional introduction of hardware and information redundancy and it is also different from program and task re-execution methods implemented on parallel systems [4, 5]. Our method exploits the redundancy that exists in a uniprocessor system comprised of multiple processing units to support the microarchitecture implementation. In our method every instruction is re-executed on another processing unit to check the results of the original program execution. is employed to check the results of the original program execution. Thus, our goal is to cover all faults that can cause a processing unit to provide incorrect results during the execution of a program.

We propose two techniques, static and dynamic task re-execution to implement fault-tolerant function and compare these schemes. Our studies demonstrate that these schemes have low performance degradation and low error latency in multiscalar architectures while covering all those transient and permanent faults in processing units that can lead to incorrect results during program execution.

This paper is organized as follows. In section 2 of this paper we briefly describe the closely related work in this area and explain the multiscalar paradigm that is being accepted as a basis of high performance computing. Section 3 introduces a multiscalar architecture and the details of a simulator [1] that are pertinent to the work presented in this paper. Section 4 describes two fault tolerant architecture models. Results of executing a number of SPEC95 benchmark programs in fault-tolerant architecture models are presented in section 5. The paper concludes with section 6.

2 Background
2.1 Related Work

New architectural innovations obtain high performance by parallelizing the execution of code [8, 9]. Current superscalar processors can issue several instructions simultaneously using multiple functional units and a dynamic scheduler [8]. However, data and control dependencies constrain the processor from fully utilizing the cycles. As a result many functional units remain idle even when multiple units issue more than one instruction per cycle. Clearly this architectural feature can be exploited to tolerate permanent and transient faults in the hardware components.

Studies of fault tolerance in superscalar processors have shown that time redundancy techniques such as instruction re-execution [5] may be implemented without much loss of perfor-

mance [3]. The techniques proposed in [3] schedule the re-execution of instructions at the "finer grain level", making it different from program re-execution. The dynamic scheduler may re-execute instructions whenever the execution of a particular instruction is stalled due to a dependency. This technique results in negligible performance degradation and low error latency, but it has low fault coverage because not all instructions are re-executed. Another technique involves duplicating all instructions to the functional units and re-executing them. Such a technique may have higher performance degradation, low error latency and high fault coverage, although some of the performance degradation can be reclaimed by nop's generated by the scheduler.

A technique called AR-SMT was proposed recently where simultaneous multithreading was exploited to implement fault tolerance in trace processors [6]. An active and a redundant instruction stream are maintained for the processor; as soon as the instructions in the active stream are committed, the data and control information are stored in a delay buffer and re-executed as the redundant instruction stream (thread). Both the active and redundant streams co-exist on the processor, resulting in low error latency, good fault coverage, and low performance degradation. A proposal similar to the above study was independently made under the Stanford ROAR project[7], a dependable adaptive computing system, suggesting simultaneous multi-threading for low performance overhead, and use of FPGA based co-processor design to achieve fault-tolerance. However neither of these schemes are implementable on a multiscalar architecture.

2.2 Multiscalar Paradigm

Current commercial microprocessors obtain high performance by exploiting instruction level parallelism. The hardware extracts parallelism by dynamically creating a window of instructions, executing instructions from this window, and communicating the result of execution to other instructions in the window. Superscalar processors are, however, limited by the size of this instruction window [9].

The multiscalar architecture takes the super-scalar architecture one step further by adding parallelism at yet another level of sequential program execution [1, 2]. A multiscalar processor divides the dynamic instruction sequence into multiple regions instead of treating it as a single region. One possible implementation of this technique is to use multiple superscalar processors so that each executes a different region of the dynamic instruction sequence at the same time. Each superscalar processor looking ahead in its region finds only as many independent instructions as is practicable. The multiple processors collectively result in looking ahead much further and finding many more independent instructions than would be feasible for a single processor.

The basic idea in the multiscalar paradigm is to divide the dynamic instruction stream into a number of contiguous regions (called tasks) using hardware, software, or the combination of the two. Each of these regions is executed in parallel on a collection of processing units. Since the regions of dynamic instruction sequence can be either control or data dependent, speculative execution is the key to this approach. Starting execution, the entry point to a program, always points to the first task to be executed. Speculating other tasks that might be executed following the first task, the multiscalar processor assigns tasks to available processing units. Once the first task completes, the speculative task execution is checked to see if it is correct. In case the speculation is correct, the task is completed and committed to the architectural state of the processor. Otherwise, all the miss-speculated tasks are squashed and the correct next task is started on the first available processor.

Figure 1 shows a portion of a control flow graph for a program. Reaching task A, a multiscalar processor may speculate task B and task D and assign B, D, and E to available processing units. In case the speculation is correct, tasks B, D and E will be completed and committed. Otherwise, all tasks following the miss-speculation (in this case all tasks following and including task B) will

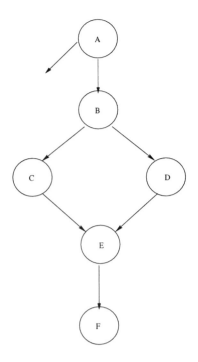

Figure 1: Control flow graph for sample execution in multiscalar paradigm.

be squashed. Figure 2 shows the architecture for a multiscalar processor with 4 processing units. Assuming that task A in the above example was assigned to *PU0*, tasks B, D, and E may be assigned to *PU1, PU2* and *PU3* to be executed in parallel with task A. In general, a multiscalar architecture is expected to have a large number of processing units. Studies conducted on multiscalar architectures thus far have considered up to 16 and more processing units [1].

3 Multiscalar Architecture

In the multiscalar architecture, the instruction supply is determined by the hierarchical predictor and the instruction memory (see Figure 2) [1]. The hierarchical predictor is made up of a single inter-task predictor (*Inter Pred*) for the entire processor and intra-task predictors (*Intra Pred*) for each of the processing units. The instruction memory is made up of the task cache (*Task $$$$*), and multiple instruction caches (*Inst $$$$*) for all the processing units.

The data supply configuration comprises of the register file (*Reg File*) and the data memory. The

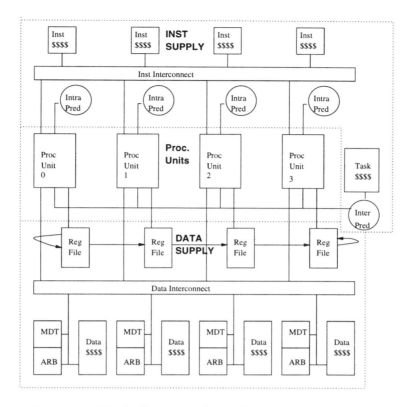

Figure 2: Block diagram of a multiscalar architecture.

register file is distributed among the processing units. Each register file contains integer and floating point registers. The data memory consists of multiple data caches (*Data $$$$*) and specialized hardware consisting of Address Resolution Buffer(*ARB*) and Memory Dependence Table (*MDT*).

The data and instruction caches are connected via crossbars to the processing units. The off-chip memory consists of a single unified cache (for the task cache, the instruction cache and the data cache) and main memory.

A simulator, written in C by Breach [1], simulates multiscalar architecture. The simulator can be reconfigured to study different architecture setups, such as cache sizes, number of processing units, and size of register files. The simulator was modified to study a number of different architecture setups with two fault tolerance mechanisms described in the next section. Table 1 highlights the simulation configuration for our experiments.

4 Fault Tolerant Architectural Model

A trivial and simple scheme can re-execute a program sequentially. But such a scheme will have very high error latency and low performance as the total program execution time will be doubled. Schemes such as instruction re-execution in the dynamic scheduler [3] belong to the other end of the spectrum of time-redundant code duplication. Such a scheme has relatively low performance degradation, and low error latency but at the expense of poor fault coverage. Below we propose two schemes, namely, static task re-execution and dynamic task re-execution for fault tolerance in multiscalar architecture. These schemes perform re-execution at a coarser grain level, providing both good fault coverage and low error latency, while maintaining near peak performance.

In the description below, we assume that a total of n processing units are partitioned into p primary units for the execution of the actual instruction stream and $r = n - p$ secondary units

Processing Units	4 to 16 used, each is 4-wide in-order
Inter - Task Predictor	Path-based DOLC=7,3,6,8 path reg., 64K-entry 2-bit counter, 4-target
Intra - Task Predictor	Global-pattern, 16 bit pattern reg., 64K-entry 2bit counter
Task Cache	1K-entry, 2-way assoc, 4 byte task desc., lru, 1bank
Instruction Cache	64K, 2 way assoc, 32 byte block interleaved, lru
Register File	32 architected regs, 1 cycle latency between adjacent register file
Data Cache	64K, 2-way associative, 32 byte block interleaved,lru
Address Resolution Buffer	128 entry per bank, 32-way associative
Memory Dependence Table	16 entry per bank, 16 way associative, lru
Unified Cache	4MB, 2-way associative, 128 byte block interleaved, lru

Table 1: Configuration parameters used in the simulation experiments.

for re-executing the instruction stream. We will denote such a configuration as $p \times (n - p)$ configuration.

4.1 Static Re-execution

In this model the number of processing units n are partitioned into a $p \times (n-p)$ configuration for a fixed value of p. Tasks completed and committed by the primary processing units are stored in a FIFO queue called the task buffer. This buffer contains the tasks completed by the primary units as well as the data for the instructions in each of the tasks. Committed tasks are added to the tail of the task buffer by the primary processing units while the secondary processing units dequeue the tasks from the head of the buffer for re-execution. The program execution (on primaries and secondaries) proceeds as follows. A task buffer is said to be full if it contains (Buffer Size $- p$) tasks. Similarly, the task buffer is said to be empty if it contains only $r = n - p$ tasks. When the task buffer becomes full, the primary units are stalled, and the re-execution units continue execution until the task buffer contains only r filled slots.

The first criteria ensures that tasks in the actual stream at the point the buffer is full can be queued once they commit. The second criteria reduces the likelihood that, at the point the buffer is empty, the secondary units will have to wait for the primary units to provide new tasks.

4.2 Dynamic Re-execution

In this case also p processing units are used to execute the actual instruction stream. How-

ever, the number of secondary units are switched between $n - p$ and n as follows. As in static re-execution, in dynamic re-execution the tasks completed and committed by the primary processing units are stored in FIFO task buffer. When the task buffer is full, the actual instruction stream executing on the p primaries is stalled and all the n processing units are used to re-execute the committed tasks from the task buffer till the task buffer is empty, at which point the processing units are reconfigured to operate in $p \times (n-p)$ configuration. Thus, this method maximally utilizes all processing units at the price of having extra hardware to provide the above re-configuration capability.

5 Experimental Results and Discussion

5.1 Performance

Instructions per clock cycle (IPC) is a commonly used measure for comparing the performance of different architectures. If an architecture commits N instructions of a given program in T clock cycles, then the corresponding IPC is N/T. Let $I_1(n)$ be the IPC obtained for a given program on a multiscalar architecture with n processing units without any re-execution. Similarly, let $I_2(p \times (n - p))$ be the IPC with task re-execution using p primary processing units in a multiscalar architecture with n total processing units. Since the total number of committed instructions to complete a given program with or without re-execution is the same and since more clock cycles will usually be required to complete the program with re-execution than without re-execution, we expect $I_2(p \times (n - p)) \leq I_1(n)$. Define the performance degradation due to re-execution as:

$$\frac{I_1(n) - I_2(p \times (n - p))}{I_1(n)} * 100.$$

Performance degradation vs. number of re-execution units

The fault-tolerant architectures proposed in the previous section were evaluated by running all SPEC95 integer benchmarks on the simulator configured to study these architectures. Figure 3(a) shows the performance degradation in the static re-execution scheme when the number of secondary processing units is varied from 0 to 16 while keeping the number of primary processing units at 16. In the 16×0 configuration, the degradation is 50% because there is no concurrent execution of the actual and the re-execution instruction streams. At the other extreme, i.e., in the 16×16 configuration, the actual and the re-execution streams can be concurrently executed on 16 processing units each, thus completing them at the same time and resulting a degradation of 0%. In the intermediate configurations, the performance degradation lies somewhere in between 0% and 50% because there are fewer processing units for the re-execution instruction stream than the actual instruction stream. Note the rapid drop in the performance degradation as the number of processing units for the re-execution stream increases from 0 to 5. Beyond 5, the performance degradation is fairly small, i.e, less than 5%. The reason for this is two-fold. First, the re-execution stream is comprised of only committed instructions. In contrast, the primary processing units speculatively execute many instructions which have to be squashed. Second, a primary processing unit is not always busy. It is often waiting for results from another processing unit. This is evident from the observation that the IPC for all the benchmarks is less than 3 (see Figure 3(b)). This means that on the average

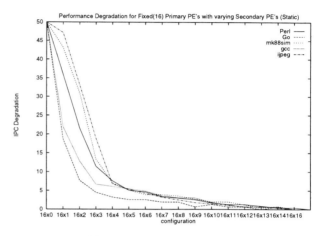

(a) Performance degradation

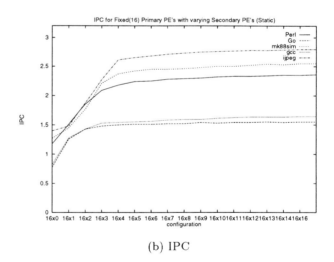

(b) IPC

Figure 3: Performance degradation and IPC in a static re-execution scheme for different re-execution PEs and constant primary PEs.

487

fewer than 3 out of the 16 processing units complete a to-be-committed instruction at any given clock cycle. Ideally this means that we do not need much more than 3 processing units for the re-execution stream to achieve close to the performance of the actual stream. However, we need more than 3 processing units for the re-execution stream to achieve this close performance because even these units cannot complete an instruction every clock cycle.

Performance degradation in static and dynamic re-execution schemes

In Figure 3, we kept the number of primary processing units constant and increased the total number of processing units. In practice, the total number of processing units is a constant. To increase the number of processing units for the re-execution stream, we must correspondingly decrease the number of primary processing units. There is, therefore, a tradeoff. If the number of re-execution units is small, the overall performance with re-execution will be poor because there will not be enough processing units for the re-execution instruction stream. At the other extreme, if too many processing units are assigned to the re-execution instruction stream, then there will be slowdown in the performance of the actual instruction stream.

Figures 4 and 5 depict this tradeoff for the five SPEC95 integer benchmarks. The three sub-graphs in each figure correspond to 8, 12, and 16 total processing units respectively. In each sub-figure, the plots show the performance degradation for different configurations of the total processing units between the actual and the re-execution instruction stream. For example, in the static re-execution scheme (i.e., in Figure 4(c)), 11×5 configuration means that 11 out of 16 processing units are for the actual instruction stream while the remaining 5 are for the re-execution instruction stream. In these plots, the minimum performance degradation occurs when about 2/3 of the processing units are assigned to the actual instruction stream. For example, in Figure 4(c), the minimum performance degradation

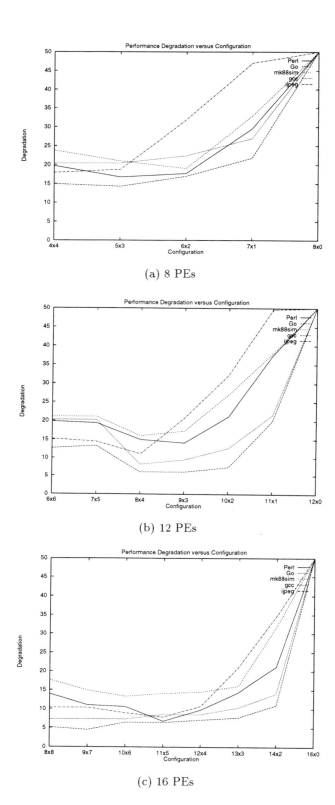

(a) 8 PEs

(b) 12 PEs

(c) 16 PEs

Figure 4: Performance degradation in static re-execution schemes for different number of total processing units.

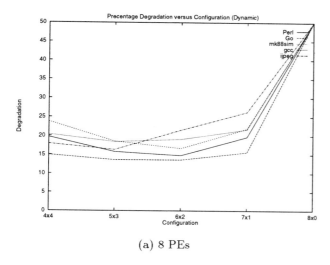

(a) 8 PEs

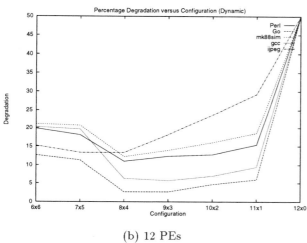

(b) 12 PEs

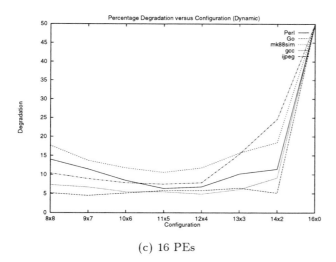

(c) 16 PEs

Figure 5: Performance degradation in dynamic re-execution schemes for different number of total processing units.

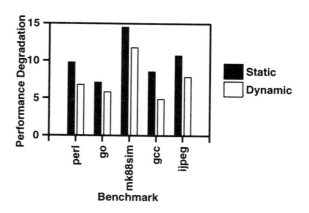

Figure 6: Comparison for performance degradation in the static and dynamic re-execution schemes for the 12×4 configuration.

for the perl benchmark occurs for the 11×5 configuration. For configurations to the left of 11×5 configuration in Figure 4(c), the performance degradation is more because there are not enough processing units for the re-execution instruction stream, whereas for the configurations to the right of 11×5, the performance degradation is more because there are not enough processing units for the actual instruction stream.

Static vs. dynamic re-execution schemes

Figure 6 compares the performance degradation for all benchmarks in the static and dynamic re-execution schemes for the 12×4 configuration. Observe that the performance degradation is smaller in the dynamic re-execution scheme than in the static scheme. This is because in the dynamic scheme there are many cycles where all 16 processing units are assigned to the re-execution instruction scheme whereas in the static scheme a fixed number of processing units, only 4, are always used for the re-execution instruction stream. This decrease in performance comes at the expense of additional hardware cost. A qualitative comparison of the hardware cost between the two schemes is presented later in Section 5.3.

5.2 Fault Coverage and Error Latency

As mentioned earlier, the static and dynamic re-execution schemes cover all the permanent and transient faults in the processing units and register files that result in incorrect program execution. By comparing the results of every instruction, incorrect results due to a fault can be detected.

The error latency depends on the size of the task buffer. The larger the buffer, the larger the latency. Figure 7 shows the latency of each task in the perl benchmark in 12×4 configuration for the dynamic re-execution scheme. The task buffer size was 100 for the results in this figure. Thus at the time the buffer was full it contained 88 filled slots. Similarly when the buffer is empty, it contained 4 filled slots. Note also that the maximum error latency never exceeded 1000 cycles.

5.3 Hardware Cost

Both, static and dynamic re-execution schemes need comparison hardware to compare the results for the actual and re-execution instruction streams. They also need a task buffer to exchange information about committed tasks and load values between the two set of processing units.

The multiscalar architecture has a distributed register file that maintains a single state for the processor. The different processing units communicate the register values in a ring. The assignment of the tasks to the processing units is in order of program execution, with the head PE executing the non-speculated task, while the tail executing the latest speculated task. Register values are communicated from the head to the tail via the distributed register file that is connected in a ring.

For the static scheme, the distributed register files are separate for both the primary and the secondary processing units, and each communicates within its own set of processing units. A flag in each processing unit can be used to maintain whether it is executing the actual or the re-execution stream. This flag can be used to ensure that secondary processing units do not update the contents of their register files when a primary processing unit sends a result and vice versa.

In contrast, in dynamic implementation both the original data values as well as the secondary re-execution data values have to co-exist in the register file. The cost for such an implementation is doubling the register file and adding a bit line to the address line to the register file. Doing so, we allocate the one half of the register file for the primary processing units, while the secondary re-execution units use the other half of the register file. We found that these hardware modifications do not effect the instruction cache misses for either of the re-execution schemes and the data caches also had no impact as the load values were passed to the secondary units through task buffer.

6 Conclusion

In this paper we introduced and studied two novel fault tolerant architectures for a state-of-the-art microarchitecture, namely multiscalar architecture. Both schemes proposed in this paper rely on re-executing all instructions in a program. The hardware cost to achieve this is very low yet the schemes cause only little performance degradation and cover transient and permanent faults in the processing units that can lead to incorrect results of computation. These studies were carried out by running a number of SPEC95 benchmark programs on a multiscalar architecture simulator. Only the integer benchmarks are reported in the paper although the results for floating point benchmarks were found to be no different. The floating point benchmarks take nearly an order more of CPU time to simulate.

We believe that the results of our study conclusively establish that new microarchitectures, such as multiscalar, can achieve fault-tolerance at very small performance loss. However, a number of issues still need to be studied. These are hardware implementation of static and dynamic re-execution methods. In particular, in the case of dynamic re-execution, the impact of switching between $n \times (n - p)$ and $0 \times n$ configuration needs to be evaluated.

References

[1] S. E. Breach, *Design and Evaluation Of A Multiscalar Processor*, PhD thesis, University

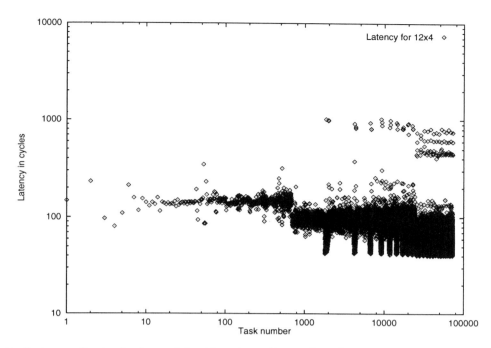

Figure 7: Latency for tasks in perl in 12×4 configuration dynamic re-execution scheme.

of Wisconsin -Madison, 1998.

[2] M. Franklin, *The Multiscalar Architecture*, PhD thesis, University of Wisconsin-Madison, 1993.

[3] M. Franklin, "A study of time redundant fault tolerance techniques for superscalar processors," In *The IEEEE International Workshop on Defect and Fault Tolerance in VLSI Systems*, 1995.

[4] C. Gong, R. Melhem, and R. Gupta, "Loop transformations for fault detection in regular loops on massively parallel systems," *IEEE Transactions on Parallel and Distributed Systems*, vol. 7, no. 12, pp. 1238–1249, December 1996.

[5] D. K. Pradhan, editor, *Fault-Tolerant Computer System Design*, Prentice Hall, 1996.

[6] E. Rotenberg, "AR-SMT: A microarchitectural approach to fault tolerance in microprocessors," In *The Twenty-Ninth Annual International Symposium on Fault-Tolerant Computing*, pp. 84–91, June 1999.

[7] N. Saxena and E. McCluskey, "Dependable adaptive computing systems - the ROAR project," In *International Conference on Systems, Man, and Cybernetics*, pp. 2172–2177, October 1998.

[8] J. E. Smith and G. Sohi, "The microarchitecture of superscalar processors," In *Proceedings of the IEEE*, pp. 1609–1624, December 1995.

[9] G. Sohi, S. Breach, and T. N. Vijaykumar, "Multiscalar processors," In *22nd International Symposium on Computer Architecture*, pp. 414–425, June 1995.

A Fault Tolerance Infrastructure for Dependable Computing with High-Performance COTS Components

Algirdas Avižienis
A. Avižienis and Associates, Inc.
2711 Washington Avenue
Santa Monica, CA 90403, USA
Fax and phone: 310-828-8821
E-mail: {aviz}@cs.ucla.edu

Abstract

The failure rates of current COTS processors have dropped to 100 FITs (failures per 10^9 hours), indicating a potential MTTF of over 1100 years. However, our recent study of Intel P6 family processors has shown that they have very limited error detection and recovery capabilities and contain numerous design faults ("errata"). Other limitations are susceptibility to transient faults and uncertainty about "wearout" that could increase the failure rate in time. Because of these limitations, an external fault tolerance infrastructure is needed to assure the dependability of a system with such COTS components.

The paper describes a fault-tolerant "infrastructure" system of fault tolerance functions that makes possible the use of low-coverage COTS processors in a fault-tolerant, self-repairing system. The custom hardware supports transient recovery, design fault tolerance, and self-repair by sparing and replacement. Fault tolerance functions are implemented by four types of hardware processors of low complexity that are fault-tolerant. High error detection coverage, including design faults, is attained by diversity and replication.

1. A Rationale for the "Fault Tolerance Infrastructure"

Presently we are witnessing a very significant and continuing reduction of failure rates for complex semiconductor devices. For example, recent Intel literature [1] quotes the failure rate of 100 FITs (failures per 10^9 hours) for their best products, with 10 FITs being the goal for the near future. The 100 FIT rate gives a device MTTF of 10^7 hours (1140 years). It may be reasonably concluded that device failures have become the least serious of dependability problems for contemporary computer systems.

At the same time we observe the increasing significance of other threats to the dependability of the hardware of computer systems. These threats are:

(1) *Susceptibility to environmental interference.* The continuing reductions in the size and power level of logic elements raises device susceptibility to *interference* by radiation and other environmental factors that cause transient faults.

(2) *Hardware design faults.* Complex devices, especially high-performance processors, contain design faults (called "errata") that are discovered after the design is completed. For example, the seven processors of the Intel P6 family in April 1999 had from 45 to 101 reported design faults, of which from *30 to 60* have remained uncorrected to the most recent versions ("steppings") of the processors, and new "errata" are announced at the rate of about one per month [2].

(3) *Uncertainty about wearout.* This threat applies to closed systems with very long life requirement. Device wearout may begin after several years, leading to an increasing failure rate in time. The FIT rate being quoted presently is based on HVEL (High Voltage Extended Life) tests and field data from millions of devices gathered over a time span of a few years.

It is evident that the benefits of very low device failure rates will only be significant if the probabilities of system failure due to transient faults and design faults can also be reduced to comparable values.

It is our goal to apply proven fault tolerance techniques to alleviate these problems. Transient fault effects are "soft" errors, eliminated by error detection and subsequent correction or rollback. Increasing failure rates are counteracted by the provision of spares. Design diversity (use of diverse devices in a redundant configuration) is an effective method to

492

detect and neutralize hardware design faults. Wearout may also be alleviated by diversity of device technologies, since some technologies may be less susceptible to wearout than others.

Two other major dependability problems are software design faults and malicious interference by humans. Analogous to the tolerance of hardware design faults, design diversity of software (e.g., N-version programming) provides software fault tolerance and supports system security as well [3–5].

The application of fault tolerance to systems that use high-performance COTS processors is severely hindered by one design deficiency. Most contemporary COTS processors have very limited error detection coverage and poor error containment provisions. For example, our recent study of Intel P6 family processors shows that error detection by parity only covers the caches and the busses, except for the data bus which has an error correcting code, as does the main memory. All the complex logic of arithmetic and instruction processing remains unchecked. Recovery choices are a set of "reset" actions of varying severity. The cancellation in April 1998 of the duplex (Master/Checker) "FRC" mode of operation has eliminated most of the error containment boundary. All internal error detection and recovery logic remains entirely unchecked [6, 7].

Similar error coverage and containment deficiencies are found in the high-end processors of most other manufacturers. The exceptions are IBM S/390 G5 and G6 processors that internally duplicate the arithmetic and instruction handling (I and E) units and provide extensive error detection and transient recovery for the entire processor [8].

The lack of error detection and recovery in hardware forces the search for software solutions that by their nature are inefficient and of limited effectiveness. The goal of this paper is to provide an alternative: a hardware based solution called the "fault tolerance infrastructure" that can provide fault tolerance for systems with processors that offer high performance, but may have low error coverage and poor containment.

The objective of the proposed "infrastructure" design is to serve as a generic "plug-in" structure with the following attributes: (1) It provides error detection and recovery support to computing systems that may employ diverse COTS hardware and software in redundant configurations for physical and design fault tolerance. (2) It provides a "shutdown-hold-restart" recovery sequence for catastrophic events such as interference by intensive radiation, temporary power outages, etc. (3) It supports the inclusion of unpowered spare system elements for long-duration missions without external repair. (4) It does not employ software and is implemented by four types of fault-tolerant controllers of very low complexity.

The following sections describe a baseline design intended for an experimental system to be built for concept validation and refinement. The last section suggests two challenging long-life applications that need the dependability that the infrastructure can assure.

2. Architecture of DiSTARS: Diversifiable Self Testing And Repairing System

2.1. The DiSTARS Concept

The structure of a system named DiSTARS (*Diversifiable Self Testing And Repairing System*) is shown in Figure 1. Conceptually, DiSTARS consists of two concentric rings: the Outer Ring and the Inner Ring. The Outer Ring is a high-performance computing system composed of *Computing*, or *C-nodes* and their *System Bus*. The C-nodes are either high-performance COTS processors (e.g., Pentium II) with the associated memory, or other COTS elements from the supporting chipset (I/O controllers, etc.), and other subsystems of a server platform [9]. The Outer Ring is supplemented with custom-designed *Decision* or *D-nodes* that communicate with the C-nodes via the System Bus. The D-nodes serve as comparators or voters for inputs provided by the C-nodes. They also provide the means for the C-nodes to communicate with the Inner Ring. Detailed discussion of the D-node is presented later.

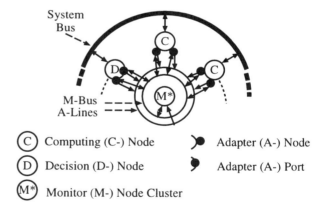

Figure 1. A Partial View of DiSTARS Two-Ring Architecture

The Inner Ring is a custom-designed system composed of *Adapter*, or *A-nodes* and a cluster of *Monitor*, or *M-nodes*, called the *M-cluster*. The A-nodes and the M-nodes communicate via the *Monitor*, or M-bus. Every A-node also has a dedicated *A-line* for one-way communication to the M-nodes. The custom-designed D-nodes of the Outer Ring contain embedded *A-ports* that serve the same purpose as the external A-nodes of the C-node chips.

The M-cluster serves as the fault-tolerant controller for the recovery management of the C- and D- nodes of the Outer Ring. The M-cluster employs hybrid redundancy (TMR with unpowered spares) to assure its continuous availability. It is an evolved descendent of the Test-and-Repair processor of JPL-STAR computer [10]. Two dedicated A-nodes are connected to every C-node, and every D-node contains two A-ports. The A-nodes and A-ports serve as the input and output devices of the M-cluster: they relay error signals and other relevant outputs of the C- and D- nodes to the M-cluster and return M-cluster responses to the appropriate C- or D-node inputs.

The custom-designed Inner Ring and the D-nodes provide a *fault tolerance infrastructure* that assures dependable operation of the COTS computing system composed of the C-nodes. The infrastructure is *generic*; that is, it can accommodate any set of Outer Ring C-node chips by providing them with the appropriate Adapter nodes and storing the proper responses to A-node error messages in the M-nodes. Fault tolerance techniques are extensively used in the design of the infrastructure's components.

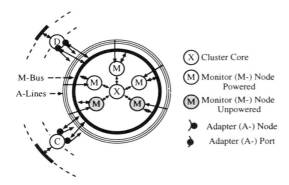

Figure 2. The Inner Ring with the M-Cluster

An expanded view of the Inner Ring is presented in Figure 2. The following discussion explains the functions and structure of the A- and M- nodes, the operation of the M-cluster, and the communication between the M-cluster and the A-nodes. Unless explicitly stated otherwise, the A-ports are structured and behave like the A-nodes. The D-nodes are discussed in Section 3.

2.2. The Adapter (A-) Nodes and A-lines

The purpose of the A-node is to connect a given C-node to the M-cluster that provides Outer Ring recovery management. The functions of an A-node are:

1. Transmit error messages that are originated by its C-node to the M-cluster.

2. Transmit recovery commands from the M-cluster to its C-node.

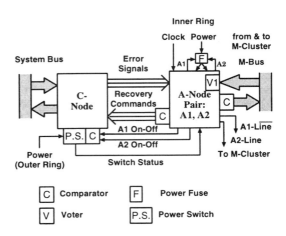

Figure 3. The Adapter (A-) Node Pair with their C-Node

3. Control the power switch of the C-node and its own fuse according to commands received from the M-cluster.

4. Report its own status to the M-cluster.

The connections of the A-node are shown in Figure 3. A self-checking pair of A-nodes (called *A-pair*) is provided for every C-node. Both A-nodes of the A-pair have a unique ID code that is associated with their C-node; otherwise, all A-nodes are identical in their design. They encode the error signal outputs of their C-node and decode the recovery commands to serve as inputs to the C-node.

For an example, consider the Pentium II processor as the C-node. It has five error signal output pins: AERR (address parity error), BINIT (bus protocol violation), BERR (bus non-protocol error), IERR (internal non-bus error), and THERMTRIP (thermal overrun error) which leads to processor shutdown. It is the function of the A-pair to communicate these signals to the M-cluster. The Pentium II also has six recovery command input pins: RESET, INIT (initialize), BINIT (bus initialize), FLUSH (cache flush), SMI (system management interrupt), and NMI (non-maskable interrupt). The A-pair can activate these inputs according to the commands received from the M-cluster.

Each A-node has a separate A-line for messages to the M-cluster. The messages are: (1) All is well, C-node powered, (2) All is well, C-node unpowered, (3) M-bus request, (4) Transmitting on M-bus; (5) Internal A-node fault. All A-pairs of the Inner Ring are connected to the M-bus which provides two-way communication with the M-cluster, as discussed in the next section.

The outputs of the A-pair to the C-node, to the C-node power switch and to the M-bus are compared in Comparator circuits. In case of disagreement, the outputs are inhibited and an "Internal fault" message is sent on the A-lines. The only exception is the C-node Power-Off command. One Power-Off command is sufficient to turn C-node power off after the failure of one A-node in the pair.

The A-pair remains powered by Inner Ring power when Outer Ring power to its C-node is off, i.e., when the C-node is a spare or has failed. The failure of one A-node in the self-checking A-pair turns off the power of its C-node. A fuse is used to remove power from a failed A-pair, thus protecting the M-bus from "babbling" outputs from the failed A-pair. Clock synchronization signals are delivered from the M-cluster. The low complexity of the A-node allows the packaging of the A-pair and power switch in one module.

2.3. The Monitor (M-) Nodes, M-Cluster and M-Bus

The purpose of the Monitor (M-) node is to collect status and error messages from all A-nodes, to select the appropriate recovery action, and to issue commands that implement recovery to the A-nodes via the Monitor (M-) Bus. To assure continuous M-node availability, they are arranged in a hybrid-redundant M-cluster with three powered M-nodes in a TMR arrangement and unpowered spares. The voting on output commands takes place in Voter logic located in the A-nodes. A built-in self-test (BIST) sequence is provided in every M-node.

The M-bus is controlled by the M-cluster and connected to all A-nodes, as discussed in the previous section. All messages are error-coded, and spare bus lines are provided to make the M-bus fault-tolerant. Two kinds of messages are sent to the A-pairs by the M-cluster: (1) an acknowledgement of A-pair request (on their A-lines) that allocates a time slot on the M-bus for the A-pair error message; and (2) a command in response to the error message.

An M-node stores two kinds of information: static (permanent) and dynamic. The *static* (ROM) data consists of (1) pre-determined recovery command responses to A-pair error messages, (2) sequences for M-node recovery and replacement in the hybrid-redundant M-cluster, and (3) recovery sequences for catastrophic events (Section 2.6). The *dynamic* data consists of (1) Outer Ring configuration status (active, spare, failed node list), (2) Inner Ring configuration status and system time, (3) a "scratchpad" store for current activity: error messages still active, requests waiting, etc., and (4) an Inner Ring activity log. The configuration status and system time is the *critical* data that is also stored in non-volatile storage in the S^3 nodes of the Cluster Core (Section 2.4).

As long as all A-nodes continue sending "All is well" messages on their A-lines, the M-cluster issues "All is well" acknowledgements. When an "M-bus request" message arrives on two A-lines that come from an A-pair with a unique

C-node ID code, the M-cluster sends (on the M-bus) the C-node ID followed by the "Transmit" command. In response, the A-pair sends (on the M-bus) its C-node ID followed by an Error code originated by the C-node. The M-nodes return the C-node ID followed by a Recovery command for the C-node. The A-pair transmits the command to the C-node and returns an acknowledgement: its C-node ID followed by the command it sent to the C-node. At the times when the A-pair sends a message on the M-bus, its A-lines send the "Transmitting" status report. This feature allows the M-cluster to detect cases when a wrong A-pair responds on the M-bus. An Error code is also sent by the A-pair if its voters detect disagreements between the three M-cluster messages received on the M-bus.

When the A-pair comparators (Figure 3) detect a disagreement, its A-lines send an "Internal Fault" message to the M-cluster, which responds (on the M-bus) with the C-node ID followed by the "Reset A-pair" command. Both A-nodes of the A-pair attempt to reset to an initial state, but do not change the setting of the C-node power switch. Success causes "All is well" to be sent on the A-lines. In case of failure to reset, the A-lines continue sending the "Internal Fault" message.

The M-cluster sends "Power On" and "Power Off" commands as part of a replacement or reconfiguration sequence for the C-nodes. They are acknowledged immediately but power switching itself takes a relatively long time. When switching is completed, the A-pair issues an "M-bus Request" on its A-lines and then reports the success (or failure) of the switching to the M-cluster via the M-bus.

When the M-cluster determines that one A-node of an A-pair has permanently failed, it sends "A-pair Power Off" message to the A-pair. The good A-node receives the message, turns C-node power off (if it was on) and then permanently opens the A-pair power fuse. The M-cluster receives confirmation via the A-lines, which assume the "no power" state. This irreversible command is also used when a C-node fails permanently and must be removed from the Outer Ring.

2.4. The M-Cluster Core

The M-cluster is shown in Figure 2, and the Cluster Core in Figure 4. The Core of the M-cluster consists of a set of S^3-nodes (S^3 stands for Startup, Shutdown, Survival) and communication links. The M-nodes have dedicated "Disagree", "Internal Error" and "Replacement Request" outputs to all other M-nodes and to the S^3-nodes. The IC (Intra-Cluster) Bus connects all M-nodes.

The purpose of the S^3 nodes is to support the survival of DiSTARS during catastrophic events, such as intensive bursts of radiation or temporary loss of power. Every S^3-node is a self-checking pair with its own backup (battery)

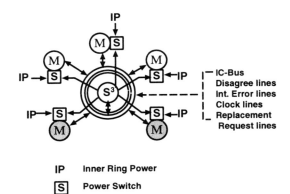

IP   Inner Ring Power

S   Power Switch

Figure 4. The Core of the M-Cluster

power. At least two S^3 nodes are needed to attain fault-tolerance, while the actual number needed depends on the mission length without external repair.

The functions of the S^3 nodes are: (1) to execute the "power-on" and "power-off" sequences for DiSTARS; (2) to provide fault-tolerant clock signals; (3) to keep System Time and System Configuration data in non-volatile, radiation-hardened registers; (4) to control M-node power switches and I-Ring power to the A-pairs in order to support M-cluster recovery. More discussion of S^3-node operation follows in Section 2.6.

Every half of the self-checking S^3 node has its own clock generator. The hardware-based fault-tolerant clocking system developed at the C.S. Draper Laboratory [11] is the most suitable for the M-cluster.

2.5. Error Detection and Recovery in the M-cluster

Initially, the three powered M-nodes are in agreement and contain the same dynamic data. They operate in the triplication-and-voting (TMR) mode. Three commands are issued in sequence on the M-bus and voted upon in the A-nodes. During operation of the M-cluster, one M-node may issue an output different from the other two, or one M-node may detect an error internally and send an "Internal Error" signal on a dedicated line to the other two M-nodes. The cause may be either a "soft" error due to a transient fault, or a "hard" error due to physical failure.

M-node output disagreement detection in the TMR mode (when one M-node is affected by a fault) is done as follows. The three M-nodes place their outputs on the M-bus in a fixed sequence. Each M-node compares its output to the outputs of the other two nodes, records one or two disagreements, and sends one or two "Disagree" messages to the other M-nodes on a dedicated line. The affected M-node will disagree twice, while the good M-nodes will disagree once each and at the same time, which is the time slot of the affected M-node.

Following error detection, the following recovery sequence is carried out by the two good M-nodes:

1. Identify the affected M-node or the M-node that sent the Internal Error message and enter *Duplex* mode of M-cluster.

2. Attempt "soft" error recovery by reloading the dynamic data of the affected M-node from the other two M-nodes and resume TMR operation.

3. If Step (2) does not lead to agreement, send request for replacement of the affected M-node to the S^3 nodes.

4. The S^3-nodes replace the affected M-node and send a "Resume TMR" command.

5. Load the new M-node with dynamic data from the other two M-nodes and resume TMR operation.

During the recovery sequence, the two good (agreeing) M-nodes operate in the Duplex mode, in which they continue to communicate with the A-nodes and concurrently execute the recovery steps (2)-(5). The Duplex mode becomes the permanent mode of operation if only two good M-nodes are left in the M-cluster. Details of the M-cluster recovery sequence are discussed next.

Step (1): Entering Duplex Mode. The simultaneous disagreement by the good M-nodes during error detection causes the affected M-node to enter the "Hold" mode, in which it inhibits its output to the M-bus and does not respond to the inputs on the A-lines. It also clears its "Disagree" output. If the affected node does not enter the "Hold" mode, step (3) is executed to cause its replacement. An M-node also enters the "Hold" mode when it issues an Internal Error message to the other two M-nodes, which enter the Duplex mode at that time. It may occur that all three M-nodes disagree, i.e., each one issues two "Disagree" signals, or that two or all three M-nodes signal Internal Error. These *catastrophic events* are discussed in section 2.6.

The two good M-nodes still send three commands to the A-nodes in Duplex mode during steps (2)-(5). During t_1 and t_2 they send their outputs to the M-bus and compare. Agreement causes the same command to be sent during t_3; disagreement invokes a retry, then catastrophic event recovery. The good M-nodes continue operating in Duplex mode if a spare M-node is not available after the affected node has been powered off in step (3). TMR operation is permanently degraded to Duplex in the M-cluster.

Step (2): Reload Dynamic Data of the Affected Node. An Intra-Cluster (IC-) bus is used for this purpose (Figure 4). At times t_1 and t_2 the good M-nodes place the corresponding dynamic data on the IC-Bus, at time t_3 the affected node compares and stores it. The good nodes also compare their outputs. Any disagreement causes a repetition of times t_1, t_2, t_3. A further disagreement between

496

good nodes is a catastrophic event. After reloading is completed, it is validated: the affected node reads out its data, and the good nodes compare it to their copies. A disagreement leads to step (3), i.e., power-off for the affected node; otherwise the M-cluster returns to TMR operation.

Steps (3) and (4): Power Switching. Power switching is the means for removing failed M-nodes and bringing in spares in the M-cluster. Failed nodes with power on can lethally interfere with M-cluster functioning, therefore very dependable switching is essential. The power switching function is performed by the S^3-nodes in the Cluster Core. They maintain a record of M-cluster status in non-volatile storage. Power is turned off for the failed M-node, the next spare is powered up, BIST is executed, and the "Resume TMR" command is sent to the M-nodes.

Step (5): Loading a New M-node. When the "Resume TMR" command of step (4) is received, the new M-node must receive the dynamic data from the two good M-nodes. The procedure is the same as the step(2).

2.6. Recovery after Catastrophic Events

Up to this point recovery was defined in response to an error signal from one C-node, A-node, or M-node for which the M-cluster had a predetermined recovery command or sequence. These recoveries are classified as *local* and involve only one node.

However, it is possible that error signals could originate concurrently (or close in time) from two or more nodes. A few such cases have been identified as *catastrophic events* (c-events) in the preceding discussion. It is not practical to predetermine unique recovery for each c-event, therefore more general catastrophe-recovery (c-recovery) procedures must be devised.

In general, we can distinguish c-events that affect the Outer Ring only, and c-events that affect the Inner Ring as well. For the Outer Ring a c-event is a crash of system software that requires a restart with Inner Ring assistance. The Inner Ring does not employ software, thus its crash cannot occur.

However, there are adverse physical events that can cause c-events for the entire DiSTARS. Examples are: (1) external interference by radiation; (2) fluctuations of ambient temperature; (3) temporary instability or outage of power; (4) physical damage to system hardware.

The predictable manifestations of these events in DiSTARS are: (1) halt in operation due to power loss; (2) permanent failures of system components (nodes) and/or communication links; (3) crashes of Outer Ring application and system software; (4) errors in or loss of M-node data stored in volatile storage; (5) numerous error messages from the A-nodes that exceed the ability of M-cluster to respond in time; (6) double or triple disagreements or Internal Error

signals in the M-cluster TMR or Duplex modes.

The current DiSTARS design employs a System Reset procedure in which the S^3-nodes execute a "power-off" sequence for DiSTARS upon receiving a c-event signal either from sensors (radiation level, power stability, etc) or from the M-nodes. System Time and DiSTARS configuration data are preserved in the radiation-hardened, battery-powered S^3-nodes. The "power-on" sequence is executed when the sensors indicate a return to normal conditions.

Outer Ring power is turned off when the S^3-node removes power from the A-pairs, thus setting all C-node switches to the "Off" position. M-node power is directly controlled by the S^3-nodes.

The "power-on" sequence begins with the S^3-nodes applying power and executing BIST to find 3 or 2 good M-nodes, loading them via the IC-Bus with the critical data, and then applying I-Ring power to the A-pairs. At this point the M-cluster commands "Power-On" followed by BIST sequentially for the C-nodes of the Outer Ring, and the system returns to an operating condition, possibly having lost some nodes due to the catastrophic event.

The present design has only the "power-off" sequence to respond to c-events. It is expected that experiments with the prototype DiSTARS system will lead to less drastic and faster recovery sequences for some less harmful c-events.

3. The Decision (D-) Nodes and Diversification

3.1. The Rationale for D-Nodes

The A-nodes thus far have been the only means of communication between the Inner and Outer Rings, and they convey only very specific C-node information. It is evident that a more general communication link is needed. The Outer Ring may need configuration data and activity logs from the M-cluster, or to command the powering up or down of some C-nodes for power management reasons. An Inter-Ring communication node is needed that acts as a link between the System Bus of the Outer Ring and the M-bus of the Inner Ring.

A second need of the Outer Ring is better error detection coverage. For example, as described in section 2.2, the Pentium II has only five error signal outputs of very general nature, and their coverage was estimated to be very limited in a recent study [6, 7]. The original design of the P6 family of Intel processors included the FRC (functional redundancy checking) mode of operation in which two processors could be operated in the Master/Checker mode, providing very good error confinement and high error detection coverage. Detection of an error was indicated by the FRCERR signal. Quite surprisingly and without explanation, the FRCERR pin was removed from the specification in April 1998, thus effectively canceling the use of the FRC mode long after the P6 processors reached the market.

In fairness it should be noted that other processor makers never even tried to provide Master/Checker duplexing for their high-performance processors with low error detection coverage. An exception is the design of the IBM G5 and G6 processors, discussed in [7]

This observation raises the need for a custom Decision (D-) node on the Outer Ring System Bus that can serve as an external comparator or voter for the C-node COTS processors. It is even more important that the D-node also can support design diversity by providing the appropriate decision algorithms for N-version programming [4] employing diverse processors as the C-nodes of the Outer Ring.

The use of processor diversity has become important for dependable computing because contemporary high-performance processors contain significant numbers of design faults. For example, our recent study shows that in the Intel P6 family processors from 45 to 101 design faults ("errata") were discovered (as of April 1999) after design was complete, and that from 30 to 60 of these design faults have remained in the latest versions ("steppings") of these processors [2].

3.2. Structure and Functions of the Decision (D-) Node

The D-nodes need to be compatible with the C-nodes on the System Bus and also embed Adapter (A-) Ports analogous to the A-nodes that are attached to C-nodes. The functions of the D-nodes are:

(1) to transmit messages originated by C-node software to the M-cluster;

(2) to transfer M-cluster data to the C-nodes that request it;

(3) to accept identical C-node outputs for comparison or voting and to return the results to the C-nodes;

(4) to provide a set of decision algorithms for N-version software executing on diverse processors (C-nodes), to accept cross-check point outputs and to return the results;

(5) to log disagreement data on the decisions;

(6) to provide high coverage and fault tolerance for the execution of the above functions.

The programs of the C-nodes have to be written with provisions to take advantage of D-node services. The relatively simple functions of the D-node can be implemented by microcode and the D-node response can be very fast. Another advantage of using the D-node for decisions (as opposed to doing them in the C-nodes) is the high coverage and fault tolerance of the D-node (implemented as a self-checking pair) that assures error-free results.

The Adapter (A-) Ports of the D-node need to provide the same services that the A-nodes provide to the C-nodes, including power switching for spare D-node utilization. In addition, the A-ports must also serve to relay appropriately formatted C-node messages to the M-cluster, then accept and vote on M-cluster responses. The messages are requests for C-node power switching, Inner and Outer Ring configuration information, and M-cluster activity logs. The D-node can periodically request and store the activity logs, thus reducing the amount of dynamic storage in the M-nodes. The D-nodes can also serve as the repositories of other data that may support M-cluster operations, such as the logs of disagreements during D-node decisions, etc.

In conclusion, it is noted that the relatively simple D-nodes can effectively compensate for the low coverage and poor error containment of contemporary processors (e.g., Pentium II) by allowing their duplex or TMR operation with reliable comparisons or voting and with diverse processors executing N-version software for the tolerance of software and hardware design faults.

4. A Proof-of-Concept Experimental System

The Two Ring concept, with the Inner Ring and D-nodes providing the fault tolerance infrastructure for the Outer Ring of C-nodes that is a high-performance COTS computer is well defined and complete. However, many design choices and tradeoffs remain to be evaluated and chosen. Our experience with the JPL-STAR, FTBBC and Dedix systems, as well as the experiences of many other system builders, have shown that essential insights are gained by building an experimental system and subjecting it to various tests and evaluations.

At this time we have initiated the construction of a prototype DiSTAR system for experimental evaluation. The prototype uses a four-processor symmetric multiprocessor configuration [12] of Pentium II processors with the supporting chipset as the Outer Ring. Two Pentium II processors will serve as C-nodes; the other two will emulate D-node behavior. The S^3-nodes, M-nodes, A-nodes and A-ports of the Inner Ring are being implemented by Xilinx FPGAs.

The next step of the development will be the FPGA implementation of the D-nodes. Other tasks are the construction of power switches and the programming of typical applications running on duplex C-nodes that use the duplex D-nodes for comparisons.

Still further ahead is the diversification of C-nodes and N-version execution of typical applications. At the present time our effort is focused on building and refining the Inner Ring that can support the Pentium II C- and D- nodes of the Outer Ring and provide a proof of the "fault tolerance infrastructure" concept.

5. Some Challenging Extensions and Applications

The Inner Ring and D-nodes of DiSTAR offer a "plug-in" fault tolerance infrastructure for contemporary high-performance, but low-coverage processors with their memories and supporting chipsets. The infrastructure was conceived as an analogy of the human immune system [13] in the context of contemporary hardware platforms [9]. DiSTARS is an illustration of the application of the design paradigm presented in [13].

A desirable advance in processor design is to incorporate an evolved variant of the infrastructure into the processor structure itself. This is becoming feasible as the clock rate and transistor count on a chip race upward according to Moore's Law. However, the external infrastructure concept remains viable and necessary to support chip-level sparing, power switching, and design diversity for hardware, software, and device technologies.

The high reliability and availability that may be attained by using the infrastructure concept in system design is likely to be affordable for most computer systems. However, there exist challenging missions that can only be justified if their computers have high coverage with respect to transient and design faults in addition to the low device failure rates.

Two such missions that are still in the concept and preliminary design phases are the manned mission to Mars [14] and unmanned interstellar missions [15].

The Mars mission is about 1000 days long. The proper functioning of the spacecraft and therefore the lives of the astronauts depend on the continuous availability of computer support, similar to the primary flight control computers in commercial airliners. Device failures and wearout are not major threats for a 1000 day mission, but design faults and transient faults caused by cosmic rays and solar flares are to be expected and their effects need to be tolerated with very high coverage, i.e., probability of success. It will also be necessary to employ computers to monitor all spacecraft systems and to perform automatic repair actions when needed [10, 16], since the crew is not likely to have the necessary expertise and access for manual repairs. Here again computer failure can have lethal consequences and very high reliability is needed.

Another challenging application for a DiSTARS type fault-tolerant computer is on-board operation in an unmanned spacecraft intended for an interstellar mission. Since such missions are essentially open-ended, lifetimes of hundreds or even thousands of years are desirable. For example, currently the two Voyager spacecraft (launched in 1977) are in interstellar space, traveling at 3.5 and 3.1 A.U.

(Astronomical Units) per year. One A.U. is 150×10^6 kilometers, while the nearest star Alpha Centauri is 4.3 light years, or approximately 63,000 A.U. from the Sun. However, the near interstellar space is being explored, and research in breakthrough propulsion physics is being conducted by NASA [15].

An interesting concept is to create a fault-tolerant relay chain of modest-cost DiSTARS type fault-tolerant spacecraft [16] for the exploration of interstellar space. One spacecraft is launched on the same trajectory every n years, where n is chosen to be such that the distance between two successive spacecraft allows reliable communication with two closest neighbors ahead and behind a given spacecraft, as shown in Figure 5. The loss of any one spacecraft does not interrupt the link between the leading spacecraft and Earth, and the chain can be repaired by slowing down all spacecraft ahead of the failed one until the gap is closed.

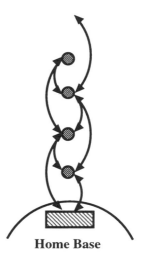

Home Base

Figure 5. A Fault-Tolerant Chain of Interstellar Spacecraft

Acknowledgments

The evolution of system fault tolerance and self-repair concepts from the JPL-STAR computer of the 1960's to the present DiSTARS computer has benefitted from the advances made in building several successful fault-tolerant systems, especially the FTMP and its successors at the C.S. Draper Laboratory and the FT BBC at JPL.

Dr. Yutao He has contributed many insights into the good and bad dependability aspects of the Intel P6 family of processors through the study of their logical structure, error coverage, and design faults ("errata").

References

[1] Intel Corp. *Intel's Quality System Databook*. January 1998. Order No. 210997-007.

[2] A. Avižienis and Y. He. Microprocessor entomology: A taxonomy of design faults in COTS microprocessors. In J. Rushby and C. B. Weinstock, editors, *Dependable Computing for Critical Applications 7*. IEEE Computer Society Press, 1999.

[3] A. Avižienis and J. P. J. Kelly. Fault tolerance by design diversity: concepts and experiments. *Computer*, 17(8):67–80, August 1984.

[4] A. Avižienis. The N-version approach to fault-tolerant software. *IEEE Trans. Software Eng.*, SE-11(12):1491–1501, December 1985.

[5] M.K. Joseph and A. Avižienis. Software fault tolerance and computer security: A shared problem. In *Proc. of the Annual National Joint Conference And Tutorial On Software Quality and Reliability*, pages 428–436, March 1989.

[6] Y. He. *An Investigation of Commercial Off-The-Shelf (COTS) Based Fault Tolerance*. PhD thesis, Computer Science Department, University of California, Los Angeles, September 1999.

[7] Y. He and A. Avižienis. Assessment of the applicability of COTS microprocessors in high-confidence computing systems: A case study. In *Digest of ICDSN 2000*, June 2000.

[8] T. J. Slegel et al. IBM's S/390 G5 microprocessor design. *IEEE Micro*, 19(2):12–23, March/April 1999.

[9] Intel Corp. *The Pentium II Processor Server Platform System Management Guide*, June 1998. Order No. 243835-001.

[10] A. Avižienis, G.C. Gilley, F.P. Mathur, D.A. Rennels, J.A. Rohr, and D.K. Rubin. The STAR (Self-Testing-And-Repairing) computer: An investigation of the theory and practice of fault-tolerant computer design. *IEEE Trans. Comp.*, C-20(11):1312–1321, November 1971.

[11] T.B. Smith. Fault-tolerant clocking system. In *Digest of FTCS-11*, pages 262–264, June 1981.

[12] Intel Corp. *P6 Family Of Processors Hardware Developer's Manual*, September 1998. Order No. 244001-001.

[13] A. Avižienis. Toward systematic design of fault-tolerant systems. *Computer*, 30(4):51–58, April 1997.

[14] Special report: Sending astronauts to Mars. *Scientific American*, 282(3):40–63, March 2000.

[15] Conference on enabling technology and required scientific developments for interstellar missions. *NASA OSS Advanced Concepts Newsletter*, page 3, March 1999.

[16] A. Avižienis. The hundred year spacecraft. In *Proc. of the 1st NASA/DoD Workshop on Evolvable Hardware*, pages 233–239, July 1999.

Synthesis of Interconnection Networks: A Novel Approach

Vijay Lakamraju, Israel Koren and C.M. Krishna

Department of Electrical and Computer Engineering
University of Massachusetts, Amherst 01003
E-mail: {vlakamra,koren,krishna}@ecs.umass.edu

Abstract

The interconnection network is a crucial element in parallel and distributed systems. Synthesizing networks that satisfy a set of desired properties, such as high reliability, low diameter and good scalability is a difficult problem to which there has been no completely satisfactory solution.

In this paper, we present a new approach to network synthesis. We start by generating a large number of random regular networks. These networks are then passed through filters, which filter out networks that do not satisfy specified network design requirements. By applying multiple filters in tandem, it is possible to synthesize networks which satisfy a multitude of properties. The filtered output thus constitutes a short-list of "good" networks that the designer can choose from. The use of random regular networks was motivated by their surprisingly good performance with regard to almost all properties that characterize a good interconnection network.

Experimental results have shown that this approach is practical and powerful. In this paper we focus on the generation of networks which have low diameter, good scalability and high fault tolerance. These generated networks are shown to compare favorably with several well-known networks.

1. Introduction

Interconnection networks (ICNs) are as much a determinant of performance and dependability in a parallel or distributed system as the processors themselves. The network impacts the cost of the architecture and the cost of communicating between processors, as well as system reliability and the extent to which the system can degrade gracefully under processor or link failures.

This paper describes a new approach to the synthesis of interconnection networks for parallel and distributed systems. The distinguishing features of our technique are that it can be tailored to the specific performance and fault-tolerance measures of interest to the designer, and that it can be used even by those who are not experts in interconnection networks. It is especially useful when seeking to synthesize a network that performs well with respect to *multiple* performance measures. For example, a designer may place a high premium on both scalability and network resilience, while simultaneously needing to constrain the degree of the network. It can also be used to study tradeoffs among several performance or dependability parameters.

A vast literature on interconnection networks exists. Networks such as the hypercube, shuffle-exchange, Banyan, bus, chordal ring, tree and others, have been extensively studied [8, 9]. However, much less has been reported on the problem of synthesizing a network to meet specific performance and reliability criteria.

In our approach, the designer specifies the performance measures of interest. These may be commonplace measures such as bandwidth, diameter, connectivity, or more exotic measures like diameter stability in the face of failure, the extent to which the network splinters as node and link failures accumulate, or scalability. A large number of random regular networks of the desired size are then generated and passed through a bank of *filters*. Each filter is associated with a per-

---

[1]This research was supported in part by DARPA and the Air Force Research Laboratory under Grant F30602-96-1-0341. The views and conclusions contained herein are those of the authors and should not be interpreted as necessarily representing the official policies or endorsements, either expressed or implied, of the Defense Advanced Projects Agency, the Air Force Research Laboratory, or the US Government.

501

formance requirement. The filters identify a subset of networks which have the desired performance with respect to the specified measures. This subset constitutes a short-list of networks from which the designer can choose.

The usefulness of this approach rests on its efficiency. That is, the number of random networks one has to generate before obtaining a useful short-list of "good" networks. This problem does not readily yield to theoretical analysis, and must be studied by simulation experiments. We have found, through extensive experimental work, that our technique is surprisingly efficient.

The rest of the paper is organized as follows. In the next section, we briefly review various desirable properties of ICNs. In Section 3, we describe our random network generation algorithm and the filtering process. Section 4 provides extensive experimental evidence to the good performance of random regular networks. It also shows the effectiveness of the filtering approach through examples. Section 5 summarizes our findings and discusses future work.

2. Preliminaries

A good interconnection network is characterized by a number of desirable properties. Some of these are listed below:

- *Small internodal distances.* One factor in the communication delay is the node-pair distances. The greater the average node-pair distance, the greater the time a message will spend in the network, the greater the energy consumed in delivering it, and the greater the chances of network congestion.

- *Small, fixed degree.* Each physical connection costs money and a small degree corresponds to reduced wiring and fewer I/O interfaces. Furthermore, if the degree is constant over all nodes, then only one basic node design may be necessary.

- *Good fault tolerance.* Many parallel or distributed systems are used in applications requiring levels of reliability that can only be achieved by making the system fault-tolerant. There are many measures of fault-tolerance: we list below a partial list of the more useful network measures.

  - Probability of network disconnection.
  - Diameter stability, i.e., how the network diameter is expected to increase as nodes or links fail.

  - Stability of the average node-pair distance as nodes or links fail.
  - How the network splinters after it gets disconnected: is it more likely to splinter into one large component which is still useful, and several small and useless components, or will all the components be too small to be useful?

- *Easy construction and good scalability.* It should be possible to construct a network of any desired size. Further, adding a few nodes to the network should not cause drastic changes in such properties as diameter or average node-pair distance. A scalable ICN should be able to accommodate small increases in size rather than only large increases.

- *Embeddability.* Some algorithms are designed to run well on certain topologies, i.e., those that map well to the communication pattern of the application. A good network should be able to embed a wide range of topologies with low dilation, thus ensuring that a large number of algorithms will run efficiently on the selected ICN.

- *Easy routing algorithms.* It is advantageous to have a simple routing algorithm, for example, one that requires only the knowledge of the destination address. Routing algorithms can have a big impact on congestion and power requirements. Networks that facilitate the use of such simple algorithms are preferable.

These measures will vary in importance from one application to another. For example, space applications may require massive levels of fault-tolerance and low power consumption, while not placing a large premium on scalability.

Interconnection networks can be represented as graphs in which the vertices correspond to processors and the edges to communication links. In this paper we use the terms networks and graphs interchangeably. We consider only undirected graphs and the size of a network refers to the number of vertices in the graph. In this paper, we mainly concentrate on networks of degree 3 and 4, though our approach is not restricted to these degrees. For comparing the performance of different measures among degree-3 networks, we use the following topologies: shuffle exchange networks [16], cube connected cycles(CCC) [14], chordal rings of degree 3 [1], Moebius trivalent graphs [12] and multi tree structures(MTS) of degree 3 [2]. In the degree-4 catogory, we use meshes, torii, chordal rings of degree 4 [7] and the wrapped butterfly networks. In the next section, we describe our approach to synthesizing networks which meet the designer's requirements.

3. Approach

Our approach to network synthesis consists of a two-step process: first, the generation of a large set of random regular networks and second, the isolation of just the right ones through a process of filtering.

3.1. Generating Random Regular Networks

We use the following definition of random regular graphs:

Definition 3.1 *A random regular connected graph of size n and degree d is a d-regular connected graph in which node pairs connected by an edge are selected at random.*

Random regular graphs of n nodes and degree d are generated as follows. We start with a set of n isolated nodes. Edges are placed between node pairs selected at random. This process continues until all the nodes in the network satisfy the following two requirements: *(i)* the degree of all the nodes is the same and equal to the specified value, d and *(ii)* no pair of nodes is joined by more than one edge, and no self-loops exist. Finally, the generated network is tested for connectedness. Algorithm 1 contains the pseudocode used to generate random regular networks.

Algorithm 1

generate_regular_random_network(size,degree,seed)

1: $A \Leftarrow \{1, \ldots, n\}$
2: **repeat**
3:     Randomly pick two nodes, u and v, from set A
4:     **if** $((u \neq v)$ *and* edge(u,v) not already present) **then**
5:         Add edge(u,v) to the adjacency matrix
6:         update A by removing nodes whose degree has been satisfied
7:     **else if** $(size(A) = 1)$ or
          (nodes in A form a fully connected subgraph) **then**
8:         discard and start all over again
9:     **end if**
10: **until** $size(A) = 0$
11: check for connectedness
12: **if** graph not connected **then**
13:     discard and start all over again
14: **else**
15:     return adjacency matrix
16: **end if**

A is the set of all nodes whose degree has not been satisfied and is initialized on line 1 to the set of all n labelled nodes. Lines 4–6 ensure that the two conditions stated above are met and lines 7–8 ensure that the algorithm does not loop infinitely. If, during construction, the nodes in A form a fully connected subgraph, then no matter which two nodes are picked, the connecting edge will always be superfluous. No attempt is made to backtrack from this situation, and so the current adjacency matrix is discarded and a new one generated.

The above algorithm generates a random regular network each time it is called with a different seed value. Note that under some conditions, such as those on lines 7 and 12, the network that is being generated needs to be discarded and the generation restarted. To estimate the runtime required to generate a valid graph, we generated a large number of random graphs for various network sizes and calculated the average runtime for each network size and for different degree networks. Results shown in Figure 1 were obtained on a 500MHz Pentium having 256MB of memory. It was observed that networks of even 2048 nodes could be generated in less than a second using this algorithm. This shows that the generation algorithm can output a random regular graph in reasonable time. It was also observed that the check for graph connectedness (line 12 of the algorithm) was almost always satisfied. It is also important that the generated networks are non-isomorphic to each other; otherwise the filtering process will not make sense. To find out how many of the generated networks are non-isomorphic, we checked the isomorphism between all pairs of networks and observed that more than 99% of the networks were non-isomorphic to each other. All these results show that the generation algorithm provides a cheap and versatile method for producing the "raw" material for the filtration process. To get a better idea of the number of distinctive networks that can be generated with size n and degree d, see [15].

3.2. The Filtering Process

The raw material for the filtering process is the set of random graphs generated. Filtering consists of identifying those networks which have the properties desired by the designer.

We use one filter for each requirement to be satisfied. Typically each requirement is associated with a single performance measure or a set of measures. A filter consists of two parts: the evaluation part calculates the value of the measure associated with the requirement, and the checking part compares the value of the measure with a *threshold* specified by the requirement. For example, if the requirement was a diameter no greater

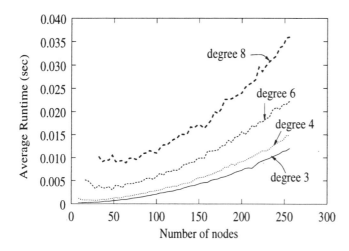

Figure 1. Average runtime of the generation algorithm

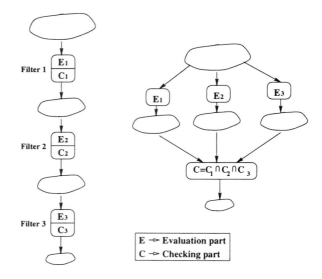

E → Evaluation part
C → Checking part

Figure 2. Sequential and Parallel Filtering

than k, then the evaluation part computes the diameter of the network and the checking part checks whether this requirement has been met. Each filter takes as input a set of random networks and outputs only those that pass the checking part. The output of one filter is used as input to the next. The filters are arranged sequentially one after the other in decreasing priority order of the measures they represent. The output at the end of the entire filtering process depends on the threshold values that have been set for each filter. If the filtering process produces no output, the designer will have to refine the threshold values. The threshold of a higher-priority filter should not be relaxed before that of every lower-priority filter has been relaxed to the maximum allowed extent. The key feature of this filtering approach is its versatility, as the set of selected filters and their order is determined by the specific application requirements.

The evaluation part is typically much more time-consuming than the checking part. In order to speed up the filtering process, the evaluation corresponding to each of the filters can be carried out in parallel and a single checking part that combines the checking parts in all filters used to sift out networks that comply with all the requirements. This approach is called parallel filtering, compared to the sequential filtering that we described earlier (Figure 2). Note that the time taken in the case of parallel filtering is bounded by the maximum evaluation time among the filters, and evaluation is carried out for all the input networks. In sequential filtering, the threshold determines the number of networks that pass through at each stage. If a stringent threshold is used, a smaller number of networks pass

through and this greatly impacts the time spent in the remaining filters. Thus, the time taken in the case of sequential filtering is dependent on the threshold set in each filter.

Some implementation details are worth mentioning. One need not store the adjacency matrices of all the input networks because they can be regenerated easily and quickly using the seed value. So, only the seed values used to generate the random networks need to be stored. Also, thresholds can be specified in relative terms rather than using an absolute threshold value (for example, take the best 5% of the input networks), although this requires sorting the input networks according to the value obtained from the evaluation part.

4. Experimental Results

In this section, we demonstrate the efficiency of our filtering approach by considering the synthesis of ICNs with required diameter, scalability and fault-tolerance characteristics.

4.1. The Diameter Filter

The diameter, Δ, which is the maximum of the node-pair distances, provides an upper-bound on the inter-task communication time, in terms of hops, and can be a decisive factor in application runtime. The problem of constructing a network of a given size and degree with the smallest possible diameter has been the focus of much research [4, 13]. While the diameter of random graphs has also been studied, the published results tend to be of an asymptotic nature, valid as the size of the graph approaches ∞. These asymptotic results provide little guidance for graph sizes that are of practical interest. In order to evaluate the diameter of random regular networks, we generated random networks sized between 8 and 256 nodes and with degrees ranging from 3 to 6 and calculated their diameters. For each size and degree, 1000 random networks were generated and the ones with the least diameter were selected. Figure 3 shows how the diameter slowly increases with size and how it reduces as the degree is increased. These results provide a lower bound to the threshold that can be set for the diameter filter. Figure 4 shows the comparison of the diameter of random networks of degree 3 with other networks of the same degree. The diameters of the networks plotted are the ones with the least diameter as specified in their respective references.

From Figure 4 it is clear that random networks perform better than such common ICNs as the mesh and the hypercube, but have greater diameter than some well-crafted ICNs such as the MTS network for some network sizes. However, graphs such as MTS are not as flexible. The MTS network is defined only for certain sizes given by $m * (d - 1)^{t-1}$ where m and t are integer parameters[1]. Among networks of degree 4 that we have considered, random regular networks performed the best. It is worthwhile to find out the number of graphs that pass through when the threshold of the diameter filter is set to different values. Figure 5 shows the frequencies of networks of degree 3 that pass through diameter filters whose thresholds have been set at the minimum diameter (as shown in Figure 3).

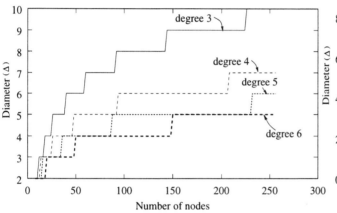

Figure 3. Diameter of random regular networks

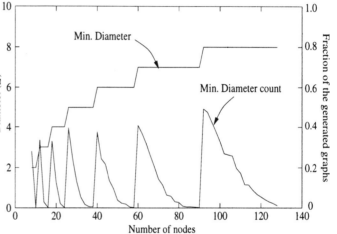

Figure 5. Frequency of minimum diameter random networks of degree 3

Figure 4 is very interesting because it shows that if we generate a sizeable number of random networks and then select the one with the smallest diameter, we will (with a high probability) get a network that is diameter-competitive with most of the interconnection networks described in the literature. It should be pointed out, however, that the size of the random graphs of a given degree and diameter tend to be greater than theoretical bounds, such as the Moore bound[3] or the bound obtained from theoretical studies of random graphs[5, 6].

Further comparisons can be carried out with the entries in the (d, Δ) table[2]. Table 1 shows some of the

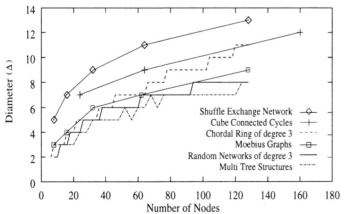

Figure 4. Diameters of different networks of degree 3

---

[1]Diameters of incomplete MTS networks have not been analyzed as yet.

[2]The (d, Δ) table gives the *state of the art* with respect to a largest known graphs with degree d and diameter Δ [10].

results. The diameter of the random graphs was at most larger by 1 than the corresponding best known diameters. It is worth pointing out that these known networks are constructed by different methods for different degrees and diameters whereas the random networks follow the same simple construction algorithm.

Size of Network	Degree	Diameter	
		Best Known	Random
10	3	2	2
15	4	2	3
20	3	3	4
70	3	5	6
364	4	5	6
532	5	5	6
740	4	6	7

Table 1. Comparison of diameter between best known networks and the best of the random networks generated in our experiments

4.2. The Scalability Filter

Some applications and situations require networks to be scalable. A network is said to have good scalability if the size of the network can be increased with minimum disruption and this does not cause a drastic change in its properties. For reasons of cost, it is better to have the option of small increments since this allows the network to be upgraded to the required size within a particular budget. The hypercube, for example, has poor scalability, in that its size cannot be increased by small increments while still maintaining its structural properties. Random graphs, on the other hand, have good scalability. They can be constructed for all sizes and degrees (as long as $n*d$ is even) and Figure 3 shows that the diameter remains constant for a considerable range of network sizes.

If regularity of the graph must be maintained even after scaling, some edges must be removed and some added to accomodate the new node. The minimum number of edges that must be removed to scale an even degree network by one node is $d/2$ whereas that required to scale an odd degree network by two nodes is $d-1$. Typically, one does not possess the flexibility of adding new nodes anywhere in the network. It may be required to attach the new node adjacent to a given set of nodes. This is typically the case in a fault-tolerant design when a spare processor must serve as a backup for a given set of processors. We define a measure for scalability in this context by the average increase in

diameter caused by connecting a new node to all possible designated sets of d nodes. The network is said to have good scalability if its diameter does not increase considerably on average.

Not all randomly generated graphs scale well. To evaluate the performance of random graphs with regard to scalability, we generated 100 random graphs of size 64 and degree 4 and diameter 5. Note that 5 is the minimum diameter obtained for graphs of size 64 and degree 4 as shown in Figure 3. For each network, we then evaluated scalability by selecting sets of four nodes at random and adding a new node adjacent to the designated nodes. If the designated nodes are connected by an edge, then this edge is removed, otherwise edges incident on the designated nodes are selected at random and removed to create connections to the new nodes as shown in Figure 6.

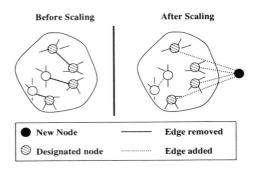

Figure 6. Example of edges that can be removed to accomodate a new node

The diameter is calculated for each set of four nodes and the increase in diameter is averaged over a large number of such runs. Figure 7 shows the cumulative distribution of the increase in diameter for the input graphs. It gives an idea of the threshold that can be set for a scalability filter, e.g., if the best 10% of the graphs are selected then we can expect that the average increase in diameter will be no more than 0.05.

4.3. The Fault-Tolerance Filter

Reliability is an important criterion in the selection of an interconnection network. Measures are required to adequately capture network qualities such as graceful degradation and robustness. Traditional measures, such as connectivity, are worst-case measures and have limited expressiveness. In this paper, we look at the following more expressive measures: the diameter stability, $\Delta(p_f)$, the average node-pair distance stability, $\overline{D}(p_f)$, the probability of disconnection, $\pi_d(p_f)$, and the size of the maximum connected component,

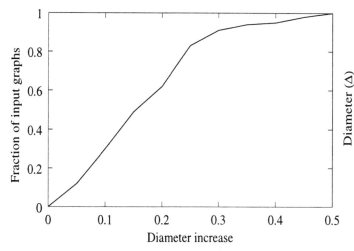

Figure 7. Cumulative frequency of the increase in diameter for random networks of size 64 and degree 3

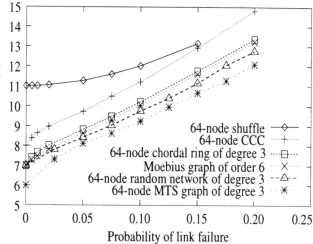

(a) Comparison among degree 3 networks

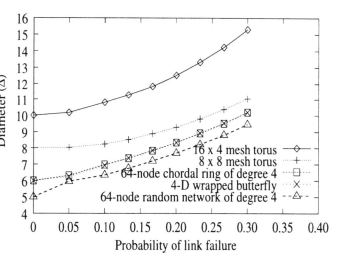

(b) Comparison among degree 4 networks

Figure 8. Diameter vs. probability of link failure

$\chi_{max}(p_f)$, all in the presence of link failures occurring independently with probability p_f. These measures were introduced in [11] and some research has already been done in characterizing various networks with respect to these measures. We performed experiments to evaluate the vulnerability of regular random networks with respect to these four measures. We used random networks of size 64 and degree 3 and 4 and compared their performance with other networks of similar size and degree. The network used was chosen at random from the set of minimum diameter networks obtained at the output of the diameter filter.

Figure 8 shows the comparison of diameter stability among degree 3 and degree 4 networks. The random regular networks of degree 4 outperform all the networks in its category whereas in the degree 3 category, it is second-best. Though Figures 9 and 11 show average node-pair distance stability and probability of disconnection for degree 3 networks only, the performance of random networks in the degree 4 category was observed to be the same as in the case of diameter stability. All these results show that random networks perform better than most of their counterparts with respect to fault tolerance as well. Careful examination of the results reveals that networks that are not regular are more vulnerable compared to those that are regular, as can be seen in the case of shuffle exchange networks and meshes.

The fault-tolerance filter that we use is a combination of four filters: one for each of the four measures. Thresholds are typically specified as a scalar

value and since each of the fault tolerant measures is given by a vector of values (corresponding to different link(node) failure probabilities), some transformation must be used to convert the vector of values to a single value. If the designer knows the exact value of the link failure probability, then the value of the measure corresponding to that failure probability can be used to do the comparison. However, it may be difficult for the designer to decide on the exact value of the failure probability. One transformation that can be applied would be to use the area under the curve obtained when plotting the values. This transformation assumes that each failure probability in the range

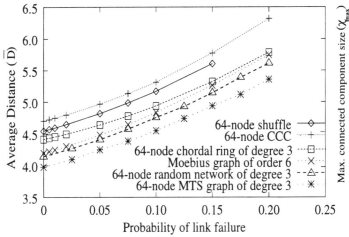

Figure 9. Average node-pair distance vs. probability of link failure

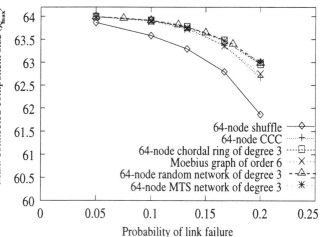

Figure 11. Maximum component size vs. probability of link failure

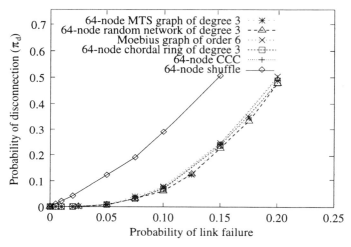

Figure 10. Probability of disconnection vs. probability of link failure

of interest is equally likely. Since this may not be the case in most situations, a more appropriate transformation would be to associate weights with each of the failure probabilities and use a weighted sum of the values corresponding to different failure probabilities.

The output at the end of the set of filters depends on the threshold values that have been set for each filter. A stringent threshold value passes a smaller number of networks through it. If the filter produces no output, the designer would have to refine the threshold values or increase the number of input graphs generated.

Experiments were performed to evaluate the ef-

ficiency of the approach by passing random graphs through a multitude of filters. Graphs of size 64 and degree 4 were generated and first passed through a diameter filter and then through a fault tolerance filter. The threshold of the diameter filter was set at 7. The networks obtained at the output of the diameter filter were tested for their fault tolerant characteristics by using two filters, the $\Delta(p_f)$ filter and the $\overline{D}(p_f)$ filter. The range of link failure probabilities of interest to us in this example was $[0.0, 0.2]$. Our initial set consisted of 1000 randomly-generated networks. After passing through the diameter filter, we were left with 33%(=330) of the networks. These networks were then evaluated for the two fault tolerance measures and then ranked according to their performance. The thresholds of the filters were set such that only those input networks that lie among the best 5% pass through it. The number of graphs obtained at the end of the filtering process was a respectable 1.5%(=15). It is important to note this "short-list" contains graphs that are better than most graphs published in the literature with regard to diameter and the two fault tolerance measures.

5. Conclusions and Future Work

Synthesizing networks that satisfy a certain set of performance or fault-tolerance requirements is difficult. In our approach, we generate a large number of random regular networks and filter out those that do not comply with the requirements. The choice of random regular networks was motivated by their ease and flexibility of construction and their surprisingly good properties. The filtering process consists of filters arranged in tandem, one for each requirement to be satisfied. Each filter removes networks that do not comply with the requirement associated with it. The strength of this approach lies in the versatility and extendability of the filtering step, in that a different set of filters can be used for a different set of requirements and new filters can be added as and when newer measures are developed. We demonstrated the effectiveness of this approach by synthesizing fault-tolerant networks with a small diameter.

Extensions to the current work are ongoing in several directions. Other filters are currently being studied, among them are the filter for embeddability and routability. Other network-generation algorithms are being developed and assessed. A graphical tool to facilitate synthesis of interconnection networks through our approach is also on the anvil.

Acknowledgement

The authors wish to thank Zahava Koren for stimulating discussions and suggestions.

References

[1] B. Arden and H. Lee. Analysis of chordal ring networks. *IEEE Trans. Computers*, C-30:291–295, Apr 1981.

[2] B. Arden and H. Lee. A regular network for multicomputer systems. *IEEE Trans. Computers*, C-31:60–69, Jan 1982.

[3] E. Bannai and T. Ito. On finite moore graphs. *J. Fac. Sci., Tokyo Univ.*, pages 191–208, 1973.

[4] J. Bermond and B.Bollobas. The diameter of graphs - a survey. *Proc. Congressus Numerantium*, 32:3–27, 1981.

[5] B. Bollobas. Random graphs. *Combinatorics Lect. Note Series London Mathematic Soc.*, pages 80–102, 1980.

[6] B. Bollobas and W. L. Vega. The diameter of random regular graphs. *Combinatorica*, 2:125–134, Feb 1982.

[7] K. Doty. New designs for dense processor interconnection networks. *IEEE Trans. Computers*, C-33:447–450, May 1984.

[8] T. Feng. *Editorial Introduction, Tutorial Interconnection networks for Parallel and Distributed Systems*. IEEE Press, Piscataway, NJ, 1984.

[9] R. Finkel and M. Solomon. Processor interconnection strategies. *IEEE Trans. Computers*, 29:360–370, May 1980.

[10] http://maite71.upc.es/grup_de_grafs/table_g.html. d-k table.

[11] V. Lakamraju, Z. Koren, I. Koren and C. M. Krishna. Measuring the vulnerability of interconnection networks in embedded systems. *Proc. First Merged Symposium IPPS/SPDP, EHPC Workshop*, pages 919–924, April 1998.

[12] W. Leland and M. Solomon. Dense trivalent graphs for processor interconnection. *IEEE Trans. Computers*, vol C-31:219–222, March 1982.

[13] J. Opatrny, D. Sotteau, N. Sitaraman and K. Thulasiraman. DCC linear congruential graphs: A new class of interconnection networks. *IEEE Trans. Computers*, C-45:156–164, Feb 1996.

[14] F. Preparata and J. Vuillemin. The cube connected cycles: A versatile network for parallel computation. *Communications of the ACM*, pages 300–309, May 1981.

[15] R. Read. The enumeration of locally restricted graphs. *J. London Math Soc.*, pages 417–436, 1959.

[16] H. Stone. Parallel processing with the perfect shuffle. *IEEE Trans. Computers*, C-20:153–161, Feb 1971.

Session 14B

Distributed System Models

The Best of Both Worlds:
a Hybrid Approach to Solve Consensus

Achour MOSTEFAOUI, Michel RAYNAL and Frédéric TRONEL
IRISA, Campus de Beaulieu, 35042 Rennes Cedex, France
{mostefao,raynal,ftronel}@irisa.fr

Abstract

It is now well recognized that the consensus problem is a fundamental problem when one has to implement fault-tolerant distributed services in asynchronous distributed systems prone to process crash failures. This paper considers the binary consensus problem in such a system.

Following an approach investigated by Aguilera and Toueg, it proposes a simple binary consensus protocol that combines failure detection and randomization. This protocol terminates deterministically when the failure detection mechanism works correctly; it terminates with probability 1, otherwise. A performance evaluation of the protocol is also provided. Last but not least, it is important to note that the proposed protocol is both efficient and simple. Additionally, it can be simplified to give rise either to a deterministic failure detector-based consensus protocol or to a randomized consensus protocol.

Keywords: Asynchronous Distributed System, Consensus Problem, Crash Failure, Fault-Tolerance, Message Passing, Randomized Protocol, Unreliable Failure Detector.

1 Introduction

The *Consensus* problem lies at the heart of a lot of agreement problems (e.g., Atomic Broadcast, Atomic Multicast, Weak Atomic commitment, etc.). This means that a solution to any of those problems can be expressed as a protocol that uses a solution to the consensus problem as an underlying building block [3, 7, 9]. Actually, the consensus problem can be seen as the *greatest common denominator* of a family of agreement problems. This encourages the following system architecture: first design a layer providing an efficient consensus protocol, and, on top of it, design protocols solving particular agreement problems.

The consensus problem can be informally stated as follows. Each process proposes a value and has to decide a value (termination property) such that (1) there is a single decided value and (2) the decided value is one of the proposed values (safety properties). This apparently simple problem is actually impossible to solve in a deterministic way in asynchronous distributed systems where (even a single) processes may crash. This is known as the Fischer-Lynch-Paterson (FLP) impossibility result [6]. Intuitively, this is due to the impossibility to safely distinguish a crashed process from a slow process or from a process with which communications are very slow.

To circumvent this impossibility result two main approaches have been investigated. One of them consists in abandoning the determinism requirement of the protocol, and allowing processes to query an oracle (R-oracle) providing them with random values [2, 4, 13, 14]. The price that has to be paid by this approach is that the termination of the randomized protocol is only *probabilistic*. Its main advantage lies in the robustness of the resulting protocol: its behavior does not depend on how the system actually behaves (but, as noted in [1], this can also be a source of inefficiency).

Another promising approach lies in the *unreliable Failure Detector* concept proposed and investigated by Chandra and Toueg [3]. In that case, each process has access to a FD-oracle that provides it with a list of processes that it suspects of having crashed. According to the properties (completeness and accuracy) a failure detector is assumed to satisfy, several classes of FD-oracles can be defined [3]. We consider here the class denoted $\diamond S$. This class is defined by the following two properties: any process that crashes is eventually suspected (completeness), and there is a time after which there is a correct process that is no longer suspected (accuracy). It is important to note that several $\diamond S$-based consensus protocols have been designed in the recent past years [3, 10, 11, 16].

As noted by Aguilera and Toueg [1], in many systems, failures are rare and failure detectors can be tuned to seldom make mistakes. This observation favors the use of a FD-based consensus protocol. But (as also noted in [1]) when a bad period occurs (i.e., when the failure detector looses its accuracy property), such a protocol can be prevented from reaching consensus until the bad period is over. So, the idea to combine unreliable failure detection and randomization to design consensus protocols has been investigated and has given rise to the notion of *hybrid* consensus protocols[1]. A hybrid protocol terminates deterministically if the failure detector is accurate, and probabilistically otherwise [1].

The issue addressed by this paper is the design of a hybrid consensus protocol. The proposed protocol is particularly simple. It combines underlying principles of Ben-Or's binary randomized consensus protocol [2] and of Mostefaoui-Raynal's $\diamondsuit S$-based consensus protocol [11]. As Aguilera-Toueg's hybrid protocol [1], the proposed protocol can be optimized to terminate in two rounds when no failure and no erroneous suspicion occurs. So, in this context, it is as time-efficient as the most efficient $\diamondsuit S$-based consensus protocols [10, 11, 16] (Moreover, the proposed hybrid protocol uses messages whose size is shorter than the size of messages used in [10, 16]). In addition to its efficiency, this protocol presents a noteworthy design modularity property. Namely, the proposed protocol can be simplified (by suppressing lines) to get either Ben-Or's protocol or an instance of Mostefaoui-Raynal's protocol. This helps to a better understanding the assumptions required to solve the consensus problem in asynchronous distributed systems prone to process crashes. Moreover, a performance analysis of the proposed hybrid protocol has been done. This performance study shows that the actual quality of service provided by the accuracy of the failure detector is a crucial parameter to get time-efficient executions of the hybrid protocol.

The modularity and the simplicity of the proposed protocol makes it attractive. They contribute to demystify the consensus problem [10, 16]. They actually set it at its right place: a basic, simple and efficient building block on top of which fault-tolerant system services can be built.

The paper is composed of eight sections. Section 2 introduces the system model, and Section 3 defines the consensus problem. Then, Section 4 presents the hybrid binary protocol. Section 5 proves it is correct. Section 6 evaluates its performances, while Section 7 discusses some improvements. Finally, Section 8 concludes the paper.

2 Distributed Computation Model

2.1 Asynchronous Distributed Systems with Crash Failures

The computation model follows the one described in [3, 6]. We consider a system consisting of a finite set Π of $n > 1$ processes, namely, $\Pi = \{p_1, \dots, p_n\}$. A process

can fail by *crashing*, *i.e.*, by prematurely halting. It behaves correctly (*i.e.*, according to its specification) until it (possibly) crashes. By definition, a *correct* process is a process that does not crash. A *faulty* process is one that is not correct. Let f denote the maximum number of processes that may crash. We assume $f < n/2$ (i.e., a majority of processes is correct)[2]. Processes communicate and synchronize by sending and receiving messages through channels. Every pair of processes is connected by a channel. Channels are not required to be FIFO, but are assumed to be reliable: they do not create, alter or lose messages. There is no assumption about the relative speed of processes nor on message transfer delays (i.e., the system is said to be *asynchronous*).

2.2 Failure Detectors Oracles

Informally, a failure detector consists of a set of FD-oracle modules, each one attached to a process: the FD-oracle module attached to p_i maintains a set ($suspected_i$) of processes it currently suspects of having crashed. Any failure detector module is inherently unreliable: it can make mistakes by not suspecting a crashed process or by erroneously suspecting a correct one. Moreover, suspicions are not necessarily stable: a process p_j can be added to or removed from a set $suspected_i$ according to whether p_i's failure detector module currently suspects p_j or not. As in other papers devoted to failure detectors, we say "process p_i suspects process p_j" at some time t, if at that time we have $p_j \in suspected_i$.

As indicated in the Introduction, a failure detector class is formally defined by two abstract properties, namely a *Completeness* property and an *Accuracy* property. In this paper, we consider the class of failure detectors denoted $\diamondsuit S$. This class includes all the failure detectors satisfying the two following properties [3]:

- **Strong Completeness**: Eventually, every process that crashes is permanently suspected by every correct process.

- **Eventual Weak Accuracy**: There is a time after which some correct process is never suspected by correct processes.

2.3 Random Oracles

Informally, a random oracle consists of a set of R-oracle modules, each attached to a process. The R-oracle module attached to p_i provides it with a bit each time p_i invokes the primitive *random*.

When it works correctly, the R-oracle module attached to p_i behaves as a random number generator: it outputs an

---

[1]The first hybrid protocols have been designed to solve agreement problems in synchronous systems where processes may exhibit a Byzantine behavior [8]. In asynchronous consensus protocols, this idea has first been investigated in [5].

[2]We will see that this requirement is necessary and sufficient for hybrid consensus protocols.

independent random bit each time it is queried. Moreover, (for simplicity [1]), we assume a uniform distribution, i.e., each value (0 and 1) has probability $1/2$ to be returned when p_i invokes *random*.

3 The Consensus Problem

In the Consensus problem, every correct process p_i *proposes* a value v_i and all correct processes have to *decide* on the same value v, that has to be one of the proposed values. More precisely, the *Consensus problem* is defined by two safety properties (Validity and Uniform Agreement) and a Termination Property [1, 3, 6]. The safety properties are:

- Validity: If a process decides v, then v was proposed by some process.

- Uniform Agreement: No two processes decide differently.

The precise statement of the Termination property actually depends on the distributed system model in which the problem has to be solved[3].

Asynchronous Systems with FD-Oracles In asynchronous distributed systems equipped with FD-Oracles, the Termination property is deterministic, namely:

- FD-Termination: Every correct process eventually decides on some value.

As indicated in the Introduction, several consensus protocols have been designed for asynchronous distributed systems equipped with FD-Oracles belonging to the class $\Diamond \mathcal{S}$ [3, 10, 11, 16]. All these protocols require $f < n/2$. It has been proved that this requirement is necessary [3]. So, all these protocols are optimal with respect to the maximum number of crashes they tolerate.

Asynchronous Systems with R-Oracles In asynchronous distributed systems equipped with R-oracles, the previous Termination property has to be weakened in order correct consensus protocols can be designed. More precisely, the Termination property is only probabilistic [1], namely:

- R-Termination: With probability 1, every correct process eventually decides some value.

The most famous randomized consensus protocol has been designed by Ben-Or [2]. It assumes $f < n/2$. As previously, it has been shown that this requirement is necessary [2].

---

[3]The FLP impossibility result states that, without additional assumptions on the model, the consensus problem cannot be solved.

Multivalued Consensus *vs* Binary Consensus Let V be the set of values that can be proposed to a consensus by processes. A consensus is *binary* when the set V is defined a priori and can contain only two values[4]. It is *multivalued* when the set V can be arbitrarily large.

Consensus protocols based on FD-oracles solve multivalued consensus, while consensus protocols based on R-oracles solve only binary consensus. Here we consider binary consensus. People interested in a transformation from binary to multivalued consensus will consult [12].

4 A Hybrid Binary Consensus Protocol

4.1 Underlying Principles

The hybrid binary consensus has to work (1) when the FD-oracle satisfies the $\Diamond \mathcal{S}$ properties (whatever the behavior of the R-oracle), or (2) when the R-oracle works correctly and the FD-oracle satisfies the strong completeness property (whatever its behavior with respect to the accuracy property can be). Actually, the protocol has to work despite some adversary power as described in [1].

To attain this goal the hybrid protocol combines in a very simple way principles from Ben-Or's randomized protocol [2] and from Mostefaoui-Raynal's $\Diamond \mathcal{S}$-based consensus protocol [11]. As those protocols, the proposed protocol proceeds in asynchronous rounds. Moreover, as in $\Diamond \mathcal{S}$-based consensus protocols [3, 10, 11, 16], to benefit from the weak accuracy property of $\Diamond \mathcal{S}$ (when it is satisfied), each round r has an initial coordinator, namely p_c, where $c = r \bmod n$ ([5]).

Each process p_i manages a local variable (est_i, initialized to its proposal v_i) that contains its current estimate of the decision value. The principles of the protocol are the following ones. As in a lot of randomized protocols, the protocol is strongly based on the fact that only two values can be proposed. It uses this fact as follows. First, as in [2], if all processes propose the same value v, then the protocol makes the processes decide on v, whatever the behaviors of the FD-oracle and the R-oracle could be. Otherwise, both values have been proposed. The protocol looks for a majority value and tries to impose it as the decision value. But due to crashes, it is possible that some processes do not see that some value is a majority value, or it is even possible that there is no majority value. The aim of the protocol is then to enforce processes to adopt the same value as their estimates. In the former case, it forces processes to adopt as their current estimate the value that has been seen as a majority value

---

[4]Usually, $V = \{true, false\}$ or $V = \{0, 1\}$.
[5]The content of local variables (e.g., the identity of the current round coordinator) cannot be corrupted by the adversary. The adversary can prevent either the eventual weak accuracy property of the FD-oracle to be satisfied, or the R-oracle to work correctly

by processes. In the latter case, it forces processes to query their R-oracle to update their current estimates, hoping that all R-oracles will provide the same value. Then, processes proceed to the next round with their new estimates.

4.2 The Hybrid Binary Protocol

The protocol is described in Figure 1. Each process p_i starts a binary consensus by invoking the function Binary_Consensus(v_i) which returns the decided value. The decision is returned at line 14. As in [1, 2], to simplify the presentation, the protocol does not include a halt statement. A process that decides a value keeps on deciding the same value forever or until it crashes. It is easy to modify the protocol to halt processes that have decided, as it is done in $\Diamond S$-based consensus protocols [3, 10, 11, 16] (this requires to use a Reliable Broadcast [3]).

From an operational point of view (Figure 1), each round r is made of three phases during which processes exchange messages (namely, PHASE1(), PHASE2() and PHASE3() messages). More precisely:

- The aim of the first phase (lines 4-7) is to (try to) force processes to have the same estimate value. This is done with the help of the FD-oracle.

  To attain this goal, the round coordinator broadcasts its current estimate value (v) to all processes. If a process receives it, it adopts it as its own estimate. Otherwise, it keeps its previous estimate.

- The aim of the second phase (lines 8-11) is to allow processes to know if there is a majority value v.

  To attain this goal, processes simply exchange the values of their current estimates. If any, the majority value (v) is kept in an auxiliary variable aux_i; otherwise aux_i is set to a default value ($\bot$). (Note that, when processes start this phase, there is a single or no majority value. So, at the end of this phase, $aux_i \neq \bot$ and $aux_j \neq \bot$ means that $aux_i = aux_j = v$ the majority value).

- The aim of the third phase (lines 12-17) is to favor the situation where all processes have the same estimate, thereby forcing them to decide without violating the agreement property.

  To attain this goal, processes exchange the value of their aux_i local variables. If a process receives a $aux_i = v \neq \bot$ value, it adopts it as its current estimate. If it receives enough (i.e., at least $f + 1$) $aux_i = v \neq \bot$ values, it also decides on v. If all the aux_i values it receives are equal to $\bot$, it knows that 0 and 1 have both been proposed; to "increase the chance" that all processes have the same estimate, it

then invokes the *random* primitive to update its current estimate.

4.3 Cost of a Round

Messages Each message carries a tag (the phase number), a round number and a value. The first phase requires one broadcast while each other phase requires n broadcasts. So, the total cost is $2n + 1$ broadcasts. Hence, when the underlying channels support broadcast operations, the message cost is $2n + 1$. If communication is point-to-point, each broadcast is implemented with n messages. More efficient implementations of the broadcasting scheme can easily be designed by taking into account the parameter f and the underlying topology (such implementations are described in [15]). But this is at the cost of increasing the broadcast latency.

Communication steps The first phase consists of one communication step when some process does not suspect the current coordinator. It requires no communication step if all processes suspect the current coordinator. The second and the third phase consists each of a single communication step. So, a round costs 2 or 3 communication steps. The cost of a round of the hybrid protocol presented in [1] is 3 or 4 communication steps (but, in this protocol, a process can decide in the middle of a round).

5 Proof

This section provides a proof of the hybrid binary consensus protocol described in the previous section. Let us note that at least $(n - f)$ processes are correct. The proof assumes $f < n/2$. Hence, $(n - f)$ processes is a majority set.

5.1 Preliminary Lemmas

Lemma 1 *Let us assume that the FD-oracle satisfies the strong completeness property. Then, no correct process blocks forever in a round.*

Proof Initially, no correct process blocks forever during the fictitious "round 0", and each starts the first round. Let us now consider any round $r > 0$. Assuming no correct process blocks forever during a round $k < r$, we show that no correct process blocks forever during r. The only lines where a correct process p_i can block forever are the lines 5, 9 and 13. We consider each case separately:

1. Line 5. There are two sub-cases.

   - p_c has crashed. In that case, due to strong completeness property of the FD-Oracle, p_i suspects p_c and progresses to the next line.

```
Function Binary_Consensus($v_i$)
(1)    $r_i \leftarrow 0$; $est_i \leftarrow v_i$; % $v_i = 0$ or 1 %
(2)    while true do
(3)        $c \leftarrow (r_i \bmod n) + 1$; $r_i \leftarrow r_i + 1$; % round $r_i = r$ %

────────────── Phase 1 of round $r$: from $p_c$ to all ──────────────
(4)        if ($i = c$) then broadcast PHASE1$(r_i, est_i)$ endif;
(5)        wait until (PHASE1$(r_i, v)$ received from $p_c \vee p_c \in suspected_i$);
(6)        if (PHASE1$(r_i, v)$ has been received from $p_c$)
(7)                    then $est_i \leftarrow v$ endif;

────────────── Phase 2 of round $r$: from all to all ──────────────
(8)        broadcast PHASE2$(r_i, est_i)$;
(9)        wait until (PHASE2$(r_i, est)$ has been received from $(n - f)$ processes);
(10)       if (a same estimate value $v$ has been received from a majority of processes)
(11)                    then $aux_i \leftarrow v$ else $aux_i \leftarrow \bot$ endif;
           % $(aux_i = v \neq \bot) \Rightarrow (v$ is maj. in $\{est_k \mid 1 \le k \le n\}$ at the end of phase 1 %
           % Hence: $((aux_i \neq \bot) \wedge (aux_j \neq \bot)) \Rightarrow (aux_i = aux_j = v)$ %

────────────── Phase 3 of round $r$: from all to all ──────────────
(12)       broadcast PHASE3$(r_i, aux_i)$;
(13)       wait until (PHASE3$(r_i, aux)$ has been received from $(n - f)$ processes);
(14)       case ($aux = v \neq \bot$ received from $f + 1 \le$ processes $\le n$) then $est_i \leftarrow v$; decide($v$)
(15)            ($aux = v \neq \bot$ received from $1 \le$ processes $\le f$)        then $est_i \leftarrow v$
(16)            ($aux = v \neq \bot$ received from no process)                      then $est_i \leftarrow$ random
(17)       endcase
(18)   endwhile

("received from $a \le$ processes $\le b$" means "received from $x$ processes with $a \le x \le b$")
```

Figure 1. A Hybrid Binary Consensus Protocol ($f < n/2$)

- p_c is correct. By assumption, it has started the round r and broadcast a PHASE1 message. As channels are reliable, p_i eventually receives this message and progresses to the next line.

2. Line 9. As, by assumption, there are at least $(n - f)$ correct processes, and as they do not block forever at line 5, each of them broadcasts a PHASE2 message. Hence, each correct process receives at least $(n - f)$ PHASE2 messages, and consequently does not block forever at line 9.

3. Line 13. The same reasoning as case (2) applies by replacing PHASE2 messages by PHASE3 messages.

$\square_{Lemma\ 1}$

Lemma 2 *If all the processes that terminate a round have the same estimate value (v) before starting the first or the second phase of this round, then they do not change the value of their estimate thereafter.*

Proof Let us first assume that all estimate values are equal to v at the beginning of a round r.

1. During the first phase, if p_c sends a message it sends PHASE1(r, v). It follows that a process p_i that receives a PHASE1 message from p_c does not modify the value of est_i. So, no estimate is changed during the first phase.

2. No estimate is updated during the second phase.

3. Due to Lemma 1, all correct processes execute r. As there are at least $(n - f) > n/2$ correct processes, participating in r, and as all processes participating in r broadcast the same estimate value (v) in PHASE2 messages, it follows that at line 11, any process p_i updates aux_i to v.

   It follows that those processes broadcast v in their PHASE3 messages. So, as any process p_i receives at least one PHASE3(r, v) message, it follows that the update of est_i to v does not change its value.

Let us now assume that all the processes that execute the second phase of r have the same estimate value before starting this phase. The Lemma follows from the previous point (3). $\square_{Lemma\ 2}$

Lemma 3 *Let r be any round. If the processes that terminate r had the same estimate value (v) at the end of the first phase of r, then they decide during r.*

Proof First, due to Lemma 1, all ($\ge (n - f)$) correct processes execute r. The lemma follows from the fact that,

517

when all estimate values are equal to v at the end of the first phase of r, any process p_i terminating r receives $(n - f)$ PHASE3(r, v) messages. As $(n - f) \geq (f + 1)$, it follows that during the third phase, p_i decides at line 14. $\square_{Lemma\ 3}$

Lemma 4 *Let r be the first round during which a process decides. All processes that terminate $(r + 1)$ decide (during r or $r + 1$).*

Proof Let p_i be a process that decides (v) during r, and p_j a process that terminates r. During r, p_i has received $(f + 1)$ PHASE3(r, v) messages. As $(n - f) + (f + 1) > n$, p_j has received at least one PHASE3(r, v) message during r, and has consequently updated est_i to v (line 14 or 15). So, all the processes that terminate r have the same estimate value. If p_j does not decide during r and terminates $r + 1$, due to Lemma 3, it will decide during $r + 1$. $\square_{Lemma\ 4}$

5.2 Validity

Theorem 1 *If a process decides v, then v has been proposed by a process.*

Proof A process p_i decides when it executes line 15. It decides the current value of est_i. To prove that the decided value is a proposed value we show the following proposition: the content of any estimate (est_i) is always a proposed value.

Let us first consider the round $r = 1$. There are two two cases.

1. Initially, all estimates values are equal. Due to Lemma 2, the theorem follows.

2. Both values (1 and 0) have been proposed by processes. The protocol manipulates three types of values, namely, proposed values, the $\bot$ value, and random values. An est_i variable is updated at lines 7, 15, 15 or 16. So, it is never set to $\bot$. It is set to a proposed value (lines 7, 15 or 15) or to a random value (line 16), but in that case whatever the result of *random* is, it is a proposed value.

Then, by induction on the round number, the proposition follows. $\square_{Theorem\ 1}$

5.3 Uniform Agreement

Theorem 2 *No two processes decide distinct values.*

Proof Let r be the first round during which a process decides. Let v be the value it has decided. We show (1) that processes that decide during r decide v, and (2) that at the

end of r, all estimates are equal to v. Then, due to Lemma 2, no other value can be decided during a next round.

First of all, let us observe that at the end of the second phase of r, any aux_i variable is equal either to a value (v) that was a majority value at the beginning of r, or to $\bot$. This means that $((aux_i \neq \bot) \wedge (aux_j \neq \bot)) \Rightarrow (aux_i = aux_j = v)$ (where v is a majority value at the beginning of r).

1. Let us prove that the processes that decide during r decide the same value.

   Let p_i and p_j two processes that decide during r. Both have received PHASE3(r, aux) messages with $aux \neq \bot$ from at least $(f + 1)$ processes. From the previous observation, the $aux \neq \bot$ value received by p_i is the same as the $aux \neq \bot$ value received by p_j.

2. Let us prove that at the end of r, all estimates are equal to v.

   This is trivially true for two processes p_i and p_j that decide during r. Let p_i be any process that decides v, and let p_j be any process that does not decide during r. As $(f + 1)$ (number of PHASE3 messages that allowed p_i to decide) + $(n - f)$ (number of PHASE3 messages received by p_j) $> n$, it follows that at least one PHASE3(r, v) message received by p_i has also been received by p_j. Consequently p_j has executed line 15, and has updated est_j to v.

$\square_{Theorem\ 2}$

5.4 FD-Termination

Theorem 3 *Let us assume that the FD-oracle satisfies $\lozenge S$ (strong completeness and eventual weak accuracy). Then, every correct process decides (whatever the behavior of the R-oracle).*

Proof If a (correct or not) process decides, then due to Lemmas 1 and 4 all correct processes decide. So, let us assume (by contradiction) that no correct process decides. Due to the eventual weak accuracy property of the FD-oracle, there is a time t, such that after t there are only correct processes and there is a correct process (let it be p_x) that is never suspected by the correct processes. Let r be the first round that starts after t and is coordinated by p_x. Due to Lemma 1, this round does exist. As during r, p_x is not suspected, it follows that during the first phase of r, each correct process p_i receives PHASE1(r, v) from p_x and updates est_i to $v = est_x$. From now on, all estimates are equal to v. Then, the theorem follows from Lemma 3. $\square_{Theorem\ 3}$

5.5 R-Termination

Theorem 4 *Let us assume that the FD-oracle satisfies the strong completeness property and the R-oracle works correctly (it is random). Then, every correct process decides with probability 1 (whatever the behavior of the FD-oracle with respect to the accuracy property).*

Proof As previously, if a (correct or not) process decides, then due to Lemmas 1 and 4 all correct processes decide. So, let us assume that no process decides. There is a time t after which there are only correct processes executing the protocol. Due to Lemma 1, correct processes keep on executing rounds after t.

As no process decides, no process executes line 15. This means that, at each round after t, each correct process executes line 15 or line 16. Let us consider such a round r. All processes that during r execute line 15, set their estimate to the same value v. The other processes execute line 16 and invoke the *random* primitive. Hence, there is a probability $p \geq 1/2^{n-1}$ that all estimates of correct processes are equal[6]. So, after t, there is a probability $P(\alpha) = p + p(1-p) + p(1-p)^2 + \cdots + p(1-p)^{\alpha-1} = 1 - (1-p)^\alpha$ that all processes have the same estimate after at most α rounds. As $\lim_{\alpha \to \infty} P(\alpha) = 1$, it follows that, with probability 1, all processes will start a round with the same estimate. Then, according to Lemmas 2 and 3, they will decide.

$\square_{Theorem\ 4}$

6 Evaluation of the Protocol

6.1 Assumptions

The performances of the proposed hybrid protocol have been evaluated[7]. This evaluation has been done with the following assumptions:

- A system of $n = 20$ processes has been considered.

- Faulty processes are assumed to be initially crashed. Their number varies from 0 to 9 ($< n/2$).

- It is assumed that the underlying failure detector satisfies the strong completeness property. As far as the accuracy property is concerned, we assume there is a probability λ that a correct process is not suspected. As an example, the case $\lambda = 1$ corresponds to a perfect failure detector, while $\lambda = 0$ corresponds to a failure detector that permanently suspects all correct processes.

Thus, λ is a measurement of the quality of service offered by the failure detector (as far as its accuracy is concerned).

- For each process p_i, each value (0 or 1) has probability $1/2$ to be chosen as its initial value, namely v_i.

- Finally, at each round, the round coordinator is randomly chosen among all processes (note that, as required by the protocol, for each round, the same coordinator is chosen by all processes[8]).

Under those assumptions, the protocol exhibits a "memorylessness" property. More precisely, this means that, during a round, the protocol behavior (in particular its termination) depends only on the values of the estimates at the beginning of the round[9]. Under these assumptions the protocol behavior can be represented by a (irreducible, finite and aperiodic) Markov chain [13]. First, an analytical study has been done to explicitly state this Markov chain (see the Appendix). This Markov chain has then been used to compute the results depicted in the next section.

6.2 Results

Figure 2 describes the results of the performance study. The number of processes that have initially crashed ranges on the x-axis. The y-axis provides the average number of rounds for the protocol to terminate. Four probabilities (λ) have been evaluated:

- $\lambda = 1$ (perfect failure detector).
  This case is represented by the curve with "." points (lowest curve).

- $\lambda = 0.9$ ("good" failure detector).
  This case is represented by the curve with "+" points (intermediate curve).

- $\lambda = 0.5$ ("half-correct" failure detector).
  This case is represented by the curve with "□" points (highest curve).

- $\lambda = 0$ (failure detector without accuracy).

For the curve associated with the probability λ, let x_λ (number of initially crashed processes) and y_λ (average number of rounds to get a decision value) denote the coordinates of its points.

It first appears that when λ is equal to 1 (i.e., when the failure detector makes no mistake) y_1 increases very slightly

---

[6]In the worst case, $p = 1/2^{n-1}$. This happens when, during r, all processes execute line 16.

[7]To our knowledge, very few papers provide analytical or experimental performance studies of consensus protocols.

[8]This can be easily achieved by applying a well-chosen hashing function to the round number.

[9]More precisely, as we consider all faulty processes have initially crashed, the protocol behavior during round r depends only on the number of occurrences of the majority value among the estimates of correct processes.

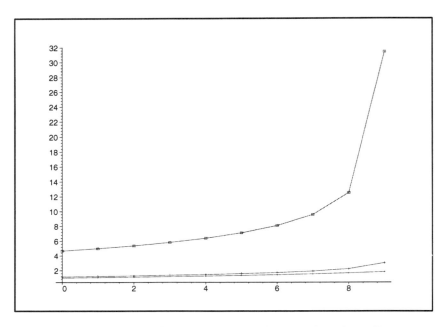

Figure 2. Performance Analysis: Varying the λ Parameter

from 1 to less than 2, when x_1 ranges from 0 to 9 (the maximal number of allowed crashes). Moreover, when λ decreases from 1 to 0.9 (i.e., when the failure detector makes very few mistakes) each value of $y_{0.9}$ is only slightly greater than its corresponding value y_1. This means that the processes converge very quickly (in number of rounds) when the failure detector is "close" to perfect.

Let us now examine the curve corresponding to $\lambda = 0.5$ (probabilistically "half-correct" failure detector). In that case, $y_{0.5}$ increases slowly from 5 to 9 when $x_{0.5}$ increases from 0 to 7. But then, when $x_{0.5}$ bypasses 7 (which is approximately the third of the total number of process, namely $20/3$), $y_{0.5}$ increases very rapidly. This means that the use of a failure detector whose probability to make mistakes is $1/2$, is efficient only when there are not "too many" crashes.

Finally, the curve corresponding to $\lambda = 0$ (failure detector without accuracy) has not been reported in Figure 2, because y_0 is always outside the figure (greater than 100). This means that the protocol converges very slowly when it relies only on its randomized behavior. This inefficiency can be easily remedied by using Rabin's technique (described in the next section).

These curves show that the closer to one λ is, (1) the smaller the number of rounds to converge is, and (2) the lesser the influence of the number of crashed processes is. So, the quality of service offered by the failure detector seems to be a factor more important than the number of actual crashes.

7 Discussion

7.1 Modularity of the Approach

As indicated, the proposed protocol relies on simple design principles. Due to this simplicity, it enjoys the following modularity property: if one suppresses some lines of it, then one gets back a pure randomized protocol, while if one suppresses some other lines, one gets back a pure $\diamondsuit\mathcal{S}$-based consensus protocol. More precisely:
- By suppressing the lines 4-7 (i.e., the first phase), one obtains Ben-Or's randomized protocol [2].
- By suppressing the lines 7-10 and 16, one obtains an instance of the generic FD-based consensus protocol proposed in [11][10].

This modularity property of the hybrid protocol help better understand the assumptions required to solve consensus in asynchronous distributed systems prone to process crashes. Moreover, it suggests a way to design hybrid binary consensus protocols: such protocols can be obtained by adding phase 1 (lines 4-7) to round-based randomized binary protocols.

7.2 Optimization

It is possible to improve the time efficiency of the protocol using techniques developed in [1, 14]. Here we sketch two of them.

---

[10]This generic protocol can be instantiated with failure detectors of different classes. Here, the instance is obtained by instantiating this protocol with the class $\diamondsuit\mathcal{S}$.

Sharing of a long sequence of random bits Let us first consider the case where the adversary never corrupts the R-oracle. In such a context, as pointed out by Rabin [14], it is possible that processes a priori agree[11] on a "constant sequence", namely, a long sequence of random bits. The protocol is then modified in the following way. All processes use the same pseudo-random number generator (namely the function *random* with the same seed). Each process p_i has an additional local variable rd_i. The statement $rd_i \leftarrow random$ is added to line 3, and the assignment in line 16 ($est_i \leftarrow random$) is replaced by $est_i \leftarrow rd_i$. So, during a round, processes that execute line 16 get the same random value. As shown in [14], this can make processes converge drastically faster.

The previous performance study has also been done with the original hybrid protocol replaced by this optimized version. It turns out that the average number of rounds for the protocol to terminate is close to 1, whatever the behavior of the failure detector and the number of failures can be.

Early decision Let us consider the "good scenario" where there are neither failures, nor erroneous suspicions. In such a scenario, the proposed protocol requires three computation steps for processes to converge to a decision value. Actually, by using the same modification as [1], the protocol can be modified to converge in two communication steps.

In a consensus protocol, each process has two types of variables. First, the variables whose scope spans the whole execution (namely, est_i and r_i); let us name them *wide scope* variables. Second, the variables whose scope is limited to a round (e.g., aux_i); let us name them *round scope* variables. The $\Diamond S$-based consensus protocols described in [10, 11] have two interesting properties. First they can be expressed using the same wide scope variables as the proposed hybrid protocol, plus their own round scope variables (Section 7.1 has shown it for a protocol of [11]). Second, they terminate in two communication steps in the previous good scenario[12]. Let $Cons$ be any of those protocols.

$Cons$ can be combined with the hybrid protocol in the following way (Figure 3). Processes have to a priori agree on a (finite or infinite) sequence K of non-negative integers $K = (k_1, k_2, \dots)$, such that the last element is $+\infty$. A process behaves in the following way: it first executes $Cons$ during the first k_1 rounds; then it executes the hybrid consensus protocol during the next k_2 rounds; then again $Cons$

during k_3 rounds; etc.

Let us examine three particular sequences. the sequence $k_1 = +\infty$ provides the underlying $\Diamond S$-based consensus protocol. The sequence $k_1 = 0$, $k_2 = +\infty$ provides the hybrid consensus protocol. The sequence $k_1 = 1$, $k_2 = +\infty$ provides a protocol corresponding to the improvement proposed in [1]: it allows processes to converge in two communication steps, in the previous good scenario. Other sequences can be used to feed the protocol described in Figure 3 ([13]).

```
Function Bin_Consensus(v_i)
(1)   r_i ← 0; est_i ← v_i; % v_i = 0 or 1 %
(2)   while true do
(3)     r_i ← r_i + 1; c ← (r_i mod n); % round r_i = r %
(4)     % Convention: 0 is even, K[0] = 0. Then K[1] = k_1, etc. %
(5)     let y be such that (Σ_{x≤y} K[x]) < r_i ≤ (Σ_{x≤y+1} K[x]);
(6)     case y is even then Text of Cons
(7)          y is odd then Text of the hybrid protocol
(8)   endwhile
```

Figure 3. General Protocol

8 Conclusion

This paper has addressed the consensus problem, which constitutes a basic building block on top of which reliable distributed services can be built in asynchronous distributed systems prone to process crash failures. Following an approach investigated by Aguilera and Toueg, the paper has presented a simple binary consensus protocol that combines failure detection and randomization. This protocol terminates deterministically when the failure detection mechanism is accurate. It terminates with probability 1 otherwise. It has been shown that this protocol can easily be improved to allow processes to terminate in two communication steps when there are neither failures, nor erroneous suspicions. Last but not least, let us notice that the protocol presented in the paper is both simple (design property) and efficient (behavior property). Interestingly, none of these properties has been obtained to the detriment of the other.

References

[1] Aguilera M.K. and Toueg S., Failure Detection and Randomization: a Hybrid Approach to Solve Consensus. *SIAM Journal of Computing*, 28(3):890-903, 1998.

[2] Ben-Or M., Another Advantage of Free Choice: Completely Asynchronous Agreement Protocols. *2nd ACM Symposium*

---

[11] In $\Diamond S$-based consensus protocols, processes have also to a priori agree on a sequence of identities for the round coordinators. Actually, this sequence is implicitly defined from the round number: all processes use the same deterministic function to compute the identity of the current round coordinator.

[12] These protocols proceed in asynchronous rounds, each round managed by a predetermined coordinator. There are other $\Diamond S$-based consensus protocols that terminate in two communication steps in this scenario [16], but they do not have the same wide scope variables as the hybrid protocol.

[13] Ideally, the idea would be to use $Cons$ in "stable" periods (i.e., when the FD-oracle satisfies the $\Diamond S$ properties) and the hybrid protocol in "unstable" periods. Then, the integers $k_1, k_3, \dots$ would be associated with "stable" periods, while $k_2, k_4, \dots$ would be associated with "unstable" periods.

on *Principles of Distributed Computing, (PODC'83)*, Montréal (CA), pp. 27-30, 1983.

[3] Chandra T. and Toueg S., Unreliable Failure Detectors for Reliable Distributed Systems. *Journal of the ACM*, 43(2):225-267, 1996.

[4] Chor M., and Dwork C., Randomization in Byzantine Agreement. *Adv. in Comp. Research*, 5:443-497, 1989.

[5] Dolev D. and Malki D., Consensus Made Practical. *Tech report CS94-7*, The Hebrew University of Jerusalem, 1994.

[6] Fischer M.J., Lynch N. and Paterson M.S., Impossibility of Distributed Consensus with One Faulty Process. *Journal of the ACM*, 32(2):374–382, 1985.

[7] Fritzke U., Ingels Ph., Mostefaoui A. and Raynal M., Fault-Tolerant Total Order Multicast to Asynchronous Groups. *Proc. 17th IEEE Symposium on Reliable Distributed Systems*, Purdue University (IN), pp.228-234, October 1998.

[8] Goldreich O. and Petrank E., The Best of Both Worlds: Guaranteeing Termination in Fast Randomized Byzantine Agreement Protocols. *Inf. Proc. Letters*, 39:45-49, 1990.

[9] Guerraoui R., Revisiting the Relationship between Non-Blocking Atomic Commitment and Consensus. *Proc. 9th Int. Workshop on Distributed Algorithms (WDAG95)*, Springer-Verlag LNCS 972, pp. 87-100, 1995.

[10] Hurfin M. and Raynal M., A Simple and Fast Asynchronous Consensus Protocol Based on a Weak Failure Detector. *Distributed Computing*, 12(4):209-223, 1999.

[11] Mostefaoui A. and Raynal M., Solving Consensus Using Chandra-Toueg's Unreliable Failure Detectors: a Generic Quorum-Based Approach. *Proc. 13th Int. Symposium on Distributed Computing (DISC'99), (Formerly WDAG)*, Springer-Verlag LNCS 1693, pp. 49-63, 1999.

[12] Mostefaoui A., Raynal M. and Tronel F., From Binary Consensus to Multivalued Consensus in Asynchronous Distributed Systems. To appear in *Inf. Proc. Letters*, 2000.

[13] Motvani R. and Raghavan P., Randomized Algorithms. *Cambridge University Press*, 476 p., 1995.

[14] Rabin M., Randomized Byzantine Generals. *Proc. 24th IEEE Symposium on Foundations of Computer Science (FOCS'83)*, pp. 116-124, Los Alamitos (CA), 1983.

[15] Rodrigues L. and Verissimo P., Topology-Aware Algorithms for Large Scale Communications. in *Advances in Dist. Systems*, Springer-Verlag LNCS 1752, pp. 127-156, 2000.

[16] Schiper A., Early Consensus in an Asynchronous System with a Weak Failure Detector. *Distributed Computing*, 10:149-157, 1997.

Appendix

The performance evaluation of the protocol assumes that, for each execution, all the faulty processes have crashed before beginning this execution. Let x be the number of faulty processes. Hence, for a given execution, in addition to n (number of processes) and f (upper bound on the number of faulty processes), x is constant.

A Markov chain.

Section 7.2 has shown that the hybrid protocol uses two types of variables, namely, *wide scope* variables and *round scope* variables. The wide scope variables of a process are its estimate value, the round number and the identity of the current round coordinator.

To carry out the performance analysis, we have considered that during each round the round coordinator is randomly selected. It then follows that the behavior of the hybrid protocol can be modeled by a Markov chain whose state is defined by the process estimate variables.

As the hybrid protocol addresses the binary consensus problem, the domain of the estimate variables is a set of two values. During a round, let n_0 and n_1 be the numbers of estimate variables set to 0 and 1, respectively. As, for each process, there is no relation between its identity and the value of its estimate variable, and as $n_0 + n_1 = n - x$ (which is a constant value), the state of the Markov chain can be defined by $max(n_0, n_1)$. Hence, the state of the Markov chain is an integer value i ($0 \leq i \leq n$) representing the number of occurrences of the majority value (among the non-faulty processes).

Modeling the current state of the protocol.

To carry out the performance analysis, the current state of the protocol execution is represented by a vector S of size $n + 1$ (from 0 to n) where $S[i]$ is the probability that $max(n_0, n_1) = i$. A round of the protocol can be represented by a transition matrix M of size $(n+1)*(n+1)$ where $M[i, j]$ is the probability that, at the end of the round, $max(n_0, n_1) = j$ assuming that it was equal to i at the beginning of the round. S_0 being the initial state vector of the protocol execution, we have the inductive definition $S_k = S_{k-1} * M$ where S_k represents the state of the protocol execution after round k.

Initially, we assume that each process has a probability $1/2$ to propose each of the two possible values 0 or 1. The vector S_0 is set to:
- (1) If $0 \leq i < (n - x)/2$ or if $i > n - x$, then $S_0[i] = 0$,
- (2): a binomial distribution is used to compute $S_0[i]$, otherwise.

The consensus is reached when the estimate values of the $n - x$ non-faulty processes are identical. Thus, the probability to reach consensus after k rounds is given by $S_k[n - x]$ ($S_k = S_0 * M^k$). The different values of the average number (m) of rounds to reach consensus given in Section 6.2 have been computed using the following inductive definition of the protocol state S_k:
- (1) Init: S_0 and $m = 0$,
- (2) Then: $S_k = S_{k-1} * M$, and
$$m = m + k * (S_k[n - x] - S_{k-1}[n - x]).$$

Synchronous System and Perfect Failure Detector: solvability and efficiency issues

Bernadette Charron-Bost
École Polytechnique
91128 Palaiseau Cedex, France
charron@lix.polytechnique.fr

Rachid Guerraoui   André Schiper
Dépt. de Systèmes de Communication
École Polytechnique Fédérale de Lausanne
1015 Lausanne EPFL, Switzerland
{rachid.guerraoui, andre.schiper}@epfl.ch

Abstract

We compare, in terms of solvability and efficiency, the synchronous model, noted $\mathcal{S}_S$, with the asynchronous model augmented with a perfect failure detector, noted $\mathcal{S}_P$. We first exhibit a problem that, although time-free, is solvable in $\mathcal{S}_S$ but not in $\mathcal{S}_P$. We then examine whether one of these two models allows more efficient solutions for designing fault-tolerant applications. In particular, we concentrate on the uniform consensus problem which is solvable in both models, and we design a uniform consensus algorithm for the $\mathcal{S}_S$ model that is more efficient than any algorithm solving uniform consensus in $\mathcal{S}_P$ with respect to some significant time complexity measure. From a practical viewpoint, the synchronous model thus seems better than the asynchronous model augmented with a perfect failure detector.

1 Introduction

The choice of a model is a fundamental issue in the design of a fault-tolerant distributed system. Since agreement protocols (e.g., atomic broadcast, atomic commit) are at the heart of such systems [3, 4, 14], one need to consider models that are strong enough to circumvent the impossibility result of [13]. For this concern, two main approaches have been proposed: the *timing-based approach* [11, 12, 10, 16, 9] and the *failure detector* approach [6, 5, 1, 2].

The first approach consists in providing processes with information about time: the resulting models are called *timing-based models*. For example, message delays and relative processes speeds are bounded, and these bounds are known in the "perfect" timing-based model, namely the *synchronous model*. In contrast, none of these bounds exist in the *asynchronous model*. Intermediate timing-based models between the syn-chronous and the asynchronous models are those in which timing information is partial or inexact.

The second approach, i.e., the failure detector approach, is based on the observation that the impossibility results in the asynchronous model stem from the inherent lack of reliable failure detection. Chandra and Toueg [6] propose to augment the asynchronous model with an external failure detection mechanism, which may make mistakes. Instead of focusing on timing features, the models of [6] are defined according to *axiomatic properties* of failure detectors. Failure detectors are classified in a hierarchy according to the correctness of their suspicions. The strongest element of this hierarchy is called the *perfect failure detector*, and is denoted by P. Roughly speaking, the failure detector P suspects a process (to have crashed) iff that process has indeed crashed.

Each approach has some advantages. On the one hand, timing-based models are more realistic than time-free models, since distributed systems do use timing information. For example, in most of real systems processes have access to almost-synchronized clocks and know approximate bounds on process step time or message delivery time. On the other hand, the abstract failure detector approach is particularly powerful for investigating the solvability of fault-tolerant problems. As an example, Chandra, Hadzilacos, and Toueg [5] determined the minimal amount of information about failures that processes require to achieve consensus. This information is simply expressed as axiomatic properties of a failure detector. In contrast, there is no analogous result for timing-based models: the minimal *amount of synchrony* required to solve consensus is still an open problem.

The motivation of our work is to explore the similarities and differences between the timing-based approach and the failure detector approach. Some relations between the system models considered in these two approaches have already been discussed in [6]. In

523

particular, it is shown that a perfect failure detector can be implemented in the synchronous model using time-outs. In the system models of [12], time-out mechanisms can also be used to implement an *eventual perfect failure detector* – one of the eight failure detectors in Chandra and Toueg's hierarchy [6]. More generally, timing assumptions can be used to implement some failure detectors, and so are translated into axiomatic properties of failure detectors. However, some features of timing-based models may be lost in this failure detector translation. Comparing the two approaches consists in the determination of the properties of the timing-based models that are not preserved by the translation.

Rather than addressing this general issue, the paper restricts the comparison to the strongest cases. More precisely, we compare the strongest timing-based model, namely the synchronous model, with the model obtained by augmenting the asynchronous model with the strongest failure detector, namely P. These two models are denoted by $\mathcal{S}_S$ and $\mathcal{S}_P$, respectively. We compare $\mathcal{S}_S$ and $\mathcal{S}_P$ assuming process crash failures and reliable links, and we address the following two questions:

1. Is the class of problems solvable in $\mathcal{S}_S$ the same as the class of problems solvable in $\mathcal{S}_P$?

2. For problems that are solvable both in $\mathcal{S}_S$ and $\mathcal{S}_P$, does one of these models allow for more efficient solutions?

We first consider question (1), about problem solvability. Since $\mathcal{S}_S$ can implement $\mathcal{S}_P$, any problem that can be solved in $\mathcal{S}_P$ can also be solved in $\mathcal{S}_S$. Conversely, there trivially exist problems that are solvable in $\mathcal{S}_S$ but not in $\mathcal{S}_P$: problems whose specifications contain timing conditions (such as the scheduled deadline of some events) might be solvable in $\mathcal{S}_S$ but cannot be solved in $\mathcal{S}_P$. This observation leads us to define a notion of "time-free" problems which captures problems whose specifications do not involve absolute and relative timing conditions. We show that even when considering this class of problems only, solvability in $\mathcal{S}_S$ does not enforce solvability in $\mathcal{S}_P$. We do so by exhibiting a time-free problem, called the *strong dependent decision* problem, that is solvable in in $\mathcal{S}_S$ but not in $\mathcal{S}_P$. The initial motivation for introducing this problem specification is theoretical. However, we show that the strong dependent decision problem is quite relevant in the context of atomic commit.

To address question (2) about efficiency, we consider the time complexity measure. For that, we introduce an adequate round-based computational model

for $\mathcal{S}_P$, denoted $\mathcal{R}_{WS}$, which is comparable to the well-known synchronous round model $\mathcal{R}_S$ for $\mathcal{S}_S$ [16]. In both $\mathcal{R}_S$ and $\mathcal{R}_{WS}$, we measure the time complexity in terms of the number of rounds until the required outputs are produced. More precisely, we consider the *latency degree* introduced in [18] and two refinements of this time complexity measure. We concentrate on the fundamental uniform consensus problem that is well-known to be solvable in $\mathcal{R}_S$ (and so in $\mathcal{S}_S$) despite failures. We show that this result still holds in $\mathcal{R}_{WS}$ (and so in $\mathcal{S}_P$). We analyze various algorithms that solve uniform consensus for $\mathcal{R}_S$ and for $\mathcal{R}_{WS}$ in the presence of up to t faulty processes. When $t = 1$, we show that the $\mathcal{R}_S$ model enables to gain one round over $\mathcal{R}_{WS}$ in failure-free runs. This result is extended to any value of t $(t < n)$ in a companion paper [7]. Therefore, uniform consensus can sometimes be reached in $\mathcal{R}_S$ sooner than in $\mathcal{R}_{WS}$. In conclusion, contrary to a fairly common idea the $\mathcal{S}_S$ synchronous model is strictly stronger than the asynchronous model augmented with a perfect failure detector $\mathcal{S}_P$, in terms of both solvability and efficiency.

The paper is organized as follows. Section 2 defines the $\mathcal{S}_S$ and $\mathcal{S}_P$ system models. Section 3 shows that $\mathcal{S}_S$ is strictly stronger than $\mathcal{S}_P$ in terms of problem solvability, even when considering only problems with time-free specifications. Section 4 compares the efficiency of uniform consensus algorithms in $\mathcal{S}_S$ and $\mathcal{S}_P$. Finally Section 5 discusses our results and summarizes our contribution.

2 System Models

In this section, we define the synchronous system model $\mathcal{S}_S$ (Sect. 2.4) and the system model $\mathcal{S}_P$ obtained from augmenting the asynchronous model with the perfect failure detector P (Sect. 2.6) in a unified framework. Our definitions are taken from [11, 6].

We consider distributed systems consisting of a set of n processes $\Pi = \{p_1, \cdots, p_n\}$. Processes communicate by exchanging messages. Communications are point to point. Every pair of processes is connected by a reliable channel. We assume the existence of a discrete global clock to which processes do not have access. The range of the clock's ticks is the set of natural numbers, and is denoted by $\mathcal{T}$.

2.1 Failures and Failure Patterns

Processes can fail by crashing. A failure pattern F is a function from $\mathcal{T}$ to 2^Π, where $F(t)$ denotes the set of processes that have crashed by time t. If $p_i \notin F(t)$, we say that p_i is *alive at time t*. Processes are assumed not to recover, i.e., $\forall t \in \mathcal{T} : F(t) \subseteq F(t+1)$. Process p_i is *faulty* if $p_i \in Faulty(F) = \cup_{t \in \mathcal{T}} F(t)$; otherwise, p_i is *correct* and $p_i \in Correct(F) = \Pi \setminus Faulty(F)$.

2.2 Algorithms

Each process p_i has a buffer, $buffer_i$, that represents the set of messages that have been sent to p_i but that are not yet received. An *algorithm A* is a collection of n deterministic automata, one for each process. The automaton which runs on p_i is denoted by A_i. A *configuration C* of A consists of:

- n process states $state_1(C), \cdots, state_n(C)$ of $A_1, \cdots, A_n$, respectively;
- n sets of messages $buffer_1(C), \cdots, buffer_n(C)$, representing the messages presently in $buffer_1, \cdots, buffer_n$.

Configuration C is an *initial configuration* if every state $state_i(C)$ is an initial state of A_i and $buffer_i(C)$ is empty. Computations proceed in *steps* of A. In each step, a unique process p_i atomically (1) receives a (possibly empty) set of messages, (2) changes its state, and (3) may send a message to a single process, depending on its state at the beginning of the step and on the set of messages received in the step. A *schedule* of A is an infinite sequence of A's steps.

System models are defined according to the way algorithms execute. In other words, a system model determines the set of runs that algorithms can produce in the model. In this way, we define the *asynchronous model*, as well as the $\mathcal{S}_S$ and $\mathcal{S}_P$ models that are both derived from the asynchronous model by restricting the set of possible runs.

2.3 The Asynchronous Model

A *run of algorithm A* in the *asynchronous model* is a tuple $<F, C_0, S, T>$, where F is a failure pattern, C_0 is an initial configuration of A, S is a schedule of A, and T is an infinite list of increasing time values of $\mathcal{T}$ (indicating when each step of S occurs), and which satisfies the following properties: (1) every correct process takes an infinite number of steps in S, (2) every process cannot take a step in S if it has crashed, and (3) every message sent to a correct process is eventually received in S.

An *asynchronous run* (or a *run*, for short) is a run of some algorithm in the asynchronous model.

2.4 The $\mathcal{S}_S$ Synchronous Model

Following [11], the synchronous model $\mathcal{S}_S$ is defined by two constants $\Phi \geq 1$ and $\Delta \geq 1$ such that any *run* $<F, C_0, S, T>$ of *algorithm A in $\mathcal{S}_S$* satisfies the two following synchrony conditions:

- *Process synchrony:* for any finite subsequence S' of consecutive steps in S, if some process takes $\Phi + 1$ steps in S' then any process that is still alive at the end of S' has taken at least one step in S'.

- *Message synchrony:* for any pair of indices k, l with $l \geq k + \Delta$, if message m is sent to p_i during the k-th step and p_i takes the l-th step, then m is received by the end of the l-th step.

Notice that these two conditions are only in terms of steps: they both refer only to schedule S and not to T. In particular, they do not specify bounds on the real time required to execute a step nor to deliver a message. In contrast, [15] defines the synchronous model in terms of real time synchrony conditions, which imply that the Φ and Δ bounds of the process and message synchrony properties exist. With respect to non-real time problems, we prefer the above definition borrowed from [11], since it does not refer to some specific operational features of systems.

2.5 Models with Failure Detectors

A *failure detector history H* is a function from $\Pi \times \mathcal{T}$ to 2^Π, where $H(p_i, t)$ represents the set of processes that p_i suspects to have crashed at time t in the history H. A *failure detector D* is a function that maps each failure pattern F to a set of failure detection histories.

In a system equipped with a failure detector, algorithms are defined in the same way as above, except that each step taken by p_i contains an intermediate *failure detector query phase* during which p_i queries and receives a value from its failure detector module. The state and the message resulting from the send phase of a step depend additionally on the value returned by the failure detector. A run r is defined as in the asynchronous model, except that one has to specify a "compatible" (cf. [5]) failure detector history H_D of D, i.e., $r = <F, H_D, C_0, S, T>$.

2.6 The $\mathcal{S}_P$ Model with Perfect Failure Detector

Roughly speaking, the so-called *perfect failure detector P* detects process crashes without any mistakes: all failures are eventually detected, and processes are never wrongly suspected to crash. The system model obtained by augmenting the asynchronous model with the perfect failure detector P is denoted by $\mathcal{S}_P$.

2.7 Problem Specifications

A *problem specification* (or a *problem*, for short) is defined as requirements on runs. Therefore, a problem may be modelled by a set Σ of runs.

We restrict our attention to specifications Σ that do not depend on failure detector histories, i.e., for any runs $r = <F, H, C_0, S, T>$ and $r' = <F, H', C_0, S, T>$, $r \in \Sigma$ implies $r' \in \Sigma$. In problem specifications, references to failure detector history are thus useless and will be omitted.

As we saw in the introduction, problems whose specifications are related to synchrony conditions lead to a trivial comparison between $\mathcal{S}_S$ and $\mathcal{S}_P$. We thereby restrict attention to problems whose specifications are insensitive to consistent schedule modifications [17]. Formally, let S_i denote the sequence of the steps taken by p_i in S. A problem Σ is *time-free* if for any runs $r = <F, C_0, S, T>$ and $r' = <F, C_0, S', T'>$ such that $S_i = S'_i$ for any process p_i, $r \in \Sigma$ implies $r' \in \Sigma$. In particular, this holds when $S = S'$ but step time lists T and T' are different. From now on, we only consider such problem specifications. The term "problems" will thus refer only to time-free problems.

For any system model $\mathcal{S}$ and any distributed algorithm A, let $Run(A, \mathcal{S}, t)$ denote the set of runs that A can produce in $\mathcal{S}$, in which at most t processes crash. Algorithm A *tolerates t crashes and solves problem Σ in $\mathcal{S}$* if $Run(A, \mathcal{S}, t) \subseteq \Sigma$.

3 $\mathcal{S}_S$ is strictly stronger than $\mathcal{S}_P$

In the synchronous model, detecting failures perfectly is easy: a simple time-out mechanism with time-out periods that depend on the Δ and Φ bounds, one can implement a perfect failure detector. This implies that any problem that can be solved with a perfect failure detector is also solvable in a synchronous system.

A widespread argument explaining why some problems (such as consensus, atomic broadcast, ...) cannot be solved in asynchronous systems is the impossibility to determine whether a process crashed or is very slow in such a system. In other words, with respect to problem solvability, asynchronous systems seem to differ from synchronous systems basically on the impossibility of achieving perfect failure detections. This leads to think that an asynchronous system becomes as "suitable" as a synchronous system for solving problems as soon as it is equipped with a perfect failure detector. So it may appear that any problem solvable in a synchronous system is still solvable in an asynchronous system where one can detect failures perfectly.

We show below that this intuition is incorrect by exhibiting a problem which can be solved in $\mathcal{S}_S$ but not in $\mathcal{S}_P$. For this problem, we consider two processes p_i and p_j. Process p_i starts with an input value in $\{0, 1\}$. The goal is for process p_j to eventually output a decision in $\{0, 1\}$. There are three conditions imposed on the decision made by p_j:

- *Integrity:* Process p_j decides at most once.
- *Validity:* If p_i has not initially crashed, the only possible decision value for p_j is p_i's initial value.
- *Termination:* If p_j is correct, then p_j eventually decides.

This problem will be referred to as the *Strongly Dependent Decision* problem (or simply, *SDD*). Note that SDD is clearly a time-free problem.

The motivation for introducing the SDD problem is not just theoretical. This problem turns out to be quite relevant in the context of atomic commit. Indeed, solving SDD provides more efficient atomic commit algorithms, i.e., algorithms that lead to the commit decision more often, while preserving the validity property: When all processes propose to commit and there is no initially dead process, processes may safely decide to commit despite failures if the SDD problem is solvable.

In $\mathcal{S}_S$, the SDD problem has a very simple algorithm: p_i sends its initial value to p_j during its first step. Process p_j executes $\Phi + 1 + \Delta$ (possibly empty) steps. If p_j receives a message from p_i during this period, p_j decides the value sent by p_i; otherwise, it decides 0.

Since the Φ and Δ bounds do not exist in the $\mathcal{S}_P$ model, this algorithm does not work in $\mathcal{S}_P$. More generally, we show that SDD cannot be solved in $\mathcal{S}_P$.

Theorem 3.1 *There is no algorithm that solves SDD in the $\mathcal{S}_P$ model and tolerates one crash.*

Proof: Suppose, for contradiction, that there is such an algorithm A. Let r_0 be a run of A where p_i's initial value is 0, p_i crashes from the beginning, and p_j suspects p_i as soon as p_i crashes. By the termination requirement, p_j eventually decides in r_0. Since messages may experience arbitrary (but finite) delays in the $\mathcal{S}_P$ model, we construct a run r'_0 of A whose first step is taken by p_i, p_i crashes just after taking one step, and except its first step, r_0' is identical to r_0 up to p_j's decision. By validity, p_j decides 0 in r_0'. From p_j's viewpoint, r_0' is indistinguishable from r_0 until p_j decides. So p_j also decides 0 in r_0. Let r_1 and r_1' be the runs of A that are the same as r_0 and r_0', respectively, except p_i's initial value is 1. By the same reasoning as above, process p_j decides 1 in both r_1 and r_1'. Clearly, r_1 is indistinguishable from r_0 with respect to p_j, and so p_j decides the same value in both r_0 and r_1 — a contradiction. □

From Theorem 3.1, it follows that there exist atomic commit algorithms for synchronous systems that are more efficient (i.e., that lead to the commit decision more often) than any atomic commit algorithm for asynchronous systems equipped with a perfect failure detector.

This result points out a fundamental difference between $\mathcal{S}_S$ and $\mathcal{S}_P$: *the delay for detecting a failure is bounded in the $\mathcal{S}_S$ model whereas it is finite but unbounded in the $\mathcal{S}_P$ model*. More precisely, if p_i is supposed to send a message m to p_j while p_j is taking its k-th step, if p_j is aware of that, and if p_i crashes and fails in sending m, then p_j can detect p_i's crash when taking its $(k + \Phi + 1 + \Delta)$-th step in $\mathcal{S}_S$. Such a bound does not exist in $\mathcal{S}_P$. Basically, the SDD problem has been specified to capture this difference.

4 Round-Based Computational Models

To address the efficiency issue, we consider the time complexity measure. For that, we introduce two round-based computational models that can be easily emulated from $\mathcal{S}_S$ and $\mathcal{S}_P$. More precisely, we show that computations in $\mathcal{S}_S$ and $\mathcal{S}_P$ can be organized in *synchronous rounds* and in *weakly synchronous rounds*, respectively. This defines two round-based computational models $\mathcal{R}_S$ and $\mathcal{R}_{WS}$, which provide a uniform framework for describing and assessing algorithms. In both $\mathcal{R}_S$ and $\mathcal{R}_{WS}$, the time complexity is measured in terms of the number of rounds until all the required outputs are produced.

4.1 The $\mathcal{R}_S$ Model.

As in Section 2, each process has a buffer denoted $buffer_i$. An algorithm A of the $\mathcal{R}_S$ model consists for each process $p_i \in \Pi$ of the following components [16]: a set of states denoted by $states_i$, an initial state $init_i$, a message-generation function $msgs_i$ mapping $states_i \times \Pi$ to a unique (possibly *null*) message, and

a state transition function $trans_i$ mapping $state_i$ and vectors (indexed by Π) of message to $states_i$. In any execution of A, each process p_i repeatedly performs the following two actions in lock-step mode:

1. Apply $msgs_i$ to the current state to generate the messages to be sent to each process. Put these messages in the appropriate buffers.

2. Apply $trans_i$ to the current state and the messages present in $buffer_i$ to obtain the new state. Remove all messages from the $buffer_i$.

The combination of these two actions is called a *round* of A.

It turns out that each round in $\mathcal{R}_S$ satisfies the *round synchrony property*: *If p_i is alive at the end of round r and does not receive a message from p_j at round r, then p_j fails before sending a message to p_i at round r.*

The $\mathcal{R}_S$ computational model can be easily emulated by $\mathcal{S}_S$. The basic idea of the emulation is the following: In each round r, every process p_i executes $n + k$ steps of the $\mathcal{S}_S$ model. The first n steps are used to send *real* messages whereas in the k last steps, p_i sends *null* messages to make sure that, before moving to round $r + 1$, p_i receives all messages sent to it by other processes in round r (k is a function of n, Δ, Φ and r).

4.2 The $\mathcal{R}_{WS}$ Model.

We define now a comparable round-based computational model $\mathcal{R}_{WS}$ for $\mathcal{S}_P$. Likewise in $\mathcal{R}_S$, the code of each process p_i is entirely determined by the state set $states_i$, the message-generation function $msgs_i$, and the state transition function $trans_i$. The difference between $\mathcal{R}_S$ and $\mathcal{R}_{WS}$ lies in the fact that the state-transition function $trans_i$ is now applied to a *subset* of messages present in $buffer_i$.

The round synchrony property is no longer guaranteed, but we assume that rounds of $\mathcal{R}_{WS}$ satisfy the *weak round synchrony property*: *If p_i is alive at the end of round r and does not receive a message from p_j at round r, then p_j crashes by the end of round $r + 1$.* Contrary to $\mathcal{R}_S$, it might be the case that a (faulty) process sends a message to p_i at round r but p_i does not receive this message although p_i is alive at the end of round r. Such a message is called a *pending* message.

The $\mathcal{R}_{WS}$ model can be emulated from $\mathcal{S}_P$. The reception of messages in round r is done as follows in $\mathcal{S}_P$: Process p_i keeps executing (possibly null) steps of model $\mathcal{S}_P$ until, for every process p_j, either p_i receives a message from p_j or p_i suspects p_j. In this emulation, it may be possible that p_j sends a pending message at round r and does not crash at round r. However, the following lemma states that p_j crashes by the end of round $r + 1$.

Lemma 4.1 *The above emulation guarantees the weak round synchrony property.*

Proof: Suppose for contradiction that some process p_j that is alive at the beginning of round $r + 2$ sends a pending message m to p_i at round r. Let t' be the time at which p_j starts round $r + 2$ and t'' be the time at which p_i starts round $r + 1$. From the emulation and the fact that m is pending, it follows that p_i suspects p_j at t'', i.e., $p_j \in H(p_i, t'')$. Since the failure detector is perfect, this implies that p_j has crashed by time t''. Therefore, we have $t' < t''$.

On the other hand, p_j is allowed to start round $r+2$ only if it has received a message from p_i at round $r + 1$ or it suspects p_i. But p_i is alive at time t'' and thus at time t'. Since the failure detector is perfect, p_j cannot suspect p_i at time t'. It follows that p_j receives a message from p_i at round $r + 1$. Let t be the time at which p_j receives this message; since a message must be sent before it is received, we have $t'' < t < t'$. This is a contradiction. $\qquad \Box_{Lemma\ 4.1}$

4.3 Runs in $\mathcal{R}_S$ and $\mathcal{R}_{WS}$

Let A be any algorithm of the $\mathcal{R}_{WS}$ model (and so of the $\mathcal{R}_S$ model). A *run of A in $\mathcal{R}_S$* is an infinite sequence of A's rounds. A *partial run of A* is a finite prefix of a run of A. Definitions of Section 2 concerning problem specifications are easily adapted to $\mathcal{R}_S$ and $\mathcal{R}_{WS}$. Note that since synchronous rounds are weakly synchronous, if an algorithm solves a problem Σ in $\mathcal{R}_{WS}$, then it also solves Σ in $\mathcal{R}_S$. The number of rounds required to solve a problem in $\mathcal{R}_S$ is thus not greater than in $\mathcal{R}_{WS}$.

5 $\mathcal{R}_S$ is More Efficient than $\mathcal{R}_{WS}$ with Respect to Uniform Consensus

We now concentrate on the uniform consensus problem. In order to measure time complexity of uniform consensus algorithms, we consider the *latency degree* introduced in [18] and various refinements of it. All these time complexity measures are in terms of the number of rounds until all the correct processes decide, and so are quite significant in practice. We prove that with regard to the most discriminating time complexity measures among the ones we consider, $\mathcal{R}_S$ allows to achieve uniform consensus faster than $\mathcal{R}_{WS}$ does.

5.1 The Uniform Consensus Specification

Let V be a fixed value set that is totally ordered. Here each process starts with an input value from V and must reach an irrevocable decision on one value of V. The *uniform consensus* specification is defined as the set of all runs that satisfy the following conditions:

- *Uniform validity:* If all processes start with the same initial value $v \in V$, then v is the only possible decision value.

- *Uniform agreement:* No two processes (whether correct or faulty) decide on different values.

- *Termination:* All correct processes eventually decide.

The uniform consensus problem for crash failures has a very simple algorithm in $\mathcal{R}_S$, called *FloodSet* [16]. Processes just propagate all the values in V that they have ever seen and use a simple decision rule at the end. More precisely, each process maintains a variable W containing a subset of V. Initially, process p_i's variable W contains only p_i's initial value. For each of $t + 1$ rounds, each process broadcasts W, then adds all the elements of the received sets to W. After $t + 1$ rounds, any still alive process decides on the minimum value of W. The complete code of *FloodSet* is given in Figure 1.[1] From the observation that if at most t processes may crash, then among $t + 1$ rounds there must be some round at which no process fails, we easily deduce that *FloodSet* solves the uniform consensus problem in $\mathcal{R}_S$ if at most t processes may crash.

Because of pending messages, *FloodSet* allows disagreement in $\mathcal{R}_{WS}$. However, we can slightly modify this algorithm by forcing any process that does not receive a message from process p_i at some round r to ignore the message that may arrive from p_i at round $r+1$. The code of the resulting algorithm called *FloodSetWS* is given in Figure 2. In a companion paper [7], we prove that *FloodSetWS* actually solves the uniform consensus problem in $\mathcal{R}_{WS}$.

Uniform consensus differs from the consensus problem in the uniform agreement condition: it prevents two processes to disagree even if one of the two processes crash some (maybe long) time after deciding. Thereby, uniform consensus, that is achievable in the context of crash failures of $\mathcal{R}_S$ and $\mathcal{R}_{WS}$, precludes undesirable runs and thus specifies the agreement problem in a more satisfactory way than consensus does. For much of system models, Charron-Bost *et al.* [8]

---

[1]In the code of *FloodSet*, as well as in the codes that follow, null messages are not specified in the $msgs_i$'s.

states$_i$
    $rounds \in N$, initially 0
    $W \subseteq V$, initially the singleton set consisting of p_i's
       initial value
    $decision \in V \cup \{unknown\}$, initially $unknown$

msgs$_i$
    if $rounds \leq t$ then send W to all processes

trans$_i$
    $rounds := rounds + 1$
    let X_j be the message from p_j, for each p_j from
       which a message arrives
    $W := W \cup \bigcup_j X_j$
    if $rounds = t + 1$ then $decision := \min(W)$

Figure 1: FloodSet Algorithm

---

states$_i$
    $rounds \in N$, initially 0
    $W \subseteq V$, initially the singleton set consisting of p_i's
       initial value
    $halt \subseteq \Pi$, initially $\emptyset$
    $decision \in V \cup \{unknown\}$, initially $unknown$

msgs$_i$
    if $rounds \leq t$ then send W to all processes

trans$_i$
    $rounds := rounds + 1$
    let X_j be the message from p_j, for each p_j from
       which a message arrives
    $W := W \cup \bigcup_{p_j \notin halt} X_j$
    for all p_j from which no message has arrived do
       $halt := halt \cup \{p_j\}$
    if $rounds = t + 1$ then $decision := \min(W)$

Figure 2: FloodSetWS Algorithm

---

show that in fact, considering the consensus specification instead of its uniform version has no bad effect: for such systems, any algorithm that solves consensus also solves uniform consensus. However, this result holds neither in $\mathcal{R}_S$ nor in $\mathcal{R}_{WS}$. Therefore, the uniform consensus problem actually differs from consensus in the system models considered here.

5.2 Latency Degrees of Uniform Consensus Algorithms

Let A be any uniform consensus algorithm of the $\mathcal{R}_{WS}$ model (and so of the $\mathcal{R}_S$ model). For any run r of A, the *latency degree of r* introduced in [18] corresponds to the number of rounds until all the correct processes decide in run r. We denote the latency degree of r by $|r|$.

Of course, any uniform consensus algorithm generates many different runs, depending for example on initial configurations or on failure histories. Given a system $\mathcal{S}$ and an integer t such that $t < n$, Schiper [18] defines the *latency degree of A* as the minimal run latency degree over all possible runs that can be produced by A when running in $\mathcal{S}$ and in the presence of at most t process failures. Namely,

$$lat(A) = \min\{|r| : r \in Run(A, \mathcal{S}, t)\}.$$

Basically, this time complexity measure captures the algorithm abilities of taking advantage of some run parameters (e.g., initial configuration, number of failures) to achieve consensus quickly.

Because of the validity condition, any process that receives n messages with the same value v at round 1

could safely decide v at the end of round 1. Based on this remark, we can slightly modify *FloodSet* and *FloodSetWS* to obtain two new uniform consensus algorithms for the $\mathcal{R}_S$ and $\mathcal{R}_{WS}$ models, respectively. Each process operates as in *FloodSet* and *FloodSetWS*, except that it decides v at round 1 if it receives n messages with value v at round 1. Formally, $trans_i$ functions are modified by substituting the following decision rule:

if $rounds = 1$ and
    a message has arrived from every process then
       if $|W| = 1$ then $decision := v$, where $W = \{v\}$
else if $rounds = t + 1$ then $decision := \min(W)$

for

if $rounds = t + 1$ then $decision := \min(W)$

We denote the resulting algorithms by $C\_OptFloodSet$ and $C\_OptFloodSetWS$, respectively. Clearly, we have

$$lat(C\_OptFloodSet) = lat(C\_OptFloodSetWS) = 1$$

This is because $C\_OptFloodSet$ and $C\_OptFloodSetWS$ both take advantage of the fact that by validity, the decision value is determined from the beginning if all the initial values are the same. A sharper comparison of $\mathcal{R}_S$ and $\mathcal{R}_{WS}$ thus requires the definition of a time complexity measure that does not focus on some runs with "too specific" initial configurations. This leads discriminating runs according

to their initial configurations. Namely, for any initial configuration C we define
$$lat(A, C) =$$
$$\min\{|r| : r \in Run(A, \mathcal{S}, t) \text{ and } r \text{ starting from } C\},$$
and
$$Lat(A) = \max\{lat(A, C) : C \in \mathcal{C}\}$$

where $\mathcal{C}$ denotes the set of A's initial configurations.

In turn, algorithms can exploit some specific failure histories to decide quickly. For example, if process p_i receives $n - t$ messages at round 1 then p_i knows the exact set of faulty processes. In this case, p_i can decide at the end of round 1 provided it notifies its decision at round 2 and this decision is then forced on other processes. According to this idea, we can modify *FloodSet* and *FloodSetWS* to design uniform consensus algorithms in which a decision is taken at the end of the first round if t processes initially crash, regardless initial configurations. We denote the resulting new versions of *FloodSet* and *FloodSetWS* by *F_OptFloodSet* and *F_OptFloodSetWS*, respectively. The formal code of *F_OptFloodSet* is given in Figure 3.

Theorem 5.1 F_OptFloodSet
and F_OptFloodSetWS *solve the uniform consensus problem in* $\mathcal{R}_S$ *and* $\mathcal{R}_{WS}$, *respectively.*

Proof: We only show the correctness of *F_OptFloodSet*. The proof for *F_OptFloodSetWS* is similar. We use the notation $W_i(r)$ to denote the value of variable W at process p_i just after r rounds.

Termination is obvious, by the decision rules. For uniform validity, suppose that all the initial values are equal to v. Then v is the only value that ever gets sent anywhere. Each set W_i is non empty, because it contains p_i's initial value. Therefore, each $W_i(t + 1)$ must be exactly equal to $\{v\}$, so the decision rules say that v is the only possible decision.

For uniform agreement, we consider two cases:

1. No process receives exactly $n - t$ messages during the first round. That is, all processes run the *FloodSet* algorithm. By uniform agreement of *FloodSet*, it follows that all processes make the same decision.

2. The set Π' of processes that receive exactly $n - t$ messages during the first round is not empty. By the round synchrony property which holds in $\mathcal{R}_S$, the set of processes from which every process in Π' receives a message at round 1 is exactly the set of correct processes. It follows that for any processes p_i and p_j in Π', we have
$$W_i(1) = W_j(1).$$

states$_i$
> $rounds \in N$, initially 0
> $W \subseteq V$, initially the singleton set consisting of p_i's initial value
> $decided \in \{false, true\}$, initially *false*
> $decision \in V \cup \{unknown\}$, initially *unknown*

msgs$_i$
>   if $rounds \leq t$ then
>   if $decided = false$ then send W to all processes
>   else send $(D, decision)$ to all processes

trans$_i$
> $rounds := rounds + 1$
>   let X_j be the message from p_j, for each p_j from which a message arrives
>   if $rounds = 1$ and $n - t$ messages have arrived then
> $W := W \cup \bigcup_j X_j$
> $decided := true$
> $decision := \min(W)$
> $decided := true$
>   else if at least one X_j equals to (D, v) then
> $decision := v$
> $decided := true$
>   else $W := W \cup \bigcup_j X_j$
>   if $rounds = t + 1$ and $decided = false$ then
> $decision := \min(W)$
> $decided := true$

Figure 3: *F_OptFloodSet* Algorithm

Then all the processes in Π' make the same decision, say v. At round 2, processes of Π' force decision v. Therefore, all the correct processes that have not decided at round 1, also decide v at the end of round 2.

□

Considering the runs of *F_OptFloodSet* and *F_OptFloodSetWS* in which t processes initially crash, we have:

$$Lat(F\_OptFloodSet) = Lat(F\_OptFloodSetWS) = 1.$$

Interestingly, this contradicts a widespread idea that minimal latency degree is typically obtained with failure free runs.

The above examples yield a new refinement of the latency degree: we now discriminate runs according to the number of failures which occur. Formally, for any integer f such that $0 \leq f \leq t$ we define

$$Lat(A, f) = \max\{|r| : r \in Run(A, \mathcal{S}, f)\},$$

and

$$\Lambda(A) = \min_{0 \le f \le t} Lat(A, f).$$

By definition of $Lat(A, f)$, we have $Lat(A, f) \le Lat(A, f + 1)$, and so $\Lambda(A) = Lat(A, 0)$. In other words, $\Lambda(A)$ is the maximal latency degree over all failure free runs.

5.3 $\mathcal{R}_S$ May Be More Efficient Than $\mathcal{R}_{WS}$

We now compare the $\mathcal{R}_S$ and $\mathcal{R}_{WS}$ models in terms of the Λ latency degree. First we restrict to the case $t = 1$, and we present a simple algorithm A_1 for uniform consensus in $\mathcal{R}_S$ that tolerates at most one crash. The A_1 algorithm is based on the following ideas: Process p_1 broadcast its initial value v_1 during the first round. Upon receiving v_1, process p_i decides v_1 at the end of round 1. Subsequently, p_i reports its decision at round 2. If p_2 does not receive a message from p_1 in the first round (because p_1 has crashed), it broadcasts its initial value v_2 at round 2. Since at most one failure may occur, every correct process has received v_1 or v_2, or both by the end of the second round. If it receives v_1, it decides v_1; otherwise it decides v_2. All the runs of A_1 have thus two rounds. The code of A_1 is given in Figure 4.

Theorem 5.2 *The A_1 algorithm tolerates one crash and solves the uniform consensus problem in the $\mathcal{R}_S$ model.*

Proof: Termination is obvious, by the decision rules. For uniform validity, suppose that all the initial values are equal to some $v_0 \in V$. Then v_0 is the only possible value of any w variable. So the decision rules say that v_0 is the only possible decision.

For uniform agreement, there are two cases to consider:

1. Process p_1 decides at round 1. Then p_1 decides on its initial value v_1. Before deciding, p_1 succeeded in sending v_1 to all processes. Therefore, any correct process receives v_1 and then decides v_1 at the end of the first round.

2. Process p_1 does not decide at round 1. In this case, p_1 crashes during the first round. Since $t = 1$, all the other processes are correct. We consider two subcases:

   (a) Process p_1 succeeds in sending at least one message to some (correct) process p_i before crashing. From the algorithm, we deduce that p_i decides v_1 at round 1 and broadcasts (p_1, v_1) at round 2. All correct processes then receive at least one message of

states$_i$
> $rounds \in N$, initially 0 ;
> $w \in V$, initially p_i's initial value ;
> $decided \in \{false, true\}$, initially $false$;
> $decision \in V \cup \{unknown\}$, initially $unknown$

msgs$_i$
> if $rounds = 1$ and $i = 1$ then send w to all
> if $rounds = 2$ then
>> if $decided = true$ then send (p_1, w) to all
>> else if $i = 2$ then send w to all processes

trans$_i$
> $rounds := rounds + 1$
> let x_j be the message from p_j, for each p_j from which a message arrives
> if $rounds = 1$ and a message has arrived from p_1 then
>> $w := x_1$
>> $decision := x_1$
>> $decided := true$
> if $round = 2$ then
>> if at least one message x_j is equal to (p_1, w_j) then
>>> $decision := w_j$
>>> $decided := true$
>> else $\qquad$ {a message $x_2 = w_2$ arrives from p_2}
>>> $decision := x_2$
>>> $decided := true$

Figure 4: The A_1 Algorithm

the form (p_1, v_1) in the second round, and so decide v_1.

   (b) No correct process receives a message from p_1 at round 1, and thus no process decides at the end of this round. At round 2, process p_2 broadcasts its initial value v_2 and all the other messages that are sent at round 2 are null. All processes, except process p_1 (that never decides), decide v_2.

$\square$

In every failure free run of A_1, each process decides at the end of the first round. We thus have $Lat(A_1, 0) = 1$, and so $\Lambda(A_1) = 1$.

Basically, the uniform agreement property is no more guaranteed by A_1 in the $\mathcal{R}_{WS}$ model. To see that, assume that at round 1, p_1 succeeds in broadcasting v_1, decides, and then crashes. In addition, suppose that all the messages sent by p_1 are pending. In this scenario, p_1 decides v_1 whereas all the other processes decide v_2. Modifications such as the one used to transform *FloodSet* into *FloodSetWS* do not preclude such disagreement. In fact, a result in [7] shows that if $n \geq 3$, then there is no uniform consensus algorithm in the $\mathcal{R}_{WS}$ model such that all correct processes decide at round 1 of all failure free runs. In other words, for any uniform consensus algorithm A in $\mathcal{R}_{WS}$ that tolerates one crash we have $Lat(A, 0) \geq 2$, and so $\Lambda(A) \geq 2$. This shows that $\mathcal{R}_S$ allows to design more efficient solutions to the uniform consensus problem than $\mathcal{R}_{WS}$ does, in the presence of one crash. Thanks to the general result stated in [7], we extend this result: we show that this discrepancy between $\mathcal{R}_S$ and $\mathcal{R}_{WS}$ still exists with any number $t < n$ of possible crashes.

6   Discussion

With regard to both solvability and efficiency concerns, we have shown that the synchronous model is better than the asynchronous model equipped with a perfect failure detector. We have pointed out some significant properties of the synchronous model that are lost when translating the synchronous timing assumptions into the axiomatic properties of a perfect failure detector. This is a first step towards the general comparison between timing-based models and models with failure detectors. This wide question is indeed a fundamental issue on which the practical relevance of the failure detector approach relies. It thus seems worthy to extend these results to other classes of timing-based models and other classes of failure detectors.

References

[1] M. Aguilera, W. Chen, and S. Toueg. Failure detection and consensus in the crash-recovery model. In *Proceedings of the 12th International Symposium on Distributed Computing*, Lecture Notes on Computer Science, pages 231–245. Springer-Verlag, September 1998.

[2] M. K. Aguilera, W. Chen, and S. Toueg. Using the heartbeat failure detector for quiescent reliable communication and consensus in partitionable networks. *Theoretical Computer Science*, 220(1):3–30, June 1999.

[3] P. A. Bernstein, V. Hadzilacos, and N. Goodman. *Concurrency Control and Recovery in Database Systems*. Addison-Wesley, 1987.

[4] K. P. Birman and T. A. Joseph. Reliable communication in the presence of failures. *ACM Transactions on Computer Systems*, 5(1):47–76, February 1987.

[5] T. D. Chandra, V. Hadzilacos, and S. Toueg. The weakest failure detector for solving consensus. *Journal of the ACM*, 43(4):685–722, July 1996.

[6] T. D. Chandra and S. Toueg. Unreliable failure detectors for asynchronous systems. *Journal of the ACM*, 43(2):225–267, March 1996.

[7] B. Charron-Bost and A. Schiper. Uniform consensus is harder than consensus. Technical Report, EPFL, Dépt. de Systèmes de Communication, April 2000.

[8] B. Charron-Bost, S. Toueg, and A. Basu. Revisiting safety and liveness in the context of failures. Technical report, LIX, École Polytechnique, January 2000.

[9] F. Cristian and C. Fetzer. The timed asynchronous distributed system model. *IEEE Transactions on Parallel & Distributed Systems*, 10(6):642–657, June 1999.

[10] F. Cristian and F. Schmuck. Agreeing on processor-group membership in asynchronous distributed systems. Technical Report CSE95-428, UCSD, 1995.

[11] D. Dolev, C. Dwork, and L. Stockmeyer. On the minimal synchronism needed for distributed consensus. *Journal of the ACM*, 34(1):77–97, January 1987.

[12] C. Dwork, N. A. Lynch, and L. Stockmeyer. Consensus in the presence of partial synchrony. *Journal of the ACM*, 35(2):288–323, April 1988.

[13] M. J. Fischer, N. A. Lynch, and M. S. Paterson. Impossibility of distributed consensus with one faulty process. *Journal of the ACM*, 32(2):374–382, April 1985.

[14] R. Guerraoui and A. Schiper. Consensus service: A modular approach for building agreement protocols in distributed systems. In *International Symposium on Fault-Tolerant Computing System*. IEEE, June 1996.

[15] V. Hadzilacos and S. Toueg. A modular approach to fault-tolerant broadcasts and related problems. Technical Report TR 94-1425, Cornell University, Dept. of Computer Science, May 1994.

[16] N. A. Lynch. *Distributed Algorithms*. Morgan Kaufmann, 1996.

[17] Gil Neiger and Sam Toueg. Simulating synchronized clocks and common knowledge in distributed systems. *Journal of the ACM*, 40(2):334–377, April 1993.

[18] A. Schiper. Early consensus in an asynchronous system with a weak failure detector. *Distributed Computing*, 10(3):149–157, April 1997.

The Timely Computing Base:
Timely Actions in the Presence of Uncertain Timeliness

Paulo Veríssimo   António Casimiro   Christof Fetzer
pjv@di.fc.ul.pt   casim@di.fc.ul.pt   christof@research.att.com
FC/UL*   FC/UL   AT&T†

Abstract

Real-time behavior is specified in compliance with time-liness requirements, which in essence calls for synchronous system models. However, systems often rely on unpredictable and unreliable infrastructures, that suggest the use of asynchronous models. Several models have been proposed to address this issue. We propose an architectural construct that takes a generic approach to the problem of programming in the presence of uncertain timeliness. We assume the existence of a component, capable of executing timely functions, which helps applications with varying degrees of synchrony to behave reliably despite the occurrence of timing failures. We call this component the Timely Computing Base, TCB. This paper describes the TCB architecture and model, and discusses the application programming interface for accessing the TCB services. The implementation of the TCB services uses fail-awareness techniques to increase the coverage of TCB properties.

1. Introduction and Motivation

A large number of the emerging services have response or mission-criticality requirements, which are best translated into requirements for fault-tolerance and real-time. That is, service must be provided on time, either because of dependability constraints (e.g. air traffic control, telecommunication intelligent network architectures), or because of user-dictated quality-of-service requirements (e.g. network transaction servers, multimedia rendering, synchronized groupware).

Real-time behavior is specified in compliance with *timeliness* requirements, which in essence calls for synchronous system models. Under this model there are known bounds for all relevant timing variables.

However, unpredictable and unreliable infrastructures are not adequate environments for synchronous models, since it is difficult to enforce timeliness assumptions. Violation of assumptions might cause incorrect system behavior. In contrast, an asynchronous model is a well-studied framework, appropriate for these environments. Informally, 'asynchronous' means that there are no bounds on timing variables, such as processing speed or communication delay. In summary, fully asynchronous models do not satisfy our needs, because they do not allow the specification nor the enforcement of timeliness specifications. On the other hand, enforcing the properties of fully synchronous models is very difficult to achieve in infrastructures with poor baseline timeliness properties. The issue that has to be addressed is: *what system model to use for applications with synchrony (i.e. real-time) requirements running on environments with uncertain timeliness?*

We propose a framework that describes the problem in a generic way. We call it the **Timely Computing Base (TCB)** model. We assume that systems can rely on services provided by a synchronous module, the TCB.

The proposed TCB is just a small part of the system and thus its properties can be implemented with high coverage. We describe an architecture that takes reliability concerns into account, enforcing the coverage of TCB synchronism properties. We show how the TCB services can be implemented and how they can be used by applications.

The paper is organized as follows. In the next section we present a brief survey of related work. Section 3 provides the definition of timing failure. The Timely Computing Base Model is introduced in Section 4, after which we present the services and application programming interface of the TCB, in Section 5. Sections 6 and 7 discuss how to implement the TCB services and improve their coverage through self-checking mechanisms. The paper concludes with some considerations about future work.

2. Related Work

Several previous papers have proposed models for systems with uncertain temporal behavior. Chandra & Toueg have studied the minimal strengthening of the time-free model [14] such that the consensus and atomic broadcast

---

*Faculdade de Ciências da Universidade de Lisboa. Bloco C5, Campo Grande, 1700 Lisboa - Portugal. Tel. +(351) 21 750 0087 (secretariat); +(351) 21 750 0103 (direct) (office). Fax +(351) 21 750 0084. Navigators Home Page: http://www.navigators.di.fc.ul.pt. This work was partially supported by the FCT, through projects Praxis/P/EEI/12160/1998 (MICRA) and Praxis/P/EEI/14187/1998 (DEAR-COTS), and by the EC, through project IST-1999-11583 (MAFTIA).

†AT&T Labs. 180 Park Ave, Florham-Park, NJ07932, USA.

problems become solvable in the presence of crash failures: they give a failure detector which will eventually stop suspecting at least one correct process and that will eventually suspect all crashed processes[6]. The present authors, in separate teams, have developed models of partial synchrony that can be seen as precursors of the present work: the timed-asynchronous model, where the system alternates between synchronous and asynchronous behavior, and where hardware clocks provide sufficient synchronism to make decisions such as 'detection of timing failures' or 'fail-safe shutdown'[8]; the quasi-synchronous model, where parts of the system have enough synchronism to perform 'real-time actions' with a certain probability[20]. All these works share a same observation: *synchronism or asynchronism are not homogeneous properties of systems*. That is, they vary with time, and they vary with the part of the system being considered. However, each model has treated these asymmetries in its own way: some relied on the evolution of synchronism with time, others with space or with both. Other works have studied the minimum guarantees for securing the safety properties of the system, assuming a time-free liveness perspective [9, 10].

3. Timing Failures

In our opinion, a general model can be devised that encompasses the entire spectrum of what is sometimes called *partial synchrony*. The common denominator of systems belonging to that realm is that *they can exhibit timing failures*, denoted as the violation of timeliness properties. Informally, timeliness properties concern the specification of timed actions, such as: P **within** T **from** t_0 (T- duration; t_0- instant of reference). Examples of timed actions are the release of tasks with deadlines, the sending of messages with delivery delay bounds, and so forth. A full discussion can be found in [22].

The bounds specified for a timed action may be violated, in which case a timing failure occurs. We base our approach on the observability of the termination event of a timed action, regardless of where it originated. If a timed action does not incur in a timing failure, the action is *timely*.

Timing Failure - *Given the execution of a timed action X specified to terminate until real time instant t_e, there is a timing failure at p, iff the termination event takes place at a real time instant t'_e, $t_e < t'_e \leq \infty$. The delay, $Ld = t'_e - t_e$, is the lateness degree*

This brings us to the central issue of this paper: the Timely Computing Base (TCB) model and its implementation and programming interface, as a paradigm for achieving timely actions in the presence of uncertain timeliness.

4. The Timely Computing Base Model

The architecture of a system with a Timely Computing Base (TCB) is suggested by Figure 1. The first relevant aspect is that the heterogeneity in system synchronism was cast into the system architecture. There is a generic or *payload* system, over a global network or *payload* channel. This prefigures what is normally 'the system' in homogeneous architectures, that is, where applications run. Additionally, there is a *control* part, made of local TCB modules, interconnected by some form of medium, the *control* channel. The medium may be a virtual channel over the available physical network or an alternative network in its own right. The second relevant aspect is that the TCB has well-defined synchronism properties. The TCB provides simple support services, such as the ability to detect failures, to measure durations, and to execute *timely* timed actions. For certain types of less critical applications, it is not necessary that all sites have TCBs. However, note that this decreases the capability of these sites to exhibit guaranteed synchronous behavior, which may be a nuisance in, e.g., fail-safe or real-time systems. So, for simplicity, and to show the virtues of the model, in this paper we assume that every site has a TCB.

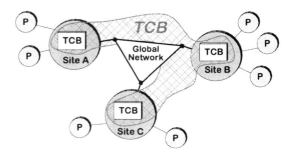

Figure 1. The TCB Architecture

4.1. Payload System Properties

We assume a system model of participants or processes (we use both designations interchangeably) which exchange messages, and may exist in several sites or nodes of the system (we use both designations interchangeably). Sites are interconnected by a communication network. The system *can have any degree of synchronism*, that is, if bounds exist for processing or communication delays, their magnitude may be uncertain or not known. Local clocks may not exist or may not have a bounded drift rate. We assume the system to follow an omissive failure model, that is, components *only have late timing failures*— and omission and crash, since they are subsets of timing failures— no value failures occur. The system model has uncertain timeliness: bounds may be violated, or may vary during system life. Still, the system must be dependable with regard to time: it must be capable of timely executing certain functions or detecting the failure thereof.

4.2. Timely Computing Base Properties

We now define the fault and synchronism model of the TCB. There is one local Timely Computing Base at every site. We assume only crash failures for the TCB components, i.e. that they are fail-silent. Furthermore, we assume that the failure of a local TCB module implies the failure of that site. The TCB subsystem, shown dashed in the figure, preserves, by construction, the properties of a synchronous system:

Ps 1 *There exists a known upper bound $T_{D^1_{max}}$ on TCB processing delays*

Ps 2 *There exists a known upper bound $T_{D^2_{max}}$ on the drift rate of local TCB clocks*

Ps 3 *There exists a known upper bound $T_{D^3_{max}}$, on the delivery delay of messages exchanged between TCB moduleFs*

Property **Ps** 1 refers to the determinism in the execution time of code elements by the TCB. Property **Ps** 2 refers to the existence of a local clock in each TCB whose individual drift is bounded. This allows measuring local durations, that is, the interval between two local events. These clocks are internal to the TCB. Property **Ps** 3 completes the synchronism properties, referring to the upper bound on the time to exchange messages among TCB modules. We assume that the inter-TCB channels provide reliable delivery, in the sense that no messages addressed to correct TCB modules are lost. The distributed TCB is the collection of all local TCBs in a system, together with the inter-TCB communication channels (*see* Figure 1). From now on, when there is no ambiguity, we refer to TCB to mean the 'distributed TCB', accessed by processes in a site via the 'local TCB' in that site. We assume nothing about how many local TCBs can fail, since under a fail-silent model this is irrelevant to the correctness of operation of the distributed TCB.

Note that having a computing base with these properties opens very interesting perspectives, in terms of turning the TCB into an oracle for applications (even asynchronous) to solve their time-related problems. Accomplishing this raises three orders of problems:

- defining the minimal services— the TCB must be kept simple;
- defining the payload-to-TCB interface— to allow potentially asynchronous applications to dialogue with a synchronous component may prove delicate;
- implementing the TCB services with the necessary coverage.

The minimal services required to satisfy a wide range of applications with timeliness requirements have essentially to do with: ability to measure distributed durations with bounded accuracy; complete and accurate detection of timing failures; ability to execute well-defined functions in bounded time.

The way applications interact with the TCB is also another important problem. Applications can only be as timely as allowed by the synchronism of the payload system. That is, the TCB does not make applications timelier,

it just detects how timely they are. However, when timing failures occur, the TCB can help implement contingency plans, such as timely fail-safe shutdown. Finally, although the TCB detects timing failures, nothing obliges an application to become aware of such failures. In consequence, applications take advantage of the TCB by construction, typically using it as a pacemaker, letting it assess (explicitly or implicitly) the correctness of past steps before proceeding to the next step. The crux of this style of operation is the application programming interface, which we discuss in Section 5, together with the TCB services.

Finally, the TCB implementation, which we discuss in Section 6. One may suggest that we are only hiding in the TCB the main problem that other systems have: achieving coverage of synchrony assumptions. We stress the fundamental architectural principle that makes the approach different from previous models— by design, there are: a larger-scale, more complex, asynchronous at the limit, payload part, where we can run the logic part of our algorithms, which can even be time-free; and a small-scale, simple, synchronous, control part, where we can run the time-related part of our algorithms, with the support of the TCB services. In consequence, the coverage of the implementation of synchronous services on the TCB can be made comparably much higher than one would achieve for the same services implemented on the payload system. In generic terms, the TCB can be seen as a *coverage amplifier* for the execution of the time-critical functions of any system (the TCB services). Still, the TCB can still fail with nasty consequences for the safety of applications no matter how small and simple it may be. In Section 7, we show how to improve the coverage of the TCB through very simple self-checking mechanisms.

5. Dependable Programming on the TCB

How can the TCB help design dependable and timely applications? We begin this section with the presentation of a simple set of services to be provided by the TCB. Then, we introduce and explain the application programming interface between payload applications and the TCB. Note that the interface must ensure correct interaction between the essentially asynchronous world of the payload applications, and the synchronous world of the TCB.

5.1. Services of the TCB

The TCB provides the following services: timely execution; duration measurement; timing failure detection. These services have a distributed scope, although they are provided to processes via the local TCB instantiations. Any service may be provided to more than one user in the system. For example, failure notification may be given to all interested users. We define below the properties of the services. The properties are defined as seen at the TCB interface. We start with timely execution and duration measurement.

Timely Execution

TCB 1 Eager Execution: *Given any function F with an execution time bounded by a known constant T_{Xmax}, for any eager execution of the function triggered at real time t_{start}, the TCB terminates F within T_{Xmax} from t_{start}*

TCB 2 Deferred Execution: *Given any function F, and a delay time lower-bounded by a known constant T_{Xmin}, for any deferred execution of the function triggered at real time t_{start}, the TCB does not start the execution of F within T_{Xmin} from t_{start}*

Eager Execution allows the TCB to execute arbitrary functions deterministically, given a feasible T_{Xmax}. Deferred Execution allows the TCB to execute delayed functions, such as those resulting from timeouts (T_{Xmin}).

Duration Measurement

TCB 3 *There exist $T_{Dmin}, T_{D^2_{max}}$ such that given any two events e_s and e_e occurring in any two nodes, respectively at real times t_s and t_e, $t_s < t_e$, the TCB measures the duration between e_s and e_e as T_{se}, and the error of T_{se} is bounded by $(t_e - t_s)(1 - T_{D^2_{max}}) - T_{Dmin} \leq T_{se} \leq (t_e - t_s)(1 + T_{D^2_{max}}) + T_{Dmin}$*

The measurement error has 1) a fixed component T_{Dmin} that depends on the measurement method, and 2) a component that increases with the length of the measured interval, i.e., with $t_e - t_s$. This is because the local clocks drift permanently from real-time as per Property **Ps** 2.

The measurement error can only be bounded a priori if the applications are such that we can put an upper limit on the length of the intervals being measured, say T_{INT}. This would bound the error by: $T_{INT}T_{D^2_{max}} + T_{Dmin}$. When it is impossible or impractical to determine the maximum length of intervals, the clocks in the TCB must be externally synchronized. In that case it is guaranteed that at any time a TCB clock is at most some known ϵ apart from real-time. In systems with external clock synchronization, the measurement error is bounded by 2ϵ. Note that internal clock synchronization for the matter would not help here. Although given properties **Ps** 1–**Ps** 3 one could implement global time, explicitly synchronized clocks would just improve some variables quantitatively, but they would not increase the power of the model. To minimize the assumptions of the model, we refrain from requiring synchronized clocks.

Timing Failure Detection

Another crucial service of the TCB is failure detection. We define a *Perfect Timing Failure Detector (pTFD)*, using an adaptation of the terminology of Chandra[6].

TCB 4 Timed Strong Completeness: *There exists T_{TFDmax} such that given a timing failure at p in any timed action $X(p, e, T_A, t_A)$, the TCB detects it within T_{TFDmax} from t_e*

TCB 5 Timed Strong Accuracy: *There exists T_{TFDmin} such that any timely timed action $X(p, e, T_A, t_A)$ that does not terminate within $-T_{TFDmin}$ from t_e is considered timely by the TCB if the local TCB does not crash until $t_e + T_{TFDmax}$*

The majority of detectors known are *crash* failure detectors. We introduce timing failure detectors. Timed Strong Completeness can be understood as follows: "strong" specifies that any timing failure is perceived by all correct processes; "timed" specifies that the failure is perceived at most within T_{TFDmax} of its occurrence. In essence, it specifies the detection latency of the pTFD. Timed Strong Accuracy can also be understood under the same perspective: "strong" means that no timely action is wrongly detected as a timing failure; but "timed" qualifies what is meant by 'timely', by requiring the action to occur not later than a set-up interval T_{TFDmin} before the detection threshold t_e. In essence, it specifies the detection accuracy of the pTFD.

5.2. Application Programming Interface

Given the baseline asynchronism of a payload application, there are no guarantees about the actual time of invocation of a TCB service by the former. In fact, the latency of service invocation may not be bounded. The same can be said of the actual time that responses or notifications from the TCB arrive at the application buffer. When considering the interface definition this is perhaps the most important problem. The interface presented in this section makes the bridge between a synchronous environment and a potentially asynchronous one.

Duration Measurement

The most basic function we have to provide is obviously one that allows applications to read a clock:

```
timestamp ← getTimestamp ()
```

The function returns a timestamp generated inside the TCB. Since the application runs in the payload part of the system, when it uses a single timestamp there are no guarantees about how accurately this timestamp reflects the current time. However, a difference between two timestamps represents an upper bound for a time interval, if the interval took place between the two timestamps. For instance, just by using this function an application is able to obtain an upper bound on the time it has needed to execute a computation step: it would suffice to request two timestamps, one before the execution and another after it. If this execution is a timed action, then the knowledge of this upper bound is also sufficient to detect a timing failure, should it occur. The TCB recognizes the importance of measuring local durations and explicitly provides interface functions to do this:

```
tag ← startMeasurement (start_ev)
end_ev,procdelay ← stopMeasurement (tag)
```

When the startMeasurement function is called, the application has to provide a timestamp to mark the start event. It gets a request `tag`. When it wants to mark the end event, and obtain the measured duration, it calls `stopMeasurement` for `tag`. The service gets a timestamp for the end event, and the difference between the two timestamps yields the duration. A very simple example of the usage of these functions is depicted in Figure 2a. Here, an application has to execute some computation in a bounded time interval (T_{spec}), on a best-effort basis. If this is achieved, the computation results can be accepted. Otherwise they are rejected. Possibly there will be subsequent (adjacent) computations also with timeliness requirements. In that case, the end event of a computation is used as the start event of the next one in order to cancel the time spent to verify the execution timeliness (shown in the far right of the figure, with `startMeasurement(B)`).

Timely Execution

The timely execution service allows the construction of applications where strict timeliness guarantees are sporadically required. In essence, timely execution means the possibility of guaranteeing that something will be executed before a deadline (eager), or that something will not be executed before a liveline[21] (deferred). This maps onto the following interface function:

```
end_ev ←
    startExec (start_ev,delay,t_exec_max,func)
```

When this is called, `func` will be executed by the TCB. The specification of an execution deadline is done through the `start_ev` and `t_exec_max` parameters. The former is a timestamp that marks a reference point from where the execution time should be measured. The latter, a duration, indicates the desired maximum termination time counted from `start_ev`. On return, the `end_ev` parameter contains a timestamp that marks the termination instant. The `delay` parameter is the deferral term, counted from `start_ev`. If it is zero, it is a pure eager execution function. The feasibility of timely execution of each function must be analyzed, for instance, through the calculation of the worst-case execution time (WCET) and schedulability analysis (*see* Section 6).

Not all eager execution requests are feasible. Depending on the specified parameters and on the instant the request is processed, the TCB may not be able to execute it and, in that case, an error status reporting this fact will be returned and made available in the interface.

The example of figure 2b illustrates the utility of the eager execution service. Suppose the application had to execute the computation of the Figure 2a with such strict timeliness requirements (instead of on a best-effort basis) that it would delegate it to the timely execution service of the TCB. The computation had a WCET and was short enough to be schedulable by the TCB. Then, instead of issuing a `startMeasurement` request, the application would call `startExec` with the appropriate `func`. `t_exec_max` would be T_{spec}. The request would always succeed, unless the delay between the `getTimestamp` call and the execution start

was so large that the execution was no longer schedulable. The application would just need to check the `startExec` return status.

Timing Failure Detection

We now present the API of the timing failure detection (TFD) service and give two short examples that illustrate how it should be used to solve concrete problems.

As introduced in section 5.1, there is logically only one TFD service, with the properties **TCB**4 and **TCB**5. However, in practice it is wise to make a distinction between the detection of timing failures in local timed actions and in distributed timed actions. This distinction is important in terms of interface, because in one case the failures are only important to one process (the one performing the action) while in the other they are important to many (all those affected by the distributed action). Therefore, the API described here has two sets of functions: for local and for distributed timing failure detection. The following two functions provide for all that is necessary concerning local timing failure detection:

```
tag ← startLocal (start_ev,spec,handler)
end_ev,procdelay,faulty ← endLocal (tag)
```

With `startLocal` an application requests the service to observe the timeliness of some execution. The TFD service takes `start_ev` as the start instant of the observed execution, and `spec` as the specified execution duration. Each request receives a unique `tag` so that it is possible to handle several concurrent requests. Since the service has to timely detect timing failures, it does not accept requests to observe executions that have already failed. The timely reaction to a timing failure can be delegated on the TCB, using the `handler` parameter. This parameter identifies one of the built-in functions of the TCB, executed as soon as the failure is detected (e.g., an orderly fail-safe shutdown procedure). Note that there would be no guarantees about the timeliness of the reaction if it were done in the payload part of the system.

When the execution finishes the application has to call the `end_local` function, with the identifier `tag`, in order to disable the detection for this action and receive information about the execution: when it finished, its duration and whether it was timely.

The relevance of this service and the importance of timely reaction to failures can be better explained with the following example. Consider a distributed system composed of a controller, a sensor and an actuator processes (Figure 3a). The system has a TCB and the payload part is asynchronous. Since processes are in different nodes, they can only communicate by message passing. The sensor process periodically reads a temperature sensor and sends the value to the controller process. When the controller receives a new reading, it compares it with the set point, and computes the new value to send to the burner, in order to keep the temperature within the allowed error interval. It then sends a command to the actuator process. The system has three classes of critical requirements: (a) the temperature

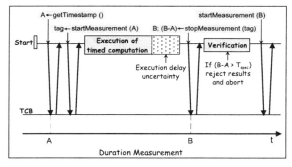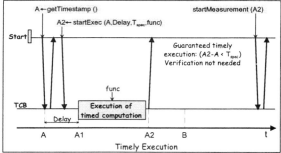

Figure 2. Using TCB services: (a) Duration Measurement; (b) Timely Execution

must remain within $\pm\varepsilon$ of a set point; (b) the control loop must be executed frequently enough (the controller must receive a valid temperature reading every $D2$ time units); (c) once the sensor value read, the actuation value must be computed and sent fast enough to the actuator to achieve accurate control. Let us neglect, for simplicity, the delay in sending the temperature reading from sensor to controller, and consider that the actuation must be acknowledged in $D1$ time units after the reading has been received. A solution for detecting delayed temperature readings is presented in [13].

Requirement (a) can be ensured by the application logic residing in the payload part. Requirements (b) and (c) can be controlled by the TCB on behalf of the application.

System safety is compromised if $D1$ or $D2$ are violated. In this case the system has to switch to a safe state. We assume the controller node to have full control of the heating device power switch and thus able to turn it off, putting the system in a safe state.

Since the system is asynchronous but has timeliness requirements, it has to rely on the TCB. In figure 3b it is possible to observe how the TFD service is used to detect local timing failures. The controller receives a new temperature reading at instant $t1$ (measured by the TCB). From this moment on the bounds $D1$ and $D2$ must be checked, and so it is necessary to invoke the `startLocal` function twice. Note the call `endLocal`(id_0) **after** the other two: the call disables detection for the previous period ($D2$ specification, not shown), since a new message arrived. The controller then sends a command to the actuator and, when it receives the acknowledgment, `endLocal` is called again, this time to terminate the execution of $id1$. Normally, neither $D1$ nor $D2$ expire. If the computation takes so long that $D1$ expires, or if a message is not received from the sensor before $D2$ expires (as depicted), the handler is immediately executed by the TCB. The handler function passed as argument can be a very simple function that is executed by the TCB, issuing a command to the actuator that turns off the heating device.

A distributed execution requires at least one message to be sent between two processes. Thus, the action to be observed for timing failure detection, in addition to local actions, is message delivery. Since a delivery delay is bounded

by a send and a receive event, the TFD service just has to intercept message transmissions. The described interface provides not only the required functionality but also allows message interceptions to be done in a very simple and intuitive manner. In the following functions we only present the TFD service-specific parameters (we omit normal parameters such as addresses, etc.).

```
tag ← send(send_ev,spec,handler)
tag,deliv_ev ← receive()
```

The meaning of the `send` function parameters is similar to the ones of the `startLocal` function. We assume it is possible to multicast a message to a set of destination processes using this `send` function. The `receive` function blocks the application until a message is received. On return, the function provides a message `tag` and a timestamp for the delivery event. The information relative to timing failures is queried by means of another function:

```
info₁ ··· infoₙ ← waitInfo(tag)
info = (delivdelay,faulty)
```

When `waitInfo` is called, the application will block until all information is available, but never more than the maximum timing failure detection latency (T_{TFDmax}). `waitInfo` returns the delivery delay and the failure result for each receiver process of message `tag`.

Using this service in the example of figure 3, we may now extend the response time control ($D1$) back to the sensor reading moment, to enforce the freshness of sensor readings. In order to achieve that, the sensor message would be sent using this interface, by specifying some maximum delivery delay. Upon message reception the `waitInfo` function could be used to detect a timing failure. There are other examples of the utility of timing failure detection in application construction [1, 12, 11].

6. Implementing TCB Services

This section provides the basic principles and guidelines to implement the TCB services. We show that despite the importance of the services, their construction can be quite simple. Likewise, their overhead on system execution is kept at a low level.

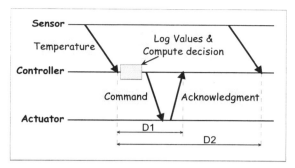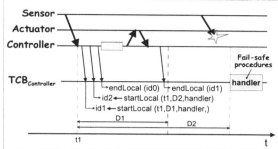

Figure 3. Using Local Timing Failure Detection: (a) Example Scenario and Timing Specifications; (b) Detecting and Handling Timing Failures with the TCB

6.1. Timely Execution Service

There are two essential functions that must be provided by the timely execution service, in order to enforce properties **TCB**1 and **TCB**2 introduced in Section 5.1: eager execution and deferred execution. They can be combined, as found in some real-time schedulers[4].

By definition, the timely execution service is designed for the execution of short-lasting time-critical application functions. These functions should not reside in the application address space. Functions have guaranteed behavior when directly called by the TCB (for instance, they can not be swapped out, otherwise it would be impossible to compute execution times). Inside the TCB, we have to assume that a number of measures have been taken a priori, such as the calculation of the worst-case execution time and the schedulability analysis of the critical albeit simple set of functions submitted to the TCB by each application. There is a body of research on the schedulability of real-time operating systems and networks that contributes to the subject of building the system support of a TCB[4, 15, 16, 17]. A more detailed discussion about the engineering principles behind the construction of a TCB can be found in [22].

Timely function execution can be explicitly triggered by an application, but can also be *implicitly triggered* as a response to some failure detected by the timing failure detection service. The former method is intended for applications where specific actions have to be executed in a bounded amount of time. The latter is mostly useful for the implementation of fail-safe orderly shutdown procedures that must be timely executed upon the occurrence of irrecoverable failures.

6.2. Duration Measurement Service

The local TCB module is trusted to provide accurate readings of time intervals, enforcing property **TCB**3 (*see* Section 5.1). Thus, when applications in the payload part have to determine durations of executions or transmissions, they delegate this task on the TCB, with the interface discussed in Section 5.

The availability of a local clock with bounded drift rate is sufficient for the measurement of *local durations*. The service has to know which are the two events that bound the time interval, so that it can determine their timestamps. The difference between the two timestamps yields the measured duration. Another way for applications to keep track of their timeliness is by using the timing failure detection service interface. This has the advantage of detecting whether a duration threshold is exceeded, besides measuring the duration.

Measurement of *distributed durations* is done differently. Given that we do not assume the existence of synchronized clocks, the methodology for measuring a distributed duration, that is, for relating timestamps of events in different sites, relies on the well-known round-trip duration measurement technique[7], which is for the matter an implicit clock synchronization action. Distributed durations are often associated to the measurement of message delivery delays. A send and a deliver event bound the measured duration. This technique produces an error associated to each measurement whose value is dictated by several factors, including the separation between the two events[13], as discussed in Section 5.1.

6.3. Timing Failure Detection Service

To construct the timing failure detection (TFD) service it is necessary to employ more elaborate algorithms than for the previously described services. The problem we have to solve is how to build a timing failure detector which satisfies properties **TCB**4 and **TCB**5 (*see* section 5.1). Timing failure detection of local actions is dealt with at the end of this section. Timing failure detection of distributed actions requires a protocol to be executed by all TFD modules on top of the control channel. Recall that we are talking about actions *in the payload system*.

For lack of space, in this paper we only provide the intuition behind this protocol. However, the protocol is available in a technical report[5]. The protocol executes in rounds, during which each TFD instance broadcasts all relevant information for the detection of timing failures. Distributed common knowledge of failure occurrences is achieved by disseminating information about locally detected failures. When an application sends a message, the TFD service uses the distributed duration measurement service to measure its delivery delay. Therefore, TFD instances in all destination sites will collect the measured value. The error associated to this measurement yields the value of T_{TFDmin} specified in property **TCB5** (*see* [5] for a proof). The TCB of the sender site logs the timed action specification of the sent message for later use. Each send request is tagged with a unique identifier, known to the TFD service and to the application. The information concerning each sent message (identifier and bound specification) is disseminated to the relevant sites during the next round.

On each receiver site, the TFD service will eventually learn the delivery delay and the specified bound of each received payload message. The bound on the timing failure detection latency, expressed by T_{TFDmax} in property **TCB4**, is enforced by timely executing a decision function after a given amount of time.

Applications that want to perform a timed action provide a timestamp for the start event (the measurement may start before the action actually starts, but that only depends on the application's own timeliness). The TFD service performs an admission test before accepting to control the action. This test is required to guarantee that timely detection of failure is achievable. In certain conditions (in the limit, if the start timestamp is already older than $t_{now} - T_{duration}$) timing failure detection is infeasible and so the request fails. For the application, this equals a timing failure.

Local actions are a subset of distributed actions, and they can be checked locally. To detect timing failures of local actions it is necessary to pre-register those actions, specifying the duration and getting a timestamp for the start instant. Again, there is an admission test and the request may be denied. The TFD service uses the timestamp, the current time and the specified duration to set a timer that counts the remaining time interval. Thereafter, either the TFD service receives an indication that the action has ended or the timer expires. The TFD service delivers the result, success in the former case, failure in the latter.

As we mentioned above, it is possible to trigger the eager execution of some function when a failure is detected. This is the way to guarantee timely reaction to failures and thus maintain correctness of the system (even when that means the orderly execution of a shutdown procedure).

7. Enforcing Synchronism Properties of the TCB

The TCB *can* be built in any way that enforces the TCB synchronism properties **Ps** 1, **Ps** 3 and **Ps** 2 stated in Section 4. The TCB *should* be built in a way that secures the above-mentioned properties with ⟨*bound,coverage*⟩ pairs that are commensurate with the time-scales and criticality of the application. In consequence, the local TCB can either be a special hardware module, or an auxiliary firmware-based microcomputer board, or a software-based kernel on

a plain desktop machine such as a PC or workstation. Likewise, the distributed TCB assumes the existence of a timely inter-TCB communication channel. This channel can assume several forms that exhibit different ⟨*bound,coverage*⟩ values for the message delivery delay ($T_{D^3_{max}}$). It may or not be based on a physically different network from the one supporting the *payload* channel. Virtual channels with predictable timing characteristics coexisting with essentially asynchronous channels are feasible in some of the current networks, even in Internet [19]. Observe that the bandwidth required of the control channel is much smaller than that of the payload channel: local TCBs only exchange control messages. In a number of local area networks, switched networks, and even wider area networks, it is possible to give guarantees for high priority messages[18, 3, 2]. In more demanding scenarios, one may resort to alternative networks (real-time LAN, ISDN connection, GSM Short Message Service, Low Earth Orbit satellite communication).

In fact, a TCB can be built out of normal hardware, and this is the scenario that we consider here, as the most adequate to show the feasibility of the model. As shown in Figure 4, the TCB is set-up on a real-time kernel that sits directly on the hardware, so that it controls all time-critical resources (e.g., clock, scheduler, network interface). The regular operating system (e.g., Linux) is layered on top of the kernel. The placement of the TCB between the O.S. and the resources allows the TCB to monitor application calls and protect the kernel activity with regard to timeliness. The TCB offers a TCB- specific application programming interface (API)— presented in Section 5— which is provided to the payload applications together with the regular O.S. and system libraries interface. The API offers access to the timely execution, duration measurement and timing failure detection services. Note however, that applications not using the TCB need not be aware of the existence of the latter.

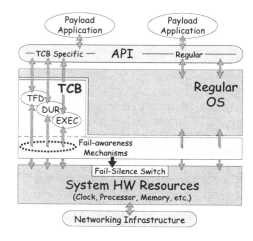

Figure 4. Block Diagram of a System with TCB

We are assuming the TCB to be fully synchronous. We are considering that the macroscopic services (timely execution, duration measurement and timing failure detection) always execute correctly. As such, we are also considering that the microscopic operations on the resources— code module executions and message transmissions— on which their correctness depends, are perfectly timely, as per the **Ps** properties. These are the foundations of a hard real-time device, which enforces the desired timeliness properties of the TCB services, namely by testing schedulability and actually scheduling computations and communication adequately.

However, there is always a risk that deadlines may be missed, mainly if sporadic or event-triggered computations take place [4]. We implement a few measures to amplify the coverage of the **Ps** properties, which consist in transforming unexpected timing failures into crash failures: we enforce fail-silence upon the first timing failure of a unit. We can afford to do that because these failures will be rare events, which could however compromise the safety of the system. Note that we *are not* allowing timing failures inside the TCB, so these are not tolerance measures, but safety measures: with this transformation, we bring some unexpected failures back into the assumed failure mode universe (crash). Note that there may be other, more sophisticated approaches to improve coverage of a TCB, and there may be distributed algorithmic approaches to a fault-tolerant TCB. Again, we wish to persuade the reader that a baseline implementation of this model can lead to very robust systems with simple mechanisms. Here is the approach and its validation:

- we only attempt to deal with unexpected failures in time (not in the value) domain;
- we assume property **Ps** 2 (clocks) to be always valid; we further assume that the same reliance can be put on clock-based operations in general, such as reading the local clock, and have the kernel set up alarms (watchdogs) that trip at a given time on the local clock;
- as such, we are concerned with the coverage of the more fragile properties: **Ps** 1 (processing) and **Ps** 3 (communication);
- we monitor the termination instants of local computations submitted to the kernel and compare them with the respective deadlines;
- we monitor the delivery instants of messages submitted to the kernel for transmission and compare them with the respective deadlines;
- should any deadline be missed, we enforce fail-silence of the unit observing the failure.

As depicted in Figure 4, the lower interface of the TCB with the system resources is under the surveillance of the monitoring mechanisms, based on fail-awareness techniques, i.e., techniques that allow the component to realize it has suffered a timing failure. As suggested in the figure, these mechanisms are hooked to a *fail-silence switch*, an abstraction whose implementation has the effect of immediately halting the whole site.

Improving the Coverage of Timely Processing

To improve the coverage of **Ps** 1 we use the local clock to measure local kernel execution durations. Recall that we assume that we can place more reliance on the timeliness of an alarm (watchdog), than on task scheduling. The kernel logs the start timestamp (T_s) of a time-critical computation with maximum termination time T_A, and sets an alarm for the desired deadline ($t_{dead} = T_s + T_A$). Either the computation ends in time, that is, until the deadline ($T_e \leq t_{dead}$) and the alarm does not trip, or else the alarm trips and causes the immediate activation of the fail-silence switch, crashing the whole site.

Improving the Coverage of Timely Communication

A similar principle can be used to improve the coverage of the bounded message delivery delay property (**Ps** 3). Message delivery delays are measured and compared to previously specified bounds. Round-trip duration measurement is used, since we are in the presence of a distributed duration. From a structural point of view, the idea is to apply the fail-awareness concept[12] to build a fail-aware broadcast as the basic kernel communication primitive to serve the TCB control channel. If a message is not delivered on time, an exception is raised that causes the immediate activation of the fail-silence switch, crashing the whole site.

Note that we cannot be as aggressive as with processing: we can only act on delivery of the message and not at the deadline instant. If we acted at the deadline point, we might be acting on either a crash or a timing failure. Whatever we did might not be appropriate in the case of crash, since we would be interfering with an assumed failure mode. For example, since we would crash a TCB that failed to receive a message until the maximum delivery time, the crash of a sending TCB (a normal event as per the assumptions) would cause all recipient TCBs to commit suicide, crashing the entire system. This would be inappropriate, since the crash of a TCB causes no safety problems, so we only crash TCBs after they receive a late message. On the other hand, with our technique, if a sending TCB or the network would cause all of the TCBs to receive a late message, then all the TCBs would crash as well. However, from a safety viewpoint this would be appropriate, in order to avoid contamination.

8. Conclusion

In essence, our paper is an attempt to provide a unifying solution for a problem that has been addressed by several research teams: how to reconcile the need for synchrony, with the temporal uncertainty of the environment. Such systems are characterized by having timeliness assumptions that may be violated, producing timing failures in components. An analysis of the effect of timing failures on application correctness shows that besides the obvious effect of delay, there are undesirable side effects: a long-term one, of decreased coverage of assumptions; and an instantaneous one, of contamination of other properties. Even when delays are allowed (e.g. soft real-time systems), any of these effects can lead to undesirable behavior of a system. Dealing with them requires some capability of acting timely at critical moments.

We have proposed an architectural construct that we have called Timely Computing Base (TCB), capable of executing timely functions, however asynchronous the rest of the system may be. Special hardware is not mandatory to achieve synchrony of the TCB. The quality of that synchrony (speed, precision) is the only thing that may be improved by special components. By implementing only a small and simple part of the system, the TCB can affordably implement stronger properties. It acts in fact as a coverage amplifier, for the execution of certain functions where high assurance is desired.

We introduced a computational model based on the TCB, generic enough to support applications (algorithms, services, etc.) based on any synchrony of the payload system, from asynchronous to synchronous. From a system design viewpoint, this is the same as saying from non real-time to hard real-time. Namely: we proposed a few services for the TCB to fulfill its role— timely execution, duration measurement, timing failure detection; and we devised an application programming interface allowing to propagate the notion of time from the TCB to payload applications. Finally, we discussed the implementation of the TCB services and the enforcement of the synchronism properties of the TCB platform, by using fail-awareness techniques.

We are currently developing an experimental prototype of a TCB. The infrastructure is composed of normal Pentium PCs, running Real-Time Linux, and communicating over a LAN. We expect to be able to publish the results of our experiments in the near future.

References

[1] C. Almeida and P. Veríssimo. Timing failure detection and real-time group communication in *quasi-synchronous* systems. In *Proceedings of the 8th Euromicro Workshop on Real-Time Systems*, L'Aquila, Italy, June 1996.

[2] R. Braden, Ed., L. Zhang, S. Berson, S. Herzog, and S. Jamin. RFC 2205: Resource ReSerVation Protocol (RSVP) — version 1 functional specification, Sept. 1997. Status: PROPOSED STANDARD.

[3] R. Brand. Iso-Ethernet: Bridging the gap from WAN to LAN. *Data Communications*, July 1995.

[4] A. Burns and A. Wellings. *Real-Time Systems and Programming Languages*. International Computer Science Series. Addison-Wesley publishers Ltd., 1996.

[5] A. Casimiro and P. Veríssimo. Timing failure detection with a timely computing base. In *Third European Research Seminar on Advances in Distributed Systems*, Madeira Island, Portugal, May 1999. Available as Tech. Report, Department of Informatics, University of Lisboa, DI/FCUL TR-99-8.

[6] T. Chandra and S. Toueg. Unreliable failure detectors for reliable distributed systems. *Journal of the ACM*, 43(2):225–267, Mar. 1996.

[7] F. Cristian. Probabilistic clock synchronization. *Distributed Computing*, 3(3):146–158, 1989.

[8] F. Cristian and C. Fetzer. The timed asynchronous distributed system model. *IEEE Transactions on Parallel and Distributed Systems*, pages 642–657, Jun 1999.

[9] D. Dolev, C. Dwork, and L. Stockmeyer. On the minimal synchronization needed for distributed consensus. *Journal of the ACM*, 34(1):77–97, Jan. 1987.

[10] C. Dwork, N. Lynch, and L. Stockmeyer. Consensus in the presence of partial synchrony. *Journal of the ACM*, 35(2):288–323, Apr. 1988.

[11] D. Essamé, J. Arlat, and D. Powell. PADRE: A Protocol for Asymmetric Duplex REdundancy. In *Proceedings of the Seventh IFIP International Working Conference on Dependable Computing for Critical Applications*, pages 213–232, San Jose, California, USA, Jan. 1999.

[12] C. Fetzer and F. Cristian. Fail-awareness: An approach to construct fail-safe applications. In *Proceedings of the 27th Annual International Fault-Tolerant Computing Symposium*, pages 282–291, Seattle, Washington, USA, June 1997. IEEE Computer Society Press.

[13] C. Fetzer and F. Cristian. A fail-aware datagram service. *IEE Proceedings - Software Engineering*, pages 58–74, April 1999.

[14] M. J. Fischer, N. A. Lynch, and M. S. Paterson. Impossibility of distributed consensus with one faulty process. *Journal of the ACM*, 32(2):374–382, Apr. 1985.

[15] F. Jahanian. Fault tolerance in embedded real-time systems. *LNCS*, 774:237–249, 1994.

[16] E. D. Jensen and J. D. Northcutt. Alpha: A non-proprietary os for large, complex, distributed real-time systems. In *Proceedings of the IEEE Workshop on Experimental Distributed Systems*, pages 35–41, Huntsville, Alabama, USA, Oct. 1990. IEEE Computer Society Press.

[17] H. Kopetz, R. Zainlinger, G. Fohler, H. Kantz, P. Puschner, and W. Schutz. An engineering approach towards hard real-time system design. *LNCS*, 550:166–188, 1991.

[18] M. d. Prycker. *Asynchronous Transfer Mode: Solution For Broadband ISDN*. Prentice-Hall, third edition edition, 1995.

[19] H. Schulzrinne, S. Casner, R. Frederick, and V. Jacobson. RTP: A transport protocol for real-time applications. Proposed Standard RFC 1889, Audio-Video Transport Working Group, Jan. 1996.

[20] P. Veríssimo and C. Almeida. Quasi-synchronism: a step away from the traditional fault-tolerant real-time system models. *Bulletin of the Technical Committee on Operating Systems and Application Environments (TCOS)*, 7(4):35–39, Winter 1995.

[21] P. Veríssimo, P. Barrett, P. Bond, A. Hilborne, L. Rodrigues, and D. Seaton. The Extra Performance Architecture (XPA). In D. Powell, editor, *Delta-4 - A Generic Architecture for Dependable Distributed Computing*, ESPRIT Research Reports, pages 211–266. Springer Verlag, Nov. 1991.

[22] P. Veríssimo and A. Casimiro. The timely computing base. DI/FCUL TR 99–2, Department of Computer Science, University of Lisboa, Apr. 1999. Short version appeared in the Digest of Fast Abstracts, The 29th IEEE Intl. Symposium on Fault-Tolerant Computing, Madison, USA, June 1999.

Reconfiguration Based Failure Restoration in Wavelength-routed WDM Networks

G. Sai Kiran Reddy   G. Manimaran*   C. Siva Ram Murthy

Dept. of Computer Science and Engineering, Indian Institute of Technology, Madras 600036, INDIA
*Dept. of Electrical and Computer Engineering, Iowa State University, Ames, IA 50011, USA
sai@hpc.iitm.ernet.in, gmani@iastate.edu, murthy@iitm.ernet.in

Abstract

Wavelength-division multiplexed (WDM) optical networks using wavelength-routing are considered to be a potential candidate for next generation wide-area backbone networks. The key component in such networks is the lightpath network (LPN) manager. The functions of the LPN manager include setting up the logical topology, sustaining the network by monitoring traffic and network parameters, and handling node and/or link failures. Failure handling in WDM networks is of prime importance due to the nature and volume of traffic these networks carry. Failure detection is usually achieved by exchanging control messages among nodes with timeout mechanisms. Failure restoration can be done either by rerouting only the failed lightpaths (LPs) or by reconfiguring all the existing LPs in the network. The reconfiguration approach involves finding new LPs in the faulty network (LP design) and realizing these new LPs by selectively removing the old LPs (LP realization) with the objective of minimizing the service disruption to the ongoing calls. The existing work on reconfiguration approach considers only the LP design and ignores the LP realization. In this paper, we first propose an architecture for the LPN manager highlighting the importance of LP realization in the reconfiguration based failure restoration, then propose performance measures and heuristic algorithms for LP realization. We evaluate the effectiveness of the LP realization algorithms through simulation studies.

1 Introduction

All-optical networks employing wavelength division multiplexing and wavelength-routing are becoming a promising candidate for future generation wide-area networks (WANs) due to their capability to provide high bandwidth, low bit error rate, and scalability [1]. A wavelength-routed WDM network consists of optical wavelength-routing nodes interconnected by point-to-point fiber links using an arbitrary topology. End nodes with a limited number of optical transmitters and receivers are attached to the routing nodes. A routing node with I input links and O output links, handling W wavelengths, consists of I wavelength demultiplexers, O wavelength multiplexers, and W optical switches one for each wavelength. A message arriving at any of the input links on some wavelength can be routed to any one of the output links on the same wavelength, without requiring any electro-optical conversion, by controlling optical switches, demultiplexers, and multiplexers.

A *lightpath* (LP) is an "optical communication path" between two nodes, established by allocating the same wavelength throughout the route of the transmitted data [2]. A lightpath is uniquely identified by a wavelength and a physical path. The requirement that the same wavelength must be used on all the links along the selected path is known as the *wavelength continuity* constraint. This constraint is unique to the WDM networks. Two lightpaths can use the same fiber link, if and only if they use different wavelengths. If two nodes are connected by a lightpath, a message can be sent from one node to the other without requiring any buffering and electro-optical conversion at the intermediate nodes. In other words, a message is transmitted in one (light) hop from the source to the destination. A good routing and wavelength assignment algorithm is critically important to improve the performance of the wavelength-routed WDM networks [3]-[6]. The routing and wavelength assignment problem on WDM networks has been addressed in [3] and a lower bound on the blocking probability for any routing and wavelength assignment algorithm was obtained.

LPs in a WDM network form a logical network over the underlying physical network. This logical network, called LP network (LPN), allows flexible management of network resources. The heart of the LPN is the LPN manager. The important functions of an LPN manager are LPN configuration (wherein the logical topology is set up over the physical network), LPN monitoring (wherein the delay, throughput and call blocking are monitored), and failure[1] handling.

Failure handling in WDM networks is of prime importance due to the nature and volume of traffic these networks carry. There are two broad approaches to handle failures in WDM networks: (i) protection based and (ii) restoration based. In *protection based* networks, dedicated protection mechanisms such as redundant LPs are established to cope with failures [7]-[10]. In *restoration based* networks, on detecting a failure, an attempt is made to restore the LPs from the failure [11]. Failure detection is usually achieved by exchanging control messages among the nodes with time-out mechanisms. Failure restoration can be done either by rerouting only the failed LPs or by reconfiguring all the existing LPs in the network. The reconfiguration approach involves finding new LPs in the faulty network (*LP design*) and then realizing these new LPs by selectively removing the old LPs (*LP realization*).

In this paper, we consider reconfiguration approach, which is a restoration based approach, for failure handling. Earlier work [12] on reconfiguration approach considers only the LP design phase and ignores the LP realization phase. In this work, we first highlight the importance of LP realization phase and then present new algorithms and performance metrics for it.

The rest of this paper is organized as follows. Section 2 first introduces the architecture of the proposed LPN manager. Section 3 deals with the second phase of the reconfiguration approach, namely, the LP realization. The problem formulation, metrics involved, and the proposed heuristics are discussed here. Section 4 evaluates the performance of the LP realization algorithms through simulation studies. Finally, in section 5, some concluding remarks are made.

2 Lightpath Network Manager

The LPN manager is the key component of the wavelength-routed WDM network architecture and is responsible for LPN configuration, LPN monitoring, and failure restoration. Fig. 1 shows the architecture of the proposed LPN manager. The LPN is present in all the nodes of the network. Although it is present in all the nodes, all of its modules (functionalities) need not be activated. For example, the *Long-term LP establishment module* is activated only at the central node, while the *Short-term LP establishment module* is active in all the nodes.

There are two main phases associated with the design and operation of WDM networks: network design and network operation. In the design phase, first, a set of LPs, known as *logical topology*, that is to be established statically over the physical topology is found, then it is implemented over the network. For finding the logical topology,

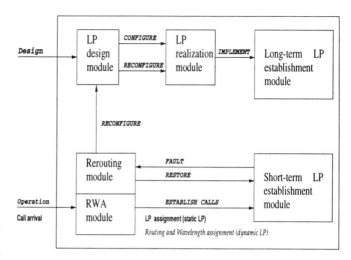

Figure 1. Architecture of LPN Manager

LP design algorithm is used which uses physical topology and information such as estimated traffic and propagation delay between nodes as inputs. The LPs are then actually implemented using the *LP realization* and *Long-term LP establishment* of which the former decides the order in which the LPs are to be established and the latter actually sets the switches along the paths of the LPs. During network design, LP realization need not be present as the order in which the LPs are implemented does not make sense when the network is not operational. However, during operational phase, LP realization plays a crucial role in minimizing the service disruption experienced by ongoing connections when the logical topology undergoes reconfiguration online. We will elaborate this aspect later.

During the operation phase, when a call arrives, a statically established LP is assigned if available; otherwise, a new LP is found dynamically [1]. For dynamically finding a route and wavelength for a given LP, *Routing and Wavelength Assignment (RWA)* component of *Assignment module* is activated. If RWA[2] succeeds, the new LP is implemented using *Short-term LP establishment module*; otherwise, the call is rejected. When a call terminates, if it is a dynamic LP, it is torn down; otherwise (static LP), it is not torn down, instead, its usage state is changed from "in use" to "not used".

During the operation phase, when a node/link failure occurs, either rerouting (rerouting only the failed LPs) or reconfiguration (reconfiguring all the existing LPs) is invoked to restore the affected LPs. For a given failure scenario, it is crucial to determine which of these techniques to use, and is beyond the scope of this paper. We believe that it may be better to use rerouting for failure restoration on a short-term

---

[1] In this paper, the term "failure" refers to "fault" in the literary sense.

[2] RWA might employ a rerouting strategy within itself. The term "rerouting" used in this paper has a different meaning.

basis (refer Fig.1) and use reconfiguration on a long-term basis, i.e., the number of failures since last reconfiguration has exceeded a threshold. The other situation to invoke reconfiguration would be when rerouting fails to restore the affected LPs even if the threshold has not reached. The reconfiguration is not only invokable for failure restoration, but also for designing a better LPN based on the current traffic demand and other dynamically varying network parameters. This is very relevant in the context of growing number of new generation applications over the Internet. Therefore, LP realization assumes a great significance during the operational phase of a WDM network.

2.1 Functions of the LPN Manager

To summarize the above discussion, the three major responsibilities of the LPN manager are LPN configuration, LPN monitoring, and failure handling.

LPN Configuration: LPN configuration involves the setting up of LPs, or the reconfiguration of the existing LPs in the network. There are two levels at which LPN configuration can be done. Long-term configuration of LPN is done during the network design phase. This phase is generally invoked by the network designer. The long-term LPN (re)configuration may also be invoked to take into account the dynamics in traffic demand and network topology. Short-term configuration of LPN is used for rerouting one or more existing LPs to accommodate a new LP or to restore faulty LPs after a failure has occurred.

LPN Monitoring: The LPN manager is also expected to monitor the LPN performance parameters (such as delay, throughput, call blocking ratio) and connectivity. Depending on the current performance and connectivity, the LPN reconfiguration phase may be triggered.

Fault-tolerance: Due to the critical nature and high volume of traffic these networks carry, the reliability expected of these networks is very high. Therefore, fault handling must be integral part of the LPN manager. To achieve this, efficient techniques for fault detection and restoration must be developed.

2.2 Failure Restoration

As stated earlier, the failure restoration becomes a key issue, bearing in mind the huge traffic load that these networks carry. There are two ways in which link failure(s) can be coped with. In the first approach, called *rerouting*, only the LPs that are affected by the link failure are routed along alternate physical paths without affecting the other existing LPs [11, 13]. But the restored LPs may take sub-optimal paths. In this approach, the number of nodes involved is a subset of all the nodes in the network. This is an advantage of this approach because most of the nodes may not be made

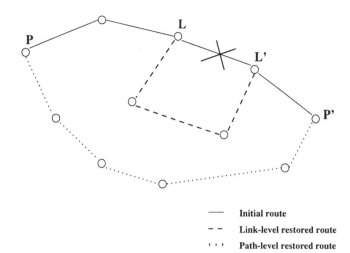

— Initial route
- - Link-level restored route
' ' ' Path-level restored route

Figure 2. Rerouting Approach for Restoring Link Failures

aware of the link/node failure and continue with their processing, unaffected. But the principal advantage is that the existing calls, which are not affected by the link failure, are never disrupted. Rerouting can be done between two nodes that terminate the failed link (LL' in Fig.2) or between all node pairs that terminate the failed LP (PP' in Fig.2). The former technique is called as *link-level* restoration and the latter is termed as *path-level* restoration [13].

A second approach, called *reconfiguration approach*, wherein services on LPs are disrupted for a short duration and an altogether new logical topology is constructed, has the potential to restore more LPs than the rerouting approach. But the drawback with this approach is that there may be a possibility of disrupting more number of LPs that are not affected by the link.

2.3 Reconfiguration Based Failure Restoration

A situation wherein the reconfiguration approach restores more number of LPs than the rerouting approach is illustrated using the following example.

Fig.3 shows a 6-node network with 7 links. Using one of the several available logical topology design algorithms, we arrive at the logical topology of the network with LPs as shown in Table 1. We shall represent the LP as $< s, d, w >$ where s and d are the end nodes of the LP and w is the wavelength on it. The calls are represented as $<< s, d >>$ where s and d represent the source and destination nodes that are communicating.

We assume a set of calls to be in the network. The calls in progress are $<< 0, 5 >>$, $<< 2, 4 >>$, $<< 2, 5 >>$,

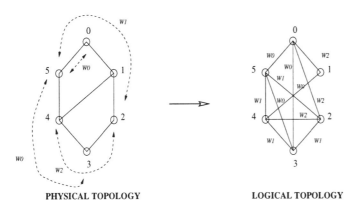

PHYSICAL TOPOLOGY   LOGICAL TOPOLOGY

3-4 LINK FAILURE   *RECONFIGURATION*

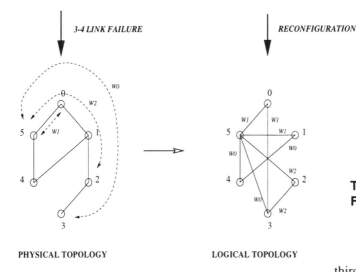

PHYSICAL TOPOLOGY   LOGICAL TOPOLOGY

Figure 3. Reconfiguration Approach for Restoring Link Failures

Lightpath	Path	Wavelength
0-1	0-5-4-1	w2
0-2	0-1-2	w2
0-3	0-1-2-3	w0
0-5	0-5	w0
1-4	1-4	w0
2-3	2-3	w1
2-4	2-3-4	w2
2-5	2-1-0-5	w1
3-4	3-4	w1
3-5	3-4-5	w0
4-5	4-5	w1

Table 1. Logical Topology of the Network in Fig.3, before the Failure of Link 3-4

Lightpath	Path	Wavelength
0-3	0-1-2-3	w1
0-5	0-5	w1
1-4	1-4	w0
1-5	1-4-5	w1
2-3	2-3	w2
2-5	2-1-0-5	w2
3-5	3-2-1-0-5	w0
4-5	4-5	w0

Table 2. Logical Topology of the Network in Fig.3, after the Failure of Link 3-4

and $<< 3, 5 >>$ (these calls are shown in the top physical topology of Fig.3). Now, if there is a link failure between nodes 3 and 4, the calls that are disrupted are $<< 2, 4 >>$ (2-3-4) and $<< 3, 5 >>$ (3-4-5). Now, our aim is to restore both these disrupted calls, if possible.

Let us first consider the rerouting approach. We search for an alternative path from the logical topology in Fig.3. The corresponding wavelengths for the LPs are shown in Table 1. For $<< 2, 4 >>$, the possible alternatives are:
$< 2, 5, w1 >< 5, 4, w1 >$,
$< 2, 0, w2 >< 0, 5, w0 >< 5, 4, w1 >$, and
$< 2, 3, w1 >< 3, 0, w0 >< 0, 5, w0 >< 5, 4, w1 >$.
The first alternative cannot be a solution because the call $<< 2, 5 >>$ is in progress and it uses $< 2, 5, w1 >$. The second alternative cannot be employed due to lack of wavelength continuity i.e., $< 2, 0, w2 >$ is on wavelength w2, $< 0, 5, w0 >$ on w0, and $< 5, 4, w1 >$ on w1. The

third alternative is also rejected for the same reason. Thus $<< 2, 4 >>$ cannot be restored.

Now, the next disrupted call is $<< 3, 5 >>$. The corresponding alternate routes are:
$< 3, 0, w0 >< 0, 5, w0 >$,
$< 3, 2, w1 >< 2, 5, w1 >$,
$< 3, 0, w0 >< 0, 2, w2 >< 2, 5, w1 >$, and
$< 3, 2, w1 >< 2, 0, w2 >< 0, 5, w0 >$.
The first alternative route cannot be used because a call $<< 0, 5 >>$ is already in progress. In the second alternative, $< 2, 5, w1 >$ is already being used by the call $<< 2, 5 >>$. Thus, the second alternative too cannot be used. The third and fourth alternatives do not satisfy the wavelength continuity constraint and therefore we summarily reject them. Thus, we observe that the rerouting approach fails to restore any of the failed LPs.

Next, we consider the reconfiguration approach for failure restoration. In this method an altogether new logical topology was arrived at and is shown in Fig.3 (bottom logical topology) and Table 2. This logical topology is obtained by employing any of the known LP design algorithm on the network, minus the failed link. That is, the LP design algorithm is run for the modified network. We see from Fig.3

that although we are not able to restore call $<< 2, 4 >>$, we do restore the call $<< 3, 5 >>$. The above example illustrates how the reconfiguration approach can better the number of LPs restored.

Henceforth, we shall concentrate on the reconfiguration approach only. The reconfiguration approach is a two-tier approach. The first phase is called the *LP design phase* which basically involves finding suitable LPs, based on the knowledge of parameters such as traffic between nodes and delay between the nodes. The subsequent phase, called the *LP realization phase*, pertains to the way that these new LPs are established onto the existing faulty network. These new LPs are established on the existing network, by selectively replacing the existing LPs with the newly computed LPs.

3 LP Realization

To the best of our knowledge, there is no prior work on LP realization. Present literature considers both LP design and LP realization phases as a single unit, the LP reconfiguration unit. Baroni [12] found that the reconfiguration (restore-all) approach yielded far better results than the rerouting (restore-only) approach in terms of the number of additional wavelengths required. But the price to pay is the complexity involved. In a network that is functioning, the usage of reconfiguration approach would hinder the working of the existing LPs. Some of the LPs which are not affected by the link failure may be disrupted. Thus, our objective is to minimize the disruption time, while restoring more number of failed LPs. The LP realization phase implements the new LPN by replacing the ongoing LPN with the objective of minimizing the service disruption. The new LPN is obtained by employing an LP design algorithm for the current network topology and traffic demand. In this section, we first propose the overall LP realization strategy and follow it up by proposing heuristics that provide the order for realizing the LPs onto the existing faulty network.

3.1 LP Realization Strategy

The following notation is used.

- *Ptot*: set of LPs in the network, before link failure(s);

- *Pfault*: set of failed LPs;

- *Pold*: set of non-disrupted LPs;

- *Pnew*: set of LPs that are currently being disrupted and need to be established;

- $dis[p]$: disruption time on the LP p. The disruption times of all the LPs are stored in the *dis* array;

- HEURISTIC(P): heuristic applied on a set P;

LP_Realization()
begin
    dis[j] = 0, $\forall$ j, j ϵ Ptot;
    Pnew = Pfault;
    While (Pnew != Φ)
        p = HEURISTIC(Pnew);
        For (i= 1 *to* hop(p))
            If e^{ip} clashes with $\exists e^{jq}$, q ϵ Pold
                release(q);
                Pnew = Pnew $\cup$ {q};
                Pold = Pold - {q};
           dis[l]++, $\forall$ l ϵ Pnew;
        Pnew = Pnew - {p};
end.

Figure 4. Lightpath Realization Strategy

- e^{ip}: i^{th} edge of the LP p;

- *release(p)*: release the resources allocated to the LP p;

- *hop(p)*: number of hops in the LP p.

In the proposed algorithm, the LP realization is carried out as follows. During the LP realization, the selection of LP, from the list of disrupted LPs, is based on a heuristic function (HEURISTIC()) which takes the set $Pnew$, as the argument. The selected LP is realized upon the existing network in the following fashion. Any *old* LPs that share the same wavelength on a link with the LP that is being realized on the network is said to *clash* with it. The *old* LPs that clash with the *new* LP are removed. These LPs are added in the set $Pnew$. The corresponding disruption times of all the LPs in the set $Pnew$ are updated. A check is enforced for finding a clash for each of the hops of the *new* LP that is to be established. After each hop, the *disruption time* for each of the LPs in the list of disrupted LPs is incremented. This way, we measure the disruption time of the LPs in terms of the hop-length units. This is repeated until the new topology completely replaces the old topology. A pseudo code for the LP realization algorithm is shown in Fig.4.

3.2 Performance Metrics

In a network which is running smoothly, if a link fails and LP reconfiguration approach is to be used, the main concern would be to reduce the disruption time of all the LPs, i.e., the LPs that are not affected by the link failure must not be disrupted for a long time and need to be restored at the earliest. To take this into account, we introduce a metric called *mean call disruption time* (MDT), which is the mean time taken for a call to be reinstated in the network. This should be as less as possible. If MDT were to be the only yardstick to measure the performance of an

LP realization algorithm, then the algorithms which restore only the short LPs will perform better. Taking this biasing aspect into consideration, we propose another metric, *Fairness Factor* (FF), which is measured as the standard deviation of the disruption times of all the LPs with respect to MDT. Ideally, one would expect this to be zero, indicating fairness to all LPs. The lesser the FF, the better is the algorithm.

3.3 Problem Formulation

In the LP realization phase of the LP reconfiguration approach, the objectives are

- to minimize the MDT, which is defined as follows:

$$MDT = \frac{\Sigma_p dis(p)}{\mid Pnew \mid}, \ p \in Pnew$$

- to minimize the FF, which is defined as follows:

$$FF = \sqrt{\frac{1}{\mid Pnew \mid} \Sigma_p \{dis(p) - MDT\}^2}, \ p \in Pnew$$

3.4 LP Realization Heuristics

We propose three heuristics for the LP realization scheme, namely, *Shortest Lightpath First* (SLPF), *Longest Lightpath First* (LLPF) and *Maximum Disrupted lightpath First* (MDF). The heuristics are invoked in Fig.4 as HEURISTIC().

SLPF: When the SLPF heuristic is invoked on the set *Pnew*, we get the disrupted LP with the smallest number of hops. This is to be realized upon the existing network. Thus, the disrupted LPs are realized onto the existing network in ascending order of the number of hops. It can be seen that there is biasing towards the LPs with shorter hop lengths. Thus, this heuristic does not perform well with respect to the FF metric. Due to the fact that LPs with shorter hop-lengths are given higher priority, the performance of this heuristic with respect to the MDT metric is expected to be very good. This is because of the fact that when an LP with small hop-length is being established, the rest of the disrupted LPs are disrupted for lesser time intervals than when an LP with large hop-length is being established.

LLPF: The mode of selection of LP in this heuristic is diametrically opposite to the one used in the previous heuristic. The disrupted LP with the largest hop-length is established first. The stigma of biasing carries on, even to this heuristic. This method supports the cause of the LPs with larger hop-lengths, neglecting the LPs with shorter hop-lengths. Thus, this heuristic is also not expected to perform well with respect to the FF metric. This may not

perform well with respect to the MDT metric too owing to the previously stated fact that when an LP with small hop-length is being established, the rest of the disrupted LPs are disrupted for lesser time intervals than when an LP with large hop-length is being established.

MDF: From the above discussion, it is clear that both SLPF and LLPF are not fair. Thus, to provide fairness to the choice of LPs, we present another heuristic, called MDF. The underlying idea behind this algorithm is to select the LP which has been disrupted for the longest time interval, i.e., the choice of LP is based not on the hop-length, like in the above two heuristics, but on the disruption time. It is expected that this heuristic will outperform the rest with respect to the FF metric.

3.5 An Example

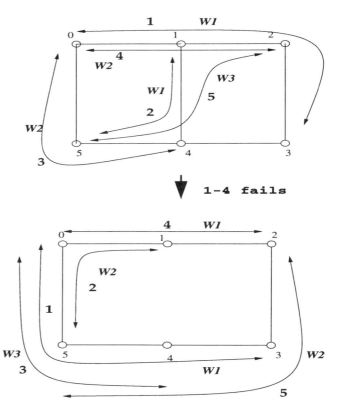

Figure 5. Example Network

Consider the network shown in Fig.5. It is a 6-node network. Table 3 shows the list of LPs on the network. Now, suppose that the link 1-4 fails. By reconfiguration approach, we have calculated the new LPs, whose path can be seen in the second column of the Table 3. We now need to realize this new set of LPs onto the existing network. To achieve this, we use the LLPF heuristic in this example.

Now, $Pnew$ consists of 2 elements namely, 2 and 5. Applying the LLPF heuristic on $Pnew$ gives 5. We now need to establish LP 5, which is the lightpath between the nodes 2 and 5 through the nodes 3 and 4. The first hop of the physical path of LP 5 is 5-4. The LP that uses this link 5-4, in the old topology is LP 3. Now, the LP 3 not only shares the common link but also the same wavelength (w2) and so LP 3 is said to clash with the new LP 5. Therefore, we disrupt LP 3 and update the $Pnew$ and $Pold$ sets. The corresponding disruption times are incremented in the $dis[]$ array. This can be seen in the third row of Table 4. Continuing, the next hop of the physical path of LP 5 is 4-3. None of the LPs on the existing networks use the link and thus only the $dis[]$ array is updated. The next link on the path of LP 5 is 3-2. LP 1 is using this link, but on a different wavelength. Therefore, LP 1 does not clash with LP 5 and is not disrupted. The $dis[]$ array is updated again. Now, the new LP 5 has been realized on the existing network with a service disruption of 3 time units (i.e., $dis[5] = 3$).

In a similar way, the rest of the LPs are also established onto the old network. The corresponding entries can be seen in Table 4.

The value of MDT is computed as,

$$MDT = (5 + 5 + 7 + 6 + 3)/5 = 5.20$$

The value of FF is computed as,

$$FF = \sqrt{\frac{1}{5}[(-.2)^2 + (-.2)^2 + (1.8)^2 + (.8)^2 + (-2.2)^2]}$$
$$= 1.497$$

LP	Path before link failure after link failure	Wavelength	Hop-length
1	0-1-2-3	w1	3
	0-5-4-3	w1	3
2	1-4-5	w1	2
	1-0-5	w2	2
3	4-5-0	w2	2
	4-5-0	w3	2
4	2-1-0	w2	2
	2-1-0	w1	2
5	5-4-1-2	w3	3
	5-4-3-2	w2	3

Table 3. List of LPs in the Example Network

4 Performance Study

We have conducted extensive simulation studies to evaluate the effectiveness (in terms of two metrics) of the pro-

Ptot : {1, 2, 3, 4, 5}
Pfault : {2, 5}
Pold : {1, 3, 4}
Heuristic Used : LLPF

Mean Disruption Time : 5.2
Fairness Factor : 1.497

p (LP)	Link	Clash (LP)	Pnew (LP)	Pold (LP)	1	2	3	4	5
			2,5	1,3,4	0				0
5	5-4	3	2,5,3	1,4	1	1			1
	4-3	-	2,5,3	1,4	2	2			2
	3-2	-	2,5,3	1,4	3	3			3
2	1-0	4	2,3,4	1	4	4	1	x	
	0-5	-	2,3,4	1	5	5	2		
3	4-5		3,4	1		x	6	3	
	5-0		3,4	1			7	4	
4	2-1	1	4,1	Φ	1		x	5	
	1-0		4,1		2			6	
1	0-5		1		3			x	
	5-4		1		4				
	4-3		1		5				
			Φ		x				

(dis[ ] (time) columns: 1, 2, 3, 4, 5)

Table 4. Implementation of the LLPF LP Realization Algorithm on the Example Network

posed LP realization algorithms for a wide variety of network parameters. The simulation experiments were conducted on randomly generated networks to avoid any influence of network topology features on the performance results. The random networks (with 20 nodes) were generated using the method described in [14]. In our simulation studies, the following parameters were varied: number of wavelengths (W), number of calls existing in the network (called the *load* (C)), maximum number of hops in a lightpath (H), and connectivity of the network topology (BETA).

4.1 Effect of Network Connectivity

When a link fails, it may not be possible to find alternate paths, if the network is sparsely connected. The necessity of reconfiguration will not arise in such situations. As the connectivity (represented by BETA) increases, the chances of invoking reconfiguration increase, thus leading to some of the existing calls being disrupted. This increase in the number of disrupted calls is reflected as an increase in the disruption time, as is seen in the initial portion of the graph in Fig.6.

Consider the situation, when the connectivity of the network is fairly high. This allows more number of alternate paths from one node to another, thus reducing the chances of disturbing an already existing call. This decrease can be observed in the latter portion of the curve. It can be intuitively visualized that in a network, there will be more number of calls with smaller number of hops. Thus, the idea of establishing a short lightpath first, will provide better dividends, as for as MDT is concerned. Conversely, the LLPF algorithm should prove less effective than its counterparts. The performance of the MDF algorithm is in-between the others. This is due to the fact that the choice of lightpath is not based on the hop-length. The argument that the need for reconfiguration is less in a sparsely connected network, holds good with reference to Fig.7 too. There is an increase in the possibility of reconfiguration as the connectivity increases. When the connectivity is fairly high, the number of disjoint alternate paths is more and thus the FF subsides. The best bet, as far as FF is concerned, is the MDF algorithm, because the underlying idea behind the algorithm is to provide fairness in the choice of the lightpaths that are to be realized. The performance of this algorithm is by far the best, in this regard. The SLPF algorithm holds an edge over the LLPF algorithm with respect to the FF metric, owing to the fact that the number of calls with less number of hops is far more than that of those with more number of hops.

4.2 Effect of Maximum LP Hop Length

Intuitively, as the constraint on the maximum allowable hop-length is reduced, i.e.,when the maximum hop-count is increased, the number of failed calls that can be reconfigured increases, thus resulting in an increase in the disruption time. This is the general trend that one can expect. This is observed in the initial portion of Fig.8. But after a certain stage, the increase in the upper limit of the number of hops does not affect the network because, although the bounds are relaxed, alternative paths may not exist. Therefore, the algorithms tend to saturate beyond maximum half length of 8. The SLPF algorithm performs better than the others with regard to the MDT, as seen in Fig.8.

In Fig.9, for lower values of the maximum number of hops, there is a steep rise in the value of the FF. This is due to the fact that the number of lightpaths that can be reconfigured, increases. After reaching a limiting value, the rise is much more gradual, owing to the fact that the mere increase in the maximum hop-count will not ensure the existence of a better path, i.e., the choice of the best path will come at the limiting value and will not change thereafter. The performance of the MDF algorithm surpasses the rest, as for as FF is concerned.

4.3 Effect of Network Load

As the number of calls existing in the network at the time of failure (called Load) increases in the network, the possibility of the calls sharing common physical links (on different wavelengths) becomes more, thus the disruption time is expected to increase as the load increases. This is the general trend that one expects. This situation is captured in

Fig.10. The initial phase on the curve, wherein the change is negligible, represents the case when the number of restored calls is less.

As expected, the SLPF algorithm performs better than the rest, with respect to MDT. With respect to the FF, as the load increases, the chances of the existence of a call with maximum number of hops is more. As such calls increase, the FF, the standard deviation of the disruption time with respect to the MDT, increases. This is observed in Fig.11. The performance of the MDF algorithm supersedes that of the other algorithms, as expected.

5 Conclusions

Wavelength-routed WDM networks are being considered as a potential candidate for next generation wide-area backbone networks. The LPN manger is the key component in such networks. In this paper, we have proposed an architecture for the LPN manager highlighting the significance of LP realization phase, and proposed performance metrics (MDT and FF) and heuristic algorithms (SLPF, LLPF, and MDF) for LP realization. From the simulation studies of the LP realization algorithms, we draw the following conclusions:

• The SLPF heuristic scores over the rest with respect to the MDT metric, followed by the MDF heuristic and lastly, the LLPF heuristic. The result confirms the intuitive idea that in general, the disrupted LPs need to wait for a lesser time when a short LP is being established, as compared to the case when a longer LP is being established.

• The MDF heuristic outperforms the rest with respect to the FF metric, thus justifying our claim. LLPF performs better than the SLPF with respect to the FF metric. This may be attributed to the combined effect of the following facts: (i) the LPs with shorter hop-lengths outnumber those with longer hop-lengths and (ii) SLPF give priority to the shorter-hop LPs. The above two facts, show that the degree of biasing of the SLPF towards the shorter LPs, is escalated by the fact that the shorter LPs outnumber the longer LPs. Thus, LLPF proves to be more fair than the SLPF heuristic.

The proposed LPN manager architecture opens up many directions for further research, which includes (i) developing sophisticated LP realization heuristics that aim at improving both the metrics, (ii) developing algorithms that integrate LP design and LP realization in such a way that both routing and disruption aspects are effectively captured, (iii) developing schemes that effectively integrate rerouting and reconfiguration, with mechanisms for finding the favorable conditions under which each of these approaches can be invoked, and (iii) devising mechanisms for triggering reconfiguration, based on network traffic dynamics.

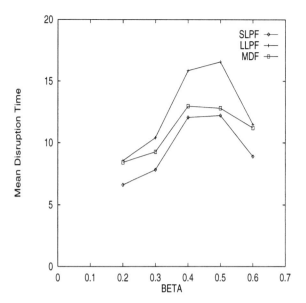

Figure 6. Performance of the LP realization heuristics with respect to the MDT metric for different values of BETA, with W=4, H=10 and C=250

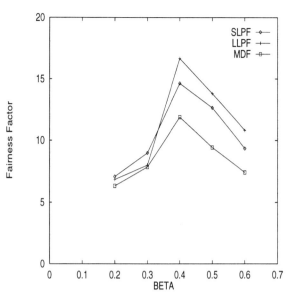

Figure 7. Performance of the LP realization heuristics with respect to the FF metric for different values of BETA, with W=4, H=10 and C=250

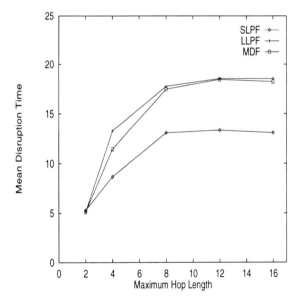

Figure 8. Performance of the LP realization heuristics with respect to the MDT metric for different values of H, with BETA=0.4, W=4 and C=250

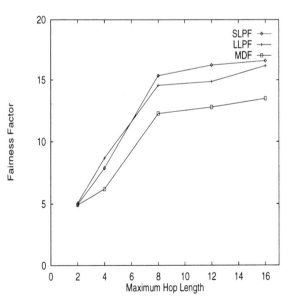

Figure 9. Performance of the LP realization heuristics with respect to the FF metric for different values of H, with BETA=0.4, W=4 and C=250

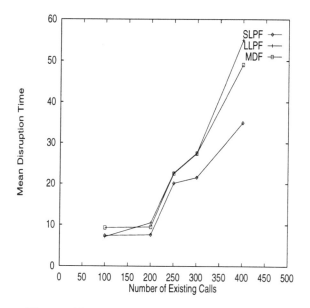

Figure 10. Performance of the LP realization heuristics with respect to the MDT metric for different values of C, with BETA=0.4, W=4 and H=10

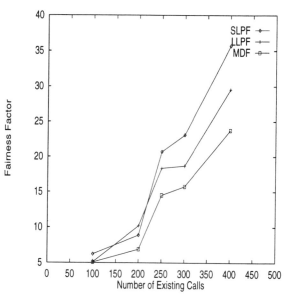

Figure 11. Performance of the LP realization heuristics with respect to the FF metric for different values of C, with BETA=0.4, W=4 and H=10

References

[1] R. Ramaswami, "Multiwavelength Lightwave Networks for Computer Communications", *IEEE Communications,* vol.31, no.2, pp.78-88, Feb. 1993.

[2] I. Chlamtac, A. Ganz, and G. Karmi, "Lightpath Communications: An Approach to High Bandwidth Optical WANs", *IEEE Transactions on Communications,* vol.40, no.7, pp.1171-1182, July 1992.

[3] R. Ramaswami and K.N. Sivarajan, "Routing and Wavelength Assignment in All-optical Networks", *IEEE/ACM Transactions on Networking,* vol.3, no.5, pp.489-500, Oct. 1995.

[4] B. Mukherjee, S. Ramamurthy, D. Banerjee, and A. Mukherjee, "Some Principles for Designing a Wide-Area Optical Network", *IEEE/ACM Transactions on Networking,* vol.4, no.5, pp.684-696, Oct. 1996.

[5] S. Baroni and P. Bayvel, "Wavelength Requirements in Arbitrarily Connected Wavelength-routed Optical Networks", *IEEE/OSA Journal of Lightwave Technology,* vol.15, no.2, pp.242-251, Feb. 1997.

[6] S. Baroni, P. Bayvel, and J.E.Midwinter, "Influence of Physical Connectivity on the Number of Wavelengths in Dense Wavelength-routed Optical Networks", in Proc. *OFC,* pp.25-26, 1996.

[7] Y. Miyao and H. Saito, "Optimal Design and Evaluation of Survivable WDM Transport Networks," *IEEE JSAC,* vol.16, no.7, pp.1190-1198, Sep. 1998.

[8] S. Ramamurthy and B. Mukherjee, "Survivable WDM Mesh Networks, Part I - Protection," *IEEE Infocom,* pp.744-751, 1999.

[9] G. Mohan and C. Siva Ram Murthy, "Routing and Wavelength Assignment for Establishing Dependable Connections in WDM Networks," in Proc. *IEEE FTCS,* pp.94-101, 1999.

[10] G. Mohan and A.K. Somani, "Routing Dependable Connections with Specified Failure Restoration Guarantees in WDM Networks," in Proc. *IEEE Infocom,* 2000.

[11] B.T. Doshi, S. Dravida, P. Harshavardhana, O. Hauser, and Y. Wang, "Optical Network Design and Restoration," *Bell Labs Technical Journal,* pp.58-83, Jan.-Mar. 1999.

[12] S. Baroni, "Routing and Wavelength Allocation in WDM Optical Networks", Ph.D. Thesis, Department of Electronics and Electrical Engineering, University College of London, May 1998.

[13] A. Jourdan, F. Bakhti, L. Berthelon, F. Bruyere, M.W. Chbat, D. Chiaroni, C. Drion, G.J. Eilenberger, M. Garnot, F. Masetti, P.A. Perrier, and M. Renaud, "Key Building Blocks for High-Capacity WDM Photonic Transport Networks," *IEEE JSAC,* vol.16, no.7, pp.1286-1296, Sep. 1998.

[14] B.M. Waxman, "Routing of Multipoint Connections", *IEEE JSAC,* vol.6, pp.1617-1622, Dec. 1988.

Session 14C

Fast Abstracts

Workshop on

Dependability of IP Applications Platforms and Networks

Introduction to the Workshop
On Dependability of IP Applications, Platforms and Networks

Welcome to the Dependability IP workshop. Today, more and more new services are using IP infrastructures to build applications. Therefore, it is very crucial to make the IP infrastructures as dependable as possible in order to provide highly reliable, scalable and secured services. This workshop intends to bring together people working on various dependability technologies of IP infrastructures and IP based applications to exchange ideas and solutions.

The workshop has three sessions. The first session focuses on new dependability IP technologies. There are four presentations in this session covering topics such as Internet applications, CORBA platforms, firewalls and routers. The second session focuses on the dependability issues of system and network layers in the IP infrastructures. There are four presentations in this session. The first presentation is on the Internet infrastructure failures and the second presentation is on the Windows 2000 dependability features. The last session discusses the dependability issues of some popular IP middleware and applications. We have three presentations in the last session including topics on CORBA, E-Speak and VoIP.

I would like to thank many people in making such a workshop possible. First, I would like to thank all authors and speakers and all PC members – Christof Fetzer, Rick Harper, Craig Labovitz, Haim Levendel, Sampath Rangarajan, Chris Smith, Falguni Sarkar, Kishor Trivedi and Yi-Min Wang – for reviewing papers and suggesting speakers. I would also like to thank the General Chair, Basil Smith, and Program Chairs, Doug Blough and Karama Kanoun, for the help in putting together the program and publication.

I invite all of you to enjoy the workshop and benefit from the wonderful papers and presentations of the workshop.

Yennun Huang
Program Chair

Towards Continuous Availability of Internet Services through Availability Domains

Nicholas Bowen[1]   Daniel Sturman[1]   Tina Ting Liu[2]

[1]IBM T.J. Watson Research Center
30 Saw Mill River Rd.
Hawthorne, NY 10532

[2]265 CSRL, MC 228
University of Illinois at Urbana-Champaign
1308 W. Main St.
Urbana, IL 61801

E-mail: {bowen|sturman}@us.ibm.com ting@crhc.uiuc.edu

Abstract

The increasing number of Internet users has caused a dramatic increase in electronic commerce. This growth is outpacing technologies for dependability causing traditional views of high availability to come under question. In particular, Internet failures are a phenomenon external to the owner of a commerce site that must be dealt with, and therefore, geographically distributed servers are a basic availability requirement for e-commerce sites. Geographic distribution provides an opportunity to view users in different roles based on those distributed components they must access. This paper presents an approach based on partitioning on-line function into domains, each of which provides service to users in a specific role. Coordination between domains is eliminated as much as possible by exploting application-specific knowledge. Once partitioned, availability techniques may be applied to each domain independently. We argue such an approach is necessary to deal with the geographic distribution of system components imposed by the nature of the Internet and maps well onto real e-commerce deployments.

1. Introduction

The Internet continues to grow at a rapid rate in terms of both the number of users and the number of Internet sites. With the increased number of users has come an increase in the amount of commerce being done over the Internet. The business need for electronic commerce (e-commerce) has been so compelling that its growth has outstripped the development of technologies for dependability. As a result, e-commerce has become a two edged sword, bringing a huge opportunity for reaching new customers but also creating a huge marketing liability in the event of outages which often become highly publicized.

Electronic commerce presents new challenges for high availability. Much of the network is out of the control of the individual business so the scope of any high availability solution must include these effects. The characteristics of the workloads are extremely non-uniform over time with many reports of peak load to average load ratios between 5:1 to 10:1. Workload variance is quite dependent on the nature of the business. For example, online financial services often experience a surge when the market opens or when a major event that impacts the market occurs. As people's home become more integrated into the Internet, there will be a strong correlation between effective advertisement and web traffic. Since availability is a function of the web server being able to handle these peak loads, businesses often purchase additional capacity above the peak loads.

The classical thinking of a single clustered server to provide high availability and scaling needs to be rethought. Geographic distribution has become a standard approach to Internet availability. For example, in the Nagano Olympics, IBM used geographically distributed servers to deal with these issues [4, 5]. Large software companies such as Netscape, Microsoft, and Sun employ extensive use of "mirrored" web sites [12, 3]. The use of multiple sites provides the ability for a business to avoid outages due to local Internet failures - either real failures or load induced outages that could be caused by high traffic to the web site in question.

However, companies are starting to provide electronic business functions such as sales, support, order processing, and supply-chain automation. These functions require coordination between disparate components, not all of which may be simply mirrored to provide geographic distribution. Traditional views of high availability designs and availability analysis come under question in this new environment. First, the complexity of the end-to-end solution make an overall availability model very difficult. The notion of a

559

availability measure for the web server (e.g., 99.9% availability) does not necessarily provide the true availability for all end users. Further, given that a single server may be involved in both B2C (Business to Consumer such as on-line sales), B2B (Business to Business such as supply-chain automation), and internal operations (such as order processing) then the availability must be mapped to these different environments. There are several important observations to make. First, Internet failures and load induced failures mean that geographically distributed servers are a basic requirement. Second, we must delineate the availability discussion with respect to the roles of various user segments (e.g., the B2B and B2C end users). Third, after these roles have been defined, their particular behavior may be leveraged to remove dependencies and enable geographic distribution.

In this paper, we present an approach to Internet availability based on partitioning on-line function into domains each of which provides service to users in a specific role. Coordination between domains is eliminated as much as possible. Where coordination cannot be eliminated, we use application-specific knowledge to convert synchronous operations into asynchronous operations. Once this partition is performed, availability techniques may be applied to each domain independently, according to acceptable expense and business need.

2. Environment

The Internet provides a unique set of challenges for building a dependable system. Central to these challenges is the fact that there is no central administration of the Internet. Because any individual can only directly control a small portion of the total infrastructure, traditional end-to-end design and failure analysis techniques cannot be applied. For example, using N-way active replication techniques to ensure constant server availability provides limited additional dependability when the service provider contracted to provide network access does not provide a similar level of resilience.

It has been shown that network failures, on average, outnumber and tend to be of longer duration than server failures [9, 10]. Specifically, network related outages can account for over half of Internet server unavailability [9]. This problem is likely to be further exacerbated given the growth patterns of the Internet [6]. As a result, Internet applications must have the following characteristics:

- Geographic distribution: geographic distribution of Internet interfaces is essential not just for response time, but minimize the impact of regional network outages.

- Loose coupling between components: A consequence of geographic distribution is that high network latencies make traditional transactional consistency techniques impractical. Asynchronous communication, such as transactional messaging, is a preferred approach. Transactional messaging systems provide a transactional guarantee for senders that messages have been sent, and for receivers that messages have been received, but do not include the entire message flight as part of a transaction. Using a transactional messaging system, messages may be guaranteed to be delivered "exactly-once", but their delivery is asynchronous and may be delayed due to system failures en route.

Where components cannot be geographically distributed, usually because of inherent synchronization, then other subsystems must be designed to operate as long as possible in the face of the components failure. Consequently, applications must be analyzed in terms of different roles such that, although one group may experience a failure, other groups may continue to operate. Thus, the system is never all-down, but may be down for users in particular roles in the organization.

3. System Design and Architecture

This section describes our proposed system design and architecture. First an example of the architecture is presented followed by a formal description of the architecture. We build off the observations about Internet services made in Section 2 and show, first with an example and then more generally, how highly available services may be built despite this environment.

3.1. Example

To illustrate our approach to factoring web applications, consider the example of an on-line store shown in Figure 1. The figure illustrates the traditional mechanism for deploying a scalable web application. A series of web servers handle requests from customers. The web servers process these order requests and modify two databases: one for order requests, and another tracking available inventory. Order handlers obtain lists of orders to be processed by accessing the databases directly.

Increased customer load is handled by increasing the number of web servers in the cluster (Database Management System (DBMS) capacity may also be scaled in a similar manner, but is not shown here). Increasing the number of servers also improves availability. However, as we will show in Section 4, Internet availability becomes the dominant factor in total system availability and, therefore, improving the availability of the web servers or DBMS alone has little impact on total system availability.

The monolithic nature of this system presents some limitations in terms of scaling and availability. In terms of scalability, static web requests can achieve a much higher raw

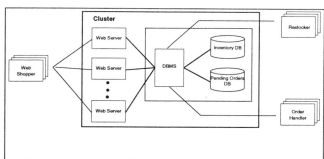

Figure 1. A traditional scalable web application deployed on a cluster.

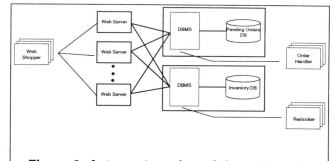

Figure 2. A *factored* version of the web application shown in Figure 1. Application characteristics are exploited to allow decoupling of components.

performance (e.g., units of work per second) that database oriented work. We calibrate this statement with some references to industry standard benchmarks. A Dell PowerEdge 6350 4-way SMP server has been benchmarked at 386 tpc-c transactions per second[1] [8]. The same hardware has been benchmarked at 13,000 SpecWeb requests per second. In this example, a comparable server is capable of performing 36 times more for static web requests than database transactions.

This difference in capability, coupled with the variability of workloads, creates significant challenges in scaling up the overall capability of web sites, i.e. the ratio between static web requests driven by browsers and DBMS activity driven by purchasing is nearly impossible to predict. This often leads to an application design where the database application is hosted on a different physical server than the web server. In this case, the application design uses a form of remote synchronous communications between the servers, *e.g.*, SQL's Distributed Relational Database Architecture (DRDA). The complexity of scaling this type of system often leads to a complicated system design where the availability of the web service is dependent on multiple physical servers and multiple software subsystems (e.g., web servers plus database servers). In an environment where geographic distribution is mandatory, these types of highly synchronous approaches become untenable.

Instead we propose the *factored* solution shown in Figure 2. Specific knowledge of the application allows us to geographically distribute components *without* reducing total system availability. In particular, we exploit the following characteristics of this application to convert synchronized interactions into asynchronous ones.

- The two database systems are used in different, non-overlapping, roles, and therefore maybe decoupled.

- Allowing some variability in inventory control allows the web servers to be decoupled from the inventory

---

[1]23,187.90 tpc-c/minute

database. This may be done in one of two ways. Either small units of inventory may be periodically allocated to each web server or *business rules* may be derived through analysis of the business process that allow web servers to optimistically sell items much as airline flights may be overbooked today. In either case, the need for a transactional database operation is eliminated.

Asynchronous operations are carried out over the Internet using a transactional messaging system. Examples of such systems include IBM's MQSeries [2] and Microsoft's MSMQ [7]. Such systems guarantee the eventual delivery of a message despite transient network outages and node failures. Guaranteed messaging systems provide a programmer the simple semantics of "PUT a message on a named queue" or "GET a message from a named queue." Program control is returned to the programmer immediately even if there are failures in other parts of the system, including failures of the link, the remote system or the receiving application. These systems use database logging techniques to ensure these qualities of service. That is, if either the remote system or the link has failed when a program attempts to PUT a message to a remote application, the message will be transactionally logged on the local system. When the link recovers and the remote system reconnects, the message will be delivered. The message delivery protocol provides an "exactly-once" guarantee that the message does not get lost in transit.

The use of guaranteed message causes the programmer to restructure the application in a fairly dramatic manner as we will discuss in Section 3.2. However, once this is done the implementors have significant flexibility in the implementation of the system. For example, Figure 3 shows a system that has multiple front end systems and multiple back end systems. The front end structure provides increased capacity and allows the system to tolerate Internet

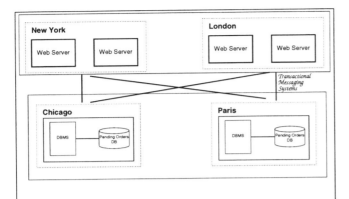

Figure 3. A web application partitioned into two availability domains. Each availability domain has a replicated sub-domain.

related outages. The multiple back end systems are for simple business reasons; that there is a requirement for a US based and European based distribution center. In addition to satisfying a business need, this back end structure could also be used to increase availability.

There are many web sites that are using geographic distribution of servers to achieve scalability. This work advances the state of the art by formalizing an architecture that

- Independently considers the availability needs of various user communities based on their roles. That is, the Internet users have different requirements than the accountants or the order handler. Many current systems view the availability of the system as the reference point while we argue that the system should be decomposed into independent units.

- The end-to-end system has faulty components. We claim that the quest to create a single highly available system is fruitless, the structure and dynamics of the Internet bring out new conditions such as load surges and network failures that require new thinking.

- Geographic distribution is a fundamental requirement for scale and availability.

3.2. System Architecture

We now propose a new architecture for highly available web sites that is based on several key principles.

- A system is partitioned into availability domains to serve the availability needs of each unique user community.

- One must independently consider the roles of various users groups.

- An information architecture that maps the aggregate data of the enterprise into availability domains.

- A strong reliance on application behavior allows a decoupling of domains and the use of guaranteed messaging technology to interconnect the availability domains in the information architecture.

Availability Domains are defined as a collection of resources (both computation and information) that are solely required to satisfy the availability requirements for a particular collection of roles. That is, availability domains are defined so that availability analysis for a particular role should be limited to the implementation of a single availability domain. The system architecture consists of a collection of availability domains that are interconnected through a persistent, transactional messaging system.

Information Architecture In situations where the information of the enterprise maps directly into the availability domains, the result is a collection of completely independent systems connected by a transactional messaging system. Unfortunately, most real life systems cannot be partitioned in such a manner.

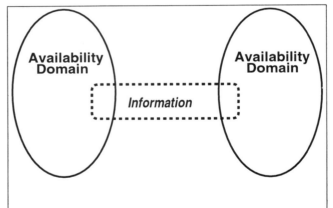

Figure 4. When information is shared across two availability domains, it creates an availability dependency that must be removed.

We define the Information Space as the total amount of data across all availability domains. An important issue is the mapping of the Information Space to availability domains. The easiest case is when the information can be partitioned to map completely inside an availability domain. For example, a particular set of static web pages is easily limited to a single availability domain: when two availability domains must share a common set of web pages, they are easily copied and treated as two sets of resources. In the cases when a file system is shared by multiple availability domains, distributed file systems such as DFS [11] can be used. DFS provides a weak consistency guarantee of eventual consistency and therefore may scale over a campus or city. The complicated situation arises when operational data, such as that stored in a relational database, overlaps multiple availability domains as is shown in Figure 4.

In general, data with high consistency guarantees requires a greater amount of synchronization and, therefore, becomes more problematic when shared across availability domains. The dependencies of such synchronization result in availability dependencies across availability domains. In such cases, our methodology dictates that application-specific information be exploited to break the dependency, that is, convert a tightly synchronous interaction on into a loosely synchronous or asynchronous one. Synchronous remote access techniques violate our basic principles of no synchronous dependencies between availability domains, as discussed in Section 3.1.

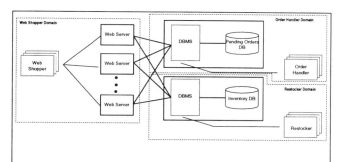

Figure 5. The *factored* **version of the web application partitioned into three domains. The web shopper domain contains several independent web server sub-domains.**

In Figure 5 we illustrate a business with three availability domains: webshopper, order handler, restocker. The webshopper role consists of the end users on the Internet. Order handlers process pending orders, bill the customer, and ship product. The restocker role periodically evaluates inventory and orders items from suppliers. The domains are designed to eliminate information dependencies between them to as great a degree as possible. For example, the webshopper is only dependent on the web cluster and failures in other availability domains will have no impact on the webshopper.

The other important aspect of defining availability domains is that each group has very different availability requirements. Although this is not a new observation, current monolithic systems are designed for the maximum of all availability requirements. In our example, the webshopper

has the highest availability requirements with an objective of 24x7 dial tone availability. The order handler has much weaker availability requirements. In fact, we could envision that the order handler has a PDA with enough orders queued up that an outage of the main system for several hours would not have an impact. Role based availability requirements fundamentally improve the overall availability in a manner that would not have been possible building around a monolithic system structure.

Sub-Domains are defined as a building block component of an availability domain. These are independent units (they could be large scalable clusters) that can be easily added into an existing availability domain to provide additional capacity, increased availability, or geographical presence (e.g., in the case of a new distribution center). A sub-domain can be the result of properly structuring the information architecture between the associated availability domains. In Figure 3, we show a case where the availability domain for the webshopper has been decomposed into two subdomains and placed in separate geographic locations. The design objective is to be able to achieve linear horizontal scaling when adding additional subdomains.

4. Analysis

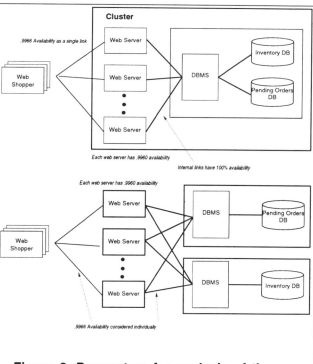

Figure 6. Parameters for analysis of the example shown in Section 3.1.

To demonstrate the effectiveness of our approach, we analyze the example discussed in Section 3.1. Two scenarios are modeled: web servers deployed in a centralized cluster, and web servers deployed in a geographically distributed configuration.

For these scenarios, we are primarily concerned with failures that cause web servers to be universally inaccessible to clients. That is, we are primarily concerned with a failure of the wide-area network, that portion of the network servicing our servers, or the failure of the servers themselves. We do not model the failure of those network resources servicing a particular client or group of clients. This assumption is justified in two ways *based on the nature of the webshopper role*. Our primary reason is that we assume a large enough number of clients that unavailability of any one client is not significant. Our secondary reason is that we are primarily concerned with presenting a high quality of service for *business* services. Consequently, client-end network failures are of less concern as they not only deny client's access to our servers, but to any competing servers.

We model the Internet connection to the cluster as a single network link, where the entire connection is either all up, or all down. The clustered servers are considered to be available when the network connection is available and at least one server in the cluster is available. For purposes of this analysis, we will ignore the availability of the DBMS (assume 100%). The availability of the cluster solution is shown in Equation 1.

$$A_{cluster} = A_{net}(1 - (1 - A_{server})^N) \qquad (1)$$

Conversely, for the distributed case, the network connection to each distributed server is assumed to fail independently of all others. The distributed servers are considered to be available when there is at least one available server whose network connection is also available. The availability of the distributed solution is shown in Equation 2.

$$A_{dist} = 1 - (1 - A_{net} \times A_{server})^N \qquad (2)$$

Values for 1 to 5 web servers in both scenarios are shown in Table 1 . We assume a network availability of 0.9966. Server availability was 0.9960. These values were derived from [9] by consolidating various classes of network failures and server failures.

The table illustrates that the limit of Equation 2 is 100% availability, but that the limit of Equation 1 is A_{net}.

The advantage of defining independent availability domains is more pronounced when you consider the availability interactions between the web servers and the DBMS. In the synchronous case, failure of the DB impacts the availability of a web server. This relationship is shown in Equation 3.

Servers	Cluster Availability	Distributed Availability
1	0.992614	0.992614
2	0.996584	0.999945
3	0.996600	0.999996
4	0.996600	0.999999997
5	0.996600	0.99999999998

Table 1. Sample values for the availability of the webshopper domain.

$$A_{cluster} = A_{net}A_{DBMS}(1 - (1 - A_{server})^N) \qquad (3)$$

In the case of the factored solution, however, the DBMS availability may be assumed to be 100% since failures of the DBMS do not affect users in the webshopper role. Table 2 shows the reduced availability of the cluster solution for three web servers based on several values for DBMS availability:

DBMS Availability	Cluster Availability
0.9	0.89694
0.99	0.98663
0.999	0.99560
0.9999	0.99650
0.99999	0.99659

Table 2. Availability of the webshopper domain in a cluster based on DBMS availability.

The level of availability achievable through the distributed solution is only possible because the database was decoupled from the web servers, and this decoupling was possible only because application specific information was exploited. By using either business rules or pre-fetching of inventory (as discussed in Section 3.1), we are able to provide clients in the web shopper role with a highly available service.

We now examine the order handler role to see if we can improve its availability in a similar manner. For this role, things are more complicated: geographically distributing a database is fundamentally more difficult than the relatively stateless web servers. However, we can exploit the following facts:

1. We "own" the application for the order handlers. Consequently, we can impose more of the burden for decoupling on the order handlers than we did for the web shoppers.

2. There are fewer order handlers and each makes requests against the database less frequently. Thus, intermittent failures are much less of a problem than long duration failures.

Based on these observations, we propose an application-specific solution. A process at the order DB periodically pushes work out the various order handlers (via a transactional messaging system). Each order processor stores work assignments in a local database so that they are not lost due a crash failure. Order processing completion is sent back to the DB and the DB uses this information to measure each order processor's service rate. Enough work is advanced to each order processor to allow for failure and recovery of the DB. A balance must be struck between continued availability for the order processor (having enough work to do) and centralized control and load balancing order processing jobs to minimize order processing time. For example, each incoming order could be immediately farmed out to an order processor, thereby providing optimal resilience to DB failures. However, if an order processor crashed in this case, those jobs would be marooned until the order processor recovered. Availability for this role is measured as the ability for the order processors to keep working and, to a lesser degree, adequate response time to orders placed.

5. Conclusion

In this paper we have presented an approach to building highly available, scalable web services. This approach is built around the observation that, fundamentally, traditional availability techniques are poorly suited to these applications because the Internet cannot be made more reliable by any single application developer. Instead, developers must use geographic distribution to improve service availability.

Applications are divided into availability domains, each of which independently provides an available service to a particular role of participants using the Internet service. Synchronization between availability domains must be reduced to a minimum to avoid availability dependencies between domains. In some cases, this naturally falls out from the application, but in other cases application-specific knowledge must be exploited to reduce a tightly synchronous interaction to a loosely synchronous or asynchronous one.

This work is complementary to other approaches to building web services such as the WebOS [14]. WebOS provides operating systems services such as naming, persistent storage, and security to applications on wide-area networks. Having universal underlying services of this nature would simplify the implemenation of availability domains.

This work is an initial step towards Internet service availability and, as such, opens many questions. A better understanding and model of Internet availability would be particularly useful. Specifically, a study comparing failure patterns based on geography would be especially useful in evaluating our approach. Such a study would provide a better understanding of the performance implications of creating availability domains and using persistent messaging techniques for communication. This analysis becomes more complex when the trend to augment traditional point-to-point messaging with many-to-many communication [1] is taken into account.

Within this work we have illustrated our ideas with one, fairly typical, example. We prototyped the factored application described in this paper. The prototype uses IBM WebSphere and DB2, with asynchronous transaction messaging provided by MQSeries. In the future, we intend to use this system evaluate our ideas against a wider number of real-world deployments. Evaluation against upcoming practices is also of interest. For example, push-based information distribution is particularly promising for certain application areas [13]. However, Internet failures may be particularly damaging to such applications. The ability to make such services highly available will significantly impact the speed of their adoption.

References

[1] G. Banavar, T. Chandra, R. Strom, and D. Sturman. A case for message oriented middleware. In *Proceedings DISC '99*, 1999.

[2] B. Blakeley, H. Harris, and R. Lewis. *Messaging & Queuing Using the MQI*. McGraw-Hill Series on Computer Communications. McGraw Hill, New York, New York, 1995.

[3] V. Cardellini, M. Colajanni, and P. S. Yu. Dynamic load balancing on web-server systems. *IEEE Internet Computing*, 3(3):28–39, May-June 1999.

[4] J. Challenger, A. Iyengar, and P. Dantzig. A scalable and highly available system for serving dynamic data at frequently accessed web sites. In *Proceedings of ACM/IEEE Supercomputing '98 (SC98)*, Orlando, Florida, November 1998.

[5] J. Challenger, A. Iyengar, and P. Dantzig. A scalable system for consistently caching dynamic web data. In *Proceedings of IEEE INFOCOM'99*, New York, New York, March 1999.

[6] R. Govindan and A. Reddy. An analysis of internet inter-domain topology and route stability. In *Proceedings of INFOCOM '97*, volume 2, pages 850–857, 1997.

[7] A. Homer and D. Sussman. *Professional MTS and MSMQ With VB and ASP*. Wrox Press Ltd., 1998.

[8] I. International. Ideas top performers - tpc-c. http://www.ideasinternational.com/benchmark/tpc/tpcc.html.

[9] M. Kalyanakrishnan, R. K. Iyer, and J. U. Patel. Reliability of internet hosts: A case study from the end user's perspective. In *Proceedings of the International Conference on Computer Communications and Networks*, Las Vegas, Nevada, 1997.

[10] C. Labovitz, A. Ahuja, and F. Jahanian. Experimental study of internet stability and backbone failures. In *Proceedings fo*

the *Twenty-Ninth Annual International Symposium on Fault-Tolerant Computing (FTCS-29)*, pages 278–285, Madison, Wisconsin, June 1999.

[11] E. Levy and A. Siberschatz. Distributed file systems: Concepts and examples. *ACM Computing Surveys*, 22(4):321–374, December 1990.

[12] D. Mosedale, W. Foss, and R. McCool. Lessons learned administering netscape's internet site. *IEEE Internet Computing*, 1(2):28–35, Mar.-Apr. 1997.

[13] V. Technologies. ebusiness: Extending the enterprise. White Paper, 1999. http://www.vitria.com.

[14] A. Vahdat, T. Anderson, M. Dahlin, E. Belani, D. Culler, P. Eastham, and C. Yoshikawa. Webos: Operating system services for wide area applications. In *Proceedings of the Seventh IEEE Symposium on High Performance Distributed Computing*, July 1998.

Issues in Interoperability and Performance Verification in a Multi-ORB Telecommunications Environment

Cheng J. Lin, Alberto Avritzer
AT&T Network Computing Services
Middletown, NJ 07748
{linch,avritzer}@att.com

Elaine J. Weyuker
AT&T Labs - Research
Florham Park, NJ 07932
weyuker@research.att.com

Sai-Lai Lo
AT&T Labs Cambridge
Cambridge, UK
S.Lo@uk.research.att.com

Abstract

The rapid change of the telecommunications environment demands that new services are developed and deployed quickly and legacy systems are integrated seamlessly. While emerging technologies and standards such as CORBA will allow rapid solution integration via shared reusable components, new issues arise for interoperability and performance assurance in a highly heterogeneous environment. In this paper, we first identify these issues in a multi-vendor and multi-ORB telecommunications environment. We then propose a systematic approach for interoperability verification using a reference ORB and industry standard test suites. We extend our interoperability-testing framework to performance verification, where the scope of the tests is detailed and the design strategy is analyzed.

Keywords: CORBA Interoperability, Performance Verification, Test Suite Design, Multi-ORB Environment.

1 Introduction

The last few years have witnessed the rapid change of the telecommunications environment driven by competition, customer expectation and new enabling technology. It has become essential to be able to rapidly develop and deploy new services while reducing business costs and improving efficiency. As a result, we have seen an increase in highly heterogeneous systems that integrate new development paradigms along with legacy systems, and we can expect to see this become even more commonplace as the telecommunications market continues to evolve, yielding ever-increasing numbers of features and new technologies that need to be rapidly integrated into the environment. Ideally, heterogeneity and open systems enable us to use the best combination of hardware and software components for each portion of an enterprise when the right standards for interoperability between these components are in place. However,

dealing with heterogeneity in a distributed telecommunications environment is by no means easy. Therefore, one of the greatest challenges for a telecommunications company today is to effectively address the problems encountered during solution integration. We expect that the seamless integration of data and systems will be a key to competitiveness in an open telecommunications market.

One of the recent shifts in software development paradigms has been the increased emphasis on sharing similar software components, using a distributed object architecture. In our organization at AT&T, we began this shift in 1996 with the adoption of CORBA as the vehicle for implementing mission-critical operations support systems. These systems are being built using flexible and reusable components that reside in accessible repositories. The expectation is that this will lead to a reduction in both development and maintenance costs, and an increase in the quality of the resulting software.

An *Object Request Broker (ORB)* is the central component of a CORBA implementation, providing the vehicle for the flow of information between objects. There are many different commercially-available ORBs addressing a variety of user needs. For example, some ORBs support multi-threading, while others use the single-threading model. Some ORBs provide high levels of security, while others are more open. In addition to the implementation differences among ORBs, there are also other reasons to use more than one ORB within an organization. The primary reason is that a large company does not want to become vendor-dependent. If that vendor was to go out of business or stop producing the particular product that the enterprise is dependent on, that could be catastrophic for the organization. Even if the ORB was still available, it might no longer be meeting the organization's quality standards, leading them to decide to migrate their systems to a different ORB.

By using multiple ORBs which have been tested and shown to interoperate, it should be possible to replace the existing ORB with another when necessary without enormous cost and disruption. For that reason, many organizations have intentionally introduced multiple ORB products into their enterprises. In addition, when dealing with a very large company like AT&T, there may be many different organizations producing software, and making their own decisions about ORB selection, independent of other organizations' decisions. It is certainly possible that even though certain systems were not initially intended to interact with each other, through organizational realignment or other reasons, it may well happen that these systems do have to be able to interact with each other. Knowing that components using different ORBs are able to interact with each other, should minimize problems associated with a new requirement that components be integrated even though they were not initially expected to interact.

The paper is organized as follows. Section 2 provides a review of related work on CORBA interoperability and performance. Section 3 discusses interoperability issues in a multi-ORB telecommunications environment. Section 4 presents a systematic approach for interoperability verification. We extend the infrastructure of the interoperability test suites to performance verification in Section 5 where some of the important performance measurements and testing strategies are discussed. Section 6 presents conclusions.

2 Related Work

In this section, we review related work in the areas of ORB interoperability and performance of distributed object systems.

The Open Group is a company that has been developing a branding program for ORB implementations to check for conformance with the CORBA 2.1 specification. CORVAL (CORBA Validation) [18] is one of its successful projects designed to facilitate and encourage multi-vendor deployment of ORB products by identifying conforming and interoperable ORB products. However, the test suites developed by the Open Group to date only support basic conformance testing. In particular, even the Internet Inter-ORB Protocol (IIOP) tests were only configured to test client/server communications within a single ORB environment, rather than a multi-system, multi-vendor environment. The CORBAnet showcase [3], developed by DSTC, demonstrates ORB interoperability to some extent by linking hardware, operating software, and ORBs from key industrial vendors. However, it does not do this comprehensively since it only shows that some ORBs can interoperate, and that the IIOP functionality is implemented by the participating vendors. In December 1998, the Distribution Object Promotion Group (DOPG) in Japan conducted some transaction level and IIOP level interoperability verification tests [12]. While the tests were rather comprehensive in terms of server/client combinations, the test items comply only with CORBA 2.0 and most of the tests cover only primitive data types and IIOP functions that

are not thorough enough to guarantee interoperability. For example, no effort was reported on testing the combination of different data types and various failure conditions and corrupted messages - an important practical problem.

While the above projects focused mainly on the functionality of the CORBA core, the Object Management Group (OMG) Interoperable Naming Service [9] addresses issues affecting interoperability with CORBA services (Naming Service), which provides a mechanism to allow multiple clients to access a common Initial Naming Context. Other research work related to interoperability in a telecommunications environment includes the evaluative framework for CORBA and WWW interoperability issues [8], interoperability in a multiple-provider telecommunications environment [4], and the interoperability metric [11] for quantitative measurements of interoperability.

There are three primary areas of research related to performance issues associated with distributed object technology.

The first area involves the development of high-performance ORB implementations, such as The ACE ORB (TAO) [16]. This project demonstrated the applicability of real-time CORBA to a wide-range of applications, particularly those having very tight timing constraints. Other ORB implementations such as the OmniORB [7] focused on exploiting the protocol and other characteristics of the CORBA specification, resulting in a high performance ORB that is also highly adaptable to a variety of network transports.

The second related research direction involves the use of design patterns which are intended to permit the widespread reuse of software architectures with the associated goal of enhancing software quality [13, 14]. Although this work is not directly related to the problems we face that are caused by the use of multiple ORBs, design patterns facilitate the development of distributed object systems.

The third area of interest involves research aimed at making an ORB a competitive programming environment in the high-performance application market. For example, significant performance gains have been reported in [5] for distributed objects via extensive runtime, transport and marshaling optimization. Other research of interest presented four Quality of Service (QoS) algorithms designed to enforce predetermined levels of service agreements between clients and objects via admission control of service requests aimed at managing the allocation of resources at a single component [2]. Although these algorithms are designed for distributed objects in general, we are investigating their use in a multi-ORB environment and preliminary indications are promising. It should be clear that the research work we surveyed above has some relevance to CORBA interoperability and performance assurance, none of it is explicitly focused on these issues. Therefore, the work we present in this paper provides a foundation for examining directly interoperability issues in a multi-ORB telecommunications environment. Our ultimate goal is to develop a systematic and thorough testing approach that can assure that ORB interoperability has been demonstrated. This will be done by using a reference ORB, industry standard test suites, and a metric developed to assure comprehensiveness. Another goal is to develop a performance testing approach using performance modeling and benchmarking.

3 Quality Issues

In this section, we will discuss various quality issues such as ORB interoperability, performance, scalability and reliability that need to be considered when a CORBA-based distributed object system is to be built using various integration approaches. It is not enough to rely on component and object technology to allow the quick development and deployment of new features for mission-critical systems, if these features cannot meet our performance and reliability standards, or cannot function properly when the workload is scaled.

There is certainly an indication that these are real issues since whereas many reusable components have been built in recent years, relatively few have been reused to a systematic and widespread degree. Our ultimate goal is to be able to easily and effectively glue existing components together to provide new services.

3.1 ORB Interoperability

The CORBA Object Model identifies various distributed transparencies that must be supported within a single ORB environment, such as location transparency. An ORB provides the mechanisms by which objects transparently make and receive requests and responses on different machines in heterogeneous distributed environments. ORB Interoperability specifies a comprehensive, flexible approach to supporting networks of objects that are distributed across and managed by multiple, heterogeneous CORBA-compliant ORBs, which can be viewed as extending transparencies to span multiple ORBs.

A general definition [10] of ORB interoperability involves the ability of a client on ORB A to invoke an OMG IDL (Interface Definition Language)-defined operation on an object on ORB B, where ORBs A and B were independently developed. For interoperability between ORBs, the ORB core and ORB services used within an ORB must be identified. It is important to recognize that CORBA interoperability is *not* synonymous with CORBA compliance. In particular, two ORBs may be fully compliant yet still not be able to interoperate. The two primary cases in which that may happen involve situations in which either something is not fully or unambiguously specified and hence different

ORB vendors will have interpreted the partial specification differently, and those situations that have been deliberately left to the vendor's discretion in the specification.

Interoperability is defined by Section 12.3.4 of the CORBA specification [10]. In addition to the fact that certain aspects of CORBA features are not defined precisely enough to ensure source code portability, whether deliberate or not, there is also no prohibitions against extensions to the CORBA specification which have led to a variety of vendor extensions further complicating interoperability among various ORBs. This too has complicated ORB interoperability. Nonetheless, since we are striving to increase the amount of component reuse that will occur, it is essential that we develop testing techniques that can be used to assure that components developed using different ORBs can safely interoperate.

3.2 Performance

Performance evaluation and verification of integrated systems are other relevant aspects of interoperability whenever performance is affected by the integration of interoperable components. When using a custom-designed development process, there are long development cycle times that are useful for identifying and fixing anticipated performance problems. In contrast, the shared distributed object approach is partly motivated by the necessity of developing new features quickly. Because components are shared, the performance degradation of one component could impact many different services. Also, conventional ORBs incur significant throughput and latency overhead [15]. These overheads stem from such things as large amounts of data copying, non-optimized presentation layer conversions, internal message buffering strategies that produce non-uniform behavior for different message sizes, and long chains of intra-ORB virtual method calls. This implies the need to protect our telecommunications infrastructure by providing performance optimization, verification and QoS guarantees that enforce response time, service request loss, and effectiveness of CPU utilization for our mission-critical applications.

A growing class of distributed applications in the telecommunications domain require end-to-end performance guarantees, involving bandwidth, latency, jitter, and level of reliability. However, no integrated solutions yet exist that provide these guarantees to distributed object applications. To rectify this situation, research efforts in the areas of design patterns [14], high-performances ORB [7, 16], and QoS enforcement [2, 15] are crucial. The advances in high-performance distributed object computing can be achieved only by simultaneously integrating techniques and tools that simplify application development, and systematically measuring performance to pinpoint and alleviate bottlenecks. These distributed applications must work as specified and deliver predictable, measurable results. Companies need to evaluate, monitor, and test these applications in disparate environments both during development and deployment.

Currently, the CORBA specification does not address load balancing [17], another complex problem that can significantly impact the performance of CORBA applications. In the CORBA world, load balancing refers mainly to the distribution of client requests over a group of servant objects that typically live on different server processes and run on different hosts. Applications that have a very high ratio of requests from clients to servers, or servers that tend to take a long time to complete, will definitely benefit from a load-balanced design. Several important factors that might influence a decision to do load balancing for an application, therefore need to be examined:

- The distribution of the workload over time

- Access and request patterns

- Granularity of components

- Runtime geographical topology

Techniques such as Application Partitioning (both horizontal and vertical) and Service Replication (location, migration, state management, concentrator, etc.) can be applied to load balance an application. However, the cost associated with each load balancing technique should also be accessed to ensure that the performance gained from load balancing is not offset by the additional cost.

3.3 Scalability and Reliability

When designing a small-scale CORBA system, there are many issues that can be safely ignored due to the nature of the system. Such systems typically support a relatively small number of users, and are typically less critical to the business with respect to performance requirements. However, developing a large-scale CORBA system presents many challenges. Large systems, such as the enterprise-wide network management systems, are generally expected to be continuously available (so-called 7 by 24 systems) and provide robust, high-performance services. For such systems, scalability issues become critical.

Scalability for an object-oriented system refers to its ability to handle an increasing number of objects. Three important aspects of scalability need to be examined:

- Speed relative to the number of objects.

- Resource consumption relative to the number of objects.

- Resource consumption relative to the number of incoming requests.

When considering the speed of a remote invocation, we recognize that both the time needed to create the proxy object and the time needed to open a connection to the object represented by the proxy vary in different ORBs. Some of the ORB operations (for example, dispatching, object reference un-marshaling, proxy creation) depend on the number of existing objects and proxies as well. In addition to CORBA scalability issues, scalability in distributed systems also needs to be addressed from the network point of view, as the number of systems increase over the network.

The reliability of the system has always been critical for the users. Building a fault-tolerant CORBA application is difficult, since CORBA specifications do not address the provisioning of reliable services. Client programs have to handle system failures including such things as communication errors between client and server, the failure of a server, and slow communication due to an overloaded server or network. The reliability of the system depends on factors such as the frequency and severity of failures, the ability to recover from failure, and the predictability of the system.

4 Interoperability Verification

As for any type of testing, it is important to select test cases that achieve the specific goals and also be able to verify that the goal has been achieved or to what degree it has been achieved when testing is complete. Thus, for interoperability testing, we have to decide what has to interoperate and then design the test cases and perform the actual testing. In addition, we have to determine how much confidence we have in interoperability through measurement.

4.1 Scope of Testing

Although ideally testing to assure ORB interoperability would consider all OMG IDL [10] types, on-the-wire protocols, various CORBA services, operating systems, compiler versions, programming languages, and various combinations of these items, that level of verification would require prohibitive amounts of resources. Therefore, we will initially restrict the scope of our interoperability testing effort to what we have determined to be the most important CORBA functionality such as the on-the-wire protocol. Future testing will consider interoperability issues existing for additional CORBA services.

4.1.1 IDL Tests

The basic element of a CORBA language mapping is the mechanism for developers to access ORB functionality from various programming languages. This includes the definitions of OMG IDL basic data types, user-defined complex data types (e.g., Structures, Unions, Sequences, Arrays and

Anys), and signatures for the ORB operations, such as the static and dynamic invocation interfaces. The tests must verify that marshaling for the various data types and combinations of data types is exercised thoroughly. The second verification effort covers the mapping of IDL constructs to a particular programming language. The role of the tests is to verify that the corresponding IDL compiler correctly implements CORBA's mapping for that language.

Our in-house interoperability verification efforts revealed that significant issues were encountered while compiling the OMG IDL of one commercially-available ORB with another ORB vendor's IDL compiler. These issues centered on OMG IDL pre-compiler directive differences and basic preprocessing discrepancies. Other issues such as marshaling of CORBA and Any types containing complex structures have also been reported in the literature [4].

4.1.2 SII Tests

The role of this set of tests is to verify the *Static Invocation Interface* (SII) implementation for certain programming languages. Using an IDL file which declares many complicated data types, and the associated client and server methods as appropriate to the mapping under test, the server side verifies the values passed to it by the client and then constructs the return and out parameters. The client then verifies that parameters contain the expected values. These tests are intended to demonstrate the ORB's capability to invoke requests on a remote object.

Our testing efforts on some Open Source ORBs demonstrated that the way that the return or out parameters are constructed and differences between interpretations of various parameters is likely to cause interoperability problems.

4.1.3 API Tests

The goal of CORBA *Application Programming Interface* (API) tests is to verify that the semantics of the ORB-under-test match those described in the CORBA specification. The tests cover a variety of CORBA module operations including the *Dynamic Invocation Interface* (DII), the *Basic Object Adapter* (BOA) (CORBA 2.1), the *Portable Object Adapter* (POA) (CORBA 2.3), the ORB Interface, and the *Interface Repository* (IR).

The POA is responsible for creating object references, activating objects, and dispatching requests from clients to their respect servants. The tests invoke various functions and verify the corresponding results.

For the Interface Repository, read operations are tested by retrieving interface definitions previously added to the repository, and verifying that they are correct. Write operations are tested by adding elements to a repository and retrieving and verifying them.

4.1.4 GIOP/IIOP Test

The CORBA specification defines the *General Inter-ORB Protocol* (GIOP) as its basic interoperability framework. The GIOP defines an on-the-wire format for each IDL data type, so the sender and receiver agree on the binary layout of data, known as the *Common Data Representation* (CDR). CDR encoding is not self-identifying. This means that CDR encoding requires explicit agreement between sender and receiver about the types of data that are to be exchanged. The receiver has no way to prevent misinterpretation of data if the agreement is violated. This could lead to significant interoperability problems since certain types of mismatch cannot be detected at run time, especially when the DII or the *Dynamic Skeleton Interface* (DSI) are being used. The *Internet Inter-ORB Protocol* (IIOP) is one concrete realization of GIOP over TCP/IP. All interoperable ORBs must support IIOP.

GIOP 1.1 supports message fragmentation that allows for more efficient marshaling of data onto the wire, while GIOP 1.2 supports bidirectional communication that permits clients and servers to communicate across firewalls over a single connection. GIOP has eight message types. To thoroughly test the interoperability between two ORBs, we need to provide a GIOP message generator that can systematically generate permutations of argument types plus all kinds of corrupted messages and failure conditions. Demonstrating that an ORB product can withstand such bombardments would likely raise one's confidence that the ORB will be sufficiently robust to stand up in a production environment.

4.2 Our Approach to Test Suite Architecture and Design

In order to verify that multiple ORBs work together satisfactorialy and conform to industry standards, we have established at AT&T, an Interoperability Lab and maintained a close relationship with the Object Management Group (OMG). This will help us to ensure close cooperation with evolving technologies and standards. In that way, when new standards and specifications are defined and products are revised and new versions released, our Interoperability Lab will serve as a point of coordination of data including standards efforts, tests suites, evaluations, and user experiences.

In the CORBA model, an application program operates in a distributed environment, composed of clients and server objects cooperating through the medium of an ORB. Figure 1 shows the general architecture of our testing environment for interoperability, where the clients and servers of two ORBs interact with each other under the control of an industry standard test suite. For example, clients of ORB-1 must be able to communicate with server objects of ORB-2, and vice versa. We propose to select one ORB that has been thoroughly tested for its compliance with the CORBA spec-

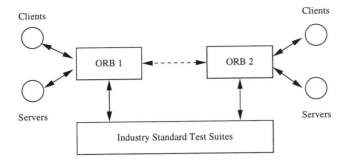

Figure 1. Interoperability Verification Prototype

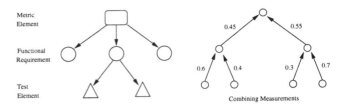

Figure 2. The Strawman Metric Decomposition Tree

ification and use it as an *oracle* or reference ORB against which other ORB products will be tested. Provided that it is possible to select an ORB in which one has sufficient confidence, there are two primary advantages to using this approach:

- It removes the problem of determining which ORB is behaving improperly when it is found that there are interoperability problems. By definition, the reference ORB is behaving properly.

- The reference ORB can provide extensive diagnostic output to help testers pinpoint what test case has failed and why it failed.

Since the goal of our testing approach is to test ORB products for conformance with the CORBA specification and interoperability with other conforming ORBs, test suites should be fully configurable and component-based. Our test suites focus on interfaces and functionality rather than implementation. This allows ORB developers to optimize and differentiate their ORB implementations for such characteristics as performance, operating environment, or marketplace, while providing a common operating interface to application clients and servers.

As indicated in the previous sections, SII and GIOP/IIOP tests require support for distributed testing. At least two distinct processes should be employed to test an ORB's SII implementation, namely the client and the server. This means that test suites must support the concept of remote systems (at least logically, if not physically.)

For functionality that is not clearly defined by CORBA, the user has to provide necessary information to the test suites. For example, CORBA does not mandate the file name that ORB implementations use to provide the definitions of CORBA interfaces and types. Therefore, it is the user's responsibility to provide ORB-specific information to the test suites. Where possible, the test suites should wrap the differences that vendor implementations exhibit due to the ambiguities in the specification. Some functional abstraction should be employed to mask these differences and enable the portability of the test suites.

4.3 Interoperability Measurement

To measure the confidence that we have in the interoperability between two ORBs, an interoperability metric [11] needs to be employed. Such a metric represents the degree to which an ORB product meets the requirement for interoperability and the confidence with which it can be asserted, taking into account the relative importance of different functions of the product based on such things as their frequency of use or their significance to the overall performance of a particular application. Therefore, differences in value need to be incorporated into the metric so that each contributing function is given an appropriate weight when deciding whether interoperability has been achieved.

The Strawman Metric Decomposition Tree (SMDT) was used in [11] as a simple but effective measurement scale. As shown in Figure 2, the tree hierarchy is decomposed as the follows: a high level operational requirement is represented in the form of a Matrix Element, which is strictly decomposed into lower level Functional Requirements and eventually into measurable Test Elements. The combination of measurement starts from the lowest level tests to form the measures of interoperability and confidence for each Test Element and Functional Requirement, and then a measure of interoperability and confidence is established for the whole Metric Element. At each point at which measures are combined, rules are established to scale the score so that it always lies between 0 and 1.0. The weight for each node in the tree represents the node's relative value to its parent node.

4.4 Value to Developers

One immediate benefit of this interoperability testing effort is that we can assess both conformance to standards and interoperability between ORB products. This can help us choose the most appropriate vendor products and reduce the time and cost that developers require for new system deployment or legacy system migration and integration. In addition, we expect that interoperability *Customer Acceptance Test* (CAT) will provide leverage with vendors, making it more likely that they will verify that their products match the standards.

Another potential benefit of doing interoperability testing is that it can help to provide coding guidelines so that portable CORBA applications can be developed. The testing helps to identify which set of APIs have the same behavior and hence are portable. ORB vendors provide different extensions to the standard. To remain portable, it is important to identify these APIs and define ORB-neutral wrappers so that portable applications can be written.

Finally, we expect that the AT&T Interoperability Lab will provide technical support such as architecture mentoring and consulting to help developers begin the process of incorporating interoperable components. We are also planning to establish an Interoperability Repository that will document and communicate our interoperability findings.

5 Performance Testing

In this section, we discuss the scope of performance testing that includes POA-specific testing and ORB implementation testing. As we have discussed in Section 4, the infrastructure of our interoperability testing environment can be extended to support performance testing. Our strategy for performance verification is through performance modeling and benchmarking.

5.1 POA-Specific Testing

The Portable Object Adapter (POA) specification provides a full suite of features and services intended to allow developers to write scalable, high-performance server applications [10, 6]. It is crucial that application developers have the ability to properly control the resources required for implementing CORBA objects and delivering requests to them. Therefore, it is essential that developers have a thorough understanding of POA features and relationships among them and be able to determine which are the most appropriate features to use under different circumstances. This will allow developers to make tradeoffs necessary for building high-performance server applications. Of course, it is also essential that the POA-specific features are thoroughly tested.

The POA is essentially a container for object-to-servant association. The lifetime of an object starts from when it is created and ends when it is destroyed. The bond between an object and a servant is initiated when the object is incarnated by a servant, and broken when the servant is etherealized. The separation between servant lifetimes and object lifetimes provides the POA with its strong support for high scalability. Depending on the number of objects an application contains, it may use a separate servant for each object, use a single servant for all of them, dynamically supply a servant for each request, or use a combination of these to best manage its resources. For example, a default servant provides the ability to support literally any number of objects in a fixed amount of memory given the tradeoff of the latency in finding the target object.

One of the key features of POA specification is that an application can contain multiple POA instances representing a group of objects that have similar characteristics. These characteristics are controlled via POA policies that are specified when a POA is created. Many POA features are directly controlled by applications through the use of POA policies. Understanding and properly using of these policies is key to using the POA to build reliable and scalable server applications.

5.2 Performance of ORB Implementation

While CORBA provides a standard framework for building distributed object systems, it is of little practical use if the ORB implementation cannot deliver adequate performance. The performance of an ORB is influenced by many factors. One of the most important factors is the effectiveness of the request/response handling mechanism that has direct impact on the latency and scalability of an ORB implementation. To test the effectiveness of request/response handling, the following items should be taken into consideration:

- Differences in invocation times when the application employs different load patterns and different invocation strategies (e.g., using SII/DII, SSI/DSI, or object colocated/distributed).

- Differences in invocation time related to different aspects of the structural complexity of IDL interfaces.

- Overall throughput of the ORB and the overhead associated with passing specific data types.

- Invocation times and resource consumption as functions of such factors as the number of objects, the number of proxies, or the number of connections.

Verifying the functional behavior of a particular ORB implementation, while important, will not guarantee its performance in a production environment. To ensure optimal application uptime, it is crucial to test the ORB and servers under expected and even unexpected load conditions. In load testing, we need to simulate traffic patterns and measure the response times and throughput of CORBA servers.

Various load generation algorithms [1] can be utilized to facilitate the tests.

5.3 Performance Modeling and Benchmarking

With the integration of legacy systems and new component-based applications, localizing a problem requires examining not only an individual object, but all the other objects with which it interacts. From a CORBA point of view, the following factors have a strong influence on the performance of a distributed system [17]:

- The number of remote method invocations that are made within the system.

- The amount of data that is transferred within each remote method invocation.

- The marshaling costs of the different IDL data types used by the system.

Meeting the QoS needs of distributed applications requires much more than defining IDL interfaces. It requires a vertically integrated architecture that can deliver end-to-end QoS guarantees at multiple levels of an entire distributed system [15]. To effectively test various performance aspects of an ORB product and its application components, we first need to have a good understanding of the application behavior and business model. Test case generation tools such as Teradyne's TestMaster are being investigated to support performance modeling and testing. These tools should have the ability to thoroughly describe application behavior from specifications or models and extract directly executable tests. For TestMaster, the controlled automation would come from its state-machine technology. The use of Extended Finite State Machines (EFSM) provides a powerful way to describe application behavior through flow and context. Other commercially-available performance modeling tools such as Segue's SilkPerformer claim to be capable of simulating a large distributed environment by spreading the load across machines and combining different load types.

After we have adequate understanding of the application model and behavior, we can develop test cases by extending our interoperability test suites to benchmark the corresponding applications. Through performance benchmarking, potential ORB users will know whether a particular ORB product is suitable for their specific application, facilitating the ORB selection process. Performance benchmarking will also help the developers locate the possible sources of performance bottlenecks or other problems existing in a particular ORB product.

6 Summary

In this paper we have investigated possible interoperability issues that could arise due to the deployment of multi-vendor ORB products in a telecommunications environment. We have considered such issues as ORB interoperability, performance, scalability and reliability. We are currently developing a systematic way for a thorough verification of interoperability and performance.

It is essential to develop a metric that is easily interpretable and indicates to both ORB vendors and users, the degree to which interoperability has been achieved.

Although our current verification effort is dedicated to the CORBA 2.3 specification, the infrastructure of our interoperability and performance testing must be easily extendible to support the testing of the forthcoming CORBA features [19] such as the notification service, messaging service (asynchronous messaging, time-independent invocation), and Object by Value, which directly address QoS requirements.

Acknowledgments

We are grateful to David Riddoch at AT&T Labs Cambridge for his invaluable input on POA specific testing.

References

[1] A. Avritzer and E. Weyuker. The Automatic Generation of Load Test Suites and the Assessment of the Resulting Software. *IEEE Trans. on Software Engineering*, 21(9):705–716, Sept. 1995.

[2] A. Avritzer and E. Weyuker. Enforcing Quality of Service of Distributed Objects. In *Proc. IEEE International Symposium on Software Reliability Engineering (ISSRE-97)*, pages 390–401, Nov. 1997.

[3] DSTC. CORBAnet. Technical report, http://corbanet.dstc.edu.au.

[4] M. Fisher, S. Rana, and C. Egelhaaf. Interoperability in a Multiple-Provider Telecommunications Environment. In *Proc. 1998 Enterprise Distributed Object Computing Workshop, (EDOC'98)*, pages 296–303, 1998.

[5] A. Forin, G. Hunt, L. Li, and Y. Wang. High-Performance Distributed Objects over System Area Networks. In *Proc. 3rd USENIX Windows NT Symp.*, pages 21–30, July 1999.

[6] M. Henning and S. Vinoski. *Advanced CORBA Programming with C++*. Addison Wesley Longman, Feb. 1999.

[7] S. Lo and S. Pope. The Implementation of a High Performance ORB over Multiple Network Transports. Technical report, AT&T Lab Cambridge, Mar. 1998.

[8] S. Mahajan and J. Chen. CORBA On WWW: Evaluative Framework for Interoperability Issues. In *Proc. 1998 Technology of Object-Oriented Languages, (TOOLS 27)*, pages 351–360, 1998.

[9] OMG. Interoperable Naming Service. Technical report, OMG TC Document orbos/98-10-11, Oct. 1998.

[10] OMG. The Common Object Request Broker: Architecture and Specification, Revision 2.3. Technical report, June 1999.

[11] J. Pridmore and D. Rumens. Interoperability - How Do We Know When We Have Achieved It? In *Proc. 3rd International Conference on Command, Control, Communications and Management Information Systems*, pages 192 –205, 1989.

[12] N. Saji. Report on the World's Largest Successful CORBA/IIOP Interoperability Verification Test. Technical report, Interoperability Working Group, DOPG, http://www.omg.org/news/pr99/5_19.html, May 1999.

[13] D. Schmidt. Experience Using Design Patterns to Develop Reusable Object-Oriented Communication Software. *Communications of the ACM, Special Issue on Object-Oriented Experiences*, 38(10), Oct. 1995.

[14] D. Schmidt. Applying Patterns to Meet the Challenges of Concurrent Software. *IEEE Concurrency, Special Edition on Software Engineering for Parallel and Distributed Systems*, 5(3), 1997.

[15] D. Schmidt. QoS for Distributed Object Computing Middleware – Fact or Fiction? In *Proc. Fifth International Workshop on Quality of Service (IWQoS '97)*, Columbia University, NYC, USA, May 1997.

[16] D. Schmidt, D. Levine, and S. Mungee. The Design of the TAO Real-Time Object Request Broker. *Computer Communications Special Issue on Building Quality of Service into Distributed Systems, Elsevier Science*, 21(4), Apr. 1998.

[17] D. Slama, J. Garbis, and P. Russell. *Enterprise CORBA*. Prentice Hall PTR, Upper Saddle River, NJ 07458, 1999.

[18] The Open Group. CORBA Validation (CORVAL). Technical report, http://www.opengroup.org/vsorb/corval.

[19] S. Vinoski. New Features for CORBA 3.0. *Communications of the ACM*, 41(10), Oct. 1998.

Algorithms for Improving the Dependability of Firewall and Filter Rule Lists

Scott Hazelhurst   Adi Attar
Raymond Sinnappan
Programme for Highly Dependable Systems, Department of Computer Science,
University of the Witwatersrand, Johannesburg,
Private Bag 3, 2050 Wits, South Africa
{scott, aattar, rsinnapa}@cs.wits.ac.za

Abstract

Network firewalls and routers use a rule database to decide which packets will be allowed from one network onto another. By filtering packets the firewalls and routers can improve security and performance. However, as the size of the rule list increases, it becomes difficult to maintain and validate the rules, and lookup latency may increase significantly. Both these factors tend to limit the ability of firewall systems to protect networks. This paper presents a new technique for representing rule databases. This representation – based on ordered binary decision diagrams – can be used in two ways: faster lookup algorithms can allow larger rule sets to be used without sacrificing performance; and algorithms for validating rule sets and changes to rule sets can be used. Overall dependability of the system is improved by allowing larger and more sophisticated rule sets, and by having greater confidence in the rule sets' correctness.

1. Introduction

Network routers and firewalls play a very important role in network traffic management. By regulating which packets are accepted by a firewall or router, both the security and performance of the network can be improved. Routers and firewalls usually have rules which indicate which packets should be accepted and which rejected.

A network manager can express many complex rules for accepting or rejecting packets. The efficacy of traffic management depends on how good these rules are. In practice, these rules develop over a period of time, and they evolve as needs change. Two problems emerge:

- As the list of rules becomes more complex, they become more difficult to understand. The person who maintains the list may leave and be replaced. For

someone to understand the rule base from scratch can be very difficult. This makes maintaining the rule base difficult if changes are made either for operational or performance needs since it may not be obvious what the effect of changing, deleting or adding a rule may be. Even changing the position of a rule in the rule list can change the semantics of the list.

- The cost of performing lookup on a rule list may become expensive, and particularly for routers, this may add significantly to latency in the network.

Terminology: To simplify notation, in the rest of the paper the term *filter* is used to cover both routers and firewalls, and the term *rule set* is used to refer to a list of rules that implement the filter's policy.

1.1. Rule sets

Filter rules come in several formats; typically these are proprietary formats. While the expressiveness and syntax of the formats differ, the following generic description gives a good feeling for what such rules sets look like. A rule set consists of a list of rules of the form **if** *condition* **then** *action*, where the action is either accept or reject.

Example 1.1. A rule in a rule list for a Cisco router might say something like [5]:

```
access-list 101 permit tcp 20.9.17.8  0.0.0.0
                          121.11.127.20 0.0.0.0
                          range 23 27
```

This says that any TCP protocol packet coming from IP address 20.9.17.8 destined for IP address 121.11.127.20 is to be accepted provided the destination port address is in the range 23 . . . 27. More detail is given later. ■

The rules are searched one by one to see whether the condition matches the incoming packet: if it does, the packet is accepted or rejected depending on the action (which will either be accept or reject); if the condition does not match the rule, the search continues with the following rules. If none of the rules match the packet is rejected.

Since the rules are checked in order, the order in which they are specified is critical. Changing the order of the rules could result in some packets that were previously rejected being accepted (and/or *vice-versa*).

This paper uses CISCO access-list format for specifying the rule set, but the methods proposed generalise to other formats.

1.2. Research goals

This paper explores the use of binary decision diagrams (BDDs) for representing rule lists, and shows the potential of using BDDs for speeding-up lookup, performing analysis, and possible hardware support. The contributions of the paper are:

- A technique for representing a rule set as a boolean expression using BDDs;

- A set of algorithms that can be used to analyse a rule set to help validate it, and to understand the effect of changes on the rule set;

- A prototype graphical interface that can be used to help analyse the rule set;

- A description of how the BDD representation can be used for fast lookup, and used as a basis for hardware support.

The use of these techniques will allow more complex and sophisticated rule sets to be used with greater confidence. This will improve both security and traffic management for two reasons: more sophisticated security policies can be used without compromising performance, and there can be greater confidence in the correctness of the access lists.

1.3. Content and structure of paper

Section 2 introduces BDDs and shows how they can represent boolean expressions. Section 3 then shows how a rule set can be converted into a BDD representation. Section 4 explores visualisation and analysis techniques that use BDD representations, and describes a simple graphical interface for a prototype filter analysis tool. Section 5.1 examines how this representation can be used for fast lookup, while Section 5.2 describes a technique for hardware support. Finally, Section 6 describes the status of the work and discusses possible future research.

2. Binary Decision Diagrams

A decision diagram is a method of representing a boolean expression. Essentially it is a directed, acyclic graph. The leaves of the graph are truth values, and the interior vertices are labelled with variable names. Each interior vertex has two outgoing edges, each of which corresponds to the truth value of the variable labelling the vertex.

To evaluate an expression given an interpretation of the variables, you start at the root and move downwards. If the variable has a 0 value, choose the corresponding edge; if the variable has a 1 value, choose the other edge. By following this rule you can easily evaluate the function.

Bryant [4] introduced the concept of reduced, ordered binary decision diagrams, which obeys the following rules.

- all duplicate terminals are removed (i.e. we shall have at most one terminal labelled 1, and one labelled 0);

- all duplicate non-terminals are removed;

- all redundant tests are removed (i.e. if both edges leaving a vertex go to the same place, you can delete that vertex since it implies that the value of the variable that that node represents is irrelevant at that point); and

- a total order is placed on the variables in the expression and for any edge (x, y), the label of x comes before the label of y in the order (variables are encountered in the same order on any path from root to leaf).

In this paper, reduced ordered binary decision diagrams are simply called binary decision diagrams and abbreviated as BDDs. Efficient algorithms are known for manipulating boolean expressions (e.g. conjunction, implication, ...). There are two important properties of BDDs. First, they are compact representations of boolean expressions (in a heuristic sense – there are expressions which are not compact). Second, for a given variable ordering, the BDD representation of an expression is canonical. (As a simple example, this means that if we build BDDs for $\neg(a \wedge (b \vee c))$ and $(\neg a \vee \neg b) \wedge (\neg a \vee \neg c)$, then we get exactly the same BDD). In practice, this means that checking equivalence can be done very cheaply once the BDD is constructed. The diagram shows the BDD representation of $(x_1 \vee x_2) \wedge x_3$: the dashed lines are followed if variable is 0, and the solid lines if the variable is 1.

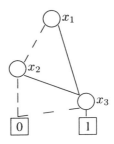

In practice it is not uncommon to work with expressions that have BDDs tens of megabytes in size. With such expressions, the efficiency benefits gained by using BDDs can make many orders of magnitude difference in the size of boolean expressions that can be manipulated.

Complexity issues: The size of the BDD is very dependent on the variable ordering chosen. Although the problem of finding an optimal BDD ordering is NP-complete [2], in practice there are good rules of thumb for finding good variable orderings and many BDD packages come with heuristic routines for dynamic variable ordering [4].

It must be emphasised that although BDDs have worked well in many application areas, they are not a panacea – after all the Boolean Satisfiability problem can easily be represented using BDDs, which immediately indicates that BDDs cannot be used to solve all boolean problems efficiently. A stronger result is in fact known — there are some problems which require exponential space [3].

3. Converting rule sets into boolean expressions

This section describes how a rule set can be converted into a boolean expression (which is represented as a BDD). Section 3.1 describes how an individual rule in a rule set can be converted into a boolean expression (and hence a BDD). Section 3.2 shows how the boolean expressions for the individual rules can be combined to give a boolean expression for the entire rule set. Some initial experimental results are given in Section 3.3.

In the description, CISCO access lists are used as illustration. However the methods can be modified to fit other approaches.

3.1. Rule conversion

A CISCO access rule is of the form

```
access-list 101 permit tcp
           20.9.17.8  0.0.0.0
           121.11.127.20 0.0.0.0
           range 23 27
```

The key components in a rule are:

- permit or reject: which indicates whether packets matching the rule are to be accepted. How this field will be used is described in the next section.
- The protocol of the packet: in this case, TCP. Other possible examples are UDP and ICMP.
- The source address: four segments, each a number in the range $0 \ldots 255$.

- The mask for the source address (also four segments).
- The destination address (in the same format as the source).
- The destination mask.
- The range of port addresses. If the port component is empty, all ports match. The eq x can be used as short-hand for range x x.

Representing numbers as bit-vectors The key technique used is that numbers can be represented as bit vectors. For example, an address segment is a number between 0 and 255. At a lower level, the address segment is just a vector of 8 bits. Using BDDs, we can represent sets of numbers symbolically and perform many operations on them efficiently.

For example, to represent the 8-bit number x symbolically, we introduce the bit-vector $\langle x_7, \ldots, x_0 \rangle$, where each of the x_is are boolean (BDD) variables. The condition that the vector of x's is equal to 3, is just $\langle x_7, \ldots, x_0 \rangle = \langle \mathbf{f}, \mathbf{f}, \mathbf{f}, \mathbf{f}, \mathbf{f}, \mathbf{f}, \mathbf{t}, \mathbf{t} \rangle$. Using the definition of equality of vectors yields the boolean expression $x_7' x_6' x_5' x_4' x_3' x_2' x_1 x_0$, (bits 0 and 1 are high, the others low). To help make the presentation of formulas more compact, unless the formula would be confusing, negation is shown using a prime or tick, and juxtaposition is used for conjunction. The condition that $\mathbf{x} = 2$ is represented by $x_7' x_6' x_5' x_4' x_3' x_2' x_1 x_0'$. The condition $\mathbf{x} = 2 \vee \mathbf{x} = 3$ is represented by

$$x_7' x_6' x_5' x_4' x_3' x_2' x_1 x_0 \vee x_7' x_6' x_5' x_4' x_3' x_2' x_1 x_0'$$

which is just $x_7' x_6' x_5' x_4' x_3' x_2' x_1$. Large expressions can be represented compactly using BDDs.

Boolean variables for the components of a rule We introduce a number of boolean variables and expressions to represent the information in the rule.

We assign each protocol a number $0, \ldots, n_p - 1$. These numbers can be represented in $m_p = \log_2 n_p$ bits, and so we introduce m_p variables $\pi_0, \ldots, \pi_{m_p-1}$ to encode the protocol used. In the examples given below, the protocols can be represented in 3 bits (in practice, 8 bits are likely to be used). For example, if the rule refers to a tcp protocol (protocol 3) packet, then this is represented by the expression $\langle \pi_2, \pi_1, \pi_0 \rangle = \langle \mathbf{f}, \mathbf{t}, \mathbf{t} \rangle$, or just $\pi_2' \pi_1 \pi_0$.

For each segment of the source address we introduce 8 variables of the form $sax[0], \ldots, sax[7]$, where x is the segment number. For example, if segment 2 of the source address refers to the number 141, this is encoded as $sa2[7] sa2'[6] sa2'[5] sa2'[4] sa2[3] sa2[2] sa2'[1] sa2[0]$.

For each segment of the destination address we introduce 8 variables of the form $dax[0], \ldots, dax[7]$, where x is the segment number. The encoding of destination addresses is similar to the encoding of source addresses.

As there can be up to 65535 ports specified, port number-s can be represented in 16 bits, so we introduce 16 boolean variables ($p[15], \ldots, p[0]$, with $p[15]$ being the most significant bit) which encode the port number. Using these variables it is possible to succinctly represent individual ports as well as ranges of ports. Examples are given below.

For the moment we ignore the effects of the mask – Section 3.1 discusses mechanisms that handle masks.

Example In the example above the source address 20.9.17.8 would be encoded by the boolean expression:

$$sa1'[7]sa1'[6]sa1'[5]sa1[4]sa1'[3]sa1[2]sa1'[1]sa1'[0]\wedge$$
$$sa2'[7]sa2'[6]sa2'[5]sa2'[4]sa2[3]sa2'[2]sa2'[1]sa2[0]\wedge$$
$$sa3'[7]sa3'[6]sa3'[5]sa3[4]sa3'[3]sa3'[2]sa3'[1]sa3[0]\wedge$$
$$sa4'[7]sa4'[6]sa4'[5]sa4'[4]sa4'[3]sa4[2]sa4'[1]sa4'[0]$$

The destination address can be encoded in a similar way.

Representing the range of ports needs a little more care. Let $\textbf{port} \stackrel{\text{def}}{=} \langle p[15], \ldots, p[0]\rangle$. Conditions can be expressed using boolean operations. Similarly to other parts of the rule, the condition that the port number must be 25 is just $\textbf{port} = int2bv\ 25$, where $int2bv$ is a function that converts a number into its bit-vector representation.

The range operations can also be represented efficiently. For example, a less-than-or-equal-to operation can easily be defined as:

$$\textbf{port} \leq n \stackrel{\text{def}}{=} \bigvee_{i=0}^{n} \textbf{port} = i$$

The port-range information in the example rule above would be encoded as:

$$(\textbf{port} \geq \text{int2bv } 23) \quad \wedge \quad (\textbf{port} \leq \text{int2bv } 27)$$

The boolean expression that represents this is

$$(p[15]'p[14]'p[13]'p[12]'p[11]'p[10]'p[9]'p[8]'p[7]'$$
$$p[6]'p[5]'p[4]) \wedge (p[3]p[2]' \vee p[3]'p[2]p[1]p[0])$$

This may appear complicated, but the BDD representation is compact.

Masks The source and destination addresses in a rule actually both have two components: a base address and a mask. The mask gives the rule specifier the flexibility to specify a number of possible matches in one rule. In effect the mask indicates which bits of the base address should be matched on and which ignored. Masks are used extensively and so any mechanism for representing the rule set must be able to deal with them.

If the base address given in a rule is $s_1.s_2.s_3.s_4$ and the mask is $m_1.m_2.m_3.m_4$, then a packet with address $a_1.a_2.a_3.a_4$ matches exactly when

$$(s_1 \textbf{ or } m_1 \ = \ a_1 \textbf{ or } m_1) \wedge (s_2 \textbf{ or } m_2 \ = \ a_2 \textbf{ or } m_2) \wedge$$
$$\tag{1}$$
$$(s_3 \textbf{ or } m_3 \ = \ a_3 \textbf{ or } m_3) \wedge (s_4 \textbf{ or } m_4 \ = \ a_4 \textbf{ or } m_4),$$

where the **or** operation is bit-wise or-ing of the two vectors.[1] The segments of the mask are typically either 0 (which means the segment must match exactly) or 255 (which means the segment is ignored). For example if the source address given is:

- 146.141.27.66 0.0.0.0: this means that the packet must match exactly as coming from the machine concave.cs.wits.ac.za;

- 146.141.27.66 0.0.255.255: this means that the packet must come from some machine in the Wits domain.

To cope with masks, the mechanism for dealing with addresses described above needs to be generalised. This is easily accomplished using a direct implementation of Equation 1.

3.2. Conversion of the entire rule set

Using the methods described above the entire rule set can in principle be represented by a boolean expression. Suppose *cvtrule* is the function that converts one rule into a boolean expression. The *cvtruleset* function can be defined recursively using *cvtrule*.

- If the rule set is empty then no packets can be accepted and so the corresponding boolean expression is **f**.

- If the first rule is an accept rule then a packet will be accepted if it matches the rule or if accepted by the rest of the rule set. So the corresponding boolean expression is the disjunction of the boolean expression representing the first rule and the boolean expression representing the rest of the rules.

- If the first rule is a reject rule then a packet will be accepted if it does not match the first rule and it is accepted by the rest of the rule set. So the corresponding boolean expression is the conjunction of the negation of the boolean expression representing the first rule and the boolean expression representing the rest of the rules.

---

[1] Here **or** binds tighter than '='.

3.3. Results

The algorithm described above has been implemented in a prototype tool built on top of the Voss system [9]. This system has a lazy functional language called FL as its front-end and uses BDDs internally to represent symbolic boolean expression. The Voss system also has heuristics for finding good BDD variable orderings. A simple Perl script processes the rule set which is then read in by the prototype tool. Then using FL as a front end, a user can analyse the rules in various ways — this is described in detail in the next section.

The algorithm for converting rule sets into a boolean formula has been tested on some synthetic test cases and a large real rule set supplied by an internet service provider. A set of just over 430 rules provided by a commercial internet service provider was converted into a boolean expressions using the simple algorithms described above. The total time taken to produce the BDD to represent this rule set was about 20s on a Sun Ultra 4, yielding a BDD of approximately 1.1K in size (the text file with the access list is about 32K in size). The maximum depth of the BDD (determined by the number of variables) is 83 which means that to check whether a packet should be accepted requires in the worst case 83 bit-operations.

This result is encouraging since it shows that the BDD representation is feasible and that lookup can be done very quickly. More experimental evidence is needed, with more rule sets and with real log data. While worst case is important, average case is much more important. What average case is depends on what real data looks like and what the pattern of incoming packets is. This is particularly important in assessing the cost of the lookup in the original rule set.

4. Analysing BDD representations of rule sets

Section 3 examined the use of BDDs for compact representation and lookup in rule sets. This section presents how the BDD representation can be used for analysis. While some of the analysis can be fully automated, the main point of the proposed tool is to provide a human user with the ability to interact with the rule set to understand it and the effect of possible changes. The tool does not act as an oracle, but a means of exploring the rule set.

4.1. Display of rule set

The cornerstone of the algorithms to analyse rule sets is the routine that, given a boolean expression representing the rule set, displays it for a human user. The BDD representation of the rule set is a compact machine-friendly way of representing the rules; however it is far from human friendly.

Therefore the tool has an algorithm that presents the boolean formula in a human readable way. A simple example of such a tabular form is shown Figure 1. The output of the algorithm displays the filter rules (or some query on the filter rules) in tabular form, with each field in the packet header being represented in a column. The user can specify the order of the columns — and the size of the table depends very much of the order of the columns. Experience has shown that listing using port and protocol first yields the smallest tables, using the addresses first leads to huge tables. By changing the order, a user can view the rules in different ways. At present, displaying the table of a large set of rules produces very large tables.

The prototype tool has two commands that can be used to display a rule set. The first called *sc* (show condition) takes two arguments:

- The first gives the order of the columns in the table. This is useful because it allows a user to view the rules from different perspectives.

  The tool provides a default order; the user specifies only the changes desired to the default ordering.

- The second gives a boolean condition that represents a rule list.

The result of the call to *sc* is a detailed table that shows the types of packets that would match the condition.

The second routine is called *gs* (give summary). It takes the same arguments but only provides a summary of the packets that match the condition – only the columns given in the first argument are used in the table. This enables the user to view the rules at different levels of abstraction.

4.2. Instantiating the conditions

One of the most useful ways of validating a rule set is to ask 'what if' questions. For example:

- Do we accept packets on port 25? If so what type of packets?

- On which ports do we accept tcp packets?

- Which packets do we accept from address y?

- What type of packets will we accept that are being sent to address y?

- And so on ...

All these queries can be expressed as boolean conditions, and depending on the user's goal, the results displayed using the routines described above. Any boolean combination of conditions is allowed. Here are some examples:

```
: sc [Port,Proto] ([Dest1<-120, NOT(Proto<-icmp)] ::: cond);

Ports Proto Src 4   Src 3   Src 2   Src 1  Dest4   Dest3   Dest2 Dest1
 0--19|  1|0--255|0--255|0--255|0--255|0--255|0--255|0--255| 120
20--21|  1|0--255|0--255|0--255|0--255|0--255|0--255|0--255| 120
       3|0--255|0--255|0--255|0--255|     3|   112|    17| 120
   22|  1|0--255|0--255|0--255|0--255|0--255|0--255|0--255| 120
       3|     9|     0|    20|   120|0--255|0--255|0--255| 120
23--24|  1|0--255|0--255|0--255|0--255|0--255|0--255|0--255| 120
......
```

Figure 1. Tabular form of some filter rules

- What type of UDP packets do we accept?

In the tool this would be asked using the following command.

```
: sc [Port,Proto] ([Proto <- udp] ::: cond);
```

This is rather cryptic at first sight, but has a simple semantics. Here, *cond* is a boolean condition representing a rule set. The command ([Proto <- udp] ::: cond) instantiates *cond* so that only the UDP packets are shown. The *sc* command then shows the packets (using port and protocol as the first two columns of the table) that match the condition and are UDP packets.

- List the packets we accept from hosts in the 120.121 domain.

```
> sc [] ([Source1<-120, Source2<-121] ::: cond);
```

- Any combination of boolean of queries using boolean operations is allowed. So, we can ask questions like: *What packets do we accept which have the first segment of the destination address of 120 and which are not icmp packets?*

```
> sc [Port,Proto] ([Dest1<-120, NOT(Proto<-icmp)] ::: cond);
```

The table in Figure 1 shows an extract from the result of this command for a sample filter list.

- Which packets are *not* accepted? As the condition for acceptance is given as a boolean expression, we can look at its negation to discover which packets are not accepted and use the *sc* and *gs* operators to show which packets are rejected.

4.3. Dealing with modifications

Probably the most useful part of the tool is the ability to analyse changes to the rule set, whether those changes are changes to a particular rule, a change in the order of the rules, or a removal or addition of a rule.

The original rule set is represented as a boolean formula, the modified rule set is represented as a boolean formula, and then the two formulas together can be used to perform any desired analysis (for example, whether they two formulas are equivalent, or whether one logically implies the other).

Suppose we have two rule sets R_1 and R_2. They may contain different rules, or orderings of rules. Here are some of the queries which can be asked, with the boolean conditions that define them formally.

- Are R_1 and R_2 equivalent? — $R_1 = R_2$.

- Are all the packets accepted by R_1 accepted by R_2? — $R_1 \Rightarrow R_2$.

- Are there packets accepted by R_2 but not by R_1? — $\neg R_1 \land R_2$

Such expressions can easily be computed by the tool. Note that an expression like $\neg R_1 \land R_2$ is a symbolic boolean expression. Its value could be **t** (which would mean that all packets are not accepted by R_1 but accepted by R_2) or **f** (which would mean no packets are rejected by R_1 and accepted by R_2). But in general, its value will be a symbolic boolean expression that describes the conditions that must be met for a packet to be accepted by R_2 and not by R_1. This expression can then be interrogated using the above routines to display such packets in a convenient form. So, using the tool, the following command will display in tabular form (with the columns ordered as given) all the packets rejected by the first rule set but accepted by the second rule set.

```
> sc [Port,Proto,Dest1,Dest2,Dest3,Dest4]
     ((NOT R1) AND R2)
```

581

4.4. Automatic validation

One automatic validation algorithm has been implemented. This routine goes through the list of rules and detects any redundant rules — this can be done efficiently, and if a redundant rule is detected it is presented to the user. A redundant rule is not necessarily an error, but it may result in slower than necessary lookup, and if the user expects the rule to be useful, then it may indicate that there is a problem with the rule set.

This detection routine was used on some synthetic examples, and on a 'real' rule set containing approximately 55 rules. In this case, about 5 redundant rules were detected. In most cases the redundant rule is caused by the same rule appearing more than once in a rule set. However, another cause of redundancies is caused by mask values in one rule covering subsequent rules.

Other automatic validation techniques are possible. For example, it would be possible to show for each (or some) deny rule in a list, which subsequent rules (if any) are affected by it.

4.5. User Interface Issues

The methods just presented in the previous sub-sections can be packaged in an easy-to-use way which hides the underlying algorithm. The first interface developed was a textual-based interface in FL, which provides the user with a simple but very expressive query language.

A prototype graphical interface has been developed using Tcl/Tk and is illustrated in Figures 2 and 3. Figure 2 shows the analysis of an access file. The user types in the name of the file in the given box. Below that is information showing how the analysis will be shown. 'Display options' shows the order in which the information will be presented. By clicking on these options the user can change the order of presentation. The user can also restrict the analysis by entering values in the boxes. In the example given, only rules pertaining to tcp packets from hosts with a 121.21 address prefix are displayed.

Figure 3 shows the results of comparing two rule sets. The user enters the file names and chooses the appropriate options for displaying the results. The differences are then displayed in the window.

For an industrial strength front-end, more care needs to be taken with the design. The ideal system would probably provide the most important functionality through the graphical interface, and then allow an advanced user to issue more powerful queries through a textual interface.

5. Current Research

The results in this paper show that BDDs are useful for representing, validating and analysing rule sets. Preliminary research presented in section 3.3 suggests that BDDs can also be used for fast lookup. Our current research is looking at how to implement lookup efficiently using both software and hardware techniques.

5.1. Software-based Lookup

Once a BDD representing a rule set has been constructed, performing lookup for a given packet is a simple matter of testing for *satisfiability*. This lookup algorithm starts at the root of the BDD, checking the value of the variable at that node and following the appropriate edge to the next node. This process is repeated until one of the terminal nodes is reached, at which point a decision can be made (accept if the terminal node reached is labelled 1, and reject if it is labelled 0).

For each incoming packet the BDD must be traversed from the root to one of its terminal nodes, and so the worst case occurs when the longest path in the BDD is chosen — when all the variables occurring in the BDD must be inspected. For a given rule list, this value is fixed and in general, this value can be no more than the sum of the bits of the packet fields the filter is interested in. If the filter considers source and destination addresses, destination port and protocol, lookup can require up to $32 + 32 + 16 + 3 = 83$ comparisons. Since nothing can be done to improve the worst case, the next obvious step is to try to improve the average case.

Improving the Average Case   One of the advantages of BDD representations of boolean expressions is that changing the variable order of a BDD changes only the shape and not the semantics of the BDD. Many BDD-based applications make use of this fact and reorder their variables, typically in an attempt to minimise the number of nodes in the BDD. Using BDDs for filtering is different in the sense that space (number of nodes) can be traded-off for average depth. So one possible optimisation involves changing the shape of the BDD in such a way that it reduces the average depth of the tree, or the time to perform lookup on average. A more useful optimisation would take into account actual traffic patterns to shape the BDD so that commonly occurring packet types have shorter paths through the BDD. A statistical analysis of traffic would indicate a variable ordering to be used that would minimise average lookup, even if worst-case lookup suffers. Doing the same with the linear representation of the rules is much more difficult because of the importance of the linear order of the access lists.

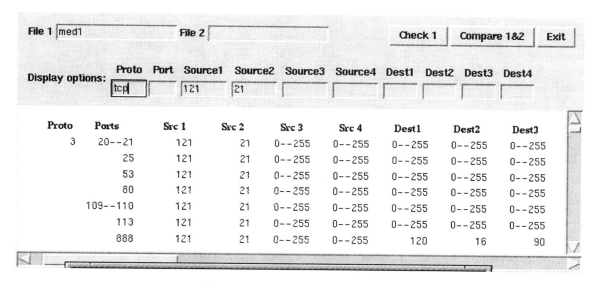

Figure 2. Analysing an access file by category

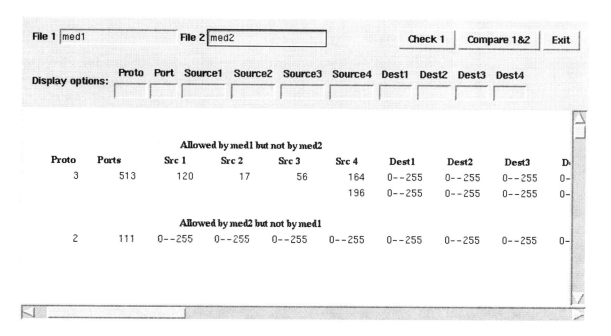

Figure 3. Analysing differences between two lists

Improving the Worst Case In its original form, a BDD is limited by the fact that in the worst case, it is possible that all its variables must be inspected before reaching a terminal node. This would require 83 bit operations in the previous example. Since on a normal computer, there is no special support for bit operations – bit operations are executed as byte operations – it seems plausible that combining several bit operations to be executed simultaneously will effectively squash the BDD lengthwise, improving lookup by a constant factor.

Experimental Work Current experimental work involves implementing a software-based packet filter that uses a BDD for its internal representation of rule lists, and comparing it to the existing packet filtering package *iptables* (the official Linux packet filter for the Linux 2.4 kernels). Experiments will compare the two filters' average and worst case performance in terms of their lookup times. Synthetic data will be used to simulate theoretical average and worst case scenarios, whereas real rule lists and packet traces (provided by local Internet and network service providers) will be used to provide evidence for how the BDD-based filter compares to existing filters in the real world.

A number of other approaches have been proposed for improving software lookup including [1, 6, 10, 11]. These approaches have had success, though they tend either not to generalise in some respects and/or have poor worst case performance, or insufficient experimental evidence has been given to allow an assessment to be made. A proper comparison between these approaches and the approach proposed here can only be done once our experimental work is complete.

5.2. Hardware-based lookup

Implementing rule lookup in hardware can reduce lookup latency significantly. One way to do this would be to implement the lookup algorithms using application specific integrated circuits (ASICs) for faster execution. Fore Systems Incorporated, for example, has used this approach in their Ethernet switches [7]. However, the BDD representation allows an even better way of implementing hardware rule lookup. Given a BDD representation of an access list, an efficient logic circuit can be constructed. This logic circuit could then be implemented on hardware, allowing extremely fast, parallel lookup to be performed.

Access lists are subject to change, and therefore, it would be inflexible to implement the logic circuit on ASICs, since they cannot be changed once fabricated. This is where programmable logic helps. Specifically, field programmable gate arrays (FPGAs) allow custom hardware to be constructed, by uploading a logic circuit design onto them [8]. And, since FPGAs are reprogrammable, the circuit can be changed when necessary. Hence, FPGAs allow changing access lists to be accommodated. An added benefit is that, while FPGAs are not as fast as ASICs, they are cheap in small quantities. Consequently, FPGAs provide a fast and low-cost solution to rule lookup.

The FPGA implementation of rule lookup is still under research and there are a number of issues to be addressed. For example, we have found that FPGA logic synthesis tools vary in the speed and size of the circuit they produce, given different input boolean expression representations (BDDs, sum-of-products, factored forms, ...). We are currently exploring different input representations to find a suitable one.

Another issue is that of logic minimisation. The method described in section 3 results in 83 different variables, which, combined with a large rule set, can result in a fairly complex logic circuit. It is necessary to optimise (minimise) the circuit to fit it on an FPGA and reduce circuit delay. However, in logic minimisation there is always a trade-off between circuit size and speed. At present, it is unclear whether it is possible to minimise the circuit sufficiently, to meet both these objectives satisfactorily. Nevertheless, preliminary research has shown promise in terms of fitting the circuit and reducing delay.

6. Conclusion

This paper has examined the problem of using filter rule sets for routers and firewalls. These rule sets are very important for both security and performance. Unfortunately as the size of the filter rule set grows it becomes more difficult to understand the rules.

This paper has shown that even large rule sets can be represented as a boolean expression in a compact way using BDDs. As a boolean expression it can easily be manipulated in various ways which allows the rule set to be manipulated and analysed.

- The rule set can be displayed at various levels of abstraction from different perspectives. This enables the user to understand what the rule set allows and does not allow.

- A range of queries can be performed on the rule set. This allows a human user to test the rule set to ensure that the behaviour of the rule set is as expected.

- The effect of changing the rule set can easily be seen. This can help reduce the possibility of errors being introduced.

- Some automatic analysis of the rule set is possible.

- A simple graphical interface to the tool enables the algorithms presented in this paper to be used easily without the user having to understand the underlying theory.

In all cases, the computational resources required are modest. By using these techniques a network manager can gain greater confidence that the rule set is correct. This will also allow larger and more complex rule sets to be used, improving both the performance and the security of the network.

There are a number of areas for future research. How to present the rules in tabular form in a compact way needs further work. A naïve algorithm works reasonably well, but the table size can grow dramatically. It should be possible to present the table more compactly. Also by integrating the tool with other tools like nslookup it should be possible present the information in a friendlier way. (From a practical point of view, a lot of work could be spent on the graphical interface.) Another possibility is using the boolean formula to generate the set of rules as a CISCO access-list (using only accept or only deny rules).

The prototype tool is not efficiently implemented (it is a collection of C, FL, Perl and Tcl/Tk code). While acceptable for a prototype, an industrial-strength tool would need to be efficiently reimplemented.

More experience and case studies could also lead to other ways of automatically analysing rule sets.

Our current research is focussed on the use of BDD representations for fast lookup, and we are tackling both software and hardware implementations. Over the next few months we plan to complete prototype implementations and to run several experiments to evaluate this technique. We also plan to do some comparative evaluations.

Acknowledgements We gratefully acknowledge the help of The Internet Solution who posed this question initially and who provided examples of real access lists to us. The work was supported by grants from the University of the Witwatersrand Research Committee and the South African National Research Foundation.

References

[1] A. Begel, S. McCanne, and S. Graham. Bpf+: Exploiting global data-flow optimization in a generalized packet filter architecture. In *Proceedings of ACM SIGCOMM 1999 Annual Technical Conference*, volume 29. ACM, ACM, Aug. 1999. Published as *Computing Communications Review*.

[2] B. Bollig and I. Wegener. Improving the Variable Ordering of OBDDs is NP-Complete. *IEEE Transactions on Computers*, 45(9):993–1002, Sept. 1996.

[3] R. Bryant. On the Complexity of VLSI Implementations and Graph Representations of Boolean Functions with Application to Integer Multiplication. *IEEE Transactions on Computers*, 40(2):205–213, Feb. 1991.

[4] R. Bryant. Symbolic Boolean Manipulation with Ordered Binary-Decision Diagrams. *ACM Computing Surveys*, 24(3):293–318, Sept. 1992.

[5] Cisco Systems Inc. Configuring IP Systems. Published at the Cisco web site, 1997. http:// www.cisco.com /univercd /cc /td /doc /product /software.

[6] P. Gupta and N. McKeown. Packet Classification on Multiple Fields. *Computer Communication Review*, 29(4), Oct. 1999.

[7] D. Newman. Firewall on a chip: Fore's FSA boosts throughput to multigigabit rates. *Data Communications*, January 1999.

[8] Z. Salcic and A. Smailagic. *Digital systems design and prototyping using field programmable logic*. Boston: Kluwer Academic, 1997.

[9] C.-J. Seger. Voss — A Formal Hardware Verification System User's Guide. Technical Report 93-45, Department of Computer Science, University of British Columbia, Nov. 1993. Available by anonymous ftp as ftp://ftp.cs.ubc.ca/pub/local/techreports/1993/TR-93-45.ps.gz.

[10] V. Srinivasan, S. Suri, and G. Varghese. Packet classification using tuple space search. In *Proceedings of ACM SIGCOMM 1999 Annual Technical Conference*, volume 29. ACM, ACM, Aug. 1999. Published as *Computing Communications Review*.

[11] V. Srinivasan, G. Varghese, S. Suri, and M. Waldvogel. Fast and Scalable Layer Four Switching. *Computer Communication Review*, 28(4):191–202, Oct. 1998.

Dynamic-Distributed Differentiated Service for Multimedia Applications

Dam Q. Hai and Son T. Vuong
Computer Science Department
University of British Columbia
Vancouver, B.C. V6T 1Z4
Email: vuong@cs.ubc.ca

Abstract

Differentiated Services (DiffServ) is a set of technologies by which network service providers can offer differing levels of network quality-of-service (QoS) to different customers and their traffic streams. In DiffServ, packets of the same QoS specification are grouped together and forwarded in the same manner, e.g. to a given subnet or set of subnets with some level of service provisioning. Thus, DiffServ scales better than the per-flow integrated service (IntServ). A major disadvantage of DiffServ in comparison with IntServ is that DiffServ does not provide a full guarantee to every application flow, especially for multimedia applications. In this paper, we propose the so-called Dynamic-Distributed DiffServ scheme that allows every DiffServ aggregate a fair chance of passing through the router in the same period of time, while guaranteeing an upper bound on the delay time and delay variations for multimedia data packets inside the DiffServ domain. The scheme is attractive in that it is simple and does not involve maintainance of complicated per-flow state information. The scheme works well for all DiffServ services, including the Premier service and the Assured Forwarding service.

I. Introduction

Recent evolution in high–speed communication technology enables the deployment of proliferating distributed multimedia applications combining a variety of media, such as text, graphics, images, voice, and full–motion video. Traditionally, network service providers provide all customers with the same level of performance (best-effort service); however, the best-effort service in the rapid expansion of the Internet has strained its current infrastructure capabilities. The support of QoS is a key challenge for the evolution of the Internet. Several players in the Internet arena are interested in QoS support. For example end users would like to send and receive their real time traffic (audio, video) with good quality; network provider would like to provide value-added services besides the pure transport of best-effort traffic; content providers are eager to have the chance to distribute their video and audio streams over the Internet.

In providing QoS guarantees, researchers have confronted technological challenges including intermedia and intramedia synchronization. This can be achieved via the so-called integrated service that supports individual flows with specific QoS requirements, e.g. RSVP flows, or via differentiated services that provide specific treatment (classification and forwarding) to packets from aggregate streams of the same QoS specification, irrespective of their individual flows.

The integrated services (IntServ) model has been proposed by IETF to provide for the support of Quality of Service in the Internet, but this model is deemed not to scale for network topologies larger that a few local routers. In this model, each "QoS flow" is identified within all routers in the path from the origin to the destination, which provide the required resources. The performance of backbone routers is severely affected by this "per-flow" approach because of the large number of the flows that must be handled by the routers. Those services also restrict the utilization of bandwidth over the network because the flow often does not use all of its subscribed bandwidth all of the time.

The Differentiated Services (DiffServ) model is a simpler approach, which handles well the scalability problems for the core routers. The basic idea is to support a set of traffic classes, e.g. premium service, assured forwarding service, besides the best effort service. In DiffServ, each packet entering a network will be marked with a DS (DiffServ) codepoint (a QoS specification). Packets of the same codepoint are grouped together and forwarded in the same manner, e.g. to a given subnet or set of subnets with some level of service provisioning. Thus, differentiated service supports a variety of qualities of services (QoS), such as premium service (PrS), expedited service (ES), and assured forwarding (AF) service; these are better than the BestEffort (BE) service, which is the only service provided by the legacy Internet. The premise of DiffServ networks is that routers within the networks handle packets in different traffic streams by applying different per-hop behaviors (PHBs) to the packet forwarding, and that services are built up from the building blocks of per-hop behaviors (PHBs). The service model is still under ongoing discussion, e.g. which kind of services can be provided, which levels of guarantees and so on.

An important difference between the IntServ and DiffServ model is that the former takes care of end-to-end behaviors in its intrinsic definition, whereas the latter basically specifies "local" (so-called "per-hop") behaviors, which must be somehow composed to achieve end-to-end significance. Much attention has been recently focused on differentiated service since it promises to provide scalable service discrimination in the Internet without the need for maintaining per-flow state and signaling at every hop.

A basic disadvantage of DiffServ in comparison with IntServ is that DiffServ does not provide a full guarantee to every application flow, especially for multimedia applications. DiffServ cannot provide a guaranteed share of the bandwidth for every flow as IntServ can. In [5] we proposed a class of so-called α-Bounded Differentiated Services that provide the guaranty of bandwidth sharing to the BestEffort packets. This scheme shows the advantage of DiffServ packet over BestEffort packet in the DiffServ domain but it does not ensure the fair sharing between the DiffServ flows. Aside from this disadvantage, the α-Bounded Differentiated Service does not lend itself to coexistence with other DiffServ schemes. In this paper we propose the so-called Dynamic-Distributed DiffServ scheme that provides a guarantee of a portion of bandwidth to each DiffServ packet at every router of the DiffServ domain. This scheme is not only simple to implement without requiring the per flow state information, but it can also co-exist with other DiffServ schemes and also guarantees the maximum delay time and delay variations for the packets moving inside the DiffServ domain. The last property is particularly suitable for the multimedia applications.

The Dynamic-Distributed scheme ensures that no single aggregate in the network can take all the bandwidth of the network for an entire period of time. It allows every aggregate a chance of passing through the router in each time period.

II. The Differentiated Services (DiffServ)

The transformation of the Internet into an important commercial infrastructure has significantly changed the user expectations in terms of performance, security, and services. While using a shared backbone infrastructure, Internet Service Providers would like to provide different services to different customers based on different service pricing or based on widely varying customer requirements.

To provide this differentiated service, service providers need some mechanisms for isolating traffic from different customers, for preventing unauthorized users from accessing specific parts of the network, and for providing customizable performance and bandwidth in accordance with customer expectations and pricing. In addition, service providers need some mechanisms that allow routing decisions to be made not just based on destination address and the shortest path to it, but also based on contracts between service providers or between a service provider and a customer.

In the differentiated service (DiffServ) model, each packet entering a network will be marked with a DiffServ codepoint (a QoS specification). Packets of the same codepoint are grouped together and forwarded in the same manner, e.g. to a given subnet or set of subnets with some level of service provisioning. Thus, the differentiated service supports a variety of qualities of services (QoS), such as premium service (PrS), expedited service (ES), and assured forwarding (AF) service; these are better than the BestEffort (BE) service, which is the only service provided by the legacy Internet.

Admission control is essential for QoS (Quality of Service) control in the presence of real-time multimedia applications such as real-time audio and video transmissions because these applications tend to consume more network bandwidth and last on a longer time scale. Forwarding engines must be able to identify the context of packets and apply the necessary actions so as to satisfy the user requirements. Such actions may be the dropping of unauthorized packets, redirection of packets to proxy servers, special queuing and scheduling actions, or routing decisions based on a criterion other than the destination address. In this paper, we use the terms *packet filtering* and *packet classification* interchangeably to denote the mechanisms that support the above functions.

The basic structure of a DiffServ domain makes a functional distinction between the edge routers and the inside (DiffServ domain internal) routers. The edge routers control DiffServ traffic entering the domain from an outside site to ensure it does not exceed the subscribed information rate (packet filtering); all excessive (out-profile) packets may be dropped or marked down to a lower class. Packet filtering functionality is required for example when a router is placed between an enterprise network and a core backbone network. The router must have the ability to block all unauthorized accesses that are initiated from the public network and are destined to the enterprise network

Once a packet has been marked with a DiffServ codepoint it should be served with the same per-hop behaviors (PHBs) by all the inside routers of the domain it traverses. It is evident that most filter rules naturally apply to a whole range of addresses, port numbers, or protocols, and not just to single predefined hosts or applications. Aggregation, for instance of addresses, is not only required because customers are usually allocated blocks of addresses, but also because it is necessary to keep the network manageable. Therefore, the specification of the packet classification policies must allow aggregations in their definitions. This means that packet classification algorithms must be able to process rules that define combinations of ranges of values. If the algorithms can only handle exact values and do not support aggregation, preprocessing is required to translate the ranges to exact values. This is infeasible since ranges can grow exponentially with length of the packet field on which the ranges are defined.

In the remainder of this subsection, we present a summary of the functions of the edge routers and the inside routers.

The functions of the edge routers:

Classifier: Classifiers select packets in a traffic stream based on some portion of the packet header.
Meter: Traffic meters measure the temporal properties of the stream of packets selected by a traffic profile.
Marker: Packet markers set the DiffServ field of a packet to a particular codepoint, adding the marked packet to a particular DiffServ behavior aggregate.
Shapers: Shapers delay some or all of the packets in a traffic stream in order to bring the stream into compliance with a traffic profile.
Droppers: Droppers discard some or all of the packets in traffic stream in order to bring the stream into compliance with a traffic profile.
Per-hop behavior (PHB): is a description of the forwarding behavior of a DiffServ router applied to a particular DiffServ behavior aggregate.

The functions of the inside routers:

Classifier: Classifiers select packets in a traffic stream based on some portion of the packet header.
Shapers: Shapers delay some or all of the packets in a traffic stream in order to bring the stream into compliance with a traffic profile.
Droppers: Droppers discard some or all of the packets in traffic stream in order to bring the stream into compliance with a traffic profile.

Per-hop behavior (PHB): is a description of the forwarding behavior of a DiffServ router applied to a particular DiffServ behavior aggregate.

The Network Simulator NS2 from UC Berkeley is used in our simulation experiments for a number of scenarios of multimedia traffic and network topologies.

III. Per-hop Behavior of the Dynamic-Distributed Differentiated Service

Generally, there are two basic approaches to admission control: *parameter-based* and *measurement-based*. The parameter-based approach seeks the worst-case or statistical analysis of the traffic based on *a priori* traffic characteristics and achieves admission decision by formal analysis. It can be used to provide *guaranteed QoS,* however, generally with the price of low network utilization. The measurement-based approach focuses on achieving higher network utilization for real-time applications that are tolerant of QoS deterioration. It relies on the measurements of actual traffic load and QoS performance in making admission control decisions.

Based on the subscriber number, the Meter determines if the packet from this customer would be on-profile or out-profile. If the packet is on-profile then it should be marked by the Marker with the appropriate DS byte and sent to the DiffServ Queue. Otherwise, the packet is out-profile and should be dropped by the Shaper. If the queue is full, the incoming packet gets dropped (this queue management is called DropTail). The BestEffort packets should be sent to the BestEffort queue and if the queue is full, the incoming packet gets dropped too. For the sake of simplicity, we assume there are only two services: BestEffort and Dynamic-Distributed DiffServ service.

In this paper, we introduce the PHB Dynamic-Distributed forwarding scheme for both the edge routers and the inside routers.

At the edge router, all packets from a customer are collected to an aggregate, but at the inside router a DiffServ aggregate contains all DiffServ packets from an incoming link. At the edge routers the DiffServ packets are classified by their flows that may number in hundreds at a router or in tens of thousands for the whole domain. At the inside router packets are classified by their aggregates, which may number in tens depending on the number of incoming links. This scheme can significantly reduce the amount of calculations at the routers of the DiffServ domain in comparison with the IntServ scheme and also ensures the fair sharing of bandwidth among DiffServ flows. This scheme is also useful for the multimedia DiffServ flows, which may have a constant rate, some time sensitivity, and a long connection time between the source and destination.

When the customers want to use the service from a DiffServ domain with some subscribing rates, they should send their packets to an edge router and all their information about the subscribing rates should be kept at this router. The customer should mark the DiffServ byte in their packets before sending them to an (ingress) DiffServ edge router. The (ingress) edge router would send those packets though the DiffServ domain to the another (egress) edge router before exiting the domain with the DiffServ PHB.

The ingress edge router aggregates all packets of each DiffServ flow from a customer into an aggregate; and the inside router aggregates all packets from each incoming link to an aggregate. Every DiffServ aggregate should get its share of bandwidth depending on the length of its queue at the beginning of the period (the subscribed bandwidth of the flow works only on the meter).

Every aggregate has its own queue, as shown in Figure 1 (all BestEffort packets constitute a BestEffort aggregate). The bandwidth is allocated to all aggregates per fixed time period, so-called *time frame*. In every time frame, the router sends all DiffServ backlogged packets at the beginning of a time frame and other aggregates would be served within the remaining time of the frame. If the total service time of the DiffServ aggregates is longer then the length of the time frame then the frame should be extended. When the router serves the DiffServ aggregates, the DiffServ packets should be sent at a tempo according to the length of their aggregate backlog.

This scheme adds some flexibility to the network in terms of routing table management. This advantage will be discussed in some future work.

This scheme provides considerable reduction in the amount of calculations at the routers of the DiffServ domain in comparison with the IntServ scheme, while enjoying the delay bound guarantee for DiffServ packets.

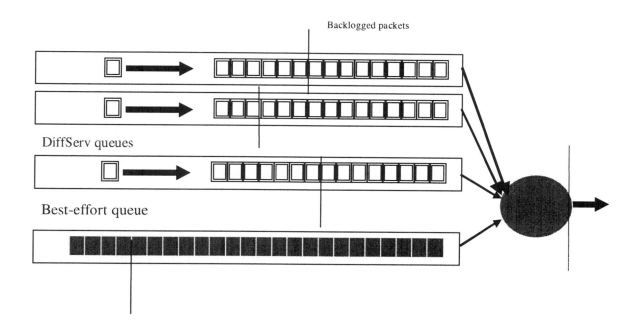

Figure 1. *Multiple-Queues in a Router of the DiffServ Domain*

Scheduling algorithm of the Dynamic-Distributed PHB

The scheduling algorithm of the Dynamic-Distributed PHB for retrieving a packet from the queues to send off to the respective outgoing line can be informally stated as follows. Every outgoing link of a DiffServ router has a fixed time slot which may be described as the number of bytes sent within the current time period. The length of the slot depends on the bandwidth of the outgoing link.

1. At the beginning of the time slot, the router looks into the DiffServ queues and takes care of all the backlogged packets first. All those packets should be sent in this time slot and all newly arrived packets must wait until the next round.
2. The router calculates the bandwidth share for each backlogged aggregate according with the backlogged number of bytes in each queue.
3. The router retrieves all backlogged packets from the DiffServ queues using the FQS (Fair queuing based on starting times) scheme [10], one packet at a time and sends them off.
4. The router returns to the BestEffort queue and uses remaining time of the slot to retrieve packets from the BestEffort queue, one packet at a time and sent them off. Go to step 1.

Thus, the BestEffort queue is served only when there are no backlogged packets in the DS queue, and the number of sending BestEffort packets depends on the size of the remainder of the slot (or until the queue becomes empty).

This scheme may be used with other DiffServ schemes such as Premier service by inserting the service time for those schemes into the time slot.

IV. Preliminary Evaluation of the Fair-Distribution DiffServ Scheme

For the preliminary evaluation of the fair-distribution differentiated service, the following assumptions are made on the DiffServ subscriber bandwidth:

1. There are two kinds of flows in the network: DiffServ flows and BestEffort flows; and the number of DiffServ flows is always less the number of BestEffort flows.
2. Two kinds of multimedia application flows are considered: CBR (Constant Bit Rate) and VBR (Variable Bit Rate).

3. Every customer S subscribes to the leaky-bucket rate with the number of bytes N_s ("bucket size") for the same time slot T.
4. The DiffServ subscribers inform the DiffServ edge router of their destinations and all flows do not change their destinations. In the future, we will consider the case where the DiffServ subscribers do not need to subscribe to the specific destinations and they can run multiple applications within their single flow.
5. The average aggregate of DiffServ packets is less than the throughput of the outgoing link, but the sum of the average aggregate of BestEffort packets and the average aggregate of DiffServ packets is greater than the throughput of the outgoing link. (The first part assumes that the router has enough resources to serve the DiffServ aggregate, the second part ensures that the capacity of the outgoing link is fully utilized).

The first conclusion is the delay guarantee of the DiffServ domain for the DiffServ packet. Let's denote PI_i as the time slot for router i on the path of the packet. We can express the total queue-waiting time of the DiffServ packet at all routers of the DiffServ domain as being lower then $\Sigma\ PI_i$.

In this the paper, we will consider the behavior of two kinds of multimedia application flows: CBR (Constant Bit Rate) and VCR (Variable Bit Rate). We assume all packets of a flow have the same length. Furthermore, we assume the traffic going through an

$$\sum_{i=1}^{s} BM_s < B$$

$$\sum_{i=1}^{s} BM_s + BM > B$$

edge router to an outgoing line comes from s DiffServ customers. The s DiffServ customers contain either CBR or bursty VBR (on-off) sources, characterized by statistical parameters such as peak rate, average transmission rate and average burst length, as well as by QoS requirements, such as packet loss probability and packet delay. We denote BN_s [bits], BT_s [s], $BM_s = BN_s/BT_s$ [bits/s], and p_s as the average burst length, the time slot, the average bit rate, and the packet length, respectively, of a source of the s-th customer. We also denote BN [bits], BT [s], BM = NB/TB [bits/s], the average burst length, the time slot, the average bit rate and respectively, of all best effort sources. Denote B [bits/s] the bandwidth of this outgoing line. From the 5th assumption above, we have:

For the nth packet of s customer which is In-profile (all out-profile packets should be dropped) we denote C_s^n, D_s^n , I_s , BL_p [bytes/s] , and DL_p the arrival time of this packet at the edge router, the outgoing time of this packet from DiffServ domain, the number of interior routers this packet must traverse, the bandwidth, and the delay time of the link from $p-1^{th}$ interior router to p^{th} interior router (if p=1 then from edge router to 1st interior router), respectively.

We have the following inequalities:

- For CBR flow

$$E[\ D_s^n - C_s^n\ ] \le \max(\ \frac{N_s}{T_s} - \frac{BN_s}{BT_s},0\ )*p_s +$$

$$\frac{(I_s+1)*N_s*p_s}{T_s} + \sum_{i=1}^{I_s}(\frac{p_s}{BL_i} + DL_i)$$

- For VBR flow

If the nth packet is the first packet of the burst, then

$$E[\ D_s^n - C_s^n\ ] \le \frac{(I_s+1)*N_s*p_s}{T_s} + \sum_{i=1}^{I_s}(\frac{p_s}{BL_i} + DL_i)$$

Else,

$$E[\ D_s^n - D_s^{n-1}\ ] \le \frac{N_s}{T_s}*p_s$$

From the above, we can guarantee the delay time to

the multimedia applications within the DiffServ domain which may combine hundreds of routers.

The numbers of calculations which must be performed by the Interior DiffServ router is many time lower then the number of calculations for the RSVP router because the number of calculations by the Interior DiffServ router is *O(number of outgoing link*) and the number of calculations for the RSVP router is *O(number of flows)*.

VI. Simulation and Results

To simulate the Dynamic-distributed Differentiated Service, we use the Network Simulator NS2 from UC Berkeley and develop some new features that support the fair-distribution DiffServ services. In our simulation experiments, every DiffServ packet has its DiffServ byte set to 1 and every BestEffort packet has its DiffServ byte set to 0.
The network topology used in our simulation experiments is shown in Figure 2.

We simulate 20 flows through each edge router (E1 to E5) all of which come out from E6. All the flows coming from E1,E2 and E3 must pass through Interior routers I1 and I2. All the flows coming from E4 and E5 must pass through interior router I2.

We simulate 10 CBR flows with the same parameters and 10 VBR flows with the same parameters for each edge router (E1 to E5), half of them is DiffServ whereas the other are BestEffort. All of the DiffServ flows go through a DiffServ edge router those implements the Dynamic-distribution Differentiated Service scheme with the predetermined subscription rates.

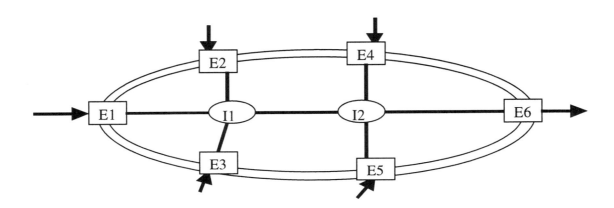

Figure 2. The DiffServ domain with 6 edge routers and 2 inside routers

The parameters of the CBR flow are as follows:
The average burst length (BN [bits]) = 6000bytes
The time slot (BT [s]) = 0.1s
The average bit rate (BM [bits/s])= 60kbytes/s
The packet size = 600 bytes.

The parameters of the VBR flow are the following:
The average burst length (BN [bits]) = 12000bytes
The time slot (BT [s]) = 0.12s
The average bit rate (BM [bits/s])= 100kbytes/s
The packet size = 600 bytes.

The parameters of the links from E1 to I1, E2 to I1,
E3 to I1, E4 to I2 and E5 to I2 are:
The bandwidth (BL) = 12Mbits/s
The delay time (DL) = 10ms
The time slot is the time used to send 200 packets (all
packets have the same length - 600 bytes)

The parameters of the link from I1 to I2 are:
The bandwidth (BL) = 30Mbits/s
The delay time (DL) = 20ms
The time slot is the time used to send 500 packets (all
packets have the same length - 600 bytes)

The parameters of the link from I2 to E6 are:
The bandwidth (BL) = 45Mbits/s
The delay time (DL) = 20ms
The time slot is the time used to send 700 packets (all
packets have the same length - 600 bytes)

Duration of the simulation is 2.9s.

With the above parameters, the simulation results are
onbtained and conveyed in Tables 1-4. The results
show a considerable difference in performance
between DiffServ flows and BestEffort flows. All
DiffServ flows do not suffer from any drop of
packets, but the BestEffort flows have about 25-30%
packets dropped. We can see that DiffServ performs
many times better than BestEffort in terms of mean
interpacket delay.

VII. Conclusions

In this paper, we propose the Dynamic Distributed
Differentiated Service scheme for the fair, simple,
flexible and efficient handling of DiffServ IP packets
within the Internet. We demonstrate its fair and
efficient performance in terms of packet dop rate,
mean packet delay and inter-packet delay, via
simulation of CBR and VBR flows of multimedia
data. In future work, we plan to investigate various
other types of multimedia application traffic such as
video teleconferencing, and experiment with various

performance measures, including delay, throughput
and jitter. Multicasting and security DS services will
also be examined.

References

1. Blake, Steve, et al., An Architecture for
   Differentiated Services. RFC 2475,
   December 1998.

2. Bradner, S., Key words for use in RFCs to
   Indicate Requirement Levels. RFC 2119,
   March 1997.

3. Floyd, S., and Jacobson, V., Random Early
   Detection gateways for Congestion
   Avoidance. IEEE/ACM Transactions on
   Networking, Volume 1, Number 4, August
   1993, pp. 397-413.

4. Nichols, Kathleen, et al., Definition of the
   Differentiated Services Field (DiffServ
   Field) in the IPv4 and IPv6 Headers. RFC
   2474, December 1998.

5. Dam Q. Hai and Son T. Vuong, A
   Simulation of α-Forwarding Differentiated
   Services for the Next-Generation Internet.
   CCBR 99, Ottawa, December 1999.

6. K. Nichols, V. Jacobson, and L. Zhang, A
   Two-bit Differentiated Services
   Architecture for the Internet?, Internet
   Draft <draft-nichols-diff-svc-arch-00.txt>,
   November 1997.

7. S. Floyd and V. Jacobson, Link-sharing and
   Resource Management Models for Packet
   Networks, IEEE/ACM Transactions on
   Networking, Vol. 3 no. 4, pp. 365-386,
   August 1995.

8. K. Poduri and K. Nichols, Simulation
   Studies of Increased Initial TCP Window
   Size, Internet RFC 2415, September
   1998.

9. K. Nichols, Improving Network Simulation
   with Feedback, Proceedings of LCN '98,
   October, 1998

10. Albert G. Greenberg, How Fair Is Fair
    queuing?, Journal of Association for

Computing Machinery, Vol 39. No 3, July 1992

11. C. Alaettiniglu, A. U. Shanker, etc. Design and Implementation of MaRS: A Routing Testbed, September 1992, http://www.ccs.neu.edu/home/matta

12. Y. Bernet, D. Durham, F. Reichmeyer, Requirements of Diff-serv Boundary Routers, Internet draft, draft-bernet-diffedge-01.txt, November 1998

13. Son T. Vuong and Dam Q. Hai, "Fair-Distribution Differentiated Services for Support of MultiMedia Applications in the Next-Generation Internet". IMMCN'2000 – the First International Workshop on Intelligent Multimedia Computing, Atlantic City, March 2000.

Flow	Type	Diff-Serv	Number of packets sent	Number of packets received	Number of packets dropped	Mean delay of first packet of Burst (s)	Mean delay between packet arrival of Burst (s)
1	VBR	Yes	400	400	0	0.26085	0.00015
2	VBR	Yes	400	400	0	0.25099	0.00014
3	VBR	Yes	400	400	0	0.26792	0.00014
4	VBR	Yes	400	400	0	0.26965	0.00015
5	VBR	Yes	400	400	0	0.27139	0.00016
6	VBR	No	400	278	122	1.04000	0.00373
7	VBR	No	400	265	135	1.05198	0.00419
8	VBR	No	400	280	120	1.04458	0.00387
9	VBR	No	400	269	131	1.04875	0.00409
10	VBR	No	400	272	128	1.05029	0.00369

Table 1: The statistics of the VBR flows through Edge router E1 to Edge router E6

Flows	Type	Diff-Serv	No of packets sent	No of packets received	No of packets dropped	Min packet delay (s)	Max packet delay (s)	Mean packet delay (s)
11	CBR	Yes	270	270	0	0.16429	0.27451	0.22987
12	CBR	Yes	270	270	0	0.16786	0.26786	0.23212
13	CBR	Yes	270	270	0	0.17098	0.27654	0.23123
14	CBR	Yes	270	270	0	0.16987	0.26987	0.23009
15	CBR	Yes	270	270	0	0.16534	0.27112	0.22876
16	CBR	No	270	175	95	0.27011	1.07107	0.69874
17	CBR	No	270	169	101	0.28576	1.09843	0.67098
18	CBR	No	270	172	98	0.27234	1.06987	0.70982
19	CBR	No	270	171	99	0.27865	1.07345	0.65687
20	CBR	No	270	162	108	0.28876	1.07129	0.66987

Table 2: The statistics of the CBR flows through Edge router E1 to Edge router E6

Flow	Type	Diff-Serv	Number of packets sent	Number of packets received	Number of packets dropped	Mean delay of first packet of Burst (s)	Mean delay between packet arrival of Burst (s)
1	VBR	Yes	464	464	0	0.10069	0.00011
2	VBR	Yes	464	464	0	0.10982	0.00012
3	VBR	Yes	464	464	0	0.10298	0.00011
4	VBR	Yes	464	464	0	0.10765	0.00011
5	VBR	Yes	464	464	0	0.10527	0.00012
6	VBR	No	464	321	143	0.61888	0.00480
7	VBR	No	464	319	145	0.62736	0.00498
8	VBR	No	464	330	134	0.60874	0.00487
9	VBR	No	464	327	137	0.63134	0.00468
10	VBR	No	464	316	148	0.61872	0.00492

Table 3: The statistics of the VBR flows through Edge router E4 to Edge router E6

Flows	Type	Diff-Serv	No of packets sent	No of packets received	No of packets dropped	Min packet delay (s)	Max packet delay (s)	Mean packet delay (s)
11	CBR	Yes	278	278	0	0.09840	0.18056	0.14192
12	CBR	Yes	278	278	0	0.09787	0.18728	0.14352
13	CBR	Yes	278	278	0	0.10982	0.17867	0.14564
14	CBR	Yes	278	278	0	0.09875	0.18374	0.14273
15	CBR	Yes	278	278	0	0.09682	0.18127	0.14437
16	CBR	No	278	202	76	0.15899	0.67216	0.41375
17	CBR	No	278	189	89	0.16758	0.68874	0.43674
18	CBR	No	278	206	72	0.15729	0.70984	0.44598
19	CBR	No	278	197	81	0.16098	0.67489	0.42365
20	CBR	No	278	191	87	0.16875	0.69808	0.43323

Table 4: The statistics of the CBR flows through Edge router E4 to Edge router E6

Workshop on

Dependability of E-Business Systems

Workshop on Dependability of e-Business Systems
Tuesday June 27, 2000

Held in Conjunction with
The International Conference on Dependability Systems and Networks
(FTCS-30 and DCCA-8)
New York city, NY, USA

Program Chair
Nick Bowen (IBM)

Program Committee
Wendy Bartlett (Compaq)
Linda Ernst (Intel)
Robert Horst (3ware)
Brendan Murphy (Microsoft)
Lisa Spainhower (IBM)
Michael Treese (Sun)

This workshop on dependability brings together technical insight of top researchers with business perspective from companies that are leaders in electronic commerce and driving significant volumes of business over the Internet. Attendees are researchers, product designers, and people deploying these systems. The day's activities provide a mixture of talks on key issues and interactive panel sessions with companies who are actively operating major e-business systems. The objective behind the panels is to engage the creators of the technology, the users of the technology, and the research community in a fruitful discussion about key issues that must be addressed in the 21rst century.

SCHEDULE:

8:30 - 9:30	"Internet Performance/Availability from an end user perspective" Eric Siegel, Keynote Systems
9:30 -11:30	Panel I: Dependability for Business to Business Systems
11:30 - 1:00	Lunch
1:00 - 2:00	"e-Business Issues for the 21rst Century," Brian Brandt, Strategic Consulting, Inc.
2:00 - 4:00	Panel II: Dependability for Consumer Based Internet Systems
4:00 - 4:30	Break
4:30 - 5:30	Forum: Key Issues for Industry, Research and System Development
5:30 - 6:30	Cocktail Hour: Meet the panelists
6:45	Depart to Dinner Cruise

Workshop on Dependability of e-Business Systems
Tuesday June 27, 2000

Invited Talks

Internet Performance/Availability from an End User Perspective, Eric Siegel, Keynote Systems

This talk provides a dose of reality by showing a view of Internet performance and availability as seen from an end users perspective. The material is based on extensive measurements of real world web sites. The company captures more than 16 million performance measurements daily using Keynote's global infrastructure of over 220 measurement computers connected to the major Internet backbones in over 90 statistically selected Internet access locations across 45 metropolitan areas worldwide.

e-Business Issues for the 21rst Century, Brian Brandt, Strategic Consulting, Inc.

This talk highlights several of the keys issues that are facing businesses as they enter the 21rst century. Particular focus is paid to those issues around providing high availability in an increasingly complex world where customer demands are constantly increasing.

Panel Sessions

There are two panels with one focused on business to business while the other is focused on consumer oriented systems. All the panelists will represent companies driving significant business over the Internet. Each panelist starts with an overview of their computing environment, issues that plague them, and suggestions for what the research and development communities should do to improve their environment. The session chair then leads an interactive and provocative session.

Panel I: Dependability for Business to Business Systems, Chair: Brendan Murphy, Microsoft

Panelists to include:

> Douglas F. Busch, Intel
> Tony Lostaglio, IBM

Panel II: Dependability for Consumer Based Internet Systems, Chair: Michael Treese, Sun Microsystems

Panelists to include:

> John Frech, Checkfree
> Carl Hutzler, AOL
> Brian Koster, Dell

Interactive Forum

Key Issues for Industry, Research and System Development

During this session participants have the opportunity to express their opinions on the critical issues that face industry, the research community and people deploying these systems. We expect a fruitful debate among this community on where the real issues lie.

Workshop on

Dependability Despite Malicious Faults

Introduction to the Workshop on Dependability Despite Malicious Faults

Current computing systems and networks are generally more vulnerable to deliberate, malicious attacks than to accidental faults, and the cost of damages produced by such attacks have increased dramatically in the recent years. Attackers' resources, competence and tenacity vary tremendously, since they range from irresponsible teenagers to criminal or terrorist organizations, from disgruntled employees to competing companies, from lonesome hackers to foreign government agencies. Compared to accidental faults, attacks are more difficult to predict, prevent and recover from. Consequently, they represent a new challenge for the researchers, designers or assessors of dependable systems. This is why this workshop takes such an important place in the first International Conference on Dependable Systems and Networks.

Considering the importance of these topics, the workshop Program Committee has chosen to select only a few of the high quality submitted papers, thus rejecting more than two thirds of the submissions. The selected papers have been assembled in two sessions devoted respectively to the analysis and the design of systems resilient to malicious attacks. Additionally, a plenary panel has been organized to address the increasing threat of "malicious code" implementing Trojan horses, logic bombs or trapdoors into innocent looking software. Exploiting new facilities to execute remotely, malicious mobile code is now changing form, from the currently numerous viruses and worms to the emerging malicious applets and mobile agents.

I wish to thank the authors who have chosen this workshop to publish their creative work and the program committee members for their thorough reviews of these submissions. Thanks to all of them, we are confident that this workshop will significantly contribute to improve the design of future dependable systems, as well as the analysis of current systems facing malicious attacks.

Yves Deswarte
Program Chair

Testing for Software Vulnerability Using Environment Perturbation

Wenliang Du
CERIAS*
1315 Recitation Building
Purdue University
W. Lafayette, IN 47907, USA
Email: duw@cs.purdue.edu

Aditya P. Mathur
Computer Science Department
1398 Computer Science Building
Purdue University
W. Lafayette, IN 47907, USA
Email: apm@cs.purdue.edu

Abstract

We describe an methodology for testing a software system for possible security flaws. Based on the observation that most security flaws are caused by the program's inappropriate interactions with the environment, and triggered by user's malicious perturbation on the environment (which we call an environment fault), we view the security testing problem as the problem of testing for the fault-tolerance properties of a software system. We consider each environment perturbation as a fault and the resulting security compromise a failure in the toleration of such faults. Our approach is based on the well known technique of fault-injection. Environment faults are injected into the system under test and system behavior observed. The failure to tolerate faults is an indicator of a potential security flaw in the system. An Environment-Application Interaction (EAI) fault model is proposed which guides us to decide what faults to inject. Based on EAI, we have developed a security testing methodology, and apply it to several applications. We successfully identified a number of vulnerabilities include vulnerabilities in Windows NT operating system.

Keywords: *Security testing, security flaws, fault injection, environment perturbation.*

1 Introduction

Security testing

Reports of security violations due to software errors are becoming increasingly common. We refer to such errors as "security errors" or "security flaws." This has resulted in security related concerns among software developers and users. All stages of software development are motivated by the desire to make the product secure and invulnerable to malicious intentions of some users. Our work is concerned with the testing of software with the goal of detecting errors that might lead to security violations.

Traditional methods for detecting security flaws include penetration analysis and formal verification of security kernels [18, 20]. Penetration analysis relies on known security flaws in software systems other than the one being tested. A team of individuals is given the responsibility of penetrating the system using this knowledge. Formal methods use a mathematical description of the security requirements and that of the system that implements the requirements. The goal of these methods is to show formally that the requirements are indeed met by the system.

A weakness of penetration analysis is that it requires one either to know or be able to postulate the nature of flaws that might exist in a system. Further, the effectiveness of penetration analysis is believed to be as good as that of the team that performs the analysis. A lack of an objective criterion to measure the adequacy of penetration analysis leads to uncertainty in the reliability of the software system for which penetration analysis did not reveal any security flaws.

Attractive due to the precision they provide, formal methods suffer from the inherent difficulty in specifying the requirements, the system, and then applying the process of checking the requirements specification against system specification.

Recently, several specific security testing techniques have been developed [4, 8, 19, 24, 22, 29]. As discussed in section 5, these techniques are either restricted to some specific security flaws or limited by the underlying testing techniques.

Another alternative for security testing is to use general testing techniques, such as path testing, data-flow testing, domain testing, and syntax testing [2]. However, the effectiveness of these techniques in revealing security flaws is still unknown and more studies are needed to justify their

---

*Center for Education and Research in Information Assurance and Security

use in testing for security flaws.

Outline of our approach

Our approach for security testing employs a well known technique in the testing of fault-tolerant systems, namely fault injection. This approach has drawn upon years of research and experience in vulnerability analysis [1, 3, 6, 17, 21]. Our approach relies on an empirically supported belief that the environment plays a significant role in triggering security flaws that lead to security violations [10, 17].

The problem

For the purpose of our discussion, we assume that a "system" is composed of an "application" and its "environment." Thus, potentially, all codes that are not considered as belonging to the application belong to the environment. However, we can reduce the size of the environment, by considering only those portions of the code that have a direct or indirect coupling with the application code. Such coupling might arise, for example, due to the application's use of global variables declared in the environment or the use of common resources such as files and network elements.

For various reasons, programmers tend to make assumptions about the environment in which their application will function. When these assumptions hold, the application is likely to behave appropriately. But, because the environment, as a shared resource, can often be perturbed by other subjects, especially malicious users, these assumptions might not be true. How to know whether a program can tolerate the environment perturbation is the key problem that we want to solve in this paper.

If we consider environment perturbations, especially malicious perturbations to be (malicious) faults, the above problem is considered as whether a program is able to tolerate various environment faults (not leading to security violations is considered toleration of such faults). In the remainder of this paper, we will use the terms "environment perturbation" and "environment fault" interchangeably where there is no confusion.

Fault injection–the deliberate insertion of faults into an operational system to determine its response–offers an effective solution to validate the dependability of fault-tolerant computer and software systems [5]. In our approach, faults are injected into environment thereby perturbing it. In other words, we perturb the application environment during testing to see how the program responds and whether there will be a security violation under this perturbation. If not then the system is considered secure.

Advantages of our approach

The use of environment fault injection technique leads to several advantages. First, in practice, it is hard to trigger certain anomalies in the environment, and knowing how to trigger them depends on the tester's knowledge of the environment. Therefore, testing software security under those environment anomalies becomes difficult. Fault injection technique provides a way of emulating the environment anomalies without having to be concerned with how they could occur in practice. Second, our approach provides a systematic way of deciding when to emulate environment faults. If we want to test whether a system will behave appropriately under certain environment anomalies, we need to set up those environments. However, the set up time is often difficult to control. If the set-up is too early, the condition might change during the test, and the environment state might not be what is expected when an interaction between the application and the environment takes place. If the environment is set up too late, the effect it has on the application's behavior might not serve the purpose for which it was set up. By exploiting static information in the application and the environment's source code, our approach can, however, decide deterministically when to trigger environment faults. Third, unlike penetration analysis, where the procedure is difficult to automate and quantify, fault injection technique provides a capability of automating the testing procedure. In addition, we adopt a two-dimensional metrics to quantify the quality of our testing procedure.

Research issues

Fault injection requires the selection of a fault model [5]. The choice of this model depends on the nature of faults. Software errors arising from hardware faults, for instance, are often modeled via bits of zeroes and ones written into a data structure or a portion of the memory [15, 26], while protocol implementation errors arising from communication are often modeled via message dropping, duplication, reordering, delaying etc. [14]. Understanding the nature of security faults provides a basis for the application of fault injection. Several studies have been concerned with the nature of security faults [1, 3, 6, 17, 21].) However, we are not aware of any study that classifies security flaws from the point of view of environment perturbation. Some general fault models have also been widely used [13, 27, 22, 29]. The semantic gap between these models and the environment faults that lead to security violations is wide and the relationship between faults injected and faults leading to security violations is still unknown. We have developed an Environment-Application Interaction (EAI) fault model which serves as the basis for the fault injection technique described here. The advantage of the EAI model is in its capability of emulating environment faults that are likely to cause security violations.

Another issue in fault injection technique is the location, within the system under test, where faults are to be injected. In the current stage of our research, we inject environment faults at the points where the environment and the application interact. In future work, we plan to exploit static analysis to further reduce the number of fault injection locations by finding the equivalence relationship among those locations. The motivation for using static analysis method is that we can reduce the testing efforts by utilizing static information from the program.

A general issue about software testing is "what is an acceptable test adequacy criterion?" [11]. We adopt a two-dimensional coverage metric (code coverage and fault coverage) to measure test adequacy.

The remainder of this paper is organized as follows: section 2 presents the fault model. A methodology for security testing is presented in section 3. In section 4 we will show the results of using this methodology in detecting real world programs. Finally a brief overview of related studies is presented in section 5 followed by summary of this research and the potential for future work in section 6.

2 An Environment Fault Model

In order to determine system behavior under various environment conditions, an engineer must be able to determine the effects of environment perturbation on a given system. Therefore, it is useful to inject faults that manifest themselves as errors in systems at the environment-application interaction level. To maintain confidence in the validity of the errors, the model used for these injections should be drawn from actual environment faults, while faults injected into the system should be able to emulate those environment faults appropriately. One assumption behind this requirement is that a security violation resulting due to the injected fault is similar to one that results due to an environment fault that arises during the intended use of the system.

2.1 Termi11ology

Definition 2.1 (*Internal State and Internal Entity*) Any element in an application's code and data space is considered an internal entity. A state consisting of the status of these entities is called an internal state.

Variable i in a application, for example, is an internal entity. The value of i is a part of an internal state. The size of a buffer used in the application is also a part of its internal state. In general, all information in this application's data space, stack space, and heap space are part of its internal state.

Definition 2.2 (*Environment Entity and Environment State*) Any element that is external to an application's code and data space is called an environment entity. A state that consists of the status of these entities is called an environment state.

For instance, file and network are treated as environment entities. The permission of a file, existence of a file, ownership of a file, real user-id of a process, and the effective user-id of process are different parts of an environment state.

A key difference between an environment and an internal entity, which makes implementation of a secure system difficult and error-prone, is the shared nature of the environment entity. An application is not the only one that can access and change an environment entity. Other objects, such as other users, may access and change the environment entity as well. Internal entity, on the other hand, is private to an application in the sense that only the application can modify and access them, assuming that the underlying operating system provides protected process space.

In concurrent programming, shared resources are handled by using the mutual exclusion and the semaphore mechanism to guarantee assumptions about the state of shared resources. However, we believe that few programmers use a similar mechanism to guarantee their assumption about the state of the environment. There are several reasons for this. First, programmers might not have recognized that the environment entities are shared resources. When, for example, an application writes to a file, it checks that it has the permission to write to that file, and then assumes that right in subsequent operations to that file without noticing that a malicious attacker could have change the environment thereby rendering the assumption false. Most security flaws resulting from race conditions [4] are caused by such dubious assumptions. Second, although some mechanisms, such as file locking, guarantee that a programmer's assumption hold on some part of the environment state, there is no general mechanism to do the same because the environment entity has various attributes and the mutual exclusion and semaphore mechanisms could handle not handle them easily. As a result, programmers often use *ad hoc* mechanisms to guarantee the correctness of their assumptions. This can lead to errors more readily than would be the case when a standard mechanism is used.

2.2 Developing a fault model

In order to provide high confidence in the validity of the security flaws caused by environment faults, the methodology described here models systems at a high level. We refer to this level as the Environment-Application Interaction (EAI) level. Fault injection at the interaction level attempts to emulate what a "real" attacker does. Since most of the vulnerability databases record the way attackers exploit a vulnerability, we transform these exploits to environment faults to be injected with little analysis on those records thereby narrowing the semantic gap between faults injected at the interaction level and faults that really occur during the intended use of the system. In contrast, other studies [22, 29] inject faults at the program statement level thereby leaving a large semantic gap between faults injected and those that might arise during the intended use of the application.

2.3 An EAI fault model

In general, environment faults affect an application in two different ways. First, an application receives inputs from its environment. The environment faults now become faults in the input, which is then inherited by an internal entity of the application. From this point onwards the environment faults propagate through the application via the internal entities. If the application does not handle the faults correctly, a security violation might occur. The direct reason for this violation appear to be faults in the internal entity. However, this violation is due to the propagation of environment faults. Stated differently, the environment indirectly causes a security violation, through the medium of the internal entity. Figure 1(a) shows this indirect way in which the environment faults affect an application.

Consider the following example. Suppose that an application receives its input from the network. Any fault in the network message related to this input is inherited by an internal entity. When the application does a memory copy from this message to an internal buffer without checking the buffer's boundaries, the fault in the network message, the fault being "message too long," now triggers a violation of security policy.

A second way in which an environment fault affects the application is that the fault does not propagate via the internal entity; instead, it stays within the environment entity and when the application interacts with the environment without correctly dealing with these faults, security policy will be violated. In this case, the environment faults are the direct cause of security violation and the medium for environment faults is the environment entity itself. Figure 1(b) shows this direct way in which the environment faults affect an application.

Let us now consider an example to illustrate this second kind of interaction. Suppose that an application needs to execute a file. There are two possibilities: one is that the file belongs to the user who runs the application. Here the environment attribute is the file's ownership. In this case the execution is safe. The other possibility is that the file belongs to some malicious user. This is an environment fault created by the malicious user. Now the individual who runs

the application assumes that the file belongs to the application. If the application does not deal with this environment fault, it might execute arbitrary commands in that file thereby resulting in a security violation.

The most error-prone interactions between an application and the environment are those that involving files. Programmers tend to use an abstraction of a file that includes only a subset of the file attributes. A file name with a location or file content, for example, is a commonly used abstraction of a file. The environment faults, such as a long file name or a file name with special characters, associated with this abstraction will propagate via the internal entity. If the application does not place appropriate checks on these internal entities, such environment faults will cause security violations such as those due to buffer overflow and the execution of an unintended command. The environment faults associated with the remaining file attributes, such as whether the file is a symbolic link, the ownership of the file, existence of the file, and the permissions associated with the file, will not propagate via an internal entity. Although these attributes are extrinsic to the application, if not dealt correctly, they are likely to directly affect the interaction between application and environment.

In summary, we have categorized the environment faults according to the way they affect applications. Environment faults which affect programs via internal entities are called *indirect environment faults*. Environment faults which affect programs via environment entities are called *direct environment faults*.

Indirect environment faults are further divided into five sub-categories according to their origins: (1) user input, (2) environment variable, (3) file system input, (4) network input, (5) process input.

Direct environment faults are similarly divided into three sub-categories: (1) file system, (2) process, (3) network.

3 Environment Fault Injection Methodology

3.1 Fault injection

Like the EAI model, which models the environment faults at the interaction level, fault injections are also done at the interaction level. The previous section classifies the environment faults into direct and indirect environment faults. These faults are injected using the following mechanisms:

1. **Indirect Environment Fault Injections:** An indirect environment fault occurs at the interaction point where an application requests its environment for an input. The input that the environment provides to the application will most likely affect the application's behavior. A secure application should tolerate an unexpected

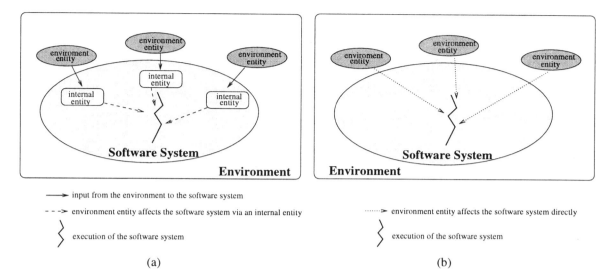

Figure 1. Interaction Model

Table 1. Indirect Environment Faults and Environment Perturbations

Internal Entity	Semantic Attribute	Fault Injections
User Input	file name + directory name	change length, use relative path, use absolute path, insert special characters such as "..", "/" in the name
	command	change length, use relative path, use absolute path, insert special characters such as "|", "&", ">" or newline in the command
Environment Variable	file name + directory name	change length, use relative path, use absolute path, use special characters, such as "|", "&" or ">" in the name
	execution path + library path	change length, rearrange order of path, insert a untrusted path, use incorrect path, use recursive path
	permission mask	change mask to 0 so it will not mask any permission bit
File System Input	file name + directory name	change length, use relative path, use absolute path, use special characters in the name such as "|", "&" or ">" in name
	file extension	change to other file extensions like ".exe" in Windows system; change length of file extension
Network Input	IP address	change length of the address, use bad-formatted address
	packet	change size of the packet, use bad-formatted packet
	host name	change length of host name, use bad-formatted host name
	DNS reply	change length of the DNS reply, use bad-formatted reply
Process Input	message	change length of the message, use bad-formatted message

anomaly in the environment input. One way to perturb the input is to use random input as in Fuzz [9, 24]. However, this approach dramatically increases the testing space, which and calls for a significantly large amount of testing effort. The Fuzz approach does not exploit the semantics of each input. Our vulnerability analysis, however, has shown that inputs most likely to cause security violations tend to have patterns according to their semantics. If, for instance, the input is a list of paths used to search for a command, then security failure will most likely occur when the order of these paths is altered, a new path is inserted or deleted, or the length of the list is increased. Other kinds of perturbations are less likely to cause security failure. Thus, by an examination of rare cases and by concentrating instead on fault patterns already observed, we reduce the

testing space considerably.

Faults injected into the application are based on patterns that are likely to cause security faults. These patterns come from our investigation of a vulnerability database and other studies reported in the literature. The faults are summarized in Table 1.

2. **Direct Environment Faults Injections:** A direct environment fault occurs at the interaction point where the application accesses an environment entity for creation, modification, reading or execution of an environment entity. Different status of environment entity attributes will affect the consequences of those interactions. Thus, the environment fault injections are used to perturb the attributes of an environment entity at points of interaction to see how the application re-

sponds to the perturbation. For example, before an application executes an `open` operation to a named `file`, several perturbations are performed on this file by changing its attributes such as its existence, permissions, ownership, and the type of the file since failure to handle these attributes is likely to cause security violations. These attributes are and their their perturbation are presented in Table 2.

3.2 Test adequacy criterion

An important issue in the management of software testing is to "ensure that prior to the start of testing the objectives of testing are known and agreed upon and that the objectives are set in terms that can be measured." Such objectives "should be quantified, reasonable, and achievable" [12].

We use *fault coverage* and *interaction coverage* measure test adequacy. Fault coverage is defined as the percentage of the number of faults tolerated with respect to that of the faults injected. Our conjecture is that the higher the fault coverage the more secure the application is. In addition to fault coverage, an additional measurement of the testing effort is the interaction coverage. Interaction coverage is defined as the percentage of the number of interaction points where we injected faults with respect to the total number of interaction points. Once again, we conjecture that the higher the interaction coverage, the more dependable the testing result are. Of course we assume that faults found during testing are removed. These two coverage criteria lead to a 2-dimensional metric for measuring test adequacy.

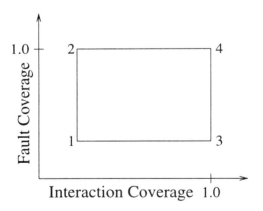

Figure 2. Test Adequacy Metric

Figure 2 shows the 2-dimensional metric and four sample points of significance. The metric serves as a quantitative evaluation of a test set. Point 1 is representative of the region where testing resulted in low interaction and fault coverage. In this case testing is considered inadequate. Point 2 is representative of the region where the fault cover-

age is high but interaction coverage is low. The test is considered inadequate since in this test, only a few interactions are perturbed, how the system behaves under perturbation of other interactions is still unknown.

Point 3 is representative of an insecure region because the fault coverage is so low that we consider the application is likely to be vulnerable to the perturbation of the environment. The safest region is indicated by point 4 which corresponds to a high interaction and fault coverage.

3.3 Procedure

The procedure of our Environment Fault Injection Methodology consists of the following steps:

1. Set **count** and **n** to 0.

2. For each test case, do step 3 to 9.

3. For each interaction point in the execution trace, decide if the application asks for an input. If there is no input, only inject direct environment faults; if there is an input, inject both direct and indirect environment faults.

4. Decide the object where faults will be injected.

5. Establish a fault list corresponding to this object using Table 1 and Table 2.

6. For each fault in the list, inject it before the interaction point for the direct environment faults; inject each fault after the interaction point for the indirect environment faults since in this case, we want to change the value the internal entity receives from the input.

7. Increase **n** by 1.

8. Detect if security policy is violated. If so, increase **count** by 1.

9. Calculate interaction coverage. If the test adequacy criteria for interaction coverage is satisfied then stop else repeat steps 3-9 until the adequacy criteria for interaction coverage is achieved.

10. Divide **count** by **n** yielding α to obtain the vulnerability assessment score (fault coverage) for the application.

3.4 Example

To illustrate the steps shown above, we consider an example of fault injection. The following code is taken from BSD version of `lpr.c`. Notice that `lpr` is a privileged application. It is a `set-UID` application which means that it runs in the root's privilege even when it is invoked by a user who does not have the same privilege as the root.

Table 2. Direct Environment Faults and Environment Perturbations

Environment Entity	Attribute	Fault Injections
File System	file existence	delete an existing file or make a non-existing file exist
	file ownership	change ownership to the owner of the process, other normal users, or root
	file permission	flip the permission bit
	symbolic link	if the file is a symbolic link, change the target it links to; if the file is not a symbolic link, change it to a symbolic link
	file content invariance	modify file
	file name invariance	change file name
	working directory	start application in different directory
Network	message authenticity	make the message come from other network entity instead of where it is expected to come from
	protocol	purposely violates underlying protocol by omitting a protocol step, adding an extra step, reordering steps
	socket	share the socket with another process
	service availability	deny the service that application is asking for
	entity trustability	change the entity with which the application interacts to a untrusted one
Process	message authenticity	make the message come from other process instead of where it is expected to come from
	process trustability	change the entity with which the application interacts to a untrusted one
	service availability	deny the service that application is asking for

```
f = create(n, 0660);
if (f<0) {
    printf(``%s: cannot create %s'', name, n);
    cleanup();
}
... (code skipped here)
if (write(f, buf, i)!=i) {
    printf(``%s: %s: temp file write error\n'',
            name, n);
    break;
}
```

Suppose that we have decided to perturb the environment at a place where the create system call is issued. This is an interaction point where lpr interacts with the file system. There is no input in this case and hence we simply carry out direct environment fault injections.

The next step is to identify the object. Here, n is a file name, and hence the object is the file referred to using this file name. Then we refer to Table 2 and get a list of attributes that need to be perturbed. This list includes 1) file existence, 2) file ownership, 3) file permission, 4) symbolic link, 5) file content invariance, 6) file name invariance and 7) working directory. A further analysis shows that attributes 5 and 6 are not applicable in this case as this is supposed to be the first time the file is encountered.

We then perturb the remaining four attributes of the file and inject the faults into the application. For example, the perturbation of the "existence" means that we make the file exist or not exist before the application creates it. The perturbation of "symbolic link" means that we make the file link to some other file, such as the password file, before the application creates it.

After fault injection, we execute the application and detect if there is any violation of the security policy. In this case the violation is detected when we perturb attributes 1, 2, 3 and 4. Doing so causes lpr to write to a file even when the user who runs it does not have the appropriate ownership and file permissions. Thus when the file is linked to

the password file, the password file is be modified by lpr. The problem here is that the application assumes that the file does not exist before the creation or assumes that the file belongs to the user who runs the application. In a real environment, this assumption could easily be false and the fault injection test points out a security vulnerability.

4   Result

4.1   Turnin

Turnin is a program used in Purdue for electronically submitting files for grading. Before students in a class can use this program, the teaching assistant (TA) for this class should have set up his account (or a dedicated course account) correspondingly. This includes creating a submit directory under the home directory of this account, creating a Projlist file under submit directory, which specifies a list of projects students could be able to turnin. Students can type "turnin -c coursename -l" to view the list of projects; students can type "turnin -c coursename -p projectname files" to turnin their project files. After submission, the submitted files will be copied to TA's submit directory.

Since turnin program allows students to copy their files to TA's protected directory, the program is running as SUID, which means its effective user is root. The program consists of 1310 lines of code.

Following our method, we have identified 8 interaction places where programmers could possibly have made assumptions about the environment. We make 41 environment perturbation to check whether programmers indeed made the assumptions, and whether the failure of these assumptions can affect program's security. Among those perturbations, 9 perturbation lead to security violation, which means the failure of assumptions on these 9 situation could lead to a vulnerability in the program. Then we investigated each assumptions by asking whether they are reasonable. For example, programmers obviously made an assumption that /usr/local/lib/turnin.cf file is trusted. Our perturbation testing found out that if this assumptions is false, the system's security will be violated. Since the turnin.cf will always be protected, so is its directory, we believe the assumption is quite reasonable, there is no vulnerability regarding to this assumption.

However, one assumption seems unreasonable to us, it turns out to be a vulnerability, and is hence exploited by us after we have known the assumption. The problematic code is list in the following:

```
if ((FILE *)0 == (fp = fopen(pcFile, "r"))) {
    printf("can not find project list file\n");
    exit(9);
}
```

Since fopen is an interaction point where potential assumption might be made, we perturb the environment status of pcFile, making it only readable by root, not by the people who is running the turnin program. The result is that by running "turnin -c coursename -l", we can successfully read the contents of the file that we are not supposed to be able to read. So, here the programmers have made an assumption that people are allowed to read file pointed by pcFile using turnin program, and its failure can cause security violation. Now, the question is: is this assumption reasonable? The result turns out to be NO since TA can make pcFile point to any file he wants, then using turnin program to read the contents of that file.

Knowing this fact, we designed a following scenario: a TA makes the Projlist a symbolic link to /etc/shadow, which is not readable by anyone except root. Then the TA runs "turnin -c coursename -l", Voila, the program prints out the content of /etc/shadow!

Another perturbation we have done is perturbing the attributes of the argument in the following code:

```
execve (acTar, nargv, environ);
```

Since *nargv* contains file names, according to table 1, we have inserted special characters, such as "/", "../", in front of the file names. The program does a good job in forbidding the "/" character, however, it does not resist the perturbation of inserting "../" in the front. Knowing this fact, a student can submit several ".login" files with different number of "../" in front of the ".login" file, such that when his TA unpacks the submitted file, the TA's ".login" will be overwritten by the student's malicious ".login" file, which can do anything evil to the TA.

The turnin program has been used in Purdue University widely since 1993, and we became the first to identify these vulnerabilities. After our discovery, the university quickly verified the problem and patched the turnin program.

4.2 Windows NT Registry

In Windows NT operation system, registry directory is a critical part to the system security. Registry directory is essentially an organized storage for operating system's and application's data which are globally shared by different applications and components. An appropriate configuration on each registry key in the registry directory is a key factor for security. Many security vulnerabilities have been reported due to inappropriate configuration of the registry keys. In the Windows NT 4.0 (SP3), there are still keys that are not protected. Our task is to test the related modules of the operating system, and find whether it is secure to leave those registry keys unprotected.

First of all, we use static analysis technique to find out where these unprotected keys are used [7], then we apply the EPA method to find if programmers have made assumptions that can fail.

We have identified 9 unprotected registry keys that could be exploited to break the system security, and indeed we came up with test cases to actually exploit the vulnerabilities. Furthermore, based on the similarities of these 9 registry keys and other 20 unprotected keys, we speculate that the same vulnerabilities exist for those 20 keys as well. However, we have not been able to perturb the modules that used the other 20 keys yet due to the lack of knowledge of how those modules work. The 9 registry keys that we have exploited are the results of applying our perturbation technique.

Due to the agreement with Microsoft, we are not revealing the exact keys and source codes that have the vulnerabilities. So, in the next discussion, we will not refer to any specific key, except the purpose of the key and the problem with the key.

One of the keys in the registry directory specifies a name for a font file. It seems pretty safe to give everybody the right to modify this registry key until we have found a module in the system that invokes a function call to actually delete this file. To know whether the program has done the correct checking before the delete or not, we did a perturbation on the properties of this file according to Table 2, making it writable only by administrator, and also making it point to a very important file (such as system configuration file) instead of just a font file. It turns out that the program fails to respond securely under this environment perturbation - when administrators run this module, they will actually delete the file specified by this registry key regardless of whether this file is a font file or a security critical file. The assumption behind this "delete" environment interaction is that the programmers assume the file name always points to a font file or a unimportant file, however, since everybody has the right to modify the value of this registry key, the assumption fail to sustain.

Another vulnerability we have found is associated with user logon module. When a user logons, the module will find the user's profile from a directory specified in a registry key. Using our EAI model, we have managed to perturb the trustability attribute of the directory, and found out that the program does not deal with the situation when the directory is not trusted, which means, whenever a user logs in, the logon module will go to the untrusted directory, and grab a specified profile for you. Therefore, by the environment perturbation, we have found out that programmers have made a fatal assumption about the trustability of the profile directory. After knowing the fact, it becomes straightforward to design a test case and fail the programmers' assumptions.

5 Related Work

A significant amount of computer security testing is performed using penetration testing. Security is assessed by attempting to break into an installed system by exploiting well-known vulnerabilities. Several researchers, including Linde and Attanasio [18], Pfleeger [25], describes the process of penetration testing. As pointed out by Pfleeger, the success of penetration testing depends on testers' skill, experience, and familiarity with the system. Moreover, the lack of well defined and tested criteria to decide when to stop penetration testing causes penetration testing difficult to use.

Our research attempts to overcome the above mentioned difficulties. It has a deterministic procedure to conduct and test, a criterion to decide when testing should stop. It overcomes the limitation of the lack of knowledge of the environment by emulating possible attacks using the faults injection technique. Finally, our approach overcomes the limitation of testers' knowledge by offering a set of concrete faults that should be injected into application.

Adaptive Vulnerability Analysis (AVA) is designed by Ghosh et al. to quantitatively assess information system security and survivability. This approach exercises software in source-code form by simulating incoming malicious and non-malicious attacks that fall under various threat classes [22, 23, 28, 29]. In this respect, our own work parallels the AVA approach. A major divergence appears, however, with respect to how incoming attacks are simulated. AVA chooses to perturb the internal state of the executing application by corrupting the flow of data and the internal states assigned to application variables. Our approach chooses to perturb the environment state by changing the attributes of the environment entity and perturbing the input that an application receives from the environment. Our

approach should be considered as complementary to AVA.

For attacks that do not affect the internal states of an application, AVA appears incapable of simulating them by only perturbing the internal states. For vulnerabilities that are caused purely by incorrect internal states, our approach cannot simulate them by only perturbing the environment. One disadvantage of the AVA is the semantic gap between the attacks during the use of an application and the perturbation AVA makes during testing. In other words, knowing that the application fails under certain perturbation, it is difficult to derive what kind of attacks correspond to this failure. This makes it difficult to assess the validity of the perturbation. Our approach narrows the semantic gap by perturbing at the environment-application level since most attacks really occur due to intentional perturbation of the environment.

Fuzz [9, 24] is a black-box testing method designed by Miller et al, which feeds randomly generated input stream to system utilities in order to test how reliable they are. The Ballista [16] testing methodology involves automatically generating combinations of exceptional and valid parameter values to be used in calling software modules. Both of these testing methods focus on the system reliability instead of security.

Bishop and Dilger studied one class of the time-of-check-to-time-of-use (TOCTTOU) flaws [4], and investigated using static analysis method to identify such type of flaws. Fink and Levitt employ application-slicing technique to test privileged applications [8]; Gligor has also proposed a security testing method using control synthesis graphs [19]. They both achieve a certain degree of success in security testing.

6 Summary and Future Work

We have presented a white-box security testing methodology using environment perturbation technique, a variant of the fault injection technique. The methodology is based on the Environment-Application Interaction (EAI) model, which captures the properties of a family of software vulnerability. We have applied this methodology to several real-world systems and applications, and we have successfully identified a number of security flaws that exist for several years without being discovered.

Future work will concentrate on applying this methodology to more applications. We are in the progress of developing and conducting a set of experiments to evaluate the effectiveness of this methodology. In the future, we hope to be able to develop a prototype tool for security testing based on this methodology.

References

[1] T. Aslam. A taxonomy of security faults in the unix operation system. Master's thesis, Purdue University, August 1995.

[2] B. Beizer. *Software Testing Techniques*. Van Nostrand Reinhold, New York, 1990.

[3] M. Bishop. A taxonomy of unix system and network vulnerabilities. Technical Report CSE-95-10, Department of Computer Science, University of California at Davis, May 1995.

[4] M. Bishop and M. Dilger. Checking for race conditions in file acesses. *The USENIX Association Computing Systems*, 9(2):131–151, Spring 1996.

[5] J. Clark and D. Pradhan. Fault injection: A method for validating computer-system dependability. *IEEE Computer*, pages 47–56, June 1995.

[6] W. Du and A. Mathur. Categorization of software errors that led to security breaches. In *21st National Information Systems Security Conference*, Crystal City, VA, 1998.

[7] W. Du and A. Mathur. Security relevancy analysis on the registry of windows nt 4.0. In *ACSAC'99 15th Annual Computer Security Applications Conference*, Phoenix, Arizona, December 6-10 1999.

[8] G. Fink and K. Levitt. Property-based testing of privileged programs. In *Proceedings of the 10th Annual Computer Security Applications Conference; Orlando, FL, USA; 1994 Dec 5-9*, 1994.

[9] B. Miller, L. Fredriksen and B. So. An empirical study of the reliability of unix utilities. *Communications of the ACM*, 33(12):32–44, December 1990.

[10] S. Garfinkel and G. Spafford. *Practical UNIX & Internet Security*. O'Reilly & Associates, Inc., 1996.

[11] J. Goodenough and S. Gerhart. Toward a theory of testing: Data selection criteria. *current Trends in Programming Methodology*, 2:44–79, 1977.

[12] H. Zhu, P. Hall and J. May. Software unit test coverage and adequacy. *ACM Computing Surveys*, 29(4):366–427, December 1997.

[13] W. Kao, R. Iyer and D. Tang. FINE: A fault injection and monitoring environment for tracing the unix system behavior under faults. *IEEE Transactions on Software Envineering*, 19(11):1105–1118, November 1993.

[14] S. Dawson, F. Jahanian and T. Mitton. ORCHESTRA: A fault injection environment for distributed systems. In *26th International Symposium on Fault-Tolerant Computing (FTCS)*, pages 404–414, Sendai, Japan, June 1996.

[15] G. Kanawati, N. Kanawati and J. Abraham. FERRARI: A tool for the validation of system dependability properties. In *Proceedings 22nd International Symposium Fault Tolerant Computing*, pages 336–344, July 1992.

[16] N. Kropp, P. Koopman and D. Siewiorek. Automated robustness testing of off-the-shelf software components. In *28th Fault Tolerant Computing Symposium*, June 1998.

[17] I. Krsul. *Software Vulnerability Analysis*. PhD thesis, Purdue University, Department of Computer Sciences, West Lafayette, Indiana, 1998.

[18] R. R. Linde. Operating system penetration. In *AFIPS National Computer Conference*, pages pp. 361–368, 1975.

[19] V. D. Gligor, C. S. Chandersekaran, W. Jiang, A. Johri, G. L. Luchenbaugh and L. E. Reich. A new security testing method and its application to the secure xenix kernel. *IEEE Transactions on Software Engineering*, SE-13(2):169–183, February 1987.

[20] E. J. McCauley and P. J. Drongowski. The design of a secure operating system. In *National Computer Conference*, 1979.

[21] C. E. Landwehr, A. R. Bull, J. P. McDermott and W. S. Choi. A taxonomy of computer program security flaws. *ACM Computing Surveys*, 26(3), September 1994.

[22] A. Ghosh, T. O'Connor, G. McGraw. An automated approach for identifying potential vulnerabilities in software. In *IEEE Symposium on Security and Privacy*, Oakland, CA, 1998.

[23] J. Voas, F. Charron, G. McGraw, K. Miller and M.Friedman. Predicting how badly "good" software can behave. *IEEE Software*, 14(4):73–83, August 1997.

[24] B. Miller, D. Koski, C. Lee, V. Maganty, R. Murthy, A. Natarajan and J. Steidl. Fuzz revisited: A re-examination of the reliability of unix utilities and services. Technical report, Computer Sciences Department, University of Wisconsin, 1995.

[25] C. Pfleeger, S. Pfleeger and M. Theofanos. A methodology for penetration testing. *Computers and Security*, 8(7):613–620, 1989.

[26] S. Han, K. Shin and H. Rosenberg. Doctor: An integrated software fault injection environment for distributed real-time systems. Technical report, University of Michigan, Department of Elect. Engr. and Computer Science, 1995.

[27] M. Hsueh, T. Tsai and R. Iyer. Fault injection techniques and tools. *IEEE Computer*, pages 75–82, April 1997.

[28] J. Voas. Testing software for characteristics other than correctness: Safety, failure tolerance, and security. In *Proc. of the Int'l Conference on Testing Computer Software*, 1996.

[29] J. Voas and G. McGraw. *Software Fault Injection: Incoculating Programs Against Errors*. John Wiley & Sons, Inc., 1998.

Survivability Analysis of Network Specifications*

S. Jha[†]   J. Wing[†]   R. Linger[‡]   T. Longstaff[‡]

Abstract

Survivability is the ability of a system to maintain a set of essential services despite the presence of abnormal events such as faults and intrusions. Ensuring system survivability has increased in importance as critical infrastructures have become heavily dependent on computers. In this paper we present a systematic method for performing survivability analysis of networks. A system architect injects fault and intrusion events into a given specification of a network and then visualizes the effects of the injected events in the form of scenario graphs. *In our method, we automatically generate scenario graphs using model checking. Our method enables further global analysis, such as reliability analysis, where mathematical techniques used in different domains are combined in a systematic manner. We illustrate our ideas on an abstract model of the United States Payment System.*

1 Introduction

Increasingly our critical infrastructures are becoming heavily dependent on computers. We see examples of such infrastructures in all domains, including medical, power, telecommunications and finance. Whereas automation provides society with the advantages of efficient communication and information sharing, the pervasive, continuous use of computers exposes our critical infrastructures to a wider variety and higher likelihood of failures and intrusions. Disruption of services caused by such undesired events can have catastrophic effects, including loss of human life. Survivability is the ability of a system to maintain essential services in the presence of undesired events. These events include malicious attacks and intrusions, and otherwise benign, but unanticipated failures [6].

In this paper we address the issue of survivability in the context of a highly distributed network of nodes. We are particularly interested in the global behavior of an asynchronous network of concurrently computing nodes and in the properties that hold of the entire network. In general, survivability is a property of the *entire network* and not just a property of a single node. Our goal is to find techniques for analyzing networks of nodes for survivability using the specifications of the individual nodes, interconnections between nodes, and of faults and intrusions to which the system is susceptible.

We believe that survivability analysis is fundamentally different from analysis techniques found in other areas (e.g., verification and analysis for fault tolerance, and reliability analysis). First, survivability analysis takes a *service view* of the system, i.e., the analysis focuses on certain key services provided by the system. Second, survivability analysis deals with *multiple dimensions* of the system with respect to a service, i.e., analysis simultaneously deals with fault tolerance, functional correctness, and reliability issues. In an abstract sense, survivability takes a *holistic view* of the system and hence is interested in a conglomerate of properties rather than an isolated one. To achieve this goal, the analytical approach described in this paper combines many different kind of analysis techniques. There are two important issues that any technique for analyzing survivability must address. Faults and intrusions should be allowed to be present simultaneously. There are many attacks that only materialize because of the interplay between faults and intrusions. For ease of analysis, the *independence assumption* (assuming that two abnormal events are independent) is prevalent in the fault-tolerant and reliability literature. We cannot make this assumption in analyzing systems for survivability. For example, if a server crashes, then it is easier for a malicious intruder to spoof the crashed server. Therefore, the chance that an intruder will succeed in spoofing a

*This research is sponsored in part by the Defense Advanced Research Projects Agency and the Wright Laboratory, Aeronautical Systems Center, Air Force Materiel Command, USAF, F33615-93-1-1330, and Rome Laboratory, Air Force Materiel Command, USAF, under agreement number F30602-97-2-0031 and in part by the National Science Foundation under Grant No. CCR-9523972. The U.S. Government is authorized to reproduce and distribute reprints for Governmental purposes notwithstanding any copyright annotation thereon. The views and conclusions contained herein are those of the authors and should not be interpreted as necessarily representing the official policies or endorsements, either expressed or implied, of the Defense Advanced Research Projects Agency Rome Laboratory or the U.S. Government.

[†] Department of Computer Science, Carnegie Mellon University, Pittsburgh, PA 15213. emails: {sjha,wing}@cs.cmu.edu

[‡] Software Engineering Institute, Carnegie Mellon University, Pittsburgh, PA 15213. emails: {rlinger,tal}@sei.cmu.edu

613

server depends on the event that the server crashes. In our method we allow users to express such dependencies. Introducing dependence between events gives rise to phenomena such as *correlated attacks* and *cascading effects*, where local attacks might not succeed, but when these attacks occur in tandem or succession can have a severe effect on the system. Distributed denial-of-service attacks is an example of a correlated attack (see CERT advisory CA-2000-0). Our framework addresses both issues.

Our main goal is to provide valuable information to the system architect during the design phase, and enable him/her to make important decisions at an early phase in the software life-cycle. Using our method a designer can visualize the global effect of local faults and intrusions. We provide the user with this information through a data structure called *scenario graphs*, which we automatically generated using model checking. By assigning probabilities to faults and intrusions of local nodes an architect can compute the reliability of the entire network. Using our method, the architect can also easily identify critical nodes in the network, i.e., where their failure would have a severe effect on the reliability of the network.

We use model checking for a very specific purpose in our method. Model checking is a technique for proving properties (expressed in a logic called the *Computation Tree Logic* or *CTL*) about specifications of reactive systems. We do not provide details of model checking here. Interested readers can refer to [4] for background material on model checking. The lack of knowledge about model checking will not impair the reader's understanding about the entire method. In this paper we use the model checker NuSMV [1].

The next section gives a general overview of our method. We describe a small example based on the United States Payment System in Section 3. We use this system as a running example throughout the remainder of the paper. Section 4 provides additional details related to each step in our method. Section 5 briefly describes a prototype tool *Trishul* that we are implementing based on our method, and describes some case studies that we have performed. Sections 6 and 7 discuss related work and conclusions respectively.

2 The General Methodology

In this section, we provide a brief overview of the general method proposed in this paper. We provide a detailed description of each step in Section 4.

2.1 Modeling the Network

First, we derive a finite state model from the specification of a network's architecture. We assume that nodes are described using a *stimulus-response* or *state machine* model.

We model a network as a set of concurrently executing finite state machines. Each node has a set of input channels and a set of output channels. We associate finite queues with the input and output channels. When an input arrives at a channel, it is appended to the associated queue. Similarly, when a system processes an output, it appends it to the relevant queue. A node can be in one of a finite set of states. In any given state, a node receives inputs from queues associated with a set of input channels, transitions to a state depending on the data it receives, and then outputs data on queues associated with a set of output channels. A network is a set of nodes and a set of *interconnections* or *couplings*. An interconnection is simply a pairing of an input channel to an output channel. The general techniques presented here can be applied to any specification language capable of modeling these basic primitives of distributed systems. In our work, we use the input language of the model checker NuSMV to specify our example network; using this model checker makes it convenient for us at later steps in our method when for additional global analysis, we need to derive information from NuSMV's output.

2.2 Injecting Faults and Intrusions

By our model of the network, we need not make a distinction between nodes and links when considering failures. That is, a link is simply a node that passes data between two other nodes. Both links and nodes may be faulty or be under attack.

For each node, the architect needs to decide the behavior of the node when a failure occurs. The exact behavior of a faulty or compromised node depends on the specific example. In practice, the nature of faults and intrusions that are injected into a node depends on the security policies and technologies deployed at that node. The specific details depend on the system being modeled.

For each module in the NuSMV specification that models a node, we introduce a special variable called `fault` that indicates whether a node is in the normal mode of operation, faulty, or compromised by an intruder. This special variable can have as many symbolic values as the user desires. For instance, the following definition in NuSMV states that there are three modes of operation for a node.

```
fault:  { normal, failed, intruded }
```

The user specifies the actual behavior of the node in each mode of operation. Transitions between various modes can be specified by the user or be completely non-deterministic. For example, a node can transition from the normal mode of operation to one of the abnormal modes (`fault` or `intruded` in our example) at any time. Figure 1 illustrates transitions between various modes of operation.

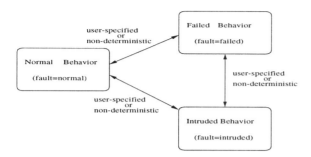

Figure 1. Transitions between different modes

2.3 Expressing Survivability Properties

Survivability properties in our methodology are expressed in the temporal logic *Computation Tree Logic* (*CTL*). We selected the Computation Tree Logic (*CTL*) because the tool we use accepts specifications in that logic. Our method would also work with other temporal logics (such as *Linear Time Logic* or *LTL* [13]). In this paper, we focus on two classes of survivability properties: *fault detection* and *transactional*. The first class of properties expresses whether the network under scrutiny can enter a faulty state. The second class of properties are related to the specific system services.

2.4 Generating Scenario Graphs

We first perform model checking to verify properties about the network. If a certain property turns out to be false, then we output a *scenario graph*. For example, if the property expresses that the network can enter a certain faulty state starting from the initial state, the model checker will output a scenario graph that encapsulates network behaviors that start in an initial state and lead to a faulty final state. A scenario graph is a compact representation of all the traces that are counterexamples of a given property. For example, suppose we want to check whether during the operation of a network a certain event (e.g., buffer overflow) never happens. If the property is not true (i.e., buffer flow can happen), the scenario graph encapsulates all sequences of states and transitions that lead the network to a state where a buffer flow occurs. We had to modify the model checker NuSMV to produce scenario graphs since this information is computed internally and not stored. We are still building tools to display the graphs to a system architect in a visually pleasing manner. In the operational security literature, scenario graphs are similar to *attack state graphs* [11].

2.5 Additional Analysis

Once we have a scenario graph, we can perform further analysis. In this paper we describe two kinds: *symbolic analysis* and *reliability analysis*.

Symbolic analysis
In this step the designer assigns symbolic probabilities, such as high and low, to events of interest (generally faults and intrusions of nodes and links). Since we do not assume independence of events, we use a formalism based on *Bayesian networks* [12] to specify the probabilities of the events. Each event has a set of events on which it depends. The probability of an event occurring depends on the past history of the set of events on which it depends. This point will become clear when we provide an example later in the paper. We combine this table of symbolic probabilities with the scenario graph, which the designer can then query. For example, the designer can ask for all scenarios that have at least one event with high likelihood of occurrence. Our tool then produces only those scenarios that satisfy the query.

Reliability analysis
Here, the designer provides numeric probabilities instead of symbolic ones. Again, we incorporate these probabilities into the scenario graph to obtain a state machine structure that has both non-deterministic and probabilistic transitions. We give an algorithm for computing system reliability on such a structure in Section 4. Later sections will provide more detail on each of these analysis.

3 Example

We consider a simplified model of the United States Payment System, depicted in Figure 2. To illustrate the architecture, we describe what happens when a bank customer deposits a check. For a detailed description of the system and this scenario see [9]. Assume that customer *A* gives a check worth 50 dollars to customer *B*. Let *Bank(A)* and *Bank(B)* denote *A*'s and *B*'s banks respectively. The following steps occur for the check to clear:

1. *B* deposits the check in his bank. If *A* and *B* have the same bank, the check is cleared in-house.

2. *Bank(B)* processes the check and bundles other checks received on the same day and sends it to the branch of Federal Reserve Bank nearest to it. To be concrete, let us assume that the Federal Reserve Bank nearest to *Bank(B)* is the Los Angeles (LA) branch.

3. The LA branch of Federal Reserve Bank sends the check written by *A* to the Federal Reserve Bank nearest *A*'s bank, say the New York (NY) Federal Reserve

Bank. The LA Federal Reserve Bank sends a bundle of checks, including *A*'s check, to the NY Federal Reserve Bank.

4. The NY Federal Reserve Bank processes the checks and sends the checks to the relevant banks. *Bank(A)* receives *A*'s check. NY Federal Reserve Bank debits *Bank(A)*'s account and credits the LA Federal Reserve Bank. The LA Federal Reserve Bank credits *Bank(B)*'s account.

5. *Bank(A)* processes the check and debits customer *A*'s account.

As illustrated in Figure 2, there is one more level between small banks and the Federal Reserve Banks. Institutions at this middle level are called *money centers*. If two banks are connected to the same money center, then transactions between them are handled by the money center; there is no need to go through the Federal Reserve Banks. For example, suppose a check with source address Bank-A and destination address Bank-C is issued. Bank-A and Bank-C are not connected through a money center, so the check is then sent to the money center MC-1. Assuming that the federal reserve bank FRB-2 is nearest to the money center MC-1, the check is transferred to the federal reserve bank FRB-2. Assuming that Bank-C is in the jurisdiction of the federal reserve bank FRB-3, the check is sent to the federal reserve bank FRB-3, and then makes it way to Bank C through the money center MC-3. We show the path of the check using dot-dashed lines.

4 Detailed Description

This section provides details about each step in our method. We give high-level descriptions of each technique and algorithm.

4.1 Modeling the Network

We model each node and link in the network as a finite state machine. The distributed network is a composition of state machines. We assume that suitable abstraction techniques have been applied to the real network to make it finite state.

In our banking example, nodes corresponding to the banks, the money centers, the federal reserve banks, and the links. Each node in the banking infrastructure corresponds to a MODULE description in NuSMV and message passing is simulated by parameter passing. We also assume the existence of a user who issues checks. The source and destination address of the checks are decided non-deterministically, i.e., the source address can be banks A, B, or C, and similarly for the destination. For simplicity,

we assume that only one check is active at any time, and the exact amount of the check is irrelevant.

4.2 Injecting Faults and Intrusions

Next we inject faults and intrusions in our model. Each node has a special state variable (called fault) associated with it. This state variable indicates the mode of operation of the node. For example, fault=normal and fault=intruded means that the node is in the normal and intruded mode, i.e., compromised by an intruder. We also specify the behavior of the node under each mode of operation.

In our example, we allow only the links between the banks and the money centers to fail and only the banks to be intruded. When a link fails, it blocks all messages and consequently no message ever reaches the recipient. We assume that a link can fail at any time; thus in our specification of a link, we allow a non-deterministic transition to the state where fault is equal to failed. We also assume that banks can sense a failed link and route the checks accordingly. Under the normal mode of operation, a bank receives a check (non-deterministically issued by the user) with its source address. Depending on the destination address of the issued check, the bank either clears it locally or routes it to the appropriate money center. For example, if a check with source address A and destination address B is issued, then it is sent to the money center MC-1 and then sent to bank B. On the other hand, a check with source address A and destination address C has to clear through the federal reserve banks (see Figure 2). If a bank is intruded, then checks are routed arbitrarily by the intruder (without paying attention to the destination address of the check). A bank can at any time non-deterministically transition from the normal mode (fault = normal) to the intruded state (fault=intruded). Once the bank is intruded it stays in that state forever.

The precise behavior of a faulty or an intruded node depends on the example, but two types of behaviors under failure conditions are common. In the case of a *stuck-at fault* the node becomes stuck, i.e., it accepts no input on its channel and consequently produces no output. A node with a *byzantine fault* exhibits a completely non-deterministic behavior, i.e., accepts any inputs and produces arbitrary or non-deterministic outputs. Byzantine fault can also be used to model an intruded node.

4.3 Expressing Survivability Properties

In this section, we model survivability properties in *CTL*. Although *CTL* is a rich logic and allows us to express a variety of properties, we focus on two classes of survivability properties. The first class is *fault detection properties* and the second is *transaction properties*.

Fault Detection Properties

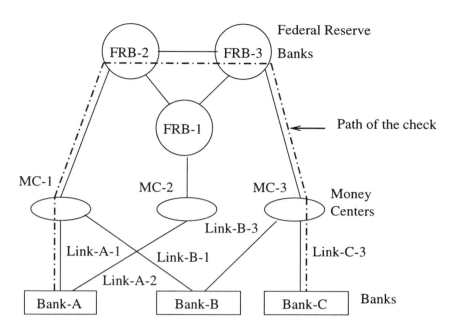

Figure 2. United States Payment System

Suppose we want to express the property that *it is not possible for a node N to reach a certain faulty state if the network starts from one of the initial states*. Let *fault* represent the atomic property that node N is in a faulty state. We can then express the desired property in *CTL* as follows:

$$\mathbf{AG}(\neg fault)$$

which says that *for all states reachable from the set of initial states it is true that we never reach a state where fault is true*. The negation of the property is:

$$\mathbf{EF}(fault)$$

which is true if there exists a state reachable from the initial state where the atomic proposition *fault* is true; in other words if the network starts in one of the initial states it is possible to reach a state where we have a fault. Suppose the desired property given above is not true in the specified model. Most model checkers will produce a counterexample, i.e., a trace or a scenario through the network that leads the node N to a faulty state. The atomic property *fault* can be as complex as we desire. It could mean that a certain critical node has entered an undesirable state (e.g., a critical valve is open in a nuclear power plant). In certain situations it could also mean that a certain unauthorized operation occurred on a critical node. For example, if a node represents a computer with a critical resource, it could represent the fact that somebody without the appropriate authority has logged onto the computer. The precise nature of a faulty state depends on the example at hand.

Transaction Properties

Many network systems are built for distributed applications. In this case we want to make sure that if a node N issues a transaction, then the transaction eventually finishes executing. Let the atomic proposition *start* express that node N started a transaction, and *finished* express the fact the transaction is finished. The temporal logic formula given below expresses that *for all states where a transaction starts and all paths starting from that state there exists a state where the transaction always finishes*, or in other words a *transaction issued always eventually finishes*.

$$\mathbf{AG}(start \rightarrow \mathbf{AF}(finished))$$

For the banking example, we verify that a check issued is always eventually cleared. This can be expressed in *CTL* as

$$\mathbf{AG}(checkIssued \rightarrow \mathbf{AF}(checkCleared))$$

We can also analyze the effect of a certain node (say N) being compromised by an intruder on the network. Assume that we have modeled the effect of an intrusion on node N (see discussion on injecting faults and intrusions). Now we can check whether the desired properties are true in the modified network. If the transaction property turns out to be true, the network is resistant to an intruder compromising the node N. This type of analysis will be very useful in determining vulnerable or critical nodes of a network with respect to a certain service. Using this analysis, if a node is found to be vulnerable or critical for a given transaction to complete, then one can deploy sophisticated intrusion detection algorithms for that node or bolster the security infrastructure around it. Thus our analysis can identify the critical nodes in a networked architecture and provide guidelines on how to make a network more survivable and robust with respect to the mission or service of the system.

4.4 Generating Scenario Graphs

This section describes how we automatically construct scenario graphs. These graphs depict ways in which a network can enter a faulty state or ways in which a transaction can fail to finish. Scenario graphs encapsulate the effect of failures on the global behavior of the network.

Fault scenario graph
Recall that we can express the property of the absence of a faulty reachable state as:

$$\mathbf{AG}(\neg fault)$$

Suppose the formula given above is not true. This means that there are states that are reachable from the initial state that are faulty. A *fault scenario graph* encapsulates all the scenarios or traces that drive the initial state of the network to a faulty state. If the architect models intrusions, the scenario graph is a compact representation of all the threat scenarios of the network, i.e., a set of sequences of intruder actions that lead the network to an unsafe state.

We briefly describe the construction of a fault scenario graph. Assume that we are trying to verify using model checking whether the specification of the network satisfies $\mathbf{AG}(\neg fault)$. Usually, the first step in model checking is to determine the set of states S_r that are reachable from the initial state. After having determined the set of reachable states, one determines the set of reachable states S_{fault} that have a path to a faulty state. The set of states S_{fault} are computed using fix-point equations [4]. Let R be the transition relation of the network, i.e., $(s, s') \in R$ iff there is a transition from state s to s' in the network. By restricting the domain and range of R to S_{fault} one obtains a transition relation R_f which encapsulates the edges of the fault scenario graph. Therefore, the fault scenario graph is $G = (S_{fault}, R_f)$, where S_{fault} and R_f represent the nodes and edges of the graph respectively. In symbolic model checkers, like NuSMV, the transition relation and sets of states are represented using *binary decision diagrams* (BDDs) [3]. All the operations described above can be easily performed using BDDs. The BDD for the transition relation R_f is a succinct representation of the edges of the fault scenario graph.

Transaction success/fail scenario graph
In the case of transactions we are interested in verifying that every transaction started always eventually finishes. Recall that we can express this property in *CTL* as:

$$\mathbf{AG}(start \rightarrow \mathbf{AF}(finished))$$

Since we allow several nodes to fail or be intruded in the network, in our experience we find that most of the time the property fails to hold. Thus more interestingly, during the model checking procedure, we derive two graphs: a *transaction success scenario graph* and a *transaction fail scenario graph*. The success scenario graph encapsulates all the traces in which the transaction finishes. The fail scenario graph captures all the traces or scenarios in which the transaction fails to finish. These scenario graphs are constructed using a procedure similar to the one presented for the fault scenario graphs. In our banking example, issuing a check corresponds to a transaction. The scenario graph shown in Figure 3 shows the effect of link failures on a check issued with source address Bank-A and destination address Bank-C (this is labeled as issueCheck(Bank-A,Bank-C) in the figure). The action of sending a check from location L1 to L2 is denoted as send-Check(L1,L2). Predicates up(Link-A-2) and down(Link-A-2) indicate whether Link-A-2 is up or down. Recall that we allow links to fail non-deterministically. Therefore, an action sendCheck(Bank-A,MC-2) is performed only if Link-A-2 is up, i.e., up(Link-A-2) is the pre-condition for performing the action sendCheck(Bank-A,MC-2). If a pre-condition is not shown, it is assumed to be true. Note that the failure of the link can also be construed as an intruder taking over the link and shutting it down using a denial-of-service attack. From the graph it is easy to see that a check clears if links Link-A-2 and Link-C-3 are up, or Link-A-2 is down and links Link-A-1 and Link-C-3 are up. We modified the model checker NuSMV to produce such scenario graphs automatically.

4.5 Additional Analysis

This subsection describes two types of further analysis that can be performed on scenario graphs, once they have been generated.

Symbolic Analysis
We first explain this analysis using the banking example and then provide a formal explanation. Assume that $A1$ and $\overline{A1}$ correspond to Link-A-1 being up and down, respectively. In general $\overline{E}$ will denote the complement of event E. Analogously, $A2$ and $C3$ denote the events corresponding to links Link-A-2 and Link-C-3 being up. Assume that event $A2$ is dependent on $A1$ and there are no other dependencies. We assume probabilities are symbolic, e.g., high, normal, and low. In order to perform computation with symbolic probabilities we need *abstract functions* corresponding to $1 - x$ and $x \star y$. Basically, we are using symbolic probabilities as an abstract domain for the real numbers. A multiplication table for symbolic probabilities is shown in Figure 4. Notice that the result of the abstract multiplication operation can be non-deterministic

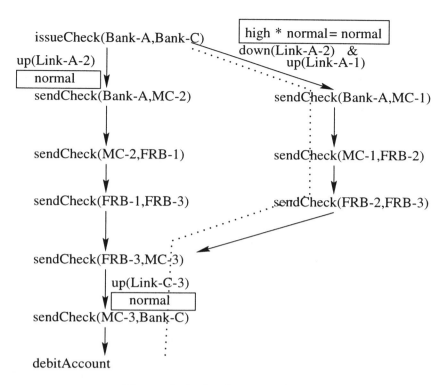

Figure 3. A simple scenario graph

⋆	high	normal	low
high	high	high	high,normal
normal	high	high, normal	normal, low
low	high, normal	normal, low	low

Figure 4. Abstract multiplication table

(see high multiplied by low), which is common in abstract interpretation. Abstract complementation operation (denoted by $1 - x$) is shown in the equations given below:

$$1 - \text{high} = \text{low}$$
$$1 - \text{normal} = \text{normal}$$
$$1 - \text{low} = \text{high}$$

Assume that probabilities $P(A1)$ and $P(C3)$ are both normal, where $P(A1)$ and $P(C3)$ are probabilities of links Link-A-1 and Link-C-3 being up. Probability of event $A2$ depends on the event $A1$ and is given in the following table.

Condition	$P(A2)$
$A1$	normal
$\bar{A}1$	low

The first row represents the probability of event $A2$ (or Link-A-2 being up) given that $A1$ is true (or Link-A-1 is up). Similarly, the second row represents the probability of event $A2$ when Link-A-1 is down. By incorporating these probabilities in the scenario graph we obtain a *annotated scenario graph*, i.e., graphs where some edges are annotated with symbolic expressions composed of high, low, and medium. The symbolic probability of the link Link-A-2 being down and Link-A-1 being up is:

$$
\begin{aligned}
P(\bar{A}2 \wedge A1) &= P(\bar{A}2|A1)P(A1) \\
&= (1 - \text{low}) \star \text{normal} \\
&= \text{high} \star \text{normal} \\
&= \text{high}
\end{aligned}
$$

These annotations are shown in Figure 3. Now suppose the designer is only interested in traces in the scenario graph that have *at least one event* with probability high. We can express this property as the following regular expression R over the alphabet of symbolic probabilities (in this case high, normal, and low):

$$(\Sigma - \{\text{high}\})^* \cdot \text{high} \cdot \Sigma^*$$

We then convert the regular expression R into a *deterministic finite automata* or *DFA* $D(R)$, and then we compose the $D(R)$ with the annotated scenario graph. Finally, we perform a reachability analysis on the composed scenario graph to eliminate states that do not have a path to the final state of $D(R)$. In our example, we would eliminate states that do not have a path to the final state which has at least one event that has probability high. Such a path is shown using dotted lines in Figure 3. Using the technique we just outlined, users obtain a specific *view* of the scenario graph in which they interested. Or, a designer can

enumerate threat scenarios that have a high likelihood of occurrence.

We now provide a formal description of the algorithm that we just outlined. Let L be the set of symbolic probabilities. We assume that there are two functions *minus* : $L \to 2^L$ and *mult* : $(L \times L) \to 2^L$. Recall that 2^L denotes the power set of L. We assume that the function *mult* is commutative. We write *minus(l)* and *mult(l, l')* as $1 - l$ and $l \star l'$ respectively. Intuitively speaking *minus* and *mult* are abstract counterparts of the operations $1 - x$ and multiplication for real numbers. First, we expand the scenario graph G by keeping the history of events with each state. We need to keep the history of events because in general the probability of an event is dependent on the occurrence of previous events. We write each state in the expanded structure, where we keep track of the history, as (s, h), where s is the state of the scenario graph and h is the history. Consider a transition $(s, h) \to (s', h')$ in the scenario graph G and let $E((s, h) \to (s', h'))$ be the set of events that occur on the transition $(s, h) \to (s', h')$. Let E be all the events of interest. In our banking example, E corresponds to link failures and bank intrusions and $E((s, h) \to (s', h'))$ are the failures and intrusions that occur on the transition. The transition $(s, h) \to (s', h')$ is labeled by the following subset of 2^L

$$\left(\prod_{e \in E((s,h) \to (s',h'))} P(e|h) \right) \left(\prod_{e \in E - E(s \to s')} 1 - P(e|h) \right)$$

The probability of an event e given history h (denoted by $P(e|h)$) can be found from the table the user provides. In the product given above we use the abstract multiplication operation for the set of symbolic values L. Therefore, in the annotated scenario graph each edge is labeled with an element of the power set 2^L. Hence the annotated scenario graph can be regarded as a non-deterministic automata over the alphabet L. Let $\mathcal{L}_G$ be the regular language corresponding to the annotated scenario graph. Next, the user provides a regular expression R over the alphabet L. Let $\mathcal{L}_R$ be the regular language corresponding to the regular expression $\mathcal{L}(R)$. We are interested in the intersection of $\mathcal{L}_G$ and $\mathcal{L}(R)$, which provides the scenarios of interest. Notice that the intersection of the two languages can be computed using the composition of the annotated scenario graph and the automata corresponding the regular language R.

Reliability Analysis

In this step, numeric probabilities are assigned to the various events. In our example, symbolic probabilities high, medium, and low can be set to 0.75, 0.5, and 0.25. The probabilities of various events are provided by the user in a tabular form as shown earlier. Again, we incorporate these probabilities into the scenario graph. Since we might assign probabilities only to some events (typically faults and intrusions) and not others, we obtain a structure that has a combination of purely non-deterministic and probabilistic transitions. In our banking example, assume a designer assigns probabilities only to the events corresponding to intrusions of banks and link failures. The user, of course, still non-deterministically issues checks. Intuitively, non-deterministic transitions are moves of the environment or the user, and probabilistic transitions correspond to the moves of the adversary. These structures are called *concurrent probabilistic systems* in the distributed algorithms literature [10].

We now explain the algorithm to compute reliability by first considering a property about transactions. Assume that we are interested in the following property:

$$\mathbf{AG}(\textit{start} \rightarrow \mathbf{AF}(\textit{finished}))$$

Let G be the transaction success scenario graph corresponding to the property. For every state s in the scenario graph G, we assign a *value* $V(s)$. We refer to V as the *value function*. In the initial step, $V(s) = 1$ for all the states that satisfy the property *finished*, and for all other states s we assume that $V(s) = 0$. A state s is called *probabilistic* if transitions from that state are probabilistic. A state is called *non-deterministic* if it is not probabilistic. For all states s that satisfy *finished* the value $V(s)$ is always 1, for all other states the value function is updated as follows: If s is non-deterministic then we update the value function $V(s)$ using the following equation:

$$V(s) = \min_{s' \in succ(s)} V(s')$$

If s is probabilistic we update the value function using the following equation:

$$V(s) = \sum_{s' \in succ(s)} p(s, s') V(s')$$

In the equations given above, $succ(s)$ is the set of successors of state s and $p(s, s')$ is the probability of a transition from state s to s'. Intuitively speaking, a non-deterministic move is made to minimize the reliability, i.e., we are computing the worst case reliability. The value of a probabilistic state is the expected value of the value of its successors. Starting from the initial state, the value function V is updated according to the equations given above until convergence. If $V^\star$ is the value function obtained after convergence and s_0 is the initial state of the scenario graph, then $V^\star(s_0)$ is the *worst case reliability metric* corresponding to the given property. If non-deterministic moves are equated with the system's environment making a decision, then the algorithm just described is similar to *policy iteration* used for optimal control of *Markov Decision Processes (MDPs)* [2]. The

proof of convergence is also similar to the one given in the context of MDPs.

Consider the scenario graph shown in Figure 3. If the symbolic probabilities `high`, `medium`, and `low` are set to 0.75, 0.5, and 0.25 respectively, then the reliability using the algorithm given above is $\frac{5}{16}$.

5 Status

We are building a tool *Trishul* based on the ideas presented in this paper. We implemented all the basic algorithms. We are finishing the visualization component and a customized editor.

We have finished two major case studies: a model of a banking system and a bond trading floor. Our model of the banking system is much more complicated than the simplified example presented in this paper. For example, we handle protocols such as *Fedwire* and *SWIFT* (used for transfer of funds and transmitting financial messages respectively) that we did not show here[1]. We have also modeled and analyzed the architecture of a bond trading floor of a major investment company in New York. The model of the bond trading floor is about 10,000 lines of `NuSMV` code and has about 100 state variables. Unfortunately, due to the propriety nature of the case study we cannot reveal additional details. We are in the process of "sanitizing" the model so that the case study can be published at a later date. Not surprisingly, we gained valuable experience during the case study. The most cumbersome part of the modeling process was the fault/intrusion injection phase because the nature of the faults/intrusions that were injected were heavily dependent on the security policies and technologies deployed at that node. We plan to automate the fault/intrusion injection process in the near future.

6 Related Work

Survivability is a fairly new discipline, and viewed by many as distinct from the traditional areas of security and fault-tolerance [6]. The Software Engineering Institute uses a method for analyzing the survivability of network architectures (called SNA) and conducted a case study on a system for medical information management [7]. The SNA methodology is informal and meant to provide general recommendations of "best practices" to an organization on how to make their systems more secure or more reliable. In contrast, our method is formal and leverages off automatic verification techniques such as model checking. Other papers on survivability can be found in the *Proceedings of the Information Survivability Workshop*.

---

[1] We thank Joe Ahearn of CSFB for clarifying the details of these two protocols.

Research on *operational security* [11] is closest to the work we presented. The attack state graph used in [11] is similar to scenario graphs we use. However, since we use symbolic model checking to generate scenario graphs, represented using *Binary Decision Diagrams (BDDs)*, we can handle extremely large graphs. Moreover, in our method a scenario graph corresponds to a particular service in contrast to the global view taken in [11]. We are currently investigating how to incorporate their concepts and analysis techniques into our method.

Allowing individual nodes to fail is similar to *injecting faults* into the specification of the network architecture. Fault injection is a well-known technique in the fault tolerance community. We allow the designer to specify any kind of fault, and thus we can consider a wider class of faults. Moreover, we allow different classes of failure events, such as faults and intrusions, to be correlated. The idea of computing reliability is not new. There is a vast literature on verifying probabilistic systems and our algorithm for computing reliability draws on this previous work [5]. The novelty of our work is that it combines a number of techniques in a systematic way and thus provides a *holistic view* of the specification of the system. This view on systems is at the core of analyzing and achieving survivability of distributed systems.

7 Conclusion

Survivability has become increasingly important with society's increased dependence of critical infrastructures on computers. In this paper we presented a systematic methodology for analyzing the survivability of networked systems. We use scenario graphs to help a system architect visualize the effect of faults and intrusions on the entire network, and we use both symbolic and numeric probabilities to reason about its reliability. The novelty of our work is in the systematic combination of a variety of mathematical techniques: model checking, Bayesian analysis, and probabilistic systems. In combination, we provide a multi-faceted view of the network with respect to a desired service.

There are several directions for future work. First, we plan to finish the prototype tool that supports our method. We are working on several case studies, including protocols used in an electronic commerce system. Since for real systems, scenario graphs can be very large, we plan to improve the display and query capabilities of our tool so architects can more easily manipulate its output. Finally, we are investigating how best to integrate operational security analysis tools such as COPS [8] into our method.

References

[1] Nusmv: a new symbolic model checker. http://afrodite.itc.it:1024/nusmv/.

[2] D. Bertsekas. *Dynamic Programming and Optimal Control*. Athena Scientific, 1995.

[3] R. E. Bryant. Graph-based algorithms for boolean function manipulation. *IEEE Trans. Comput.*, C-35(8):677–691, Aug. 1986.

[4] E. M. Clarke, O. Grumberg, and D. Peled. *Model Checking*. MIT Press, 2000.

[5] C. Courcoubetis and M. Yannakakis. The complexity of probabilistic verification. *Journal of ACM*, 42(4):857–907, 1995.

[6] R. Ellison, D. Fisher, R. Linger, H. Lipson, T. Longstaff, and N. Mead. Survivable network systems: An emerging discpline. Technical Report CMU/SEI-97-153, Software Engineering Institute, Carnegie Mellon University, Pittsburgh, PA 15213, November 1997.

[7] R. Ellison, R. Linger, T. Longstaff, and N. Mead. Survivability network system analysis: A case study. *IEEE Software*, 16/4, July/August 1999.

[8] D. Farmer and E. Spafford. The cops security checker system. In *Proceedings Summer Usenix Conference*, 1990.

[9] J. Knight, M. Elder, J. Flinn, and P. Marx. Summaries of three critical infrastructure applications. Technical Report CS-97-27, Department of Computer Science, University of Virginia, Charlottesville, VA 22903, December 1997.

[10] N. Lynch, I. Saias, and R. Segala. Proving time bounds for randomized distributed algorithms. In *Proceedings PODC*, pages 314–323, 1994.

[11] R. Ortalo, Y. Deswarte, and M. Kaaniche. Experimenting with quantitative evaluation tools for monitoring operational security. *IEEE Transactions on Software Engineering*, 25/5:633–650, Sept/Oct 1999.

[12] J. Pearl. *Probabilistic Reasoning in Intelligent Systems: Networks of Plausible Inference*. Morgan Kaufmann, 1988.

[13] A. Pnueli. A temporal logic of concurrent programs. *Theoretical Comput. Sci.*, 13:45–60, 1981.

Benchmarking Anomaly-Based Detection Systems

Roy A. Maxion

Department of Computer Science
Carnegie Mellon University
5000 Forbes Avenue
Pittsburgh, PA 15213 USA
Tel: 1-412-268-7556
Email: maxion@cs.cmu.edu

Kymie M.C. Tan

Department of Computer Science
Carnegie Mellon University
5000 Forbes Avenue
Pittsburgh, PA 15213 USA
Tel: 1-412-268-3266
Email: kmct@cs.cmu.edu

Abstract

Anomaly detection is a key element of intrusion-detection and other detection systems in which perturbations of normal behavior suggest the presence of intentionally or unintentionally induced attacks, faults, defects, etc. Because most anomaly detectors are based on probabilistic algorithms that exploit the intrinsic structure, or regularity, embedded in data logs, a fundamental question is whether or not such structure influences detection performance. If detector performance is indeed a function of environmental regularity, it would be critical to match detectors to environmental characteristics. In intrusion-detection settings, however, this is not done, possibly because such characteristics are not easily ascertained. This paper introduces a metric for characterizing structure in data environments, and tests the hypothesis that intrinsic structure influences probabilistic detection. In a series of experiments, an anomaly-detection algorithm was applied to a benchmark suite of 165 carefully calibrated, anomaly-injected datasets of varying structure. Results showed performance differences of as much as an order of magnitude, indicating that current approaches to anomaly detection may not be universally dependable.

Keywords: Anomaly detection, benchmarking, computer security, empirical methods, intrusion detection.

1. Introduction

Detection of anomalies in data is a core technology with broad applications: detection of clandestine nuclear blasts using seismic data [17], detection of cardiac arrhythmias in ECG data [1], detection of bridge failures (e.g., cracks, structural deteriorations, etc.) from vibration data, discovering semiconductor defects from plasma-etch data, detecting network faults from traffic data [11], ascertaining user-interface design defects from user data [10], etc. Over the last dozen years, another application has emerged: detection of unauthorized or malicious users on computer hosts and networks, often called intrusion detection.

Intrusion-detection systems have become available commercially over the past few years [2, 4, 14]). Although their deployment in the marketplace suggests that these systems benefit their users, there is almost no data measuring their effectiveness. The same paucity of evaluation results plagues the research arena [7, 8, 13, 20].

Evaluating detection systems is a difficult undertaking, complicated by several common practices. For example, most evaluations are done according to a black-box testing regime (e.g., [7]). While black-box testing can demonstrate the overall performance capabilities of a detection *system*, it reveals almost nothing about the performance of components inside the black box, such as how phenomena affecting the components (e.g., a feature extractor or an anomaly detector) or the interactions among them will influence detection performance. If the performance aspects of components like anomaly detectors are not fully understood, then the performance aspects of any system composed of such elements cannot be understood either.

This paper proposes benchmarking as an approach toward understanding the performance characteristics of anomaly-detection algorithms applied to categorical data. Because operational environments are unlikely to be identical in their characteristic signal and noise structures across different application enterprises, the benchmarking scheme incorporates datasets that vary in these characteristics, as measured by entropy, across a continuum from zero to one. The paper shows how a series of benchmark datasets was constructed, both for training and test data, and illustrates how the datasets were varied across a continuum of intrinsic structure to reveal the influence of that structure on the performance of an anomaly detector.

2. Problem and approach

The principal problem addressed here is the expectation that an anomaly detector will perform uniformly, irrespective of the environment in which it is deployed. Benchmarking seeks to address the problem of evaluating detectors across different environments.

Environment variation. All anomaly-detection algorithms operate on data drawn from some kind of computing domain or environment, e.g., a process-control environment, an e-commerce environment, an air force base environment, etc. Embedded in each type of environment is a particular structuring of the data that is a function of the environment itself. Because most, if not all, anomaly-detection algorithms depend on the intrinsic structure embedded in the data upon which they operate, it seems reasonable to assume that differences in such structure would influence detector performance. Structure can be conceptualized as regularity, or the extent to which a sequence is either highly redundant or highly random. High-regularity data contain redundancies that facilitate predicting future events on the basis of past events; low-regularity data impede prediction.

Approach. Benchmarking is proposed as a methodology that can provide quantitative results of running an anomaly detector on various datasets containing different structure. Sets of benchmark data, each set with its own regularity, measured in ten equal steps from 0 to 1, were constructed and used to test anomaly-detection capabilities. Calibrated anomalies were injected into test sets at specified intervals.

Hypotheses. The work described in this paper tests the hypotheses that (1) differences in data regularities, *do* influence detector performances, and (2) such differences will be found in natural environments. If the working hypotheses are true, there are certain implications for anomaly detection, particularly in an information-assurance regime such as intrusion detection. First, the common practice of deploying a particular anomaly detector across several environments may have unintended consequences on detection outcomes, such as increasing false-alarm rates; second, detecting masqueraders by training on a user's behavior in one time period, and testing against that same user's behavior in another time period, may encounter difficulties if the environmental characteristics differ significantly among the several time periods. The extent to which such differences influence detector outcomes may be a function of the environment itself.

Anticipated results. If the first hypothesis is true (differences in data regularities do influence detector performances), then testing an anomaly detector across a range of environmental or behavioral regularities should produce a range of relative operating characteristic (ROC) curves; otherwise, the ROC curves should all be superimposed upon one another. If the second hypothesis is true (characteristic differences will be found in natural environments), then there is convincing evidence that a given anomaly detector cannot be moved arbitrarily from one environment to another without accommodating the differences in regularity (provided that the first hypothesis is true).

3. Structure in categorical data

The idea of intrinsic structure, or regularity, in a categorical data sequence is intuitive. A structured sequence has a definite organizational pattern. That a sequence's structure is intrinsic means that it is the essential nature of the sequence to contain such structure, on the basis of regularities in the process that generated the sequence. Such structure spans a continuum from highly irregular (e.g., random, no apparent structure) to highly regular (e.g., perfectly systematic, readily apparent structure). Examples of sequences with systematic, or regular, structure are: A A A A ... or A B A B A B ... . The most interesting examples lie somewhere between the extremes of perfect regularity and perfect randomness.

The usual measure of randomness (uncertainty) in a sequence, X, of categorical data, is entropy, sometimes called the Shannon-Wiener Index [18]. Because entropy has no upper bound (in terms of bits), and because it is desirable to measure the randomness of a sequence on a 0-1 scale, relative entropy is used. Relative entropy is simply the entropy of the sequence divided by the maximum entropy for that sequence.

Some events in data sequences necessarily precede others, introducing a notion of sequential dependence amongst the elements of the sequence. Conditional relative entropy reflects this sequential dependency by accounting not only for the probability of an event, but also for the probability of its predecessor. These concepts are covered in most texts on information theory, such as [3]. Conditional relative entropy is used to measure the structure present in the benchmark datasets presented in this paper.

Many anomaly-detection systems depend on the presence of regularities in data (e.g., [5, 6, 15, 20]). In the remainder of this paper, the terms *regularity* or *regularity index* refer to the sequential dependencies of sequences as measured by entropy. A regularity index of 0 indicates perfect regularity (or redundancy); an index of 1 indicates no regularity, i.e., random.

4. Constructing the benchmark datasets

This section provides details of the benchmarking process, followed by an experiment validating the hypothesis that detector performance is influenced by intrinsic structure in background data.

In general, three kinds of data need to be generated: training data (normal background), testing data (background plus anomalous events), and the anomalies themselves. In benchmarking parlance, the training and testing data constitute the anomaly-detector workload. Several factors influence the composition of a sequence: alphabet size, alphabet symbols, regularity or randomness, sequential dependencies among symbols or subsequences, and length. This section describes how the datasets were generated and subsequently combined with anomalies to form the benchmark datasets.

4.1. Defining the sequences

The benchmark training datasets are made up of five suites of eleven files each, totaling 55 files. Each suite used a predetermined alphabet size whose constituency was held constant within the suite. Each suite contained eleven unidimensional datasets with regularities (conditional relative entropies) equally spaced at 0.1 intervals, from 0 to 1 inclusive.

Alphabet size. Alphabet sizes were 2, 4, 6, 8, and 10, yielding the five aforementioned suites. Low-order alphabets have the advantage that almost all operations on them are computationally easy; high-order alphabets, e.g., 10 or more, require significantly more computation, and hence the experiment was limited to a maximum alphabet size of 10.

Alphabet symbols. Symbols for categorical data can be almost anything. In this experiment, symbols were drawn from the standard English alphabet (e.g., A, B, C, D, E, F for alphabet size 6) for simplicity's sake. The symbols could have been system kernel-call names, but such names are longer than a single element, and hence slightly clumsier to handle.

Regularity. Regularity (conditional relative entropy) for a sequence is determined by the transition matrix from which the sequence is generated. There were eleven such matrices, one for each regularity level from 0 to 1 in steps of 0.1.

Sequence length. Because the detector (described later) used in this experiment is based on a moving window that encompasses n sequence elements at once, the datasets needed to be long enough to contain all possible n-grams for a given alphabet to guarantee equiprobable occurrence of n-grams. When the sequence does not contain all possible n-grams, empirical regularity (calculated from the data) will reflect this, and the equiprobable case will be impossible to obtain. For this reason, all datasets contained 500,000 characters (or events).

4.2. Defining the anomalies

An anomalous event is a surprising event. An event is a subsequence of one or more symbols. The extent to which an anomaly is considered surprising is determined by the anomaly detector itself, often on the basis of the expected probability of encountering the event. The anomalous events defined here are considered to be juxtapositional anomalies -- events juxtaposed in unexpected ways. Another type of anomaly, not considered here, is the temporal anomaly, which manifests as unexpected periodicities. Benchmark datasets could be built for either type of anomaly. Several types of juxtapositional anomalies are defined for this study:

Foreign-symbol anomalies. A foreign-symbol anomaly contains symbols not included in the training-set alphabet. For example, any symbol, such as a Q, not in the training-set alphabet comprised of A B C D E F would be considered a foreign symbol. Detection of such anomalies should be relatively simple.

Foreign n-gram anomalies. An n-gram that contains a sequence not found in any n-gram in the training dataset (but not containing a foreign symbol) is considered a foreign n-gram, because it is foreign to the training dataset. A foreign n-gram anomaly contains n-grams not present in the training data. For example, given an alphabet of A B C D E F, the set of all bigrams would contain AA AB AC ... FF, for a total of $6^2=36$ (in general, for an alphabet of α symbols and an n-gram of size n, total possible n-grams = α^n). If the training data contained all bigrams except CC, then CC would be a foreign n-gram. Note that if a foreign symbol appears in an n-gram, that would be a foreign-symbol anomaly, not a foreign n-gram anomaly. In real-world data it is quite common that not all possible n-grams are contained in the data, partly due to the relatively high regularity with which computers operate, and partly due to the large alphabets in, for example, kernel-call streams.

Rare n-gram anomalies. A rare n-gram anomaly contains n-grams that are infrequent in the training data. In the example above, if the n-gram AA constituted 96% of the events in the sequence, and the n-grams BB and CC constituted 2% each, then BB and CC would be rare n-gram anomalies. An n-gram whose exact duplicate is found only rarely in the training dataset is called a rare n-gram. The concept of *rare* is determined by a user-specified threshold. A typical threshold might be .05, which was the threshold used to generate the data sets for the present work. A threshold of .05 means that a rare n-gram would have a frequency of occurrence in the training data of not more than 5%. The selection of this threshold is arbitrary, but should be low enough for "rare" to be meaningful.

4.3. Generating the training and test data

The training data are generated from 11 transition matrices that produce the desired regularities for the sequences such that the regularity indices of the sequences run, in increments of .1, from 0 to 1 inclusive. The transition matrix is entered at a random point, determined by a random number generator. Once inside the transition matrix, each transition is determined by a random number between 0 and 1. To permit using any random number generator, particularly one that has been certified to be as random as technically possible [9], the 500,000 random numbers are computed first, stored in a table, and then used in determining the matrix transitions. In this way, the random-number sequence can be retained, if need be, to enable perfect repetition of the experimental sequence. The seed used for generation is different from the one used to enter the table, simply to go as far as possible to eliminate dependencies in the generation scheme. A single seed is used to generate data for all regularities. The seed is a 4-digit random integer produced from the Perl rand() function. Test data were generated in the same way in which the training data were generated, except that different random-number-generator seeds were used for generating the test data. Using new seeds for the test data guarantees that the generated sequences will retain the same intrinsic structure as seen in the training data, while ensuring that the specific order of symbols is not identical to that in the training data.

4.4. Generating the anomalies

A pool of anomalies is generated independent of generating the test data. A separate pool is generated for each anomaly type. After the pool is prepared, anomalies are drawn from the appropriate pool, and injected into the test data in accordance with the plan detailed in Section 4.5. Each of the anomaly types is generated in a different way, although the size of each anomaly is selected according to common criteria that reflect experimental goals. In the present case, the anomaly size was chosen to be 4, because the window parameter of the detector was set to 4. The paragraph below details the injection process for the various anomaly types.

4.5. Injecting anomalies into test data

The test data were generated without anomalies, as described in Section 4.3, and anomalies were injected into the test data later. The system determines the maximum number of anomalies to inject. This number is arbitrary, but is kept low enough so that the injected anomalies do not change the regularity of the test data. In practice, a heuristic is used that limits the number of injection replacements to not more than .24% of the uninjected test data. As a simple example, if the test data contains 500,000 elements, then .24% of these would be 1200 events which could be replaced by anomalies. If the anomaly size is 4, then only 300 4-gram anomalies could be injected into the test data. An injection interval is selected that determines the minimum and maximum spacing between anomalies. An anomaly is selected at random, with replacement, from the anomaly pool (foreign symbol, foreign n-gram or rare n-gram) and injected according to the constraints imposed by the injection interval. Each injected n-gram anomaly replaces n elements of the test sequence. After the injections have been done, the regularity of the test sequence is recalculated. If the recalculated regularity differs from the target regularity by more than .05, the injections are backed out, and the process is repeated using a broader spacing interval. Of course it is expected that the change in regularity will be larger when injecting foreign symbols.

5. Experiment one: synthetic benchmarks

This experiment tests the hypothesis that the performance of an anomaly detector is influenced by intrinsic structure (i.e., regularity as measured by conditional relative entropy) in data sequences; that is, the hypothesis that the nature of "normal" background noise affects signal detection. If the hypothesis is correct, then the same anomalies, injected into datasets that differ only in regularity, would be expected to generate different hit, miss and false-alarm rates; i.e., the ROC curve for a given regularity should not be superimposed on the ROC curve for any other regularity. If the hypothesis is not true, then all ROCs should be superimposed on one another. A noteworthy implication of this hypothesis, if true, is that if intrinsic structure does influence anomaly-detection capability, the performance of a given anomaly detector will vary across datasets of differing regularity, and as such it cannot be expected that the observed performance on one dataset will extend to datasets of other regularities, even if the detector is retrained. This means that one cannot use the same detector in different computational environments (e.g., research enterprises, educational enterprises, commercial enterprises, military bases, etc.) where different dataset regularities prevail, and expect to obtain results of the same level of accuracy for each environment. Simple retraining will not suffice. This is in absolute contrast to current practice.

5.1. Data sets

The data used were the calibrated benchmark datasets described in Section 4. The rare-4-gram anomalies had less than 5% occurrence in training datasets. For each alphabet size, all variables were held constant except for dataset regularity. There were 275 benchmark datasets total, 165 of which were anomaly-injected.

5.2. Description of anomaly detector

The anomaly detector used in this experiment was designed to detect anomalous subsequences embedded in longer sequences of categorical data. The choice of anomaly detector was arbitrary among the class of detectors that are probabilistically based. It works in two phases: a learning phase and a detection phase. Simply described, in the learning phase it constructs an internal table containing the probability of occurrence of every unique n-gram in the training sequence (e.g., normal background data), where n is user-specified. In the detection phase, it is given a test sequence consisting of normal background data (noise) mixed with injected anomalous-event subsequences (signal.) As the detector scans the test sequence, it raises an alarm each time it encounters an unusual event. The extent to which an event is unusual is the extent to which the probability of an event (i.e., subsequence) exceeds the probability of that event as stored in the table constructed during the training phase. A user-specified threshold between 0 and 1 determines the boundary above which an event is considered anomalous. The tunable parameters of the anomaly detector are window size (set to 4) and anomaly threshold (varied through the range 0-1). A window size of 4 means that the detector determines the level of surprise at a particular event, given the three events that preceded it; i.e., the detector is sensitive to sequential dependency in the data. A similar anomaly detector was reported by Nassehi [15]. Note that this kind of detector is designed to detect juxtapositional anomalies; it may be blind to certain kinds of temporal anomalies, unless a different encoding of input data stream is used. The same anomaly detector was used in all experiments.

5.3. Training the detector

Training, for any probabilistically-based detector, consists of establishing a representation of normal behavior in the detector's tables or data structures. Training the detector was done by running the training portion of the detection program on each of the 11 training datasets in each alphabet size; a total of 55 training sessions were conducted. Resultant data structures for each of the training sessions were stored for later use in detection.

5.4. Testing the detector

Testing the detector on test data consists of running the trained detector, with its data structures fully populated from the normal (training) data, on the test datasets. The detector is expected to indicate the presence of the injected anomalies, without falsely indicating subsequences that are not anomalous, and without missing any of the injected anomalies. Training and testing were done on data sets of the same regularity. Detection thresholds were swept through the range of 0.0 to 1.0 to yield different outcomes, depending on the detector's sensitivity at each threshold. For each of the 5 alphabet sizes, the detector was run on 33 test datasets, 11 for each anomaly type. Outcomes are presented in Section 5.6.

5.5. Scoring the detection outcomes

Several aspects of scoring are considered: exact determination of event outcomes, ground truth, detection threshold, anomaly scope, and presentation of results.

Event outcomes. The primary scoring task is to determine whether or not each event in the input datastream is correctly identified by the detector output in terms of hits, misses and false alarms. This is done by matching detector outcomes against a ground-truth oracle, or key.

Ground truth. Ground truth is ascertained automatically by the injection program, which produces a key to be compared against detector outcomes. The key identifies each event in the test dataset, showing the positions of injected events, their types (foreign-symbol, foreign n-gram, etc.), and their scope, as discussed above.

Threshold. The anomaly threshold determines the magnitude above which the anomaly is taken seriously (i.e., an alarm is raised), and below which the anomaly is disregarded. The magnitude, or surprise level, of an anomaly can vary from 0 to 1, where 0 is completely unsurprising and 1 is astonishing. In practice, one may decide that somewhere in between is the best set point for a particular environment coupled with a particular anomaly detector. For the detector used in the present study, the anomaly threshold was varied through its 0-1 range.

Scope. The scope of an anomaly refers to the locations in the test data where an anomaly would be detected. For example, if a 4-element anomaly had been injected at test-data location 101, then the basic scope of the anomaly would cover the four locations actually covered by the injected anomaly (101, 102, 103, and 104). For detectors that are sensitive to sequential dependencies, the scope of the anomaly may extend beyond the basic scope to cover residual anomalies. For example, the 4-gram AAAA would not only be anomalous by itself, but also in juxtaposition with whatever followed it in the data sequence. The residual anomalies would cover the distance that the detector window extends past the actual injected 4-gram; if the detection window was set to 4, then the scope would extend 3 elements beyond the actual anomaly, for a total scope of 7. Any detection within the basic scope or extended scope is considered a correct detection.

A correct detection, or hit, occurs when any point in the basic or extended scope of an injected anomaly is identified as anomalous. A false alarm is any detection that falls outside the total scope of the injected anomaly. A stricter scoring would count only detections in the basic scope, in which case detections in the extended scope would be regarded as false-alarm errors. A miss is the absence of a detection within the basic (not extended) scope of the injected anomaly.

Presentation of results. Experimental outcomes were analyzed graphically, using a technique from signal detection theory called ROC analysis -- the preferred method for measuring the accuracy of diagnostic systems [19]. Note that diagnosis is a classification process that assigns outcomes to predetermined classes; in the current case there are exactly two alternatives: each event in the test sequence is either anomalous or it is not. ROC analysis compares two aspects of detection systems: percent correct detections and percent false detections (sometimes called hits and false alarms, respectively, or true positives and false positives). The methodology, based on statistical decision theory, was originally developed in the context of electronic signal detection (e.g., radar) [16]. A detector operates through a range of sensitivities; the higher the sensitivity, the more likely the possibility of confusing signal and noise (e.g., anomaly and background), resulting in decisions that either identify noise as signal (false alarm) or, at the other extreme, fail to identify signal for what it is (miss). One wishes to find the point, between these extremes, at which to set the sensitivity; this is achieved by incrementing through a series of operating sensitivities, thereby sweeping out a relative operating characteristic (ROC) curve, with false alarms on the X-axis and hits on the Y-axis. As can be seen in Figure 5-1, the best operating point lies at the upper left (100% detection, 0% false alarms), and the worst at the lower right (all events falsely identified). The diagonal from [0,0] to [100,100] is the line indicating random guessing. Selecting the best operating point on the ROC curve is a matter of determining the relative cost of the two kinds of errors -- false alarms vs. missed detections, but this is outside the scope of the present work.

5.6. Results

A total of 165 separate tests was conducted, using 5 alphabets, 3 anomaly types, and 11 regularities. Results were graphically very similar across all alphabets and all regularities. Consequently, only one result, typical of the 165, will be presented. Figure 5-1 shows the ROC curve family for alphabet 6. Notice in the figure that the ROC curve for regularity index 0 (completely regular) would be a point at coordinate [0,100], indicating perfect performance, if there had been any rare-n-gram anomalies at regularity 0; by definition there could not have been. Also, the ROC curve for regularity-index 1 (completely random) is the 45-degree diagonal that, in signal-detection theory, represents pure guessing.

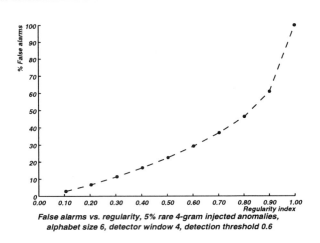

Figure 5-2: Synthetic benchmark data; false alarms vs. regularity index; detection threshold held constant at 0.6, 100% hit rate, no misses, rare-4-grams, detection window 4.

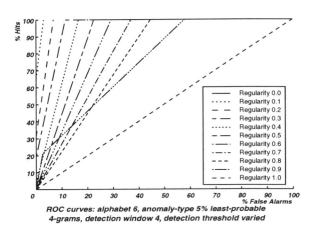

Figure 5-1: Synthetic benchmark datasets: ROC curve family; anomalies drawn from 5% least-probable 4-grams; alphabet 6, detector window 4, detector thresholds swept 0.0 to 1.0, data regularity (measured as entropy) indices 0.0 to 1.0. Different line types (dotted, dashed, etc.) are for visual aid only. Line across top appears solid only because many lines overlap.

It is noteworthy that none of the curves overlap until they reach the 100% hit rate, demonstrating that regularity does influence detector performance. If regularity had no effect, the fan effect clearly evident in the figure would not be present. What appears to be a solid line across the top of the figure is not actually solid; it's the superimposition of several curves at the 100% detection level. The hypothesis that regularity influences detector performance is confirmed.

Figure 5-2 shows the same results from another

perspective: the false-alarm rate rises as the regularity index grows (i.e., the data become more and more random). Each point on the graph indicates the false alarm rate for each of the 11 datasets of increasing regularity index (increasing randomness), with detection threshold held constant, using the lowest value at which 100% hits could be achieved. As regularity degrades from highly regular (at the left) to highly irregular (at the right), the false alarms rise sharply, even though the detector did not miss any anomalous events. The deterioration in detector performance manifests as an increase in the false-alarm rate. It is important to note that the deterioration in detector performance is attributed solely to changes in regularity; nothing else in these experiments was manipulated.

These results demonstrate, starkly, that training and testing on datasets of the same regularity will facilitate a particular hit vs. false-alarm ratio; and that that ratio may not be similarly achieved when the same detector (using the same parameters) is trained and tested on datasets of different regularities. The results achieved on one set of data are very different from those achieved on another, and this difference grows substantially as the regularity index increases. The same detector cannot be expected to achieve the same results when used on datasets of differing regularities. Note that if regularity in a single dataset is nonstationary, detector performance will vary even within the dataset. This suggests that regularity needs to be tracked in real time, possibly changing either the nature of the detector in response to changes in regularity, or shifting confidence in the detector's results. Although these particular results are for the probabilistically-based detector used in this work, other detector architectures may produce similar differences, possibly manifested in different ways.

6. Experiment two: using real-world data
Experiment one demonstrated that intrinsic structure in data, as indicated by the regularity index, influences anomaly-detection performance. The results, however interesting, are of little use unless they can be grounded in naturally-occurring data; i.e., if natural data show differences in regularities, then perhaps regularity can be used as one predictor of detection performance. The results shown in this section demonstrate clearly, based on data obtained from a natural domain, that regularity is a characteristic of natural data, and that regularities can be different even within a single environment.

6.1. Natural dataset: undergraduate machine.
BSM[1] audit data were taken from an undergraduate student computer running the Solaris operating system. System-call events were extracted for each user session in the 24-hour monitoring period. Most users produced only a single session, but in cases for which multiple sessions existed for the same user, these sessions were concatenated into one session for the purpose of calculating regularities over a 24-hour period. These data were examined with the objective of determining whether or not data in different user enterprises exhibit different regularities.

Results. The regularities of the 58 user sessions active on one day are illustrated in Figure 6-1. The regularities differ considerably with respect to one another, illustrating that different users have different behaviors, at least with respect to the regularities of their system-call streams. Although there has long been an intuitive understanding that user behaviors differ, measures of regularity show these differences quantitatively. Note that the range of differences among user-session regularities equates to a difference in detector performance in the synthetic data in terms of a false-alarm range of about 10%, suggesting that using the same detector in different conditions may not yield the expected results.

7. Conclusion
The principle objective of this paper has been to show that intrinsic structure in data, as measured by conditional relative entropy, will affect the performance of anomaly detectors. This has been demonstrated experimentally through the use of synthetic benchmark datasets, generated so that each dataset had a different, carefully measured regularity. Regularity was manipulated in these datasets so that anomaly detectors could be evaluated at the com-

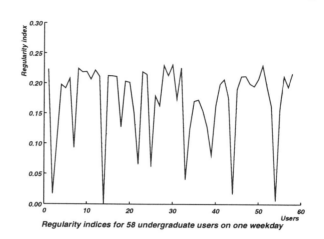

Figure 6-1: Natural dataset: Solaris BSM data; undergraduate machine; regularity indices for 58 undergraduate users.

ponent level, not at the system level. In the experiments conducted here, all variables were held constant except regularity, and it was established that a strong relationship exists between detector accuracy and regularity.

Both of the main hypotheses were affirmed: regularity does influence the performance of a probabilistic detector in that false alarms rise sharply as the regularity index rises; and regularity differences were found to occur in natural data. There are important implications of this work. First, an anomaly detector cannot be evaluated on the basis of its performance on a dataset of one regularity, and be expected to perform similarly on datasets of different regularities, in contrast to current practice. Second, differing regularities do not necessarily occur only between different users or different environments; they also occur within user sessions and among users, indicating that shifting regularities may prevent effective anomaly-detection performance even within one dataset. Overcoming this obstacle may require a mechanism to swap anomaly detectors or change the parameters of the current anomaly detector whenever regularity changes.

Although it is beyond the scope of this paper, it can be shown [12]that other types of anomaly detectors (e.g., decision trees, neural networks, etc.) are similarly affected by shifts of intrinsic structure in data. In general, at least one of the quadrants of signal detection theory (hits, misses, false alarms or correct rejections) is affected by changes in regularity.

---

[1]BSM is the Sun SHIELD Basic Security Module; it provides a security-auditing subsystem for Solaris-based computers.

8. Acknowledgements

It is a pleasure to acknowledge the contributions of David Banks (U.S. Bureau of Transportation Statistics) and Robert Olszewski (CMU), both of whom participated in a number of fruitful discussions. We are especially grateful to Robert Olszewski, who implemented the detector used in the demonstration experiment. The authors thank the Defense Advanced Research Projects Agency for their support of this research through contracts F30602-96-1-0349 and F30602-99-2-0537.

References

[1] Akhavan, S. and Calva, G., "Automatic Anomaly Detection in ECG Signal by Fuzzy Decision Making", In *Proceedings of 6th International Conference on Fuzzy Theory and Technology*: Association for Intelligent Machinery, 23-28 October 1998, pp. 96-98, Research Triangle Park, North Carolina.

[2] Amoroso, Edward, *Intrusion Detection*, Intrusion.Net Books, Sparta, New Jersey, 1999.

[3] Cover, Thomas M. and Thomas, Joy A., *Elements of Information Theory*, Wiley, New York, 1991.

[4] Debar, Herve; Dacier, Marc and Wespi, Andreas, "Towards a Taxonomy of Intrusion-Detection Systems", *Computer Networks*, Vol. 31, No. 8, 23 April 1999, pp. 805-822.

[5] Forrest, Stephanie; Hofmeyr, Steven A. and Somayaji, Anil, "Computer Immunology", *Communications of the ACM*, Vol. 40, No. 10, October 1997, pp. 88-96.

[6] Lane, Terran and Brodley, Carla E., "Temporal Sequence Learning and Data Reduction for Anomaly Detection", In *5th ACM Conference on Computer and Communications Security*. New York: Association for Computing Machinery, 3-5 November 1998, pp. 150-158, San Francisco, California.

[7] Lippmann, Richard P.; Fried, David J.; Graf, Isaac; Haines, Joshua W.; Kendall, Kristopher R.; McClung, David; Weber, Dan; Webster, Seth E.; Wyschogrod, Day; Cunningham, Robert K. and Zissman, Marc A., "Evaluating Intrusion Detection Systems: The 1998 DARPA Off-Line Intrusion Detection Evaluation", In *Proceedings of the DARPA Information Survivability Conference and Exposition: DISCEX-2000, Volume 2*. Los Alamitos, California: IEEE Computer Society, 25-27 January 2000, pp. 12-26, Hilton Head Island, South Carolina.

[8] Lunt, Teresa F.; Tamaru, Ann; Gilham, Fred; Jagannathan, R.; Neumann, Peter G. and Jalali, Caveh, "IDES: A Progress Report", In *Annual Computer Security Applications Conference*. Tuscon, Arizona: IEEE Computer Society Press, 3-7 December 1990, pp. 273-285.

[9] Marsaglia, George, "A Current View of Random Number Generators", In *Computer Science and Statistics: Proceedings of the Sixteenth Symposium on the Interface*, L. Billard (Ed.): Elsevier Science Publishers, 1984, pp. 3-10.

[10] Maxion, Roy A. and deChambeau, Aimee L., "Dependability at the User Interface", In *25th International Symposium on Fault-Tolerant Computing*. Los Alamitos, California: IEEE Computer Society, 27-30 June 1995, pp. 528-535, Pasadena, California.

[11] Maxion, Roy A. and Feather, Frank E., "A Case Study of Ethernet Anomalies in a Distributed Computing Environment", *IEEE Transactions on Reliability*, Vol. 39, No. 4, October 1990, pp. 433-443.

[12] Maxion, Roy A. and Tan, Kymie M.C., "Comparing Anomaly-Detection Algorithms". Forthcoming.

[13] Me, Ludovic, "Security Audit Trail Analysis Using Genetic Algorithms", In *International Conference on Computer Safety, Reliability and Security*, Janusz Gorski (Ed.). Poznan-Kiekrz, Poland: Springer-Verlag, 27-29 October 1993, pp. 329-340.

[14] Mukherjee, Biswanath; Heberlein, L. Todd and Levitt, Karl N., "Network Intrusion Detection", *IEEE Network*, Vol. 8, No. 3, May/June 1994, pp. 26-41.

[15] Nassehi, Mehdi, "Anomaly Detection for Markov Models", Tech. report RZ 3011 (#93057), IBM Research Division, Zurich Research Laboratory, 30 March 1998.

[16] Peterson, W.W.; Birdsall, T.G. and Fox, W.C., "The Theory of Signal Detectability", *Transactions of the IRE Professional Group on Information Theory*, Vol. PGIT-4, 1954, pp. 171-212.

[17] Ringdal, Frode, "Teleseismic Event Detection Using the NORESS Array, with Special Reference to Low-Yield Semipalatinsk Explosions", *Bulletin of the Seismological Society of America*, Vol. 80, No. 6, December 1990, pp. 2127-2142.

[18] Shannon, Claude E. and Weaver, Warren, *The Mathematical Theory of Communication*, University of Illinois Press, Urbana, Illinois, 1949.

[19] Swets, John A., "Measuring the Accuracy of Diagnostic Systems", *Science*, Vol. 240, No. 4857, 03 June 1988, pp. 1285-1293.

[20] Teng, Henry S.; Chen, Kaihu and Lu, Stephen C-Y., "Adaptive Real-Time Anomaly Detection Using Inductively Generated Sequential Patterns", In *IEEE Computer Society Symposium on Research in Security and Privacy*. Oakland, California: IEEE Computer Society Press, 7-9 May 1990, pp. 278-284.

Avoiding Loss of Fairness Owing to Process Crashes in Fair Data Exchange Protocols

Peng Liu
Department of Information Systems
University of Maryland, Baltimore County
Baltimore, MD 21250
pliu@umbc.edu

Peng Ning   Sushil Jajodia
Center for Secure Information Systems
George Mason University
Fairfax, VA 22030
{pning, jajodia}@gmu.edu

Abstract

Fair exchange between two or more potentially mutually distrusted parties has been identified as an important issue in electronic commerce. However, the correctness (fairness) of the existing fair exchange protocols that use a Trusted Third Party (TTP) is based on the assumption that during an exchange there are no failures at any of the local systems involved in the exchange, which is too strong in many situations. This paper points out that (1) system failures could cause loss of fairness, and (2) existing fair exchange protocols that use TTPs cannot ensure fairness in presence of system failures. We present a systematic way to develop such data exchange systems that can recover from system failures without losing fairness. We identify a set of fairness loss risks caused by local system failures. We identify a fault tolerance correctness criteria for fair data exchange, denoted fairness-lossless recoverability. A fairness-lossless recoverable fair exchange system is immune from the set of fairness loss risks. Standard message logging approaches are then studied and extended to achieve fairness-lossless recoverability with good performance.

Key Words: Fair Exchange, Fairness, Recoverability, Electronic Commerce

1 Introduction

Experience with electronic commerce has shown that an *exchange* of one data item for another between mutually distrusted parties is usually the crux of an electronic transaction [6, 10, 11, 19]. A desirable requirement for exchange is *fairness*. An exchange is *fair* if at the end of the exchange, either each player receives the item it expects or neither player receives any additional information about the other's item. Fair data exchange has been used in many applications such as non-repudiation of message transmission [19], certified mail [11], contract signing [6], and electronic payment systems [10].

1.1 Fair Data Exchange Protocols

Existing practical fair exchange protocols that use a Trusted Third Party (*TTP*) [2, 3, 4, 12, 19] can be summarized by Figure 1 [1] where two players, *A* and *B*, and two communication channels between *A* and *B*, the *normal channel* and the *trusted channel*, are involved in an exchange. The normal channel models the direct communication between *A* and *B*. Since *A* and *B* mutually distrust each other, exchanges which are solely dependent on this channel cannot be assured to be fair. The trusted channel between *A* and *B* is therefore established with the help of the *TTP* [2]. Items sent via the trusted channel are first sent to the *TTP* and then forwarded by the *TTP* to the recipient. Exchanges performed in the trusted channel can be considered fair because of the mediation of the *TTP*. Note that *A* and *B* are interchangeable.

Although exchanging items using the trusted channel is fair, it is usually undesirable since the *TTP* will then be the performance bottleneck and the main target of attacks. Due to this consideration, one of the design goals for fair exchange protocols is to minimize the use of *TTPs* as much as possible. There are also some other design goals which are identified: (1) Tolerating temporary communication failures without losing fairness [3]; (2) Relaxing the extent to which *TTPs* can be trusted without losing fairness [12]; (3) Relaxing the fairness requirement to further reduce the overhead of the *TTP* [3]. Note that these goals may conflict with each other, thus trade-offs are needed in some situations.

---

[1] *Gradual exchange* protocols [6], another main class of fair exchange solutions, do not need a *TTP*; however, they are impractical due to the high communication overhead. Issues related to these protocols are out of the scope of the paper.

[2] A semi-trusted *TTP* is allowed in [12], where it may misbehave on its own but will not conspire with either of the players.

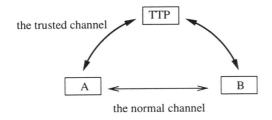

Figure 1. Fair Data Exchange using a *TTP*

Fair data exchange protocols that use a *TTP* can be classified into two categories in terms of how *TTPs* are exploited:

Exchange with On-line *TTPs*: An exchange cannot be completed without using the trusted channel, even if both players play honestly [3]. Semi-trusted *TTPs* can be supported in some cases [12]. Protocols proposed in [10], [12], and [19] fall into this class.

Exchange with Off-line *TTPs*: An exchange can be completed without interference of the *TTP* if the two players play honestly. If one player realizes that they cannot fairly exchange the items as expected, another exchange will be carried out in the trusted channel. Protocols proposed in [2], [3], and [4] fall into this class. In some cases, only *weak fairness* [4] can be achieved.

1.2 Loss of Fairness due to System Failures

Existing fair exchange protocols that use a *TTP*, however, depend on certain strong assumptions about the communication channels and/or the local systems. Specifically, all of the protocols assume that during an exchange no failures will happen at the local systems of either the players or the *TTP*. Although all of the protocols can achieve certain degree of fairness under these assumptions, none of them can ensure fairness in presence of system failures, such as process crashes. The goal of this paper is to present techniques that can enable a data exchange system to survive system failures without losing fairness.

Consider the following fair non-repudiation protocol which is adapted from [19], an efficient non-repudiation protocol which can ensure fairness when there are no system failures. Relevant notations of the protocol are summarized in Figure 2. Note that the protocol is different for that presented in [19] where message 4 and 5 are retrieved by *A* and *B* instead of being delivered by

the *TTP*. The impact of this difference on fairness is addressed in Section 4. The protocol consists of five messages. Note that message 4 and 5 are interchangeable. The purpose of this protocol is for *A* to exchange a message together with a non-repudiation of origin (*NRO*) token, denoted $\{m, S_A(B, m.id, E_k(m))\}$, for a non-repudiation of receipt (*NRR*) token for the message from *B*, denoted $\{S_B(A, m.id, E_k(m)), S_{TTP}(A, B, m.id, k)\}$.

1. $A \rightarrow B : \quad B, m.id, E_k(m), S_A(B, m.id, E_k(m))$
2. $B \rightarrow A : \quad A, m.id, S_B(A, m.id, E_k(m))$
3. $A \rightarrow TTP : \quad B, m.id, k, S_A(B, m.id, k)$
4. $TTP \rightarrow B : \quad A, B, m.id, k, S_{TTP}(A, B, m.id, k)$
5. $TTP \rightarrow A : \quad A, B, m.id, S_{TTP}(A, B, m.id, k)$

Based on the assumption that there are no local system failures, and the assumption that each communication channel is *reliable*, that is, the messages inserted into the channel by the sender can always be received by the recipient within a known, constant time interval, fairness of the protocol can be proved in a way similar to [19]. However, system failures, e.g., process crashes, can cause loss of fairness. To illustrate this, consider an exchange instance during which no player (process) stores any data item into the stable storage, if the process on behalf of player *B* crashes after message 2 is sent out, then message 1 which has been delivered to the process is lost. As a result, when the protocol terminates, *A* will get the expected item, but *B* cannot, even if the process on behalf of *B* restarts instantly after the failure and gets message 4. Similar problems can also be caused by failures at the local systems of player *A* and the *TTP*.

This example raises several questions on how to survive system failures without losing fairness in data exchange, which to the best of our knowledge have not yet been clearly answered. We believe that answering these questions is important because it gives developers a much clearer understanding of the relationship between security (fairness) and fault tolerance (recoverability) in data exchange, which will not only help to develop secure and fault tolerant fair exchange systems, but also help to develop other kinds of secure and fault tolerant electronic commerce applications.

- Besides the problem identified in the example above, how many kinds of security problems caused by local system failures are with current fair data exchange protocols?

- Can traditional fault tolerance mechanisms for distributed computing, such as *message logging*, be directly applied to fair exchange systems to avoid the loss of fairness caused by system failures? How can they be applied to the fair exchange problem in a better way?

- What is the fault tolerance requirement for fair exchange systems?

---

[3] We say a player *plays honestly* if he or she will send his or her own item even after he or she receives the other party's item.

[4] We say an exchange protocol achieves weak fairness if in some cases the players will have to use some specific affidavits in an external dispute resolution system, such as a court, to achieve fairness.

m	message sent from A to B
k	message key used by A
$E_k(m)$	m encrypted with k
$m.id$	unique identifier of m
$S_X(y)$	text y signed with the private key of party X

Figure 2. Notation

1.3 Contributions

Existing fair exchange protocols that use a *TTP* cannot ensure fairness in presence of system failures. In this paper, we present a systematic way to develop such data exchange systems that can recover from system failures without losing fairness. We identify a new design goal for fair exchange systems, i.e., surviving local system failures without losing fairness. We formally model a data exchange system as a specific distributed system and identify a set of security risks caused by local system failures. We identify a fault tolerance correctness criteria for fair data exchange, denoted *fairness-lossless recoverability*. A fairness-lossless recoverable fair exchange system is immune from the set of security risks. Standard message logging approaches are then studied and extended to achieve fairness-lossless recoverability with good performance.

The remainder of this paper is organized as follows. Section 2 identifies a set of security risks caused by local system failures. Section 3 studies how to avoid loss of fairness caused by process crashes, assuming there is no *TTP* failures. Issues on how to survive *TTP* failures are described in Section 4. Section 5 extends our solutions to exchange with off-line *TTPs*. Section 6 discusses (1) the impact of output and communication failures, and (2) the usefulness of transactions. Section 7 concludes the paper.

2 The Model

In order to make the presentation clearer, we deal with only protocols with on-line *TTPs* in Sections 2 - 4. Protocols with off-line *TTPs* are addressed in Section 5. Moreover, in order to focus on the impact of system failures on fairness and for simplicity of presentation, we first assume a point-to-point communication and a reliable communication channel. Issues about communication failures are later addressed in Section 6.

Fair exchange protocols with on-line *TTPs* can be modeled with Figure 3(a) where player A exchanges an item X for an item Y from player B. Each player splits its item into two parts: one is to be sent via the trusted channel, and the other via the normal channel. The item should be split in such a way that the other player cannot restore any useful information about the item from only the part sent via

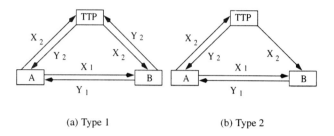

(a) Type 1   (b) Type 2

Figure 3. Fair Data Exchange with On-line *TTPs*

the normal channel. In the model, $X = f(X_1, X_2)$ and $Y = g(Y_1, Y_2)$, and no useful information about X (Y) can be derived from X_1 (Y_1). Here f and g are two specific functions. For better performance, the part sent via the trusted channel should be as small as possible. As a result, the exchange of X for Y is split into two exchanges: the exchange of X_1 for Y_1 via the normal channel followed by the exchange of X_2 for Y_2 via the trusted channel. The fairness of the exchange is ensured by the fairness of the *TTP* in forwarding X_2 and Y_2. Sometimes, Y_2 can be generated by the *TTP* [19]. This situation is shown in Figure 3(b). Notice that the example specified in Section 1 falls into this class. To be more concrete, a protocol modeled by Figure 3(a) is specified as follows. A protocol modeled by Figure 3(b) can be specified in the same way except that in step 3 B does not send Y_2 to the *TTP*.

1. $A \rightarrow B: X_1$
2. $B \rightarrow A: Y_1$
3. $A \rightarrow TTP: X_2; \quad B \rightarrow TTP: Y_2$
4. $TTP \rightarrow A: Y_2; \quad TTP \rightarrow B: X_2$

2.1 Site Failures

To study the impact of system failures on fairness, we must first specify what kinds of system failures we are trying to overcome. The simplest failure model is the *crash model*. In the model, the only kind of failure is that a processor may suddenly halt and kill all the processes that are executing there. We say these processes *crash*. Operational processes never perform incorrect actions, nor do they fail to perform correct actions. Moreover, all operational processes can *detect* the failure of a processor. For the rest of the paper we assume that only process crashes can occur. There are a couple of reasons for restricting our attention to crash failures. First, the abstraction of crash failures can be implemented on top of a system subject to more complex failures by running an appropriate software protocol [8]. Second, techniques are available to automatically translate a protocol that tolerates crash failures into protocols that tolerate larger classes of failures [16].

2.2 Fair Exchange Systems

We view an exchange as a set of interactions among three processes: P_A, P_B and P_{TTP}, which are running on behalf of player A, player B, and the *TTP*, respectively. Although the *TTP* usually serves multiple exchanges at the same time, we assume that different *TTP* processes are being used for different exchanges for clarity.

Processes interact by sending and receiving messages. An arriving message is buffered. A buffered message is delivered when the receiver process is ready to receive a message.

Each process has a local *state* and performs computation based on the current state which is kept in the volatile storage. For example, during an exchange modeled by Figure 3(a), the actions which P_A will take after receiving a message from P_B or P_{TTP} are dependent on the state variable indicating which phase P_A is currently in the exchange.

Processes execute events, including *send* events, *receive* events, and *local* events [1]. Each event transforms one process state to another. Therefore, a process can be viewed as an interleaved sequence of events and states. A local event is *deterministic*, if based on the same current process state (and the same message used in the event), the event does the same state transformation and outputs the same message to the following send event (if there is any). An exchange system is *deterministic* if the local events of P_A, P_B, or P_{TTP} are all deterministic.

Note that the fair exchange protocols modeled by Figure 3 are deterministic. One may question that the event of splitting X (Y) into X_1 (Y_1) and X_2 (Y_2) is nondeterministic, since an item is usually split using a randomly chosen cryptographic key to make the split unpredictable. However, the algorithm that split an item is deterministic and the splitting event is also deterministic if we consider the random key as a message.

Events within an exchange are ordered by the irreflexive partial order *happens before* that represents potential causality [15]. For example, a send event of process P_1 happens before a receive event of process P_2, if the mes-

sage sent out by the send event is the message received by the receive event.

2.3 Security Risks Owing to Process Crashes

Process crashes could cause the following types of fairness loss in a fair exchange protocol modeled by Figure 3(a). Here we assume that no data item is stored to the stable storage during an exchange.

Type 1.1 If P_A (P_B) crashes after X_2 (Y_2) is sent out, then P_B (P_A) can get X (Y), but P_A (P_B) cannot get Y (X) since Y_1 (X_1) is lost.

Type 1.2 If P_{TTP} crashes after it delivers X_2 (Y_2), but before it delivers Y_2 (X_2), then P_B (P_A) can get X (Y), but P_A (P_B) cannot get Y (X) since Y_2 (X_2) is lost.

Types of fairness loss risks for a protocol modeled by Figure 3(b) are as follows. Note that in this protocol no loss of fairness will be caused when P_{TTP} crashes after X_2 is delivered, but before Y_2 is delivered because P_A can get Y_2 later on by resending X_2 to the restarted P_{TTP}.

Type 2.1 If P_B crashes after Y_2 is sent out, then P_A can get Y, but P_B cannot get X.

Type 2.2 If P_A crashes after X_2 is sent out, then P_B can get X, but P_A cannot get Y.

Type 2.3 If P_{TTP} crashes after Y_2 is delivered, but before X_2 is delivered, then P_A can get Y, but P_B cannot get X. Since P_{TTP} is usually stateless, so after P_{TTP} restarts P_{TTP} has already forgot X_2. And P_{TTP} is unable to force P_A to provide X_2 again in many cases because P_A may lie that it has not got Y_2 and it wants to abort the exchange.

The classification of fairness loss risks presented above indicates that fairness loss could be avoided if we store some messages (or data items) to the stable storage during an exchange. For example, the loss of fairness caused by Type 1.1 risks can be avoided by storing Y_1 (X_1) to the stable storage before X_2 (Y_2) is sent out. Indeed, this implies that recoverability is important to the correctness of fair exchange protocols.

3 Avoiding Loss of Fairness

Message logging is the standard method in the literature of distributed systems to achieve recoverability. In this section, we study the application of message logging to fair exchange protocols, trying to use the technique in an appropriate way. For clarity, in this section we assume there are no *TTP* failures. Surviving *TTP* failures is addressed in Section 4.

3.1 Message Logging

A message is *logged* if both its content and sequence number have been saved on stable storage. Assuming that each local event executed by a process is *deterministic*, it is then always possible to reconstruct the current process state from the set of messages delivered. Occasionally a process takes a *checkpoint*, a snapshot of it local state, and writes it to the stable storage to reduce recovery time. A process state is *recoverable* if every message delivered after the latest checkpoint is logged.

In our model, a *global state S of an exchange system* is a collection of three process states: s_A, s_B and s_{TTP}, one for each process. Viewing processes as sequences of events and states, a global exchange system state S can also be viewed as a collection of three subsequences: (1) the subsequence of P_A ended with s_A; (2) the subsequence of P_B ended with s_B; and (3) the subsequence of P_{TTP} ended with s_{TTP}. A global exchange system state S is *consistent* if and only if every message received via a receive event of S has been sent out via a sent event of S. A consistent global exchange system state S is *recoverable* if s_A, s_B and s_{TTP} are all recoverable.

3.1.1 Pessimistic Message Logging

A naive approach to achieve recoverability of a fair exchange protocol is to use *pessimistic message logging*, which has been applied in many systems to support transparent, application-independent recovery [5, 9]. The mechanism is *pessimistic* because it never rolls back process computations.

The application of pessimistic message logging to fair exchange is straightforward. In a data exchange system modeled by Figure 3, a buffered message m is always first logged before being delivered to another player. The log record may have the structure $(p.id, m.id, m)$, where $p.id$ denotes the unique identifier of the player process and $m.id$ denotes the sequence number of the message. The logging operation may be performed by a specific separate process which is responsible for delivering m to P_A (or P_B) when P_A (or P_B) is ready to receive m. Process P_A (or P_B) may also take checkpoints periodically.

When P_A (P_B) crashes, P_B (P_A) and P_{TTP} can continue their normal computations after detecting the crash if their computations are not affected by P_A, otherwise, they need to wait for P_A (P_B) to recover. When a crashed process P_A (P_B) restarts, it first restores its current state from the corresponding inputs and the logged messages, then it can continue its computation.

If the fair exchange system is deterministic, pessimistic message logging ensures that the current system state is recoverable because P_A and P_B can always restore its current

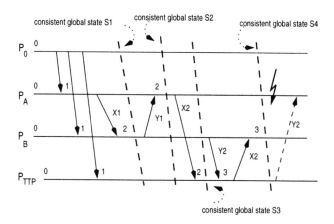

Figure 4. Recoverable State with Loss Of Fairness

state from the information on the stable storage no matter there are checkpoints or not. Therefore, every type of fairness loss risks that is identified can be immunized from the system when there are no *TTP* failures. However, it should be noticed that logging messages regardless of whether they can contribute to the fairness of an exchange or not will inevitably result in performance penalty, especially when most of the messages are unnecessary to ensure the fairness.

3.1.2 Optimistic Message Logging

The advantage of pessimistic approaches is the absence of cascading rollback, since there always exists a *non-decreasing* consistent system state constructible from the most recent checkpoint and the logged messages. However, the writing time for a message to be logged before processing can be significant, compared with the computation. This is unacceptable in an environment where a large number of messages are exchanged. This results in the *optimistic message logging* approach [14, 17].

Optimistic message logging allows messages to be processed independent of when they are logged, in an asynchronous manner. In the absence of failures, the only overhead is the asynchronous logging of messages.

Optimistic message logging ensures that a *maximal* recoverable system state is reconstructible after a failure [5]. However, this kind of recoverability does not ensure fairness. Consider the example shown in Figure 4 where P_0 denotes an external process that generates inputs for P_A, P_B, and P_{TTP}. We view these inputs as the 1st messages delivered to P_A, P_B, and P_{TTP}, respectively. And we as-

---

[5]Readers can refer to [14] for the definition of maximal recoverable system states and the algorithm to compute such states. Details are omitted here for space reason.

sume that only the input delivered to each process is logged but all the other messages are not. See that Figure 4 depicts the message interactions of an exchange modeled by Figure 3(a). When P_A crashes after P_{TTP} sends X_2 to P_B, according to optimistic message logging, all volatile messages delivered to P_B and P_{TTP} will be logged. At this time, although S_4 is the current system state, it is not recoverable because the second message delivered to P_A is lost. In fact, the maximal recoverable state is S_1. However, the ability to find the maximal recoverable state does not imply the ability to ensure fairness. In particular, before we roll back the system state to S_1 the fairness may have already been lost because after getting X P_B may reject to continue the exchange process from state S_1.

3.2 Semantics-Based Message Logging

The previous two subsections show that pessimistic message logging can ensure fairness in fair data exchange but may result in unacceptable performance, while optimistic message logging cannot even ensure fairness. This is due to ignorance of the semantics of fair exchange protocols. In this section, we identify the semantics of fair exchange protocols that can be exploited to ensure both fairness and good performance.

Definition 1 A state of player process P_A (P_B) is called the *point-of-no-return* of P_A (P_B) if P_B (P_A) can get X (Y) without further information provided by P_A (P_B) after P_A (P_B) enters the state, and there are no other such states which P_A (P_B) can enter before it enters the state.

Intuitively, the point-of-no-return of a player in a data exchange represents the stage after which the player cannot take back his or her data item even if the exchange is stopped. Thus, in order to avoid losing the fairness due to process crashes, the player process has to *remember* what has happened so that it can continue the exchange even after a crash. Semantics of points-of-no-return has been informally mentioned in some specific exchange protocols such as [10].

It is easy to see that fair exchange protocols modeled by Figure 3 have the following points-of-no-return: (1) for Type 1 protocols, the point-of-no-return of P_A is the state which P_A enters by sending out X_2; the point-of-no-return of P_B is the state which P_B enters by sending out Y_2; (2) for Type 2 protocols, the point-of-no-return of P_A is the state which P_A enters by sending out X_2; the point-of-no-return of P_B is the state which P_B enters by sending out Y_1.

Definition 2 An exchange system state S is *fairness-lossless recoverable* if whenever a failure happens all the messages delivered to P_A (P_B) before P_A (P_B) enters its point-of-no-return are logged.

Based on our discussion on traditional message logging approaches, it should be easy to show that fairness-lossless recoverability can generally ensure the fairness of fair exchange systems. See that the correctness of pessimistic message logging can also be justified by the fact that it achieves fairness-lossless recoverability.

Theorem 1 Given a fair data exchange system modeled by Figure 3, assuming that P_{TTP} will not crash, if the system is deterministic and can ensure fairness when there are no process crashes, then if the system can ensure fairness-lossless recoverability when there are process crashes, it can ensure fairness, that is, it can be immunized from every type of fairness loss risks that is identified.

In the following, we propose a semantics-based message logging algorithm to achieve fairness-lossless recoverability, thus the algorithm can ensure the fairness of fair exchange systems in presence of process crashes. We assume that (1) there is a *recovery manager*, a process responsible for logging, at each player's local system; and (2) whenever a message is delivered to a player it is also delivered to the recovery manager. We augment optimistic message logging systems with a specific facility, called *message filter*, a process responsible for detecting points-of-no-return, at each player's local system. We assume that every message sent out by a player process is forwarded by the message filter to communication channels.

Algorithm 1 Semantics-Based Message Logging
For a data exchange system modeled by Figure 3

1. Before the data exchange system starts to function, each player registers its point-of-no-return with the Message Filter.

2. When player process P_A (P_B) is sending out a message, the Message Filter checks if sending out the message will make P_A (P_B) enter its point-of-no-return. If the answer is YES, the Message Filter will inform the Recovery Manager to log all the messages that have already been delivered to P_A (P_B). The message will not be sent out to the channel until the Recovery Manager succeeds. If the answer is NO, the message will be forwarded to the channel.

3. The recovery actions taken by the system when a set of messages are logged, the method to compute the maximal recoverable state after a crash, and the rolling back process are the same as those performed in a normal optimistic message logging system, such as [14].

4. After P_A (P_B) rolls its state back to the corresponding one specified in the maximal recoverable global system state, it continues its computation.

The correctness of Algorithm 1 is shown in the following theorem.

Theorem 2 Given a fair data exchange system modeled by Figure 3, assuming that P_{TTP} will not crash, if the system is deterministic, then Algorithm 1 ensures that the system is fairness-lossless recoverable.

Similar to pessimistic message logging, the semantics-based approach is application independent. The only information that a data exchange protocol needs to inform the recovery system is the point-of-no-return of each player. Since this interaction is finished by an offline registration process, the codes of the protocol need not be tailored. As a result, recovery facility can be provided by the system and transparent to the fair exchange protocols. With almost no modifications, current fair exchange protocols, which assume no system failures, can be directly performed on a platform where the semantics-based approach is enforced to immunize themselves from fairness loss risks caused by process crashes.

3.3 Application Specific Approaches

Although having the advantage of being transparent, the application-independent methods usually cannot achieve optimal performance in terms of the amount of computing resources used. Better performance is usually achievable by incorporating recovery semantics into fair exchange protocol code. The drawback is that the developing cost, and the possibility of incurring faults can be substantially increased.

Consider the example introduced in Section 1, before P_B enters its point-of-no-return in step 2, it may log only the *NRO* token, namely $S_A(B, m.id, E_k(m))$, instead of the whole message sent by P_A (message 1), after verifying the token. Similarly, P_A can only log the data item $S_B(A, m.id, E_k(m))$ instead of the whole message when it receives message 2. In this way, the I/O costs can be reduced. Note that no general application specific approaches can be presented here because they are dependent on application semantics thus different from one application to another.

4 Surviving *TTP* Failures

So far we assume that there are no *TTP* failures. *TTP* failures may also cause loss of fairness though *TTPs* are usually more reliable than player systems. As addressed in Section 2.3, *TTP* failures in a fair exchange protocol modeled by Figure 3 could cause Type 1.2 and Type 2.3 loss of fairness. Indeed, similar to the player systems, there is also a critical state for P_{TTP}.

Definition 3 A state of process P_{TTP} is called the *point-of-fair-delivery* of P_{TTP} if after P_{TTP} enters the state only

X_2 or Y_2 is delivered but not both, and there are no other such states which P_{TTP} can enter before it enters the state.

Similar to the discussion in Section 3.2, we can see that when P_{TTP} enters its point-of-fair-delivery if all the messages which have already been delivered to P_{TTP} are logged, then Type 1.2 and Type 2.3 fairness loss can be avoided.

It is easy to see that both application-independent and application-specific approaches which we have just presented to deal with player process crashes can be directly applied or adapted to handle *TTP* failures. The corresponding algorithm and correctness proof are omitted here since they are very similar to those dealing with player process crashes.

In some practical fair exchange protocols such as [19], fault tolerance of P_{TTP} is achieved in a different way where X_2 and Y_2 are retrieved by P_A and P_B instead of being delivered by P_{TTP}, thus the fairness can be ensured by logging X_2 and Y_2 before any of them can be queried.

Now it is the time to consider the situations where more than one process among P_A, P_B, and P_{TTP} crash at the same time. Fortunately, we found that multiple failures (at the same time) do not cause more security problems (see Theorem 3).

Definition 4 In a fair exchange system where P_A, P_B, or P_{TTP} may crash at the same time, a global exchange system state S is *fairness-lossless recoverable* if whenever a failure happens: (1) all the messages delivered to P_A (P_B) before P_A (P_B) enters its point-of-no-return are logged; and (2) all the messages delivered to P_{TTP} before P_{TTP} enters its point-of-fair-delivery are logged.

Theorem 3 Given a fair data exchange system modeled by Figure 3, if the system is deterministic and can ensure fairness when there are no process crashes, then if the system is fairness-lossless recoverable, it can ensure fairness even if P_A, P_B, or P_{TTP} may crash simultaneously.

5 Dealing with Exchange with Off-line *TTPs*

Although the protocols used in exchanges with off-line *TTPs* are different from those used in exchanges with on-line *TTPs*. These protocols suffer from similar security problems caused by process crashes.

Fair exchange protocols with off-line *TTPs* can be modeled by Figure 5(a) [2, 3]. For simplicity, only the normal exchange procedure is specified. If player A and player B play honestly, then they can exchange fairly without the interference of the *TTP*. Otherwise, if P_A cannot get Y after X is sent to P_B, then messages 3 (X) and 4 (Y) will be re-exchanged under the supervision of the *TTP*. The (weak) fairness is ensured by the following property:

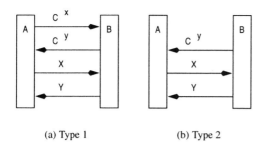

(a) Type 1   (b) Type 2

Figure 5. Fair Data Exchange with Off-line *TTPs*

$\exists f$ such that $f(C^x, C^y) = 1$ indicates that P_A plays honestly; and $\exists g$ such that $g(C^x, X) = 1$ indicates that X is valid; $g(C^y, Y) = 1$ indicates that Y is valid.

Sometimes, message 1 (C^x) need not be sent and the re-exchange of X and Y can be avoided even if P_B does not play honestly, instead, P_{TTP} can extract Y from C^y for P_A but P_A cannot do this by itself [4]. This situation is shown in Figure 5(b). However, in order to ensure fairness, the following property must be satisfied:

$\exists g$ such that $g(X, C^y) = 1$ indicates that P_A plays honestly; and $\exists f$ such that $f(C^y, K_{TTP}) = Y$. Here, K_{TTP} is the private key of the *TTP*.

The set of fairness loss risks caused by process crashes in a fair exchange protocol modeled by Figure 5 can be identified in a way very similar to what we have done in Section 2.3. Details are omitted here for space reason.

It is clear that the fair exchange system model proposed in Section 2 can model exchange systems with off-line *TTPs*. And it is clear that points-of-no-return also exist in exchange with off-line *TTPs*. In particular, sending out X lets P_A enter its point-of-no-return, and sending out Y lets P_B enter its point-of-no-return. The following theorem shows that fairness-lossless recoverability can also ensure fairness in exchange with off-line *TTPs*. The difference is that there are no recoverability requirements on P_{TTP} when P_{TTP} is involved in an exchange even if P_{TTP} crashes during the exchange. The main reason is that there is no point-of-fair-delivery for P_{TTP} since P_{TTP} on behalf of an off-line *TTP* can be stateless during an exchange.

Definition 5 A global state S of a fair data exchange system modeled by Figure 5 is *fairness-lossless recoverable* if whenever a failure happens (P_{TTP} may also crash) all the messages delivered to P_A (P_B) before P_A (P_B) enters its point-of-no-return are logged.

Theorem 4 Given a fair data exchange system modeled by Figure 5, if the system is deterministic and can ensure fairness when there are no process crashes, then if the system is fairness-lossless recoverable, it can ensure fairness in presence of process crashes.

The mechanisms we have presented for exchange systems with on-line *TTPs* to survive process crashes can be directly applied to exchange systems with off-line *TTPs* except that P_{TTP} needs no recovery services. See that protocols with on-line *TTPs* and protocols with off-line *TTPs* share the same system model and have very similar fault tolerance requirements.

6 Discussion

6.1 Output Failures

Previous presentation implies the following assumption: that process P_A (P_B) gets Y (X) implies that player A (B) gets Y (X). However, in practice, P_A (P_B) needs to output Y (X) to player A (B) after it gets Y (X).

Failures during the output procedure can cause loss of fairness. For example, in a protocol modeled by Figure 3(a), if P_A crashes after it gets Y_2, but before it outputs Y, then player A cannot get Y but player B may have already got X.

There can be several solutions for the problem. For example: (1) letting P_A (P_B) output Y_2 (X_2) before acknowledging receiving Y_2 (X_2); or (2) letting P_A (P_B) log Y_2 (X_2) before acknowledging receiving Y_2 (X_2). In both methods, P_{TTP} will continue to be active unless player A (B) is assured to be able to get Y (X).

6.2 Communication Failures

Two levels of quality of a communication channel which can be used in a fair exchange system are defined in [3]: (1) a communication channel is *reliable* if the messages inserted into it by the sender are received by the recipient within a known, constant time interval; and (2) a communication channel is *resilient* if messages inserted in it will eventually be delivered although the messages can be delayed by an arbitrary, but finite amount of time. Some fair exchange protocols, such as [3], can use resilient channels, but some other protocols, such as [2], can only use reliable channels.

When we apply our mechanisms to implement a fair data exchange system to survive process crashes without losing fairness, whether the exchange system will suffer from fairness loss risks caused by communication failures is primarily dependent on the underlying exchange protocol itself instead of how we implement the protocol. For example,

[3] shows that changing an exchange protocol from synchronous to asynchronous can enable the protocol to use resilient channels. Therefore, our mechanisms are orthogonal to the techniques that can enable a fair exchange protocol to survive communication failures.

6.3 On Transactions

Transactions have been widely used in database systems and distributed computing to provide reliability, availability, and performance [7, 13]. A transaction can be considered a sequence of system-state-changing operations with the ACID properties, namely atomicity, consistency, isolation, and durability. Atomicity allows us to run a transaction as a single unit, that is, when a transaction is executed, atomicity can ensure that either all the operations involved in the transaction are executed or none or them are. Therefore, atomicity can mask all the failures that may happen during the execution of a transaction.

As a distributed system with specific goals, i.e., achieving fairness in exchanges, fair data exchange systems can surely use transactions to help improve reliability. However, we found that although transactions can effectively mask the failures that may happen during an exchange, they cannot guarantee fairness.

To illustrate, consider a protocol modeled by Figure 3(a), it is easy to see that if delivering X_2 and Y_2 is atomic, then Type 1.2 fairness loss can be avoided. Grouping these two message delivering operations into a single distributed transaction can technically provide such atomicity. In particular, according to the 2PC (two phase commit) protocol, a standard mechanism to ensure the atomicity of distributed transactions, the transaction *commits* only if both P_A and P_B get the item they want and vote YES; and if P_{TTP} crashes during message delivery, the transaction will *abort* and P_A and P_B will discard (or return) whatever they have received and stop.

However, in an environment where the processes involved in a transaction do not mutually trust each other, this type of atomicity is not enough to ensure fairness. In the above example, when the transaction aborts, that both P_A and P_B will discard (or return) whatever they have received does not mean that the items they have received will be kept confidential to the players they are working for before the abort. In fact, before a received item is discarded (or returned), players A or B may have already had a look of the item or even have made a copy of the item if they do not play honestly, because they have the ability to check the memory space of every process that works for them whenever they want. As a result, although the atomicity in terms of delivering messages to processes is achieved, the atomicity in terms of delivering messages to players is lost thus the fairness is lost.

The above discussion indicates that technical atomicity in terms of processes cannot guarantee fairness, and high level atomicities in terms of players, such as the atomicity of delivering messages to players, are required for data exchange systems. For example, in [18], Tygar identifies three levels of atomicity requirements for payment systems, namely, money atomicity, goods atomicity, and certified delivery. However, it should be noticed that these high level atomicity requirements usually cannot be satisfied by normal transaction processing.

7 Conclusion

In this paper, we systematically identified and studied the negative impact of system failures on the fairness of existing fair exchange protocols that use a *TTP*. We investigated the application of message logging techniques to remove the impact. In addition to standard message logging approaches, including pessimistic and optimistic message logging, we proposed an application-independent, semantics-based approach to achieve both fairness and good performance. Better performance can be achieved by looking into application semantics and logging only the data items necessary for maintaining the fairness.

Acknowledgement

We would like to thank the anonymous reviewers whose detailed and insightful comments and suggestions have significantly improved this paper.

References

[1] L. Alvisi and K. Marzullo. Message logging: Pessimistic, optimistic, causal and optimal. *IEEE Transactions on Software Engineering*, 24(2):149–159, 1998.

[2] N. Asokan, M. Schunter, and M. Waidner. Optimistic protocols for fair exchange. In *4th ACM Conference on Computer and Communications Security*, pages 8–17, Zurich, Switzerland, April 1997.

[3] N. Asokan and V. Shoup. Asynchronous protocols for optimistic fair exchange. In *Proceedings of IEEE Symposium on Research in Security and Privacy*, pages 86–99, Oakland, CA, May 1998.

[4] F. Bao, R.H. Deng, and W. Mao. Efficient and practical fair exchange protocols with off-line ttp. In *Proceedings of IEEE Symposium on Research in Security and Privacy*, pages 77–85, Oakland, CA, May 1998.

[5] J. F. Bartlett. A 'nonstop' operating system. In *Proceedings 11th Hawaii International Conference on System Sciences*, Hawaii, 1978.

[6] M. Ben-Or, O. Goldreich, S. Micali, and R. L. Rivest. A fair protocol for signing contracts. *IEEE Transactions on Information Theory*, 36(1):40–46, January 1990.

[7] P. A. Bernstein, V. Hadzilacos, and N. Goodman. *Concurrency Control and Recovery in Database Systems*. Addison-Wesley, Reading, MA, 1987.

[8] K. P. Birman and T. A. Joseph. Reliable communication in the presence of failures. *ACM Transactions on Computer Systems*, 5(1):47–76, 1987.

[9] A. Borg, J. Baumbach, and S. Glazer. A message system supporting fault tolerance. *Operating System Review*, 17(5):90–99, October 1983.

[10] B. Cox, J.D. Tygar, and M. Sirbu. NetBill security and transaction protocol. In *the First USENIX Workshop on Electronic Commerce*, pages 77–88, New York, July 1995.

[11] R. H. Deng, L. Gong, A. A. Lazer, and W. Wang. Practical protocols for certified electronic mail. *Journal of Network and System Management*, 4(3), 1996.

[12] M.K. Franklin and M.K. Reiter. Fair exchange with a semi-trusted third party. In *4th ACM Conference on Computer and Communications Security*, pages 1–7, Zurich, Switzerland, April 1997.

[13] J. Gray and A. Reuter. *Transaction Processing: Concepts and Techniques*. Morgan Kaufmann Publishers, Inc., 1993.

[14] D. B. Johnson and W. Zwaenepoel. Recovery in distributed systems. *Jounal of Algorithms*, 11(3):462–491, September 1990.

[15] L. Lamport. Time, clocks, and the ordering of events in a distributed system. *Communications of the ACM*, 21(7):558–565, 1978.

[16] G. Neiger and S. Toueg. Automatically increasing the fault-tolerance of distributed systems. In *Proceedings Seventh ACM Symposium on Principles of Distributed Computing*, Toronto, Ontario, August 1988.

[17] R. E. Strom and S. Yemini. Optimistic recovery in distributed systems. *ACM Transaction on Computer System*, 3(3):204–226, August 1985.

[18] J. D. Tygar. Atomicity versus anonymity: Distributed transactions for electronic commerce. In *Proceedings 24th VLDB Conference*, pages 1–12, New York, 1998.

[19] J. Zhou and D. Gollmann. A fair non-repudiation protocol. In *Proceedings of IEEE Symposium on Research in Security and Privacy*, pages 55–61, Oakland, CA, May 1996.

A Formal-Specification Based Approach for Protecting the Domain Name System

Steven Cheung
Department of Computer Science
University of California
Davis, CA 95616
cheung@cs.ucdavis.edu

Karl N. Levitt
Department of Computer Science
University of California
Davis, CA 95616
levitt@cs.ucdavis.edu

Abstract

Many network applications depend on the security of the domain name system (DNS). Attacks on DNS can cause denial of service and entity authentication to fail. In our approach, we use formal specifications to characterize DNS clients and DNS name servers, and to define a security goal: A name server should only use DNS data that is consistent with data from name servers that manage the corresponding domains (i.e., authoritative name servers). To enforce the security goal, we formally specify a DNS wrapper that examines the incoming and the outgoing DNS messages of a name server to detect messages that could cause violations of the security goal, cooperates with the corresponding authoritative name servers to diagnose those messages, and drops the messages that are identified as threats. Based on the wrapper specification, we implemented a wrapper prototype and evaluated its performance. Our experiments show that the wrapper incurs reasonable overhead and is effective against DNS attacks such as cache poisoning and certain spoofing attacks.

1. Introduction

This paper presents a detection-response approach for protecting the domain name system (DNS). DNS manages a distributed database to support a wide variety of network applications such as electronic mail, WWW, and remote login. For example, network applications rely on DNS to translate between host names and IP addresses. A compromise to DNS may cause denial of service (when a client cannot locate the network address of a server) and entity authentication to fail (when host names are used to specify trust relationships among hosts). For example, if DNS is compromised to cause a client to use incorrect DNS data, the client may be unable to obtain the IP address of a mail server and thus cannot communicate with it. As another example, if the DNS mapping for www.cnn.com is compromised, an attacker may be able to direct a web browser looking for the news web site to one that gives out counterfeit news. If the web browser does not authenticate the server, the user may use the counterfeit news as if they were genuine. Some applications (e.g., Unix *rlogin*) use name-based authentication. Attacking DNS could change the name-to-address mapping, and hence may allow an attacker's machine to masquerade as a trusted machine. Thus protecting DNS is security critical.

Our approach for protecting DNS is driven by formal specifications. The use of formal specifications enables reasoning, thus providing assurance for our solution. Formal methods have not been used in connection with an intrusion detection approach. Using Vienna Development Method (VDM), we developed formal specifications to characterize DNS clients and DNS servers, and to define a security goal as an invariant: A DNS server should only use DNS data that are consistent with those disseminated by the corresponding authoritative sources. We designed a DNS wrapper, also characterized by formal specifications, that enforces the security goal. Our DNS wrapper examines DNS messages entering and departing a protected name server to detect those messages that could lead to violations of our security goal. If the wrapper does not have enough information to determine whether a DNS message represents an attack, it collaborates with the name servers that manage the relevant part of the DNS name space. If the DNS wrapper cannot verify the data of the DNS message to be trustworthy, the wrapper logs the message and prevents it from reaching the protected name server.

Section 2 reviews the basics of the domain name system. (Readers are referred to [1, 13, 14] for more details about DNS.) Section 3 describes some known DNS vulnerabilities. Section 4 presents our system model. Section 5 presents a DNS wrapper that enforces our security goal for DNS. Based on the wrapper specification, we implemented a wrapper prototype. Section 6 describes our experiments for evaluating the performance of the wrapper implementation and their results. The results show that the DNS wrapper incurs reasonable overheads and is effective against some known DNS attacks. Section 7 concludes, compares our work with related work, and suggests future work. For the sake of brevity, we omit the formal specifications for DNS clients, DNS servers, and the DNS wrapper in this paper. See [7] for details of this work.

2. Overview of DNS

2.1. What is DNS?

DNS manages a distributed database indexed by *names*. The database has a hierarchical structure. A name (e.g., cs.ucdavis.edu.) has a structure that reflects the hierarchical name space, which is depicted in Figure 1.

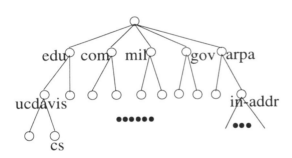

Figure 1. Hierarchical Structure of DNS Name Space

A *zone* is a contiguous part of the domain name space that is managed together by a set of machines, called *name servers*. The name of a zone is the concatenation of the node labels on the path from the topmost node of the zone to the root of the domain name space. The name servers that manage a zone are said to be *authoritative* for this zone. Every subtree of the domain name space is called a *domain*. The name of a domain is the same as the zone name of the topmost node of the corresponding subtree.

One of the main design goals for DNS is to have distributed administration. The distribution is achieved by delegation. For instance, instead of storing all the information about the entire edu domain, which is a very large domain, in a single name server, the responsibility of managing the ucdavis.edu domain is delegated to the authoritative name servers of UC Davis. The authoritative name servers of the edu zone are equipped with the names of the authoritative name servers of the ucdavis.edu zone. Thus if the edu servers need information about the ucdavis.edu domain, they know which servers to contact.

Clients of DNS are called *resolvers*, which are usually implemented as a set of library routines. Whenever an application on a machine needs to use the name service, it invokes the resolver on its local machine, and the resolver interacts with name servers to obtain the information needed. The most common implementations of resolvers are called *stub resolvers* (e.g., BIND[1] resolvers are stub resolvers). Stub resolvers only do the minimal job of assembling queries, sending them to servers, and re-sending them if the queries are not answered. Most of the work is carried out by name servers.

2.2. How does DNS Work?

The process of retrieving data from DNS is called *name resolution* or simply *resolution*. Suppose the host h1.cs.ucdavis.edu needs the IP address of h2.cs.foo.edu. The resolver will query a local name server in the cs.ucdavis.edu domain. There are two modes of resolution in DNS: *iterative* and *recursive*. In the iterative mode, when a name server receives a query for which it does not know the answer, the server will refer the querier to other servers that are more likely to know the answer. Each server is initialized with the addresses of some authoritative servers of the root zone. Moreover, the root servers know the authoritative servers of the second-level domains (e.g., edu domain). Second-level servers know the authoritative servers of third-level domains, and so on. Thus by following the tree structure, the querier can get "closer" to the answer after each referral. Figure 2 shows the iterative resolution scenario. For example, when a root server receives an iterative query for the domain name h2.cs.foo.edu, it refers the querier to the edu servers. Eventually, the querier will locate the authoritative servers of cs.foo.edu and obtain the IP address. In the recursive mode, a server either answers the query or finds out the answer by contacting other servers itself and then returns the answer to

---

[1]BIND stands for Berkeley Internet Name Domain, which is the most common implementation of DNS.

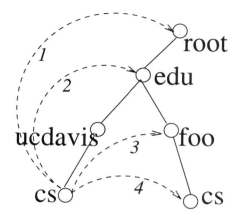

Figure 2. Iterative Name Resolution

the querier.

The above resolution process may be quite expensive in terms of resolution time and the number of messages sent. To speed up the process, servers store the results of the previous queries in their *caches*. Consider the above example. If h1.cs.ucdavis.edu asks its local server to resolve the same name twice, the server can reply immediately based on the information stored in its cache the second time. Also, if in a subsequent query h1.cs.ucdavis.edu asks its local server to find out the IP address of h3.cs.foo.edu, the local server can skip a few steps and contact a cs.foo.edu server directly. If the querier gets an answer from an authoritative server, the answer is called an *authoritative answer*. Otherwise, it is called a *non-authoritative answer*. Because there may be changes to the mapping, servers do not cache data forever. Authoritative servers attach time-to-live[2] (TTL) tags to data. Upon expiration, a name server should remove the data from its cache.

2.3. DNS Message Format

A DNS message consists of a header and four sections: *question, answer, authority,* and *additional*. A *resource record* (RR) is a unit of information in the last three sections. Here is a list of common resource record types [13]:

---

[2]There is no single "best" TTL value for all resource records. The TTL value of a resource record is based on a tradeoff between consistency and performance. A small TTL will increase the average name resolution time because remote name servers will remove the resource record earlier and need to query the corresponding name servers more often. If a resource record is changed, a small TTL enables other name servers to purge the stale data and to use the new data earlier. One should reduce the TTL before the resource record is changed. A common TTL value is one day (e.g., the cs.ucdavis.edu zone), although some high-level zones (e.g., the root zone) use a multi-day TTL.

- An A record contains a 32-bit IP address for the specified domain name.

- A CNAME record lists the original (or *canonical*) name of the specified domain name. In other words, a CNAME resource record maps an alias to the canonical domain name.

- An HINFO record contains host information such as the operating system used.

- An MX record contains a host name acting as a mail exchange for the specified domain.

- An NS record contains a host name that is an authoritative name server for the specified domain.

- A PTR record contains a domain name corresponding to the specified IP address.

- An SOA record contains information for the entire specified domain such as the domain administrator's mail address.

The header has a query id field, which is used to facilitate requesters' matching up responses to outstanding queries. The question section carries a target domain name (QNAME), a query type (QTYPE), and a query class (QCLASS). For example, a query to find the IP address of the host h2.cs.foo.edu has QNAME=h2.cs.foo.edu, QTYPE=A, and QCLASS=IN (which stands for the Internet). The answer section carries RRs that directly answer the query. The authority section carries RRs that describe other authoritative servers. For instance, the authority section may contain NS RRs to refer the querier to other name servers during iterative resolution. The additional section carries RRs that may be helpful in using the RRs in the other sections. For instance, the additional section of a response may contain A RRs to provide the IP addresses for the NS RRs listed in the authority section.

3. DNS Vulnerabilities

Bellovin [3, 4], Gavron [10], Schuba and Spafford [15], Vixie [17], and CERT advisory CA-98.05 [5] discuss several security problems of DNS. In the following, we describe two well-known problems of DNS that are relevant to this paper—*cache poisoning* and failure to authenticate DNS responses.

In the cache poisoning attack, an attacker can trick a name server S_1 to query another name server S_2. If S_2 is a compromised name server, the attacker can have S_2 to return a DNS response that contains faked RRs.

Otherwise, the attacker can masquerade as S_2 and send the DNS response to S_1 (see below). Recall that a name server caches the results of previous interactions with other servers to improve performance. When S_1 uses its contaminated cache to resolve a name, it may use the incorrect DNS data supplied by the attacker.

The message authentication mechanism used by most implementations of DNS is weak: A DNS server (or a DNS client) attaches an id to a query, and uses it to match with the id of the corresponding response. Suppose a server S_1 sends a query to another server S_2. If an attacker can predict the query id used by S_1, the attacker can send a forged response that has a matching query id to S_1. When S_1 receives the response that claims to be from S_2, S_1 has no way to verify that the response actually comes from S_2. If S_2 is unavailable when the query is sent, the attacker can just masquerade as S_2 and send the forged response to S_1. If S_2 is operational, the attacker can mount a denial of service attack against S_2 to prevent S_2 from responding to S_1's query. Also, if a name server receives multiple responses for its query, it uses the first response. Thus even if S_2 can reply to S_1, the attacker can still succeed if the forged response reaches S_1 before S_2's response does.

4. System Model

In our model, there are two types of processes: DNS servers and DNS clients (or resolvers). These processes communicate with each other through message passing. Resolvers only communicate with servers; servers can communicate with other servers in addition to communicating with resolvers. These two types of processes are denoted by *Server* and *Resolver* respectively. Basically, we model DNS clients and DNS servers as an object that maintains a view on DNS data. The view may be changed only through communicating with other DNS components (i.e., sending DNS requests and receiving DNS responses) or by timeouts for DNS data.

We use the Vienna Development Method (VDM) to specify our system model, because VDM provides a formal language for specifying data and the associated operations, and includes a framework to perform refinements of data and operations. Another reason is that VDM provides a basis for performing formal verification, which makes it more convenient to extend our work in the future. Most of the symbols used in VDM are standard mathematical symbols. We will describe the non-standard or less commonly used ones as we need them. Readers are referred to [11, 2] for more details on VDM.

In the following, Section 4.1 presents our DNS data

model. Section 4.2 defines our notion of a process' view on DNS data. Section 4.3 formalizes the DNS concept of authority. Section 4.4 discusses our assumptions about DNS. Section 4.5 presents our security goal for DNS.

4.1. DNS Data

DNS messages (of type *Msg*) are either a query (of type *Query*) or a response (of type *Resp*).

$$Query \cup Resp = Msg$$
$$Query \cap Resp = \emptyset$$

A message m of type *Msg* consists of the following sections: header, question, answer, authority, and additional. We denote these sections of m by $Hdr(m)$, $Q(m)$, $Ans(m)$, $Auth(m)$, and $Add(m)$ respectively. The header section includes a query id, an opcode[3], a truncated message flag[4], and a response code[5]. We denote these fields of m by $id(m)$, $opcode(m)$, $tc(m)$, and $rcode(m)$ respectively. The question section consists of a domain name, a query type, and a query class. The answer, the authority, and the additional sections consists of resource records (RR). We denote the set of resource records of a message m by $RRof(m)$. A RR consists of a domain name, a type, a class, a 32-bit TTL (in seconds), and a resource data field. For a resource record r, we denote these fields by $dname(r)$, $type(r)$, $class(r)$, $ttl(r)$, and $rdata(r)$ respectively.

DNS manages a distributed database. The database is indexed by a tuple (dname, type, class) of type *Idx*. The range of the database is a set of resource records, abbreviated as RR. To denote this database type in VDM, we use a map type $DbMap : Idx \xrightarrow{m} RR-\text{set}$. A *map* type $T = D \xrightarrow{m} R$ has domain D and range R. The domain and the range of T are denoted by $\mathsf{dom}(T)$ and $\mathsf{rng}(T)$ respectively. A map of type T is a set that relates single items in D to single items in R.

$$
\begin{aligned}
RRType &= \{\mathsf{A}, \mathsf{PTR}, \mathsf{NS}, \mathsf{CNAME}, \mathsf{MX}, \mathsf{SOA}, \\
&= \mathsf{HINFO}, \dots\} \\
RRClass &= \{\mathsf{IN}, \dots\} \\
TTL &= \{0 \dots 2^{32} - 1\}
\end{aligned}
$$

---

[3]The opcode of a DNS message distinguishes between different types of queries—standard queries and inverse queries. A standard query looks for the resource data given a domain name. An inverse query looks for the domain name given resource data.

[4]The truncated message flag indicates whether the DNS message is truncated. Message truncation occurs when the message length is greater than that allowed on the transmission medium.

[5]The response code field is used to indicate errors and exceptions.

$$
\begin{aligned}
Idx \quad &:: \quad \text{dname} \ : \ DName \\
& \quad \text{type} \ \ : \ RRType \\
& \quad \text{class} \ : \ RRClass \\
RR \quad &:: \quad \text{dname} \ : \ DName \\
& \quad \text{type} \ \ : \ RRType \\
& \quad \text{class} \ : \ RRClass \\
& \quad \text{ttl} \ \ \ : \ TTL \\
& \quad \text{rdata} \ : \ RData \\
DbMap &= Idx \xrightarrow{m} RR\text{-set}
\end{aligned}
$$

Db represents the data managed by DNS. $SubDomain$ captures the domain-subdomain relationships. Given a domain d, the set of all the sub-domains of d is represented by $SubDomain(d)$. A zone contains the domain names and the associated data of a domain, except those that belong to a delegated domain. A zone is a contiguous part of the domain name space that is managed together by a set of name servers. A zone may have a set of delegated subzones, represented by the function $SubZone$. (In VDM, a *function* specification consists of two parts. The first part defines the argument types and the result type, which are separated by the symbol "$\rightarrow$". The second part gives the function definition.) For a zone z, $ZoneData(z)$ contains all resource records whose domain names belong to zone z, the *zone cut data*, and the *glue data*. The zone cut data describe the cuts around the bottom of zone z: In particular the NS resource records of the name servers for the delegated zones of z. If there are name servers for the delegated zones residing below the zone cut, the glue data contain the addresses of these servers.

$$
\begin{aligned}
&Db : DbMap \\
&SubDomain : Domain \xrightarrow{m} Domain\text{-set} \\
&ZoneData : Zone \xrightarrow{m} DbMap \\
&SubZone : Zone \rightarrow Zone\text{-set} \\
&\forall z \in Zone \cdot SubZone(z) \ \underline{\triangle} \\
&\quad \{cz \mid \exists rr \in \mathsf{rng}\,ZoneData(z) \cdot type(rr) = \mathsf{NS} \wedge \\
&\quad\ dname(rr) \neq z \wedge cz = dname(rr)\}
\end{aligned}
$$

4.2. View

Every process maintains its view of the database. The view of a server s can be partitioned into the authority part (denoted by $View_{auth}(s)$) and the cache part (denoted by $View_{cache}(s)$), where the former takes precedence over the latter. The *map overwrite* operator $\dagger$ takes two map operands and returns a map that contains all the elements in the second operand and those in the first operand whose domain does not appear in the domain of the second operand. For a server that is not authoritative for any part of the database

and for a resolver, the corresponding $View_{auth}$ is $\emptyset$.

$$
\begin{aligned}
&View_{auth} : Process \xrightarrow{m} DbMap \\
&View_{cache} : Process \xrightarrow{m} DbMap \\
&View : Process \rightarrow DbMap \\
&\forall p \in Process \cdot View(p) \ \underline{\triangle} \\
&\quad View_{cache}(p) \dagger View_{auth}(p)
\end{aligned}
$$

4.3. Authority

Some servers are said to be authoritative for a zone; their views on the zone data define them. $AuthServer$ maps a zone to the list of authoritative servers. $AuthAnswer$ defines the mapping from an index to the *authoritative answer*, defined by the view of the an authoritative server on the index. $Authoritative$ returns true if and only if every resource record in the input resource record set is authoritative.

$$
\begin{aligned}
&AuthServer : Zone \xrightarrow{m} Server\text{-set} \\
&AuthAnswer : Idx \rightarrow RR\text{-set} \\
&\forall i \in dom(Db) \cdot AuthAnswer(i) \ = \\
&\quad \mathsf{let}\ z \in Zone \wedge p \in Process \wedge \\
&\quad i \in \mathsf{dom}\,ZoneData(z) \wedge p \in AuthServer(z)\ \mathsf{in} \\
&\quad View_{auth}(p)(i) \\
&Authoritative : RR\text{-set} \rightarrow Boolean \\
&\forall rrs \in RR\text{-set} \cdot Authoritative(rrs) = \\
&\quad \forall rr \in rrs \cdot rr \in \\
&\quad AuthAnswer((dname(rr), type(rr), class(rr)))
\end{aligned}
$$

4.4. Assumptions

In this section, we explicitly list our assumptions for DNS. They concern with how name servers prioritize RR sets, the accuracy of authoritative DNS data, the effect of changes on DNS data, the accuracy of delegation data, and the power of attackers on eavesdropping DNS packets.

Assumption 1 *Protected servers do not add an RR to the $View_{cache}$ of a process if an RR that corresponds to the same index already exists in the $View_{cache}$. Moreover, protected servers prefer authoritative data over cache data.*

Both of them hold for "good" servers (i.e., servers that behave according to the DNS RFC [13, 14]). Some server implementations rank data from different sources at different credibility levels. Moreover, data from a higher credibility level can preempt data from a lower credibility level. We do not model data credibility levels in our work for the sake of simplicity. Because our DNS wrapper only allows authoritative data to reach a protected name server, this simplification does not affect the validity of our results.

Assumption 2 *Data from an authoritative server are correct.*

For example, if a server is authoritative for a machine h and the server says the IP address of h is i, then we believe that the IP address of h is i.

Assumption 3 *When a server attaches a TTL with t seconds to a resource record for which the server is authoritative, the resource record will be valid for the next t seconds.*

We state this assumption because there is no revocation mechanism in DNS. Without this assumption, one cannot determine the validity of DNS data as soon as they leave their authoritative servers. We argue that this assumption is reasonable. When a resource record needs to be changed, the TTL of this resource record is usually decreased before the changeover so that incorrect/stale records will timeout shortly after the changeover.

Assumption 4 *For every zone, the delegation data and the glue data of its child zones correspond to the NS RRs and the A RRs of the name servers of the child zones.*

An example violation of this assumption is called *lame delegation*. Lame delegation is caused by operational errors: A system administrator changes the name servers for a zone without changing the corresponding delegation information in the parent zone or notifying the system administrator of the parent zone about the change.

Assumption 5 *Attackers cannot eavesdrop on the DNS packets sent between our protected servers and the legitimate name servers.*

This is a limit we place on the attackers; if attackers can monitor the communication, our scheme may fail to cope with spoofing attacks. In the future, when the use of the DNS security extensions [8] (DNSSEC)— which employs digital signatures to authenticate DNS data—is widespread, we may drop this assumption. An implication of this assumption is that by randomizing the query id used, the probability that an attacker can forge a response whose id matches the randomized query id is small. Thus attempts for sending forged responses by guessing the query id used can be detected by the wrapper.

4.5. Our Goal

Our goal is to ensure that the view of a protected name server agrees with those of the corresponding authoritative name servers. This goal is specified using a VDM data invariant. A *data invariant* of a data type specifies the predicates that must hold true during the execution of a system. Our name server specification, which reflects the minimal functionalities of DNS servers among existing implementations, does not satisfy this data invariant because it allows non-authoritative DNS data to be used by a name server. Thus for a name server s, $Authoritative(\text{rng } View(s))$ may not hold. In the next section, we will present our solution—a security wrapper for protecting name servers. Our DNS wrapper filters out DNS messages containing resource records that cannot be verified as authoritative. Therefore, a protected name server that satisfies the data invariant can be constructed by composing a name server and our DNS wrapper.

> state *DNS* of
> $\qquad$ *protectedNS* : *Server*$-$set
> $\ldots$
> inv *mk-DNS(protectedNS)* $\triangle$
> $\qquad \forall s \in protectedNS \cdot Authoritative(\text{rng } View(s))$
> end

5. Our DNS Wrapper

We use *security wrapper* (or simply wrapper) to refer to a piece of software that encapsulates a component, such as a name server, to improve its security. Using wrappers to enhance the security of existing software is not a new idea. Related work includes TCP wrapper [16] and TIS' generic software wrappers [9]. However, our work is different in that it addresses problems that are DNS specific and it involves the use of formal specifications.

Consider a wrapper w. Wrapper w checks DNS response packets going to a name server and ensures that they are authenticated[6] and they agree with authoritative answers. If a resource record in the response does not come from an authoritative server, wrapper w locates an authoritative server and queries that server for the authoritative answer. To locate an authoritative server for a zone, say z, the wrapper starts with a server, say s, that is known to be an authoritative

---

[6]Data authentication checks can be performed by matching the query id's of queries to those of responses, or by using DNSSEC. However, the query id generation process used in some implementations of name servers is quite predictable. Before DNSSEC is widely deployed, we need a means to protect these name servers from spoofing attacks.

server for an ancestor zone of z, and queries server s for authoritative servers of the child zone that is either an ancestor zone of z or z itself. The search is performed by traversing the domain name tree, one zone at a time, until an authoritative server for the DNS data being verified is located. Recall that the zone data maintained by a server include the name server data of the delegated zones. Moreover, the zone data, including the zone cut data and the glue data, take precedence over RRs obtained from outside sources. Thus the delegation data is immune from cache poisoning attacks. Our scheme exploits this fact to securely locate the authoritative servers.

Let ns denote the name server protected by wrapper w. Our wrapper consists of two main parts: $Wrapper_s q$ for processing queries, and $Wrapper_s r$ for processing responses. (The subscript s stands for "server".) Wrapper w processes queries generated by ns before they are sent out, and processes queries destined for ns. Wrapper w also processes responses destined for ns; those that are accepted by w will be forwarded to ns.

When ns sends a query, wrapper w generates a random query id and uses it to replace the original query id (used by ns). We use a translation table to track the mapping between the random query id's used by w and the original query id's used by ns.

$Wrapper_s q$ processes queries that involve ns. These queries can be partitioned into two types. The first type corresponds to the queries that are sent to ns. The second type corresponds to the queries that are generated by ns. These two types of queries are treated differently. For the first type, wrapper w checks the queries to determine whether they are well-formed (e.g., the answer, the authority, and the additional sections for a standard query should be empty). For the second type, the wrapper generates a random query id, replaces the query id used in the original query by this randomly generated query id, and updates the local query id translation table.

$Wrapper_s r$ processes responses that are received by the wrapper. $Wrapper_s r$ has two components: $Wrapper_s r1$ and $Wrapper_s r2$. $Wrapper_s r1$ screens out forged response messages. In other words, response authentication is hardened. $Wrapper_s r2$ verifies the response messages to ensure that they agree with authoritative answers, and copes with cache poisoning attacks. There are two types of responses received by a wrapper: responses for queries generated by the protected name server ns, and responses for queries generated by the wrapper itself (for message diagnosis purposes). When a response for a query generated by ns is received, the wrapper uses the query id translation table to restore the query id (to the one used by ns) before passing the response to $Wrapper_s r2$.

6. Experiments

6.1. Overview

We conducted experiments to evaluate the response time (i.e., the elapsed time between sending a query to a name server and receiving a response from it) of a wrapped name server, and to evaluate the false positive rate, the false negative rate, and the computational overhead (i.e., CPU time used) of our wrapper.

Based on the DNS wrapper specification, we implemented a prototype of the DNS wrapper for BIND release 4.9.5, which was the latest release for BIND when we started our implementation. The DNS wrapper was written in C. We modified the BIND name server source code to invoke the DNS wrapper upon receiving queries and responses and upon sending queries to other name servers.

In this section, we describe two sets of experiments and their results. In Experiment A, we examined the response time, the false positive rate, and the computational overhead of our wrapper using a trace of DNS queries received by a name server in an operational setting. In Experiment B, we examined the false negative rate of our wrapper with respect to four attacks: three cache poisoning attacks and one spoofing attack.

6.2. General Experimental Setup

In these experiments, our name servers (BIND 4.9.5) listened to port 4000 instead of port 53 (the *de facto* standard port number for name servers) for DNS queries to prevent queries outside our experiments from affecting our results.

In every run of our experiments, we started a fresh copy of our name server because name servers maintain a cache for DNS information obtained through interacting with other name servers. The behavior of a name server can be quite different depending on whether the DNS information queried can be found in the cache. Restarting name servers can avoid interference between consecutive runs of the experiment.

We used a modified version of *nslookup* as the DNS client in our experiments. (See [1] for a good tutorial on *nslookup*.) We chose *nslookup* because it is a convenient tool for generating DNS queries and displaying DNS responses. Moreover, *nslookup* can be easily configured to use a specified name server port number and to query a specified name server. Our modified *nslookup* uses Unix *gethrtime()* system calls to record the time when a query is sent and when the corresponding response is received. Unless otherwise specified, we will use *nslookup* to refer to this modified version of *nslookup*.

Our experiments were performed on a lightly loaded Sun SPARC-5 running Solaris 2.5.1. We ran our name servers and *nslookup* on the same machine to eliminate the network latency for the communication between them, thus reducing the influence of the local area network load on the experimental results.

Because we did not have control over external name servers, and the inter-network links between our name server and external name servers, we performed Experiment A multiple times and calculated the average response time.

6.3. Experiment A

6.3.1   Data Set

The data set for Experiment A consisted of a trace of 1340 DNS queries received by a name server in a "real world" setting. To gather the trace of DNS queries, we modified a name server to log all DNS queries it received and ran it for two days. We also modified the local BIND resolver configuration file to direct all DNS queries to this name server. In the resolver configuration file, the *search list* was consisted of cs.ucdavis.edu., ucdavis.edu., and ucop.edu. When a BIND resolver is invoked to resolve a *relative* domain name—a domain name that does not have a trailing dot—it appends the domain names in the order specified in the search list and attempt to resolve them until a positive response is received. If none of them results in a successful resolution, the resolver then generates a query for the relative domain name itself. For example, when the BIND resolver is invoked for domain name dn, it attempts to resolve for dn.cs.ucdavis.edu., dn.ucdavis.edu., dn.ucop.edu., and dn in that order until a successful resolution is obtained.

6.3.2   Experimental Procedure

1. Start a wrapped name server.

2. Run *nslookup* to query the wrapped name server for resolving the 1340 DNS queries sequentially.

3. Record the total system CPU time and the total user CPU time used.

4. Terminate the wrapped name server.

5. Repeat the above procedure using an unmodified name server instead of a wrapped name server.

6.3.3   Experimental Results

Table 1 shows the statistics related to response times recorded by *nslookup* based on 33 runs of this experiment. The mean response time for the wrapped server was 0.12 second per query, and that for the unmodified server was 0.08 second per query. We examined the trace segments that correspond to "steep" increases in the response times (e.g., 400th-600th query), we found that they could be explained by DNS queries generated by web surfing sessions, which involved mostly remote and distinct domain names. Specifically, the trace segment for the 400th-600th query included 43 remote and distinct domain names. The average total response times for those 43 queries for the unmodified server and the wrapped server were 28.29 seconds and 47.54 seconds respectively, which accounted for 83% and 88% of the total response times for that interval respectively.

Table 2 shows the CPU times used by the unmodified server and the wrapped server. The figures show that the average CPU times used are a small fraction (8% for the unmodified server and 7% for the wrapped server) of the total response time. Thus the response time overhead of the wrapper reported in Table 1 was largely due to waiting for the response messages in the message diagnosis process. The average total CPU time increased from 9.33 seconds to 11.29 seconds (i.e., a 21% increase).

The number of false positives ranged from 2-10 per run, with the mean being 5.85 and the standard deviation being 1.89. Among the false positives, 80% of them were caused by name server behaviors that violate our name server specification or to a violation of our assumptions. For example, false positives caused by misconfigurations of name servers are in this category. The remaining 20% of the false positives were generated when the wrapper gave up on diagnosing a DNS message after the amount of resources spent (e.g., the number of DNS queries issued) had reached a threshold. The threshold is used to ensure that the amount of resources used for verifying a message is bounded, thus protecting the wrapper from problems like denial of service attacks.

6.4. Experiment B

The main goal of Experiment B is to examine the detection rate of malicious attacks of a wrapped name server (i.e., false negative rate). We investigated the following four types of attacks:

- *Sending incorrect resource records for a remote domain name to the target*: This is accomplished by

Table 1. Cumulative Response Time (in Sec.) for the "Two-day trace" Data Set.

# queries	Unmodified Name Server				Wrapped Name Server			
	Mean	Min	Max	Std Dev	Mean	Min	Max	Std Dev
200	6.24	3.75	19.78	3.62	8.83	4.27	24.52	4.66
400	11.63	7.44	23.99	4.06	19.56	10.48	34.53	6.37
600	45.59	22.29	147.99	28.31	73.42	40.66	270.41	45.65
800	59.71	35.60	171.83	28.99	94.66	58.53	312.98	49.46
1000	74.15	40.28	263.69	50.93	111.69	70.72	332.60	62.77
1200	96.71	55.36	370.10	75.22	145.10	85.13	396.51	87.50
1340	111.05	70.52	392.48	78.75	165.96	102.38	439.51	91.96

Table 2. System and User Times Used (in Sec.) for the "Two-day Trace" Data Set.

Type	Unmodified Name Server				Wrapped Name Server			
	Mean	Min	Max	Std Dev	Mean	Min	Max	Std Dev
System	4.01	3.43	4.90	0.36	5.32	4.59	5.82	0.33
User	4.35	3.73	4.90	0.26	6.94	6.31	7.90	0.43

using a CNAME resource record in the answer section of a response message to introduce (in the resource data field) an arbitrary domain name for which the target server is not authoritative, and then including incorrect resource records for this remote domain name in the additional section of the response message.

- *Sending incorrect resource records that conflict with the zone data for which the target is authoritative*: In particular, the attacker uses a CNAME resource record to link to an A resource record for which the target is authoritative.

- *Sending resource records that correspond to a non-existing domain name that lives in the target server's zone.*

- *Sending a response with a guessed query id*: In this attack, one queries the target server to trigger it to send a query to the attacker, whom records the query id used. A second query is then issued to trigger the target to query the attacker again. Instead of using the query id of the second query, the attacker adds one to the query id used in the first query and uses the result as the query id in its second response.

The first three types of attacks correspond to sending incorrect DNS data to a name server (i.e., cache poisoning attacks). The fourth type of attacks corresponds to masquerading attacks. Our wrapper used randomized query id's for outgoing queries. Thus attackers who do not have access to those queries will have to guess the query id's used for their forged response messages. As a result, their forged messages will be detected with high probability.

6.4.1 Data Set

In Experiment B, we modified the data set used in Experiment A by inserting two queries that correspond to each of the four types of attacks at random locations in the two-day trace. Moreover, we also inserted four queries at random locations in the trace as controls. These queries correspond to different domain names in the domain for which a malicious name server is authoritative but do not trigger an attack.

6.4.2 Experimental Procedure

1. Start a malicious name server for a new subdomain dns.cs.ucdavis.edu. When that malicious name server is asked to resolve for certain domain names that reside in the dns.cs.ucdavis.edu. domain, depending on the domain names queried, it will either return incorrect DNS resource records or send out response messages with an incorrect query id or a predicted query id.

2. Start a wrapped name server.

3. Run *nslookup* with the modified trace of DNS queries as input and send the queries sequentially

to the wrapped name server.

4. Terminate the wrapped name server.

5. Terminate the malicious name server.

6. Repeat the above procedure using an unmodified name server instead of a wrapped name server.

6.4.3 Experimental Results

We ran the experiment five times. In all five runs, all eight attacks (i.e., two from each of the four attack types) were reported correctly by the wrapped name server, and none of the response messages corresponding to the control queries were misclassified as attacks.

When we applied these four types of attacks to an unmodified name server, the first type of attacks succeeded in planting incorrect DNS data into the cache of the target server. For the second and the third type, the unmodified name server did not cache the incorrect DNS data for domain names that belong to its authoritative domain. However, the name server did forward the entire response message received, including those incorrect resource records for which the name server was authoritative, to its client. That did not make much difference for our experiments because the client used was *nslookup*, which did not perform caching. However, if the client was another name server that was not authoritative for those incorrect DNS data, the cache of the client would be corrupted. This situation may occur when the client is a *caching-only server*[7] that uses another name server as a *forwarder*[8]. The fourth type of attacks succeeded for an unmodified name server. It was because the query id used by the unmodified name server was predictable: the query id used in successive queries always differed by one.

7. Conclusions and Future Work

This paper presents a detection-response approach for protecting DNS. Our approach consists of the following steps. First, we define a security goal—name servers only use DNS data that are consistent with the corresponding authoritative data. Second, we declare the threats, namely cache poisoning and spoofing attacks. Third, we develop a DNS model, which includes formal characterizations of DNS clients and

---

[7]A caching-only server is a name server that is not authoritative for any domain.

[8]A forwarder is a name server to which other name servers forward their recursive queries. A forwarder is useful for building a large cache for remote DNS data, especially when communication between local machines and remote machines is slow or restricted.

DNS servers. Fourth, we design a DNS wrapper with the objective that the composition of the specification for a protected name server and that for the wrapper satisfies our security goal for DNS. If the DNS wrapper receives a DNS message that may cause violations of the security goal, the wrapper drops the message instead of forwarding it to the protected name server. Fifth, we use the formal specification for the wrapper to guide our implementation of a wrapper prototype.

To counter cache poisoning, Vixie [17] presents enhancements to BIND. Briefly, BIND version 4.9.3 checks the input resource records more carefully before caching them. Moreover, it implements a credibility level scheme in which resource records from a more credible source take precedence over those from a less credible one. Cheswick and Bellovin [6] present a design for a DNS proxy (*dnsproxy*). In their design, the domain name space is partitioned into regions called *realms*. A realm is served by a set of servers. Depending on the query name of a DNS request, *dnsproxy* forwards the request to the servers responsible for the corresponding realm. Certain resource records in response messages—those that do not refer to realm to which the query name belongs, and those that satisfy a set of filtering rules—are removed to protect the queriers. Eastlake and Kaufman [8] present security extensions to DNS (DNSSEC) that uses digital signatures to support data authentication for DNS data. In DNSSEC, new resource record types are introduced for public keys and digital signatures. Security-aware servers and security-aware resolvers can use zone keys, which are either statically configured or learned by chaining through zones, to verify the origins of resource records. Compared to the prior work for protecting DNS, our DNS wrapper has the following advantages:

- Provides assurance by employing formal specifications (written in VDM) to characterize DNS components, to state the security goal, and to characterize our solution.

- Effective against cache poisoning attacks and certain spoofing attacks (i.e., query id guessing) when the assumptions in Section 4.4 are met.

- Compatible with existing DNS implementations.

- Does not require changes for the DNS protocol.

- Incurs reasonable performance overhead.

- Can be deployed locally; does not depend on changes to other remote DNS components.

In November 1998, a company called Men & Mice surveyed the status of name servers on the Internet

[12]. Among 4184 randomly picked com zones, 1344 of them (i.e., 32.1%) were found to be vulnerable to cache poisoning attacks. In other words, the name servers of those zones could be compromised and gave out incorrect information about other domains, including its delegated domains. We note that the effectiveness of our DNS wrapper is not affected by attacks against external name servers as long as our assumptions are met.

There are several directions for future research.

- To further raise the assurance level of our wrapper, one may perform a complete formal verification from specification to implementation. The VDM specifications developed can be used as the basis for conducting the formal verification.

- Results from Experiment A show a 0.437% false positive rate for the DNS wrapper. Because the majority of these false positives were caused by misconfigurations of external name servers, a non-trivial modification for the DNS wrapper may be needed to significantly reduce the false positive rate.

- We have not discussed protecting DNS resolvers. If the communication path between a resolver and its trusted local name server is secure, and the name server is protected by the DNS wrapper, the DNS data received by the resolver is "safe" because a wrapped name server only uses DNS data that are consistent with the corresponding authoritative answers. Future research may be conducted to protect DNS resolvers when the resolver-server communication path is insecure. A possibility is to adapt the DNS wrapper to protect resolvers.

- One may apply our approach to protect other network services and privileged processes.

8. Acknowledgments

This work was supported by DARPA under grant ARMY/DAAH 04-96-1-0207.

References

[1] P. Albitz, and C. Liu, "DNS and BIND." O'Reilly and Associates, Inc., 1992.

[2] D. Andrews, and D. Ince, "Practical Formal Methods with VDM." McGraw-Hill, 1991.

[3] S.M. Bellovin, "Security Problems in the TCP/IP Protocol Suite." *Computer Communications Review*, Vol.19, No.2, April 1989, pp.32-48.

[4] S. Bellovin, "Using the Domain Name System for System Break-ins." *Proc. of the 5th UNIX Security Symposium*, June 5-7, 1995, pp.199-208.

[5] CERT Coordination Center, "Multiple Vulnerabilities in BIND." CERT Advisory CA-98:05, April 8, 1998.

[6] B. Cheswick, and S. Bellovin, "A DNS Filter and Switch for Packet-filtering Gateways." *Proc. of the 6th UNIX Security Symposium*, July 22-25, 1996, pp.15-19.

[7] S. Cheung, "An Intrusion Tolerance Approach for Protecting Network Infrastructures." Ph.D. Dissertation, University of California, Davis, September 1999.

[8] D. Eastlake, 3rd, and C. Kaufman, "Domain Name System Security Extensions." RFC 2065, January 1997.

[9] T. Fraser, L. Badger, and M. Feldman, "Hardening COTS Software with Generic Software Wrappers." *Proceedings of the 1999 IEEE Symposium on Security and Privacy*, Oakland, California, May 5-7, 1999, pp.2-16.

[10] E. Gavron, "A Security Problem and Proposed Correction with Widely Deployed DNS Software." RFC 1535, October 1993.

[11] C.B. Jones, "Systematic Software Development using VDM." Prentice-Hall, 1990.

[12] Men and Mice, "Domain Health Survey." http://www.menandmice.com, November 1998.

[13] P. Mockapetris, "Domain Names – Concepts and Facilities." RFC 1034, November 1987.

[14] P. Mockapetris, "Domain Names – Implementation and Specification." RFC 1035, November 1987.

[15] C.L. Schuba, and E.H. Spafford, "Addressing Weaknesses in the Domain Name System Protocol." Technical Report, Department of Computer Sciences, Purdue University, 1994.

[16] W. Venema, "TCP Wrapper: Network Monitoring, Access Control, and Booby Traps." *Proc. of the 3rd UNIX Security Symposium*, September 1992, pp.85-92.

[17] P. Vixie, "DNS and BIND Security Issues." *Proc. of the 5th UNIX Security Symposium*, June 5-7, 1995, pp.209-216.

Author Index

IEEE Computer Society Publications

The world-renowned IEEE Computer Society publishes, promotes, and distributes a wide variety of authoritative computer science and engineering texts. These books are available from most retail outlets. Visit the Online Catalog, *http://computer.org*, for a list of products.

IEEE Computer Society Proceedings

The IEEE Computer Society also produces and actively promotes the proceedings of more than 141 acclaimed international conferences each year in multimedia formats that include hard and softcover books, CD-ROMs, videos, and on-line publications.

For information on the IEEE Computer Society proceedings, send e-mail to *cs.books@computer.org* or write to Proceedings, IEEE Computer Society, P.O. Box 3014, 10662 Los Vaqueros Circle, Los Alamitos, CA 90720-1314. Telephone +1 714-821-8380. FAX +1 714-761-1784.

Additional information regarding the Computer Society, conferences and proceedings, CD-ROMs, videos, and books can also be accessed from our web site at *http://computer.org/cspress*

Revised 9 November 1999